Systematic Instruction of the Moderately and Severely Handicapped

Second Edition

Martha E. Snell, editor

University of Virginia

Charles E. Merrill Publishing Co.
A Bell & Howell Company
Columbus   Toronto   London   Sydney

For all the "first and second priority" individuals—
those who are not yet served and those for whom services
are still inadequate—their current teachers, and their
teachers-to-be.

And for my mentors, Ed Keller and Don Burke.

Published by Charles E. Merrill Publishing Company
A Bell and Howell Company
Columbus, Ohio 43216

This book was set in Bembo
Cover design: Tony Faiola

Photographs courtesy of: p. 84, Linda Burkhart; p. 151,
Dan Grogan; pp. 187, 189, 191, 192, 194, 195, Philippa
H. Campbell; pp. 206, 216, 217, Linda K. Bunker and
Sherril Moon; pp. 244, 246, 248, 249, Kathleen Davey;
pp. 293, 296, 297, 303, 307, 308, Dan Grogan; pp. 384,
401, 403, 404, Martha E. Snell; pp. 511, 520, Frank
Rusch.

Library of Congress Catalog Card Number: 82–62497
International Standard Book Number: 0–675–20035–0
Printed in the United States of America
5 6 7 8 9 10/87 86

Preface

Regardless of the sophisticated computer technology that runs our lives today, there exists in our society an overwhelming ignorance about moderately and severely handicapped citizens and about what they are capable of accomplishing. Now that the purse strings of our economy have been tightened, some citizens are scrutinizing public education spending more than ever. That scrutiny is healthy when it coexists with accurate information. But more often it is accompanied by extensive misinformation about some groups of school-aged students and a greedy bias toward the "rights" of other groups (regardless of who these groups include). Irresolvable battles are the likely outcome, with students being the victims.

The severely handicapped have been the last to obtain the right to appropriate educational services. Most of them still have obtained little more than a legal right. At least three factors are responsible: (*a*) the lag in preparation of needed personnel, (*b*) the absence of adequate models for service provision, and (*c*) defeatist attitudes in school systems and communities toward the value of educating the severely handicapped.

Historically parents with severely handicapped children have been the primary force in the effort to obtain services for this group of citizens. However, in this and upcoming years even these hard-won rights and services are threatened by our economic difficulties. The success or failure of teachers working with severely handicapped students is likely to determine whether their educational rights will continue to be protected by law. The burden of proof rests more upon the demonstration that educational intervention leads to defensible benefits for severely handicapped students—that it is worthwhile to learn to swallow and chew, wash and bathe, greet others socially, cross the street, make a bed, communicate your basic needs, and perform a payable skill. It is the intent of this text and its contributors to describe some of what we know about successful intervention with the moderately and severely handicapped. It is your responsibility as its readers to master and apply these ideas, questioning when necessary and improving when possible. Your success is urgent.

I would like to express my sincere thanks for the constructive and detailed reviews provided by Luanna M. Voeltz and Robert York. Other helpful reviewers included Elaine Francis, David Gast, James Tawney, Gerald Mahoney, Cheryl Hansen, Nathan H. Azrin, Fred Orelove, William Heward, and Carolee Mountcastle. Acknowledgment must also be given to the many publishers and authors who have granted permission to quote their work and reprint their illustrations. This same gratefulness is extended to the parents who granted permission for photographs of their children to be printed in this text.

Contents

13

14

15

16

17

Educational services for moderately and severely handicapped people have progressed during the last decade; these services are now legally required and thus are no longer uncommon. Their quality, however, still requires careful scrutiny. Often there is great discrepancy between what we know about appropriate education and what is actually practiced. In this first chapter, Nicholas Certo will finetune your critical focus as he portrays the flaws we must correct in our efforts to provide appropriate educational programs.

As in other complex organizations, progress in school systems is tedious, since it ultimately depends on interrelated changes in human behavior. For example, eliminating the widespread practice of segregated schooling for the severely handicapped in states like Missouri can only be accomplished through the courts. While individual parents or school systems may provide powerful pro or con arguments, progress toward less restrictive services will depend on a legal mandate that school systems change their ways.

Progress is also slowed by our individual resistance to adopting new behavior, to moving away from familiar routines and taking the risk of error that comes with new behaviors. This resistance often takes the form of defensiveness about our "old ways." For example, when reading this and later chapters, you will quickly note the recurring criteria of "functionality" and "chronological-age suitability." Once these criteria are absorbed, you may find yourself bristling in reaction. Sure you put up Santas for your adolescent students around Christmas, but doesn't everyone else? You teach counting with play money or with colored pegs, but what's the harm? Rather than defensive reaction, our goal must be objective self-evaluation with the intent of professional improvement. We must not confuse our current practices with the "best practices," since the meaning of the best practices will change as our knowledge advances. Even the most skilled teachers will confess to instructional practices they now find embarrassing and indefensible.

On the other hand, since improvement does not necessarily accompany all change, you must determine which educational innovations are sound and which are merely faddish bandwagons. Thus I urge you to challenge requests for educational change with reason and data rather than personal defensiveness. Changes in educational practices affect our students much more than us, and these ultimate effects must be the yardsticks by which we measure their desirability.

Introduction to Chapter 1

1

Characteristics of Educational Services

Nicholas Certo is at the University of Maryland. This manuscript was supported in part by Grant No. G00-80-01719 to the University of Maryland, College Park, from the United States Department of Education, Special Education Programs, Division of Innovation and Development, Handicapped Children's Model Programs, Washington, D.C., and by Grant No. G00-81-01732 from the Special Education Programs' Division of Personnel Preparation. The opinions expressed herein do not necessarily reflect the position or policy of the U.S. Department of Education, and no official endorsement should be inferred.

It is heartening to note that most of the severely handicapped students in the United States are now educated in public schools. Although the transition from private schools and institutions has evolved over an extended period, Public Law (P.L.) 94-142 certainly has been a catalyst increasing the speed of this transition. Along with public education for severely handicapped students has come the Individualized Educational Program (IEP), an unprecedented tool mandated by P.L. 94-142 for managing service delivery and objectively verifying student change. Furthermore, educational services predicated on social kindness have been replaced by services based on a recognition of student rights, assured by student- and parent-oriented procedural safeguards delineated in the law. The delivery of crucial related services, such as occupational therapy, speech and language therapy, and vocational education, has been increasing through this transition.

Public education also means that severely handicapped students are to be extended the same privileges as nonhandicapped citizens, including being educated by individuals who have met state certification standards. In large part because of the astute use of federal funds by the special education programs of the United States Department of Education, many people have been encouraged to enter this field, either to take newly created university course sequences to meet state certification requirements or to conduct relevant applied research. Finally, public education for severely handicapped students has meant a public funding base and an increased ability to assure adequate basic services. This change has resulted in a significant shift in financial security over that provided by the typical sources available to private agencies, such as combinations of the United Fund, Catholic Charities, United Jewish Appeal, and a sundry assortment of bake sales; rummage sales; bird cage, pot holder, and ashtray marketing campaigns; and infrequent quasibenevolent donations.

As a result, most severely handicapped students today attend schools, though the majority are segregated for at least 5 hours a day. They are no longer transported to these settings at parent expense and sacrifice, but rather at public expense on public vehicles. The schools they attend are generally well lighted, heated, and maintained. Some of these schools have swimming pools, libraries with record players and audiovisual equipment, vocational training areas with related tools and equipment, fully equipped home economics rooms, carpeted classrooms, adapted bathrooms in each class, and even an occasional greenhouse.

In addition, rolled up, discarded pillows from home have been replaced with more appropriately designed, professionally manufactured bolsters, wedges, and mats. The number and variety of available instructional materials and equipment have gradually expanded. And severely handicapped students are receiving the benefits of these facility and service improvements within the context of low, state-controlled student-teacher ratios.

With all of this available to varying degrees around the country, it is time to ask ourselves one basic question: Why is it that, given apparently adequate levels of service, severely handicapped students still graduate at the age of 21 (or older, depending on state laws) without being able to shop, use public recreation facilities or public transportation, hold down a job, engage in sociopolitical gossip with peers, wash clothes, cook, or clean windows? Is it, as some have suggested (e.g., Burton & Hirshoren, 1979; Kauffman & Krouse, 1981), that severely handicapped students can be expected to benefit only minimally from educational services? Or are we educators failing to organize service delivery systems that maximize the probability that severely handicapped students acquire, through 21 years of public education, functional, age-appropriate skills that result in at least partial participation in integrated community and school environments (Brown, Branston, Hamre-Nietupski, Pumpian, Certo, & Gruenewald, 1979)? It is our position that severely handicapped students can acquire these functional, age-appropriate skills. And it is the purpose of this chapter to highlight some factors that may be inhibiting the delivery of effective educational services for severely handicapped students and inadvertently reducing the overall effect of 21 years of public school education to that of a richly endowed baby-sitting service.

SEGREGATED SCHOOLS

Public school education for severely handicapped students typically is provided in schools separate from those used for nonhandicapped students. Most of these are both physically and socially isolated from general elementary and secondary schools. Some have been recently built, while others are older facilities that often were unoccupied before the initiation of educational services for the severely handicapped students.

There is some variation throughout the country in the physical proximity of segregated schools for severely handicapped students to those for nonhandicapped students. Some school systems place these segregated schools on the same grounds as elementary schools. The assumption there is that the severely handicapped students gradually can feed into the elementary school. Unfortunately, this assumption usually translates into placing one or two self-contained classes, composed only of students who are inappropriately classified as severely retarded, into the adjoining elementary school without regard for the potential benefits of integrated placements for lower functioning and multiply handicapped students. To compound the problem further, in several years, when these students are too old for the elementary setting, their placement continues, since it is considered to be developmentally appropriate in spite of their chronological age.

Another variation is the establishment, through construction, renovation, or administrative reorganization, of a segregated section or wing of a school building. Although the actual physical isolation of these wings varies, the overall effect of *clustering* a large (small or moderate) number of severely handicapped students in a designated portion of a school building emphasizes the *presumed* need to keep severely handicapped and nonhandicapped students separate to provide equal education. In short, regardless of the degree of physical isolation, there is a prevailing assumption that separate education is necessary to provide equal education.

In a comprehensive analysis of the issue of segregated schooling for severely handicapped students, Gilhool and Stutman (Note 1) conclude that, from five different related perspectives, there is neither a legal nor an educational basis for maintaining segregated schools for severely handicapped students. In drawing this conclusion, the authors go well beyond the typical right-to-education cases, such as *PARC v. Commonwealth of Pennsylvania* (1972), *Mills v. D.C. Board of Education* (1972), and *Lebanks v. Spears* (1973), by delineating the constitutional basis for integration found in the 14th Amendment. From an historical perspective, they show how United States courts have systematically denied the practice of separate education on the grounds of the 14th Amendment, related to such varied issues as the right to learn German in public schools (*Meyer v. Nebraska*, 1923); the right to attend integrated graduate schools (*McLaurin v. Oklahoma Board of Regents*, 1950); the right to attend integrated professional schools (*Sweatt v. Painter*, 1950); and the right to attend integrated public elementary and secondary schools (*Brown v. Board of Education*, 1954).

Furthermore, in reviewing the findings of fact entered into the Congressional Record and the statements of the Congressional sponsors, P.L. 94-142 is based on a clear legislative intent for integrated educational services for all handicapped individuals with an opportunity for interaction with nonhandicapped peer models. Both the legislative intent of P.L. 94-142 and the integration imperative of the 14th Amendment have been subsequently upheld in litigation following the enactment of P.L. 94-142. Court cases such as *Armstrong v. Kline* (1979) and *Campbell v. Talladega County Board of Education* (1981) have forcefully required functional and integrated educational services for severely handicapped students.

As an example, in *Campbell v. Talladega County Board of Education,* Judge Vance's court decree states:

it is necessary that Joseph's new IEP provide for significantly increased contact with nonhandicapped students. One means by which this may be accomplished is to place Joseph's class into the main high school building at Munford High School or Talladega County High School. Alternatively, the school may choose to educate nonhandicapped students in the Munford Center so that the center ceases to be an isolated enclave for the handicapped. If defendants choose neither of these approaches, they bear the heavy burden of insuring that Joseph's interaction with nonhandicapped students will be substantially equal to that he would enjoy were his classroom located in the main school building. (pp. 13–14)

Certainly there is sufficient legal and practical support for integrated educational services for severely handicapped students. Why, then, are segregated schools the most common educational service "model" for severely handicapped students? Although there are many reasons for the perpetuation of this disenfranchisement of severely handicapped students, one possible explanation lies in the commonly cited assumption that these students need to be grouped together to receive appropriate educational services. This assumption has been referred to as the "logic of homogeneity" (Brown, Nietupski, & Hamre-Nietupski, 1976). It is used to justify the appropriateness of segregated schools by assuming that all students placed in these schools have similar educational *needs,* when in reality it facilitates placement decisions on the basis of similarities in student *disabilities.*

For example, in many segregated schools for severely handicapped students, those students with additional motoric disabilities are grouped together in several classrooms. Often these classes group students with total disregard for chronological age. It is not uncommon to see an 18-year-old student in a class with primarily 5- through 10-year-old class-

mates. On the other end of the activity spectrum, those students with severe behavior problems are frequently grouped in the same class or classes.

There are several possible effects of these homogeneous placements. First, they encourage educators to make programming decisions and judge student progress in reference to a peer group that in no way approximates the diversity of the culture in which those students should function. If you were to ask a teacher of all motorically involved, severely handicapped students why he or she was not attempting to teach softball to the class, the teacher would probably seriously challenge your competence. However, it is my contention that it is *not* the consideration of an adaptive version of a sport such as softball that is absurd; rather, it is the consideration of softball within the homogeneous class of motorically involved students that renders it absurd. If you were to place the same class of severely handicapped students in a general elementary school, the experience of watching six students sit passively in wheelchairs during daily recess would increase the relevance of the question. In addition, the availability of ambulatory nonhandicapped peers significantly alters grouping possibilities. Furthermore, placing students with similar problems in the same school, and then subgrouping them into classes of the physically handicapped, behavior problems, receptive signers, Blissymbol designees, and so on, simply multiplies the teachers' problems.

These schools are organized under the assumption that homogeneity produces a better learning environment. However, the difficulty of managing high frequency self-stimulatory behavior in eight students concurrently; the difficulty of positioning, lifting, carrying, and feeding six immobile students daily; or the difficulty of continuously stopping the flow of instruction to correct inappropriately signed articulation of eight other students can actually minimize the overall effectiveness of a teacher and an aide on a class. On the other hand, these classes can accelerate, to the maximum extent possible, teacher burnout.

Another implicitly and occasionally explicitly stated reason for segregated schools for severely handicapped students is the cost effectiveness of serving a low-incidence population at one school site. Although rationalizations like this appeal to the conservative, property-tax-paying constituency, they rarely hold up to careful examination. For example, it is widely assumed that severely handicapped students need architecturally barrier-free environments. As a result, it is considered logical and cost effective to pay for the renovation (or construction) of one such school within a district (Burton & Hirshoren, 1979). However, neither the logic nor cost effectiveness holds up under closer scrutiny. First of all, a large portion, possibly as high as 75% (Snell, 1982), of severely handicapped students have the necessary motor skills to negotiate obstacles generally considered to be architectural barriers; yet they are religiously placed alongside their more motorically impaired counterparts within barrier-free segregated schools. In addition, for the remaining nonambulatory students, what is the overwhelming obstacle recalcitrantly lurking within all school buildings? Although responses to that question would vary, a frequently cited example is stairs. It is interesting to note that public school systems still persist, possibly with the encouragement of some experts in the field (cf., Burton & Hirshoren, 1979), in spending money to make one or two schools barrier-free for severely handicapped students, when most public schools built in the last 25 years have only one floor. Other than the need to check the boiler, there are few, if any, occasions to negotiate steps. Certainly, someone firmly ensconced in today's economic slashings would be able to recognize that we may not need to renovate one school when so many naturally "renovated" buildings may already exist. And, from a legal perspective, as court cases such as *Lloyd v. Regional Transportation Authority* (1977), in reference to Section 504 of the Vocational Rehabilitation Act of 1973 indicate, requiring all severely handicapped students to attend school in one barrier-free building, rather than making the school system barrier-free, is unacceptable under the equal protection clause of the 14th Amendment.

A second frequently cited economic factor in serving severely handicapped students is the cost of related services, such as physical and occupational therapy. As Brown, Branston, Hamre-Nietupski, Johnson, Wilcox, and Gruenewald (1979) point out, it is assumed that placing all students who need related services in the same school increases the delivery of direct therapy by eliminating the time it would take for therapists to travel across school sites. However, as these authors also indicate, these students require 24-hour therapeutic intervention. Therefore, even if they receive 2 hours of direct therapy services a day, it is insufficient.

One way to increase therapeutic services is to train teachers, parents, and others to deliver them in consultation with a therapist (Sternat, Messina, Nietupski, Lyon, & Brown, 1977). However, simple arithmetic shows that having one full-time physical therapist available to consult for even as a few as 30 students (a luxury in most school systems) results in only approximately 1 hour of consultation per student per week. If you subtract travel time across school sites, it becomes even more disheartening. How then could it be less costly to integrate severely handicapped students throughout a school system?

One often overlooked factor is the cost of heating, lighting, and maintaining a segregated school when there are empty classrooms in the school system. For example, the Prince George's County School District in Maryland closed 31 schools in the fall of 1981 and another 10 schools in the fall of 1982. In neighboring Montgomery County, a plan of similar scope was slated for the fall of 1982. Furthermore, many of the elementary and middle schools that remain open in Prince George's County have empty classrooms. All of these schools were closed because their enrollments dwindled to a point where they no longer justified their operating costs. At a cost of up to $150,000 a year for heat, light, and maintenance alone, as cited in a recent article in the *Washington Post,* it is easy to see why these schools were closed.

Taking this situation one step further, suppose the segregated schools operated for severely handicapped students were closed, and these students were dispersed into *existing* open classes within their respective consolidated school systems. The savings in recurring heat, light, and maintenance costs could be transposed into additional therapy services without increasing overall system operating costs. If the figure of $150,000 is accurate, it could pay for at least ten more physical therapists each year. With that increase, using the same figures, every three students could have their own therapist. Obviously this analysis is not completely accurate, but it does highlight one very important point. For all the lamenting that is heard across the country in school board meetings, congressional hearings, newspaper exposés, and television documentaries about the high cost of special education, an exorbitant unnecessary amount of money is being willingly spent to maintain a segregated system for severely handicapped students based on a questionable educational and legal foundation. The remaining sections of this chapter will consider some of the educational problems inherent in the segregated school "model" being perpetrated with the severely handicapped population.

ADMINISTRATIVE CONVENIENCE

Although P.L. 94-142 requires educational decisions to be based on individual student needs, many educational decisions are unwittingly based on administrator or teacher convenience. As Gilhool and Stutman (Note 1) point out, least restrictive environment (LRE) decisions are made in reference to existing, available placement and program options within a system and not solely in reference to student needs. These decisions rarely lead to the initiation of needed new services. Instead, they perpetuate a tacit acceptance of providing services that meet only some of the needs of handicapped students. Severely handicapped students lose many things in these decisions, the most important being interactions with nonhandicapped peers.

In addition to the convenience of having available classroom space, segregated schools conveniently cluster severely handicapped students so that therapists and other specialists do not suffer the inconvenience of travelling across school sites within a system. Apparently, the inconvenience experienced by the students—who often spend up to 3 hours a day riding school buses to and from centralized segregated schools (Brown, et al., 1976b)— is considered minor compared to the therapists' inconvenience. In questioning these practices, you might be told that the inconvenience, stoically endured, builds character, and character building is a frequent IEP objective for severely handicapped students.

Other administrator and teacher convenience decisions include feeding physically handicapped students in their classrooms instead of cafeterias, since it is more convenient than taking feeding equipment to a cafeteria every day. Often it can take as long as 2 hours for a teacher and two assistants to prepare, feed, and clean up for as few as six physically involved students. In addition, the students spend most of this time waiting passively while other students are being fed. If these students were fed in a school cafeteria, there would be other peers and instructional personnel available to interact with them or assist in feeding, eliminating the long waiting periods.

Other convenience examples include the use of a single "whatever works" criterion for instruction. If a severely handicapped student responds to edible reinforcers, use them. If tokens are effective with another student, use them. If you need to teach a 16-year-old student an independent leisure skill, and he shows an interest in a toy designed for a toddler, such as a Busy Box, use it. If you need to develop work skills, and a heat sealer has been donated to your school, use it.

There are many problems with these examples. The overall issue is that they are shortsighted. They are solutions to immediate problems without regard for the students' long-term development. Edible reinforcers may be effective in controlling a student's on-task behavior, but how and when do you move on? And the real question is: *Why* should you set up instructional expectations that will require transition later if they can be avoided? You could attempt to increase a severely handicapped student's rate of stacking clean dishes at a dish-washing job training site with an artificial token reinforcement system. The question is: Why add an artificial reinforcer (that is, one that is not a natural consequence of the task)

that eventually must be eliminated when it may not be absolutely necessary? Through a careful analysis of the consequences and cues that are natural components of functional tasks (Falvey, Brown, Lyon, Baumgart, & Schroeder, 1980), you can find instructional procedures that are more situationally appropriate. In our vocational example, the racks could be stacked against a wall with a marker added for every fifth rack. After stacking five racks, the student begins another row. This procedure could eventually function as self-reinforcement for dish-washing. Although adding the *marker* to cue the student is not a completely natural consequence, it provides immediate feedback without creating dependence on instructor feedback. In addition, it is closer to other workers' behavior, since workers in these situations usually use some similar cue to pace their work.

In our leisure example, preschool toys are frequently used not only because teachers consider them developmentally appropriate (a point that will be discussed later), but also because they are *available*. If the teacher attempted to order leisure materials that might be more appropriate for a 16-year-old, there would be few items to choose from in a typical educational catalogue. But the simple substitution of a Sears catalogue could greatly enhance the age-appropriate leisure options available to the teacher. And the acquisition of age-appropriate leisure skills by severely handicapped students can significantly increase their opportunities to interact with nonhandicapped peers. As a result, severely handicapped individuals might be prepared to interact with people other than infants, toddlers, and preschool teachers.

Finally, on occasion, instruction is not conducted because it is inconvenient. For example, a group of severely handicapped students are being taught to buy one drug-store item that their families need on a weekly basis. The teacher will need to send weekly reminders to parents to determine the item they want purchased and secure the money. Clearly, the teacher must be highly organized and persistent. It is much simpler—that is, more convenient—to simulate purchasing at school and hope for community performance. Unfortunately, the "train and hope" method of generalization facilitation rarely works (Stokes & Baer, 1977).

PROGRAMMED DEPENDENCE

One common sight in a self-contained class or segregated school is instructional personnel helping severely handicapped students. They are regularly helped off and on buses, carrying trays to tables in cafeterias, taking their coats off in the morning, and in a variety of other situations. In addition, when students do not comply with a teacher's request to sit, line up, go to a specified area of the room, or walk (not run) at a mall, they are helped to perform these responses. Although in these situations the students unquestionably may need help, it becomes a problem when the assistance is always provided and independent responding is not an instructional target. It is not unusual to observe students who are physically capable of at least *partially participating* (Brown, Branston, Baumgart, Vincent, Falvey, & Schroeder, 1979) automatically receiving complete assistance. Often this assistance occurs at instructional transition points such as when students are getting ready to board a school bus. In these situations, given difficult logistical demands and tight time constraints, even the most dedicated teacher will probably provide some help rather than wait for independent performance. And providing extra training for incorrect student responses is even more difficult to consider.

Frequently, these problem times are neither identified nor made targets for instruction. If we would recognize that we may inadvertently teach severely handicapped students to wait for our assistance, it might give us some incentive to reorganize instructional scheduling. More time could be set aside for these situations so that instructional personnel would be able to correct student performance. If it is important for severely handicapped students to put on their coats independently before they leave school at 3:00, then starting dressing at 2:50 is a questionable practice.

A component of this problem is that many severely handicapped students need assistance because they have not learned the basic responses required for routine tasks—opening a milk carton at lunch, hanging coats on arrival, or independently boarding a school bus. Even under legitimate circumstances, severely handicapped students should at least be taught to request assistance. These requests, of course, could fill two purposes—decreasing passive dependence while increasing student interactions (Certo & Kohl, in press). Further dependence is created by selecting instructional materials or arranging tasks that automatically lead to correction (Halle, Baer, & Spradlin, 1981). For example, if you want students to learn to put lunch items on a cafeteria tray, and the items are organized so that the plates are last, there is a good chance that the students will need help, since there probably will be no room for the plate.

Finally, we program for dependence by systematically avoiding instruction in areas we assume to be dangerous. Sometimes severely handicapped students are not taught to cook, cross streets, or play with leisure materials they could swallow because of potential injury. But avoiding instruction in these areas in order to avoid injury will never lead to the development of instructional procedures that maximize independence and minimize injury.

STUDENT DEFICITS

Another issue is the criteria used to select instructional objectives. Students with motor problems generally have IEP objectives that focus on equilibrium and righting reactions, improved head control, grasping, and wheelchair transferring. Nonverbal students have IEP objectives slanted toward developing formal communication skills and building the motor and cognitive prerequisites of those skills. Students with added sensory losses have IEPs oriented toward using alternate senses or increasing the functional use of residual vision or hearing. In short, instructional objectives are often selected primarily in reference to the student's obvious handicapping conditions.

It is interesting to note what may not be selected for instruction when such a single criterion is used. Severely handicapped students may not learn to cook, clean, do laundry, make purchases at stores, eat at restaurants, cross streets, go to recreation centers, ride buses to work, or play Pac Man at a convenience store. Of course, as mentioned earlier, selecting an electronic game for instruction probably would be considered unimportant in reference to the student's problems in head control, grasping, and righting. In addition, it might be considered unethical to spend the student's time or tax dollars so frivolously when the chance of correctly operating an electronic game may be minimal.

However, if you forget about the rules of an electronic game and view it as a machine that provides reliable, immediate visual and auditory feedback following a variety of responses (many of which my colleagues and I have found to be well within the range of motion of many physically involved students with proper positioning or simple adaptive devices), it becomes similar to using a microswitch to turn on a record player in the classroom. Yet manipulating the electronic game has many distinct advantages over operating a record player in the classroom. Electronic games naturally require the repeated performance of motor responses. Performing those motor responses when operating the game in the community may be more intrinsically reinforcing than swiping at a microswitch manipulandum that turns on a *Sesame Street* record—especially when the record player is arbitrarily turned off every 2 minutes by the teacher in order to require repeated motor responses artificially. Furthermore, operating an electronic game makes the student engage actively in a normalized leisure skill in settings with nonhandicapped peers and adults, which can lead to many unanticipated interactions.

We need to judge instructional objectives against the performance of nonhandicapped individuals engaged in functional skills in natural settings (Brown, et al., 1979c). Only when we begin to recognize the importance of normalized performance standards will we be forced to confront the discrepancies between the repertoires of severely handicapped and nonhandicapped individuals. Confronting these discrepancies can lead to instructional solutions. Solving these problems not only can lead to improved head control, but more importantly can assure the acquisition of functional, age-appropriate, community-referenced skills.

Many individuals who have tried to ignore student handicapping conditions have been successful in teaching many difficult, critical, normalized skills. Schleien, Kiernan, and Wehman (1981) taught a severe motorically involved student the leisure skill of using a Polaroid camera by adapting the camera's shutter button and modifying the typical method of focusing. Schleien, Wehman, and Kiernan (1981) taught severely handicapped adults (one with severe spasticity) to play darts as a leisure skill by adapting the board height and throwing distance during training. Learning this skill let these adults participate in dart games at local bars, giving them access to typical adult leisure environments. Nietupski, Certo, Pumpian, and Belmore (Note 2) taught severely handicapped students to buy groceries in supermarkets by using a picture shopping card that eliminated the need to read labels and automatically calculated money. Other researchers have taught severely handicapped students to shop in supermarkets using pocket calculators (Wheeler, Ford, Nietupski, Loomis, & Brown, 1980). A variety of creative procedures and adaptive devices have been used to teach bus riding to severely handicapped students (Certo, Schwartz, & Brown, 1977; Coon, Vogelsberg, & Williams, 1981; Neef, Iwata, & Page, 1978; Sowers, Rusch, & Hudson, 1979). Vending machine (Sweet, Shiraga, Ford, Pumpian, & Brown, Note 3) and restaurant skills (Marholin, O'Toole, Touchette, Berger, & Doyle, 1979; van den Pol, Iwata, Ivancic, Page, Neef, & Whitley, 1981; Christopher, Nietupski, & Pumpian, Note 4) also have been taught by simplifying task requirements. Finally, Schleien, Muccino, and Certo (Note 5) taught a severely handicapped adolescent to bowl, order a drink, and use a vending machine at a bowling alley by substituting picture cards for verbal responses and using predetermined amounts of money.

We cannot stress enough that we must make full use of the educational opportunities created by P.L. 94–142 for severely handicapped students. To do this we must discipline ourselves to look at a physically handicapped student not as someone who can not *move*, but as someone who must *learn* to shop; we must look at a nonverbal student not as someone who can not interact, but as someone who must learn to engage in interactive leisure skills with nonhandicapped peers. We must exercise caution in selecting these skills for instruction, to avoid committing the single criterion error by using nonhandicapped performance as our sole reference point. Certainly other factors need to be considered. Ford, Brown, Pumpian, Baumgart, Nisbet, Schroeder, and Loomis (in press) list 19 criteria for leisure-skill selection that are applicable to most functional skill domains. However, we must not avoid selecting age-appropriate skill objectives because of the cognitive, physical, or sensory disabilities of our students. It is our responsibility, as educators, to compensate creatively for any interference presented by their disabilities.

SKILL APPROXIMATIONS

Shaping, the technique of teaching successive approximations of a terminal skill (cf., Skinner, 1953), is a widely accepted instructional strategy for severely handicapped students. Observations of severely handicapped students probably would show that approximations pervade most skill domains. Students acquiring manual signing skills typically form signs with wide variations. In the self-help area, many different approximations of hand washing can be observed. Other students assemble packages of utensils or toys or drive screws into blocks of wood to approximate work skills. Skill approximations are justified by assuming that simpler versions must be acquired before more complex, terminal skills. But it is curious that while many skill approximations are observed in segregated schools, few final skills are seen. Often skills remain approximations. There are two issues here, both of which interact with previously raised points. One involves an open acceptance of performance standards that are lower than the minimal standards for nonhandicapped individuals. The other involves an assumption that a simulated version of a skill is both necessary and sufficient for skill acquisition.

Regarding the issue of lower standards, inconsistent approximate responses are accepted for a variety of well-intended reasons that are not easily open to empirical verification. For example, it is assumed that a particular student does not have sufficient motor control to articulate the sign for "play" precisely. As a result, five distinctly different approximations of this sign are accepted for this student. Another explanation, commonly cited in reference to the inconsistent performance of students with physical impairments, is that a student is not feeling well on a particular day or exhibits muscle fatigue, which is impairing typical movements.

Certainly, there is some validity to these explanations. However, we do a disservice to our students to accept an approximate performance when the accepted response is only understandable to a small, select number of people. Skills that are not complete or understandable, that require additional assistance for completion, or that require constant attention to avoid problems should not be accepted. If approximations are necessary, then transition points leading to the terminal skill should be determined in advance and implemented when indicated by data. If a teacher is continuously correcting what amounts to an approximation of a skill, then instruction should be assumed to be ineffective and should be modified. The problem is compounded further when these approximate skills are not targets for systematic instruction and simply receive intermittent feedback from instructional personnel.

Regarding the simulation issue, approximations of many community skills are taught in school settings. For example, against all odds many severely handicapped students have learned how to buy toys and trinkets valued between 1¢ and 10¢ in cardboard stores located in public school classrooms (Certo & Swetlik, Note 6). Other severely handicapped students have had the distinct privilege of riding cardboard replicas of public buses in public school cafeterias (Certo, Schwartz, & Brown, 1977). The assumption is that the simulated skill will generalize to the target community setting. Unfortunately, there have been very few studies that demonstrate that effect (Stokes & Baer, 1977). Although early work (Neef et al., 1978; Page, Iwata, & Neef, 1976) showed that simulation could result in transfer to community settings for skills such as street crossing and bus riding, later work by van den Pol et al. (1981) and Coon et al. (1981) indicates that extensive exposure in community settings may be necessary for simulation to have any effect. Another qualification is that the skills targeted for instruction in these studies generally were simplified versions of community skills. For example, in Neef et al. (1978), students learned to travel to only one destination along one bus route. Teaching severely handicapped students more comprehensive functional bus riding skills that will relate to their complete travel needs may make simulation impractical.

As the complexity of the skill increases (e.g., going to five places along eight bus routes and transferring) or the complexity of the community environment increases (e.g., supermarket, shopping mall), the discrepancies between the simulated skill and the final community skill widen. Obviously, purchasing a toy car for 8¢ cents at school is very different from buying as few as four grocery items at a supermarket. Even learning how to find the same four grocery items on four different shelves in a classroom with other distracting items present is very different from attempting to find the Campbell's tomato soup, among all the other Campbell's soups, among all the other soups, among all the other canned goods, among all the other rows, across stores from different supermarket chains. It is not that simulated training is totally ineffective, but with such highly discrepant settings, extensive community training may be the only way to produce useful skills. This need certainly was found by Coon et al. (1981) with only a simplified version of bus riding, in an attempt to replicate Neef et al. (1978).

From a slightly different point of view, it is critical to teach skills in community settings for two additional reasons. First, critical component skills will not be ignored. For example, with severely handicapped students in public school classrooms, my colleagues and I used a simulated cleaning task to teach them to move all desks, chairs, and tables to one side of the room before sweeping the floor. When these students were finally placed in an actual custodial position during on-the-job training, we discovered that the custodians did not have the luxury of moving furniture before sweeping. Given the fact that each custodian had more desks in his or her first five classrooms than we had in our entire segregated school, the need for a shortcut was apparent. Therefore, the skill that we taught was nonfunctional in the community environment. Furthermore, even if we had been astute enough to observe the custodians and incorporate the actual sweeping responses in our simulated training, it is questionable whether we could ever simulate the qualitative aspects of the skill, such as the rate and duration of sweeping, under the actual job conditions. Responding inappropriately to these qualities sometimes can lead to failure more quickly than any other job-related factors. If the only way to build these qualitative dimensions is through community training, simulation, regardless of its value, postpones the real training.

Severely handicapped students often behave inappropriately in community settings. For anyone who has attempted community-based instruction with severely handicapped students, behaviors such as attempting to grab food from a passing waiter's tray, screaming in an echo-prone enclosed mall, knocking over a candy display, engaging in a tantrum in the middle of a department store, or urinating with excitement in a drugstore checkout lane should sound familiar. It is extremely important to expose severely handicapped students to community settings systematically, beginning when they enter the school system, not only to teach functional age-appropriate skills in natural environments, but to build appropriate community-referenced social behavior. Only when we are forced to confront these problem behaviors in a community environment will we have the incentive to develop management solutions. Unfortunately, many severely handicapped adolescents currently are excluded from community-based instruction because they are difficult to control in nonschool settings. Our exclusionary practices do little to change the predictable course of 21 years of segregated public school education, namely custodial care in postschool years to compensate for independent community living skills that were never acquired.

NONRECURRING FIELD TRIPS

The primary technique used to provide community-based instruction for severely handicapped students is infrequently scheduled, generally nonrepeated, large group bus excursions at nonpeak times to community settings of questionable value, such as the Ice Follies, circuses, fire stations, Special Olympic events, and bowling alleys. Systematic daily or weekly direct instruction in community settings such as restaurants and supermarkets that continues until some predetermined criterion is reached is rarely used by public school systems in educating severely handicapped students. Given the well-documented problems in generalization and the growing number of demonstrations of community skills, either acquired directly or verified in community settings, it is hard to understand why systematic community-based instruction is so rarely found.

There are many possible explanations for this disheartening situation. One possibility is a traditional view that education is a school-based event. This assumption, of course, is at variance with the individual educational needs of severely handicapped students, who require a gradual increase of community-based training and decrease in school-based training over their school years (Brown et al., 1979a). Another possible inhibiting factor is the fear that the students will be injured if they are brought to the dangerous, hostile settings that lie beyond the protective shield of segregated schools. This view often is espoused by both parents and administrators. It is unfortunate that by organizing protective segregated environments for severely handicapped students, we systematically *deny* their parents the experiences our parents encountered when we were gradually exposed by the school system to more and more "dangers" in moving from elementary to secondary schools and on. It is understandable that a parent (or administrator) should react negatively to the idea of community-based instruction, when for the first time their child is 18 years old and the school system is finally beginning to think about vocational training. Generally this decision is compounded by the fact that the student has learned so few skills that are functional in community settings that the parent's fears are real. However, it would seem that the logical solution would be to teach functional skills in community settings systematically well before the age of 18.

A third possible factor involves cost. Daily or weekly trips to community settings require transportation, usually in school buses. The thought of increasing transportation costs seems unthinkable in today's economy. However, the cost of transporting severely handicapped students long distances to one centrally located segregated school site, when those same buses pass schools with unused classrooms in students' neighborhoods, is apparently not considered unreasonable by the majority of public schools in the country. The savings that would result from closing segregated schools—both in terms of daily transportation and maintenance costs—easily could provide the funds necessary for extensive, long-term community-based instruction. However, it is unnecessary to wait for segregated schools to close before initiating community-based instruction.

Using school bus transportation to and from community training sites is a single solution approach to this problem. It is *convenient* to use these buses, but not necessarily economically efficient or instructionally beneficial. From an instructional point of view, to maximize interactions with nonhandicapped individuals and best use limited instructional time, small numbers of students should be trained at any one time in a community setting. To make maximum use of yellow school buses, the buses should be filled. If viewed this way, the instructional needs of the students and the cost-effective use of school buses are incompatible. From a strictly economic point of view, there are many available alternative modes of transportation. Generally, these forms of transportation are not used because they are inconvenient to arrange, may require frequent monitoring to assure availability, or raise the specter of potential liability problems. For example, some schools for severely handicapped students are within walking distance of stores and services, yet fear of street-crossing injuries keeps educators from using this option. Other schools have easy access to public buses or subways. In addition, students can receive reduced public transportation rates in many cities. Certainly, the cost of eight roundtrip public bus rides at a rate of $1.20 for a 15-mile roundtrip is lower than spending approximately $40 to use a school bus for the same distance. In addition, depending on the distance, taxi cabs generally are less expensive than school buses. If you are able to supplement the use of one taxi with a parent who is willing to drive, you can easily accommodate a class of severely handicapped students. Although it is difficult to find a large number of parents available, finding only one per week would add great flexibility to a school's transportation options, without requiring parents to subsidize a service that should be provided by the school system. Teachers could be reimbursed for using their own cars and for securing additional liability insurance available through unions or professional organizations. Finally, if a relationship can be established with a local state university, fleet cars or vans can be used for transportation. The state vehicle option is particularly appealing, since most state vehicles have liability coverage that is at least equal to public school coverage. Finally, you should *not* necessarily assume that every student who uses a wheelchair will need to be transported in a bus with a lift. In consulting with parents of these students, we often find that they are transported in car seats or collapsed travel chairs. These options are not too difficult to use with smaller severely handicapped students, but larger students are more difficult to lift or transfer. However, confronting the problem of alternatives to lift buses is the only way to develop alternatives. If even one severely handicapped student learns to transfer from a wheelchair to a car seat, the new mobility options that become available to that student are worth the effort. Therefore, the potential benefits of using multiple solutions to the problem of providing community-based instruction for severely handicapped students far outweigh the administrative inconvenience.

SEGREGATED SCHOOL SKILLS

It is well-established that environment has a controlling effect on behavior (Skinner, 1954). This principle forms the foundation of the instructional methodology used with most severely handicapped students. However, an issue that receives less attention is the environmental influence of teacher behavior, especially in terms of skills selected for instruction. Some segregated school-based skills are functional across other school and nonschool settings, while others are functional only in segregated settings. Examples of skills or instructional arrangements that are often found in segregated schools but are only infrequently encountered in nonsegregated settings include going to the bathroom in a potty chair in a corner of a classroom, brushing teeth at a utility sink in class, loading a cart with lunch food and utensils to prepare to eat in class, waiting in a separate classroom ("busroom") to be taken to a school bus in a group, sending lunch money in advance to the cafeteria so students do not

need to "worry" about paying the cashier, teaching several students to use the same nonportable communication board stationed in the classroom, teaching language content that relates primarily to school events, and teaching severely handicapped students to use leisure equipment or materials not found in their homes. We must be very careful as educators to avoid selecting skills or adding response requirements or materials that are functional only in segregated settings. If we do not scrutinize tasks from this perspective, we may not adequately prepare our students to function in later nonsegregated environments.

Another aspect of this issue involves qualitative response characteristics. Often, for even those skills that could be functional in integrated settings, the criterion levels of performance accepted in segregated schools render the skill nonfunctional. Some examples have been discussed earlier as they relate to simulation. Examples highlighting this kind of discrepancy include requesting food items in a cafeteria with signs, when in community restaurants or integrated schools no one will understand signs; teaching severely handicapped students to balance on a slowly moving merry-go-round, when nonhandicapped peers will spin it faster, requiring a totally different position to maintain balance; discriminating Crest toothpaste from Post Raisin Bran, when in a supermarket you will need to discriminate Crest Mint from Crest Gel; and allowing students to buy candy for 1¢ or a 6-pack of soda for $1.00 at school, assuming that exchanging money is more important than the amount exchanged. If severely handicapped students were educated in integrated school and community environments, the discrepancies between populations would be more noticeable and the selection of such nonfunctional skills or response characteristics could be more easily controlled.

DEVELOPMENTAL ZEITGEIST

A predominant view in the field is that severely handicapped students are very slowly developing people who, regardless of their chronological age, need to replicate the growth patterns of nonhandicapped individuals. As Brown et al. (1979c) point out, not only does this assumption lack empirical documentation, but it encourages such inappropriate and nonfunctional activities as having 18-year-old severely handicapped students manipulate Busy Boxes or place toy trucks under, on top of, and in small plastic tubs. Developmental approaches to instruction lead to the selection of isolated instructional objectives, like grasping, taken from a domain organized around motor development. Traditional developmental domains compartmentalize the student. They reference skills against the presumed total physiological and psychological makeup of an individual. They do not reference skills against normalized requirements for functioning in integrated environments. As a result, grasping is selected for instruction without regard for the functional context in which it is performed or its relationship to the repertoires of nonhandicapped individuals of the same chronological age.

It may be simpler and less stressful for a teacher to select skills from developmental domains, since these skills are substantiated by normative data, validated with nonhandicapped individuals. It may be more difficult and more stressful to accurately predict the skills a severely handicapped student needs to function in the environments he or she encounters, and even more difficult to predict the subsequent environments and related skills the student will need in the future. In summary, using a developmental approach with severely handicapped students inevitably means that instruction will focus on acquiring the skills demonstrated by nonhandicapped children ranging from birth to approximately 4 years old. As severely handicapped students become older, this approach simply *increases* rather than decreases the developmental discrepancies between severely handicapped and nonhandicapped people. In addition, focusing on replicating the behavior of infants and toddlers does not provide the incentive to develop methods to teach students to participate at least partially (Brown et al., 1979a) in performing age-appropriate and functional skills in natural environments. Rather, it justifies 21 years of extensive training focusing exclusively on presumed prerequisite skills, regardless of their functional use. This feeds into the skill approximation problem cited earlier.

PRESCHOOL MODEL

An issue closely aligned to the developmental dominance in the field is the use of the preschool classroom model beyond the preschool years. Regardless of chronological age, many classes for severely handicapped students have, for example, morning "opening" where students are introduced to each other daily and teachers dress felt school children on felt boards according to the weather; daily snacks, regardless of weight problems; afternoon naps; seasonal or holiday bulletin boards with related craft activities; designated "play" areas where students spend copious free time engaging in a variety of non-functional leisure activities such as mouthing toys, lying on the floor, and engaging in self-stimulation; large group story times; and twice weekly gatherings where two classes of severely handicapped students are brought together to bang, shake, or drop musical instruments, whether they are physically capable or not, in cadence to archaic French folk songs. With so many complex community-referenced skills needing to be acquired, and so few daily direct instructional hours to use, it is difficult to understand how so much time can be spent regularly engaging in even some of these activities beyond a student's preschool years.

INTERPERSONAL INTERACTIONS

Severely handicapped student interactions are generally confined to exchanges with teachers during instruction or with parents at home. These task-related interactions simply meet the response requirements for a particular skill being taught. They are not necessarily selected to increase the student's total interaction skill repertoire. In addition, the restricted focus ignores interactions with context-appropriate individuals, such as clerks, when performing functional skills in natural community environments.

Certo and Kohl (in press) speculate that several factors contribute to a lack of emphasis on teaching interpersonal interactions to severely handicapped students. First, interactions are generally considered to consist of conversations. Since most severely handicapped students are nonverbal or have limited verbal skills, conversational exchange, even with acquisition of formal nonverbal communication skills, is difficult. Second, interactions are equated with *social skills,* while *task-related* exchanges when performing functional skills with other people are equally important. As a result, most interactions selected for instruction focus on things such as moving from isolative to cooperative play. This emphasis, of course, is reinforced by a developmental view of instruction. Third, instruction often is organized to minimize exchanges, especially with peers. Finally, interactions, when consciously selected for instruction, are usually chosen as the vehicles to expand formal communication skills, rather than being selected because of their functional value in the community.

Certo and Kohl (in press) have developed a category system, designated the *Interpersonal Interaction Hierarchy,* to help teachers determine the interaction instructional content that relates to the performance of skills in various school and community environments. This hierarchy is broken into *(a)* mandatory task-related interactions, *(b)* contextual social interactions, *(c)* optional task-related interactions, and *(d)* optional social interactions. Mandatory task-related interactions are those exchanges with others that must occur in order to complete a task—handing money to a cashier at a supermarket in response to a request to pay. Contextual social interactions are exchanges that occur during or following a mandatory task-related interaction. An example would be acknowledging a cashier in a supermarket after receiving your change. Optional task-related interactions are exchanges involved in a task that do not need to be performed to complete the minimum requirements of the task. Buying an item from a delicatessen counter at a supermarket would be an example. Finally, optional social interactions are exchanges that can occur either following an optional task-related exchange or independent of other exchanges. An example of the former would be thanking the clerk for the delicatessen item; the latter might be picking up a grocery item dropped by another customer.

By using this simple, four-category system to analyze the responses that must or can occur between people while performing age-appropriate skills, you can determine the content for functional interaction instruction. Teaching severely handicapped students to perform even simple interaction responses with nonhandicapped peers and adults in community and school settings can enable them to become active participants in their environments, reducing their passive dependence.

EDUCATIONAL SERVICES: MINIMUM CRITERIA

There are many factors that affect educational services for severely handicapped students. Some of those that can impair the overall effect have already been discussed. Regardless of the extent to which these characteristics exist in a public school system, their negative impact on the acquisition of functional skills can only be minimized by careful monitoring and adhering to a set of standards upon which services are predicated. Certainly, future discoveries and unanticipated needs of your students will lead to new expectations and criteria that go beyond the minimum standards listed here. At this point the criteria listed below, developed from a variety of sources (Brown et al., 1979a, 1979b, 1979c; Brown et al., 1976; Certo, Brown, Belmore, & Crowner, 1977; Certo & Kohl, in press; Sontag, Certo, & Button, 1979), should be given serious consideration.

1. Severely handicapped students should be educated in self-contained classes within general elementary and secondary schools, with accompanying planned systematic contact with nonhandicapped peers.
2. The educational convenience of students should be given priority over administrative inconvenience in service system decisions.
3. Instruction should be organized to program consciously for independence.
4. IEPs should be jointly developed by parents and educators to reflect the needs of students to function in a variety of current and subsequent integrated school and community environments.
5. Instructional content should be referenced against functional, age-appropriate skills required for performance in integrated environments selected from at least the following domains: domestic living, vocational, stores/services, transportation/mobility, and leisure.
6. Regardless of presumed physical, sensory, or cognitive deficits, students should be taught, through skill adaptations when necessary, to participate at least partially in integrated environments.
7. Interpersonal interaction instruction should assure that students interact realistically with other individuals in integrated settings.
8. Community-related functional skills should be systematically trained in community environments, with the amount of training time increasing with chronological age.

The purpose of this chapter has been to highlight some of the factors that may be impeding the overall effectiveness of public school education for severely handicapped students. Subsequent chapters will amplify these eight criteria, in addition to providing relevant information in other important areas. In conclusion, when questioning an employee of a local restaurant regarding his interest in working with severely handicapped students, a colleague recorded the following statement: "I don't mind. I work at IHP (i.e., International House of Pancakes) with a Mongoloid guy and another guy who had some sort of problems mentally and looked kind of different, and *they* helped train *me*." Through the implementation of the ideas in this and later chapters, not only will the impact of 21 years of public school education for severely handicapped students be enhanced, but we hope statements like this will become commonplace.

REFERENCES

Armstrong v. Kline, 476 F. Supp. 583 (E.D. Pa. 1979), Aff'd CA 78-0172 (3rd cir. July 15, 1980).

Brown, L., Branston, M.B., Baumgart, D., Vincent, L., Falvey, M., & Schroeder, J. Utilizing the characteristics of a variety of current and subsequent least restrictive environments as factors in the development of curricular content for severely handicapped students. *AAESPH Review,* 1979, *4,* 407–424. (a)

Brown, L., Branston, M., Hamre-Nietupski, S., Johnson, F., Wilcox, B., & Gruenewald, L. A rationale for comprehensive longitudinal interactions between severely handicapped students and other nonhandicapped and other citizens. *AAESPH Review,* 1979, *4,* 3–14. (b)

Brown, L., Branston, M., Hamre-Nietupski, S., Pumpian, I., Certo, N., & Gruenewald, L. A strategy for developing chronological age appropriate and functional curriculum content for severely handicapped adolescents and young adults. *Journal of Special Education*, 1979, *13*, 81–90. (c)

Brown, L., Nietupski, J., & Hamre-Nietupski, S. The criterion of ultimate functioning and public school services for severely handicapped students. In *Hey don't forget about me: Education's investment in the severely, profoundly and multiply handicapped.* Reston, Va: Council for Exceptional Children, 1976.

Brown v. Board of Education, 347 U.S.483 (1954).

Burton, T.A., & Hirshoren, A. The education of severely and profoundly retarded children: Are we sacrificing the child for the concept? *Exceptional Children*, 1979, *45*(8), 598–602.

Campbell v. Talladega County Board of Education, U.S. Dist. Ct., March 31, 1981.

Certo, N., Brown, L., Belmore, K., & Crowner, T. A review of secondary level educational service delivery models for severely handicapped students in the Madison Public Schools. In E. Sontag, J. Smith, & N. Certo (Eds.), *Educational programming for the severely and profoundly handicapped.* Reston, Va: Council for Exceptional Children, 1977.

Certo, N., & Kohl, F. Strategies for developing interpersonal interaction instructional content for severely handicapped students. In N. Certo, N. Haring, & R. York (Eds.), *Public school integration of severely handicapped students: Rationale, issues, and progressive alternatives.* Baltimore: Paul H. Brookes, in press.

Certo, N., Schwartz, R., & Brown, L. Community transportation: Teaching severely handicapped students to ride a public bus system. In N.G. Haring & L.J. Brown (Eds.), *Teaching the severely handicapped* (Vol. II). New York: Grune & Stratton, 1977.

Coon, M.E., Vogelsberg, R.T., & Williams, W. Effects of classroom public transportation instruction on generalization to the natural environment. *Journal of the Association for the Severely Handicapped*, 1981, *6*, 46–53.

Falvey, M., Brown, L., Lyon, S., Baumgart, D., & Schroeder, J. Strategies for using cues and correction procedures. In W. Sailor, B. Wilcox, & L. Brown (Eds.), *Methods of instruction for severely handicapped students.* Baltimore: Paul H. Brookes, 1980.

Ford, A., Brown, L., Pumpian, I., Baumgart, D., Nisbet, J., Schroeder, J., & Loomis, R. Strategies for developing individualized recreation/leisure plans for adolescent and young adult severely handicapped students. In N. Certo, N. Haring, & R. York (Eds.), *Public school integration of the severely handicapped: Rationale, issues, and progressive alternatives.* Baltimore: Paul H. Brookes, in press.

Halle, J.W., Baer, D.M., & Spradlin, J.E. Teacher's generalized use of delay as a stimulus control procedure to increase language use in handicapped children, *Journal of Applied Behavioral Analysis*, 1981, *14*(4), 389–409.

Kauffman, J.M., & Krouse, J. The cult of educability: Searching for the substance of things hoped for; the evidence of things not seen. *Analysis and Intervention in Developmental Disabilities.* 1981, *1*(1), 53–60.

Lebanks v. Spears, 60 F.R.D. 135 (E.D. La. 1973).

Lloyd v. Regional Transportation Authority, 548F. 2d 1277, 1280–84 (F. cir. 1977).

Marholin, D., II, O'Toole, K.M., Touchette, P.E., Berger, P.L., & Doyle, D.A. "I'll have a Big Mac, large fries, large coke, and apple pie" . . . or teaching adaptive community skills. *Behavior Therapy*, 1979, *10*, 236–248.

McLaurin v. Oklahoma Board of Regents, 399 U.S. 637, 641–642 (1950).

Meyer v. Nebraska, 262 U.S. 390, 399–401 (1923).

Mills v. D.C. Board of Education, 348 F. Supp. 866 (D.D.C. 1972).

Neef, N.A., Iwata, B.A., & Page, T.J. Public transportation training in vivo versus classroom instruction. *Journal of Applied Behavior Analysis*, 1978, *11*, 331–344.

Page, T., Iwata, B., & Neef, N. Teaching pedestrian skills to retarded persons: Generalization from the classroom to the natural environments. *Journal of Applied Behavior Analysis*, 1976, *9*, 433–444.

PARC v. Commonwealth of Pennsylvania, 343 F. Supp. 279 (E.D. Pa. 1972).

Schleien, S.J., Kiernan, J., & Wehman, P. An age-appropriate leisure skills program for moderately retarded adults. *Education and Training of the Mentally Retarded*, 1981, *16*, 13–19.

Schleien, S.J., Wehman, P. & Kiernan, J. Teaching leisure skills to severely handicapped adults: An age-appropriate darts game. *Journal of Applied Behavior Analysis*, 1981, *14*, 513–519.

Skinner, B.F. *Science and human behavior.* New York: Macmillan, 1953.

Snell, M.E. Characteristics of the profoundly mentally retarded. In P.T. Cegelka & H.J. Prehm (Eds.), *Mental retardation: From categories to people.* Columbus, Ohio: Charles E. Merrill, 1982.

Sontag, E., Certo, N., & Button, J.E. On a distinction between the education of the severely and profoundly handicapped and a doctrine of limitations. *Exceptional Children*, 1979, *45*(8), 604–616.

Sowers, J., Rusch, F.R., & Hudson, D. Training a severely retarded young adult to ride the city bus to and from work. *AAESPH Review*, 1979, *4*(1), 15–23.

Sternat, J., Messina, R., Nietupski, J., Lyon, S., & Brown, L. Occupational and physical therapy services for severely handicapped students: Toward a naturalized public school service delivery model. In E. Sontag, J. Smith, & N. Certo (Eds.), *Educational programming for the severely and profoundly handicapped.* Reston, Va.: Council for Exceptional Children, 1977.

Stokes, T.F., & Baer, D.M. An implicit technology of generalization. *Journal of Applied Behavior Analysis*, 1977, *10*, 349–367.

Sweatt v. Painter, 339 U.S. 629, 634 (1950).

van den Pol, R.A., Iwata, B.A., Ivancic, M.T., Page, T.J., Neef, N.A., & Whitley, F.P. Teaching the handicapped to eat in public places: Acquisition, generalization and maintenance of restaurant skills. *Journal of Applied Behavior Analysis*, 1981, *14*(1), 61–69.

Wheeler, J., Ford, A., Nietupski, J., Loomis, R., & Brown, L. Teaching adolescent moderately/severely handicapped students to shop in supermarkets using pocket calculators. *Education and Training of the Mentally Retarded,* 1980, *15,* 105–112.

REFERENCE NOTES

1. Gilhool, T.K., & Stutman, E.A. Integrating severely handicapped students: Toward criteria for implementing and enforcing the integrative imperative of P.L. 94-142 and Section 504. In *Developing criteria for the evaluation of the least restrictive environment provision.* Washington, D.C.: United States Office of Education, Bureau of Education for the Handicapped, Division of Innovation and Development, State Program Studies Branch, 1978.

2. Nietupski, R., Certo, N., Pumpian, I., & Belmore, K. Supermarket shopping: Teaching severely handicapped students to generate shopping lists and make purchases functionally linked with meal preparation. In L. Brown, N. Certo, K. Belmore, & T. Crowner (Eds.), *Madison's alternative for zero exclusion: Papers and programs related to public school services for secondary age severely handicapped students* (Vol. VI, Part 1). Madison, Wisc.: Madison Metropolitan School District, 1976.

3. Sweet, M., Shiraga, B., Ford, A., Pumpian, I., & Brown, L. Curricular strategies to teach severely handicapped adolescent and young adult students to perform chronological age appropriate and functional vending machine use skills in instructional and natural environments. In L. Brown, M. Falvey, D. Baumgart, I. Pumpian, J. Schroeder, & L. Gruenewald (Eds.), *Strategies for teaching chronological age-appropriate functional skills to adolescent and young adult severely handicapped students* (Vol. IX, Part 1). Madison, Wisc.: Madison Metropolitan School District, 1979.

4. Christopher, D., Nietupski, J., & Pumpian, I. Teaching severely handicapped adolescents and young adults to use communication cards to make purchases at a fast food counter. In L. Brown, M. Falvey, D. Baumgart, I. Pumpian, J. Schroeder, & L. Gruenewald (Eds.), *Strategies for teaching chronological age-appropriate functional skills to adolescent and young adult severely handicapped students* (Vol. IX, Part 1). Madison, Wisc.: Madison Metropolitan School District, 1979.

5. Schleien, S., Muccino, A., & Certo, N. Teaching a severely handicapped adolescent to functionally use a bowling alley. In F. Kohl, N. Certo, & L. Moses (Eds.), *Teaching interpersonal interactions to severely handicapped students: Conceptual issues and educational programs.* College Park: University of Maryland, Department of Special Education, 1982.

6. Certo, N., & Swetlik, B. Making purchases: A functional money use program for severely handicapped students. In L. Brown, N. Certo, K. Belmore, & T. Crowner (Eds.), *Madison's alternative to zero exclusion: Papers and programs related to public school services for secondary age severely handicapped students.* (Vol. VI, Part 1). Madison, Wisc.: Madison Metropolitan School District, 1976.

As teachers we often refer to the students in our classrooms possessively as "our kids." Yet during a student's years in school, we, as teachers, are responsible for only about 20% of that student's waking hours. By comparison, 80% of the student's life is under the influence of the home—parents, siblings, relatives, family friends—the neighborhood, and the community. The home influence has a greater advantage than simple frequency. It tends to be consistent for most students; that is, interactions are with a small, constant number of family members. By contrast, the school's influence fluctuates from one teacher to another every year and across a variety of classroom aides, supplementary staff, and classmates.

My point is that often we hastily claim to understand the parents of our handicapped pupils, to know what feelings they have about their child and his or her performance. We may categorize them nonchalantly into accepting and rejecting parents, and we may think we know what the 80% year-in and year-out influence and responsibility is, but we cannot easily know this. Our aim must be to foster and cultivate that understanding.

In this next chapter Ann Turnbull discusses the power of positive teacher-parent interactions. She purposefully avoids the term "parent training." While it is true that some parents may allow us to share with them our talents in teaching the handicapped, more often we need to occupy a variety of other roles. The most common role involves listening rather than telling, to understand what most of us have not actually experienced—the day-to-day trials of having a severely handicapped child. Another role is to answer questions as best we can on the causes of handicaps and the reasons for "peculiar" behaviors, such as self-stimulation or the absence of speech. Other interactions with parents may consist primarily of trying to establish trust between the parent and the school.

We must understand the intent and language of P.L. 94-142. Consistent with its requirements, we must set instructional goals for students with the help of their parents and discuss with them ways to achieve these goals and to maintain and generalize that learning once it has been acquired. As you read "Parent-Professional Interactions," your concept of the potential ties that may be established between the teacher and the home will expand and come into better focus.

Introduction to Chapter 2

2

Parent-Professional Interactions

Ann P. Turnbull is Associate Professor, School of Education, and Acting Associate Director, Bureau of Child Research at the University of Kansas.

In the following passage Roos (1978), a parent of a mentally retarded child, raises issues that have, in the past, characterized many of the interactions among parents of moderately and severely handicapped children and educational professionals.

Val's early months were characterized by colic, hyperactivity, inattentiveness, total absence of social response, and sleep disturbances. During the latter part of her first year, she became increasingly hyperactive, would spend hours banging her head against her crib, and failed to reach the typical landmarks in sensorimotor development. As I repeatedly pointed out these indications of developmental anomalies to our pediatrician, he would gaze at my wife and me with obvious disbelief and assure us that the baby was quite normal; we were anxious parents. This and subsequent episodes led me to formulate the concept of professional ignorance: the unfortunate fact that many professionals simply do not know about mental retardation and have failed to recognize it or misdiagnose it and, all too often, give parents misinformation or fallacious advice. . . . Clinging stubbornly to the conclusion that our daughter was "probably just fine," our pediatrician next referred us to a neurologist. Since this worthy was a consultant to the large state institution for the retarded of which I was the superintendent, I felt confident that he would immediately recognize the obvious signs of severe retardation in our child. Imagine my consternation when, after failing to accomplish even a funduscopic (vision) examination on Val due to her extreme hyperactivity, the learned consultant cast a baleful eye on my wife and me and informed us that the child was quite normal. On the other hand, he continued, her parents were obviously neurotically anxious, and he would prescribe tranquilizers for us. I had suddenly been demoted from the role of a professional to that of "the parent as patient": the assumption by some professionals that parents of a retarded child are emotionally maladjusted and are prime candidates for counseling, psychotherapy, or tranquilizers. My attempts to point out the many indications of developmental delays and neurological disturbances were categorically dismissed as manifestations of my "emotional problems." I was witnessing another captivating professional reaction—the "deaf ear syndrome": the attitude on the part of some professionals that parents are complete ignoramuses so that any conclusion they reach regarding their own child is categorically ignored. Later I found that suggestions I would make regarding my own child would be totally dismissed by some professionals, while these same suggestions made as a professional about other children would be cherished by my colleagues as professional pearls of wisdom. Parenthetically, when I wrote to the neurologist years later to inform him that Val's condition had been clearly diagnosed as severe mental retardation and that she had been institutionalized, he did not reply.

This interchange also illustrated another problem faced by parents; namely, professional omniscience and omnipotence; the myth that professionals possess the source of all ultimate knowledge and can make wise decisions affecting other people's destinies. This unfortunate myth has been frequently perpetrated by professionals as well as by parents. (pp. 14–15)

As professionals, we must be aware of some problems that have interfered with positive parent-professional relationships in order to understand fully today's emphasis on establishing a new partnership.

Parents have often been analyzed, criticized, and blamed for the problems of their handicapped children. In the past, many parents were encouraged to place their handicapped child in a residential institution immediately after diagnosis. The implicit message was that rearing the child required coping skills and attitudes the parents did not possess.

Some educational programs have required parental involvement such as serving as a classroom aide, attending therapy sessions, following through on training at home, and attending formal training sessions to learn new child management skills. If parents became overwhelmed with all their extra responsibilities, they have at times been viewed as unresponsive and uncaring. The mother who fights for services for her severely retarded, multihandicapped child may be turned down by every agency she contacts. If she, herself, rejects her child, she may be viewed by professionals as needing psychiatric help.

Some attempts to establish interactions among educational professionals and parents are doomed to failure from the start. Some failures relate to an unwillingness to listen to the parents' concerns or to respond to problems in their order of priority. Parents who are wondering where their next meal is coming from are not likely to be very interested in a teacher's home visit to explain positive reinforcement. One parent trainer was describing his home-based training program for low-income parents. He commented, "On the first visit to the parents' home, we spend about 5 minutes making small talk and listening to their problems. Then we introduce our new parent training manual and ask them to turn to chapter one." This trainer questioned why he had few parents agreeing to finish the prescribed 12 weekly home visits. His hypothesis was that the parents were not concerned about the development of their children.

Some parents of handicapped children describe their interactions with professionals as characterized by a superiority (professional)–inferiority (parent) status. One parent involvement program used the slogan "Parents are Educable." In the jargon of special education, the literal translation of this slogan is "Parents have IQs roughly between 55 and 70." Of course, this was not their intent; yet parents viewed it as an insult.

Just as professionals have sometimes slighted parents of moderately and severely handicapped children, the attitudes and behaviors of the parents have also contributed to negative interactions. There is no easy way to tell a mother and father that their child is substantially handicapped. Some parents want to hear the hard truth; others want to be eased into it. Professionals may carefully choose their words with the greatest sensitivity, yet still offend the parents. Sometimes parents are unforgiving and do not realize the difficult position of the professional. They may vent their anger at the professional and discuss the professional's "gross lack of sensitivity" with family and friends. Frequently, parents of handicapped children have been highly critical of the professionals with whom they and their children have worked. Professionals are sometimes totally or socially excluded from community interest groups on the grounds that it is impossible for them to understand parents' feelings and needs. Parents sometimes form tight cliques with the primary goal of ostracizing and criticizing professionals. There are situations in which parents have fought long and hard for services for their handicapped child; after the services are found and the child is receiving an appropriate education, the parents continue their intensive advocacy to the point that minor issues become the basis for major confrontation. This type of posture is likely to lead to unproductive interactions among parents and professionals.

Why has the important relationship of parents and educators frequently been counterproductive? Negative interactions have resulted largely from a lack of awareness and sensitivity of both groups to the other's roles and responsibilities. Only in the last decade has significant national attention been focused on the importance of a parent-professional partnership based on mutual respect and decision making. Some of the reasons contributing to the recognition of the importance of this partnership include:

1. The experimental evidence that parents can positively influence the development of their children through teaching them at home (Bronfenbrenner, 1974; Gordon, 1971; Karnes, Teska, Hodgins, & Badger, 1970; Schaefer, 1972).
2. The encouraging results of early intervention in ameliorating the developmental deficits associated with actual and "at-risk" handicaps (Bronfenbrenner, 1974; Consortium for Longitudinal Studies, 1979; Horowitz & Paden, 1973; Tjossem, 1976).

3. The success of parents in bringing litigation to establish the educational rights of their children (*Armstrong v. Kline,* 1979; *Fialkowski v. Shapp,* 1975; *Hines v. Pittsburgh County Board of Education,* 1980; *Mills v. Board of Education,* 1972; *Pennsylvania Association for Retarded Children v. Commonwealth of Pennsylvania,* 1972).

4. The resulting federal legislation, P.L. 94-142 (Education for All Handicapped Children Act), which sets forth clear standards for parent involvement in the educational process.

Since P.L. 94-142 provides statutory guidelines for the interaction among parents and educational professionals, we will review the six major principles of the legislation concerning parental rights and responsibilities. Their implementation is providing the basis for new relationships among educators and parents.

P.L. 94-142: PARENT RIGHTS AND RESPONSIBILITIES

P.L. 94-142 was passed by Congress in November, 1975. Its essential purpose is to insure that all handicapped children receive a free, appropriate education. The six major principles that contribute to the provision of a free, appropriate public education include:

1. Zero reject,
2. Nondiscriminatory assessment,
3. Individualized Education Programs,
4. Least restrictive alternative,
5. Procedural due process,
6. Parent participation.

The regulations adopted to implement each principle clearly set forth requirements for parent involvement. These regulations, summarized below, were issued in the August 23, 1977 *Federal Register.*

We must recognize that there have been attempts by the Reagan administration and some members of Congress to repeal P.L. 94-142. Although these attempts have been unsuccessful to date, future efforts to obtain cutbacks are anticipated. P.L. 94-142 will probably survive and not be substantially cut back; however, there may be some changes in the federal requirements. Undoubtedly the law has brought an unprecedented degree of parental involvement into the education of handicapped students. The six principles of P.L. 94-142 represent good educational practice, as well as legal mandates. In a recent survey I conducted with directors of special education in local education agencies, 75% of the directors surveyed reported that they would maintain the requirement to conduct the IEP conference and involve parents in decision making even if it were not required by federal and state law. Thus, threats to P.L. 94-142

should not be interpreted as negating the value and utility of the six principles.

In addition to federal law, you should also be aware that each state except New Mexico has legislation pertaining to the education of handicapped students addressing these same six principles. State legislation also has accompanying regulations outlining specific rights and responsibilities. We encourage you to obtain a copy of your state legislation and the accompanying regulations from your state educational agency.

Finally, some local school districts have policies on parent rights and responsibilities that exceed the requirements of both federal and state law. At the school district level, each teacher should discuss local practices with the director of special education and the building principal.

The six principles are summarized below. They provide a foundation for many of the interactions among educators and parents.

Zero Reject

Zero reject assures that *all* handicapped children will receive a free, appropriate public education. Timelines were set requiring states to provide full educational opportunity to all handicapped children between the ages of 3 and 18 by no later than September 1, 1978, and to all handicapped children between the ages of 3 and 21 by no later than September 1, 1980. There is an exception to this requirement: states do not have to provide educational services to handicapped students between the ages of 3 through 5 and 18 through 21 if a state law or practice or a court order is inconsistent with the requirements of educating students in these age groups. Basically, this means that states that do not provide education to nonhandicapped students in these age groups (3–5 and 18–21) are not required to serve handicapped students in these age ranges.

The legislation requires that each state education agency (SEA) and local education agency (LEA) conduct an annual child-find program to identify, locate, and evaluate all handicapped children residing in their jurisdiction who need special education and related services. Federal aid to SEAs and LEAs complying with the requirements of P.L. 94-142 must be used first for two "service priorities": *(a)* all handicapped children previously excluded from school and *(b)* handicapped children with the most severe handicaps within each disability area who are not receiving an appropriate education.

When there is no suitable program for a handicapped child in the LEA in which he resides, the LEA may refer him for placement in a private program. In these instances, the private program must meet all requirements of P.L. 94–142, and the LEA must assume full financial responsibility for the room, board, and educational expenses (not medical expenses) of the student. In some cases, the LEA may choose to create a new program to serve the student rather than pay the cost of a private program.

Not only must handicapped students be admitted to school, they must also have a relevant and appropriate curriculum. This issue will be discussed in the section on Individualized Education Programs.

The implication of zero reject for parents of moderately and severely handicapped children is that they can be *assured* that educational services must be provided. With the service priorities covering handicapped children previously excluded from school and the more severely handicapped children, parents of moderately and severely handicapped students are in the best position to receive appropriate services for their children. In the past, negative interactions among educational professionals and parents have developed when parents were in the position of having to beg for programs and often feeling the frustration of finding no publicly financed programs. Private schools have been tremendous financial burdens for parents and have led to feelings of further alienation from the public schools. Many educators have been similarly frustrated, wanting to provide for moderately and severely handicapped children, but realizing the constraints posed by school budgets. Zero reject requirements are creating new relationships among educators and parents, based on the premise that appropriate educational services will be provided at public expense. Interactions can begin by defining the types of curricula and services that constitute an appropriate education rather than by deciding whether or not the school will provide services for the student.

Nondiscriminatory Assessment

The requirements for nondiscriminatory assessment focus on insuring that evaluation procedures are broadly based, fairly administered, and given only with the parents' informed consent. Obtaining informed consent of parents throughout the evaluation process will be discussed under due process. In regard to broadly based and fairly administered evaluation procedures, tests must be sensitive to cultural factors (e.g., administered in the child's native language, validated for the specific purpose for which they are used) and a variety of measures must be used (a minimum of two tests and information from sources other than tests, including data on physical condition, sociocultural background, and adaptive behavior in home and school). To gather this information, parents should contribute to the evaluation.

Although not specifically required by the law, parents may be members of the evaluation team charged with interpreting educational data. If they are not formal team members, the professionals on the evaluation team should conduct a parent conference or solicit information from them, possibly through a questionnaire on relevant topics.

Parents have other rights related to evaluation, such as challenging the appropriateness of particular data and obtaining formal evaluations of their children from private sources to be considered in making placement decisions. Since these rights are classified as procedural safeguards, they also will be discussed under due process.

Thus, P.L. 94–142 gives parents fuller opportunities than they have had in the past to be involved in collecting and interpreting evaluation data. As parents participate in evaluation, they begin to interact with professionals in making important educational decisions. No longer are they merely recipients of information collected on their children. The intent of P.L. 94–142 is to assert parents' rights for active participation.

Individualized Education Programs

The Individualized Education Programs (IEP) are a primary mechanism set forth by P.L. 94–142 to insure that handicapped children receive a meaningful education appropriate to their needs and abilities. The required components of the IEP include:

1. A statement of the child's present level of educational performance;
2. Annual goals expected to be achieved by the end of the school year;
3. Short-term instructional objectives representing the intermediate steps between the present performance and the annual goal;
4. Special education and related services needed by the student;
5. Date of initiating services and anticipated duration of services;
6. Specification of the extent of time the student will participate in the regular educational program;
7. Evaluation procedures (criteria and schedules) for determining at least annually whether the short-term objectives are being met.

IEPs must be developed at the beginning of the year for all handicapped students receiving special education. For a handicapped child not receiving special education, a meeting must be held to develop the IEP within 30 days of the determination that the child is handicapped. The required participants on the IEP committee include:

1. An LEA representative, other than the child's teacher, who is qualified to provide or supervise special education services;
2. The child's teacher (or teachers) who has direct responsibility for implementing the IEP;
3. One or both of the child's parents;
4. The handicapped child, when appropriate.

When the child is classified as handicapped for the first time, the evaluator or a representative familiar with evaluation results must also attend the IEP committee. Others may also be included on the committee at the discretion of the parent or LEA.

Recent clarifications of IEP requirements were issued by the Office of Special Education in the Department of Education. These clarifications were printed in the January 19, 1981, *Federal Register*. Currently they are being reviewed by the Reagan administration and they may or may not become effective policy. (At the time this book went to press, a final decision had not been made.) These clarifications were developed in response to questions by professionals and parents regarding the original intent of the regulations. The clarifications clearly support the strong role parents are expected to assume in the IEP conference. One of the major purposes of the IEP, as stated in the clarifications, is as follows:

The IEP meeting serves as a communication vehicle between parents and school personnel, and enables them as equal participants, to jointly decide what the child's needs are, what services will be provided to meet those needs, and what the anticipated outcomes may be. (Federal Register, 1981, p. 5462)

Thus, the expectation is that parents should assume an active decision-making role in the conference rather than being passive receivers of information shared by professionals.

The implications of parent involvement in developing the IEP are tremendous. This requirement brings parents to the forefront in specifying what is an appropriate curriculum for their children and significantly influences the interactions of educators and parents in mutual decision making and shared responsibility. Some parents of handicapped children have complained that the educational professionals working with their children neither solicited their opinions nor considered the child's needs they felt were most pressing. The IEP conference provides an opportunity for parents to state what they want for their child. In one recent IEP conference, the mother of a moderately retarded child questioned why her son was being taught to label prehistoric animals verbally. The parent asked the teachers what type of job they expected the child to have as an adult. The teachers replied that they had never really considered job opportunities for the child since he was only 10. To the teachers, 10 seemed young; to the parents, 10 meant that almost half of his formal education was completed. As the meeting progressed, it was clear that the parents were specifying objectives related to independence as an adult (telling time, reading survival words, sex education) that were different from the more traditional curriculum proposed by the teachers. Through sharing evaluation data, goals for the child, and special problems, all parties involved created a curriculum that met everyone's approval.

Educational professionals must provide either an oral or written notice to parents informing them of the purpose, time, location, and names of persons who will be in attendance at the IEP conference. The policy clarifications (*Federal Register,* 1981) also recommend that parents be informed that they may bring their handicapped child or other persons, such as an advocate or friend, to the conference. The meeting must be scheduled at a time and place convenient for the parents.

All communication at the conference must be understandable to the parent. Thus an interpreter must be provided for parents who are deaf or whose native language is not English. If it is impossible for parents to attend a meeting, their participation can be achieved by an individual or conference telephone call.

According to P.L. 94-142, the only exception to parental involvement in the IEP conference is in cases in which parents refuse to be involved. In these cases, school officials must document attempts to encourage the parents to be involved, including detailed records of telephone calls, copies of letters, and visits to the parents' home or place of employment.

The membership of parents on IEP committees strongly influences the interactions of parents and professionals. They must meet at the beginning of the school year to define the child's total educational program. If all parties agree that the IEP is appropriate, the specified instructional objectives and educational services are implemented. Since the parents know what progress to anticipate, they can monitor implementation, which can result in increased accountability for both the professionals and the parents. Some IEP committee meetings will not result in complete consensus. If either the professionals or parents object to the opinions of the other to the point of being deadlocked, either may initiate a due process hearing to resolve the conflict. One point of conflict is likely to be the related services needed by the student. For example, parents may think that their severely handicapped child needs daily physical therapy. The professional members of the IEP committee may disagree (perhaps because they know it is impossible for the school to provide it). If consensus cannot be reached, the IEP cannot be officially approved and either party can initiate a due process hearing. The P.L. 94-142 requirements related to IEPs clearly result in curriculum decisions that are a shared responsibility among professionals and parents rather than the singular responsibility of professionals. Specific guidelines for involving parents in IEP meetings are included later.

Least Restrictive Alternatives

P.L. 94-142 states that, to the maximum extent possible, handicapped children, including those in public and private facilities, should be educated with children who are not handicapped. They should be removed from regular schools only when the nature or severity of the handicap is such that education in regular classes, with supplementary aids and services, cannot be successful. The placement decisions are made by the IEP committee. Thus, parents interact with professionals in deciding what constitutes the most appropriate environment for the child.

There are significant implications of this doctrine for parents of handicapped children. For example, consider parents who institutionalized their child shortly after birth and never established strong ties with him. The institution now recommends that the child, age 15, be returned to his family, based on the concept of least restriction. The parents may be psychologically unable to provide a home for their child and make the tremendous adjustments posed by deinstitutionalization. Presently, the legal assumption is in favor of parental custody; yet many parents are unprepared to discharge these duties (Turnbull & Turnbull, 1975).

Avis (1978), a social worker in a residential institution, shared this example:

An elderly couple . . . came to see me during a regular visit to see their daughter in the institution. Their daughter is a woman of nearly forty who has Down's Syndrome. They had seen a television show on which an enthusiastic proponent of the community movement was a guest. They perceived his message as a promise. The message was that all clients from a given area who resided in the institution would be returned to the homes of their families or to their home area, preferably "down the street," within the year. This plan was given greater color by dramatic stories of institutional abuse.

These parents were considerably upset. They had placed their daughter in the institution as a newborn infant. This decision had been made upon the recommendation of a much respected physician. The prognosis was that the baby would live less than a year and would not develop beyond the most infantile stage. They were also told that family and friends should be told that the baby would not be coming

home from the hospital and the conclusion would be that the baby had died.

Through forty years they had visited faithfully, had assumed financial responsibility, and had an affectionate relationship with their daughter. They felt they had made the only choice for her and had acted in good faith by the standards of the time.

They tearfully asked if some consideration could be given to their daughter's remaining in the institution, as it had always been her home. They feared that there would not be adequate protection and care for her in any place but the institution. They also found it difficult to imagine how they could cope with explaining their daughter's existence after all of these years if she were placed "down the street." (pp. 170-171)

Although this example deals with the deinstitutionalization of a retarded adult, parents of institutionalized school-aged children have many of the same concerns. Professionals should understand that the decision to institutionalize a child is based on a complex set of factors that may include family stress, degrees of family support, availability of community alternatives, and competing needs of other family members. That decision can best be made by parents and professionals working together to identify the placement that is in the best interest of the handicapped individual and other family members.

We must devise educational models focusing on preparation for both the handicapped individual and his family who are in the midst of deinstitutionalization (Turnbull, Tyler, & Morrell, Note 1.). Parents of institutionalized children are organizing into interest groups in many states to delay deinstitutionalization until community alternatives are developed. Professionals and parents should interact carefully in planning the movement of moderately and severely handicapped children from residential institutions to community environments. The process must be systematic, manageable for the family, and sensitive to the unique needs of the child.

Many parents also have concerns about placing their children in regular schools. Parents of nonhandicapped children may have concerns about whether severely handicapped children will be a negative influence on their children or about whether severely handicapped children might engage in inappropriate behavior such as aggressiveness. On the other hand, parents of the handicapped students may fear placing their child in a regular school because of the possibility of teasing and rejection. Professionals and parents need to cooperatively devise a system for moving handicapped students from more to less restrictive environments. Parents of both handicapped and non-handicapped students might serve on advisory boards or help specify needs and identify strategies to meet those needs. Paul, Turnbull, and Cruickshank (1977) describe a procedure for collaborative planning among professionals and parents for mainstreaming and point out the roles and responsibilities of both groups. Since it is both educationally sound and legally required that parents of handicapped students be involved in making placement decisions, the positive interaction of professionals and parents on this important task is crucial.

Due Process

Due process can be viewed as a means for holding both professionals and parents accountable for the educational decisions they make on behalf of the handicapped child. Basically, due process safeguards include these requirements.

1. Parental consent must be obtained before the preplacement evaluation is conducted. *Evaluation* is defined as a procedure used to determine whether a child is handicapped and to identify the nature of needed special education services. According to the regulations, parental consent must be obtained only when selective tests are used with an individual child, not for basic tests given to all children in a school, grade, or class.

2. Parents of a handicapped child may examine all relevant records with respect to the identification, evaluation, and educational placement of the child.

3. Parents may obtain an independent evaluation (conducted by a certified or licensed examiner who is not employed by the school system and who does not routinely provide evaluations for the SEA or LEA) at public expense and have it considered by the system in determining what constitutes a free, appropriate public education for the child.

4. Written notice must be provided to the parents before initiating or changing the identification, evaluation, or educational placement of a child or the refusing to make such a change. The notice must include: (*a*) a full list of due process safeguards available to the parent; (*b*) a description of the action proposed or refused, including an explanation of the rationale for the decision, a description of other options considered, and reasons that the other options were rejected; (*c*) a description of each evaluation procedure, record, or report upon which the decision was based; and (*d*) a description of any other factors related to the agency's decision.

   Further requirements specify that the notice must be written in language understandable to the general public and in the native language or other mode of communication of the parent (if not, the notice must be translated orally into the parents' native language or some other mode of communication must be used). In essence, the educational agency must insure that parents understand the content of the notice.

5. The SEA must insure that a child's rights are protected when his parents are unknown or unavailable or when he is a ward of the state. In these cases, a determination must be made as to whether the child needs a surrogate parent; if necessary, a surrogate parent must be assigned. The surrogate parent has all responsibilities of representing the interests of the child in obtaining a free, appropriate public education. The surrogate parent must: (*a*) have no interests that conflict with the interest of the child, (*b*) have knowledge and skill that will insure adequate representation, and (*c*) not be an employee of the SEA or LEA responsible for providing an education to the child.

6. The parents (including the guardian and surrogate) or the LEA may initiate a due process hearing to present complaints concerning the child's identification, evaluation, placement, or right to a free, appropriate public education. Any party may be advised by counsel or by individuals with expertise related to the education of handicapped students, present evidence, cross-examine, obtain a written or electronic verbatim record of the hearing, and obtain written findings of facts and decisions. The hearing officer must not be an employee of the SEA or LEA or have any personal or professional interests that would bias his or her opinions.

   All hearings must be conducted within 45 days after receipt of the complaint, except when all parties agree to an extension. While the proceedings are being conducted, the child should remain in his present educational placement unless the SEA or LEA and the parents agree to another placement. If the complaint involves the child's initial admission to public education, the child must be placed in the public school program until the proceedings are completed.

   Any party dissatisfied with the findings of the hearing conducted by the LEA may appeal to the SEA for an impartial review of the hearing. If parties are further aggrieved by the decisions of the reviewer, any party may file a civil action in either a state or federal district court.

Obviously, due process stipulations create significant opportunities for parents to have access to educational information and to influence or change educational decisions. The opportunity for due process hearings provides a system of checks and balances for both the parents and educators. Due process requirements most certainly provide new chances for parents and professionals to interact and to have increased accountability in their interactions. As stated already, many parent-professional relationships have been characterized by dissatisfaction with the behavior of one party by the other. Due process hearings provide an opportunity to examine these issues objectively and systematically. Thus, due process requirements can be viewed as a method of resolving conflict. Undoubtedly due process will significantly influence the interactions of professionals and parents, making both parties more accountable to each other and to the best interests of the handicapped child. A model for professional and parent participation in the due process hearing is included in Turnbull and Strickland (1981).

Parent Participation

The P.L. 94-142 regulations pertaining to parent participation extend the opportunity to parents to have access to educationally relevant information and to be involved in educational decisions. The parents must receive (a) a summary of policies in regard to the storage, release to a third party, and the protection of personally identifiable information, (b) a description of all the rights of parents and children regarding personally identifiable information, and (c) a description of the children on whom the SEA will maintain information, the methods to be used in gathering the information, and the uses to be made of the information.

Parents are entitled to inspect and review all educational records (unless they are prevented from doing so under state laws pertaining to matters such as guardianship, separation, and divorce) within a maximum period of 45 days after their request to record access. They may ask for an interpretation of the information and may ask that the information be amended. If the agency refuses to amend the information according to the parents' request, the parents must be advised of their right to a due process hearing. The hearing will determine whether or not the information in the record is to be amended. All opportunities must be made available to parents to review or inspect the records, including providing copies if they are unable to come to school to review them. Finally, parents may request from the LEA a list of the types and locations of information it has collected, maintained, or used.

Access to records is another way of equalizing the power to make educational decisions among professionals and parents. Before the legal establishment of this parental right, a common educational practice

was not to fully report the results of evaluation of moderately and severely retarded children to their parents. Some school policies even prevented the release of IQ scores to parents. Another practice has been to write subjective opinions in school records. These opinions can become very debilitating to handicapped students if future teachers and employers read them. In the past, there has been limited accountability for professionals, because usually they were the only ones who read the records. By extending the opportunity to parents not only to read their child's records but also to receive an explanation of the contents and request an amendment, a new forum is established for interaction. Thus, there are no private sanctions off limits to the parent-professional partnership. The implications for professionals are that they will be held accountable for the manner in which they collect and maintain student data.

Before personally identifiable information is released to anyone other than authorized agency officials, parents must consent. Each agency must train everyone who uses personally identifiable information in the state's policies and procedures pertaining to confidentiality and must maintain a current list of names and positions of employees who have access to the information. The list must be available for public inspection. Further, the agency must inform parents when a need no longer exists for the collection, maintenance, and use of the confidential information; however, parents should also be informed that records may be needed in the future to obtain Social Security and tax benefits. Upon the request of the parents, all confidential information must be destroyed when the agency no longer needs it. A permanent record of name, address, phone number, grade, attendance record, classes attended, grade level completed, and year completed may be maintained.

Parent participation is also addressed in P.L. 94-142 by encouraging their participation at public hearings and membership on advisory panels. Before it adopts the annual state program plan, the SEA must conduct public hearings at times and in locations that would permit interested parents to attend. A notice of the hearings and the purpose of the plan must be provided in the newspaper or other media with enough advance time to inform the public of the upcoming hearing. At the public hearing on the annual program plan, the SEA must provide information on its programs to interested parties and solicit their favorable and critical comments. Prior to the final adoption of the plan, modifications must be made to incorporate the educationally significant public comments. Further, LEAs are required to develop a process for giving parents of handicapped students the opportunity to participate in the development of the application for P.L. 94-142 funds. After the application is developed, it must be made available to parents and the general public.

The SEA is required to establish an advisory panel with parental representation to establish guidelines for meeting educational needs of the handicapped population and commenting publicly on rules and regulations. Panel meetings are to be open, and minutes must be shared. Thus, parents who are not members of the panel can still stay informed and monitor the proceedings of the meetings.

By having public hearings and advisory meetings as arenas for the interaction of professionals and parents, parents have the chance to influence the initial development of policy and to monitor its implementation. This provides the opportunity to interact on system issues, whereas other parental rights, such as membership on the IEP committee, affect interaction on child issues.

From the discussion of parental rights and responsibilities as they relate to the six principles of P.L. 94-142, it is obvious that a parent-professional alliance is a critical component of the provision of a free, appropriate public education to handicapped students.

PARENTS AS EDUCATIONAL DECISION MAKERS

The many requirements for parent involvement in P.L. 94-142 are integrated into a systematic process involving the identification, evaluation, and placement of handicapped students. This process is summarized in Figure 2.1. Many parents are interested in being involved in all functions from the point of referral to reviewing and revising the IEP. Other parents may prefer a less active role. Frequently, professionals view parents of handicapped students as homogeneous rather than heterogeneous. They assume that all parents have similar interests and capabilities for particular types of involvement. In fact, recent research on parent involvement from the perspectives of parents reveals diverse opinions and preferences in assuming an active decision-making role (Winton & Turnbull, 1981). Professionals have a responsibility to insure that parents have opportunities for decision making; however, in the end each parent must be allowed the freedom to decide the degree to which he or she will assume the role and responsibility of an educational decision maker. Special attention will be given here to two types of decision making for parents—involvement in evaluation and in IEP development.

Parent Involvement in Evaluation

Involving parents in the evaluation of their child can help give educators access to the parents' view of the child's developmental level and needs. Thus, a more complete assessment of the child will be available. Active parent involvement also enhances the probability that the parents will, indeed, understand the information they receive. Parents should have the opportunity to share information with educators and also to receive information and interpretations from them.

Marion (1980) has stated that, compared to other issues, evaluation has caused the most friction between schools and culturally diverse populations. Parents of culturally diverse children have been concerned about the disproportionate number of these children assigned to classes for handicapped children. By comprehensively involving parents in sharing and receiving information, educators can minimize their concern over the potential discrimination in evaluation.

In regard to the sharing of information by parents, valuable information can be obtained from them immediately after referral and before the initial educational evaluation of the student (McLoughlin, Edge, & Strenecky, 1978). At this point, parents can provide information on the child's developmental history, previous diagnostic reports, and any special concerns that should be considered in planning the evaluation procedures. Guidelines for constructing a behavioral inventory to use with parents to pinpoint the child's strengths and weaknesses are provided by Heward, Dardig, and Rossett (1979).

Parents also can share useful information on topics such as the child's adaptive behavior, self-help skills, peer interaction in the neighborhood, medication schedule, and language development. This information can be collected through a variety of formats, including informal discussions, structured interviews, and written questionnaires. Some standardized tests on adaptive behavior, such as the *Vineland Social Maturity Scale* (Doll, 1965) and the *AAMD Adaptive Behavior Scale* (Nihira, Foster, Shellhaas, & Leland, 1974), can be administered to the parent or a third person in order to obtain information on the child's functioning. These instruments provide an opportunity for parents to provide systematic information to educators.

In order to be informed appropriately of the child's needs as a basis for planning an IEP tailored to his or her strengths and weaknesses, parents also need to receive information from educators on the child's performance on the evaluation instruments. Most moderately and severely handicapped children are initially diagnosed before they enter the educational system. Thus, their parents typically do not learn that their child has some serious problems from school personnel. Rather, the educational evaluation typically reconfirms the presence of the handicap and provides additional information on the child's pre-academic and academic performance. Rockowitz and Davidson (1979) present a model for discussing diagnostic findings with parents, which is included in Table 2.1. General guidelines for communication style during such an interpretative conference include listening to the parents' concerns and gearing the interpretation of the data to their concerns, being willing to answer their questions, using examples to illustrate developmental concepts (e.g., visual tracking), minimizing or eliminating the use of jargon, and insuring comprehensiveness in sharing information rather than withholding aspects that are unpleasant or difficult to discuss.

Although practical concerns such as time must be considered in sharing evaluation information with parents, it can be extremely helpful to parents to have a fairly immediate follow-up meeting to the interpretative conference (e.g., a week later) in which they can ask for clarification or interpretations after they have had the chance to reflect on what was said. Regardless of how many times parents have been told about the developmental deficits of their children, interpretative sessions are usually stressful. They need time to comprehend the information they have received, which sometimes can be clouded by the stress they feel.

When handicapped students are re-evaluated (P.L. 94-142 requires re-evaluation every 3 years), some parents may prefer to receive a written summary of the evaluation results before the conference set up for interpreting them. This advance information allows parents to identify parts of the report that are unclear and make notes on information to share and questions to ask, and it generally provides them a boost of confidence in knowing they will not be caught by surprise when they meet face-to-face with educators.

Parent Involvement in IEP Development

As stated earlier, parents are required members of IEP committees for their handicapped child. Further, the IEP policy clarifications state that parents should be "equal participants to jointly decide what the child's needs are" (*Federal Register*, 1981, p. 5462). A review of the research on parent participation in the IEP meeting suggests that to date parents have been passive rather than active. The National Committee for Citizens in Education (Note 2) surveyed approx-

imately 2,300 parents from 438 school districts. Slightly over half the parents indicated that the IEP was completed before the meeting. Observations of IEP conferences for mildly handicapped elementary school students revealed that a typical conference involved a resource teacher's describing an already developed IEP to the parent (Goldstein, Strickland, Turnbull, & Curry, 1980). The mean length of these conferences was 36 minutes. Gilliam and Coleman (1981) surveyed participants at IEP meetings to determine the status ranking of roles in regard to influence and contributions. The four most highly ranked positions were psychologist, special education teacher, special education director, and supervisor. Parents were perceived to be low in actual contribution and influence.

These data suggest that definitive intervention is necessary to insure that parents have a real opportunity for active decision making. One strategy is to provide group training sessions to prepare parents for participation. I have conducted training with parents that breaks the IEP conference into six components.

1. *Preconference preparation*—Advance planning prior to the conference to help insure meaningful parent participation during the conference.
2. *Initial conference proceedings*—Establishing rapport at the beginning of the meeting; insuring that the purpose of the meeting is understood and the agenda is organized.
3. *Interpretation of evaluation results*—Identifying the student's strengths and weaknesses as a foundation for planning an appropriate IEP.
4. *Development of the curriculum portion of the IEP*—Specifying the student's current level of performance, annual goals, short-term objectives, and evaluation procedures to be used in measuring progress.
5. *Placement decision and related services*—Determining the least restrictive appropriate setting and the necessary related services to insure that the child will be able to benefit from special education.
6. *Conclusion of the meeting*—Summarizing the decisions made, the methods to be used in maintaining communication between parents and professionals, and the nature of follow-up responsibility.

Table 2.2 includes parental suggestions for each of the six components of the conference. Training sessions using this model have been most effective when video tape examples and role play are used to enrich the didactic content. More information on this model can be obtained from Turnbull and Strickland (1981) and Turnbull, Strickland, and Brantley (1982).

FIGURE 2.1.

Sequence and Functions of Committee Activities

Responsible Agent	Function	Activities
special services committee	Coordination of Process from Referral to IEP Review	development of organizational plan appointment of committees insurance of compliance with law and regulations intervening when obstacles prevent other committees from carrying out assignments
special services committee	Reviewing the Referral	referral reviewed all available information examined questions generated by committee need for further assessment determined appointment of multidisciplinary evaluation team
special services committee	Providing Notice Obtaining Consent	parents informed of rights and of proposed actions parental consent obtained for further assessment
multidisciplinary evaluation team	Collecting Evaluation Information	responsibilities assigned for obtaining evaluation (consulting members named) evaluation scheduled and completed evaluation summaries received evaluation summaries reviewed as to appropriateness and completeness documentation of any biasing factors during evaluation
special services committee multidisciplinary evaluation team	Sharing Evaluation Information	parents informed of meeting and invited to attend all available information and evaluations examined oral reports made on all obtained information classification and documentation of needs related to program planning appointment of IEP committee by special services committee parents informed of evaluation results and IEP involvement in written notice
special services committee	Informing Parents of Evaluation Results & IEP Involvement	parents informed of rights proposed or refused actions, reasons for decisions made, description of evaluation procedures used, and any other relevant information parents invited to attend IEP conference

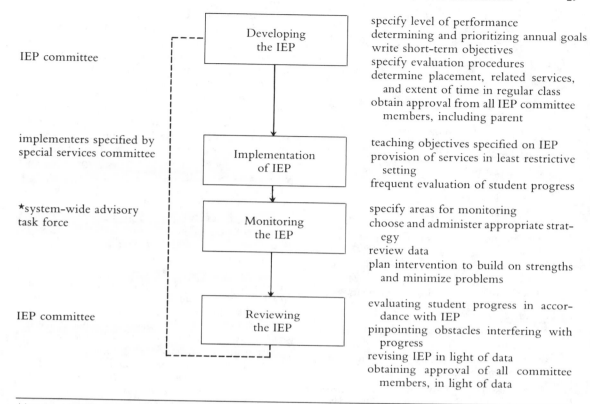

IEP committee	**Developing the IEP**	specify level of performance determining and prioritizing annual goals write short-term objectives specify evaluation procedures determine placement, related services, and extent of time in regular class obtain approval from all IEP committee members, including parent
implementers specified by special services committee	**Implementation of IEP**	teaching objectives specified on IEP provision of services in least restrictive setting frequent evaluation of student progress
★system-wide advisory task force	**Monitoring the IEP**	specify areas for monitoring choose and administer appropriate strategy review data plan intervention to build on strengths and minimize problems
IEP committee	**Reviewing the IEP**	evaluating student progress in accordance with IEP pinpointing obstacles interfering with progress revising IEP in light of data obtaining approval of all committee members, in light of data

★Appointed by IEP administrator rather than special services committee.

SOURCE: From *Procedures for Identification, Evaluation, and Placement of Exceptional Children,* Frankfort, Ky.: Bureau of Education for Exceptional Children, Kentucky Department of Education, 1977. Reprinted by permission.

Research corroborates the effectiveness of two other intervention strategies in increasing parent participation. Goldstein and Turnbull (1982) examined the effectiveness of having school counselors serve as parent advocates at IEP meetings and sending parents questions before the meeting. The counselors were given five guidelines to follow: introducing the parent at the beginning of the meeting, clarifying jargon, directing questions to parents, verbally reinforcing parents for their contributions, and summarizing the decisions made at the conclusion of the conference. The counselors were given a sheet of instructions to follow and were not included in any formal training. The second strategy involved sending these questions to parents to consider before the meeting:

- What skills would you most like your child to learn?
- Is your child having problems at home that we could help with at school?
- Are there any areas in which you feel that your child's behavior could be improved?

- What things does your child have a hard time doing?
- What punishments and rewards have you found that work well with your child?
- How do you feel about your child's classroom and resource room placement this year?
- What type of special services would you most like for your child to receive next year?

Forty-five IEP meetings (15 with the counselor as advocate, 15 with questions in advance, and 15 as a control group) of mildly handicapped students at the elementary level were observed. The speaker and the topic being discussed were recorded at 15-second intervals. The results indicated that a significant increase in the number of parent contributions was made in the group that had the counselor serving as a parent advocate. Although the questions in advance did not result in significantly more parent contributions, a post hoc analysis revealed an unanticipated finding. Significantly more fathers attended the conference along with their wives when questions were

TABLE 2.1. Interpretive Conference Format Outline

I. Entry pattern
  A. Introductions
  B. Review of evaluation procedures
  C. Parents' perceptions of child's functioning
  D. Restatement of parental concerns
    1. Main worry
    2. Additional concerns
II. Presentation of findings
  A. Encapsulation: Brief overview
  B. Reaction by parents and child
  C. Detailed findings
    1. Strengths
      a. Reactions
    2. Deficits
      b. Reactions
III. Recommendations—Only after time has been allowed for reactions
  A. Restatement of concerns with both parents
  B. Recommendations—one at a time
  C. Reactions after each recommendation
  D. Sharing with child
IV. Summary
  A. Repetition of findings, in varied wording if possible
  B. Restatement by parents or patient
  C. Planning for future contacts

SOURCE: "Discussing Diagnostic Findings with Parents" by R.J. Rockowitz and P.W. Davidson. © 1979 by The Professional Press, Inc. Reprinted with permission from JOURNAL OF LEARNING DISABILITIES, 11 East Adams, Street, Chicago, Illinois 60603. Vol. 12, No. 1, January 1979, page 4.

sent in advance. Alternative explanations for this finding include an increased recognition of the importance of the IEP meeting and a possible intimidation on the part of some parents when they received the questions, causing them to come to the meetings in pairs rather than alone (e.g., mother only).

Dardig and Heward (1981) provide an excellent model for helping parents and professional prioritize annual goals in IEP meetings. This procedure includes individually ranking suggested goals against eight specified criteria (e.g., child's demonstrated interest in skill, skill as prerequisite for more complex skills). See their article for detailed guidelines on implementing this ranking procedure.

DEVELOPMENT OF A PARENT PROGRAM

In addition to the nature and scope of interactions among professionals and parents established by P.L. 94-142, there are many other ways interactions can occur. Many educational programs for moderately and severely handicapped children have a concurrent parent program with particular expectations for parental involvement. Programs funded for preschool and school-aged handicapped children through the Handicapped Children's Early Education Program (Office of Special Education) are required to have parent involvement components, though the direct effect of parent involvement on programmatic success with severely handicapped children has yet to be consistently and objectively documented (Bricker & Casuso, 1979). In spite of the lack of scientific documentation, parent involvement is a widely accepted practice in programs serving handicapped children (Karnes & Teska, 1980; Lillie, 1981; Shearer & Shearer, 1972; Shearer, 1976).

When a parent program is begun, one of the most important considerations is to clearly identify the rationale for parent involvement. Parent programs are probably most frequently designed as a strategy for improving child outcomes (e.g., parents are trained in behavior management so they can in turn teach the child). In addition to child outcomes, parent programs have been justified in the literature in terms of promoting family adjustment and functioning (Bristol & Gallagher, in press; Lillie, 1981) and in increasing personnel for programs (Shearer & Shearer, 1972). The rationale for parent involvement for a given program may not be limited to just one dimension—it may also be a combination of factors. Identifying the particular rationale for parent involvement is important, since the goals and strategies of the program should be largely influenced by the rationale.

Another important consideration in developing a parent program is to tailor the program to the individual needs and interests of the parents. Meeting individual needs is a concept that applies to adults as well as children. Porcella (1980) describes a method of individualizing parent services used at the Exceptional Child Center, Utah State University. Parents of the severely handicapped children served by the project are presented with a "menu of home services," including training in behavior management or in teaching a specific skill, lending equipment for toilet training, lending books, parent meetings, field trips to group homes or sheltered workshops, and legal rights information. Parents can also choose the format for training, including phone calls, home or school visits, and group meetings. The Chapel Hill Outreach Project recommends the use of an assessment form such as the one shown in Figure 2-2 as a method of identifying individual needs and interests of parents. This form (Cansler, Martin, & Valand, 1975) or a similar one could be completed by parents on the first day of school or sent to them by mail. Eliciting parental views from the beginning sets up a

TABLE 2.2.
Parental Suggestions for the IEP Conference

1. Preconference Preparation
   a. Check to see if written notice contains required components: time of meeting, purpose, location, and participants.
   b. Insure that time of meeting is convenient.
   c. Reschedule meeting if time suggested by the school personnel is inconvenient.
   d. Obtain any information you believe will be helpful at the meeting, including your child's school or medical records.
   e. If possible, plan for both parents to attend the meeting.
   f. Ask an advocate or friend to attend the meeting with you if their presence would make you more comfortable.
   g. Consider the possibility of including your child in the meeting. If you decide it is appropriate for him to attend, discuss the purpose and procedures of the meeting with him.
   h. List any questions you would like answered at the meeting.
   i. Inform the school of your intent to attend the meeting and the persons whom you will bring with you.
   j. State your eagerness to be involved in the decisions pertaining to your child's program.
2. Initial Conference Proceedings
   a. If you are not introduced at the meeting to any persons you do not know, introduce yourself to all committee members.
   b. Make a note of the names and positions of everyone at the meeting.
   c. Ask questions to clarify the particular role of other committee members if not explained initially.
   d. If you bring friends or an advocate, introduce them and explain their role.
   e. If you have a time limit for the meeting, let other committee members know.
   f. Ask the chairperson to state the purpose of the meeting and review the agenda, if this is not done.
   g. If you have any questions about your legal rights, ask for a clarification.
3. Interpretation of Evaluation Results
   a. Insure that the teacher or psychologist states all tests that were administered and the specific results of each.
   b. You may make a record for yourself or ask for a written copy of the test results and evaluation of your child. This may become an important part of your records on your child.
   c. Insure that the classroom and educational im-

plications of the evaluation results are identified.
   d. If any professional jargon is used that you do not understand, ask for a clarification.
   e. Ask how your child was classified in regard to a particular handicapping condition (e.g., mental retardation).
   f. If you disagree with evaluation findings or classfication, state your disagreement.
   g. If your disagreement cannot be resolved within the meeting, ask for an independent evaluation to be administered by a psychologist or appropriate professional outside the school.
   h. Do not proceed with the development of the IEP until you and the school personnel agree on your child's evaluation data.
4. Development of the Curriculum Portion of the IEP
   a. If the school's description of your child's performance is not as you perceive it, *do give* your description of his or her performance level.
   b. State the skills and content areas you believe are most important for your child's program.
   c. If you question the goals and objectives suggested by the school, ask for justification. Your ideas are also valid.
   d. Insure that *all* subjects requiring specially designed instruction are included in the IEP.
   e. If your child receives instruction from two different teachers, clarify how the responsibility for teaching the objectives will be shared.
   f. If you are willing to assume responsibility for teaching or reviewing some of the objectives with the child, make this known to the committee.
   g. Insure that the procedures and schedules for evaluation of goals and objectives are specified.
5. Placement Decision and Related Services
   a. State the placement (regular classroom, resource program, special class, special school) you believe is most appropriate for the child.
   b. Be sure all necessary related services (speech therapy, physical therapy, transportation) you believe your child needs are included. Remember that the school is not obligated to provide related services that are not written into the IEP.
   c. If the school does not agree with you on placement and related services and you are convinced you are right, *do not sign the IEP*. Ask for the procedural guidelines for mediating a disagreement or initiating a due process hearing.
   d. If you agree on a placement and you are unfa-

TABLE 2.1. (CONTINUED)

miliar with the teacher, ask about the teacher's qualifications (training and experience) in regard to handicapped students.

e. Insure that your child has appropriate opportunities to interact with nonhandicapped children (placement in the least restrictive setting).

6. Conclusion of the Meeting

a. If the chairperson does not initiate it, ask for a summary of the meeting to review major decisions and follow-up responsibility. Make a written record of this summary.

b. If follow-up responsibility has not been specified, ask who is going to be responsible for each task.

c. Specify what responsibility (teaching objectives, increasing socialization opportunities during after-school hours) you will assume.

d. Insure that a tentative date is set for reviewing the IEP on at least an annual basis and preferably more frequently.

e. State in what ways and how frequently you would like to communicate with the teacher. Negotiate for these in light of the teacher's preferences.

f. State your desire and intent to work in close cooperation with the school.

g. Express appreciation for the opportunity to share in decision making and for interest of the school personnel in your child.

SOURCE: Adapted from A.P. Turnbull, and B. Strickland, in *Understanding and Working with Parents of Children with Special Needs,* J. L. Paul (Ed.). New York: Holt, Rinehart & Winston, 1981.

FIGURE 2.2
Sample Form for Parents to Rate their Needs for Service

It is our feeling that a child's progress in school is greatest when staff and family form a cooperative team with common goals. To have an effective family-staff team, parents should be given the opportunity to express what they feel are their expectations and limitations in relation to such a program. Will you please rate the following areas for service according to their importance to you.

Please check:	Not Important	Some Importance	Very Important
1. Training in classroom activities and teaching methods.			
2. Interpretation of test results.			
3. Counseling for family problems.			
4. Suggestions of other available services in the community.			
5. Help with managing behavior of children (temper tantrums, toilet training, eating habits, etc.)			
6. Transportation			
7. Suggestions for home activities for child.			
8. Training for brothers and sisters of child.			
9. Meetings for groups of parents.			
10. Suggestions for inexpensive or homemade learning and play materials.			

What do you think would be the most helpful format for parent-staff contacts? Check one or more.

__Group meetings with information-sharing (lecture-discussion) on general areas of interest
__Small-group discussion on topics selected by participating parents
__Periodic individual conferences between parent(s) and staff member(s). How often?
__Visits to families' homes by staff member
__Classroom observation and participation by parents
__All of the above, depending on need at the time
__I do not feel that parents should be involved in child's education program
__Other

Thank you for your comments.   Name_____

SOURCE: *Working with Families,* by D.P. Cansler, G.H. Martin, and M.C. Valand. Winston-Salem, N.C.: Kaplan Press, 1976, p. 15.

communication pattern of respect for what parents have to say. An outgrowth of this communication is tailoring the objectives of the parent program to the preference of parents. Thus, parental interest and active participation are likely to be enhanced.

Parent programs can be described or categorized in many ways, including by focusing on the various roles and responsibilities of the parents. These include parenting, teaching, and advocating. The remainder of this chapter focuses on those areas, with emphasis on various parental roles and responsibilities and strategies to help them meet these responsibilities.

PARENTS AS PARENTS

Sometimes parent programs overemphasize the roles of parents as teachers of their own children and as advocates for their children and deemphasize their role as parents. To be the parent of a moderately or severely handicapped child requires tremendous emotional adjustment, additional time devoted to parenting, and often excess financial burdens in comparison to the cost of rearing nonhandicapped children (Moroney, 1981). Parents can be assisted in carrying out their responsibilities by a program aimed at providing support, knowledge, and access to resources. Some of the particular issues that might be addressed include:

1. The adjustment process,
2. Socialization for the child,
3. Addressing concerns related to siblings,
4. Estate planning and guardianship.

Adjustment Process

Parents of handicapped children experience tremendous emotional pain from the first recognition that something is wrong with their child until they are at the point of realistically planning for his or her education. Cansler et al. (1975) describe three phases of emotional adjustment: (a) denial; (b) intellectual awareness of the handicap with emotional reactions of anger, guilt, depression, and grief; and (c) intellectual and emotional adjustment.

The process of moving through these stages and adjusting to the fact that a child is handicapped is somewhat different for each parent; yet in almost every situation parents can be helped by supportive and sensitive friends and professionals (Schlesinger & Meadow, 1976). Educational professionals might work in conjunction with organizations such as the Association for Retarded Citizens and the Society for Autistic Children in developing parent-support groups. The major purpose of these groups is for par-

ents with similar problems to have opportunities to offer support to one another. It can be extremely helpful for parents to know that other parents have similar problems, questions, and concerns. The support groups often initially need a facilitator. If parents have trouble discussing their feelings, perhaps a parent speaker or a film dealing with adjustment could be used to elicit reactions. Parents need to be encouraged to express their feelings. Active, nonjudgmental listening can create a trusting atmosphere for parents (Coletta, 1977). If more intensive support is needed, educational professionals should discuss with the parents the possibility of receiving counseling and might help them obtain these services.

Socialization for the Child

A frequent source of concern for parents of moderately and severely handicapped children is the sometimes negative reaction of the nonhandicapped population toward their child. Michaelis (1981), the mother of a child with Down syndrome, expressed this concern as follows:

When Jim was learning to walk he walked into the neighbors' yards and houses. Some didn't mind, but Jim couldn't tell which ones were which; he just followed the other kids. When he wandered away from the immediate neighborhood I would get phone calls telling me that they had seen Jim walking by. If they were concerned about him, I wondered why they didn't stop him and keep him there or even bring him home. In the small town everyone knew that I had four other children that I had to leave or bring when I came to get Jim. The implied message was that he was not welcome even on the sidewalk in front of their house and that they didn't want to touch him or help me train him. (p. 13)

It can be exasperating for parents to be out in public with their moderately or severely handicapped child and to be aware of stares and sometimes even to receive insensitive questions such as "Why does Joe look so funny?" It is difficult to know the most appropriate way to respond in these situations. Some parents are more comfortable trying to ignore the situation, and others feel strongly that a reply is in order. Schulz (1978) described her typical response to a stranger who stares at her son, who has Down syndrome. She looks squarely at the stranger and says, "You seem interested in my son. Would you like to meet him?" She reports that this comment frequently ends the staring and creates an opportunity to provide information.

Another related problem can be in helping the child to be socially accepted by neighborhood peers. Some handicapped children are automatically accepted; others need assistance in making friends. Parents can feel disappointed and helpless if they see all the other children in the neighborhood frequently playing together while their child remains isolated at home with few friends. Parents might share their experiences and, working with educational professionals, plan a systematic procedure to help nonhandicapped children be comfortable around and get to know their child. The procedure for increasing socialization should be based on successive approximation and could include the following steps.

1. Invite one or two neighborhood children over to the house to play (the house of the handicapped child). In choosing which neighborhood children to invite first, consider choosing children who are already sensitive to individual differences and who have influence with other neighborhood children. The parents of the handicapped child should be available to answer the children's questions about the nature of the handicapping condition. For example, one neighborhood peer asked of a new friend who had hydrocephaly, "Why is his head so big?" It is important to have open and honest communication with nonhandicapped children in responding to questions resulting from natural curiosity. The visit should be brief and supervised by the handicapped child's parents. If the handicapped child has any special problems such as seizures, the parents should look for an appropriate time to explain the nature of seizures to the nonhandicapped peers and again to answer their questions.

2. Expand the length of visits with the one or two neighborhood children and begin to phase out the parental supervision.

3. Add a new child to the invitation to visit or to go on a family outing with the handicapped child. Use the older neighborhood friends as models for the new friend.

4. Have the parents of the nonhandicapped peers over to the house to allow them the opportunity of getting to know the handicapped child. Communicate very openly concerning the needs of the handicapped child. (Step 4 may occur before Step 1 in some cases.)

5. Ask the parents of the nonhandicapped children if it would be agreeable with them for the children (handicapped and nonhandicapped) to play together at their homes.

6. Reinforce nonhandicapped peers for including the handicapped child in activities away from his house and yard. Encourage independence in the neighborhood.

Parents might be interested in having group meetings with educators and other parents to devise strategies to resolve problems with socialization and to role play particular resolutions. Further, educational professionals might work with handicapped children at school in encouraging friendships that can generalize from the school setting to the neighborhood. As pointed out by Heward et al. (1979), a key to positive socialization is to insure that handicapped students are systematically prepared to initiate and maintain friendships. Preparation of students for this responsibility should be one goal of parents and teachers.

Addressing Concerns Related to Siblings

The brothers and sisters of handicapped children often need special help in understanding their handicapped sibling. They may have concerns related to the cause of the handicapped sibling's problems, whether their friends will understand, the educational and vocational potential of the sibling, the likelihood of producing a handicapped child themselves, and whether they will have responsibility for their handicapped sibling after their parents die.

Sibling problems that have been documented in the literature are time-consuming care-taking responsibilities resulting in feelings of resentment toward the handicapped family member (Grossman, 1972) and psychological needs to overachieve to compensate for the limitations of the handicapped brother or sister (Cleveland & Miller, 1977). Parents may request help from educational professionals in dealing with some of these concerns.

Strategies that can be used by educators include parent meetings with a panel discussion by younger and older siblings of handicapped persons, setting up a library with books for siblings, organizing a sibling support group, planning for siblings to observe the classroom, and conducting a workshop for siblings of handicapped children enrolled in the educational program. Cansler et al. (1975) describe a sibling workshop conducted by the staff of a developmental center serving moderately and severely retarded children. This workshop was a full week in length and included sessions on causes of mental retardation, making educational materials, principles of behavior modification, and observation of the classroom program.

Estate Planning and Guardianship

Parents of moderately and severely handicapped children understandably have concerns about planning for their child's future. How should their will be devised? Whom should they ask to assume the responsibilities of serving as a guardian should one be needed? What is the procedure for appointing a guardian? Should a trust fund be established?

Estate planning and guardianship are embroiled with many intricate issues that must be fully explored before parents make important decisions in regard to their child's future. For example, in many states, guardianship is declared on an "all-or-none" basis. For a guardian to be appointed, the severely handicapped individual must be declared incompetent by the courts; that declaration generally results in the handicapped person's losing all legal rights and privileges including, as a rule, the power to give consent, vote, obtain a driver's license, enter into contracts, and decide where he will live. A few states have passed limited guardianship legislation that provides degrees of guardianship according to the level of independent functioning of the handicapped individual. In these states, the handicapped person does not have to be declared incompetent to receive the services of a guardian. Since state laws to a large extent determine the best course of action for a parent to take, the first step in making decisions on estate planning and guardianship is to become informed on these topics.

If parents need help in exploring these issues, educational professionals and parents might plan a group parent meeting devoted to discussing various alternatives associated with estate planning and guardianship. A lawyer and a trust officer of a bank might be asked to present information pertaining to state laws and specific options under these laws. A discussion of the pros and cons of various options should be included.

Parents who have strong concerns about their moderately or severely handicapped child's future may not be able to concentrate fully on his or her present educational needs. Helping parents alleviate concerns about the future can significantly help them fulfill their parenting roles and responsibilities.

PARENTS AS TEACHERS

Parents have been recognized as valuable instructional resources in meeting the developmental and educational needs of handicapped children. There are many valid reasons for encouraging parents to teach their handicapped child, including these: (a) parents typically are powerful reinforcing agents; (b) parents know their children better than others and generally spend more time with their children than do professionals; (c) the effectiveness of intervention can be increased if parents follow up at home on the skills being taught at school; and (d) parents receive gratification from contributing to the development of their child. To date, the majority of demonstration projects aimed at training parents as teachers have involved early intervention with handicapped infants and preschoolers; however, the procedures involved in the development of these programs are applicable also to parents of elementary-age and adolescent individuals.

Karnes and Teska (1980) enumerated the competencies needed by parents as follows:

Generally speaking, parents need to acquire knowledge or information about the provisions of P.L. 94-142 and state rules and regulations; principles of child's development and the special needs of a handicapped child; the availability of special programs; financial assistance, and counseling services; relevant parent organizations; ways of coping with others' attitudes and behaviors toward the handicapped child and the variety of ways in which they can be involved in their child's program.

More specifically, the parental competencies required for direct teaching of the handicapped child at home involve interacting with the child in ways that promote positive behavior; reinforcing desired behavior; establishing an environment that is conducive to learning; setting up and maintaining a routine for direct teaching; using procedures appropriate for teaching concepts and skills; adapting lesson plans to the child's interests and needs; determining whether the child has mastered knowledge and skills; keeping meaningful records, including notes on child progress; participating in a staffing of the child; communicating effectively with others; and assessing the child's stage of development.

Finally, it is important for parents to have knowledge of the services that are available to handicapped children and the rights of handicapped children. They need help in locating and assessing services in the community, region, and state that exist to facilitate the growth and development of the handicapped child and to serve other members of the child's family. They need help in interpreting federal and state legislation on the handicapped and in understanding how such legislation is administered. Parents need training if they are to become effective advocates for the handicapped child throughout his or her life. (pp. 98–99)

This comprehensive list of skills is very similar to the competencies generally associated with a masters degree in special education. Is the development of competencies in all of these areas realistic for parents? Obviously, priorities for training must be established for each family, considering criteria such as their interests, needs, and available time and resources. Many professionals automatically assume that parent training is necessary and valuable. This assumption, however, needs to be critically examined. Winton and Turnbull (1981) interviewed mothers of preschool children in regard to their perspectives on preschool services and parent involvement; 65% of the mothers indicated that their most preferred parent involvement activity was maintaining informal contact with their child's teacher; 13% chose parent training opportunities as their most preferred activity. One of the contradictions to the assumption on the value of parent training was expressed by a mother in this study, who is also an elementary teacher.

> I think you have to be removed as a parent from the situation . . . living with a child like this and trying to train them is just about an impossibility. It's just the constant supervision of a child like this that really gets to you after a while. It's frightening enough without having to teach them too.

A need to turn their child's education over to competent professionals so that they could take a break from educational problems was expressed by 65% of the mothers. This should not be interpreted as a total lack of interest in helping their child develop skills at home; rather, parents were expressing the view that they were not interested in being the primary teacher of the child.

Another consideration of parent as teacher model is the effect it has on the child. As will be discussed in this section, many parent training programs have resulted in substantial skill development for handicapped children. Parent training may, however, have unanticipated consequences on the parent-child relationship. Sondra Diamond, a physically handicapped psychologist, has written an insightful chapter entitled "Growing Up With Parents of a Handicapped Child" (1981). She made the following comments pertaining to the personal impact of "home training" she experienced.

> Something happens in a parent when relating to his disabled child; he forgets that they're a kid first. I used to think about that a lot when I was a kid. I would be off in a euphoric state, drawing or coloring or cutting out paper dolls, and as often as not the activity would be turned into an occupational therapy session. "You're not holding the scissors right," "Sit up straight so your curvature doesn't get worse." That era was ended when I finally let loose a long and exhaustive tirade. "I'm just a kid! You can't therapize me all the time! I don't think about my handicap all the time like you do!" (p. 30)

Severely handicapped children need time to be children—to play, to be "unprogrammed," to relax. Sometimes parents need help in learning to give their children the right to be different, as well as the right to be normalized.

Some parents become excellent teachers of their handicapped children, and others are not inclined to develop these skills. The individuality of parents requires that their priorities and interests be respected.

Home Training

One approach to parent training is to teach intervention skills to the parents in their home. This approach has the greatest utility with parents of preschoolers who are providing direct care to their child during the day.

Home training is not a substitute for providing severely handicapped children a free appropriate public education once they reach school age. Certainly, however, training parents in the home can be a *supplement* to public school services. In home training, the trainer who goes into the home can work with both the parent and the handicapped child and, furthermore, can observe the parent interacting with and teaching the child.

A model home-based instruction program, the Portage Project, was developed by Shearer and Shearer (1972). The Portage Project serves preschool handicapped children in south central Wisconsin. Rather than having a classroom program, all teaching is done in the home by the parents. A home teacher is assigned to each family and has the responsibility of teaching the parents skills in specifying objectives, methods of instruction, and principles of behavior management. The home teacher is assigned 15 families and visits with each family 1 day per week for an hour and a half. During each weekly visit, an individualized curriculum is planned for the child in language, self-help, cognitive, motor, and socialization skills. The project incorporates the following behavioral model.

1. Three behaviors are targeted each week to be accomplished by the next weekly visit.
2. Baseline data are recorded by the home teacher.
3. The home teacher models teaching techniques for the parent and then observes the parent teaching the child.
4. Written directions are provided to the parents.
5. The parents follow through on the teaching sequences during the week.
6. The home teacher records post-baseline data to determine if the child has mastered the objectives.

Boyd (1979) reports that one goal of the project is to make parents as independent as possible in instructional planning and implementation. Individual needs of parents are identified through the use of a Parental Behavior Inventory, which allows targeting of specific areas for systematic skill development. In addition to direct instruction from the home teacher, parents are also given a set of readings on various topics in teaching and home management. By the end of training, all parents were writing their own activity charts with varying degrees of help from the home teacher.

Although the majority of home training programs have been conducted with parents of preschool children, this model applies to parents of older severely handicapped persons as well. Fowler, Johnson, Whitman and Zukotynski (1978) reported on a successful program to teach behavior management skills to the mother of a 24-year-old profoundly retarded woman. Evening sessions were conducted in the home to train the mother to teach self-help (e.g., hair brushing, tooth brushing, face washing), preacademic (e.g., bead stringing and ring stacking), and compliance skills. Results documented the success of the program in changing the mother's behavior, which in turn produced positive changes in the daughter's behavior.

When professionals make home visits, basic courtesy should be extended. For example, teachers should ask the parents in advance for permission to visit them at home, be prompt, listen attentively to the family's concerns when they might conflict with the purpose of the meeting, and respect the family's privacy. Many parents of handicapped children feel threatened by home visits and may believe that the visitor (professional) is evaluating their lifestyle or standard of living. Establishing rapport from the beginning is essential. Giesey (1970) offers valuable "how-to" suggestions for readers desiring more information on the mechanics of home visits.

A drawback to home training often occurs when parents work during the day and are at home only in the evenings. When both parents have busy jobs in which they interact with people all day, they might prefer "time-out" from professional interactions in the evening. Some families are large and live in crowded conditions. Disruptions during home sessions can make it virtually impossible to concentrate on training. Another drawback happens in situations in which the handicapped child is in a school-based program during the day. In these circumstances, the training might best be delivered in the same setting as the program attended by the child.

Group Training

Group training of parents in teaching competencies can be conducted in a variety of ways. Bricker and Bricker (1976) trained mothers of handicapped children in the four curriculum areas of language, cognitive, motor, and social development. As a component of the Infant, Toddler, and Preschool Research and Intervention Project, mothers were requested to spend half a day each week at the center, which provided the educational program to their handicapped child. Mothers attended weekly training groups that focused on a single skill. Emphasis in training sessions was given to specifying target behaviors, discussing training strategies, and reviewing evaluation data collected by the mothers. In demonstration sessions the mothers' teaching strategies were observed

by the trainer. These sessions let the trainers help the mothers refine their teaching skills.

Another model for group training of parents is described by Baker and Heifetz (1976). This program is part of a behavior modification residential camp for retarded children (Baker, 1973). Parents meet in groups of 6 to 12 families with a preprofessional trainer. The instructional program is packaged into an assessment booklet with instructional manuals entitled "Basic Skills," "Early Self-Help Skills," "Advanced Self-Help Skills," "Toilet Training," "Beginning Speech," "Speech and Language," "Early Play Skills," "Play Skills," and "Behavior Problems." The trainer uses the manuals as the basis for instruction. Each manual includes content related to pinpointing behaviors, teaching principles, using rewards, and recording progress. The manuals are enhanced by case studies, explanatory illustrations, and specific program outlines. This model comprises nine training sessions, and parents receive a $50 tuition refund if they attend at least eight of them.

Baker (1978) reported on a similar parent training model at Kansas Neurological Institute. Ten modules were developed and taught to parents in evening sessions, with one session each week. Five modules covered behavior management principles and techniques, two focused on teaching self-help skills, and the remaining ones covered a range of topics including legal rights, positioning, and adaptive equipment. A particularly interesting incentive used to maintain parent interest was the incorporation of audience participation games that were entertaining as well as instructional. At the end of the training, parents were also given an 8 × 10 color photograph of their child and a certificate indicating the achievement of "master parent." Pre- and post-test data showed that parents made significant gains in knowledge.

A comprehensive and systematic parent training program has been developed by Embry and her colleagues (Embry, Schilomoeller, Kelley, & O'Malley, Note 3; Embry, Kelley, Herbert-Jackson, & Baer, Note 4). They have developed a training curriculum for a 10-week course focusing on behavior management skills. Parents attend a group training session for 2½ hours 1 evening per week in which behavioral principles are discussed and an opportunity for sharing ideas and support is provided. In addition, a staff member makes a weekly "home-check" to observe parent-child interactions in two settings—instructional training and free play. Data indicate that parents do make some changes in their use of behavior management principles in both settings as a result of the formal training. These changes, however, do not always result in sufficient improvement in the child's behavior. When in-home feedback was added during the homechecks, generalization from group training to home was substantially increased. Embry's model of combining group training and home follow-up represents an exemplary approach.

A distinct advantage to group training models is that parents have the chance to learn from one another and to share their successes. Many parents benefit from this type of group involvement. In planning group training sessions, groups should be relatively small (12 persons or fewer) to increase the likelihood of meeting individual members' needs. Professionals and parents should jointly plan sessions to consider the schedules of the parents who will be attending. If the majority of the parents work, evening meetings may be the most convenient. The number and frequency of the meetings should be determined according to parent preferences. Practical obstacles, such as baby-sitting and transportation, can prevent parent participation. These problems can be eliminated by working out car pools and arranging for a baby-sitter at the same location as the group meeting. Meetings should use a variety of training strategies, including ones emphasizing active involvement of parents, and each session should end with an evaluation.

In the group training sessions, a procedure should be devised that meets the approval of both the educators and the parents to coordinate the instructional program of the handicapped child after the training is completed. Efforts at school and home should be simultaneously directed toward the same objectives, using similar teaching strategies. Coordination can partly be handled as the professionals and parents work together to develop the child's IEP. Once the IEP is developed, all parties have agreed on the appropriate goals and objectives for the child. However, further coordination is required to determine exactly what to teach at a given time. Professionals and parents might agree that weekly or biweekly home activity sheets would be helpful. These activity sheets, developed by the teacher, could include suggestions for ways the parents can follow up at home on specific skills and concepts currently being taught at school. Teachers must be reasonable in suggesting activities that can be accomplished within limited time constraints and typically without special instructional materials.

Group training sessions must be directed at the day-to-day concerns of parents. To insure the relevance of training, parents should help choose the topics of instruction. As parents recognize that they can teach their children effectively, their interest in more advanced training is likely to increase. Additional guidelines for implementing group training are provided by Cansler et al. (1975) and Auenback (1968).

Classroom Helper

A third alternative for training parents as teachers is to involve them in the classroom program as helpers (e.g., Hayden & Haring, 1976; Wiegerink & Parrish, 1976). Participation in the classroom gives parents the chance to observe their child and other handicapped children in an educational setting and to model the teaching strategies used by the teacher. An additional advantage is that this approach provides the teacher with some valuable assistance.

Parents served as classroom helpers in the Regional Intervention Program (RIP) in Nashville, Tennessee (Wiegerink & Parrish, 1976). In this preschool program, parents were expected to spend from 6 to 9 hours per week at the program working with their child. The first phase included working with their child in individual tutoring sessions or on special behavioral problems under the supervision of a case manager. Parents learned skills that enabled them to work successfully with their child at home. In addition to learning essential behavior modification skills, they received information on social, language, and motor development. As the skills of the child and parent progressed, the handicapped child was transferred to a preschool class in the program. Parents were expected to volunteer in the class for 6 months. This opportunity to be in the classroom enabled parents to learn competencies that prepared them to be effective teachers of their children. At the conclusion of the 6-month volunteer period, some parents assumed other duties in the program, such as conducting admission interviews with new families or administering assessment procedures. Parents had a significant role both as providers and recipients of the RIP services.

The classroom participation of parents requires careful and systematic planning. Serving as a classroom helper may be the outgrowth of home-based training or group training sessions. Parents should be given the back-up support to feel confident with this new role. In order to provide this support, educators and parents might jointly establish the expectations for parent involvement. Expectations might differ for individual parents, depending upon their schedules, time commitment, prerequisite teaching skills, and interest in being in the classroom.

When parents first start to work in the classroom, professionals should arrange frequent conferences to answer questions and provide feedback on performance. The most careful attention must be given to the interpersonal style of the professional-parent interactions in these conferences. It is important for parents to feel the gratification and satisfaction that results from being successful. At the same time, the professionals must help the parents refine their teaching skills. Parents should be encouraged to evaluate themselves.

Many working parents will be unable to participate in the classroom program. Alternative methods will have to be developed for increasing their competency in working with their children. Home-based instruction and group parent meetings should be considered. Additional information on parent training models has been reported by Snell and Dunkle (1979).

PARENTS AS ADVOCATES

The term *advocacy* has many different meanings; however, it is generally used to refer to advancing or securing the rights and interests of a client. Advocacy can take many directions but is mainly directed at federal or state laws, state agency regulations, local policies of school boards or county commissioners, community service agencies, or potential employers.

Many interactions among professionals and parents are advocacy oriented as they try to advance or secure the rights and interests of handicapped persons and their families. A parent program with advocacy as a primary objective might focus on (a) legal advocacy, (b) citizen advocacy, or (c) locating professional, community, family, and financial resources.

Legal Advocacy

Legal advocacy may take the form of instituting a lawsuit, lobbying for legislation, participating in a due process procedure, or seeking to influence administrative decisions. Parent-professional coalitions have been extremely successful in advancing the rights of handicapped persons through legal advocacy. Right-to-education litigation and the passage of P.L. 94-142 are two results of these efforts. In addition, every state except New Mexico has passed mandatory education legislation for handicapped individuals that establishes the right to education in the state law. Since legal rights to education have already been established for handicapped students, the question of whether legal advocacy efforts are still necessary is sometimes raised. Unquestionably, legal advocacy for the handicapped population must continue in order to enhance the educational, vocational, personal, and recreational quality of life.

Some of the particular issues requiring legal advocacy include insuring that P.L. 94-142 and state legislation is not repealed, mandatory educational services for handicapped individuals between the ages of 3 and 5 and 18 and 21, increased financial appropriations for the education of handicapped students, pro-

vision of meaningful career education, increased enforcement of nondiscriminatory employment practices, revision of guardianship legislation in accord with the principle of normalization, and review and revision of sterilization legislation.

Professionals and parents can organize group meetings to explore issues requiring legal advocacy. If there is strong interest, training sessions should be planned for all concerned parties. The purpose would be to define exactly what goals need to be accomplished and to plan strategies for accomplishing them. Since many professionals and parents alike are unsure of the best method of influencing legislation or administrative decisions, the training leader should have direct experience with legal advocacy and be knowledgeable in the organization of advocacy coalitions.

One of the most successful advocacy associations is the PACER Center, the Parent Advocacy Coalition for Education Rights (Goldberg & Goldberg, 1979). PACER was organized in 1977 as a coalition of 18 Minnesota organizations. A variety of workshops is provided by PACER staff, who are mostly parents of handicapped children. A major objective of many workshops is advocacy training. Biklen (1974) has prepared a manual that could be an excellent training tool for legal advocacy groups. It outlines step-by-step procedures for various strategies, including demonstrations, letter writing, public hearings and fact-finding forums, communication, symbolic acts, negotiation, lobbying, and boycotts. The National Association for Retarded Citizens (1973) and Paul, Neufeld, and Pelosi (1977) also provide practical assistance to persons planning advocacy campaigns. Other sources of information in regard to legal assistance and support include:

- Closer Look
  Box 1492
  Washington, D.C. 20013
- The National Center for Law and the Handicapped
  1235 North Eddy Street
  South Bend, Indiana 46617
- Council for Exceptional Children
  Governmental Relations Unit
  1920 Association Drive
  Reston, Virginia 22091
- American Civil Liberties Union
  84 Fifth Avenue
  New York, New York 10011
- Reed Martin, J.D.
  Public Law Division of Research Press
  2612 N. Mattis Ave.,
  Champaign, Ill 61820

When educational professionals and parents in a particular program decide to collaborate in legal advocacy, they should communicate with other local, state, and national advocacy groups. The addresses above provide national contacts. At the local and state levels, contact should be made with interest organizations (associations for retarded citizens), advocacy councils, interagency coalitions, and special commissions established by local or state agencies to advocate for handicapped individuals. Advocacy efforts that are coordinated and speak with singular purpose for a substantial number of people are likely to be more successful in accomplishing their goal than multiple splinter groups. This kind of effort provides a meaningful forum in which parents and professionals can interact.

Citizen Advocacy

Wolfensberger (1972) describes citizen advocacy as individualized short- or long-term relationships that may include formal roles (adoptive parenthood, guardianship) or informal roles (friend). The functions of the advocate will depend upon the needs of the client. Citizen advocacy is largely distinguished by the personal relationship between two or more people in overcoming some of the complex life problems associated with handicapping conditions (Turnbull, 1977). Citizen advocacy relationships might be structured so that the advocate spends a specific amount of time with the handicapped individual each week. The shared time might be directed at personal communication about concerns or problems, developing leisure-time hobbies, taking advantage of community recreation (swimming, shooting basketball), going shopping, or developing social skills. Informal citizen advocacy may be likened to Big Brother or Big Sister programs.

The need for moderately and severely handicapped persons to have personal relationships cannot be overstated. Sometimes, in the desire to provide systematic training programs, we overemphasize skill development and underemphasize humanistic concerns such as developing personal relationships with others.

Parents and professionals might jointly establish a community citizen advocacy program. They would need to identify interested volunteers to serve as advocates and to train the volunteers to prepare them for their advocacy roles. Volunteers might be recruited from civic or service clubs, religious organizations, nearby colleges or universities, senior citizens' groups, or the citizenry at large. Since the volunteers may have had limited previous exposure to handicapped persons, training sessions should involve an overview of handicapping conditions, prin-

ciples of behavior management, and principles of normalization. The volunteers could be assigned a particular handicapped individual with whom they will develop a relationship, considering preferences such as age and degree of disability. After individual assignments have been made, each advocate needs more detailed information about the associate, such as level of skill development, special interests, and behavioral needs identified by the parents and professionals. This type of background information can enable the advocate to approach the new relationship with confidence. More detailed guidelines are provided to professionals and parents by the Texas Association for Retarded Citizens (1973).

Locating Professional, Community, Family, and Financial Resources

Many parents of moderately and severely handicapped children are unsure of where to go for specialized professional help (pediatricians, speech therapists, physical therapists, ophthalmologists, orthopedists, psychiatrists, dentists, audiologists, and others), community recreation services, religious opportunities, baby-sitting, respite care services, or financial aid. Advocacy efforts are required in helping to locate or sometimes instigate resources and services.

Parent meetings can be scheduled to give an overview of this information. A panel presentation could be made on obtaining various professional services, or a representative from an interagency council might speak to the group on the particular services of various agencies set up to help handicapped persons and their families. Parents should also be encouraged to share information with each other related to the particular professionals and agencies with whom they have had positive interactions. Educational professionals might start a community service file or directory, which would need to be updated regularly. This file or directory could be made available to parents when they have particular questions.

Many parents of moderately and severely handicapped children find that the child is excluded from many community recreation services and religious opportunities. If these are problems, educators might work with parents in trying to locate services or work directly with the personnel of recreation and church programs to increase their awareness of the needs and to prepare them with skills to serve moderately and severely handicapped individuals.

Another major area in which parents often need help is in locating baby-sitting and respite care services. Some parents of moderately and severely handicapped children have an extremely difficult time finding persons who feel comfortable and confident in assuming responsibility for their child. Educators might encourage high school service clubs or community volunteer groups to consider taking on such projects. When lists of baby-sitters and/or respite care providers are generated, professionals and parents might jointly plan and conduct some training sessions on topics such as behavior management, feeding problems, language stimulation, medication, and handling special problems. Training can help insure the success of baby-sitters and respite care providers. Parents of children in an educational program might consider setting up a baby-sitting cooperative in which they agree to take care of one another's children. If parents are interested in such a strategy, a group parent meeting might be devoted to planning the logistics.

The final resource that requires advocacy is locating and obtaining financial aid. There can be extreme excess cost associated with moderate and severe handicapping conditions. Often the lack of awareness of financial resources results in many eligible persons receiving no assistance. This unfortunate situation can be prevented by active advocacy efforts directed at compiling accurate information on available financial resources. Educators and parents might work on a collaborative project of compiling a financial directory. The purpose of this directory would be to identify financial sources, including supplemental security income (Social Security Administration), Crippled Children's Services, Easter Seals, and Vocational Rehabilitation. Information should also be compiled on possible income tax deductions related to handicapping conditions.

For each source of financial aid, information should be compiled on criteria for eligibility, including the age of qualifying handicapped individuals, level of family income, type of disability, severity of disability, and manner in which the money can be spent. After the information has been collected, it should be shared with all parents and continually updated to remain useful. If it becomes known that a potential financial source, such as supplemental security income, is turning away parents who should qualify for help according to the specified regulation, professionals and parents might work together to secure the rights of parents who qualify for support.

SUMMARY

Historically, parent-professional interactions have not been as positive and productive as they might have been. The passage of P.L. 94-142 has established new ground rules for both educational professionals and parents in interacting with one another. Associated with each of the six major principles of P.L. 94-142—zero reject, nondiscriminatory assessment, Individualized Educational Programs, least restrictive alternative, due process, and parent participation—are requirements for shared decision making and responsibility in insuring that handicapped students receive an appropriate education.

In addition to the interaction required by P.L. 94-142, educators and parents frequently interact in parent programs developed as an integral part of the educational services delivered to the handicapped child. Suggestions for these interactions were made according to the various roles and responsibilities associated with being the parent of a handicapped child, including parents as parents, parents as teachers, and parents as advocates.

Regardless of the particular issue being addressed, the key to successful parent-professional interactions is mutual respect and open communication. Appropriately preparing moderately and severely handicapped individuals with the academic, social, emotional, and vocational skills to function in society is a complex process. It requires the best efforts of parents and professionals working together as partners to accomplish mutually defined goals.

REFERENCES

Armstrong v. Kline, 476 F. Supp. 583 (E.D. Pa. 1979).

Auenback, A. *Parents learn through group discussion: Principles and protection of parent group education.* New York: John Wiley, 1968.

Avis, D.W. Deinstitutionalization jet lag. In A.P. Turnbull & H.R. Turnbull (Eds.), *Parents speak out: Views from the other side of the two-way mirror.* Columbus, Ohio: Charles E. Merrill, 1978.

Baker, B.L. Camp Freedom: Behavior modification for retarded children in a therapeutic camp setting. *American Journal of Orthopsychiatry,* 1973, *43,* 418–427.

Baker, B.L., & Heifetz, L.J. The read project: Teaching manuals for parents of retarded children. In T.D. Tjossem (Ed.), *Intervention strategies for high risk infants and young children.* Baltimore: University Park Press, 1976.

Baker, D. *Project Learn parent training manual.* Lawrence, Kans.: Bureau of Child Research, 1978.

Biklen, D. *Let our children go: An organizing manual for advocates and parents.* Syracuse, N.Y.: Human Policy Press, 1974.

Boyd, R.D. Systematic parent training through a home based model. *Exceptional Children,* 1980, *45*(8), 647–650.

Bricker, D., & Casuso, V. Family involvement: A critical component of early intervention. *Exceptional Children,* 1979, *46*(2), 108–115.

Bricker, W.A., & Bricker, D.D. The infant, toddler, and preschool research and intervention project. In T.D. Tjossem (Ed.), *Intervention strategies for high risk infants and young children.* Baltimore: University Park Press, 1976.

Bristol, M.M., & Gallagher, J.J. A family focus for intervention. In C. Ramey & P. Trohanis (Eds.), *Finding and educating the high risk and handicapped infant.* Baltimore: University Park Press, 1982.

Bronfenbrenner, U. *A report on longitudinal evaluations of preschool programs: Is early intervention effective?* (Vol. II). Washington, D.C.: United States Department of Health, Education and Welfare, 1974.

Cansler, D.P., Martin, G.H., & Valand, M.C. *Working with families.* Winston-Salem, N.C.: Kaplan Press, 1975.

Cleveland, D., & Miller, N. Attitudes and life commitments of older siblings of mentally retarded adults: An exploratory study. *Mental Retardation, 1977, 15*(3), 38–41.

Coletta, A.J. *Working together: A guide to parent involvement.* Atlanta: Humanics Limited, 1977.

Consortium for Longitudinal Studies. *Summary report: Lasting effects after preschool.* Washington, D.C.: United States Department of Health and Human Services, 1979.

Dardig, J.C., & Heward, W.L. A systematic procedure for prioritizing IEP goals. *The Directive Teacher, 1981, 3*(2), 6–8.

Diamond, S. Growing up with parents of a handicapped child: A handicapped person's perspective. In J.L. Paul (Ed.), *Understanding and working with parents of children with special needs.* New York: Holt, Rinehart & Winston, 1981.

Doll, E.A. *Vineland Social Maturity Scale: Condensed manual of directions* (Rev. ed.), Minneapolis: American Guidance Service, 1965.

Federal Register. Washington, D.C.: U.S. Government Printing Office, August 23, 1977.

Federal Register. Washington, D.C.: U.S. Government Printing Office, January 19, 1981.

Fialkowski v. Shapp, 405 F. Supp. 946 (E.D. Pa. 1975).

Fowler, S.A., Johnson, M.R., Whitman, T.L., & Zukotynski, G. Teaching a parent in the home to train self-help skills and increase compliance in her profoundly retarded adult daughter. *AAESPH Review, 1978, 9,* 151–161.

Giesey, R. (Ed.). *A guide for home visitors.* Nashville: George Peabody College, DARCEE, 1970.

Gilliam, J.E., & Coleman, M.C. Who influences IEP committee decisions? *Exceptional Children, 1981, 47*(8), 642–644.

Goldberg, P., & Goldberg, M. PACER Center: Parents learn about special education laws. *Education Unlimited, 1979, 1*(4), 34–37.

Goldstein, S., Strickland, B., Turnbull, A.P., & Curry, L. An observational analysis of the IEP conference. *Exceptional Children, 1980, 46*(4), 278–286.

Goldstein, S., & Turnbull, A.P. The use of two strategies to increase parent participation in the IEP conference. *Exceptional Children, 1982, 48*(4), 360–361.

Gordon, I.J. A home learning center approach to early stim-

ulation. Gainesville, Fl.: Institute for Development of Human Resources, 1971. (Grant No. MH 16037-02)

Grossman, F.K. *Brothers and sisters of retarded children.* Syracuse, N.Y.: Syracuse University Press, 1972.

Hayden, A.H., & Haring, N.G. Early intervention for high risk infants and young children: Programs for Down's syndrome children. In T.D. Tjossem (Ed.), *Intervention strategies for high risk infants and young children.* Baltimore: University Park Press, 1976.

Heward, W.L., Dardig, J.C., & Rossett, A. *Working with parents of handicapped children* . Columbus, Ohio: Charles E. Merrill, 1979.

Hines v. Pittsburgh County Board of Education. 497 F. Supp. 403 (E.D. N.C. 1980).

Horowitz, F.D., & Paden, L.Y. The effectiveness of environmental intervention programs. In B.M. Caldwell & H.N. Ricciuti (Eds.), *Review of child development research* (Vol. 3). Chicago: University of Chicago Press, 1973.

Karnes, M.B., & Teska, J.A. Toward successful parent involvement in programs for handicapped children. In J.J. Gallagher (Ed.), *New directions in exceptional children: Parents and families of handicapped children.* (#4). San Francisco: Jossey-Bass, 1980.

Karnes, M.B., Teska, J.A., Hodgins, A.S., & Badger, E.D. Educational intervention at home by mothers of disadvantaged infants. *Child Development, 1970, 41,* 925–935.

Lillie, D. Educational and psychological strategies for working with parents. In J.L. Paul (Ed.), *Understanding and working with parents of children with special needs.* New York: Holt, Rinehart & Winston, 1981.

Marion, R.L. Communicating with parents of culturally diverse exceptional children. *Exceptional Children, 1980, 46*(8), 616–625.

McLoughlin, J.A., Edge, D., & Strenecky, B. Perspective on parental involvement in the diagnosis and treatment of learning disabled children. *Journal of Learning Disabilities, 1978, 11*(5), 32–37.

Michaelis, C.T. Mainstreaming: A mother's perspective. *Topics in Early Childhood Special Education, 1981, 1*(1), 11–16.

Mills v. Board of Education of the District of Columbia. 348 F. Supp. 866 (D.C.D.C., 1972).

Moroney, R.M. Public social policy: Impact on families with handicapped children. In J.L. Paul (Ed.), *Understanding and working with parents of children with special needs.* New York: Holt, Rinehart & Winston, 1981.

National Association for Retarded Citizens. *Action guidelines: Evaluating and monitoring education services for mentally retarded persons.* Arlington, Tex.: National Association for Retarded Citizens, 1973.

Nihira, K., Foster, R., Shellhaas, M., & Leland, H. *AAMD Adaptive Behavior Scale: Manual* (Rev. ed.). Washington, D.C.: American Association on Mental Deficiency, 1969.

Paul, J.L., Neufeld, G.R., & Pelosi, J.W. (Eds.). *Child advocacy within the system.* Syracuse, N.Y.: Syracuse University Press, 1977.

Paul, J.W., Turnbull, A.P., & Cruickshank, W.M. *Main-*

streaming: A practical guide. Syracuse, N.Y.: Syracuse University Press, 1977.

Pennsylvania Association for Retarded Children v. Commonwealth of Pennsylvania, 343 F. Supp. 279 (E.D. Pa. 1972).

Porcella, A. Increasing parent involvement. *Education and Training of the Mentally Retarded,* 1980, *15*(2), 155–157.

Rockowitz, R.J., & Davidson, P.W. Discussing diagnostic findings with parents. *Journal of Learning Disabilities,* 1979, *12*(1), 11–16.

Roos, P. Parents of mentally retarded children—misunderstood and mistreated. In A.P. Turnbull & H.R. Turnbull (Eds.), *Parents speak out: Views from the other side of the two-way mirror.* Columbus, Ohio: Charles E. Merrill, 1978.

Schaefer, E.S. Parents as educators: Evidence from cross-sectional longitudinal and intervention research. *Young Children,* 1972, *27*, 227–239.

Schlesinger, H.S., & Meadow, K.P. Emotional support for parents. In D.L. Lillie & P.L. Trohanis (Eds.), *Teaching parents to teach.* New York: Walker, 1976.

Schulz, J.B. The parent-professional conflict. In A.P. Turnbull & H.R. Turnbull (Eds.), *Parents speak out: Views from the other side of the two-way mirror.* Columbus, Ohio: Charles E. Merrill, 1978.

Shearer, D.E., & Shearer, M.S. The Portage Project: A model for early childhood intervention. In T.D. Tjossem (Ed.), *Intervention strategies for high risk infants and young children.* Baltimore: University Park Press, 1972.

Shearer, M.S. A home-based parent training model. In D.L. Lillie & P.L. Trohanis (Eds.), *Teaching parents to teach.* New York: Walker, 1976.

Snell, M.E., & Dunkle, M. A review of established programs for training parents of young handicapped children. *Education Unlimited,* 1979, *1*(5), 54–58.

Texas Association for Retarded Citizens. *Citizen advocacy: A manual for local implementation and operation.* Austin: Texas Association for Retarded Citizens, 1973.

Tjossem, T.D. (Ed.). *Intervention strategies for high risk infants and young children.* Baltimore: University Park Press, 1976.

Turnbull, A.P. Citizen advocacy in special education training. *Education and Training of the Mentally Retarded,* 1977, *12*, 166–169.

Turnbull, A.P., & Strickland, B. Parents and the educational system. In J.L. Paul (Ed.), *Understanding and working with parents of children with special needs.* New York: Holt, Rinehart & Winston, 1981.

Turnbull, A.P., Strickland, B., & Brantley, J.C. *Developing and implementing Individualized Education Programs* (2nd ed.). Columbus, Ohio: Charles E. Merrill, 1982.

Turnbull, H.R., & Turnbull, A.P. Deinstitutionalization and the law. *Mental Retardation,* 1975, *13*, 14–20.

Wiegerink, R., & Parrish, V. A parent-implemented preschool program. In D.L. Lillie & P.L. Trohanis (Eds.), *Teaching parents to teach.* New York: Walker, 1976.

Winton, P., & Turnbull, A.P. Parent involvement as viewed by parents of preschool handicapped children. *Topics in Early Childhood Special Education,* 1981, *1*(3), 11–19.

Wolfensberger, W. *The principle of normalization in human services.* Toronto, Can.: National Institute on Mental Retardation, 1972.

REFERENCE NOTES

1. Turnbull, A.P., Tyler, D.K., & Morrell, B.B. *An educational model for deinstitutionalization.* Proceedings of the Council for Exceptional Children Institute on Right to Education, CEC National Topical Conference, 1976.

2. National Committee for Citizens in Education. Unpublished manuscript serving as basis for Congressional testimony, 1979.

3. Embry, L.H., Schilomoeller, G.L., Kelley, M.L., & O'Malley, J. *A parent class for training parents as their children's therapists.* Paper presented at the meeting of the American Psychological Association, Chicago, August, 1975.

4. Embry, L.H., Kelley, M.L., Herbert-Jackson, E., & Baer, D.M. *Group parent training: An analysis of generalization from classroom to home.* Paper presented at the meeting of the American Association of Behavior Therapy, Chicago, November, 1978.

Introduction to Chapter 3

The right to obtain appropriate educational services is meaningful only if a student actually obtains those services. Two of the initial steps in this process are identifying the handicaps that a student displays and matching services to the student's needs. By designation, persons with moderate and severe handicaps are more "visible" than those with mild handicaps. Thus the process of identification is less tedious than is the purposeful translation of those identification results into an appropriate educational program.

In this chapter Rebecca Fewell and John Cone describe the typical procedure for identifying and placing moderately and severely handicapped students in public educational programs. Teachers and parents are essential contributors to these procedures; thus their grasp of the process—its rationale, terminology, and the instruments employed—is likely to influence the ultimate outcome and impact on the student. Once a student is placed into a suitable special classroom, the teacher's role becomes central. Identification and placement data will serve as broad-spectrum information, somewhat narrowing the focus for classroom assessment. However, to develop an individualized educational program (IEP), many more steps must be taken; these are described generally in chapters 4 and 5 and more specifically in the remainder of the text.

3

Identification and Placement of Severely Handicapped Children

Rebecca R. Fewell *is at the University of Washington and* **John D. Cone** *is at West Virginia University.*

The identification of a child's impairment is usually confirmed before the child is 18 months of age. In fact, many children today are diagnosed before birth and begin to receive treatment, even surgery. The impact of prenatal development on the child's future is of critical importance to his long-term outcome. Hagberg (1975) reports that 85% to 90% of severe intellectual and neurological problems result from prenatal causes. These problems must be identified and addressed early. Alarming as it may seem, the United Cerebral Palsy Foundation reports that if you wait for a pediatrician to refer a cerebrally damaged infant to an early intervention program, the mean age at referral is 14 months; if the parents refer their child, the mean age at referral is 4 months (Brazelton, 1981). Thus, the younger the child, the greater the chance for severe developmental problems. Children with severe problems should be identified while they are quite young and, if possible, placed in programs designed for young handicapped infants. For some moderately handicapped children, identification may not take place until some years later, possibly as late as their entrance into public schools. Regardless of when initial identification occurs, the process and procedures need to be clearly understood by the responsible staff, the child's family, and the agency or classroom staff that will eventually serve the child.

In this chapter, we clarify the classifications of severely and moderately handicapped, the target populations of this book, and then describe how children with severe handicaps are identified and how placements are selected. Throughout the chapter, we emphasize the role and responsibility of the identification team in initial assessment. Other chapters in this book describe the more extensive assessment process that occurs once a child has been placed in a classroom or program. Because severely handicapped children are identified during their early years, this chapter describes procedures and processes usually associated with very young children.

DEFINITIONS AND CLASSIFICATION

Before describing the identification process, we must identify the populations with whom we are concerned. This text addresses the instructional needs of moderately and severely handicapped students, who have traditionally been referred to as "trainable" (TMR). This term was meant to describe their potential to learn self-help tasks, basic communication skills, some functional academics, basic daily living skills, and vocational skills. The results of research (reported later in this volume) show that these individuals can master these skills with appropriate instruction. Unfortunately, when we label the moderately and severely retarded "trainable," the underlying implication is that the profoundly retarded are not capable of learning much at all. This, of course, is erroneous. The profoundly retarded are, however, the most varied of all retarded groups in terms of additional motor or sensory impairment and serious medical problems (such as seizures), as well as the group most frequently institutionalized. These factors contribute more to our difficulty in teaching them than to their potential for learning, which we are only beginning to recognize.

We still need to classify students according to some criteria to determine their eligibility for services. Unfortunately, classification criteria have been slow to change over the years. Past definitions have described a child's impairments rather than the kinds of services and instructional environments needed. Educators and policy makers must rely upon earlier definitions until we can persuade those who create classification standards that definitions based on services needed are more appropriate and functional and less demeaning. Fortunately, we are beginning to see slight changes in definitions (originally formulated in the 1970s) that reflect an awareness of more functional considerations.

Moderately Handicapped

"Moderately handicapped" has been defined in terms of retardation rather than handicap, stemming from Grossman's (1977) definition of moderate retardation as performance of 3.01 to 4.00 standard deviation units below the mean on a standardized intelligence test. If the test used for classification is the *Stanford-Binet Intelligence Scale* (Terman & Merrill, 1973), then intelligence scores falling between 36 and 51 would be considered in the moderate retardation range. On the *Wechsler Intelligence Scale for Children* (WISC) (Wechsler, 1949, 1974), the equivalent scores would be 40 to 54. A measurement of adaptive behavior must also be included in any classification of mental retardation. In *Manual on Terminology and Classification in Mental Retardation* (Grossman, 1977), mental retardation is defined as "significantly subaverage general intellectual functioning existing concurrently with deficits in adaptive behavior, and manifested during the developmental period" (p. 5). The phrase "existing concurrently" shows that the deficits in intelligence and adaptive behavior must occur simultaneously. Compared to previous definitions, the 1977 definition delineated more precisely and narrowly the population of individuals falling into the retarded range. To be considered moderately retarded, the individual must show a measured intelli-

gence score of 54 or below *(Wechsler Scale)* or 51 *(Stanford-Binet) and* exhibit adaptive behaviors inappropriate for his or her age and cultural group.

The fact that definitions of "moderately handicapped" have their formal roots in definitions of "moderate retardation" does not mean there are no such classifications, for indeed this book's title attests to the widespread use of the term "handicapped." The lack of a clearly specified definition of "moderately handicapped" reflects the awakening interest during the 1970s in a previously unserved group, the severely handicapped. Several definitions are currently used to designate this group.

Severely Handicapped

Perhaps the most widely used definition of "severely handicapped" is the one adopted by the Bureau of Education for the Handicapped (U.S. Office of Education, 1975):

Severely handicapped children are those who because of the intensity of their physical, mental, or emotional problems, need educational, social, psychological and medical services beyond those which are traditionally offered by regular and special education programs, in order to maximize participation in society and self-fulfillment. Such severely handicapped children may possess severe language or perceptual-cognitive deprivations and evidence a number of abnormal behaviors including failure to attend to even the most pronounced stimuli, self-mutilation, manifestations of durable and intense temper tantrums, and the absence of even the most rudimentary forms of verbal control. They may also have extremely fragile physiological conditions. (Sec. 121.2)

Dollar and Brooks (1980) point out three essential characteristics of severely handicapped children identified through this definition: "(a) they must have a 'severe' or 'intense' handicap; (b) they need an educational program requiring greater resources than are normally provided by traditional programs; and (c) they need programs that focus on skills necessary for greater independent functioning and 'self-fulfillment' " (p. 88). This definition would certainly include children often classified as *deaf-blind, multiply handicapped, autistic, cerebral palsied, neurologically impaired, brain-damaged, schizophrenic,* and *mentally retarded,* but in no way would it be limited to these groups.

Members of the Southeastern Regional Coalition (SERC) debated the problem and finally arrived at a definition that they felt described the population they were serving, while also reflecting the more traditional measurement requirement included in several states' official definitions. SERC's (1979) definition is:

The severely handicapped individual is defined for educational purposes as 1) having serious primary disabilities that are cognitive (e.g., -4 standard deviations below a normal IQ on a standardized test of intelligence such as the Revised Stanford-Binet Test of Intelligence*) and/or behavioral (e.g., autistic or childhood schizophrenic), 2) having the high probability of additional physical and/or sensory handicaps, and 3) requiring significantly more resources than are provided for the mildy and moderately handicapped in special education programs.* (p. 39)

The SERC definition adds specificity to previous definitions in order for states to have a quantifiable measure for decision making. At the same time, it includes other disabilities besides or in place of cognition; finally, it notes the importance of additional services. Although this definition has no nationwide recognition, it has been officially adopted by several states.

In synthesizing the descriptions of the children whose needs are addressed in this text, we can say that the target population will include (*a*) all moderately, severely, and profoundly retarded individuals; (*b*) all severely and profoundly emotionally disturbed persons; (*c*) all moderately to profoundly retarded or disturbed individuals who have at least one additional impairment (i.e., deafness, blindness, crippling condition).

Clearly, additional handicaps do not have an additive effect on the child; the effect is multiplicative. A child's severe handicaps in one area cannot be measured or treated separate from their impact on skill development in general. For example, the inability to see interferes with the acquisition of fine and gross motor skills; the inability to express yourself in ways that others understand can interfere with social development or bring on behavior management problems.

We are not trying here to devise a classification system that encompasses all handicapped persons. We do hope that future systems will focus on different aspects from those of the past. Individuals whose behavior was different from the majority were first identified and classified with the intention of providing them the services and help they needed. Today the intent remains the same; more problematic are the procedures for determining who needs what services and how these services can be delivered most effectively.

INCIDENCE AND PREVALENCE

The actual number of individuals identified as mentally retarded is not known. However, the consensus is that the incidence of mentally retarded persons is

3% and the prevalence is 1% (Tarjan, Wright, Eyman, & Keeran, 1973); that is, 100 persons in a town of 10,000 are mentally retarded. The U.S. Office of Education (1975) reports 2.3% of the school-aged population as mentally retarded, with 0.8% falling into the moderate to severe range. Dunn (1973) and Penrose (1966) estimate that the ratio of EMR to TMR to S/PMR is 12:3:1 or 75%:20%:5%. Thus, in the town of 10,000, we have 100 retarded persons, 75% of whom would be mildly retarded, 20% moderately and severely retarded, and 5% in the severely/ profoundly retarded range. We can assume that the population of severely handicapped is even greater than these figures suggest because these estimates do not include people with severe emotional disturbance. Phillip Roos, in a publication for the National Association for Retarded Citizens (1976), remarks upon the size of this population.

We are dealing with the most severely handicapped members of the human race—individuals whose nervous systems have been seriously damaged, or never developed properly. The severely and profoundly retarded include approximately the lowest 5% of the retarded population. More than 99% of all persons learn more easily than they do. Many have IQs that may be termed "unmeasurable." (p. 5)

While numbers are a concern of administrators and do influence dollars, teacher–pupil ratios, and length of instructional time, the ways in which people are identified as moderately or severely handicapped are more critical to the issues addressed in this book. We will now describe the process and procedures for decisions that identify children as handicapped.

THE IDENTIFICATION TEAM

The team of professionals that designates a child as moderately or severely handicapped is seldom the same group that decides what should be included in the child's instructional program. The reason for this relates to both timing and responsibilities. Because severely impaired people are usually identified during infancy and have physiological problems, a team in a medical center is the most likely team to make the initial identification. If the problem is not detected until the child enters the public schools, then not only is the team quite different, but there is a greater focus on aspects of the assessment process that are more readily translated into actual intervention strategies. In this section, we briefly describe characteristics that apply to all teams and process models that describe how members relate to one another.

Characteristics of Service Teams

In any field (for example, business, religion, medicine, or education), professionals who work together contribute their particular expertise in order to bring about better service. We have all benefitted from such teamwork, which has existed for years. Regardless of the field, all teams operate according to certain underlying principles. These principles may or may not be clearly articulated and may be simply learned as individuals begin to work as a team (Fewell, 1982). Golin and Ducanis (1981) describe three attributes that characterize team organization: composition, functions, and task. The *composition,* or membership, will depend on the task. For example, a newborn Down syndrome infant may require a medical team including a geneticist and other health services personnel. However, a child who is to be identified and placed in an appropriate educational setting may have a psychologist, therapist, parents, and special educator on the team.

The *functions* of the team are identified in terms of the organizations for which they operate and the services they provide. Teams in a community-based mental health center would be likely to focus on problems related to the family, the environment, and other similar concerns. In contrast, a team in a vocational rehabilitation center would emphasize employment concerns. While there is, of course, some overlap in functions, the major functions of each team are distinctive because of its association with a particular institution.

A team may limit its concern to a single *task* (medical diagnosis, for example); once this task has been completed, the case is referred to another team. When very clearly defined tasks exist, there is usually role delineation within the team. Each member is there to contribute specific knowledge and skills. In cases where the team's function is to oversee the assessment and the implementation of educational services, the team is far more likely to have a long-term relationship with the family; team members tend to know much about each other's roles and can help one another in both assessment and intervention.

Process Models for Team Services

The ways in which team members relate to one another, to the handicapped child and the parents, and to other care providers can be described through three team models: multidisciplinary, interdisciplinary, and transdisciplinary. Because a handicapped child will probably be served by several teams, each child is likely to be exposed to teams that operate with different models. If team members have a clear understanding of the model they are following, their work together will be smoother. Likewise, families will know what to expect from team members, both individually and collectively.

The Multidisciplinary Team

The multidisciplinary approach to the delivery of services has evolved from a medical model in which people with expertise in various areas contribute to the common good of the patient (Hart, 1977). This model has been used most frequently (as you might expect) in the initial identification of handicapped children. In this model, team members are expected to be competent in their discipline and to work independently of other team members. For example, a social worker may take a family history, a psychologist may give a mental measure, a pediatrician may provide a medical exam, and an audiologist may test the child's hearing. Each person may provide some oral feedback to the parents, then file a written report for the child's permanent clinical record. In these cases, there is a minimum of communication across disciplines (Sirvis, 1978). In the multidisciplinary model, one person may be responsible for scheduling the various appointments, but there is no formal attempt to allocate resources by prioritizing the child's needs, by considering the overlap between disciplines, or by providing coordinated feedback to the family (McCormick & Goldman, 1979).

The Interdisciplinary Team

The interdisciplinary team functions very similarly to the multidisciplinary team; individual examiners see the client independent of each other. However, team members get together to discuss the case and to make recommendations (Hart, 1977). McCormick and Goldman (1979) indicate the importance of a clearly specified case manager in this model. The case manager prevents fragmentation and directs information flow; however, there is no provision for monitoring services. Holm and McCartin (1978) describe the interdisciplinary team slightly differently. According to Holm and McCartin, there is considerably more interchange between team members during the service period; members are likely to ask one another for additional information, to work together to provide a particular diagnosis, or to design a procedure for solving a particular problem. Holm and McCartin also perceive more mutual trust and respect between team members who rely on each other to improve and add to the skills of the whole team.

The Transdisciplinary Team

In the transdisciplinary team, each member is prepared to assume responsibility for other team members and represent them to the child and family (Hart,

1977). This is not to say that one member actually does the work of other team members, who in fact continue to make their own contributions in the initial diagnosis. However, one or two appropriate team members assume the responsibility for seeing that the recommendations of other team members are successfully put into effect (McCormick & Goldman, 1979). Because of the emphasis on program implementation, the transdisciplinary team model is especially useful for classroom assessment, program planning, and implementation. In addition, this model is extremely functional for teams that serve moderately and severely impaired children, where contributions from ancillary services and staff supplement the roles of teachers and other direct care personnel.

The ways in which transdisciplinary assessment teams operate vary considerably. Sailor (1977) advocates a model in which team members, working through the teacher, carry out their tasks in the classroom context.

We favor a self-contained, integrated model, rather than an isolated model. We would have the people from other disciplines doing what they do in the classroom, training the teachers or at least including the teacher as part of the educational process, and becoming a consultant more than a hands-on therapist for the handicapped. We do foster the idea of a team, but it's a team of consultants to the teacher. The teacher is the hub and focus of the activity, whatever the therapy. (p. 18)

Role of Parents on Service Teams

In addition to their disciplinary make-up and ways of operating, teams also vary in terms of the parents' role. Historically, teams were composed of professionals who evaluated children while parents waited anxiously in reception rooms. In the 1970s, some centers began including parents as observers and participants. As we have seen, P.L. 94-142 calls for the explicit participation of parents in the assessment process. In the 1980s, teams began to consider the transactional influence of the environment on the child and the child on the environment, described quite eloquently by Sameroff and Chandler (1975) as existing in both the continuum of reproductive casualty and the continuum of care-taking casualty. Today, team members within and across disciplines are translating research into practice as they measure these child–environment transactions and intervene with the aid of the parents, who are such critical parts of the child's environment. The participation of parents as full-fledged team members is most apparent in the IEP team, which may be an outgrowth of the original diagnostic team. Chapter 2 described the

parent role on this team in more detail. The diagnostic team responsible for determining the cause and immediate status of a child's impairments relies upon parental input, but conclusions about the specific nature of a child's condition remain primarily the responsibility of professionals.

Referral Decisions

Once a medical center team has identified a newborn child as severely handicapped, it must consider several factors to reach a decision about referral. First, there is a body of data that team members have obtained about the child and his or her parents. On the basis of these data, the child's needs will be specified and addressed. Second, there are state laws in regard to services required or possible for the child and the family. Third, there are available resources in the community. A team may identify multiple needs that require immediate action, such as correctional medical procedures, applications to a state developmental disabilities agency to qualify the child for certain financial assistance programs, or referral to an infant stimulation program.

While only large medical centers have infant education programs affiliated with a university-based medical complex, the number of these programs has increased dramatically in the last few years. The book *The Health Care/Education Relationship* (Gilderman, Taylor-Hershel, Prestridge, & Anderson, 1981) describes many of these programs; the authors describe the differences in expectations and services between medically-based infant programs and other community-based programs. If the identification team is located in a medical complex that includes an infant program, then an infant educator would very likely be included on the team and referral of the child to the hospital's infant program would be probable. If the medical identification team does not have ready access to an infant program, then the team will rely heavily on its social worker or placement specialist to identify community facilities to meet the infant's needs.

Identification teams that operate within public schools have different concerns and procedures for referral and placement. If the initial assessment team determines that a child qualifies for services because of a moderate or severe handicap, that team may (a) extend its services to include more intensive diagnosis and assessment; (b) recommend placement in a diagnostic classroom for a limited time so that specific programmatic needs and instructional strategies can be identified, tested, and adjusted; or (c) place the child in a classroom for an in-class assessment by the direct service team. This process may include further parent interviews or the evaluation of past records;

however, its primary emphasis is upon a functional, curriculum-based assessment that relies on informal observations in many settings and allows the teacher and other team members to validate the presence of skills and behavior problems (Snell & Renzaglia, 1982). This process and the steps that follow are described in detail in Chapter 4. The data gathered during this assessment are translated into an IEP. If any of the initial identification data (including results from standardized tests) are meaningful and appropriate for identifying the child's present educational performance, the IEP team may use this information and later include posttest data as one element in the evaluation plan.

Placement Decisions

P.L. 94-142 specifies how placement priorities are determined by LEAs. The most important concern is that each child be placed in the least restrictive environment. The impact of this requirement can be quickly seen by examining the educational placement of handicapped children since P.L. 94-142 was enacted. Until recently, about 10% of the handicapped children in the United States were receiving special education in residential schools (Haring, 1982). This figure has decreased dramatically as the number of handicapped children served in local public schools has increased. The regular education classroom is the preferred placement today; any other decision must be justified by specific circumstances.

Many placement decisions are temporary to allow time to determine the child's exact needs and instructional priorities. For example, if the child is placed in a diagnostic or trial classroom, the staff can learn about the child's idiosyncrasies and the conditions for optimal learning. In this environment, several prospective teachers can spend time with the child before reassignment, avoiding the stress of multiple placements.

These data are extremely valuable to those team members who are responsible for the permanent placement. When temporary placements are not possible, team members must be more aware of local resources and how well they can be used to meet needs. Nevertheless, as required by P.L. 94-142 and confirmed by the courts, the team must make its recommendations based on the child's needs, not on the basis of what is available.

The final placement decision is frequently made by the team that has been involved in the child's education during the trial placement or by those who conducted the functional assessment. Parents who have participated in this process since it began must agree in writing with the proposed placement. Their consent is voluntary and can be withdrawn at any time

(Turnbull & Turnbull, 1982). The placement decision is made after data have been gathered and analyzed, and the least restrictive educational options identified. White (1980) specifies three steps in the placement decision process: "1) the verification that the pupil does, indeed, require some form of special education or related service (as opposed to continuation in the regular education program alone); 2) the identification of the specific needs which must be met; and 3) the selection of actual placements and services to meet those needs." (p. 56)

The first step is actually accomplished during the initial identification and referral but is not verified until after the classroom assessment. The second step occurs during the trial placement or in-depth assessment; finally, the third step is manifested in the IEP.

IDENTIFICATION OF HANDICAPPED CHILDREN

Screening

Once someone has suggested that some aspect of a child's development may be different enough to merit further attention, the child is referred for screening. Screening is the process of determining the presence of atypical development. It is a broad level testing that separates development or behavior that is normal from that which is not normal. It does not identify why a problem exists, nor does it specify the characteristics of the behavior; it does determine the existence of atypical behavior and in some cases the general nature of typical behavior. Screening can cover several domains, such as language, ambulation, fine motor, and personal-social skills, or it can be restricted to a single domain such as vision.

Interviews and observations are more likely to be used as screening measures than is direct testing. Thus, very few materials are necessary, and many screening procedures can be completed in less than an hour. Screening can take place in a variety of settings; however, a parent or person familiar with the child is almost always needed. Results are quickly tabulated; in a matter of minutes, the presence of atypical development can be determined.

General screening can be done by people in any discipline related to child development. Relevant disciplines would include, but are not limited to, health care, child development, education, social work, and therapy. Frequently, screening is carried out by the first professional notified by the referral source. More recently, Child Find Teams have been assigned screening responsibilities; when possible, these team members do screening to determine the need for further assessment or services.

Screening outcomes either confirm the initial suspicion of delayed or abnormal development or verify normally developing behavior. The results of a screening measure given to the child or an interview with the parent(s) are compared to a normative sample of chronological age-mates. If these results clearly indicate atypical development, the child is referred to an assessment team with members representing the areas where skill deficits are suspected. In cases where there is some question as to the outcome of the screening, a second screening is usually scheduled some weeks later.

Severely handicapped children or children with physiological or genetic problems are likely to be screened during infancy by medical professionals. The screening procedures used with newborns are not used when screening occurs later. In the next section we will discuss some screening measures used to identify infants at risk, as well as some that are more appropriate for older children.

Apgar Scoring System

The Apgar Scoring System (Apgar, 1953) is a measure of a newborn's physical responsivity, development, and health. Pulse (heart rate), respiration (breathing effort), reflex responsiveness (response to stimulation), activity (muscle tone), and appearance (color) are scored as 0 (sign not present), 2 (sign in the best possible condition), or 1 (given for all conditions between 0 and 2). The optimal Apgar score is 10. The system can be initiated at 1 minute and repeated at 3, 5, and 10 minutes after birth.

Severely handicapped infants and infants in life-stressing conditions have very low Apgar scores; however, the relationship between Apgar scores and later intelligence is not clear. Serunian and Broman (1975) compared Apgar scores to Bayley (1969) mental and motor scores at 8 months of age and found that infants with Apgar scores between 0 and 3 had significantly lower mental and motor scores than infants with Apgar scores between 7 and 10. Yet Shipe, Vandenberg, and Williams (1968) compared children with Apgar scores of 5 or below to a matched sample of controls at 3 years and found no differences between the groups. One value of the Apgar system is that it quickly and easily identifies infants in immediate life-stressing situations. Richards, Richards, and Roberts (1968) compared infants with low Apgar scores (0–4) to infants with high Apgar scores (9–10) matched for sex, parity, and social class. A neonatal mortality rate of 16% was found for the low Apgar group compared with no deaths in the control cases. The study included 47 infants. Because low Apgar ratings have virtually no validity for long-term outcomes, it is important they not be used as reliable long-term outcome measures.

Brazelton Neonatal Behavioral Assessment Scale

The *Brazelton Neonatal Behavioral Assessment Scale* (BNBAS) (Brazelton, 1973) was designed to assess the newborn's responses to and effect on the environment. The scale is divided into 20 elicited items and 27 behavioral items. The elicited (neurological) items include reflexes such as the plantar grasp, automatic walking, placing, Moro (startle), rooting, and sucking, and passive movements of the arms and legs. The behavioral scale consists of state measures, general measures, and specific behavioral measures. State measures consist of six stages ranging from deep sleep to crying. The general measures include degree of alertness, cuddliness, activity, irritability, lability of skin color, self-quieting activity, number of smiles, and so on. The specific behaviors include response to light, rattle, bell, and pinprick, inanimate visual and auditory orientation responses, animate responses, and so forth.

The neurological items are rated on a 3-point scale and the behavioral items are each rated on a 9-point scale, with the midpoint of each scale denoting the behavior expected of a 3-day-old infant.

After appropriate theoretical and practical training, those who give this instrument consistently report an interrater reliability of above 90%. In perhaps the most extensive study of the predictive validity of the BNBAS (Tronick & Brazelton, 1975), it was administered to 53 newborns who had been labeled *neurologically abnormal* (having more than two minor or one major abnormality) or *suspect* (having two minor abnormalities) at 3 days. Infants labeled *suspect* demonstrated neurological signs such as tremulousness, clonus, restricted motor movements, and irritability. Infants labeled *abnormal* showed signs such as an abnormal Moro, seizures, high pitched cries, or abnormal vestibular responses. These infants were also given two Brazelton behavioral exams between days 2 and 6 by two different examiners. These early examination scores were compared to outcome measures 7 years later, when the children were again classified as suspect, abnormal, or normal on the basis of neurological signs. The neurological exam correctly diagnosed 13 of the 15 newborns, and the BNBAS correctly identified 12 of the 15 newborns as abnormal. However, the false positive rates for the BNBAS and the neurological exam were quite different. The neurological exam classified 80% of the newborns as suspect/abnormal who later were normal, while the BNBAS classified 24% as suspect/abnormal who later were found to be normal. Thus, the BNBAS correctly detected 80% of the abnormal infants without mislabeling as many normal infants as the neurological exam.

In one study that examined the relationship between Brazelton scores and later intelligence, 1-week and 4-week Brazelton scores of low birth-weight babies were positively correlated with Cattell (1940) IQ at 1 year (Scarr & Williams, Note 1).

The Apgar and Brazelton scales are important in that they call attention to infants in distress. As infants mature, their usefulness as predictors of future outcome diminishes substantially. The more seriously impaired the infant, the more likely these scales will alert the medical team to special needs.

The Denver Developmental Screening Test

The *Denver Developmental Screening Test* (DDST) (Frankenburg, Dodds, & Fandal, 1975) was developed to quickly determine developmental deviations in children. Based on the *Gesell Developmental Schedules* (Gesell & Armatruda, 1947), it yields a profile that includes gross motor, language, fine motor, adaptive, and personal-social skills in children birth to 6 years. Approximately 20 age-appropriate items are given to a child, and performance is scored as normal, abnormal, or questionable. Reliability results on the DDST are comparable to those of longer diagnostic tests even though they have been administered by nonprofessionals. For example, in a study comparing children's DDST scores to the *Bayley Scales* or *Stanford-Binet,* the DDST identified 92% of children with development quotients below 70 and 97% of those with DQs or IQs of 70 and above (Frankenburg, 1981). In another study of 1,292 children, the predictive validity of a negative test was 100% (Frankenburg, Goldstein, & Camp, 1971; Stangler, Huber, & Routh, 1980).

It is apparent from these findings that the DDST will quickly and accurately identify those children whose performances are abnormal and who are likely to be moderately or severely handicapped. Because of its high predictive value, this test has been widely used; at some time in their lives, most severely handicapped children have received it.

Developmental Profile II

The *Developmental Profile II* (Alpern, Boll, & Shearer, 1980) uses interviews to screen development in physical, self-help, social, academic, and communication skills. The interview can be completed in 20 to 40 minutes. The scale, which provides a profile of behavior between birth and 9 years, is divided into 13 age levels, most of which contain three items per area.

The *Developmental Profile II* has often been used to screen children for services. Its wide age base and the areas covered make the scale particularly appropriate for moderately and severely impaired children.

In addition to the more widely used screening tests described here, several other screening measures are used by local agencies responsible for locating and screening children with special needs. It is likely that these children will be mildly as opposed to moderate-

ly or severely handicapped. Nevertheless, these additional screening measures (as well as those discussed in more detail) are noted in Table 3.1.[1]

The Measurement of Mentation

Once a child has been screened and abnormal development confirmed, the next process is to identify the behavior contributing to this condition. This identification process can be completed through a few measures or an extensive battery of tests. The identification addressed in this chapter is whether a child is moderately or severely handicapped. We will focus on the traditional ways of determining whether children are mentally retarded and fit the standard classifications. We will briefly describe other areas of development that might be included in the identification if a multidisciplinary team makes the initial identification. The identification of mental retardation requires the measurement of two domains: mentation and adaptive behavior.

Our classification systems grew out of a need to conceptualize homogeneity in large groups of individuals. Individual variability was regarded as a form of error. In the late 1800s, a few experimental psychologists began conducting psychological experiments involving the individual's reaction time to sensory stimuli. Alfred Binet, a Frenchman, felt that these early tests were too largely sensory and focused unduly on simple abilities. Instead, functions such as memory, imagination, attention, comprehension, suggestibility, and aesthetic appreciation must be tested to focus upon the complexity of individual differences. Rather than revealing an absolute measure of ability, tests should compare persons to each other (Binet, 1898). In 1905, with Theophile Simon, Binet published the first Binet-Simon scales, which in 1908 were revised to include the concept of "mental age." The Binet-Simon tests were quickly adapted and translated into many languages and within a few years were recognized as the first major tests of intelligence. In the United States, a revision by L. M. Terman at Stanford University became known as the *Stanford-Binet* (Terman, 1916). After 10 years of research, the second revision appeared in 1937. It consisted of two equivalent forms, L and M (Terman & Merrill, 1937). In an attempt to eliminate obsolete items and to adjust items because of cultural and time changes, the authors published a third revision in 1960. It combined forms L and M into a single (L-M) form.

David Wechsler has developed a number of intelligence scales similar to the Binet scales. His scales are

---

[1]For a more comprehensive review of screening measures, see Stangler, et al. (1980) and Kemper and Frankenburg (1979).

TABLE 3.1 General Screening Measures

Test	Age Range	Description	Score
Developmental Indicators for the Assessment of Learning (DIAL) (Mardell & Goldenberg, 1975)	30–66 months	Gross motor, fine motor, concepts, communication, social-emotional development	Developmental Quotient Age
Revised Developmental Screening Interview (DSI) (Knobloch, Stevens, & Malone, Note 2)	1–36 months	Adaptive, gross motor, fine motor, language, personal-social	Developmental Quotient
Developmental Activities Screening Inventory (DASI) (DuBose & Langley, 1977)	6–60 months	Adaptive, fine motor, object relations, causality, discrimination, seriation	Developmental Age
Denver Developmental Screening Test (DDST) (Frankenburg, Dodds, & Fandal, 1975)	1–72 months	Personal-social, fine motor, adaptive, language, gross motor	Normal Abnormal Questionable
Carolina Developmental Profile (Lillie & Harbin, 1975)	2–5 years	Fine motor, gross motor, visual perception, reasoning, receptive language, expressive language	Criterion-Referenced; Developmental Age Ceiling
Developmental Profile II (Alpern, Boll, & Shearer, 1980)	0–9 years	Physical, self-help, social, academic, communication	Developmental Age or Quotient
Vineland Social Maturity Scale (Doll, 1965)	0–adult	Adaptive, self-help, communication, self-direction, socialization, locomotion, occupation	Social Quotient and Age Equivalent
Preschool Attainment Record (Doll, 1966)	0–84 months	Ambulation, manipulation, rapport, communication, responsibility, information ideation, creativity	Attainment Age and Quotient
TMR Performance Profile for Severely and Moderately Retarded (DiNola, Kaminsky, & Sternfeld, 1963)	Criterion-referenced	Social behavior, self-care, communication, basic knowledge, practical skills, body usage	0–4 ratings of behaviors

grouped into subtests arranged in increasing order of difficulty. Subtest grouping allows for the computation of verbal and performance IQs. Wechsler has developed three scales: one for adults, the *Wechsler Adult Intelligence Scale* (WAIS) (Wechsler, 1955); one for school-aged children, the *Wechsler Intelligence Scale for Children* (WISC) (Wechsler, 1949) and *Revised Edition* (WISC-R) (Wechsler, 1974); and one for preschool and primary levels, the *Wechsler Preschool and Primary Scale of Intelligence* (WPPSI) (Wechsler, 1967).

Types of Assessment Measures

The scales referred to above are *norm-referenced tests,* the type of test most often used in the identification process to verify the results of screening and to determine the extent of deviation from the norm. *Criterion-referenced measures* are used primarily to determine the extent of deviation from skill levels necessary for independent functioning; these measures form the core for assessment within the classroom. The characteristics of these measures are presented in Table 3.2.

Because the assessment of severely handicapped children is extremely complex, multiple methods are required to generate the data needed for each of the variety of decisions to be made about the child. In addition to describing the child's current status relative to his or her peers, norm-referenced measures are commonly used to certify the child for program eligibility. Though they have been subjected to much criticism (e.g., Bailey & Harbin, 1980; Jenkins & Pany, 1978; Jones, 1973; Salvia & Ysseldyke, 1978; Tallmadge, 1977; White & Haring, 1980), norm-referenced measures are nonetheless important, primarily because program eligibility criteria have traditionally been specified in terms of degree of deviation from normal or typical behavior. If 90% of the state departments of education require *Stanford-Binet* and *Adaptive Behavior Scale* (Nihira, Foster, Shellhaas, & Leland, 1974) information to place children in special education programs and to report census data to the U.S. Department of Education to justify funding, then there are immediate and practical reasons for gathering this information. Moreover, if certain norm-referenced measures are commonly used when

TABLE 3.2 Norm-Referenced and Criterion-Referenced Assessment Procedures*

Characteristic	Norm-Referenced Measure	Criterion-Referenced Measure
Primary purpose	To reveal differences between individuals to permit interindividual comparisons with respect to some measure of central tendency (mean, median) for a particular reference group. Permits determination of normal-nonnormal status vis-à-vis that group.	To reveal a person's status in cumulative skill acquisition relative to an absolute standard of performance. Permits determination of mastery-nonmastery vis-à-vis that particular standard.
Instructional relevance	Limited; measures not designed to lead to specific instructional pinpoints and often contain content not intended to be taught in school.	Variable but usually high, since purpose is to establish what has been acquired relative to some absolute standard and items are selected from a task analysis of skills taught in school.
Source of content	Domains of interest are specified, and items are generated to represent them. Items showing differences between individuals during field tests are retained as the content of the measure.	Skills of interest are specified and task-analyzed to determine their component responses. These responses become the content of the measure.
Meaning of a score	Derives from comparing it with the mean of the appropriate reference group.	Derives from comparing it with the level of performance set as the absolute standard.
Importance of standardization	Very important; representative samples of persons against whom the student is being compared must have been used in developing the norms; standardized procedures for test administration must be clearly stipulated.	Very important; representative samples for comparison are not required, but standardized procedures for test administration must be clearly stipulated.
Type of score	A number expressed in standard score form (z, T, etc.) or presented with mean and standard deviation for appropriate reference group to permit its interpretation relative to scores of other persons.	A number expressed in percentage form or some fraction of the score representing the absolute standard of performance (e.g., "70% of mastery;" "20 of 35 steps in the task analysis") against which the student is being compared.
Applicable psychometric criteria	Generalizability of scores over scorer, item, time, setting. Correlations between scores on the measure and others (validity); construct and convergent validity sometimes important; content validity is important for some types (e.g., achievement tests) but less so for others (e.g., intelligence tests).	Accuracy of scores as well as their generalizability over scorers; content validity; sequential validity; instructional validity; sensitivity to change produced by instruction.
Identifiable subtypes	Age-referenced (e.g., developmental scales); grade-referenced (e.g., achievement tests); stage-referenced (e.g., measures of Piagetian concept development).	May be identified in terms of the criterion being referenced (e.g., home-referenced, school-referenced, work-referenced), and in terms of the specificity of their content (e.g., goal-referenced, objective-referenced).

*Similar tables comparing norm- and criterion-referenced measures can be found in Livingston (1977) and Wilcox (1979).

describing the subjects of research projects, communication among researchers (and between them and consumers) is facilitated if they describe their subjects with identical measures. Many of the criticisms are unfounded if norm-referenced measures are used for administrative and descriptive purposes. The most important characteristics of norm-referenced measures used for these purposes are the adequacy of their standardization samples and the reliability with which they are scored.

Characteristics other than consistent administration and reliable scoring would be important if the measures were to be used for making other decisions about a child. For example, decisions about program effectiveness require consideration of a measure's sensitivity to change. Decisions about intervention priorities would have to consider educational relevance. Norm-referenced measures are not likely ever to lead to specific instructional objectives for individual children. Furthermore, as presently constructed, they are not sensitive enough to change to be used in evaluating programs for severely handicapped students. Thus, as has frequently been noted, they are not appropriate for these uses.

Thus, use of norm-referenced measures should be limited to administrative/communicative functions. Problems arise when efforts are made to derive educationally relevant information from them or to use them for program evaluation and other purposes for which they are not designed. For those purposes, the judicious use of other measures that are part of a carefully organized, comprehensive, and coherent assessment system will alleviate some of the problems associated with norm-referenced approaches.

Measuring Mentation in Children

Scales of infant intelligence are frequently given to severely handicapped children. The scales most commonly used are the *Cattell Infant Intelligence Scale* (Cattell, 1940), a downward extension of the 1937 *Stanford-Binet,* and the *Bayley Scales of Infant Development* (Bayley, 1969). Lewis (1976) has seriously questioned the value of infant tests. Correlations of infant test scores with later scores over long periods of time are negligible. However, when the tests are given to children with clearly identified handicaps, the IQs from infant tests have proven to be good predictors of later performance (Bierman, Connor, Vaage, & Honzik, 1964; DuBose, 1977; Illingsworth, 1961; Werner, Honzik, & Smith, 1968). The value of these measures appears to be in identifying moderately, severely, and profoundly handicapped youngsters for whom additional educational services will be needed. A major disadvantage of these measures is the misuse of the information derived from them:

they are used to make decisions about persons and services based on a very limited set of data, and they become the yardstick for measuring progress, which is inappropriate.

More recently, service providers have turned to ordinal scales to measure behavior. These scales are bridging the gap between the inappropriate norm-referenced tests and the functional assessments needed by classroom staff. Ordinal scales provide a sequence in which a schema develops. They do not yield IQ or DQ scores; however, by comparing the child's chronological age to the highest item passed on each subscale, we can find the extent to which a child's performance is like that of age mates. These scales are valuable because each step sequentially follows another; thus programming objectives are more readily identified. We discuss ordinal scales in more detail later in this chapter in connection with other tests given by team members.

In the next sections, we describe the two infant mental tests noted above because they are the ones most frequently used to identify severely handicapped children. We will also describe three measures used as moderately and severely handicapped children get older and their performances and ages exceed the limits of the infant tests.

Cattell Infant Intelligence Scale (Cattell, 1940)

This instrument was designed to measure the intelligence of children between the ages of 2 and 30 months. The items are consistent with those in similar instruments, that is, stacking rings, placing pegs in boards, stacking cubes, manipulating objects. A mental age and an IQ are computed.

Standardization was completed on 294 children tested at 3, 6, 9, 12, 18, 24, 30, and 36 months. The subjects' family status was described as lower middle class. Test-retest correlations ranging from .06 to .52 were reported by Cavanaugh, Cohen, Dunphy, Ringwall, and Goldberg (1957) for both normal and premature infants. Gallagher (1953) found correlations ranging between .77 to .83 when adoption cases were retested 7 to 8 months later.

Higher reliability coefficients result in cases where the test has been given to handicapped populations. Matheny (1957) tested children with central nervous system (CNS) disorders and obtained a .75 test-retest coefficient 18 months later. Fishman and Palkes (1974) tested children with CNS problems at 6, 12, 18, and 24 months and obtained coefficients ranging from .63 to .95.

The Cattell test has been used to identify estimated mental ages of persons functioning at the ages covered by this scale. The limited number of verbal items makes it appealing for low-functioning children.

Bayley Scales of Infant Development (BSID) (Bayley, 1969)

The *Bayley Scales* are an outgrowth of the California First Year Mental Scale, Bayley's first formal test. There are two scales, a motor scale and a mental scale, and an Infant Behavior Record. The *Bayley Scales* were standardized on 1,262 term and normal infants between birth and 30 months of age. Items are arranged in terms of age placement by determining at what point at least half the children tested passed the item. However, none of the items are arranged according to a developmental sequence of maturation. Reliability and validity information is provided in the manual. Correlations between the Bayley mental scale and the *Stanford-Binet* have ranged from minimal to moderate.

Of the infant scales, the Bayley has been used most frequently with severely impaired children, although none were included in the standardization sample. The BSID proved useful to examiners testing severely handicapped children, regardless of whether the children's ages were appropriate, because the scales included a sufficient number of items (mental scale, 163; motor scale, 81) for obtaining a reasonable estimate of abilities (Haskett & Bell, 1978). The raw score on the scales yields separate developmental indices expressed as standard scores with a mean of 100 and a standard deviation of 16. No indices are provided below 50; thus, examiners of severely handicapped children must estimate these scores on the basis of the mental ages of the items passed. Others find the raw scores to be desirable measures for the pre-posttest assessment of severely and profoundly handicapped children whose changes are not large enough to be detected by the traditional procedures. Recently, Naglieri (1981) responded to the need of examiners for a more quantifiable expression of Bayley performances by preparing extrapolated raw scores and psychomotor developmental indices below 50. We caution you of the increased probability of error that is embedded in the tables; nevertheless, it is apparent that these extrapolations and the adjusted social age scores on the *Vineland Social Maturity Scale* provided by Song and Jones (1982) will be widely used in the next few years.

Stanford Binet Intelligence Scale (Terman & Merrill, 1973)

This scale was designed for persons age 2 through adult. It is given individually by a psychologist and takes about an hour. The test yields two scores, a mental age and an intelligence quotient. It does not include subtests; however, Sattler (1965) divides the test into seven categories: language, memory, conceptual thinking, reasoning, numerical reasoning, visual motor, and social intelligence.

The standardization sample was over 2,000 and included people from all ability levels. The 1973 manual reports reliability and validity data for earlier versions but does not include data on the 1973 edition.

Wechsler Scales

Perhaps the most widely used tests of intellectual performance are the Wechsler tests. The *Wechsler Intelligence Scale for Children–Revised* (Wechsler, 1974) is given to school-aged children ages 6 to 16, who are able to sustain attention for extended time periods. It requires 50 to 75 minutes and has many timed items. The age span it covers, the attention required, and the fact that it is a timed test make it highly impractical for severely handicapped children. However, older moderately handicapped children may be given this test when identification, classification, and placement decisions must be reevaluated.

The *Wechsler Preschool and Primary Scale of Intelligence* (WPPSI) (Wechsler, 1974) is the Wechsler scale that covers the age span that is more appropriate for the early identification of handicapped children. This test, standardized on 1,200 children, covers the 4 years to 6 years, 6 months age span and is administered in 60 to 90 minutes. The administration of the WPPSI is similar to that of the WISC-R; while it can be administered over a 2-day period, this is not encouraged. The WPPSI contains 10 separate tests, five verbal and five performance. The test yields a verbal score and a performance score. These scores are summed to produce a full scale score. All scores are converted into deviation IQ scores based on a mean of 100 and a standard deviation of 15. No validity is reported in the manual. Studies describe concurrent criterion-related validity. For example, when 50 6-year-old children were given both WISC-R and WPPSI, a correlation of .80 was found between both the verbal and the performance IQs, while an .82 was observed between full scale IQs. Other studies have compared the WPPSI to the *Binet,* the *Peabody Picture Vocabulary Test* (PPVT) (Dunn 1965), and the *Pictorial Test of Intelligence* (PTI) (French, 1964). When slightly under 100 students between 5 and 6 years of age took all three tests, the WPPSI full scale IQ correlated .75, .58, and .64 with the IQs derived from the Binet, PPVT, and PTI (Goodwin & Driscoll, 1980). Goodwin and Driscoll, in an evaluation of the WPPSI, report that the data in support of its reliability are both impressive and convincing.

The tests described here are used to assess development or mental abilities in children. While the tests are used with handicapped children, none included handicapped samples in their standardization. Invariably, one or more of these tests will be used in the identification process. The inappropriateness of these tests for moderately and severely handicapped children has led to the development of tests of adaptive behavior as well as other tests which are far more helpful for making decisions about initial identification and placement.

The Concept of Adaptive Behavior

As we have noted, adaptive behavior is a critical factor in determining who is retarded. Grossman (1977) defined adaptive behavior as "the effectiveness or degree with which an individual meets the standards of personal independence and social responsibility expected for age and cultural group" (p. 11). Adaptive behavior is difficult to measure because the interpretation of responses is subjective.

The inclusion of the popular, yet vague and ill-defined, term *adaptive behavior* has been the subject of severe criticism (Adams, 1973; Baumeister & Muma, 1975; Cleary, Humphreys, Kendrick, & Wesman, 1975; McIntosh & Warren, 1969). Baumeister and Muma point out that "it is a problem in adaptive behavior that first brings the child to the attention of those responsible for labeling him" (p. 302). The responsible agent will probably use the *Vineland Social Maturity Scale* (Doll, 1965) to verify that a problem exists. Investigating the role played by the *Vineland* in the classification of the level of mental retardation and its relationship to measured intelligence, Adams (1973) found a statistically significant relationship between IQs and social quotients (SQs), which indicates that they are not independent but aspects of the same behavior. Furthermore, his findings support his hypothesis that physicians were more likely to use IQs than SQs when classifying individuals with mental retardation. Baumeister and Muma comment that "adaptive behavior scales often turn out to be a poor man's intelligence test, and they generally enjoy such high correlations with standardized intelligence tests as to suggest that these are functionally redundant measures" (p. 303).

Confusion over the meaning and measurement of adaptive behavior arises because the definition is so broad as to be barely meaningful. Skills that allow you to function adequately in a narrow, restrictive environment are likely to be poorly correlated with the ability to cope in other settings (Cleary et al., 1975).

Responses on these measures come from parents, ward attendants, and other primary care providers. Neither the questions nor the answers are subjected to critical tests of reliability and validity. Some tests of adaptive behavior are limited to self-care and social maturity performances (e.g., *Vineland Social Maturity Scale*); others include measures of negative behaviors such as violent and destructive behavior or sexually

aberrant behavior (*AAMD Adaptive Behavior Scale, Part Two,* Nihira et al., 1974); while a more recent measure reflects a systems approach that includes measures of intelligence and adaptive behavior, then relates these to the child's cultural background and provides an estimate of the child's learning potential. We hope that this system, the *System of Multicultural Pluralistic Assessment* (SOMPA) developed by Jane Mercer (1979), will prove to be a valuable and long overdue aid to psychologists who have been responsible for measuring adaptive behavior but have not had the tools with which to do it.

Vineland Social Maturity Scale (VSMS) (Doll, 1965)

This scale, first published over 40 years ago, was designed to evaluate progress in social maturity and responsibility from birth to maturity. The 117 items are divided into eight categories of social maturity: self-help general, self-help eating, self-help dressing, self-directions, occupation, communication, locomotion, and socialization. The scale is administered as an interview with either the subject or someone who knows the subject well.

The major validation study of the VSMS was completed on institutionalized mentally retarded children in 1939–40. These scores were compared with the norms established for normal children. The institutionalized children demonstrated far less social maturity than that reported for normal children. The correlation between VSMS and Binet scores was .84 (Doll, 1953).

The reliability of the VSMS is reported for a sample of 250 subjects. A correlation of .98 between social age scores over a 2-year period was obtained. Other studies report similar correlations.

Because the VSMS was specifically developed for use with mentally retarded persons, it has been widely used as one measure in the identifying process. The emphasis placed on functional skills as opposed to cognitive concepts and processing is appropriate as a measure of adaptive behavior. Although several other tests have emerged since the VSMS to evaluate similar skills (e.g., *Developmental Profile, Adaptive Behavior Scale for Children*), this test continues to be widely used to assess the adaptive skills of moderately and severely handicapped persons.

AAMD Adaptive Behavior Scale, Public School Version (ABS) (Lambert, Windmiller, Cole, & Figueroa, 1975)

This is a rating scale designed as a questionnaire to be completed by a professional familiar with the typical performance of the student. Standardized and norm-referenced, it was designed for use with students aged 7 to 13 and requires about 1½ hours to complete. Norms are presented for different class placements such as EMR and TMR. The ABS is divided into two parts. Part I includes 10 subtests of daily living skills and some other domains. Part II assesses maladaptive behavior using 14 subtests. The ABS yields percentile rank scores for each subtest but no overall test score. Student performance is compared with age peers in several educational placements. There are no reliability data for this edition, although reliability on an earlier version is cited. Validity is demonstrated by comparing the student's class placement to domain scores.

Adaptive Behavior Inventory for Children (ABIC) (Mercer & Lewis, 1977)

This is a parent interview scale designed to assess the adaptive behavior of children from different ethnic groups. It is included in the *System of Multicultural Pluralistic Assessment* and was standardized and norm-referenced on children in one state. It is appropriate for children 5 to 11 years of age; the interview requires approximately 30 minutes. Seven types of questions are included for such areas as family, community, peer relations, nonacademic school roles, and self-maintenance. A raw score is computed and then converted to scale scores through norm tables. A total test score, the Average Scaled Score, is calculated and plotted onto a profile which also contains percentile ranks. The classification of "At Risk" is given to students whose scores fall approximately two standard deviations below the mean.

Reliability is described in the manual and coefficients are generally in the .80's and .90's. The validity of the ABIC, although not systematically determined, is (according to the test authors) shown by the instrument's ability to reflect accurately the extent to which the child meets the expectations of members of the social system to which he or she belongs.

Team Assessment for Educational Placement and Planning

The multidisciplinary team is likely to have responsibilities beyond identifying who is handicapped. Team members gather information that contributes to placement decisions and educational planning. In gathering this information, most team members use tests or procedures common to their disciplines. The information is shared across disciplines and used in making placement decisions. Further, these data are included in the team report that usually accompanies the child to the placement setting.

It is beyond the scope of this chapter to provide in-depth coverage by discipline of all assessment tools appropriate for moderately and severely impaired children. However, we will describe a few additional measures that might be used in making placement decisions. These measures might be particularly useful to the teacher or team of direct service providers who will perform the classroom assessment and make instructional recommendations that will probably become an integral part of the IEP. Our discussion is limited to tests that are commercially available and easily obtained. In a few cases, we note tests that team members appear to use in the assessment of severely impaired children; however, the tests are less readily available and have been subject to less research than other, better known instruments. Checklists, more extensive criterion-referenced measures, and teacher-made assessment procedures are more likely to be used by the placement setting (classroom) staff (particularly the teacher). Table 3.3 provides information on a few of these tests that you may find helpful in comparing the test capabilities with their needs.

Communication Measures

The communications disorders specialist (CDS) (states use different titles for this team member) is likely to use two or more assessment tools as well as to rely upon informal observation. However, there are few well-tested measures that assess communication in nonverbal children. Many specialists resort to articles and experimental scales that appear in scholarly journals, monographs, and books. Two trends in communication assessment are evident. First, many specialists find it inappropriate to try to separate communicative intent from sensorimotor schemes; they are resorting to Piagetian-based scales such as the *Uzgiris-Hunt Ordinal Scales of Psychological Development* (Uzgiris & Hunt, 1975) to pinpoint behavior that forms the basis for later symbolic language. Second, in the last few years the importance of play and its relation to early language development has resulted in a surge of articles and experimental scales comparing play and cognition sequences to those of language (e.g., McCune-Nicolich & Carroll, 1981; Westby, 1980).

Unfortunately, few of these newer assessment measures have been thoroughly tested and they are not readily available to specialists. The advantage of these scales is that they provide a basis for examining communication in children whose skills are developmentally young. The communication instruments noted in Table 3.3 provide scores that permit the team to measure the child's progress during the intervals between one assessment and the next. While the information indicates some of the skills in a child's repertoire at a given time, the scales provide little

TABLE 3.3. Assessment Measures Used With Severely Handicapped Children

Instrument and Publisher	Type of Reference			Assessment Methods			Ages Covered			Content Areas										Score Produced			Remarks
	Norm-Referenced	Age/Stage-Referenced	Criterion-Referenced	Interview	Observation	Direct Testing	0–3 Yrs	3–6 Yrs	6+ Yrs	Sensory	Gross Motor	Fine Motor	Language	Cognition/Academic	Social/Emotional	Self-Help	Independent Living	Vocational	Recreation/Leisure	Quotient	Mental Age	Binary or Criterion	
Communication Development																							
Peabody Picture Vocabulary Test — American Guidance Service Publishers Building Circle Pines, MN 55014	X					X	X	X	X				X							X	X		Book of pictures and recording forms, available at low cost; requires no verbal response and minimal motor response
Environmental Prelanguage Battery — Charles E. Merrill 1300 Alum Creek Drive Box 508 Columbus, OH 43216		X	X			X	X						X							X	X	X	For use with children below or at the single word level; comes with program manual; adaptable.
Environmental Language Inventory — Charles E. Merrill 1300 Alum Creek Drive Box 508 Columbus, OH 43216		X	X			X	X	X					X							X	X	X	Assesses early semantic-based grammar through imitation, conversation, and play

60

											Description
Receptive-Expressive Emergent Language Scale University Park Press 300 North Charles Baltimore, MD 21201	X			X	X				X	X X	Low-cost instrument that may be completed by interview; six items for each month for the first year, six items for 2-month intervals the second year, and six for every four months the third year; yields a language age, both receptive and expressive
Preschool Language Scale Charles E. Merrill 1300 Alum Creek Drive Box 508 Columbus, OH 43216	X			X	X X X			X	X X	To be used as an evaluation instrument, not as a test; requires picture book, record book, and manual, available at low cost; includes sections on Auditory Comprehension, Verbal Ability, and Articulation; not standardized; no information on validity or reliability
Sequenced Inventory of Communication Development University of Washington Press Seattle, WA 98195	X			X	X X			X	X X	"Fairly elaborate" kit of materials needed to examine and determine both the receptive and expressive language capabilities of the child
Test for Auditory Comprehension of Language Teaching Resources Corporation 50 Pond Park Road Hingham, MA 02043	X			X	X X			X	X	Moderate cost

TABLE 3.3. (CONTINUED)

Instrument and Publisher	Norm-Referenced	Age/Stage-Referenced	Criterion-Referenced	Interview	Observation	Direct Testing	0–3 Yrs	3–6 Yrs	6+ Yrs	Sensory	Gross Motor	Fine Motor	Language	Cognition/Academic	Social/Emotional	Self-Help	Independent Living	Vocational	Recreation/Leisure	Quotient	Mental Age	Binary or Criterion	Remarks
Motor Development																							
Bayley Scales of Infant Development — The Psychological Corporation, 304 East 45th Street, New York, NY 10017	X					X	X				X	X								X	X		Includes mental and motor scales and infant behavior record; good for very low functioning SPH children
Milani-Comparetti Motor Development Test — Meyer Children's Rehabilitation Institute, University of Nebraska Medical Center, 444 South 44th Street, Omaha, NE 68131		X				X	X				X												A rapid (5–10 min.), standardized neurodevelopmental examination for early detection of neuromotor deficits in children with cerebral palsy, motor delay, asymmetry, or mental deficiency; provides direct assessment of child's spontaneous behavior (motor control) and evoked response (reflexes); requires no special equipment to administer
Newington Children's Hospital (M. R. Fiorentino: Reflex testing methods for evaluating CNS development, 2nd edition, 1973) Charles C Thomas Springfield, IL		X				X	X	X	X		X	X										X	Manual presents procedures for testing and recording reflex responses of children with neurophysiological dysfunctions; to be administered by physicians, neurologists, or therapists.

Test / Publisher	Comments
Peabody Developmental Motor Scales Teaching Resources 50 Pond Park Road Hingham, MA 02043	Scales are accompanied by developmental activities for each area assessed.
Bruninks–Oseretsky Test of Motor Proficiency American Guidance Service Publishers Building Circle Pines, MN 55014	Requires special kit of materials; Complete Battery (45–60 min.) and Short Form (15–20 min.) available; satisfactory test-retest reliability for both versions; validity established through comparison of test content with research findings in motor development
Cognitive Development Bayley Scales of Infant Development (see above) Cattell Infant Intelligence Scale The Psychological Corporation 304 East 45th Street New York, NY 10017	Low validity and reliability of this instrument means that it should be used in conjunction with other assessments and observations of the child's development, by those knowledgeable about infant behavior in general.
Uzgiris–Hunt Ordinal Scales of Psychological Development University of Illinois Press Urbana, IL	Concerned with the hierarchical interrelationships of achievements at different levels; intended primarily as a research tool, yet can be used reliably and validly with SPH children

TABLE 3.3. (CONTINUED)

Instrument and Publisher	Norm-Referenced	Age/Stage-Referenced	Criterion-Referenced	Interview	Observation	Direct Testing	0–3 Yrs	3–6 Yrs	6+ Yrs	Sensory	Gross Motor	Fine Motor	Language	Cognition/Academic	Social/Emotional	Self-Help	Independent Living	Vocational	Recreation/Leisure	Quotient	Mental Age	Binary or Criterion	Remarks
	Type of Reference			Assessment Methods			Ages Covered			Content Areas										Score Produced			
Stanford–Binet Intelligence Scale (Third Revision) Houghton Mifflin Company 666 Miami Circle N.E. Atlanta, GA 30324	X					X		X	X					X						X	X		Usually not appropriate for delayed preschool children; basal age performance level dependent on intact sensory and motor systems; moderately high cost
Wechsler Intelligence Scale for Children–Revised The Psychological Corporation 304 East 45th Street New York, NY 10017	X					X		X	X					X						X	X		Yields information for both verbal and performance skills; not recommended for hearing impaired
McCarthy Scales of Children's Abilities The Psychological Corporation 304 East 45th Street New York, NY 10017	X					X		X	X				X	X						X	X		Subtest scores in five areas: General Cognitive (3), Motor, Memory; excellent reliability
Woodcock–Johnson Psychoeducational Battery Teaching Resources Corporation 50 Pond Park Road Hingham, MA 02043	X					X		X	X					X						X	X		Intended to measure cognitive ability, achievement, and interest; reliability and validity established, but with normal subjects

Instrument	Comments
Haeusserman's Psychoeducational Evaluation of the Preschool Child Grune & Stratton 381 Park Avenue South New York, NY 10016	Emphasis on matching and short-term memory; not recommended for determining child placement, but as a screening device for discovering problem areas
Merrill-Palmer Scale of Mental Tests Stoelting Co. 1350 South Kostner Chicago, IL 60623	Good for low functioning nonverbal children because test items largely measure performance; high initial cost
General Development Behavioral Characteristics Progression VORT Corporation P.O. Box 11132 Palo Alto, CA 94306	Provides a comprehensive checklist of behavioral objectives to assist in the design of individual-education programs; not really an assessment
Learning Accomplishment Profile Kaplan Press 600 Jonestown Road Winston-Salem, NC 27103	Measures changes in rate of development; can be used to develop curriculum
Callier Azusa Scale Callier Center for Communication Disorders University of Texas/Dallas 1966 Inwood Road Dallas, TX 75235	Low-cost instrument designed for assessment and development of an individualized educational program for deaf-blind and multihandicapped children

TABLE 3.3. (CONTINUED)

Instrument and Publisher	Type of Reference: Criterion-Referenced	Age/Stage-Referenced	Norm-Referenced	Assessment Methods: Direct Testing	Observation	Interview	Ages Covered: 0–3 Yrs	3–6 Yrs	6+ Yrs	Content Areas: Sensory	Gross Motor	Fine Motor	Language	Cognition/Academic	Social/Emotional	Self-Help	Independent Living	Vocational	Recreation/Leisure	Score Produced: Quotient	Mental Age	Binary or Criterion	Remarks
Adaptive Performance Instrument, Department of Special Education, University of Idaho, Moscow, ID 83843	X			X	X	X	X			X	X	X	X	X	X	X						X	Recently developed (1980); consists of three sections or "domains" assessed: Physical Intactness, Self-Care, Sensorimotor; the latter is based on Piaget's theory of sensorimotor development.
Uniform Performance Assessment System, Charles E. Merrill Publishing, 1300 Alum Creek Drive, Box 508, Columbus, OH 43216	X			X	X		X	X	X		X	X	X	X	X	X						X	Sequenced according to normal patterns of child development; two forms: birth–age 6, age 6–12
Pennsylvania Training Model: Individual Assessment Guide, Pennsylvania Dept. of Education, Bureau of Special Education, Harrisburg, PA 17111	X			X	X		X	X		X	X	X	X	X	X	X						X	Concerned with both gross assessment of major skill areas and more specific assessment within these areas; has been field-tested to establish content validity for its items, determine its interrater reliability, and develop norms for subgroups within SPH population

Instrument / Publisher																		Description
Inventory of Early Development Curriculum Associates 6 Henshaw Woburn, ME 01801	X	X						X	X	X	X	X	X	X		X	X	Norm-referenced but not independently standardized
Self-Care/Adaptive Development																		
Lakeland Village Adaptive Behavior Grid Lakeland Village Medical Lake, WA 99022	X		X		X	X	X	X	X	X	X	X	X	X	X	X	X	Allows evaluator to derive developmental levels for skills such as eating, grooming, dressing, mobility, recreation, socialization, and behavior control, all of which are task analyzed
Adaptive Behavior Scales American Association on Mental Deficiency 5201 Connecticut Avenue N.W. Washington, DC 20015	X	X	X		X	X	X	X	X	X	X	X	X	X	X	X	X	Comprehensive, providing ratings in many areas
Camelot Behavioral Checklist Camelot Behavioral Systems P.O. Box 607 Parsons, KS 67357	X	X			X	X	X	X	X	X	X	X	X	X	X	X	X	Checklist of behaviors that fall into ten behavior domains (Self-help, Independent Travel, etc.)
Balthazar Scales of Adaptive Behavior Consulting Psychologists Press 577 College Avenue Palo Alto, CA 94306	X		X		X	X	X	X	X	X	X	X	X	X		X	X	Two sections: Functional Independence, Social Adaptation

TABLE 3.3. (CONTINUED)

Instrument and Publisher	Type of Reference			Assessment Methods			Ages Covered			Content Areas											Score Produced			Remarks
	Norm-Referenced	Age/Stage-Referenced	Criterion-Referenced	Interview	Observation	Direct Testing	0–3 Yrs	3–6 Yrs	6+ Yrs	Sensory	Gross Motor	Fine Motor	Language	Cognition/Academic	Social/Emotional	Self-Help	Independent Living	Vocational	Recreation/Leisure	Quotient	Mental Age	Binary or Criterion	
TARC Assessment Inventory for Severely Handicapped Children PRO-ED 5341 Industrial Oaks Blvd. Austin, TX 78735	X		X		X			X	X		X	X	X	X	X	X	X					X	Especially discriminatory at lower ranges of retardation; designed to be administered by the classroom teacher
The Pyramid Scales PRO-ED 5341 Industrial Oaks Blvd. Austin, TX 78735			X	X	X	X	X	X	X	X	X	X	X	X	X	X	X	X	X			X	Curriculum-referenced; leads directly to more than 5,000 skills and specific instructional procedures found in curriculum available from publisher; highly reliable, valid

information to help teachers plan communication programs.

Motor Measures

Both physical and occupational therapists have roles to play on multidisciplinary teams. The age of the child may be a factor in determining whether one or both therapists participate on a particular case. Today, there is increasing overlap between these roles, as both therapists share in the activities. This is an excellent example of a transdisciplinary model. In some centers these roles have been completely merged and the therapist is known as a "developmental therapist." The focus, described by Banus, Kent, Norton, Sukiennicki, and Becker (1979), has been encouraged through the joint training provided for therapists in both neurodevelopmental therapy training and sensory integration training, two very popular approaches to therapy delivery in the United States today. (See chapter 7.)

Developmental therapists include at least two kinds of instruments in their assessment batteries, supplemented by locally developed measures or their own observational systems. A measure of normal motor development that lets therapists identify the degree of delay is usually included in a battery even though it may be of little value in the assessment of a very severely involved physically impaired child. In addition, to assess the severity of motor impairments, some means of determining the presence or absence of primitive reflexes is used. Both primitive reflex tests and tests of motor development have contributions to make; however, after an in-depth review of the predictive power of both kinds of measures, Campbell and Wilhelm (1982) recently concluded: "the appropriate appearance of motor milestones and emerging postural reactions in high-risk infants may be more important predictors than the failure to suppress primitive reflexes as early as this is accomplished by low-risk children" (p. 123). Table 3.3 includes developmental scales and reflex profiles. We also include one assessment tool developed specifically for use with older, severely handicapped persons. Other procedures are described in Hoskins and Squires (1973) and Harris and Tada (1983).

Unfortunately, we do not have, in readily available form, materials that describe the process or procedures for identifying persons appropriate for neurodevelopmental therapy training (now being prescribed by some teams and included on IEPs of severely handicapped children) or for measuring progress as a result of treatment. However, Pip Campbell, in chapter 7, does provide a means for assessing movement difficulties.

Cognition and Achievement

We already noted those tests of mental development that are frequently used as the basis for identification and classification, and they are included in Table 3.3. Depending on the age of the child, the psychologist may want to use an ordinal assessment measure in addition to the required, less functional measures. Ordinal scales are helpful in programming for handicapped infants (Dunst, 1980; 1981). This is logical because the administrative instructions are more flexible in ordinal scales, permitting the examiner to use a variety of materials and to elicit situations to determine performance in each domain. Spontaneously observed behaviors are permitted on selected scales. In ordinal scales, the goal is to elicit the highest level performance on each scale. Unfortunately, there are few ordinal scales based on a Piagetian model to assess preoperational and concrete operational skills. Beyond the sensorimotor stage of development, psychologists and diagnosticians turn to tests of basic skills, developmental checklists, curriculum- and criterion-referenced measures to determine a child's skill knowledge in areas that will be addressed by the placement site. The multidisciplinary team reassessing a child after 3 years is likely to use tests listed in Table 3.3 although they may not have been included in the original battery. In addition, Corry Robinson's adaptations of sensorimotor measures, in chapter 8, will supplement those listed in Table 3.3.

General Measures

Some teams prefer to administer one test that is very comprehensive. These tests have emerged because other tests were ineffective in providing specific information on the skills of severely impaired children. Many of these tests grew out of locally identified needs and are used in local areas. In some cases, these locally developed tests have been officially approved or mandated by states. Examples include *Pennsylvania Training Model* (Somerton-Fair & Turner, 1979), the *Oregon Student Progress Record* (Oregon State Mental Health Division, 1977), and the *West Virginia Assessment and Tracking System* (Cone, 1981). Others, developed in a single locale, have been published commercially and are more widely distributed. These tests include the *Uniform Performance Assessment System* and *Learning Accomplishment Profile* (see Table 3.3). With these measures we obtain more specific information on self-care behavior and social skills.

One instrument developed specifically for very young or very severely impaired functioning children under 2 years of age is the *Adaptive Performance Instrument* (McCartan, Note 3). This instrument, developed by the Consortium on Adaptive Performance Evaluation, is designed to test performances in eight broad curricular areas using adapted procedures for deaf/blind, visually impaired, hearing impaired, and motorically impaired children. The test measures functional skills that are necessary for performance in the environment and are possible targets for educational programming. Although the scale has not been completely field tested and work on it continues, the test is gaining more recognition as an appropriate criterion-referenced measure for use by identification and placement teams.

Physical and Health Care

Nurses or other health care team members may be called on to provide information on functional hearing and vision, nutritional needs, or other concerns related to medical management within the placement setting. Several tools have emerged in recent years to assess the sensory functioning of severely impaired children. One example is the *Functional Vision Inventory for the Multiply and Severely Handicapped* (Langley, 1980).[2] Though these instruments cannot take the place of more complete examinations provided by ophthalmologists, audiologists, and so on, they do provide information helpful to teachers as they plan instructional programs.

Health care workers and some social and family workers are asked to provide assessments of the home environment. In the past, this has been done through a case study approach with very little quantitative assessment. New research findings are supporting the transactional model (Sameroff & Chandler, 1975) and showing the importance to child outcome of contributions from the environment as well as physical factors. The need to examine these factors is leading to broader test batteries, such as those described by Brooks-Gunn and Lewis (1981); Simeonsson, Huntington, and Parse (1980); Simeonsson, Huntington, Short, and Ware (1982), and Fewell (1982). These batteries describe assessments that include mother-child, father-child dyads, stress, knowledge of resources, depression, auditory and visual responsivity, rhythmic habit patterns, state, and a host of other areas that researchers have found to be closely related to current and future child status. It is quite apparent that assessment is in a state of change; today's best practices may not be evaluated as best tomorrow.

Placement Decisions

Identification teams within educational settings have a responsibility to make placement recommendation decisions. P.L. 94-142 ensures that the child must be placed in the least restrictive environment in which his or her educational needs can be met.

Placement decisions are considered once the data have been gathered and needs determined. The parents and the most likely recipient agency representatives are active in placement decisions. For example, one of the child's needs may be for physical therapy, yet that service may not be available in the agency that can provide the child a less restrictive environment. In these cases, the agency explores ways in which the needed services can be coordinated through other means.

Placements are reviewed regularly to determine whether the child–environment fit continues to be appropriate. The law requires the identification team to review its decision completely in 3 years, at which time the student must be assessed and again classified to determine whether his or her status or classification has changed.

CONCLUSION

This chapter has focused on the initial step in the service model, assessment for the purpose of identification and placement. The steps that follow (described in detail in later chapters) concern procedures more directly related to the instructional program. While information gathered during identification contributes to the total plan, it cannot substitute for the actual classroom assessment that teachers complete in their efforts to make appropriate instructional decisions. Nevertheless, identification is the essential beginning for the entire assessment process.

REFERENCES

Adams, J. Adaptive behavior and measured intelligence in the classification of mental retardation. *American Journal of Mental Deficiency*, 1973, *78*(1), 77–81.

Alpern, G.D., Boll, T.J., & Shearer, M.S. *Developmental Profile II manual* (Rev. ed.). Aspen, Colo.: Psychological Development Publications, 1980.

Apgar, V. A proposal for a new method of evaluation of the newborn infant. *Current Researches in Anesthesia and Analgesia*, 1953, *32*, 260–267.

Bailey, D.B., Jr., & Harbin, G.L. Nondiscriminatory evaluation. *Exceptional Children*, 1980, *46*, 590–596.

Banus, B.S., Kent, C.A., Norton, Y., Sukiennicki, D.R., & Becker, M.L. *The developmental therapist* (2nd ed.). Thorofare, N.J.: Charles B. Slack, 1979.

Baumeister, A.A., & Muma, J.R. On defining mental retardation. *The Journal of Special Education*, 1975, *9*(3), 293–306.

Bayley, N. *Bayley Scales of Infant Development*. New York: Psychological Corporation, 1969.

---

[2]See Paget and Bracken (1983) for a more thorough discussion of the assessment of many of these areas.

Bierman, J.M., Connor, A., Vaage, M., & Honzik, M.P. Pediatrician's assessments of the intelligence of two-year-olds and their mental test scores. *Pediatrics*, 1964, *34*, 680–683.

Binet, A. La mesure en psychologie individuelle. *Revue Philosphique*, 1898, *46*(2), 113–123.

Brazelton, T.B. *Neonatal Behavioral Assessment Scale*. Philadelphia: Lippincott, 1973.

Brazelton, T.B. Assessment in early infancy as an intervention. In D. Gilderman, D. Taylor-Hershel, S. Prestridge, & J. Anderson (Eds.), *The health care/education relationship*. Monmouth, Ore.: WESTAR, 1981.

Brooks-Gunn, J., & Lewis, M. Assessing young handicapped children: Issues and solutions. *Journal of the Division of Early Childhood*, 1981, *2*, 84–95.

Campbell, S.K., & Wilhelm, I.J. Developmental sequences in infants at high risk for central nervous system dysfunction: The recovery process in the first year of life. In J.M. Stack (Ed.), *The special infant*. New York: Human Sciences Press, 1982.

Cattell, P. *Infant Intelligence Scale*. New York: Psychological Corporation, 1940.

Cavanaugh, M.C., Cohen, I., Dunphy, D., Ringwall, E.A., & Goldberg, I.D. Prediction from the Cattell Infant Intelligence Scale. *Journal of Consulting Psychology*, 1957, *21*, 33–37.

Cleary, T.A., Humphreys, L.G., Kendrick, S.A., & Wesman, A. Educational uses of tests with disadvantaged students. *American Psychologist*, 1975, *30*(1), 15–41.

Cone, J.D. *The West Virginia Assessment and Tracking System* (Rev. ed.). Morgantown: West Virginia University, 1981.

DiNola, A.J., Kaminsky, B.P., & Sternfeld, A.E. *TMR Performance Profile for the Severely and Moderately Retarded*. Ridgefield, N.J.: Reporting Service for Children, 1963.

Doll, E.A. *The measurement of social competence: A manual for the Vineland Social Maturity Scale*. Circle Pines, Minn.: American Guidance Service, 1953.

Doll, E.A. *Vineland Social Maturity Scale: Condensed manual of directions*. Circle Pines, Minn.: American Guidance Service, 1965.

Doll, E.A. *Preschool Attainment Record* (Research ed.). Circle Pines, Minn.: American Guidance Service, 1966.

Dollar, S., & Brooks, C. Assessment of severely and profoundly handicapped. *Exceptional Educational Quarterly*, 1980, *1*(3), 87–101.

DuBose, R.F. Predictive value of infant intelligence scales with multiply handicapped children. *American Journal of Mental Deficiency*, 1977, *81*(4), 388–390.

DuBose, R., & Langley, B. *The Developmental Activities Screening Inventory*. Hingham, Mass.: Teaching Resources, 1977.

Dunn, L.M. *Peabody Picture Vocabulary Test*. Circle Pines, Minn.: American Guidance Services, 1965.

Dunn, L.M. Children with moderate and severe general learning disabilities. In L.M. Dunn (Ed.), *Exceptional children in schools* (2nd ed.). New York: Holt, Rinehart & Winston, 1973.

Dunst, C.J. *A clinical and educational manual for use with the Uzgiris and Hunt States of Infant Psychological Development*. Baltimore: University Park Press, 1980.

Dunst, C. *Infant learning: A cognitive-linguistic intervention strategy*. Hingham, Mass.: Teaching Resources, 1981.

Fewell, R.R. *Fathers and their young handicapped children: Assessment of intervention impact*. Paper presented at the annual meeting of the American Association on Mental Deficiency, Boston, June, 1982.

Fishman, M.A., & Palkes, H.S. The validity of psychometric testing in children with congenital malformations of the central nervous system. *Developmental Medicine and Child Neurology*, 1974, *16*, 180–185.

Frankenburg, W.K. Early screening for developmental delays and potential school problems. In C.C. Brown (Ed.), *Infants at risk*. Palm Beach, Fla.: Johnson & Johnson Baby Products, 1981.

Frankenburg, W.K., Dodds, J., & Fandal, A. *Denver Developmental Screening Test: Reference manual* (Rev. ed.) Denver: LADOCA Project and Publishing Foundation, 1975.

Frankenburg, W.K., Goldstein, A.D., & Camp, B.W. The revised Denver Developmental Screening Test: Its accuracy as a screening instrument. *Journal of Pediatrics*, 1971, *79*(6), 988–995.

French, J. *Pictorial Test of Intelligence*. Atlanta: Houghton-Mifflin, 1964.

Gallagher, J.J. Clinical judgement and the Cattell Infant Intelligence Scale. *Journal of Counseling Psychology*, 1953, *17*, 303–305.

Gesell, A., & Armatruda, C.S. *Developmental diagnosis*. New York: Paul B. Hoeber, 1947.

Gilderman, D., Taylor-Hershel, D., Prestridge, S., & Anderson, J. *The health care/education relationship*. Monmouth, Ore.: WESTAR, 1981.

Golin, A.K., & Ducanis, A.J. *The interdisciplinary team*. Rockville, Md.: Aspen Systems Corporation, 1981.

Goodwin, W.L., & Driscoll, L.A. *Handbook for measurement and evaluation in early childhood education*. San Francisco: Jossey-Bass, 1980.

Grossman, H.J. (Ed.). *Manual on terminology and classification in mental retardation*. Washington, D.C.: American Association on Mental Deficiency, 1977.

Hagberg, B. Pre-, peri- and postnatal pediatric handicaps. *Neuropaediatric*, 1975, *6*, 331–338.

Haring, N.G. Introduction. In. N.G. Haring (Ed.), *Exceptional children and youth* (3rd ed.). Columbus, Ohio: Charles E. Merrill, 1982.

Harris, S.R., & Tada, W. Providing developmental therapy services. In S.G. Garwood & R.R. Fewell (Eds.), *Education of handicapped infants: Issues in development and intervention*. Rockville, Md.: Aspen Systems Corporation, 1983.

Hart, V. The use of many disciplines with the severely and profoundly handicapped. In E. Sontag, J. Smith, & N. Certo (Eds.), *Educational programming for the severely and profoundly handicapped*. Reston, Va.: Council for Exceptional Children, 1977.

Haskett, J., & Bell, J. Profound developmental retardation: Descriptive and theoretical utility of the Bayley Mental Scale. In C.E. Meyers (Ed.), *Quality of life in severely and profoundly mentally retarded people: Research foundations for improvement*. Washington: American Association on Mental Deficiency, 1978.

Holm, V.A., & McCartin, R.E. Interdisciplinary child development team: Team issues and training in interdisciplinariness. In K.E. Allen, V.A. Holm, & R.L. Schiefelbusch (Eds.), *Early intervention—A team approach*. Baltimore: University Park Press, 1978.

Hoskins, T.A., & Squires, J.E. Developmental assessment: A test for gross motor and reflex development. *Physical Therapy*, 1973, *53*(2), 117–125.

Illingsworth, R.S. The predictive value of developmental tests in the first year with special reference to the diagnosis of mental subnormality. *Journal of Child Psychology and Psychiatry*, 1961, *2*, 210–215.

Jenkins, J.R., & Pany, D. Standardized achievement tests: How useful for special education? *Exceptional Children*, 1978, *44*, 448–456.

Jones, R.L. Accountability in special education: Some problems. *Exceptional Children*, 1973, *39*, 631–642.

Kemper, M.B., & Frankenburg, W.K. Screening, diagnosis, and assessment: How do these types of measurement differ? In T. Black (Ed.), *Perspectives in measurement: Proceedings of TADS Conference*. Chapel Hill, N.C.: TADS, 1979.

Lambert, N., Windmiller, M., Cole, L., & Figueroa, R. *AAMD Adaptive Behavior Scale, Public School Version* (1974 Rev.). Washington, D.C.: American Association on Mental Deficiency, 1975.

Langley, M.B. *Functional vision inventory for the multiply and severely handicapped*. Chicago: Stoelting, 1980.

Lewis, M. What do we mean when we say "Infant intelligence scores"? A sociopolitical question. In M. Lewis (Ed.), *Origins of intelligence*. New York: Plenum Press, 1976.

Lillie, D.L., & Harbin, G.L. *Carolina Developmental Profile*. Winston Salem, N.C.: Kaplan Press, 1975.

Livingston, S.A. Psychometric techniques for criterion-referenced testing and behavioral assessment. In J.D. Cone & R.P. Hawkins (Eds.), *Behavioral assessment: New directions in clinical psychology*. New York: Brunner/Mazel, 1977.

Mardell, C., & Goldenberg, D. *Developmental Indicators for the Assessment of Learning*. Edison, N.J.: Childcraft Education Corporation, 1975.

Matheny, A.P. Improving diagnostic forecasts made on a developmental scale. *American Journal of Mental Deficiency*, 1957, *62*, 330–333.

McCormick, L., & Goldman, R. The transdisciplinary model: Implications for service delivery and personnel preparation for the severely and profoundly handicapped. *AAESPH Review*, 1979, *4*(2), 152–161.

McCune-Nicolich, L., & Carroll, S. Development of symbolic play: Implications for the language specialist. *Topics in Language Disorders*, December, 1981, 1–15.

McIntosh, E.I., & Warren, S.W. Adaptive behavior in the retarded: A semi-longitudinal study. *The Training School Bulletin*, 1969, *66*, 12–22.

Mercer, J.R. *System of multicultural and pluralistic assessment (SOMPA)—Technical manual*. New York: Psychological Corporation, 1979.

Mercer, J., & Lewis, J.F. *Adaptive Behavior Inventory for Children*. New York: Psychological Corporation, 1979.

Naglieri, J.A. Extrapolated developmental indices for the Bayley Scales of Infant Development. *American Journal of Mental Deficiency*, 1981, *85*(5), 548–550.

National Association for Retarded Citizens. *Educating the twenty-four hour child*. Arlington, Tex.: National Association for Retarded Citizens, 1976.

Nihira, K., Foster, R., Shellhaas, M., & Leland, H. *Adaptive behavior scales: Manual* (Rev. ed.). Washington, D.C.: American Association on Mental Deficiency, 1974.

Oregon State Mental Health Division. *The student progress record*. Salem, Ore.: Oregon State Mental Health Division, 1977.

Paget, K., & Bracken, B. (Eds.) *The psychoeducational assessment of preschool children*. New York: Grune & Stratton, 1983.

Penrose, L.S. *The biology of mental defect* (2nd rev. ed.). New York: Grune & Stratton, 1966.

Richards, F.M., Richards, I.D.G., & Roberts, C.J. The influence of low Apgar rating on infant mortality and development. In R. MacKeith & M. Box (Eds.), *Studies in infancy: Clinics in developmental medicine* (No. 27). London: Spastics Society (Heinemann), 1968.

Sailor, W. Telephone communication: Conference call interview. In R. Perske & J. Smith (Eds.), *Beyond the ordinary*. Seattle: American Association for the Education of the Severely/Profoundly Handicapped, 1977.

Salvia, J., & Ysseldyke, J.E. *Assessment in special and remedial education*. Boston: Houghton Mifflin, 1978.

Sameroff, A.J., & Chandler, M.J. Reproductive risk and the continuum of caretaking casualty. In F. Horowitz (Ed.), *Review of child development research* (Vol. 4). Chicago: University of Chicago Press, 1975.

Sattler, J.M. Analysis of functions of the 1960 Stanford-Binet Intelligence Scale, Form L-M. *Journal of Clinical Psychology*, 1965, *21*, 173–179.

Serunian, S.A., & Broman, S.H. Relationship of Apgar scores and Bayley mental and motor scores. *Child Development*, 1975, *46*, 696–700.

Shipe, D., Vandenberg, S., & Williams, R.D.B. Neonatal Apgar ratings as related to intelligence and behavior in preschool children. *Child Development*, 1968, *39*, 861–866.

Simeonsson, R., Huntington, G., & Parse, S. Assessment of children with severe handicaps: Multiple problems—multivariate goals. *Journal of the Association for the Severely Handicapped*, 1980, *5*(1), 55–72.

Simeonsson, R.J., Huntington, G.S., Short, R.J., & Ware, W.B. The Carolina Record of Individual Behavior: Characteristics of handicapped infants and children. *Topics in Early Childhood Special Education*, 1982, *2*(2), 43–55.

Sirvis, B. Developing IEPs for physically handicapped students: A transdisciplinary viewpoint. *Teaching Exceptional Children*, 1978, *10*, 78–82.

Snell, M.E., & Renzaglia, A.M. Moderate, severe and profound handicaps. In N.G. Haring (Ed.), *Exceptional children and youth* (3rd ed.). Columbus, Ohio: Charles E. Merrill, 1982.

Somerton-Fair, E., & Turner, K.D. *Pennsylvania Training Model: Individual assessment guide* (Rev. ed.). Harrisburg: Pennsylvania Department of Education, 1979.

Song, A.Y., & Jones, S.E. Vineland Social Maturity Scale norm examined—The Wisconsin experience with 0- to 3-year old children. *American Journal of Mental Deficiency*, 1982, *86*(4), 428–431.

Southeastern Regional Coalition. Issues in certification for teachers of the severely handicapped. In National Association of State Directors of Special Education, *Special education programs for severely and profoundly handicapped individuals: A directory of State Education Agency services*. Washington, D.C.: National Association of State Directors of Special Education, 1979, 32–50.

Stangler, S.R., Huber, C.J., & Routh, D.K. *Screening growth and development of preschool children: A guide for test selection*. New York: McGraw-Hill, 1980.

Tallmadge, G.K. *The joint dissemination review panel ideabook*. Washington, D.C.: U.S. Department of Health, Education, and Welfare, 1977.

Tarjan, G., Wright, S.W., Eyman, R.K., & Keeran, C.Y. National history of mental retardation: Some aspects of epidemiology. *American Journal of Mental Deficiency*, 1973, *77*, 369–379.

Terman, L.M. *The measurement of intelligence*. Boston: Houghton Mifflin, 1916.

Terman, L.M., & Merrill, M.A. *Measuring intelligence*. Boston: Houghton Mifflin, 1937.

Terman, L.M., & Merrill, M.A. *Stanford-Binet Intelligence Scale*. New York: Houghton Mifflin, 1973.

Tronick, E., & Brazelton, T.B. Clinical uses of the Brazelton Neonatal Behavioral Assessment. In B.Z. Friedlander & L. Rosenblum (Eds.), *Exceptional infant* (Vol. III). New York: Brunner/Mazel, 1975.

Turnbull, H.R., & Turnbull, A. Public policy and handicapped citizens. In N.G. Haring (Ed.), *Exceptional children and youth* (3rd ed.). Columbus, Ohio: Charles E. Merrill, 1982.

United States Office of Education. *Estimated number of handicapped children in the United States, 1974–75*. Washington, D.C.: Bureau of Education for the Handicapped, 1975.

Wechsler, D. *Wechsler Intelligence Scale for Children*. New York: Psychological Corporation, 1949.

Wechsler, D. *Wechsler Adult Intelligence Scale*. New York: Psychological Corporation, 1955.

Wechsler, D. *Wechsler Preschool and Primary Scale of Intelligence*. New York: Psychological Corporation, 1967.

Wechsler, D. *Wechsler Intelligence Scale for Children–Revised*. New York: Psychological Corporation, 1974.

Uzgiris, I.C., & Hunt, J. McV. *Assessment in infancy: Ordinal scales of psychological development*. Chicago: University of Illinois Press, 1975.

Werner, E.E., Honzik, M.P., & Smith, R.S. Prediction of intelligence and achievement at ten years from twenty months pediatric and psychologic examinations. *Child Development*, 1968, *39*, 1063–1075.

Westby, C. Assessment of cognitive and language abilities through play. *Language Speech and Hearing Services in the Schools*, 1980, *11*, 154–168.

White, O.R. Basic considerations in child assessment: Not quite everything you wanted to know . . . and more. In C.L. Hansen (Ed.) *Child assessment: The process and the product*. Seattle: Program Development Assistance System, 1980.

White, O.R., & Haring, N.G. *Exceptional teaching* (2nd ed.). Columbus, Ohio: Charles E. Merrill, 1980.

Wilcox, B. Severe/profound handicapping conditions: Instructional considerations. In M.S. Lilly (Ed.), *Children with exceptional needs*. New York: Holt, Rinehart & Winston, 1979.

REFERENCE NOTES

1. Scarr, S., & Williams, M.L. *The assessment of neonatal and later status in low birthweight infants*. Paper presented at meeting of the Society of Research in Child Development, Minneapolis, 1971.

2. Knobloch, H., Stevens, F., & Malone, A.F. *The Revised Developmental Screening Interview*, 1980. (Available from Dr. Hilda Knobloch, Albany Medical College, Albany, NY 12208.)

3. McCartan, K. *The Adaptive Performance Instrument*. Unpublished test. Moscow: University of Idaho, 1980.

The next two chapters describe informal educational assessment and intervention strategies for the severely handicapped. For many of you these pages will be reminders of familiar concepts; for others this content will be new. Regardless, the basic elements of systematic instruction covered here represent essential information. All the colorfully packaged materials, commercial teaching kits, curriculum guides, test manuals, and fancy media sets cannot begin to substitute for the readily available mastery of these techniques.

To develop an IEP for a severely handicapped student, you must thoroughly survey his or her performance-relevant environments—the home neighborhood, the school's cafeteria, the nearby supermarket, the local group home. You cannot simply guess which objectives to set, nor can you pull "packaged" IEPs from curriculum guides, nor can you write one IEP for all your students, nor can you just use last year's. Because severely handicapped students learn slowly and generalize poorly, even with quality teaching, we must invest a lot of care in selecting IEP objectives. This annually constructed teaching plan dictates what the student is exposed to. After 18 to 20 IEPs, a student is finished with schooling. Each successive IEP should mesh with the last, and thus build predictably toward increased independence and community survival.

Once written, a functional IEP must be implemented and monitored. The talent of translating well-written IEP objectives into systematic, quality teaching is one special educators must strive for daily. Seemingly small aspects of an interaction are, in fact, important. For example, how will you ask a student to perform the targeted task? Where and when will you teach? What happens to the other 4 to 11 or so other students you're responsible for? What will you do if the student doesn't respond at all to your request, or if he or she makes a mistake or performs correctly, or kicks you in the shins? What will you do? While a battery of effective procedures can be drawn upon to answer each question, there is no simple formula to apply in isolation of a particular student. Performance data—before and during instruction—provide the measure you must consult to judge the ultimate adequacy of your methods.

Enormous talents are required to effectively teach severely handicapped students, but the results are clearly cost effective. Unlike many other educators, teachers of this group cannot assume that their students will learn appropriately in spite of the teacher's errors or ignorance.

Introduction to Chapters 4 and 5

4

Developing the IEP: Selecting and Assessing Skills

Martha E. Snell is at the University of Virginia. This chapter was written with *Deborah D. Smith,* who is at the University of New Mexico.

The process of developing a relevant IEP for a severely handicapped student, as diagrammed in Figure 4.1, involves many steps but always yields long- and short-term objectives that are functionally suited to a specific student. Goals and objectives lock both the student and the teacher into a series of structured activities that may extend over a long period. Years can be spent mastering the many minor and major objectives comprising one goal. If that goal is inappropriate for the learner, the time spent is wasted. And if an IEP is appropriate but is not used to guide daily instruction, precious time is lost. This chapter focuses upon four topics relevant to the IEP development process. First we address some basic assumptions about the IEP process, already touched upon in chapter 1. Next, the means for determining and prioritizing instructional goals are described. Then procedures by which a teacher evaluates student performance are set forth. Finally, the process of using evaluation results to set instructional objectives is explained.

SOME BASIC ASSUMPTIONS

Learning Is Slow; Time Is Dear

Mentally retarded individuals generally take longer to learn skills that nonretarded persons learn quickly. Stated broadly, the greater the retardation, the more likely learning is slowed. Approximately 48% of the moderately to profoundly retarded have one or more additional handicap, whether it be physical or emotional (Hill & Bruininks, 1981). When the retarded person's vision or hearing is less than perfect and cannot be corrected, accurate perception of the surroundings is less likely. An inability to control or move your limbs voluntarily adds greatly to difficulty in acquiring skills. Frequent aberrant behavior also has a negative impact on learning.

However, there is widespread documentation (e.g., Whitman & Scibak, 1979) that, when provided with appropriate instruction, the majority of this difficult-to-teach population can learn functional skills. At the same time, there is almost no documentation of skill acquisition for a small fraction of the severely handicapped, who generally have serious motor impairments. Yet, as noted by Donald Baer, the lack of documentation does not prove that the students cannot be educated.

All this implies that there is no way to be sure that a given behavior is unteachable in a given child. The set of procedures to be tried is too large and not yet totally invented; the set and sequence of possible reasonable prereq-

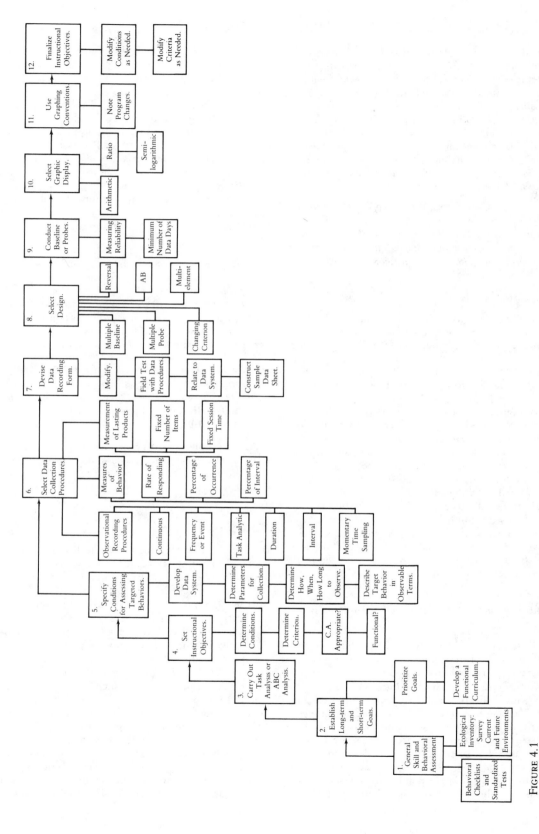

FIGURE 4.1 *Developing the IEP: Selecting and Assessing Skills*

uisite skills that, if taught first, would then render easy the teaching of the original target, is too large with even a moderately imaginative behavior analyst. A child cannot be declared unteachable in fact until teaching has been tried and has failed; teaching is too large a set of procedures (even in its known world) to have been tried and to have failed in its entirety, within the lifetimes of the child and the child's teachers. The point can also be stated in more mundane terms: The cost of truthfully affirming a child to be unteachable is no less than the cost of continuing to attempt teaching the child. (Baer, 1981, p. 96–97)

This first assumption, then, may be stated as follows: *All severely handicapped persons can learn, though learning is likely to be slow in contrast to the less severely handicapped; in order to attain the highest level of self-sufficiency, instructional time must not be wasted.*

Functional Skills

"The schools' responsibility," according to P.L. 94-142, "is to teach whatever skills a student needs to optimize his or her independent, responsible functioning in society" (Hawkins & Hawkins, 1981, p. 13). For the severely handicapped, these functional skills are chosen from a group of tasks and activities that have a high probability of being required and that will increase self-sufficiency (Brown, Branston, Hamre-Nietupski, Pumpian, Certo, & Gruenewald, 1979). Because of cultural and geographic differences from one family and setting to another, all skills that are relevant for one student cannot be assumed to be relevant for another. Functional curricula *must* be determined individually. Thus, commercially developed lists of IEP objectives or state curriculum guides must be used cautiously, as they will not be relevant for all students. Assumption two may be stated as follows: *Teach skills that are relevant to a student's daily life—skills that are or will be required in the home and community.*

Establish Early and Continued Contact with Parents

While most parents or guardians of handicapped children are not professional educators, if given the opportunity, they will almost always make critical contributions to their child's education. This cooperation should not be restricted by the child's chronological age. Whether a student is at the beginning or end of his or her public schooling or is involved in postschool programming, parents are more constant in a child's life than are teachers. Thus functional skills are most easily selected, assessed, and taught from the parents' vantage point. Parent-teacher interaction also should not be limited by the phase of instruction. When a teacher draws up plans for teaching, identifies effective reinforcers, or is interested in assessing "typical" or generalized performance, it is only logical to involve parents.

In Figure 4.1, this initial step in programming is called the "ecological inventory." Besides parent interviews and home visits, it involves a survey of other relevant environments, such as potential work or living settings, present and subsequent schools, and parts of the community the student visits frequently (e.g., grocery stores, neighborhood). *Involvement* of parents is based upon mutual understanding and repeated interactions. Hawkins and Hawkins (1981) emphasize the meaning of this involvement.

In our experience it is not unusual for teachers to write IEP goals, objectives, or procedures that sound important and relevant, but that are too vague or jargon-filled to actually be evaluated by most parents. Thus it is insufficient to ask whether a parent agrees with a particular goal, objective, or procedure written on an IEP—to which parents are likely to respond affirmatively out of respect for the educator and fear of looking ignorant—and it is even insufficient to ask whether they understand the goal, objective, or procedure. The teacher must see that the parent understands. This may require that the teacher demonstrate as well as discuss the contents of the IEP, or even that the teacher get the parents to do so. (p. 20)

Assumption three may be stated as follows: *To make the most impact, teachers must interact meaningfully and continuously with the parents and guardians of the students they teach.*

Behavioral Principles

Behavioral principles, more specifically principles of operant conditioning, "describe the relationship between behavior and environmental events (antecedents and consequences) that influence behavior" (Kazdin, 1980, p. 27). What occurs *before* a behavior (instructional cues, materials, prompts to respond) or *after* a behavior (reinforcement, extinction, or punishment) will ultimately affect whether that behavior is acquired, is forgotten, or occurs more or less frequently. When behavioral principles are used with humans in natural settings, such as the home and school, to modify socially significant problems, then the term "applied behavior analysis" is appropriate. This approach rests firmly upon direct and frequent measurement of behavior, individual rather than group analysis of behavior, replicable teaching procedures, and single-subject rather than group experimental control. Stated as an assumption and as a well-documented fact, *behavioral principles are almost universally applied with the severely handicapped as the method of choice* (Berkson & Landesman-Dwyer, 1977).

Low Reliance upon Norm-Referenced and Developmental Assessment Devices

Traditional assessment approaches with the severely handicapped include norm-referenced or informal developmental tests. This approach tries to identify which tasks normally performed by nonhandicapped infants and young children are failed by severely handicapped students. Failed items then are rewritten as instructional goals, based upon the assumption that all retarded students should acquire the same orderly progression of skills the nonretarded do. Unfortunately, this approach to selecting objectives is rarely functional for teaching. In fact, if the handicapped student is much beyond infancy, a developmentally-based curriculum is likely to have little impact upon the ultimate attainment of self-sufficiency (Holvoet, Guess, Mulligan, & Brown, 1980). Therefore, more consistent with the assumption that functional skills should be taught is the complementary practice of informal but precise assessment of a person's ability to perform practical skills in realistic settings.

Some norm-referenced instruments, such as the AAMD *Adaptive Behavior Scales* (Lambert, Windmiller, Cole, & Figueroa, 1975) and TARC (Sailor & Mix, 1975), may be useful for teachers of the severely handicapped for two purposes. First, these tools may provide a global picture of a student's abilities, thereby giving direction for later informal assessment. Thus, as shown in Figure 4.1, the teacher's first task often is to use such a test to grossly define a student's entry skills and begin the list of long- and short-term goals.

Second, because these published tests have wide familiarity among special educators and psychologists, the results, if considered accurate, provide common ground for reporting performance levels. Since they are not intended to detect small changes in behavior or do not address all areas where instruction is likely, they cannot be used to evaluate IEP performance. Thus, with the limited exception of some norm-referenced assessment tools, most educational testing for the severely handicapped will be informal. It will contrast observed performance with a specified criterion rather than with a comparison group. While this approach is more tedious, the teacher cannot simply rely on commercially available tests. Thus, assumption five: *Precise informal measurement of the very behaviors a teacher wishes to instruct is the only assessment approach consistent with a functional and behavioral philosophy.*

Social Validation of Goals, Procedures, and Effects

In every society, the moderately and severely handicapped are an incredibly small subgroup. Most people know little of their existence and have false notions about their potential. Still, as noted by Kazdin (1977, 1980) and Wolf (1978), regardless of which people receive behavioral intervention, every society has certain concerns and constraints that ultimately affect (*a*) the objectives of intervention; (*b*) the acceptability of intervention procedures; and (*c*) the utility of the intervention results.

In our society, as in most, self-sufficiency is worked toward and rewarded. Being able to care for or, at the very least, assist with your most basic daily living needs is regarded as an indisputably essential skill. Perhaps second-most important is socially appropriate behavior—the absence of uncalled-for aggressiveness, bizarre behaviors, or disruptiveness. A close third in this list of assumed essentials might be productivity, or the interest in and ability to partially or wholly support yourself. Thus, the notion of functionality is quite consistent with socially validated goals. In other words, if the *goals of instruction* address behaviors judged to be practical and acceptable in a given community rather than irrelevant or deviant, then we might say those goals have social validation.

Similarly, if *treatment techniques* are regarded as being highly objectionable to those who must use them (parents and teachers) or to those with whom they will be applied, then they lack social validation and are likely not to be used. Noteworthy examples include aversive conditioning procedures, which often conflict with personal beliefs as well as with legal regulations. Likewise, when techniques are perceived as too complicated or unnecessarily time consuming, the users may reject them for simpler procedures. Etzel and LeBlanc (1979) present a strong argument for selecting the simplest *but still effective* methods for teaching the difficult-to-teach student.

Also of interest is the social validation of actual *intervention outcome*. That is, once the targeted behavior has been learned, is it clinically relevant for the client? Kazdin (1980) addresses two methods of socially validating treatment results: social comparison and subjective evaluation.

In the first method, the student's posttreatment performance may be contrasted with that of nonhandicapped peers. For example, before setting standards to teach retarded women to color coordinate their clothing, Nutter and Reid (1978) observed the color combinations worn by over 600 women in nearby public settings. Similarly, O'Brien and Azrin (1972) contrasted the frequency of retarded students' eating errors with that of nonhandicapped people in a local restaurant to evaluate the effects of a training program geared toward establishing proper eating behavior.

A second means of socially validating performance is eliciting the opinion of consumers or people qualified to judge or to set standards. If, for example, an adult was so slow counting change that grocery shoppers in the line behind him were irritated, then his skills would be judged inadequate.

Assumption six may be stated as follows: *Instructional objectives and procedures, as well as the resultant changes in the student, exist in a social medium far greater than a single classroom, school, or community; teachers must be able to defend instructional objectives as practical and important; they must be able to justify teaching procedures as being humane, usable, and effective; and they must be able to teach until behavior changes meaningfully.*

SELECTING AND PRIORITIZING INSTRUCTIONAL GOALS.

We have already said that IEP objectives must be appropriate for a particular student. This means that:

1. Objectives address practical or functional skills that are most likely to be needed currently or in the near future;
2. Objectives span four instructional domains: domestic, leisure-recreational, community, and vocational;
3. Objectives are suitable for the student's chronological age;
4. Objectives must not be so difficult that they cannot be accomplished in a year's time or so simple that they are already in the student's repertoire.

It is surprising how often IEP objectives written for this population fall short on one or more counts. Because of the importance of IEP goals, we will address each of these characteristics.

Functional Skills

Instruction should focus upon partial or total independence in those skills *most often required* at home, in school, at work, or in the community. Again, a teacher cannot assume that the skills functional for one student will also be functional for another. Objectives therefore must be selected individually. This procedure involves surveying the student's current and future environments to identify needed domestic, leisure-recreation, community, and vocational skills (Brown et al., 1979b; Vincent, Salisbury, Walter, Brown, Gruenewald, & Powers, 1980). This

practice contrasts strongly with a developmental approach, which identifies instructional objectives from the "bottom up"—starting with skills normally performed by infants and proceeding to more advanced motor, social, and cognitive skills. Brown and his colleagues refer to their functional survey for objectives as a "top-down" approach to skill building. That is, they *begin* with the requirements of independent adult functioning in four skill categories.

The *domestic domain* includes skills performed in and around the home: self-care, clothing care, housekeeping, cooking, and yard work. To the extent that an adult might be paid for performing domestic tasks, this domain has some overlap with vocational skills (e.g., janitorial or hotel maid jobs). In the *leisure-recreational domain* are the skills needed to engage in spectator or participant activities performed to enjoy yourself. Skills required in the *community domain* include street crossing, using public transportation, purchasing in stores, eating in restaurants, and using other public facilities (such as movies and parks). Finally, *vocational domain* skills include those involved in attaining sheltered and competitive employment. Functional academics are likely to play a part in all four domains.

The process of developing a functional curriculum for a given student has been precisely defined by Brown and his colleagues (1979b); we will summarize its six phases with a case illustration.

Consider Rose Mary, an ambulatory 17-year-old young woman in her final few years of public schooling. Rose Mary functions in the severely retarded range. She lives in an institution, as she has since the age of 9 months, but is scheduled to move into a group home when she is 21. Currently she lives in a dormitory with 28 others, aged 11 to 22 years. At the institution she attends a self-contained classroom for eight severely handicapped students. Rose Mary can carry out all her own personal hygiene, though she has not had any instruction in clothing care, food preparation, or cleaning. Currently she is learning to eat "family style" in the dorm cafeteria. She has received no relevant vocational training, even though she would be eligible for placement in a workshop when she moves. She cannot use public transportation nor does she occupy her leisure time appropriately. Rose Mary has learned manual signs and uses them more effectively to express herself than speech, which is limited and generally unintelligible. Because she has not had the opportunity to learn, she is deficient in most of the daily living skills that will be expected of her in the group home. Unless Rose Mary can demonstrate more self-sufficiency, her teachers have been told that she will not qualify for the up-coming community placement.

Rose Mary's teachers have little choice at this point but to develop a functional curriculum sequenced to address the most needed skills first. They must proceed through six phases of curriculum development:

1. Identify curriculum *domains;*
2. Identify and survey current and future natural *environments;*
3. Divide the relevant environments into *subenvironments;*
4. Inventory these subenvironments for the relevant *activities* performed there;
5. Examine the activities to isolate the *skills* required for their performance;
6. Design and use instructional *programs* to teach the identified skills (Brown, et al., 1979b).

1. *Identify curriculum domains.* For most students, including Rose Mary, all four domains will be relevant. It is possible, however, that very young students will focus most on domestic, leisure, and community skills, while leaving the vocational domain until after preschool. These curriculum domains rather than the traditional academic or developmental categories are used because they (*a*) represent the major life areas, (*b*) lead to the selection of practical skills, and (*c*) emphasize the functional goals of self-sufficiency. This practice does *not* mean that skills such as "language" or "fine motor" are forgotten.

2. *Identify and survey current and future natural environments.* Working closely with the student's parents, guardians, or residential staff, the teacher will identify and examine the settings in which the student presently lives, works, and plays. To prepare the same student to function in the settings he or she eventually will be placed in, these *future* environments also must be added to the inspection list. The intent here is to make a student's entry into alternate schools, residences, workshops, and so forth possible by guaranteeing that he or she can perform as required. Without future planning, there is no guarantee whatsoever for entry.

In Rose Mary's case (as shown in Figures 4.2 and 4.3), natural environments were identified for both the institution and the community setting. To teach Rose Mary the skills needed for a successful transition to the community in 4 years, her teachers made an *ecological inventory*—they visited the proposed group home, workshop, and town. After conversing with her community services social worker, the houseparents of the group home, and the workshop director and staff, the curriculum development could be completed. Even though they were aware of the environmental differences between the community and the institution, Rose Mary's teachers decided to create opportunities in and around the institution to teach skills needed in the future. For example, they would teach restaurant-related skills (community domain) in two places: the institution canteen, which Rose Mary could easily and frequently use, and a nearby McDonald's.

3. *Divide the relevant environments into subenvironments.* Further subdivision of environments is necessary to isolate the activities most likely to be required (which constitutes the fourth step in curriculum development). For example, "restaurants," a community environment selected for Rose Mary, was divided into fast-food ordering area, eating area, and bathroom. Although many other public use areas are possible in restaurants, these subenvironments were the most relevant for Rose Mary.

4. *Inventory these subenvironments for the relevant activities performed there.* What are the essential clusters of behaviors you are required to perform in these settings? At this stage of curriculum development, critical activities should be listed. The teacher should identify only those activities necessary for basic successful functioning, rather than isolating every possible activity. Furthermore, in selecting activities, extensive consideration should be given to the student's current skills, his or her interests, the priorities of the parent, and the specific physical characteristics of the setting which dictate behaviors required there. For example, there was no washer and dryer on the institutional living unit where Rose Mary lived. However, there was one at the group home which Rose Mary would need to operate. Her teachers decided that the machines available at the institution school building (generally used only by housekeeping staff) would be reserved some time each day for instruction. Because many leisure and recreation activities were possible, those actually selected were determined by: (*a*) activities available both at the institution and in the community setting, (*b*) activities suited most to Rose Mary's chronological age, (*c*) interests, and (*d*) skill level.

5. *Examine the activities to isolate the skills required for their performance.* At this phase, activities are analyzed into teachable units. These units or separate skills are likely to be further task-analyzed into sequences of behaviors. While each skill is separated for measurement and teaching, the teacher must not lose sight of the end goal—*clusters* of *related skills* must be performed together in the natural environment. Rose Mary's success in using a fast-food restaurant will rely on her ability to enter the restaurant, stand in the order line, select the desired food, state her order, pay, find seating, eat, dispose of her trash, and leave. At some point, either during acquisition or after, this sequence of skills must be performed in combination.

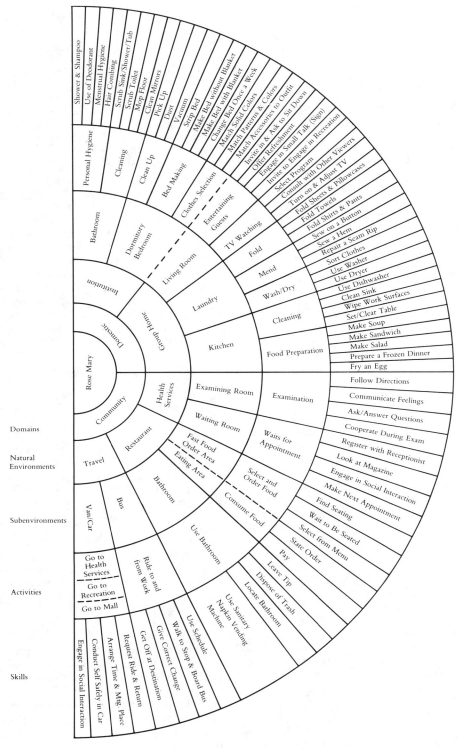

Domains

Natural Environments

Subenvironments

Activities

Skills

FIGURE 4.2

A Functional Curriculum in the Community and Domestic Domains for a 17-Year-Old Young Woman

SOURCE: Credit for this manner of displaying a functional curriculum must be extended to Kathy Steward. The content was developed by Kathy Steward and Joan Miller.

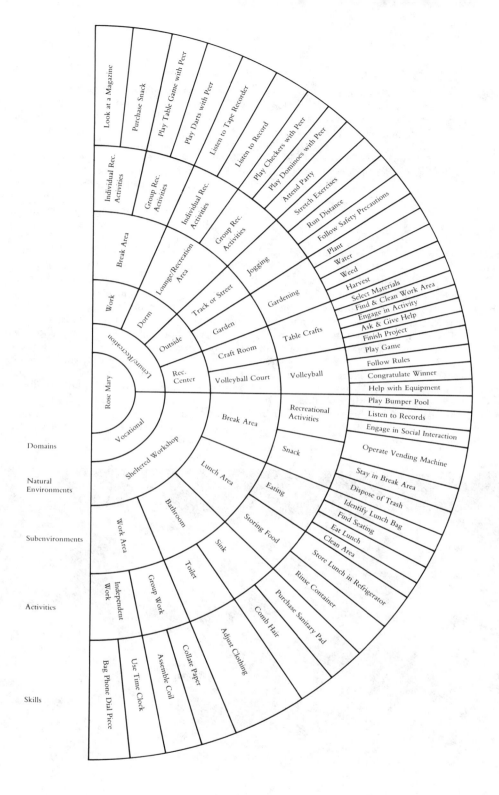

FIGURE 4.3
A Functional Curriculum in the Vocational and Leisure/Recreation Domains for the Same Young Woman

6. *Design and use instructional programs to teach the identified skills.* It almost goes without saying that a curriculum of functional objectives, no matter how good, is useful only if intervention follows. Basic characteristics of informal assessment will be addressed later in this chapter, as will task analysis. We will discuss instructional procedures in the next chapter.

Difficulty Level

What are the motor and thinking requirements of a particular activity or skill? Can they be simplified by physically modifying the materials involved? When a raised plastic overlay is used to cover a row of manually operated switches (for a communication board, an automatic game, etc.) it is easier to select and push only the desired switch, which significantly reduces the difficulty of the task. When a 3-year-old can apply light pressure to a homemade flipper switch and activate a toy, as shown in Figure 4.4, he realizes the pleasures that result from controlling his environment. Adjusting a functional task to enable performance has been referred to as the *principle of partial participation* (Brown, Branston-McClean, Baumgart, Vincent, Falvey, & Schroeder, 1979a).

Simplifying the thinking requirements of a task without changing its ultimate intent is another way to reduce difficulty and permit partial participation. Picture directions may remind a person completing a complex housekeeping task or a cooking chore. Changing the rules for croquet or checkers might make playing easier to learn. Teaching a student to prepare cookies from frozen premade cookie dough and to mix a drink from canned, frozen concentrated juice is simpler than starting from scratch, and still practical. A nonvocal student can be taught to order at fast-food restaurants with minimal confusion by showing photos of desired items. Since all of these task simplifications still require instruction, the teacher must "field-test" or validate the task simplification beforehand to guarantee its ultimate value in the natural environment. For example, can others look at the photos of the fast-food items and tell what foods they represent? Is the flipper switch that operates the toy car reliable? How much and what type of pressure does it require, and do these simplified motor requirements match the student's abilities? This validation must be thorough and completed before instruction begins to avoid wasting the student's time.

Another comment on difficulty level relates directly to *how long* it will take for a student to master a

FIGURE 4.4
A Young Boy Activates a Toy Train by Pressing Down on a "Flipper" Switch. When he releases the lever, the switch turns off.
SOURCE: "Homemade Battery Powered Toys and Educational Devices for Severely Handicapped Children" by L.J. Burkhart, Millville, Pa., 1980, p. 7.

specific skill stated as the short-term objective. Objectives must not be so difficult that they cannot be accomplished in year. Thus the teacher must make accurate predictions both about the student's learning rate and about the success of the intervention program. These predictions are validated with data, since the teacher will monitor progress by regular observation of the student performing the skill *without any assistance*. These probe results are then graphed, as will be described later. At times performance data will indicate that little or no learning is occurring and that a program change is needed. More often, performance data will indicate steady acquisition of the skill. IEP objectives that are not accomplished should be modified rather than simply carried over to the next IEP. Modifications may include (*a*) a change in instructional techniques (reinforcement, prompt, materials, etc.), (*b*) a change in the teaching conditions (setting or materials, frequency of instruction, length of session, number of students involved in group positioning, etc.), (*c*) a change in the criterion for performance, (*d*) a change in the test or probe procedure, or (*e*) a change in the behavior or skill targeted for instruction.

Chronological Age

Traditionally, teachers of the retarded have put more stock into the mental age of their students than into their chronological age. In fact it has been common for teachers to ignore a severely handicapped student's chronological age (CA). Indiscriminately, in April each year Easter bunnies appear on the walls of many such classrooms, whether the students are 5 or 15 years old. These practices only emphasize the handicap of mental retardation, as Brown and his colleagues have expressed:

If one goal of education is to minimize the stigmatizing discrepancies between the handicapped and their nonhandicapped peers, it is our obligation to teach the former the major functions characteristic of their chronological age using materials and tasks which do not highlight the deficiencies in their repertoires. (Brown et al., 1979b, p. 86)

However, it certainly *is* true that not all materials, activities, or instructional objectives suited to nonhandicapped persons are also appropriate for severely handicapped persons of the same chronological age.

It is apparent to even the most optimistic professionals that there are a substantial number of skills that these students will never acquire. Translating from Spanish to English, selling life insurance, and driving a bus are but a few. At the same time, however, there are many chronological-age-

appropriate skills that they can indeed acquire. Eating, communicating, and turning on a television set are but a few. (Brown et al., 1979b, p. 86)

Thus, in addition to difficulty level and function, a teacher must consider the student's chronological age when selecting skills for instruction. Applying these three considerations requires some careful thought. Consider, for example, the 21-year-old person who has mixed spastic-athetoid involvement in all four limbs and trunk. Instead of teaching her to enjoy a weighted musical infant toy, any of the following activities might be selected:

1. Operating a cassette tape recorder with popular music with a mercury head control switch;
2. Listening to a transistor radio by operating a cheek switch;
3. Viewing slides with an adapted carousel projector.

Functionality is also addressed in this example when the teacher selects an *available* leisure activity. If the student's living environment does not have a projector and slides available (and cannot afford one), then teaching a 21-year-old to enjoy that task is very nonfunctional, as its use will be limited to the few remaining months in school.

To select objectives that address all three criteria—function, CA appropriateness, and difficulty level—it is probably best to satisfy the requirements of function and CA appropriateness first, dealing with difficulty level last.

Prioritization of Goals

When a "top-down" approach to curriculum development is used, an abundance of functional activities and skills is the likely outcome. The skills selected for Rose Mary (in Figures 4.2 and 4.3) were limited to three or four per activity for purposes of illustration. However, instruction cannot begin simultaneously on all 112 objectives and be very effective. Some choices must be made about which skills to teach before others. The main guide for prioritizing skills is *to select for immediate instruction those skills the student requires most often to function more independently in current and subsequent least restrictive settings.* Informants in this process include those persons already questioned: parents or guardians; workshops or other vocational training staff; group home or foster care parents, or other residential living staff; teaching staff in the *upcoming* educational settings; interdisciplinary staff (occupational and physical therapists, speech therapists, etc.); and individuals familiar with community programs for which the student is or may be eligible. Time is saved if the teacher asks each informant to prioritize activities and skills *as* the curriculum is being developed. In addition, there are likely to be repetitions in activities and skills recommended for a given student across both domains and informants. Skills repeatedly isolated as being critical would logically be given higher priority.

There is no magic or "appropriate" number of IEP objectives, but a balance of skills should be drawn from all relevant domains. In addition, teaching clusters of related skills makes instruction more efficient *and* the resulting performance contributes more to self-sufficiency than teaching fragments of skills.

Before we describe data collection procedures in the next section, we should relate our discussion to IEP development (refer to Figure 4.1). After identifying functional skills a student needs to learn and establishing priorities for these skills, the teacher may restate these priorities as the long- and short-term IEP goals. Short-term goals are expanded into instructional objectives when the teacher has obtained a clear grasp of the target behavior through ABC analysis or task analysis.

When *skills* are to be taught (rather than *inappropriate behavior* being reduced), task analysis defines guidelines for both assessment and instruction. *Most IEP objectives for most students will relate to learning new skills or generalizing already learned skills;* however, some students will require intervention to reduce excessively maladaptive or harmful behavior. An ABC analysis is useful when teachers, parents, and others are trying to sort out the relationship between a student's inappropriate behavior and the environment.

ABC Analysis

"ABC Analysis" refers to a descriptive analysis of behavior—"listing all environmental events subsequent and antecedent to or during a recurring behavioral event or the general setting in which that behavior occurs with the purpose of attempting to identify possible discriminative and reinforcing stimuli" (White, 1971, p. 7). In an ABC analysis, you examine the causal relationships between the stimulus events preceding or antecedent to the behavior (response or movement) and events following or consequential to it. The particular arrangement or contingency by which consequential events are made available to the behaving individual is directly related to the strength and frequency of the behavior.

Antecedent events include commands, instructions, teaching materials and setting, prompting, and behavior modeling; consequential events may be reinforcing (food, praise, tokens, activities), punishing (angry look and words, removal of toys), or neutral. Both antecedent and consequential events are often a result of staff (teacher, aide), parent, or peer behavior.

Although the questions a teacher must answer about the target behavior during an ABC analysis depend upon the teaching problem, the following questions are of general concern.

1. Antecedent conditions
   A. In what situation(s) does the target behavior occur (e.g., setting, time of day or night, peers or adults present)?
   B. What adult or peer behaviors occur just prior to the targeted behavior (e.g., teacher requests, presentation or removal of certain toys, change in schedule)?

2. Behavior
   A. How often does the individual independently perform the target behavior and how much of the target behavior can the individual currently perform without assistance (i.e., baseline level)?

3. Consequential conditions
   A. What comments are made or actions taken by staff and peers as the behavior is occurring or during the moments following the behavior?
   B. Approximately how often do these particular consequences occur in relation to the behavior (i.e., arrangement or contingency of the consequences)?

Once these preliminary questions are answered, you have a more accurate picture of the student's behavior. This information in turn enables you to identify what needs to be taught, to set instructional objectives, and to assess these targeted behaviors more precisely (steps 4, 5, and 6 in Figure 4.1).

Task Analysis

There are a variety of methods to analyze tasks (e.g., Becker, Engelmann, & Thomas, 1975; Resnick, Wang, & Kaplan, 1973; Smith, Smith, & Edgar, 1976; Gaylord-Ross, Note 1); while some involve more extensive procedures than others, most require the following three steps.[1]

1. Identify a skill suitable for a particular student in terms of function, chronological age, and difficulty level.
2. Select the setting and materials most suited to the natural performance of the skill.
3. Perform the task in the selected setting using the chosen materials; watch others (handicapped and nonhandicapped) who are skilled at the task perform. Validate the task analysis.

---

[1]For a more thorough discussion of task analysis, consult Gaylord-Ross (Note 1).

Although we have already addressed the first step, some additional comments are needed regarding steps 2 and 3. First, if a student is physically handicapped, materials and setting may need to be individually adapted. These modifications, if permanent rather than temporary, should be made before finalizing the task analysis, as any change in the task analysis will change the assessment as well. Results obtained from assessing a skill with one task analysis are not comparable with those obtained when a different task analysis of the same task is used. The differences will be in the number, order, or type of steps that constitute the task analysis.

A related point concerns the setting where the task will ultimately be performed. While it generally is best both to teach and assess a skill in its natural setting, some skills may be more efficiently or safely *taught* in artificial or simulated settings. For example, Page, Iwata, and Neef (1976) found it was safer to teach moderately retarded students pedestrian skills using a tabletop street model. This simulated situation permitted much more training time, since training could take place in bad weather and time was not lost traveling to and from the classroom. However, it is important to know that Page et al. (1976) regularly tested the students' street-crossing skills in the real environment. Without regular checks for generalization, a teacher of the severely handicapped cannot guess whether simulated training is of value. If tests under simulated conditions indicate skill gains but tests in the actual environment do not, then training conditions must be made more realistic or the acquired skill will not be useful. The general rule is to use natural environments for training whenever possible; however, if safety or efficiency is a problem, training under simulated conditions should be used as long as probes in the natural environment indicate that the training is being generalized.

Finally, the task analysis must be validated or "field-tested." During these repeated performances, a teacher will identify and sequence the behaviors involved from task beginning to end. You must not lose sight of which student or students are to be taught the skill being analyzed and adapt the steps and sequence accordingly. For example, while most of us would load, play, and empty a cassette tape recorder in a manner dictated mainly by the tape recorder's construction, a person with spastic involvement of both arms will need a modified task analysis or materials.

At least two people should observe the actual behavior and independently state the steps involved (Cuvo, 1978). Since there are likely to be some disagreements, the task analysts should resolve their differences by (a) discussing the differences, resolving them verbally, and repeating independent modified task analysis until agreement is obtained; (b) resolving the differences through repeated observa-

tion of the behavior with revision of the task analysis; or (c) consulting a third person more skilled in the selected behavior. Cuvo and his coworkers (e.g., Cronin & Cuvo, 1979; Cuvo, Leaf, & Borakove, 1978; Johnson & Cuvo, 1981) found that consultation with "experts" was necessary to validate task analyses. For example, Cuvo et al. (1978) observed the school janitor (as well as videotapes of his performance) to validate task analyses for six bathroom-cleaning tasks. (See Table 4.1 for an example.) Cronin and Cuvo (1979) asked a home economist to evaluate preliminary task analyses of mending skills and then to perform each task using the steps to verify (or improve upon) their inclusion and order. (See Figure 4.5 for a task analysis of stripping a bed.)

Most tasks can be performed in more than one way, depending upon both materials selected and method used. For example, when a contour bottom sheet is used, the steps involved in putting it on the mattress are quite different from those needed with a flat sheet. Some bedmakers miter the corners to tuck in the bed covers neatly. The extra moves involved in mitering are not essential, but may be desired. Method, material, and quality decisions must be made before you can finalize a task analysis. Many

TABLE 4.1 Task Analysis for Cleaning the Sink

1. Take spray cleaner from container.
2. Shake spray cleaner.
3. Spray entire sink with back-and-forth sweeping motions.
4. Replace cleaner in container.
5. Reach over to towel dispenser.
6. Pick up two paper towels.
7. Put paper towels together.
8. Wipe sink sides and edges with back-and-forth strokes.
9. Wipe between faucets with back-and-forth strokes.
10. Wipe faucets by lightly grasping them with towel and twisting back-and-forth.
11. Wipe sink bowl with circular and back-and-forth motions.
12. Turn on cold water.
13. Swish water around bowl with towel.
14. Turn off cold water.
15. Wipe sink bowl again with towel, using circular and back-and-forth motions.
16. Bend over wastebasket which is located under sink.
17. Throw dirty towels in wastebasket

SOURCE: "Teaching Janitorial Skills to the Mentally Retarded: Acquisition, Generalization, and Maintenance," by A.J. Cuvo, R.B. Leaf, & L.S. Borakove. *Journal of Applied Behavior Analysis,* 1978, *11,* 347. Copyright 1978 by the Society for the Experimental Analysis of Behavior, Inc. Reprinted with permission.

revisions will probably be made before producing a task analysis that works for a particular student.

The examples in Table 4.1 and Figure 4.5 have the following characteristics:

1. The target behavior is specified (e.g., hemming).
2. Steps are stated in terms of observable behavior.
3. Steps are written with adequate detail (not too many or too few behaviors per step).
4. Each step results in a visible change in the product or process.
5. Steps are ordered from first performed to last performed.
6. Steps are worded in the second person so, when spoken, could serve as a verbal prompt.

Often task analyses need adjustment after being used with a given student. Points 3 and 5 are likely to need modification at these times. For some students, a single step can include a cluster of related behaviors (e.g., step 10 in Table 4.1: wipe faucets by lightly grasping with a towel and twisting back and forth); for other students, fewer behaviors per step are more appropriate. The order of the steps or the actual method of performing the task may also change, depending upon the student's additional physical or sensory impairments.

Finally, it may be necessary to provide so much detail when describing a step that the entire step is too complex in its wording to serve as a verbal prompt. In these cases only the words used as the verbal prompt are underlined, as shown in Figure 4.5.

Latticing is an alternate form of task analysis. Rather than a simple vertical listing of steps, the lattice displays skill components and the sequence of steps leading to each skill (Smith et al., 1976). A lattice for table setting is shown in Figure 4.6. This analysis identifies eight skill components, each of which have one or more steps. However, lattices, like vertical-list task analyses, are not instructional programs in and of themselves, since neither outlines teaching strategies.

Both task analysis and ABC analysis yield information that lets the teacher formulate intervention strategies and specify conditions and performance criteria more accurately.

SETTING INSTRUCTIONAL OBJECTIVES

Many teachers have relied upon behavioral objectives to plan individualized curricula for their students since their popularization in the early 1960s. Behavioral objectives provide clear and precise goal statements and are worded to assure agreement on the description of the behavior—its topography and oc-

currence. The key is that behavioral objectives must be stated in reliable and observable terms: the behavior specified can be demonstrated to the observer.

It is relatively easy to translate behaviors chosen for instruction into a series of behavioral objectives. Since reliably observable behaviors are stated precisely in all ABC and task analyses, merely expanding them into behavioral statements produces at least simple behavioral objectives.

Monitoring students' achievement of skills specified in a series of behavioral objectives may substitute for a checklist and record of their progress. If, however, sequenced behavioral objectives indicate student progress, more information is required. Thus objectives must exactly describe the *criteria* for mastery as well as the environmental *conditions:* the setting, time, and materials. The criteria for mastery must indicate aim scores: quantifiers (that is, percentage scores, correct and error rates, frequency count) with which to determine and judge the acceptability of performance, such as 100% within a specific time period. In addition, the teacher needs to indicate where and when the behavior is expected to occur. If, for example, John's objective is "to select and punch his time card at work," the teacher expects that, after instruction, "each time John enters the workshop he will select his card from a group of about 30 cards and operate the time clock with 100% accuracy over 3 consecutive days according to the steps in the task analysis of that skill."

By having objectives which indicate all parameters of the desired response, the teacher may use them during all phases of instruction: acquisition, maintenance, and generalization. If objectives indicate what will be considered proficiency, they indicate mastery during acquisition and maintenance. The teacher, then, will know when to terminate direct instruction and begin maintenance or generalization. A notion of when to shift from one situation to another makes teaching more efficient.

After writing the instructional objectives, the teacher selects suitable data collection procedures and devises recording sheets to assess the student's pretreatment of baseline performance (steps 4, 5, 6, and 7 in Figure 4.1). Finally, the instructional objectives are re-examined after observing the student's baseline performance to check the suitability of the behavior, criteria, and performance conditions.

DATA COLLECTION PROCEDURES

Behavior measurement is arduous, and data-based analyses are complex. For example, you may examine (*a*) direction of change (increase, decrease, no change), (*b*) rate of change, (*c*) stability of change, and (*d*) amount of change in a behavior. Recently effec-

Instructional Cue: "Strip the whole bed" (point to bed and hamper).

Teacher: Gina Student: Bert

Assessment Method: Single Opportunity

Target Behavior: Stripping a Bed

Target Behavior: Stripping a Bed	3/4	3/5	3/6	3/7
1. Pull bed out from wall at least 6 in.	+	+	+	+
2. Remove pillowcase from pillow.	+	-	+	+
3. Put pillowcase in hamper.	-	-	+	+
4. Put pillow on chair, other bed or dresser.	-	-	+	+
5. Remove spread.	-	-	-	-
6. Put spread on chair, other bed or dresser.	-	-	-	-
7. Remove blanket.	-	-	-	-
8. Put blanket on chair, other bed or dresser.	-	-	-	-
9. Remove top sheet.	-	-	-	-
10. Put sheet in hamper.	-	-	-	-
11. Stand at top and nearside, grasp sheet at corner pull up and off.	-	-	-	-
12. Go to far side, grasp sheet at corner pull up and off.	-	-	-	-
13. Continue around to other end of bed, grasp sheet at lower edge pull up.	-	-	-	-
14. Put sheet in hamper.	-	-	-	-
15. Push bed into wall	-	-	-	-
% correct	13%	7%	27%	27%

Recording Key: + Correct C Error correction
 − Incorrect M Model prompt
 P Physical prompt

Criterion: 100% correct over three consecutive probes

Materials: Begin with bed partially unmade (top sheet, blanket, & spread pulled down and wrinkled), bed pushed into wall, contour bottom sheet, clothes hamper & empty chair near bed.

Response Latency: Allow 6 seconds to respond. Stop probe after 10 seconds inappropriate behavior or 6 seconds no response.

FIGURE 4.5
Task Analytic Data Sheet for Stripping a Bed

89

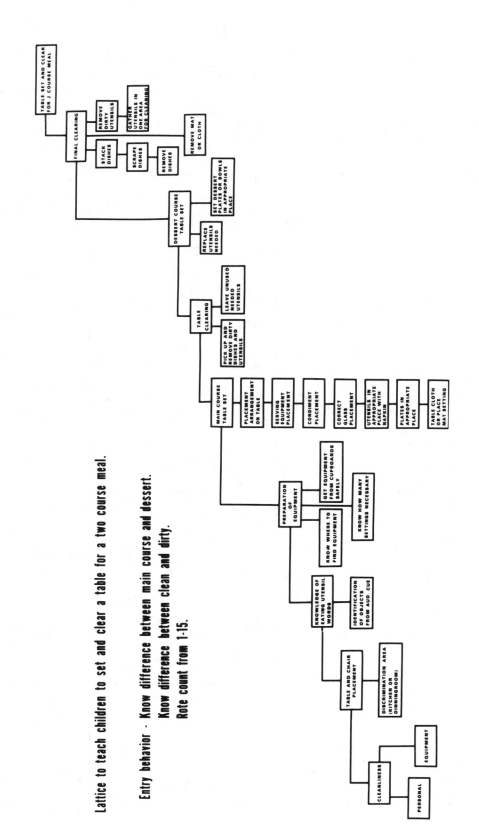

Lattice to teach children to set and clear a table for a two course meal.

Entry behavior - Know difference between main course and dessert.
Know difference between clean and dirty.
Rote count from 1-15.

FIGURE 4.6

A Lattice for the Skill of Table Setting

Source: "Research and Application of Instructional Material Development" by J.O. Smith and D.D. Smith. In N.G. Haring (Ed.), *Annual Report: A Program Project for the Investigation and Application of Procedures of Analysis and Modification of Behavior of Handicapped Children.* Washington, D.C.: National Institute of Education, 1974.

tive procedures have been developed which help us measure the behavior of young children and adults in applied settings. These procedures can be classified as either direct observation of behavior, of which five types will be described, or measurement of permanent products.[2] To apply these behavior measurement procedures, the observer must proceed meticulously through this sequence.

1. Clearly describe the target behavior in observable terms.
2. Specify the conditions for observation that will yield accurate measurement (e.g., when, where, and for how long the behavior will be observed).
3. Identify the characteristics of the target behavior (i.e., its duration, frequency, etc.), and select the appropriate measurement procedure.
4. Select a design that adequately tests the effect of the intervention on the behavior.
5. Construct a data-recording form or specify the way data will be recorded.
6. Collect the data through observation.
7. Estimate the reliability of the measurement procedure.
8. Graph the data.

Clearly Describe the Behavior

Once a behavior is defined precisely, it may be measured. All observable behaviors can be quantified by counting, timing, or some combination. The wording of the behavior definition should specify the observable characteristics so that two or more observers can agree on the occurrence or nonoccurrence of the behavior. Behavior is defined independently of the specific person; that is, what constitutes an instance of the behavior for one individual must constitute an instance for any other individual.

Definitional terms are functional guides for measurement only when they specify both the observable action, activity, or movement constituting the behavior and the behavior's onset or beginning and its offset or ending. The behavior identified for change must be discrete enough that it is repeatable, but not so discrete as to obviate measurement. For instance, "toilet trained" is too "large." It is better stated as specific portions of the chain of behaviors involved (e.g., approaches toilet, removes pants, urinates in toilet, or wets pants). Conversely, targeting "says

words" for a highly verbal student will make measurement quite difficult. You may limit an expressive target to specific response classes, such as pronouns or the use of appropriate greetings, depending upon the person's expressive skills and deficiencies.

Specify the Conditions for Observation

Each measurement must be carried out in the same way. Measurements taken under changing conditions cannot be compared meaningfully. Conditions that affect behavior include not only environmental conditions (such as physical setting, people present, assessor's familiarity with measurement procedure, materials, comments and assistance provided) but also less obvious physiological conditions, such as the presence of a fever or changes in medications (Breuning & Davidson, 1981; Singh & Aman, 1981). Once the targeted behavior is defined, the teacher can identify when and where measurement will be conducted (step 5 in Figure 4.1) and select an appropriate procedure (step 6). Behaviors should be assessed before they are taught or treated to identify realistic performance criteria and to evaluate the effects of intervention. Pretreatment assessment results are *baseline performance* (step 9 in Figure 4.1) and will be addressed in detail later. Once baseline assessment is finished and graphed, and objectives with behavior, conditions, and performance criteria are completely specified, intervention may begin. The assessment procedure used during baseline will be repeated regularly throughout intervention to determine the effect of the treatment. These assessments often are called *probes*. They are performed in the same manner as baseline assessment, so the results can be compared. Generally the time and place selected for assessment should be natural to the behavior. Since there are somewhat different considerations for measuring *skills* rather than *social behaviors* or *inappropriate behaviors,* we will cover these behavior classes separately.

Skill Performance

Besides identifying the most natural times and places to assess skills, a variety of additional measurement conditions must be addressed:

1. What verbal or instructional cues, *if any,* will be provided?
2. What materials will be provided?
3. How will the materials be arranged?
4. What will happen when the student makes an error, stops performing, or behaves inappropriately?
5. What will happen once the student completes the task or indicates that he or she has finished?

---

[2]For further expansion of behavior measurement techniques, see Hall, Hawkins, and Axelrod (1975), Hersen and Barlow (1976), Kazdin (1980), Sulzer-Azaroff and Mayer (1977).

The behavior of the teacher during assessment differs in a few important ways from that during instruction. Generally speaking, the teacher does not provide assistance or performance feedback during assessment.

During skill testing, the teacher must identify the materials and instructional cues, if any, that will be provided, as well as the setting for assessment. These conditions are the same as those described in the instructional objective. For example, in a study on bed-making skills (Snell, 1982), when subjects were tested on making a partially unmade bed, each student was asked to "Make the bed." The experimenter simultaneously pointed toward a bed that had its top sheet, blanket, and spread pulled down at least halfway and wrinkled. Assessment during baseline and intervention always took place in the school training area; but once the student met criteria, the setting was changed to include the student's own bed, so that skill generalization could be checked. The experimenter also specified a procedure for errors and nonperformance. A single opportunity task analytic method of observation (discussed in the next section) was used to measure performance. When the student stopped performing for 10 consecutive seconds, inappropriately undid a successfully completed step, excessively repeated a step, or destroyed materials (ripped a sheet), testing was stopped and all remaining steps scored as errors. If the student indicated he was finished before the bed was actually made, nothing was said and the test ended 10 seconds after the student had stopped performing. Specifying test conditions precisely allows all five questions to be answered and thus enables more accurate skill measurement.

Consider the assessment of expressive use of manual signs. A teacher may want to teach and test different sets of signs in the actual locations where the student will use them. Therefore, a set of food and eating signs (e.g., drink, eat, milk, spoon, sandwich) might be assessed in the cafeteria during lunch. Each item or activity could be shown in random order and the student asked once "Show me the sign for this." The student might be given 5 seconds to initiate the response, with a lack of performance beyond 5 seconds scored as an error. The first response made within the 5-second period would be scored as either correct or incorrect. Each response must be defined precisely, so that poor quality responses can be scored as errors. At intermittent intervals, when the student is attending, the teacher may praise the general effort, although no comment would be provided for a specific sign response. No assistance such as showing the student part or all of the motion, manually assisting the student, or giving verbal instructions is provided.

In both the bed-making and the signing tests, the teacher addressed each of the five test condition questions before the first use of the assessment. In this way the test could be repeated with comparable results.

Inappropriate Behavior

Some low-frequency behaviors occur only during specific activities (for example, sloppy eating during snack at a classroom table and during lunch time in the cafeteria). Observation and modification strategies can be implemented only when and where the behavior occurs. If observation is easier at one time than another, a teacher may decide to limit baseline and intervention to that setting.

For behaviors occurring frequently throughout the day, a teacher should select times and places for observation which meet several requirements:

1. When and where the behavior or its absence is most troublesome;
2. When and where the teacher or aide is able to observe and record the behavior;
3. When and where it will be possible to intervene.

The first consideration may be best decided after observing the behavior over several periods during the whole day and determining whether the performance varies. Whenever possible, observations should be made at various times during the day so the data more accurately reflect the behavior. These initial observations are part of the ABC analysis.

Next, the teacher must answer two related questions: How frequently should data be collected and how long should each observation period last? As a general guideline, behaviors should be observed as often as possible—daily or every other day. The length of each observation must be determined by the behavior's frequency and topography. To obtain an adequate representation of low-frequency behaviors, longer observation periods are required (e.g., 1 hour), while shorter periods (10 to 15 minutes) are sufficient for higher frequency behaviors.

There must be enough baseline observations to give an accurate picture of the behavior, whether it is appropriate or inappropriate. For example, since a child's aggressiveness may fluctuate after weekends or vacations, the baseline measurement should extend beyond these atypical days. Cooper (1974) suggests having at least five measurement sessions before beginning intervention. If the data collected are relatively stable and individual scores are not discrepant, baseline measurement may stop and intervention procedures begin. Note that the data may either descend or ascend and be considered stable. Stability is achieved when the scores are predictable. When there is an unstable baseline trend in the same direction as the aim of the intervention (perhaps a disruptive behavior begins to decrease), it is best to wait to intervene until stability is achieved (Hall, 1971). Without relative baseline stability, it is difficult to evaluate the actual effect of the intervention. Hall (1971) described two variations in this general rule. Intervention may be initiated if the baseline of a desirable behavior is descending or if the baseline of an undesirable behavior is ascending. If the target behavior is dangerously self-destructive or destructive to others, the period of baseline observation must be shortened considerably, sometimes by taking a series of measurements over a single morning and afternoon.

Identify the Behavioral Characteristics and the Measurement Procedure

If a teacher is able to identify the relevant aspects of the target behavior, selecting the method of observation is simplified. The seven observation procedures summarized in Table 4.2 are detailed below.

Measurement of Lasting Products

Frequently with academic, domestic, and vocational skills, student performance results in a product (correctly set table place, objects matched to pictures, number of plastic dinnerware and napkin combinations properly packaged, etc.). This tangible evidence may be measured more conveniently after the student has completed the task—an advantage over behavior observation techniques. Also teachers may examine products for error patterns and thus select remedial teaching procedures. However, the specific product or bit of tangible evidence still must be identified clearly. For example, when teaching ironing, a piece-rate measurement—number of articles correctly ironed per unit of time—could be the measurement procedure. Daily piece-rate data would be essential to evaluate the instructional program for someone who has learned to iron, but is so meticulously slow that the skill is not functional.

Measurement of Observed Behavior

Unfortunately, many behaviors do not result in tangible products and, therefore, are most difficult to measure. Transitory behavior must be measured as it occurs; these behaviors may be appropriate and targeted for instruction (staying on-task, street-crossing, requesting needed materials, etc.), or they may be inappropriate or aberrant behavior to be reduced and replaced (e.g., hitting, stereotypic movements, masturbation in public). The method of measurement selected will vary depending upon (a) the duration of the behavior, (b) its visibility, (c) the number of other behaviors being recorded simultaneously, (d) the level of measurement precision required, and (e) the time and attention available for measurement (Hall, Hawkins, & Axelrod, 1975).

Frequency or Event Recording

Frequency measures have wide use in the classroom with both appropriate and inappropriate behavior. For a specified, constant period of time, the observer counts the number of times a particular behavior occurs. Behaviors measured this way must be relatively uniform in length, readily divided into discrete units with a beginning and end, and easily visible. These behaviors may be inappropriate and too frequent: talks during class discussion; pinches, hits, kicks, swears; makes errors in labeling tasks; gives the wrong value for a coin; requests the wrong materials when asked "what do you need?" Some behaviors may be appropriate but too infrequent and in need of acceleration: hand raising prior to speaking, toy sharing, quantities correctly counted, responses to "come here" commands, correct motor imitations, coat hanging, clearing dishes from cafeteria tables. Since frequency provides a direct measure of the amount of behavior occurring, it is sensitive to changes produced by intervention.

When a behavior occurs at a very high rate or is ongoing and lasts for an extended time, frequency recording is not generally used. The first case increases the probability of error due to difficulties in counting. However, if you substitute hand-held counters or wrist-worn golf counters (Lindsley, 1968) for the typical paper-and-pencil tally, you can count these rapidly occurring behaviors more accurately. For recording the frequency of several behaviors, multiple channel manual counters are useful (Cooper, 1974). With behaviors emitted at a high rate (such as sorting parts or self-stimulatory behaviors like rocking or hand waving), an easier recording procedure is to total duration or sample rate across time. (These procedures—duration and interval recordings—are discussed later.)

When behaviors of long duration (e.g., out of seat for entire class periods) are measured with a frequency count, the result is deceiving. These data, reported as frequency or as rate (number of behaviors per minute), will be so small that changes will not be detected. In these cases, duration or interval records are more descriptive than rate or frequency.

If the opportunity for the behavior occurs only a fixed number of times per observation (the opportunity to brush your teeth is made available only two times per day at school; the total number of correct

Table 4.2 Classroom Evaluation Measurement Procedures

Procedures for the Measurement of Behavior	Advantages	Disadvantages	Examples of Behaviors Measured
Direct measurement of lasting products—A frequency record from appropriate or inappropriate behavior	1. Measurement is taken after behavior has occurred 2. Specification of a tangible behavior is easier	1. Behavior must have a tangible result 2. Inaccurate measurement may occur for individual counts when others are producing similar products during period before measurement	*Appropriate*—Number newsletters folded and stapled, places set at the dinner table *Inappropriate*—Number of buttons ripped from clothing, wet diapers
Observational recording 1. *Frequency or event*—a running tally of a given target behavior	1. Useful with a wide variety of discrete classroom behaviors 2. Often part of the regular classroom routine 3. Often only paper and pencil are needed 4. May be converted to rate	1. Necessitates continuous attention during observation period 2. Yields less accurate results with very high rate behaviors and/or behaviors taking varying amounts of time 3. Inappropriate for long-duration behaviors	*Appropriate*—Accurate ball throws, hand raising, spontaneous requests for needed materials, all types of *correct* responses *Inappropriate*—talk-outs, hits, obscene gestures, all types of *incorrect* responses
2. *Task analytic*—A frequency record of correct and incorrect responses made for each step in a sequence of behaviors comprising a task	1. Useful for most skills in domestic, vocational, leisure/recreational, and community domains 2. May be used to guide instruction 3. Enables the measurement of each behavior that comprises a skill 4. Meaningfully reported as percentage *or* number of steps	1. Requires a good task analysis of skill 2. Not suitable for measuring inappropriate behaviors	*Appropriate*—Bedmaking, playing a record, hair combing, mopping floors, assembly tasks *Inappropriate*—Not suitable
3. *Duration*—The total amount of time a targeted behavior was engaged in	1. Yields precise record of a behavior's length of occurrence 2. May be used to record total duration of each incident of behavior as well as response latency	1. Necessitates continuous attention during observation period 2. For best accuracy requires a stop watch 3. Inappropriate for high-rate behaviors of short duration	*Appropriate*—Attending, completion of tasks (eating, dressing, cleaning), work production, physical fitness activities *Inappropriate*—Temper tantrums, stereotypic behavior

TABLE 4.2 (CONTINUED)

Procedures for the Measurement of Behavior	Advantages	Disadvantages	Examples of Behaviors Measured
4. *Interval*—The occurrence or non-occurrence of a target behavior during a defined amount of time	1. Requires less effort than continuous event or duration procedures 2. Yields sufficiently precise duration and frequency data 3. Does not require definition of a precise unit of behavior 4. Applicable to a wide variety of behaviors	1. Difficult to use with less visible behaviors 2. Low-frequency behavior 3. Size of interval must be appropriate to behavior frequency. Accuracy is facilitated by timers or a tape-recorded counting of intervals	Any of those listed for frequency or duration
a. *Whole interval*—continuous occurrence throughout an interval	Useful when it is important to know that the behavior is not interrupted.	Underestimates magnitude of target behavior	More useful with appropriate behaviors such as toy sharing or attending
b. *Partial interval*—occurrence at any time in an interval	Useful for behaviors that may occur in fleeting moments.	Overestimates magnitude of target behavior	
5. *Momentary time sampling*—occurrence or nonoccurrence of a target behavior during a randomly timed check	Useful for behaviors that tend to persist for a while	Must be frequent, random, and relatively short intervals	

sight words possible in a list of 25 words is 25), then the frequency recording may be expressed as the percentage of behaviors observed out of the total possible or as rate (number of behaviors per minute, hour, etc.). When the number of behaviors emitted is the variable, the observer cannot predict the frequency ceiling or the maximum behaviors possible per unit of time. These data are reported either by a *simple frequency*—the total number of behaviors observed each day or in a 20-minute teaching session—or by *rate*—number of behaviors per minute or hour—but *not* by percentage.

Frequency measures must be taken for equal units of time which are long enough to obtain a representative behavior sample. If the observation time cannot be uniform, then frequency counts cannot be used as they would not be comparable (the number of opportunities to perform in a 1-minute period cannot be equated with a 30-minute period). In these cases, frequency must be converted into rate per standard unit of time. For example, if a child vocalizes 15 times during a 10-minute observation and 60 times during a 30-minute observation, the vocalization rate per minute is calculated by simple division: number of behaviors observed divided by number of minutes observed. The resultant rates are 1.5 and 2 vocalizations per minute.[3] However, with the severely handicapped, attention span and fatigue may make this "equation" practice unwise when the observation

[3]See White and Haring (1976) and Haring, Liberty, and White (1980) for in-depth discussions of the use of rate recording and charting procedures with handicapped students.

periods are widely discrepant (White & Haring, 1976). Therefore, observation periods should be equal whenever possible.

Task Analytic Assessment

Task analytic assessment is a variation of a frequency measure in that a sequence of behaviors is measured at one time. It is probably the most valuable method for assessing skill performance informally. Unlike a frequency method, it is not useful for assessing inappropriate behavior. It is appropriate for most of the skills isolated in Figures 4.2 and 4.3 as being relevant for Rose Mary. The first, and perhaps most difficult, step is to analyze the sequence of behaviors involved in completing a given task. To assess with a task analysis, the task steps are entered on a data sheet (as shown in Table 4.2) and used to guide the observation. The student is asked to perform the task and judgments are made about his or her performance. A symbol for correct or incorrect performance is entered on the data sheet beside each step. Before assessment, the teacher selects one of three task analytic procedures: (a) single opportunity, (b) multiple opportunity, or (c) a variation.

The *single opportunity method* is carried out as follows.

1. Materials are readied as described on the data sheet.
2. The instructional cue is given when the student is attending (e.g., "Strip the whole bed").
3. The student's responses to each step in the task analysis are recorded as correct or incorrect (performed incorrectly or not performed at all). One or more of these rules are used to handle errors, periods of no response, and inappropriate behavior.
   a. Testing is stopped after the first error, and all remaining steps are scored as errors.
   b. Testing is stopped after two or more consecutive errors, and all remaining steps are scored as errors.
   c. After a specified period of no response (e.g., 6 seconds), testing is stopped and all remaining steps are scored as errors.
   d. After a specified period of inappropriate behavior (e.g., 10 seconds) or after a single inappropriate response (e.g., ripping a sheet), testing is stopped and all remaining steps are scored as errors.
   e. All steps performed are scored as correct (if they correspond to the task description) regardless of the order in which they are carried out. However items (c) and (d) are specified so that testing is stopped following a period of no

response or inappropriate behavior. In addition a maximum length of time might be specified for testing.

The single opportunity method can be illustrated using the task of stripping a dirty bed and the data-recording sheet shown in Figure 4.5.

The teacher first readied the bed by pulling down the spread, blanket, and sheet as if the bed had been slept in; the bed was pushed into the wall. Bert was then asked to stand by the bed and, once he was attending, was told "Strip the whole bed," as the teacher pointed toward the bed and the clothes hamper nearby. On the first assessment day (March 4) Bert hesitated after the request, but not for more than the 6-second limit, approached the bed, and pulled the bed roughly 12 inches from the wall. The teacher scored a plus for the first step. Then, again in less than 6 seconds, Bert moved toward the pillow and took off the pillowcase, thus receiving a plus score on step 2. However, Bert tried to put the pillowcase back onto the pillow. After 10 seconds of this inappropriate behavior, the teacher stopped him, thanked him for his effort, and scored the remaining steps as errors. On the second day Bert was stopped after step 1 because he performed the steps out of order—he tried to remove the spread before taking off the pillowcase. On days 3 and 4 Bert hesitated for longer than 6 seconds after placing the pillowcase into the clothes hamper. His four days of test performance resulted in the percentage scores shown in Figure 4.5.

The single opportunity method generally is completed quickly and provides a conservative estimate of the student's skills. Learning is less likely to occur during testing, which is regarded as an advantage over other methods for experimental conditions. One disadvantage is that you cannot observe the steps occurring late in a task analysis unless the preceding steps are performed. Thus probes (testing done once intervention has started) will not initially reflect learning on later steps because testing always ends before the student reaches the learned steps. If the teacher is using a backward chaining progression (i.e., last step following second-to-last step and so on), then the single opportunity probe will not reflect any progress until training advances to the first step in the chain. In these cases, the multiple opportunity probe or some variation would produce more information.

The *multiple opportunity method,* while started in the same way as the single opportunity method, differs in a number of ways.

1. Materials are readied as described on the data sheet.
2. The instructional cue is given when the student is attending.

3. The student's responses to each step in the task analysis are recorded as correct or incorrect.
4. Whenever an error occurs or after a specified period of no response or inappropriate behavior, the step is then completed by the assessor, using as little effort as is needed. The student is positioned for the next step.
5. This procedure is repeated after each incorrectly performed step. The examiner may or may not wish to repeat the instructional cue with each opportunity, but should be consistent in this practice.

The multiple opportunity method may be used in a variety of ways. First, it may be used for all assessments. However, since its biggest disadvantage is being time-consuming, you can also use this method only part of the time (i.e., on alternate days) to have an idea of progress on steps later in the chain. In this case, the results of the multiple opportunity assessment would be graphed separately from those of the single opportunity.

To understand the process of multiple opportunity assessment better, examine Table 4.3. This task analysis was used by Tucker and Berry (1980) to both assess and teach six students to put on their hearing aids. Because different types of aids and harnesses were used, the steps relevant to a given student are indicated by numbers horizontally aligned with the master list of steps. Consider Susan and the 13 steps required to put on her aid. Tucker and Berry (1980) used single opportunity method to assess all six students. Using Susan as an example, they began by placing hearing aid equipment in front of Susan, who was then told: "Susan, please put on your hearing aid." Tucker and Berry scored as correct any steps

TABLE 4.3 Hearing Aid Program Task Analysis

Component	Step	Susan	Tom	Matthew	Billy	Randy	Steve
Universal	1. Open container	1	1	1	1	1	1
	2. Remove harness (or other)	2	2	2	2	2	2
Commercial	3. Harness over head	3		3			
Harness	4. Fasten side strap 1	4		4			
	5. Fasten side strap 2	5		5			
Modified	6. Arm 1 through strap 1		3		3		3
Harness	7. Arm 2 through strap 2		4		*		4
	8. Harness over head		5		4		5
	9. Fasten harness		6		5		6
T-shirt	10. Pull T-shirt over head					3	
	11. Arm 1 through sleeve 1					4	
	12. Arm 2 through sleeve 2					5	
	13. Pull hem down to waist					6	
Vest	14. Wrist 1 through hole 1						
	15. Vest to shoulder						
	16. Wrist 2 through hole 2						
	17. Vest to shoulder						
	18. Fasten vest						
Universal	19. Unsnap pocket	6	7	6	6	7	7
	20. Remove aid from container	7	8	7	7	8	8
	21. Insert aid into pocket	8	9	8	8	9	9
	22. Snap pocket	9	10	9	9	10	10
Body-type	23. Pick up earmold	10	11		10		11
Air Aid	24. Insert earmold into ear	11	12		11		12
Body-type	25. Pick up headband			10		11	
Bone Aid	26. Place headband on head			11		12	
Ear Level	27. Pick up aid & earmold						
Aid	28. Place aid behind & over ear						
	29. Insert earmold into ear						
Universal	30. Turn on aid	12	13	12	12	13	13
	31. Set gain control	13	14	13	13	14	14

*Billy's harness contained only 1 strap to accommodate an orthopedically impaired arm.
SOURCE: "Teaching Severely Multihandicapped Students to Put on Their Own Hearing Aids" by D.J. Tucker and G.W. Berry. *Journal of Applied Behavior Analysis*, 1980, 13, 69. Copyright 1980 by the Society for the Experimental Analysis of Behavior, Inc. Reprinted with permission.

Teacher: Bill

Target Behavior: Putting on Hearing Aid

Student's Name: Susan

Instructional Cue: "Susan, please put on your hearing aid."

Method of Assessment: Multiple opportunity

Student Name and Date

	%/12																			
1. Open the box	−																			
2. Remove the harness	+																			
3. Put the harness over your head	+																			
4. Fasten the first side strap	−																			
5. Fasten the second side strap	+																			
6. Unsnap the pocket	−																			
7. Take the aid from the box	+																			
8. Put the aid into the pocket	+																			
9. Snap the pocket	+																			
10. Pick up the ear mold	+																			

Materials: Aid in container, harness

Response Latency: 5 seconds

Recording Key: + correct   − incorrect

Criterion: 100% correct performance over two consecutive sessions

FIGURE 4.7
Multiple Opportunity Assessment

Student Name and Date:

11. Put the ear mold into your ear	−																			
12. Turn on the aid	−																			
13. Set the control	−																			
	7/13																			
Percent Correct	54%																			

Materials: Aid in container, harness

Response Latency: 5 seconds

Recording Key: + Correct   − incorrect

Criterion: 100% correct performance over two consecutive sessions

FIGURE 4.7 (CONTINUED)

99

performed according to the criteria for the 13 steps listed for Susan, regardless of the sequence in which she performed them. Since they taught all steps simultaneously, beginning with the first step, this assessment was time-efficient and likely to reveal progress once training was begun.

The following description and Figure 4.7 show how a *multiple opportunity method* would work with Susan.

The teacher placed the box of hearing aid equipment in front of Susan, saying "Susan, please put on your hearing aid." After 3 seconds of no response the teacher opened the container (step 1); Susan removed the harness and lifted it over her head (steps 2, 3). The teacher scored a minus for step 1 and pluses for steps 2 and 3. Three seconds passed with no response by Susan, so the teacher fastened side strap #1 and recorded a minus by step 4, while counting 3 seconds to himself. Susan fastened strap 2 within the 3-second period and then unfastened strap 1 (a step already scored as an error). Step 5 was scored correct, and the teacher refastened the first strap as it should have been. Next he waited for step 6, which Susan did not perform. Therefore, he unsnapped the pocket (step 6) and recorded an error. Susan then performed steps 7, 8, and 9 correctly—removed the hearing aid from the container, inserted it into the pocket, and snapped the pocket closed. Pluses were recorded by steps 7 through 9, and the teacher waited 3 additional seconds for Susan to perform the 10th step. She picked up the ear mold (step 10 was scored correct), but inserted it only partially into her ear (step 11 was scored as an error). The teacher reinserted the ear mold and waited for step 12. Since Susan did not perform, the teacher turned on the aid, recorded a minus by step 12, waited 3 seconds, and then set the volume control. A minus was recorded for step 13. Susan was thanked for her work and the assessment was complete.

A third possibility is to use a variation of *multiple opportunity assessment*. With this alternative, the student would initially be given the instructional request and expected to perform the first step in the chain. In other words, the single opportunity method is given, and results are recorded. If performance stops *before* reaching the step on which there had been clear progress during training sessions, then the student is readied for that particular step (all prior steps are completed or omitted by the assessor, depending on the task) and a second opportunity is given at the critical step. This method allows the examiner to observe whether the student can perform one or more steps under test conditions (in an otherwise unmastered series) on which progress has been observed during training.

As we stated earlier, no feedback is provided to the student on performance of the targeted skill in order to separate the process of testing and teaching. In the multiple opportunity method, the student is *not physically assisted* through incorrectly performed steps, but rather the step *is performed by the examiner for the student,* again to avoid teaching during testing.

To select the most suitable method of task analytic assessment, you should consider the particular task, the testing time possible, and the amount and type of assessment information needed to evaluate performance before and during instruction as well as after instruction has ended and skill maintenance or generalization needs to be assessed.

Duration Recording

Duration may be used to assess the length of time a particular behavior is performed. Response latency—the time taken for an individual to begin a response once the controlling stimuli are presented—is also measured by duration. Duration measures have been used to measure length of time spent engaged in classroom assignments (Konarski, Johnson, Crowell, & Whitman, 1980), cooperative play (Redd, 1969), thumb-sucking (Skiba, Pettigrew, & Alden, 1971), and social responses (Whitman, Mercurio, & Caponigri, 1970).

Duration is recorded by accumulating the number of seconds or minutes of behavior observed. For example, whenever a child initiates off-task behavior during instruction (that is, looking away from teacher, teaching materials, or seatwork; making inappropriate verbalizations unrelated to the task), a teacher could start an unobtrusively held stopwatch. As soon as the child is on-task, the watch would be stopped but *not* returned to zero. Each time the child is off-task, the stopwatch would again be started and stopped. At the end of the session, the total time accumulated on the stopwatch would be the total duration of off-task behavior during a single observation. Though duration recording may sound simple, accuracy rests upon precise delineation of what constitutes the behavior's onset and termination.

Duration may be reported in terms of the total number of minutes or the percentage of time a behavior is engaged in during each observation. Percentage reporting is especially useful if the observation sessions vary in length, since the resulting percentages are roughly comparable. The percentage of time a behavior occurs during a given observation is calculated by a simple percentage formula,

$$\frac{A}{B} \times 100 = X.$$

If A equals the total amount of time a behavior occurs and B equals the total length of observation, then X is the percentage of time the behavior occurred during observation.

Duration records also may be kept when a teacher is interested in the amount of time a student takes to begin or to complete a specific task for which no minimum or maximum time has been set. For example, meal eating may range from 5 minutes to more than an hour, yet there still may be no time limitation set. A slow-eating child's baseline duration over 5 lunches, measured in minutes, could consist of 75 minutes, 50 minutes, 67 minutes, 43 minutes, and 70 minutes. Behaviors for which no time criteria are set are reported in time units (seconds, minutes, etc.), since percentages are meaningless without a maximum or minimum criterion.

Duration recording, like event recording, requires the observer's complete attention during each observation. Duration records are most appropriate for behaviors which either have a high or even rate or which simply may be variable in length from onset to end, making frequency less meaningful. Time out of seat, for example, may vary in length from a few seconds to long periods. Although stopwatches facilitate more accurate duration measurements, wall clocks or wristwatches with second hands may be used, as long as the observer can write down the duration of each occurrence of the behavior. These separate occurrences are later totaled to yield a single duration for each unit of observation. Since interval measures are more adaptable to a variety of behaviors and are also time-based, they are often used in place of duration measures.

Interval Recording

There are two different types of interval recording: partial and whole interval. In both procedures, the observer divides the observation unit (2 minutes, 10 minutes, etc.) into equal periods (5 seconds, 10 seconds, etc.) and notes for each smaller period whether or not the behavior(s) under observation occurred. With *whole interval* recording, an interval is checked only when the target behavior occurs continuously throughout the entire interval. With *partial interval* recording, an entire interval is checked even if the behavior occurs for only part of the interval; in addition, regardless of the number of times a target behavior occurs during any single interval, only one tally is recorded for that unit (see Figure 4.8). Interval recording gives both a measure of the behavior's duration and its frequency. More than one behavior may be observed simultaneously. As with frequency and duration recording, the teacher's total attention must be directed toward the behavior during the entire observation period. In addition, the observer must have some method of timing each interval to move from one interval to the next. Generally a watch or clock with a second hand is used to time the intervals. If available, a portable tape recorder with prerecorded interval counts and an ear plug is less obtrusive, though a timer with a light or sound flashing at regular intervals may also be used. For longer

intervals (3 to 5 minutes), inexpensive egg timers, kitchen timers (with cotton taped around the bell to muffle the sound), and Memo-Timers (Foxx & Martin, 1971) have been used effectively. Interval recording may be applied to many behaviors—discrete, continuous, or sporadic—as long as the behavior can be classified as observed or not observed during any interval.

How do you decide whether to use whole or partial interval recording? At times, with appropriate behavior in particular, it is important that the behavior is continuous, not interrupted. For example, either attending or appropriate use of toys could not be meaningfully measured with a 10-second partial interval, since the data would not reflect repeated interruptions during intervals. A whole interval method (or a duration procedure) would be more suitable to measure these two behaviors. As noted in Table 4.2, the whole interval method tends to deflate or underestimate the amount of the target behavior, since occurrence of the behavior during only part of an interval is regarded as nonoccurrence.

Brief or fleeting behaviors are more suitably measured by a partial interval procedure. Partial interval measurement tends to overestimate or inflate the magnitude of the observed behavior since any instance of the behavior results in an entire interval being scored.

The length of the interval depends on both the behavior being observed (its average length and frequency) and the observer's ability to record and attend. The more frequent the behavior, the smaller the interval for observation should be, so the observation may be an accurate measure of behavior frequency. For example, if "talking out" were measured in 30-minute intervals, a tally in one interval would not begin to reflect the behavior's density (i.e., did 35 talk-outs occur or 3?). However, with infrequently occurring behavior, longer intervals are practical for classroom use but remain inadequate for experimental purposes. Also, the more obvious the behavior, the easier it is to record; behaviors that can be heard and seen (e.g., talking out versus attending to work) are more easily detectable. The reliability of interval measurement in the classroom increases when the teacher has good behavior management, observes during independent work periods or observes more obvious behaviors, uses an unobtrusive interval timer, and selects smaller intervals (5 to 15 seconds).

Repp, Roberts, Slack, Repp, and Berkler (1976) compared the accuracy of observations taken by interval procedures with frequency measures of the same behavior for the same time period. Low and medium rates of responding were accurately measured with 10-second intervals, but high rate response patterns (either continuously high rate or with bursts of high rates) were grossly underestimated by interval measurements. They recommend using intervals less than 10 seconds or frequency procedures to measure high rate behaviors.

Momentary Time Sampling

Another type of interval measurement, momentary time sampling, has many of the advantages of time interval recording plus additional convenience, with little or no reduction in accuracy (Hall et al., 1975). As in interval recording, the observer divides the observation unit into intervals, but the behavior is observed and recorded only at the end of each interval rather than continuously.

Time samples need not be taken at regular intervals. Hall et al. (1975) suggest that, after determining the number of samples to take during each observation session, a teacher may set a timer randomly, record the student's behavior immediately upon hearing the timer, reset the timer, and repeat for the predetermined number of times.

In an alternate type of time sampling, reported by Quilitch and Risley (1973), a teacher could assess participation of an entire class in an activity. Placheck (Planned Activity Check) requires the teacher to carry out a series of three steps.

1. Define the planned activity or behaviors (on-task during math period, engaged in aggressive behavior, etc.) the teacher wants to measure in a group;
2. At given intervals (e.g., 5 minutes, 10 minutes), count and record how many students are engaged in the activity.
3. Immediately count and record the total number of students present in the area of the activity.

The total number engaged in the planned activity is divided by the total number present and multiplied by 100, which yields the percentage of the group engaging in the defined behavior during the sampled interval. When used with longer activities, it is best to sample once in the middle or at equally spaced points (beginning, middle, and end of activity). If attending or on-task behavior is observed, this procedure will provide a rough indication of a group's length of interest in a particular activity.

For classroom data collection, momentary time sampling is generally efficient, though not so accurate as continuous interval observation or frequency observations. Because it does not require continuous observation, time sampling is more easily used by teachers than interval or duration recording. One difficulty arises when using time sampling to measure low-frequency or short-duration behavior—the results may indicate that the behavior never occurred because the samples were too infrequent. With both low-frequency and short-duration behavior, the intervals must guarantee enough observation samples to obtain an adequate measure of the behavior.

Continuous and time-sampling interval records have a number of advantages in common. Besides being appropriate to observe a wide variety of behaviors in individuals, they may be used to observe one or multiple behaviors across a group of people. This is done very effectively by sequentially rotating the brief interval observation across each member of the group until all have been observed, and repeating this sequence until the observation period is over (Thomson, Holmberg, & Baer, 1974). The simple recording form illustrated in Figure 4.8 may be used with partial or whole interval, though the example illustrates partial interval procedures. This form may also be adapted to fit differing numbers of individuals, intervals, and behaviors. For example, in Figure 4.8, when recording data for a group of students, the observer records from the top to the bottom of the page, observing each subject for the first interval, then uses the second column of intervals, and so on. The appropriate symbol is recorded in each interval depending upon whether the behavior occurred (a) anytime during the interval (for partial interval recording), (b) during the entire interval (for whole interval recording), or (c) during the end of the interval (for momentary time sampling).

An additional advantage of interval methods is the convenient conversion of the data into percentages for graphing. Interval percentages are calculated simply by dividing the total number of intervals observed and multiplying by 100. When data are reported as "the percentage of intervals an individual engaged in a particular behavior," they are easier to understand.

Devise Data Recording Form

Data-recording forms must be constructed to conform to the constraints set by:

1. The measurement procedure selected—e.g., permanent products, interval, frequency;
2. The number of individuals observed—Sufficient space should be allowed so data for each individual are clearly separated and identifiable;
3. The number of behaviors observed—Intervals or observation periods (as with frequency and duration) need to be subdivided and coded so tallies or times recorded are identified with the behavior they measure;
4. The length of each observation period—When frequency measures are used, enough space must be allowed for recording the more frequent behavior.

Target Behavior:

Student engages in self-abusive behavior consisting of biting the thumb joint of either hand, hitting her head with either or both fists, and slapping one or both thighs with her opened hand.

Date	Times		10-Second Intervals										Total Intervals	Percentage Intervals
	Start	End	1	2	3	4	5	6	7	8	9	10		
2/20	10:00		−	−	+	+	+	−	−	+	+	+		
			+	+	−	−	−	−	−	−	−	+		
		10:05	+	+	+	−	−	+	+	+	−	−	15/30	50
2/21	9:30	9:31	−	+	+	+	−	+					4/6	67
2/21	10:45	10:46	+	+	+	−	−	−					3/6	50
2/21	12:05	12:06	−	−	−	−	+	+					2/6	33
2/21	1:15	1:16	+	+	−	−	+	+					4/6	67
2/21	2:30	2:31	−	−	−	+	+	+					3/6	50

+ = yes   − = no

FIGURE 4.8
Interval Data-Recording Form Using a Partial Interval Procedure
SOURCE: Credit for this figure must be given to Joan Miller.

A rough draft of the data collection form should be field tested, modified, and converted to a ditto master for easy reproduction since its repeated use will be necessary before, during, and following the intervention. Data forms may be constructed so several days' observation can be recorded on one form.

Every data form, regardless of the measurement procedure used, should include space for basic information: name of individual(s) observed; observer's name; date, time, and place of observation; length of each observation period; behavior(s) observed (with brief definition); data totals and/or percentages; and perhaps comments.

SELECT A DESIGN

Once the type of measurement system is selected, the design must be determined. Although there is similarity between the designs used by researchers and those recommended for use by teachers or clinicians, there are some critical differences.

Researchers must determine the functional relationship between specific behaviors and intervention strategies. This is important, for it is only through researchers' careful and meticulous efforts that prac-

titioners will have the basic knowledge necessary to select the most efficient and effective teaching strategies for their students. For researchers to provide this information with any certainty, they must control the environment carefully and systematically and consistently apply the procedure(s); insure the reliability of measurement; and determine the functional relationship of the treatment and behavior in question. This stringent attention to details is not the role of the practitioner.

Teachers must teach students new skills and help them remain proficient on skills already mastered. Their responsibility is to select techniques proven effective with the population, to schedule interventions in accord with their students' performance, and to evaluate the effectiveness of their teaching. They need not, however, employ methods as rigorously as the researcher. Several available "teaching" designs facilitate the evaluation of consistent instructional techniques. We will describe only those designs suitable for classroom use.[4]

---

[4]For a more thorough discussion of single subject designs, see Hersen and Barlow (1976), Kazdin (1980), Kratochwill (1978), Murphy and Bryan (1980), and Sulzer-Azaroff and Mayer (1977).

AB or Baseline-Intervention Design

In an AB design, intervention is initiated on one or more behaviors or in one or more students or places after baseline assessment. An AB design is *not* an experimental design, because baseline followed by intervention cannot yield experimental control. If, after baseline, the target behavior changes in the desired direction and criterion is met, you cannot be sure that the intervention procedure was the cause of the behavior change. Since experimental control is not obtained and the influence of a specific instructional tactic cannot be validated, this design is not fruitful for researchers unless a reversal or a direct replication is added. However, for teachers using procedures already shown to be effective, the baseline-intervention design can be functional. Student performance is monitored before teaching (baseline) and during different phases of teaching (acquisition, maintenance, and generalization), which generally is adequate to demonstrate whether a student has learned and retained a skill or an IEP objective. Thus, with the majority of students and objectives, most teachers will employ the simple baseline-intervention design.

Often the first intervention strategy selected does not change the target behavior in the desired direction or does not produce enough change. In this case, a second intervention strategy should be added to or substituted for the first. Teachers should predetermine criteria for changing from one condition to the next. When using either the AB or multiple baseline designs (described next), only 1 or 2 days is not long enough to determine the influence of an intervention. However, it is not advisable to leave a student in an intervention beyond what is efficient or effective. When modifying inappropriate behavior, this decision *probably* can be made after collecting data on the behavior for 5 to 7 days. When teaching a new skill, the "trial" period is *often longer*—2 to 3 weeks. Nevertheless, it is beneficial to have some idea of when an intervention shall be discontinued and another scheduled.

Regardless of the design employed, it is also helpful to have some preconception of the level of performance needed to determine mastery. This will help the teacher determine when to change conditions (either to schedule another intervention or to discontinue instruction). Many teachers believe that 3 consecutive days of 100% performance should be noted before a student moves to maintenance. This, however, may be too stringent for some learners on certain tasks, and teaching will not be efficient because the teacher is waiting too long for mastery before moving onto another skill. The teacher must determine when enough is enough.

Multiple Baseline

In some instances, a teacher may wish to demonstrate the impact of a particular treatment upon one or more behaviors or students or across a variety of settings. To do so, one of at least four single subject experimental designs might be selected. Any of these may be more easily applied in the classroom than other single subject designs. The first of these, a multiple baseline design, provides (*a*) data across several behaviors of the same individual; (*b*) data for the same individual across a variety of situations (e.g., classroom, school cafeteria, and the home); or (*c*) data from a number of students in the same situation exhibiting the same class of behavior. In each case, several baselines are developed. Using the multiple baseline across behaviors as an example, a behavior modification procedure is applied to one of the behaviors until it changes. Then the same intervention procedure is applied to a second behavior until the desired change is obtained, then to the third behavior, and so forth. If in each instance the target behavior alters when the treatment begins, a functional relationship between the experimental variable and the dependent behavior is demonstrated. Note that the baseline or assessment phases are initiated on the same day, but the intervention is scheduled at different times, staggered across several days or even weeks. Figure 4.9 illustrates a multiple baseline design implemented both across students and behaviors.

Multiple Probe Design

An alternate to multiple baseline design is the multiple probe (Horner & Baer, 1978). This design is quite similar to multiple baseline in that baseline is taken simultaneously on three behaviors (or on one behavior for three people) before intervention begins with the first behavior or person. An example of a multiple probe for bed-making skills is shown in Figure 4.10.

When the multiple probe design (in Figure 4.10) is contrasted with a multiple baseline design (in Figure 4.9), we see a number of differences. Fewer data points are required in a multiple probe; intermittent rather than continuous baseline measurement is used. In some cases, extended measurement of behavior without intervention leads to the development of reactions that make intervention less likely to succeed. For example, Horner and Keilitz (1975) used a multiple baseline design across subjects and reported that, before training, subject 4 (the last to receive tooth-brushing training after weeks of baseline assessment only) began behaving inappropriately, such as playing in the water and with the toothpaste. In

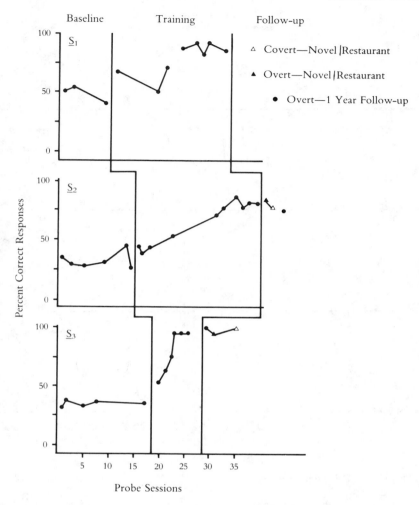

FIGURE 4.9
Multiple Baseline Across Subjects and Restaurant Skills
SOURCE: "Teaching the Handicapped to Eat in Public Places: Acquisition, Generalization, and Maintenance of Restaurant Skills," by R.A. van den Pol, B.A. Iwata, M.T. Ivancic, T.J. Page, N.A. Neef, and F.P. Whitley. *Journal of Applied Behavior Analysis,* 1981, *41, 66.* Copyright 1981 by the Society for the Experimental Analysis of Behavior, Inc. Reprinted with permission.

cases where a reactive baseline is likely, a multiple probe design is a better choice. Other reasons for selecting a multiple probe design include the time-consuming or impractical nature of taking continuous baseline and the certainty of stability in baseline performance—when teaching a series of skills and the later skills are successive approximations of the earlier skills (e.g., supported sitting with head steady, sits self-supported by arms, sits no support). A multiple probe technique features (a) "one initial probe of each step in the training sequence," (b) "an additional probe of every step after criterion is

reached on any training step," and (c) "a series of 'time' baseline sessions conducted *just* before the introduction of the independent variable" (intervention procedure) "to learn training step" (Horner & Baer, 1978, p. 189).

Changing Criterion Design

This design, originally described by Wolf, Risley, and Mees (1964) and discussed in some detail by Kazdin (1980) and Hartmann and Hall (1976), comprises three general phases: baseline, changing criterion,

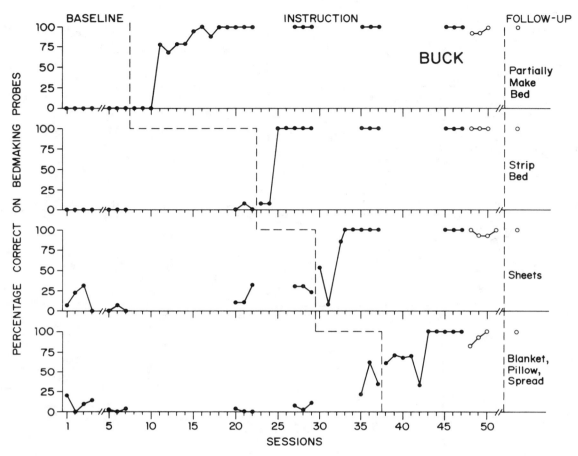

FIGURE 4.10
A Multiple Design Across Behaviors in which a Severely Handicapped Adolescent was Taught Bedmaking Skills

SOURCE: "Analysis of Time Delay Procedures for Teaching Daily Living Skills to Retarded Adolescents," by M.E. Snell. *Analysis and Intervention in Developmental Disabilities*, 1982, *2*, 150. Reprinted with permission.

and follow-up. After a traditional baseline or assessment period, an intervention (usually a contingency) is scheduled. In the beginning of the intervention, minimal behavior change is required. Gradually, however, closer and closer approximations of the target behavior or attainment of the criterion is demanded. This design is particularly appropriate when shaping procedures are used in intervention. For example, in Figure 4.11, a student's work production rate for assembling a drapery pulley is increased stepwise as the criterion for obtaining *self-administered* reinforcement gradually changed from .07 completed pulleys per minute to 2.2 pulleys per minute, a rate well beyond that required for sheltered employment (Bates, Renzaglia, & Clees, 1980).

Multielement or Alternating Treatments Design

In this design, the effects of two or more treatments on a single behavior are compared. Typically, following a baseline period two treatments are quickly alternated (e.g., one in the morning, one in the afternoon). However, conditions are balanced so neither treatment is always associated with a single time of day, location, or therapist (Barlow & Hayes, 1979). For example, Murphy, Doughty, and Nunes (1979) compared the effect of music given contingent on head control in four cerebral palsied adolescents (treatment 1) with music given noncontingently (regardless of the student's head control) (treatment 2).

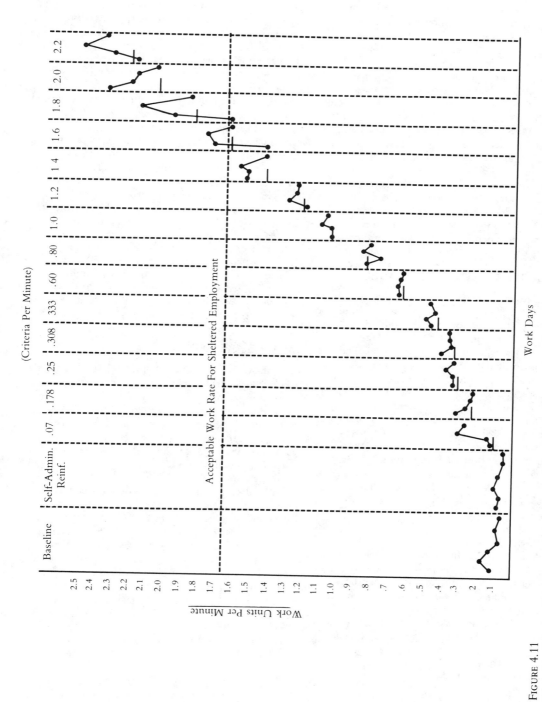

FIGURE 4.11

Changing Criterion Design Applied to a Severely Retarded Woman's Production Rate of Assembling Drapery Pulleys

SOURCE: "Improving the Work Performance of Severely/Profoundly Retarded Young Adults: The Use of a Changing Criterion Procedural Design," by P. Bates, A. Renzaglia, and T. Clees. *Education and Training of the Mentally Retarded*, 1980, *15*, 95–104. Reprinted with permission.

Contingent music led to increases in the time during which the students maintained head control. This design is particularly useful for assessing the effects of various treatments on social behavior (smiling, interaction), inappropriate behavior (mouthing, hitting), and skill maintenance (brushing teeth regularly).

Regardless of the design employed, there are several recommendations which we need to make. First, data collection procedures should be simple so that many data collectors—teachers, aides, volunteers, or students—can be used. Second, a period of baseline assessment must be scheduled before the intervention begins. In this way, the teacher can determine whether the student needs direct instruction on the target and begin to identify the best strategy for the first attempts. Third, an intervention procedure should be selected and consistently applied daily. Performance must be evaluated after some time to determine whether mastery will be achieved soon, or another kind of intervention will be required. After this, the student's behavior should be monitored periodically to check for retention of mastery.

CONDUCT BASELINE OR PROBES

Accurate data are collected when the observer is both unobtrusive and consistent. The observer should be familiar with the situation and the individual being observed or the individual's performance may change merely as a result of the observation. The ultimate purpose of data collection is to measure the influence of an intervention on a behavior. Occasionally, prebaseline observations are recommended. They serve two purposes: to "desensitize" the individual to the observation procedure and to familiarize the observer with the measurement methods.

The baseline period occurs before intervention (or whenever intervention is withdrawn). *Probes* are measurements or informal assessments carried out during the intervention period. However, the measurement procedures used for both baseline and probes must be precisely the same so that the results are comparable.

Sometimes the observer can both collect data and interact with the individual who is the target of the program. At other times, however, the observer should be a passive bystander. In both cases the place, time, teaching materials, and basic teaching methods must be held constant during any given phase of the program (that is, baseline, intervention, changes in the intervention, follow-up, maintenance, generalization).

Minimum Number of Data Days

The minimum time over which baseline data are collected is *generally* 3 days, unless the data collected are unstable. In other words, if a student's performance is fairly consistent over three observations, then the teacher can be confident that a representative and accurate picture of that student's performance has been obtained. During intervention, the target behavior is probed either until the specified criterion is attained (e.g., 3 consecutive days at 100% accuracy) *or* until it appears that the intervention is not affecting the behavior as planned and needs to be modified. This may mean that (*a*) the behavior shows little change in the desired direction, (*b*) it does not change at all from its baseline level, or (*c*) it changes in the opposite direction (for instance, a partially known skill is forgotten). We have already given general guidelines for how long to wait before changing the intervention. However, it is impossible to state sure and fast rules for making these decisions. The behavior selected (whether it is a skill or a maladaptive behavior), the intervention procedure and conditions, the teacher's instructional skills, and the student's learning history, current repertoire of skills, and current reinforcement conditions all influence treatment effects. Two prime considerations in the decision to change an intervention procedure are that instructional time not be wasted by waiting too long before modifying the program and that interventions be given a fair chance to have their effect by not changing the program too quickly.

Measuring Reliability

Reliability, a keystone of the behavior analytic approach, addresses whether or not the planned intervention strategy actually causes behavior change. Reliability includes both the consistency of a measurement instrument over time and the concept of observer agreement and observer accuracy. In research, regardless of the design, it is imperative that reliability measures be taken consistently across all conditions.

Probably the most obvious difference between research and teaching lies with the issue of reliability. Reliability is required for research projects. Typically, it necessitates extra personnel trained in data collection and analysis. Usually extra people are not available to clinicians or teachers, whose energies need to be directed entirely to remediation. Therefore, although desirable for all projects, the frequency of reliability checks by teachers certainly can be reduced; in many instances, they might even be eliminated. But, because it is still important for the teacher to be sure that student behavior is being measured accurately, some reliability checks are a good idea.

When reliability measures are taken, it is best if the "outside observer" not be an active participant in the project. One important reason for teachers to check reliability is to insure that the changes noted actually occurred. Often, when working daily with students, we become accustomed to unusual behaviors, and the data recorded may not reflect the actual occurrence and topography of the target behavior. In addition, others working with the students may also experience this change in expectations. Therefore, another teacher or aide (rather than the usual classroom personnel) might well be the best reliability checker.

One method for determining reliability of measurement is to obtain the percentage of agreement for two observers. In this case, a fraction is derived by using the smaller frequency of observations as the numerator and the larger score as the denominator. A percentage of agreement is then obtained by multiplying by 100. Basically, the formula used to arrive at this reliability statement is:

$$\frac{\text{smaller frequency}}{\text{larger frequency}} \times 100 =$$
$$\text{percentage of agreement.}$$

If duration data are taken, merely dividing the larger duration score into the smaller and multiplying by 100 suffices. Reliability scores obtained this way must, however, be viewed cautiously, for only total frequency scores of two observers are considered and not the specific instances of the occurrence of the target behavior.

When interval recordings are used, a different formula for reliability is required. If A equals the number of intervals of agreement, B equals the number of intervals of agreements and disagreements, then X is the percentage of agreement according to this formula:

$$\frac{A}{B} \times 100 = X$$

In this instance, the number of intervals in which both observers noted the occurrence of a behavior is the numerator and that number plus all those instances in which only one person recorded the behavior (disagreements) is the denominator. However, if the behavior occurred but neither observer recorded it, it is not indicated as an error.

At what point should data be considered unreliable? There is not a standard answer to this question. In part, the type of measurement and kind of target behavior must be considered. Data obtained from permanent products should be 100% accurate; when agreement for counting permanent products is less than 100%, the products simply may be recounted and the data made accurate. If data are gathered from observations, 100% agreement is rarely achieved.

Lower percentage-of-agreement scores indicate a need to increase the number of reliability checks. Usually 80% is considered the minimal reliability acceptable (Kazdin, 1980).

SELECT GRAPHIC DISPLAY AND GRAPH BEHAVIOR

Changes in a behavior's duration, frequency, and rate are much more visible when graphed. This is true for most people using the data: teachers, administrators, aides, parents, and even students. Basic behavior graphs are simple, equal interval graphs on which days of the week or sessions are plotted along the horizontal line (abscissa). The scores or behavior measurement totals are stated in percentage, duration, rate per minute, or frequency and are plotted in equal intervals along the vertical line (ordinate).

Both the horizontal and the vertical axes are labeled before the data are plotted. In Figure 4.10, the abscissa is simply labeled *sessions* to indicate probes generally taken daily on the four bed-making skills. The ordinate is labeled *percentage correct on bed-making probes,* with each of the graphs marked in percentage units from 0 to 100. Generally, the vertical axis must be divided into units that allow measurement of the entire range of behaviors possible, from zero to the highest possible score (e.g., 100%). This range extends from the behavior's baseline level or below to somewhat beyond the targeted level. Space should be allowed for extreme variability in the data. Depending on whether the behavior needs to be increased or decreased, the targeted level in the first case will be above and in the second case below the baseline level.

Data points for each phase of a program are connected by straight lines. However, plots are not connected across phase changes (baseline, intervention 1, intervention 2). Each phase is identified concisely across the top (e.g., baseline, intervention 1: modeling). Vertical lines separate the different treatment or program phases. If more than one behavior (or if the same behavior, in more than one individual) is being measured simultaneously in the same units, these may be plotted on a single graph. Different shaped data points or solid and broken lines indicate the various behaviors or individuals. When these graphing conventions are used, the graph will be interpreted more accurately by parents and often educators.

We can state some general rules of data interpretation for behavior graphed conventionally.[5]

---

[5]For more detail on this and related graphing procedures, consult Cooper (1974), Hall (1971), Parsonson and Baer (1978), and White and Haring (1976).

1. An upward slope indicates an increase or an acceleration in the behavior.
2. A downward slope indicates a decrease or a deceleration in the behavior.
3. A flat or horizontal line indicates no measurable change but a maintenance of the behavior.
4. The degree of the slope (upward or downward) indicates the speed with which the behavior is changing.

Another type of graph is the ratio chart or standardized semilogarithmic grid. It is used to present daily rate data stated in movements or behaviors per minute. Although ratio charts may seem somewhat more confusing than interval charts, they may be mastered quickly and appear to permit more accurate instructional decisions to be made (Haring, Liberty, & White, 1980). For example, ratio charts offer greater precision and flexibility in recording the rate changes of a wide range of behaviors from very slow (0.01 behaviors per minute) to very fast (1,000 behaviors per minute).

CONCLUDING COMMENTS

The selection of IEP objectives often starts with the combined use of standardized assessment instruments and behavioral checklists. At the same time, an individualized functional curriculum is generated for each student with the help of parent interviews and visits to settings the student *participates* in *regularly* and *will participate* in *subsequently*. The outcome of this assessment must be the determination of the student's current functioning level (entry level) across a number of skill categories. It should lead to the establishment of pragmatic long-term and short-term general goals designed specifically for each learner, based on those strengths and weaknesses revealed in the assessment.

Task analysis and ABC analysis contribute further definition to these general goals. Next, the teacher must select which goals are to be rewritten as IEP objectives, narrowing the specific skills to focus on. Criteria and learning conditions are determined so that each IEP objective can be stated completely and measurably. At the same time, each objective must be "tested" for its functional value to the specific student as well as its suitability to his or her chronological age.

Once objectives are written, more precise measurement of the targeted behaviors begins and continues through all phases of learning each targeted behavior. The selection of the appropriate measurement system depends largely on the target behavior. If, for example, tantrums are the target, the teacher might choose to measure duration. If, however, street-crossing is the target, a task analytic approach would be the best measurement system. Various measurement systems and related data-collection procedures are available. The selection of the approach to use depends on each learning situation and the kind of information the teacher needs. Once the measurement procedure is chosen, data collection is facilitated by developing a recording form that summarizes the information gathered during teaching.

Data gathered during a teaching project are not only entered on raw data sheets but also plotted on a graph for visual display and quick analysis. Most often, arithmetic graphing procedures are selected for rate, duration, frequency, and percentage information. Regardless of the type of graph paper, standard graphing conventions are used to insure consistent interpretation of the graph. The most obvious advantage of converting a student's behavior to a statistical form and graphically presenting it centers on educational evaluation and decision making. By visually summarizing each student's classroom performance, the teacher can assess the influence of the scheduled intervention strategies against both the initial performance level and the criterion.

The next chapter focuses upon intervention strategies to build skills as well as to increase and reduce existing behaviors. Program revisions are discussed—what does the teacher do when programs don't work as planned? Finally, the concepts and related teaching strategies of learning stages (acquisition, maintenance, and generalization learning) are addressed.

REFERENCES

Baer, D.M. A hung jury and a Scottish verdict: "Not proven." *Analysis and Intervention in Developmental Disabilities*, 1981, *1*, 91–97.

Barlow, D.H., & Hayes, S.C. Alternating treatments design: One strategy for comparing the effects of two treatments in a single subject. *Journal of Applied Behavior Analysis*, 1979, *12*, 199–210.

Bates, P., Renzaglia, A., & Clees, T. Improving the work performance of severely/profoundly retarded young adults: The use of a changing criterion procedural design. *Education and Training of the Mentally Retarded*, 1980, *15*, 95–104.

Becker, W.C., Engelmann, S., & Thomas, D.R. *Teaching 2: Cognitive learning and instruction.* Chicago, Science Research Associates, 1975.

Berkson, G., & Landesman-Dwyer, S. Behavioral research on severe and profound mental retardation (1955–1974). *American Journal of Mental Deficiency*, 1977, *81*, 428–454.

Breuning, S.E. & Davidson, N.A. Effects of psychotropic drugs on intelligence test performance of institutionalized mentally retarded adults. *American Journal of Mental Deficiency*, 1981, *85*, 575–579.

Brown, L., Branston, M.B., Baumgart, D., Vincent, L., Falvey, M., & Schroeder, J. Using the characteristics of current and subsequent least restrictive environments as factors in the development of curricular content for severely handicapped students. *AAESPH Review*, 1979, *4*, 407–424. (a)

Brown, L. Branston, M.B., Hamre-Nietupski, S., Pumpian, I., Certo, N., & Gruenewald, L. A strategy for developing chronological age appropriate and functional curricular content for severely handicapped adolescents and young adults. *Journal of Special Education*, 1979, *13*, 81–90. (b)

Cooper, J.O. *Measurement and analysis of behavior techniques.* Columbus, Ohio: Charles E. Merrill, 1974.

Cronin, K.A., & Cuvo, A.J. Teaching mending skills to retarded adolescents. *Journal of Applied Behavior Analysis*, 1979, *12*, 401–406.

Cuvo, A.J. Validating task analyses of community living skills. *Vocational Evaluation and Work Adjustment Bulletin*, 1978, *11*(4), 13–21.

Cuvo, A.J., Leaf, R.B., & Borakove, L.S. Teaching janitorial skills to the mentally retarded: Acquisition, generalization, and maintenance. *Journal of Applied Behavior Analysis*, 1978, *11*, 345–355.

Etzel, B.C. & LeBlanc, J.M. The simplest treatment alternative: The law of parsimony applied to choosing appropriate instructional control and errorless-learning procedures for the difficult-to-teach child. *Journal of Autism and Developmental Disorders*, 1979, *9*, 361–382.

Foxx, R.M. & Martin, P.L. A useful portable timer. *Journal of Applied Behavior Analysis*, 1971, *4*, 60.

Hall, R.V. *Managing behavior. Part 1 - Behavior modification: The measurement of behavior.* Lawrence, Kans.: H & H Enterprises, 1971.

Hall, R.V., Hawkins, R.P., & Axelrod, S. Measuring and recording student behavior: A behavior analysis approach. In R.A. Weinberg & F.H. Wood (Eds.), *Observation of pupils and teachers in mainstream and special education settings: Alternate strategies.* Minneapolis: University of Minnesota, Leadership Training Institute, 1975.

Haring, N.G., Liberty, K.A., & White, O.R. Rules for data-based decisions in instructional programs. In W. Sailor, B. Wilcox, & L. Brown (Eds.), *Methods of instruction for severely handicapped students.* Baltimore: Paul H. Brookes, 1980.

Hartmann, D.P., & Hall, R.V. The changing criterion design. *Journal of Applied Behavior Analysis*, 1976, *9*, 527–532.

Hawkins, R.P., & Hawkins, K.K. Parental observations on the education of severely retarded children: Can it be done in the classroom? *Analysis and Intervention in Developmental Disabilities*, 1981, *1*, 13–22.

Hersen, M., & Barlow, D.H. *Single case experimental designs: Strategies for studying behavior change.* New York: Pergamon, 1976.

Hill, B.K., & Bruininks, R.H. *Physical and behavioral characteristics and maladaptive behavior of mentally retarded people in residential facilities.* Minneapolis: University of Minnesota, Department of Psychoeducational Studies, 1981.

Holvoet, J., Guess, D., Mulligan, M., & Brown, F. The

Individualized Curriculum Sequencing model (II): A teaching strategy for severely handicapped students. *Journal of the Association for the Severely Handicapped*, 1980, *5*, 337–351.

Horner, R.D., & Baer, D.M. Multiple-probe technique: A variation of the multiple baseline. *Journal of Behavior Analysis*, 1978, *11*, 189–196.

Horner, R.D., & Keilitz, I. Training mentally retarded adolescents to brush their teeth. *Journal of Applied Behavior Analysis*, 1975, *8*, 301–319.

Johnson, B.F., & Cuvo, A.J. Teaching mentally retarded adults to cook. *Behavior Modification*, 1981, *5*, 187–202.

Kazdin, A.E. Assessing the clinical or applied importance of behavior change through social validation. *Behavior Modification*, 1977, *1*, 427–452.

Kazdin, A.E. *Behavior modification in applied settings* (2nd ed.). Homewood, Ill.: Dorsey Press, 1980.

Konarski, E.A., Jr., Johnson, M.R., Crowell, C.R., & Whitman, T.L. Response deprivation and reinforcement in applied settings: A preliminary analysis. *Journal of Applied Behavior Analysis*, 1980, *13*, 595–609.

Kratochwill, T.R. *Single subject research: Strategies for evaluating change.* New York: Academic Press, 1978.

Lambert, N., Windmiller, M., Cole, L., & Figueroa, R. *AAMD Adaptive Behavior Scale: Public school version* (1974 rev.). Washington, D.C.: American Association on Mental Deficiency, 1975

Lindsley, O.R. A reliable wrist counter for recording behavioral rates. *Journal of Applied Behavior Analysis*, 1968, *1*, 77.

Murphy, R.J. & Bryan, A.J. Multiple-baseline and multiple-probe designs: Practical alternatives for special education assessment and evaluation. *Journal of Special Education*, 1980, *14*, 325–335.

Murphy, R., Doughty, N., & Nunes, D. Multielement designs: An alternative to reversal and multiple baseline evaluation strategies. *Mental Retardation*, 1979, *17*, 23–27.

Nutter, D., & Reid, D.H. Teaching retarded women a clothing selection skill using community norms. *Journal of Applied Behavior Analysis*, 1978, *11*, 475–487.

O'Brien, F., & Azrin, N.H. Developing proper mealtime behaviors of the institutional retarded. *Journal of Applied Behavior Analysis*, 1972, *5*, 389–399.

Page, T.J., Iwata, B.A., & Neef, N.A. Teaching pedestrian skills to retarded persons: Generalization from the classroom to the natural environment. *Journal of Applied Behavior Analysis*, 1976, *9*, 433–444.

Parsonson, B.S., & Baer, D.M. The analysis and presentation of graphic data. In T.R. Kratochwill (Ed.), *Single subject research: Strategies for evaluating research.* New York: Academic Press, 1978.

Quilitch, R.H., & Risley, T.R. The effects of play materials on social play. *Journal of Applied Behavior Analysis*, 1973, *6*, 573–578.

Redd, W.H. Effects of mixed reinforcement contingencies on adults' control of children's behavior. *Journal of Applied Behavior Analysis*, 1969, *2*, 249–254.

Repp, A.C., Roberts, D.M., Slack, D.J., Repp, C.F., & Berkler, M.S. A comparison of frequency, interval, and time-sampling methods of data collection. *Journal of Applied Behavior Analysis,* 1976, *9,* 501–508.

Resnick, L.B., Wang, M.C., & Kaplan, J. Task analysis in curriculum design: A hierarchically sequenced introductory mathematics curriculum. *Journal of Applied Behavior Analysis,* 1973, *6,* 697–710.

Sailor, W., & Mix, B.J. *The TARC assessment system.* Lawrence, Kans.: H & H Enterprises, 1975.

Singh, N.N., & Aman, M.G. Effects of thioridazine dosage on the behavior of severely mentally retarded persons. *American Journal of Mental Deficiency,* 1981, *85,* 580–587.

Skiba, E.A., Pettigrew, L.E., & Alden, S.E. A behavioral approach to the control of thumbsucking in the classroom. *Journal of Applied Behavior Analysis,* 1971, *4,* 121–125.

Smith, D.D., Smith, J.O., & Edgar, E.B. Prototypic model for the development of instructional materials. In N.G. Haring & L.J. Brown (Eds.), *Teaching the severely handicapped* (Vol. 1). New York, Grune & Stratton, 1976.

Snell, M.E. Analysis of time delay procedures for teaching daily living skills to retarded adolescents. *Analysis and Intervention in Developmental Disabilities,* 1982, *2,* 139–155.

Sulzer-Azaroff, B., & Mayer, G.R. *Applying behavior-analysis procedures with children and youth.* New York: Holt, Rinehart & Winston, 1977.

Thomson, C., Holmberg, M., & Baer, D.M. A brief report on a comparison of time-sampling procedures. *Journal of Applied Behavior Analysis,* 1974, *7,* 623–626.

Tucker, D.J., & Berry, G.W. Teaching severely multihandicapped students to put on their own hearing aids. *Journal of Applied Behavior Analysis,* 1980, *13,* 65–75.

Vincent, L.J., Salisbury, C., Walter, G., Brown, P., Gruenewald, L.J., & Powers, M. Program development and curriculum development in early childhood/special education: Criteria of the next environment. In W. Sailor, B. Wilcox, & L. Brown (Eds.), *Methods of instruction for severely handicapped students.* Baltimore: Paul H. Brookes, 1980.

White, O.R. *A glossary of behavioral terminology.* Champaign, Ill.: Research Press, 1971.

White, O.R., & Haring, N.G. *Exceptional teaching.* Columbus, Ohio: Charles E. Merrill, 1976.

Whitman, T.L., Mercurio, S.R., & Caponigri, V. Development of social responses in two severely retarded children. *Journal of Applied Behavior Analysis,* 1970, *3,* 133–138.

Whitman, T.L., & Scibak, J.W. Behavior modification research with the severely and profoundly retarded. In N.R. Ellis (Ed.), *Handbook of mental deficiency, psychological theory and research* (2nd ed.). Hillsdale, N.J.: Lawrence Erlbaum, 1979.

Wolf, M.M. Social validity: The case for subjective measurement or how applied behavior analysis is finding its heart. *Journal of Applied Behavior Analysis,* 1978, *11,* 203–214.

Wolf, M.M., Risley, T., & Mees, H. Application of operant conditioning procedures to the behavior problems of an autistic child. *Behavior Research and Therapy,* 1964, *1,* 305–312.

REFERENCE NOTE

1. Gaylord-Ross, R.J. *Task analysis and the severely handicapped.* Unpublished manuscript, San Francisco State University, 1981.

Martha E. Snell *is Associate Professor, Department of Special Education at the University of Virginia.*

When teaching is systematic, it is a defined, replicable process which reflects currently accepted "best" practices, uses performance data (both probe and instructional) to make modifications, and proceeds from acquisition to proficiency, maintenance, and finally generalization learning. Though systematic instruction is complex, it appears to be the most certain route to learning for severely handicapped students. Trial and error and "hit or miss" approaches are not defensible with this population. With severely handicapped students, the ultimate goals of learning are functional skills performed so well that mere passage of time or variations in materials, setting, and people present will not cause a failure in performance.

Figure 5.1 shows an abbreviated analysis of systematic instruction that starts with program development and ends with generalized skills. This chapter reviews some intervention strategies found successful with the severely handicapped and thus used to implement and monitor the IEP.[1]

CHARACTERISTICS OF APPROPRIATE INSTRUCTION

In chapter 4 we saw that skills taught must be functional and age appropriate. We will now look at other characteristics of instruction that can serve as guidelines for applying intervention strategies both to build skills and to reduce inappropriate behavior.

Planning and Writing Programs

While it may seem to many teachers that paperwork saps too much of their time, some written documents are essential and cannot be ignored. At the very *minimum* these include:

1. Emergency and medical information (chapter 7),
2. A complete IEP (chapters 2, 3, and 4),
3. Descriptions of probe and teaching procedures for each objective being taught (see chapter 4 for probe procedures),
4. Dated graphs of baseline and probe performance data for each objective being taught (chapter 4),
5. Daily instructional schedule.

Teaching procedures, often referred to as *lesson plans,* also need certain ingredients to be complete guides for implementing a program. Written program procedures must specify the:

---

[1]The reader interested in more detailed information on behavior modification and applications with mentally retarded and emotionally disturbed individuals should consult Azrin and Besalel (1980); Hall and Hall (1980a, 1980b, 1980c); Kazdin (1980); Leitenberg (1976); Sulzer-Azaroff and Mayer (1977).

5

Implementing and Monitoring the IEP: Intervention Strategies

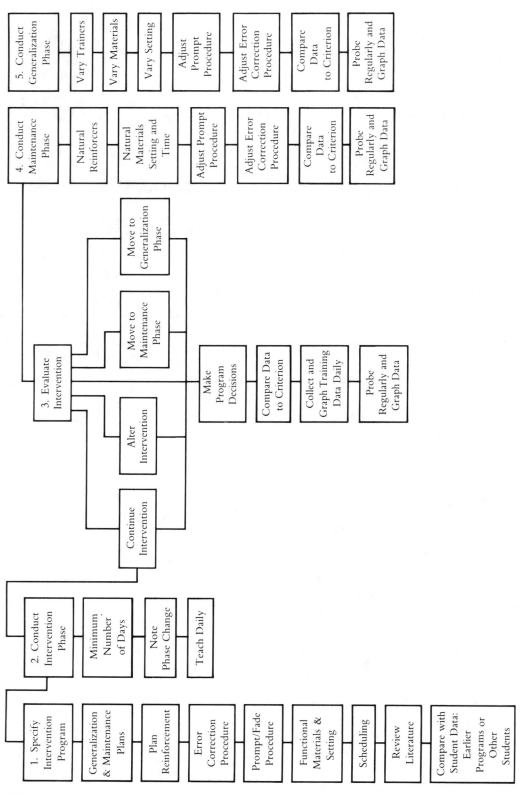

114

FIGURE 5.1
Implementing and Monitoring the IEP

1. Instructional objective;
2. Student or students being taught;
3. Scheduled time and place;
4. Instructor;
5. Date initiated;
6. Instructional materials needed;
7. Baseline and probe procedure and schedule;
8. Teaching procedure:
   a. Discriminative stimulus,
   b. Prompt/fade methods,
   c. Error correction procedure,
   d. Reinforcers,
   e. Reinforcement schedule;
9. Skill maintenance plan;
10. Skill generalization plan;
11. Task analytic data collection sheets (if task analyses are used to teach the skill).

If programs are written out in this detail, they are more likely to be consistently implemented regardless of the instructor. Programs that lead to learning thus can be replicated, while those that yield little or no learning can be modified more precisely.

Stage of Learning

Research (Ayllon & Azrin, 1964; Csapo, 1981; Smith & Lovitt, 1976; White & Haring, 1976; White & Liberty, 1976) indicates that there is more than one stage of learning and that the influence of intervention strategies depends on stage. Since one tactic might be influential in one learning stage but not another, it is important to determine which learning stage an individual is in before interventions begin.

There are at least four distinctly different stages of learning: acquisition, fluency, maintenance, and generalization. During acquisition, the learner cannot perform the skill accurately. Initially the percentages correct are zero, indicating the need to acquire competency in the target skill. Once the learner can perform the task correctly, the fluency stage begins. Here, the teacher must program for fluent performance. In addition to accuracy, speed of performance (proficiency) is the aim. Once the learner can accurately perform the task fast enough to indicate fluency, the performance level must be maintained. Using the skill under changing conditions is generalization. Generalization learning may refer to the variation of teaching materials, settings, or trainers.

In many cases, accuracy is the only target in instructional programming. Through the following example, you can see why this is not sufficient. In one vocational training program, moderately and severely handicapped students were learning to work as busboys. They needed to learn to set a table correctly before they could receive on-the-job training. The teacher conducted a task analysis of the target skill, assessing each student's abilities to clear a table. She then initiated an instructional program, carefully measured daily performance, and kept daily records. She determined that 3 consecutive 100% days would indicate mastery. Finally all the students reached this goal and were ready to enter their job-training situation; or were they? After the first day on the job, all but one student returned with an indication that their skills were not sufficient for on-the-job programs.

What was the cause of this apparent failure? Simply that the teacher had not completed her instruction. Two very important phases were omitted. First, apparently only one student was fluent at the target task. In a work situation, speed of performance as well as accuracy is vital. The teacher should have asked the potential employer how quickly employees needed to clear tables and this time should have been added to the mastery criteria. For some students, even more instruction will be required. Some students demonstrate skill fluency in the classroom, but require further instruction to transfer or generalize that skill to a different setting. So, in addition, our teacher should have probed her students' newly acquired, fluent table-clearing skills at the job site as well and trained in that setting in the first place if at all possible.

Clearly, there are two important reasons for attending to the stage of learning. First, moderately and severely handicapped students will not succeed in least restrictive environments unless they perform fluently. Second, tactics selected for instruction should match the stage of learning. For example, while instruction obviously is needed to establish a brand new behavior, fluency learning such as increasing the speed of an already learned skill may be managed by simply manipulating reinforcement.

Natural versus Simulated Training Conditions

Retarded learners do not easily retain known skills or transfer them to new situations; the more severely handicapped the learner, the more critical are the problems of maintenance and generalization (Liberty, Haring, & Martin, 1981). If students are taught functional skills, their natural daily performance helps to maintain them. If students are taught to perform skills using *real materials* (e.g., wall clocks, groceries in a store) rather than simulated or teacher-made materials (e.g., paper plate "clocks," empty food cartons, and pictured groceries), they are more likely to be able to perform the skill outside the classroom.

When the training setting itself is natural, skill generalization is even further facilitated. For example, when teaching a student to cross streets, the skill will more likely be usable if instruction takes place on a nonbusy side street and then is moved to a busier street as students gain independence. While simulated training in the classroom *is* safer, skill generalization is likely to be more difficult since the classroom differs drastically from a real street. Thus actual use of pedestrian skills learned under simulated conditions may ultimately be more dangerous.

If a teacher adopts the principle of teaching in the natural setting whenever possible, then less time will be spent in the classroom. This is especially true as students grow older and vocational and community skills become priorities (Brown, Nisbet, Ford, Sweet, Shiraga, & Loomis, Note 1). Realistic training settings available in and around most schools include cafeterias (eating skills and janitorial skills), a variety of bathrooms (self-care and janitorial skills), sidewalks (pedestrian skills), school buses (loading and unloading), and hallways (social interaction and mobility). Thus, while the teacher concerned with skill generalization will *not* be spending the bulk of the day in the classroom, it also is not essential to leave the school to teach all generalized skills.

Planning for Interaction with Nonhandicapped Peers

P.L. 94-142 requires education in the least restrictive setting possible, regardless of the degree of handicap. Some researchers have set about to show the positive outcome of interactions between severely handicapped and nonhandicapped students. Three studies (McHale & Simeonsson, 1980; Voeltz, 1980, 1982a) show that favorable attitude changes in nonhandicapped students can result from carefully planned integration of the severely handicapped in public schools. Others are currently investigating the reciprocal effects of integration on the severely handicapped. These benefits should include more age-appropriate social skills, better skill generalization due to freer movement in the school and community, and ultimately more acceptance in the local community, which would lead to job opportunity and more certain acceptance of local residential facilities.

But mere mixing of the handicapped with their normal peers in school buildings will not yield attitude changes as positive as that obtained from structured interactions (Voeltz, 1980; 1982a). Instead, formal and informal efforts must be made to promote integration (Voeltz, 1982b). Hamre-Nietupski and Nietupski (1981) reported on a variety of integration methods used in the Milwaukee Public School to mingle 80 severely handicapped students into an elementary school, two middle schools, and a high school. These included the following strategies:

1. A faculty member was employed to plan and conduct integration activities.

2. Before integration began, faculty, administrators, and students were given sensitization sessions and information on integration and the severely handicapped.
3. Preintegration planning with faculty and administration facilitated scheduling, cafeteria and gym use, hall movement, use of home economics area, and other school facilities.
4. Severely handicapped students were taught the age-appropriate behavior expected of them in the regular school.
5. Parents were included in the planning.
6. Faculty were given sensitization media to use with nonhandicapped students.
7. An "open-door" visitation policy was initiated for special education classrooms.
8. Special teachers mixed regularly with regular teachers.
9. Severely handicapped students were involved in school jobs and participated in school activities.
10. Nonhandicapped students served as partners or tutors of handicapped students, assisted in conducting sensitization sessions for their peers, and wrote articles for school paper on integration.

Group Versus One-to-One Instruction

One-to-one instruction has not proven to be as beneficial for severely handicapped students as many had thought. Recent investigations show that groups of 2 to 6 moderately to severely handicapped students acquire a variety of skills at rates *comparable to* or *even better than* one-to-one instruction (Alberto, Jobes, Sizemore, & Doran, 1980; Biberdorf & Pear, 1977; Favell, Favell, & McGimsey, 1978; Frankel & Graham, 1976; Kohl, Wilcox, & Karlan, 1978; Storm & Willis, 1978). Since group instruction maximizes instructional time, those findings are encouraging.

Furthermore, as emphasized both by these studies and by Brown, Holvoet, Guess, and Mulligan (1980), group instruction promotes opportunities not available in one-to-one instruction. These include "(*a*) increased control of motivational variables; (*b*) opportunities to facilitate observational learning, peer interaction, and peer communication; and (*c*) generalization of skills" (p. 353). For example, in motivation, timeout from reinforcement for a nonresponsive student in a group allows the teacher to work with a responsive student rather than creating unproductive time. Learning by observation is more likely to occur when intentionally arranged and reinforced in groups. Students, rather than teachers, present cues and consequences to other students in the group, as group independence work in showering (Matson, DiLorenzo, & Esveldt-Dawson, 1981) and family style eating (Matson, Ollendick, &

Adkins, 1980) has so successfully demonstrated. Students are actively involved in the learning process even during the "turns" of other students. Finally, groups create more natural reinforcement conditions. These "natural" conditions include learning to take turns, to attend to others, to wait for teacher and peer attention, to obtain a turn contingent on responsiveness, to tolerate intermittent attention, to receive reinforcers and cues from peers rather than only adults. All these conditions approximate the real world and prepare students to perform under those conditions.

Other Learning Considerations

There are numerous other characteristics of appropriate programming; only a few other important ones will be emphasized.

Principle of Parsimony
Some teaching methods for the difficult-to-teach student can be tedious to use effectively. Etzel and LeBlanc (1979) recommended the principle of parsimony: select the simplest but still effective treatment first and move to more rigorous techniques if easier techniques are not effective. In other words, don't risk planning programs that won't or can't be skillfully implemented when easier procedures are defensible.

Low Error
Related to this first principle is the ideal learning condition of keeping student error at a minimum. Research with retarded learners indicates that the best learning occurs when the student makes few or no errors. Thus while a teacher must incorporate techniques to keep errors low, he or she must not select procedures that are so complex they cannot be applied correctly.

Massed, Distributed, or Spaced Trial Learning
Most teachers use a 15- to 30-minute daily teaching slot to teach each program. During that time, the student has many trials on the same skill. If the skill is a discrete trial skill (e.g., request or label objects, identify prices, use signs), the repetitions are often *massed*—one right after the other. Group instruction (where students take rotating turns) breaks up these trials, creating a *spaced* trial situation; but because students take turns, no teaching time is lost. When the skills taught are chained or multiple-step sequences, as are most functional skills such as ironing and folding clothes, then performance of the skill is actually a *distributed* performance of a series of subskills rather than massed practice on a single response. Other possibilities for distributed trials include teaching one

student a cluster of related discrete behaviors or teaching in a group but involving students in cue and reinforcer presentation during the turns of other students, thus eliminating the "wait" time.

A review of trial scheduling by Mulligan, Guess, Holvoet, and Brown (1980) emphasizes the *distributed* trial schedule as a more efficient use of time than either massed or spaced trials. Evidence available thus far suggests to:

1. Use distributed trials rather than spaced to minimize "down time";
2. Use massed trials initially to obtain speedier acquisition or to correct errors and change to distributed trials to maintain and generalize skills.

Massed trials should be used mainly when learning time is critical, while most instruction should distribute trials across tasks, to yield fewer actual trials required for learning each separate skill.

INTERVENTION STRATEGIES AIMED AT INCREASING BEHAVIOR

When a behavior increases because specific consequences (reinforcers) consistently follow all or most instances of that behavior and are not available without that behavior, a reinforcement contingency is in operation. This interdependent or contingent arrangement between behaviors and consequences lets us change behaviors purposefully. This is commonly called *contingency management*. As illustrated in Figure 5.2, positive reinforcement occurs when the presentation of rewarding consequences (called *positive reinforcers*), made contingent upon a behavior, leads to an increase in the performance of that behavior. To reinforce behavior means to strengthen behavior—increase its frequency, its duration, or its intensity.

Positive Reinforcement

Selection of Positive Reinforcers
Particular items or events in and of themselves do not serve as positive reinforcers for everyone. Reinforcers are defined by their effect upon an individual's behavior. The test is whether the object or event, when made contingent upon a behavior, causes an increase in that behavior. If the behavior does not increase, the object or event is not a positive reinforcer. Because of past experiences or personal preference, what is reinforcing to one individual may not be to others. For example, many youngsters do not initially like carbonated beverages; with repeated tastes, however, they learn to like them. Some children learn to fear water, though most learn to enjoy it. In addition, secondary reinforcers (e.g., money)

TYPE OF EVENT

OPERATION PERFORMED AFTER A RESPONSE

Presented Positive Reinforcement Effect: frequency of positively reinforced behavior *increases*	Punishment Effect: frequency of punished behavior *decreases;* other side effects may occur
Removed, Withdrawn Punishment Effect: frequency of punished behavior *decreases;* other side effects may occur	Negative Reinforcement Effect: frequency of negatively reinforced behavior *increases*
Withheld, Not Presented Extinction Effect: frequency of behavior placed on extinction *decreases*	

FIGURE 5.2
The Influence Principles of Operant Conditioning
SOURCE: Adapted with permission from *Behavior Modification in Applied Settings* (Rev. ed.) by A.E. Kazdin. Homewood, Ill.: Dorsey Press, 1980, p. 35.

are effective only if the learner knows that they are associated with primary reinforcers.

Reinforcers should not be determined by guessing. This information can be gained precisely with four general techniques.

1. Ask the student directly about his or her likes and dislikes. Direct questioning, while often effective with verbal individuals, is nonfunctional with many severely handicapped learners because it relies upon communication.

2. Ask others familiar with the individual's likes and dislikes for a list of potential reinforcers. When asking other teachers, parents, siblings, or relatives to identify reinforcers for a student, it is especially important to verify their responses with one of the other three methods. While both questioning methods may seem to be efficient, they can yield limited information, because what is reinforcing in one setting may be impractical, ineffective, or unavailable for use in another.

3. Observe the individual over a period of days in the natural setting and list observed reinforcing events. If carried out systematically for long enough, direct observation of a person's preferences for foods, beverages, toys, songs, people, classroom and playground activities, clothes, and so on probably yields the most accurate list of reinforcers. A teacher may use any of the measurement procedures described in chapter 4 to record these preferences (e.g., duration of time spent in various activities, frequency of selecting various toys). In addition, Wuerch and Voeltz (1982) suggest using picture choices to determine preferred similar leisure activities.

4. Structure the environment to observe a period of reinforcement. As with natural observations, structured observations do not depend upon language skills—an advantage with many severely handicapped students. Structured observation lets a teacher observe the reaction to potential reinforcers that are normally unavailable. Ayllon and Azrin (1968) used a strategy called *reinforcer sampling,* in which they allowed handicapped adults limited "free" exposure to novel activities, such as participation in social evenings, religious services, and musical activities. The adults were exposed to activities not otherwise available to teach them the reinforcing value of the events before making that event contingent upon certain behaviors. In a structured observation, an individual is first allowed to sample briefly a small group of similar items (foods, beverages, toys) or events suitable to his or her chronological age (listening to a tape recorder, looking at magazines, being pushed in a wagon). Then he or she is given the entire group of potential reinforcers and the frequency of duration of choices is recorded. After a group of possible reinforcers is sampled and the free-choice observation is recorded, other groups may be

observed similarly. The best time to observe response to food groups is just prior to a meal.

Primary and Secondary Reinforcers

Although reinforcers have unlimited range and vary from tangible items and activities to abstract thoughts of self-approval, all reinforcers are of two general types: primary (unlearned or unconditioned) or secondary (learned or conditioned). The first category includes the "universal" or automatic reinforcers to which everyone responds (though not continuously) without instruction. Primary reinforcers for someone who is hungry, thirsty, or uncomfortably chilled include food, drink, and warmth.

Secondary reinforcers are those that have developed reinforcing value through conditioning. Secondary reinforcers begin as neutral pairings with already existing (primary or other secondary) reinforcers. Eventually these events take on reinforcing value in and of themselves. For example, students learn to value playing with toys, riding a bike, listening to music, receiving pay for work, receiving praise, and accomplishing a goal.

Generalized reinforcers are highly effective secondary reinforcers that acquire their reinforcing power by association with many other primary and secondary reinforcers. Money, affection, attention, and approval by others are all generalized reinforcers because each requires learning and is associated with many additional reinforcers (for instance, money purchases food, various activities, clothes, toys, etc.).

Generalized reinforcers commonly used in educational settings include attention, approval, money, and *tokens*. A token system or economy is analogous to a currency-payment system, except that the value of a token is limited to the immediate setting and is controlled by the person who implements the system. Tokens come in many forms—coins, washers, poker chips, checkers, slips of specially marked paper—and may even simply be checkmarks on an "official" checksheet. As with other reinforcers, tokens are given contingent upon target behaviors and, in turn, are exchangeable for the "purchase" of back-up primary and secondary reinforcers. Tokens have advantages over many other reinforcers because they may be distributed in classrooms conveniently and, because of their exchange power, are durable in reinforcing quality. Unlike money, tokens have no value outside the intervention program, and the exchange value within the program may be easily and quickly adjusted. Tokens have been used in combination with praise as reinforcers to modify a wide variety of behaviors in the moderately and severely handicapped (Kazdin & Bootzin, 1972): math skills (Baker, Stanish, & Fraser, 1972; Dalton, Rubino, & Hislop, 1973), language skills (Baer & Guess, 1973; Baker et al., 1972), bed-making (Snell, 1982), signing (Renzaglia & Snell, Note 2), and social skills (Bates, 1980).

Most token economies have a specific and additive exchange value. Some use a variety of tokens with their own specific values, much like our own currency system. Although counting may be taught with a token system, many severely handicapped students may be unprepared to learn counting and the concept of purchasing. In these cases, the usual token economy may be modified. First, and most common, is the use of counters. The student places earned pennies on a card with circles or squares or a wooden block with coin-sized holes. When all the spaces are filled with coins, the student can purchase a reinforcer. In other cases a token economy based on varying rather than specific values may be used (Kent, 1974). With varying value systems, tokens are given contingent upon specific behavior(s) but are exchanged for back-up reinforcers singly or, more often, in varying amounts whenever the teacher feels a more tangible reinforcer is necessary to maintain the generalized reinforcing value of the tokens. The individual is "token trained" before implementing such a system. This type of token system has been used effectively with nonverbal, profoundly retarded learners (Snell, 1979).

The steps listed next comprise token training and can establish an association between tokens and their back-up reinforcers.

1. Identify a behavior or class of behaviors easily performed by the individual (e.g., imitation of movements, following simple commands like "Show me the ball").
2. Prepare a choice of known back-up reinforcers (arranged on a tray or cupcake pan), a token container (one-pound coffee can), and a uniform set of at least 30 tokens at a training table.
3. Ask the individual to perform the behavior and:
   a. Reinforce immediately following the behavior with a single token placed in the individual's hand and with enthusiastic praise, or
   b. Prompt if the behavior is not forthcoming, and then reinforce with a token and praise immediately following the behavior.
4. Immediately hold out a hand to collect the token (with prompting, if necessary) and present the reinforcer tray. Prompt the student to select one reinforcer.
5. Repeat this cycle—request for behavior, praise and token reinforcement, immediate exchange—until the individual, without any prompts, shows evidence of making the association between tokens and token exchange. For example, the stu-

dent may reach for the tokens after a response to speed up the exchange process. Increase the exchange schedule gradually from one token to an accumulation of four or five tokens before exchange.

6. While remaining at four or five tokens, introduce the token container to facilitate the collection and exchange process. Tokens are then dropped into the can by the teacher and the student is shown how to lift and empty the contents at exchange time.

7. Increase the exchange ratio gradually over the remainder of the token-training session, which should not last beyond 15 to 20 minutes.

8. At this point, tokens can be used as reinforcement during actual teaching sessions. Initially, a brief review (a few immediate or low ratio exchanges) may be necessary to remind the student of the tokens' exchange value.[2]

Reinforcer Schedules and Durability

Schedules of reinforcement indicate how many and which responses are reinforced. Thus they affect the response pattern. Reinforcement schedule is the "A" or "arrangement" element in Lindsley's (1964) operant framework: $E^A \rightarrow B \rightarrow A \rightarrow E^C$. Reinforcement may be given according to the number of responses performed (ratio schedules) or the passage of time in relation to the performance (interval schedules). Both types of schedules may be based either upon absolute numbers of responses or amounts of time (fixed schedules) or upon averaged responses or time (variable schedules). For example, the presentation of one reinforcer for every occurrence of the target behavior is a fixed ratio schedule of one (FR:1). This is commonly called *continuous reinforcement*. All other schedules may be generally called *intermittent reinforcement*. An FR:5 would be a fixed pattern of reinforcement for every fifth response; in a VR:5 schedule, reinforcement would be variable rather than regularly applied to an average of every fifth response. This VR: 5 pattern might consist of three occurrences of a target behavior, reinforcement, seven occurrences of the same target behavior, reinforcement, two occurrences of the target behavior, reinforcement, eight occurrences of the target behavior, etc. In interval schedules, the first target response occurring after a regular time period of so many seconds or minutes (fixed interval or FI) or an averaged period (variable interval or VI) is reinforced.

In many regular classrooms, reinforcement schedules are time-based (at the end of a class period), and teacher-dispensed social reinforcers may be as meager as one per minute. In a classroom of 30, this converts to a schedule of one reinforcement every half-hour—a rather sparse schedule. Classroom schedules are more often variable than fixed. Teachers may provide reinforcement when they judge enough "work" has been done or sufficient time has passed. Because "sufficient" and "enough" tend to vary from one day to the next, a variable schedule results. If the students are unaware of the reinforcement schedule, they probably will not learn as predictably as if schedules are planned. For example, increasing speed in counting money is facilitated by using fixed ratio schedules that the teacher adjusts as the student improves (e.g., initially one reinforcement per correct counting, later one reinforcement every other counting, then one reinforcement every correct third, fifth, and so on).

Differential reinforcement of high rates of behavior (DRH) is a useful schedule that also requires the teacher to conscientiously identify a target rate of performance that may be gradually achieved over a period of instruction. DRL or differential reinforcement of low rates of behavior is another ratio reinforcement schedule, the complement of DRH. DRL is used to reduce undesirably frequent misbehaviors.

Satiation results from the overuse of a reinforcer. It is quite possible to tire of an event so that it is no longer reinforcing, especially if the reinforcer is given too frequently or is given less often but in large amounts. For instance, if too much of an edible reinforcer is given or if food is offered too frequently, the reinforcing effect may be lost. After extensive involvement with certain toys or activities, the novelty lessens and the desired behavior is no longer effectively reinforced. This same outcome occurs when reinforcers are given freely or noncontingently—the person has unlimited access to certain events, which devalues their contingent effect on the target behavior. Because of satiation, a teacher must take care to preserve the "special" quality of objects or activities selected as reinforcers.

Due to the powerful influence of reinforcement schedules upon behavior, some related considerations on scheduling reinforcement should be applied when arranging the learning conditions for instruction.

1. Reinforcers should be available only when they are contingent upon the performance of appropriate behavior or a realistic approximation of that behavior.

2. During the acquisition stage of learning, every instance of behavior should be encouraged by the continuous provision of small amounts of contingent reinforcement (e.g., small bits of food, a few seconds of music, etc.) rather than larger amounts less often. Continuous reinforcements yields a high rate of performance.

---

[2]The reader interested in more detailed readings on token systems should consult Ayllon and Azrin (1968) and Stainback, Payne, Stainback, and Payne (1973).

3. After a higher rate of behavior has been established (in fluency or maintenance stage), reinforcers should be provided on an intermittent schedule. That is, the reinforcement schedule should be thinned slowly so that more behavior is required for each reinforcement. This will "strengthen" the behavior; the individual will learn to tolerate periods of nonreinforcement rather than to abruptly "give up" and stop responding when reinforcement is not forthcoming.

4. Intermittent reinforcement also avoids satiation because of the efficient use of fewer reinforcers for more behavior while using less training time administering reinforcers.

5. Variable schedules generally produce more even patterns of behavior than fixed schedules because the individual cannot predict the occasions for reinforcement.

6. To avoid satiation, a variety of reinforcers should be used instead of a single reinforcer, and, whenever feasible, the student should select the reinforcer.

7. Reinforcers should be arranged in order from the most preferred/most powerful to the least preferred/least powerful. This allows the teacher to match reinforcers with the effort required by the student to perform a particular behavior and to reserve the most powerful reinforcers for more "difficult" teaching programs (behaviors on which the student, after a lot of instruction, has shown minimal progress).

Reinforcer Hierarchy

Besides arranging reinforcers from most to least preferred, reinforcers can be arranged along a continuum from less natural or immature (unlearned, primary) to more natural or mature (conditioned, secondary, and generalized). At more mature levels of reinforcement, the individual has learned to expect less immediate and less frequent reinforcement. The following hierarchy is arranged from primary to secondary and generalized reinforcers.

1. Food;
2. Toys and leisure activities;
3. Tokens with back-up reinforcers from categories 1 and 2;
4. Letter grades which indicate progress;
5. Parental, peer, or teacher approval;
6. Self-praise for accomplishment of a goal.

Within the level of reinforcement preferred, the teacher should select actual reinforcers that are appropriate to the individual's chronological age. For example, if observation indicates that an adolescent boy likes food and preschool toys best, the teacher probably would want to:

1. Reinforce with food less often and eventually not at all until other reinforcers are established;

2. Select suitable "toys" or leisure activities that are liked and easily used (e.g., tape-recorded music, magazines);
3. Using understandable praise, reinforce before every instance of tangible reinforcement, while gradually reducing tangible reinforcement;
4. Teach the use of new, potentially reinforcing, age-appropriate activities (e.g., the Simon electronic game by Milton Bradley, velcro dart boards, pinball, and video games)[3] which would replace the tangibles;
5. Teach the use of tokens so that the frequency of activity reinforcers can be reduced.

The teacher and parents must reduce the excessive use of reinforcers, eliminate inappropriate reinforcers, and encourage students to function at more natural levels of reinforcement suitable to their chronological age.

Immediacy of Reinforcement

Effective positive reinforcement is hardly simple. As we have seen, it is influenced by the schedule used and the quality or intensity of the reinforcers. A third factor which affects the degree of behavior change is timing. The relationship is direct—the more immediately the reinforcers are presented after the behavior, the greater their effect. Immediacy promotes the association of reinforcement with performance of the target behavior; that is, understanding of the contingency used by the teacher. Immediacy is especially important for children and adults with limited language skills. They are less able to learn contingencies from verbal contracts (that is, "after you perform a certain behavior, you may do or have a particular reinforcer"). Immediacy also decreases the chance that intervening behaviors, not targeted for positive reinforcement, will be reinforced accidentally.

Immediacy is more essential during acquisition than during the later stages of learning, when the behavior is performed more reliably. Further, after a behavior is in the fluency or the maintenance stage of learning, the student should be taught to tolerate delays as well as a reduction in reinforcement, thus lessening the dependency on reinforcement.

Antecedent Techniques

In chapter 4 we discussed the ABC arrangement of the antecedent conditions, the behavior, and the consequences. Intervention strategies used to build skills frequently involve careful programming not only of the consequences for various responses, but also of the antecedent stimuli that precede performance of the target behavior.

---

[3]Refer to Wuerch and Voeltz (1982) for instructional techniques.

Discriminative Stimulus

Learning is primarily a process of understanding how to respond in the presence of specific signals or cues and how to respond differently when these stimuli change. A student who has learned to ask for things she wants at meals finds that sitting (*a*) in the presence of food (*b*) at the dining room table (*c*) when she is hungry all serve as discriminative stimuli for the behavior of saying "Want *milk*" (or some other food). This behavior in the presence of these stimuli has been reinforced long enough to have been learned. Discriminative stimuli (more commonly referred to as S^Ds) may include the natural cues of the setting, the materials, the time of day, the weather, or a full bladder. They may also include a teacher's request or various assists or prompts provided to get the student responding. In other words, some stimuli are *known* S^Ds for a given individual, while other S^Ds are still to-be-learned and therefore have not yet been discriminated by the learner. For example, when first teaching a student to clean a bathroom mirror, the instructional cue or S^D of "clean the mirror" is not likely to be meaningful. Because he is unsure of what has been requested, the student may not respond. The stimulus "clean the mirror" has not become associated with the behavior of mirror cleaning, so it is a to-be-learned S^D. However, if the teacher provides some meaningful S^Ds for this student, such as a model of the first step plus directions (teacher says "Get the glass cleaner" and then reaches into cupboard and removes the spray bottle), the student can perform the first step in the task. If similar meaningful S^Ds are provided over time for all the remaining steps in the task, the student eventually will come to respond on his own to the S^Ds provided by the request "clean a mirror" and the situation.

Eventually students must be able to respond in the presence of natural cues rather than artificial or teacher-applied stimuli (see Falvey, Brown, Lyon, Baumgart, and Schroeder, 1980, for more comment). For example, in the mirror-cleaning example, the student should respond by cleaning mirrors that are dirty rather than only when requested by the teacher. Similarly we would like students to initiate requests for materials needed or desired rather than only respond after the teacher asks "What do you want?" To have natural S^Ds control a behavior, a teacher must incorporate them into the instructional plan. Teaching in natural settings and at natural times lets the teacher use environmental cues. Initially, however, for most tasks the *instructional cues* (which constitute one or more of the to-be-learned S^Ds):

1. Should be stated in terms easily understood by the student;
2. Should be phrased as commands, not questions ("Tie your shoes");
3. Should be provided only when the student is attending;
4. Should be given only once at the beginning of the task rather than repeated over and over (prompts, which will be described next, are used when the student is unable to follow the instructional cue);
5. Should reflect the conditions stated in the instructional objective (e.g., "Given the request 'Clean the mirror,' a dirty mirror, and a cabinet with cleaning materials inside. . .");
6. May include the presentation of materials (cleaning materials handed to the student) or may require the students to locate them on their own;
7. Should include the natural cues provided by realistic settings (real bathrooms with mirrors) and materials (dirty mirrors and actual glass cleaner).

Stimulus and Response Prompting

Behavior must occur before it can be shaped. To insure that a new behavior will occur, various types of assistance can be given before the response to increase the likelihood that the learner will perform the desired behavior or a better approximation. This assistance, in the form of directions, models, cues, or physical prompts, primes the desired behavior—hence Skinner's term *response priming*.

The term *prompting* often is used interchangeably with *priming*. Prompts may be associated primarily with the task stimuli or materials or with the response. The former, *stimulus prompts*, would include color coding various parts of bicycle brake pieces to make the assembly task easier (Gold, 1972). The retarded worker simply color matched the parts that are to be joined. The use of a picture to prompt reading is another stimulus prompt. Response prompts include verbal instructions, gestures or pointing movements, models, and physical assists.

Prompts help students make unknown responses, which in turn can be reinforced and eventually learned. However, prompts are generally introduced only to "get the behavior going" and must be removed so that the student learns to respond independently. Thus stimulus and response prompts are only temporary means to obtain behavior during *acquisition*. Eventually, this guidance must be eliminated so that stimulus control transfers from the priming stimuli to the appropriate natural discriminative stimuli (S^Ds)—those stimuli in the presence of which the target behavior is appropriate and results in reinforcement. Let us illustrate. If a pupil is always reminded that five pennies equal a nickel, then she will not learn a nickel's value. The teacher must fade the support gradually so the student can practice independence in performance and thus gain mastery. Knowing when and how to help a student perform and when and how to withhold help constitute a large portion of the skill of effective teaching.

Falvey et al. (1980) suggest that most prompts used in teaching are artificial rather than natural. Artificial prompts are more likely to foster excessive dependence upon a trainer and to slow the assistance-fading process. Directing the learner's attention toward the cues inherent in the natural setting where the task is performed ultimately promotes self-prompting and self-correction. When instruction takes place in unnatural settings—teaching street crossing in the classroom—instructional procedures are not likely to focus on natural cues to correct or prompt the student (seeing and hearing cars as they drive by the street edge of the sidewalk). However, it is also true that less "natural" procedures, such as verbal instructions, can and have been successfully applied to teach a new skill in a natural setting. Why do natural procedures appear to be used less frequently? One difficulty with relying solely on natural cues to prompt and correct responses is that they are less systematic; that is, the trainer has less control over their presentation. Another problem with using natural procedures is the wide variety of cues present across every step in a task-analyzed skill. A prompt hierarchy such as system of *least intrusive prompts* is rather easily used across steps in a task—first wait for independent performance, then give verbal instructions; next, if needed, give a model plus verbal prompts; finally, if still necessary, give physical assistance along with instructions. When natural cues are used, the teacher must vary the prompts (or correction procedure) by focusing the learner's attention on different cues related to each step in a task, so instruction becomes much more complex. Clearly more research is needed to develop and test natural prompt and correction procedures to resolve these difficulties since *independent performance in natural settings is the only defensible goal of teaching.*

Teachers still may promote the presence of natural cues during teaching by:

1. Careful validation of each task analysis, so that all necessary steps are included and appropriate methods are selected to complete the task (chapter 4);
2. Matching verbal prompts with the actual terminology used in the setting where the skill ultimately will be performed (Liberty et al., 1981);
3. Emphasizing the type of prompt (models, verbal directions, pictorial instruction) most prevalent in the natural setting (watching others use dryers at a laundromat);
4. Using natural prompts and correct procedures whenever possible, but especially during the fluency, maintenance, and generalization phases when performance is more complete;

5. Teaching students in the later phases of learning to ask for assistance when no prompts are forthcoming.

Types of Instructional Prompts

Verbal directions offered before and during the performance of a behavior often serve as guides for responding. For example, when a teacher asks a student to select seven forks and knives from a tray of silverware by saying, "Count out forks and knives," many different behaviors are being requested. The discriminative stimuli, which come to control the individual's behavior, demand action, number selection, and object discrimination. Initially, the teacher may need to assist with additional directions that prompt the correct behavior. If the student begins to count out spoons, the teacher might repeat the word *forks*. If the student miscounts, the teacher might say the numerical sequence for the student; if he hesitates, the teacher could prompt to "count faster." The most important thing to remember when using verbal directions to prompt is that the student must understand the directions. Sometimes the teacher must speak slowly and use simple word combinations and vocabulary, and even use accompanying gestures, signs, or cues.

Instructions provided for moderately and severely handicapped individuals may be given in a variety of modes and formats: verbal, verbal with gestures, verbal with models or demonstrations, by means of a single picture or a sequentially arranged set of pictures, with text, and text alone. Pictures and text promote independence from the teacher and create opportunities to practice the more cognitively demanding skills of picture and word comprehension. Of course the learner must have a variety of prerequisite skills (picture-object association and word-object association) before illustrated and written instructions will be appropriate.

Cuvo and Davis (1980) list three different methods of verbal instruction that have been proven successful with moderately to severely handicapped learners:

1. Stating the response (reminding a student to "Set the table");
2. Asking questions (asking a student who has hesitated 5 seconds "What is next?");
3. Procedural description (for the first step in table wiping, "Go get the sponge").

Procedural descriptions will be most helpful as prompts when teaching new tasks to students who have some ability to understand simple verbal instructions. Once a student has partially or completely mastered a task, questioning prompts may act as less intrusive but still very helpful prompts. Initially, verbal instructions that simply state the response will be used as the to-be-learned S^D for the entire task ("Cross the street when it's safe"). However, once the skill has been mastered, students should be taught to respond to natural S^Ds such as the need to get to the other side of a street. At these times, if a student hesitates, stating the response then serves as a verbal prompt.

However the teacher decides to provide instructions, certain qualitative aspects of the instructions must match the learner's language abilities (Berman, 1973). These include the number of specific instructions given simultaneously, the length of instruction, the complexity of language in the instructions, and whether gestures and demonstrations accompany them.

Modeling consists of demonstrating part or all of the desired behavior to the learner and having the learner imitate or repeat the action immediately. The modeled response may be performed by the teacher or by peers, or it may be represented more permanently through illustrations (copying a printed name card; using a coin equivalency card to make change; following a series of pictures to make iced tea or soup).

Since the learner must see the demonstration in order to imitate, visual-attending skills are important and imitative skills are essential. The effectiveness of modeling as a prompt with severely handicapped individuals is increased when:

1. The individual's attention is gained prior to presenting the model. If the student attends part of the time, verbal or physical prompts may be used along with shaping to improve attending behavior.
2. The individual readily imitates movements and sounds and this imitative behavior is under stimulus control.
   a. If the individual imitates part of the time, physical prompts may be used after the model is presented in conjunction with shaping to encourage better imitations.
   b. If the individual does not imitate or imitates only infrequently, imitation skills must be taught before using modeling as a method to prompt behavior.
3. If direction of the response is important, the orientation of the viewed model is the same as it will be when the individual performs the skill (Parton, 1976).
4. The length of complexity of the modeled response or the chain of responses is short and simple. When errors occur in a student's imitations, the task analysis of the skill may need revision.

Cuing a behavior, at times similar to modeling, is different from manual guidance in that cuing directs the learner's attention to the teaching materials without physical contact. For example, in a multiple-

choice object location task, a child is taught to associate a coin with a particular prize card made from vending machine photos, in the presence of the instruction (S^D), "Which coin goes with this price?" The correct choice may be cued in a variety of ways.

1. Movement cues—Pointing to, touching, or tapping beside the correct choice;
2. Position cues—Placing the correct choice closest to the student;
3. Redundancy cues—Pairing one or more dimensions of color, shape, size, or position (as in position cues) with the correct choice (e.g., color: a white piece of paper is always placed under the correct choice while other choices all have red paper or perhaps no paper; size: the correct choice is always physically larger than the other choices as with some coins).

In an effort to learn more about cuing, Gold (1972) compared the effectiveness of color-redundancy cuing with form cuing for severely handicapped individuals learning to assemble bicycle brakes in a sheltered workshop. Color cues were placed on one side of every part so that when assembled correctly the colored part faced the worker. The presence of color cues led to significantly faster acquisition and longer retention of the task than did cues provided only by the form or shape of the individual brake parts.

A fourth type of cuing, *match-to-sample,* is similar to modeling. When prompting by means of match-to-sample, the teacher simply gives the instruction (S^D) ("Find the nickel") and cues the correct response by showing the learner a sample of the correct choice. The learner merely must select a matching object from a group of choices. While movement cues rely only upon attending and imitation skills to successfully prompt a response, redundancy and match-to-sample cues depend upon the ability to discriminate visually between dimensions such as color, size, and shape. In addition, the ability to use match-to-sample cues requires that the learner to distinguish similarities between stimuli. If a student has difficulty discriminating between different samples of a single dimension (e.g., different shapes of the same color and size), additional redundant cues should facilitate the discrimination (Fisher & Zeaman, 1973; Zeaman & House, 1963). That is, a person will learn to select the circular shape more quickly when it is represented as a large, red circle shown with a plain, small square. The difference between the choices is made more obvious by adding additional redundant stimuli. Likewise, difficulties in matching may be overcome by offering fewer choices and, more importantly, by making all the nonmatching choices differ widely from the stimulus object to be matched (Gold & Scott, 1971).

Manual guidance, sometimes referred to as *molding* a behavior or *physical prompting,* consists of various degrees of "putting the learner through" the response. The difference between "putting through" and "doing for" is subtle but important. For example, complete manual guidance during dressing may mean standing behind a child, taking the back of his hands and moving his fingers to grasp the top of his pants, and pulling upward. The child's pants are not simply pulled up for him.

As with other types of response primes, when manual guidance is being faded, it may simply consist of a small portion of the actual response—touching the back of a learner's elbow to begin an arm-moving forward or touching the bottom lip rather than molding the lips to prompt an "m" sound. At this fading stage, the stimulus control is being transferred from a manual guidance S^D to more natural stimuli, often in the form of verbal commands or situational stimuli. In other words, a learner is made to attend to stimuli that have more relevance to the behavior than the artificially applied prompting stimuli. This fading process is illustrated in Figure 5.3.

Prompts Systems.   Prompts may be used singularly, in combination, or as part of a hierarchy of prompts. If prompts are arranged in order of complexity and reliance upon prerequisite skills, manual guidance is the least complex because it relies primarily on cooperation and minimal attention. Manual guidance is also the *most* intrusive in that the learner performs very little of the response alone. Manual guidance would be followed in *decreasing* intrusiveness and *increasing* difficulty by cuing (movement cues, position cues, and match-to-sample cues), modeling, verbal direction (oral, then written), and naturally occurring prompts and cues.

At each level of complexity, an individual prompt may range from complete assistance (serving to evoke the complete response) to partial assistance (serving to evoke less than the complete response). Complete and partial manual guidance prompts are illustrated in Figure 5-3.

Prompt hierarchies consist of a sequence of two or more "levels" of prompts arranged and used in a *least to most intrusive order* or a *most to least intrusive order.* Lent and his colleagues (Lent & McLean, 1976) have used a prompt hierarchy in which a teacher advances to increasing levels of instructional assistance depending upon the learner's ability to respond in a task. Since their first use of this least-to-most system, many other researchers have applied this specific three-level hierarchy of (a) verbal instructions, (b) verbal instructions plus a model, and (c) verbal instructions plus physical assistance. As shown in Figure 5.4, the *system of least intrusive prompts* is applied one level at a time until the student is able to complete the response successfully. A short latency period (usually from 3 to 5 seconds but longer or shorter depending on the task or student) is allowed for the response after the instructional cue is pre-

FIGURE 5.3.

Stages in the Acquisition of Eye Contact from a Completely Guided Response to Total Fading of the Prompt

| Stage of Behavior Acquisition | Antecedent Stimuli | | Behaviors | Consequence |
	Instructions	Manual Guidance		
Beginning	"Look at me."	Turns head with both hands	Child's head is manually turned to face teacher and held until the eyes approximate contact	Praise, 5 seconds music (continuous schedule)
Middle	"Look at me."	Touches cheek and applies gentle turning pressure	Child turns head toward teacher after touch on cheek and looks at teacher	Praise, 5 seconds music (continuous schedule)
Final	"Look at me."		Child turns and looks at teacher	Praise, 5 seconds music (Music faded to intermittent schedule after criterion of 10 consecutive correct responses is met.)

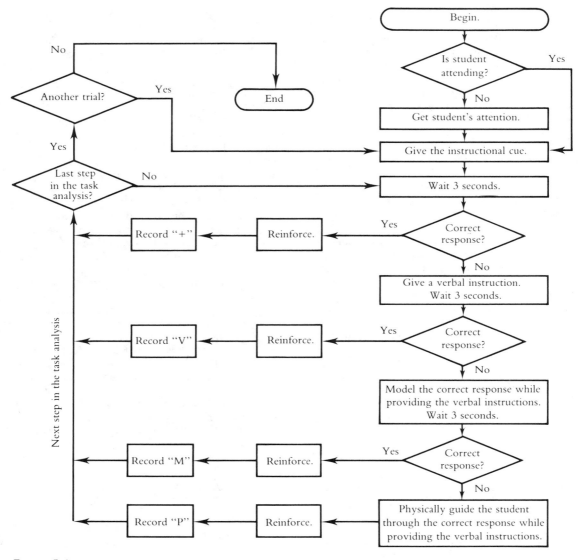

FIGURE 5.4.
System of Least Intrusive Prompts
SOURCE: Credit for this illustration must be given to Joan Miller, University of Virginia, 1981.

sented, as well as after each successive prompt. If no response occurs during this time, the next, more intrusive prompt is provided. If an error is made it is interrupted immediately and the next level of prompt is given. The responding student usually receives verbal reinforcement regardless of what level of prompt was required.

Tucker and Berry (1980) used this least prompt system to teach six severely handicapped students to put on their hearing aids. Cuvo and his colleagues have used "least prompts" to teach moderately to severely retarded students janitorial skills (Cuvo, Leaf, & Borakove, 1978), cooking skills (Johnson & Cuvo, 1981), and sewing and mending (Cronin & Cuvo, 1979). Labeling with signs and playing a simple board game were taught using least prompts to six severely handicapped students (Renzaglia & Snell, Note 2).

The least prompt system of verbal, model, and physical prompts lends itself well to a variety of tasks (and will be referred to in later chapters of this book). However, it must be matched carefully to the student's level of functioning. For example, students who do not imitate generally will be unable to use the first two prompt levels. For these students, variations using two or three simpler prompts may be employed. Those students who do not respond well to verbal cues but do imitate or follow gestural prompts (such as pointing) might be given prompts in the following order:

1. Model plus verbal (or gestural plus verbal depending upon the behavior being prompted),
2. Partial physical plus verbal (less than half of the behavior prompted),
3. Full physical plus verbal (the entire behavior prompted).

It would be possible to omit a partial physical and use only two prompt levels. Students unskilled in using model prompts might be given two or three levels of physical plus verbal prompts ranging from partial to complete assists. The same general procedures used with the verbal-model-physical prompt hierarchy and shown in Figure 5.4 would be applied with these simpler systems (that is, always allow an independent response first, interrupt errors with the next level of prompt, wait the latency period between prompts, etc.).

Cuvo et al. (1978) used two interesting variations of this prompting system when teaching janitorial tasks. On a few steps that proved extra difficult, a most-to-least order of prompts was employed; thus physical plus verbal prompts were used first. At some point, the trainer switched to model plus verbal prompt; later a verbal prompt was used, followed finally by no prompts at all. (It would also be possible to further task analyze these difficult steps, creating more steps, and continue the least-to-most intrusive system.)

A second novel variation of this prompt system by Cuvo et al. (1978) included the use of two even more minimal prompts during maintenance training, after the student had met acquisition criteria. That is, before using the verbal-model-physical sequence, a teacher would first try a confirmation prompt and secondly a nonspecific question prompt.

1. Confirmation;
2. Nonspecific question ("What's next?");
3. Verbal;
4. Verbal plus model;
5. Verbal plus physical assistance.

Confirmation consisted of saying "yes" to a student who had begun but not completed a step in the task. If this didn't work or there was no opportunity to use a confirmation prompt, then the student would be asked, "What's next?" Remaining prompts in the hierarchy would be used only if necessary.

Graduated guidance is a second response prompt system. Unlike the system of least intrusive prompts, graduated guidance uses most intrusive to least intrusive prompts. A few variations of graduated guidance have been described to teach eating (Azrin & Armstrong, 1973; O'Brien & Azrin, 1972; Richman, Sonderby, & Kahn, 1980; Stimbert, Minor, & McCoy, 1977); dressing (Azrin, Schaeffer, & Wesolowski, 1976; Foxx, 1981); aspects of toileting; and physical fitness exercises (Moon, Renzaglia, Ruth, & Talarico, Note 3).

The most frequently applied version of graduated guidance uses "constant contact" physical assistance applied by the teacher to the student first at the hand, then the wrist, the forearm, the elbow, and finally the shoulder. This order gradually reduces the physical prompt. Initially the student is guided through the steps of the task—the teacher's hand over the student's hand—with *only as much physical assistance as is necessary for the student to complete the task.* Over successive trials, the teacher reduces the physical assistance by shifting her hand to the student's wrist. The teacher will return her hand to the student's hand when more control is necessary or if errors or long hesitations occur. Next, for as many steps as possible, the teacher's guiding hand is shifted upward further, first to the forearm, then to the elbow and shoulder, as the student continues to successfully perform the task.

Thus graduated guidance moves the student forward through all the steps in the task, like most applications of a least intrusive prompt system. However, both prompt systems can be applied singly to one step in a task, as in backward chaining. The two systems differ in the fading procedure. In least prompts, because the student is given an opportunity to respond on every step with increasing assistance, the student is generally given only as much prompting as he or she needs. Over successive trials, the student uses less and less assistance as learning occurs. In graduated guidance, the teacher must gauge the reduction in physical assistance mainly on the moment-to-moment, subtle pressure cues between her guiding hands and the student's. While it might be possible to systematize fading by designating a certain number of trials at each level of prompt (20 trials at hand, 20 at wrist, 20 at forearm, etc.), this schedule is difficult to guess. There is no research to substantiate this use of graduated guidance.

A second type of graduated guidance (Foxx, 1981) uses the following progression of physical prompts:

1. *Full graduated guidance*—Teacher holds hands over student's hands using as little physical guidance as

is needed to guide student through the steps in the task.

2. *Partial graduated guidance*—Teacher maintains only thumb and forefinger contact with the student's hands, requiring, for example, the student to grasp a spoon alone.

3. *Shadowing*—Teacher keeps hands within one inch of the student's hands but does not actually touch the student's hands.

Moon et al. (Note 3) used three levels of graduated guidance to teach severely handicapped young adults sit-ups, push-ups, sit, bob and reach, chin-up, and squat thrust exercises. The levels all included a verbal prompt—(a) full hand prompt (molding of the hand around the body part involved in the movement); (b) fingertip guidance using little force; (c) verbal prompt alone.

In most forms of graduated guidance, verbal reinforcement is given continuously for steps completed. In many applications, an edible or an activity reinforcer is provided at the end of the chain. Whenever the student resists or tries to pull away from the physical guidance, the trainer holds the student's resistive hand in place until the student relaxes. No movement is prompted by the trainer until the student stops "fighting" the physical assistance.

Physical guidance may be a mild irritant to the student (Foxx, 1981). To avoid the irritant of being guided, the student begins to imitate independent movement on various steps in the chain. If avoidance learning partially or wholly explains fading, it is critical for the teacher to be sensitive moment-by-moment to any pressure cues indicating the student is performing more independently; these cues should result in immediate reduction of physical assistance.

Fading and Prompts

Fading is the gradual changing of the stimulus "controlling an organism's performance to another stimulus, reinforcer, or contingency usually with the intent of maintaining the performance without loss or alteration, but under new conditions" (White, 1971, p. 63). To maintain performance, fading must be gradual, moving for example from complete prompts to partial prompts. Fading may also include reducing the number of prompts provided (demonstration and instructions faded to just instructions) and substituting more complex prompts for less complex prompts as long as the individual has the necessary skills (see Figure 5.3).

Elimination of prompts or fading may be done systematically. If prompts are removed "cold turkey," the learner may fail, which impedes performance. Thus fading is best if it is a planned and

orderly transfer of control from prompts to the natural cues. Above all, prompts should be faded as rapidly as possible without excessive error or loss of the behavior.

Moving Through a Prompt Hierarchy. In a system of least prompts and more structured forms of graduated guidance, prompts are faded naturally. On every teaching trial, the student has an opportunity to perform without assistance and then with increasing amounts of help. For example, first a verbal prompt is given, then verbal instruction plus a model, and finally verbal instructions and physical assistance. The sooner the student responds correctly, the sooner he or she receives reinforcement, which contributes to fading. At times, especially in different steps and after lapses in training sessions, students will require more assistance than usual or will need help on steps that had been performed before without help. This apparent backtracking should be only temporary, until the student returns to the earlier performance level. Some times, however, learning can be assisted by analyzing a difficult step again—breaking it down further or selecting an alternate method and eliminating the difficult step altogether.

When using a system of least prompts and recording training data, the teacher will discover that, over successive sessions, less intrusive prompts (verbal instructions and models) are used more often than more intrusive ones (models and physical assistance). The number of unprompted or independent responses will gradually increase.

At times the teacher may want to provide more intrusive reinforcement for responses made independently than for prompted responses. This strategy, which can apply to any prompt procedure, is called *differential reinforcement*. It may be used most effectively when students seem to rely on verbal prompts or least prompts that are less intrusive. Differential reinforcement motivates students who have already made progress to perform without prompts. However, students who appear to rely on physical prompts over a period of more than a week or two are likely to need more reinforcement, a simplification of the difficult step or steps, or more training each day rather than differential reinforcement.

It is possible that the task is simply too hard, and easier or prerequisite skills should be taught first. The student who has made no progress in training (perhaps intervention data show little or no change over baseline) and consistently relies on physical prompts may be engaging in behavior that is incompatible with learning (Etzel & LeBlanc, 1979). For example, poor visual attention and excessive self-stimulation may need to be modified as part of the skill instruction procedure.

With any least prompt system, training criteria can be set to facilitate fading. This procedure is illustrated in Table 5.1 and Figure 5.5 with a task analysis of playing a cassette tape recorder.

Reducing the Saliency of the Stimulus Prompts. When color, picture, or word cues are used to prompt a response, these too must be faded. Stimulus prompts used in the classroom are more commonly faded by gradually reducing their visibility. For example, if words are taught by pairing a picture cue with each word, the teacher can use three to six successively less obvious variations of the picture while providing perhaps five trials with each of the levels of picture fading (see Figure 5.6). It is critical that the student attend to the S^D (in this case, the word) rather than simply the picture. Otherwise the S^D will be meaningless when the picture is finally faded. Because fading of stimulus prompts this way requires a variety of materials (six different versions of each picture prompt), prompting procedures like these are less common in classrooms than response prompts.

Time Delay. Progressive time delay procedures are another means of gradually fading prompts (Touchette, 1971). In time delay, the customary prompt is

TABLE 5-1. Plan for Fading and Error Correction for Teaching the Skill of Playing a Tape Recorder

Method of Instruction: System of least prompts
1. Verbal (V)
2. Verbal plus model (M)
3. Verbal plus physical (P)

Plan for Fading:
For a given behavior.
1. After 3 consecutive corrects no prompts are allowed; treat as an error (see step 9 in the task analysis).
2. After 3 consecutive V (see steps 8 and 11) or M (see step 7), no prompts of greater "strength" are allowed; if needed treat as an error.
3. After 4 consecutive days (minimum of 5 training trials per day) of P scores on a given behavior (step) (with errors also recorded on the probe for that behavior) that behavior (step) should be task analyzed into smaller steps.

Error Correction: Firmly say "No, that's not how you play the tape recorder"; then physically put the student through the step saying nothing. Record behavior as a "—" with a C for correction. During reading do not look or talk to student; then continue with next step.

delayed by gradually increasing increments of time, allowing the learner to anticipate the correct response without assistance. Though less frequently used than other prompt-fading procedures, time delay has been applied to teach severely handicapped learners to follow instructions (Striefel, Bryan, & Aikins, 1974; Striefel, Wetherby, & Karlan, 1976); to read manual signs (Smeets & Striefel, 1976a) and to sign (Browder, Morris, & Snell, 1981; Kleinert & Gast, 1982; Smeets & Striefel, 1976b; Stremel-Campbell, Cantrell, & Halle, 1977); to sign and play a table game (Renzaglia & Snell, Note 2); to request lunch (Halle, Marshall, & Spradlin, 1979) and other activities (Halle, Baer, & Spradlin, 1981); and to make beds (Snell, 1982).

For example, in sign training the teacher must first decide whether physical or model prompts are best, since a single prompt is used more easily with time delay. (However, more than one prompt—a hierarchy of prompts—may be used, as illustrated in Browder, Morris, and Snell, 1981, and Snell, 1982). If the student is a good imitator, a model is best, with physical assistance used only to correct errors. However, if a student cannot accurately reproduce a modeled sign, a physical prompt is appropriate.

After selecting functional signs and reinforcers, the teacher identifies the amounts or levels of time delay in seconds. As described in more detail in Snell and Gast (1981), there are many possibilities. However, a no-delay or 0 seconds level is always used initially—the prompt is swiftly given after the S^D—when the student first begins instruction. Next, gradually increased increments are introduced, delaying the prompt and giving the student more time to respond independently. Delay levels may consist of 0, 2, 4, 6, 8 seconds; 0, 1, 2, . . . 8 seconds; 0, 4 seconds; or other combinations. It is important to end with a delay period long enough for the student to respond, which for some motorically impaired learners may be longer than 8 seconds.

Once delay levels are chosen, the teacher may specify the number of trials to be carried out at each level. Although a wide variety of tasks have been taught, the number of trials have included 1 trial per delay level, 3, 5, and 10 trials. Other teachers may wish to be less structured and simply advance to the next delay level after several successive prompted corrects and backtrack to the previous delay level after any error made before the prompt is presented.

Signs can be taught in *serial training order* one at a time to a set criterion, adding a second, then mixing the two; adding a third, then mixing the three; and so on. However, a number of researchers have made a good case for *concurrent task sequencing,* where two or more skills are taught at the same time (Holvoet,

Teacher: _____

Instructional Cue: "Play music"

Target Behavior: Inserting and playing a tape in a battery operated tape recorder

STUDENT NAME AND DATE

	10/15		
	1	2	3
1. Push the button to open the lid.	M	M	V
2. Pick up the tape.	+	+	+
3. Put the tape in.	P	P	M
4. Push tape down.	M	+	V
5. Close lid.	+	V	+
6. Press play.	+	+	+
7. Press stop (after listening to whole 10 second segment)	V	V	V
8. Press rewind.	M	M	M
9. Push the button to open the lid.	V	V	V
10. Take out tape.	V	V	V
11. Put tape on table.	+	V	+
12. Close lid.	V	+	V

Recording Key: + for correct, – for incorrect or no response within 3 seconds.

Training: + for independ. V for verbal, M for model, and P for physical.

Criterion: 100% accuracy with no prompts for 3 consecutive days.

Materials: Tape recorder (either battery-operated or with plug already plugged in); tape with a 10-second segment of student's preferred type of music.

Response Latency: 3 seconds

Figure 5.5.
Task Analysis Data Sheet for Playing a Cassette Tape Recorder

FIGURE 5-6.
Fading Levels for a Picture Cue
SOURCE: *Teaching Sight Words to the Moderately and Severely Mentally Retarded* by D.M. Browder. Unpublished doctoral dissertation, University of Virginia, 1981. Used with permission.

Guess, Mulligan, & Brown, 1980; Panyan & Hall, 1978; Waldo, Guess, & Flanagan, 1982). Using this approach, signs would be taught in groups of two to four, with multiple trials on each sign and rotating across the group in a mixed fashion. In either case, each sign is taught using the planned procedure—for example, five trials at delay levels 0, 2, 4, 6, and 8 seconds. The general method illustrated in Figure 5.7 describes the teacher's behavior and Table 5.2 illustrates the signing application more specifically.

As the teacher gives each additional trial after the 0 delay level, he must count the number of seconds silently to delay the prompt and allow the student to

respond. Research with signing indicates that moderately to severely handicapped students correctly anticipated the delayed prompt (responded correctly before the prompt) at increments from 2 to 8 seconds. Generally successive signs were learned more quickly (Renzaglia & Snell, Note 2). At the longest delay level, unlimited trials are often allowed, though students may learn the sign before getting to this level.

Time delay requires rather different teacher responses from other instructional procedures. It is an effective procedure to teach students with a minimum of errors.[4]

Strategies Involving Consequences

Shaping

Shaping and chaining are two major reinforcement strategies used to build new behaviors and to improve or expand present behaviors. Both involve selectively providing reinforcing consequences for certain improvements in behavior or for specific amounts of behavior. The teacher must focus carefully on the learner's responses and make instant judgments about any particular response in comparison to earlier occurrences and the targeted criterion level.

Shaping consists of reinforcing successive approximations or better and better "attempts" at the target response. Every behavior or response actually exists within a larger response class—slight variations of the same basic movement. For example, you do not always sit in exactly the same way; however, we may think of each variation of "resting primarily upon the buttocks or haunches" as being within the sitting response class. When a response is not in the student's repertoire, the teacher must use prerequisite response classes—earlier approximations which lead to the target response. To teach walking to delayed children, these prerequisites would include (*a*) weight bearing, or standing while holding onto a table, and (*b*) "cruising," or moving in a side-step fashion while holding onto a table. Knowing which response

[4]For further background on time delay of prompts, see Snell and Gast (1981) or any of the other studies cited.

TABLE 5.2 Concurrent Task Sequencing of Signing

S^D or To-Be-Learned Stimuli	Delay	Prompt	Response	Reinforcement
Point to a glass of Coke. "What is this?" (Also teach signs for *cracker, glass,* and *napkin*)	0 sec. 2 sec. 4 sec. 6 sec. 8 sec. (5 trials of each level)	Teacher models sign for *pop*.	Student signs *pop*.	Teacher praises student, saying "Good, you made the sign for *pop*," and gives her a sip.

NOTE: The skills of preparing snacks and cleaning up, requesting and passing food, pouring Coke from can to glass, and opening a pop can are taught along with the 4 signs.

Time Delay

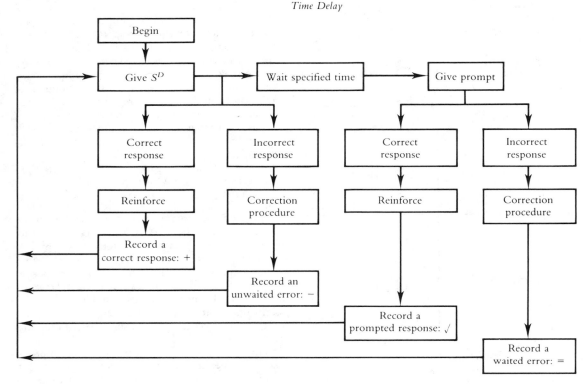

FIGURE 5.7

Flow Chart Illustrating Time Delay Procedure

SOURCE: Credit for this illustration must be given to Sherri Owen, University of Virginia, 1981.

classes represent earlier approximations of a target behavior is part of the skill of shaping.

A closer examination of shaping reveals that extinction plays a complementary role to reinforcement. As each successively closer approximation of the desired response is reinforced, the earlier, less precise approximations are no longer reinforced. They are thereby placed on extinction. Thus shaping leads to the development of new behaviors that often do not resemble earlier approximations.

Response Chaining

At times called *forward* and *backward shaping,* response chaining differs from shaping. While shaping is used to develop new behaviors, chaining is used (usually with shaping) to "link together" a series of functionally related responses. Most skills actually consist of a chain of smaller component responses. For example, self-care behaviors (toileting, eating), daily living skills (vacuuming a room, grocery shopping), and vocational tasks (parts assembly, "punching in" at work) provide many examples of response chains. Learning a chain or sequence of responses means that

the student must attend to the stimuli in each successive step as the S^D for the next step in the chain.

To teach these chains, the response is first divided into an ordered list of separate "teachable" behaviors, usually through task analysis. Since chaining may proceed forward or backward across the sequence of behaviors, the teacher must select the order in which the components will be taught. In Figure 5.8, face washing is analyzed into steps arranged backward from the bottom of the graph to the top. Face washing could be divided into 10 steps or 40 steps, depending on how finely the chain is separated. The number of responses any given chain is divided into, though somewhat arbitrary, will vary for different levels of beginning skills. It must meet the following general criteria.

1. Each step must be observable and easily measured.
2. The chain must be divided finely enough that the addition of each successive step does not result in an excess of errors.
3. There must not be too many steps, or instruction

becomes inefficient. If chaining proceeds *forward,* one of at least three methods may be used.

Either all steps are taught simultaneously in their natural order of performance, or steps are taught one at a time in a forward progression. A third method may include dividing an excessively long chain into several shorter chains, and teaching each shorter chain in a forward all-steps-at-a-time manner. Once the first component chain is mastered, the second would be taught but preceded by independent performance of the first segment, and so on until all components are learned and successively linked together.

When teaching a student to perform *one step at at time,* the first unmastered step in the chain is identified through baseline observations. Instruction be-

gins at that point, with the student performing earlier steps independently. If the baseline performance is inconsistent and only some nonsequential steps are mastered, instruction should start with the first step. It may be necessary to shape this first behavior until no errors occur or to prompt the learner. Successive approximations are reinforced until the student can adequately perform the first teaching step without assistance. Then he or she is taught to perform the next step by shaping or prompting, yet is expected to continue to correctly complete the preceding, already mastered, step. The student is reinforced only after completion of the *teaching step.* The individual may or may not be assisted through all the remaining steps in the chain, but is not expected to perform them independently until each successive step in the sequence is

FIGURE 5.8.

Graph Especially Useful in Recording Frequency of Correctly Chained Responses in Forward and Backward Chaining

This figure records an individual's performance in face-washing skills, taught by backward chaining. Note that steps 8 and 9 proved unnecessary during later performances and were omitted from the chain.

Forward Sequential Order in Performance	Backward Teaching Order
1.	20. Turn on water
2.	19. Pick up wash cloth
3.	18. Wet cloth and squeeze out
4.	17. Wet entire face with cloth
5.	16. Pick up soap & soap cloth
6.	15. Wipe soapy cloth across face
7.	14. Scrub face with cloth
8.	13. Rinse cloth & squeeze out
9.	12. Wipe face with cloth
10.	11. Rinse cloth & squeeze out
11.	10. Open eyes, look in mirror for soap
12.	9. Wipe face with cloth
13.	8. Rinse cloth & squeeze
14.	7. Wipe face clean with cloth
15.	6. Rinse cloth & squeeze
16.	5. Hang face cloth on rack
17.	4. Rinse sink
18.	3. Turn off water
19.	2. Dry face on towel
20.	1. Straighten towel

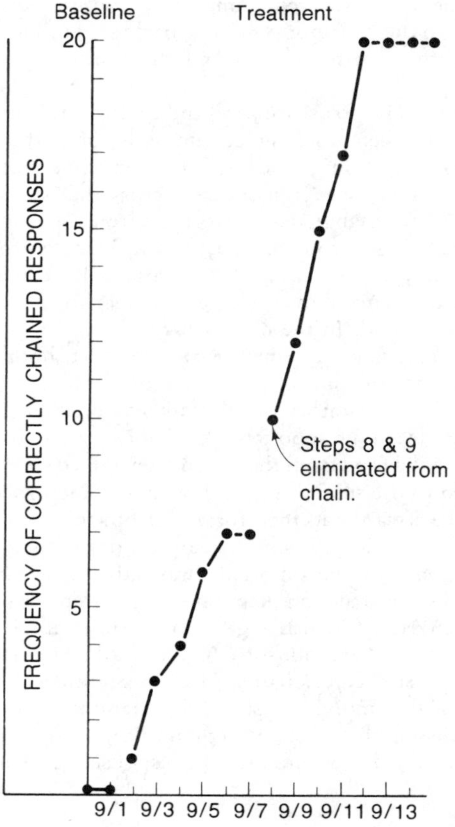

mastered. If, for example, the skill of shoe tying is to be taught through forward chaining, the first skill in the sequence to be mastered is the half-knot (or just crossing the two shoelaces). Later, the bow loop and then the remaining steps in the chain are taught.

In backward chaining, teaching generally begins with the last step and progresses toward the beginning of the chain. Sometimes baseline performance indicates that the learner has mastered one or more steps at the end of the chain. For example, in Figure 5.8, the student was able to straighten the towel during baseline testing. Teaching therefore would begin with the 19th step—drying face—but the learner would be expected to continue unprompted performance of the last step—straightening the towel. With some behaviors (eating, toileting, dressing), the individual actually may be guided through the preceding steps in the chain until the teaching step is reached. At other times, the learner may simply be started at the teaching step. Then, by shaping or prompting, this unmastered step is taught. Reinforcement is given only after the *last step* in the chain is completed. When you teach steps that precede the last step, the student may be prompted to perform the target step but is expected to perform all remaining steps in the chain without assistance. He then receives reinforcement. Eventually, as the remaining steps are learned and added to the behavior chain in a backward order, the entire chain is performed and the learner is reinforced.

It is possible to use forward and backward chaining together when teaching certain skills or particular students, including students whose baseline performance shows scattered success across the behavior chain (that is, ability to perform more than a single step or a single group of steps). Both chaining procedures may also be combined when a skill's primary behavior occurs in the middle of a longer chain rather than at its end. In the basic self-care skills of eating with a spoon and elimination on the toilet, both the eating and toileting responses are preceded and followed by preparatory or related behaviors. The first step in teaching spoon use probably would be to remove the food from the spoon after a filled spoon is guided to the student's lips. Teaching could proceed both backward and then forward from this step.

Teaching all steps simultaneously, or teaching the whole task, can be a more natural and perhaps faster method of instruction than training one step at a time (e.g., Azrin & Armstrong, 1973; Azrin et al., 1976; Cuvo et al., 1978; Johnson & Cuvo, 1981). However, some researchers (Bellamy, Horner, & Inman, 1979) suggest that individual steps, for example on vocational assembly tasks, be taught until an accuracy rate of 80% is achieved and then the responses be chained together.

Functional Response-Reinforcer Relationships

Learning in the severely handicapped may be facilitated by establishing functional relationships between the response to be learned and the reinforcer (Janssen & Guess, 1978; Litt & Schreibman, 1981; Saunders & Sailor, 1979; Williams, Koegel, & Egel, 1981). That is, when reinforcement is either specifically matched to a given response (reinforcer specificity) or is the natural outcome of performing a behavior (functional reinforcement), more rapid learning of the response appears to result. For example, Saunders and Sailor (1979) found that severely handicapped students were reinforced with immediate access to the specific toy they were asked to label; furthermore, toy labels were learned more quickly this way than when a student was given either a toy whose label was not being taught or a training toy that had not just been labeled. Based upon these findings, Goetz, Schuler, and Sailor (1979) suggested that the instruction of words associated with reinforcing events (such as *music, eat,* or *swing*) would be successful more quickly than with words not so associated (such as *house, table,* or *shoe*). Furthermore, simply using different reinforcers for different responses leads to faster learning than using a single reinforcer across responses or randomly presenting reinforcers.

Premack's Principle

This principle (Premack, 1959), often referred to as "Grandma's Law," follows the common childhood dictum, "First you eat your vegetables; then you can have your dessert." In other words, if the opportunity to perform a high probability behavior (HPB) is contingent upon the performance of a low probability behavior (LPB), the frequency of the LPB will increase as a result of positive reinforcement. HPBs are simply activities that are reinforcing to an individual (riding bikes, recess, listening to music on earphones, even being allowed to run and yell for 3 minutes) that may be parceled out following the completion of less popular activities (sorting bolts of varying sizes, collating and stapling, finishing a specific clean-up task). HPBs can be readily identified as those activities a child consistently selects when given the opportunity to do what he prefers.

HPBs have an advantage over tangible reinforcers in that they tend to be readily available, free of cost, and naturally occurring instead of artificially applied—a feature important in maintaining learned behaviors. However, HPBs also tend to be time-consuming, disruptive, and not easily turned on and off. Each of these disadvantages can delay reinforcement, which, in turn, may mean accidental reinforcement of intervening behaviors. To counteract these potentially disastrous side-effects, a teacher can immediately reinforce the target behavior with tokens or activity "pictures/tickets" to exchange at a more convenient time. Both procedures remind the learner of the appropriate behavior and the delayed reinforcement, thus bridging the delay between behavior and reinforcement with a HPB. Kitchen timers may facilitate a student's understanding and cooperation, for they structure the beginning and end of a HPB.

Finally, it is not ethical to identify essential activities or use basic possessions as HPBs. Of course, the ethical issues surrounding the application and withdrawal of all intervention strategies must always be considered. As emphasized by Kazdin (1980),

The ideology of presenting activities and other potentially reinforcing events (e.g., meals and sleeping quarters) noncontingently was developed to ensure that individuals would not be deprived of basic human rights. Institutionalized clients are usually deprived of many amenities of living simply by virtue of their institutionalization. Withholding or depriving individuals of the already limited number of available reinforcers is viewed as unethical. (p. 139)

The solution lies in introducing a variety of novel, optional events as HPBs (special snack, use of a new bedspread, extra leisure time, etc.)

Error Correction Procedures

When a severely handicapped student responds with the wrong response, it is generally better to correct the error than simply to ignore it (Denny, 1966). If the student is acquiring the skill, the teacher will prompt the student and reduce the probability of error. However, errors are still possible and can be interrupted and corrected in any of a number of ways.

One way is to repeat the S^D immediately, giving another opportunity to perform but increasing the amount of assistance provided. For example, give a least intrusive but still effective prompt. This could include verbal instructions, a model, a pointing cue, physical assistance, etc.

The teacher holds up a clock that reads 4:30 and asks "What time is this?" The student replies "Four o'clock." The teacher moves the clock a little closer, points to the minute hand, and says "What time is this? Be sure to look at the minute hand." "It's 4:30," says the student. "Right, it reads 30 when the minute hand points straight down."

A second procedure is to simply interrupt the error and follow it immediately with the least amount of assistance needed to obtain a correct response; do not repeat the S^D.

A student is learning to set the table while the teacher prompts him through the steps using a system of least

prompts. On the first step (go into the kitchen) a verbal prompt was required. The student erred on the second step (open the dish cupboard) by opening the wrong cupboard. The teacher saw this error develop and stopped the student's hand as he tried to open the wrong cupboard. Next she immediately gave the verbal prompt "Open the dish cupboard" and waited 5 seconds. The student did not respond and looked confused. The teacher then repeated the verbal while modeling which cupboard to open. The student responded correctly and was praised.

A third approach is to interrupt the error and follow it immediately with a verbal prompt plus *physically assisted repeated practice.* Using the vocational assembly task illustrated next, Close, Irvin, Prehm, and Taylor (1978) demonstrated this correction procedure to be more effective than a single verbal-physical prompt or a verbal-gestural correction.

A student is learning a nut and bolt assembly task which requires: (a) picking up an axle nut from one compartment in the left hand; (b) rotating the nut with the right hand until the raised side faces up; (c) picking up an axle post from the other compartment with the right hand; (d) inserting it into the flat side of the nut; and (e) placing the completed assembly between the compartments. When the student forgets to rotate the nut the trainer says "Flat side in," and physically prompts the correct response, saying "Good." Then the nut is replaced in the bit flat side up and the student is assisted in picking it up. The trainer then prompts ("Flat side in") and physically assists the correct positioning of the nut in the student's hand. After five repetitions of this correction procedure in steps (a) and (b), the nut and bolt are assembled with physical assistance given only as needed. (pp. 272–273)

Once the student has learned all or most of the skill and moved to the fluency or maintenance stage, slightly different error correction procedures may be used. Because the student is more proficient at the skill, errors are infrequent and may be caused by distraction or carelessness rather than not knowing what to do. In these cases, one of the following procedures may be chosen.

1. The student who makes an error or hesitates may simply be given a brief period of time (10 to 15 seconds) to self-correct. Some errors, if uninterrupted, will provide natural correction cues. If a correction is not forthcoming, then one of the other procedures can be tried.
2. The error *might* be followed by a mild reprimand ("No," or "That's not right") plus a request to try the step again. If a second error results, some assistance would be given.
3. A minimal prompt—"What's next?" or verbal rehearsal of the last step correctly performed

("You just finished getting the plates, now what's next?")—may be applied as soon as the error is stopped. If the student stops before a step is complete, the teacher may confirm and urge him to continue ("That's right, keep going.").

4. Provide a mildly aversive statement ("No, that's not how you empty the trash"), possibly mention that the reinforcement will be withheld ("You can't be paid this time"), and physically assist the student through the step. This procedure should always be followed by an opportunity to repeat the task with reinforcement. If the same error is repeated for two to four consecutive trials, the teacher may want to reinstitute the prompt procedure.

There are other possible methods of correcting errors. However, to be effective, error correction procedures must:

1. Be matched to the learner's present level of functioning;
2. Be applied immediately and consistently;
3. Provide enough help to correct the error quickly;
4. Be suited in their amount of assistance and aversiveness (if any) to the student's stage of learning for that task; and
5. Be followed by additional opportunities to respond on the same task or step.

INTERVENTION STRATEGIES AIMED AT DECREASING BEHAVIOR

Is There Really a Problem?

As coherently illustrated by Gaylord-Ross (1980) and Voeltz, Evans, Derer, and Hanashiro (Note 4) in their models for the treatment of aberrant behavior, careful assessment of the so-called "behavior problem" must precede any intervention. "Not all excess behaviors are priority targets" suggest Voeltz et al. (Note 4, p. 2). Gaylord-Ross suggests that the teacher and parent first answer the following four questions and decide whether the problem behavior is severe or obtrusive enough to require intervention.

1. *Is the behavior causing physical harm to the student or others?*
2. *Is the behavior disrupting overall classroom instruction to a significant degree?*
3. *Does the behavior appear to be triggering collateral emotional reactions, e.g., excessive crying or screaming, extreme withdrawal?*
4. *Is the behavior so contextually inappropriate that it is leading to social exclusion and a limitation in the number of places and experiences in which the student can engage?* (p. 140)

If any of these questions is answered yes, baseline data must be collected to further substantiate the problem (see chapter 4). If the data do verify that a problem exists, Gaylord-Ross suggests that one further step be taken before planning an intervention—eliminating illnesses or other medical explanations for the behaviors. For example, chronic ear infections, fevers, and changes in medications are likely to result in visible behavioral changes. If medical factors can be identified as causing the problem, a corresponding medical intervention is the logical solution.

If medical causes are ruled out as the problem's source, then a behavioral analysis is continued until causative or maintaining factors are identified and corresponding intervention procedures selected. The best way to *decrease a behavior problem* is generally to *increase* one or more related skills. The student's IEP would therefore reflect those new skills prioritized to replace that student's severe deficits instead of merely including behavior reduction objectives (Voeltz et al., Note 4).

Withholding reinforcement (extinction), reinforcing other behaviors, removing reinforcers (punishment), and presenting aversives (punishment) are four different classes of consequences that can be provided contingent upon a behavior to reduce or eliminate that behavior. For many severely handicapped students, the antecedent application of classroom rules may also prevent undesirable behavior from occurring in the first place. Environmental modifications (such as changes in temperature, noise, amount of space available, number of activities or toys available) may make a strong and positive impact upon aberrant behavior. Finally, and generally most often, improvements in a student's curriculum may be needed to reduce inappropriate behaviors. These intervention procedures vary considerably in complexity, ease of implementation, and suitability to various students, behavior problems, and environments. They cannot be selected haphazardly or based on personal whim or preference. Procedures selected to reduce inappropriate behavior must meet four criteria:

1. Proven effective with the moderately and severely handicapped;
2. Matched to the likely causative or maintaining factors;
3. Simplest to use but still effective;
4. Least intrusive; in other words, the least punitive and most normalized and socially accepted procedure.

If intervention procedures have been carefully chosen and planned and competently and consistently applied, but the programs still fail to reasonably reduce the behavior after adequate trial, modifications must be made. The four criteria are still applied. *Either* a change is made in the existing intervention *or* the next most intrusive, but still effective, procedure is used.

Extinction

Extinction is the intentional withholding of positive reinforcement by the teacher (parent or peer) as a consequence of an individual's response (Figure 5.2). Reinforcement is not withdrawn, which would constitute punishment; rather it simply is not presented. To ignore a behavior that formerly was rewarded consistently places that behavior on extinction. The effect is a decrease in the frequency of the behavior. Because it is fairly easy to use and is less intrusive than most other behavior reduction procedures, extinction is the first treatment of choice when the behavior problem appears to be maintained by others' positive reinforcement of it.

With extinction, the rate of decrease of a behavior's frequency relates directly to its reinforcement history—its earlier schedule(s) of reinforcement. For example, if a behavior was always continuously reinforced, the change to extinction would be abrupt and highly noticeable to the individual and the behavior would extinguish rapidly. As few as one or two unreinforced instances of a behavior may lead to total cessation. However, an individual who performs well on an intermittent schedule (perhaps reinforcement of every 10th response) has learned to perform a number of times without reinforcement. During extinction, that person will continue with these bursts of performance before an eventual decline in frequency. Histories of gradually developed, variable, lean schedules (with many responses occurring before each reinforcement) lead to the strongest responses and are most resistant to extinction.

Some other factors combine with reinforcement history to affect the speed of extinction.

1. The *amount of reinforcement* presented during the learning or acquisition of the behavior: the greater the reinforcement for each behavior provided prior to extinction, the greater the resistance;
2. The *length of the learning period* before extinction is initiated: longer periods of reinforcement yield more extinction-resistant behaviors;
3. The *number of times* a behavior is placed on a lengthy extinction schedule: the more exposures to extinction the faster the behavior will extinguish during each successive schedule.

Although extinction is useful to reduce a large range of undesirable behaviors, there are some situations and some classes of behavior for which extinction is not recommended. First, extinction is not effective unless the reinforcers that are maintaining the undesirable behavior are known and can be controlled by the teacher. In classrooms, controlling peer reinforcement is difficult, which makes extinction ineffective for reducing mildly annoying behaviors such as swearing, burping, and showing off. When the mere performance of the behavior produces the reinforcement, such as with self-stimulation (i.e., rocking, arm movements, hand waving), the teacher cannot control reinforcement and therefore cannot contingently withhold the reinforcers.

Second, because extinction is slow, it is not recommended for use with destructive behaviors or self-injurious behaviors. Although extinction may eventually decrease the frequency of self-aggressive behavior, irreversible physical harm may occur before the behavior is eliminated. Clearly the use of extinction would be unethical here.

Because most seriously undesirable behaviors tend to have a long, varied reinforcement history, the rate of extinction may be very slow. Since consistency in the use of extinction is essential for its effectiveness, the teacher must determine his or her ability to tolerate the behavior. If the behavior occurs frequently, the need for consistency can become taxing. In addition, if the behavior is particularly disruptive and annoying to others in the classroom, even if it is not destructive, then using extinction is demanding for the teacher and the entire class. The requirement for consistency is strongly threatened in these situations.

In general, extinction is used easily and effectively as a contingent consequence with less frequently occurring misbehaviors when performance will not endanger the individual or others and is not self-reinforcing. In addition, the effects of extinction are greatly magnified when one or more desirable behaviors are reinforced. Reinforcing a student for all efforts made toward completing a task while ignoring her when she screams and pushes away her task materials will be more effective than simply ignoring the inappropriate behavior.

When extinction is first applied, the target behavior may become worse before it gets better. That is, before the frequency of the behavior declines it may increase. This effect, called *extinction burst,* appears to be due simply to the individual's prior learning that the behavior was followed by reinforcement. For example, temper tantrums and whining are shaped when we "give in" to the increased demands (the extinction burst) of a child placed on extinction. Reinforcing behavior during extinction bursts makes the effects of extinction take longer and may even render it ineffective for that behavior. If extinction for a period of roughly 5 to 10 days does not eliminate the behavior or reduce it to an acceptable level, another intervention procedure should be selected.

The "Fair Pair"

Although strengthening or shaping desirable behaviors is clearly the goal of education, teachers are also concerned with the reduction of behaviors that upset classroom routine. The "fair pair" rule (White & Haring, 1976) states that when it is necessary to decrease an undesirable behavior, you should select one or more desirable behaviors to increase at the same time. This procedure results in a repertoire of appropriate behaviors, providing the student with alternative responses rather than merely eliminating behavior. More opportunities to reinforce students positively are also created.

The desirable half of the "fair pair" of behaviors may simply be the behavior opposite of that to be eliminated (out-of-seat and in-seat; incorrect labels and correct labels). However, if this rule of thumb produces the absence of behavior (excessive crying and no crying), a better strategy might be to select a behavior that can be accelerated and cannot occur at the same time as the undesirable behavior. Depending upon the child's abilities, the positive half of "excessive crying" could be "requests items by name"; "handwaving and staring" could be paired with "eye contact with teacher and objects presented by the teacher." Teachers or parents using these procedures are differentially reinforcing behavior that is incompatible with the problem behavior while ignoring (or placing on extinction) the problem behavior. This procedure is called *differential reinforcement of incompatible behavior* or *DRI*. It is especially useful when the amount of reinforcement the target student obtains during an average day is fairly low *and* the behavior problem is either reinforcing in and of itself (e.g., stereotypic behavior) or results in attention from others (Gaylord-Ross, 1980).

A second procedure similar to DRI is *DRO* or *differential reinforcement of other behavior*. In this procedure the student is reinforced for performing other appropriate behavior which may not necessarily be incompatible with the problem behavior, but provides an alternative means for obtaining adult and peer attention. For example, when a 5-year-old sucks his thumb, both his tooth formation and social acceptance in the school and neighborhood may be affected. Giving the child praise or tokens to exchange for favorite activities for periods of time when he is not sucking his thumb is a DRO strategy.

Classroom Rules

When reinforcement for misbehavior cannot be controlled because it is given by the student's peers, classroom rules are a more effective means of behavior management than extinction. Inevitably there are *rules* to guide the effective use of rules in the classroom. First and most essential, the rules describe behavior in ways understandable to the students. In many situations, pictures and simple wording yield comprehensible rules; with other classrooms, role playing will result in more complete understanding. Invariably, however, it is the consistent enforcement of the rules that leads to this comprehension. In classrooms where comprehension skills are only in beginning stages, the use of simply stated rules is still justifiable for two reasons. First, even in early stages of language development, the child learns to associate an adult's facial expressions, tone of voice, and some words like "No!" or "Good!" with punishing or reinforcing consequences. Second, the rules may increase the teacher's consistency in applying various contingent consequences to behavior.

In addition to the verbal statement of rules in comprehensible terms, (*a*) rules should be stated positively whenever possible, so that appropriate behavior is described; (*b*) the number of rules should be limited so they can be enforced; and (*c*) the teacher should review new classroom rules daily until infractions decrease. Rules must be periodically revised if they are to remain relevant to the specific school situation, the classroom curriculum and individuals within that class. Whenever possible, class members should help formulate new rules and revise old rules.

If a rule is stated positively ("We eat with a spoon"), the teacher should attempt to reinforce those who follow the rule, restating the rule as they are praised ("Good eating with a spoon"). If positively stated rules are broken, the teacher may choose either to punish the behavior ("No, use the spoon," removal of food for 30 seconds) or to ignore it. If a rule is stated negatively ("No swearing in class"), infractions cannot be ignored but must be punished in some way or the rule becomes meaningless. However, with both types of rules, whenever an individual is punished for an infraction, the teacher should ask the child to restate the rule before punishment. Prompts should be offered if the child cannot state the rule. This verbal rehearsal of rules before punishment will help the child understand the contingency. The eventual self-rehearsal of rules is critical in self-control. Finally, if punishment is used, the teacher must determine the punishing consequences in advance as well as when they will be applied in relation to rule infractions (that is, whether a single warning will be given before punishment is applied or whether the child will be punished after the first infraction of the rule). The discussion of punishment below should aid in answering these questions.

Ecological Considerations

Gaylord-Ross (1980) provides good arguments for examining the effect of ecological variables on a student's misbehavior. Factors such as amount of space per student, heat, light, noise, and interesting activities or objects available all may influence behavior. For example, when the living environment of five profoundly retarded women in a rather austere institutional setting (many residents and few engaging objects) was enriched with activities and manipulable objects and differential reinforcement for engaging with these items, the women exhibited more adaptive behavior and far less maladaptive behavior (Horner, 1980).

Curriculum Modifications

Another important set of variables that may cause or maintain behavior problems are related to instructional curriculum. Possible modifications in curriculum should be investigated if the targeted misbehavior increases when certain instructional tasks are engaged in (Gaylord-Ross, 1980). There are at least four types of curriculum problems.

Task Is too Difficult. A student making many errors is obtaining little or no reinforcement. If the task is a high priority (e.g., toilet training) and there are no medical or physical reasons that it cannot be learned (e.g., the student is older than 2 years and does not have damage to the nerves controlling the bladder and bowel sphincters), then the task should be retained but the teaching procedure changed. For example, the task analysis may need more steps, prompts could be used to get the student responding, and possibly more time could be spent daily on the task. In other cases, the task may simply be too difficult and should be preceded by easier but still functional skills or taught in smaller fragments. At other times, a student may have a long history of failure on a given task and come to dislike it even though it is still unmastered. In these cases, it may be best to ask first whether the task is actually needed for the particular student. If it cannot be dropped altogether, it may be best to simply postpone work on it since it is associated with failure.

Task Is too Simple. In some cases skills students have already mastered are still actively "taught" by teachers rather than simply maintained through natural use. Boredom or unmotivated performance often results and in turn may lead to behavior problems during instruction.

Task Is not Preferred by Students. Is the task actually needed by the student? Will its mastery contribute to the student's immediate increased independence more than other tasks? If it is important, then the next area of concern is the reinforcement. Reinforcers may need to be changed completely; perhaps a new reinforcer hierarchy needs to be developed. A choice of reinforcers could be offered to avoid satiation. The task could be altered so that it is more game-like, with other peers possibly competing. For example, new manual signs can be taught with a gameboard (Renzaglia & Snell, Note 2), while functional sight words can be taught with a *Language Master* machine.

There Is Little or no Instruction. The obvious solution here is to develop and implement a functional curriculum. No matter how handicapped a student, boredom as a result of excessive down time is likely to cause inappropriate behavior.

Punishment

Punishment is defined by its effect on behavior; that is, it decreases the behavior which it follows. Figure 5.2 identifies two different punishing operations: the presentation of an aversive event (reprimand) and the removal of positive reinforcers (loss of privileges, removal of tokens, isolation from an enjoyable situation) immediately following a behavior. The first type of punishment includes aversive conditioning, overcorrection, and firm verbal statements: the second includes response cost and timeout. Both types of punishing consequences decrease the frequency of a behavior. If the behavior is not decreased, punishment has not occurred—the "aversives" presented actually were not aversive to that person or the events or objects removed were not reinforcing in the first place. As with reinforcers, punishers range along a hierarchy from primary to secondary and must be identified individually.

Along with a reduction in the punished behavior, other, less desirable effects may also occur. These may include a suppression of unpunished behaviors (desirable or undesirable); emotional reactions such as counteraggressive behavior, avoidance, escape, or anxiety in the punishment situation or in the presence of the punisher; a future reoccurrence of the punished behavior; and failure to suppress the behavior completely. Because of these potential side effects and because some forms of punishment are unacceptable, it is essential that teachers know and follow guidelines when seeking to decelerate behavior. Whenever punishment is used, the teacher should monitor any side effects and be prepared to revise or drop the program if they become extreme.

MacMillan, Forness, and Trumbull (1973) identified seven variables which alter the effects of punishment, discussed next.

Timing. The punishment should be delivered immediately after the misbehavior. The longer the delay between the undesirable act and the punishment, the less effective the punishment is in inhibiting the behavior. If a student has completed the behavior and punishment is delayed for some reason, it may be best to wait for the next instance of the behavior rather than risk punishing the wrong behavior or a desirable behavior.

Consistency. Punishment must be consistently applied for every instance of the behavior and by all persons involved with the student. Consistency includes carrying out threats. The contingency of punishment for a behavior will be learned most quickly if the same punishing consequence is applied every time the misbehavior occurs, at a point early in its performance or immediately after its termination.

Intensity. The initial administration of the punishment should be at full intensity, rather than escalating the intensity with each successive occurrence of the behavior. First the teacher must determine the intensity that constitutes punishment for an individual and then always apply that level of punishment. For example, if brief removal of dessert is not sufficiently aversive to control food stealing, then perhaps the entire meal must be removed temporarily. When using verbal aversives, intensity involves firmness, not loudness. In fact, soft, firm reprimands directed toward the appropriate person are more effective in a classroom than loud reprimands and avoid any spillover effect—the suppression of behavior in others located near the punished individual. In implementing the intensity rule, you must be careful not to overpunish.

Adaptation or satiation lessens the effects of a punisher upon a behavior and is related to both consistency and intensity. Escalating the intensity of a punisher often allows the student to adapt to each degree of punishment. The use of the same specific punishers to the exclusion of others can lead to satiation. Varying aversive consequences of the same intensity tends to increase awareness of the contingency.

Alternatives to the Behavior. Whenever punishment is used to reduce a behavior's frequency, alternatives to the punished behavior should be provided (see "Fair Pair"). This can be done by reinforcing behavior that competes with the punished behavior. When the competing behaviors are not in the student's repertoire, various prompts and shaping procedures should be used so that alternative behaviors can be learned and thus compete with undesirable or inappropriate behaviors.

Prior Relationship. The more positive the prior relationship of the one who punishes with the individual being punished, the more immediate the effects. When teachers who are "liked" by the students apply punishment (either present an aversive or withdraw reinforcement), they also automatically withdraw the reinforcing consequences of their attention and affection. This increases the effectiveness of the punishment.

Cognitive Variables. Finally, cognitive variables are of utmost importance in influencing the effects of punishment upon the severely handicapped. Since the goal of punishment is to decrease a behavior by teaching the recipient to associate aversive consequences with it, the student obviously must understand which behavior is being punished. Either the teacher should use simple terms to identify the behavior being punished at the time or the student should be asked to state the classroom rule which was broken. Furthermore, if punishment must be delayed, these simple verbal explanations become essential.

Selection of a Punishment Procedure

Aversive conditioning using strong primary aversives (such as electric shock and slapping) to eliminate behavior is only defensible in two general instances: when the behavior is so dangerous or self-destructive that positive reinforcement and extinction are not feasible and when all other intervention methods (reinforce competing response, extinction, milder punishment forms) have been applied competently and have been documented as unsuccessful. In most districts and public school settings, use of these procedures may be illegal. Clearly these procedures cannot be used without formal agency review and consultation with experienced professionals.

Firm Verbal Statements. A common punishment consists simply of firm verbal statements made as soon as the misbehavior occurs. Verbal punishment and threats are often overused, ineffective, and may even be reinforcing. However, when backed up by other methods (restraint, overcorrection, response cost, or timeout) and combined with positive reinforcement of appropriate behavior, firm verbal statements may serve as effective immediate aversives.

Generally these statements are short negative imperatives ("No!" "Stop!") or brief restatements of the broken rule ("No hitting!" "Stop eating with your hands!"). In addition, the teacher may firmly, but nonpainfully, grasp the child's shoulders to get his attention and stop or restrain the behavior. As the punishment for object banging and string twirling, Pendergrass (1972) combined verbal aversives ("No, don't bang!") with 2-minute timeouts and eliminated the behaviors. In a program to teach proper mealtime behavior, O'Brien and Azrin (1972) decreased incorrect responses such as touching food with hands, taking oversized bites, and drooling by use of an "interruption-extinction" procedure. The trainer said "No!" while returning the food to the plate and wiping the student's hand or mouth. After acquisition training, a timeout procedure, which consisted of food removal for 30 seconds, was combined with verbal punishment and the interruption of the response.

The teacher must be careful to prevent peers from thinking the punishment is intended for them. Statements should be brief, matched to the individual's comprehension, and accompanied by a frown or other nonverbal sign of disapproval. For some individuals, verbal punishment alone or in combination with brief restraint is sufficiently aversive to maintain low rates of a misbehavior. In sum, verbal statements may be employed primarily to stop and identify a misbehavior, but might also accompany an additional punishing consequence.

Response Cost. This procedure removes reinforcers the learner already has through a fine or penalty for the misbehavior. Fines may include the removal of money, tokens, points, stars, food, free time, or privileges. The removal of colored slips of paper on which the individual's name had been written constituted an effective punisher for emotionally disturbed boys (Hall, Axelrod, Foundopulos, Shellman, Campbell, & Cranston, 1971). For response cost to be used as a decelerating strategy, the punished individual must already have a valued commodity that can be removed and the economy must be planned carefully so that he does not go into debt, in which case motivation to perform can be severely dampened. Response cost is easily used as part of a primary positive intervention program in which the students earn reinforcers, such as in a token economy. As with other forms of punishment, the effectiveness of response cost increases when careful attention is given to the seven variables described earlier.

Timeout from Positive Reinforcement. Timeout achieves its punishing effects by the removal of positive reinforcers, generally teacher and peer attention. Applied contingent upon misbehavior, timeout eliminates social interaction and opportunities to obtain positive reinforcement. As a method to reduce inappropriate behaviors in the severely handicapped, timeout has been applied successfully to self-destructive behavior (Lucero, Frieman, Spoering, & Fehrenbacher, 1976), aggressiveness (Bostow & Bailey, 1969; White, Nielson, & Johnson, 1972), and disruption during mealtime (Barton, Guess, Garcia, & Baer, 1970).

In the simplest form of timeout, the teacher merely turns away from the misbehaving child and refuses to interact or present instructional stimuli for a brief time. As a more complex punishment, the misbehaving individual is removed from a reinforcing situation and taken or sent to a neutral place for some period. Return to the reinforcing situation is contingent upon the absence of misbehavior. A neutral place can be as simple as a chair facing the wall or a screened corner of a room. However, for students unlikely to remain in a chair, a small, empty room with adequate lighting and ventilation may be necessary. Although the ultimate effectiveness of timeout as a deceleration depends upon the consistency and immediacy of application, the user should follow these specific guidelines.

1. Use a neutral timeout area which is neither reinforcing nor punishing. Generally this means that no books, windows, toys, or peers are available but that the space is comfortable, well-lighted, and ventilated.

2. When the individual is sent or accompanied to the timeout area, the teacher should neither use angry words nor give positively reinforcing attention. Interaction should be limited to a simple restatement of the broken rule or the reason for timeout ("No hitting").

3. To facilitate immediacy of punishment, the timeout area should be close to but visually isolated from the teaching areas.

4. The length of timeout may vary. With moderately and severely retarded individuals, White et al. (1972) found that short timeouts (1 minute) were as effective as longer timeouts (15 to 30 minutes). However, if a teacher first used 1-minute timeouts and then switched to longer timeouts, the reapplication of 1-minute timeouts lessened their punishing effect. Therefore, it is best to select shorter timeouts (1 minute, 3 minutes) and, with a kitchen timer, apply them consistently so that more time is left for instruction and the chance to obtain positive reinforcement.

5. After the timeout has ended, the individual returns to the reinforcing situation *only* if he is not disruptive. If tantrums or other inappropriate behavior are still occurring at the end of the timeout, the teacher should wait until the first quiet moment available to remove the individual from timeout.

6. When a timeout booth or room is being used with a resistive student and an outside lock is needed, it is *especially* important to measure the duration of timeout. *Whenever punishment of any type is used, you must keep exact records of the occurrence of the target behavior to insure that the punishment is not abused or inconsistently applied and to make program changes.*

7. For timeout to be successful, there must be an ongoing program of positive reinforcement from which the individual is removed. Although this last point is obvious, it cannot be overstated.

Timeout relies upon the individual's perception of the contrast between the neutral conditions of timeout and the reinforcing conditions that precede and follow it.

Overcorrection. In this punishment procedure, the individual must either correct the consequences of a misbehavior by restoring the disrupted situation to a "better-than-normal" state (restitutional overcorrection) or practice an exaggerated form of the behavior after each performance of the misbehavior (positive practice). Restitutional overcorrection has been used to eliminate food stealing (Azrin & Wesolowski, 1974), in toilet training (Azrin & Foxx, 1971), and to reduce self-stimulatory behaviors such as rocking, head weaving, and hand staring (Azrin, Kaplan, & Foxx, 1973). There is also evidence, however, that overcorrection can have negative side effects and may not produce consistent effects on the target behavior.

. . . *(a) overcorrection procedures, applied contingently on the occurrence of stereotyped behavior, may produce deceleration in rate of that behavior, but the magnitude of the effect varies considerably between subjects: (b) punishment and nonpunishment conditions are well discriminated by the subject, partly on the basis of trainer proximity; (c) increased collateral stereotypic and emotional responding may accompany deceleration of target behaviors; (d) no spontaneous generalization of suppression is observed from training to living areas; and (e) suppression effects obtained under the procedures employed here are not durable. In general, we may conclude that the overcorrection procedure is actually a very complex package of contingencies and that the effects on behavior may also be complex.* (Rollings, Baumeister, & Baumeister, 1977, p. 42–43)

These authors suggested the use of overcorrection procedures of shorter duration (2 to 3 minutes), training sessions with a variety of teachers and settings to help generalize the suppressed behavior, and a strong plan to promote an increase in desirable behaviors.

Conclusions

In summary, there are a number of variations of punishment, all designed to decrease the frequency of undesirable behavior. These strategies should be implemented only if positive tactics such as instruction or reinforcement of incompatible behaviors alone are not successful. Even in these cases, a positive program to increase appropriate behaviors should be initiated with the punishment program. Accurate data records (taken prior to and during each day of intervention) must be kept to make program decisions and to prevent abuse of the student. Clearly written program procedures must be posted and understood by all staff concerned. Punishment procedures should be chosen and implemented in a least-to-most intrusive order. While parental participation in program planning is especially important, it is critical that parents be consulted and give their permission when an instructional program uses any form of punishment. Furthermore, use of more intrusive punishment procedures often requires formal examination by a professional review board or expert consultation. Teachers should be aware of procedures in their school district and insure due process for students whenever more intrusive punishment is considered.

SUMMARY

This chapter reviews basic intervention strategies to increase and decrease behavior and provides, whenever possible, research-based guidelines for their classroom application with the moderately and severely handicapped. Positive reinforcement is described and its parameters outlined—reinforcer selection, types of reinforcers, scheduling, and procedures. Methods available to begin behaviors which do not readily occur are explained, as are the means by which these response primes may be ultimately faded to promote independence in skill performance. Extinction, classroom rules, and punishment are described as strategies to decrease inappropriate behavior. Specific methods of punishment—overcorrection, timeout, response cost, and firm verbal statements—are described. Cautions in the application of all three deceleration strategies are emphasized and guidelines for their use are provided.

REFERENCES

Alberto, P., Jobes, N., Sizemore, A., & Doran, P. A comparison of individual and group instruction across response tasks. *Journal of the Association for the Severely Handicapped,* 1980, 5, 285–293.

Ayllon, T., & Azrin, N.H. Reinforcement and instructions with mental patients. *Journal of Experimental Analysis of Behavior,* 1964, 7, 327–331.

Ayllon, T., & Azrin, N.H. Reinforcer sampling: A technique for increasing the behavior of mental patients. *Journal of Applied Behavior Analysis,* 1968, 1, 13–20.

Azrin, N.H. & Armstrong, P.M. The "mini-meal"—A method for teaching eating skills to the profoundly retarded. *Mental Retardation,* 1973. 11(1), 9–11.

Azrin, N.H., & Besalel, V.A. *How to use overcorrection.* Lawrence, Kans.: H & H Enterprises, 1980.

Azrin, N.H., & Foxx, R.M. A rapid method of toilet training the institutionalized retarded. *Journal of Applied Behavior Analysis,* 1971, 4, 89–99.

Azrin, N.H., Kaplan, S.J., & Foxx, R.M. Autism reversal: Eliminating stereotyped self-stimulation of retarded individuals. *American Journal of Mental Deficiency*, 1973, *78*, 241–248.

Azrin, N.H., Schaeffer, R.M., & Wesolowski, M.D. A rapid method of teaching profoundly retarded persons to dress by a reinforcement-guidance method. *Mental Retardation*, 1976, *14*(6), 29–33.

Azrin, N.H., & Wesolowski, D.M. Theft reversal: An overcorrection procedure for eliminating stealing by retarded persons. *Journal of Applied Behavior Analysis*, 1974, *1*, 241–248.

Baer, D.M., & Guess, D. Teaching productive noun suffixes to severely retarded children. *American Journal of Mental Deficiency*, 1973, *77*, 498–505.

Baker, J.G., Stanish, B., & Fraser, B. Comparative effects of a token economy in nursery school. *Mental Retardation*, 1972, *10*(4), 16–19.

Barton, E.S., Guess, D., Garcia, E., & Baer, D.M. Improvement of retardates' mealtime behaviors by timeout procedures using multiple baseline techniques. *Journal of Applied Behavior Analysis*, 1970, *3*, 77–84.

Bates, P. The effectiveness of interpersonal social skills training on the social skills acquisition of moderately and mildly retarded adults. *Journal of Applied Behavior Analysis*, 1980, *13*, 237–248.

Bellamy, G.T., Horner, R.H., & Inman, D.P. *Vocational habilitation of severely retarded adults*. Baltimore: University Park Press, 1979.

Berman, M.L. Instructions and behavior change: A taxonomy. *Exceptional Children*, 1973, *39*, 644–650.

Biberdorf, J., & Pear, J. Two-to-one vs. one-to-one student-teacher ratios in the operant verbal training of retarded children. *Journal of Applied Behavior Analysis*, 1977, *10*, 586.

Bostow, D.E., & Bailey, J.B. Modification of severe disruptive and aggressive behavior using brief timeout and reinforcement procedures. *Journal of Applied Behavior Analysis*, 1969, *2*, 31–37.

Browder, D.M., Morris, W.W., & Snell, M.E. The use of time delay to teach manual signs to a severely retarded student. *Education and Training of the Mentally Retarded*, 1981, *16*, 252–258.

Brown, F., Holvoet, J., Guess, D., & Mulligan, M. The Individualized Curriculum Sequencing Model (III): Small group instruction. *Journal of the Association for the Severely Handicapped*, 1980, *5*, 352–367.

Close, D.W., Irvin, L.K., Prehm, H.J., & Taylor, V.E. Systematic correction procedures in vocational-skill training of severely retarded individuals. *American Journal of Mental Deficiency*, 1978, *83*, 270–275.

Cronin, K.A., & Cuvo, A.J. Teaching mending skills to retarded adolescents. *Journal of Applied Behavior Analysis*, 1979, *12*, 401–406.

Csapo, M. Comparison of two prompting procedures to increase response fluency among severely handicapped learners. *Journal of the Association for the Severely Handicapped*, 1981, *6*(1), 39–47.

Cuvo, A.J., & Davis, P.K. Teaching community living skills to mentally retarded persons: An examination of discriminative stimuli. *Gedrag*, 1980, *8*(1), 14–33.

Cuvo, A.J., Leaf, R.B., & Borakove, L.S. Teaching janitorial skills to the mentally retarded: Acquisition, generalization, and maintenance. *Journal of Applied Behavior Analysis*, 1978, *11*, 345–355.

Dalton, A.J., Rubino, C.A., & Hislop, M.W. Some effects of token rewards on school achievement of children with Down's syndrome. *Journal of Applied Behavior Analysis*, 1973, *6*, 251–259.

Denny, M.R. A theoretical analysis and its application to training the mentally retarded. In N.R. Ellis (Ed.), *International review of research in mental retardation* (Vol. 2). New York: Academic Press, 1966.

Etzel, B.C., & LeBlanc, J.M. The simplest treatment alternative: The law of parsimony applied to choosing appropriate instructional control and errorless-learning procedures for the difficult-to-teach child. *Journal of Autism and Developmental Disorders*, 1979, *9*, 361–382.

Falvey, M., Brown, L., Lyon, S., Baumgart, D., & Schroeder, J. Strategies for using cues and correction procedures. In W. Sailor, B. Wilcox, & L. Brown (Eds.) *Methods of instruction for severely handicapped students*. Baltimore: Paul H. Brookes, 1980.

Favell, J.E., Favell, J.E., & McGimsey, J.F. Relative effectiveness and efficiency of group vs. individualized training of severely retarded persons. *American Journal of Mental Deficiency*, 1978, *83*, 104–109.

Fisher, M.A., & Zeaman, D. An attention-retention theory of retardate discrimination learning. In N.R. Ellis (Ed.), *The international review of research in mental retardation* (Vol. 6). New York: Academic Press, 1973.

Foxx, R.M. *Effective behavioral programming: Graduated guidance and backward chaining*. Champaign, Ill.: Research Press, 1981.

Frankel, F., & Graham, V. Systematic observation of classroom behavior of retarded and autistic preschool children. *American Journal of Mental Deficiency*, 1976, *81*, 73–84.

Gaylord-Ross, R. A decision model for the treatment of aberrant behavior in applied settings. In W. Sailor, B. Wilcox, & L. Brown (Eds.), *Methods of instruction for severely handicapped students*. Baltimore: Paul H. Brookes, 1980.

Goetz, L., Schuler, A., & Sailor, W. Teaching functional speech to the severely handicapped: Current issues. *Journal of Autism and Developmental Disorders*, 1979, *9*, 325–343.

Gold, M.W. Stimulus factors in skill training of the retarded on a complex assembly task: Acquisition, transfer and retention. *American Journal of Mental Deficiency*, 1972, *76*, 517–526.

Gold, M.W., & Scott, K.G. Discrimination learning. In W.B. Stephens (Ed.), *Training the developmentally young*. New York: John Day, 1971.

Hall, R.V., Axelrod, S., Foundopulos, M., Shellman, J., Campbell, R.A., & Cranston, S.S. The effective use of punishment to modify behavior in the classroom. *Educational Technology*, 1971, *11*(4), 24–26.

Hall, R.V., & Hall, M.C. *How to use planned ignoring (extinction)*. Lawrence, Kans.: H & H Enterprises, 1980. (a)

Hall, R.V., & Hall, M.C. *How to use systematic attention and approval (social reinforcement)*. Lawrence, Kans.: H & H Enterprises, 1980. (b)

Hall, R.V., & Hall, M.C. *How to use time out*. Lawrence, Kans.: H & H Enterprises, 1980. (c)

Halle, J.W., Baer, D.M., & Spradlin, J.E. Teacher's generalized use of delay on a stimulus control procedure to increase language use in handicapped children. *Journal of Applied Behavior Analysis*, 1981, *14*, 389–409.

Halle, J., Marshall, A., & Spradlin, J.E. Time delay: A technique to increase language usage and facilitate generalization in retarded children. *Journal of Applied Behavior Analysis*, 1979, *12*, 431–439.

Hamre-Nietupski, S., & Nietupski, J. Integral involvement of severely handicapped students within regular public schools. *Journal of the Association for the Severely Handicapped*, 1981, *6*(2), 30–39.

Holvoet, J., Guess, D., Mulligan, M. & Brown, F. The Individualized Curriculum Sequencing Model (II): A teaching strategy for severely handicapped students. *Journal of the Association for the Severely Handicapped*, 1980, *5*, 337–351.

Horner, R.D. The effects of an environmental "enrichment" program on the behavior of institutionalized profoundly retarded children. *Journal of Applied Behavior Analysis*, 1980, *13*, 473–491.

Janssen, C., & Guess, D. Use of function as a consequence in training receptive labeling to severely and profoundly retarded individuals. *AAESPH Review*, 1978, *3*, 246–258.

Johnson, B.F., & Cuvo, A.J. Teaching mentally retarded adults to cook. *Behavior Modification*, 1981, *5*, 187–202.

Kazdin, A.E. *Behavior modification in applied settings*. Homewood, Ill.: Dorsey Press, 1980.

Kazdin, A.E., & Bootzin, R.R. The token economy: An evaluative review. *Journal of Applied Behavior Analysis*, 1972, *5*, 343–372.

Kent, L.R. *Language acquisition program for the severely retarded*. Champaign, Ill.: Research Press, 1974.

Kleinert, H.L., & Gast, D.L. Teaching a multihandicapped adult manual signs using a constant time delay procedure. *Journal of the Association for the Severely Handicapped*, 1982, *6*(4), 25–32.

Kohl, F.L., Wilcox, B.L., & Karlan, G.R. Effects of training conditions on the generalization of manual signs with moderately handicapped students. *Education and Training of the Mentally Retarded*, 1978, *13*, 327–331.

Leitenberg, H. (Ed.). *Handbook of behavior modification and behavior therapy*. Englewood Cliffs, N.J.: Prentice-Hall, 1976.

Lent, J.R., & McLean, B.M. The trainable retarded: The technology of teaching. In N.G. Haring & R.L. Schiefelbusch (Eds.), *Teaching special children*. New York, McGraw-Hill, 1976.

Liberty, K.A., Haring, N.G., & Martin, M.M. Teaching new skills to the severely handicapped. *Journal of the Association for the Severely Handicapped*, 1981, *6*(1), 5–13.

Lindsley, O.R. Direct measurement and prosthesis of retarded behavior. *Journal of Education*, 1964, *147*, 62–81.

Litt, M.D., & Schreibman, L. Stimulus-specific reinforcement in the acquisition of receptive colds by autistic children. *Analysis and Intervention in Developmental Disabilities*, 1981, *1*, 171–186.

Lucero, W.J., Frieman, J., Spoering, K., & Fehrenbacker, J. Comparison of three procedures in reducing self-injurious behavior. *American Journal of Mental Deficiency*, 1976, *80*, 548–554.

MacMillan, D.L., Forness, S.R., & Trumbull, B.M. The role of punishment in the classroom. *Exceptional Children*, 1973, *40*, 85–89.

Matson, J.L., DiLorenzo, T.M., & Esveldt-Dawson, H. Independence training as a method of enhancing self-help skills acquisition of the mentally retarded. *Behavior Research and Therapy*, 1981, *19*, 399–405.

Matson, J.L., Ollendick, T.H., & Adkins, J. A comprehensive dining program for mentally retarded adults. *Behavior Research and Therapy*, 1980, *18*, 107–112.

McHale, S.M., & Simeonsson, R.J. Effects of interaction on nonhandicapped children's attitudes toward autistic children. *American Journal of Mental Deficiency*, 1980, *85*, 18–24.

Mulligan, M., Guess, D., Holvoet, J., & Brown, F. The Individualized Curriculum Sequencing Model (I): Implications from research on massed, distributed, or spaced trial training. *Journal of the Association for the Severely Handicapped*, 1980, *5*, 325–336.

O'Brien, F., & Azrin, N.H. Developing proper meal time behavior of the institutionalized retarded. *Journal of Applied Behavior Analysis*, 1972, *5*, 389–399.

Panyan, M.C., & Hall, R.V. Effects of serial versus concurrent task sequencing on acquisition, maintenance, and generalization. *Journal of Applied Behavior Analysis*, 1978, *11*, 67–74.

Parton, D.A. Learning to imitate in infancy. *Child Development*, 1976, *47*, 14–31.

Pendergrass, V.E. Timeout from positive reinforcement following persistent, high-rate behavior in retardates. *Journal of Applied Behavior Analysis*, 1972, *5*, 85–91.

Premack, D. Toward empirical behavioral laws: 1. Positive reinforcement. *Psychological Review*, 1959, *66*, 291–333.

Richman, J.S., Sonderby, T., & Kahn, J.V. Prerequisite vs. *in vivo* acquisition of self-feeding skill. *Behavior Research and Therapy*, 1980, *18*, 327–332.

Rollings, J.P., Baumeister, A.A., & Baumeister, A.A. The use of overcorrection procedures to eliminate the stereotyped behaviors of retarded individuals. *Behavior Modification*, 1977, *1*(1), 29–46.

Saunders, R., & Sailor, W. A comparison of three strategies of reinforcement on two-choice learning problems with severely retarded children. *AAESPH Review*, 1979, *4*, 323–333.

Smeets, P.M., & Striefel, S. Acquisition and cross modal generalization of receptive and expressive signing skills in a retarded deaf girl. *Journal of Mental Deficiency Research*, 1976, *20*, 251–260. (a)

Smeets, P.M., & Striefel, S. Acquisition of sign reading by transfer or stimulus control in a retarded deaf girl. *Journal of Mental Deficiency Research*, 1976, *20*, 197–205. (b)

Smith, D.D., & Lovitt, T.C. The differential effects of reinforcement contingencies on arithmetic performance. *Journal of Learning Disabilities*, 1976, *1*, 32–40.

Snell, M.E. Retarded residents as language trainers of profoundly retarded students. *Education and Training of the mentally Retarded*, 1979, *14*, 77–84.

Snell, M.E. Analysis of time delay procedures in teaching daily living skills to retarded adults. *Analysis and Intervention in Developmental Disabilities*, 1982, *2*, 139–156.

Snell, M.E., & Gast, D.L. Applying delay procedure to the instruction of the severely handicapped. *Journal of the Association of the Severely Handicapped*, 1981, *5*(4), 3–14.

Stainback, W.C., Payne, J.S., Stainback, S.B., & Payne, R.A. *Establishing a token economy in the classroom*. Columbus, Ohio: Charles E. Merrill, 1973.

Stimbert, V.E., Minor, J.W., & McCoy, J.F. Intensive feeding training with retarded children. *Behavior Modification*, 1977, *1*, 517–530.

Storm, R.H., & Willis, J.H. Small-group training as an alternative to individual programs for profoundly retarded persons. *American Journal of Mental Deficiency*, 1978, *83*, 283–288.

Stremel-Campbell, K., Cantrell, D., & Halle, J. Manual signing as a language system and as a speech initiator for the nonverbal severely handicapped student. In E. Sontag, J. Smith, & N. Certo (Eds.), *Educational programming for the severely and profoundly handicapped*. Reston, Va.: Council for Exceptional Children, 1977.

Striefel, S., Bryan, K.S., & Aikins, D. A transfer of stimulus control from motor to verbal stimuli. *Journal of Applied Behavior Analysis*, 1974, *7*, 123–136.

Striefel, S., Wetherby, B., & Karlan, G. Establishing generalized verb-noun instruction-following skills in retarded children. *Journal of Experimental Child Psychology*, 1976, *22*, 247–260.

Sulzer-Azaroff, B., & Mayer, G.R. *Applying behavior-analysis procedures with children and youth*. New York: Holt, Rinehart & Winston, 1977.

Touchette, P.E. Transfer of stimulus control: Measuring the moment of transfer. *Journal of the Experimental Analysis of Behavior*, 1971, *15*, 347–354.

Tucker, D.J., & Berry, G.W. Teaching severely multihandicapped students to put on their own hearing aids. *Journal of Applied Behavior Analysis*, 1980, *13*, 65–75.

Voeltz, L.M. Children's attitudes toward handicapped peers. *American Journal of Mental Deficiency*. 1980, *84*, 455–464.

Voeltz, L.M. Effects of structured interactions with severely handicapped peers on children's attitudes. *American Journal of Mental Deficiency*, 1982, *86*, 180–190. (a)

Voeltz, L.M. Program and curriculum innovations to prepare children for integration. In N. Certo, N. Haring, & R. York (Eds.), *Public school integration of the severely handicapped: Rational issues and progressive alternatives*. Baltimore: Paul H. Brookes, 1982. (b)

Waldo, L., Guess, D., & Flanagan, B. Effects of concurrent and serial training on receptive labeling by severely retarded individuals. *Journal of the Association for the Severely Handicapped*, 1982, *6*(4), 56–65.

White, G.D., Nielsen, G., & Johnson, S.M. Timeout duration and the suppression of deviant behavior in children. *Journal of Applied Behavior Analysis*, 1972, *5*, 111–120.

White, O.R. *A glossary of behavioral terminology*. Champaign, Ill.: Research Press, 1971.

White, O.R., & Haring, N.G. *Exceptional teaching*. Columbus, Ohio: Charles E. Merrill, 1976.

White, O.R., & Liberty, K.A. Behavioral assessment and precise educational measurement. In N.G. Haring & R.L. Schiefelbusch (Eds.), *Teaching special children*. New York: McGraw-Hill, 1976.

Williams, J.A., Koegel, R.L., & Egel, A.L. Response-reinforcer relationships and improved learning in autistic children. *Journal of Applied Behavior Analysis*, 1981, *14*, 53–60.

Wuerch, B.B., & Voeltz, L.M. *Longitudinal leisure skills for severely handicapped learners*. Baltimore: Paul H. Brookes, 1982.

Zeaman, D. & House, B.J. The role of attention in retardate discrimination learning. In N.R. Ellis (Ed.), *Handbook of mental deficiency*. New York: McGraw-Hill, 1963.

REFERENCE NOTES

1. Brown, L., Nisbet, J., Ford, A., Sweet, M., Shiraga, B., & Loomis, R. *The critical need for nonschool instruction in educational programs for severely handicapped students*. Unpublished manuscript, University of Wisconsin, 1982.

2. Renzaglia, A., & Snell, M.E. *Manual sign training for the severely handicapped: Time delay and a system of least prompts*. Manuscript submitted for publication, 1982.

3. Moon, S., Renzaglia, A., Ruth, B., & Talarico, D. *Increasing the physical fitness of the severely mentally retarded: A comparison of graduated guidance and a hierarchy of prompts*. Unpublished manuscript, University of Virginia, 1981.

4. Voeltz, L.M., Evans, I.M., Derer, K.R., & Hanashiro, R. *Targeting excess behavior for change: A decision model for the selection of priority goals*. Manuscript submitted for publication, 1982.

Introduction
to Chapter 6

As a teacher of the moderately to severely handicapped, you will be confronted with many health-related problems and information needs. Some of your students may have seizures you will need to recognize, handle, record, and report. Many will be on medication you will dispense during the school day. Others will have bowel and bladder disorders that require special attention. Controlled movement will be very limited in some students, and thus their positioning and transfer will require special skills on your part. In some cases these muscular control problems, such as with cerebral palsy, will be so extensive that chewing and swallowing will be slow and ineffective, making choking and food aspiration a daily risk. In addition to these unusual problems, your students will be exposed to the usual: vaccines for measles and mumps, strept throat, ear infections, head lice, nose bleeds, burns, and broken bones.

While you are a teacher and *not* a nurse or doctor, your responsibilities do not end with teaching. In this chapter, Toni McCubbin explains some of the essential information you will need to carry out the routine and emergency medical procedures presented by your students. In her nursing practice Toni interacts every day with handicapped children and adolescents, their parents, and teachers. The chapter is an abbreviated resource filled primarily with the basics. Your preparation in this area should extend beyond this resource, probably including training in feeding, lifting, and positioning of CP students; a Red Cross course in cardiopulmonary resuscitation (CPR); and further instruction in classroom medical procedures.

6

Routine and Emergency Medical Procedures

Toni McCubbin is a registered nurse and Pediatric Nurse Practitioner in a clinic serving handicapped children.

Because of recent legislation and a developing philosophy promoting the educational rights of the developmentally disabled, handicapped individuals are moving out of their homes and institutions into their communities. Schools are facing medical concerns beyond their routine scope of expertise. Teachers are handling seizures and intermittent clean catheterization as well as chicken pox and skinned knees. Many schools do not have a full-time nurse, so the immediate responsibility for emergencies is shifted to the teacher.

As handicapped students attend school regularly, the teacher becomes a critical observer of behaviors that may be the first indications of serious medical problems. It is important that the family, school, and medical professionals work together as a team. The teacher needs some knowledge of the child's disability to plan an appropriate educational program, as well as to recognize potential problems and deal with medical emergencies. It is not our purpose to make teachers diagnosticians, but rather to help you understand and manage medical concerns in the classroom.

SCHOOL PROTOCOL

The legal implications of medical management in the classroom vary according to state laws and individual policies within each school system. Of primary concern are policies regarding bowel and bladder management in the school and administration of prescription medications. The teacher should clarify specific guidelines on these issues with the school administration. Issues like intermittent clean catheterization should be included in the child's IEP, and it should be determined at the IEP meeting who will carry out this procedure and how and where it will be done.

Planning a school protocol for emergencies is critical. Phone numbers of the rescue squad, emergency room, and poison control center should be posted. Every child should have an emergency card in a central office, listing the child's full name, parents' names, address, home phone number, parents' work phone numbers, the name and phone number of another person who may be contacted in an emergency, and the name and phone number of the child's doctor. In addition, any disability or chronic disease should be noted along with particular related concerns. All known allergies should be recorded. Medications should be listed with the prescribed dosage, the time it is given, the prescribing physician's name, and pertinent side effects. Any medications taken at school should have this information on the bottle and should be kept in a locked cabinet. It may also be useful to keep the child's immunization record on this card.

All responsible citizens should be trained in cardiopulmonary resuscitation (CPR) and in the care of a choking victim. This training, available through the American Red Cross, is especially important for people who work with the handicapped population. These individuals are frequently at higher risk for cardiac or respiratory compromise. For example, many students with Down syndrome have an associated cardiac defect; cerebral palsied children often have oral dysfunction, which may result in aspiration and choking. We strongly recommend that teachers become certified by the American Red Cross in CPR and in first aid. These emergency techniques are briefly described later in this chapter.

SPECIFIC CONDITIONS

Cerebral Palsy

Cerebral palsy describes a nonprogressive insult to the brain that results in motor dysfunction. It is *not* a disease. Vining, Accardo, Rubenstein, Farrell, and Roizen (1976) state that 50% to 70% of children with cerebral palsy are mentally retarded, though there is a wide range of intellectual impairment. Any child who suffers a brain insult, such as anoxia prenatally, during the birth process, or postnatally, is at risk for cerebral palsy.

There are three types of cerebral palsy classified according to muscle tone and motor characteristics: spastic, extrapyramidal, and mixed. The spastic group is further classified by the area of the body involved:

1. *Hemiplegia*—the arm and leg on the same side are involved;
2. *Paraplegia*—only the legs are involved;
3. *Quadriplegia*—all four extremities are involved;
4. *Diplegia*—the lower extremities are more involved than the upper extremities; and
5. *Double hemiplegia*—the upper extremities are more involved than the lower extremities and often one side is more involved than the other (Peterson & Cleveland, 1975).

Spastic cerebral palsy implies hypertonicity in the affected muscles. These children are prone to joint contractures. Extrapyramidal cerebral palsy usually involves all four extremities and may involve variable muscle tone. Rigidity, choreoathetosis (writhing movements), ataxia, or tremor may be noted. Mixed cerebral palsy involves components of both spastic

and extrapyramidal abnormalities (Vining et al., 1976). Children with cerebral palsy may have a variety of other, related disabilities such as oral dysfunction resulting in feeding and language problems, hearing loss, poor visual acuity and strabismus, seizures, mental retardation, and behavior problems.

Drug therapy is sometimes used to minimize hypertonicity and involuntary movements. Valium and Dantrolene have been used to reduce the tone of hypertonic muscles. Fonazine has been used to minimize severe rigidity but can have a sedative effect (Vining et al., 1976).

Orthopedic surgery is frequently used to improve ambulation and self-care and may be necessary to prevent deformity. Bracing, casting, and intensive physical therapy are often combined with the efforts of the orthopedic surgeon.

Myelomeningocele

The child with a neural tube defect has an anomaly of the spinal column. There are several types of neural tube defects:

1. *Myelomeningocele*—an anomaly of the vertebral column allowing the spinal cord and its covering (the meninges) to protrude through the bony defect into a sac on the back;
2. *Meningocele*—a bony defect in the vertebral column with protrusion of the meninges, but not the spinal cord itself, into a sac on the back;
3. *Spina bifida occulta*—a bony defect in the vertebra.

Myelomeningocele is more common than meningocele. There is marked sensory impairment over and below the level of the myelomeningocele, resulting in motor impairment, immobility, poor circulation, and osteoporosis (brittle bone) (Holt, 1980).

Hydrocephalus

Hydrocephalus, sometimes referred to as "water on the brain," is a condition seen in 85% to 90% of children with myelomeningocele and less frequently with other disorders. Hydrocephalus is due to an obstruction such as a cyst in the brain, an overproduction of cerebrospinal fluid (CSF), or poor reabsorption of cerebrospinal fluid. The excess fluid causes dilation of the ventricles (the cavities in the middle of the brain), resulting in increased intracranial pressure and compression of the brain's cortex. This increased pressure, if left untreated, can cause illness and even death. Surgical intervention is necessary to insert a plastic tube, called a *shunt,* into the brain to drain the excess fluid.

The teacher must be alert to the signs of increased intracranial pressure in the child with hydrocephalus and a shunt. These signs indicate increasing intracranial pressure that is usually progressive and requires prompt attention:

1. Headache;
2. Irritability, restlessness;
3. Drowsiness, lethargy;
4. Behavior/personality changes;
5. Tense or bulging fontanelle in an infant;
6. Swelling, redness at shunt site;
7. Fever, if infection is present;
8. Decreased appetite;
9. Prominent forehead veins;
10. Ataxis (clumsiness);
11. Diplopia (double vision);
12. Change in muscle tone;
13. "Sunset eyes";
14. Twitching, seizures.

The signs may be subtle and noticeable only to those who know the child well, such as a teacher and parents. The teacher, as part of the team involved with the child, can share with the physician and parent vital information like changes in behavior and academic achievement that may indicate a shunt malfunction.

The child with a shunt does not require any special handling or management in the classroom. Head gear that may compress the shunt tubing should be avoided. Use of one-way valves in the shunt eliminates the concern of backflow of fluid into the brain, so activity and exercise need not be restricted.

Bowel and Bladder Management

Most children with a neural tube defect have permanent bowel and bladder incontinence. Lack of appropriate innervation and sensation leads to urinary tract infections and fecal impaction. There are several options for managing the incontinent bowel and bladder to prevent long-term complications. Goals for management should include preservation of a healthy urinary tract and bowel, skin integrity, social acceptance, and maximum independence.

The incontinent bladder may be spastic or flaccid, depending on innervation. Either situation may result in incomplete emptying of the bladder, resulting in urinary stasis. Stagnant urine acts as a medium for bacterial growth, resulting in frequent urinary tract infections. Poor sphincter control may allow urine to leak, which irritates the skin in the perineal area.

Several alternatives to bladder management are outlined in Table 6.1. Initially, a child with bladder incontinence should receive a complete urological evaluation and recommendation for management. Intermittent clean catheterization has become popular recently with physicians and individuals with spinal cord defects. A child functioning on a 5-year level may be able to catheterize himself, allowing more independence and an improved self-image. This is a clean rather than sterile procedure, making it relatively convenient. Most importantly, the bladder is completely emptied, discouraging urinary stasis and infection. Table 6.2 shows one protocol for intermittent clean self-catheterization.

Bowel management should be initiated at the time toilet training would normally begin. Prevention of constipation is a major goal. Chronic constipation may lead to fecal impactions with leaking stool, distended bowel, hemorrhoids, foul breath, abdominal pain, and vomiting. Continued use of diapers with frequent stooling results in skin irritation, odor, and poor self-concept.

Constipation can frequently be managed with dietary adjustments and increased activity. Constipating foods (rice, bananas, applesauce, milk products) should be avoided, and whole grains, fiber foods (leafy vegetables, fruits) and fluids should be encouraged. Dependence on laxatives is not desirable. Table 6.3 lists some alternatives for bowel management. A bowel program such as the sample in Table 6.4 is the most generally desirable alternative because it promotes a total bowel evacuation routine, allowing the individual to discard diapers, avoids accidents and odors, and enables independence in bowel management. This protocol takes advantage of the gastrocolic reflex, the increased bowel activity after the individual has eaten or drunk a large amount. It is imperative that a convenient daily routine be established. Patience, perserverance, and motivation are critical to the success of a bowel routine. Many people are able eventually to discontinue the suppositories and maintain the routine. Stool softeners may become unnecessary with adequate fluids intake.

Genetic and Metabolic Disorders Associated with Developmental Disability

There are multiple chromosomal disorders that result in significant handicaps and retardation. Down syndrome is the most widely known and most commonly diagnosed cause of retardation (Peterson & Cleveland, 1975). Many manifestations of Down syndrome may be significant in the classroom, including cardiac defects.

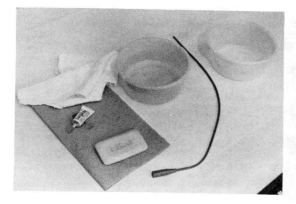

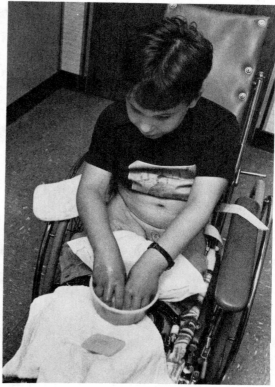

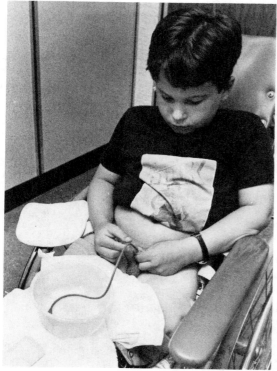

FIGURE 6.1

This boy with myelomeningocele is catheterizing himself to empty his bladder, eliminating the need for diapers. He carries the equipment in a clean container and clean, rather than sterile, technique is used. Jimmy is quite proud of this step toward independence.

SOURCE: Photos by Dan Grogan, Children's Rehabilitation Center, University of Virginia Medical Center.

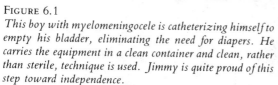

TABLE 6.1 Bladder Management Alternatives

Options	Implications	Problems
Diapers or pads	Requires constant use of absorbent pads or diapers to catch leaking urine	Skin irritation Odor Poor social acceptability
Toilet	Requires scheduled potty times combined with straining or "grunting" to increase intra-abdominal pressure onto the bladder	Poor success rate Requires additional protection (e.g., diapers, pads)
Credé	Use firm pressure above the pubic bone to press in and down on the bladder to express urine. May be used together with techniques to increase intra-abdominal pressure (e.g., sitting up, straining)	Should not be done on individual with an abnormal urinary tract (e.g., reflux of urine from bladder to ureters)
External devices for males (e.g., penile sheath)	Requires constant use of device and collecting bag	Skin irritation Leaking Odor Poor social acceptability
Intermittent clean catheterization	A painless, nonsterile procedure requiring insertion of clean catheter through the urethra into the bladder to drain urine	Requires equipment (catheter container, wash cloth, soap water, toilet, or container for urine) and privacy Should be done every 2–4 hours depending on the individual May use credé to assist in complete bladder emptying May need pads between catheterizations to absorb dampness if bladder leaks urine
Ileal conduit	Ureters are detached from the bladder and joined to a segment of bowel. One end of the bowel is attached to the abdominal wall to form a stoma. Urine drains from the kidneys to the bowel segment and through the stoma into a collecting bag attached to the skin	Surgical procedure Surgical revision of stoma may be needed throughout life Skin irritation Odor Poor social acceptance Potential kidney damage Interference with bracing and appliances

Metabolic disorders are variable in their clinical presentation and implications for the classroom. Some, such as phenylketonuria, are controllable. Others, such as Lesch-Nyhan syndrome and the mucopolysaccharidoses (e.g., Hurler's syndrome), imply progressive loss of function, mental deterioration, and severe behavior problems. Seizures and dysmorphic features are not uncommon.

Complete descriptions of these disorders are beyond the scope of this text. *Recognizable Patterns of Human Malformation: Genetic, Embryologic and Clinical Aspects* (Smith, 1976) may be a useful resource. It is especially important with these children that the team of school, parents, and medical professionals work together closely to share concerns and recommendations, and frequently reassess the children's capabilities and needs.

ROUTINE PEDIATRIC CONCERNS

Several routine health-related concerns for the handicapped child are important to the teacher. Vision and hearing screening should be done for every preschool child, more frequently for children at risk for vision or hearing impairments as part of their disability. Communicable diseases are a concern in any group setting and particularly with handicapped children. The responsibility for disease control frequently falls into the hands of the teacher, who must be aware of the symptoms and contagious periods for the more common communicable diseases. We have purposefully listed seizures with routine concerns to emphasize the nonemergency nature of a convulsion in a child with a known seizure disorder.

TABLE 6-2. Sample of Clean Intermittent Self-catheterization Program

1. Collect all the things you need: catheter, soap and washcloth or towelettes, lubricant, container for urine, absorbent pads, paper towel, clean container for storing catheter, and mirror. If you catherize yourself in your wheelchair or on the toilet, you probably won't need a urine container or absorbent pads. A mirror is only necessary when first learning to catheterize.

2. Wash your hands with soap and water. Rinse well.

3. Get yourself into a comfortable position, lying on an absorbent pad if you're on the bed. Arrange equipment so you can reach it easily.

4. *Girls:* Clean between your legs with a washcloth and soap and water. Rinse. Remember to clean from front to back, wiping at least 3 times.
   Boys: Retract the foreskin (if not circumcised) and wash penis with soap and water. Rinse with clean water.

5. Apply lubricating jelly to small end of catheter (girls may prefer not to use lubricant).

6. *Girls:* Open labia with one hand and insert catheter gently with the other—do not force it.
   Boys: Grasp the penis on the sides (not top and bottom) with one hand and hold it up straight; use the other hand to insert the catheter gently into the urinary opening. When the catheter comes to an area where it meets resistance, use gentle but firm pressure until the internal muscle relaxes.

7. Direct your urinary stream into the toilet; if you're on the bed, use the container.

8. When the urine stops flowing, strain as though you were having a bowel movement and then press firmly on your bladder to make sure there is no more urine. Remove the catheter gently, stopping if urine flows again.

9. *Boys:* If uncircumcised, pull foreskin back to normal position.

10. Wash your hands and the catheter with soap and water, rinsing catheter carefully. Shake catheter to remove water inside it; then dry very well.

11. At home you may hang catheter up to dry. Otherwise, place it in a clean container such as plastic sandwich bag, envelope, or small covered jar.

12. Collect your equipment and put it away. Throw away soiled absorbent pad and empty urine container. Rinse out container and wash cloth.

SOURCE: Adapted with permission from Barbara Deaver, OTR, Children's Rehabilitation Center.

TABLE 6.3 Bowel Management Alternatives

Option	Implications	Problems
Diaper	Requires the individual to wear diaper constantly to catch stool	Skin irritation Constipation/fecal impaction Poor social acceptance Odor
Toilet	Requires scheduled potty times combined with straining or "grunting" to increase intra-abdominal pressure	Low success rate Requires continued use of diapers Frequent accidents Constipation/fecal impaction Poor social acceptance
Bowel Program	Combined use of scheduled potty times, straining, and suppository with daily stool softener to insure complete emptying of bowel	May require occasional enemas or digital evacuation Takes time to regulate the bowel
Colostomy	Lower bowel is brought out to abdominal wall to form a stoma. Stool is collected in bag attached to the skin.	Surgical procedure Skin irritation at stoma site Odor Poor social acceptance Interference with bracing and appliances

TABLE 6.4 Sample Bowel Program

1. Well-balanced diet
     3 quarts of liquid per day (water, fruit juices)
     Raw fruits (with peels), stewed or dried apricots, figs, prunes, dates, raisins
     Vegetables
     Whole grain cereals and bread
     (Avoid constipating foods—rice, bananas, milk, and milk products)
2. Plenty of exercise.
3. Fleets enema until clear first night
4. Colace—50 mg (age 2–8 years) before bed *each* night.
     100 mg (age 8 years +).
5. Ducolax Suppository—½–1 suppository ages 2–8 years.
     1+ suppository ages 8 years +

   given at the *same time* every *other* night after eating a big meal or drinking large amounts of fluids
   Retain suppository 20–40 minutes (it may be necessary to pinch the buttocks together), then sit on the toilet, massage abdomen, rock back and forth and strain to aid in expelling the stool.
6. If no bowel movement (BM) after 30 to 40 minutes, use digital stimulation (insert lubricated finger into rectum and rotate) to evacuate the bowel manually.
7. If no BM for 3 days, give milk of magnesia.
8. To establish a bowel habit:
     Routine should be done every night with suppository every other night regardless of any stooling during the day or lack of results after routine. It may take several weeks for a routine habit to be established.

Vision Screening

Every child with developmental delays or perceptual problems deserves screening for visual impairments. Delayed diagnosis of significant visual impairments may lead to social and intellectual delays and permanent visual disorders. Any child with cerebral palsy, myelomeningocele, or many of the chromosomal disorders such as Down syndrome or metabolic disorders such as Hurler's syndrome is at risk for visual impairment.

Acuity and muscle imbalance problems are frequently found in handicapped people. The following disorders are commonly found:

1. *Strabismus*—commonly called "squint"; an imbalance of the eye muscles;
2. *Esotropia*—a type of strabismus in which the eye turns inward;
3. *Exotropia*—a type of strabismus in which the eye turns outward;
4. *Amblyopia*—a functional decrease in acuity in one eye due to untreated strabismus, where the child becomes dependent on one eye for vision and suppresses vision in the amblyopic eye;
5. *Nystagmus*—abnormal rapid eye movements in either the horizontal or vertical plane;
6. *Hyperopia*—poor acuity for close vision; and
7. *Myopia*—poor acuity for distance (Vaughan & McKay, 1975).

Strabismus is commonly found in children with abnormalities of the central nervous system, as cerebral palsy and myelomeningocele.

Early detection and treatment of all of these disorders are critical. The teacher should be alert to symptoms of visual impairment such as squinting, unusual positioning of the head, unusual eye movements, and inappropriate distance between eyes and toy (Langley & DuBose, 1976). The teacher can then notify the parents and recommend evaluation by their pediatrician or ophthalmologist. There are several tools that may be used for different developmental ages. The well-known Snellen chart requires a knowledge of the alphabet. The "illiterate E" chart requires some manual dexterity or verbal expression to describe the direction of the E. However, the Lighthouse Vision Test[1] uses simple pictures and matching flash cards for the very young or nonverbal child. See Langley and DuBose (1976) for further discussion of informal screening tests. In addition to acuity, peripheral fields should also be evaluated. The local Commission for the Visually Handicapped is an excellent resource for screening, assessing, and managing visual impairments. Specific concerns should be referred to an ophthalmologist for further assessment and management. Patching, lenses, and surgery are all possible interventions.

Hearing Screening

In addition to vision screening, any child with developmental delay deserves a hearing screening. Far too many hearing impaired children have been misdiagnosed as mentally retarded or hyperactive.

Causes for hearing impairments may be congenital, as with maternal rubella, or acquired, as with chronic ear infections. There are four types of hearing losses:

1. *Conductive*—Usually a temporary loss resulting from some obstruction, e.g., ear wax or middle ear pathology that interferes with the transmission

---

[1]Available through the New York Association for the Blind, 111 E. 59th St., New York, NY 10022.

TABLE 6.5 Children with High Risk of Hearing Impairment

POSITIVE FAMILY HISTORY for deafness
CONGENITAL ANOMALIES—CRANIOFACIAL
EAR, NOSE, OR THROAT including cleft palate.

Prenatal	Postnatal
Maternal toxemia	Birth trauma
Maternal alcoholism	Hypoxia
Congenital infections	Jaundice
Rubella	Prematurity
Toxoplasmosis	Low birth weight (1500 gram)
Cytomegalic virus	Ototoxic drugs
Syphillis	Gentamycin
Herpes	Streptomycin
Rh incompatibility	Infection
Chromosomal abnormalities	Meningitis
Trisomy 21—Down syndrome	Measles (Rubeola)
Trisomy 13-15	Mumps
	Acoustic nerve tumor
	Chronic ear infections
	Head trauma
	Trauma to the acoustic nerve

of sounds to the inner ear. Most cases of conductive hearing loss can be corrected medically or surgically.

2. *Sensorineural*—A permanent loss involving damage to the eighth cranial nerve due to disease processes (e.g., maternal rubella, anoxia at birth, excessive jaundice) or ototoxic drugs. This type of loss may be progressive, is irreversible, and may benefit from a hearing aid.

3. *Mixed*—A combination of sensorineural and conductive losses.

4. *Central auditory dysfunction*—An impairment in the central nervous system (the brain), resulting in poor auditory comprehension despite normal audiogram and a healthy ear (Northern & Downs, 1978).

The teacher should be alert to signs of hearing impairment, including poor articulation, poor response to verbal instructions, frequent requests to repeat what has just been said, inattention and distractibility, and hyperactivity.

Hearing screening ascertains the intensity level at which sound is perceived as well as the capacity for speech discrimination. The pediatrician or audiologist may use several different tools. A tuning fork is useful for gross assessment. An audiometer gives a quantitative measure of hearing by determining hearing level in decibels. Impedance audiometry or tympanometry evaluates middle-ear function. Electro-physiological audiometry, including brain stem-evoked responses and cortical-evoked response, measures the brain's response to auditory stimuli and may be needed to evaluate children who cannot cooperate with more standard procedures (Northern & Downs, 1978; Wolfson, Aghamohamadi, & Berman, 1980).

Children should be routinely screened during the preschool period, and children at risk (Table 6.5) should be followed closely by an audiologist.

Seizures

Epilepsy is abnormal, unpredictable, yet temporary paroxysmal discharge of neurons resulting in alterations of consciousness (Sharpe, 1975). It is perhaps one of the most feared and least understood disorders of handicapped individuals. In fact, the social stigma may be more disabling than the seizures. Teachers should educate themselves and their students about epilepsy, thereby alleviating the mystery around the student with a seizure disorder.[2]

There are many known causes of seizures, including head trauma, infection, poisoning, metabolic disorders, and fever; but there are many seizure disorders that have no known etiology. The types of

[2]It is not the purpose of this chapter to describe fully the history, etiology, symptoms, or treatment of seizures. Those readers desiring further information should refer to publications by the Epilepsy Foundation of America, 1828 L. Street, N.W., Washington, DC 20036.

seizures are even more varied than their causes. Seizures are classified primarily according to their clinical picture as well as the age of the child and characteristic electroencephalographic (EEG) patterns.

The EEG is an often misunderstood diagnostic tool. Small electrical discharges within the brain are amplified through electrodes placed over the head and recorded graphically. Abnormalities may be localized, but the EEG is not conclusive and may record a transient event. There is certainly no relation between the EEG tracing and measurement of intelligence. The EEG may be normal in individuals who have a documented history of seizures (Peterson & Cleveland, 1975) as well as abnormal in individuals with no history of seizures.

A well-recorded history of seizure activity is the most important aspect of diagnosis. The teacher who sees the child every day can make critical observations of atypical behaviors such as staring spells, nodding, picking at one's clothes, or lip smacking, that can lead to early diagnosis and treatment.

Any child with a known seizure disorder should have information on file as to the type of seizure, severity, average length of seizure activity, and length of recovery period. Prodromal, or anticipatory, signs of the seizure should be noted, as well as individual precautions and instructions for emergency care. Medications, dosages, side effects, and the prescribing physician should be listed (Bryan, Warden, Berg, & Hauck, 1978).

Children with disorders of the central nervous system are at risk for seizure disorders. The seizures may become evident at any age or may remain subclinical or barely noticeable to the untrained eye. The char-

TABLE 6.6 Common Characteristics and Treatment of Seizures

Seizure Type	Characteristics	Drugs
Partial seizures Partial with elementary symptomatology	Focal Includes Jacksonian; motor, sensory, and/or autonomic symptoms	Phenobarbital Depakene Dilantin Tegretol Mysoline
Partial with complex symptomatology	Includes psychomotor; confusion, behavioral symptoms	Phenobarbital Zarontin Depakene Dilantin Tegretol Mysoline
Generalized seizures Absence	Bilateral, symmetrical Includes petit mal; sudden onset; brief unresponsiveness	Clonopin Depakene Zarontin
Myoclonic	Sudden, uncontrolled, severe jerking; brief loss of consciousness; associated with severe mental retardation	Depakene Clonopin Valium ACTH Ketogenic diet
Infantile spasms	Sudden flexion and extension of extremities; associated with severe and progressive mental retardation	Clonopin ACTH Ketogenic diet
Tonic-clonic	Massive contraction then rhythmic jerking of muscles followed by CNS depression	Phenobarbital Depakene Dilantin Tegretol Mysoline
Akinetic	Complete relaxation of muscle tone	Depakene Clonopin Valium Ketogenic diet

acteristics or type of seizure may change as the child grows older. Table 6.6 briefly summarizes some of the more common seizure types described in the International Classification of Epileptic Seizures.

Partial seizures, also called *focal* seizures and *temporal lobe* seizures, begin in a particular area of the brain and exhibit symptoms related to that area. Included in this category are seizure types previously known as *Jacksonian* seizures, with the familiar "marching" of motor activity up the body, and *psychomotor* seizures, with more complex behavioral symptoms including chewing, lip smacking, picking at clothes, and other purposeless activity. It is important to differentiate between partial seizures with complex symptoms and emotional disturbances.

Generalized seizures involve more diffuse electrical activity in the brain, resulting in symptoms that involve both sides of the body. One of the best known types of generalized seizures is the simple *absence* seizure, including the *petit mal* seizure. This type most frequently occurs in school-aged children. It is characteristically very brief, lasting only a few seconds, and frequently goes unnoticed. Changes in behavior and academic performance may be the only indications. The child is often described as daydreaming or inattentive. Some children may exhibit some mild motor involvement such as eye blinking or a loss of muscle tone.

Tonic-clonic seizures, previously called *grand mal* seizures, are what most people identify when someone mentions epilepsy. Witnessing a tonic-clonic seizure may be frightening. There is sudden loss of consciousness as the individual falls to the ground, the entire body becomes extended and rigid, and the extremities jerk rhythmically. The individual may cry out at the beginning of the tonic phase. There may be loss of bowel or bladder control. Often respirations cease, and the individual may be cyanotic or bluish. Following the seizure activity (the postictal or recovery phase), the individual may remain unconscious or sleep for a long period of time.

Febrile seizures are not considered a type of chronic epilepsy. These are generally tonic-clonic in nature and occur in children 6 months to 5 years old following an abrupt onset of high fever. Febrile seizures are frequently associated with viral infections, upper respiratory infections, and immunizations, often with a family history of febrile seizures. Children who are normal before the incident rarely have any sequelae, though they are at a slightly higher risk for future febrile seizures and epilepsy. Prompt treatment of fever is preferable to anticonvulsant therapy in this distinctly different population.

Status epilepticus is prolonged seizure activity without regaining consciousness. It is important to know the average length and severity of an individual's seizures to determine if he is in status epilepticus as there is no fixed definition for the condition. This is the one situation with seizures which is a medical emergency and requires immediate transportation to a hospital for treatment with intravenous anticonvulsants.

First aid for seizures consists primarily of protecting the individual from injuring himself and protecting his privacy. Some people may benefit from helmets to prevent head injuries from falling. If a student begins to have a seizure with major motor components, allow or help him to lie down, move away any nearby furniture, loosen restrictive clothing, and tilt his head to one side if possible to allow saliva to drain out. Never try to hold the child, stop the seizure, or force any object in the child's mouth. Try to provide privacy during and after the seizure. Accurate observation and recording of the seizure are of utmost importance (Table 6.7). This information may help the medical team classify and therefore appropriately treat the seizure.

The primary goal of anticonvulsant therapy is to achieve maximum control with the fewest possible drugs and side effects (Hawken & Ozune, 1979). Drug therapy is based on the seizure type, emphasizing the importance of accurate observation and recording of seizures. The teacher should be alert to symptoms, behavior changes, and possible side effects of anticonvulsant medication. Table 6.8 lists some common anticonvulsants by trade name with generic name in parenthesis, the seizure type most frequently treated by the drug, and the more common side effects. Some of the side effects are transient, some are related to dosage or blood levels of the drug, and some are idiosyncratic. Blood levels of the drug are monitored regularly to prevent toxicity and evaluate compliance. Some drugs, such as Valproic Acid, require blood tests of liver and other organ function to monitor adverse effects. As a general rule, it seems the greater the number of drugs used in combination, the longer the individual has been on drug therapy, and the poorer the general state of health, the greater the risk of significant side effects.

Communicable Diseases

Infectious diseases are an integral part of growing up. Rarely does a child survive his first 10 years without contracting chicken pox. Medicine has provided us with immunizations (Table 6.9, page 161) against many of the viral illnesses, significantly reducing childhood morbidity and mortality. The communicable disease chart (Table 6.10, page 162) may be used as a reference for some of the more common infectious diseases found in schools.

TABLE 6.7 Describing and Recording Seizure Activity

Why It's Important to Be Accurate

Anticonvulsants are prescribed according to seizure type; therefore, it is necessary to know the type and frequency of seizure(s) to determine appropriate treatment and control.

Few people are trained in observing seizure behavior, and it is essential for all those who come in contact with the child (teachers and allied health professionals) to be aware of the importance of their observations and to know specifically what to look for and record.

I. Activities Prior to Seizure.
  A. Environmental or situation.
    1. Fatiguing (too much exercise; not enough sleep night before)
    2. Stressful (argument with parent, sibling)
II. Seizure Activity
  A. Warning (part of the seizure; begin recording time)
    1. Fear
    2. Headache
    3. Specific smell
    4. Specific noise
    5. Visual impression, experience
    6. Unusual feeling (butterflies in the stomach)
  B. Record in proper sequence
    1. Where did activity begin: face, extremities (can begin as blank stare and be missed)?
    2. Did the individual fall, thrash, go limp, jerk?
    3. Did the individual lose consciousness?
    4. Did the individual make strange sounds or cry out?
  C. What parts of the body were involved?
    1. Arms: right, left, both
    2. Legs: right, left, both
    3. Head: drop, turned to left or right, ache
    4. Eyes: turn to right, left, up, down, blinking; were pupils dilated? did they react to light?

    5. Autonomic system: gastric disturbances, flushing of the face
  D. Did any of these activities take place during the seizure?
    1. Talk
    2. Walk
    3. Pick at clothes
    4. Demonstrate any purposeless movement
  E. Miscellaneous activities
    1. Teeth clamped, bite tongue
    2. Incontinent of urine or feces
    3. Characteristic of respirations
    4. Skin changes during seizure
    5. Vomiting
    Record time activity ends
III. Postictal Phase (after seizure)
  A. Degree of alertness—oriented to person, place and things
  B. Degree of confusion—how long
  C. Was sleep necessary—for how long
  D. Any weakness in the extremities
    1. Where?
    2. Degree?
    3. Length of time until full strength returned?
  E. Did the child remember anything unusual occurring prior to seizure?
IV. Did This Seizure Vary from Past Seizures?

1. Record date and time of day each seizure occurs.
2. All who come in contact with an individual having seizures should be taught how to describe and to keep seizure records accurately. It is necessary for the clinician, the family, and the school to have this information on seizure activity and frequency.
3. If you are not sure an individual is having seizures, observe that person for 5 minutes out of every hour for a day or two. (This is very helpful when identifying absence seizures.)

SOURCE: "Screening for Seizures" by Nancy Santilli and Stephen Tonelson. *Pediatric Nursing,* March/April, 1981, 7(2), 14. Reprinted with permission.

Cast Care

The physically handicapped child may undergo frequent orthopedic surgery requiring casting. Prolonged periods of postoperative or therapeutic casting make casts a common concern in the classroom. The primary concerns here are continued adequate circulation and maintenance of a clean dry cast. Swelling or pressure may impair circulation at any time during casting and result in severe problems.

Skin breakdown due to rubbing and pressure is a significant concern with sensorily impaired children. The cast checklist below provides guidelines for daily assessment.

1. Can the child wiggle the toes/fingers?
2. Are the toes/fingers pink and warm to touch?
3. Does the child notice any tingling or numbness?
4. If you pinch the nail beds, do they quickly become pink again?

TABLE 6.8 Common Anticonvulsants Used with Seizure Disorders

Drug	Seizure Type	Side Effects
Clonopin (clonazepam)	Absence Infantile spasms Myoclonic Akinetic	Ataxia Hypotonia Muscle weakness Aggression Hyperactivity Irritability Attention deficits Drowsiness Slurred speech Confusion Psychosis Increased salivation
Depakene (valproic acid/sodium valproate)	Absence Partial elementary Partial complex Tonic-clonic Myoclonic Akinetic	Drowsiness Irritability Aggressive behavior Hyperactivity Resting tremor Anorexia Nausea, vomiting, alopecia—transient Alteration in bleeding time Hepatotoxicity Abdominal pain
Dilantin (phenytoin)	Tonic-clonic Partial elementary Partial complex	Ataxia Nystagmus Diplopia Vertigo Dysarthria Gum hypertrophy Coarse facial features Hirsutism Metabolic problems Skin rash
Mysoline (primidone)	Tonic-clonic Partial elementary Partial complex	Drowsiness Ataxia Nausea, vomiting—transient Hyperactivity Psychosis Anemia
Phenobarbital (luminal)	Tonic-clonic Partial complex Partial elementary Febrile Status epilepticus (I.V.)	Drowsiness—transient Agitation Irritability Behavior problem Ataxia Nystagmus Dysarthria (slurred speech) Paradoxical excitement
Tegretol (carbamazepine)	Tonic-clonic Partial elementary Partial complex	Nausea, vomiting Drowsy Dizziness Ataxia Diplopia

Table 6.8 (continued)

Drug	Seizure Type	Side Effects
		Hypotension Skin rash Blood dyscrasias
Valium (diazepam)	Myoclonic Akinetic Status epilepticus (I.V.)	Drowsy Ataxia Dullness Vertigo Hypotension Irritability
Zarontin (ethosuximide)	Absence Partial complex	Nausea, vomiting Drowsiness Headache Dizziness Behavior changes Photophobia Parkinson-like symptoms Blood dyscrasias
ACTH & Corticosteroids	Myoclonic Infantile spasms	Hypertension Muscle weakness Osteoporosis Cushingoid symptoms Glaucoma Cataracts
Ketogenic diet	Myoclonic Infantile spasms	

5. Is there any odor or drainage?
6. Is there any redness or blistering around the edges of the cast?

Any change in status requires immediate evaluation by a physician.

The child in a cast, especially body casts and hip spica casts that limit mobility, should change position frequently to avoid pressure areas. Pressure sores are most common at bony prominences, ankles, heels, hip bones, spine, and ribs. The skin area around the edges of the cast are subject to irritation from rubbing and pressure. Moleskin, a special soft nonabrasive fabric, may be used to protect the edges of the cast. Alcohol may be rubbed on the skin which is irritated to toughen it, preventing blistering and skin breakdown. Never use lotions on the skin around the cast!

The child may itch under the cast. Coat hangers, toys, and other items should never be pushed under the cast. It is best to divert the child's attention from this discomfort.

Efforts should be made to keep the cast clean and dry, which is a particular problem for the incontinent child in a hip spica or body cast. Plastic wrap may be tucked in around the perineum and used to funnel urine into a bedpan when the child is on a special frame. If diapers are used, they should be changed frequently.

Frequent change of position, usually every 30 minutes during the day, is recommended to prevent pressure areas and ulceration (e.g., decubitus ulcers) under the cast. Any skin breakdown should be reported to the physician. The *Manual of Orthopedics* (Hilt & Cogburn, 1980) is recommended for a more in-depth discussion of orthopedic concerns.

ACUTE PEDIATRIC CONCERNS

This section deals briefly with various emergency situations the teacher may encounter in the classroom, focusing on identification and management.

Cardiopulmonary Arrest

Cardiopulmonary arrest is the cessation of spontaneous respiration and heart activity, resulting in a lack

TABLE 6.9 Recommended Immunization Schedule

Age	Immunization
2 months	DPT (Diphtheria-Pertussis-Tetanus)
	OPV (Oral Polio Vaccine)
4 months	DPT
	OPV
6 months	DPT
	OPV (variable)
9–12 months	Tuberculine test
15 months	MMR [Measles (Rubeola)-Mumps-Rubella]
18 months	DPT
	OPV
4–6 years	DPT
	OPV
Every 10 years thereafter	TD (Tetanus-Diphtheria)
	OPV

of oxygen to vital tissues, including the brain. This is a life-threatening emergency requiring prompt intervention by trained individuals. Cardiopulmonary resuscitation (CPR) is a technique that requires discussion and hands-on training beyond the scope of this chapter. Specialized instruction in CPR for the adult and child is available through the American Red Cross and the American Heart Association and should be incorporated into school in-service programs. Yearly recertification is recommended to keep these skills current.

For the teacher who is not trained in CPR, the American Red Cross ABC—*Airway Breathing Circulation*—assessment of the collapsed victim should serve as a guideline for intervention. The first step is to be sure there is an open airway (clear the mouth of any debris); listen or feel for air exchange to assess spontaneous breathing; and check the carotid pulse in the neck as well as for severe bleeding. The teacher untrained in CPR should immediately call for help in any situation of cardiopulmonary arrest.

Choking

If a child appears to be choking on a foreign object, the teacher should first assess for air transfer and the degree of effective breathing. If the child appears cyanotic, very pale, or cannot talk, he may need help expelling the foreign body. Check the child's mouth to see if the object can be removed with your fingers. If not, place the child over your knees or have him bend over at the waist, and give a sharp blow between the shoulder blades. This may need to be repeated several times. If the child continues to choke, the Heimlich maneuver or thrust should be used. Standing behind the child or sitting him in a chair, place your fists between the umbilicus and sternum or breastbone, and thrust sharply inward and upward. This may be alternated with the back-slapping technique. The American Red Cross publication on *First Aid for Foreign Body Obstruction of the Airway* (1978) has a more detailed discussion.

Bleeding and Hemorrhage

Nose bleeds are perhaps the most common bleeding injury and can be frightening. The child should sit quietly and apply direct pressure to the bleeding nostril. Ice packs to the nose may alleviate pain or swelling if the bleed is due to trauma and may hasten clotting. Severe nose bleeds may require the nostril be packed with gauze in an emergency room.

Bleeding from a laceration is usually most effectively managed by direct pressure over the wound with a clean bandage. If possible, the extremity should be elevated. Only severe, life-threatening bleeding should be treated with a tourniquet. In an emergency, a scarf, necktie, or strip of cloth may be used as a tourniquet and applied above the bleeding site. Once applied, never release the tourniquet. It is very important to mark somewhere on the person the time the tourniquet was applied.

Musculoskeletal Problems

Children with gait disturbances, seizures, and hypotonia are subject to frequent falls and therefore at risk for bony and soft tissue injuries.

Fractures involve some type of break to a bone. A child may have pain, swelling, and deformity at the fracture site. *Crepitus,* a grating noise, may be noted if the bone ends rub together when moved. The child should lie down and the extremity be supported and kept immobile. A splint should be applied to insure immobility during transfer to a hospital. Popsicle sticks for fingers, pillows for arms, or padded broomsticks for legs are possible splints. If the bone is exposed, bleeding should be controlled and the wound covered.

Sprains are injuries to the soft tissue (ligaments, and tendons) around a joint. Symptoms (rapid swelling, pain, discoloration) are similar to those of a fracture and require X-ray to differentiate. Elevation of the extremity, cold, and immobilization are necessary before diagnosis.

A *strain* due to overstretching of a muscle results in a sharp pain or spasm. The muscle becomes stiff and sore but requires no emergency treatment.

Dislocations of bones in a joint result in severe pain and sudden swelling. Deformity is usually obvious. There is loss of joint function and shortening of the extremity may be observed. The individual may

TABLE 6.10 Communicable Disease Chart

1. *Chicken Pox*
   AGE: 2–8 years.
   SYMPTOMS: Malaise, mild fever followed in approximately 2–3 days by sudden onset of small raised pimples beginning on the head and mucus membranes and spreading to the extremities. Pimples become filled with clear fluid. Later formation of scabs. Successive crops of pox appear. Itching.
   INCUBATION: 14–21 days.
   CONTAGIOUS: From 24 hours before onset fever until rash vessels are dry—approximately 5–7 days from appearance of rash.
   TRANSMISSION: Highly communicable. Direct or indirect contact. Droplets spread by airborne transmission; direct contact with lesions.
   PREVENTION: No vaccine available. Immune after one attack.
   COMPLICATIONS: Rare; occasionally encephalitis, pneumonia, or secondary to bacterial skin infection, conjunctivitis.

2. *Rubella* (German measles or 3-day measles)
   AGE: School age and older.
   SYMPTOMS: Mild fever, sore throat, runny nose, conjunctivitis, headache, and malaise. May perceive tiny rose-colored rash that begins on face and progresses onto the body. Rash fades on pressure. Enlarged glands at back of neck and behind ears. Highest incidence in spring.
   INCUBATION: Approximately 2–3 weeks.
   CONTAGIOUS: From 1 week before to 5 days after rash appears.
   TRANSMISSION: Droplets or direct contact with infected person or articles freshly contaminated with nasal pharyngeal secretions, urine, or feces.
   PREVENTION: Vaccine recommended at 15 months of age. Immune after one attack.
   COMPLICATIONS: Rare in children; in adolescents and young adults, grave concern for fetus of infected mother.

3. *Rubeola* (Measles)
   AGE: 1 year through school age.
   SYMPTOMS: Mounting fever, harsh dry cough, runny nose and red eyes for 3–4 days prior to brownish red rash that begins at hair line and spreads down the body in blotches. Small, red spots with white centers may be seen in the mouth before the rash. Decreased appetite, swollen glands.
   INCUBATION: 7–14 days.
   CONTAGIOUS: 5–6 days before first symptom appears until 5–7 days after the rash appears.
   TRANSMISSION: Direct contact with droplets from infected persons.
   PREVENTION: Vaccine recommended at 15 months of age. Gamma globulin if injected shortly after exposure may lighten or prevent the disease.
   COMPLICATIONS: Otitis media, pneumonia, laryngitis, bronchitis, hearing loss, encephalitis.

4. *Mumps*
   AGE: 5–12 years.
   SYMPTOMS: Fever, headache, vomiting. Glands below the ear at jawline swollen and painful. Anorexia.
   INCUBATION PERIOD: 12–26 days.
   CONTAGIOUS: 7 days before swelling appears till swelling subsides.
   TRANSMISSION: Direct contact with saliva of infected person or droplet transmission.
   PREVENTION: Vaccine recommended at 15 months of age. Immune after one attack.
   COMPLICATIONS: Rare in childhood. Occasional deafness. Adult males may become very ill with involvement of the testes. Sterility is uncommon.

5. *Infectious Hepatitis*
   AGE: School age.
   SYMPTOMS: Abrupt onset of fever, headache, abdominal pain, mild upper respiratory infection, dark urine, sluggishness, fatigue, anorexia, nausea, vomiting. Jaundice is a later symptom.
   INCUBATION PERIOD: 14–40 days.
   CONTAGIOUS: As long as 2 months.
   TRANSMISSION: Oral fecal contact.
   PREVENTION: Injection of gamma globulin gives temporary immunity if exposed.
   COMPLICATIONS: Hepatic failure, fluid retention, blood disorders, hemorrhage. Usually mild in childhood.

6. *Strep Throat*
   AGE: 5–16 years.
   SYMPTOMS: Sudden onset of severe sore throat, high fever, headache, nausea, sometimes vomiting. Sometimes followed by a fine red rash on body (scarlatina) or scarlet fever.
   INCUBATION PERIOD: 2–5 days.
   CONTAGIOUS: Throughout the acute stage; 7–10 days.
   TRANSMISSION: Direct or indirect contact with nasal phalangeal secretions.
   PREVENTION: None.
   COMPLICATIONS: Glomerulonephritis approximately 1–2 weeks after disease. Rheumatic fever 2–3 weeks after disease. Peritonsillar abscess, pneumonia, otitis media.

8. *Syphilis*
   AGE: Any age.
   SYMPTOMS: Primary syphilis—painless chancre

TABLE 6.10 (CONTINUED)

on mucus membranes. Secondary syphilis—rash, sores in mouth, fever, sore throat, headache.
INCUBATION PERIOD: 10–60 days.
CONTAGIOUS: Until cure.
TRANSMISSION: Sexual contact, transplacental and congenital.
PREVENTION: Sexual discretion; premarital serology.
COMPLICATIONS: Multiple and severe including the cardiovascular system, central nervous system, and skeletal system as well as congenital syphilis.
9. *Impetigo* (Streptococcus, Staphylococcus)
AGE: Toddler through preschool.
SYMPTOMS: Blisters with pus that later become crusted. Usually on face or extremities.
INCUBATION PERIOD: 1–5 days.
CONTAGIOUS: While lesion is active.
TRANSMISSION: By direct or indirect contact.
PREVENTION: Cleanliness.
COMPLICATIONS: Acute glomerulonephritis, rheumatic fever.
10. *Ringworm*
AGE: Toddler through school age.

SYMPTOMS: Round or oval lesion with red scaly ring and central clearing. Border spreads very slowly.
TRANSMISSION: By contact with infected animals or humans.
11. *Scabies* (Itch Mite)
AGE: Any age.
SYMPTOMS: Small, raised, red bumps in linear lesions, especially at fingers, wrist, skin folds. Severe itching especially at night or after bath.
INCUBATION PERIOD: Symptoms appear approximately 1 month after infestation.
TRANSMISSION: By direct contact with infected persons or indirect contact with bedlinens, clothing, etc.
12. *Lice*
AGE: Any age.
SYMPTOMS: Itching scalp. Tiny, white eggs (nits) fasten to the hair shaft. Red pimples seen on scalp. Itching.
INCUBATION PERIOD: 1 week to 1 month.
TRANSMISSION: By direct contact with infected person or indirect contact with infected person's articles.

show signs of shock (pallor, cold and clammy skin) and should be encouraged to lie down with the feet slightly elevated, if possible. The joint should be immobilized and a cold pack used to minimize swelling. No attempts should be made to realign the joint before transporting to a hospital.

Closed head injuries due to falls and trauma may present an emergency situation. Care should be taken to be certain there is no cervical spine injury. Be certain the individual is breathing effectively and the airway is open. Table 6.11 describes assessment and management of head injuries.

TABLE 6.11 Advice on Head Injuries

1. The head injury is considered trivial or mild if the child falls, hits head, cries a few moments, and resumes normal activity.
   A. No loss of consciousness, no vomiting, or change of color is present.
   B. May complain of a mild headache.
   If the abrasion is minor, clean with antiseptic. If necessary, come into the ER for sutures. Apply cold compresses to slight swelling and observe closely for 24 hours.
2. The head injury is moderate if:
   A. There is brief loss of consciousness and return to normal alert state.
   B. There is a decreased level of consciousness for some time and the child needs rousing.
   C. There are one or two episodes of vomiting shortly after the injury.
   The decision of whether the child should be seen in the hospital depends on how far away the child is and whether the parent/guardian is competent

to observe accurately for a 48-hour period for:
   Persistent vomiting
   Unequal pupil size
   Excess drowsiness or lethargy
   Weakness of an arm or leg
   Continuous crying
   Change of color from normal to pale
3. The severe head injury that requires immediate hospitalization is one in which the child has:
   A. Loss of consciousness and remains unconscious.
   B. Persistent vomiting.
   C. Convulsions.
   D. Irregular respirations.
   E. Pale color.
   F. Bleeding from the external ear canal (basal skull fracture).
   G. Worsening of any of the symptoms of moderate head injury.

SOURCE: *Assessment and Intervention in Emergency Nursing* by Nedell Lanros. Bowie, Md.: Robert J. Brady, 1978, p. 324. Reprinted with permission.

Burns

Burns may be caused by heat, scalding water, chemicals, or electricity. They are described as partial thickness or full thickness burns, referring to the extent of tissue damage. *Partial thickness* burns are pink or red, sensitive to pain, and may blister. Of greater concern are *full thickness* burns, which may be white, red, brown, or black. They become edematous or swollen, feel leathery to touch, and are not painful. Children with electrical burns should be transported immediately to the emergency room because the burn is always more severe than it appears. Chemical and thermal burns should be immediately flushed with cold water. Oils, ointments, or lotions should never be applied to a burn. A dry, clean dressing may minimize the sensitivity.

Foreign Objects in the Eyes, Ears, and Nose

Beans and small toy pieces frequently become lodged in ears and nostrils of little children. Tweezers may be used to grasp and remove a very superficial object, but referral to an ENT (Ear, Nose, and Throat) specialist may be necessary. Foreign particles in the eye are painful and cause profuse tearing. The child may effectively wash the particle out on his or her own, or a damp, clean swab may be used to carefully remove the particle. Flushing the eye with warm water may rinse away the particle. If there is any concern that the particle is embedded in the eye, cover the eye and transport immediately to the emergency room.

Anaphylactic Shock

Anaphylactic shock is a severe allergic reaction (e.g., to drugs and insect bites) resulting in respiratory distress, low blood pressure, swelling, and collapse. This is an emergency situation that may require CPR. The child should immediately be transported to an emergency room. Children with known severe allergic reactions to insect bites should have an emergency kit with injectable epinephrine with them at all times.

Poisoning

Because of mouthing behaviors, impulsiveness, and indiscretion, developmentally delayed children are at high risk for poison ingestion. Many substances are potentially poisonous—drugs, plants, cleaning solutions, and other household items. The school should post the phone number of the local poison control center at a central location. Syrup of Ipecac, which can be purchased at a drug store, should be on hand to give at the recommendation of a physician to induce vomiting. Do not routinely induce vomiting after a suspected poison, as some chemicals may be severely caustic.

Vomiting, Diarrhea, and Fever

Teachers of the handicapped are especially concerned with episodes of vomiting, diarrhea, and fever because these problems may be far more threatening to handicapped children than they are to normal, healthy children. For example, a fever may be due to an ear infection or a viral illness, or it might be due to an infected shunt, a serious urinary tract infection, or a decubitus ulcer under a cast. The teacher should always be alert to the signs of dehydration. Prolonged vomiting, diarrhea, or fever should be evaluated by a physician.

Child Abuse and Neglect

The handicapped child is at a significantly higher risk for abuse and neglect than the normal population. Bonding and parental expectations are frequently inappropriate. Marital and financial stresses are prevalent, and sexual abuse is more common with retarded children. The teacher should be alert to physical signs of abuse such as unexplainable bruises, lacerations, or burns; bruises on the head, back, and shoulders in various stages of healing; and repeated fractures. The child may demonstrate behavior changes or give verbal cues about the home environment. The teacher should document specific occurrences and observations. Each state has guidelines for reporting suspected abuse or neglect. The teacher should be well aware of the state and school policy and not hesitate to follow up accordingly on any suspicions of abuse or neglect.

SUMMARY

Medical problems in the classroom are of particular concern to the special educator. The teacher should be aware of the diagnosis and its implications before the child's entrance into the classroom. Thereafter, the teacher's ongoing relationship and daily contacts with the child make him or her an integral part of the team providing optimal comprehensive care for the disabled child.

Regular communication between all members of the team—teacher, parents, and medical professionals—cannot be emphasized strongly enough. The nature of the disability and the impact of the child's environment on development require frequent reassessment of medical, educational, and psychosocial goals.

This chapter briefly touched upon some of the more common routine and acute problems encountered by the teacher. The discussion should serve as a guideline for identification, management, and referral of specific concerns. We encourage you to seek out further indepth medical and educational information on specific concerns.

REFERENCES

American Red Cross. *First aid for foreign body obstruction of the airway.* American Red Cross, 1978.

Bryan, E., Warden, M., Berg, B., & Hauck, G. Medical considerations for multiple-handicapped children in the public schools. *Journal of School Health,* 1978, *48*(2), 84–90.

Hawken, M., & Ozuna, J. Practical aspects of anticonvulsant therapy. *American Journal of Nursing,* June 1979, 1062–1068.

Hilt, N.E., & Cogburn, S.B. *Manual of orthopedics.* St. Louis: C.V. Mosby 1980.

Holt, K. Neurological and neuromuscular disorders. In S. Gabel & M. Erickson (Eds.), *Child development and developmental disabilities.* Boston: Little, Brown, 1980.

Langley, B., & DuBose, R.F. Functional vision screening for severely handicapped children. *The New Outlook,* 1976, *8*, 346–350.

Northern, J., & Downs, M. *Hearing in children.* Baltimore: Williams and Wilkins, 1978.

Peterson, R., & Cleveland, J. *Medical problems in the classroom: An educator's guide.* Springfield, Ill.: Charles C Thomas, 1975.

Sharpe, K. Epilepsy and diseases of the nervous system. In R. Peterson & J. Cleveland (Eds.), *Medical problems in the classroom.* Springfield, Ill.: Charles C Thomas, 1975.

Smith, D.W. *Recognizable patterns of human malformation: Genetic, embryologic, and clinical aspects* (2nd ed.). Philadelphia: W.B. Saunders, 1976.

Vaughan, V., & McKay, R.J. (Eds.). *Nelson textbook of pediatrics* (10th ed.). Philadelphia: W.B. Saunders, 1975.

Vining, E., Accardo, P., Rubenstein, J., Farrell, S., & Roizen, N. Cerebral palsy: A pediatric developmentalist's overview. *American Journal of the Disabled Child,* 1976, *130*, 643–649.

Wolfson, R., Aghamohamadi, A., & Berman, S. Disorders of hearing. In S. Gabel & M. Erickson (Eds.), *Child development and developmental disabilities.* Boston: Little, Brown, 1980.

Controlled movement is the bedrock for most other behaviors. Moderately and severely handicapped infants, children, and adults may have permanent, though manageable, movement difficulties as a result of muscle or neurological damage. Motor problems, which may also be caused by programmatic neglect, can lead to poor posture, overweight, weakness, or the absence of recreational skills. In either case, educational programs should reflect goals and objectives in motor learning, though they will vary widely from one student to the next.

The next three chapters provide rather different perspectives on movement and motor learning. In chapter 7, Pip Campbell, an occupational therapist, describes a framework for understanding and programming for the motor difficulties typically associated with neurological disorders such as cerebral palsy. Because of the enormous variety of movement problems associated with cerebral palsy alone, Pip and many of her colleagues profile student's difficulties in terms of high or low muscle tone. The student's performance changes as a result of treatment may be compared to this baseline profile.

In contrast, chapter 8 addresses motor learning in the "more typical" severely handicapped student who has thinking problems, but generally does not have permanent movement deficiencies. As physical educators, Linda Bunker and Sherril Moon trace the interdependencies of locomotor and manipulative skills with fundamental motor skills. They use the model of functional curriculum development described in chapter 4 to view motor skill instruction, from body management to physical fitness and recreation.

Finally, in chapter 9, Corry Robinson and Jacques Robinson explain sensorimotor skill learning—a model for teaching young severely handicapped students the basics of movement and thinking skills. This model, rooted in Jean Piaget's work, with the more recent influences of Uzgiris and Hunt, encompasses the emergence of language and problem solving from such basic movement skills as hand watching, visually directed grasping, visual tracking of objects as they move in and out of view, emptying and filling containers, navigating around barriers to reach a desired goal, and imitating motor and vocal responses. When young severely handicapped students have movement problems such as cerebral palsy, their acquisition of these basic movements and skills is threatened. The training procedures detailed in this chapter are the product of extensive field-testing with multiply handicapped infants and young children at the Meyer Children's Rehabilitation Center at the University of Nebraska.

Introduction to Chapters 7, 8, and 9

7

Basic Considerations in Programming for Students with Movement Difficulties

Philippa H. Campbell, an occupational therapist, is Director, Early Intervention Program, at the Children's Hospital Medical Center of Akron, Akron, Ohio. The development of material presented in this chapter was supported in part from USOE/BEH Grant No. G007900506 to Children's Hospital Medical Center of Akron.

Movement difficulties can result from genetic causes; damage to the infant before, during, or after birth; or various traumatic events such as gunshot wounds, automobile accidents, or child abuse. The conditions that produce movement problems can *generally* be classified into one of two basic origins. The first group includes disorders (such as polio) that originate from damage to the anterior horn cell and the nerves leading to the muscles. These conditions are lower motor neuron lesions. A second group, upper motor neuron lesions, derives from damage to the structures of the brain, including the cerebral cortex, the spinal cord, and the cerebellum. Cerebral palsy is the single largest category of diagnosed upper motor neuron problems in children.[1]

Lower motor neuron problems typically involve weakened muscles with limited or no power to move. In contrast, the motor impairment in cerebral palsy is not initially characterized by weak muscles or decreased strength. Rather, the child's ability to move in response to events is limited by atypical muscle tone and poor coordination among muscle groups. The ways in which the environment is represented motorically to the infant or young child with motor dysfunction may include distortions characterized or defined by the limitations of the movement. For instance, a child with poorly coordinated movement patterns may develop a representation of shaking a rattle that is quite different from the representation of shaking produced by the infant with normal movement. And the infant with severely limited movement may develop no representation of a rattle as a shakeable object simply because the limitation of movement prevents shaking actions.

In cerebral palsy as well as in other conditions involving disturbance to the central nervous system (CNS), all of the child's movements may be atypical. However, not all students with deviations in movement show overt CNS dysfunction. Down syndrome students frequently demonstrate deficient movement, as do students with labels of psychomotor retardation or developmental delay. Movement may also be atypical in children with genetic abnor-

---

[1]See Bleck and Nagel, 1975, or Bigge, 1982, for further discussion of conditions producing impaired motor functioning.

malities or degenerative diseases or conditions of the central nervous system. The movement produced may be atypical in terms of quality (or form) and quantity (or amount), but will relate to deviations in the postural or muscle tone, on which all movement is based.

BASIC PROCESSES UNDERLYING MOVEMENT COMPETENCE

Three fundamental dimensions underlying the performance of motor activities have been represented in scale form (Bricker & Campbell, 1980; Campbell & Bricker, 1980) such that the *extent* and *direction* of deviations from a standard can be determined. The most critical of these three basic processes is postural tone or the degree of tension in the body musculature. Related to this very basic process are measures of the quality and the amount of movement performed in both structured and nonstructured situations. Each of these basic processes, as well as secondary processes of mobility, hand transport, manipulation, oral-motor/eating, and oral-motor/vocalization, can be represented in a way that allows us to not only measure initial performance, but also to indicate methods of intervention.

The relationship among the various types of movement required for everyday living and the basic processes underlying movement production is outlined as a model for intervention with motor handicapped students in Figure 7.1. All movement can be classified as either automatic, primary, or goal-directed. However, no movement is produced without a stimulus. For this reason, movement difficulties are often described as sensorimotor disturbances to emphasize the relationship between the sensory and the motor systems in producing movement. The function or purpose of each type of movement is unique. Automatic movements result from disturbances to the body alignment in relation to gravity. These movements realign body parts and institute and maintain balance against gravity. Primary movements are very simple schemes involving a stimulus and a movement response that produces a consequence. This type of movement is the initial basis from which goal-directed (voluntary) movements are generated (Piaget, 1952). Goal-directed movement also results from a stimulus and produces a consequence. However, it results from a complex organization where simple movement schemes are grouped together, often in unique combinations, to attain a predetermined end.

The basic motor processes of tone, movement quality, and movement quantity provide the basis on which automatic, primary, and goal-directed movement is produced. Disturbances in any of the three basic processes will cause all movements to be atypical. However, the student must have a reason to generate goal-directed movement, since it is not rooted in only motoric competence. Rather, a significant component of goal-directed movement is intention (Bower, 1979) expressed in relation to people, events, and objects in the student's environment. *Intention* can be defined as the coordination of two existing schemes in order to obtain a pre-existing and desired goal (Bricker, Macke, Levin, & Campbell,

FIGURE 7.1.
Intervention Model for Children with Sensory and Motor Impairments

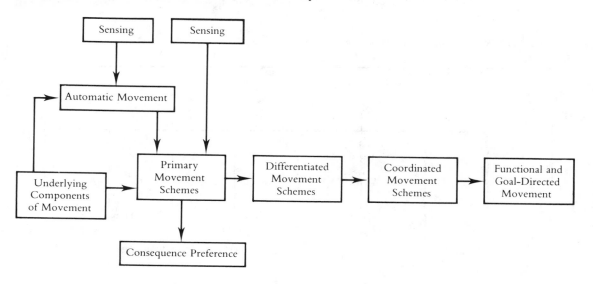

1981). Many students with dysfunction in tone and movement quality and quantity may use movement intentionally and to attain a goal. However, there are other students whose movement is not goal-directed with or without disturbance in the basic underlying processes. This differentiation is critical when choosing intervention strategies since techniques designed to alter the underlying processes of movement will not, in and of themselves, produce goal-directed motor behavior.

UNDERLYING PROCESSES

Tonicity

Postural tone is a measure of the tension in the muscles throughout the body. It is the basis on which both automatic and goal-directed movements are produced. Normal postural tone allows postural stability with mobility; that is, the head can remain stable when the arm moves forward or the wrist remains stable while the fingers move. Deviations in postural tone range from an absence or severe limitation in tone (hypotonia or too little tone) to too much postural tone (hypertonus or spasticity). An individual with hypertonus may have difficulty with motor skills because of stiffness in involved parts of the body. Adequate muscle tension to move against gravity is absent or limited in students with hypotonia.

Other children have unstable postural tone which fluctuates even when the child is not performing motor actions. These students may show relatively low postural tone at one moment and be severely hypertonic the next moment. Postural tone fluctuations from one extreme in the range to the other are the most dramatic, but fluctuations can occur anywhere on the continuum from hypotonic to hypertonic. Fluctuating tonicity inhibits movement in that muscle tone is not only atypical but also constantly changing. The child, therefore, has not only an atypical but also an unstable base from which to generate motor patterns necessary to interact with the environment.

Basic tone can be represented on a continuum such as the scale illustrated in Figure 7.2 by using ratings of 1 for hypotonic students and 9 for those students who are so severely hypertonic as to be labeled *rigid*. These initial ratings reflect the *underlying tone* under conditions of rest or limited to no goal-directed activity. Observations of the student when resting, lying down, or sitting quietly provide the necessary information.

The measurement of *underlying tone* is essentially a rating of postural tone under conditions as inactive as possible. More critical to developing and implementing intervention methods to normalize postural tone are measurements of tone under varying conditions of stimulation. Postural tone can be modified systematically by using intervention methods to increase tone (facilitation) or decrease tone (inhibition). However, it is more important to realize that postural tone can also be changed nonsystematically as a functional response to influences from the environment. A severely hypertonic child may tighten up even more when someone speaks to him or attempts to pick him up, or simply because someone else in the classroom coughs or makes a sudden noise. Those children with fluctuating basic tone may show even greater fluctuations in response to a favorite toy or when attempting to vocalize or talk. Some children even show changes in postural tone in *anticipation* of something that is going to occur but has not yet actually happened. The point here is that postural tone is not

FIGURE 7.2.
Two-dimensional Representation of the Domain of Tonicity

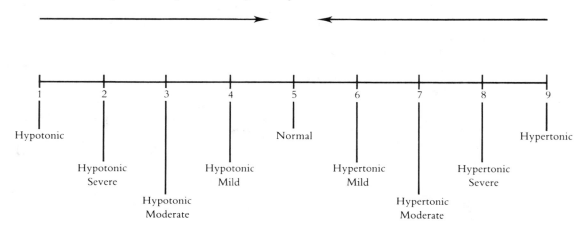

fixed, is changeable, and does change in uncontrolled (or nonsystematic) situations as well as under the controlled and systematic conditions of intervention.

The measurement of *underlying tone,* then, provides the teacher or therapist with an initial assessment that leads into general intervention strategies. The intervention strategies appropriate for the child with a tonicity rating of 9 are those that will normalize tone by decreasing hypertonicity. For the child who scores 1, the intervention strategies will produce normalized tone by increasing basic postural tone. However, when the postural tone changes significantly in response to events, a more precise measurement or individual definition of tone must be used to determine which intervention strategies are most effective for that individual student. Structured observation of the student's motor performances in the classroom will produce information about what types of events alter postural tone.

There are many situations which potentially can occur in the classroom to alter the postural tone of individual students. In fact, unless they receive intervention to normalize tone or stay in situations where the amount or type of stimuli are controlled, students with atypical tone are likely to respond motorically to almost any event with changes in postural tone. Techniques that normalize tone (without requiring any movement response from the student) are relatively easy to implement successfully. However, maintaining that state of normalized tone as part of some type of functional movement is far more difficult. We will now look at some conditions which can potentially alter postural tone.

Preferred/Nonpreferred Toys, People, or Activities

Students with atypical postural tone still have preferences in relation to environmental events. They may prefer certain foods or liquids (and not prefer others), may prefer their mother over the teacher, or may have particularly favored toys or activities. Changes in postural tone frequently occur as an expression of preferred or nonpreferred events. For instance, a student with high underlying tone is likely to have even higher tone when crying and still even higher tone when tantruming. Similarly, significant tonal changes may occur during toilet training if the student is uncomfortable or if the activity is not highly desirable. The student may become quite stiff each day when being dressed to go home if going home is motivating.

Transitional Movements

Lifting, carrying, transferring, positioning, repositioning, dressing, and other activities routinely done with physically handicapped students to move them from one instructional situation to another frequently alter tone. Tonal changes can be dramatic if the child is not handled appropriately. In addition, where position changes are associated with particular activities, postural tone may change significantly. For instance, if the child is motivated to eat and is always fed in the same chair, putting the child in that chair may alter tone, both because of the movement transition and because the transition is associated with a preferred activity.

Performance Requirements

The movement competence required by a particular task, activity, or material can alter postural tone generally but can also change tone specifically in one or more extremities. Increased tone is predictable when the movement required is extremely difficult for the student. For instance, the tone may significantly increase in the left hand and arm when the student is required to use fine manipulations of the fingers in his right hand. Tone may increase in the left leg when the student is required to balance on the right leg.

The observer can list each of these events and record data on the extent to which tone is changed and the stimuli related to those changes. Information about the student's postural tone under stimulation or typical environmental influences can also be represented on the scale of tonicity. A rating of 2–7 can be used to describe a student whose basic tone is hypotonic but changes to moderate hypertonicity under stimulation. A more complete recording of this situation could state: "Rating 2–7: favorite toys; eating ice cream; positioned prone for head control." Even this general information provides more concise information about those stimulating situations which will require modification and intervention if the student is to be taught to move with more normalized postural tone.

All developmental milestone skills have some component of motor behavior regardless of whether required performances are classified as language, social, or cognitive. The preverbal student, for instance, has only movement as a means for responding to the environment. Postural tone must be as normalized as possible for the student to acquire the functional movements necessary to perform developmental skills such as sitting, walking, and self-feeding and even problem-solving skills such as object permanence or means-end relationships. The results of programming for tone normalization provided through basic therapy alone or without regard for the tone changes that occur in nonspecific intervention situations will not be as significant as when postural tone is viewed as an essential component of all of the student's activity. Teachers, therapists, and parents of students with postural tone deviations must not lose sight of the relationships between the motor system and environmental interaction. Intervention strategies can only be as effective as the assessment on which the selection of those strategies is based. If the teacher fails to identify that the tone of a particular student changes when the child is provided with a specific toy and therefore continues to provide the toy, the intervention might teach the student to be more hypertonic. No teacher, therapist, or parent would intentionally instruct a student that way. However, these instructional situations often occur when observational assessment has not been careful or precise or when postural tone is viewed as a fixed and unchangeable dimension of behavior.

Qualitative Movement

Most assessments or observations of motor skills focus on the number of motor milestone skills performed by a student (Campbell, 1978). However, most physical and occupational therapists are also interested in determining the patterns of movement the student uses to perform both automatic and goal-directed movements. A description of the patterns of movement provides an operational definition of *how* the student moves under varying conditions.

Historically, patterns of movement have been globally classified as normal, abnormal, primitive, or mixed (Bobath & Bobath, 1975). *Abnormal* patterns of movement are typically associated with hypertonus, can be described as stereotypic, and generally are not observed in any phase of normal movement. Abnormal patterns are sometimes referred to as *reflexes* or *abnormal reflexes*. Several guides have been published that measure these patterns by a standard method of eliciting the patterns under fixed situations (Fiorentino, 1972). Often, therapists will label these patterns as *obligatory,* to describe observations where the student appears to use the same patterns in a variety of situations. Examples of movement patterns often classified as *abnormal* are the total extension pattern, where the head is back, the shoulders retracted (or pushed back), the hips extended, the legs turned in, and the feet pushing downward (Figure 7.3); and the total flexion pattern, where the head is forward, the shoulders protracted (or hunching forward), the hips and knees bent, and the legs in a neutral position (Figure 7.4). These are both examples of total abnormal patterns of movement that traditionally have been observed in cerebral palsied children with increased postural tone.

Primitive patterns of movement are those characteristic of infant movement that are retained by older children past the time in the normal sequence of development when they would have been integrated or replaced by more complex ways of moving. For

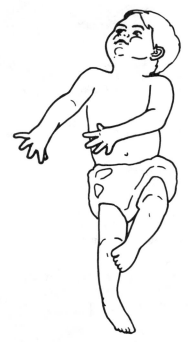

FIGURE 7.3.
Total Extension Pattern

instance, young babies grasp objects placed in their hands (grasp reflex or tactile grasp pattern) until about 3 or 4 months of age. This primitive pattern disappears in a sense, but more accurately, becomes replaced with far more complex hand movements the infant uses to interact with the variety of objects in the environment. A tactile grasp pattern observed in an 8-month-old child would be a primitive pattern of movement. The movement is not abnormal because it is observable in normal infants or young children. Primitive patterns may be noted under a variety of conditions of postural tone. Students with increased tone are as likely to show primitive patterns of movement as those with hypotonicity.

Patterns of movement have been classified into these global categories as a means of understanding differences in movement between the movement pat-

FIGURE 7.4.
Total Flexor Pattern

terns of children with dysfunctional postural tone and the patterns exhibited by children with normal tone. This classification does not differentiate or imply a differentiation of treatment goals and methods; both primitive and abnormal movement patterns require intervention to inhibit or integrate both types of movement. Some cerebral palsied children perform all movements in ways that can be labeled abnormal, but these students typically also display severe discrepancies in postural tone. Correspondingly, students with moderate disturbances in postural tone (such as motor-delayed or Down syndrome students) may perform most movements with primitive organizational patterns. However, most students with motor difficulties will perform some patterns normally, some abnormally, and some primitively, depending upon postural tone states, the complexity of the task requirements, and other environmental factors.

A more precise method for analysis of movement patterns has been derived from the work of Kong and Quinton in Switzerland (Hanson & Campbell, in press) and is outlined in Figure 7.5. This analysis is based on a notion of the *function* of both normal and atypical movement rather than on the specific milestone *forms* of movement that result from motor development.

The purpose or function of movement is to provide coordinated interaction with various aspects of the environment. Gravity is the primary factor with which the very young infant must learn to contend. Muscle activity provides the force necessary to enable the human body to move against gravity, to perform actions that resist the influence of the pull of gravity. For instance, lifting the head in a prone (stomach-lying) position is an antigravity movement; the muscles of the head and neck must contract to provide the force necessary to move the head upward against the downward pull of gravity. This movement would be classified as an active motion, one performed through activation of the muscle movers of head extension. Once moved to this position, if the head is held upright, both the muscles that extend the head and those that bend the head must cocontract to provide stability against the gravitational pull. This type of movement would be called *head control prone,* or more specifically, *postural stability of the head in a prone position.* However, when the child then moves his head, for instance turns it to the side, the result is *activation* (mobility) of the neck rotator muscles against a background of postural stability achieved through cocontraction. Therefore, all normal function movement is the result of a coordinated relationship of muscle activity that allows for active

Figure 7.5.
Progression of Motor Development

Muscle Tone
↓
Movement for Postural Stability (Cocontraction)
↓
Movement for Mobility Against Postural Stability (Activation)
↓
Practice for Refined Coordination

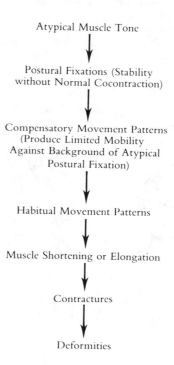

Atypical Muscle Tone
↓
Postural Fixations (Stability without Normal Cocontraction)
↓
Compensatory Movement Patterns (Produce Limited Mobility Against Background of Atypical Postural Fixation)
↓
Habitual Movement Patterns
↓
Muscle Shortening or Elongation
↓
Contractures
↓
Deformities

movement (mobility) in combination with postural control (stability).

Postural tone provides the background for both active and cocontracted movements. However, postural tone is deficient or atypical in most types of movement disorders because of CNS damage. Therefore, the resultant movement, whether functional for stability or mobility, will also be atypical. In infancy, many variations in postural tone may be seen. The majority of infants are believed to have hypotonic (rather than hypertonic) tone variations. The infant's initial movements are likely to be those which gain some degree of stability against gravity (such as head control). But when postural tone is deficient, cocontraction for stability may not be possible. Postural stability, however, may still occur. However, stability will be achieved through an atypical *fixation* rather than through normal cocontraction of the muscles. These fixes compensate for lack of cocontraction and insufficient tone artificially, allowing for the function, postural stability, to be achieved through atypical means. The *fix* provides stability but does not allow for ranges of movement in any one position.

An example may help to clarify the concept of fixing. One fix that is commonly observed in low-toned students is described as turtling of the head into the shoulders. The shoulders are elevated (raised) toward the ear lobes and the neck is subsequently "shortened." The result is a change in the relationship of gravity to movement. The amount of balance required to maintain the head in relationship to the shoulders is significantly decreased (see Figure 7.6). However, the resultant movement pattern depends on *and is restricted to* stability rather than characterized by stability with mobility, as are normal movement patterns.

The progression of abnormal motor development (see Figure 7.5) is sequential and is built upon the fixations resulting from movement that performs the function of postural stability without normal tone and without normal muscle cocontraction. These fixations are atypical and severely limit (or prevent) subsequent movement patterns involving mobility and stability. Compensatory patterns that are not normal in form and are seldom efficient in function derive directly from atypical postural fixations. If repeated or practiced, they become habitual; the student spontaneously produces these restricted patterns in a variety of conditions. The habitual patterns are frequently characterized by limited range of motion of involved joints. When untreated or unaltered, they can lead to secondary problems of muscle shortening or elongation. These problems with muscle length are sometimes referred to as *muscle tightness, muscle lengthening,* or *contractures.* Contractures must be stretched out through directed exercise to return muscles to their correct and optimal length. As shown in Figure 7.7, when unaltered, contractures become *deformities* that can only be changed through surgery. Thus, the original postural tone helps produce atypical postural fixations which, in turn, force the production of compensatory (atypical) movement patterns. Practiced or repeated patterns become habitual, produce secondary muscle tightness due to movement being restricted, and result in the formation of deformities that are correctable only through surgery.

Some therapists (e.g., Bly, Note 1) refer to certain types of postural fixations as *blocks* to distinguish

FIGURE 7.6.
Change in the Relationship to Gravity in Head Control with and Without Atypical Postural Fixation

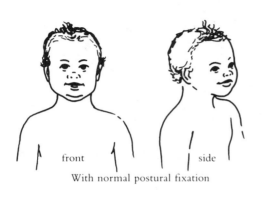

With normal postural fixation

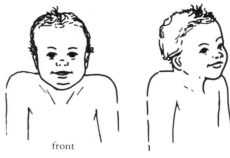

With atypical postural fixation
of elevated shoulders to
compensate

SPASM ⟶ CONTRACTURE ⟶ DEFORMITY

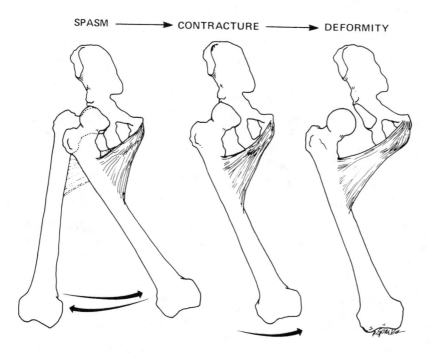

FIGURE 7.7.
Progression from Tightness to Deformity in the Hip Joint with Resultant Deformity of Dislocation of the Hip
Source: *Physically Handicapped Children: A Medical Atlas for Teachers* by Eugene Bleck and Donald Nagel (New York: Grune & Stratton, 1982), p. 64. Reprinted by permission.

those fixations that block (or prevent) the development of normal patterns of movement. However, the number and types of fixes that can be considered blocks are unknown, and the differentiation itself does not relate to treatment goals or intervention methods. Therefore, we have eliminated the terminology of movement block, recognizing that, in fact, some postural fixations (particularly habitual ones) will severely limit normal movement (Hanson & Campbell, in press). The greatest number of postural fixations (normal or atypical) occur at the proximal joints—head/neck, scapula, shoulder, hip, and pelvis. These joints represent the areas of the body where the largest bulk muscles are placed and where motor actions require little fine coordination and control. Movement that occurs, for instance, at the head/neck or the shoulder is gross motor controlled in contrast to the finely coordinated movement performed by muscles in the hands or in the oral-motor region. The very young baby's first attempts to move against gravity involve the head/neck and the shoulders. Therefore, initial postural atypical fixations are likely to occur in these proximal areas. For instance, in the head/neck movement described earlier, the turtling produces a compensatory pattern of neck extensor hyperextension. The neck hyperextension (without balanced flexion necessary for cocontraction) results in a limited function of head control prone that is restricted to an atypical movement form. In other words, the purpose of the activity is

met with a qualitatively atypical movement form. As a result, the muscles of the head/neck may become shortened and elongated, and contractures may develop if this pattern is practiced and becomes habitual. (See Figure 7.8.) Furthermore, though head control may seem to be present, the movement is restricted to only one *form*. The student may be prevented from using the neck extensors/flexors and rotators to flex the head laterally or to turn through rotation. Or flexion of the head forward (e.g., chin tucked toward neck) may be prevented through elongation of the neck flexor muscles. The full range of head movement is therefore prevented by a pattern of fixation that originally produced stability against gravity.

The quality of movement of a particular student or group of students can be rated numerically with a variety of mechanisms. A global system based on presence/absence of abnormal movement patterns may be satisfactory for older students with muscle tightnesses or contractures and deformities. However, additional assessment will be needed to provide a basis for intervention (Figure 7.9). A more precise rating system that quantifies the number and degree of postural fixations may be more appropriate for younger children where movement patterns (normal and atypical) are still developing and have not yet fully reached the habitual level.

Table 7.1 and Figure 7.10 illustrate a format and process that is used by therapists to generate treat-

FIGURE 7.8.
Shortening/Elongation of Flexor and Extensor Muscles in the Neck Hyperextension Movement Block

ment based on an analysis of movement patterns. The therapist not only records observations of atypical fixations but also notes the resulting compensatory movement patterns. The potential implications of limited patterns are determined to better relate the child's movement functioning to the sequence of abnormal movement development as well as to relate difficulties with movement in one body area to those in another area. Table 7.2 shows an example of the analysis completed for a student with underlying hypotonic tone that fluctuates to ranges of hypertonus (particularly in the shoulders and pelvic/hip areas).

Intervention provided by a physical or occupational therapist is typically directed at normalizing postural tone and simultaneously improving the quality of movements, particularly the automatic movements. Educational programming more often is aimed at primary or goal-directed movements required for functional skills. However, in order for both the therapists and the teachers to be effective, postural tone must be normalized as part of all movement training (whether automatic, primary, or goal-directed) and the student must be taught to perform each type of movement with patterns as normal as possible. Therefore, the teacher must be skillful in observing patterns of movement and determining whether they are normal or atypical in order to effectively train functional skills such as eating, toileting, communicating, and manipulating.

Movement Quantity

The amount of movement present is a dimension that is seldom evaluated by teachers or therapists. However, deviation on this dimension has significant implications for the intervention provided for a motor handicapped individual, particularly where the other movement processes of tone and movement quality

are normal. Furthermore, movement quantity or rate acts to bridge the underlying processes with mobility, manipulation, and other movement-based functional skills.

Some students with relatively normal postural tone and with primitive-to-normal patterns of movement are seldom observed to move. For instance, many severely handicapped students with long histories of institutionalization or lack of programming have not been placed in situations requiring movement. In fact, many custodial care environments inadvertently foster immobility since immobile people are easier to care for than mobile ones. These students often show a lack of movement quantity that we cannot account for on the basis of deviations in postural tone or movement quality. Seligman (1975) refers to this type of situation as *learned helplessness*—which implies not just that the student had not had the opportunity to learn to move, but rather that the opportunities provided for the student have taught *lack* of movement even when the motor capability for producing the movement was present. Students with long histories of no intervention are not the only ones who learn to be helpless when movement is required. Younger children can also inadvertently be taught not to move by receiving passive motor intervention (such as range of motion exercises) or by being prevented from performing movement activities through management routines such as carrying, dressing, or feeding.

All types of movement—automatic, primary, and goal-directed—result in response to incoming stimuli and produce a consequence to the movement. However, each isolated movement pattern must occur often enough to be incorporated into the more complex organizations of movement patterns, to be functional for the student, and to be practiced enough that the response is strengthened and maintained. For instance, the consequence of turning the head from midline to the side is viewing or listening to something. In other words, a child is not likely to turn her head from midline to the side for the sake of head turning alone. The movement is present for some purpose or function. If a student were able to turn her head from midline with balance between the neck flexors/extensors and with normal postural tone, a movement response of head turning to the side would be said to be present in the student's repertoire. However, if the student performed this movement only once per day or once per hour, the rate or the quantity of the movement would be insufficient for functional use without intervention. Furthermore, the movement of head turning would not be likely to be strengthened or increased without intervention to provide repeated practice under functional and motivating conditions.

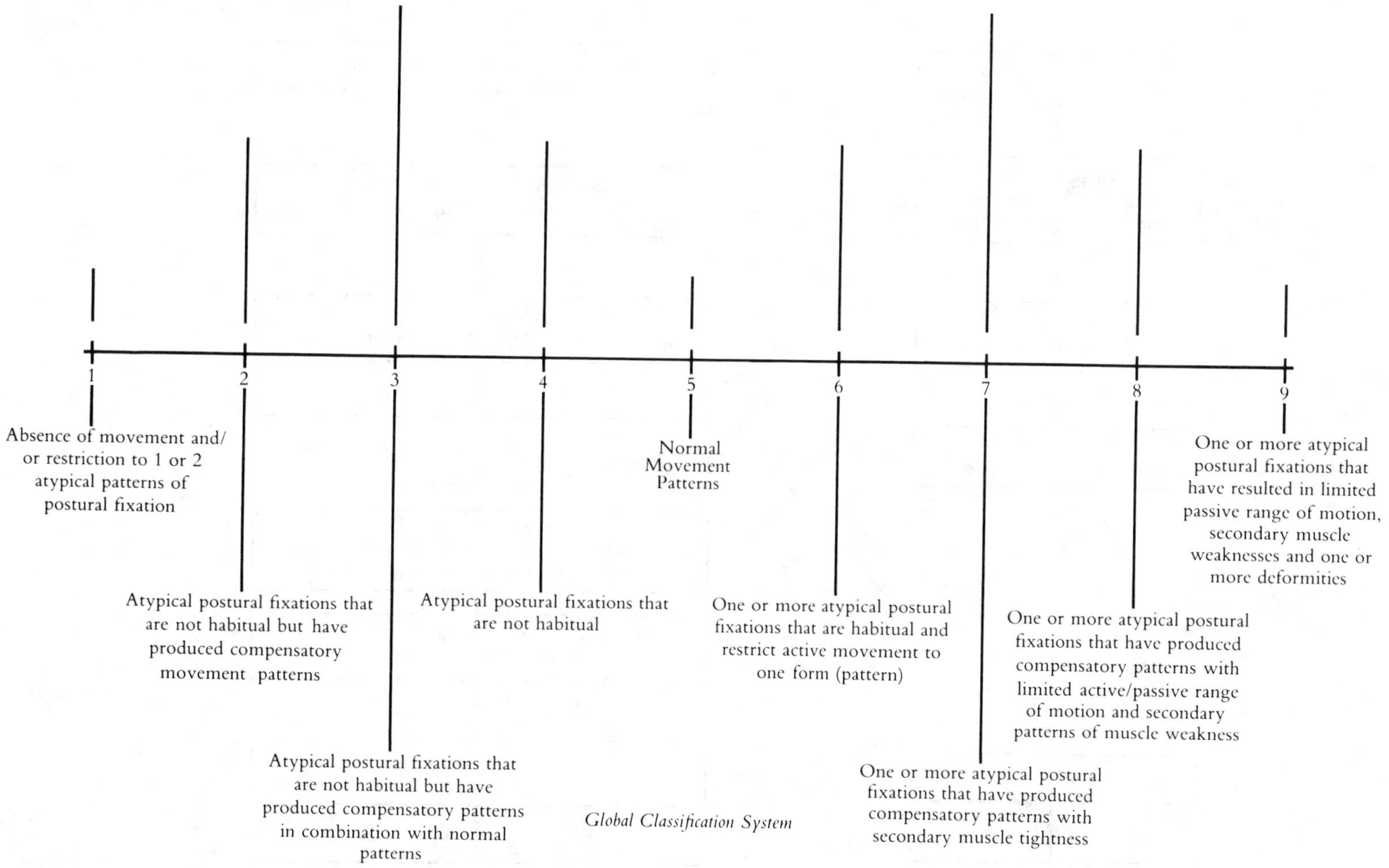

Absence of movement and/or restriction to 1 or 2 atypical patterns of postural fixation

Atypical postural fixations that are not habitual but have produced compensatory movement patterns

Atypical postural fixations that are not habitual but have produced compensatory patterns in combination with normal patterns

Atypical postural fixations that are not habitual

Normal Movement Patterns

One or more atypical postural fixations that are habitual and restrict active movement to one form (pattern)

One or more atypical postural fixations that have produced compensatory patterns with secondary muscle tightness

One or more atypical postural fixations that have produced compensatory patterns with limited active/passive range of motion and secondary patterns of muscle weakness

One or more atypical postural fixations that have resulted in limited passive range of motion, secondary muscle weaknesses and one or more deformities

Global Classification System

FIGURE 7.9.
Classification of Patterns of Movement

177

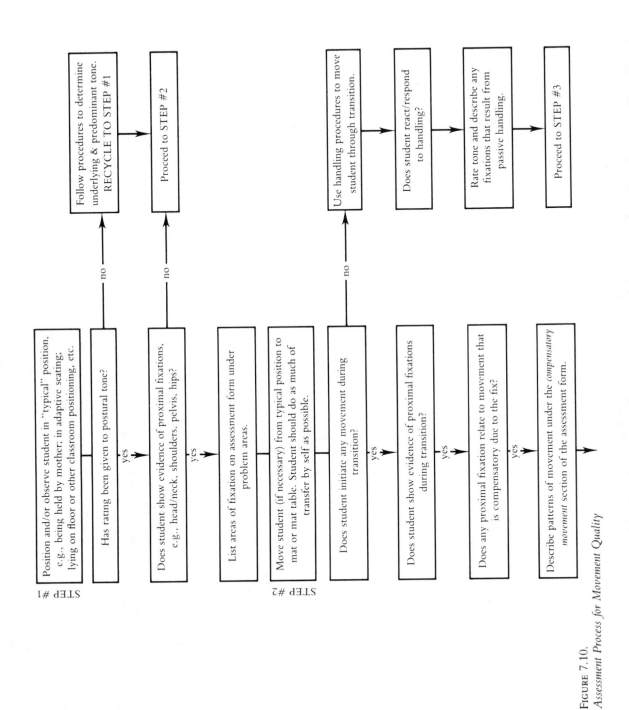

STEP #1

Position and/or observe student in "typical" position, e.g., being held by mother; in adaptive seating; lying on floor or other classroom positioning, etc.

Has rating been given to postural tone?

no → Follow procedures to determine underlying & predominant tone. RECYCLE TO STEP #1

yes

Does student show evidence of proximal fixations, e.g., head/neck, shoulders, pelvis, hips?

no → Proceed to STEP #2

yes

List areas of fixation on assessment form under problem areas.

STEP #2

Move student (if necessary) from typical position to mat or mat table. Student should do as much of transfer by self as possible.

Does student initiate any movement during transition?

no → Use handling procedures to move student through transition.

Does student react/respond to handling?

Rate tone and describe any fixations that result from passive handling.

Proceed to STEP #3

yes

Does student show evidence of proximal fixations during transition?

yes

Does any proximal fixation relate to movement that is compensatory due to the fix?

yes

Describe patterns of movement under the *compensatory movement* section of the assessment form.

FIGURE 7.10.
Assessment Process for Movement Quality

178

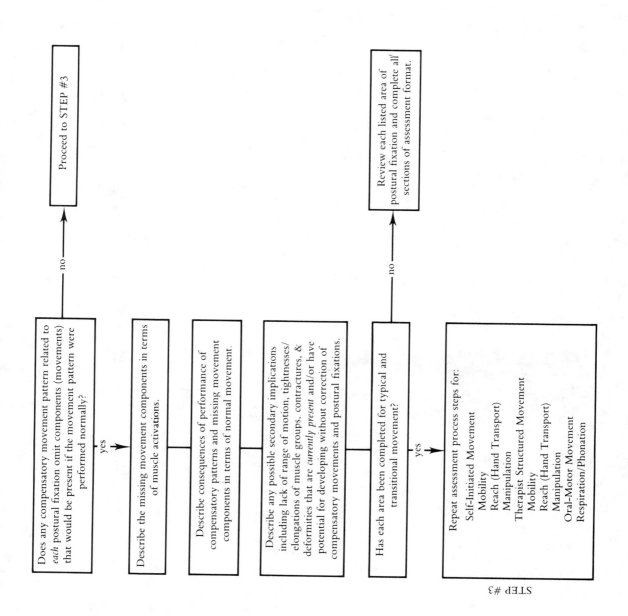

Proceed to STEP #3

no

Does any compensatory movement pattern related to *each* postural fixation omit components (movements) that would be present if the movement pattern were performed normally?

yes

Describe the missing movement components in terms of muscle activations.

Describe consequences of performance of compensatory patterns and missing movement components in terms of normal movement.

Describe any possible secondary implications including lack of range of motion, tightnesses/elongations of muscle groups, contractures, & deformities that are *currently present* and/or have potential for developing without correction of compensatory movements and postural fixations.

Has each area been completed for typical and transitional movement?

no

Review each listed area of postural fixation and complete all' sections of assessment format.

yes

Repeat assessment process steps for:

Self-Initiated Movement
    Mobility
    Reach (Hand Transport)
    Manipulation
Therapist Structured Movement
    Mobility
    Reach (Hand Transport)
    Manipulation
Oral-Motor Movement
Respiration/Phonation

STEP #3

FIGURE 7.10.
(CONTINUED)

179

TABLE 7.1 Format for Part of a Neurodevelopmental Assessment

Neurodevelopmental Assessment

Child's Name: _____ C.A. _____ Assessment Completed By _____ Date(s): _____

Problem Area(s)	Compensatory Patterns	Missing Components	Direct Consequences	Secondary Implications
Standard Position: 1. 2. 3. 4. 5. 6.				
With Movement on Floor or Mat: 1. 2. 3. 4. 5. 6. 7. 8. 9. 10.				

Assessments of movement quantity are most typically made in relation to primary or goal-directed movements and, therefore, are frequently confounded with other variables such as opportunity to perform or consequence preferences. For instance, when a student does not move his head from midline to the side more frequently than once per minute, the teacher can say that the rate of movement is atypical but cannot determine the reason for the low rate. This same student may motorically be able to perform at a higher rate, but not do so because he does not prefer the resultant consequence of looking or listening or does not see or hear well enough for the consequence to be relevant. The consequences of primary and goal-directed movements are likely to be positive and not punishing or aversive, where the consequences of not performing automatic movement patterns may be more aversive in terms of causing discomfort or pain if the student falls rather than maintains balance. Therefore, some students may show better rates of automatic movements than primary or goal-directed movements.

Movement quantity can be rated using the same system described for postural tone and for movement quality. A student with a lack of or limited observable movement under any conditions would be rated as 1 or 2, and the student with severely excessive movement would score a 9. Each type of movement can be rated if the therapist or teacher thinks that there are differences in rates of movement in each of these situations. Discrepancies between ratings on automatic and goal-directed movements may indicate difficulties with motivation, nonpreferred consequences to movement, or sensory problems including deficient visual, hearing, or tactile-kinesthetic/vestibular processes. Intervention can then be started to increase or decrease the rate of movement, as appropriate. However, specific baseline measures must often be taken to assess precise rates for particular movement patterns under varying conditions of postural tone and movement quality so that intervention can be fully effective. The baseline measurements of rate of performance of a particular movement allow the teacher to manipulate variables of opportunity and motivation systematically to increase or decrease movement quantity. Often, physical and occupational therapists, because of their orientation to consider movement development maturational or neurological, do not systematically consider the relationship of consequences to desired movement patterns. Therefore, movement patterns that are neurologically present may not become sufficiently strengthened or increased because the consequences of the movement are not manipulated.

Figure 7.12 graphs the relationship between consequences of performing a desired movement and the rate (or quantity) of performance of that movement

Table 7.2. Partially Complete Neurodevelopmental Treatment (NDT) Assessment Form

Child's Name: ___B.J.___   C.A.: ___9-8___

Assessment Completed By ___LM___   Date(s): ___1/13, 14/1982___

Problem Area(s)	Compensatory Patterns	Missing Components	Direct Consequences	Secondary Implications
In adaptive chair 1. Head/neck extension.	Neck hyperextension for extension Lateral flexion (with extension) for rotation/diagonal movement	Symmetrical strength/endurance in the extensor muscles Strength in head flexors Coordinated lateral/diagonal movement	Head falls forward/ backward Shoulder elevation Increased extension with lateral movement Lack of rotary head movement	Decreased visual range Lack of shoulder/ arm disassociation Tightness in right neck musculature
2. Scapular elevation/ adduction	Trunk movement (lateral flexion) for arm extension	Controlled trunk extension	Extension reinforced by scapular adduction & UE flexion/retraction	Weak shoulder depressors Tightness of the scapular humeral muscles Tightness of elbow flexor Tightness of finger flexors Weak upper extremity extension
	Upper extremity abduction for forward flexion Asymmetry	Scapular stability Scapular mobility on trunk Isolated/coordinated combined shoulder muscle activation Controlled elbow extension Active forearm movement	Achieved only with retraction and shoulder elevation Lack of range of motion for reaching Decreased functional manipulation Limited unilateral arm use	

with an 18-month-old child with Down syndrome and ratings in postural tone of 3 and movement quality of 4. This student had achieved mobility by crawling and was able to move well inside. However, walking was inhibited by lack of weight bearing on the legs, regardless of the amount of support provided for weight bearing. When placed on a prone standing board, the child cried and withdrew the legs from the supporting surface unless well strapped. Baseline measurements of standing, in the initial segments of the graph, show that weight bearing on the legs was virtually absent. However, the staff judged that weight bearing was physically and neurologically possible and not prevented by postural tone or movement fixations. Therefore, they instituted an intervention program that provided highly preferred consequences for weight bearing in a supported standing position. The student was given his favorite foods (which he fed himself) for increasingly long periods of weight bearing. The second segment of the graph illustrates the effectiveness of

highly preferred foods in increasing the rate of weight bearing. To validate the effectiveness of this strategy, the highly preferred consequences for standing were eliminated and social praise was provided. The third section of the graph shows the *decrease* in rate of movement as a function of altering the consequences this way. The remaining sections document the progression from supported weight bearing to independent weight bearing once food reinforcement was reinstated.

This example emphasizes the importance of the consequences of movement quantity, both in terms of increasing and decreasing rate of movement. However, more important is the relationship of sufficient rate to the acquisition of additional, more complex movement patterns. The student in this illustration was prevented from acquiring the complex movement patterns required for walking, but not because of insufficient postural tone or inability to perform a specific movement pattern (weight bearing on the legs in standing). Rather, insufficient

FIGURE 7.11.
Two-dimensional Representation of the Domain of Movement Quantity

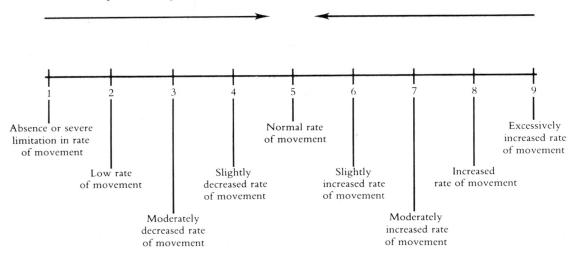

PROCESSES INVOLVED IN AUTOMATIC, PRIMARY, AND GOAL-DIRECTED MOVEMENT

The general purpose of all intervention with motorically impaired students is to promote the acquisition of functional skills that will enable them to be as independent as possible in both current and future environments. Separate measurements of postural tone, movement quality, and movement quantity are essential to generate intervention strategies to both help students move (improve postural tone and movement quality) and teach both automatic and goal-directed movement. Many parents and teachers of motorically impaired students who do not know that tone can be modified do not construct home or classroom environments that allow or systematically program for movement. These negative expectations can limit the quantity and type of movement of the severely involved student (because movement is not expected) or restrict available movement to atypical compensatory or abnormal patterns.

Each of the descriptors used to identify both underlying and secondary motor processes refers to the *function* of a particular behavior rather than to its specific *form*. For instance, the function of postural tone is to maintain sufficient muscle tension to allow for a variety of movements against gravity. However, postural tone may take many forms, ranging from

consequences for weight bearing in standing prevented him from developing the necessary *rate*—a critical component from which other, more complex movement patterns required for walking develop.

severely limited to severely excessive. Similarly, the purpose of movement quality is to allow for the performance of smooth, well-coordinated, efficient ways of moving in and around the environment. The forms of patterns of movement, however, can range from primitive to abnormal or from compensatory movements to movement abnormalities as a result of contractures or deformities.

The secondary motor processes of mobility, manipulation, hand transport, and oral-motor proficiency are based on necessary and sufficient postural tone, movement quality, and movement quantity. The phrase *necessary and sufficient* is important; it does not imply "normality" in basic motor processes but rather denotes a concept relative to secondary motor processes. For instance, hypotonia can in fact be sufficient for the production of certain motor patterns, even though it is not "normal." *Necessary and sufficient,* therefore, directly relates to the function of the dimension under consideration in certain circumstances. Hypotonia in the head/neck and shoulders may be sufficient to produce postural *fixes* that allow head control in a prone position but insufficient to allow head control in a standing position.

Further, the function of mobility is to go from place to place, but the form of that mobility can include many behaviors. Thus, forms of mobility include rolling, creeping, crawling, knee walking, walking, running, and jumping, or hopping on one foot. All these ways of moving would be present in the repertoires of most normal children. However, other mobility forms such as scooting on one's bottom in a sitting position, "frog leaping" or "bunny hopping" in a hand-knee position, or walking up on

FIGURE 7.12.
Relationship between Motivation and Length of Standing

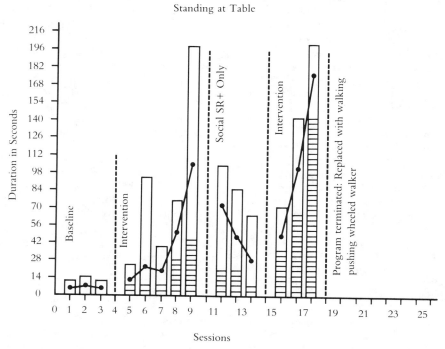

Series of 10 opportunities to stand per session. Solid bar represents the shortest time in standing of any trial. Hatched bar represents the longest time in standing of any trial. Solid line indicates the mean time in standing per session.

one's toes with the legs turned in and scissoring would be less likely to be observed in a normally developing child. Still others, such as moving a wheelchair by pushing the wheels or using a mouth stick to operate a switch to activate an electric wheelchair, would probably not be observed with normal children. Forms of mobility that are typically observed in developing children without movement disorders can be classified as normal in relation to particular chronological age ranges. Other mobility forms can be categorized as primitive in relation to chronological age ranges. For instance, a 5-year-old student who uses crawling as the primary form of mobility has a primitive form of mobility, since walking is the primary form of mobility of a typical 5-year-old. Still other forms of mobility, such as walking up on the toes, might be described as atypical; where using a walker or crutches, or being mobile in a sitting position in a wheelchair, provide the function of mobility through abnormal or unusual behavior forms.

Using the hand to interact with and manipulate objects in the environment with precise and con-

trolled movements is one behavior that differentiates humans from lower animals (see Bower, 1979; Bruner, 1974; Piaget, 1952; and other writers). The use of the hand as a tool for object manipulation precedes the normally developing infant's use of other tools in relation to objects. Within this context, upper extremity skills or arm movements have two primary functions in relation to movement. The first is to move the arms to bring the hand to a particular location to manipulate objects. This function is typically referred to as *reach* or *hand transport* (Bower, 1979). The second function is *manipulation*, typically described as *grasp* or by Piaget (1952) and Uzgiris and Hunt (1975) as *schemes of prehension*. The forms of behavior that perform the functions of hand transport or manipulation are varied and relate both to competence in underlying motor processes and experience.

Using the oral musculature for eating and for vocalization are two separate behavioral functions that may be related. The forms of behavior used to perform these functions of eating and vocalizing (speech and nonspeech sounds) are differentiated in relation to purpose. Oral-motor movements to obtain liquid from a straw are different from those that produce sound or word production. The literature is confusing, and research is limited in documenting specific relationships between movement competence in eating functions and in speaking functions. One hypothesis holds that young children practice coordination of the oral musculature in eating and that coordination developed in relation to eating facilitates the coordination required for later sound, word, and sentence production.[2] These dimensions are represented as separate functions, since we cannot assume that programming in eating skills will, in fact, carry over to or influence oral motor coordination in relation to sound production.

Forms of behavior for each of these dimensions—hand transport, manipulation, oral-motor/feeding, and oral-motor/vocalization—are varied and show changes in organizational form during infancy. Specific forms of behavior demonstrated by older students will relate directly to necessary and sufficient basic motor processes as well as to movement forms used by the student (perhaps long before school age). As with mobility, the range of response forms in each of these behavioral functions can be defined as any motoric organization that allows the behavioral function to be realized. These forms subsequently can be judged in relation to chronological age range expectations and rated normal, primitive, atypical, or unusual. Behavioral forms for each of these dimensions can also be rated with older (noninfant) students in terms of functional competence. Unusual forms of behavior which allow for the function may well enable the handicapped student to perform competently. For instance, the severely motorically impaired student who is mobile with an electric wheelchair would be competent in mobility even though the form is unusual. Similarly, a student who is able to use a head wand or electronic switches to point would be using unusual forms of hand transport, but the forms allow the performance of certain manipulatory functions. Functional competence on each dimension is the end goal of programming, whether the chosen response form is normal or unusual.

Each of these movement dimensions can be rated in relation to a standard of normal (direct relationship with chronological age range expectations) or of competence. The relationship to competence is more appropriate for older students. However, it implies that, with known methods of treatment consistently and systematically applied, the behavior form used by the student is not likely to change significantly (not likely to be able to be made normal). There are, in fact, many forms of motor behavior which we do

not know how to normalize in terms of tone, movement quality, and movement quantity. However, knowledge and application of innovative approaches are emerging (e.g., Campbell, 1978; Campbell, Bricker, & Esposito, 1981; Inman, 1979) and being systematically tested with students with varying types of motor impairment. Where competence is used as the rating standard, students who have no form of behavior or who are severely restricted to one form of behavior would be rated as 1. Examples include the student who is totally tube fed (oral-motor/feeding); who is not observed to use the arms for automatic, primary, or goal-directed movement (hand transport); or who is unable, under any circumstances, to hold or manipulate an object (manipulation). Excessive forms of behavior would rate 9 and might include a student who constantly vocalizes stereotypically (oral-motor/vocalization) or who is frequently observed running around the environment without direction or purpose (mobility).

IMPLICATIONS FOR PROGRAMMING

Use of a rating system to document the student's current functioning on each behavioral dimension directly relates the assessment to programming in two significant ways. The initial information derived from dimensional ratings further defines which specialists are necessary to insure comprehensive programming. For instance, a student who is rated atypical on tone, movement quality, movement quantity, and other motoric dimensions would require services from a physical or occupational therapist. Students with atypical scores on oral-motor dimensions would also require speech and language services. However, a student without oral-motor difficulties or without atypical motor ratings could probably be provided with adequate programming by a teacher, alone.

The second relationship of a rating system to programming concerns the directional judgments made about a student's movement difficulties in comparison to attained necessary or sufficient competence, the middle values on the scale. This representation defines the initial functional goals of programming as well as the class of intervention approaches needed to influence behavior on each dimension. A student with a rating of 8 or 9 on postural tone would require programming to normalize tone and any intervention techniques that *reduce* tone would be effective. Similarly, normalization of postural tone would also be an appropriate goal for a student with a tonicity rating of 1 or 2. However, the intervention approaches required would be those that *increase* tone. A rating of 9 on mobility would signal intervention to reduce or structure mobility in the environment,

---

[2]See Campbell, 1979, for further discussion.

FIGURE 7.13.
Model of Intervention for Children with Motor Impairments

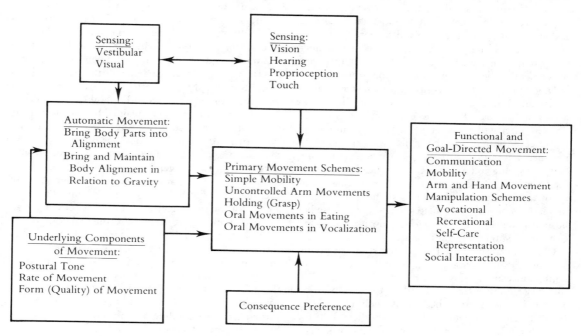

where a rating of 1 would indicate approaches to produce some form of mobility.

Specific and individualized programming goals for motor-handicapped students can be derived directly from the ratings on underlying movement processes in relation to the types of movement expected (see Figure 7.13). The physical therapist is typically most interested in the basic underlying movement processes of tone, quality, and quantity, and thus focuses intervention on improving automatic movement patterns by modifying these processes. The occupational therapist, speech/language therapist, and educator must have knowledge of these basic processes, but the major emphasis of their intervention is likely to be on primary and goal-directed movements.

Automatic Movement Patterns

Automatic movement patterns have been traced to specific areas of the brain through animal studies severing brain fibers at various CNS levels (Talbott & Humphrey, 1979). To a certain extent, automatic righting reactions can be considered reflexive behavior because they result from response to a specific set of stimulus conditions, are integrated at neurological levels lower than the cortex, and include patterns of movement that are typically very similar from person to person. Equilibrium (or balance) reactions are

an embellishment of righting reactions because the body must be righted in relation to gravity before the equilibrium reactions can function. These automatic movements also result from disturbances of body alignment in relation to gravity but are thought to be cortical functions and not the result of confining stimulus conditions. The resultant components of movement, however, are similar from person to person (Weisz, 1938).

The possibility of responding motorically (governed by postural tone and muscle action) in ways which right the body and keep it upright against gravity probably occurs as a function of genetic expression and, in infant development (under 6 months of age), of CNS maturation. However, the maintenance and elaboration of responses are probably a function of sensorimotor coordination. Head control provides a simple example. The very young infant may "discover" that if she keeps her head to the side of her body as opposed to downward in the pillow, the side position is more comfortable (and certainly relates to survival in that it is easier to breathe if her head is not held directly downward when she is on her stomach). The infant may happen to raise her head at a time when interesting events are occurring and "discover" a new relationship of "seeing" what is going on around her. The initial response of prone head raising is related to certain levels of motor competence present as a function of genetic expression. The initial movement is automatic and reflexive head righting. However, all subsequent responses, increase in the rate of head raising, and maintenance of the newly discovered relationship between seeing and head raising occur as a function of the consequences to that behavior (primary movement). The subsequent behavior, labeled a *head righting reaction,* actually is *strengthened and maintained* under the control of the consequences to the behavior—not because of genetic expression or maturation. In other words, as long as interesting and novel events are going on, the child will continue to produce temporary discoveries of the relationship between seeing and movement of the head. Head raising then comes under the control of antecedent conditions. When the child hears something interesting or someone visually stimulates her, she will raise her head in a goal-directed sense for the purpose of seeing or hearing something motivating.

Children can be placed in positions but, at young ages or with inexperience, may not be able to maintain balance in those positions. For instance, when the very young infant is placed in a sitting position and his balance is disturbed, he is likely to fall over (or to be caught by an adult!). Later, the child may catch himself with his arms with what has been described as protective responses of the arms (Milani-Comparetti & Gidoni, 1967). Using the arms for balancing allows the child to stay upright without having to use the muscles in the trunk and the legs (Figure 7.14). However, the function of the protective responses of the arms is the same as the function of equilibrium reactions in sitting; both movements allow the individual to remain upright when the body is displaced in relation to gravity. Using the arms for protection from falling also prevents use of the arms for reaching and manipulation. The arms are not released from protective functions until the

child develops equilibrium reactions that allow maintenance of balance without the arms (Figure 7.15).

The use of the trunk and body extremities for balancing in each position (Figure 7.16) developmentally follows maintenance of the position. That is, equilibrium reactions in standing follow the ability to maintain standing with support when placed in that position. These reactions have traditionally been viewed as largely maturational. However, from a sensorimotor perspective, the ability to balance against gravity might be explained by saying that the very young child acquires competence in balance by experimenting with the properties of gravity just as the young infant experiments with properties of objects (such as size, weight, color, shape, and function). These automatic movement responses may become sophisticated and precise because the child adapts for the varying effects of gravity. Gravity is an important and significant environmental component relating to movement competence. Movements performed against gravity are far more difficult than those performed when gravity is either neutral or assisting the movement. For instance, a head turn to the side performed lying supine (on the back) is gravity assisted (turning head to side) but the head is turned back to midline against effects of gravity. Similarly, the effects of gravity are less when maintaining the head upright in a prone-lying position than in standing independently. A very young baby has had no experience with gravity (in fact, gravity is reduced in the womb by the fluid environment) and must acquire not just the ability to move but to perform movements against varying and changing conditions of gravity.

Primary and Goal-Directed Movement

Primary movements are demonstrated by babies soon after birth and consist of simple stimulus-response behaviors. The function of this type of movement is to receive interesting consequences. However, the child with atypical postural tone may not have enough basic competence to perform even the simplest form of primary movement. The child may find noise from a rattle interesting when the rattle is moved by somebody else, but may not subsequently shake the rattle because rate of arm movement is too low to produce sufficient noise. Other students with disturbances in the underlying processes of movement may generate interesting consequences with qualitatively deficient patterns of movement. Perhaps rather than shaking the rattle up and down, as most infants would, the student waves his arms back and forth with atypical patterns of movement. However, as long as the arm movements generate a reinforcing consequence, the student will

FIGURE 7.14.
Protective Reactions of the Arms in Sitting

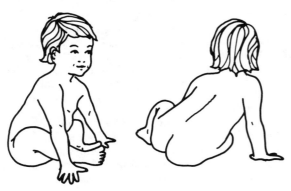

FIGURE 7.15.
Equilibrium Reactions in Sitting

increase those arm movements (along with the atypical patterns of movement). Even the simplest form
of movement must be viewed in relation to the sensorimotor processes involved and the environmental
conditions under which the response is performed. If
not, the student will acquire atypical postural tone,
quantity of movement, and movement quality.

Primary movement is important because it is the
most primitive form of movement organization in
relation to environmental events and objects.
Through this type of basic movement organization,
the child has chances to practice various kinds of
muscle coordinations. These coordinations are refined into more complex and goal-directed movement organizations. For instance, the very young
infant, if properly positioned, is able to reach for an
object within the visual field. In fact, the infant can
anticipate the movement of the object and move the
arm toward where the object will be at the end of the
movement (Von Hefstein & Lindahagen, 1979).
However, the quality of the organization of the
movement is poorly coordinated. The organization
of this primary movement increases in precision and
coordination with practice and precedes the organized control of the motor system required for adult
reaching. The student with atypical underlying motor processes may not generate a reaching motion
and therefore may lack practice in learning to organize primary motor behaviors into goal-directed
movement. This lack of experience with normally
organized patterns of movement will effect acquisition of goal-directed and intentional motor behavior.

The relationships between tone, movement quantity, and movement quality and primary and goal-

directed movement are such that the basic processes
are present or absent in varying degrees in relation to
genetic expression and CNS functions. Only the initial and most primitively organized unit of motor
behavior (whether head righting, sucking, arm
movement, or grasping) is related to genetic expression. All responses which follow develop as a function of cognitive processes of assimilation and accommodation producing more elaborately organized
and more precise forms of motor interaction with the
environment. Basic therapeutic procedures that normalize tone and make some degree of movement
organization possible can be effective in facilitating
the initial production of the movement. However,
once the movement has been initiated and produced,
elaboration and maintenance of the response can be
best facilitated by constructing and arranging the
environment systematically.

INTERVENTION APPROACHES

There are many ways of intervening to improve the
functioning of students with movement disorders.
Traditionally teachers and parents have been taught
methods that manage or maintain postural tone
through passive techniques such as range of motion,
carrying, positioning, or generalized "relaxation"
techniques (Finnie, 1975). These approaches derive
from the therapy professions and focus on techniques
that simultaneously make possible (facilitate) normal
tone and movement while preventing (inhibiting)
atypical tone and patterns of movement. Primary
among these approaches is *neurodevelopmental
treatment* (or the Bobath approach), which focuses
on changing tone and patterns of movement through

FIGURE 7.16.
Equilibrium Reactions

 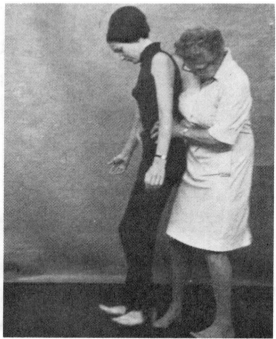

proper positioning and handling (see Bobath & Bobath, 1975; Connor, Williamson, & Siepp, 1978; Hanson & Campbell, in press). One reason for the wide use of this approach is that it can be successfully applied without conscious cooperation from the student. These methods can be used even with preverbal students who are severely handicapped or with very young infants.

Neurodevelopmental treatment (NDT) approaches require careful analysis of patterns of movement (movement quality) and apply intervention techniques designed to alter the form of movement by making the pattern as normal as possible. Therapists task analyze the components of movement required to perform a particular task. Intervention is then directed toward developing the muscle actions required by each component and organizing these isolated actions into an overall pattern. Basic handling techniques are used to facilitate more normally organized movement and to practice use of required muscle actions in automatic, primary, and goal-directed movement situations.

Critical to both tone normalization and facilitation of more normal movement forms are *proper positioning and handling* of the motor impaired student. For

NDT to be maximally effective, the student must be consistently positioned and handled in ways that normalize postural tone, inhibit atypical patterns of movement, and facilitate normally organized movements. The consistent management of the student is so essential to neurodevelopmental treatment that instructing parents and teachers who are in daily contact with the child is as important as the direct, hands-on intervention provided by the therapist. Where the student is not managed consistently, the sensorimotor feedback necessary for normal movement is not sufficiently practiced and an internal scheme of normal movement organization may not be acquired.

The vast majority of techniques practiced by therapists and taught to others can be classified as management programs rather than as specific instructional programs. In other words, these methods are designed to maintain postural tone at levels as normal as possible and to encourage or make possible normal movement patterns. Proper lifting, carrying, positioning, use of adaptive equipment, and other procedures generally are not specifically instructional. Antecedent and consequent conditions are seldom defined, nor is the exact response desired from the student described operationally. Instructional programs may be implemented by a teacher, parent, or therapist and are differentiated from management programs in that specific responses are being trained and evaluated with systematic data. Management programs include passive programs and instruction where ongoing data are not maintained and where specific responses are not systematically trained. For instance, a self-feeding program would involve training the student to move his hand to his mouth with tone as normal as possible, at an adequate rate, with normal upper extremity movements (Campbell, 1982a). Carrying a student in a specific way or moving that student from one position to another using appropriate techniques to normalize tone would both be management programs. These procedures should help the student acquire more normal movement. However, more normal movement is not being specifically trained in these situations. Programming for students with movement disorders should include both instructional and management programs. However, general procedures related to managing movement are not emphasized here because they have been widely described in other materials (e.g., Campbell, 1982a, 1982b; Connor et al., 1978; Finnie, 1975; Galka & Fraser, 1980; Hanson & Campbell, in press).

Equipment

There are several basic principles of neurodevelopmental treatment that can be implemented by parents and teachers. The first is to apply those approaches that will normalize the student's tone as much as possible throughout the day. One method of maintaining tone normalization is to use equipment both to prevent atypical responses and to facilitate normal movement responses (see Figures 7.17 and 7.18).

Several precautions must be taken with adaptive equipment meant to normalize tone and facilitate normal movement patterns. Equipment will not *produce* these results. Well-selected and well-fitted equipment will only *maintain* normal tone if appropriate methods have first been used to increase or decrease tone. A second precaution is careful and systematic observation of the student in the selected piece of equipment over time. Just because the equipment is advertised to produce a specific effect does not mean that the outcome will be produced with every student placed in it. The teacher, parent, or therapist must carefully observe the student over time and in a variety of situations using the equipment to see if it is performing the desired function (see Figure 7.19). A third precaution involves length of time the student is placed in a piece of equipment. Many motor impaired students are relatively immo-

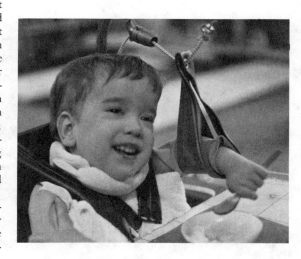

Figure 7.17.
Student Positioned for Self-feeding

bile and lack the postural adjustments necessary to remain in the static positions generated through equipment for long periods of time. Restricting the student to one type of position can produce secondary problems of skin ulcerations, muscle tightness, and contractures leading to deformities. Every motor impaired student should have a minimum of two (and preferably more) ways of being positioned in the classroom. All equipment used in each of those two positions should be *appropriate and well-fitting*. Teachers and parents should ask therapists to specify the length of time the student can be positioned in the equipment. Some children can sit or stand with adaptive equipment for long periods of time (2 to 3 hours). Other students should be repositioned as frequently as every 20 to 30 minutes.

Many types of adaptive equipment have been designed to be built or are manufactured and distributed by a variety of commercial companies. However, despite the innumerable resources for procuring appropriate equipment, no one piece of equipment, whether home-made or commercially distributed, is appropriate for all students (Campbell, Green, & Carlsen, 1977). Equipment varies in purpose, cost, and durability, and all these factors must be considered when selecting the piece of equipment to be used with a student. Some students need equipment that is highly durable and will last for many years. Others need equipment that will be used temporarily or until the student acquires the skills that will make another piece of equipment more appropriate. In addition, equipment selected should be the most appropriate for the student's chronological age and the most normalized in appearance. For instance, some prone

FIGURE 7.18.
Student Positioned for Language Activity

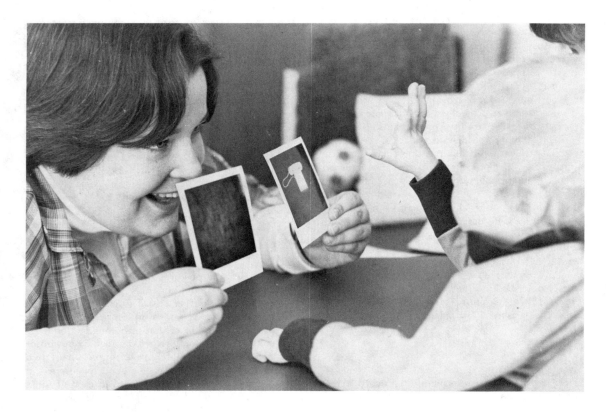

boards work to perfectly align posture and fully normalize tone, but also isolate the student from peers and group classroom activities (see Figure 7.20). Adaptive chairs can simultaneously position a student appropriately while preventing movement outside the classroom due to lack of durability or wheels. Equipment should be selected so that the student is neither over- nor underequipped, not isolated from peers, and not prevented from experiences because of its limitations. Table 7.3 lists some of the major equipment manufacturers and the types of equipment available for motor impaired students. Figure 7.21 illustrates some of the basic types of adaptive equipment that can be helpful for children with movement difficulties. However, listing all manufacturers or illustrating all types and variations of available equipment would be impossible, since new developments emerge regularly. A teacher, therapist, or parent should explore all possible manufacturers and design sources, the financial resources available for purchase or building, and the uses for the equipment in terms of durability, before deciding on the types of equipment needed by an individual student.

Programming for Normalized Tone and Patterns of Movement

A second method for maintaining tone normalization and normal motor patterns is to incorporate postural tone and patterns of movement in every instructional and recreational activity. Too often, motor impaired students receive "motor programs" for part of the classroom day and other programs for the rest of the day. The basic motor processes affect every skill the child may be learning—regardless of whether that skill is classified as language, vocational, self-help, cognitive, leisure, affective, or recreational. Before the student is asked to put the spoon in his mouth in self-feeding or to point to a symbol in nonverbal communication training, the teacher should be sure that the postural tone is as normal as possible and that appropriate facilitation/inhibition techniques have been used to allow the required goal-directed behavior. The specific techniques that are appropriate and effective with a given student must be picked considering individual characteristics of tone and movement. Facilitation and inhibition, viewed from the

7.19.
Proper and Improper Positioning

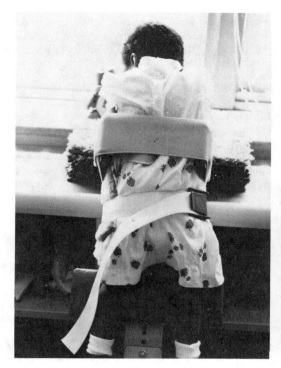 

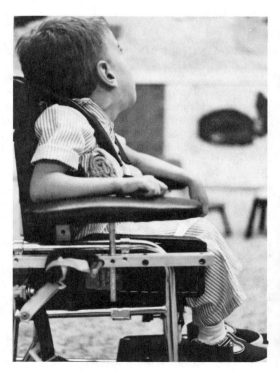 

FIGURE 7.20.
Prone Board Positioning, which Socially Isolates Student

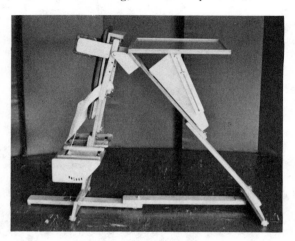

standpoint of overall learning, are simply precise forms of physical guidance. However, rather than just to physically manipulate or guide the movement response, the therapist or teacher must carefully manipulate the movement, using key points of control. The key points of control are the joints of the body which are most proximal (i.e. head, shoulders, hips), but movement can also be guided from the hands and feet by a skillful and well-trained therapist (Bobath, Note 2). Appropriate use of facilitation/inhibition procedures requires precise knowledge of normal movement. Figure 7.22 illustrates some general principles of facilitation/inhibition of patterns of movement. Table 7.4 outlines basic approaches.

Teachers and therapists who have had training in neurodevelopmental treatment can provide more suggestions for teaching motor handicapped students more normal patterns of movement. However, all suggested techniques may not be appropriate for or effective with a particular student. When implemented, they should be systematically observed to insure effective outcomes.

The most difficult aspects of providing appropriate programming for motorically impaired students are instating and maintaining normal tone, movement quantity, and movement quality in primary and goal-directed movement. A suggested format for determining where facilitation/inhibition techniques and appropriate positioning are required for a student is illustrated in Tables 7.5 and 7.6. The planning format outlines the form (quality) of behavior expected from the student in terms of long-term outcomes and specifically describes the movement processes involved, the requirements for adequate performance in each of those processes, and the potential problems an individual may demonstrate with movement.

This information is incorporated into instructional programming and management programs to teach the student the expected form of behavior. The purpose is to help the teacher and therapist relate movement competence and areas of classroom curricular emphasis, as outlined on the intervention model in Figures 7.1 and 7.13. The physical or occupational therapists are typically most interested in underlying components of movement and automatic movement patterns. Goal-directed movement related to mobility is often an emphasis of physical therapy, where occupational therapists concentrate on facilitating functional movement related to self-care, vocational, and recreational-leisure skills. Obviously, the speech/language therapist emphasizes communication skills, where the teacher must concentrate on classroom programming that emphasizes all these areas in addition to social interaction. Where therapists, teachers, and parents work together as a team, the interrelatedness of the movement dysfunction for a student can be analyzed so that task requirements are appropriate. For instance, practicing balance in sitting (an automatic movement pattern) would not be appropriate to teach at the same time as use of the shoulders/arms for a skilled movement such as dressing if the student has to use the arms for balance. Therapists can help teachers identify appropriate positions for particular educational activities by using the format illustrated in Tables 7.5 and 7.6.

DETERMINING PROGRAM EFFECTIVENESS

The effectiveness of any instructional or therapeutic program with a motor handicapped student must be judged on the basis of change in the student. Many techniques have been suggested as appropriate, but have been only clinically judged as effective. Therefore, the teacher or therapist must individually evaluate the effectiveness of the techniques with each student with whom they are used. Decisions on when to alter programming techniques can then be made objectively (Bricker & Campbell, 1982).

As an example, an interdisciplinary team established a goal for a 6-year-old student of instating controlled movement of the head and neck muscles. This student scored at 8 on tonicity, 1 on movement quantity, and 9 in movement quality (presence of postural fixations at the head/neck, shoulders, hips and pelvis). An asymmetrical turning of the head to the right combined with increased extension was the predominant movement demonstrated by this youngster, who made no voluntary arm or leg movements. The student was unable to grasp objects unless placed in his hands, could not bear weight on his legs, had lim-

TABLE 7.3. Major Commercial Equipment Distributors

Company Name and Address	Types of Products
ACHIEVEMENT PRODUCTS FOR CHILDREN P.O. Box 547 Mineola, NY 11501	Transporters Corner chairs; Potty chairs Crawlers Self-feeding equipment Head pointers
ADAPTIVE EQUIPMENT COMPANY 175 Parker Court Chardon, OH 44024	Booster chair/table Standing tables Pony scooters Positioning vests
COMMUNITY PLAYTHINGS Rifton, NY 12471	Corner, preschool/toddler chairs Standing boards Mobility tricycles; Kiddie car
EQUIPMENT SHOP P.O. Box 33 Bedford, MA 01730	TrippTrapp chair with attachments Corner chairs Standing boards Scooter boards; tricycles Self-care equipment
KAYE PRODUCTS, INC. 1010 E. Pettigrew Street Durham, NC 27701	Seat inserts for strollers Booster; Corner chairs Standing boards Toilet aids
L. MULHOLLAND CORPORATION 215 N. 12th Street Santa Paula, CA 93060	Mulholland Growth Guidance Positioning Systems (Adaptive chair) Prone board/Standing system
J.A. PRESTON CORPORATION 60 Page Road Clifton, NJ 07012	Wheelchairs/transporter chairs TumbleForms positioning aids/scooter Rehabilitation equipment Self-care aids Educational materials
FRED SAMMONS, INC. Box 32 Brookfield, IL 60513	Self-care aids/Feeding & dressing Toileting aids Scooter boards Misc. rehabilitation devices/Materials

ited vocalizations, and had difficulties eating solid foods. Therefore, controlled movement of some form to use for mobility, communication, and limited "manipulation" (head stick or adaptive equipment) was identified as a priority. A therapy program was initiated using slow rocking and traction on the neck musculature to facilitate normal movement of the head from side to side. Specific desired responses were movement from midline to right, right to midline, midline to left, and left to midline. Progress was measured after each therapy session by placing the student on his back on a wedge to facilitate neck flexion and inhibit neck hyperextension and asymmetry. An auditory or visual stimulus was used to encourage head turning to a visual or sound source

(Figure 7.23). Responses were measured in rate per minute calculated over the 15-minute measurement session. However, initial data indicated no increase in right to midline head movements and considerable movement in midline to right head movements with hyperextension (Figure 7.24). Therefore, an additional intervention of saying "no!" and preventing head movement from moving into hyperextension and asymmetry was instituted. It effectively decreased the atypical movement.

Additional examination of data indicated that while movement rate was increasing (see blocks 1–3, Figure 7.23), the rate of increase was slow and variable. Visual examination indicated that head movement was somewhat under the control of atypical

FIGURE 7.21.
Types of Adaptive Positioning Equipment

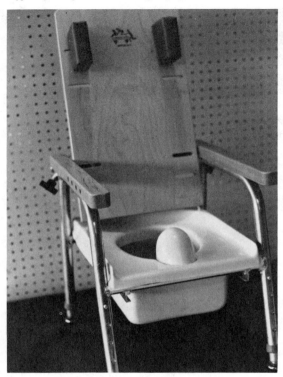

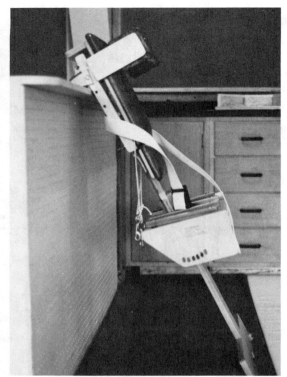

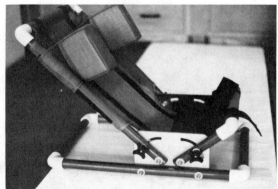

Figure 7.22.
General Principles of Facilitation and Inhibition

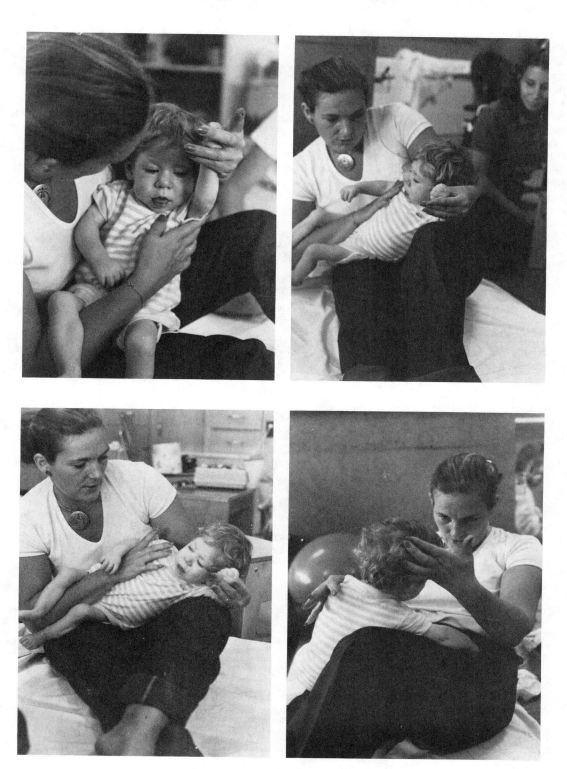

visual functioning. Vision was assessed to be some-what decreased in the left eye (possibly limited to light/dark discriminations) and poor in the right eye. The strategies were then changed so that only audi-tory stimuli were used to elicit the head turning, and the eyes were patched during treatment and measure-ment sessions. The interesting aspect of this is that while the rate of head turning significantly increased with the eye patching, elimination of vision itself had no effect. Rather, the effect of the conditions of eye patches on or off produced an increase in behavior that can only be explained by novelty or changing conditions (rather than the condition itself). To fur-ther validate the increase in head turning over time and with therapy, the rates of head turning in supine and in sitting (head supported) were compared. The comparison indicated that, while this student had not been trained to hold his head up and turn in sitting, the increased rate of movement was generalized to this position. Subsequently, this primary form of movement was changed into a more goal-directed movement (Figure 7.25), where head turning could

be functionally elicited by the antecedent condition of a light.

This illustration shows only one example of preci-sion measurement and programming with therapeu-tic intervention designed to normalize tone, inhibit atypical patterns of movement (specifically the asym-metrical head/neck fix), and facilitate more normal patterns of movement. Use of the neck flexor mus-cles along with the neck extensors in a coordinated interplay is necessary for normal head movement from side to side. Data indicated that therapeutic intervention procedures in combination with applied behavior analysis were effective in altering postural tone, movement rate, and movement quality in this student. Without data, however, the effects of thera-peutic procedures would have been less evident, and other programming aspects (such as the patching) might not have been systematically added. There-fore, collecting data and making programming de-cisions on that basis are essential if effective in-structional programming is to be designed and implemented with motor handicapped students.

TABLE 7.4. Examples of Treatment Strategies

Atypical postural tone	Normalize tone by decreasing tone or increasing tone, for exam-ple:
	    Slow movement (decrease)
	    Fast, controlled movement (increase)
	Graded sensory input (multiple stimulus control procedures) for adaptive normalized response
	Proper positioning
	Proper adaptive equipment

Atypical postural fixations	Provide more normal fixation through guidance (facilitation) and adaptive equipment Facilitate cocontraction for stability Activate weak muscles Strengthen weak muscles
Compensatory movement patterns	Obtain normal postural fixation and normalized postural tone Facilitate normal movement components Activate weak muscles Strengthen weak muscles
Habitual movement patterns	Accelerate normal movement while decelerating atypical pat-terns through incorporating applied behavior analysis tech-niques
Tightness/elongation of muscles	Passive range of motion within normal movement compo-nents Active range of motion within normal movement compo-nents Stretching Positioning and adaptive equipment
Deformities	Bracing, splints, other devices to maintain Surgery

FIGURE 7.23.
Head Turning in Supine Position

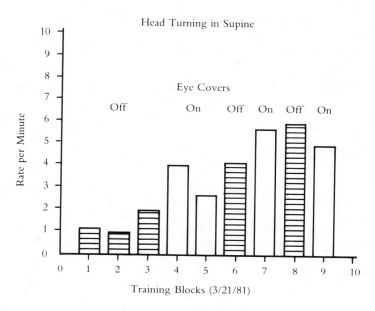

CONCLUSION

The purpose of this chapter has been to introduce methods and approaches that can be used both to identify problems with movement and to generate intervention strategies that will be effective in altering those processes. Traditional approaches to motor development and programming have focused on the acquisition of motor milestone skills and on manage-

FIGURE 7.24.
Decrease in Atypical Head-Neck Hyperextension

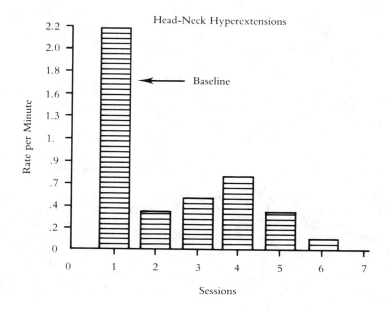

TABLE 7.5. Program Planning Sheet Incorporating Movement into Reach-Grasp Skill

Individual Educational Planning Sheet

Child's Name: __F.G.__   Individual Completing Sheet: __K.J.C.__   Date: __5/4/81__

Long Range Goal: __Upper extremity movement—reaching for hand transport to object manipulation.__

Form(s)	Required Processes	Requirements	Problems
Controlled forward movement directed from shoulder	A. Muscle tone	A. Normalized	A. 1. Increased humeral/scapular adduction hypertension, elbow flexion 2. Increased shoulder elevation, head/neck hyperextension 3. Increased crying 4. Increased seizure activity
	B. Movement quality	B. 1. Symmetrical positioning 2. External head/neck support 3. Adequate external trunk and scapular support 4. Upper extremities supported so movement not influenced by gravity 5. Humerus anterior to trunk 6. Hands open 7. Gradation of stimulus	B. 1. Increased tone as above 2. Resistance to positioning 3. Resistance to facilitation 4. Startle to tactile input 5. Increased crying 6. Seizures 7. Scapular-humeral tightness
	C. Movement quantity	C. 1. Adequate external support 2. Hierarchy of consequency preference 3. Gradation of stimulus and consequences 4. Frequency of movement increased 5. Primary circular reactions move to secondary circular reactions	C. 1. Increased tone as above 2. Nonsystematic stimulus control 3. Nonsystematic consequence control 4. Decrease rate of behavior 5. Increased crying 6. Increased seizure activity 7. Scapular humeral tightness
	C. Consequence preference	D. Preferred: illumination, movement, auditory source Nonpreferred: stimuli without movement, bright color or illumination	D. 1. Nonsystematic development of hierarchy

ment programs, often ignoring the modifiability of postural tone, patterns of movement, and movement quantity. In contrast, the system of indexing behavior presented here focuses on the processes which underlie the production of movement and enable those organizations of movements to be performed efficiently with coordination. The use of this assessment system along with the intervention program-

ming model allows an interdisciplinary team to identify the areas in which a student requires specialized services and to determine the initial programming emphasis. The motor system does not function in isolation but rather provides each of us with a means of interacting with our environments. Neurodevelopmental treatment approaches, when combined with behavior analysis techniques and carefully eval-

TABLE 7.5. (CONTINUED)

Suggested Instructional Activities

Data-Based Training Activities

Preparation Strategies:	Slow movement to decrease muscle tone, shaking to decrease tone in shoulder girdle, passive forward movement to upper extremities.
Antecedent Conditions:	Decreased muscle tone
	Adequate external support
	Hands open and on object
Responses:	Forward arm movement from shoulder
	Hand movement
	Maintain grasp on object greater than 10 seconds
Consequences:	Gentle rocking
	Verbal interaction
	Patting on chest
	Stimulus consequence
Training Consequences:	Reinforce independent movement of any degree
	Prevent increased tone/scapular/humeral tightness
	Position in chair post preparation
Data:	Baseline three data points, mean length grasp right/left hand with normalized tone; frequency data to percent of hand movement, upper extremity movement, visual fixation on object; Duration: Time upper extremity maintained forward.

General Management Programs (Informal)

1. Record seizure activity frequency, duration and antecedents
2. Manage seizure activity as stated
3. Maintain normalized tone throughout day as possible

uated through ongoing data collection, provide one approach to help motor handicapped students to function appropriately in academic, leisure, vocational, and self-care areas, critical for independence as adult members of society.

REFERENCES

Bigge, J.L. *Teaching individuals with physical and multiple disabilities* (2nd ed.). Columbus, Ohio: Charles E. Merrill, 1982.

Bleck, E., & Nagel, D.A. *A medical atlas for teachers.* New York: Grune & Stratton, 1975.

Bobath, B., & Bobath, K. *Motor development in the different types of cerebral palsy.* London: William Heinemann, 1975.

Bower, T.G.R. *Human development.* San Francisco: W.H. Freeman, 1979.

Bricker, W.A., & Campbell, P.H. Interdisciplinary programming. In W. Sailor, L. Brown, & B. Wilcox (Eds.), *Teaching the severely handicapped.* Baltimore: Paul H. Brookes, 1980.

Bricker, W.A., & Campbell, P.H. *Individualized educational programming.* Akron, Ohio: Children's Hospital Medical Center of Akron, 1982.

Bricker, W.A., Macke, P.R., Levin, J.A., & Campbell, P.H. The modifiability of intelligent behavior. *Journal of Special Education,* 1981, 15(2), 145–163.

Bruner, J. The organization of early skilled action. In M. Richards (Ed.), *The integration of a child into a social world.* London: Cambridge University Press, 1974.

Campbell, P.H. Measuring motor behavior. In P.W. Bailey (Ed.), *Ongoing data collection in the classroom.* Seattle: WESTAR, 1978.

Campbell, P.H. Assessing oral-motor skills in severely handicapped persons: An analysis of normal and abnormal patterns of movement. In R.L. York & E. Edgar (Eds.), *Teaching the severely handicapped* (Vol. IV). Seattle: American Association for the Education of the Severely/Profoundly Handicapped, 1979.

Campbell, P.H. *Teaching eating skills: A problem-oriented approach.* Akron, Ohio: Children's Hospital Medical Center of Akron, 1982. (a)

Campbell, P.H. *Teaching self-care skills: A problem-oriented approach.* Akron, Ohio: Children's Hospital Medical Center of Akron, 1982. (b)

Campbell, P.H., & Bricker, W.A. Programming for the severely handicapped person. In J. Gardner, L. Long, R. Nichols, & D. Iagulli (Eds.), *Program issues in developmental disabilities.* Baltimore: Paul H. Brookes, 1980.

TABLE 7.6 Program Planning Sheet Incorporating Movement in Head/Neck Muscles into Primary Movement Scheme

Individual Educational Planning Sheet

Child's Name: __L.L.__   Individual Completing Sheet: __K.J.C.__   Date: __5/4/81__

Long Range Goal: __Head/neck control for visual auditory attention.__

Form(s)	Required Processes	Requirements	Problems
Graded head movements in sitting and supine	A. Muscle tone	A. Normalized	A. 1. Increased or decreased tone, fluctuation 2. Increased left elbow extension 3. Increased shoulder elevation 4. Shoulder internal rotation, adduction with elbow extension 5. Neck hyperextension 6. Increased crying 7. Scapulo-humeral tightness 8. Random upper extremity movement 9. Resistance to facilitation
	B. Movement quality	B. 1. Symmetrical positioning 2. Shoulders not elevated 3. Adequate trunk and scapular support 4. Head/neck control 5. Shoulders in neutral → external rotation 6. Coactivation of flexors and of extensors	B. 1. Abnormal tone as above 2. Head falls forward if decreased tone and no support 3. Resistance to support 4. Random upper extremity movement 5. Increased crying/sleeping behavior
	C. Movement quantity	C. 1. Visual stimuli with properties of illumination and/or movement 2. Adequate external support 3. Secondary circular contigency management 4. Decreased extraneous movements	C. 1. Nonsystematic control of stimuli 2. Minimal increase in rate of behavior 3. Increased tone as above, fluctuation resulting in no graded movement
	D. Consequence preference	D. Preferred: illumination/movement Nonpreferred: auditory stimuli alone	D. Difficulty shaping antecedent control of light to auditory stimuli

Campbell, P.H., Bricker, W.A., & Esposito, L. Technology in the education of the severely handicapped. In B. Wilcox & R. York (Eds.), *Quality education for the severely handicapped*. Washington, D.C.: U.S. Office of Special Education, 1981.

Campbell, P.H., Green, K., & Carlsen, L. Approximating the norm through environmental and child-centered prosthetics and adaptive equipment. In E. Sontag, N. Certo, & J. Smith (Eds.), *Educational programming for the severely and profoundly handicapped*. Reston, Va.: Council for Exceptional Children, 1977.

TABLE 7.6 (CONTINUED)

Suggested Instructional Activities

Data-Based Training Activities

Antecedent Conditions:	Symmetrical positioning
	Normalized muscle tone
	Adequate external trunk support
	Positioned supine on wedge at phase one of training
	Shoulders in neutral position in contact with surface
	Illuminated stimulus presented at side of desired head turn
Response:	Head turn in direction data reflects needs strengthening
	Once criteria is reached, trainer will counter balance alternating head turn response
Consequences:	Phase one: Music (10) seconds
	Phase two: Mother's voice and face; social interaction with primary caretaker
Training Considerations:	Reinforce only head turn to appropriate side
	Phase one block incorrect response
	Prompt correct response after 5 second latency
	See flow chart for Phase one specifics
	Once criteria is reached on Phase one of training, Phase two begins by shaping the antecedent conditions to auditory cues "L.", and altering consequences to social interaction with primary caretaker. After established criteria are reached on Phase two, position will be shaped through successive approximations from supine to supported sitting.
Data:	Record independent response/prompted response; compute percent correct, and trials to criteria.

General Management Programs (Informal)

Behavior management plan implemented daily/frequency and duration data on crying/extension and sleeping behavior. Data plotted daily.

Connor, F., Williamson, G., & Siepp, J. (Eds.). *Program guide for infants and toddlers with neuromotor and other developmental disabilities.* New York: Teachers College Press, 1978.

Finnie, N. *Handling the young cerebral palsied child at home.* New York: E.P. Dutton, 1975.

Fiorentino, M.R. *Normal and abnormal development: The influence of primitive reflexes on motor redevelopment.* Springfield, Ill.: Charles C Thomas, 1972.

Galka, G., & Fraser, B.A. *Gross motor management of severely multiply impaired students* (Vol. II). Baltimore: University Park Press, 1980.

Hanson, M., & Campbell, P. *Teaching your motor delayed child.* Baltimore: University Park Press, in press.

Inman, D.P. Gaining control of tension in spastic muscles. In L.A. Hamerlynck (Ed.), *Behavioral systems for the developmentally disabled: Institutional, clinic and community environments.* New York: Brunner/Mazel, 1979.

Milani-Comparetti, A., & Gidoni, E.A. Routine developmental examination in normal and retarded children. *Developmental Medicine and Child Neurology,* 1967, *9,* 631–638.

Piaget, J. *The origins of intelligence.* New York: W.W. Norton, 1952.

Seligman, M.E. *Helplessness: On depression, death and development.* San Francisco: W.H. Freeman, 1975.

Talbott, R.E., & Humphrey, D.E. *Posture and movement.* New York: Raven Press, 1979.

Uzgiris I., & Hunt, J. McV. *Assessment in infancy: Ordinal scales of psychological development.* Chicago: University of Illinois Press, 1975.

Von Hofstein, C., & Lindahagen, K. Observations on the development of reaching for moving objects. *Journal of Experimental Child Psychology,* 1979, *28,* 158–173.

Weisz, S. Studies in equilibrium reaction. *Journal of Nervous and Mental Disease,* 1938, *88,* 150–162.

REFERENCE NOTES

1. Bly, L. *Abnormal motor development.* Paper presented in the Neurodevelopmental Treatment course, Akron, Ohio, March, 1980.

2. Bobath, B. *Key points of control.* Mimeographed materials. London, England, Western Cerebral Palsy Centre, 1972.

FIGURE 7.25.
Graph Showing Differences between Training A and Training B: Training A included a light antecedent cue with music as a reinforcer for correct turns; Training B included a light antecedent with a movement cue in front of the light with music as a reinforcer. Student's performance was under the control of the movement cue (and not the light antecedent).

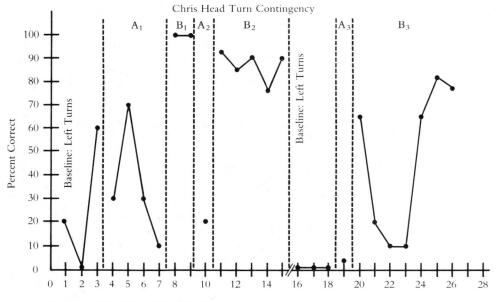

Sessions (4/16–5/15   9/8–10/1/81)

Graph showing differences between Training A
and Training B: Training A included a light antecedent
cue with music as a reinforcer for correct turns;
Training B included a light antecedent with a movement
cue in front of the light with music as a reinforcer.
Student's performance was under the control of the movement
cue (and not the light antecedent).

// = 3 month absence in training.

Linda K. Bunker is at the University of Virginia. *Sherril Moon* is at Virginia Commonwealth University.

8

Motor Skills

Training motor skills, which is essential for teachers of severely handicapped students, is one of the most difficult instructional areas in which to take a remedial or functional approach because motor development is highly sequential and interdependent. Teaching motor skills is even more challenging as students become older or when they are physically handicapped.

Because of the range of individual differences within this population, it is impossible to deal adequately with the total spectrum of motor skills. For example, some severely handicapped students have cerebral palsy or other central nervous system (CNS) disorders that may make independent locomotor skills especially difficult for them. Motor skills training for these students will probably involve the goals and procedures discussed in chapter 7.

This chapter focuses on the development of motor skills, including recreational and physical fitness activities. Objectives in these areas are relevant for all handicapped children, including those with multiple handicaps. Most severely handicapped students whose major impairments are mental retardation or behavior disorders have the physical potential to develop fine and gross motor skills, including the complex patterns necessary for participating in sports. The needs of these severely handicapped students will be the focus of this chapter.

Choosing the most appropriate skills for instruction is difficult, even for those students who have the basic motor skills prerequisite to locomotion and prehension. We have little data-based information on the most efficient skill sequences and training techniques in any motor skill area for the severely handicapped (Haavik & Altman, 1977). Nonetheless, training specific motor skills is important since fine and gross movement is involved in accomplishing all other skills across all domains.

Several factors must be considered in training motor skills to students with severe handicaps. One issue is how closely to follow the typical developmental patterns of motor behavior in nonhandicapped children. All fundamental and advanced fine and locomotor abilities depend on the acquisition of body awareness, posture, and physical fitness. Therefore, we cannot overlook developmental sequencing of some skills. When a student's functional needs, chronological age, and physical readiness and experience conflict, the teacher must examine the instructional program from many angles.

The normal sequence of motor development is highly predictable, yet individual variations may be

quite large. Some children may show a rather preco-
cious ability to crawl, sit, or stand, and yet the development of walking may be on-age or delayed. For
example, many severely retarded children make no
attempt to stop crawling without prompting and
reinforcement (O'Brien, Azrin, & Bugle, 1972). Retarded children may also lag behind in functional
motor skills in one or more areas of body management or fundamental skills. Their deficiences may
include general body awareness, development of spatial concepts, and control of body actions that should
be developed very early in life (Levy, 1973). In addition to these basic skills, some children may also have
difficulty with efficient locomotor patterns such as
skipping, hopping, and jumping, and with both
gross and fine motor manipulative skills such as
grasping, throwing, striking, kicking, and catching.
These basic deficiencies may be compounded by not
participating in vigorous activities that require them
to use their skills.

Considering these basic deficiencies, it is no won-
der that there has been so little research on or programming for the participation of the severely handicapped in recreational activities involving complex
motor behaviors. However, there is evidence that
even the most profoundly retarded can be taught not
only fundamental gross and fine motor activities, but
complicated fitness and sports skills through systematic, operant procedures (Bates & Renzaglia, 1979;
Haavik & Altman, 1977; Loynd & Barclay, 1970).
The remainder of this chapter focuses on the variety
of motor skills that should be considered for instruction and techniques useful in training these skills to
the severely handicapped.

A MODEL FOR CURRICULUM DEVELOPMENT

Goals and objectives for motor skills programs
should be established within the context of the
assumptions and principles of sound educational programs explained in chapters 4 and 5. Specific instructional objectives will depend on many factors, particularly the individual's age and the most deficient
motor skill area. Before describing the various skill
areas, we will discuss some general guidelines for
selecting and prioritizing instructional goals.

Spanning the Four Instructional Domains

To insure the instruction of functional motor skills, a
teacher must first proceed through the six phases of
curriculum development to identify domains, environments, activities, and skills that are most relevant
to a student's current and future environments (refer
to chapter 4). Motor skills that most often occur
across leisure, domestic, vocational, and community
domains should be emphasized. For example, if independent ambulation has been identified as necessary
in all four domains, it should be a priority gross
motor skill. Other skills, such as buttoning and zipping, using a pencil, and performing certain vocational tasks involving a pincer grasp, may also be
targeted. In this case, instructional programs for
training this particular grasp must be designed.

One of the most important domains involving
complex motor skills is recreation. Recreational skills
involving complex behavior, such as sports, are selected and developed like all other instructional objectives. An example of how the six-phase curriculum development strategy can be used to establish
functional recreational motor skills for a severely
handicapped adolescent is shown in Figure 8.1.

Chronological Age of the Student

The student's age will help determine the skills chosen for instruction. For example, it may be appropriate to spend time teaching a preschooler to walk by
working on the following skill sequence: (a) righting
and equilibrium responses, (b) standing from a sitting
position, (c) crawling, (d) creeping, (e) walking with
support, (f) independent stepping, (g) walking with
balance, and (h) maneuvering with obstacles, height
barriers, etc. However, this same skill sequence
would be inappropriate for a 16-year-old profoundly
retarded boy who prefers to crawl though he has no
major physical disabilities. A more efficient program
for this older student would be similar to that proposed by O'Brien et al. (1972), in which crawling is
restrained and walking is primed by physical assistance to a standing position and then reinforced
appropriately.

The student's age will also determine whether basic fine and gross motor and body management skills
are instructed in isolation or within the context of
other activities. It is reasonable to work on advanced
locomotor skills such as running, jumping, and
climbing with preschool and early elementary aged
children by task analyzing these skills and training
them in a variety of settings. Figure 8.2 shows how
these skills can be taught to young children during a
physical education program. These same locomotor
skills should be taught to adolescents and adults in the
context of age-appropriate recreational activities,
vocational, and community mobility skills. If certain
skills, such as hopping, skipping, and galloping, are
not necessary for adaptation to probable adult environments, they probably should not be included in
the curriculum.

FIGURE 8.1
Six-Phase Curriculum for Recreational Skills

DOMAIN:	Recreation (Physical Activities)	

ENVIRONMENT:		
	I. School playground	VI. City bowling alley
	II. School gym	VII. Neighborhood park
	III. Home backyard	VIII. YMCA
	IV. Home living room	IX. City pool
	V. City rec center	X. Group home

SUBENVIRONMENTS:

I. Playground: ball diamond, jungle gym, track, swings, tennis courts, basketball courts, volleyball court
II. School gym: racquetball courts, pool, track, basketball court, weight room, locker room
III. Home backyard: swings, basketball goal, horseshoe area, grass area
IV. Home living room: furniture, television area
V. City rec center: weight room, racquet courts, pool, track, courts, gymnastics area, locker rooms

VI. Bowling alley: Pinball area, bowling lanes
VII. Park: softball fields, horseshoe area, jogging trails, lake, swings, tennis courts
VIII. YMCA: weight room, racquet courts, pool, track, courts, gymnastics area, locker rooms
IX. Pool: swimming area, locker rooms
X. Group home: recreation room, living room, bedroom, backyard

ACTIVITIES:

I. Softball, climbing, jogging, walking, swinging, tennis, basketball, volleyball
II. Racquetball, squash, handball, swimming, jogging, walking, basketball, weight lifting, rope jumping, stationary cycling, exercises, showering, using lockers
III. Swinging, basketball, horseshoes, croquet, pitching softball
IV. Exercises, table games, sewing, painting

SKILLS:

I.

Softball	*Basketball*	*Walk (on track)*
underhand throw	catch basketball	move with support 20 yards
overhand throw	chest pass	move with support 100 yards
catch with glove	overhead pass	move alone 100 yards
batting pitched ball	bounce pass	move alone 220 yards
running bases	dribble	move alone 440 yards
throwing to person at base	dribble and walk	move alone 880 yards
tagging runner	two-hand shot	
hitting pitched ball	dribble-pass-shoot on move	
catching hit ball	jump and tap ball	
playing softball game	play one-on-one half-court	
	play three-on-three half-court	
	play five-on-five half-court	
	play five-on-five full-court	

TASK ANALYSES:

I. *Softball—underhand throw*

1. Curl fingers around ball
2. Wrap thumb around opposite side of ball
3. Apply inward pressure between thumb and fingers to grasp ball firmly

FIGURE 8.1 (CONTINUED)

4. Bend elbow, bringing ball to waist level
5. Extend elbow, bringing arm outward to dominant side of body
6. Extend elbow, moving arm backward behind body, forming a 45-degree angle with back of body

7. Rotate wrist so that palm of hand is facing forward
8. Extend elbow, swinging arm forward to front of body in a pendular motion, while shifting weight to forward foot (foot opposite the throwing hand)
9. When arm is extended forward, pointing at target, release ball in forward direction

NOTE: Only a few of the possible activities and skills have been included.

Difficulty Level of the Motor Skill

Most motor activities can be broken into sequential skills or components, which in turn can be task analyzed for instruction (see Figure 8.1) without further adaptations. However, for some complex activities such as team sports or skills involving equipment like a bicycle, changes in rules or mechanical adaptations may be necessary. A teacher must first decide whether or not the student will be able to participate independently, even with certain adaptations. Second, if you decide to adapt equipment or rules, the change must be validated so that the adaptations still allow later participation in the same or similar activities with nonhandicapped peers. In most cases, it is probably best to select age-appropriate activities that

do not require major changes. For a profoundly retarded 18-year-old who has never been taught any recreational motor skills, bowling, jogging, and archery are probably more appropriate than tennis, volleyball, or basketball, which have more complicated rules and movement patterns.

Assessment

Specific priorities for motor-skill training for each student must be identified by individual assessment across all motor skill areas. The first step in this assessment process involves some general evaluation instrument, such as that shown in Figure 8.3. An evaluation of this nature is helpful in identifying the absence or presence of particular skills, as well as the sequential development of skills within each motor category. Refer to the individual sections of this figure as the various motor skill categories are described in this chapter.

The second and most important assessment procedure involves task analyzing the skills chosen for instruction. The task analytic assessment methods described in chapter 4 are applicable to all motor skills. Specific examples of task analyses of motor skills are provided in this chapter as well as in several other sources, including Wehman and Schleien (1980). Each task analysis should be validated to match the specific student characteristics, materials, and setting variables.

FIGURE 8.2

This Young Student along with his Classmates is Learning to Climb up a Sliding Board. Note that both handicapped and nonhandicapped students are having physical education together. Motor skills programs are excellent for carrying out integrated programming.

FUNDAMENTAL MOTOR SKILLS

The motor skills discussed here depend on the earlier, more fundamental motor responses that usually develop in nonhandicapped children before the age of 1 year. For example, each child must have adequate

FIGURE 8.3
Motor Skills Checklist

1. *Gross Locomotor Skills*
   _____ Stands alone
   _____ Walks forward with support (holds someone's hand)
   _____ Walks forward alone
   _____ Walks in a straight line between two objects 50 yards apart
   _____ Walks sideways 5 steps
   _____ Walks backwards 10 steps
   _____ Ascends stairs in upright position by taking each step with a dominant foot (marking time—immature pattern)
   _____ Ascends stairs in upright position by taking each step, alternating lead feet (mature step)
   _____ Runs without support, 25 yards
   _____ Transfers weight during walking from heel to toe
   _____ Descends stairs, same foot leading
   _____ Descends stairs, alternating feet
   _____ Jumps up with two-foot take off and two-foot landing
   _____ Maintains balance when standing on one foot for 3 seconds
   _____ Jumps down from object 1 foot from ground
   _____ Jumps over rope at least 6 inches from ground
   _____ Executes 5–10 consecutive jumps
   _____ Jumps forward and moves through air 1 foot before landing on both feet
   _____ Hops forward on one foot
   _____ Executes 4 consecutive hops on same foot
   _____ Runs in a straight line between two objects 50 yards apart, turns around, and runs back
   _____ Walks a circular path 20–25 feet without stepping out of bounds
   _____ Steers tricycle (or bicycle with training wheels) and manages turns.
   _____ Manages two-wheeled scooter
   _____ Propels (pushes) object such as grocery cart forward while walking
   _____ Pulls object such as wagon while walking
   _____ Gallops forward
   _____ Slides to right from middle position without going more than 2 feet forward or backward from middle position.
   _____ Slides to left from middle position
   _____ Skips forward by making 10 consecutive steps on alternating feet without losing skipping rhythm

2. *Gross Manipulative Skills*
   _____ Pushes large ball distance of 2 feet while sitting with legs fully extended
   _____ Rolls large ball distance of 2 feet while sitting
   _____ Rolls ball distance of 4 feet toward objects while in sitting position
   _____ Rolls ball to partner seated 4 feet away
   _____ Extends arms to retrieve rolled ball while in sitting position
   _____ Throws ball with both hands from chest
   _____ Throws ball with both hands over head
   _____ Throws with underarm pattern
   _____ Throws with overarm pattern
   _____ Throws with sidearm pattern
   _____ Throws basketball into hoop 6 feet tall
   _____ Catches large ball with arms extended in front of body
   _____ Catches bounced ball by scooping it into body
   _____ Catches thrown ball by scooping it into body
   _____ Catches smaller ball with scooping motion
   _____ Catches ball by running to meet it and using only hands for initial contact
   _____ Strikes stationary ball or tee with open palms (suspended on string)
   _____ Strikes stationary ball with fisted hand

FIGURE 8.3 (CONTINUED)

_____ Strikes stationary ball with paddle (large hitting surface or short handle)
_____ Bounces large ball with both hands
_____ Bounces smaller ball with both hands
_____ Bounces ball with one hand
_____ Bounces smaller ball (basketball-size) with one hand 5 consecutive times
_____ Kicks stationary ball (soccer size)
_____ Kicks thrown ball (thrown at ground level)
_____ Place kicks ball to height of 5 feet
_____ Punts ball to height of 5 feet
_____ Strikes moving ball with hand
_____ Strikes moving ball with paddle or racquet
_____ Holds ball in one hand and strikes it with other
_____ Hits volleyball over net
_____ Hits small ball or birdie over net with paddle or racquet
_____ Hits tennis ball over net with regulation-size racquet
_____ Hits stationary ball with bat
_____ Hits thrown ball with bat
_____ Rides tricycle or bicycle with training wheels
_____ Rides two-wheel bicycle
_____ Jumps rope 10 consecutive jumps (alternate or both feet)

3. *Fine Motor Skills*
   _____ Crude reach with no contact
   _____ Fisted hands
   _____ Reaches for object and pushes object with open hand
   _____ Brings hands to mouth
   _____ Reaches and grasps object with palmer grasp
   _____ Transfers objects from one hand to another
   _____ Grasps object, holds object for at least 10 seconds, and voluntarily releases object
   _____ Grasps spoon with *cylindrical* grasp
   _____ Brings spoon to mouth, maintaining grasp
   _____ Grasps glass with *spherical* grasp
   _____ Grasps small ball with *spherical* grasp
   _____ Grasps small four-sided object with *three-jaw check* grasp
   _____ Picks up narrow object with *lateral pincer* grasp
   _____ Picks up pencil with *pincer* grasp
   _____ Uses pencil functionally with pincer grasp
   _____ Zips coat using pincer grasp
   _____ Holds toothbrush using *hook* grasp
   _____ Holds hammer or racquet using hook grasp
   _____ Cuts with scissors using *scissors* grasp
   _____ Uses color paints appropriately by grasping crayon/brush in one hand and using other to hold paper
         when necessary
   _____ Uses both hands simultaneously
   _____ Uses fingers, individually, especially index finger
   _____ Uses thumb to push, fasten, press
   _____ Places small object in container
   _____ Places lids or tops on containers
   _____ Carries objects using both arms and hands
   _____ Uses both hands and arms to stir, mix, pour
   _____ Turns door knobs and faucets

4. *Body Management and Physical Fitness Skills*
   _____ Identified body parts
   _____ Understands body planes (front, back, side)

FIGURE 8.3 (CONTINUED)

—— Knows concepts of right and left
—— Greets people appropriately
—— Responds to greetings and salutations appropriately
—— Can move to designation in a crowd or on a curb
—— Can walk on a 2 × 4 balance beam

Refer to a physical fitness testing manual (e.g. American Association . . ., 1980) for age-norms for the following items. In order to receive credit, the skill must be performed at a level that has been determined to be average or above average for that student's age group.

—— 660-yard run/walk
—— 330-yard run/walk
—— 50-yard dash
—— Sit-ups
—— Chin-ups or flexed arm hang
—— Shuttle-run
—— Squat-thrusts
—— Softball throw
—— Sit, bob, and reach
—— Push-ups
—— Standing broad jump

The skill sequences shown in Figure 8.3 were developed from Renzaglia, 1979; Bayley, 1935; Espenschade & Eckert, 1980; Frankenberg & Dodds, 1976; Gesell, 1940; Johnson, 1978; Sherrill, 1981; Sinclair, 1973; Wellman, 1937; Wild, 1938; and Halverson & Robertson, Note 1.

equilibrium and body control skills to progress to more advanced motor skills such as standing, walking, and manipulating objects. Many severely handicapped persons with CNS disorders do not have even the most fundamental motor functions. This may be further complicated by the presence of nonfunctional, primary reflexes. This population of CNS-involved, severely handicapped individuals also needs physical education experiences, as emphasized in chapter 7.

Primitive reflexes generally persist for a number of weeks in all children, and then gradually disappear as corresponding functional voluntary reflexes and reactions are acquired. When these reflexes do not disappear, they can interfere with normal movement, and the child needs programs to inhibit and integrate these primitive responses. The most commonly seen reflexes in this category include the tonic labyrinthine reflex (TLR), asymmetrical tonic neck reflex (ATNR), the symmetrical tonic neck reflex (TNR), primitive neck righting reflex (PNRR), grasp reflex, and the Moro (head turn to startle) reflex. Whenever these reflexes persist, a program should be implemented in conjunction with occupational or physical therapy to modify them or accommodate their presence.

Righting and equilibrium responses are automatic responses that facilitate balance and support as the body moves from one position to another. Children need a wide variety of experiences to learn to control the head, arms, and total body as it moves from aligned to off-balance positions. For example, you must be able to shift the head, trunk, or extremities from side to side, forward to backward, to create all forms of body positions (Johnson, 1978).

Head control is the first major accomplishment that ultimately contributes to total movement control. Normal development moves downward from the head (cephalocaudal) and outward from the center of the body (proximal-distal). Head control refers to the ability to stabilize the head in space. It is the alignment of the head with the rest of the body, without excessive sideward tilt, flexion forward, or extension backward.

Trunk control is the second ability necessary for independent movement. The ability to control the position and movement of the trunk in relation to the rest of the body is essential for sitting as well as all locomotor skills, including crawling, standing, and walking.

Trunk control can be assessed by observing the quality of alignment and trunk rotation. These questions may be asked: Can the child roll from side to side while lying on the ground? Does the whole trunk rotate when the shoulders turn from side to side in a seated position? If the student has both trunk and head control while upright, he or she should be ready to attain a sitting position.

Rolling is actually the first locomotor movement to develop. By 6 months of age, an infant should be able to roll from back to back or abdomen to abdomen without assistance (Sherrill, 1981). Mature rolling is segmental in nature and involves turning the head first, followed sequentially by the shoulders, pelvis, and legs.

Sitting is a total body response which requires not only trunk and head control, but also the ability to use the legs, feet, and arms for balance. Prerequisite skills for sitting can be tested by having the child sit on the floor, receiving support at the lower back; on a large beach ball while held at the thighs; or on a tilt board, as you observe the balance responses as the surface is slowly tilted from side to side (Finnie, 1975).

Crawling and Creeping

The rudiments of locomotor behavior can be observed in reflex form in neonatal crawling movements. These early patterns support the concept that the basic movements necessary for locomotion are innate and are developed through normal maturation. The first volitional locomotor movement occurs as the child begins to crawl. Often the first movements are accidental, as the prone child tries to reach for a distant object. If the object is out of reach, the child's chest will return to the floor, causing a forward slide as the arms attempt to pull. This early crawling behavior uses the arms exclusively. As the child progressively involves both arms and legs, two forms of quadripedal locomotion may develop. The crawling pattern may show a well-coordinated, oppositional action of the arms and legs (e.g., right arm and left leg move simultaneously). At approximately the same point in development, the child may also have a hand-knee position and characteristic knee rock. In this position, the child may rock back and forth in a steady forward-backward sway. The hand-knee position represents a definite attempt to creep even though there is no actual motion through space.

Once the child has mastered the hand-knee position, locomotion is almost inevitable. Early creeping movements show high intraindividual variation, as well as interindividual variation such as erratic arm and leg coordination with unilateral, bilateral, and crosslateral movements randomly interspersed.[1]

TRAINING GROSS MOTOR SKILLS

Larger gross movements include both locomotor and manipulative skills. Locomotor skills involve coordi-

nating perceptual motor abilities such as walking and running that are primarily designed to transport the body through space. These skills allow us to interact with the environment, where manipulative skills allow us to act on the environment. The fundamental locomotor skills of rolling, crawling, creeping, and walking provide the foundation for advanced activities, including climbing, running, leaping, hopping, jumping, galloping, sliding, and skipping. All other locomotor movements are combinations or variations on these patterns. Manipulative motor skills can be categorized as throwing, striking, catching, object bouncing, kicking, and manipulating objects, as in bicycle riding (Espenschade & Eckert, 1980; Wickstrom, 1980). Because all recreational and mobility activities are composed of one or more of these basic gross motor skills, teachers of the severely handicapped must understand how these individual skills can be most efficiently trained.

Locomotor Skills

Creeping

Although profoundly retarded people sometimes creep and crawl rather than walk, this is inappropriate and unnecessary in most older students. In most cases, crawling can be replaced with walking in adolescents through operant training (O'Brien et al., 1972). If creeping is to be targeted for a young severely handicapped child, the teacher must first be sure that the child has lost the symmetrical tonic neck reflex and can maintain balance on three body parts. At that point, crosslateral movement (right arm and left leg moving simultaneously, etc.) can be primed. Sherrill (1981) suggests that scooter boards, movement on mirrored surfaces, and creeping over and through hoops can facilitate this crosslateral patterning.

Walking

Most children's first locomotor patterns are crawling and creeping, though some do bypass these patterns in favor of seat sliding or scooting or begin to move directly from an upright posture. Attaining a standing position is in itself a task worth noting because it depends upon a rather complex combination of basic physical abilities, including balance, strength, and flexibility. To reach a standing position, most children roll from their front and then rise to stand. Children first learn to sit and later to be pulled to standing either by being pulled by some other person or by pulling themselves up on a stable object. Once upright, they then proceed to walk with the assistance of a stable object such as a chair or an adult's hand.

Truly independent stepping develops after both an upright posture and initial bipedal locomotion re-

---

[1]Sherrill (1981) provides an excellent explanation of these movement principles as well as others that guide motor development.

quiring hand support are achieved. The first independent steps are hesitant, irregular in length and rate, and quite unstable. Early walking is generally characterized by a wide stance with knees flexed. The toes are usually turned out to increase the base of support. The initial, irregular steps sometimes appear to consist of a few running steps with arms held high, for safety or to counteract gravity. This arm action progresses through a series of developmental changes. During the intermediate stages, the arms may swing with the legs unilaterally, where in the mature walk the arms swing in opposition to the legs to help counterbalance hip rotation.

The walk of many mentally retarded people is unnecessarily characterized by a shuffle step and somewhat stooped posture. In contrast, the well-integrated mature walk is characterized by a narrow

and more rhythmic gait, with the feet pointed straight ahead and a heel-toe progression of weight bearing. The feet move as if the inner borders of each foot were placed on opposite sides of a line rather than directly in front of each other, as in the "model's walk." As the walk matures, arm-leg opposition becomes obvious and up-down motion decreases.

Several recent studies show how applied behavior analysis can be used to develop independent walking in both physically impaired and nonimpaired severely and profoundly mentally retarded children and adolescents. Loynd and Barclay (1970) used positive reinforcement to teach walking in the sequence of (a) cruising along a table; (b) walking around a table; (c) crossing a gradually increasing space; and (d) fading of the table by using other objects such as broomsticks, a person's hand, tape, and a piece of

TABLE 8.1 Shaping Sequence for Walking

Objectives	Methodology
Level I	
Child takes alternating steps in a forward direction with adult holding one hand.	Child should walk a few steps holding an adult's hand. As child gains skill, distance should be gradually increased.
Level II	
Child takes alternating steps in a forward direction holding onto a rope.	Child grasps taut rope, with the adult's hand directly adjacent to the child's hand. Then, the length of the rope between the adult and the child is gradually increased (maximum of 12 to 18 inches). Ropes with decreasing diameters may be used. Initially, rope is held taut; rope slackens, allowing a momentary experience of independent walking. In this way, support by the taut rope can be alternated with increasingly longer periods of the slackened rope following a schedule dictated by the child's level of acquisition.
Level III	
Child takes independent, alternating steps in a forward direction.	After placing the child in the standing position, have him walk to an attractive positive consequence. Gradually increase distance. A large, open environment should be selected, with no intervening physical barriers.
Level IV	
Child will initiate independent walking towards an attractive object, and/or when verbally instructed to walk at random periods during a treatment session when given a verbal or visual cue.	Environment should be arranged so that attractive and/or necessary objects are far enough from the child to require walking. Placing objects higher makes crawling less functional. Crawling should be stopped immediately if it occurs and followed by placement in the standing position and a short physical prompt to initiate walking. A successful trial is immediately followed by a positive consequence.

SOURCE: Reprinted with permission of authors and publisher from Haavik, S., & Altman, K. Establishing walking by severely retarded children. PERCEPTUAL AND MOTOR SKILLS, 1977, 44, 1107–1114, Table 1.

string. Similar positive reinforcement and shaping procedures have been used with severely handicapped children by Chandler and Adams (1972), Horner (1971), O'Brien et al. (1972), and Westervelt and Luiselli (1975). Haavik and Altman (1977) used positive reinforcement, a physical prompting-to-walk procedure to stop crawling, and a four-step sequence of skills to train independent walking. These steps, along with their corresponding behavioral objectives, are shown in Table 8.1. This kind of sequence could be easily adapted for any student, regardless of age.

Once independent walking is established, students must practice on a variety of surfaces. Only through practice can the proper balance and posture be obtained. Teachers should also encourage increasing or decreasing speeds until the rate stabilizes at approximately 115 to 145 steps per minute (Sherrill, 1981).

Stair Climbing

Once the initial walking pattern is developed, walking up and down stairs requires only a modification of the fundamental pattern. Stair walking demands the integration of sufficient strength, control, and balance to support the body weight on one foot while moving forward and either downward or upward. Most first attempts at stair climbing are a "marking time" movement, where one foot advances a step, the trailing foot comes to rest on that step, and then the lead foot again advances one step. The task analysis in Table 8.2 shows both this form and mature stair climbing. Either one may initially be appropriate for a severely handicapped student who has no stair-climbing experiences.

When children are learning to negotiate stairs, it is common to have them climb up and then require help because they cannot descend. Other, intermediate solutions for descending stairs are used by those who have not mastered climbing down. For instance, you can either walk or crawl backward down the stairs or sit down on the steps and scoot down.

Most studies investigating developmental sequences indicate that climbing up stairs develops before climbing down stairs, that shorter flights of stairs are negotiated before longer flights, and that stairs with lower risers are mastered before higher and deeper stairs (Bayley, 1935; Gesell & Thompson, 1929; Shirley, 1933; Wellman, 1937). Some variations have been reported, but the basic sequence remains consistent, suggesting that stairs should be scaled to meet the child's physical abilities (Espenschade & Eckert, 1980).

Other climbing skills develop similarly. For example, ladder climbing is characterized by "marking time" followed by the more mature, alternate foot pattern. Many other activities require either the basic walking pattern or a modification. It is, therefore, particularly important that young children have a wide range of environmental stimuli, including stairs, ladders, lofts, and bridges, to climb.

Ultimately, however, locomotor skills must be taught in the natural settings where the behavior will occur. It is never enough to train stair climbing on a simulated five-step staircase during physical education class, if the stairwell between the two floors of the school is the current environment in which the student needs to maneuver. In this case, it would be more efficient to train on the school stairwell whenever possible during the day, or at least regularly probe performance on the stairwell to check for generalization.

Running

Running is primarily an adaptation and extension of the basic walking movement. The basic walking pattern is modified to produce a run in which there is a

TABLE 8.2 Task Analyses for Training Stair Climbing

Immature Pattern	Mature Pattern
1. Stand at bottom of stairs	1. Stand at bottom of stairs
2. Grasp handrail (hook grasp)	2. Grasp handrail
3. Lift one foot to first stair	3. Lift one foot to first stair
4. Put weight on foot on first stair	4. Put weight on foot on first stair
5. Bring other foot to first stair	5. Bring other foot to second stair
6. Lift first foot to second stair	6. Put weight on foot on second stair
7. Put weight on foot	7. Lift first foot to third stair
8. Bring other foot to second stair	8. Put weight on foot
9. Continue lifting one foot and then the other to stair until all stairs are climbed	9. Lift other foot to fourth stair
	10. Continue lifting alternating feet to stairs until all steps are climbed

NOTE: The immature pattern may have to be trained initially in very young children or older students with little locomotor training.

period of nonsupport (a flight phase), in contrast to the walk, in which one foot is always in contact with the ground. Arm and leg opposition are critical in both the well-balanced and efficient walk and run.

A significant maturational step occurs in running as the arms are moved in opposition to the legs. In the early run, arms and legs move unilaterally (i.e., right arm and right leg forward simultaneously), causing a great deal of upper body rotation. During this stage, the arms are extended and swing through a very short arc, in a pattern similar to the leg action. As the knee and leg action increases, the arm swings more rapidly, often swinging across the middle of the body (Wickstrom, 1980). Finally, in the mature run, the arms are flexed to approximately 90 degrees at the elbow and swing up and down in the vertical plane, remaining synchronized in opposition to the legs (Corbin, 1980).

Other Advanced Locomotor Skills

A wide variety of upright locomotor skills develop from the basic walking pattern. There are eight basic upright locomotor movements, each of which can be identified by a specific sequence of foot movements and by the underlying rhythm of the movement (see Figure 8.4). Of these eight locomotor patterns, there are five even locomotor patterns (²⁄₄ or ⁴⁄₄ time) that are all modifications of the walk.

1. Walk—The transfer of weight from one foot to the other while moving forward or backward. One foot must always be in contact with the floor.
2. Run—The transfer of weight from one foot to the other (as in the walk) but with a momentary loss of contact with the floor, providing a period of flight when neither foot is in contact with the ground.
3. Leap—The transfer of weight from one foot to the other foot as in the run, but with a more sustained period of flight and greater height and distance. In the mature leap, the toe of one foot is the last to leave the floor and the toe on the opposite foot is the first to land.
4. Hop—The transfer of weight from one foot to the same foot, with the opposite foot never touching the surface. In the mature form, the toe is the last to leave the floor and the first to contact again on the downward flight.
5. Jump—The transfer of weight from one or both feet, with a landing on both feet.

These five even locomotor patterns are combined with three uneven locomotor patterns (sometimes called *two-part* or *long-short* rhythms). These uneven locomotor skills develop later and provide fundamental skills for many recreational activities.

1. Gallop—Moving with the same foot in front, in a step-close sequence.
2. Slide—Moving sideward with the same foot always leading. The weight is sequentially transferred from the lead foot to the closing foot and back to the same lead foot.
3. Skip—Moving forward with a combination of long step-hop patterns during which the lead foot is alternated.

The skip and slide are both rather complex. The slide is quite difficult for some children, since it requires moving in one direction while facing another. However, it is necessary for many functional behaviors, since it occurs in many recreational activities such as dancing and most sport skills such as tennis and basketball.

Gross Motor Manipulative Skills

Manipulative or purposeful skills are primarily designed to allow the individual to have an effect on some external object. They may involve both fine and gross motor skills. Throwing, catching, and bouncing a ball are three different manipulative movements. The first requires the production of force, the second requires the absorption or reception of force, and the third requires the sequential combination of both production and reception of force. Throwing, catching, striking, and kicking a ball are propulsive skills that require eye-hand or eye-foot coordination. Coordination problems may be magnified as the child begins to move through space while executing propulsive movements (i.e., running and kicking or catching a ball, pushing and pulling objects through space). Other gross motor manipulative skills include riding a tricycle and eventually a bicycle. These skills are particularly complex because they require you to coordinate both arms and legs, while simultaneously integrating the changing visual environment. Although gross motor manipulative skills are very complex, they are the foundation for most recreational and functional living skills.

Rolling and Pushing

Manipulating objects by rolling or pushing is often prerequisite to more mature throwing and catching. Teaching these patterns can be particularly beneficial to very young children who are not physically ready to catch. Rolling and pushing balls, for example, are also good ways to encourage partner or group participation. In older students, these skills should be taught in the context of bowling or shuffle board or vocational activities such as pushing tables, carts, brooms, and so on.

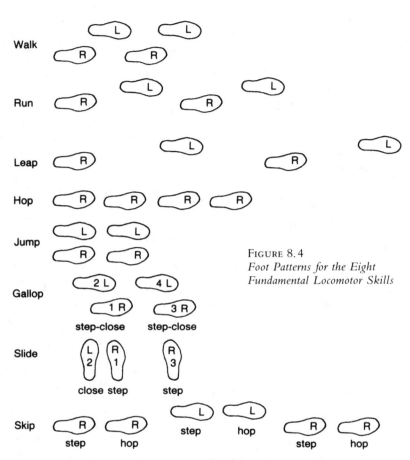

FIGURE 8.4
Foot Patterns for the Eight
Fundamental Locomotor Skills

Throwing Patterns

The three basic throwing patterns—overhand, underhand, and sidearm—form the foundations for many functional skills. The overarm pattern, for example, is the basic movement in hammering, swimming, and throwing objects. It also occurs in nearly every sport involving ball playing.

The basic developmental sequence for overhand throwing progresses through four distinct phases of movement: monoplanar action, whole body rotation, unilateral action, and sequential, crosslateral movement (Bunker, 1975; Deach, 1950; Hanson, 1961; Jones, 1951; Wickstrom, 1980; Halverson & Roberton, Note 1).

The development of the underarm pattern is very similar to that of the overarm throw. It typically progresses from a single plane action to crosslateral movement. A task analysis of an underhand softball throw, shown in Table 8.3, illustrates how this pattern can be broken down for instruction.

Catching

Catching and throwing skills are sometimes thought to be linked. However, they are actually quite different. Throwing and catching develop independently, with throwing skills generally thought to precede catching by as much as 12 to 24 months (Gutteridge, 1939; Wickstrom, 1980).

Like throwing, catching can involve several different types of movements and can be affected by many external variables. Wickstrom (1980) and Ridenour (1975) have pointed out six major variables affecting both the performance and analysis of catching patterns: the size of the ball, the speed of the ball, the distance the ball travels before it is caught, the method of projecting the ball, the direction of the ball in relation to the catch, and the arm action of the catcher. Several other factors should also be considered: the shape of the ball, the trajectory of the flight, and the position of the catcher (e.g., moving or stationary). The most important variables are ball ve-

TABLE 8.3. Task Analysis for Softball Underhand Throw

1. Curl fingers around ball.
2. Wrap thumb around opposite side of ball.
3. Apply inward pressure between thumb and fingers to grasp ball firmly.
4. Bend elbow, bringing ball to waist level.
5. Extend elbow, bringing arm outward to dominant side of body.
6. Extend elbow, moving arm backward behind body, forming a 45-degree angle with back of body.
7. Rotate wrist so that palm of hand is facing forward.
8. Extend elbow, swinging arm forward to front of body in a pendular motion, while shifting weight to forward foot (foot opposite the throwing hand).
9. When arm is extended forward, pointing at target, release ball in forward direction.

locity and direction (Bruce, 1966; Ridenour, 1975; Williams, 1968). The actual skill of catching may be further divided into three aspects: the visual perception of the moving object, the preparatory movements of the body, and the actual stopping and controlling of the moving object (Bruce, 1966; Seefeldt, Note 2).

The three basic developmental stages of catching include (a) nesting, in which the ball is scooped or trapped against the body, (b) hands-only catch, in which arm flexion allows the hands to capture the ball, (c) mature catching, in which upper body action joins hands and arms to absorb force to catch the ball. This sequence implies that shaping procedures may be needed to develop mature catching gradually from nesting and hands-only catching.

In the first stages of catching, children are most likely to try to trap objects against the chest, suggesting that large, soft objects are more likely to be caught successfully than small, hard objects. The importance of using large objects in learning to catch must not be confused with the need for smaller objects for early throwing experiences. The size of the object to be caught can affect the type of catching behavior that develops. For example, the same person may catch a large ball by using an arm-trapping motion, but may use a hand clasp catch when a small ball is tossed (Halverson & Roberton, Note 1). Similarly, during the initial attempts, catchers should be encouraged to "make a nest for the ball, and hold it close to your chest." During later stages, they should be more successful at catching a ball which has been allowed to bounce first (Pedersen, 1973).

Striking Patterns

The developmental sequences for striking behaviors are similar in direction and rate to the progress of throwing skills. Part of this association is no doubt due to the similarity of the three movement patterns:

overarm, sidearm, and underarm. In addition, striking skills are affected by the same variables, namely, the size of the object being struck, the speed of the object, the direction and trajectory of the object, the source of force for the object, anticipatory adjustments required (spatial and locomotor), and the weight of the object. In addition to these object-related considerations, other factors related to the implement and the performer must be considered. For example, the striking surface may be part of the body (hand, foot, head, etc.) or an external object (bat, racket, paddle, stick, etc.) whose weight, size, and shape must also be considered. A third consideration concerns the interaction of the object and implement. There are two basic combinations: (a) the object is at rest and the implement is moving (croquet, hammering) or (b) both the object and the implement move, which requires more complex visual-motor integration for coincident timing (in batting, playing tennis, etc.). Striking skills therefore involve not only the physical skill of striking but also visual-motor integration.

Watching children's striking behavior gives a dramatic example of individual variability influenced by external factors. For example, the weight and size of the striking implement may significantly affect the movement. When a child is given a heavy, large object, such as a wooden paddle, the movement patterns may regress from a more mature sidearm swing to a poking, overarm action (Halverson & Roberton, Note 1; Seefeldt & Haubenstricker, Note 3).

Leverage also affects striking. The shorter the lever, the easier it is to strike with accuracy and control. Therefore, striking with the hand in games like volleyball or with very short implements when learning softball or tennis can be helpful (Sherrill, 1981).

The basic developmental sequence for striking is similar for all children and all three striking patterns. The mature patterns of each skill contain three essential components: (a) the body weight shifts forward, usually onto the opposite foot, (b) the trunk rotates rapidly to add to the sequential force production, and (c) the arm action follows at the moment of maximum speed of rotation or force. The difference in the striking patterns are quite obvious, but these three underlying similarities will be critical in each pattern.

Ball Bouncing

Ball bouncing is somewhat unusual in that it requires the sequential combination of both the production and reception or redirection of force. The first instance of bouncing probably occurs when a ball is accidentally dropped. Later a series of taps upon the ball is added until control is lost. The mature ability to control successive bounces requires accurate visual-motor integration, since the hand must meet the ball during the upward portion of the bounce and then redirect it downward. Bouncing a basketball, illustrated in Figure 8.5, to a partner is another form of this skill.

The immature pattern shows the difficulty children have coordinating the movement of the object with their hand movements. This problem can be seen when a child tries to "catch up" with the ball when it is already moving downward. The mature ball bounce also seems to require that the ball and the child's hand are proportionate in size, to allow some degree of directional control (Espenschade & Eckert, 1980). Small balls should be used with small hands.

Kicking

The kick is a unique manipulative skill because it is a propulsive movement pattern requiring a sophisticated interaction of the visual system with the legs and feet. Because of the requirement of balancing on one foot while striking an object, the individual must be able to run and balance effectively before being asked to kick.

In the early stages of kicking, balance may be a major problem. Children often merely push the ball forward to avoid losing their equilibrium. The first actual kicking consists of moving the leg forward only, as in pushing. Children appear to be able to execute this rudimentary kick soon after they are able to run effectively. The second stage merely adds some preliminary backward leg action in a pendular motion, to provide for a more powerful leg swing. It is later accompanied by a compensatory action of the opposite arm (a rather difficult skill). The mature kick is characterized by the addition of a sequence of preliminary hip extension and knee flexion, followed by forceful leg extension and a backward trunk lean (Dohrman, 1967; Wickstrom, 1980). This is often combined with a preparatory phase, including an approach to the ball while walking or running.

FIGURE 8.5
Bouncing a Basketball to a Partner Is a Complex Skill That Is Fun to Do with Friends.

Bicycle Riding

Cycle riding is very self-rewarding and pleasurable. It is particularly dependent upon appropriate early experiences. For this reason, the use of training wheels attached to the rear axle to aid in balance will benefit most learners. These aids may be used temporarily but should either be removed or raised off the ground as soon as the rider is familiar with the bicycle and has learned the basic skills. Most children will need some actual physical experience with a pusher, rather than training wheels, to learn to ride a bicycle (Ridenour, 1975). Seats and pedals may need to be adapted initially for small children who do not have good sitting balance and locomotor skills (see Figure 8.6).

Figure 8.3 provided a review of gross motor skills and their general developmental sequence. Once skills have been selected for instruction, it is crucial to (a) focus on individual skills within the context of functional activities and (b) teach in the natural environment whenever possible. Specific methods for training gross motor skills to the severely handicapped are no different from any other skills. Applied behavior analysis techniques such as those described in chapter 5 have been used successfully to teach gross locomotor and manipulative skills to profoundly retarded children and adults (Hardiman, Goetz, Reuter, & LeBlanc, 1975).

DEVELOPING FINE MOTOR SKILLS

The fundamental skills of locomotion and manipulation are essential for all motor behavior. In addition, many specific tasks required for daily living and economic sufficiency depend upon fine motor skills. For example, cafeteria workers are more efficient if their work is performed with competent locomotor and manipulative skills.

FIGURE 8.6
Two severely retarded adolescents (first and third boys from the left) participate in a high school physical education class with nonhandicapped adolescents. The weight training activities are part of a daily physical fitness program.

The value of fine motor skills in the vocational and self-care training of moderately and severely handicapped students cannot be overestimated. Of particular importance are object control skills that encourage independence and self-expression and provide information about the external world. These skills are based on the development of manual dexterity and reaching, grasping, holding, and releasing. For example, the ability to grasp and hold objects provides the key to controlling and producing in this world. Each individual needs experiences with handling different objects to learn to identify and discriminate size, shape, texture, weight, and firmness. The fine motor skills involved in reaching, grasping, and manipulating objects develop sequentially, based upon a combination of experiences, chronological and physiological age, handicapping conditions, and the establishment of hand preference.

The early foundation for fine motor as well as gross motor manipulative skills lies in the ability to voluntarily reach, grasp, and release objects, which typically develops before the age of 1 year. The typical sequence of development of these early skills is shown in Figure 8.3.

Grasping

The most important fine motor skills involve different types of grasps. There are seven fundamental grasping patterns (Halverson, 1931; Kamin, 1972), each of which is used to accomplish specific types of tasks, as shown in Figure 8.7.

The palmer grasp is the most fundamental and primitive of all grasps. It involves raking objects into the palm without using the thumb. As soon as a student is able to reach, grasp, and release objects independently, this grasp should be discouraged and thumb use encouraged through shaping. *The cylindrical grasp* is usually the next to develop. It involves use of the thumb in wide opposition to the fingers. This kind of grasp is typically used by youngsters who are just beginning to spoon feed or for grasping wide objects that do not require much thumb usage.

The cylindrical grasp is usually replaced by the *spherical grasp,* in which the thumb is not in direct opposition to fingers, but in wide abduction. This is a functional grasp that can be used for handling (throwing and catching) recreational materials or for holding any two-dimensional objects such as a glass.

The *pincer grasp* is the most sophisticated and functional of all grasps. It involves using the thumb in abduction to the index finger. The *three-jaw chuck* is a more fundamental pincer grasp involving the thumb and first two fingers. It is usually used for grasping wide objects. The *lateral pincer* or scissors grasp involves the use of the thumb to the side of the index finger. It is necessary for actions such as using scissors or tongs and is best developed by practicing with

FIGURE 8.7
Typical Grasps

1. Palmer Grasp

2. Cylindrical Grasp

3. Spherical Grasp

4. Three Jaw Chuck

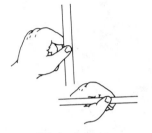

5. Lateral Pincer

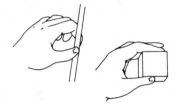

6. Pincer

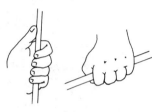

7. Hook or Shovel

these implements. The refined pincer involves use of thumb and index finger with the index finger exhibiting tip control. This grasp is necessary for writing, painting or drawing, zipping, sewing, and many vocational tasks.

The last type of grasp is the *hook or shovel,* in which the fingers serve as a hook to wrap around an object without involvement of the thumb. The thumb can serve as a lever or work with the fingers by wrapping over or under them. This type of grasp is used in tooth brushing, hammering, and most racquet sports.

Whenever possible, the various grasps should always be developed within the context of functional skills. A teacher should be able to analyze the grasps involved in vocational, self-care, and recreational activities to determine which of the seven fundamental grasps is appropriate for a specific activity.

Other Fine Motor Skills

Most fine motor skills other than grasping can be categorized as (*a*) finger use, (*b*) eye-hand precision coordination, and (*c*) simultaneous use of both arms and hands. Table 8.4 outlines these skills along with corresponding functional examples.

TABLE 8.4. Fine Motor Skills

Skill	Example
1. Fingers move in any direction and with control	Turning book pages
2. Individual finger use	Dialing telephone
3. Individual thumb use	Clothes snaps
4. Coordinated finger use	Typing; playing musical instrument; shoe tying
5. Arm placement	Placing arm on small table or in water basin
6. Placing objects in or on other objects	Jar lids, box tops
7. Using both arms for holding and carrying	Carrying cafeteria tray
8. One hand holding, one hand manipulating	Painting, stirring, gardening

TRAINING BODY MANAGEMENT AND PHYSICAL FITNESS SKILLS

Each person's motor performance is affected by the fundamental level of perceptual functioning and the body's physiological capabilities. Many underlying physical and anatomical factors help determine a child's ability to perform perceptual-motor tasks. For example, bicycle riding depends on many factors, including the use of force to maintain speed, sufficient balance to remain upright, an understanding of space and speed, and the complex interaction of the visual-motor system for steering. Similarly, sewing a button on a coat requires finger dexterity to hold the button, flexibility and agility to manipulate the needle, strength to pull the needle through the cloth, and rather sophisticated visual integration to guide the needle through the holes in the button. Each of these skills develops as a result of sound body management, including accurate body awareness and functional physical fitness.

Body Awareness

Body management skills are the most fundamental motor abilities, providing the means for acquiring basic body awareness and understanding the capabilities of the body in motion. In addition, body management skills help children acquire an awareness of their posture and control over body movements.

Movement permits children to explore their own capabilities, including identifying body parts and their functions in both locomotor and nonlocomotor movement. These body management skills help them understand and discover their movement capabilities and the relationship of the body to other objects and people. As body awareness improves, children should have experiences that let them develop concepts of space-time relationships and either cooperate or compete with others. Probably the best way to train body awareness in severely handicapped students is to make sure they have adequate opportunities for normalized activities involving a wide variety of movement patterns and social interactions. Two training programs that incorporate body awareness include learning to greet classmates appropriately at the beginning of the school day and playing games such as "twister" and "Simon says."

Basic Physical Fitness Abilities

Each individual's motor performance is based in part on body awareness skills and the ability to cultivate and use the basic physical abilities which underlie the actions of the body. Physical fitness is essential to the acquisition of efficient motor skills. It is also important for controlling weight and for overall health. In addition to these physical benefits, activities designed to build physical fitness also encourage social interactions.

All motor activities involve one or more physical fitness variables and can be analyzed in terms of relative importance. Thus tasks can be specifically analyzed in terms of physical fitness requirements. A careful understanding of these physical variables will help teachers develop sound educational programming to enhance the health of each learner. Although these variables cannot be described in detail here, we will briefly introduce them.

Strength is the ability to exert force by a specific muscle group, as in gripping or by the entire body, as in lifting a weight or running. Strength is a critical component in almost everything you do, from the first attempts at lifting your own head, to sitting, crawling, climbing, sitting, jumping, throwing, and almost all vocational skills.

Three basic types of strength have been identified: static, dynamic, and ballistic. Static strength is the ability to exert force against an immovable object. Dynamic strength refers to controlled force applied through a range of motion, such as pushing a large object or lifting a box. Finally, ballistic or explosive strength is the ability to propel a relatively heavy object using a rapid, powerful movement followed by a continuous, momentum-produced movement, such as is required to throw a basketball.

Flexibility, or the range of motion present at a given joint, refers to the ability to move the body and its parts through a maximum range or motion without undue strain. Typically, flexibility is measured in degrees of motion, in either flexion (where the angle of the body and its articulations are decreased through movement, as in bending at the elbow) or extension (where the angle is increased, as in straightening the arm). Various aspects of flexibility are obvious in activities like bending and stretching and may easily be observed in children's posture and in their play.

Agility is the ability to change body positions or direction rapidly. It is particularly important in such activities as moving in crowds of people, dancing, and playing most sports. The term *agility* is often confused with *flexibility* and *speed* because it involves the ability to make rapid, successive movements in different directions. The concept of agility emphasizes the directional shifting of the body.

Balance refers to the ability to maintain equilibrium relative to gravity. There are three types of balance: static, dynamic, and object balance. Static balance refers to the maintenance of equilibrium in a stationary position and is necessary for many skills, including standing and sitting. Dynamic balance is even more difficult because it involves locomotion and may vary from walking and running, to skipping, climbing bleachers, riding a bicycle, or traveling on a rapid transit vehicle. Object balance is slightly different; it refers to the ability to balance an external object such as an armful of dishes, a stack of boxes, or a tray of glasses.

Endurance is the ability to sustain activity over a relatively long period. There are two distinct types of endurance: muscular endurance and cardiorespiratory endurance.

Muscular endurance refers to the ability of a muscle to repeat identical movements to maintain tension over a period of time. It is manifested in such situations as doing continuous sit-ups or working on your feet all day. Lack of muscular endurance is not a very dramatic limitation in physiologically normal people unless they are forced to continue activity beyond their limits (Campbell, 1973).

The second type of endurance, cardiorespiratory, refers to the ability of the body to supply oxygen to the working muscles and the ability of the muscles to use this oxygen. Cardiorespiratory endurance is enhanced by placing stress on the body for an extended time through activities such as running, swimming, cycling, or repeated exercise.

In addition to the five health-related physical fitness abilities (strength, flexibility, agility, balance, and endurance), three other fundamental physical fitness abilities are needed for more complex motor skills: power, speed, and coordination. These may be considered combinations of the five fundamental abilities. A powerful individual is one who can combine the basic abilities of strength and speed to produce an explosive movement. Rapid or explosive strength produces *power* and is critical to many forms of motor tasks.

Speed involves rapid muscular contraction required to move from one place to another quickly. Speed may demand other abilities such as strength, flexibility, and power. The use of speed involves responding to some specific stimulus (i.e., starting gun for a race or an assembly line) and then executing a prescribed movement.

The key to efficient motor behavior is the ability to coordinate individual physical fitness capacities meaningfully. The development of *coordination* results in rhythmic, synchronous movement of the entire body. It is ultimately reflected in smooth-balanced, flowing movements and in the principles of opposition (e.g., hand and foot opposition in walking), rotation, and sequential joint action in many perceptual-motor skills. The concepts of opposition and symmetry are critical to human movement because of the use of both sides of the body. These skills must be carefully taught to and reinforced in handicapped students.

Health and motor fitness can be worked on specifically in individual exercises and sporting events and

TABLE 8.5 Examples of Functional Activities Related to Physical Fitness Abilities

	Preschool Elementary	Junior/Senior High	Adult	Individual Exercises
1. Strength	Building Blocks Climbing Objects	Carrying Objects	Moving Objects Bowling	Flexed Armhang
2. Flexibility	Tying Shoes Tumbling Activities	Swimming	Picking up Objects	Sit and Reach Shoulder Rotation
3. Agility	Tag Games	Moving through Crowds	Square Dancing	Squat Thrust Obstacle Course
4. Balance	Walking on Curbs Riding Bicycle	Waiting on Tables	Carrying Supplies	Stork Stand Stick Balance Test Balance Beam Walk
5. Cardiorespiratory Endurance	Running	Jumping Rope Bicycling	Aerobic Dance Hiking Stair Climbing Carrying Objects	Running in Place Run-Walk
6. Power	Hammering Skills	Baseball Batting	Chopping Wood	Softball Throw Vertical Jump
7. Speed	Games of Chase	Discus	Assembly Line Work	50-yard Dash
8. Coordination	Bouncing Balls	Swimming	Bowling	Jumping Jacks

within the context of domestic, community, and vocational activities. Table 8.5 indicates a variety of activities that incorporate physical fitness. When training these and similar activities, the fitness variables involved should be analyzed and emphasized.

Posture

One of the most important body management abilities is the integration of body awareness and physical fitness to produce a pleasing functional posture. *Posture* refers to the manner in which you stand, sit, move, and perform daily activities. It is generally judged by the relationship of various body parts to one another. Posture may be affected by the relative strength and flexibility of various muscle groups and by the visual and proprioceptive perception of verticality.

Body posture is a key in all motor skills, for it provides the basic starting position for all movement. Good body alignment is important not only for proper functioning of internal organs but also because it reflects the general health and psychological well-being (self-image) of the individual. It contributes not only to static, nonlocomotor behavior but also to dynamic, moving activities, which contribute to all aspects of daily living.

The functional posture of many mentally retarded individuals is stereotyped by slumped shoulders and a downward gaze. This posture is *not* permanent and can be modified with careful teaching. A child's functional posture may be evaluated with respect to the relationship between the base of support and the five main weight centers of the body: head, chest, shoulders, pelvis, and knees and feet. The most typical posture problems involve misalignment of these weight centers. If you were to hold a plumb line next to a child, a good standing posture would be indicated by the line passing slightly behind the ear, through the shoulder, through the hip, behind the knee, and in front of the ankle (see Figure 8.8).

Two of the most common postural problems, *kyphosis* and *lordosis*, are illustrated in Figure 8.8. Kyphosis is a postural problem generally characterized by rounded shoulders and a somewhat forward head. This change in thoracic curvature of the spine may be

FIGURE 8.8

Erect Standing Posture Should be Characterized by Well-Balanced Body Centers. A plumb line hung along the body should fall slightly behind the ear, through the shoulder, through the hip, behind the knee, and in front of the ankle.

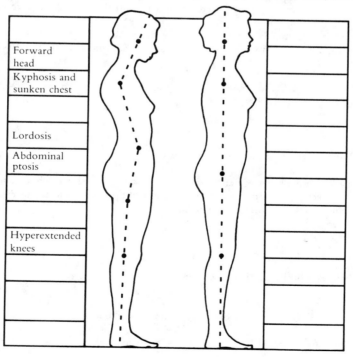

Forward head

Kyphosis and sunken chest

Lordosis

Abdominal ptosis

Hyperextended knees

Bad posture   Good posture

caused by an imbalance of the musculature, with the anterior chest muscles too tight and the posterior (upper back muscles) too loose. To reduce the problem, it would be important to strengthen the muscles of the upper back and stretch the muscles on the front or chest side.

Lordosis is a very common problem in children, teenagers, and adult females. It is characterized by an increased forward curvature of the lumbar spine, often referred to as a *hollow back* and accompanied by a "protruding tummy." As in the case of kyphosis, it may be alleviated (in nonpathological cases) by a conscious effort to strengthen the abdominal muscles and stretch the muscles of the lower back.

Conditions such as lordosis and kyphosis often combine to produce a kind of zig-zag alignment that stretches certain muscles and ligaments while others must work constantly to maintain balance. In addition, these misalignments may also place undue stress on joint structures such as the hips and knees. For example, our students frequently stand with their toes pointed outward and their knees "locked" to maintain a counterbalanced position. The posture assessment in Table 8.6 can serve as a good check for potential postural problems.

It is especially critical that classroom teachers of severely handicapped students screen for postural abnormalities. The awareness of the students' postural needs can provide important information about needed services and programming direction for specialists in physical education (Sherrill, 1980).

RECREATIONAL ACTIVITIES INVOLVING MOTOR SKILLS

There are several categories of recreational activities, some of which do not require complex motor skills. These have been categorized as cultural and social (Bates & Renzaglia, 1979). Most of these activities are spectator events like enjoying music, theater, movies, and dining out. Most other recreational activities can be categorized as either physical, outdoor, or hobbies and can be participatory or spectator in nature. Practically all the participatory activities involve combinations of the many locomotor, gross manipulative, and fine motor skills we have discussed. Although all groups of recreational activities are important, we will address only the physical category since they are based on the motor skills discussed earlier.

TABLE 8.6 Posture Self-Assessment

Award 3 points if correct; 2 points if slight deviation; and 1 point if moderate to severe.

I. Side View: Partner Observing

Hang a plumb line from ceiling or some object away from the wall.

Place sideward-facing subject behind the plumb line and check the following points.

		Score
A. Head Erect	A. _____
B. Shoulders	B. _____
C. Lumbar Spine	C. _____
D. Pelvis	D. _____
E. Knees	E. _____
F. Ankles	F. _____
G. Body Lean (Total body tilted forward or backward)	G. _____

II. Back View

Subject bends forward and observer marks spineous process of each vertebrae with colored chalk or washable marker. Subject stands and is evaluated in an upright position. (It may be easier to do this with *S* facing a grid or wall which has horizontal markings).

H. Head Square (versus tilted)	H. _____
I. Shoulders even	I. _____
J. Hips even	J. _____
K. Spine Straight	K. _____

Check for simple or compound lateral curves.

TOTAL:_____

Rating Scale

Total Score:	33	Excellent
	29–31	Very Good
	26–28	Marginal
	23–25	Poor
	less than 22	Very Poor

Recreational physical activities include exercises and individual and team sports such as those listed in Table 8.7. These activities are targeted because they (a) have been shown to increase or help maintain physical or motor fitness and (b) are functional activities in which nonhandicapped people participate in the community. Any recreational physical activity considered for instruction for the severely handicapped should meet these two criteria.

Prioritizing Functional Recreational Activities

Many factors, including those discussed in chapter 4, must be considered in deciding what skills are necessary for participating in age-appropriate recreational activities. First, the six-phase curriculum development strategy (see Figure 8.1) should be used to choose the physical activities most relevant to the student's current and future environments. Once these potential functional activities and skills have been identified, parent and student preferences should be considered. This is particularly critical in recreation since these activities are often performed with other family members (Wehman & Schleien, 1980; Ford, Brown, Pumpian, Baumgart, Schroeder, & Loomis, Note 4).

Fitness Considerations

The student's general health and physical fitness will also influence the choice of activities and skills.

Matching functional recreational activities to the student's strengths and weaknesses requires the instructor to understand the relationship of the various fitness variables to exercises and sports and be able to assess the student's level of fitness. The teacher who is not familiar with the fitness variables discussed earlier and particular activities related to each should refer to any physical education measurement and evaluation text. A student's fitness level across all the categories can be assessed by using a published fitness test such as the *AAHPERD Health Related Physical Fitness Tests* (American Association . . . , 1980).

Generally, severely handicapped people have below-desirable fitness levels in all health and motor fitness variables (Campbell, 1973; Moon & Renzaglia, in press). When this is the case, activities that increase all fitness components should be included in the recreational program. Sports and exercises like swimming, jogging, and rope jumping that build cardiovascular endurance are particularly important. On the other hand, if a student shows deficiencies in a specific area such as strength, activities to increase it must be emphasized. For example, the student with very low strength could benefit from a daily exercise program including sit-ups, pull-ups, and weight or strength training.

Level of Difficulty of the Activities Chosen

After identifying beneficial functional activities, the teacher must decide which skills to train first. At this

TABLE 8.7 Recreation Activities

Individual Activities		
Yoga	Aerobics programs	Diving
Walking	Exercises	Cycling
Swimming	Weight training	Dancing
Tumbling	Horseback riding	Archery
Skating	Using playground equipment	Jogging
Hiking	Baton twirling	Climbing
Dancing	Jumping rope	
Dual Activities		
Boating	Racquet sports	Golf
Bowling	Horse shoes	Darts
Boxing	Martial arts	Handball
Croquet	Gymnastics	Fencing
Team Sports		
Hockey	Basketball	Soccer
Softball	Volleyball	Rugby
Lacrosse	Water sports	Baseball
Kickball	Dodge ball	Stickball

NOTE: Many of these activities can be included in more than one category.

SOURCE: Adapted from "Community-Based Recreation Program" by P. Bates & A. Renzaglia in P. Wehman (Ed.), *Recreation Programming for Developmentally Disabled Persons*, Baltimore: University Park Press, 1979.

point, task components must be analyzed in terms of the locomotor, gross manipulative, fine motor, and body management skills involved. For example, the skills involved in playing softball and basketball are quite complicated, encompassing running, sliding, catching, all forms of throwing, bouncing, striking, and a host of rules.

Some of these games may be too complex for a severely handicapped student who has not had ample opportunity to practice the motor skills involved. In this case, other functional activities should be trained first. Volleyball is an easier activity because it primarily entails only striking, jumping, sliding, running, and fewer rules than basketball or softball. Another example of selecting activities according to skill complexity is the choice of aerobic weight lifting rather than rope jumping to improve cardiovascular endurance. For a student with enough strength to work with weights, this activity is probably less difficult because it entails lifting with variations of the hook grip and pushing and pulling with the arms and legs. Rope jumping, on the other hand, demands many more skills, including balance, jumping with both feet, and eye-hand and eye-foot coordination.

This discussion should not discourage teachers from teaching complex sports to severely handicapped individuals. If activities are broken into component skill sequences, task-analyzed, and taught systematically, many individual and team sports can be chosen. However, it is important that these activities are pleasurable since they are primarily recreational. With this in mind, activities that are the least difficult to acquire but still age-appropriate should probably be taught first.

Structuring Competition in Recreational Activities

Motor skills provide a natural avenue for students to test their physical abilities and learn to appreciate their own capabilities. For the retarded individual, the competition provided through recreation can be particularly important. Competition, in its broadest sense, refers to matching skills or abilities against a standard. This matching of performance can involve individual challenges to "do the best that you can" or direct interpersonal challenges against other individuals or standards.

An example of four students may help to illustrate the two types of healthy competition. David, Sue, Mike, and Sandy are in a community-based exercise program. David can presently do 12 sit-ups in a minute, Sue can do 13, Mike can do 8, and Sandy can do 9. One technique might be to establish a direct competition between the four students in which one with the highest number of sit-ups by May 1 will

receive a prize. This direct competition means that only one of the four can "win." In contrast, a more appropriate challenge would be to encourage each of them to "do 5 more sit-ups by May 1 than you can do today." This indirect competition allows each person to be challenged and to "win" (Bunker, 1980).

There is an important distinction between being successful and winning. Working to be "better than you are today" is possible and desirable for everyone. It requires that each person know his or her present performance level and establish a goal toward which to work. Everyone can be successful because success does not require besting someone else; it requires doing better than you have done before.

Another competitive outlet for athletes who are mentally retarded is the Special Olympics. This competition was envisioned as an opportunity for individuals to learn the value of a challenge and the joy of winning. Unfortunately, if misused, the Special Olympics can become an egocentric quest for only one goal—"the Gold!" Special Olympics *does* provide a good opportunity for organized competition. Learners are encouraged to compete against others in order to test their own skills. It also provides an opportunity for a group of mentally retarded children and adults to meet in a situation that is both social and competitive. However, Special Olympics should not become the focus of a physical education or recreation program. Like anything else, it represents only one aspect of a program and should not be emphasized at the expense of other motor skills or recreational activities.

Teaching Recreational Skills to the Young Severely Handicapped Child

It is critical that young children have adequate chances to learn the fundamental locomotor and manipulative skills that comprise individual and team sports. Just like nonhandicapped children, these students should have regular daily physical education instruction. It is normal for younger children to receive some isolated training and practice in various motor skills, as shown in Figure 8.2. However, because severely handicapped children are not likely to generalize motor skills learned in isolated settings to game or sports situations, motor skills must be trained in the context of sports activities as much as possible. Therefore, teachers of younger children should devote time to both fundamental motor skill development and to simple, modified games and sports. For example, a child can learn to roll a ball by aiming it at bowling pins or similar objects. Once this can be done from a sitting position, it can be learned from a kneeling and then standing position. Eventually the distance away from the pins can be increased to the length of a bowling alley. Striking patterns can be developed using the same shaping procedures. A very large racquet made of heavy cardboard or a coat hanger with nylon stretched over it can be used to swing at nerf balls. An oversized striking area and a very short handle can be used initially as the child assumes a comfortable stance in a sitting, kneeling, or standing position. The ball can be suspended with string so that the child can practice without the fear of being hit and with a greater probability of success. Once proficiency at this level is attained, smaller racquets with less striking surface and more handle can be introduced as the object is thrown and finally struck by a partner or teacher. It is also possible to change entire motor patterns within the context of a game or sport. For example, kicking a ball (which is generally easier than striking a ball in the air) can gradually be replaced by hitting a ball with a bat in a game involving base runners.

Regardless of the chronological age of a severely handicapped student, the teacher must never lose sight of the relationship of fundamental motor skills and functional recreation activities that optimize the student's health and fitness and facilitate integration with nonhandicapped peers. Movement patterns such as skipping, galloping, and hopping, which may not directly increase participation in individual and team sports, will probably be a lower priority than skills such as throwing, catching, kicking, striking, running, jumping, and cycling. Similarly, functional fine motor skills should be a priority in systematically designed programs for acquiring motor skills (Wehman, Schleien, & Porter, 1979).

SUMMARY

The development of functional motor skills is essential for all children. Each individual's unique abilities and past experiences must be considered in planning optimal learning experiences. Once initial assessments have been completed, a well-rounded curriculum can be designed to train posture, locomotor skills, fine motor skills, and physical fitness abilities to improve not only functional skills, but also social interactions and self-concepts.

REFERENCES

American Association for Health, Physical Education, Recreation, and Dance. *Health related physical fitness tests*. Reston, Va.: American Association for Health, Physical Education, Recreation, and Dance, 1980.

Bates, P., & Renzaglia, A. Community-based recreation program. In P. Wehman (Ed.), *Recreation programming for developmentally disabled persons*. Baltimore: University Park Press, 1979.

Bayley, N. The development of motor abilities during the first three years. *Monographs of the Society for Research in Child Development*, 1935, No. 1.

Bruce, R. *The effects of variations in ball trajectory upon the catching performance of elementary school children*. Unpublished doctoral dissertation, University of Wisconsin, 1966.

Bunker, L.K. Nature-nurture, and the future of co-ed sports. *The Proceedings of the National Association for Physical Education in Higher Education* (Vol. II). Champaign, Ill.: Human Kinetics Press, 1980.

Campbell, J. Physical fitness and the MR: A review of research. *Mental Retardation*, 1973, *11*(5), 26–29.

Chandler, L.S., & Adams, M.A. Multiple handicapped child motivated for ambulation through behavior modification. *Physical Therapy*, 1972, *52*, 399–401.

Corbin, C. *A textbook of motor development*. Dubuque, Iowa: Wm. C. Brown, 1980.

Corbin, C.B., Dowell, L.J., Lindsey, R., & Tolson, H. *Concepts in physical education*. Dubuque, Iowa: Wm. C. Brown, 1981.

Deach, D. *Genetic development of motor skills in children two through six years of age*. Unpublished doctoral dissertation, University of Michigan, 1950.

Dohrman, P. Throwing and kicking ability of eight-year-old boys and girls. *Research Quarterly*, 1967, *35*, 464–471.

Espenschade, A.S., & Eckert, H.M. *Motor development*. Columbus, Ohio: Charles E. Merrill, 1980.

Finnie, N. *Handling the young cerebral palsied child at home*. New York: E.P. Hutton, 1975.

Frankenberg, W.K., & Dodds, J.S. The Denver Developmental Screening Test. *Journal of Pediatrics*, 1976, *71*, 181–191.

Gesell, A. *The first five years of life*. New York: Harper & Row, 1940.

Gesell, A., & Thompson, H. Learning and growth in identical twin infants. *Genetic Psychology Monographs*, 1929, *6*, 1–24.

Gutteridge, M. A study of motor achievements of young children. *Archives of Psychology*, 1939, *34*, 1–244.

Haavik, S., & Altman, K. Establishing walking by severely retarded children. *Perceptual and Motor Skills*, 1977, *44*, 1107–1114.

Halverson, H.M. An experimental study of prehension with infants by means of systematic cinema records. *Genetic Psychology Monographs*, 1931, *10*, 107–286.

Hanson, S.K. *A comparison of the overhand throw performance of instructed and non-instructed kindergarten boys and girls*. Unpublished master's thesis, University of Wisconsin, 1961.

Hardiman, S.A., Goetz, E.M., Reuter, K.E., & LeBlanc, J.M. Primes, contingent attention, and training: Effects on a child's motor behavior. *Journal of Applied Behavior Analysis*, 1975, *8*, 399–409.

Horner, R.D. Establishing use of crutches by a mentally retarded spina bifida child. *Journal of Applied Behavior Analysis*, 1971, *4*, 183–189.

Johnson, J.L. Programming for early motor responses within the classroom. *AAESPH Review*, 1978, *3*, 4–14.

Jones, R.A. *A descriptive and mechanical analysis of throwing skills of children.* Unpublished master's thesis, University of Wisconsin, 1951.

Kamin, P. Fine motor development and the grasp function. In J.S. Malloy (Ed.), *Trainable children: Curriculum and practices.* New York: John Day, 1972.

Levy, J. *The baby exercise book.* New York: Pantheon, 1973.

Loynd, J., & Barclay, A. A case study in developing ambulation in a profoundly retarded child. *Behavior Research and Therapy,* 1970, *8,* 207.

Moon, M.S., & Renzaglia, A. Physical fitness in the mentally retarded: A critical review of the literature. *Journal of Special Education,* in press.

O'Brien, F., Azrin, N.A., & Bugle, C. Training profoundly retarded children to stop crawling. *Journal of Applied Behavior Analysis,* 1972, *5,* 131–137.

Pedersen, E.J. *A study of ball catching abilities of first, third and fifth grade children on twelve selected ball catching tasks.* Unpublished doctoral dissertation, Indiana University, 1973.

Ridenour, M.D. Bicycles and tricycles for preschool children. *Physical Education,* 1975, *32,* 71–73.

Sherrill, C. Posture training as a means of normalization. *Mental Retardation,* 1980, *18,* 135–138.

Sherrill, C. *Adapted physical education and recreation: A multidisciplinary approach.* Dubuque, Iowa: Wm. C. Brown Co., 1981.

Shirley, M.M. *The first two years: A study of twenty-five babies* (Vol. 2). Minneapolis: University of Minnesota Press, 1933.

Sinclair, C.B. *Movement of the young child, ages 2–6.* Columbus, Ohio: Charles E. Merrill, 1973.

Wehman, P., & Schleien, S. Assessment and selection of leisure skills for severely handicapped individuals. *Education and Training of the Mentally Retarded,* 1980, *15,* 50–57.

Wehman, P., Schleien, S., & Porter, R. *Leisure skills curriculum for developmentally disabled persons: Virginia model-LSCDD training model.* Richmond: Virginia Commonwealth University, 1979.

Wellman, B.L. Motor achievements of preschool children. *Childhood Education,* 1937, 311–316.

Westervelt, J.D., & Luiselli, J.K. Establishing standing and walking behavior in a physically handicapped, retarded child. *Physical Therapy,* 1975, *55,* 761–765.

Wickstrom, R.L. *Fundamental motor patterns.* Philadelphia: Lea and Febiger, 1980.

Wild, M. The behavior patterns of throwing and some observations concerning its course of development in children. *Research Quarterly,* 1938, *9*(3), 20–24.

Williams, H.G. *The effects of systematic variation of speed and direction of object flight and of skill and age classifications upon visual-perceptual judgments of moving objects in three dimensional space.* Unpublished doctoral dissertation, University of Wisconsin, 1968.

REFERENCE NOTES

1. Halverson, L.E., & Roberton, M.A. *A study of motor pattern development in young children.* Paper presented at American Alliance of Health, Physical Education and Recreation research conference, Chicago, March 1966.

2. Seefeldt, V. *Developmental sequence of catching skill.* Paper presented at the National Convention of the American Association of Health, Physical Education and Recreation, Houston, March 1972.

3. Seefeldt, V., & Haubenstricker, J. *Developmental sequence of striking.* Unpublished material from Motor Development Conference, Michigan State University, July 1974.

4. Ford, A., Brown, L., Pumpian, I., Baumgart, D., Schroeder, J., & Loomis, R. *Strategies for developing individualized recreation/leisure plans for adolescent and young adult severely handicapped students.* Unpublished manuscript, University of Wisconsin, 1980.

Cordelia C. Robinson is at Meyer Children's Rehabilitation Institute, University of Nebraska Medical Center, and *Jacques H. Robinson* is at Special Education Department, Kent State University.

9

Sensorimotor Functions and Cognitive Development

PART I: SENSORIMOTOR FUNCTIONS AND COGNITIVE DEVELOPMENT

This chapter describes a model of systematic instruction designed to foster the development, in the handicapped, of the sort of sensorimotor and cognitive processes that undergird the behavior of the normal child during the first 2 years of life. Of course, the severely or profoundly handicapped individual may or may not mature beyond the performance levels of the sensorimotor period. But we cannot know this unless we try. The fact that a child does not show the usual autonomous development must not be taken as evidence that growth cannot be stimulated. Often, we must redefine "success" in learning. But we cannot permit our adjustments in instructional targets to form the basis for the self-validating premise that the severely handicapped cannot respond to systematic instruction or that efforts to enhance more normal development are not worthwhile.

Our general approach will be to examine the implications of two psychological schools of thought, or traditions, associated with the works of B.F. Skinner and Jean Piaget. Neither of these men has been concerned directly with the handicapped. However, their work, and that of their coworkers and students, is of profound import to those of us who do work with the developmentally disabled. We will examine this work within a frame of reference supplied by (*a*) our basic task, the systematic instruction of the handicapped, and (*b*) some fundamental ideas and observations about the development of the human infant.

The early parts of this chapter stress the work of Piaget, particularly his views on early human development. Applied behavior analysis, which follows from the Skinnerian tradition, and its implications for systematic instruction of the disabled will not be developed so fully. This imbalance does not imply relative importance. Rather, we assume that you have prior knowledge of applied behavior analysis and systematic instruction. (For a review of these topics, see chapters 4 and 5).

Education involves a dynamic interplay between curriculum decisions and instructional decisions. Curriculum decisions relate to the *ends,* the goals, of education and are directed to answering the question "what to teach." Instructional decisions relate to the *means* of education and are concerned with answering the question "how to teach." In this context, Piaget's work is extremely useful in determining *what to teach* the child. The concepts and principles of applied behavior analysis are particularly relevant to problems of *how to teach* the child.

It is useful here to separate and contrast *instruction* (means) and *curriculum* (ends). In the real world, however, means and ends cannot be separated in other than a very arbitrary and abstract sense. Rather, "real world" educational processes reflect emphases, temporary and dynamic balances or imbalances between means and ends.

Thus, it is an oversimplification to say that Piaget offers an answer to "what to teach" and behavior analysis an answer to "how to teach it." More precisely, Piaget's explanation and synthesis of the scope and sequence of early human development is a fundamental basis for the *curriculum* decision. On the other hand, his observations of the concrete behavior of children, particularly his own, is a rich source of help in determining *instruction,* how to foster development.

Applied behavior analysis offers a powerful model to modify behavior and is most useful when the behavior is available, observable, and occurs at a reasonable rate or when precursor or substitute behaviors can be shaped into the desired behavior. Thus, the concepts and strategies of applied behavior analysis also are relevant to structuring and modifying short-term and intermediate goals and confirming readiness (both motivational and cognitive). Such concerns, of course, relate to curriculum as well as to instruction.

In summary, Piaget offers us useful advice on long-term curricular goals and sequences as well as immediate instructional strategies. Applied behavior analysis offers a major generalized instructional technology and strategies related to modification of behavior, but is also relevant to the definition of readiness and the structuring and modification of short-term goals.

A Frame of Reference: Human Values and Human Development

This section will establish a frame of reference, based upon the early development of the normal human infant, within which to view instructional programming for the handicapped in general and the role of applied behavior analysis and Piaget in particular. The first issue has to be: "Why this normative frame of reference?" Why can we not accept handicapped people as individuals, at face value, without fracturing our image of them through the prism of "normal development"?

In the first place, words such as *handicapped* (severe or otherwise), *abnormal, deviant,* etc. have no meaning except in relationship to *normal.* Yet, in the absence of such terms, we assume normalcy. This assumption is not a value judgment. It does not imply that normal is better, even if this is a value frequently espoused in our culture and by many special educators. Further, to characterize an individual as either "normal" or "handicapped" is *not* to deny that person's individuality.

But why label at all? When it is so easy for some to depersonalize and devalue the disabled, why provide the target that a label offers? The immediate response to this question is that labeling cannot be prevented or labeling can also be a means of marshaling unusual resources to meet the needs of the handicapped. These responses may seem too pat and simpleminded; and yet, who can say they are not true?

Our stress on normal human development should not be taken to imply that normal is *good* and abnormal is *bad.* The more salient distinction is between *deviance* and *incompetence.* Both of these terms are defined in contrast to *normality.* However, *incompetence* connotes the absence of a potential for choice to be normal or abnormal.

As teachers, we must accept responsibility for all the unnecessary incompetencies of our students. Likewise, we must accept responsibility for complete, appropriate curricula directed toward reversing the incompetencies of our students. Piaget offers a model of the development of human competence as a biological process. This model offers a goal structure which reflects our value posture.

Early Human Development: Fundamental Features

Certain features of early human behavior and development are outstanding, and any account of human development must deal with them. Among these features are:

1. The striking dependency of the human neonate relative to other species.
2. The autonomous character of human development.
3. The accelerating acquisition of systems of behavior that are highly organized, flexible, and adaptable.
4. The startling capacity of the child to develop symbolic processes and abstract thought.
5. The dynamic interplay between maturation and learning in human development.
6. The vast range of individual differences in human behavior.

The writings of Hebb (1949) and Hunt (1961) are particularly illuminating in validating and defining these features with respect to normal development. Further discussion is beyond the scope of this chapter. However, these features supply a basic context for us. It is in this context, first, that the lack of normal development has such import and, second, that the diagnosis of severe handicap and its associated prognosis is so devastating. Thus, it is in the context of normal human development that the instruction of the handicapped finds its meaning.

A number of theories have been offered to account for different aspects of cognitive development. All these models focus upon the development of *concepts* or classifications of environmental events and develop *strategies* for responding to those events.

There are some differences in various definitions of the term *concept*. Most involve the idea that a concept is the basis for responding to stimuli as "the same" even if they are quite different in some ways. For example, a child learns to say "cup" when she sees one. Maybe the cup is her own, which is short, wide, white, and plastic. When she can verbally identify that cup, she has acquired a response. But not until she can label a cup she has never seen before, maybe a yellow china cup, do we say that the child has acquired the concept of "cup." The concept, of course, is an idea, not a cup and not a label, and cannot be seen or heard. We infer the "existence" of the concept from her *generalized response*. The child also may *overgeneralize* and say that glasses and jars are cups too. On the other hand, she may omit all blue cups from the class of cups by attending to an irrelevant dimension (color) and cue (blueness). Thus, it is not enough that the child identify the cups she has seen before. She must discriminate or identify new cups, and only cups, before we say that she "has the concept." These features, of course, hold for the child's response to most of the objects and events in her world. However, there are radical differences in the complexity and abstraction involved between concepts. Having a cup is not the same as having a cup of milk or a cup of water, nor the same as drinking milk, interacting with mother, having an apple or an orange, having an orange cup or a plastic cup, etc.

Assume that a mother wishes her child to develop a generalized response of labeling all cups (and only cups) as "cups." Some basic principles of applied behavior analysis are relevant to any attempt to instruct the child systematically. In this situation the discriminative factor which will be the stimulus to evoke the child's behavior is known. As soon as it is clear that there is a stable relationship between a specific training stimulus (say, the child's cup) and the appropriate response, it is possible to start generalization training. The procedure is to introduce many other cups, of different sizes, shapes, and colors as stimuli and model the response "cups." It is also appropriate to contrast the cups with stimuli which are "not-cups" to inhibit overgeneralization. It

might, or it might not, be necessary to reinforce the child's imitation of mother's modeling with tangible reinforcement. Generally it is not.

Another fundamental idea used to describe and explain the organization and adaptability of the young child's behavior is *strategy*. A strategy is much more than a concept, though concept learning is involved. Strategies may be addressed to either attaining or using concepts at various levels of complexity and abstraction. It implies intent and planning and is generally manifest in the child's behavior. But strategies generally are rather complex and difficult to interpret.

The example of the cup may highlight the problems in inference. If, after generalization has begun, the child seeks out a new cup, brings it to mother, and says, "Cup?", this is a strategy. In fact, it is several strategies. One strategy relates directly to the display of concept or label generalization. Another involves a request for confirmation of the generalization—the child is seeking feedback. Still another strategy might be to obtain a smile, a hug, or even a drink from mother.

After strategies are well practiced, they may become *routines*. They become so well integrated that they may be used in the service of still higher-order strategies. In that case, they become *subroutines*. For instance, the child may have used a "climb-up-on-the-chair-and-get-it-because-it's-high" subroutine in getting the cup to show to mother.

One of the problems with strategies is that they may, through unanticipated generalizations, be used at times or directed at goals that mother may not be inclined to reinforce. Suppose that the cup the child gets is a valuable, irreplaceable, fragile family heirloom. And suppose that mother, all too humanly, responds negatively and "reinforces" by screaming, "No! No! That's a NO-NO!" What are apt to be the consequences of this? First, the child might drop, or even throw, the cup. But what might she learn? That it is not a cup? That mother punishes confirmation behavior or punishes concept generalization? That it is one of those days to avoid mother? Or that my cup is the only cup? Or my cup is the only cup I can touch? Or I can't touch any cup anymore? It is difficult to say. Only careful observation can validate the appropriate inferences.

Following the precepts of applied behavior analysis, mother would be advised not to use any verbal punishment at all. The first move might be to get the cup. The associated delay in reinforcement might well be appropriate. Then it might be best to respond to the generalization/confirmation strategies and confirm that it is indeed a cup. She could then switch to modeling a new discrimination, "MY cup, not your cup."

The bulk of the preschool curriculum consists of learning specific and basic content (e.g., recognition and identification of colors, shapes, numerals) and applying strategies to that content (classification by color and shape, matching numerals to quantities). While the use of strategies enhances knowledge of the content, it also reinforces generalization of the strategy to other classes of objects on some dimension of similarity (function, size, etc.). These strategies become increasingly important as the child gets older and as what she can do, and is expected to do, becomes more complex. Thus, it is important to develop strategies as well as content skills systematically to enhance later learning.

Piaget's Theory of Human Development

It is not our purpose to provide a detailed discussion of Piaget's approach to studying development. Such material is available in Furth (1969), Hunt (1961), and Flavell (1963). Piaget (1954, 1963) and Uzgiris and Hunt (1966, 1975) provide more detail on the descriptions of the tasks that form the basis of the activities included here.

Piaget uses the terms *mental structure* and *scheme* to refer, globally, to what we call *concepts* and *strategies*. Concepts and strategies or mental structures represent two sides of the same coin, the organizational and adaptive patterns of the child's developing cognition. Piaget organizes this development into a sequence of cognitive stages. Each stage may be characterized in terms of a set of recurrent observable behaviors that reflect a system, a mental structure, or a pattern of concepts and strategies. These structures synthesize prior learnings and form the basis for further development. This leads to a new, qualitatively different pattern or stage in development. For example, relatively early, in the sensorimotor period, the child uses systematic search behaviors directed toward recovering partly or completely hidden objects. This search behavior serves as a basis for the inference that the child has developed "object permanence." At age 5 or 6, the child displays "the conservation of mass" which presupposes object permanence and is characterized as the ability to explain adequately how it is that one of two clay balls, if transformed into a sausage shape, without any addition or removal of clay, is still equal in mass to the other ball.

We use the terms *concept* and *strategy* to emphasize the relevance shaping and learning have to the sensorimotor (SM) stage. However, as we will establish later, *intention* or purposeful use of a strategy is a result of SM development. Further, Piaget sees SM development as preconceptual, occurring before the development of cognition. The issue is one of definition and convention. In any event, SM functions (*a*)

are qualitatively different from cognitive functioning in later periods and (*b*) appear to be absolutely essential to subsequent cognitive development.

Each of Piaget's stages are characterized by the acquisition of specific content. Environmental experiences provide the material for learning. Development takes place as a function of the complementary processes of *assimilation* and *accommodation*.

The function of assimilation is the integration of new information or experience into the organism's existing behavioral repertoire. During assimilation the input is changed by the child's existing way of thinking; during accommodation the child changes thinking processes to align more closely with the input. Therefore the function of accommodation is to modify and elaborate existing thinking processes (schemes, concepts, and strategies) so that they will have greater applicability. Accommodation leads to the emergence of a more advanced level of thinking processes.

In his writing, Piaget uses many concepts from biology, one of which is *equilibration*. For Piaget, development reflects the dynamic processes of assimilation and accommodation. Each fluctuates in dominance. When one process predominates, a state of disequilibrium exists. The course of these two processes coming back into more equal balance is equilibration and the state is one of equilibrium.

When the child has adjusted (accommodated) to the newness of the situation and integrated (assimilated) the new information to existing schemes, a period of repetition of the newly formed scheme usually follows. This incorporates the new form of behavior into the child's repertoire more completely. In a sense, the child "practices" the new behavior; this practice is not boring but rather appears to be self-reinforcing.

Piaget's descriptions of stage and sequences in the development of specific concepts can be used in constructing instructional sequences for handicapped as well as for normal children. Stephens (1971, 1977) has developed an excellent overall summary of Piaget's developmental stages (Table 9.1).

This chapter focuses upon development during the sensorimotor period—a period from birth to about 2 years in children of average development. During the SM stage, practical or motoric intelligence develops rapidly. Much of the child's accumulation of "mental structures" during this period comes about through active physical exploration and manipulation of the environment. It is only toward the very end of this period that the child can use language to guide behavior. Among the early developments of this period are the recognition of the permanence of objects, the use of objects as tools to solve problems, the functional use of objects, and increasing competency in motor imitation. All these developments occur, for the typical child, as a function of daily interactions during

TABLE 9.1 Piaget's Stages of Intellectual Development

Stage and Approximate Age	Characteristic Behavior
I. Sensory-motor operations	
A. Reflexive (0–1 month)	Simple reflex activity; example: kicking.
B. Primary circular reactions (1–4.5 months)	Reflexive behavior becomes elaborated and coordinated; example: eye follows hand movements.
C. Secondary circular reactions (4.5–9 months)	Repeats chance actions to reproduce an interesting change or effect; example: kicks crib, doll shakes, so kicks crib again.
D. Coordination of secondary schema (9–12 months)	Acts become clearly intentional; example: reaches behind cushion for ball.
E. Tertiary circular reactions (12–18 months)	Discovers new ways to obtain desired goal; example: pulls pillow nearer in order to get toy resting on it.
F. Invention of new means through mental combinations (18–24 months)	Invents new ways and means; example: uses stick to reach desired object.
II. Pre-operational	
A. Preconceptual (2–4 years)	Capable of verbal expression, but speech is repetitious; frequent egocentric monologues.
B. Intuitive (4–7 years)	Speech becomes socialized; reasoning is egocentric, "to the right" has one meaning—to his right.
III. Concrete operations (7–11 years)	Mobile and systematic thought organizes and classifies information; is capable of concrete problem-solving.
IV. Formal operations (11 years upward)	Can think abstractly, formulate hypotheses, engage in deductive reasoning, and check solutions.

SOURCE: B. Stephens, The appraisal of cognitive development. In B. Stephens (Ed.), *Training the Developmentally Young.* New York: John Day, 1971, p. 48. Reprinted from J.H. Flavell, *The Developmental Psychology of Jean Piaget.* Princeton, N.J.: D. Van Nostrand, 1963. Copyright © 1963 by Litton Educational Publishing, Inc. Reprinted by permission of D. Van Nostrand Company.

the first 2 years of life. For the severely handicapped, this development will be much more gradual, its rate being a product of teachers, parents, and the learners themselves.

There have been a number of demonstrations that the sequences of the Uzgiris-Hunt (1975) sensorimotor scales, which were theoretically derived and empirically validated on nonhandicapped infants, can be reliably administered to severely handicapped individuals (Kahn, 1976; Silverstein, Brownlee, Hubbell, & McLain, 1975). In addition, in the case of those scales which yield higher coefficients of ordinality when administered to nonhandicapped children, we also see evidence of ordinality when used with severely handicapped persons (Wohlheuter & Sindberg, 1975).

As can be seen in Table 9.2, Piaget divides the SM period into six substages involving increasingly complex applications of the sensorimotor schemes. These areas of application, which progressively differentiate during the SM period, involve object permanence, means-ends relationships, causality, spatial organizations, schemes in relation to objects, and verbal and motor imitation schemes.

Table 9.2 contains a matrix of the sensorimotor concept areas and the level of the concept corresponding to each substage. The substages and major accomplishments for each are noted. Some of these brief descriptions are expanded upon later.

Functional Adaptation of Observation and Instruction to the Needs of the Handicapped

Before describing the SM instructional program, we need to discuss some questions and problems associated with systematic instruction for severely disabled individuals functioning at the SM level. Of particular importance are concerns about observing and measuring SM behavior and accommodating instructional goals and methods to the child's disabilities.

The content of chapter 10 is of immediate relevance to the observation and recording of SM behavior and the shaping of task attention, imitation (motoric and vocal), action patterns, and the discriminative use of objects. Because the focus in chapter 10 is on shaping early language behavior, a skill area that dovetails with SM behavior, there is little point in describing these prelanguage skills here (Dunst, 1977; Kahn, 1975, 1979; Lobato, Barrera & Feldman, 1981).

The focus in this section is on accommodating to the handicap. In implementing a program to induce more normal development, certain basic questions

TABLE 9.2 Sensorimotor Stages and Accomplishments

Stages	Months	Visual Pursuit Object Permanence	Means-End	Causality
I. *Reflexes:* Slight modifications of initial reflexes	0–1			
II. *Primary Circular Reactions:* Reflexes undergo adaptations to environmental experience beginning coordination e.g. look at grasped object	1–4	Visual fixation and tracking Tracks 180 Maintains gaze briefly at point object disappears	Coordination of schemes/ hand watching Sustained object grasp Repetition of accidental movement producing spectacle e.g. batting Reaches and grasps object when object and hand in view Reaches and grasps when object is in view	Coordination of schemes/ hand watching Repetition of accidental movement producing spectacle e.g. batting Uses a procedure to repeat spectacle caused by adult
III. *Secondary Circular Reactions:* Schemes are repeated producing systematic effect on environment	4–8	Look/reach for partially covered object Anticipates reappearance of disappearing object	Purposefully pulls support (e.g. cloth pillow) to obtain object out of reach Holding two objects, purposefully drops first to reach for third	Directed action towards object or person to repeat spectacle in game situation, person spectacle (e.g. funny face) an adult acting on object
IV. *Coordination of Secondary Circular Reactions:* Schemes are used together for intended results	8–10	Searches for visibly displaced object	Locomotes to get objects out of reach Reaches directly to object out of reach held above support	Elaboration of stage III behaviors Replicates action of toy to repeat spectacle
	10–12	Searches for visibly displaced objects with two or more screens	Purposefully pulls horizontal string to get object out of reach	
V. *Tertiary Circular Reactions:* Through Trial and error solution to problems child expands skills	12–15	Sequential visible displacement of object with two or more screens	Uses vertical string to obtain toy out of view	Hands toy back to adult to repeat spectacle or guides adult's hand to toy
	15–18	Invisible displacement of object with one screen Invisible displacement of object with two or more screens Sequential invisible displacement with two screens	Uses unattached tool to obtain an object out of reach	Imitative attempt to activate mechanical toy
VI. *Invention of New Means through Mental Combination:* Child is assumed to solve problems representationally and then applies a solution to the problem situation	18–24	Systematically retraces sequential invisible displacement of object with three screens	Foresightful problem solving, i.e., using mental combinations Necklace in cylinder problem Solid ring stacking problem	Explores to activate mechanical toy before demonstration

Schemes for Relating Objects	Spatial Relations	Verbal Imitation	Motor Imitations
		Vocalizes without distress Positive response to "own" sounds when made by another person Repeats sounds, when adult imitates child.	
Incidental use e.g., mouthing	Slowly alternates glance between two objects		
Attention to object e.g., momentary hold and look	Rapidly alternates glances between 2 objects	Repeats similar sounds when adult initiates child's own sound	
Systematic use of object e.g., hitting, banging, shaking	Localizes sound e.g., turns head and fixates	(Produces a variety of consonant syllable sounds.)	Makes a motor response on seeing own movement
Beginning Differentiation of Simple Schemes e.g., shakes bell; bangs stick	Visually follows object trajectory and looks where object falls in view	(Vocalizes in response to hearing own sounds (Elaboration of babbling) multiple syllables	Imitates movement response to familiar scheme when:
Investigating properties/Examining e.g., Visual and tactile			child must start cycle e.g., movement or object schemes
Complex schemes derived from object properties e.g., slide, push, squeeze, stretch. New Complex Schemes e.g., purposefully drops, throws objects	Searches for dropped object fallen from view. (Takes objects out of container)	Vocalizes in response to hearing "own" babble not similar sound Repeats similar babble sound if adult initiates	adult can start cycle Imitates expansion of familiar scheme Partial imitation of visible novel movement.
Beginning representation of functional use of familiar objects (self-directed) e.g., cup , spoon (Relates objects functionally; e.g., stir in cup)	Places single object in and out of container	Imitates babble sound accurately	Imitates visible novel movement through gradial approximation. Imitates visible novel movements (e.g., body movements or object schemes) Responds with movement but cannot imitate facial gesture
Expansion of representation of functional use of familiar objects e.g., brush, shoe (Includes another person in representational play)	Sequences objects in and out of containers (Dumps objects out of container) Experiments with gravity e.g., inclined plane, dangling string	Imitates novel sounds by gradual approximation	
Refers to object in shared interaction e.g., shows, gives, points Spontaneous words associated with object play	Moves to get object visible behind barrier Moves to get object invisible behind barrier	Repeats most simple words Imitates novel sounds directly Repeats most simple new words	Imitates novel invisible facial gesture
(Representational play sequences with doll based on familiar experiences)	Remembers whereabouts and recognizes absence of familiar people and objects (Put simple series together (3-4 cups) using trial and error)	(Repeats more complex new words and short phrases)	Imitates many novel facial actions which child can't see himself perform

must be addressed. Among these concerns are: What reinforces the child? Are the response criteria appropriate for a given child? Are the instructional objectives appropriate? Are the instructional methods appropriate? Are the procedures to evaluate learning appropriate for a given child? Each of these questions will be considered in turn.

What Reinforces the Child?

In the sensorimotor activities described in this chapter, the functional definition of a reinforcer is assumed (see chapter 5). When confronted with a child who does not demonstrate the desired behavior, you must determine whether the consequences of the behavior do not reinforce the child by observing the effect of other stimuli as reinforcers. The intrinsic functional value of the behavior is particularly important during the SM period when the child depends upon a physical or spatial connection between two events to relate them. For example, the reinforcer for uncovering an object is getting that object; the reinforcer for pulling on a string attached to a toy is the access to the toy. It has been our experience that to superimpose a primary reinforcer, an edible, upon these tasks is not functional. Primary reinforcers can be effectively used within the tasks themselves, as the hidden object or the goal object in the means–end problem. Karlan (1980) found higher levels of object permanence performance among severely handicapped people when preferred objects were hidden than when nonpreferred objects were hidden.

Are the Response Criteria Appropriate for a Given Child?

Various developmental researchers have identified particular tasks as criteria for assessing whether a child has grasped certain concepts. From the Piagetian descriptions of sensorimotor intelligence, we have identified concepts that are part of the young child's accomplishments during the first years of life. These conventional tasks also make demands upon the child's physical abilities. The child's increasing physical abilities and problem-solving abilities usually correspond closely. When working with severely handicapped children, we inevitably encounter some with multiple handicaps, both physical and sensory. Thus, often the conventional behavioral criteria which validate an inference about the child's stage of cognitive development are inappropriate in light of some handicapping conditions.

One of the advantages of the Piagetian approach to cognitive development is that it gives us a sequence of concepts rather than simply an empirical arrangement of tasks. Thus, we have conventional tasks to use as operational definitions of the SM concepts of object permanence, means–end, and causality. How-

ever, by identifying specific concepts, we can then define them to accommodate a task to a particular individual's response capabilities if the conventional criterion cannot be used.

Object permanence, for example, typically has been operationally defined as uncovering and obtaining a covered object. This operation cannot be demonstrated by many severely handicapped students because they have not mastered the prerequisite skills of visually directed reach, grasp, and visual tracking. These responses may be impossible due to visual defects or abnormal persistence of certain early reflex patterns such as the asymmetric tonic neck reflex that prevent coordination of reach and grasp or visual tracking. If we were to persist with only one operational definition of object permanence, we still would be working on the prerequisite behaviors for that operation. But return to the concept of object permanence. It involves the recognition, in the absence of sensory contact with an object, that the object still exists. There must be *some* alternate responses in the person's repertoire from which we may infer that he recognizes the existence of the object despite a loss of sensory contact with it. The behavior from which we infer object permanence does not have to be visually directed reach, uncover, and grasp of the object. Perhaps the child who cannot reach and uncover and grasp could tell someone else "it is under the cup over here." However, if in addition to physical limitations, the child lacks speech, the recurrent response of looking in the direction of the object may be substituted.

This strategy of adapting a response to the person's physical abilities can be applied to any content area. It is possible to carry it out more readily when the curriculum is organized around the teaching of concepts. Working through a behavioral checklist of skills arranged in an empirically determined hierarchy, such as the items in standardized infant assessments, presents problems. While infant assessments can be adapted, the concept the item is measuring must be analyzed first in order to select an alternate response.[1]

Based upon our experience over the past several years, we have concluded that the most successful strategy of adaptation will vary depending upon the child's substage of development. For example, during SM substage IV, the strategy of a directed look

---

[1] Since this chapter was originally published in 1978, several authors have argued for adapting evaluation procedures and response criteria for severely handicapped learners (Duncan, Sbardellati, Maheady, & Sainato, 1981; White, 1980). Others have attempted to look at the effects of task adaptations upon performance systematically (Ilmer, Rynders, Sinclair, & Helfrich, 1981).

appears to be too complex for the child to master. Uzgiris (1976) thoroughly discusses the SM organizational levels and their possible import and Robinson (1984) discusses how SM organization levels may relate to the strategy of adapting tasks.

Are the Instructional Objectives Appropriate for a Given Child?

The primary question to be answered when identifying instructional objectives for any child concerns the functional utility of a particular behavior for that child. Before including any objective and the activities for meeting it in a child's IEP, you must ask whether it will increase this child's competence in daily interactions at home, school, and play. At one level we might say that all typical preschool activities increase a child's competence. However, if pressed for specifics regarding how puzzles, bead stringing, and color sorting relate to activities that come later in the curriculum, we are frequently unable to provide them.

Time spent teaching behaviors that may not be physically possible for a child and that are questionable prerequisites to later tasks is wasted. Any activity chosen for instruction should lead toward a skill that gives the child additional control over either the *physical* environment or the *social* environment. If it does not meet one of these criteria, it should be excluded from the child's program.

Our emphasis upon increasing the child's control over the physical environment stems from a growing body of literature on "learned helplessness" (Seligman, 1975). This term refers to behaviors that provide no opportunity to control the environment, typically an aversive situation. After 5 years of work with moderately to severely handicapped infants and toddlers, we are finding that this term frequently applies to situations in which we place these children. In some cases, limited mobility, sensory capabilities, motivation, or combination of the three results in a child with few opportunities to act upon the environment systematically even if the act is something as simple as swatting at a musical hanging toy. With such children, the overall rate of movement is low and the number of repetitions necessary to bring a response under control is often great. Therefore, every possible opportunity for learning a response should be taken. For example, when a child shows no ability to voluntarily repeat a response (arm wave, foot kick, or head turn) that results in a visually interesting or sound-producing event, our first major goal is to teach some form of this behavior. The specific stimulus or response is not important. What is critical is establishing a relationship between a behavior on the child's part and some predictable occurrence in the environment. While it may initially be related to

only a very minute aspect of the environment, the child will have some opportunity to exercise control. This basic relationship can be then extended by planning other activities over which the child can exercise control. It is our experience that before long the child will be inventing opportunities for generalizing this strategy. The response strategy can then be extended over an increasing number of daily events. This provides a series of very predictable occurrences throughout the day. In the context of these predictable events, which require specific action from the child, the concepts of object permanence, means-ends activities, causality, specific actions on objects, and spatial relationships can then be taught.

The second criterion for the inclusion of objectives and activities relates to the child's social environment. Although similar to the development of control over the physical environment, the two are separated to emphasize the need for both types of control. During the initial development of our curriculum activities at the Meyer Children's Rehabilitation Institute, more emphasis was placed upon the manipulation of the physical environment than upon social interaction. After many hours observing and working with children, we have begun to recognize this as a problem and now are trying to correct our mistakes. Specifically, we see communication as a basic strategy that develops and takes a number of forms (gesture, vocal, communication board). By not restricting communication to one specific mode, we immediately create more opportunities to require a child to use some mode of communication to act upon the environment.

There are opportunities for communication in every interaction with the child. Consider the young child who enjoys moving up and down in a bouncy seat. The activity is provided, it stops, and the child continues to bounce a little. A father interprets the child's bouncing as "make it happen again," and he does make it happen again. This sequence can be the beginning of a communication strategy. After going through this sequence many times, the child starts to bounce as soon as she is put in the seat. Once that occurs, the parent may require the bounce first from the child before he makes the seat "go." In general terms, this routine involves interpretation of the child's use of a procedure for reproducing an interesting event as a request for the event to happen again. This routine can be applied to any event during the child's day. It is a very early form of communication, requiring much shaping and interpretation on our part. But it is the material from which a formal communication system will be developed.

Again, instructional objectives must focus upon behavior relevant to the child's control over the environment. In addition, however, objectives also must be adapted to the child's specific handicaps, potential for development in a given area, and the physical requirements of the task. Often predicting a child's future performance will be difficult, and we must extrapolate "educated guesses" from the child's performance data with the assistance of program therapists.

To use the example of object permanence again, if a child seems to have some difficulty in hand use but the eventual development of functional reach and grasp is feasible, the teacher may assess object permanence with the conventional task. The child must reach, uncover, and grasp the hidden objects. The task provides a natural consequence for use of reach and grasp. It is, therefore, a good activity for two objectives—refinement of reach and grasp and object permanence. If, however, reach and grasp are so difficult for the child that any effort to reach with accuracy results in a distraction from the object permanence task, it would be better to use an alternative response, such as a directed gaze, during assessment and training. The question of the best response system for a given child must be determined according to the characteristics of the individual child. The decision is based upon current child data and may be revised as more information becomes available.

A task analysis of skills involved in any one objective will often provide guidelines for adapting tasks to a child's physical and sensory capabilities. Sometimes the child shows delay in a particular area of prerequisite skills. In this case, the task can be modified to substitute an alternate skill for the delayed one and keep the skills which he can do as part of the task. For example, if visual tracking is poor but reach and grasp are adequate, the teacher may wish to construct the object permanence task so that the child can use alternate glancing or tactile following of the movement of an object in the sequential search tasks. Alternate strategies for the development of communication, which include communication boards or signing systems, provide excellent examples of adapting tasks to a particular child's conceptual and motor capabilities.

Are the Instructional Methods Appropriate for a Given Child?

The sensorimotor period has been referred to as the *period of practical intelligence* because the tasks learned are based upon direct sensory and motor experience. *Practical intelligence* reminds us that the tasks are most likely to be accomplished by the child at the current level of functioning and during the course of naturally occurring events. *Naturally occurring* does not, however, mean that the teacher should function as an ecological psychologist and wait for events to occur to record the child's response. Rather, instructional

events must be arranged using the daily routine and the problems the child encounters during daily activities as the instructional method.

We are generally accustomed to dividing instructional time into segments according to content areas (e.g., language time, arithmetic skills, art time, and gross motor activities). This scheduling, however, is not appropriate for the child functioning at the sensorimotor level. If you try to require children to search for different objects for 5 trials and then switch to 5 trials of tool use and then 5 trials of putting objects into a container, you typically end up with very exasperated children. This is probably because you are constantly taking objects away from them. A more successful approach is to intersperse the activities so that after the child finds an object or uses a tool to get an object, you allow time to examine it. During this time you may record the scheme with that object. Then you might demonstrate a new scheme and try to get the child to imitate you. Go on to another object only after interest in the first seems exhausted for a time.

Instruction in causality objectives generally requires some form of gesture. This need not be a formal sign, but a movement that has been associated with a particular consequence. Development of this early gesture system is best accomplished by making daily events center around routines such as eating, dressing, toileting; these and other favored events would be made contingent upon the designated "gesture." For example, the child is not picked up unless she moves her hands up. She does not get another bite of food unless she touches the hand of the person feeding her. She doesn't get rocked in the rocking chair unless she taps the arm of the chair. These gestures, the beginnings of communication, indicate an understanding of causality.

To stimulate ambulation, the child might be expected to walk (roll, scoot, or crawl) to her favorite activities, which may include snack or music time. This exemplifies the Premack principle (Premack, 1962), using a more highly preferred activity to reinforce the occurrence of a less probable behavior. It is critical to provide many very brief opportunities to respond rather than lengthy periods directed toward instruction in isolated content areas. The antecedent events, the response, and the consequence must occur together during the sensorimotor period.

Are the Procedures to Evaluate Learning Appropriate for a Given Child?

Procedures for evaluating cognitive learning are essentially the same as those for any other content area. Generally, there are two measurement levels to consider. The first is simply the presence or absence of the skill. The assessment sequences from Uzgiris and

Hunt's work (1966, 1975) on sensorimotor development are included later in this chapter to provide an example of this type of evaluation. To set goals for any child, we must begin with an assessment of the child's performance on a series of tasks. The child is given tasks in an increasing order of difficulty until the point of initial failure. Both the child's responses to that task and the task itself are analyzed to determine whether failure may be caused by the physical or the cognitive requirements of the task. If the particular response mode has contributed to the child's failing performance, then the task is modified to meet the child's capabilities. If the child is unable to respond correctly in another mode, the task is presented using different antecedent conditions (cues and prompts), in an effort to find some condition under which the child demonstrates the response. Teaching activities should use the antecedent conditions that resulted in the initial correct performance. The usual goal is to teach the student to perform under standard task conditions.

Initial assessments are meant to determine the presence or absence of a behavior. Eventually, however, we must use a second level of assessment and examine the proficiency with which the child demonstrates the behavior. Proficiency can refer to the generalizability of the response across a variety of stimuli as well as to the rate at which the response is performed.

In cognitive development we are particularly concerned with the generalizability of the response across stimuli. In fact, generalization of a response to new stimuli constitutes the operational definition of a concept and the underpinnings of cognitive development. The eventual goal in working on all SM areas is to develop the concept involved, not simply the isolated behaviors of searching under cups or pulling on strings. We want the child to learn the general principles that objects still exist when we cannot see them and that objects and events can be used as tools to solve problems in the environment. How a generalized response will be accomplished must be answered individually for each child. One of the characteristics we can expect in the severely retarded is difficulty in skill generalization. Research indicates that retarded individuals need many, many examples from one class of antecedent events before the response is spontaneously generalized to a new example of that same class of stimuli. Deficiencies in skill generalization have been particularly evident in training motor imitation and learning set in the severely retarded (Bricker, 1970). Experimental interventions to train SM developments such as object permanence with severely retarded individuals have resulted in initial acquisition but lack of long-term retention and generalization of results (Brassel &

Dunst, 1976). Kahn (1978), who used a longer training period (6 months), demonstrated retention of object permanency training results with four low-functioning children. Indeed, some have suggested that the amount of training required to achieve generalization is a better means of assessing retardation than the sum of a person's accumulated knowledge.

When working with a child on a particular activity, such as the simple object permanence problem, we begin with several different objects for hiding and perhaps two different screens with which to hide objects. We start with variety in order to facilitate generalization. If we find a very low rate of searching, we reduce to one screen but still use whatever variety we can in the hidden object. Once the child searches under one screen, we introduce a second, third, fourth, and fifth screen. This goes on until we see correct responding within several trials of the first introduction of a new screen. Generally we find that a change in the form of the screen (towel, cup, box) is more likely to result in a breakdown in behavior than a change in a screen characteristic such as color.

The physical location or task setting is another important factor to consider in response generalization. For example, one child we worked with would search diligently for a completely covered object placed in front of her. However, if the object was moved partly out of sight to the side, she would not pursue the search, suggesting that adequate generalization training had not been provided for physical location.

Since, for any one task, it may not be possible to test adequately for generalization, problems at the next level of difficulty in the sequence may help to identify gaps in generalization training. The best test for skill generalization includes placing a child in a natural situation where the newly learned concept is required to solve an immediate problem. With successful performance under these conditions we can have confidence in the adequacy of the response as a generalized strategy.

For Whom Is SM Instruction Appropriate?

You may question the appropriateness of SM instruction for older severely handicapped students, particularly given that the illustrations in this chapter are all of children under 3 years of age and of preschool and infant toys. Because the concepts and strategies that comprise Piagetian SM development are basic to intellectual development beyond a mental age of 2 years, in our own work with severely handicapped school-aged children we use the content of sensorimotor development as the guide for developing instructional objectives. We select materials and strategies to accomplish those objectives that are more age-appropriate. Our priority in selecting objectives is based upon matching the level of difficulty to the individual's SM level. In addition, we are likely to emphasize SM content areas that appear to be directly related to the development of the form of communication most likely to be used by the given individual. Fieber (Notes 1 and 2) elaborates on this point. When older children and young adults do not have basic SM concepts and strategies, any SM instruction that is provided still must satisfy the criteria of skill functionality and age-appropriate materials. These criteria may be less easily satisfied at older ages. However, the skills still must be useful for a given person and the instructional materials need to match the student's age. For example, a bedridden, 19-year-old, severely retarded cerebral palsied young woman with no reliable communication system and no independence in self-care skills is likely to benefit from some instruction in causality, particularly if a simple communication system is part of this instruction. Depending upon the extent and location of her voluntary movement, she might be taught to move her head to the right to indicate which of three activities (record player, television, cola) she wants when presented all together and then one at a time. Ficociello, Stoddard, and Ogden (Note 3) have developed a cognitive curriculum based upon SM development specifically for the prevocational level deaf-blind child that may be useful in working with severely handicapped preadolescents and adolescents.

PART II: INSTRUCTIONAL SEQUENCES

The remainder of this chapter provides suggested instructional sequences for a number of the SM actions presented in Table 9.2, organized into four content areas. Table 9.3 outlines these content areas and the SM tasks under each content area that are treated in detail.

Each of these tasks, in turn, is described as an instructional sequence for the purpose of providing information necessary for teaching. Our comments, organized in a standard format, are directed to terminal objective, rationale, conditions, and task sequence. Included under task sequence are the following topics which provide further teaching suggestions for each task: child characteristics, positioning, materials, subsequent tasks, test for generalization, and general comments.

Object Permanence

The final goal for object permanence within the sensorimotor period is for the child to search systematically for an object when the exact location is unknown. There are, however, many steps in the development of this goal that can be defined and used as individual objectives. It is convenient to classify these objectives into three task sequences: (1) prerequisite object permanence skills, (2) simple object permanence skills, and (3) complex object permanence skills. Each task will be discussed separately. (See Tables 9.4, 9.5, and 9.6.)

Task 1: Prerequisite Object Permanence Skills

Terminal Objective: The final step in the development of skills prerequisite to object permanence involves search for a partly covered object. In this situation, the child is shown (and perhaps allowed to hold) an object which is then *partly* covered (with a cloth, cup, paper, box, etc.). The child may either take the cover off the object and pick it up or obtain the object by pulling it from under the screen.

Rationale: The objectives in this task sequence provide opportunities for further development of the visual-tracking skills. These skills are important to the solution of later object permanence problems.

TABLE 9.3 Instructional Sequences

Content Area	Tasks
1. Object Permanence	1. Prerequisite Object Permanence Skills
	2. Simple Object Permanence Skills
	3. Complex Object Permanence Skills
2. Development of Means for Achieving Environmental Events and Operational Causality	4. Repetition of Early Schemes for Environmental Effect
	5. Visually Directed Reach and Grasp
	6. Attached Tool Use
	7. Unattached Tool Use
	8. Operational Causality
3. Spatial Structuring	9. Localization of Objects in Space
	10. Examining and Relating Objects
	11. Container Play

TABLE 9.4. Task Summary 1: Prerequisite Object Permanence Skills

Task Description	Response Description	Criteria/Specific Commentary
Level A Check reinforcement value of the stimuli. Tracking and anticipation.		
Visual tracking: Teacher selects an object in which the child has demonstrated interest and moves it in a trajectory from one side of the child's head to the other.	Child smoothly and completely tracks movement of an object through a horizontal 180° trajectory.	Child tracks a variety of objects through at least a 180° trajectory on 4 out of 5 opportunities on 5 occasions. A variety of objects should be used for this activity.
Anticipation of trajectory of a slowly moving object: Teacher presents an object suspended from a string in front of the child and moves it out of view to one side of the child's head and continues movement in back of child's head, bringing object back in front of the child, slightly above the child's eye.	2 levels of responding indicating different levels of development may be noted: (1) Child's gaze lingers at point where the object disappears. (2) After several presentations, child turns gaze to point of reappearance before object reappears.	The first is a transition response which should be replaced by a second level response after some experience with the task. Child turns in anticipation of reappearance of the object when presented to each side on 4 of 5 trials on 5 occasions.
If child does not turn in anticipation of appearance of the object, teacher may present a sound cue to bring the child's attention to the object.	Child turns and visually localizes object by sound cue.	Presentation for only one direction should be continued until the sound cue can be faded. A variety of objects should be used for this activity.
Level B Reach and grasp. Check reinforcement value of the stimuli.		
Movement to maintain object in visual field: Teacher presents an object to the child and moves the object (that the child is tracking visually) out of view.	Child has to rotate the torso as well as the head in order to maintain gaze on object moved out of view to side.	Child moves to keep object in view when it is moved to either side on 4 of 5 trials on 5 occasions. A variety of objects should be used in this activity.
Search for partly covered object: Teacher presents an object to the child.	Child reaches for or picks up the object.	By doing this the teacher has confirmed the probable reinforcement value of the object.
Teacher retrieves the object from the child and partially covers the object.	Child removes cover and picks up object or reaches under cover and picks up object. The child who can reach and grasp must pick up the object to be credited as correct.	Child retrieves partly covered object on 4 of 5 opportunities on 5 occasions. A variety of different objects and covers should be used for this activity.
		Child at this level will also begin to enjoy peek-a-boo with the game being covering and uncovering of the child by the adult, and then the child can uncover herself when covered.

Conditions and Task Sequence—Child Characteristics: The prerequisite sequence begins with visual tracking at the primary circular reaction stage and continues into the substage of secondary circular reactions. The child typically develops increasing trunk control during this period, which makes it possible to pursue objects visually through greater distances. Another development during this period is visually directed reach and grasp, which are prerequisite skills for the conventional object permanence task.

Positioning of Child: The basic position for the prerequisite tasks is "supported sitting." For the activities in Level A of Task 1, as much support is provided as is necessary for the child to have maximum head control. For Level B (partly covered objects), support is given so that the child has maximum use of the hands.

For the child with special neuromotor problems, adaptations of the task to side-lying or supported sitting positions may be appropriate.

Materials: Use a variety of objects in which the child has shown interest. Yarn or string will be needed to suspend the object when the task involves anticipation of a trajectory.

Subsequent Task: After achieving criterion performance on the task of the partly hidden object, the child will be ready for the problem of the completely hidden object described in Task 2.

Generalization Test: The child picks up a variety of different objects partly covered with a variety of different screens. He should also be playing peek-a-boo by pulling the cover off a person's face or peeking around the edge of the screen the person is behind. There should also be an attempt to initiate peek-a-boo by pulling a piece of clothing up to the child's face.

Other related tasks can be found in the spatial development sequence. These include turning the head to look toward a falling object.

Task 2: Simple Object Permanence Skills

Terminal Objective: The most difficult problem among the simple object permanence problems requires that the child (a) visually track the movement of an object moved through three locations and then (b) search for and recover the object in the last location. The teacher selects an object in which the child is interested, then moves the object under the first two screens (allowing the child to see it between each location). The object is left in the last location. If the child searches in either of the first two locations, the response is considered incorrect. This problem is not ambiguous if the child visually tracks the movement of the object. He should reach directly to the last location and recover the object.

Rationale: The problems in this sequence are "simple" because the exact location of the hidden object is not ambiguous if the child uses a visual-tracking strategy. This series of simple object permanence problems gives the child the experiential basis of searching for, and recovering, hidden objects. This prepares him for more complex problems in which the exact location of the object is unknown. Thus, the child must engage in a systematic search to recover the object in the case of complex problems.

Conditions and Task Sequence—Child Characteristics: The child is able to solve the first simple object permanence problem toward the end of the substage of secondary circular reactions. The remainder of the tasks are accomplished during the substage of coordination of secondary circular reactions. To learn even the simple object permanence problems, the child will need to master three prerequisite skills: (a) visually directed reach and grasp for objects on a surface, (b) recovery of partly covered objects, and (c) smooth visual tracking of objects through interrupted trajectories.

Positioning of Child: These activities will typically be worked on with the child in a sitting position. He should be offered as much support as is necessary for optimal use of the hands. That is, he should not have to use the hands for balance, as this makes it less probable that he will be able to reach and grasp well.

Materials: The goal object on a given trial can be anything in which the child shows interest. A child of this developmental age usually indicates interest by reaching for an object that is within reach or prolonged looking at an object that is out of reach. Edibles may be used as the goal object if the child is not initially interested in very many other objects. If edibles are used, they should be faded as quickly as possible. In addition to changing goal objects, a variety of covers are needed—cups, boxes, cloth, cushions, etc. Anything that can be used to hide another object will do.

Subsequent Task: Once the child meets criterion on the series of simple object permanence problems he is ready to begin looking for objects in more complex problem situations (Task 3).

Generalization Test: As the child meets criterion on each of the problem situations, sufficient variability in goal objects and screens has been introduced so that he has a generalized search strategy for a specific situation. The ultimate generalization criterion is reached when the child uses the search strategy in daily play situations as objects go out of sight.

General Comments: When the child first is responding to the single screen problem, there may be a number of limitations on the search behavior. For example, the child may uncover and retrieve the

TABLE 9.5 Task Summary 2: Simple Object Permanence Skill

Task Description	Response Description	Criteria/Specific Commentary
Level A Check the reinforcement value of the stimuli.		
The teacher should place an object presumed to be interesting to the child before her and observe whether the child tries to pick it up.	Child shows interest in the object by reaching for it, looking at it, and smiling or behaves in some way that indicates interest in the object.	Child searches for an object on 4 of 5 opportunities on 5 occasions. Trials should include a variety of objects under at least 3 different covers.
Finding an object which is completely covered: The teacher may then hide that object under a screen (cloth, cup, box, chair cushion, etc.) in such a way that the object is not showing. The object should be moved under the screen as opposed to setting the object down and placing the screen over the object.	Child uncovers and picks up hidden object. Alternate responses: 1. Child grabs both screens. 2. Child does not pick up object.	Teacher allows child to play with object. Strategies: 1. Teacher moves screens farther apart so child has to choose one or other. 2. Use another object
Level B Finding a completely covered object which is hidden alternately between 2 places: Teacher selects an interesting object and hides it under screen on one side of the work surface. Teacher then hides object under screen on opposite side of work surface.	Correct response: Child uncovers and obtains object. Alternate response: Child pulls correct screen but does not pick up object.	Teacher allows child to play with object. Teacher encourages child to pick up object; count trial as prompted.
Level C Finding an object after 2 sequential visible displacements: Teacher selects an "interesting" object. The object is visible in the teacher's hand as she moves the object under one screen and out the other side and under the second screen, leaving the object under the second screen and bringing her empty hand out to show to the child.	Correct response: Child goes directly to location where the object was left, uncovers it, and picks up the object. Incorrect responses: 1. Child grabs both screens. 2. Child does not visually track movement and child searches under first screen. 3. Child uncovers correctly but does not pick up object.	The child should search for a variety of objects under a variety of screens on 4 of 5 opportunities on 5 occasions. Trials should involve random variation between 2 locations. Strategies: 1. Teacher places screens farther apart. 2. Teacher calls child's attention to reappearance of object after passing under one screen. 3. Teacher tries a new object since child's interest in first probably has waned. Objects may be varied from trial to trial as necessary to maintain the child's interest.
Level D Finding an object after 3 sequential visible displacements:	Correct response: Child searches directly under	The child should search for a variety of objects under a vari-

TABLE 9.5 (CONTINUED)

Task Description	Response Description	Criteria/Specific Commentary
Teacher does the same as in the 2 screen displacement problem, merely adding a third location with the object left under third screen.	third screen and picks up object.	ety of screens for 4 of 5 opportunities on 5 different occasions. Once the child searches correctly several times in this problem, the direction used (right to left or left to right) can be varied from trial to trial. Child is expected to achieve same criterion as in the 2-screen problem. This problem merely requires an increased level of skill in visual tracking and makes greater demands on the child's memory.

object only if he was already reaching for it as it was covered. Searching for an object that is covered while sitting on a surface is simpler than searching for an object that is moved across the surface and then placed under a cover. Sometimes the child only searches for objects he had just before they were hidden. All of these conditions may affect performance at the first introduction of the completely covered object problem.

It appears that the dimension of difficulty involves the length of time between the moment that the object is removed from sight and the point when the child can physically begin to search for the object. Mastery of the simple object permanence problem implies that search behavior should be reliable under all the situations described. That is, the child will search whether or not he has just held the object, whether it is placed on the surface and covered or is moved under the cover. We expect the child to be able to seek out and retrieve any object in which he demonstrates interest in a variety of hiding situations and up to about 5 seconds between the time the object is removed from sight and the child starts to uncover and retrieve the object.

Some of the cues that were originally thought by researchers to facilitate searching for completely hidden objects, such as making a sound with the object or leaving a lump under the screen, are ineffective as cues at this level of development. In order for a lump or a noise to serve as a cue, each must represent the hidden object for the child. Children at this stage of cognitive development are not capable of such representation (Piaget, 1954).

Task 3: Complex Object Permanence Skills

Terminal Objective: The terminal objective in this task sequence is that the child search for an object when its precise location is ambiguous. This situation involves showing a child an object, then hiding it in your hand, passing your hand through three hiding locations, and leaving it under one of the screens. The child is then expected to continue looking in those locations until he uncovers the object.

Rationale: The ability to search systematically for a missing object is a culminating feature of sensorimotor development. It requires the child to remember the successive displacements of an object and, in essence, reproduce the displacements by looking in several locations. Some degree of object permanence has been consistently observed in young children before they begin to develop functional use of objects or object-name associations (Bayley, 1969). This is not to suggest that a necessary and sufficient relationship of object permanence to receptive language has been established. Rather, object permanence skills consistently appear to precede the development of receptive understanding of object and action names.

Conditions and Task Sequence—Child Characteristics: The ability to solve this sequence of more complex problems begins during the subperiod of tertiary circular reactions. The child begins with trial-and-error to discover new solutions. Development extends into the sixth subperiod—invention of new means through mental combinations. At that time the child is assumed to solve problems through representational thought.

Typically, before the child can solve the first problem in this complex sequence, he will have solved the means-end problem of attached tool use and also will engage in simple container play. This is the usual situation, assuming the typical kinds of infant and toddler age-appropriate experiences. However, there is likely to be considerable variability in this pattern as the child's development and experience deviate from the typical.

Positioning and Materials: The positioning of the child and materials used as stimuli are essentially the

TABLE 9.6 Task Summary 3: Complex Object Permanence Skill

Task Description	Response Description	Criteria/Specific Commentary
Check the reinforcement value of the stimuli.		
Level A Invisible displacement of object with 1 screen: Teacher shows the child an interesting object and then hides the object in her hand. Next she moves her hand under a screen leaving the object under that screen.	The child uncovers the object and picks it up. The child may check the teacher's hand to look for the object there first.	The child is allowed to play with the object.
Invisible displacement of object with 2 screens: Teacher shows child an interesting object and then hides the object in her hand. Next she moves her hand under 1 of 2 screens, leaving the object under 1 of the screens.	The child searches only under the correct screen and uncovers the object and picks it up. The child may check the teacher's hand first.	The child is allowed to play with the object. The child searches correctly on 4 of 5 opportunities on 5 occasions. Trials should be alternated randomly between the 2 locations. A variety of objects and screens should be used.
Sequential invisible displacement with 2 screens: Teacher shows child an interesting object and then hides the object in her hand and moves her hand under 1 screen and out the other side and then under a second screen, leaving the object under the second screen.	Alternative correct responses: 1. Child picks up second screen and recovers object. 2. Child picks up first screen, the object is not there; she then picks up second screen and recovers the object. Incorrect response: Child stops searching after not finding it under first screen.	Child is allowed to play with object. Child searches correctly using either pattern on 4 of 5 opportunities on 5 occasions. Again a variety of objects and screens are used.

Show her where it is and cover it again, encouraging her to continue to search. |
| *Level B* Sequential invisible displacement with 3 screens: Teacher does same as in 2-screen problem with the only change being that a third screen is present and the object is left under the third screen. | Alternate correct responses: 1. Child picks up third screen and recovers object. 2. Child picks up first and second screen, not finding the object. Child picks up third screen and recovers the object. | Child is allowed to play with object. Same criterion. If the child searched from the first to last screen during the preceding activity, this activity is not necessary. However, it is unlikely that a child would persist with that strategy once she found the object in the last location several times. |
| *Level C* Representation of sequential invisible displacement: Teacher shows child an interesting object and hides object in her hand. Then moves hand through the 3 locations, reappearing after each screen. But the object is left in the first location. | Child searches systematically from the last screen to the first in the order of last, middle, first, and picks up object. | Child is allowed to play with object. Same criterion as other responses.

If the child has difficulty with the 3-screen problem it can be simplified by going back to 2 screens first. The goal is to teach systematic search behavior. After she accomplishes the 3-screen problem, she can be presented with 4- and 5-screen problems. |

same as in the simple skill sequence, with the exception that the child does not require as much physical support in sitting.

Subsequent Task: Accomplishment of the representational search problem marks the final point of sensorimotor development in the object permanence sequence. Object permanence is now a generalized concept available in combination with other concepts and strategies for solutions of preoperational problems—the next stage of cognitive development.

Development of Means for Achieving Environmental Events and Operational Causality

The steps in this sequence are described as means-end developments. The child learns successively more complex ways of acting upon the environment to cause desired events. From the Piagetian point of view, this sequence involves the development of intentionality. Others would describe this sequence as the development of operant responding. From either perspective, it marks an extremely important refinement in the child's behavioral repertoire.

The means-end sequences are organized into the following tasks: (4) repetition of early schemes for environmental effect (systematic repetition), (5) visually directed reach and grasp, (6) development of attached tool use, (7) use of separated object as a tool, and (8) development of operational causality. (See Tables 9.7, 9.8, 9.9, 9.10, 9.11, and 9.12.)

Background

The first step in the sequence involves the child's repeating an early motor movement scheme (hitting or shaking) and systematically keeping an object, such as a bell, rattle, wind chime, or rolling musical toy, active. Piaget's description (1963) of his children between 2 and 4 months old provides an excellent example. He suspended a toy above his child's crib and tied a string from the toy to the child's wrist. Since a child of that age usually plays by moving the arms and legs, it was not long before the child's movement made the toy move. Then the child quieted and looked at the animal. After a brief period, the animal stopped swinging and the child started to fuss and in doing so moved again. The animal was in turn activated, the child quieted and watched, and then the animal stopped again. This cycle continued for some time, the child's behavior changed from flailing arms and legs to systematic movement of one arm with gaze directed at the object. Once this response was firmly established, Piaget switched the string from the child's right wrist to his left. The child would continue to move his right wrist but the animal did not move. After a time the child again became fussy and returned to the flailing movements of both arms. After a period of time he again isolated his movement to one arm, this time the left arm. This isolation of the response to the second limb typically occurred in less time than the isolation to the first limb when the activity was started. This increase and differentiation of responding characterizes learning in the means-end sequence. It is not restricted to arm movements. The response can be of any form as long as it can be described and reliably counted. Therefore, foot kicks, head turns, vocalizations, open or shut mouth, or movement of one finger may qualify. Once the response is selected, it is necessary to arrange some environmental event so that it occurs contingent upon the child's response.

In addition to Piaget's work, there is a growing body of literature suggesting the importance of contingent stimulation in learning in infants. This work

FIGURE 9.1.
This Child Is Using the Alternate Response Strategy of Directing his Gaze at the Correct Location in an Object Permanence Problem

includes that of Ramey and Watson (1972) and Watson (1971), who studied the learning rates of three groups of 8-week-old infants exposed to a mobile in their own homes. One group experienced mobile turns contingent upon a head-turning response. The second group saw a nonmovable hanging stimulus, a "stabile" (the same visual stimulus as the mobile, but it did not turn). The third group experienced noncontingent mobile turns. The contingent group was the only group that showed a reliable change in head-turning behavior. Six weeks later all three groups were exposed to a different mobile that turned contingently for all three groups. The original contingent and stabile groups demonstrated reliable responding. Thus, they controlled the movements of a new mobile in the laboratory situation. The original noncontingent group did not show this same change in their rate of responding. The authors suggest that a positive learning effect results from a contingent experience, whereas a maladaptive effect results from experience with random responsiveness of environmental events.

More recently, Finkelstein and Ramey (Note 4) demonstrated that infants who had learned a lever-pressing response to control stimulation in the treatment phase of a study later learned to vocalize to control the presentation of the stimulation slides used in the previous contingent situation. Infants in a noncontingent group who were presented with the same amount of visual stimulation, but who did not have to give a specific response for the stimulation to occur, did *not* demonstrate the vocalization response on the posttest. Thus, experience with contingent stimulation may be more than simply learning a single response. Rather, infants who receive contingent stimulation may become, in general, more competent and efficient learners (Finkelstein & Ramey, Note 4). These results suggest that contingent experience produces a "learning-to-learn" phenomenon.

Another line of research suggests that noncontingent stimulation may have equally potent negative effects. Seligman (1975) emphasizes the importance of experiencing predictability in, and control over, environmental events. When you have no control over positive or negative events, this lack of control or "helplessness" often leads to nonresponsiveness in situations where access to positive reinforcers or avoidance of noxious stimuli is controllable. Seligman specifically cites as an example the baby's first opportunity to control contingent stimulation from her caregivers. Helplessness can be prevented or, in some cases, overcome with careful arrangement of contingent experiences.

In his work with retarded children and young adults, Cromwell (1963) posited a lower expectancy for success in retarded learners, particularly when they are confronted with failure experiences. There are many parallels between Cromwell's work, Seligman's work on learned helplessness, and Watson's research on contingency awareness and the negative effects of noncontingent stimulation. All warrant much more investigation. Further research may provide information regarding the optimal characteristics of learning environments for the severely handicapped.

The greater the number of daily events contingent upon the child's responses, the more adequate will be the educational experience. The limitations on arranging contingent experiences are practical ones which may be overcome by examining a child's response potentials and daily activities and then arranging these events to maximize contingent experiences. For example, if the child is dependent during eating or dressing, a teacher may make every bite of food contingent upon a response from the child. This response may be as simple as touching the hand of the person feeding her. The same type of sequence may be established in dressing. When the learner is shown a sock, he moves his foot. When he is shown a shirt, he lifts his arms to the extent possible. For the severely physically involved child, the objective may not be an approximation of the feeding or dressing skill movements. Rather, a very simple response (either vocal or motor) becomes a signal that the child anticipates the next event that will happen. In a sense, he is requesting the occurrence of the next event in a learned sequence.

Task 4: Repetition of Early Schemes for Environmental Effect

Terminal Objective: The terminal objective for the initial means-end level of responding requires the child to display a variety of different responses, each specific to producing a particular environmental effect.

Rationale: The ability to differentially respond to stimuli (such as wind chimes, shaking a bell or rattle, or kicking to get the teacher to activate a bouncing seat) serves as the basis for providing the child with strategies for acting on the environment. Uzgiris and Hunt (1966; 1975) refer to this as a learning set of "If I act, I can make interesting things happen and can find interesting things to do" (p. 40). This learning set results in a variety of responses and provides behaviors that then can be shaped into more elaborate responses.

Conditions and Task Sequence—Child Characteristics: Repetition of responding is observed in the typical baby during the 2nd to 4th month. In fact, infant researchers requiring less elaborate motor responses have begun to document evidence of primary circular reactions during the neonatal period (Bower, 1977). Consequently, we recommend arranging some type of response-contingent experience as soon as possible for the child who does not already have an "if I act" response. There are no observable prerequisites for beginning this activity except that the child must have some voluntary response. It can be any response—an arm wave, a foot kick, any vocalization. By the time the child achieves the differentiated responding described in the terminal objective, he will have progressed to the level of secondary circular reactions (Piagetian terminology) and discriminated operant responding (terminology of applied behavior analysis).

Position of Child: In order to work on the level of initial means-end development, the child must display some response. First, the response that is to be increased is selected. The position in which the child displays that response most frequently is the position in which to place the child.

Materials: There is not a particular set of materials to use for these activities. Any object in which the child shows interest and to which he can apply a response that produces an effect will do. Materials such as wind chimes, mobiles, toys that turn when batted, bells, and rattles are especially good. In addition, some brightly colored yarn may be used to construct a mobile (see Figure 9.2).

General Comments: There are several important points to consider when working on the early means-end objective with a child. For the child to learn the concept "If-I-act-I-can-make-interesting-things-happen," the consequence for the selected response must be an effective reinforcer. It may take a number of trials with different sound, visual, or tactile events to find a reinforcer. Once a reinforcing event is determined, it is not advisable to assume that that event will remain a reinforcer indefinitely. After mastering a particular event, the child may become bored with it. Thus boredom is inferred from a decrease in responding. Therefore, it is necessary to vary the consequence and, perhaps, even the response. Because of this satiation, it is essential that particular environmental events be arranged for only selected periods during the day. Further, the child's behavior should be observed to detect any evidence of decrease in responding. If a decrease is observed, potential explanations such as satiation, seizure activity, and physical discomfort can be considered and modifications made. If the child has had a seizure or is physically uncomfortable, we might not change the task or consequence. However, if the child is satiated with the activity, we would change the consequence. If an increase in activity is still not observed, perhaps the response should be changed.

With this objective, the particular response or reinforcing event used is irrelevant. The objective is not that the child move an arm or leg or turn his head or

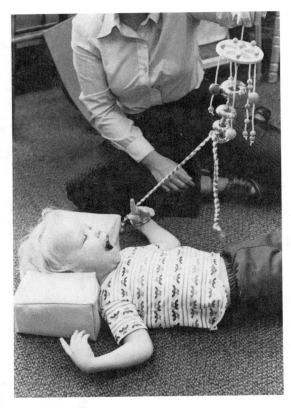

FIGURE 9.2.
Child Demonstrates Beginning Level of Means-End Behavior

vocalize, but that the child have a variety of responses to produce corresponding responses in the environment. As a generalized response, the child should use these behaviors by testing them in new situations until a behavior is found that produces a spectacle. Very often teachers stop working on an activity when the child masters one response in one specific setting. One response in one setting is not a sufficient level of competence on this objective.

Generalization Training and Subsequent Tasks: The development of generalized responding involves showing different movements appropriate to different situations. At the level of repetition of an early scheme, the child is likely to begin demonstrating movement to an object that is out of reach, the next task to be described.

Locomotion as a Means-End Response: Once a child demonstrates a generalized means-end repertoire (the repetition of responses which produce environmental events) and visually directed reach and grasp (if physically possible), the next step in the means-end sequence involves the use of some means of locomotion to obtain an object that is out of reach. Again, the important aspect of this response is not the form

TABLE 9.7 Task Summary 4: Repetition of Early Scheme for Environmental Effect (Systematic Repetition)

Task Description	Response Description	Criteria/Specific Commentary
Check reinforcement value of stimuli. Teacher takes data on movements occurring in the absence of stimuli. Without presenting any toys or objects, teacher observes child in a variety of positions, recording movements such as arm waves, foot kicks, head turns, etc. This observation should be done for 3-5-minute periods on several occasions.	Possible responses: 1. Child moves arms at a fairly high rate (more than 10 per minute). Follow procedure under Level B. 2. Child moves arms at a low rate (less than 10 per minute). Follow procedure under Level A; after rate has increased, follow Level B procedure.	Child is lying on floor with firm pillow under head and shoulders. This keeps the child's shoulders somewhat rounded, making it easier for her to move. 1. This rate is sufficiently high so that simply presenting a stimulus such as a wind chime will be possible. 2. If child's rate is low and amplitude of movement is slight (lifts arms only a slight amount), teacher may decide to "rig" environment to facilitate movement (see Figure 9.2).
Level A Low-baseline arm movement rate. Teacher ties piece of yarn, one end to child's wrist and other end to wind chimes suspended over child.	Child moves arm slightly, wind chimes are activated, child quiets and looks at chimes, chimes stop; child moves again and cycle is repeated.	Child shows an increase in the rate of arm movements over baseline rate. Example of repetition of early scheme behavior (arm movement) at advanced level.
Teacher shows child the toy and activates it, then presents toy successively to each of the child's limbs. Toy may be wind chime, roly-poly ball, mobile, etc.	Child moves all limbs and gradually isolates movement to limb where toy is placed.	The child demonstrates a generalized primary circular reaction means-end strategy when she isolates the movement to each limb appropriately.
Level B High-baseline arm movement task. Teacher presents wind chimes in a position close to child's arm which she moved most frequently during baseline and records child's arm movements.	Child waves arm and most arm movements come into contact with chimes. The child alternates between moving arm and quieting and looking at chimes. This is an early phase, however, so hitting and looking do not occur together.	Initially the child may move both arms during no stimulus and stimulus conditions. After several weeks the child's overall rate of movement is less. But she moves the arm closest to the chimes more frequently. She has become more efficient in controlling the chimes. After another 2 weeks her rate is closer to her initial rate of responding in stimulus condition but is predominately unilateral movement (indicating greater efficiency of responding).

of the specific motor locomotion. Rather, the question is, will the child use any available method of locomotion to secure an object? For the child who is developing typically, the mode of locomotion is likely to be crawling. With the handicapped child, it may vary from rolling to walking. In the case of the severely physically involved child, we do not want to confuse the motor ability to locomote with the concept that the body can be used as a tool to obtain objects that are out of reach. For some, locomotion as a means-end response may begin with only a turn from back to side to obtain the object. Then the distance that the child must travel to retrieve the object (or to have physical contact with a person) is gradually increased. The ability to persist over a great distance correlates with increasing competence in visual pursuit of a disappearing object and search for the partly covered object.

Task 5: Visually Directed Reach and Grasp

Terminal Objective: The final objective in this sequence requires the child to lift the hand when it is out of the visual field and grasp an object that is in the visual field. Optimally, the child anticipates the shape of the object to be grasped.

Rationale: This task is an important component motor skill of many of the later sensorimotor concepts. There is, apparently, a concept of hand as a "tool object" learned during the development of reach and grasp. In this sense, it is a prerequisite skill to subsequent use of other objects as tools.

Conditions and Task Sequence—Child Characteristics: The development of reach and grasp begins during the reflexive subperiod of development. However, development of the final objective involves refinements during the primary and secondary circular reaction subperiods. For the child who does not have specific neuromotor problems or visual deficits, the development of reach and grasp is very likely to follow the sequence outlined in Table 9.8. The child with neuromotor problems may have difficulty with voluntary control of arm and hand movements. For example, a child that has abnormal persistence of the asymmetric tonic neck reflex (ATNR) may begin reaching by looking at the object but will lose visual contact with the object as he extends his arm. This occurs because the ATNR reflex dominates his movement. This pattern is illustrated in Figure 9.3. The side position (as illustrated in Figure 9.4) facilitates visually directed reach and grasp, for such a child. When physical handicaps are encountered, the teacher should consult with a physical or occupational therapist to select the most appropriate conditions for working on reach and grasp.

Difficulties in learning to reach and grasp are further complicated when the child is visually impaired and lacks opportunity to coordinate visual and tactual input. This coordination seems to provide the experiential basis for learning to use the hand as a tool.

Materials: The materials needed for working on reach and grasp objectives include items that are easily grasped. However, during the period when the child's reach takes the form of swatting at an object, any visually interesting object is a good stimulus. During this period brightly colored patterned cloth, chimes, and brightly colored roly-poly toys often work well as stimuli.

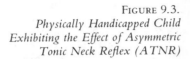

FIGURE 9.3.
Physically Handicapped Child Exhibiting the Effect of Asymmetric Tonic Neck Reflex (ATNR)

TABLE 9.8 Sequence of Child Behavior in the Development of Visually Guided Reach and Grasp

1–1½ months	Child is in asymmetric tonic neck reflex (ATNR) position but does not regard his hand(s). Grasping, looking, sucking, are all schemes that the child has, but each is done in isolation. Hands are generally fisted.
1–2 months	Child tends to be in ATNR position and gaze is occasionally fixed on hand facing eyes (head is turned to one side and child regards hand on same side for period up to 5–10 seconds).
2–2½ months	Child is able to keep head closer to midline position; eyes converge and focus on stimulus at 5″. Swipes or bats at stimulus to side with near hand (beginning eye-arm coordination). Hand is fisted and child makes no attempt to grasp object. If object is placed in hand, child brings grasped object to mouth and may suck object.
1½–3 months	Child's head is often in midline and limbs are symmetrical in their position. Child regards hand for sustained periods. Converges and focuses on stimulus at 3″. Visual accommodation is increasing. Child swipes at objects with alternate looking between object at which she swipes and her hand.
3–3½ months	Child's head is mostly in midline. The hands are predominately open. Child continues hand regard and also plays with hands at midline. Occasionally he looks at hands while playing. The child moves hands to grasp at object he is sucking. The child is beginning to look at object he is holding. When an object is presented in front of child, a bilateral or one-handed reach up is elicited.
3½–4 months	Head is in midline with little or no asymmetric tonic neck reflex observed. Child looks at own hand play. Stimulus object presented to child's midline evokes a bilateral grasp. When the child is reaching, he also orients torso toward object.
4–4½ months	When an object is presented within reach at midline, the child reaches up with both hands or one while the other hand remains at midline. Grasp results when hand and object are both in view. Child raises hand slowly with alternate glancing at hands and object, grasping on contact is awkward.
4½–5 months	Reaching at the criterion level involves the child rapidly lifting his hand from out of view to an object which is in view. Hand opens in anticipation. Increased looking at grasped object.

SOURCE: Adapted from an unpublished table prepared by Nancy Fieber (1975, Meyer Children's Rehabilitation Institute), based upon research of White, Castle, and Held (1964) and White, Held, and Castle (1967).

FIGURE 9.4.
This Child is in a Sidelying Position, Which is Used to Facilitate Hand Use

TABLE 9.9 Task Summary 5: Visually Directed Reach and Grasp

Task Description	Response Description	Criteria/Specific Commentary
Level A Swiping at objects. Check reinforcement value of the stimuli. Teacher observes child.	Child engages in hand watching play in ATNR position. That is, when lying down with head turned to side, child watches hand on that side.	This behavior indicates a good time to place a visually interesting object close to that hand.
Teacher places visually interesting object several inches from child's head with the child lying on her back.	Child looks at and swipes or bats at object, but does not attempt to grasp object.	Child needs many opportunities on this activity with each hand. After the batting response is learned, she begins more direct reaching for object suspended over head.
Teacher presents visually interesting object at a point closer to child's midline.	Child swipes at objects, looking alternately at hand and at object.	As child becomes more proficient, an object is presented closer to and finally at midline. Gradual movement toward midline should take place alternately from both sides to the middle.
Teacher observes child's response.	1. Child plays with her hands in midline position; occasionally she is also looking at her hands while playing with them. 2. Child moves hand to grasp at object she is sucking.	This is a behavior that systematically precedes the direct visually guided reach. Side-lying position may facilitate the occurrence of this behavior for some children.
Level B Reach and grasp without accommodation for object shape. Teacher physically guides child's arm to assist bringing a held object into visual range.	Child looks at the object in her hand. On subsequent occasions she brings hand and object into view spontaneously.	This behavior may also be facilitated with side-lying for some children. The child should be bringing almost all grasped objects into view.
Teacher presents an object in front of the child in such a way that both the object and the child's hands are in her visual field.	Child reaches out with one or both hands to object but does not accommodate hand(s) to shape of object before touching object. Child engages in midline play with hands while also looking at her hands.	The child should demonstrate this behavior with a variety of objects. This coordination of visual and tactile schemes typically precedes the next development in reach and grasp.
Teacher presents an interesting object to child with both object and child's hand in her visual field.	Child grasps object with both hands and also orients toward object if it is not presented at midline.	Child should be doing this with a variety of objects. Objects should be presented for grasping rather than being put in her hands at this stage.
Teacher presents object to child but at a greater distance from child.	Child raises hand slowly, glancing alternately between her hand and the object. When she	Child should have many opportunities for this activity. Include times when objects are sus-

Table 9.9 (continued)

Task Description	Response Description	Criteria/Specific Commentary
	grasps the object, her accommodation to its shape is often awkward.	pended in easy reach over the child as she is lying down or sitting in a chair.
Level C Reach and grasp with hand accommodation anticipated. Teacher presents object to child at a distance which requires reaching for it.	Child lifts hand which is out of her visual field directly to object. She accommodates the position of her hand to the object's shape.	Child should be able to do this with a variety of objects. Following this accomplishment, she will be able to reach for and grasp objects on a surface in the same manner.

Task 6: Attached Tool Use

Background: The development of tool use occurs in two steps. Initially, for the child to use one object (the means) to obtain another object (the end), the means and end must be physically connected. Examples might be a string attached to a toy or an object resting on a piece of cloth. This ability comes about as part of the subperiod of secondary circular reactions and becomes a generalized skill through coordination of various secondary circular reactions. The second step in the means-end developmental sequence involves the ability to use an object that is *not* connected to the goal object. An example would be the use of a stick to pull a box off a shelf. This type of problem-solving ability begins during the fifth sensorimotor subperiod (tertiary circular reactions) and becomes generalized during the subperiod of invention of new means through mental combinations.

Terminal Objective: The terminal objective for the solution of attached tool problems requires that the child be able to use a variety of objects (string, pillows, pieces of cloth, box tops, etc.) as tools for bringing desired objects into reach. The child should be able to differentiate when a tool is functional or not functional. Evidence of differentiation could be the child who does not pull on strings that are not attached to a goal object or does not pull on a cloth that does not have a goal object sitting on it.

Rationale: The use of tools attached to objects is an intermediate step between using the hand as a tool and the final step, locating and using an unattached tool to obtain a desired object.

Conditions and Task Sequence—Child Characteristics: This sequence of tool use begins during the subperiod of secondary circular reactions. Children typically show some evidence of search for the partly covered object at least before they begin to use supports or strings as tools. Also, the typical tool-use situation requires good visually directed reach and grasp. It is important, again, to separate the motor requirements of the task from the problem itself. The use of some type of intermediary to obtain an object that is out of reach is the goal and the problem to be solved. Sometimes a very simple modification, such as tying a wooden bead to the end of a string or attaching some similar type of handle to a cloth, can make the tool more useable for a physically handicapped child with poor grasp.

Materials: Materials for this type of activity are objects in which the child has demonstrated some interest. Pieces of yarn, cloth, paper, or any other object may serve as the attached tool.

Subsequent Task: Once the child has demonstrated generalized use of attached tools (including the vertical use of the string) and is able to alter his own behavior according to whether a given tool is functional, he is ready for problems requiring use of an unattached tool.

Generalization Test: A child should be able to use a variety of tools to obtain a number of goal objects at this level. In addition, he should spontaneously employ (without demonstration) a tool not previously used on the first presentation of that new tool.

Task 7: Unattached Object as a Tool

Terminal Objective: By the end of the sensorimotor period, the child should be using objects within reach (rakes, sticks, chairs, etc.) in order to obtain objects which are out of reach (toys, cookie jars on counters, etc.).

Rationale: It is the novel combination of means and ends that marks the child's increasing readiness for representational problem solving. Experience with situations in which the child has to use tools to obtain desired ends (rather than simply having goal objects brought to him) is the final elaboration of the

TABLE 9.10 Task Summary 6: Attached Tool Use

Task Description	Response Description	Criteria/Specific Commentary
Check reinforcement value of the stimuli.		
Level A Use of support as tool. Teacher presents an object to the child.	Child reaches for the object.	Teacher feels confident that object is interesting.
Teacher moves the object out of reach and sets it on a support which is within reach. Possible supports include a towel, pillow, box top, string, etc.	Possible responses: 1. Child begins to pull forward onto table surface, falls back, but object is now within reach.	Child is likely to become gradually more direct and efficient in her response.
	2. Child does not pull support but may request help.	Child should begin to pull spontaneously on new trials after several demonstrations.
If child does not pull support, teacher demonstrates.	3. Child pulls support after demonstration. 4. Child has pulled in past but does not now.	Teacher probably needs to change goal object.
	5. Child pulls support directly and obtains object.	
Test for understanding of the "unattached" tool problem (object held above support making support useless as tool). This test is given only after child successfully uses the support as a tool to obtain an object resting upon it. Teacher allows child to play with object, then takes it out of reach and holds it a few inches above the "tool" support the child has just used.	Possible responses: 1. Child pulls pillows and looks surprised.	Teacher moves pillows back, sets object on pillow, and encourages child to reach for object.
	2. Child pulls pillow, stops, and then immediately reaches up for the object. 3. Child reaches up for object and does not touch pillow support.	Teacher gives child the object if it is likely that she will soon start reaching directly. This problem should then be presented with other tool situation.
Level B Use of string as tool on surface (vertical string problem). Teacher presents an object to the child.	Child reaches for the object.	Teacher feels confident that object is interesting.
Teacher moves the object out of sight over edge of table but leaves string tied to the object within reach. Teacher makes point of showing child where object has gone.	Possible responses: 1. Child plays with string and, while playing, object comes within reach; then child picks up the object.	Child is likely to become more efficient on repeated trials.
	2. Child does not pull string but requests help.	Child should begin to pull spontaneously on new trials after demonstration. Teacher should change goal object.

252

Table 9.10 (continued)

Task Description	Response Description	Criteria/Specific Commentary
	3. Child pulls string after demonstration. 4. Child has pulled string in past but does not now. 5. Child pulls on string directly and obtains the object, either with hand-over-hand motion or a quick jerking motion.	Child should begin to pull spontaneously on new trials. Teacher needs to try new goal object. This is the level of response desired. Child should demonstrate this behavior on at least 5 different occasions.

means-end skill. That is, the child must act in increasingly complex ways in order to make interesting things happen.

Conditions and Task Sequence—Child Characteristics: Before the child solves this type of problem, he is likely to have demonstrated some systematic search behavior for the object that has just been hidden. He will engage in sequential container play—putting a series of objects into a container—as well as attempt to activate some mechanical toys.

Position of Child: It is very important to construct the situation so that there is not an alternative means of obtaining an object. For example, we find that children are unlikely to use the unattached tool if they are seated on the floor or even at a table where they can readily reach the object by stretching. They seem more likely to use a tool when an object is out of reach and higher. At any rate, it is important that there be a functional necessity for use of the tool rather than the whim of the teacher. This is a form of problem solving best observed when the child is moving around the environment rather than in a structured situation.

Materials: Again, this type of tool-use problem requires some fine motor skills the physically handicapped child may not have. In a successful effort to modify this task for a physically handicapped child, one teacher attached a magnet to the end of a stick.

Subsequent Task: Use of an unattached tool is the highest skill in the tool-use realm of means-end cognitive development. Uzgiris and Hunt (1975) describe an extension of the means-end problem-solving tasks which requires more foresight by the learner. The problem situations include placing a long string of beads in a tall, narrow container and the problem of the solid ring (pp. 173–175). In the first situation, the child will be unsuccessful because of the container's unsteadiness unless he invents a means to stabilize the container (e.g., holding the glass and dangling the necklace over it, rolling up the necklace first, etc.). In the second problem, the child is provided with a set of rings and a rod for mounting them; however one ring is made solid by taping over

the hole. The foresightful youngster will not attempt to stack the solid ring but instead will set it aside.

Generalization Test: Once the child demonstrates (a) using a new tool spontaneously, (b) subsequently using other tools in situations where he may have to move a short distance to obtain the tool, and (c) returning to the problem and using the tool to obtain the goal, he has reached criterion for invention of a means to obtain desired ends.

Task 8: Operational Causality

Background: The development of causality involves the ability to separate actions from the results which they produce. This separation occurs in a sequence which begins similarly to the means-end sequence. In the first steps the child examines his hands. Next he repeats actions which produce an interesting result. The next activity involves showing the child an interesting spectacle such as a toy top, a wind-up toy, or any event which he cannot reproduce by direct action on the object. We can then observe the child and record the level of response. Does he make some kind of gesture that suggests he wants to experience the spectacle again (e.g., hitting his hand on the table or bouncing up and down)? Does he use a more formal gesture such as pushing the object toward you or bringing your hand toward the object? Does he try to recreate the spectacle by manipulating the toy manually such as by sliding a friction toy back and forth without removing his hand from it? Finally, does he explore various means to reproduce the spectacle such as turning the key on a wind-up toy? There is not a correct or an incorrect response on this sequence. Rather, different skill levels correlate with different stages in the child's development of causality. The level of searching for a means to reproducing the spectacle, such as winding the key on a mechanical toy, is the terminal objective described for the sensorimotor period.

Rationale: The first step in this series of skills is a very opportune point to begin establishing a basis for communication. This is accomplished by reinforcing the rudiments of a gesture system. Think of the 7- or

TABLE 9.11. Task Summary 7: Unattached Tool Use.

Task Description	Response Description	Criteria/Specific Commentary
Check reinforcement value of stimuli. Teacher arranges a situation in which an object the child has requested (through word or gesture) is out of reach, but a tool (rake, chair, stool, etc.) is available to obtain the object.	Possible responses: 1. Child uses tool to obtain the object only after demonstration. 2. Child uses the tool to obtain the object spontaneously.	Once the child (1) uses a new tool spontaneously, (2) subsequently uses other tools in situations where she may have to move a short distance to get the tool, and (3) returns and obtains the goal, she has accomplished the generalized criterion for invention of a new means to obtain desired ends.

8-month-old baby being bounced on her father's lap. When the bouncing stops, the baby is likely to continue the bouncing and do some additional wiggling. Dad is likely to interpret this movement as "Oh, you want more." Dad then resumes the bouncing. This continuing movement on the child's part is not initially a response to make Dad bounce her some more. However, this interpretation on the father's part typically results in the development of a more explicit gesture by which the child indicates that she wants more. Thus, in this example, we have the roots for a communication system with the child. This type of situation offers a number of opportunities throughout the day to require the child to use a rudimentary gesture system.

An example of the process was illustrated by one of our teachers and a student who liked to bounce on the teacher's lap. The teacher used this event as a reinforcer after the child engaged in less preferred activities. In addition, the teacher worked toward rudimentary communication by requiring that the child request the bouncing. After initially bouncing the child on his lap, the teacher stopped and asked the child whether he wanted more. The response that had been selected for this child to indicate that he wanted "more" is an "ah" sound. In a period of 4 days, the number of times the teacher had to ask a child if he would like more before the child responded appropriately decreased from a mean of 3.2 to 1 on individual trials. The next step in this objective might be to require the "ah" sound before the first bounce in response to the question, "Do you want to bounce?" The teacher is working toward the point when the child not yet on the teacher's lap responds positively (and by now the response may be a head nod for "yes") to the question, "Do you want to bounce?", before he is even allowed on the teacher's lap. The progression is to move gradually to situations where the child must use gestures or sounds in the presence of fewer and fewer contextual cues.

This shapes the child's progress closer to that expected in situations which require communication in a representational context.

Conditions and Task Sequence—Child Characteristics: The initial step in the causality sequence is differentiated from the means-end sequence in that it requires the child to repeat a gesture (hitting hand on surface, kicking, vocalizing, etc.) when a spectacle, such as a moving toy, stops. This level of responding typically begins during the subperiod of primary circular reactions. Prerequisite behavior is the repetition of motor schemes that produce an interesting effect.

Subsequent Task: The remaining steps in the development of a generalized concept of causality represent refinements in the type of action required to produce particular consequent events. This results from experience with a variety of mechanisms, wind-up toys, tops, light switches, strings to pull, and keys to insert. In many cases, the means for activating the spectacle may be physically impossible for a particular person. This should not limit opportunities to experience this type of control over the environment. Observe a person's response to an interesting event such as a wind-up toy. Then select some component of that response (e.g., reaches toward the key when it stops) and require that response in subsequent situations before reproducing the event.

General Comments: Again, specific examples have been given to illustrate operational causality. The context, the response, and the reinforcer for each level of causality, however, are each examples of entire classes. This is not an objective that you work on for 15 minutes out of the day. Rather, it is a principle—that of requiring some form of communication from the child before every event that occurs during the day. The limitations in applying this principle are, as has been previously emphasized, of our own making. It is our responsibility to organize the child's daily activities to create a match between response capabilities and environmental demands.

To use this principle, begin with only a few situations during the school day. Gradually introduce new sequences of context (antecedent events), required responses, and reinforcing consequences as the child masters the previous sequences. If meals are generally positive for a child, training should begin in that context. Perhaps initially the child is expected to open his mouth when he sees the spoon. Or perhaps he has to touch your hand before he receives another bite. Whatever the response, the essential characteristic of the situation is that the child must do something consistently in order for a specific event to occur.

Nancy Fieber, who is training coordinator in the M.C.R.I. Infant Program, has designed a process teaching format she calls a *script* (Figure 9.5) in which she uses this principle of integrating strategies for eliciting communication into daily events. Fieber uses a recording tool shown in Figure 9.6 as a basis for systematically recording the child's behavior which she interprets for communicative intent. These observations serve as the basis for the design of an individual child's script (Fieber, Note 5).

In the examples used so far, the child has been asked to respond to contextual cues (e.g., being on the teacher's lap or the filled spoon) as the discriminative stimulus for a "gesture." With some children, tactile prompts are necessary during beginning work. For example, a touch on the child's chin to get the mouth open or a tap on the shoulder to cue sitting down may work. Additional information about the use of tactile cues for the beginnings of communication work may be sought if this means-end communication does not develop (Fieber, Notes 1 and 2).

Once the child begins to use these primitive gestures spontaneously, a tremendous step in the development of communication has been accomplished. The child now uses responses as a means to control events which he cannot directly manipulate. This separation of action and consequent events is the essence of operational causality.

Spatial Structuring

"Localization of objects in space" is the phrase Uzgiris and Hunt (1975) use for a collection of skills typically observed in the toddler's repertoire. These skills include items that we feel may be divided into three task sequences: (9) localization of objects in space, (10) examining and relating objects, and (11) container play. (See Tables 9.13, 9.14, and 9.15.)

Task 9: Localization of Objects in Space

Terminal Objective: The terminal objective for this task requires the child to follow the path through which an object is moved to a point some distance away before it is removed from view. The child must then move around any barriers to that object and retrieve it.

Rationale: This series of behaviors develops in parallel with object permanence skills. It represents coordination of the concepts of object permanence and understanding of the consistency with which objects move in space. The steps in this sequence represent a generalization of the object permanence concept as the child must pursue hidden objects over greater distances and, consequently, over longer periods of time.

Conditions and Task Sequence—Child Characteristics: This series of items begins during the subperiod of primary circular reaction. The learned behaviors include alternating gaze, localization of sounds, and anticipation of horizontal trajectories. Development proceeds into the subperiod of secondary circular reactions when the child learns to follow rapidly falling objects and to rotate his body to retrieve objects. Pursuit of objects around barriers (first tranparent, then opaque) is accomplished during the later subperiod of tertiary circular reactions.

The initial behavior in this series, alternate glancing, typically follows the development of visual fixation and visual tracking. For the physically involved child, however, this actually may be more feasible than visual tracking. Anticipating the direction of a horizontal trajectory is an accomplishment that comes about along with the activities prerequisite to object permanence (e.g., anticipation of the trajectory behind the child's head). Trunk rotation to pursue objects and localization of a fallen object lag slightly behind the ability to search for objects in the single screen situation. Finally, pursuit of objects around barriers follows, in developmental sequence, the accomplishment of the complex object permanence skills.

Any one of these tasks might be too motorically complex for the physically handicapped child. For example, recall what happens when you try to pursue an object moved behind you without using your hand for support as you turn. Modifications, both in the response and the consequences, may be necessary. With the barrier problems, locomotion may be difficult for a child who moves by rolling without much directional control. If the child cannot ambulate, you may have to act out the situation with a doll. This involves asking the child to indicate whether the doll or puppet is going the "right way" to get the object. If it is necessary to use a "pretend" situation, the concepts involved will be more difficult. Considerable initial teaching centered on the object of the game will be required before you can feel confident that the child has the concept.

Materials: Materials used in these activities are, most importantly, objects in which the child has

PRELIMINARY CUES
Helping Mom

Position Erica on bean-bag in kitchen to keep you company as you prepare meal. The surround may begin to signify eating time. Picking up cues-verbal/touch sides. Tell her you are going to put her in chair. Show her bib, "Here's your bib. I'm going to put your bib on," with touch cue to chest. Guide her to feel bib. Look for anticipation.

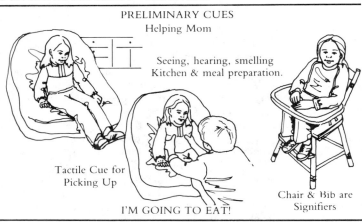

Seeing, hearing, smelling Kitchen & meal preparation.

Tactile Cue for Picking Up

Chair & Bib are Signifiers

I'M GOING TO EAT!

FEEDING PROGRAM
Guided EAT sign

Guide her in eat sign & drink sign approximations. Show her spoon or glass each time you change & move slowly toward mouth to see if she visually recognizes. Touch to mouth as cue. Use manual techniques to help lip closure, fade as feasible. Introduce textures gradually. Use food mill. Place bits of food on lateral teeth—touch cue to open & chew.

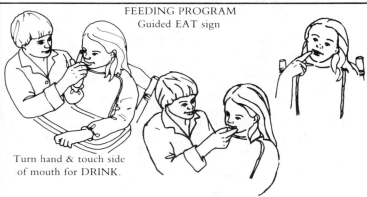

Turn hand & touch side of mouth for DRINK.

EQUIPMENT: Cup cut-out, plastic-tipped spoon.

OTHER LEARNING OPPORTUNITIES

Cognition: Object Schemes. Guide Erica in holding spoon & glass a bit in feeding so that she acquires haptic meaning. We do not expect her to feed herself yet.

Cognition: Causality. Pause & ask if she wants more, holding spoon or glass in front, also touching to her mouth. Accept any signal behavior she uses such as move head, vocalize.

So that's what it is!

Tying the feeling & action of spoon & cup to experience at mouth.

Guide a bit.

Ask "More" Guiding hands in more sign.

FINISHING

Cue Erica to hold damp washcloth to wipe her face, then wipe face & hands. Tell her "All done," guiding hands in approximation of finish sign.
Cue with hands to each side of trunk when you pick her up. We expect all cues will also be verbal and that strong intonation will accompany cues.

Touch washcloth to face as cue.

All done!

Guide a bit.

Cue with touch to sides prior to picking up.

FIGURE 9.5.
Situational Script for a Multiply Handicapped Child

Source: *A Process Teaching Approach Applied to Mealtimes: Derived from the Individual Educational Plans of Two Multihandicapped Children* by N.M. Fieber. Omaha: Meyer Children's Rehabilitation Institute, 1981. (unpublished)

FIGURE 9.6

Procedure for Analyzing Child Behaviors as to Communication Intent

Eliciting Situation	Child's Signal	Function	Meaning to Adult
1. Child for long period in chair.	Fuss and extend	Personal—unhappy, uncomfortable	He wants out of chair
2. Adult offers verbal cues "Want out?" Touch to child's sides.	Arm movement & head movement	Instrumental Responsive	He means yes, he wants out
3. Adult guides child through favored activity e.g. pat-a-cake. Pauses, asks "more?" Touches child's hand.	Child gives eye contact, smiles, moves hands to adult's hand.	Instrumental Responsive	He wants to play patacake again
4. Adult activates See "N" Say, pauses, says, "more?"	Child hits at See "N" Say	Instrumental Responsive	He wants me to activate it again
5. Child is bounced on back on ball. Adult asks "more" and moves ball as cue.	Child kicks, kicks and smiles, kicks and smiles and vocalizes and gives eye contact.	Instrumental Responsive	He wants to bounce again
6. Adult places child on tummy on ball, then begins to rock child.	Fuss	Personal—unhappy	He doesn't like this.
Mom takes child's hand forward & sings, "See Saw" as rocked on ball.	Child stops fuss, smiles and lifts head slightly	Personal, OK	This way is OK. He feels safe with his mom.

SOURCE: Based upon recording tool developed by Nancy Fieber for use in Parent Instruction in Infant Development Program. Omaha: Meyer Children's Rehabilitation Institute.

shown some interest. Barriers may be simply pieces of furniture placed in the room.

Subsequent Task: Following the accomplishment of object pursuit around barriers in immediate situations, the child should be able to learn to search systematically for objects played with and left alone as much as an hour earlier (and, eventually, several hours earlier). This degree of memory indicates that the child is using object names to mediate actions in time. He may not be able to tell you what he is looking for. Once he finds it, however, he knows he has accomplished what he set out to do. This behavior is the culmination of the sensorimotor stage and serves as a transition to the initial phases of the preoperational functioning.

Task 10: Examining and Relating Objects

Terminal Objective: This category of spatial relationship activities involves two accomplishments: examining objects in such a way as to note different parts and bringing together functionally related objects in a manner that indicates understanding of the conventional functional relationships.

Rationale: Accomplishment of these two behaviors may be monitored by observing a child's schemes (movements and actions with objects) in relation to objects. These schemes are typically observed before the child displays understanding of action and object names. Demonstration and training in functional use of objects forms one of the bridges between sensorimotor "cognitive" and language developments.

Conditions and Task Sequence—Child Characteristics: Examination of objects typically begins during the subperiod of secondary circular reactions. This coincides with the solution of single-screen object permanence problems and the use of attached tools in the means-end sequence. Conventional, functional object use typically begins during the coordination of secondary circular reactions subperiod. Functional use is then generalized across more complex combinations of objects through the remaining subperiod. The beginning of functional use typically follows the abil-

TABLE 9.12. Task Summary 8: Operational Causality

Task Description	Response Description	Criteria/Specific Commentary
Check reinforcement value of stimuli.		
Level A Actions to prolong interesting events. Teacher performs a spectacle such as swinging a toy, spinning a top, or rocking the child, playing peek-a-boo or pat-a-cake.	Levels of responding: 1. Child responds in some way when the spectacle stops; it may be a foot kick, hitting, hand on table, or vocalizing.	Teacher selects most useful future behavior for the child and requires that behavior from the child before she reproduces a desired spectacle. Once the child uses the gesture upon seeing the object used in the spectacle or the person who produced the spectacle, she has developed expressive communicative response. At this level it is likely to be limited to perhaps one or two events.
Teacher initiates a familiar spectacle or game as described above and stops abruptly.	2. Child attempts to restart the activity with an action that is part of the game.	While this type of responding initially occurs in only one or two situations, with repeated contingent experience it will become a generalized strategy for acting in the environment.
Level B Actions to reinstate interesting spectacles.		There is not a correct or incorrect response in this series, rather different responses indicate different levels of understanding on the part of the child.
Teacher presents some type of mechanical toy (wind-up toy, jack-in-the-box, etc.) but initially does not permit the child to see the means by which it is activated.	Levels of responding: 1. Child touches the object or the teacher's hand as a gesture to the teacher to make the event happen again. (Teacher should do so this time, showing the child how it was activated.)	1. Subperiod of secondary circular reactions.
	2. Child makes the mechanical toy perform its activity manually. (Child should be allowed to do so.)	2. Subperiod of coordination of secondary circular reactions.
	3. Child hands object back to the teacher and waits.	3. Subperiod of tertiary circular reactions.
	4. Child explores for a way to activate the toy.	4. The child does not have to succeed but merely try, since many toys are very difficult to activate. The most difficult type of toy is one which requires combining events such as inserting a key into the toy and then turning it. This solution does not come about until the sixth subperiod.
	5. Child attempts to imitate means for activating the toy.	

Table 9.13 Task Summary 9: Localization of Objects in Space

Task Description	Response Description	Criteria/Specific Commentary
Check the reinforcement value of the stimuli. *Level A* Alternate glancing between objects. Teacher presents two interesting visual stimuli in front of the child, holding them about 12 inches apart.	Child switches gaze from one visual stimulus to another 4–5 times in 10 seconds.	This achievement typically follows in sequence the development of visual tracking. Its occurrence denotes a significant development in sensory organization skills—that of voluntary control over visual attention. The younger infant has difficulty selecting what stimuli to look at and can frequently shift her attention only by closing out stimuli altogether.
Localization of an object by its sound: Teacher presents auditory stimulus outside of the child's visual field.	Child turns and focuses gaze on object.	This objective was discussed in more detail in the sensory organization sequence.
Anticipation of trajectory of an object moved behind a screen: Teacher: (1) selects an object that the child has tracked visually, (2) shows the child the object, (3) begins moving it in a horizontal plane behind an opaque screen, and (4) then moves the object out from behind the screen on the other side. The teacher should begin the trajectory of the object at least 8–10 inches from the first side of the screen and keep an even pace of movement throughout the maneuver. This should always be done from the same direction (i.e., right to left) until the child is responding correctly.	Child tracks the object to the point of disappearance and then immediately shifts gaze to the other side of screen. The child may not do this on the first trial but begins to after several presentations.	The child has reached criterion level of responding when she anticipates the trajectory on at least 4 of 5 opportunities on 5 occasions for each direction used.
If child does not shift gaze immediately, a sound cue may be used to draw her attention to the other side of the screen.	Child shifts gaze when sound cue is provided.	Continue activity until child shifts gaze to other end of screen without a sound cue. Once child is shifting gaze correctly without a sound cue, the same task can be presented with trajectories that follow other directions—left to right etc.

ity to search in the two-screen situations and more complex tool use (use of the vertical string).

Subsequent Tasks: The "appropriate" functional use of objects—such as using a cup to drink from or stirring with a spoon in a cup—systematically precedes evidence of the understanding of the object's name. Do not be unduly constrained, however, by the word *appropriate*. In a given context, for example

TABLE 9.13. (CONTINUED)

Task Description	Response Description	Criteria/Specific Commentary
Level B Following trajectory of a rapidly falling object. Teacher selects an object in which the child has shown interest. Teacher holds the object above the child's head and calls the child's attention to the object.	Child looks up at the object.	
Teacher drops object in such a way that it makes very little noise when dropped. (This may be because it is a "quiet" object such as a ball or paper or aluminum foil or because it falls on a padded surface.)	Child follows the trajectory of the object to the point where it disappears, such as below the table surface and then moves to look for it. The child may locate it visually or with a pointing response, or behave in some consistent manner from opportunity to opportunity so that the teacher is confident that the child is trying to locate the object.	This behavior is most likely to be seen as the child plays with objects and drops them. While we would establish an arbitrary criterion of demonstrating the behavior on 4 of 5 trials on 5 occasions, when we see the child use the strategy of visually pursuing and then using that information to locate a fallen object, we are confident that the child has reached an appropriate level of generalization of the response.
Level C Motoric pursuit of a moving object. Level 1 Teacher takes an object with which the child has been playing and moves it behind the child. The teacher moves the object in such a way that the child visually follows the object for a portion of the trajectory.	Child searches with her hand behind herself and retrieves the object or rotates her trunk about 45° in the direction of the object and retrieves the object.	Criterion performance means the child retrieves the object when it is moved to either side on 2 of 3 opportunities (for each side) on 5 occasions. This problem is at about the same level of complexity as the object permanence problem with one screen.
Level 2 Teacher takes an object with which the child has been playing and moves it behind the child in such a way that she cannot visually pursue the object during the movement.	The child is correct if she rotates her trunk or actually turns around and retrieves the object. She may turn in either direction.	Criterion performance means the child retrieves the object on 2 of 3 opportunities when it is moved to each side on 5 occasions. This problem is at about the same level of complexity as the object permanence problem with two screens.
Level D Pursuit of objects around barriers. Level 1: Transparent barriers. Teacher takes an object child has been playing with and moves it behind a transparent barrier (such as plexiglass	Child moves (creeps or walks) around barrier and retrieves the object within 10–15 seconds. (For a child whose movement is very slow, a longer period may	Criterion performance means the child moves around a variety of barriers to obtain an object on 4 of 5 opportunities on 5 occasions. Some of these op-

TABLE 9.13. (CONTINUED)

Task Description	Response Description	Criteria/Specific Commentary
screen) situated behind a chair, that the child can see under but cannot crawl under.	be allowed but the teacher should feel confident that the child is pursuing the object all along.)	portunities may be observed incidently during the course of play.
Level 2: Opaque barriers. Teacher takes an object that the child has been playing with and moves it behind an opaque barrier such as a door or table or chair that the child cannot see under.	Child moves (creeps or walks, etc.) around barrier and retrieves the object within 10–15 seconds.	Criterion is same as that for Level D1.

when playing with hats, a cup or bowl might make an appropriate hat. At the culmination of this objective, we hope to observe the child engaging in pretend play with a variety of objects in a variety of situations. The pretend play at this point generally will be a single action. The child may do a series of things but they may not relate to one another functionally.

Comments: In the "relating objects" task sequence, we begin by observing the child to see if he examines objects by turning them over, poking fingers in holes, or feeling individual parts. When children at this point in their development do not examine objects, modeling that behavior produces little change in the child's behavior. Imitation skills have not been developed adequately. A better method to teach examining and other complex motor schemes is simply to provide the child with many different objects. These might include different containers, different kinds of paper or cloth, balls, pieces of yarn, and small toys which have movable but firmly attached parts. As the child shows evidence of trying out new schemes with objects, the teacher can begin to use the familar schemes to initiate motor imitation activities. Then, slight variations on these familiar movements are introduced to expand the child's repertoire to include relating two objects (a stick and a xylophone, a cup and spoon, a crayon and paper, and sliding a car with wheels on a surface, for example).

In Figure 9.7, Uzgiris and Hunt (1975) depict the developmental hierarchy of schemes for relating to objects. Functional use of objects corresponds to socially instigated actions (item *h*). If a child is deficient in those earlier, more basic behaviors for manipulating objects, he will not be successful in learning to use objects functionally.

TABLE 9.14 Task Summary 10: Examining and Relating Objects

Task Description	Response Description	Criteria/Specific Commentary
Check reinforcement value of stimuli. Recognition of reverse side of objects. Teacher positions a desired object in an upside-down orientation and observes for appropriate child behavior.	Child grasps an object which has a definite front and back, or top and bottom (i.e. doll, baby bottle, cup) and turns it to the "right side" or examines the object by turning it over several times.	This behavior should be observed with at least 10 different objects before one is confident that the child has this scheme well established. The 10 occasions may be accounted for over a period of time.
Relate functionally related objects. Teacher presents 2 functionally related objects such as cup and spoon, drum and drumstick, close to each other.	Child relates the 2 objects in an appropriate manner, stirring in the cup, hitting the drum, feeding a doll a bottle, etc.	Criterion level of responding would be for the child to relate appropriately 10 different pairs of objects in a functionally appropriate manner. The 10 occasions may be accumulated over a period of time.

FIGURE 9.7
Developmental Hierarchy of Schemes for Relating to Objects

Name:
Birthdate:
Date of Examination:

Schemes Shown	For Example:	1 Rattle	2 Doll	3 Plastic Fish	4 Foil	. . .	15
a. Holding		___	___	___	___	. . .	___
b. Mouthing		___	___	___	___	. . .	___
c. Visual inspection		___	___	___	___	. . .	___
d. Simple motor schemes:							
1. Hits or pats with hand		___	___	___	___	. . .	___
2. Hits surface with object		___	___	___	___	. . .	___
3. Hits two together		___	___	___	___	. . .	___
4. Shakes		___	___	___	___	. . .	___
5. Waves		___	___	___	___	. . .	___
Other:		___	___	___	___	. . .	___
e. Examining							
f. Complex motor schemes:							
1. Slides		___	___	___	___	. . .	___
2. Crumples		___	___	___	___	. . .	___
3. Swings		___	___	___	___	. . .	___
4. Tears or stretches		___	___	___	___	. . .	___
5. Rubs or pats		___	___	___	___	. . .	___
Other:		___	___	___	___	. . .	___
g. "Letting go" actions:							
1. Drops		___	___	___	___	. . .	___
2. Throws		___	___	___	___	. . .	___
Other:		___	___	___	___	. . .	___
h. Socially instigated actions:							
1. Drinks		___	___	___	___	. . .	___
2. Wears		___	___	___	___	. . .	___
3. Drives		___	___	___	___	. . .	___
4. Builds		___	___	___	___	. . .	___
5. Hugs		___	___	___	___	. . .	___
6. Dresses		___	___	___	___	. . .	___
7. Sniffs		___	___	___	___	. . .	___
8. Making "walk"		___	___	___	___	. . .	___
Other:		___	___	___	___	. . .	___
i. Showing		___	___	___	___	. . .	___
j. Naming		___	___	___	___	. . .	___
(List names used by infant)							

SOURCE: *Assessment in Infancy: Ordinal Scales of Psychological Development,* by I. Uzgiris & J. McV. Hunt. Urbana: University of Illinois Press, 1975, p. 221.

Task 11: *Container Play*

Terminal Objective: The terminal objective for container play (at the sensorimotor level of development) is that the child continue placing objects into a container or place nested containers together until the play sequence is completed (i.e., all beads in a cup; all cups properly nested).

Rationale: Container play is an activity in which the young child frequently engages spontaneously.

Often mothers of toddlers describe their children as getting into cupboards and playing with pots and pans for long periods of time. The gradual increase in the number of objects the child will place into containers relates to the ability to work with more materials (greater levels of distraction) without losing sight of the initial task. The development of dumping out filled containers represents the child's functional understanding of gravity. This concept forms the basis for much active experimenting at the sensori-motor and preoperational levels.

Conditions and Task Sequence—Child Characteristics: This sequence of container play typically begins during the subperiod of coordination of secondary circular reactions. The child consistently searches for hidden objects before he shows reliable interest in container play. Progression to the point of placing large numbers of objects into containers is not accomplished until the end of the sensorimotor period. When working on container play objectives, the teacher should remember that the first step is *taking objects out of a container one at a time.* We have no simple explanation for this; it is simply an observation. At this point, try to give the child manipulation experience with a variety of containers: cups, boxes, pots, bowls, measuring cups, boxes with holes in the sides, or cellophane windows. Demonstrate placing objects into various containers and allow the child to take the objects out. Expect imitation of putting *in* only after numerous demonstrations of putting an object into a container. In the development of container play, the severely handicapped child is likely to remain for several months at the level of putting only one or two objects in a container (even if many objects are available) and then taking them out again, one at a time. Usually after several months, the child begins to place all of the available objects in the container, with 12 being the approximate limit. Up to this point, the child typically places objects in and takes them out of a container one at a time. After an experience with putting a series of objects into a container one by one, the child will group several objects together and then pick them up and put them into a container. Next the child learns to dump the contents rather than taking objects out one at a time.

This gradual skill building also occurs with putting pegs in a pegboard and pieces into a formboard. However, it is often ignored when teachers try to teach container and form concepts. When the objective includes using a covered container, another frequently ignored prerequisite is object permanence. We often meet resistance from a child when he is asked to place objects in a container he cannot see into. If the child is without object permanence, objects cease to exist once he no longer sees or touches them.

Materials: Again, the primary characteristics to consider when selecting objects to go into containers (and the containers themselves) is that the child be interested in them. Experience with a variety of containers and materials should be provided.

Subsequent task: Culmination of the container play sequence means that the child is prepared for more difficult tasks involving matching objects according to specific physical characteristics and, later, sorting. This takes us into the preoperational period.

Comments: For the child with moderate to severe physical involvement of the upper extremities, container play does not make a good deal of sense as an educational activity. The physical constraints make it unlikely that the child will do the activity with any facility. The time involved does not seem worthwhile. It is possible, however, to demonstrate filling and dumping to the child and give him the opportunity to indicate with a signal when there are still objects to go into a container or when it is filled and perhaps even tip it over himself. Again the task difficulty is slightly increased by this modification.

With formboard activities, you may adapt the task by putting handles on the form pieces or having the child indicate their placement and then helping him place the form. It is not necessary to physically place something in order to know its correct location. For the child who cannot physically indicate the location for an object, we can match the form to different locations and ask him to use a yes/no system for indicating whether the match is correct or incorrect.

A note of caution is in order here. You may find that a child, responding correctly to the task, begins to say yes to incorrect locations and no to correct locations on very familiar items. The child usually giggles after the "error" and the teacher has the impression that the child is teasing. While this behavior can be annoying, it is important to recognize the achievement it heralds. The child is now sure of the correct response and can make intentional errors for their effect on the teacher or parents. Before becoming annoyed, consider the importance of this development for a child who has few opportunities to engage in the usual forms of teasing available to pre-schoolers. This kind of teasing may occur in any of the task situations described thus far. It is likely to occur as the child advances to more complex cognitive and language concepts, and it is probably a good indication that he is ready for concepts at the preoperational level. However, so as not to encourage the child it is best to say, "No," and correct the response matter-of-factly.

IMITATION AND SCHEMES FOR RELATING TO OBJECTS

In their sensorimotor assessment series, Uzgiris and Hunt (1975) include identification of schemes in relation to objects and verbal and gestural imitation among the skill sequences. These sequences are two extremely important developments during the sensorimotor period. In this book, these two developments are discussed and strategies for training them are described in chapter 5. They are extremely important prerequisites to later cognitive and language development.

TABLE 9.15. Task Summary 11: Container Play

Task Description	Response Description	Criteria/Specific Commentary
Check reinforcement value of stimuli.		
Level A Stacking blocks	Levels of responding:	
Teacher provides some blocks and demonstrates stacking them.	1. Child combines blocks in air. 2. Child stacks 2 blocks. 3. Child stacks 3 blocks. 4. Child stacks 4 or more blocks.	Step (1) usually precedes putting objects into a container and usually comes after child has started putting 1–3 blocks into a container. This step usually follows child putting a series of 3 or more objects into a container.
Sequence of steps in putting objects into a container and removing them.	Levels of responding:	
Teacher presents objects and a container into which the object may be placed and demonstrates putting objects in and taking them out.	1. Child takes 1 or 2 objects out of container 1 at a time. 2. Child places 1 or 2 objects into the container singly and takes them out singly. 3. Child places a series of 3 objects into container and then takes them out singly. 4. Child places a series of 4 or more objects into a container 1 at a time and opens the container to try to remove the objects. 5. Child picks up a couple of objects at a time and places them into container and will place as many as a dozen objects into the container. Removes the objects by dumping the container if she physically can or up-ending the container if it is too big for dumping.	Children typically spend a great deal of time at each of these levels. The teacher will find the best teaching strategy is to provide opportunities for playing with appropriate materials and demonstrate responding at a step just ahead of child's current level. This is the most advanced level of container play and is typically accomplished before the child is ready for formboards or form boxes.
Level B Arrangement of nested objects in a series.		
Teacher presents a series of 4 nested containers (round containers initially).	Child places smaller container inside larger for 3 insertions. However, she does not necessarily get the 2 closest in size together. If she tried to nest all 4 and made an incorrect insertion, she cannot correct it by removing only the incorrect piece; she must take all pieces apart, start again, and is likely to make the same error over.	By the end of the sensorimotor period the child may have started using a systematic strategy for placing 3–4 pieces together but working successfully with more than 4 at one time is an indication that the child has started the transition to the preoperational period.

SUMMARY

In summary, by the end of the sensorimotor period of intelligence (as conceptualized by Piaget), we see a child who has accomplished a number of very important steps in cognitive growth. As Piaget puts it:

The elaboration of the universe by sensorimotor intelligence constitutes the transition from a state in which objects are centered about a self which believes it directs them, although completely unaware of itself as subject, to a state in which self is placed, at least practically, in a stable world conceived as independent of personal activity. (1954, p. 395)

For the child, the culmination of stage six in the sensorimotor period has the following results. In the area of *object permanence* the child now sees objects as things separate from himself, subject to movement in space independent of himself. He still has not learned all there is to know about the invariant properties of objects. These refinements come during the preoperational and concrete operational periods. But the foundation for concepts such as conservation lies in the sensorimotor concept of object permanence (Flavell, 1963).

Stage six sensorimotor behavior with respect to *causality* results in two new achievements: "the child can, through representation, infer a cause, given only its effect; and foresee an effect, given its cause" (Flavell, 1963).

Imitation is also influenced by the stage six development of representation. The child begins to imitate objects as well as persons. This includes combinations of behaviors he cannot see himself perform. Also in the culmination of the sensorimotor period, the child begins to demonstrate what Piaget calls "deferred *imitation:* the child reproduces an absent model through memory" (Flavell, 1963, p. 126).

Spatial concepts for the child in stage six mean "he is able to keep a running tab on his own movements in space, internally representing his own previous displacements relative to those of other bodies. And . . . he is able to represent the invisible displacement of external objects" (Flavell, 1963, p. 141).

Thus, the accomplishments of the sensorimotor period result in a child who can, not only through trial-and-error but also through representation, solve problems involving differentiation of cause and effect and who has begun to construct an external reality through the beginnings of the concepts of object, space, and time permanence.

The next phase in development, in Piaget's conceptualization, is the subperiod of preoperational thought. This superiod extends from 1.5–2 years (the sensorimotor period) to 6–7 years (the beginnings of concrete operations). The primary accomplishment of this period is the child's growing independence of the need for the physical presence of objects and events in order to act. During the preoperational period, the child becomes capable of symbolic functioning whereby he can assign "a signifier (a word, an image, etc.) to objects and events which symbolizes a perceptually absent event" (Flavell, 1963, p. 151) and thus act upon them in their absence. In the sensorimotor period the child behaved in such a way as to acknowledge the permanence of objects. In the preoperational period the child can extend that concept to more active manipulations of the environment.

REFERENCES

Bayley, N. *Manual for the Bayley Scales of Infant Development.* New York: Psychological Corp., 1969.

Brassel, W.R., & Dunst, C.J. Comparison of two procedures for fostering the development of the object construct. *American Journal of Mental Deficiency,* 1976, *80,* 523–528.

Bower, T.G.R. *A primer of infant development.* San Francisco: W.H. Freeman, 1977.

Bricker, W.A. Identifying and modifying behavioral deficits. *American Journal of Mental Deficiency.* 1970, *75,* 16–21.

Cromwell, R.L. A social learning approach to mental retardation. In N.R. Ellis (Ed.), *Handbook of mental deficiency.* New York: McGraw-Hill, 1963.

Duncan, D., Sbardellati, E., Maheady, L., & Sainato, D. Nondiscriminating assessment of severely physically handicapped individuals. *Journal of the Association for the Severely Handicapped,* 1981, *6(2),* 17–22.

Dunst, C.J. *An early cognitive-linguistic intervention strategy.* Morganton, N.C.: Western Carolina Center, 1977.

Flavell, J.H. *The developmental psychology of Jean Piaget.* Princeton, N.J.; Von Nostrand, 1963.

Furth, H.G. *Piaget and knowledge: Theoretical foundations.* Englewood Cliffs, N.J.: Prentice-Hall, 1969.

Hebb, D.O. *The organization of behavior.* New York: Wiley, 1949.

Hunt, J. McV. *Intelligence and experience.* New York: Ronald Press, 1961.

Ilmer, S., Rynders, J., Sinclair, S., & Helfrich, D. Assessment of object permanence in severely handicapped students as a function of motor and prompting variables. *Journal of the Association for the Severely Handicapped,* 1981, *6,* 30–40.

Kahn, J.V. Relationship of Piaget's sensorimotor period to language acquisition of profoundly retarded students. *American Journal of Mental Deficiency,* 1975, *79,* 640–643.

Kahn, J.V. Acceleration of object permanence with severely and profoundly retarded children. *AAESPH Review,* 1978, *3,* 15–22.

Kahn, J.V. Applications of the Piagetian literature to severely and profoundly mentally retarded persons. *Mental Retardation,* 1979, *17,* 273–280.

Karlan, G.R. The effects of preference for objects and repeated measures upon the assessed level of object permanence and means/end ability in severely handicapped students. *Journal of the Association for the Severely Handicapped*, 1980, *5*, 174–193.

Langer, J. *Theories of development*. New York: Holt, Rinehart & Winston, 1969.

Lobato, D., Barrera, R.D., & Feldman, R.S. Sensorimotor functioning and prelinguistic communication of severely and profoundly retarded individuals. *American Journal of Mental Deficiency*, 1981, *85*, 489–496.

Piaget, J. *The construction of reality in the child*. New York: Ballantine, 1954.

Piaget, J. *The origins of intelligence in children*. New York: W.W. Norton, 1963.

Premack, D. Reversibility of the reinforcement relation. *Science*, 1962, *136*, 255–257.

Robinson, C. A strategy for assessing motorically-impaired infants. In I. Uzgiris & J. McV. Hunt (Eds.), *Research with Scales of Psychological Development in Infancy*. Urbana: University of Illinois Press, 1984.

Seligman, M.E.P. Helplessness: On depression, death and development. San Francisco: W.H. Freeman, 1975.

Silverstein, A.B., Brownlee, L., Hubbell, M. & McLain, R.E. Comparison of two sets of Piagetian scales with severely and profoundly retarded children. *American Journal of Mental Deficiency*, 1975, *80*, 292–297.

Stephens, B. The appraisal of cognitive development. In B. Stephens (Ed.), *Training the developmentally young*. New York: John Day, 1971.

Stephens, B. A Piagetian approach to curriculum development for the severely, profoundly and multiply handicapped. In E. Sontag, J. Smith, & N. Certo (Eds.), *Educational programming for the severely and profoundly handicapped*. Reston, Va.: Council for Exceptional Children, 1977.

Uzgiris, I. Organization of sensorimotor intelligence. In M. Lewis (Ed.), *Origins of intelligence: Infancy and early childhood*. New York: Plenum Press, 1976.

Uzgiris, I., & Hunt, J. McV. *Instrument for assessing infant psychological development*. Urbana: University of Illinois Press, 1966.

Uzgiris, I., & Hunt, J. McV. *Assessment in infancy: Ordinal Scales of Psychological Development*. Urbana: University of Illinois Press, 1975.

Watson, J.S. Cognitive-perceptual development in infancy: Settings for the seventies. *Merrill-Palmer Quarterly*, 1971, *17*, 139–152.

Watson, J.S., & Ramey, C.T. Reactions to response contingent stimulation early in infancy, *Merrill-Palmer Quarterly*, 1972, *18*, 219–227.

White, B.L., Castle, P., & Held, R. Observations on the development of visually directed reaching. *Child Development*, 1964, *35*, 349–364.

White, B.L., Held, R., & Castle, P. Experience in early human development. Part I. Observations on the development of visually directed reaching. In J. Hellmuth (Ed), *Exceptional infant, Vol. I: The normal infant*. New York: Brunner/Mazel, 1967.

White, O.R., Adaptive performance objectives. In W. Sailor, B. Wilcox, & L. Brown (Eds.), *Methods of instruction for severely handicapped students*. Baltimore: Paul H. Brookes, 1980.

Wohlheuter, M.J., & Sindberg, R.M. Longitudinal development of object permanence in mentally retarded children: An exploratory study. *American Journal of Mental Deficiency*, 1974, *79*, 513–518.

REFERENCE NOTES

1. Fieber, N.M. *Movement in communication and language development of deaf-blind children*. Paper presented at National Deaf-Blind Workshop of Physical Occupational and Recreational Therapists, Dallas, August 1975.

2. Fieber, N.M. *The profoundly handicapped child assessing sensorimotor and communication abilities*. Paper presented at Nebraska Conference for Teachers of Severely/Profoundly Handicapped and Deaf-Blind Children. Cozad, Nebraska, 1978.

3. Ficociello, C., Stoddard, A., & Ogden, J. *A cognitive approach to prevocational and daily living skills training*. Denver: Mountain Plains Regional Center of Services to Deaf Blind Children, 1978.

4. Finkelstein, M.W., & Ramey, C.T. *Learning to control the environment in infancy*. Unpublished manuscript, University of North Carolina, 1976.

5. Fieber, N.M. *A process teaching approach applied to mealtimes: Derived from the individual education plans of two multihandicapped children*. Unpublished manuscript, Meyer Children's Rehabilitation Institute, Omaha, 1981.

In classrooms for the moderately and severely handicapped, you often find a language period scheduled in which the teacher is the only one who speaks in sentences or even uses words. In other classes, students speak or sign during a structured teaching period, but are nonexpressive in times of actual need. Despite the prevalent absence of communication skills, our goal is to teach all handicapped individuals to communicate, if not by voice, then by manual language or through the use of communication boards, symbol systems, and yes-no motions.

When faced with students severely deficient even in the prerequisites for communication, what can be done? How do you facilitate the emergence of functional speech in a young child who appears lethargic, takes no interest in toys or people, and seldom makes noise except to cry? If allowed, this child will spend most of the day rocking or waving his hands in repetitive, meaningless motions. How do you teach the adolescent who speaks in phrases but primarily imitates others and who only rarely demonstrates comprehension of simple requests? What about the student whose extensive motor problems prevent speech? While most special educators feel that all handicapped persons can learn some form of communication, however simple, it is the teacher on the front lines who must determine when and how to start teaching communication. Recently a few authors have provided clear guidelines for making these complex decisions. Some of these choices include (a) whether to focus upon language prerequisites (attending, imitation, etc.) or to begin with expression of wants; (b) whether to teach a vocal or nonvocal system of communication; (c) what nonvocal system to select if this route is chosen; and (d) what vocabulary to teach (Alpert, 1980; Musselwhite & St. Louis, 1982; Sailer, Guess, Goetz, Schuler, Utley, & Baldwin, 1980; Waldo, Barnes, & Berry, 1981). Generally these decisions depend upon how much schooling time is left for a student and what communication capabilities, if any, he or she reliably performs.

In chapter 10, Diane Bricker describes a sequence of steps for training verbal behavior. This sequence is not a simple conglomeration of other language programs nor is it an untested review of the literature. Instead, the training steps reflect years of application and revision on populations of moderately and severely handicapped young children, first at the J.F. Kennedy Experimental School at George Peabody College, then in the Debbie School at the Mailman Center for Child Development of the University of Miami, and finally in the Center on Human Development at the University of Oregon. This chapter traces a developmental sequence of skills leading to vocal communication. The order of instruction is dictated by the interdependence of the skills in the sequence. This chapter gives a striking impression of

Introduction to Chapters 10 and 11

the complexity of language skills as contrasted with the common view that these skills are simple, easily developed, and necessarily present in all children.

Bricker's language program is particularly relevant for younger handicapped children, as is the *Environmental Language Program* developed by MacDonald and Horstmeier (1978). Other developmentally based programs leading to speech include one by Kent (1974) and another by Stremel and Waryas (Stremel & Waryas, 1974; Waryas & Stremel, 1978) and will serve as useful references.

A four-part language program by Guess, Sailor, and Baer (1976) details a validated 60-step training sequence which focuses primarily upon more practical expressive abilities. Unlike the programs just mentioned, the *Functional Speech and Language Program* takes a remedial approach, teaching comprehension, for example, only if it is not already acquired once expression is taught—an order reversed from a developmental approach but still supported by research (Cuvo & Riva, 1980; Guess, Sailor & Baer, 1978; Keller & Bucher, 1980).

Chapter 11 describes nonvocal approaches to communication along with the vast array of related programmatic decisions. Teaching a person to communicate nonvocally is not simply a matter of choosing between manual signs or pictures. Jan Allaire and Joan Miller address the basic considerations for matching the type of augmentative system to the particular student, for selecting a response mode, for developing instructional procedures, and for choosing a functional vocabulary. Their background in language with the moderately and severely handicapped population provides a firm empirical support for this discussion.

Neither chapter alone nor both together will equip you to teach communication skills. The topic of communication in the severely handicapped is too complex for such brevity to suffice. However, their coverage, along with the references cited, furnishes a rich resource of validated methods you are encouraged to pursue and apply.

REFERENCES

Alpert, C. Procedures for determining the optimal nonspeech mode with the autistic child. In R.L. Schiefelbusch (Ed.), *Nonspeech language and communication*. Baltimore: University Park Press, 1980.

Cuvo, A.J., & Riva, M.T. Generalization and transfer between comprehension and production: A comparison of retarded and nonretarded persons. *Journal of Applied Behavior Analysis*, 1980, *13*, 315–331.

Guess, D., Sailor, W., & Baer, D. *Functional speech and language training for the severely handicapped*. Lawrence, Kans.: H & H Enterprises, 1976.

Guess, D., Sailor, W., & Baer, D.M. Children with limited language. In R.L. Schiefelbusch (Ed.), *Language intervention strategies*. Baltimore: University Park Press, 1978.

Keller, M.F., & Bucher, B. The influence of receptive training on rate of productive language acquisition in mentally retarded children. *Behavior Research of Severe Developmental Disabilities*, 1980, *1*, 93–103.

Kent, L. *Language acquisition program*. Champaign, Ill. Research Press, 1974.

MacDonald, J.D., & Horstmeier, D. *Environmental language intervention program*. Columbus, Ohio: Charles E. Merrill, 1978.

Musselwhite, C.R., & St. Louis, K.W. *Communication programming for the severely handicapped: Vocal and non-vocal strategies*. Houston: College Hall Press, 1982.

Sailor, W., Guess, D., Goetz, L., Schuler, A., Utley, B., & Baldwin, M. Language and severely handicapped persons. In W. Sailor, B. Wilcox, & L. Brown, (Eds.), *Methods of instruction for severely handicapped students*. Baltimore: Paul H. Brookes, 1980.

Stremel, K., & Waryas, C. A behavioral psycholinguistic approach to language training. *American Speech and Hearing Monographs*, 1974, *18*, 96–214.

Waldo, L.J., Barnes, K.J., & Berry, G.W. *Total communication checklist and assessment*. Lawrence, Kans.: Kansas Neurological Institute, 1981.

Waryas, C.L., & Stremel-Campbell, K. Grammatic training for the language delayed child. In R.L. Schiefelbusch (Ed.), *Language intervention strategies*. Baltimore: University Park Press, 1978.

*This chapter was written by **Diane Bricker**, Center on Human Development, University of Oregon. Support for preparation of this chapter comes in part from Grant No. G008002235 from the Office of Special of Education, USOE.*

10

Early Communication: Development and Training

INTRODUCTION

This chapter is directed to any professional, paraprofessional, parent, or student involved in language programming with the developmentally young. *Developmentally young* in this context refers to two specific populations: (*a*) infants and children who have not acquired the early behaviors that appear to precede the acquisition of language, and (*b*) school-age severely handicapped children who have multiple problems that interfere with the acquisition of communication. The training sequence and content outlined here may not be appropriate for older severely handicapped learners. This program is child-oriented and assumes that intervention will occur while the child is in the early and formative period.

This chapter focuses on communication processes rather than only language or linguistic behavior. The terms *communication* and *language* are often incorrectly interchanged. *Communication* is more inclusive. It encompasses all behavior generally used for the transfer of information, be it social or informative, between a sender and receiver. There is controversy about the parameters of communication (for example, see deVilliers, in press) but for our purposes, *communication* is any gestural, vocal, or facial-body response used to control another's behavior or convey information. *Language* is a form of communication based on a referential or representational system. That is, language is a formal system that uses symbols, generally words, to stand for objects, people, and events (Bloom & Lahey, 1978).

Finally, the orientation of this chapter is pragmatic; it focuses on practical aspects of communication development and intervention and does not discuss controversies surrounding theories of language acquisition and training regimes.[1]

Rationale

The communication training program presented in this chapter has been derived from a synthesis of clin-

---

[1]For more theoretical discussions of psycholinguistic theory and application, see Dale, 1976; deVilliers and deVilliers, 1978; Morehead and Morehead, 1976; Schiefelbusch and Bricker, 1981.

ical experience, research, and relevant literature fo-cusing directly or indirectly on language interven-tion. This synthesis has led to a program rationale based on four assumptions:

1. The content of effective early communication programs must extend beyond formal linguistic behavior and attend to selected early sensorimotor and social-communication processes.
2. The developmental progression of communi-cation acquisition reported for nonhandicapped infants and young children provides useful guide-lines for designing a training sequence for com-municatively impaired children.
3. Program objectives can be reached most effi-ciently by flexible use of operant training tech-niques.
4. Programming should occur under conditions that are ecologically valid for the child. The primary emphasis should be on targeting responses that enhance the child's functional communication repertoire.

Program Content

Language deficits are a major handicapping condition associated with mental retardation (Bricker & Bricker, 1974). In addition, children with motor and sensory handicaps often have trouble acquiring and producing functional language. With the more seri-ously impaired infant and child, the basic deficits may extend to the underlying communicative, affec-tive, and cognitive processes. Controversy exists as to the relationship between the development of the language and sensorimotor development (Leonard, 1978).[2] However, from an interventionist's perspec-tive, it is apparent that language dysfunctions do not begin during the 2nd year. Language problems arise, in part, because the child has failed to develop the necessary foundation for acquisition of representa-tional behavior (Bricker & Carlson, 1981). Thus lan-guage intervention for the moderately to severely handicapped child should begin by focusing on early social-communication and sensorimotor responses. Therefore, this program includes selected sensorimo-tor and social-communication processes that appear to affect the acquisition of a functional communica-tion system.

Program Training Sequence

The second assumption which has shaped this train-ing program is that the developmental sequences

generally observed in nonhandicapped children cur-rently provide the most useful guidelines for de-signing a communication training sequence for handicapped children. It is reasonable to conclude that children typically follow general patterns of de-velopment because they are useful. Early learning appears to provide a necessary foundation for pro-gressively more complex behavior. As Piaget (1970) has argued, children do not arrive at the stage of for-mal operations through maturation alone. Rather, they seem to acquire new perceptions and more com-plex problem-solving abilities that produce gradual changes in cognitive organization and overt response patterns. This gradual change appears likely for com-munication acquisition as well. Therefore, it seems sensible to design a training program beginning with targeting simple response forms that can be gradually shaped into progressively more useful communica-tion behavior. In many instances these developmen-tal sequences are logical progressions.

Adopting training sequences that follow typical developmental progressions is useful for two rea-sons. First, attention to the typical development may alert us to behaviors that might otherwise be over-looked. For example, the reciprocal vocal behavior between many caregivers and their nonhandicapped infants may have important implications for the handicapped infant who does not engage in this behavior. Without attention to the nonhandicapped child's behavior, this and other potentially important behaviors could go unnoticed because they do not occur regularly in impaired infants. Second, develop-mental sequences map movement from response to response or level to level. Without such a map, train-ing regimes may be less systematic, increasing the possibility that certain response forms will be exclud-ed or inefficient training sequences followed. Cur-rently we do not have data proving that training pro-grams that follow typical developmental sequences are the most efficient or effective for handicapped children; however, given the available options, adop-tion of a typical developmental pattern seems to offer a most useful route.

Using typical developmental progressions for se-lecting training objectives does not require slavish adherence to those sequences. Even nonhandicapped children demonstrate great variety and individuality in growth and learning patterns. Instead, we use the typical communication development sequence as a general set of benchmarks adapted to the needs of individual children.

Instructional Strategies

Typical development provides valuable information for designing and sequencing program content; how-

---

[2]For different theories, see Bates 1979; Cromer, 1981; and Leonard, 1978.

ever, this information does not tell us how to teach this content. An effective behavioral technology has been developed for communication training. It includes attention to arrangement of antecedent events, objective descriptions of target responses, and delivery of salient consequences to provide appropriate feedback. In addition, many principles of effective programming such as task analyses, shaping, and prompting make communication training more effective.

Careful consideration should be given to the training tasks selected to reach a target objective. The goal should be to help the child acquire general strategies and concepts that can be used across different settings, people, and objects. Learning the label "cup" for only small white cups is not nearly as useful as being able to label all cylindrical containers with handles as cups regardless of size, color, texture, or location.

Selecting tasks with multiple targets is important for efficient training. Language activities can often be superimposed on the training of other skills. In some cases, this might be done by structuring communication training to coincide with learning a new motor or cognitive skill; for example, while rolling a ball, the child could be encouraged to label the ball as well as the action.

The strategies used in teaching the selected content of a program will account, in large measure, for the efficiency with which responses are acquired and in many instances whether responses are acquired at all.

Functional Programming

Our final assumption concerns the usefulness of the selected training objectives. That is, the training context, the personnel, and the selection of objectives should be guided by whether they will enhance the child's ability to communicate in the environment every day. Training activities should be conducted in settings where the communication is appropriate; for example, asking for juice during snack time. To assure that the objectives are functional for the child, the primary caregiver should be integrally involved. This helps us select communication targets that will enhance the child's efforts as well as enhance generalization of acquired responses.

Communication will become intrinsically rewarding if it provides the child with a means for obtaining desired objects, events, or people; that is, if it helps the child at least partially control the environment. (See chapter 9.) If a point and vocalization produces a cookie more quickly than crying, then the frequency of that gesture will increase and crying for cookies will decrease. This training program focuses on targeting those behaviors which will enhance communication in the child's social environment.

COMMUNICATION DEVELOPMENT

As we have said, the content for our communication training program is based on communication development in nonhandicapped infants and children. Thus we must describe the "normal" acquisition of communication skills. This description should help orient and organize program users. In particular, it should help you understand the inclusion of the selected content and the reason for the suggested sequence. In addition, P.L. 94-142 mandates placement of the handicapped child in the least restrictive environment. Successful mainstreaming requires, in part, knowledge of environmental expectations. Being familiar with typical communication behavior should help you design programs that maximize the possibility of the least restrictive placement for the handicapped child.

Although this chapter focuses on communication, the separation of behavior during early periods of development into discrete domains is artificial and does not reflect the interrelationships of affective, sensorimotor, and social-communicative responses (Saarni, 1978; Bricker & Carlson, 1981). We will assume their interrelatedness and recognize the artificiality of presenting communication as a singular line of development. In addition, you should recognize that development often occurs in parallel fashion and varies across children.

Early Vocal Development

During the first few months of an infant's life, vocal behavior is not like speech but is composed primarily of vowel-like sounds (Oller, Wieman, Doyle, & Ross, 1976). The infant seems to be learning to operate the sound production mechanisms and can produce noises and sounds that adults have difficulty imitating. The infant learns to differentiate vocal activity into "pleasurable" (i.e., cooing) and "distressful" (i.e., crying) vocalizations. At this early age, infants can discriminate or perceive differences between certain speech sounds and a number of non-speech variables such as duration, intensity, and pitch (Trehub, Bull, & Schneider, 1981).

Other behaviors that appear to precede language acquisition begin to develop at this early age. Infants learn to attend to objects in the environment and gaze at them for long periods of time. They learn to shift their gaze from object to object and turn their heads to locate an object. Around the 4th month, they begin to vocalize when they hear sounds produced by the caregiver. Infants also learn to locate sound sources at this stage. An indication that they are becoming aware of their social-communication environment is their apparent attempt to synchronize their activities or engage in actions similar to adults (Condon & Sander, 1974). For example, if an adult waves an arm, an infant, if watching, will often move his or her arm (Uzgiris & Hunt, 1975).

Between 7 and 10 months most infants become adept at vocalizing the same speech-like sounds repeatedly. This vocal behavior is babbling and can be reduplicated (e.g., "ba, ba, ba") or variegated (e.g., "ba, da, ta"). The relationship of babbling to the mastery of speech sounds is unclear (deVilliers & deVilliers, 1978). Nonetheless, it appears to offer opportunities to learn control of the vocal mechanism and to elicit feedback from the environment (Bricker, Ruder, & Vincent, 1976). Around the 10th to 11th month, the infant's babbling has many features of adult inflection. The force, quality, and pitch of vocal behavior are called *prosodic features,* and acquisition of early prosodic features coincides developmentally with the acquisition of speech sounds (Reese & Lipsitt, 1970). Prosodic features can be thought of as the "melody" of language, while the content or words are the "lyrics." Ruder and Smith (1974) suggest that prosodic features seem to be so basic a behavior that children, beginning with the acquisition of their first words to the time they are producing adult-like sentences, use subtle features of inflection as part of their communication behavior.

Early Social-Communication Development

Early social interactions between infants and their caregivers apparently provide a basis for the acquisition of language (Bruner, 1975). Through these social exchanges, infants acquire many skills needed when they begin to express meaning through language. In the first few months of life, the young child learns to attend to the mother's speech and in time to wait before responding to her utterances. By following her gaze, the infant can discover the mother's focus of attention and establish the same reference point. Likewise, the infant learns to direct the adult's gaze by visually focusing on objects to which the adult subsequently attends. Mothers often interpret their infant's intent by assigning meaning to the child's actions and vocal patterns. If the infant tries to retrieve a dropped teething ring by reaching and vocalizing, the attentive mother will help by getting the ring. Mothers also make it easier for their infants to interpret signals, both gestural and vocal, by standardizing certain action formats for games (e.g., peek-a-boo). These ritualized activities have a regular structure, giving the baby a chance to anticipate what the mother is going to do next and to align his or her attention.

Prior to 9 months, the baby's vocalizations and primitive gestures appear as unconventionalized schemes. That is, their form and purpose (or intent) are not mutually agreed upon by familiar persons (Bates, 1979). During this period, the child's signals often seem oriented more toward direct goal-attainment than social purposes. When the 7-month-old child plays with objects, his actions tend to be directed solely toward the objects themselves (e.g., banging two blocks together and then dropping them into a container) or solely toward a person (e.g., vocalizing and reaching toward the adult). Instances in which a person and an object are involved in a social exchange are rare (Bricker & Carlson, in press; Sugarman, 1978). Around 9 months, however, significant shifts are seen as infants start to coordinate actions with people and objects. As their behavior becomes coordinated, they are demonstrating the capacity for social tool use; they use a person as a means for obtaining an unreachable desired object and use an object to gain adult attention. A baby showing coordinated schemes is apt to look and point to a favorite toy beyond reach, shift his or her gaze to the adult, vocalize, and look back to the goal. If further social bidding is necessary, the baby might add a tug at the adult's clothing and then mark the toy with a vocal or hand gesture. Coordination is also apparent in the behavior of a baby who holds a toy up to the father, looks at him, gestures, and vocalizes. The father in turn takes the toy and vocalizes, looking at the baby. At the same time, important changes in the baby's communicative signals may be observed. Existing sound/gesture schemes gradually become more conventional. The meaning the baby is trying to convey through signals is more explicit and takes a form that can easily be interpreted by others (e.g., pointing to desired objects; calling for attention). Thus, by the end of the 1st year, the infant is increasingly capable of integrating social interactions with object schemes, using conventional gestures, and showing an interest in social interaction.

Development of Referential Language

After conventional sound/gesture schemes develop, the child makes the transition to early referential language, that is, uses words symbolically. Conventional communication becomes symbolic when the child realizes that a word (symbol) can be substituted for its referent for certain purposes, and the symbol and its referent are not one and the same. To be considered referential, a word must approximate mature forms phonetically and be appropriately used across a variety of contexts (e.g., "ca" is used for cars, including the family's car and the sound of a car moving down the street). Once referential capacities are developed, one word may serve several purposes for the child, including calling, greeting, protesting, labeling, and requesting (Dore, 1975).

Children's receptive language skills become more overt toward the end of the 1st year. They will stop and turn when their names are called, will stop when an adult says no, and will produce gestures with a familiar request, such as "Wave bye-bye." Although most children can produce a variety of sounds during their 1st year, it is not until the 2nd year that they produce conventional words. Studies of initial word acquisition suggests these words serve two broad functions for the child: social-communicative and referential. Social-communicative functions include requests, demands, greetings, and so forth, while referential language is used to name, classify, and comment on the world (Nelson, 1979).

The production of early words clearly shows the interrelated nature of early communication processes. That is, when the child says "car," the function as well as the referential meaning must be interpreted by the listener. The sequence of early word production suggests that young children focus on those aspects of the environment that hold the greatest saliency for them—that is, they talk about what they want, see, and do (Greenfield & Smith, 1976). In the early productions of young children, both overextension and underextension of word meaning have been reported (Bowerman, 1976). However, no consistent pattern has been reported, suggesting that word meaning acquisition may begin as a rather idiosyncratic undertaking (Nelson, 1978). Attention to salient aspects of the environment elicits words that are either in the child's repertoire or provided by the adult. The element or characteristic of the person, object, or event the child focuses on will, in part, determine how the word will be used subsequently and to what items or events the child will attach the word. Further, the types of lexical items used initially by children also vary. For example, Greenfield and Smith (1976) have reported the two children in their study initially predominantly used either entity words or relational words. Nelson (1973) found that children tended to be either expressive or referential, coinciding with the aspect of the environment their mothers stressed.

Since labels for persons, objects, actions, and events are arbitrary, a child's word acquisition depends on the label the parent provides. It has been suggested that parents provide labels "at an intermediate level of generality" (deVilliers & deVilliers, 1978). When indicating a cat to a young child, an intermediate term such as *kitty* or *cat* is offered instead of *Siamese* or *animal*. This strategy implies that the child's semantic understanding must be expanded downward to the more specific (e.g., *Siamese*) and upward to the more general (e.g., *animal*). The words a child initially acquires and the labels provided vary from family to family. However, acquisition of a single word for persons, objects, and events is obviously not sufficient. Both comprehension and production expansions and limitations will be necessary if the child is to proceed past primitive communication.

Between 18 to 24 months, most toddlers begin sequencing words (Prutting, 1979). Producing two-word utterances is generally considered the initial stage of syntactic development. Sequencing words implies that the child has a rudimentary organizational system that uses rules. These rules let the child convey intentions and be understood by members of the language community. Bellugi (1972) and others have shown that young children produce sentences on the basis of generative rules. That is, they learn that words are sequenced systematically rather than randomly. Many of the two-word utterances produced by young children can be classified as representing a variety of semantic relations. Brown (1973) reports that children whose mean length of utterance is between 1.0 and 2.0 words use the following semantic relations for the majority of their utterances: agent-action, action-object, agent-object, action-locative, entity-locative, entity-attribute, demonstrative-entity, and possessor-possession. With the addition of more formal linguistic elements to these basic semantic relations, further development of the phonologic system, the assimilation of more complex pragmatic functions, and acquisition of syntactic rules, the child's linguistic competence gradually expands until he can understand and generate an almost infinite variety of appropriate and acceptable sentences.

GENERAL TRAINING PROCEDURES

Target Population

Again, our target population includes infants and young children who show significant developmental problems and older children whose impairments have severely restricted the acquisition of basic communication skills. The form and structure of this program is appropriate for both groups if the goal is the development of a *vocal language system*. Of course, the suggested training procedures may need to be modified depending on child characteristics and program objectives.

Target Goal

This training program focuses on establishing fundamental communication behaviors (e.g., speaker-listener roles) followed by acquiring formal language skills (e.g., word production and comprehension). The terminal goal is the production and comprehension of simple grammatical sentences. To reach this goal the following objectives are targeted:

Phase 1. Establish visual and auditory attention.
Phase 2. Establish reciprocal actions.
Phase 3. Establish appropriate and functional use of objects and people.
Phase 4. Establish social-communication signals.
Phase 5. Establish multiword comprehension.
Phase 6. Establish multiword production.

These training objectives and their associated targets appear in Figure 10.1 in a lattice format. This format was chosen for two reasons. First, it can display the entire composite of target behaviors that are the focus of training—in this case, the six training phases with associated subobjectives. These targets are displayed hierarchically from simple to increasingly more complex. Second, in providing an overview, the lattice displays the potential horizontal and vertical training sequences to consider. Horizontal lines imply that parallel training on these targets is appropriate. Vertical lines imply that the first target should be trained before advancing to the next one. Again, individual variation is frequent and therefore the lattice is only a general plan subject to modification.

General Principles of Training

Several important points should be remembered and used throughout this training program. First, determine the child's general functioning level before training. Observations of the child in the classroom or at home and use of adaptive or behavioral measures will be necessary. Second, once the child's general level of functioning has been established, assess specific behaviors to determine precisely where to begin training. A suggested assessment format is specified for each training step in this program. Using assessment before and periodically throughout training helps establish the child's level of functioning before and during intervention. If a child's repertoire in a specific area is unknown, evaluation of progress is impossible. Third, carefully select and define the behaviors that are assessed and targeted for training. For example, when assessing the frequency of a child's vocalizations, the responses to be counted must be precisely defined. Do you include crying? Does whining count? The more precisely a behavior is defined, the more accurate the assessment is likely to be. Fourth, specify the length of the training sessions and nature of the data to be collected. The number of trials, duration, and frequency (as in language samples) per session should be relatively constant. The time of the day assessment data are taken may be

important. Assessments given periodically throughout training are called *probes*. Each probe should be given without cues, prompts, or assistance (unless carefully specified) to objectively determine progress. Fifth, always remember the importance of generalizing the skills the child has learned in a specified training situation to a broad range of objects, environments, and people. For example, if a child learns to use a particular cup appropriately, this activity should occur with many types of cups. Finally, whenever possible, train children in small groups. Group training allows children to stimulate each other, generally fosters more efficient use of a trainer's time, and approximates natural learning environments (Bricker, 1978; Bricker, Seibert, & Casuso, 1980).

Training throughout this program is based on a developmental approach; difficult skills are built on simpler skills. Most behavior is acquired in a developmental pattern in which simple basic skills are modified into more complex response ones. For example, a child apparently must learn to vocalize before producing words or to produce single words before producing word strings or sentences. Consequently, we believe a child should master simpler communication and language processes before training a more difficult skill. Following the developmental sequence outlined here should let the child systematically acquire an increasingly complex repertoire.

Though developmental in its approach, the skills taught in this training program should be intentionally selected to suit the particular student's language needs and environment. They must also fit the child's physical and sensory capabilities or disabilities. Clearly, a blind child cannot be taught to visually attend, for example. Instructions for that child might begin with auditory attention. Thus functional skills are chosen for instruction—language skills that are practical for a given student in his or her daily life.

TRAINING PROGRAM

Phase 1. Establish Visual and Auditory Attention

In this program, *attention* is any behavior that facilitates the acquisition of a new response or modification of an existing one. For example, if you are attempting to teach motor imitation, it is essential the child attend to you. Attempting to teach any response to a child who is not focusing on you or the training materials is difficult at best.

The objectives of this phase enable the child to attend to the teacher and engage in behaviors that will facilitate the process of learning language. These

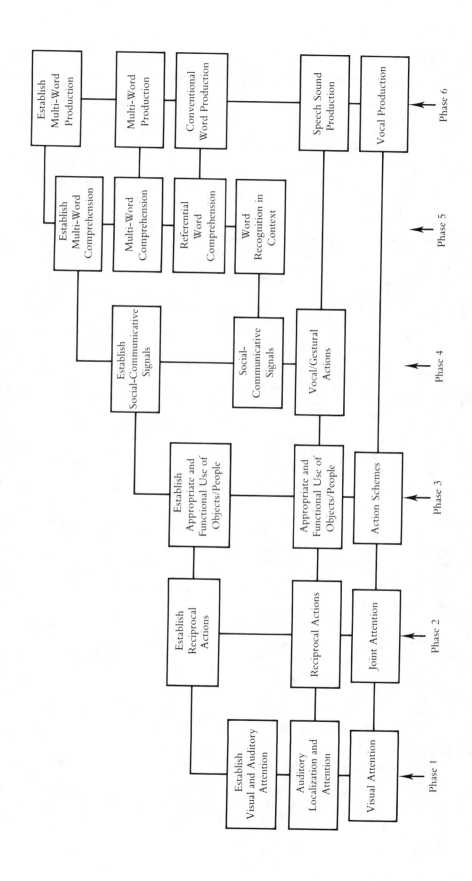

FIGURE 10.1
Program Objectives and Associated Training Targets

responses include visual attending and auditory attending.

As we said, before choosing specific training criteria, the developmental level of the child must be considered. Expecting a child who is developmentally very young to sit in a chair and attend to a task for 10 minutes is unrealistic; however, those responses may be appropriate for a child who is more competent. Therefore, the length of time established as criterion will vary. The training location may also vary. A child who is quite young developmentally might begin training cradled in your lap. A mobile, active child might begin seated on the floor if that is more appropriate.

Once you have established appropriate training targets, take a baseline measure on these responses. Baseline data should be collected until a consistent rate of behavior is recorded. The child who attends for 10 minutes in a 10-minute training period on Day 1, 59 second on Day 2, and 4 minutes on Day 3 is not presenting a stable rate of behavior. Baseline data should be collected until a stable rate of activity is recorded. However, this rule, like most, has exceptions. If the child's behavior rate does not stabilize but the general trend indicates the need for training, begin programming.

While reading through the following sections, you can formulate objectives for a child, taking into account developmental level and the particular training situation which would be most appropriate. Establish criterion behavior by specifying the task, the time period, and the locaion.

Step 1. Visual Attention

To begin, obtain objective information on the child's ability to visually attend to a person, object, or task. You can determine visual ability by appropriately positioning the child and saying "Look at _____." Do this for a predetermined number of trials, recording the child's response each time. If the child does not look when asked on at least 75% of the trials, begin training.

Take the child's head and gently direct the face toward the person, object, or task. If the child gives even the most fleeting glance, provide some positive feedback. Gradually lessen the prompts and reward the child for longer and longer gazes. Talk to the child while he or she is attending. If the child does not look following a verbal command or respond to physical prompting, search for an alternate method that may be more successful.

After a predetermined number of training sessions, reassess the child's ability to attend visually and compare the results with the baseline performance. If the child is attending appropriately at least 75% of the time, move on to the next step.

Step 2. Auditory Localization and Attention

The infant or young child must learn to orient to relevant sounds. Orientation is the selection of particular content from the child's "blooming, buzzing" world and the subsequent attempt to position the body, or a portion of the body, to locate the source of the stimulation. Once this basic skill is acquired, the child must learn to sustain interest in objects, people, or situations that, for whatever reason, warrant further scrutiny. If a child lacks auditory localization and attending skills, systematic intervention is in order.

The key to training is selecting an object/sound that has saliency for the child. That is, select objects or events that will attract the child's attention. This may require considerable exploration with a variety of sound-producing stimuli. Using a variety of objects or events that elicit attention is preferable to finding only one or two. Variations in pitch and intensity may attract some children, while others may respond better to sustained sounds. For children difficult to engage, accompanying tactile stimulation may be useful. For example, pair the presentation of a pleasurable sound with a stroke on the cheek that is toward the sound source. You may have to explore a variety of events and presentation sequences before finding combinations that elicit consistent attempts to localize.

As before, baseline data should be collected to determine if intervention is necessary. Place the child in a comfortable position that allows maximum mobility in body orientation, eye movement, and head turning. Present the selected sound and record whether the child tries to locate and attend to it by some body movement (e.g., eyes shift, head turns). Present the stimuli a predetermined number of trials.

Although during initial training the objective is attention and localization to any sound, the ultimate target is to have the child orient to speech production. That is, the objective is to help the child locate the person who is speaking. With some children, you may begin training with a sound produced by the teacher rather than an inanimate object such as bells or drums. For many children, the human face and voice are a powerful elicitor of attention. Exploration during baseline should provide the necessary information to select the most appealing stimuli.

For the child who does not localize and attend, training can be conducted with a variety of techniques. The key to success rests with the child finding the location of the sound a pleasurable event. The sound should be produced, and then the child prompted to locate the sound. Physical prompting or tactile stimulation to elicit a head turn may be necessary. When the head turn or eye shift occurs, the child should find an event which is rewarding.

Systematic probes should be used to monitor progress toward the established criterion. These probes should resemble the baseline condition. The criteria should be turning toward a sound source at least 75% of the time.

Phase 2.   Establish Reciprocal Actions

The major objective of this training sequence is to establish a synchrony of action between the infant/child and the teacher/caregiver. This interaction can be conceptualized as a jointly or mutually regulated system in which each member modifies and adapts his or her behavior to dovetail with the other. For communication to occur, the child and adult must assume the roles of initiator and responder, each influencing the other's behavior. The balance of reciprocity changes over time, with the child's participation increasing with age. The adult becomes less dominant as the child becomes capable of initiating. The handicapped child may either introduce unexpected variability or fail to initiate interactions. Either of these patterns inhibits the establishment of a mutually rewarding reciprocal relationship if the adult does not make adjustments.

Most children and adults display organized interactions which appear as structured cycles of affective and attentional responses. These cycles reflect periods of adult–child activity and engagement as well as inactivity and disengagement. In striking a balance between the mode and intensity of the behavior of both partners, these cycles typically consist of the following sequence of responses:

- Initiation—Child vocalizes while looking at adult to attract attention.
- Mutual orientation—Child vocalizes and adult focuses on his or her face.
- Recognition—Child smiles when seeing adult, establishing a joint reference.
- Reciprocal play-dialogue—Adult vocalizes and child vocalizes.
- Disengagement—Adult vocalizes and child looks away (Brazelton, Koslowski, & Main, 1974).

The disengagement phase probably reflects the child's need to control the amount of stimulation he or she can process during an intense social interaction. These cycles or response sequences do not have a fixed pattern or behavioral content. That is, both children and adults can enter the cycle at any point with widely varying behavioral content.

To successfully interact, certain prerequisites are required of both participants. Adults must contribute their unique sensitivities and environmental experiences to the interaction when reading and responding to the child's signals. Equally important, the child must clearly and predictably signal his or her state and needs as well as remain receptive and responsive to the adult's feedback. Without a match between initiator and respondent, the relationship may not evolve into a healthy context for the child's social-communication development.

Step 1.   Joint Attention

Joint attention or a mutual topic between speaker and listener is essential to communication. Communication is predicated on some mutual focus. Once the child is able to locate a sound source, the next step is to help him focus on an object, event, or person that is the topic of the adult's "conversation." Establishing joint attention helps the child understand that the adult's words are related to "here and now" events. In addition, joint attention helps establish the relationship between words and their associated object, event, or person.

Baseline data can be collected in a variety of ways. Two strategies are marking an object or event by shaking or pointing in the appropriate direction and gazing at an object or event. If the child generally looks toward the marked object or follows the adult's eye gaze, training is not necessary; however, if he does not, training is required.

Again, the selected event and training strategies will need to be individualized; however, we can outline a general procedure. While seated beside the child, select a desired object and place it in front of the child. Look at the object and comment on it. If the child looks toward the object, make sure some pleasurable activity occurs (give the object to the child or activate it). The comments should be relevant to the most salient aspects of the object and should be relatively redundant. If the child does not look toward the object for any sustained period, point to it and shake it if necessary. If the child still does not focus on the object, gently prompt the response by turning the child's head. If this is unsuccessful, follow the child's gazes. That is, notice what attracts the child's attention, point to that object, and label it. For example, before giving a child a glass of juice, hold it up and say, "This is juice." Get the child to focus on the cup before offering it. Activities that involve objects are particularly useful for establishing joint attention.

The terminal objective here is to have the child consistently focus on the topic of conversation. Periodic probes should monitor the child's progress towards this objective.

Step 2.   Reciprocal Actions

As the child and adult interact, their social-communication exchanges should be associated and should

be mutually contingent. Social stimulation successfully elicits feedback from the child just as the child's
expanding repertoire effectively elicits adult attention
and responses. The contingent feedback provided by
the adult to the child's signals appears to be instru-
mental in fostering the development of communication just as it increases the child's ability to control
the environment.

Child-Initiated Imitation.   The objective of this training step is to have the child respond reciprocally to
the adult's actions. To reach this target, use the following procedure. When the child responds, wait
briefly and then imitate the child's response.[3] After
imitating the child, provide a positive social response
and then wait for the child to respond again. When
the next response occurs, again imitate the response
and give some positive affective behavior. For example, if the child says, "Ah" when waving an object,
immediately copy the child's behavior by using the
same vocalization while waving a similar object. If
the child reproduces the action, imitate the sequence
and then demonstrate obvious pleasure by smiling or
laughing while looking at the child. This paradigm
should be effective for a number of reasons. First, to
imitate the child, you must attend closely to his or
her behavior. Second, the child's behavior precedes
yours and forces the following of the child's lead.
Third, since we assume the child is engaging in self-
reinforcing behavior, we are considering the child's
motivation. Fourth, the child will begin to get a sense
of control. That is, the child is discovering that his or
her behavior elicits some systematic, predictable effect from the environment. Fifth, the child can control the timing of the interactions. Getting the child
to control the speed of responses should establish a
flow that is optimal for producing and assimilating
responses.

Adult-Initiated Imitation.   Once you have established
a chain of reciprocal responses, try to expand the
child's repertoire. For example, if you and the child
have initiated and maintained a vocal imitation pattern, you may introduce a minor variation in the imi-
tated response, from "ba-ba" to "be-be," and watch
to see if the child responds differently. When retriev-
ing objects that are being dropped, you might introduce slightly different ways of returning the desired
object so the child will have to accommodate the
reach-and-grasp response a little each time. Other

simple extensions of the imitation method are easily
developed.

Following training on reciprocal chains of interaction, social ritual games can be introduced. Games
such as "up we go," "pat-a-cake," and "peek-a-boo"
(other, more appropriate games need to be selected
for older children) provide opportunities for the child
to learn to participate in activities in which partners
have mutually reciprocal roles. The games should be
individually chosen based on the child's age, motor
skills, and their reinforcement value. The form is
unimportant, but the child should be helped to gradually assume independence in participating in more
and more of the activity. Introduce systematic variation to enhance the child's imitative repertoire.

The collection of baseline data and subsequent
monitoring of progress should be tied to the activities
selected for training. Assessment strategies should
reflect the nature of the specific training targets.

Phase 3. Establish Appropriate and Functional Use of Objects

For most children, environmental interaction
produces the ability to differentiate objects and
events.[4] Initially a child's interactions with the environment are simple; objects are banged, waved, or
mouthed. Activity or action patterns used with most
objects are similar. As children engage in an activity
with a variety of objects, they learn that some
objects, because of their properties or characteristics,
are better to bang and wave, such as a rattle (which
makes noise); and others are better to mouth, such as
a spoon (which is ideal for putting in the mouth).
Children learn to differentiate activities based on the
object's properties.

As children develop more experience with the environment, they begin to engage in more complex
activities based on objects' unique characteristics. For
example, the child may drop a set of beads into a
bowl, swirl them around inside the bowl, pluck the
beads from the bowl, bang them on the chair, and
then throw them on the floor. The child is learning
many things while playing this way—including the
beads' weight, texture, contour, and reactions; and
distance in relation to weight and size. By combining
several action patterns with the same object and with
different objects, the child learns the different characteristics of objects and how to differentiate between
them.

---

[3]Initially choose responses that are visible to the child; imitation of visible behavior (e.g., hands together) is easier for
most children than imitation of invisible behavior (e.g.,
hands on head).

[4]As discussed by Kopp and Shaperman (1973) and Gratch
(1982), children are able to acquire cognitive concepts
through observation of others and attention to perceptual
cues.

Children's use of objects generally follows a hierarchical sequence (Zelazo & Kearsley, 1980):

1. Simple undifferentiated action patterns;
2. Relational play—using two objects together in some fashion;
3. Functional—using objects based on their physical properties;
4. Symbolic—using an object to represent another object or action.

Training should assist children in moving through this sequence.

Step 1. Establish Different Action Patterns

The primary objective here is to teach the child a variety of action patterns to be used with different objects. Before taking baseline, do some structured observation to determine if intervention is necessary. Select several objects around the house or classroom that are unbreakable and are usable in a variety of ways (a plastic bowl, a pan with a lid, a box with a top, some spoons, beads, a drum and stick, some aluminum foil, keys, a toy car or truck, some small blocks, a pull toy). Place a few of them in front of the child and record the responses. Do this several times over a period of a few days until you determine the child's usual interaction with these items.

Intervention is necessary only if the child engages in the same activities with all or many of the objects. For example, does the child only mouth each item? Does he or she only wave and bang objects? If so, then intervention is appropriate. If the child engages in different activities with many of the objects (for example, shaking the keys, banging the blocks together, and tearing the aluminum foil), then go to the next training step.

To initiate training, select five or six items that are interesting to the child and choose one or two appropriate activities for each item. Decide the criterion performance for each item and the criterion for exit from this step.

Record the child's activity with each item as appropriate, inappropriate, or an approximation. Over a period of a day, present and score each item the same number of times. If the child does not meet criterion, begin training. Intervention can be informal and may consist of playing with selected objects with the child. Place a few of the items in front of the child and demonstrate some activity with one object. For example, place a truck in front of the child, give the truck a big push, and say "go truck" or "push truck." Then give the child the truck and observe the response. If the child imitates you, you can turn it into a game of imitation. If the child does not imitate you, observe the response. Is it the same activity performed during baseline? If so, gently prompt a differ-

ent, yet easy activity. If the activity is new, encourage novel interaction, even if it is not the same as your demonstration. The actions that are demonstrated for the child and those done spontaneously need not be restricted to a training activity only. A white paper cup is interesting to drink from, to put on your head, to cover your eye, and to roll in a circle. While playing with the cup, talk about the activity. For example, talk about drinking milk from the cup (even if it is "pretend milk"), or making the cup into a hat by putting it on your head. A string of beads becomes a train when it is pulled across a table; when wiggled, it becomes a snake. This type of play, using different actions with many objects, coupled with simple verbalizations describing the events, may be important for later generative language. While playing, encourage the use of objects in many different ways and model new interactions. This exploratory play can involve all the senses. Making sounds into an old milk carton will slightly alter the sounds, which can be interesting. Looking down through the base of an empty glass distorts vision. Encourage the child to manipulate the objects to learn about them.

The child is ready to move on when he or she meets the criterion by demonstrating the new activities being trained or by engaging in novel activities he has constructed. Remember the goal is to use different action patterns with objects. If the child meets criterion by demonstrating untrained actions, this is acceptable. Also, the child may perform some of the same actions across several objects. As long as he or she engages in some activities that are unique to the properties of the object, criterion is met satisfactorily.

Step 2. Appropriate and Functional Use of Objects

Children learn about objects and their characteristics by developing action patterns that are unique to particular objects, people, and events. Following this differentiation of objects, the child begins to demonstrate activity that reflects the culture and people-object interactions that have been observed. The objective of this training step is to encourage the child to interact or play appropriately and functionally with objects. Some different training settings and object combinations are listed here; however, choose any object or location suitable to the child.

Setting	Objects
Kitchen	Cup, spoon, pan, doll, plastic tumbler, teapot, plate, table, chair
Bedroom	Shoe, hat, comb, soap, bed, dress, shirt, doll, pillow, chair
Outdoors	Truck, car, shovel, pail, box, toy dog, doll, boat

These objects are commonly found in most environments. In addition, a doll is included so the children can model feeding, drinking, and other caretaking activities they often experience. The kitchen is an ideal setting because it is familiar to most children. Many of their first words are objects or events that can be found there, such as "cup," "cookie," "drink," or "spoon."

To begin, select four training items. Determine what responses are acceptable as a demonstration of appropriate use. Table 10.1 describes some appropriate and inappropriate responses for the suggested items. After selecting the objects, define the appropriate response(s) for each item and administer a probe. If a child can use each object in two appropriate ways or has at least one appropriate use of each object which is demonstrated at least twice within a predetermined time, training in this phase is probably unnecessary.

Training should capitalize on the child's ongoing interactions with the environment. Seize every opportunity to enhance the child's functional use of objects. As children explore, play, or manipulate objects, instigate training to shape more functional activities with the self-selected items. A more formal approach to training may be appropriate as well. Take a manageable group of children into the kitchen or kitchen area of the classroom and have them sit around a small table. Place the items to be trained in front of each child. Show the children one appropriate use of an item and then have them imitate you. For example, if the item to be trained is a cup, take a drink from the cup and prompt or encourage the children to imitate by drinking from their cups. If any child does not respond, physically prompt the response. If the children imitate or attempt to imitate, praise them, hug them, or otherwise reinforce them. Once they are imitating actions reasonably well, move on to other uses of the item. Be alert to self-initiated appropriate activities the child might perform with the object and be sure to reinforce these responses.

At this point, begin to incorporate other items so the children learn to combine two objects into a single action, such as holding the cup with one hand and stirring with a spoon with the other hand. Introduce only a few new actions at a time. Gradually teach the children the functional or appropriate use of each item. As the children are able to produce the action without an immediate model, begin to encourage variation so they learn to use the items appropriately in several different ways. Although the children are not required to understand or verbalize the names of the objects in this step, name the objects frequently and talk about what is happening in simple, short sentences.

Children need to practice new responses outside the training situation; therefore, when possible, take

TABLE 10.1 Description of Appropriate and Inappropriate Use of Suggested Objects

Object	Sample Appropriate Responses	Sample Inappropriate Responses
Cup	Drink from cup Dipping liquid with cup Giving baby drink Stirring with spoon in cup Pouring from cup into another container	Banging cup Putting cup on head Throwing
Spoon	Spooning objects into a container Stirring with spoon in a container Feeding self Feeding doll	Beating table or other surface with spoon Throwing Sitting on spoon
Pan	Placing lid on pan Stirring in pan Drinking from pan Pouring from pan into another container	Throwing Spinning pan Banging
Jacket	Putting jacket on Taking jacket off Buttoning up jacket Hanging up jacket	Chewing on jacket Throwing jacket

them to a different location to practice their new skills. Use different examples of the items targeted for training. For example, when playing, use several different types of cups and let them drink from each one.

Administer probes regularly. When the child demonstrates criterion performance, move on to the next phase if training is not already underway in this area.

Phase 4. Establish Social-Communication Signals

Before they comprehend and produce referential words, most children use nonconventional and conventional vocalizations or gestures for a variety of communicative functions. Because these vocalizations and gestures are not conventional symbols (e.g., words), they are called social-communication or prelinguistic communication signals. These prelinguistic signals generally precede the initial referential language.

Step 1. Develop Vocal/Gestural Actions
In this initial step the form of the vocalization/gesture is unimportant; rather, the objective is to elicit vocal and gestural responses that ultimately can be used for communication. For example, the responses might include a pointing response that can eventually be shaped to indicate a desired object or a vocalization that can be used to gain an adult's attention. The most useful assessment data can be obtained by observing the child in the environment. Record the frequency and form of any systematic vocalization or gesture produced by the child. It is also useful to specify the conditions present when the vocalization/gesture was produced. If the child reaches the predetermined criteria, move on to Step 2; if not, begin training.

Choose training strategies that are appropriate for the target child and setting. Although it may be preferable to have a simultaneous vocalization and gesture, initially either is acceptable alone. The baseline data should suggest responses for likely training targets. For example, if the child tends to look towards a desired object and wave, this might be an appropriate target. Encourage any looking, vocalization, or gesture that can be shaped into a social-communication signal. Even children with serious motor impairments may have simple signals such as eye pointing. Discovering these may require sensitive observation of the child in a variety of settings and events. For the non-motor-impaired child, pointing is often an appropriate target. This response tends to occur "naturally" and is easy to prompt physically. The most important aspect of training is establishing a contin-

gent relationship between the child's vocal/gestural action (e.g., pointing) and some response from the environment (e.g., receives the object pointed at). If pointing has been selected, place favorite or desired objects around the room. Keep these objects visible but out of the child's reach. When the child indicates a desired object, be sure to retrieve it immediately. When the signal occurs regularly, shape it into a more conventional form.

Give periodic probes to determine when the child has reached the predetermined criterion for the initial targets. Two dimensions of the child's vocal/gestural action repertoire should be considered for expansion: frequency and diversity of actions. Training on this step should continue until the child reaches the predetermined criteria.

Step 2. Use of Social-Communication Signals
In the previous steps the vocal/gestural actions may be idiosyncratic to the child and the setting, and may be rather general in nature. That is, the child may use the same vocalization to obtain your attention and to have you retrieve a desired object. In this phase the objective is to help the child develop conventional social-communication signals and discriminate the use of signals across settings or changing conditions (e.g., the signal used to gain attention is different from that used for refusal). Table 10.2 lists some possible social-communication training targets.

Again training should be embedded into the child's ongoing activities. Arranging the environment so the child must use a variety of signals is necessary for the child to learn their discriminated use. In addition, you should gradually demand more explicit communicative gestures and vocalizations over time. For example, initially the child may point and say "da" when requesting an object. Once this pattern is established, change the criterion so the child must begin to say "want [or "wa"] da" or may be asked to imitate the name of the requested object such as "ball" rather than "da." If the initial refusal signal was a head shake, require the child to add the vocalization "no" or "na." The child who is using a standard vocal production such as "na" to indicate label-seeking and denial should be encouraged to discriminate between those two functions. "Na" or "no" can be paired with a head shake to indicate denial or rejection, while an alternative sound combination such as "What's this" ("dis") with a visual point might be encouraged for seeking object names.

Data for this training step can be recorded on a form similar to the one in Table 10.3. Table 10.4 lists social-communication signals that may be appropriate targets. Select several of these signals or others that are appropriate for the child, and begin training. Use every opportunity to elicit or shape a communi-

TABLE 10.2 Early Social-Communication Signals

Social-Communicative Signal		Communicative Function
Gesture	Vocalization	
Head shake	Negative vocalization	No
Pointing	Attention-getting vocalization	Look; obtain object, etc.
Giving objective	Marking vocalization such as "ta" or "da"	I give this to you
Showing or shaking object	As above	See this; look
Raise arms	Demand or attention vocalization such as "ah" or "up"	Pick me up
Move adult's hand	Demand vocalization	Do this or get this
Push or pull adult	Demand vocalization	Come here or go there
Waving arm	Calling or greeting	Hi; notice me

cation signal. Again, observation of the child's interactions with the environment may offer useful clues about structuring training activities. Monitor progress with systematic probes.

Phase 5.   Establish Multiword Comprehension

For the child to associate sounds in the environment with persons, objects, and actions; names of objects, people, and events should be used while the child is interacting with them. For language to be meaningful to the child, it must be relevant and directly related to ongoing experience. Therefore, it is essential to talk about what the child sees and does in simple, consistent language.

Initially, the child appears to learn that certain events tend to occur with certain other events. For example, Joe's shoes are associated with Joe, car keys are associated with going for a ride in a car, and a coat is associated with going outside. We know that children begin to make these associations by their demonstrated anticipatory behavior. The sight of car keys will often bring about excitement; the sight of dinner preparation will often lead to anticipatory behavior such as sitting at the table.

When the child is demonstrating the association of one event with another, he or she should hear language that is appropriate and relevant to the occasion. Thus, the child begins to associate sounds (words and phrases) with their referents. The goal of this training phase is to teach the child to respond appropriately to words and phrases.

Step 1.   Word Recognition in Context

Before training, spend time observing the child's environmental interactions. From these observations, select a group of words for training. First, select words that represent objects, persons, or

TABLE 10.3 Sample Recording Form for Social-Communicative Signals and Words

Name: _____   Date: _____   Observer: _____

Context	Form of Social-Communication Signal		Consequence	Function of Response					
	Vocal	Gesture		Request	Refusal	Labeling	Social Ritual	Other	Unclear
In kitchen with Mom	ah	Points to cracker	Mother gives cracker	X					
Looking at book; teacher across room	po	Points to picture	Teacher says, What?			X			
Peer enters room	Squeal	Clap hands	Peer smiles				X		
Teacher offers object	None	Shakes head	Object removed		X				
Looks at teacher; holds book	ua	None	Teacher ignores						X

TABLE 10.4 Selected Social-Communication Signals, Definitions, and Examples

Signal/Function	Definition	Examples
Request	Child signals that he/she wants to obtain some object or goal; Child signals he/she wants another person to obtain some goal for him/her to intervene for him/her in some way; Social tool use. May make gesture regarding desired object.	"Uh?" While pushing pegs into hole, looks at mother. Mother responds by helping. "jee" or "mm" holding empty cup to teacher for more juice. Child vocalizes to adult, reaches toward chair—adult places adult in chair.
Refusal	Child signals dislike of a person's social bid or another person's actions involving him/herself; Child signals to register protest. May gesture regarding spurned object.	"Nee!" for "no I don't want that food, take it away," or other emphatic vocalization for "no I don't want my shoes on right now." Throws shoes.
Labeling	Child names objects or attributes with non-standard, idiosyncratic forms. Early labeling; Child comments on the disappearance of an object that had existed in context; Child comments that some activity has ceased.	"Duh" as child touches picture in book, expecting no response; Ball stops rolling child says, "oh."
Social Ritual	1) *Calling*—addresses adult by saying adult's name loudly (may be idiosyncratic in form); waits for response. 2) *Greeting*—attends to adult or object. 3) *Ending*—child terminates "conversation."	"Mama!" when mother is in next room fixing coffee. "Hi!" as teacher enters the room. "Bye"—usually idiosyncratic in form.

events with which the child has frequent contact. Frequent opportunities to hear the word in relation to its referent should facilitate training. Second, select words that refer to objects, persons, or events, or that are important to the child—favorite toys or foods. Third, select words that have functional value. Learning names of common items and events should aid in the child's adaptation to the environment and so should provide some intrinsic reward. Finally, select words that have relatively easy-to-produce sound combinations. Although the objective of this training phase is comprehension, training of word production follows or occurs simultaneously. Selecting easy-to-produce words may enhance production training.

Using these criteria, select a group of training items (e.g., words) such as those in Table 10.5. Enter each of these items several times on an appropriate recording form. Determine what responses will be classified as appropriate, inappropriate, or approximations for each item.

Collect baseline data over a period of at least 2 days. If these data indicate the child has not reached the established criteria, begin training. Training involves teaching the child to respond appropriately to selected words or commands. For example, if training the response to the word "up," prompt the child to raise his or her arms when you say, "Do you want up?" Do not forget to pick the child up if genuine communication is to occur.

Remember that the primary objective of this phase is not production, it is comprehension or word recognition; therefore, do not expect the child to repeat the words or sounds, but encourage any expression that occurs. Administer probes regularly. When the child has met criterion by indicating appropriate activities in response to your words and commands in context, he or she has completed this training step.

Step 2.   Referential Word Comprehension
The primary objective of this training step is to help the child understand a verbal label without contextual cues. That is, the child must recognize that the word "dog" stands for Fido even if the animal is not present. In most cases the words chosen may be the same as those used in Step 1 of this training phase. They may also be those items used in Phase 3.

Before initiating training, collect baseline data and enter them on an appropriate form.[5] You can collect baseline data formally by placing objects, pictures, or the actual item in front of the child and saying, "Give

---

[5]With slight modifications, the form in Table 10.3 could be used.

TABLE 10.5 Suggested Comprehension Items for Word Recognition Training

Comprehension Items	Suggested Responses
Hi	Wave or smile.
See the _____ (familiar object such as dog or person. Be careful not to point)	Child looks in direction, searches for object, e.g., dog, or looks at a closely related item, e.g., looks at water dish.
Up or down	Child indicates anticipation of being picked up or put down.
Time to go outside	Child indicates anticipation of going outdoors.
I'm gonna tickle you	Child smiles, laughs, or indicates the tickle game is about to follow.
Do you want some _____ (favorite food)?	Child looks or points in direction of food, cupboard, refrigerator, etc.

me (show me, point to, touch, etc.) the (object label)." Request each of the four objects three times in random order as listed on the recording form. However, though it is more difficult, it may be preferable to conduct the assessment while observing the child's daily contact with the environment. For example, when asked to retrieve the ball without other additional cues, can the child follow the command?

Likewise, training can use a formal structured approach or a more naturalistic approach, or both. In formal training, the child can be seated around a table with the selected training objects. Ask the child to select the objects one at a time, varying requests to include such phrases as "touch," "point to," "show me," "get," "take," "give me," or "find." You may begin teaching a new word-object association by placing only one item in front of the child and asking him or her to touch it. Imitation and physical prompts should be used if necessary. After the child has touched the first training object on command, place a second object on the table so the child must make a choice. The child should be allowed and encouraged to play with the objects in a functionally appropriate way after selecting the correct object, and you should continue to label the items frequently as the child plays with them. Once a child has learned to attach a verbal label to an object, you can begin to expand the class of objects encompassed by that label. For example, if the object used to train "cup" has been a white coffee cup, other cups of varying size, shape, and color should be used to broaden the child's concept of "cup."

Baseline assessment and training action words (verbs) or events may differ somewhat. Collect baseline data on the selected training items as suggested for objects, persons, and events. For example, if targeting the verbs "eat" and "ride," place a cookie, apple, boat, and wagon on the table and give the child a dog and doll. Say "Make it eat" or "Make him ride." Test each of the verbs three times, varying the order of the verbs and actions randomly. The assessment can also be conducted with less structure.

Training should entail using motor imitation and physical prompts until the child shows the ability to discriminate between, for example, "eat" and "ride" by manipulating the items appropriately based on your command. Again attempt to maximize the child's learning by having alternative training stimuli available (e.g., other dogs and boats) in the form of objects and pictures. By having these stimuli available, opportunities should arise when you can ask a child to get the "apple," point to the "boat," or bring the "wagon." The child can collect pictures of people and animals eating different foods and riding in various types of vehicles. When the child has learned to make appropriate discriminations, use group time to generalize the concepts. For example, each child could hold a picture that depicts eating and a second that depicts riding. You then could ask the children to hold up the picture of eating or riding. Each child would hold up the appropriate picture depending on the verbal cue.

Step 3. Multiword Comprehension

Collect baseline data on the child's ability to comprehend action words (verbs) with content words (nouns). Place a preselected number of items on the table and say, for example, "Roll the truck" or "Feed the baby." Be sure the items necessary to carry out the activity are available. Again, training can use a less structured approach, in which you observe the child's ability to comprehend multiword sequences during daily activities.

Training the comprehension of multiword phrases or sentences should be embedded in daily classroom and home routines. In both group time and snack time, give children simple requests to carry out. For example, a child can be asked to demonstrate "Johnny kick ball" or "push bus." Older children can be used to demonstrate or give commands.

Games of "Follow-the-Leader" or "Simon Says" can be played. Many outdoor activities lend themselves to training multiword comprehension, such as "Sally, empty the pail" or "push the bike."

Once the child is under the control of simple two- and three-word sequences, gradually expand these basic agent-action, action-object, agent-action-object kernels to include:[6]

1. Attributives (color, size, texture, etc.)—"Get the blue car"; "Point to the big apple."
2. Prepositions—"Push the car under the table"; "Put the block in the cup."
3. Locatives—"Put the chair here"; "Go over there."
4. Possessives—"The baby's dress"; "The car's wheel."
5. Pronouns—"Open it"; "Give the book to him."
6. Negatives—"The boy will not run"; "Johnny will not sing."
7. Questions—"Does Sharon want the ball?" "Do you want a snack?"

Phase 6. Establish Multiword Production

This final phase of training focuses on oral production. The ability to control the environment in both a social and informational sense largely rests with facility with language. In our culture the most desirable form of communication is oral language. It should be the target for the child unless it is barred by serious sensory or motor problems.

Step 1. Vocal Production

Initially a child who does not talk may make only a small variety of sounds—crying, whimpering, coughing, or making little noises. Therefore, in this phase the primary objective is to get the oral muscle complex working by increasing the number of vocalizations in general and the throat and mouth noises in particular.

Baseline data on the number of times a child vocalizes during a certain period of the day are necessary before attempting to train. First, identify the time of day the child seems to vocalize most often. Some children seem to vocalize more in the mornings; others are more vocal in the afternoon. Second, specify exactly what counts as a vocalization. For example, with some children coos and whines may be counted; other children may have vowel sounds targeted for measurement. Third, schedule a block of time and count the number of vocalizations during this period.

Do this until a consistent pattern emerges. This procedure will provide a rough estimate of the average number of vocalizations during the given period. Fourth, set the criterion level or goal for the child in terms of the number of vocalizations per minute or hour.

Start intervention by attending to any appropriate vocalizations. Do this by imitating the child's vocalizations or attending to them. Try to increase the child's opportunity to vocalize. Schedule training periods in which you make concentrated efforts to evoke vocal responses. Make the situation as pleasant as possible since making noises and sounds should be enjoyable. Appropriate times for this training are those that are part of the child's normal routine, such as mealtime or bathroom time. Physical stimulation seems to be an important part of increasing vocalization. By increasing the child's activity levels through physical stimulation, the number of vocalizations may increase. While you are performing these activities, make pleasurable sounds. These vocalizations may stimulate the child to make "happy" vocalizations, such as laughing and babbling. These vocalizations can then be rewarded with more tickling, touching, or rough-housing. Repeat the sounds the child makes; sometimes this will stimulate him or her to make the sound again.

Schedule regular probe periods. Compare the number of vocalizations produced during the probe with the criterion level. If the child reaches criterion, move on to the next training step. If the number of vocalizations does not meet the criterion, continue training, or consider developing an alternative, non-speech communication system with the child.

Step 2. Speech Sound Production

Over time, the child should begin to produce closer approximations to English sounds such as "ma" and "da." The child may also begin using intonation patterns that match mature patterns. The objective is to have the child produce sounds that make up the phonemic components of English.

To establish the items to use for baseline assessment, it is helpful to know which English sounds are generally easiest for children to produce. Table 10.6 lists English consonant sounds and their ease of production. Although children may vary, this sequence offers a general hierarchy that will be appropriate for most children.

The most efficient assessment and training strategy for this step may be imitation; however, some children may be restive with this approach and you may need other strategies. Select the number of trials that will constitute your probe, set the criterion, and begin the baseline sessions. Over a period of a few days, when the child is alert and vocalizing, stand or

---

[6]For a more detailed description of these modifications and expansions, see Bricker, Ruder, and Vincent (1976).

Table 10.6 Ease of Consonant Production

Level	Consonant	Representative Word
1	b	*boy*
	w	*way*
	m	*man*
	t	*toy*
	d	*dog*
2	h	*hot*
	n	*no*
	k	*cut*
	p	*pipe*
3	g	*go*
	s	*see*
	f	*fat*
	d_3	*jump*
4	ʃ	*shoe*
	r	*run*
	l	*lamp*
	tʃ	*church*
	z	*zoo*
5	ʒ	*measure*
	ð	*that*
	θ	*thin*
	v	*vest*
	j	*yellow*
	ŋ	*sing*

sit where the child can see and touch your face. Wait until the child has been silent for a few seconds and then present one of the baseline sounds. Record whether or not the child imitates you. If the imitation is similar to the model, count it as appropriate. If the child vocalized, but the vocalization did not sound at all like the model, count it as an attempt. If the child does not imitate, count it as inappropriate. Present the items a consistent number of times over a few days and record the responses.

Training consists of teaching the child to produce new sounds. At first, begin by working only with sounds the child can already say. Gradually introduce new sounds one at a time. Remember to work on vocal imitation during caretaking and other routine activities. A mirror may help focus a child on oral motor movements.

Administer probes regularly. The decision to continue training or to move to the next step should be based on an objective evaluation of the child's performance. If the child appears motivated and has been working on some specific sounds without reaching criterion for several days, it may be wise to re-examine the sounds selected for training and the training procedures.

Step 3. Production of Conventional Words

The target words selected for training should generally be the same words used in Phase 5. Baseline assessment can be conducted using a formal or informal procedure or both. If a formal approach is used, hold up the item and ask, "What's this?" Set a pre-established criterion such as two out of three correct responses per item. As in previous steps, an informal or less structured approach could be used.

Use every opportunity throughout the day to ask the child the names of the objects targeted for training. Most of the activities suggested in the earlier steps are also appropriate here.

In assessing and training production of action words (verbs), you can determine the child's skill level by demonstrating an activity (e.g., the dog eating dog food) and then asking, "What's the dog doing?" The child should respond with some form of the correct verb such as "eating," "eat," or "eats." Each verb should be tested three times following a random presentation. If the child does not give at least two appropriate responses for each verb, continue training.

By now it should be clear that generalization of a response learned in a training session to other settings is a major focus of this program. Once the child can produce the correct label for an object without prompting, the next step is to help generalize the use of the label to other objects in the class, home, and other environments. You must be alert to all opportunities for the child to vocalize his or her desires. In other words, the child's speech production should be made functional so he or she has a reason to talk.

Step 4. Use of Multiword Productions

The baseline assessment procedures are the same as used in previous steps except that the stimulus items are different and the length of the target response has increased. Each target verb should be presented in combination with each target object three times in random order. Demonstrate an activity (push truck) and then ask the child, "What am I doing?" or "What's happening?" The child's response should be some form of the correct verb combined with the correct object (e.g., "pushes truck," "pushing truck," or "push truck"). The child's responses should be recorded on a form similar to the one in Table 10.3. If the child does not give at least two appropriate responses for each verb-object combination, begin training. Again the assessment may be less structured.

Table 10.7 lists some two- and three-word utterances that are appropriate targets for training. These utterances include the major linguistic kernels that give the child the structure to communicate a wide

TABLE 10.7 Training Targets for Multiword Productions

Semantic Structure	Example
Agent-action	boy runs
Action-object	throw ball
Possessor-possession	Susy's book
Demonstrative entity	that boy
Recurrence entity	more cookie
Nonexistent entity	no doll
Attribute entity	red train
Locative entity	there book
Agent-action-object	Joe drinks juice
Agent-action-location	dog sleeps there
Action-object-location	put dish here

variety of observations, requests, statements, and questions.

You can begin to demonstrate the activity and then ask "What am I doing?" Or you can let one child demonstrate the action with the same object and ask the other children what is happening. Appropriate responses can be prompted with imitation. Begin by using one object and one verb, then one object and two verbs, and so on; then introduce another object with one verb, two verbs, etc. The two objects should be alternated with the four verbs. The third and fourth objects should be added in the same way until the children can identify any of the four objects with any of the four verbs.

The children must be taught to generalize production of multiword responses to other environments. One advantage of the two-word action-object phrase is that it constitutes a command that can be reinforced. At group time, choose one child to be a leader for the day, and devise a game in which the other children follow his or her requests. Toys and snacks should only be given if the children verbalize their wants. If a child is unable to do so, provide the appropriate response that should be gradually faded over time.

SUMMARY

Each individual is entitled to the assistance needed to acquire fundamental skills that result in independence. The ability to communicate is surely a vital skill; for children in our culture, oral language is the primary form of communication. Assisting the severely impaired child to develop language is difficult. The enormity of the undertaking is probably responsible for the historic unwillingness of speech language therapists, educators, and psychologists to involve themselves in such a "doomed" venture.

Humane reasons being insufficient, recent legal agreements and legislation have mandated changes in the willingness of professionals to educate all children.

This chapter has described an intervention program to teach the developmentally young child the responses necessary for production and comprehension of referential language. The primary strategy is to shape simple response forms through systematic environmental interaction into successively more complex response forms. The training content is derived from cognitive and linguistic theory of development. The focus of this approach necessarily is on training communication skills; however, the recognition of the interrelated nature of early social, sensorimotor, and communication development is obvious throughout this program. Early social, sensorimotor, and communication skills must be synthesized into a repertoire that provides the foundation for the development of more complex systems such as language.

REFERENCES

Bates, E. *Emergence of symbols: Cognition and communication in infancy.* New York: Academic Press, 1979.

Bellugi, U. Development of language in the normal child. In J.E. McLean, D.E. Yoder, & R.L. Schiefelbusch (Eds.), *Language intervention with the retarded.* Baltimore: University Park Press, 1972.

Bloom, L., & Lahey, M. *Language development and language disorders.* New York: Wiley, 1978.

Bowerman, M. Semantic factors in the acquisition of rules for word use and sentence construction. In D. Morehead & A. Morehead (Eds.), *Normal and deficient child language.* Baltimore: University Park Press, 1976.

Brazelton, B., Koslowski, B., & Main, M. The origins of reciprocity: The early mother-infant interaction. In M. Lewis & L. Rosenblum (Eds.), *The effect of the infant on its caregiver.* New York: Wiley, 1974.

Bricker, D. Early intervention: The criteria of success. *Allied Health and Behavioral Sciences Journal,* 1978, *1,* 567–582.

Bricker, D., & Carlson, L. Issues in early language intervention. In R. Schiefelbusch & D. Bricker (Eds.), *Early language: Acquisition and intervention.* Baltimore: University Park Press, 1981.

Bricker, D., & Carlson, L. The relationship of object and prelinguistic social-communicative schemes to the acquisition of early linguistic skills in developmentally delayed infants. In G. Edgar, N. Haring, J. Jenkins, & C. Pious (Eds.), *Mentally handicapped children: Education and training.* Baltimore: University Park Press, 1982.

Bricker, D., Ruder, K., & Vincent, L. An intervention strategy for language-deficient children. In N. Haring & R. Schiefelbusch (Eds.), *Teaching special children.* New York: McGraw-Hill, 1976.

Bricker, D., Seibert, J., & Casuso, V. Early intervention. In J. Hogg & P. Mittler (Eds.), *Advances in mental handicap research*. London: Wiley, 1980.

Bricker, W., & Bricker, D. An early language training strategy. In R. Schiefelbusch & L. Lloyd (Eds.), *Language perspectives: Acquisition, retardation, and intervention*. Baltimore: University Park Press, 1974.

Brown, R. *A first language: The early stages*. Cambridge, Mass.: Harvard University Press, 1973.

Bruner, J. The ontogenesis of speech acts. *Journal of Child Language*, 1975, *2*, 1–19.

Condon, W., & Sander, L. Synchrony demonstrated between movements of the neonate and adult speech. *Child Development*, 1974, *45*, 456–462.

Cromer, R. Reconceptualizing language acquisition and cognitive development. In R. Schiefelbusch & D. Bricker (Eds), *Early language: Acquisition and intervention*. Baltimore: University Park Press, 1981.

Dale, P. *Language development*. New York: Holt, Rinehart & Winston, 1976.

deVilliers, J. Functional categories in early language. In D. Bricker (Ed.), *Intervention with at-risk and handicapped infants: From research to application*. Baltimore: University Park Press, 1982.

deVilliers, J., & deVilliers, P. *Language acquisition*. Cambridge, Mass.: Harvard University Press, 1978.

Dore, J. Holophrases, speech acts and language universals. *Journal of Child Language*, 1975, *2*, 1–19.

Gratch, G. Piaget, the notion of action, and assessing intelligence in handicapped infants. In D. Bricker (Ed.), *Intervention with at-risk and handicapped infants: From research to application*. Baltimore: University Park Press, 1982.

Greenfield, P., & Smith, J., *Structure and communication in early language development*. New York: Academic Press, 1976.

Kopp, C., & Shaperman, J. Cognitive development in the absence of object manipulation during infancy. *Developmental Psychology*, 1973, *9*, 430.

Leonard, L. Cognitive factors in early linguistic development. In R. Schiefelbusch (Ed.), *Bases of language intervention*. Baltimore: University Park Press, 1978.

Morehead, D., & Morehead, A. *Normal and deficient child language*. Baltimore: University Park Press, 1976.

Nelson, K. The role of language in infant development. In M. Bornstein & W. Kessen (Eds.), *Psychological development from infancy: Image to intention*. Hillsdale, N.J.: Lawrence Erlbaum, 1979.

Oller, D., Wieman, L., Doyle, W., & Ross, C. Infant babbling and speech. *Journal of Child Language*, 1976, *3*, 1–12.

Piaget, J. Piaget's theory. In P. Mussen (Ed.), *Carmichael's manual of child psychology* (Vol I). New York: Wiley, 1970.

Prutting, C. Process: The action of moving forward progressively from one point to another on the way to completion. *Journal of Speech and Hearing Research*, 1979, *44*, 3–23.

Reese, H., & Lipsitt, L. *Experimental child psychology*. New York: Academic Press, 1970.

Ruder, K., & Smith, M. Issues in language training. In R. Schiefelbusch & L. Lloyd (Eds.), *Language perspectives: Acquisition, retardation, and intervention*. Baltimore: University Park Press, 1974.

Saarni, C. Cognitive and communicative features of emotional experience, or do you show what you think you feel? In M. Lewis & L. Rosenblum (Eds.), *The development of affect*. New York: Plenum Press, 1978.

Schiefelbusch, R., & Bricker, D. (Eds.). *Early language: Acquisition and intervention*. Baltimore: University Park Press, 1981.

Sugarman, S. Some organizational aspects of pre-verbal communication. In I. Markova (Ed.), *Social context of language*. New York: Wiley, 1978.

Trehub, S., Bull, D., & Schneider, B. Infant speech and nonspeech perception. In R. Schiefelbusch & D. Bricker (Eds.), *Early language: Acquisition and intervention*. Baltimore: University Park Press, 1981.

Uzgiris, I., & Hunt, J. McV. *Assessment in infancy: Ordinal scales of psychological development*. Urbana: University of Illinois Press, 1975.

Zelazo, P., & Kearsley, R. The emergence of functional play in infancy: Evidence for a major cognitive transition. *Journal of Applied Developmental Psychology*, 1980, *1*, 95–117.

Janet H. Allaire is with The Children's Rehabilitation Center of the University of Virginia. *Joan M. Miller* is with the University of Virginia.

When two people need to exchange information, the most efficient, rapid method is speech. Most humans speak at an average rate of 190 words per minute (Enderby & Hamilton, 1981). The ability to speak requires rapid and specific movement of the lips, tongue, jaw, and palate coordinated with breath and voice production. This complex motor task must be integrated with thought to communicate orally using speech.

Because of the complexity of speech, many severely handicapped people have difficulty using it as a primary form of communication. Specifically, meaningful, articulate speech is lacking in approximately 50% of autistic children (Carr, 1982; Ratusnik & Ratusnik, 1974), 75% of cerebral palsied persons (Eisenson & Ogilvie, 1977), and 75% of the profoundly and severely retarded adolescents studied by Naor and Balthazar (1975).

Although speech may be the preferred form of communication, it is often necessary to supplement and augment it. Over 100 different systems are available for this purpose (Silverman, 1980), known as augmentative, auxiliary, nonvocal, or nonspeech systems of communication. Those commonly used with moderately to profoundly handicapped persons are visual-graphic and gestural systems. Visual-graphic systems usually involve a board or chart containing pictures, drawings, symbols, or printed words selected in some way by the message-sender (Harris & Vanderheiden, 1980). Thus, these systems are based on adaptive devices or communication prostheses (Harris, 1982) which must be available to the student to express messages. In contrast, gestural systems do not generally involve prosthetic devices. Rather, they are used to transmit messages visually through patterned muscle movements, usually the arms and hands (Silverman, 1980). Sign language, natural gestures, and communication codes are different types of gestural systems. These systems, as well as the various visual-graphic systems available, offer many possibilities for providing the severely handicapped student with a reliable, unambiguous means of expression.

WHEN TO CONSIDER AUGMENTATIVE COMMUNICATION

Before we look at alternative communication systems themselves, we must consider the initial question: How do we know when to train a student to use augmentative communication? For example, one standard that has been applied is that the individual

11
Nonspeech Communication

demonstrate intent or the desire to communicate in some way, through vocalizing, gesturing, or some other form of expression (e.g., Harris-Vanderheiden, Brown, MacKenzie, Reinen, & Scheibel, 1975; Hobson & Duncan, 1979; Kladde, 1974). A second suggested criterion is that the student be able to use symbols; that is, to recognize that symbols such as words, pictures, or signs may be used to represent objects and events (e.g., Harris-Vanderheiden et al., 1975; Chapman & Miller, Note 1). In this vein, several investigators have reported that cognitive functioning at Stages V–VI of Piaget's sensorimotor phase is needed before meaningful expressive language develops (Greenwald & Leonard, 1979; Kahn, 1975; Lobato, Barrera, & Feldman, 1981). A third indicator that has been frequently used is the failure to develop intelligible speech despite prolonged training. According to this position, an alternative system is not introduced until speech training is proven ineffective (e.g., Carr, Binkoff, Kologinsky, & Eddy, 1978; Faw, Reid, Schepis, Fitzgerald, & Welty, 1981; Reid & Hurlbut, 1977).

Viewed collectively, these suggested prerequisites resemble goals of communication training. For example, one important goal is to understand that communication provides a means of controlling other people and environmental events. Unless the individual learns that he or she can use communication to obtain preferred objects or events, cause other events not to happen, or gain attention or aid from another person, he or she will have little need or desire to communicate (Harris-Vanderheiden & Vanderheiden, 1977). Similarly, it would be advantageous for the student to use spoken language as the primary communication mode. Since speech is the expressive mode used by most people, the handicapped person who uses speech will be able to converse in a wide variety of settings and activities (Nietupski & Hamre-Nietupski, 1979). Furthermore, the student who can use the symbols and rules of spoken language will be able to express a vast number of messages (Sailor, Guess, Goetz, Schuler, Utley, & Baldwin, 1980). He or she will be able to use words to represent objects or events not necessarily present, as well as concepts for which there is no physical referent, such as *again* or *have*. Without a symbolic base such as language, the student can refer only to observable objects and events available in a given setting at a given time.

Clearly, goals such as understanding the power of communication, using language, and using speech are desirable. But these qualities are long-term goals of communication, rather than prerequisites for training. It is more reasonable to teach students the skills they need to progress toward increasingly advanced and independent communication behaviors.

There is substantial support for this view in the literature. For example, several strategies have been developed to facilitate proactive or interactive skills in the passive or noncommunicative student, targeting such basic skills as showing a consistent gross body movement to sensory stimuli (e.g., Hamre-Nietupski, Stoll, Holtz, Fullerton, Ryan-Flottum, & Brown, 1977; Scheuerman, Baumgart, Sipsma, & Brown, 1976; Sternberg, Battle, & Hill, 1980; Keogh & Reichle, Note 2) or choosing between preferred objects (e.g., Keogh & Reichle, Note 2; Klein, Wulz, Hall, Waldo, Carpenter, Lathan, Myers, Fox, & Marshall, Note 3). A strategy that might be used with a student who already shows a preference for certain objects or events is to select initial vocabulary to reflect these preferences and require the student to communicate in order to obtain them (Nietupski & Hamre-Nietupski, 1979). At a more advanced level, if the student already has some communication skills but does not use them to initiate an exchange, the trainer might conduct "spontaneity sessions" (Carr, 1982). The trainer might also use strategies to foster a desire to communicate among oral language users (Hart & Risley, 1975; Sosne, Handleman, & Harris, 1979).

For the student who does not associate symbols such as pictures, signs, or words with the referent objects or events, instruction may begin at the present level of concreteness and gradually move to more symbolic representations. For example, a first "communication board" might be a tray containing several items from which the student is trained to make a selection. Once the student demonstrates this skill reliably, a requirement may be added to point to a visual symbol for "want" before being given access to the tray (Keogh & Reichle, Note 2). At a slightly more advanced level, a communication board comprised of tactile representations of objects can be used, such as the bowl of a spoon for "eat," pieces of a milk carton and a pop tab for "drink," and a piece of toweling for "bathroom" (Karel, Galloway, Brankin, Pajor, & Freagon, 1981). Yet another frequently used approach is to train object-picture or object-sign matching directly (e.g., Carr, 1982; Faw et al., 1981; Kucherawy & Kucherawy, 1978). As a specific example, Dixon (1981) found that using figures cut from photographs was associated with greater acquisition of photo-object matching skills than using the complete photograph. While these suggestions all pertain to training highly concrete, object-bound communication, they nevertheless are strategies by which a student can acquire a reliable expressive response. As the student learns to associate specific symbols with their referents, he or she may gradually be introduced to a specific symbolic system of graphics, signing, or speech.

The same position applies to the issue of restricting programming to speech training for an extended period. Rather than leaving students without any way to express themselves while trying to determine whether speech training will eventually be profitable, it is more appropriate to give them systems they can use in the interim or even permanently to augment their speech (McDonald, 1976). This does *not* preclude concurrent speech training. Indeed, Wells (1981) found greater gains in articulation skills when signs were paired with speech than when speech was used by itself for training. There is widespread support for continuing to develop speech to whatever extent is possible whenever an augmentative system is introduced (e.g., Hamre-Nietupski et al., 1977; Harris-Vanderheiden & Vanderheiden, 1977; Waldo, Barnes, & Berry, 1981).

Using this perspective, then, programming decisions do not concern issues such as which students are ready for training or when training should begin. Rather, they focus on the immediate target skills and strategies through which the teacher, therapist, or other interventionist may best facilitate purposeful use of communication, the ability to use symbols, and unambiguous, reliable expression of messages for each learner. Developing an initial system based on the student's current skills, the teacher can establish a basis for meeting immediate needs and working toward more functional, expandable, and symbolic systems as the student becomes more competent.

As the student progresses toward this goal, the teacher should consider several systems rather than concentrating on just one. For example, Hamre-Nietupski and her colleagues (1977) have advocated that, depending on the individual's specific abilities, all severely handicapped students should learn to use communication aids, signs, natural gestures, and speech to increase the number of listeners with whom they may interact. While this may not be possible for some physically disabled students, a variety of modes may still be appropriate for them, such as using a communication device, vocalizing, and gesturing (Harris, 1982). Similarly, if a student can control eye movements, an initial system might use directed eye gaze for looking at specific referents or their symbols. Separate training might be conducted concurrently for a different skill, such as hand-pointing, so that another response mode may later be added (Bottorf & DePape, 1982; Hamre-Nietupski et al., 1977). To extend communication skills for students who have learned to use a communication board, you can develop separate "miniboards" to use in specific settings or activities, with vocabulary chosen to fit those environments (Bottorf & DePape, 1982; Hamre-Nietupski et al., 1977; Shane, Lipschultz, & Shane, 1982).

A communication system, then, does not necessarily or even probably consist of a single mode. Rather it begins with an initial system to establish basic interaction and then may grow into a whole constellation of modes, with one being used most frequently. Thus, it is not sufficient to identify one mode for which the learner already has the necessary motor, visual, or representational skills and to neglect other possibilities. With training in certain responses, the student may develop the skills necessary to add another mode to his or her system.

CHOOSING SYSTEMS OF AUGMENTATIVE COMMUNICATION

The ultimate criterion for a nonverbal communication system is the extent to which it is used by the handicapped person to interact with others (Bottorf & DePape, 1982; Harris, 1982; Shane et al., 1982). This standard requires not only that we find an efficient means of communication for the severely handicapped student, but also that we train the student to use the system in daily interactions (Bottorf & DePape, 1982; Shane et al., 1982) and evaluate it on a continuing basis (Yoder, 1982).

From the very inception of planning a communication system, then, a standard of functionality must be applied. An important step in designing a functional system is assessing the student's communication needs (Hamre-Nietupski et al., 1977). This entails listing all environments in which the student participates regularly to identify the situations in which the student needs to communicate, the individuals with whom he or she interacts, and the vocabulary needed in particular situations (Bottorf & DePape, 1982; Shane et al., 1982). This analysis should focus on skills the student uses during real activities and across all daily situations (Bottorf & DePape, 1982).

For example, using this approach, Hamre-Nietupski and her colleagues (1977) identified playing, eating, and toileting as important activities in three relevant environments—home, school, and community. They then tried to identify possible opportunities for training during naturally occurring events. For example, training during mealtime might involve placing a preferred food within sight but out of reach of the student, who would be prompted to request the food using the communication system. Another opportunity would be available during music period, when the student would be required to request a specific instrument in order to play it. In addition to identifying functional activities, these authors generated vocabulary lists of nouns, pronouns, verbs, adverbs, prepositions, and adjectives used by people in the target environments and activities. Using all this information, they selected the most appropriate communication content for each student.

In keeping with a standard of function, a top-down curriculum (Brown, Branston, Hamre-Nietupski, Pumpian, Certo, & Gruenewald, 1979) is suited to the task of analyzing a communication environment to identify common situations and listeners. For each of the four major domains cited by Brown and colleagues (domestic, community, vocational, and leisure/recreation), both immediate and future environments are identified for the student. For each of these environments, subenvironments are listed and then analyzed for the activities the student is likely to engage in when in each setting. Finally, each activity is examined for its essential skills, which, in turn, become targets for instruction. (See chapter 4 for a more complete explanation of this process.) A partial top-down curriculum generated through this process is shown in Table 11.1, on page 302. It will be used later in an example of choosing appropriate systems for a student.

TYPES OF NONSPEECH COMMUNICATION SYSTEMS

Once the student's communication needs have been identified, specific systems must be chosen to meet those needs. To make appropriate selections, the teacher needs to understand the nature and relative advantages of both visual-graphic and gestural systems. The student's motor and sensory skills will be considered. The teacher may also wish to train certain motor or sensory skills along with communication. Several programs have been developed for this purpose, teaching skills such as visual discrimination (Cress, Spellman, DeBriere, Sizemore, Northam, & Johnson, 1981; Newsom & Simon 1982) and tracking, scanning, and making selections (Hamre-Nietupski et al., 1977; Scheuerman et al., 1976).

Visual-Graphic Systems

The wide array of visual-graphic systems available differ according to how they look, how the student uses them, and whether they use pictures, printed words, or some other symbol system. Two systems may look very similar and yet require different motor responses from the student. Others may look quite different, but both use line drawings for vocabulary. Thus, you need to consider the most appropriate type of device, method of responding, and set of vocabulary symbols to develop a visual-graphic system.

Types of Devices

Nonelectronic Devices. Simple communication boards may be constructed from any type of flat, sturdy material such as paper, cardboard, plexiglass, or wood. The symbols to be used, such as drawings, letters, or printed words, are affixed to the board and often covered with plastic to protect them from wear and tear. The student communicates by selecting one of the symbols in some way, using a predetermined method of responding (described later in this section).

Several formats for nonelectronic communication devices are possible. For example, a single sheet may be used to display all symbols used by the student, as shown in Figure 11.1. According to Vicker (1974), the single-sheet display is easiest for the student to use and easiest for the practitioner to make and mount within a frame. Single-sheet displays may be fitted beneath plexiglass on the student's lap tray (Silverman, 1980), folded in half and equipped with handles for carrying (Detamore & Lippke, 1980), or reproduced several times so that one copy may be kept in each location frequented by the student, such as the home, classroom, cafeteria, or workshop. If the vocabulary begins to exceed the space on the board, several versions of a single-sheet display may be used, each with vocabulary appropriate for a given setting (McDonald & Schultz, 1973).

Alternatives to single-sheet displays are possible for students whose vocabulary is large and who are able to turn pages or cards in some way. Multiple displays may be combined into one unit, such as a flip chart (Vicker, 1974), notebook (Detamore & Lippke, 1980), or set of wallet-sized cards attached to a key chain or metal ring (Silverman, 1980). Each sheet may be tabbed to help turn the pages or cards. Using a similar arrangement, Karel and her associates (1981) developed a wallet-sized set of flipcards for one student, grouping them in categories such as recreation activities and vocational items. The student was required to scan the tabs separating the categories, select the correct one, and then point to the desired drawing.

The arrangement of symbols on either single-sheet or multiple displays will depend, in part, on the motor response to be used. If there are no constraints, symbols may be grouped according to syntactic function, such as subjects-verbs-prepositions-modifiers-objects or so that frequently used words are most easily indicated.[1]

---

[1] For more complete descriptions of display format and construction, see McDonald and Schultz, 1973; Silverman, 1980; and in particular, Vicker, 1974.

FIGURE 11.1

A Single-Sheet Design Illustrates the Learner's Wants and Needs. This board combines line drawing, Blissymbols, and photographs.

SOURCE: Photo by Dan Grogan

Nonelectronic communication aids have several advantages:

1. Availability, since they are easily and economically constructed;
2. Adaptability, since they may change as the user's skill increases; and
3. Flexibility, since they allow the use of many different symbol systems (Harris & Vanderheiden, 1980).

However, they have a serious disadvantage because they provide only temporary visual output. Therefore, a listener must attend carefully and remember the message, as it is constructed piece by piece.

Electronic Devices. Electronic communication systems allow various types of output, using devices such as a video screen, voice synthesizer, or a display like those used on calculators. They also allow for various types of input, such as a magnetized pointer, a push-switch, or a keyboard. Electronic systems are based on three components (Silverman, 1980): a switching mechanism, control electronics, and a display. Thus, they can be adapted to meet the individualized needs of the nonvocal communicator.

One commonly used input device is a switch of some sort. An electronic switching mechanism is activated by muscle or nerve innervation. Various switches are available, so that at least one switch may be found for the severely physically disabled student. Figure 11.2 shows a variety of switches.

Electronic switches should be tried to facilitate accuracy, reduce delay of response, and decrease fatigue. These switches are easily obtained from local electronics stores or built by anyone familiar with wiring. Burkhart (1980) has developed a manual for teachers describing methods for constructing and using a variety of switches. Community hobby groups or high school clubs may also be helpful in procuring switches. These switches not only interface with many electronic communication systems, but also with tape recorders, record players, radios, slide projectors, and mechanical toys. This offers the student a means of selecting leisure-time activities and of gaining more control over the environment. They may also be used to facilitate increased gross motor responses, such as correct posture or head control (Ball, McCrady, & Hart, 1975).

The second component of these systems is the control electronics. Each system must have some means

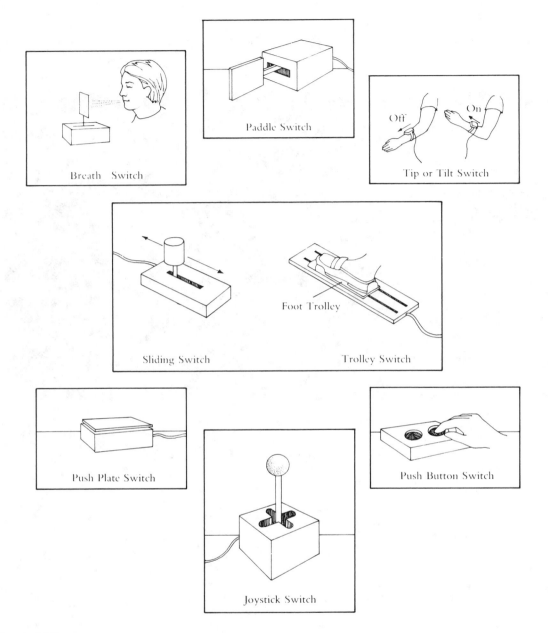

FIGURE 11.2
Various Types of Switches May Be Used to Activate Electronic Communication Systems or Battery-Powered Leisure Materials such as Toys or Tape Recorders. If a student has a reliable motor response, a switch may be found.

SOURCE: "Interface Switch Profile and Annotated List of Commercial Switches," by C. Holt, D. Buelow, & G. Vanderheiden. In G. Vanderheiden (Ed.), *Nonvocal communication resource book*. Baltimore: University Park Press, 1978. Reprinted with permission.

of controlling what happens after the student activates the switch. To accomplish this, commercially available systems use the same technology found in personal computers. For example, a basic light-scanning device may be connected to a speech synthesizer. If the student selects the symbol for "drink" on the light scanner, the control electronics will send the proper signals to the output device in the correct order. This results in the word being spoken by the synthesizer.

Finally, the display or output mode should be considered. Displays may be visual-graphic or auditory. For example, a display could be taped speech, cathode-ray tube (TV screen), light crystal display (used in digital clocks), or synthesized speech. Even a hospital call button has a display in its beep.

Many commerical devices are available specifically for communication purposes, such as those described in the newsletter *Communication Outlook* (Note 4). One such device, the Autocom, has been used successfully by severely cerebral palsied students (Harris, 1982; Wendt, Sprague, & Marquis, 1975).

When and if an electronic system is chosen for communication, funding can be a concern. Potential funding sources include private insurance and government programs such as Medicaid, Crippled Children's Services, or Vocational Rehabilitation. In addition, religious organizations, community clubs, and fund-raising events can help fund devices. A child with whom one of us worked needed an electronic device which was ultimately provided through a Christmas bazaar sponsored by the operators of the local telephone company. After the device was secured, the child got extra practice using it by communicating her thanks individually to the fund raisers. Parents should not be forgotten when determining resources for funding. Even if families contribute only a small amount of money toward the system, their contribution often gives them a vested interest in it and results in greater cooperation using the system with their child.

Should finances dictate, electronic devices can also be constructed rather than purchased. For example, Kucherawy and Kucherawy (1978) constructed a rotary scanner for a nonambulatory woman classified as profoundly retarded. The woman first learned picture-object association and gradually developed to using printed words. Silverman (1980) describes the materials and procedures needed to build some of the more basic electronic scanning devices. Local hobby groups, such as high school science clubs, can be another source of procuring electronic devices at reduced cost.

Personal or microcomputers may also be adapted with various switching mechanisms, giving access to a vast vocabulary tailored to the student's needs or to a series of questions or statements listed according to the frequency of use (McDonald, 1981). Local "users' groups," sometimes associated with home computer stores, may be available in the community to provide specific programming aid.

Manner in Which the Student Responds

Just as there are many types of electronic and non-electronic devices, there are several methods through which the student can select the intended message. The teacher must identify the most efficient, fastest, and least tiring response, using data obtained through systematically investigating the student's performance across a variety of tasks.

It is not sufficient to determine whether the student can complete a given response within a certain time period, however. Other factors are important. For example, the speed of the response may decrease the listener's motivation as the length of time needed to communicate increases. When single-word responses require 15 seconds or more, it is laborious for both the speaker and listener to attend. The fatigue of the nonvocal communicator may show up in the inability to attend to the conversation, maintain valid and reliable responses, or remain active in the conversation.

Associated but sometimes undesirable motor responses may also accompany the response. For example, hand-pointing may be accompanied by increased thrusting of the lower jaw or increased drooling. Headstick-pointing may increase hyperextension of the head and promote abnormal swallowing. The teacher should observe these responses and modify them as necessary. Thus, it is particularly important to obtain assistance from physical and occupational therapists in choosing the most efficient response method.

We will discuss the three most common methods of responding—direct selection, scanning, and encoding—with suggested screening tasks for each. Remember, however, that some students might be able to use a combination (Karel et al., 1981) and others might begin with one but learn to use a more efficient one after specific training (Bottorf & DePape, 1982).

Direct Selection. Vanderheiden and Grilley (1976) describe this response as one in which the user directly indicates the message, usually by moving one body part, such as a fist or arm, in a pointing motion. For those students with adequate motor control, it offers the important advantage of being efficient and rapid. However, direct selection requires more refined motor skills than does scanning (Vanderheiden & Grilley, 1976).

You may think of pointing with the index finger as being the most common way to select a bit of information on some type of direct selection system. However, variations in pointing can be achieved using certain electronic systems or other body parts. A student could use an optical head pointer which, by using a small light and a specialized light-sensitive board, allows for efficient direct selection by lateral and vertical head movement. Reid and Hurlbut (1977) used nonelectronic stylus-type head pointers with three nonambulatory, severely retarded adults, who were able to move their heads until the pointer rested on the intended square on single-sheet communication boards. Another possibility for direct selection is for the student to use the eyes to focus on the symbol that needs to be communicated. This type of eye-pointing (Connor, 1978) works when a clear piece of plexiglass is placed vertically before the student with various symbols around its outside border. (See Figure 11.3 for a variation of eye-pointing.) This simple response can be used when motor deficits prevent valid and reliable pointing with the hands or arms. Elder and Bergman (1978) used directed eye-gaze successfully with five mildly to profoundly retarded students, who learned to discriminate among a variety of Blissymbols.

To determine the feasibility of using direct selection, you must find the most efficient motor activity for indicating choices by analyzing the task and collecting data systematically. For example, to use a nonelectronic visual-graphic system, consider the following procedure.

FIGURE 11.3
Using Dots of Various Colors around the Periphery of a Plexiglass Sheet, a Student Learns to Use Eye Pointing to Encode a Given Message, Matching the Colored Dot to the Color Outlining Each Picture.
SOURCE: Photo by Dan Grogan.

1. Establish a rectangular board divided into 10 areas with each area numbered as a pointing board (Waldo et al., 1981). Place it in front of the student with the extremity being tested having easy access to it.
2. Test the student's ability to touch each area, presented in random order. Suggested methods are to model the response, while saying "Point here" (Reid & Hurlburt, 1977) or to place a small reinforcer in the square and say, "Get _____" (Sailor et al., 1980).
3. If the student gives the correct response, record the number of seconds required. In addition, record whether the response required so much concentration and effort that it would be fatiguing over time. Finally, record if the student was able to maintain the response for at least 2 full seconds without tremor or extraneous movements (Waldo et al., 1981).
4. If the student achieved accuracy in all squares, use another piece of lap-board sized paper, dividing it into more squares. Repeat the testing process.
5. If the student is unable to complete the task in fewer than 20 seconds, try to modify the task using another body part or larger squares. For example, a right hand or a left hand or a lower extremity may be tried.

Adequate vision and conjugate gaze, where both eyes focus together, are particularly important in considering eye-pointing system. Screening for an eye-gaze response might be similar to this.

1. Choose two objects known to be reinforcing to the student.
2. To determine the visual field within which the student responds reliably, systematically vary the distance of the objects in front of the student. Indicate one object and say, "Look at the _____."
3. Randomize the presentation.
4. After the student has shown competency with objects, make line drawings of the same objects and place them around the outside border of a clear piece of plexiglass 12" × 24".
5. Repeat the trials as for the objects.

Scanning. Scanning systems, which are quite common, may or may not be electronic. Nonelectronic scanning systems require another person to serially present information to the communicator. This person may be the listener and wait for a message. It's easy to picture a teacher slowly presenting the items on a picture communication board and waiting for the student's response after saying, "What is it that you want?" "Is it _____?" The student's signal acts like a yes/no answer in this situation. If a student with severe physical disability makes an error, he or she may become so excited that muscle tone increases and it is impossible to use the prearranged signal so the series must be repeated. (See Figure 11.4)

Electronic scanning systems rely most frequently on a light which systematically scans information when a switch is activated. The speed of the scan can be adapted to meet the individual's need. Thus if the communicator makes an error, the scan can go backwards quickly, slow down when the message gets near, and then proceed as before. This electronic option makes scanning more efficient. A variation of this idea (Vanderheiden, 1981) uses very rapid scanning until the user stops it near the target response, when a normal rate is used to backtrack to the intended message.

Electronic, switch-activated scanning offers a major advantage of requiring only one reliable motor response, such as pressing a lever, tilting the head, or pushing a foot pedal. Thus, scanning can be used by almost any severely handicapped person. However, compared with direct selection, it is more time-consuming, especially if the intended message is among the last to be scanned.

The ability to scan can be determined with a task in which the student surveys an organized sequential visual array. A predetermined signal to stop, such as vocalizing, moving the head, or hitting a bell, would be the expected response, or the teacher might watch the student's eye movements.

1. Choose five pairs of common objects that are familiar or reinforcing to the student, such as drink, shoe, sunglasses, or a disco record. Arrange one set on a tray in front of the student.
2. Choose one item from the matched set and move it sequentially along the array in front of the student slowly and regularly. Say for each, "Is this a _____?"
3. Wait for a signal from the student when the correct match has been determined.
4. Repeat the process using pictures in the array.

Encoding. With encoding, information is translated by the student with a predetermined code that is then interpreted by the listener. This code may be memorized or placed on a chart that is visible to both parties. For example, a child could indicate two separate numbers on a chart that are interpreted by the adult to mean "thirsty." A useful type of encoding is ETRAN. ETRAN uses a piece of plexiglass mounted vertically opposite the student with a code system of numbers, letters, or colors displayed around the glass. Using eye-pointing, the student indicates the appropriate letter, color, or numbers, which each refer to a specific message. For example, if a student is using a symbol board with 100 vocabulary items, each item could be coded with a color and a number. If the student looks at number 5 and then red, he would be communicating symbol 5-red. The listener would then consult the vocabulary chart to find that 5-red means "thirsty."

A strategic advantage of encoding is that it allows for a much larger vocabulary than do most direct selection or scanning systems, since a set of 10 numbers, letters, and colors may be used to code many different words or messages. However, encoding requires a multistep response with rather complex representational and sequencing skills, and therefore will be inappropriate for many students.

To determine whether a student can encode information, a very elementary task can be used. The student is required to associate an object with one isolated attribute of that object.

1. Determine if the student could discriminate color and match for color.
2. Choose colored objects known to the student, such as a banana, apple, and pear.

FIGURE 11.4
When Simple Electronic Scanning Is Used, as in the Zygo Communicator Model 16, a Light Moves Serially across the Squares until the User Selects One by Activating a Switch.
SOURCE: Photo by Dan Grogan.

3. Give the student an array of three different colors and present an apple.
4. Say, "Show me one that means this" to determine whether the student can use one isolated aspect such as color to represent an object.
5. After the student can successfully complete this task, use a similar procedure with numbers.

Determining the Symbol System

Various options including objects, photos, line drawings, abstract symbols, and words may be used to represent messages. The visual-graphic symbols for an augmentative communication system should be chosen systematically. First, the student's ability to determine object-to-symbol association should be clarified.

Matching Objects to Pictures. To determine whether the student can associate two-dimensional representations of objects with actual objects, these steps may be helpful.

1. Choose a small group of items that are reinforcing to the student or are used frequently.
2. For each trial, place two or more simple line drawings, each on a separate card, in front of the student. Hold up the object and give an instructional cue such as, "Show me (the picture of) _____." The expected response can be touching the picture or using eye pointing to indicate it.
3. If the student cannot match the line drawing with the object, repeat the process with photographs.
4. If photographs do not yield the appropriate response, training may need to proceed using real objects.
5. For functionally blind students, object-object matching can be screened or trained first, perhaps followed by matching of three-dimensional abstract shapes or shapes differentiated by texture.

Objects. When learners have not made the association between objects and related symbols such as pictures, it may be advisable to place objects on the display, which may be temporary for many learners. However, for visually impaired learners, a three-dimensional tactile display may be a highly functional beginning communication device. For example, Karel and colleagues (1981) have used a tactile board with a visually impaired student, teaching him a systematic row-scanning system.

Pictures. Pictures with orthographic symbols printed below are one of the most common visual displays used in nonvocal communication systems. They may be hand drawn, cut from old magazines, or taken from a commercially available set. When choosing among photos, line drawings, or cut-out pictures, it is important to consider the ease with which the board can be reproduced for use in a variety of settings.

Blissymbolics. Blissymbolics is a symbol system used by many nonvocal people. Developed by Charles Bliss for the purpose of international communication, it is a logical visual-graphic system that is semantics- or meaning-based (as opposed to phonetics- or sound-based). McNaughton (1975) suggests the following prerequisite skills for using Blissymbols: (a) good visual discrimination, (b) visual representational skills, and (c) a reliable method of indicating choices. This language-based system uses standardized symbols that in some cases are similar to the objects or events they represent. For example, standardized line drawings of a house, a chair, and a heart are used. However, additional symbols are combined to denote specific states of other symbols. For example, a wheel is placed under a chair to convey "wheelchair"; a verb marker placed over a circle means "to eat" rather than the noun "food." (See Figure 11.5.)

Rebus Symbols. Rebuses are symbols that represent entire words or parts of words. They may be concrete, such as the picture of a girl's face to mean "girl"; relational, such as a ball on top of a box to mean "on"; or abstract, such as a dash (—) to mean "is." Suffixes such as "-ing" and "-s" are written orthographically with this system.

Developed in 1974 and distributed by the American Guidance Company, these symbols may be beneficial for students who do not read, and in fact are sometimes used with the mildly handicapped to introduce reading. Clark, Davies, and Woodcock (1974) have published a standardized set of more than 800 rebuses.

Determining the Size of the Symbols

When line drawings, photographs, or cut-out pictures are being considered, the size of the image is important. To determine how large symbols must be for a given student, use a series of identical sets of pictures graded in size in a match-to-sample format (Waldo et al., 1981).

1. If a student can label receptively or match pictures to familiar objects, such as ball, cookie, and juice, prepare drawings of these objects in an intermediate size, e.g., 2 inches.
2. Presented with the correct picture, shown one of the objects, and given the instructional cue, "Show me the _____," the student should select the correct picture.
3. The response chosen should be easy to perform and valid and reliable to insure that visual skills are not confounded. Do not confuse a slow or unreliable motor response with poor visual skills.

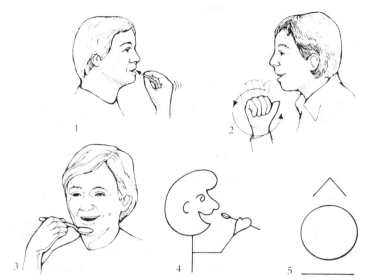

FIGURE 11.5
The Word Eat *Is Shown in (1)
American Sign Language (the
Amer-Ind Sign for* Eat *Is
Similar), (2) Signing Exact
English (SEE₂), (3) a Line
Drawing, (4) Rebus, and (5)
Blissymbols.*

SOURCE: Illustration by John Owen.

4. If the student cannot respond correctly, use a series of larger pictures until the minimum size required is identified.

5. If the student does respond correctly, use a series of smaller pictures until the smallest recognizable picture is found.

6. If an abstract system such as Blissymbolics, rebuses, or written words is to be used, the search for the appropriate size should focus on that system.

Gestural Systems

As we said earlier, gestural systems are a second major category of augmentative systems. The three types of gestural systems—sign language, natural gestures, and communication codes—vary according to the range of messages that can be expressed and the degree of fine motor skill required.

Sign Language Systems

Sign language systems offer several advantages, including (a) portability, since no adaptive equipment is required (Nietupski & Hamre-Nietupski, 1979); (b) similarity to the fluid and spontaneous nature of spoken language (Hopper & Helmick, 1977); (c) unrestricted vocabulary (Waldo et al., 1981); and (d) for many concepts, similarity between sign and the object or event represented (Scheuerman et al., 1976). However, signing systems also have disadvantages, foremost among which are the need for complex fine motor skills and the restricted number of people who will know the particular system being used (Nietupski & Hamre-Nietupski, 1979; Waldo et al., 1981; Chapman & Miller, Note 1). Of particular concern is the student's ability to use signs with persons outside

current school and home environments (Shane et al., 1982).

Vision.   The student's ability to see signs formed by others will affect the ability to imitate them during learning and to understand messages expressed through sign. According to Sailor and colleagues,

If a student is severely visually impaired in addition to showing severe, functional retardation, and visual efficiency cannot be substantially improved with prosthetic devices, then manual signing, above the level of gross gestures may not be successfully taught. (1980, p. 88)

Therefore, it is important to consider the results of an optometric evaluation.

Motor Skills.   To determine accuracy of motor response for signing, it is useful to test signs according to hand configurations, arm/hand movements, and position in space. For example, in their *Total Communication Checklist and Assessment,* Waldo, Barnes, and Berry (1981) group sample signs according to whether they use (a) one-handed movements, (b) two-handed movements, (c) touching movements, (d) nontouching movements, and (e) different hand configurations.

Students may be tested either for the ability to imitate a model of the sign or for willingness to be physically guided through the sign. In either case, careful criteria for each sign should be predetermined so that data can be collected on each aspect, i.e., configuration, position in space, and movement. If the student does not perform the signs accurately, even with physical prompting, the ability to convey messages will be impaired. Accuracy will also be impaired for the student who has limited use of one hand. Because there are many two-handed signs, Waldo and colleagues (1981) suggest that signing should automatically be excluded as a possible system if the student cannot use both hands.

Selecting a Specific Signing System

If it appears that signing will meet many of the student's communication needs and that he or she is visually and motorically capable of using manual communication, a specific signing system must be selected. Three systems that have been used with severely handicapped people are Amer-Ind, American Sign Language, and systems based on English language structure. We will describe each of these briefly.[2]

Amer-Ind. Amer-Ind is a manual system developed by Skelly (1979) for modern clinical use with communicatively handicapped people. Derived from American Indian Hand Talk (Skelly, 1979), Amer-Ind is a manual code that has no grammatical or structural rules and thus is not a language (Kirschner, Algozzine, & Abbott, 1979; Skelly, 1979). Amer-Ind signs are based on actions rather than words and are highly concrete. In addition, each sign has several related meanings. For example, the sign that represents the action "throw" also represents the concepts "ball," "game," "play," and "projectile" (Skelly, 1979).

Amer-Ind signs have been found more understandable than signs from American Sign Language for college students who were unfamiliar with any sign language (Kirschner et al., 1979). They have been taught successfully to severely and profoundly mentally retarded children (Daniloff & Shafer, 1981) in a school setting.

American Sign Language. Also known as ASL and Ameslan, American Sign Language was reported in 1975 to be the third most frequently used non-English language in the United States (Wilbur, 1976). Derived from a sign language developed in France and then brought to this country (Moores, 1974), ASL is *not* a manual version of the English language, nor is it a worldwide sign language. It is a separate, self-contained language that differs from English and other languages in many significant ways, including: (*a*) it does not use English word order; (*b*) it has no form of the verb *to be;* (*c*) it has no passive voice; (*d*) it uses no articles; (*e*) it marks verb tense for a whole conversation or segment of conversation, not for individual verbs; (*f*) it does not have signs for pronouns, but establishes the intended referent(s) in space; and (*g*) it can use movement in space to convey in one sign a subject + verb + object statement that would require three words in English (Mayberry, 1976; Moores, 1974; Fristoe & Lloyd, Note 5). Thus,

the syntactic and semantic rules of ASL differ greatly from those of English.

Signs taken from ASL have been taught successfully to autistic children (Cohen, 1981) and moderately to profoundly retarded students (Stremel-Campbell, Cantrell, & Halle, 1977). In both of these studies, signing and speech were used simultaneously for single or two-sign responses. Beyond a one- or two-word level, ASL could not be taught simultaneously with speech since its word order and grammar are different from English. Instead, one of the sign languages that parallels English word order might be more appropriate.

Systems that Parallel English. Several signing systems were specifically developed to parallel the English language. Referred to as *pedagogical systems* (Moores, 1974), these alternatives include Seeing Essential English (SEE$_1$), Signing Exact English (SEE$_2$), Signed English, Linguistics of Visual English (LVE or LOVE), and Manual English. Usually drawing their signs from those used in ASL, these systems differ significantly from ASL in that they use English word order and reflect English syntax and morphology (Mayberry, 1976; Wilbur, 1976). Thus, these systems incorporate signs for affixes such as "-s" and "-ed," pronouns, and usually articles. However, these systems differ from each other in the rules used to reflect English structure and morphology. Other differences include rules for forming past participles, contractions, and plurals; the number of signs borrowed from ASL; the extent to which fingerspelling is allowed; the number of affixes included; and the rules for choosing or creating signs (Mayberry, 1976; Wilbur, 1976; Fristoe & Lloyd). See Figure 11.5 for example of the word *eat* in various signing systems.

Of these systems, Signed English appears to have been used most extensively. Vocabulary from Signed English has been taught both to severely mentally retarded students (Browder, Morris, & Snell, 1981; Kohl, 1981; Linville, 1977) and autistic adolescents (Carr et al., 1978). However, other systems have also been used with severely retarded students. For example, one adolescent learned to form phrases and simple sentences using SEE$_1$ and began to communicate spontaneously in both school and home (Brookner & Murphy, 1975). SEE$_2$ signs have formed the basis of a sign language training program used with several severely handicapped students (Waldo, Riggs, Davaz, Hirsch, Eye, & Marshall, Note 6), though any signing system that parallels English word order may be used in this program.

Choosing Among Signing Systems. Because most studies on the use of signing with the severely handicapped investigated only one- and two-word signing skills, they do not offer any empirical evidence

---

[2]For more complete descriptions, see Mayberry (1976), Moores (1974), and Wilbur (1976).

for selecting one signing system over another. On the basis of these studies, we do not know which system, if any, would facilitate the greatest acquisition of complex language skills or which one might be mastered most easily.

Using considerations other than research, however, we can offer some recommendations. For example, Mayberry (1976) suggests that, with populations such as the severely mentally retarded, the manual system should be selected after the student has acquired a repertoire of one- and two-sign utterances. In selecting the initial vocabulary, then, the teacher could choose individual signs from ASL, SEE₂, or Signed English. Once students have initial signing skills, it makes intuitive sense for people "with near-normal nonverbal intelligence scores, motor skills, and social interaction that either SEE₂ or Signed English should be chosen" (Mayberry, 1976, p. 226). These systems parallel spoken English, may facilitate acquisition of English syntax, and do not require people in the student's environment to learn a new syntax or vocabulary as part of the signing system.

For students with multiple handicaps, such as the mentally retarded deaf or profoundly mentally retarded, Kopchick and Lloyd (1976) and Fristoe and Lloyd (Note 5) recommend Signed English because (a) it allows the message to be given orally and manually at the same time, (b) it incorporates more advanced skills as the learner develops competence, and (c) there are storybooks and other printed materials available. However, Kopchick and Lloyd qualify their position by advising that initial training not include inflectional markers for tense and plurality, such as "-s," "-ed," and "-ing."

Natural Gestures

Commonly understood gestures constitute one viable mode through which the severely handicapped student may communicate. Hamre-Nietupski and her colleagues (1977) have listed over 160 natural gestures that are understandable to untrained persons, such as shaking a fist to express anger or shivering and rubbing crossed arms to indicate being cold. These gestures are commonly used by handicapped and nonhandicapped people alike to supplement speech.

As an augmentative system, natural gestures offer the same advantage as sign language of not requiring equipment. However, unlike signing systems, natural gestures are generally understandable to most untrained observers and require relatively few fine motor skills (Hamre-Nietupski et al., 1977). Therefore, they are useful with a broad population of listeners and can be used by some students with motor and visual impairments. Despite these advantages, however, natural gestures have a serious disadvantage: the number of ideas that can be expressed is limited (Nietupski & Hamre-Nietupski, 1979).

Support for the use of natural gestures is available from several sources. For example, Hamre-Nietupski and colleagues (1977) strongly suggest that students learn to use natural gestures, as well as other modes, to increase the number of people with whom they will be able to communicate. Taking a different perspective, Sailor and colleagues (1980) suggest that training in use of natural gestures may help refine motor skills so that a formal sign language system becomes possible later. In addition, Reich (1978) provides empirical support for gestures, in a study showing that nonverbal retarded preschoolers used significantly more spontaneous words when they were trained through gestures paired with speech than when taught solely through speech. Finally, Harris (1982) found that severely cerebral palsied nonretarded students used gestures and vocalizations most frequently for spontaneous communication, despite being supplied with and trained in the use of an electronic direct selection aid.

Thus, there is ample reason to consider natural gestures as one form of augmentative communication. Screening similar to that used for sign language may be used to determine whether the student can imitate or be physically guided into forming natural gestures.

Communication Codes

Communication codes generally involve asking a series of yes/no questions to which the student makes some sort of predetermined response, such as eye movement or foot-tapping (Nietupski & Hamre-Nietupski, 1979). For example, when asked such questions as "Do you want to listen to this record?" or "Do you want to play this card?" during a recreational activity, the student might use a code such as blinking or moving the arm to answer yes and not responding to signify no. Since communication codes require only reliable motor response (Scheuerman et al., 1976), they can be used by almost any severely handicapped student. However, because the student must rely on the questioner to ask the right questions, codes are highly restrictive and make the student very dependent. Therefore, codes should be considered only in extreme cases of physical impairments (Nietupski & Hamre-Nietupski, 1979).

MATCHING THE NONSPEECH SYSTEM TO THE STUDENT: AN EXAMPLE

Given the many augmentative systems available, their relative advantages and disadvantages, and the types of motoric and sensory skills needed to use them, choosing appropriate communication modes for a given student is a complex and long-range process. To illustrate this process, let us look at one student. However, this example illustrates only the *types* of factors and decisions involved; it is in no way intended to represent the "right" answers for all severely handicapped students.

Susan, a 12-year-old girl, is cerebral palsied and retarded. She is not ambulatory and has better use of her arms and hands than her legs. She uses a wheelchair, a standing table, and an adapted chair during her school day in a severely and profoundly handicapped classroom in a regular public school. Three of Susan's classmates use speech to communicate their functional needs. Another uses gesture and is learning Signed English, while another uses Signed English exclusively. One student has no communication system but is being trained to use a nonelectronic, direct selection communication board with pictures. Susan's class is self-contained but is integrated with 6th grade for lunch and recess. She lives with her parents and two siblings (age 10 and 4) in a suburb. Table 11.1 gives a partial list of the subenvironments, activities, and skills that might be generated for Susan through a top-down curriculum strategy.

Table 11.1 shows several natural contexts for communication. For example, in the cafeteria, Susan may ask for help in opening her milk carton or cutting her meat. On the playground, she might ask schoolmates to play catch or push her over a bump in the grass. Susan would need to respond if asked to join in a game, but would also need to ask for assistance. At home, Susan will at least need to understand directions for wiping the table, drying dinner utensils, and getting dressed or undressed. She will need to ask for food to be passed to her and may want to tell her family about children at school or in the neighborhood. She may need to tell her brother to stop teasing her or may want to ask to listen to the stereo in the evening.

Thus Susan will require a system available in her kitchen and bedroom at home and in the cafeteria and playground area at school. In addition, were Susan's complete curriculum presented in Table 11.1, we would see that she will need to communicate in many other areas as well, such as her living room and backyard at home; the classroom, school bus, and gymnasium at school; her grandparents' home; a neighbor's swimming pool; and a restaurant frequented by her family. Thus, Susan needs a highly portable means of communicating. It is also apparent that she needs to communicate with her family, classmates, and nonhandicapped peers every day. Thus, her method of communicating must be understandable to many others, at least some of whom will not know sign language or how to read.

We can also see that Susan needs an expandable

TABLE 11.1 A Partial Top-Down Curriculum

Domain:	Community
Environment:	School
Subenvironment:	1. Cafeteria
Activity:	1.1 Getting lunch
Skills:	a. Get a tray of food
	b. Put napkin, utensils, straw, and milk on tray
	c. Present meal card
Activity:	1.2 Eating
Skills:	a. Find a place to sit
	b. Open milk carton
	c. Eat with fork and spoon
	d. Use napkin
	e. Clean up
Subenvironment:	2. Playground Area
Activity:	2.1 Playing group games
Skills:	a. Catch/throw a ball
	b. Play adapted volleyball
Activity:	2.2 Playing alone
Skills:	a. Move wheelchair over grass
	b. Take pictures with a camera
Domain:	Domestic
Environment:	Home
Subenvironment:	1. Kitchen
Activity:	1.1 Eating with family
Skills:	a. Pass food to others
	b. Cut meat
Activity:	1.2 Cleaning
Skills:	a. Assist in clearing table
	b. Dry and store dinner utensils
Subenvironment:	2. Bedroom
Activity:	2.1 Getting dressed/undressed
Skills:	a. Take off slacks
	b. Take off pullover shirt
	c. Put on pullover shirt
	d. Put on slip-on shoes

system. Examination of Susan's completed top-down curriculum would show many words and word chains she will need. Since she will not learn all of these words at once, her communication system must allow for expansion of vocabulary as she acquires trained items and as additional subenvironments, activities, and skills become relevant.

In short, then, as possible communication systems are considered for Susan (or any other severely handicapped student), they must be evaluated for their utility in those settings, with those listeners, and for those purposes specified by the student's present and future communication needs.

In choosing communication systems for Susan, immediacy would be the first concern. Therefore, we would institute a temporary nonvocal system that could be used to gather information for a more permanent system. This initial system would be undertaken after initial screening to determine the most effective response. Screening on imitation of signs indicated that Susan could neither imitate two-handed signs nor repeat them immediately after several trials of physical prompting. Therefore, sign was judged to be impractical for immediate use. Furthermore, it did not appear to be the best choice because the symbol system should be easily interpreted by classmates and family.

In screening for a visual-graphic system, the teacher found that 1-inch square images would be appropriate. Line drawings were chosen because Susan could associate at least some with their referents, because they are easily produced, and because most peers and family members would be able to recognize them. Each picture would be labeled with its word underneath. Since screening revealed that Susan could use direct selection using one-finger pointing, these pictures could be placed in a small notebook under sheets of clear plastic. The notebook could be placed in a side pocket on her wheelchair to move from place to place, but would be on her lap tray at other times. (See Figure 11.6.)

In addition, a wallet-sized packet of the same line drawings would be given to Susan's parents for use at home or in the community. Information on frequency of use, need for expandability, and feasibility of the symbol system would be gathered while Susan used this initial system. Later Susan might be considered a likely candidate for an electronic system using synthesized speech, to communicate in her classroom, home, grandparents' home, and community.

However, because of the limitations imposed by a visual-graphic system (i.e., it must be immediately available, other people must be able to interpret pictures, and it must be as acceptable as possible in various settings), a second form of communication, natural gestures, would accompany it. Thus, Susan could learn the gestures for "stop," "give me," and "come here" (described by Hamre-Nietupski et al., 1977). Therefore, she would have a second way to make her needs known when her communication book was unavailable. Finally, Susan would be trained to say "ah" to signal people to come over and

FIGURE 11.6
Susan Might Use a Conversation Notebook Like This, Though Probably Smaller.
SOURCE: Photo by Dan Grogan.

interact with her. The student using an augmentative system always benefits from having a signal such as vocalizing or hitting a bell to initiate exchange with others. Thus, Susan's initial modes of communication would include a picture conversation book, natural gestures, and vocalizing. These systems may be temporary and only give her instructors data about other plausible systems. Nevertheless, they allow her to learn the power of communication and language rules and, most importantly, provide her with a reliable, unambiguous means of communicating here and now.

TEACHING COMMUNICATION SKILLS TO USERS OF AUGMENTATIVE SYSTEMS

Once a primary communication mode has been selected, the question of how the person will communicate has been answered. However, of at least equal importance are the questions of what the person will communicate and how he or she will learn to use the communication system. Thus, teaching language to a nonvocal learner is a two-fold task. Target skills and strategies will concern both (a) message content or vocabulary and (b) means of expressing this content.

Choosing Vocabulary

Initial Vocabulary
As stated earlier, one efficient way to identify vocabulary is to analyze the settings and activities relevant for the individual student (Bottorf & DePage, 1982; Hamre-Nietupski et al., 1977; Shane et al., 1982). Since the student cannot learn all possible vocabulary at once, the teacher must choose an initial core of words. It is particularly important to select words that are functional and reinforcing (Carlson, 1981; Carr, 1982; Nietupski & Hamre-Nietupski, 1979; Sailor et al., 1980). Thus, for some students, "need" words such as "eat," "drink," "toilet," and "coat" may be inappropriate for initial instruction (Bottorf & DePape, 1982; Waldo et al., 1981). For example, if a young child is used to having all basic needs met, he or she may have little motivation to communicate about them. In this case, initial training might better focus on "want" words that provide novel reinforcement or control over the environment. For example, the student might initially learn to request favorite toys, foods, events, or persons (Nietupski & Hamre-Nietupski, 1979), with training in "needs" words later. Considering the example of Susan, the words "ball" and "camera" might be more appropriate as initial vocabulary than "tray" and "spoon."

In addition to being interesting and functional for the student, initial vocabulary words should be ones the student will frequently need, as determined by an inventory of the environment (Carlson, 1981; Sailor et al., 1980). Words that can be used across settings and activities, such as "yes," "want," and "more," are particularly relevant (Scheuerman et al., 1976).

Factors Related to the Learning of Signs
When sign language has been selected as an augmentative system, the choice of initial vocabulary items should consider research indicating that the manner in which signs are made influences the ease and rate with which they are learned. Specifically, faster learning is obtained on signs in which (a) one hand comes in touch with the other; (b) both hands form identical configurations or shapes and move independently; (c) the target sign differs from other signs on at least three of the following: hand configuration, location in relation to the signer's body, movement through space, and direction faced by the palm; (d) both hands make the sign at the same location relative to the body; and (e) the hand configuration or movement closely resembles the actual object (Griffith & Robinson, 1980; Kohl, 1981; Stremel-Campbell et al., 1977).

When choosing initial signing vocabulary, then, teachers must analyze functional, reinforcing, and frequently used words to identify the way each word is signed. They may then choose the order in which signs will be introduced according to the ease with which they are likely to be learned.

Choosing Settings and Times for Training

Communication training should take place in natural settings across a variety of instructional activities (Karel et al., 1981; Kopchick & Lloyd, 1976; Nietupski & Hamre-Nietupski, 1979; Scheuerman et al., 1976). In part, this position stems from findings that severely handicapped people fail to generalize communication skills spontaneously beyond training conditions, both for verbal language (Harris, 1975) and for augmentative systems (Faw et al., 1981; Kopchick, Rombach, & Smilovitz, 1975). In addition, normal language development shows that children acquire communication skills through interactions in natural social contexts, such as conversing, exchanging questions and answers, and requesting aid or attention (Nietupski, Scheutz, & Ockwood, 1980). Because the home and school provide natural social contexts and activities for severely handicapped students, they provide the most likely settings for communication training.

Training in Natural Settings
Augmentative communication skills can be taught successfully in natural settings, including the classroom (Harris, 1982; Karel et al., 1981; Reich, 1978; Richardson, 1975) and home living units of institu-

tionalized students (Faw et al., 1981; Kopchick et al., 1975; Reid & Hurlbut, 1977). Of particular interest is a study by Kohl, Wilcox, and Karlan (1978) of the learning of signs by three moderately retarded children. Comparing training in the classroom with that conducted in a separate therapy room, they found that the highest number of correct responses for a given set of words occurred in the setting where those words had been trained. It seems most efficient, then, to train communication skills in the setting where they will be needed.

For some specific communication needs, a simulated environment may be effective for training if followed by generalization probes, and if necessary, training in the actual setting. Christoph, Nietupski, and Pumpian (1980) used this approach to teach five severely retarded students to order a snack in a fast-food restaurant using a wallet-sized communication card. Using a simulation in several classrooms for initial teaching, the trainers probed regularly for generalization in actual shopping plazas and found that four of the students met criteria in the natural setting, while the fifth mastered all skills but did not perform them within the 60-second limit. Thus, a simulated training environment provided an efficient use of instructional time for a community skill and proved to be valid when complemented by testing and further training in the natural setting.

Training Across a Variety of Activities

Closely related to the issue of training in the natural setting is the need for training across a variety of naturally occurring activities. Many daily routines provide suitable opportunities for developing communication skills. For example, during meals, the student might be required to ask for a preferred food before receiving it; in the family room with a sibling, he might be asked to choose between listening to a record or watching television (Hamre-Nietupski et al., 1977). Similarly, the student might be asked to watch a peer or sibling during sports to improve visual-tracking skills or might be required to look at a picture of a bicycle before being allowed to use it to improve attending skills (Scheuerman et al., 1976). As proficiency increases, the student might be required to expand the length of messages by pointing to the words "I want" and then the desired item (Karel et al., 1981) during meals, leisure activities, or shopping trips. He or she might be prompted to ask for assistance in a task like shoe-tying by having the teacher model the request and then requiring the student to imitate it before aid is given (Linville, 1977). Analysis of the student's daily environments and activities will reveal many additional natural opportunities for training.

Incorporating communication training into daily activities does not preclude the use of instructional sessions devoted to communication skills. Indeed,

many studies show that skills in signing or using communication boards may be mastered during regularly scheduled communication training (e.g., Bricker, 1972; Carr et al., 1978; Cohen, 1981; Elder & Bergman, 1978). However, unless specific programming takes place during other activities, as well, it is not likely that students will generalize their communication skills to other activities, materials, or trainers (Guess, 1980).

Group Interaction

When communication training is provided across activities in school, it is important for the student to interact with his or her peers. Waldo and colleagues (Notes 6, 7) include training sequences specifically for this purpose in their manuals for teaching sign language and for teaching the use of communication boards. Each step of the nine instructional skills taught in these programs includes sequential training to vary the type of input provided. First, the step is taught with the teacher's speaking and using the board or signing, depending on the system being trained. Then the step is retaught with the teacher using speech alone. Finally, the step is repeated with the teacher using the new system alone. In this way, the student is prepared to converse with peers who use similar augmentative communication systems, as well as with others who use oral language.

Other means for enhancing communication are appropriate during group instruction. For example, Detamore and Lippke (1980) describe a large wallboard for the teacher to use during group instruction. By using speech and the wallboard to present instruction and conversation, along with signing if appropriate, the teacher can model the use of augmentative systems frequently and naturally, facilitating students' use of these modes.

Commercially made scanning devices are also available to accommodate groups of students, with each student using his or her own switch to convey a message on a large, central display (News on aids, 1978). In this way, students can participate fully in a group activity, conversing with each other as well as the teacher.

Involving the Family

Of critical importance in developing functional, generalized communication skills with a severely handicapped student is family support for the augmentative system (Hamre-Nietupski et al., 1977; McDonald & Schultz, 1973; Nietupski et al., 1980; Vicker, 1974). Several studies reporting spontaneous generalization of augmentative communication skills also indicated that the subjects' parents cooperated in using the system, whether sign language (Brookner & Murphy, 1975; Linville, 1977) or a communication board (Ratusnik & Ratusnik, 1974).

When engaging the support of a student's family, it is important to set realistic expectations. The duties and obligations of parents to provide for the physical needs of their handicapped child comprise a lengthy and time-consuming list. Compounding it with numerous training requests may mean that these requests are not met. The parents feel guilty for not meeting the professional's expectations and blame themselves for their child's lack of progress. Sensitivity to the parents' other obligations can alleviate the difficulties of unrealistic home programs.

In addition to helping family members learn the particular system being used, it is important to help them learn to recognize natural opportunities for training or reinforcing communication skills. Both at home and in the community, parents and siblings will have many opportunities to ask the student to express choices or make requests. Bottorf and De-Pape (1982) have recommended strategies that would be useful here. For example, symbols of important household items, such as "glass," "water," "chair," and "hot," could be taped to the actual objects. Parents and siblings could then use these symbols when discussing the items or asking the student to express a message about them. Similarly, symbols referring to outdoor objects or events might be placed along the bottom edge of a window, so that family members can use them to converse about such items as "car," "play," "tree," "go," and "lawnmower." Within the "augmentative atmosphere" created by a family's use of such strategies, the student would see others using the system and would be more likely to use similar behaviors (Bottorf & DePape, 1982).

Enhancing Conversations

While it is important for the severely handicapped person to use the augmentative system to obtain desired objects or events and learn the power of communication, it is also important for him or her to engage in social conversations under appropriate circumstances (Harris, 1982). Unfortunately, it is easy to lose sight of the need for social conversation with people who use augmentative systems. According to Harris (1982), people rarely interacted with the cerebral palsied, nonretarded children in her study unless they were seeking specific information or unless the child initiated an exchange. Small talk, general interest conversations, and exchanges of anecdotes occurred rarely. According to Harris, "a general atmosphere seemed to be created in which communicative interaction was gotten over with as soon as possible" (1982, p. 32).

Obviously, that atmosphere is counterproductive to the development of communication skills. Several strategies are available to provide a communication-enhancing environment. First, teachers, family members, and others who interact with the student should communicate for enjoyment as well as instructional or need-oriented purposes. Students should be expected to participate in these exchanges and should be given enough time to respond without being interrupted by additional questions or second-guessing from the listener (Harris, 1982). Second, other people interacting with the severely handicapped person should avoid asking questions with obvious or limited answers. For example, rather than asking "What are you drinking?" when the student is obviously drinking a Coke, it would be more appropriate to make some statement such as "I see you are drinking a Coke. I like Coke, too," while pointing to the words *I like Coke* on the student's board (Bottorf & DePape, 1982). Similarly, after a trip to the bowling alley, the teacher could ask, "Do you like bowling?" or "Do you want to go again?" and elicit only a limited or one-word response. A more useful approach would be to pose questions such as "How did you do?" or "Why do you want to go again?" as a stimulus for an expanded answer. In this way, interactions may become conversations rather than redundant or stilted exchanges of questions and one-word answers.

Third, when the student does converse, it is important that the listener reinforce the content of the message rather than the use of the augmentative system, unless the individual student needs the latter as well (Bottorf & DePape, 1982). Instead of saying, "Good; you used your system to tell me," the listener would provide greater reinforcement by commenting on or expanding the student's message or sharing a good joke. (See Figure 11.7.)

Instructional Strategies

Group versus Individual Training

While most studies on the use of alternative communication modes with severely handicapped children have relied on one-to-one training, a comparison of individual and small-group training by Kohl and her colleagues (1978) indicates that the latter is effective and may be advantageous. They compared (*a*) learning in a group instructional setting where each child received training on his or her own set of words and thus was exposed to signs being taught to the other students with (*b*) learning during individual instruction, with all children learning the same set of signs. The study indicated that individual training had no advantage over small-group training. Furthermore, during group instruction, each child learned the three sets of words taught to the other students about as well as those taught specifically to him or her. Thus, group instruction was a more efficient use of training

Using an Augmentative System, a Severely Handicapped Child Can "Ham It Up" as Well as the Next Person. In this case, a pocket chart used in the home provides an easy means of altering vocabulary as needs dictate.

time and a greater number of signs was acquired by each child.

Input Modes

Several studies of teaching signing or communication device use to severely handicapped learners have used "simultaneous communication," i.e., simultaneous use of spoken language and the alternative communication mode, when presenting the stimulus to be labeled (e.g., Carr et al., 1978). Others have also used the augmentative system to praise the student or to expand upon the response (e.g., Linville, 1977; Stremel-Campbell et al., 1977).

Noting that there is some disagreement over the advisability of using a simultaneous approach, Nietupski and Hamre-Nietupski (1977) concluded that there is little empirical basis for knowing whether that approach actually facilitates initial skill acquisition. However, the simultaneous approach may ultimately allow students to function more effectively in highly verbal natural environments.

There is some empirical basis for determining the effects of a simultaneous approach on the development of receptive language. For example, verbal imitation skills of autistic children predict the modality in which signs will be acquired more rapidly (Carr, 1982). Specifically, students with good imitation skills acquired signs receptively with equal facility for spoken or signed input, while those with poor verbal imitation skills met criterion more quickly when words were signed without speech.

Kohl, Karlan, and Heal (1979) investigated the question of whether sign should be paired with each spoken word in a sentence or only with certain key words. For receptive learning of verb-noun chains (e.g., *fold sock*) and put-noun-preposition-article-noun sentences (e.g., *put milk in the cup*), there was no significant difference between complete signing (the trainer's signing each word in the statement) and partial signing (signing only key elements). Furthermore, a third condition in which no words were signed was associated with significantly lower scores.

Thus, complete and partial signing were equally effective in facilitating reception of two- and five-word statements, and both were significantly better than using oral input alone.

Prompting Systems

Many prompting systems have been used successfully to teach signing to severely handicapped students, including (a) hand-shaping or molding the student's hands into the correct sign and then gradually fading this prompt (Browder et al., 1981; Carr et al., 1978; Cohen, 1981; Stremel-Campbell et al., 1977); (b) a system of least intrusive prompts in which successively more intrusive prompts are provided only as needed (Browder et al., 1981; Hobson & Duncan, 1979; Kohl, 1981; Renzaglia & Snell, Note 8); and (c) time delay, which places a systematically increased number of seconds between the instructional cue and a specific prompt (Browder et al., 1981; Kohl et al., 1978; Stremel-Campbell et al., 1977; Renzaglia & Snell, Note 8; see chapter 5 for more complete descriptions of these prompting systems). In these studies, the maximum latency allowed after the instructional cue and between levels of prompts ranged from 3 to 5 seconds.

All of these systems were effective in facilitating the acquisition of signing skills. It is difficult to determine their relative effectiveness because of differences among subjects, training settings, and the exact prompts used. However, two systems were compared directly in one study. Renzaglia and Snell (Note 8) compared a system of least prompts, consisting of verbal, verbal plus model, and verbal plus physical prompts given in order as needed, with a system of time delay, consisting of either a physical or a model prompt based on students' needs and presented at delays of 0, 2, 4, 6, and 8 seconds. They found that (a) students acquired signing skills in the first phase of the study regardless of the prompt system; (b) there were no significant differences between the systems in the number of errors produced; and (c) significantly fewer physical prompts were required than model or verbal prompts within the system of least prompts.

In studies in which students learned to use communication devices, physical guidance was generally used to prompt the correct response and was faded gradually as proficiency increased (Harris-Vanderheiden et al., 1975; Kucherawy & Kucherawy, 1978; Song, 1979). (See Figure 11.8.) In a somewhat different approach, Reid and Hurlbut (1977) used a different prompting system for each of two target skills. First, they trained students to use a reliable pointing response, with a blank grid as the visual stimulus. If the student did not point to the designated square within 10 seconds, they were physically guided and given corrective feedback as needed. After students met criterion on this skill, they were trained in expressive labeling of photographs. However, verbal rather than physical guidance was provided during this phase. Students met criteria for both target skills and were able to generalize the photographs to the actual locations they represented. Thus, both prompting systems were effective.

None of these studies used time delay as a prompting system. Since this strategy would appear to be viable for teaching communication board use, empirical comparisons of various delay levels and types of prompts would be interesting.

CLOSING STATEMENT

In closing, developing appropriate communication systems for severely handicapped persons is a demanding, dynamic process, one which focuses as much on the purposes and circumstances under which the individual communicates as it does on the

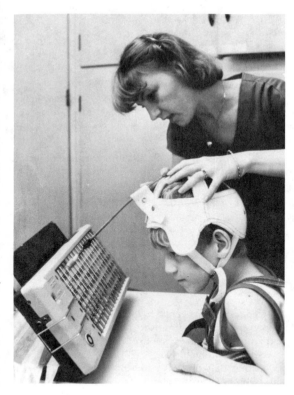

FIGURE 11.8
The Teacher Uses Physical Guidance to Prompt a Correct Head-Pointing Response on a Visual Display with Synthesized Speech. A Handvoice 110 is shown.
SOURCE: Photo by Dan Grogan.

mode of expression. Success can be measured against only one criterion—the extent to which the severely handicapped person is able to and does communicate within his or her unique environment.

REFERENCES

Ball, T., McCrady, R., & Hart, A. Automated reinforcement of head posture in two cerebral palsied retarded children. *Perceptual and Motor Skills*, 1975, *40*, 619–622.

Bottorf, L., & DePape, D. Initiating communication systems for severely speech-impaired persons. *Topics in Language Disorders*, 1982, *2*, 55–71.

Bricker, D. Imitative sign training as a facilitator of word-object association with low-functioning children. *American Journal of Mental Deficiency*, 1972, *76*, 509–516.

Brookner, S., & Murphy, N. The use of a total communication approach with a nondeaf child: A case study. *Language, Speech, and Hearing Services in Schools*, 1975, *6*, 131–137.

Browder, D., Morris, W., & Snell, M. Using time delay to teach manual signs to a severely retarded student. *Education and Training of the Mentally Retarded*, 1981, *16*, 252–258.

Brown, L. Branston, M., Hamre-Nietupski, S., Pumpian, I., Certo, N., & Gruenewald, L. A strategy for developing chronological-age-appropriate and functional curricular content for severely handicapped adolescents and young adults. *Journal of Special Education*, 1979, *13*, 81–90.

Burkhart, L. *Homemade battery powered toys and education devices for severely handicapped children.* 8315 Potomac Ave., College Park, Maryland, 1980.

Carlson, F. A format for selecting vocabulary for the nonspeaking child. *Language, Speech, and Hearing Services in Schools*, 1981, *12*, 240–245.

Carr, E. Sign language. In R. Koegel, A. Rincover, & A. Egal (Eds.), *Educating and understanding autistic children*. San Diego: College Hill Press, 1982.

Carr, E., Binkoff, J., Kologinsky, E., & Eddy, M. Acquisition of sign language by autistic children. I: Expressive labeling. *Journal of Applied Behavior Analysis*, 1978, *11*, 489–501.

Christoph, D., Nietupski, J., & Pumpian, I. Teaching severely handicapped adolescent and young adults to use *communication cards* to make purchases at a fast food counter. In L. Brown, M. Falvey, D. Baumgart, I. Pumpian, J. Schroeder, & L. Gruenewald (Eds.), *Strategies for teaching chronological age appropriate functional skills to adolescent and young adult severely handicapped students.* Wisconsin: University of Wisconsin–Madison and Madison Metropolitan School District, 1980.

Clark, C. Davies, C., & Woodcock, R. *Standard rebus glossary*. Circle Pines, Minn. American Guidance Service, 1974.

Cohen, M. Development of language behavior in an autistic child using total communication. *Exceptional Children*, 1981, *47*, 374–379.

Conner, P. Appendix 11: Eyepointing. In H. Silverman, S. McNaughton, & B. Kates (Eds.), *Handbook of Blissymbolics*. Toronto: Blissymbolics Communication Institute, 1978.

Cress, P., Spellman, C., DeBriere, T., Sizemore, A., Northam, J., & Johnson, J. Vision screening for persons with severe handicaps. *Journal of the Association for the Severely Handicapped*, 1981, *6*, 41–50.

Daniloff, J., & Shafer, A. A gestural communication program for severely and profoundly handicapped children. *Language, Speech, and Hearing Services in Schools*, 1981, *12*, 258–267.

Detamore, K., & Lippke, B. Handicapped students learn language skills with communication boards. *Teaching Exceptional Children*, 1980, *12*, 104–106.

Dixon, L. A functional analysis of photo-object matching skills of severely retarded adolescents. *Journal of Applied Behavior Analysis*, 1981, *14*, 465–478.

Eisenson, J., & Ogilvie, M. *Speech correction in the schools.* New York: Macmillan, 1977.

Elder, P., & Bergman, J. Visual symbol communication instruction with nonverbal multiply-handicapped individuals. *Mental Retardation*, 1978, *16*, 107–112.

Enderby, P., & Hamilton, G. Clinical trials for communication aids? A study provoked by the clinical trials of SPLINK. *International Journal of Rehabilitation Research*, 1981, *4*, 181–195.

Faw, G., Reid, D., Schepis, M., Fitzgerald, J., & Welty, P. Involving institutional staff in the development and maintenance of sign language skills with profoundly retarded persons. *Journal of Applied Behavior Analysis*, 1981, *14*, 411–423.

Greenwald, C., & Leonard, L. Communicative and sensorimotor development of Down's syndrome children. *American Journal of Mental Deficiency*, 1979, *84*, 296–303.

Griffith, P., & Robinson, J. Influence of iconicity and phonological similarity on sign learning by mentally retarded children. *American Journal of Mental Deficiency*, 1980, *85*, 291–298.

Guess, D. Methods in communication instruction for severely handicapped persons. In W. Sailor, B. Wilcox, & L. Brown (Eds.), *Methods of instruction for severely handicapped students*. Baltimore: Paul H. Brookes, 1980.

Hamre-Nietupski, S., Stoll, A., Holtz, K., Fullerton, P., Ryan-Flottum, M., & Brown, L. Curricular strategies for teaching selected nonverbal communication skills to nonverbal and verbal severely handicapped students. In L. Brown, J. Nietupski, S. Lyon, S. Hamre-Nietupski, T. Crowner, & L. Gruenewald (Eds.), *Curricular strategies for teaching functional object use, nonverbal communication, problem solving, and mealtime skills to severely handicapped students.* Madison, Wisc.: Madison Metropolitan School District, 1977.

Harris, D. Communicative interaction processes involving nonvocal physically handicapped children. *Topics in Language Disorders*, 1982, *2*, 21–37.

Harris, D., & Vanderheiden, G. Augmentative communication techniques. In R. Schiefelbusch (Ed.), *Nonspeech language and communication*. Baltimore: University Park Press, 1980.

Harris, S. Teaching language to nonverbal children—With emphasis on problems of generalization. *Psychological Bulletin*, 1975, *82*, 565–580.

Harris-Vanderheiden, D., Brown, W., MacKenzie, P., Reinen, S., & Scheibel, C. Symbol communication for the mentally handicapped. *Mental Retardation*, 1975, *13*, 34–37.

Harris-Vanderheiden, D., & Vanderheiden, G. Basic considerations in the development of communicative and interactive skills for non-vocal severely handicapped children. In E. Sontag, J. Smith, & N. Certo (Eds.), *Educational programming for the severely and profoundly handicapped*. Reston, Va: Council for Exceptional Children, 1977.

Hart, B., & Risley, T. Incidental teaching of language in the preschool. *Journal of Applied Behavior Analysis*, 1975, *8*, 411–420.

Hobson, P., & Duncan, P. Sign learning and retarded people. *Mental Retardation*, 1979, *17*, 33–37.

Hopper, C., & Helmick, R. Nonverbal communication and the severely handicapped: Some considerations. *AAESPH Review*, 1977, *2*, 111–116.

Kahn, J. Relationship of Piaget's Sensorimotor Period to language acquisition of profoundly retarded children. *American Journal of Mental Deficiency*, 1975, *79*, 640–643.

Karel, P., Galloway, A., Brankin, G., Pajor, M., & Freagon, S. Alternate forms of communication to increase successful interactions. In S. Freagon, M. Pajor, G. Brankin, A. Galloway, D. Rich, P. Karel, M. Wilson, D. Costello, W. Peters, & D. Hurd (Eds.), *Teaching severely handicapped students in the community: Processes and procedures*. DeKalb: Northern Illinois University–DeKalb and DeKalb County Special Education Association, 1981.

Kirschner, A., Algozzine, B., & Abbott, T. Manual communication systems: A comparison and its implications. *Education and Training of the Mentally Retarded*, 1979, *14*, 5–10.

Kladde, A. Nonoral communication techniques: Project summary # 1. In B. Vicker (Ed.), *Nonoral communication system project*. Ames: University Hospital School, The University of Iowa, 1974.

Kohl, F. Effects of motoric requirements on the acquisition of manual sign responses by severely handicapped students. *American Journal of Mental Deficiency*, 1981, *85*, 396–403.

Kohl, F., Karlan, G., & Heal, L. Effects of pairing manual signs with verbal cues upon the acquisition of instruction-following behaviors and the generalization to expressive language with severely handicapped students. *AAESPH Review*, 1979, *4*, 291–300.

Kohl, F., Wilcox, B., & Karlan, G. Research implications: Effects of training conditions on the generalization of manual signs with moderately handicapped students. *Education and Training of the Mentally Retarded*, 1978, *13*, 327–335.

Kopchick, G., & Lloyd, L. Total communication programming for the severely language impaired: A 24-hour approach. In L. Lloyd (Ed.), *Communication, assessment, and intervention strategies*. Baltimore: University Park Press, 1976.

Kopchick, G., Rombach, D., & Smilovitz, R. A total communication environment in an institution. *Mental Retardation*, 1975, *13*, 22–24.

Kucherawy, D., & Kucherawy, J. An electrical communication system for a nonverbal profoundly retarded spastic quadriplegic. *Education and Training of the Mentally Retarded*, 1978, *13*, 342–344.

Linville, S. Signed English: A language teaching technique with totally nonverbal, severely retarded adolescents. *Language, Speech, and Hearing Services in Schools*, 1977, *8*, 170–175.

Lobato, D., Barrera, R., & Feldman, R. Sensorimotor functioning and prelinguistic communication of severely and profoundly mentally retarded individuals. *American Journal of Mental Deficiency*, 1981, *85*, 489–496.

Mayberry, R. If a chimp can learn sign language, surely my nonverbal client can too. *ASHA*, 1976, *18*, 223–228.

McDonald, E. Language foundations. In G. Vanderheiden & K. Grilley (Eds.), *Nonvocal communication techniques and aids for the severely physically handicapped*. Baltimore: University Park Press, 1976.

McDonald, E., & Schultz, A. Communication boards for cerebral palsied children. *Journal of Speech and Hearing Disorders*, 1973, *38*, 73–78.

McDonald, J. The microcommunicator. *Journal of Courseware Review*, 1981, *1*, 6–10.

McNaughton, S. *Blissymbolics Communication Foundation symbol teaching guidelines*. Toronto: Blissymbolics Communication Foundation, 1975.

Moores, D. Nonvocal systems of verbal behavior. In R. Schiefelbusch & L. Lloyd (Eds.), *Language perspectives—Acquisition, retardation, and intervention*. Baltimore: University Park Press, 1974.

Naor, E., & Balthazar, E. Provision of a language index for severely and profoundly retarded individuals. *American Journal of Mental Deficiency*, 1975, *79*, 717–725.

News on aids. *Communication Outlook*, 1978, *1*(3), 4.

Newsom, C., & Simon, K. Vision testing. In R. Koegel, A. Rincover, & A. Egal (Eds.), *Educating and understanding autistic children*. San Diego: College Hill Press, 1982.

Nietupski, J., & Hamre-Nietupski, S. Nonverbal communication and severely handicapped students: A review of selected literature. In L. Brown, J. Nietupski, S. Lyon, S. Hamre-Nietupski, T. Crowner, & L. Gruenewald (Eds.), *Curricular strategies for teaching functional object use, nonverbal communication, problem solving, and mealtime skills to severely handicapped students*. Madison, Wisc.: Metropolitan School District, 1977.

Nietupski, J., & Hamre-Nietupski, S. Teaching auxilliary communication skills to severely handicapped students. *AAESPH Review*, 1979, *4*, 107–123.

Nietupski, J., Scheutz, G., & Ockwood, L. The delivery of communication therapy services to severely handicapped students: A plan for change. *Journal of the Association for the Severely Handicapped*, 1980, *5*, 13–23.

Ratusnik, C., & Ratusnik, D. A comprehensive communication approach for a ten-year-old nonverbal autistic child. *American Journal of Orthopsychiatry*, 1974, *44*, 396–403.

Reich, R. Gestural facilitation of expressive language in moderately/severely retarded preschoolers. *Mental Retardation*, 1978, *16*, 113–122.

Reid, D., & Hurlbut, B. Teaching nonvocal communication skills to multihandicapped adults. *Journal of Applied Behavior Analysis*, 1977, *10*, 591–603.

Richardson, T. Sign language for the SMR and PMR. *Mental Retardation*, 1975, *13*, 17.

Sailor, W., Guess, D., Goetz, L., Schuler, A., Utley, B., & Baldwin, M. Language and severely handicapped persons: Deciding what to teach to whom. In W. Sailor, B. Wilcox, & L. Brown (Eds.), *Methods of instruction for severely handicapped students*. Baltimore: Paul H. Brookes, 1980.

Scheuerman, N., Baumgart, D., Sipsma, K., & Brown, L. Toward the development of a curriculum for teaching nonverbal communication skills to severely handicapped students: Teaching basic tracking, scanning, and selection skills. In L. Brown, N. Scheuerman, & T. Crowner (Eds.), *Madison's alternative for zero exclusion: Toward an integrated therapy model for teaching motor, tracking, and scanning skills to severely handicapped students*. Madison, Wisc.: Madison Public Schools, 1976.

Shane, H., Lipschultz, R., & Shane, C. Facilitating the communicative interaction of nonspeaking persons in large residential settings. *Topics in Language Disorders*, 1982, *2*, 73–84.

Silverman, F. *Communication for the speechless*. Englewood Cliffs, N.J.: Prentice-Hall, 1980.

Skelly, M. *Amer-Ind gestural code based on Universal American Indian Hand Talk*. New York: Elsevier North Holland, 1979.

Song, A. Acquisition and use of Blissymbols by severely mentally retarded adolescents. *Mental Retardation*, 1979, *17*, 253–255.

Sosne, J., Handleman, J., & Harris, S. Teaching spontaneous-functional speech to autistic-type children. *Mental Retardation*, 1979, *17*, 241–244.

Sternberg, L., Battle, C., & Hill, J. Prelanguage communication programming for the severely and profoundly handicapped. *Journal of the Association of the Severely Handicapped*, 1980, *5*, 224–233.

Stremel-Campbell, K., Cantrell, D., & Halle, J. Manual signing as a language system and as a speech initiator for the nonverbal severely handicapped student. In E. Sontag, J. Smith, & N. Certo (Eds.), *Educational programming for the severely and profoundly handicapped*. Reston, Va. Council for Exceptional Children, 1977.

Vanderheiden, G. Technically speaking. *Communication Outlook*, 1981, *3*(2), 15.

Vanderheiden, G., & Grilley, K. (Eds.). *Nonvocal communication techniques and aids for the severely physically handicapped*. Baltimore: University Park Press, 1976.

Vicker, B. Advances in nonoral communication system programming: Project Summary #2, August 1973. In B. Vicker (Ed.), *Nonoral communication system project*. Ames: University Hospital School, The University of Iowa, 1974.

Waldo, L., Barnes, K., & Berry, G. *Total communication checklist*. Topeka: Kansas Neurological Institute, 1981.

Wells, M. The effects of total communication training versus traditional speech training on word articulation in severely mentally retarded individuals. *Applied Research in Mental Retardation*, 1981, *2*, 323–333.

Wendt, E., Sprague, M., & Marquis, J. Communication without speech. *Teaching Exceptional Children*, 1975, *8*, 38–42.

Wilbur, R. The linguistics of manual language and manual systems. In L. Lloyd (Ed.), *Communication, assessment, and intervention strategies*. Baltimore: University Park Press, 1976.

Yoder, D. Foreword. *Topics in Language Disorders*, 1982, *2*, x.

REFERENCE NOTES

1. Chapman, R.S., & Miller, J.F. *Analyzing language and communication in the child*. Paper presented at the Conference on Nonspeech Language Intervention, Gulf State Park, Alabama, March 1977.

2. Keogh, J., & Reichle, J. *The comprehensive communication curriculum*. Paper presented at Second Annual Statewide Conference for Educators of the Severely and Profoundly Handicapped, Huntington, West Virginia, May 1980.

3. Klein, M.D., Wulz, S.V., Hall, M.K., Waldo, L.J., Carpenter, S.A., Lathan, D.A., Myers, S.P., Fox, T., & Marshall, A.M. *Comprehensive communication curriculum guide*. Lawrence: Early Childhood Institute, Haworth Hall, University of Kansas, 1981.

4. *Communication Outlook*, Artificial Language Laboratory Computer Screener Department, Michigan State University, East Lansing, Michigan 48824.

5. Fristoe, M., & Lloyd, L. *The use of manual communication with the retarded*. Paper presented at the Gatlinburg Conference on Mental Retardation, March 1977.

6. Waldo, L., Riggs, P., Davaz, K., Hirsch, M., Eye, R., & Marshall, A. *Functional sign training for the severely multiply handicapped*. Kansas Neurological Institute, 3107 West 21st Street, Topeka, Kansas.

7. Waldo, L., Riggs, P., Davaz, K., Hirsch, M., Eye, R., & Marshall, A. *Functional communication board training for the severely multiply handicapped*. Kansas Neurological Institute, 3107 West 21st Street, Topeka, Kansas.

8. Renzaglia, A., & Snell, M. *Manual sign training for the severely handicapped: Time delay and a system of least prompts*. Unpublished manuscript, University of Virginia.

The social behavior of moderately and severely handicapped people is often primary in determining their success in community-based employment and living. Skills in independent toileting, communication, self-feeding, street-crossing, and even time-telling, for example, are often important steps toward increasing self-sufficiency. However, when a person routinely exhibits obvious deficiencies in the basics of social interaction (appropriate eye contact, smiling and laughing, vocal or nonvocal social greeting), or engages in excessive maladaptive behavior (such as aggressiveness or self-stimulatory responses), no amount of independence in grooming, bed-making, performing janitorial tasks, or handling money will surmount the inadequacies in socially appropriate behavior. Researchers studying the community experiences of this population have repeatedly cited behavioral problems and little or no participation in social activities as critical factors when these persons were either returned to institutional settings or placed there initially (Gollay, 1981; Gollay, Freedman, Wyngaarden, & Kurtz, 1978; Schalock & Harper, 1981; Moon & Snell, Note 1).

In the next chapter, Adelle Renzaglia and Paul Bates address the task of teaching socially appropriate behavior to moderately and severely handicapped people. The primary instructional strategy they put forth is one of building social skills. Frequently as social skills are learned and used, problem behaviors decline without any direct intervention. On the other hand, if the sole focus of intervention is on eradicating inappropriate behavior, the student still may be left with little or no talents for naturally obtaining approval from others. The authors detail guidelines for implementing social skill programs as well as intervention directed toward behavior reduction.

Introduction to Chapter 12

REFERENCES

Gollay, E. Some conceptual and methodological issues in studying the community adjustment of deinstitutionalized mentally retarded people. In R.H. Bruininks, C.E. Meyers, B.B. Sigford, & K.C. Lakin (Eds.), *Deinstitutionalization and community adjustment of mentally retarded people.* Washington, D.C.: American Association of Mental Deficiency, 1981.

Gollay, E., Freedman, R., Wyngaarden, M., & Kurtz, N. *Coming back: The community experiences of deinstitutionalized mentally retarded people.* Cambridge, Mass.: Abt Books, 1978.

Schalock, R.L., & Harper, R.S. A systems approach to community living skills training. In R.H. Bruininks, C.E. Meyers, B.B. Sigford, & K.C. Lakin (Eds.), *Deinstitutionalization and community adjustment of mentally retarded people.* Washington, D.C.: American Association on Mental Deficiency, 1981.

REFERENCE NOTE

1. Moon, M.S., & Snell, M.E. *Deinstitutionalization of the severely and profoundly retarded: Facts, figures, and misconceptions.* Paper submitted for publication, 1982.

12

Socially Appropriate Behavior

*This chapter was written by **Adelle M. Renzaglia**, University of Virginia, and **Paul Bates**, Southern Illinois University.*

An individual's social competence determines to a large degree his or her acceptance by the community. Leland (1977) has suggested that the ability of retarded people to succeed in the community is partially a function of the ability to maintain "social invisibility." Social invisibility implies that an individual avoids being labeled *deviant* by emitting socially appropriate behavior and refraining from high rates of socially inappropriate behavior.

Unfortunately, many retarded people are noted for their extremely limited social skills and excessive socially unacceptable behaviors. Follow-up studies of retarded people placed in community settings conducted to evaluate long-term results have revealed that social skill deficits consistently interfere with vocational success and community integration (Goldstein, 1964; Greenspan & Shoultz, 1981; Stanfield, 1973). In fact, the most frequently cited reason for failure is lack of appropriate social skills (Gaylord-Ross, 1979).

Although we often see inadequate social skills and excessive inappropriate behaviors in moderately and severely handicapped people, we must remember that many of them have lived in segregated environments and have hardly been exposed to community settings and appropriate models. Further, the social acceptance of handicapped persons by their nonhandicapped peers is also influenced negatively by lack of exposure and ongoing interactions. The limited interactions coupled with the lack of social competence of the severely handicapped often result in a perception of the severely handicapped as unrewarding social partners. Consequently, nonhandicapped people may come to actively avoid the severely handicapped (Kelly, Furman, Phillips, Hathorn, & Wilson, 1979). Given this pattern, severely handicapped people have limited exposure to socially effective models and their social contacts are primarily restricted to others with similar handicaps. Thus we have a self-perpetuating cycle which is in part responsible for the impoverished social skill repertoire and high rate of socially inappropriate behavior of handicapped persons.

Before addressing the issues surrounding the development of social skill training programs, we need to have an overall concept of social competence. Social competence is a complex phenomenon, encompassing both the existence of socially effective responses and the absence of high rates of socially unacceptable behavior. A concentrated investigation in this area has been deterred by lack of agreement by both researchers and practitioners on the parameters of social competence and a failure to define the many components of social behavior operationally. Failure to arrive at specific definitions has precluded accurate measurement and made evaluation of instructional procedures difficult. As a result, curriculum and instructional technology in social skills has lagged behind other areas such as vocational training, academics, and language instruction (Wehman, 1979).

In the past few years, several studies have been reported in which specific social skills have been operationally defined and directly influenced by systematic intervention. These studies have reported efforts to increase behaviors such as block passing (Whitman, Mercurio, & Caponigri, 1970), cooperative ball rolling (Morris & Dolker, 1974), and pulling peers in a wagon (Paloutzian, Hasazi, Streifel, & Edgar, 1971). More recently, severely handicapped students have been trained in more sophisticated social-interpersonal behaviors such as table games (Bates & Renzaglia, 1982; Marchant & Wehman, 1979), conversational speech (Kelly et al., 1979a; Matson & Andrasik, 1982), pinball (Hill, Wehman, & Horst, 1982), darts (Schleien, Wehman, & Kiernan, 1981), and job interviewing (Hall, Sheldon-Wildgen, & Sherman, 1980). In addition, a large body of literature is accumulating on the effectiveness of various environmental manipulations in reducing maladaptive social behaviors. These studies have included aberrant behavior such as pica (e.g., Ausman, Ball, & Alexander, 1974), habitual vomiting (e.g., Azrin & Wesolowski, 1975), noncompliance (e.g., Doleys, Wells, Hobbs, Roberts, & Cartelli, 1976), aggression (e.g., Bostow, & Bailey, 1969), self-injury (e.g., Favell, McGimsey, & Jones, 1978), and stereotypical behavior (e.g., Rollings, Baumeister, & Baumeister, 1977).

Despite the increasing specificity and sophistication of the training programs cited, we still have not agreed upon an overall conceptualization and delineation of the parameters of social competence. In this chapter we view social competence as the complex set of verbal and nonverbal behavior emitted in response to the unique stimuli of specific interpersonal situations. These behaviors include social skills requiring interaction with other people as well as isolated skills that occur within a social context (a situation in which other people are present). Within this conceptualization, we will discuss the following parameters: decoding, social communication, nonverbal behavior, and independent social skills. These parameters comprise the curriculum of behavioral objectives required for an individual to think critically and act independently in social situations. We will present each of these parameters and identify

curriculum examples as they relate to the overall development of social competence. Following this discussion, we will detail programmatic issues involved in the direct instruction of social skills. Finally, we will identify intervention procedures for remediating excessive maladaptive behaviors. Since maladaptive behaviors are often the result of a limited social skill repertoire (Gardner, 1977; Gaylord-Ross, 1979; 1980), social competence-building techniques are presented first and reductive techniques second.

PARAMETERS OF SOCIAL COMPETENCE

Social Decoding

Social decoding is the ability to discriminate social cues and interpret relevant information. These skills are prerequisite to all social interaction and are essential for effective interpersonal functioning. To use appropriate social skills under a variety of different conditions, the socially competent individual must be able to identify the critical aspects of specific situations and alter the response accordingly. Discrimination problems result in the failure to interpret signals used in the adult world to direct and regulate behavior accurately (Edmonson, Leland, & Leach, 1967). Many handicapped people do not adjust their interpersonal behaviors in response to unique situations. For example, some fail to respond differently to familiar persons and strangers. Failure to socially decode this information may result in indiscriminate physical displays of affection (such as hugging strangers). We can create objectives specifying situations requiring social decoding, such as:

1. When a *familiar person* (e.g., mother, father, sibling, teacher) makes *eye contact* with Terry, Terry will visually fixate on the person's face and smile on four of five occasions across 5 consecutive days.
2. When approached by a *peer* and *greeted with "Hi"* or "Hello," Tim will verbally reciprocate this greeting within 2 seconds on four of four trials across 5 consecutive school days.
3. During *church*, Jon will sit quietly with his family for the 45-minute Sunday service without requiring a verbal reprimand for four consecutive Sundays.

The socially relevant information highlighted in these examples includes the interpersonal partner, verbal message, nonverbal message, and physical setting. Since the social context consists of unique combinations of many variables, social competence is largely determined by social decoding skills. The importance of accurate discrimination and interpretation of relevant stimuli is obvious. However, these skills are irrelevant if the individual does not have a repertoire of socially effective responses from which to choose the most effective response for a unique situation. Thus if an individual is to function optimally in social situations, he or she needs a fairly sophisticated repertoire of social-interpersonal behaviors, including the range of verbal and nonverbal behaviors required in interpersonal and independent social activities.

Social Communication Content

Assertiveness training research has identified several component skills within social communication. These include the delivery of and response to greetings, praise, positive information, neutral information, criticism, demands, requests, and questions. Table 12.1 presents simple and complex examples of social communication behaviors for these skill areas.

Typically, social communication implies the use of a fairly high-level repertoire of verbal skills. However, given the verbal communication problems of many moderately and severely handicapped students, abbreviated verbal responses or augmentative communication modes need to be identified. (See chapter 11.)

The "style" in which the response is delivered is another powerful variable affecting social competence (Serber, 1972). Eisler, Hersen, and Miller (1973) investigated interpersonal verbal content and response style. They found that assertive and nonassertive subjects could be differentiated on the basis of duration of reply, latency of response, and loudness of speech. Thus we can surmise that the socially competent person responds fairly quickly to the verbal initiations of others (short response latency), uses a pleasant speaking voice (proper volume), with appropriate intonation (modulation) and smoothness of delivery (fluency).

Recently there have been several studies of the success of social skills training programs for verbal effectiveness of moderately retarded learners (Bates, 1980; Kelly et al., 1979; Kelly, Laughlin, Claireborne, & Patterson, 1979; Matson & Andrasik, 1982; Rychtarick & Bornstein, 1979). These studies have looked at many different skills, such as refusing requests, asking for help, and requesting change. We will discuss the instructional procedures used in these studies later in this chapter.

Nonverbal Behaviors

Social competence is frequently demonstrated by nonverbal behaviors, including certain qualitative aspects of interpersonal situations, physical contact, and cooperative interactions mediated by work and leisure materials.

If social communication refers to the *content* or *what* of social competence, qualitative variables refer to *how* you communicate. Clinicians have long recognized that *how* you communicate is as important as *what* you say. According to Serber (1972), the ineffective person often lacks command of style rather than knowledge of what to say. Style or qualitative variables include eye contact, facial expression, posture, hand gestures, interpersonal distance, physical appearance, and hygiene. The following examples of social competence objectives include one or more of these behaviors.

1. When introducing himself to a nonhandicapped peer, Ted will stand at a *distance of arm's length, smile,* and make *eye contact,* for five consecutive introductions.
2. Before leaving on a community recreation outing, Carol will independently *tuck in her blouse* and *comb her hair* for three consecutive community trips.
3. While visiting his rehabilitation counselor, Carl will *sit up* in his chair and maintain *eye contact* at an acceptable level (as judged by his counselor) for five consecutive visits.

Unfortunately, very few programmatic efforts have focused on qualitative variables of social interaction (Bates & Harvey, 1978). When they have been incorporated into research with handicapped populations, only one or two of the variables have been studied. Although initial investigations might appropriately study a limited number of variables, coordinated delivery of several of these behaviors is usually required. Future research should be directed toward various combinations of verbal and nonverbal behavior that result in effective interpersonal functioning.

Another important nonverbal behavior is the physical contact that may be part of social-interpersonal relationships. Physical contact can be analyzed by response form, ranging from touching and shaking hands to the more intimate involvement that may be associated with an emotional/sexual relationship. The appropriateness of physical contact depends on cultural and interpersonal standards. In specific interactions, the appropriate amount of physical contact

TABLE 12.1 Simple and Complex Social Skill Behaviors

Content Area	Delivery of (Initiation)	Response To (Receive)
Greetings	Simple: Nod and smile as a peer approaches Complex: Sign or verbally state "Hi, how are you today?"	Simple: Smile in response to greeting Complex: Reciprocate with sign or verbal response (e.g., "Hi, I'm fine. How have you been?")
Praise	Simple: Smile and pat peer on back. Complex: Specifically communicate what you like (e.g., "I like your new coat. It really looks good on you.")	Simple: Smile and sign or say "Thank you." Complex: Communicate your appreciation for the praise and elaborate briefly (e.g., "Thank you. I appreciate you noticing.")
Positive Information	Simple: Show your parent what you purchased on a community shopping trip. Complex: Communicate excitement about a positive event (e.g., "I got my first job!")	Simple: Smile and nod. Complex: Acknowledge the information in a positive way and request additional information (e.g., "That's wonderful! When do you start?")
Neutral Information	Simple: Inform others of actions (e.g., going to the bathroom). Complex: Provide information about current events (e.g., "I watched the game last night.")	Simple: Acknowledge reception of message by nodding or affirming. Complex: Acknowledge reception of message and either provide relevant information or inquire further (e.g., "So did I. Can you believe they won!")
Negative Information (Criticism)	Simple: Shakes head left to right to signal no. Complex: Communicates negative information and provides reason (e.g., "Don't change the channel. I was watching my show.")	Simple: Stops engaging in behavior that is the target of criticism. Complex: If criticism is perceived as justified, student might respond with "OK, I won't do that anymore." If unsure, student might respond with inquiry such as "Why do you say that?"
Demands/Requests	Simple: Gesture toward object and communicate need for assistance (e.g., point to catsup bottle and indicate need for assistance removing the top). Complex: Communicate need for assistance in a store situation: "Excuse me, I'm looking for the magazines. Would you please tell me where they're located?"	Simple: Nod yes or shake head no. Complex: Ask for more information or respond yes and request more information, or respond no and provide simple reason (e.g., "No, I don't lend money to strangers.")
Questions	Simple: To determine someone's name, point to the individual and shrug shoulders. Complex: Communicate question in a specific and polite manner (e.g., "Would you please tell me what time it is?")	Simple: In response to name request, state first name, sign name, or point to name log. Complex: Answer question fully and possible follow-up question on a related topic (e.g., "It's 4:00 p.m. Do you need to go now?")

will depend on the social context and the relationship of the partners.

One of the more controversial aspects of physical contact involves the sexual behavior of moderately and severely handicapped persons. Since sex, marriage, and family are integrally tied together in our culture, it is difficult to evaluate the appropriateness of a sexual relationship for someone who may be marginally capable of independent living. However, moderately and severely handicapped adolescents and adults are sexual beings. Professionals and parents must come to grips with this issue and seriously discuss masturbation, homosexuality, heterosexuality, birth control, and other related topics. As fuller participation in community life becomes a reality for these individuals, heterosexual opportunities will increase. Handicapped persons will be better able to handle these opportunities if they are at least taught the less intimate skills along the continuum of physical contact.

Hamre-Nietupski and Williams (1977) have described a social skills and sex education program used with severely handicapped adolescents in a public school. The students in this program were taught skills in (a) a bodily distinctions related to sex and growth, (b) premenstrual training, (c) social manners (e.g., alternative hand and leg placements to avoid suggestive posture), (d) growth distinctions and reproduction, (e) menstrual training, and (f) appropriate response to inappropriate and appropriate verbal and physical interaction. These skills represent the less intimate skills and behaviors involved in physical contact.

One final category of nonverbal social behavior is interaction that involves people and leisure materials. In the literature on handicapped populations, more studies with the term social in the title involve leisure activities than any other topic. These studies have covered toy manipulation, doll play, cooperative block passing, and table games. Most of these studies involved younger learners or used materials designed for young normal children. There is a distressing lack of play/leisure materials appropriate for moderately and severely handicapped adolescents and adults. Their involvement in play/leisure activities with their nonhandicapped peers is just as limited. Recently, Wehman and Schleien (1981) and Wuerch & Voeltz (1982) have published curriculum materials for severely handicapped populations emphasizing age-appropriateness and interaction with the nonhandicapped. These recent contributions contain some excellent suggestions for leisure materials and integrated activities.

Independent Social Skills

When not involved directly with other people, the socially competent person can function independently in a social context without drawing undue attention. This person can sit in a theatre, walk in a store, jog through a park, watch television, play solitaire—all in the presence of other people, without generating negative responses or avoidance behaviors. One method for determining individual social skill objectives in this area is to watch students in a variety of these situations and note those behaviors that make them more noticeable.

DETERMINING SOCIAL COMPETENCE OBJECTIVES

A first step in designing a social skill training program is to identify priority objectives. The assessment should involve analyzing the environments in which the student interacts to identify the behavioral expectations for successful performance. Included among these behavioral expectations are standards specifically relevant to social competence. Brown, Branston, Hamre-Nietupski, Pumpian, Certo, and Gruenewald (1979) have described how an ecological inventory can be used for generating relevant curriculum objectives (see chapter 4 for an in-depth discussion).

Directly related to this assessment is social validation, the process of involving significant persons in a particular community in establishing training objectives, determining particular teaching procedures, and evaluating the program's results (Kazdin, 1980a; Wolf, 1978). Social validation maximizes the chances that important behaviors will be selected for instruction and that the resulting behavior changes will be interpreted as socially competent by members of a given community.

Assessment

As in any other instructional area, after priority objectives have been identified, an assessment must be conducted to determine individualized social competence objectives and to provide a baseline for later evaluation of effectiveness of instruction. The most useful and valid assessment of social competence is direct observation. Criterion-referenced assessment is one direct observation method that is highly versatile and appropriate here.

In criterion-referenced assessment, the standards for competent social performance in specific environments are described in measureable terms, and students are evaluated regarding their progress toward meeting these criteria. Criterion-referenced assessment in the area of social behavior may include:

1. Number of steps completed independently in a leisure task (e.g., task analytic assessment of pinball);
2. Frequency of topic repetitions in a conversation;
3. Latency of responding to a request for information (e.g., "What is your name?");
4. Duration of time of involvement in cooperative leisure activity;
5. Percentage of time intervals that an individual maintains eye contact during a 10-minute conversation.

With all criterion-referenced assessment, the behavior(s) of interest must be operationally defined, observational procedures specified, recording forms developed, and interobserver agreement demonstrated. By conducting initial assessment and collecting ongoing performance information, data are collected from which the effectiveness of specific instructional procedures can be evaluated. (Chapter 4 elaborates upon these topics.)

INSTRUCTIONAL PROCEDURES

The social competence of moderately and severely handicapped individuals can be significantly influenced by planned manipulations of both antecedent and consequent events. We will describe several antecedent and consequence instructional strategies, and then discuss combinations of these variables.

Antecedent Arrangements

In comparison to consequence procedures, the manipulation of antecedent variables has received relatively little attention in the literature on social competence instruction. This is unfortunate, since manipulating antecedents is potentially economical and effective. A few of these antecedent variables are integration of handicapped with nonhandicapped, physical location of social interaction, presentation of materials, scheduling of activities, task analysis of objectives, and teacher cues and corrections.

Integration of Handicapped with Nonhandicapped
Recent litigation and legislation have created an imperative for integration (Gilhool & Stutman, in press), which has led to increased efforts to integrate handicapped and nonhandicapped people in school and other community settings. The instructional value of integration is supported by research on the value of peer modeling (Bandura, 1969). Further, integration must start with educational opportunities for severely handicapped children to acquire skills needed to adjust over time to integrated community placements (Brown et al., 1979).

Peterson and Haralick (1977) documented social benefits for handicapped preschool children when given opportunities to integrate. Other research suggests that additional instruction may be necessary to obtain optimal benefits from integration. Along this line, Voeltz (1980, 1982) has conducted extensive attitude studies with nonhandicapped youngsters who have had varying amounts of contact with severely handicapped children. Contact (integrated school experiences) was associated with increased acceptance of individual variations in performance and behavior. Attitude differences were also found in students from integrated schools who had different amounts of contact and interaction with severely handicapped students. Those students enrolled in schools with an interaction program (orientation activities and structured interaction experiences) had more accepting attitudes than those students attending an integrated school with no planned program.

Brown and his colleagues (1979) have delineated several dimensions of interaction possible within integrated school settings. *Proximal interactions* are social contacts and increased familiarity that develop when handicapped and nonhandicapped people attend the same schools, use the same community services, and live in the same neighborhoods. In integrated schools, handicapped and nonhandicapped students can be in close proximity on the bus, in the hallway, on the playground, at school assemblies, and during lunch.

With increased contact (proximal interactions), *helping interactions* are possible. Helping interactions are situations in which nonhandicapped youngsters help handicapped students participate in school and community activities. These interactions may be formal (e.g., peer instruction on how to use a vending machine) or informal (e.g., accompany a child to a bowling activity). Finally, *reciprocal interactions* are those naturally occurring, freely chosen interactions that mutually benefit both the handicapped and nonhandicapped. Examples of these include conversing together, taking a walk, and attending a party. As integrated settings become more prevalent and training with nonhandicapped students increases, the social value of proximal, helping, and reciprocal inter-actions may soon be realized.

Related to the topic of integration is integration of severely handicapped people with those with less severe handicaps. Morris and Dolker (1974) demon-strated that a higher functioning handicapped peer was able to facilitate cooperative ball rolling with a profoundly retarded child. Matson and Andrasik (1982) were able to use retarded peers as models of appropriate social interaction for other moderately retarded people.

As classrooms for severely handicapped students are more frequently located in regular public school buildings, the opportunity for peer modeling by less severely handicapped and nonhandicapped students will be increased. From these various mixtures, se-verely handicapped students are likely to benefit in terms of increased social competence.

Physical Setting

Different social competence skills may be required in different physical settings. For example, a unique set of social behaviors will be appropriate in church and another set at an outdoor concert. Severely handi-capped persons must have the opportunity to experi-ence a wide variety of community settings. Without exposure to regular public schools, restaurants, stores, and so on, a person's social competence will most certainly be impoverished.

Materials

Recreation/leisure behavior and the materials that a person uses are often used as a measure of social com-petence. For instance, the play materials' age-appro-priateness, reactivity, and need to cooperate may promote different degrees of social competence.

If a moderately retarded young adult is only provided with infant toys (e.g., jack-in-the-box, Fisher-Price radio), it is unlikely that he will be judged socially effective by other community members. However, if he is exposed to a variety of age-appropriate materials (e.g., pinball machine, transistor radio), there is a greater likelihood that he will use more advanced social skills and be perceived as more competent by others.

In addition to selecting social leisure materials on the basis of age-appropriateness, the reactivity of the materials should be considered. Reactive materials are toys or games that light up, make noises, or move when manipulated. According to Granger and Weh-man (1979), reactive materials may elicit movement from multiply handicapped students and facilitate independent action. Reactive materials may be par-ticularly valuable for those who have not previously engaged in appropriate social/leisure behavior.

Materials that can be used by more than one person can encourage cooperation. If materials are presented that can be used by *only* one person, severely handi-

capped people have no need to interact. However, planned presentation of materials that require or en-courage cooperation can promote the development of more advanced social behaviors (Quilitch & Ris-ley, 1973).

Scheduling of Activities

Social competence development can be enhanced by careful scheduling. At a minimum, opportunities for social interaction should be scheduled daily and weekly. These opportunities may include recreation/leisure game period, social conversation time, inter-action with nonhandicapped, and special outings. If a student prefers isolated activities over social activi-ties, a Premack arrangement may increase the attrac-tiveness of the social events (Premack, 1965). This can be accomplished by scheduling a lower probabil-ity behavior (e.g., small talk conversation) before a higher probability behavior (e.g., listening to a record.) A student's access to a desired activity is made contingent on engaging in a less preferable behavior.

One environmental arrangement used with se-verely retarded children which resulted in more so-cial play behavior involved scheduling sociodramatic activities before a free play period (Strain, 1975). The sociodramatic activities consisted of the teacher read-ing a story to the children and requiring each student to act out the various characters in the story. The social play of these students increased during the free play period that immediately followed.

As we mentioned social competence is unlikely to develop if there is no scheduled opportunity for peo-ple to interact. Careful inspection of the schedule of activities may reveal possible changes that can pro-mote more appropriate social behavior.

Task Analysis

Task analysis has been used to facilitate skill acquisi-tion by handicapped populations in virtually all cur-ricular areas. However, it has only recently been used to improve social competence skills. Sample task analyses for a cooperative table game and an interper-sonal communication appear in Tables 12.2 and 12.3. Acquisition of specific social skills can be furthered by systematic use of other instructional strategies (e.g., response prompting, chaining, and contingent reinforcement). As an antecedent strategy, task anal-ysis promotes structure and specificity of instruction, which both facilitate acquisition for severely handi-capped students.

Teacher Instructions (Cues and Corrections)

Verbal directions are potentially efficient and effec-tive for teaching social interpersonal behavior. Ver-bal instructions differ in degree of specificity, ranging from general commands to engage in social behavior ("Jerry, ask someone to play a game") to specific

TABLE 12.2 Task Analysis of Cooperative
Table Game

Step 1.	Ask peer to play game
Step 2.	Get game from storage area
Step 3.	Set up game (organize materials)
Step 4.	Select moving piece (token)
Step 5.	Place moving piece (token) on "go"
Step 6.	Pick one card
Step 7.	Place card on table (face up)
Step 8.	Move token to first matching picture
Step 9.	Wait turn
Step 10.	Repeat steps 6 through 9 until one player reaches "win" circle
Step 11.	Congratulate winner
Step 12.	Put away game materials
Step 13.	Thank peer for playing game
Step 14.	Return game to storage area

TABLE 12.3 Task Analysis of Communication
Content (Differing with Others)

Step 1.	Get attention (e.g., "Excuse me")
Step 2.	State position (e.g., "I was watching TV")
Step 3.	Request change in behavior (e.g., "Please turn back to channel 12")
Step 4.	Suggest alternative (e.g., "After this, you can watch what you want")
Step 5.	Thank the person for compliance

directions for a particular step of a task analysis ("Sarah, say hello").

Although verbal instructions have been used to increase prosocial behavior and decrease inappropriate social behavior of handicapped students, they may need to be supplemented with other, more explicit prompts. For instance, in working with severely handicapped individuals with limited receptive language, relying on verbal instruction alone is inappropriate. In these cases, gestural/model prompts are more explicit and have been used successfully with verbal instructions. Pairing verbal directions with gestural/model demonstrations of the desired behavior has resulted in improved skill acquisition with severely handicapped students (Nelson, Gibson, & Cutting, 1973; Wehman, 1977). These gestural/model prompts range from pointing cues to full demonstrations of the desired behavior. For example, gestural prompts can be used to provide feedback on eye contact; a demonstration can be used to model how to introduce yourself to a new person.

Since some students do not imitate very well, model/gestural prompts may not provide enough information. In these cases, additional prompts are necessary. Graduated physical guidance is an instructional prompt that has led to social competence acquisition by people who do not have well-developed receptive language or imitation skills. With graduated physical guidance, the teacher provides only as much physical assistance as is necessary to ensure that the student performs the targeted behavior. This technique is appropriate for nonverbal behaviors (e.g., manual sign social communication) and social skills involving interaction with materials (e.g., operation of a cassette tape player).

Combinations of verbal, gestural, and physical cues and corrections can also be sequenced together

systematically. For example, if you select an instructional objective such as "waves greeting to peer who approaches in corridor," the first thing to do would be to set up the natural situation and give the student the opportunity to perform independently. If the student does not wave independently, you might provide a verbal direction ("Tom, wave to Karla"). Failure to wave following the verbal direction would lead to combining the verbal command with a modeled demonstration of hand waving. Finally, if these prompts are unsuccessful, you could repeat the verbal instruction and provide physical assistance to wave the hand. With this system, handicapped learners have been taught a variety of functional skills. Once the student responds, other consequation procedures are necessary.

Conclusion

Systematic manipulation of antecedents may prove to be very effective for facilitating social skill acquisition. A major advantage is that the resulting social behaviors may be more spontaneous and not under the control of artificial reinforcers (Wehman, 1979). Far too often antecedent environmental arrangements are overlooked in instructional programming with handicapped individuals. (Chapter 5 discusses these antecedent strategies.)

Consequence Arrangement

Once appropriate social competence behaviors are performed, the teacher must make sure that they reoccur. Systematic manipulation of consequences (e.g., positive reinforcement) is the instructional component used most frequently to strengthen social-interpersonal behavior. Response feedback, external reinforcement, and self-reinforcement are consequence arrangements that have increased the use of appropriate social behaviors. (Again, chapter 5 further delineates consequence strategies.)

Response feedback refers to providing factual information contingent on performance. For example, Bates (1980) had moderately retarded persons role-play interpersonal situations (e.g., handling criticism) and then provided feedback regarding content, eye contact, fluency, facial expression, and voice volume. To maximize the value of response feedback, feedback should be (a) given immediately after performance, (b) presented objectively, and (c) followed by immediately opportunity for additional performance.

Performance can also be increased by following social skill behaviors with contingent reinforcers. A hierarchy of potentially reinforcing events may consist of primary reinforcers (food, water), tangible reinforcers (jewelry, record album), activity reinforcers (going for a walk), token reinforcers (money), and social praise ("Congratulations!").

For social-interpersonal behaviors, the ideal reinforcement conditions are those that naturally occur as a result of the activity. For example:

1. After you hold a door open for a stranger, the stranger says, "Thank you."
2. After you ask a friend to play a card game, the friend agrees to play.
3. After you smile at a person passing by, the person smiles at you.

To have these natural consequences maintain specific social behaviors, these natural events may need to be established as being reinforcing. Reinforcement pairing is a technique that has been effective here. For example, for initiating a request to play cards, token incentives could be paired with the partner's willingness to play. Once the social skill behaviors are being emitted consistently, the additional reinforcers are gradually faded until the behaviors are maintained by the natural event.

By pairing established reinforcers with other consequent events and then fading the already established reinforcers, new reinforcing events can be developed. In social competence instruction, natural consequence events need to be identified and strengthened as reinforcing events by pairing and fading.

Self-Reinforcement

Self-delivered consequences can influence behavior just as externally provided reinforcers do (Thoresen & Mahoney, 1974). An advantage of self-delivered reinforcement is that immediate consequences for socially appropriate behavior can be delivered without a teacher. Since the social-interpersonal behavior of moderately and severely handicapped individuals will most likely occur with peers rather than with experimenters, self-reinforcement should be developed. Matson and Andrasik (1982) used self-recording and self-delivered token reinforcement to establish higher rates of appropriate social interaction. Target behaviors in this study included introductions, greetings, requests, asking favors, asking questions, sharing, complimenting, and talking politely.

Conclusion

Relying only on consequence arrangement as an instructional strategy is based on an assumption that is often erroneous with handicapped students. This assumption is that the targeted skills are already in the learners' repertoires and that reinforcement of these skills will increase their occurrence under appropriate conditions. However, many handicapped students have learning and performance deficits. Not only must they be encouraged to perform, but they must learn the appropriate responses. In cases involving learning deficits, consequence arrangement strategies must be used along with antecedent environmental arrangements and response instruction techniques.

Instructional Combinations

Since moderately and severely handicapped persons are frequently socially deficient and have significant learning difficulties, powerful instructional programs are usually necessary to change their social-interpersonal behavior. Programs may include various combinations of antecedent and consequence arrangements. For example, in Wehman's (1978) investigation, the play behavior of severely handicapped adolescents and adults was strengthened by manipulating the proximity of play materials to the learners, using modeling and physical guidance to prompt responses, and giving reinforcers for appropriate activity. This combination yields a powerful instructional strategy that can help promote a wide variety of social-interpersonal behaviors with a wide range of handicapped learners.

Several common instructional components have been included in most training programs in verbal interaction. This treatment regimen consists of verbal instruction, modeling, rehearsal, feedback, and practice in the natural environment. In these programs, verbal directions are used to direct specifically the desired action or content of a response. Following the verbal instructions, an explicit *model* demonstration of the target behavior is provided by the teacher. Once the student has had the opportunity to observe the modeled demonstration, he or she is encouraged to rehearse by practicing the behavior several times. After demonstrating particular aspects of the target response, the student receives feedback in the form of *social and token incentives*. If the skill is being taught in the classroom, the student should *practice in natural environments* where the behavior is to be used.

In the past 2 years, several instructional programs have been reported that used variations of this regimen with moderately and severely handicapped individuals. This training model was used to teach skills in asking questions, providing information, and giving compliments to moderately and mildly retarded adolescents (Kelly et al., 1979a). It was also used to teach mildly retarded adults to answer questions, ask questions, and make social invitations to a peer (Rychtarik & Bornstein, 1979). An adolescent and adult population of moderately and mildly retarded given a similar social-interpersonal skills training program improved significantly on trained and untrained situation role-play items (Bates, 1980). However, these gains failed to generalize to a more natural setting (i.e., local grocery store). This result highlights the need to emphasize those procedures that maximize maintenance and generalization of behavior change.

In response to the need to plan for maintenance and generalization, Matson and Andrasik (1982) added self-reinforcement and self-monitoring to a social skills training program. In this study, appropriate social interaction skills were taught by presenting specific scenes, prompting performance (role play), providing feedback, and modeling appropriate responses. Clients were also taught to self-reinforce (with tokens) for appropriate behavior and to monitor their own appropriate behavior. As a result, several clients learned socially effective responses and generalized these gains to a nontraining environment.

Generalization Program Procedures

As the Matson and Andrasik (1982) study demonstrated, social skill gains can generalize beyond the training setting with proper planning and instruction. In this curriculum area, we must establish a variety of responses used with different people, in different places, across different time periods. Several program procedures for accomplishing these objectives are presented in Table 12.4.

EXCESSIVE MALADAPTIVE BEHAVIOR

In addition to vast deficits of appropriate social skills, severely handicapped people frequently have excessive maladaptive behaviors. Aberrant behaviors identified as characteristic of the severely handicapped include aggressive/disruptive acts, self-mutilation, vomiting and rumination, self-stimulation, and temper tantrums (Forehand & Baumeister, 1976; Sontag, Burke, & York, 1973; U.S. Office of Education, 1974). As we have said, the lack of appropriate social skills may contribute to the excessive time severely handicapped people spend engaging in aberrant behavior. However, due to the high frequency and

TABLE 12.4 Procedures to Enhance Generalization of Social-Interpersonal Skills

Procedure	Examples
Fade Incentives	After using continuous teacher-praise to teach a student to compliment his friend's appearance, begin reinforcing less often and attempt to establish the peer's response (e.g., "Thank you") as the natural maintaining consequence.
Use Different People to Establish New Social Skills and Serve as Interpersonal Partners	When instructing students to give social greetings (e.g., "Hi, how are you today?"), teach this response with different teachers so that the student learns to greet many people appropriately. Initially, the student may be taught to greet the teacher and later this could be expanded to the teacher's aide, other teachers, handicapped peers, nonhandicapped peers, family members, etc.
Vary the Instructions That Are Used to Establish Social-Interpersonal Responses	In teaching a student to provide information in a conversation (e.g., "What is your name?"), vary the requests that should control the same response. These variations may include direct requests (e.g., "Who are you?", "What's your handle?", etc.) and indirect requests (e.g., "Hi, my name is Don.").
Conduct Instruction in Several Locations Where the Social Skills are Required	After a student has learned to ask for assistance in a grocery store, conduct instruction in other grocery stores and in different kinds of stores. For example, in several stores students should be taught to identify store personnel, get their attention (e.g., "Excuse me") and make polite and specific requests (e.g., "Please help me find _____.").
Teach a Variety of Different Responses To Similar Social Situations	In response to a compliment ("Your hair looks nice today"), students could be taught a variety of responses, including "Thanks," "I appreciate you saying that," "I just washed it," etc.
Teach Self-Instruction and Self-Reinforcement for Socially Effective Behavior	When making a social contract to ask someone to go on a date (e.g., attend a movie), the person could be taught to self-instruct "good eyes and smile." These self-verbalizations may help the individual to have eye contact and appear pleasant when making the request. Self-reinforcement could be delivered by treating oneself to a soda for making the social initiation.

intensity of these behaviors, in addition to teaching appropriate social skills, attention must be focused on eliminating maladaptive behavior. *Maladaptive* or *aberrant* behavior can be defined as those behaviors considered abnormal due to response form, frequency, intensity, or the environment in which the behavior occurs (Gaylord-Ross, 1980). Severely handicapped people may engage in maladaptive behaviors that are dangerous to themselves (e.g., rumination, self-abuse) or to others (e.g., aggression) and that consequently need immediate attention. In an instructional setting, excessive nonfunctional behaviors interfere by making attention to instructional stimuli difficult and thus decreasing acquisition rate (Gaylord-Ross, 1980). In addition, these behaviors frequently disrupt the learning of other students in the classroom.

Before developing an elaborate program to reduce a behavior, the behavior must be established as a problem (Sulzer-Azaroff & Mayer, 1977). Goals and objectives for reducing aberrant behavior are environmentally determined. An ecological survey should be conducted to determine the degree to which a behavior may be exhibited before it is considered excessive or problematic. For example, a certain amount of aggressive verbal behavior (e.g., yelling, cursing, name calling, or a loud refusal to participate in activities) may be tolerated and even expected in a particular child's home. Eliminating all verbal aggression from the child's repertoire may be inappropriate. Perhaps aggressive verbal behavior is seen as a necessary survival skill by the child's parents for living in the household and in the neighborhood. In another setting (e.g., school), however, aggressive verbal behavior may be totally inappropriate and not be tolerated to any degree. It therefore would warrant intervention.

If a behavior has been determined to be excessive by a number of people in the student's environment, further attention and perhaps systematic intervention may be warranted (Sulzer-Azaroff & Mayer, 1977). Teachers, parents, or other significant persons must ask: (*a*) what *does* the learner do in the environment and (*b*) what is the minimum the learner *should* do in that environment? Once these questions are answered, the discrepancy between learner behavior and environmental expectations has been identified, and the degree to which a problem exists becomes evident (Gardner, 1977). The goal of intervention, then, is to eliminate this discrepancy, so that the behavior meets at least the minimum environmental expectations.

Considerations for Establishing Priorities for Intervention

Even though there is a discrepancy between a handicapped student's behavior and the expectations of the environment, intervention is not necessarily warranted. Since so many behaviors of severely handicapped students are problematic (either excessive or deficient), the teacher must systematically select those problems targeted for immediate intervention and those considered for future intervention. A number of considerations will help in establishing priorities. The first step should be identifying problems needing immediate intervention. The following questions can be asked (Gaylord-Ross, 1980; Sulzer-Azaroff & Mayer, 1977).

1. Is the problem causing physical harm to the misbehaving person?
2. Is the problem threatening physical harm to others?
3. Is the problem disrupting the entire class and prohibiting others from learning?
4. Does the problem require an inordinate amount of the teacher's (or parents') time so that other responsibilities are overlooked?

Answering yes to at least one of these questions identifies an immediate priority for intervention.

Problematic behaviors that are not so severe that immediate intervention is necessary should also be prioritized systematically for future intervention. Frequently, however, as appropriate social skills are acquired, these problematic behaviors may decrease without direct intervention. For this reason, skill acquisition programs designed to teach socially appropriate skills must be implemented before behavior reduction programs. If maladaptive behaviors persist, however, a number of other factors can be considered for establishing intervention priorities (Sulzer-Azaroff & Meyer, 1977). First, do parents, community, or administrative staff support an intervention program for the targeted behavior? Without their support, the likelihood of a successful intervention is minimal. If they do not support the intervention program, significant people in a child's environment may interfere with success. Furthermore, priorities should be established through agreement among everyone who interacts with the child. No one should make unilateral decisions.

Another factor to consider is the likelihood of successful intervention (Sulzer-Azaroff & Mayer, 1977). Likelihood of success may be judged by the teacher's past successes or by the past successes of others with intervention programs designed to reduce the same or similar behaviors of other severely handicapped people. Through a thorough review of relevant literature, potentially effective intervention techniques can be identified. The required steps can be obtained by reading descriptions of successful applications of these techniques with the targeted behaviors.

Another consideration is the competence of the person who will conduct the behavior reduction program. Past experience with similar problems will affect program success. If a teacher has had no past experience with similar maladaptive behaviors, a consultant may be needed to assist in program development and implementation (Sulzer-Azaroff & Mayer, 1977).

Finally, practical matters, such as the number of staff members available to conduct intervention programs, resources, and amount of space available, may all affect the decision to intervene as well as the procedure selected. An aberrant behavior that is not an *immediate* priority, but which would require the full-time attention of one staff member in a setting with only two staff persons for eight students, for example, may not be high on the priority list. Until a time when one staff member can be freed of other responsibilities and made available solely to attend to the targeted behavior, the problem behavior may not reach the top of the list.

Once all of these factors have been considered, problem behaviors can be ranked for intervention. As one problem is alleviated, intervention can begin on the next problem on the list. In fact, in many instances the elimination of one aberrant behavior may result in reduction of other behaviors that are lower on the list. Consequently, intervention may not be required for all maladaptive behaviors. Establishing priorities based on immediate needs, support of significant others, likelihood of success, trainer competence, and practical limitations is a systematic method for working through problems and will help the teacher avoid situations in which he or she makes commitments that cannot possibly be kept.

Functional Analysis

Once a problem has been targeted for intervention, an assessment should be initiated, beginning with a functional analysis of the problem behavior (Gardner, 1977; Sulzer-Azaroff & Mayer, 1977). This analysis identifies the relationship between environmental events and the occurrence of the problem behavior. The results should help the teacher identify environmental variables that may be influencing or aggravating the problem. In addition, potentially effective intervention techniques can be selected based on the results.

A functional analysis of a specific aberrant behavior involves observing the child in the natural environment and recording the situation surrounding an occurrence of the target behavior. The antecedent events, including the setting, the people present, the activities, and the type of interactions occurring at the time the misbehavior began, should be noted. The topography of the misbehavior should also be described, as well as any consequences. Information including who delivers the consequence, when con-

sequences are presented, and type of consequence should be described.

The antecedents, behavior, and consequences (ABC) should be recorded on numerous occasions across days until a pattern develops, if one exists. A behavior log (see Table 12.5) will increase ease and consistency of recording. With this information, the teacher can specifically define the problem behavior, determine whether maladaptive behavior occurs with any consistency given certain antecedent events, and identify consequences that may be maintaining or increasing the frequency of the aberrant behavior.

In addition to analyzing the ABC events, the functional analysis should evaluate the student's natural environment to determine the number and frequency of positive and negative events available to the student. If people in the student's environment frequently use negative or aversive techniques, perhaps increasing the amount and frequency of positive reinforcers will decrease the misbehavior. In addition, observing how the student spends his or her free time and the events the student avoids should also provide pertinent information. Free time behavior should reveal potential natural reinforcers. If the student has no functional behavior, but only maladaptive behavior, during free time, teaching alternative appropriate behavior may be the basis for future reduction of aberrant behavior.

Since a functional analysis of the maladaptive behavior is an anecdotal, preliminary step to program development, it should not take the place of specific observational data collection. The functional analysis provides information on the aberrant behavior (what, when, where, with whom, under what circumstances, for what effect) that is relevant to the selection of appropriate data collection and intervention techniques.

Assessment

Following the functional analysis of the aberrant behavior, specific data collection procedures can be selected for preintervention assessment and program monitoring. The choice of data collection procedures depends on (a) the estimated frequency and duration of the problem behavior as determined by preliminary observations, (b) the number of staff members available for data collection, and (c) the type of intervention procedure most likely to be used. These variables should be considered when selecting from the following data collection procedures:

1. A simple *frequency count,* used to record the occurrences of behaviors that are discrete, have distinct beginnings and ends, and are of inconsequential duration (e.g., number of chairs thrown);

Student's Name _____   Target Behavior _____

Observer _____

| Date | Setting | Behavior Topography | Time | | Antecedents | Consequences | Comments |
			Starts	Stops			

TABLE 12.5 Behavior Log

SOURCE: Adapted from *Behavior Modification*, 2nd ed., by James Walker and Thomas M. Shea. St. Louis: C.V. Mosby, 1980, p. 110. Reprinted with permission.

2. A record of *behavior rate,* used instead of a simple frequency count when observation periods vary in length;
3. A record of *behavior duration,* used to assess behaviors of varied lengths (e.g., temper tantrums);
4. *Time sampling* techniques, used as a manageable alternative to continuous data collection, which involve selecting times through the day which *represent* the times and settings in which measurement of the behavior is desired;
5. *Interval data* collection techniques, used to assess behaviors that do not have distinct beginnings and ends (e.g., self-stimulatory behavior) and are difficult to count or record in terms of duration. (Refer to chapter 4 for an in-depth discussion of observational data collection techniques.)

The baseline assessment establishes the extent of the problem and the degree to which the behavior needs to change. Baseline assessment must be continued until the pattern of aberrant behavior has become stable. This will provide a record against which change can be measured. Ongoing assessment throughout intervention is necessary to evaluate program effectiveness and to make program changes based on objective evaluation (Haring, Liberty, & White,

1980). Especially when targeting maladaptive behavior, intervention data are necessary. Frequently, change does not occur or occurs very slowly. Continuous data collection reveals the lack of acceptable change and, therefore, indicates the need to change the program. Since aversive techniques are frequently used to reduce maladaptive behavior, continuous program monitoring is very important both for programming and for ethical and legal justification.

A Conceptual Framework for Intervention

Before developing an elaborate intervention program, a teacher should investigate relevant and potentially important alternatives for behavior change. The medical status of a misbehavior is of foremost concern and should be evaluated before any behavior/environmental intervention (Gaylord-Ross, 1980; Sulzer-Azaroff & Mayer, 1977). Perhaps illness, allergy, or some other form of physical discomfort is responsible for aberrant behavior. Excessive crying or aggression, for example, may be the means by which a nonverbal, severely handicapped 10-year-old tries to say that he is in pain. Medical factors must be explored before any other intervention begins.

If an examination does not reveal any medical problems, other approaches to behavior reduction must be explored. Frequently, when teachers, parents, and other behavior managers are faced with selecting techniques to decrease aberrant behaviors, aversive techniques come to mind. Spanking, yelling, timeout through isolation in a bedroom, and withdrawal of privileges are techniques that can often be observed in home and at school. These techniques, though often effective, are not always the most efficient and certainly do not always result in long-lasting effects (Kazdin, 1980b; Sulzer-Azaroff & Mayer, 1977). In addition, aversive techniques are very intrusive and are easily overused and abused.

Before selecting aversive or punishing events to consequate a problem behavior, a teacher should try a range of less intrusive techniques. In fact, a conceptual framework for selecting behavior reduction techniques systematically involves picturing the techniques along a continuum of least intrusive and, in most cases most natural, to most intrusive and least natural. The degree of intrusiveness can be determined by evaluating (a) the extent to which a procedure can be applied in the natural environment without interfering with learning, (b) the necessity for involving artificial or prosthetic devices, (c) the amount of staff time required, (d) the potential for abuse of the technique, (e) the potential for increasing appropriate behaviors as alternatives to the aberrant behavior, and (f) the degree to which the people required to carry out the program feel comfortable with the techniques selected.

Ecological Variables

Ecological variables such as the number of students in the training environment (Rago, Parker, & Cleland, 1978), the specific setting in which training occurs, the materials used for instruction, and the amount of free, nonstructured time the student has for misbehavior should be evaluated first. Perhaps modifying one or a number of these variables will decrease the aberrant behavior (Gaylord-Ross, 1980; Sulzer-Azaroff & Mayer, 1977). The functional analysis of behavior will help identify ecological variables that may be increasing the likelihood of misbehavior and consequently should be modified.

Reinforcement Variables

If modifying ecological variables does not effectively reduce the behavior, reinforcement variables should be examined. The functional analysis of the problem should reveal patterns of reinforcement (or lack of it) that may be contributing to the high rates of aberrant behavior. Positive reinforcement (attention, presentation of desired events, or presentation of desired objects) may be delivered when a student misbe-haves, thus increasing the occurrence of the problem behavior. For example, if attention is paid to a student each time she disrupts the class, the attention may be maintaining that disruptive behavior. Consequently, when she wants attention, she will become disruptive. Therefore, attention as a positive reinforcer should no longer be provided when she is disruptive, and a reduction in disruptive acts should result. However, using extinction to reduce maladaptive behavior leads to a very slow decrease in behavior over time (Gardner, 1977; Kazdin, 1980b; Sulzer-Azaroff & Mayer, 1977). Therefore, behaviors that are harmful or that cannot be tolerated to any degree may require an alternative approach. In addition, a burst in maladaptive behavior frequently occurs immediately after beginning extinction. If a burst in frequency or intensity cannot be tolerated, extinction alone should not be used. For example, though extinction has been effective with self-abusive behavior (e.g., Lovaas & Simmons, 1969), due to the severity of self-abuse and the necessity for immediate reduction, extinction is not recommended unless it is used in combination with a more direct technique.

Environments in which aversive events are more prevalent than positive events may negatively reinforce aberrant behavior as a means of escape. Often students who engage in excessive problem behavior are removed from the learning environment when they misbehave. If the environment is not a pleasant, rewarding setting, the students may misbehave more to escape from the nonreinforcing or perhaps aversive classroom. If an analysis of the situation reveals a lack of reinforcers in the learning environment, successful reduction of aberrant behavior may depend on increasing the availability and amount of positive reinforcement for appropriate behavior. In addition, the aberrant behavior should not result in removal from the learning situation (Gaylord-Ross, 1980). Once a student has experienced positive learning in the classroom, escape should cease to be a goal; and aberrant behavior used initially as a means for escape should decrease.

Another variable that may influence the occurrence of aberrant behavior is the reinforcing value of the behavior itself. Repetitive, stereotypic behaviors may be intrinsically reinforcing and persist without external encouragement. For example, the rhythmic motion involved in body-rocking or head-weaving may "feel good," thus increasing the likelihood of those behaviors. Under these circumstances, the intrinsic reinforcers of the maladaptive behavior compete with the external reinforcers available for appropriate alternative behaviors. Reduction of self-reinforcing maladaptive behaviors, therefore, may depend on increasing the external reinforcers so that appropriate social behavior is more rewarding than the maladaptive behavior. Differential reinforcement of other behavior (DRO) and reinforcing incompatible behavior (DRI) (Gardner, 1977; Kazdin, 1980b; Sulzer-Azaroff & Mayer, 1977) are two techniques that involve targeting and reinforcing behavior alternatives to inappropriate self-stimulatory behavior. These methods of reducing inappropriate behavior are positive and constructive; they emphasize increasing the reinforcement in the environment, which strengthens appropriate alternative behaviors. Since reinforcement is essential to successful acquisition, maintenance, and generalization of behavior, its parameters should be evaluated and manipulated in relationship to excessive maladaptive behavior.

Aversive Consequences

If positive approaches to behavior reduction are not successful, perhaps punishment of the aberrant behavior will be necessary. To review, punishment includes the removal of positive events or the presentation of negative or unpleasant events contingent on the maladaptive behavior. Before selecting an aversive consequence, a teacher should (a) *establish the need for aversive consequences either by documenting the severity of the aberrant behavior or previous unsuccessful attempts to reduce the maladaptive behavior through less intrusive means;* (b) *be fully aware of the rules* of the system in which the procedure will be used (e.g., Is timeout in an isolated setting permissible? Is corporal punishment prohibited?); (c) *obtain informed consent* from administrators and the student's parents; and (d) *evaluate the ethical and legal parameters* of using specific aversive techniques (e.g., shock or physical punishment as an aversive consequence) (Gaylord-Ross, 1980; Sulzer-Azaroff & Mayer, 1977).

Aversive consequences can also be pictured along a continuum from least to most intrusive and should be evaluated this way. For example, response cost and timeout both involve removing positive events. Response cost involves removing a reinforcer from the student, while timeout most frequently involves removing the student from the learning environment. Although the intrusive nature of these procedures must be evaluated in each specific instance, timeout would generally seem to be more intrusive than response cost. During timeout, the student is pulled out of the instructional interaction; there is no opportunity for learning. Response cost, on the other hand, does not require interruption of instruction. In most instances the opportunity to learn and earn positive reinforcers is ongoing.

When delivering aversives, the intrusiveness of the procedure also must be evaluated. A verbal reprimand (e.g., "No!" or "Stop hitting!") is usually less intrusive than presenting a noxious smell (e.g., ammonia) or distasteful liquid (e.g., tabasco sauce) and requires much less time than overcorrection procedures, which combine a number of behavior reduction techniques including aversive components.

On the extreme end of the continuum is the use of electric shock as an aversive consequence. Electric shock is never a natural consequence for aberrant behavior. It can be easily abused by the punisher, does not teach constructive alternatives, and is frequently unpleasant to those who must deliver it. For these reasons, shock is very intrusive and should be used only in emergency situations or as a last resort. It must be used conscientiously to avoid physical damage. For example, if less intrusive procedures have been ineffective with *life-threatening*, self-abusive behavior and the self-abuser is in 24-hour restraints, shock may be defensible. If contingent delivery of shock successfully reduces self-abuse, the student may have increased freedom to live and learn. However, the effects of shock must be closely monitored. If the behavior does not decrease within a short time, the procedures should be modified and perhaps abandoned.

If any punishment is employed, the opportunity for positive reinforcement for appropriate behavior should be provided. Punishment in combination with positive reinforcement for appropriate alternatives is less intrusive and more defensible than the use of aversive consequences alone.

A number of excessive maladaptive behaviors are characteristic of severely handicapped persons. However, the frequently cited, high prevalence maladaptive behaviors may be specific to institutionalized populations, since the majority of studies have been conducted in institutions. The nature of institutions, including the large amounts of "down time" and the lack of alternative socially appropriate behaviors, are very likely to contribute to aberrant behavior. As deinstitutionalization is realized, perhaps these frequently cited problems will become less "characteristic." Until that time, it is likely that punishment will be necessary in at least some instances. Fortunately, teachers have a wide range of punishment procedures from which must choose. These techniques must be carefully evaluated to determine potentially successful approaches to alleviating a particular problem behavior of a specific student.

Review of Characteristic Problems

Specific classes of aberrant behavior characteristic of severely handicapped persons include stereotypic behavior, self-injurious behavior, aggression, chronic vomiting, and pica (Forehand & Baumeister, 1976). Since these maladaptive behaviors are chronic problems that occur frequently in the severely handicapped, we will discuss specific techniques for reducing them. Tables 12.6 through 12.9 provide representative samples of techniques used to alleviate these behaviors. The specific studies in each table are grouped by categories of intervention procedures, arranged from least to most intrusive.

Stereotypic Behavior

Stereotypic behaviors are also called *self-stimulatory behaviors* and include "highly consistent and repetitious motor or posturing behaviors which are not outer directed in the sense of being explicitly disruptive and harmful to others" (Forehand & Baumeister, 1976, p. 226). They are among the most striking maladaptive behaviors of severely handicapped persons (Baumeister & Forehand, 1974). In fact, stereotypic behaviors have been observed in approximately two-thirds of institutionalized retarded persons (Berkson & Davenport, 1962; Kaufman & Levitt, 1965).

Stereotypic behaviors includes (a) repetitive body movements such as body-rocking, head-weaving, hand-flapping, and finger- or palm-staring; (b) repetitious and meaningless manipulation of objects such as spinning, banging, or staring at toys or other materials; and (c) repetitive vocalizations including screaming, hooting, throat or tongue sounds, and excessive laughing. These behaviors, though not always disruptive to others in the classroom, disrupt the misbehaver's learning environment and prohibit participation in educational activities. As a consequence, intervention to reduce their occurrence is usually required.

Table 12.6 lists studies designed to reduce the stereotypic behavior of severely handicapped people. Studies using differential reinforcement procedures (DRO) are listed first, since DRO is an unintrusive and constructive approach. The success of DRO depends on selecting strong reinforcers that are more powerful than the intrinsic reinforcement of the self-stimulatory behavior. Although in some cases this is possible, frequently it is very difficult to select external reinforcers that overpower the intrinsic value of self-stimulation. Consequently, it may be necessary to use alternative intervention techniques or techniques that can be used in combination with DRO.

A second category of intervention techniques involves sensory extinction (e.g., Rincover, 1978; Rincover, Newsom, & Carr, 1979). Sensory extinction is based on the premise that the reinforcement for stereotypic behaviors is inherent in the aberrant behavior itself. Sensory extinction removes the reinforcing value of the stereotypic act. For example, Rincover (1978) used sensory extinction with three subjects who engaged in plate-spinning, object-twirling, and finger-flapping, respectively. The sensory extinction involved removing the reinforcing feedback of the stereotypic act. Since the reinforcing value of plate-spinning had been assessed to be the sound produced by the spinning plate, Rincover decided to carpet the surfaces on which the child spun the plate, thus removing the reinforcing sound. Similarly, the movements involved in object-twirling and finger-flapping were assessed to be the reinforcers for those behaviors. Consequently, a vibrator was taped to the back of the misbehaver's hand, which interfered with the positive value of the movements involved in self-stimulation. These procedures effectively eliminated the self-stimulatory behaviors.

Although the results of the few studies using sensory extinction are positive, more research is needed. In addition, the logistical or practical limitations of sensory extinction should be evident. Carpeting surfaces, modifying equipment so that its not operational (e.g., light switches), using vibratory stimulation, or removing lights from the learning environment may be expensive and might interfere with instruction.

Response cost procedures have potential for effective elimination of self-stimulation, but successful application depends on identifying a strong reinforcer in the environment that can be removed. In addition, the reinforcers withdrawn must be stronger than the self-reinforcing value of the stereotypic act. Similarly, successful application of timeout depends on the timeout environment being less reinforcing than the time-in environment. This is often difficult to accomplish when consequating stereotypic behaviors because self-stimulation can usually be performed in the time-out setting.

Overcorrection procedures have been developed in recent years to eliminate chronic self-stimulatory behavior. Overcorrection usually involves a number of components that make up a treatment package. In addition to an aversive component which serves as a punisher, overcorrection also includes an educational or constructive component. This component usually involves repeated practice of an appropriate behavior that is an alternative to the maladaptive behavior.

The results of the use of overcorrection are somewhat mixed. For example, Foxx and Azrin (1973) and Azrin, Kaplan, and Foxx (1973) are very successful in decreasing stereotypic behavior, while Rollings, Baumeister, and Baumeister (1977) failed to replicate their results. One explanation for this inconsistency may be the different length, type, and application of specific procedures across studies (Axelrod, Brantner, & Maddock, 1978). In addition, the degree to which overcorrection can be used depends on the staff available to carry out the often extensive procedures.

Use of aversive consequences in the form of liquids, physical punishment, and finally electric shock

(Text continues on page 336.)

TABLE 12.6 Decreasing Stereotypic Behavior: Representative Intervention Studies

Reference	Subjects	Target Behavior	Treatment Technique	Design	Results
Differential Reinforcement of Other Behaviors (DRO)					
Weisburg, Passman, & Russell, 1973	28-year-old male severely retarded 23-year-old male profoundly retarded	hand flicking and hand staring	differential reinforcement of imitative gestures, differential control of imitative and non-imitative behavior reinforced, contingency and instruction reversal, differential control over non-gesturing and contrast response, fading of nongestural cues, fading of food, maintained by social	reversal (ABCA$_2$DEF)	SSB decreased; the incompatible behavior which replaced SSB was a functional task
Repp, Deitz, & Spier, 1974	12-year-old female severely retarded 22-year-old female severely retarded 23-year-old male severely retarded	lip flapping, body rocking, hand motions	baseline conditions included a verbal "No" for self-stimulatory behavior; intervention: predetermined time interval was established and if no self-stimulatory behavior occurred throughout interval, teacher hugged and praised subject; if behavior occurred, teacher said, "No," and reset timer.	reversal	"No" by itself was not effective for any of the 3 subjects; DRO plus "No" was effective for all 3 subjects
Sensory Extinction					
Rincover, 1978	14-year-old male profoundly retarded severely visually impaired	plate spinning while listening	auditory extinction: carpeting of surfaces	reversal, multiple baseline across subjects	behavior decreased from 72% during baseline to a range of 0–7% during extinction
	7-year-old autistic female	twirling objects	proprioceptive extinction: vibrator taped to back of hand		behavior decreased from 95% during baseline to an average of 49% during extinction
	10-year-old autistic male	finger flapping	proprioceptive extinction: vibrator taped to back of hand		behavior decreased from 83% during baseline to an average of 0–12% during extinction

Study	Subject	Behavior	Procedure	Design	Results
Rincover, Cook, Peoples, & Packard, 1979	9-year-old male retarded severely visually impaired	plate spinning while listening	carpeting of surfaces	reversal	reduced self-stimulation, which remained low; appropriate play increased for all subjects
	8-year-old male retarded	hand flapping	vibrator taped to hand		
	10-year-old female retarded	dust flicking/watching	overhead lights turned off		
	8-year-old female retarded	finger flapping	vibrator taped to hand, blindfold		
Rincover, Newsom, & Carr, 1979	8-year-old male profoundly retarded severely visually impaired	ritualistic light switching	auditory extinction: carpeting switch and adjacent wall	reversal, multiple baseline across subjects	behavior decreased from 11% during baseline to 3% during extinction
	8-year-old female schizophrenic	excessive light switching	visual extinction: making light switch nonoperational		behavior decreased from 14% of observation intervals to 4% during extinction
Response Cost Murphy, Nunes, & Ruprecht, 1977	18-year-old male institutionalized severely retarded legally blind partially deaf	stereotyped hyperventilation	withdrawal of vibratory stimulation contingent upon hyperventilation	reversal	hyperventilation decreased from mean of 39% to mean of 6% during extinction
	20-year-old female institutionalized severely retarded	mouthing	withdrawal of hand massager contingent upon mouthing for 15 seconds	multiple baseline across settings	mouthing decreased to 0–1% in all settings
Time Out Sachs, 1973	13-year-old male autistic-like	hand waving, spinning, jumping, repetitive sounds	"No" delivered upon self-stimulation, subject removed from learning interaction and let stand out of sight, 30 seconds quiet time with trainer's back to seated subject	reversal	baseline average was 6 SSB per 5 minute period, "No" increased SSB, out of sight time had to be terminated due to disruptive behavior but 30 sec. of quiet time with no trainer interaction was successful.

Table 12.6 (CONTINUED)

Reference	Subjects	Target Behavior	Treatment Technique	Design	Results
Overcorrection Foxx & Azrin, 1973	8-year-old female severely retarded	mouthing objects, hand	punishment: slapping, painting thumb with distasteful solution, free reinforcement, overcorrection: oral hygiene technique beginning with "No!", then brushing teeth and gums with toothbrush immersed in antiseptic for 2 minutes	modified reversal: use of free reinforcement to provide baseline before beginning each treatment	least effective techniques were free reinforcement and reinforcement for non-mouthing; distasteful solution reduced mouthing to 50/hour; punishment to 4/hr.; overcorrection to 0/hour
	3 severely retarded females and 1 autistic male, ages 7–8 years	mouthing, hand weaving, clapping	positive practice for 5 minutes, commands were in random sequence	reversal: A-baseline B-overcorrection A-baseline B-overcorrection C-verbal warning to facilitate generalization	Rate of SSB: A-SSB more than 80% B-SSB virtually ceased A-SSB more than 40% B-zero level C-maintenance at zero level
Azrin, Kaplan, & Foxx, 1973	9 adults in state hospital ward severely/profoundly retarded	any SSB engaged in longer than 2 seconds including hand postures, body rocking, pill rolling, string twisting, paper flipping	positive practice for 20 minutes, verbal instructions and guidance used as needed, fading by reducing time to 10, then 5 and 2 minutes, then just a verbal warning when SSB rate less than 2 on the previous day	reversal: A-nonreinforcement B-reinforcement A-nonreinforcement C-reinforcement plus positive practice	rates of SSB: A-SSB 75% of the time B-SSB 25% A-SSB 60% C-SSB 10% or less
Wells, Forehand, & Hickey, 1977	2 males 10-years-old severely retarded severely emotionally disturbed	mouthing	verbal warning alone, overcorrection: appropriate toy play as positive practice component	multiple baseline	suppression of self-stimulation with overcorrection
Newman, Whorton, & Simpson, 1977	8-year-old male autistic functionally retarded	self-stimulatory verbalizations	overcorrection: 30 seconds of hand over mouth with praise for being quiet, intermittent reinforcement for quiet	modified reversal: A-baseline B-verbal warning plus overcor.	mean occurrences of SS verbalizations: A-196 B-156

Study	Subject	Target behavior	Procedure		Design		Results
Kissel & Whitman, 1977	14-year-old male profoundly retarded	mouthing, head back	package of play training and overcorrection to occur without SSB, hand overcorrection applied to each behavior across situations	C-overcor. alone A-baseline C-overcor. alone	multiple baseline across settings	C-13 A-more than in intervention C-8	overcorrection was effective in reducing SSB but with no generalizing effects unless treatment was being conducted with the specific behavior, hand overcorrection found effective with all behaviors dealt with but topographically variant
Rose, 1979	38-year-old female severely retarded	pinching and touching face	overcorrection: 3 positions maintained for 30 sec. over a 2-minute period: arms in front of chest, apart on thighs, folded resting on thighs, verbalization: "you are touching your face" intervention only during 20 minute work breaks		reversal, multiple baseline across settings (3 at workshop, 1 at home)		SSB decreased in the 3 work settings but not at home, generalization seemed to occur in settings similar to the treatment setting
Rollings, Baumeister, & Baumeister, 1977	(unspecified)	head weaving	replication of Foxx & Azrin (1973)		none specified		only once during study did behavior decrease below baseline, also examined effect of proximity of trainer: the subject exhibited a longer latency for engaging in head weaving when engaged in head weaving
	35-year-old male profoundly retarded	head nodding, self-hitting, body rocking	20 minute sessions of overcorrection procedures, type of overcorrection not specified		multiple baseline across behaviors, 6 month follow-up		baseline: high rates of body rocking, low rates of other behaviors; treatment: overcorrection reduced body rocking to 0, head nodding increased and there was a burst of self-hitting; follow-up showed body rocking at a higher rate than final days of intervention, head nodding lower and self-hitting no different

TABLE 12.6 (CONTINUED)

Reference	Subjects	Target Behavior	Treatment Technique	Design	Results
Roberts, Iwata, McSween, & Desmond, 1979	3 adults profoundly retarded	mouthing, grabbing, clapping, growling, inappropriate finger movements, table hitting, grimacing	overcorrection that did not physically prevent occurrence of the target behavior: called attention to the behavior, verbal instruction to engage in overcorrection, manual guidance if needed, ranging from 1–2 minutes depending on behavior	reversal	target behaviors seemed to decrease when overcorrection was used, with incompatibility of behavior and overcorrection not a critical factor
Harris & Wolchik, 1979	4 males autistic severely retarded ages 4–12 years	unspecified self-stimulation	treatments included overcorrection, DRO, and time out	reversal with treatments varying	with one subject overcorrection decreased SSB, DRO increased SSB, and timeout decreased; with another boy reversal after overcorrection was difficult and results inconclusive
			same as above but DRO and timeout randomly assigned and overcorrection made the final treatment due to reversal problem	multiple baseline across work and play settings as well as reversal	DRO had little effect, timeout seemed to increase behavior and overcorrection dramatically decreased the SSB, no generalization from work to play settings unless overcorrection used
			same as above, examining relation between frequency and duration data	reversal	visual inspection showed consistency in both data collection methods (DRO not as consistent)

Presentation of Aversive Consequences—Aversive Liquids

Reference	Subjects	Target Behavior	Treatment Technique	Design	Results
Lamal, 1976	school setting, subjects unspecified	sucking/chewing	Listerine in a spray bottle administered on every occurrence of behavior, faded by decreasing frequency of treatment to every other and then every third occurrence of behavior, verbal reprimand paired with Listerine	none specified	reported effective at school but did not generalize to home

Presentation of Aversive Consequences—Physical Punishment

Study	Subjects	Target behavior	Intervention	Design	Results
Koegel & Covert, 1972	3 mute autistic children	general SSB	verbal "No!" and slap contingent upon SSB during discrimination acquisition	none	when SSB decreased, correct responses in discrimination increased
Koegel, Firestone, Kramme, & Dunlap, 1974	8-year-old male, 6-year-old female, both autistic	exhibition of up to 31 different self-stimulatory behaviors	verbal "No!" and slap or holding body part engaged in SSB, one experimenter responsible for behaviors occurring from the waist up, another from the waist down	reversal (ABA)	during intervention SSB decreased and appropriate toy play increased, behaviors reversed at reintroduction of baseline conditions; toy play did not occur in isolation from punishment, indicating that toy play and SSB are not necessarily incompatible

Presentation of Aversive Consequences—Shock

Study	Subjects	Target behavior	Intervention	Design	Results
Baumeister & Forehand, 1974	3 males 19–33 years institutionalized severely retarded	body rocking	shock contingent on body rocking	none: baseline intervention (AB)	decreased body rocking, 10 month follow-up showed durability but no generalization
	6 males institutionalized severely retarded	body rocking	verbal commands contingent on body rocking	reversal	A-17 rocks/minute B-near 0 rocks/min. A-9.7 rocks/min. B-near 0 rocks/min.
Risley, 1968	6-year-old female autistic	body rocking	verbal command: "stop that!" while shaking subject	none: baseline intervention (AB)	behavior decreased from baseline of 25% of the time to under .7% during intervention

should be the last resort. Whenever these procedures are used, an opportunity for positive reinforcement for alternative behavior should be provided. Furthermore, even though shock has successfully eliminated stereotypic behavior (e.g., Baumeister & Forehand, 1974; Risley, 1968), the need for such an intrusive procedure for nonthreatening behaviors is very difficult to justify.

More research is needed to compare the relative effectiveness of different techniques in decreasing stereotypic behavior. In addition, research identifying the effective components of treatment packages such as overcorrection and the parameters (e.g., length) of successful applications would facilitate effective programming.

Self-Injurious Behavior

Self-injurious behavior is any behavior or behavior pattern that a person repeats in an attempt to inflict injury to himself or herself (Horner & Barton, 1980; Smolev, 1971; Tate, 1972). Other terms referring to the same behavior include *self-abuse, self-mutilation, self-destruction,* and *self-punishment.* Included in the category are head-banging, face-slapping, hair-pulling, self-biting, scratching, eye-gouging, banging body against objects, pinching, and burning parts of the body (DeCatanzaro & Baldwin, 1978; Frankel & Simmons, 1976; Horner & Barton, 1980). A surprisingly large number of severely handicapped persons engage in self-injurious behavior. The figures on prevalence of self-injury range from 4% to 6% (Bachman, 1972) to 10% (Schroeder, Schroeder, Smith, & Dalldorf, 1978). However, these figures refer to an institutionalized population and therefore may be inflated. In any case, self-injurious behaviors frequently pose a real threat to life. Physical damage to the body, infection, and sensory impairment can directly result. Therefore, self-injurious behaviors are high priorities for intervention.

Table 12.7 lists studies representative of those designed to reduce self-injurious behavior. Although extinction procedures have been successful in reducing this behavior (Horner & Barton, 1980), they have not been included in the table because of the potential problems that may occur. These problems include the slow decline in target behaviors and the expected increase in the target when extinction is first initiated. Since many self-injurious behaviors are intolerable because they threaten life, a *slow* decrease is not acceptable, and certainly any increase could not be tolerated.

The first technique presented in Table 12.7 involves modifying stimulus conditions. Specifically, Carr, Newsom, and Binkoff (1976) evaluated a subject's learning environment and determined that placing him in high-demand situations might result in

self-injurious behavior. They altered antecedents to evaluate the effect of demands on self-injury. Self-injury increased when verbal demands also increased, and self-injury decreased when positive events were most prevalent in the learning environment. This study exemplifies an ecological evaluation and modification of environmental events.

Differential reinforcement has also been effective with self-injurious behavior. However, if self-injury occurs at very high rate, the opportunity to reinforce other behavior may be minimal (Horner & Barton, 1980). A combination of DRO and other procedures is perhaps a stronger but more intrusive alternative (e.g., DRO plus timeout, Peterson & Peterson, 1968). Timeout, response cost, or other aversive techniques are more justifiable if paired with differential reinforcement of alternative behaviors.

Overcorrection has also been effective with self-injurious behavior (e.g., DeCatanzaro & Baldwin, 1978; Measel & Alfieri, 1978). However, as with stereotypic behavior, more research is needed to define effective procedures as well as the relative contribution of the specific components of the package.

Since self-injurious behavior is many times life-threatening, the use of aversive consequences including noxious odors and liquids or electric shock may be justifiable. In many cases, people who engage in frequent self-injury are restrained for large portions of their day. This restraint prohibits their involvement in any habilitative programming. Therefore, using more intrusive aversive consequences may be justifiable in that their effects are usually rapid, resulting in increased freedom for the individual (Kazdin, 1980b). In fact, some advocates consider use of aversive consequences a part of a self-injurious person's right to freedom (Horner & Barton, 1980). Once self-injury is eliminated, an individual has access to habilitative programming, free movement, and the opportunity for positive interaction with the environment.

More comparisons of treatment techniques are needed, as well as thorough evaluations of the parameters of specific techniques. In addition, we need methodologically sound research. Many of the available studies failed to evaluate program effectiveness with an experimental design. Therefore, their results must be interpreted carefully, and no conclusions can be drawn.

Aggression/Disruption

Aggressive/disruptive acts explicitly disrupt the environment adversely or threaten physical harm to others (Forehand & Baumeister, 1976). Aggression includes attacks toward people, attacks toward objects, abusive language, and tantrums that combine two or more disruptive behaviors such as crying,

(Text continues on page 341.)

TABLE 12.7 Decreasing Self-Injurious Behavior: Representative Intervention Studies

Reference	Subjects	Target Behavior	Treatment Technique	Design	Results
Modifying Stimulus Conditions					
Carr, Newsom, & Binkoff, 1976	3-year-old boy educable mentally retarded schizophrenic institutionalized	head hitting	alter antecedent conditions that could effect SIB by putting subject in demand and nondemand situations	multiple schedule with reversal within each setting	SIB increased when verbal demands given; with demand situations SIB decreased when demands positive; antecedents just as important as consequence in maintaining SIB
Differential Reinforcement of Other Behavior					
Lovaas & Simmons, 1969	9-year-old girl institutionalized schizophrenic	multiple SIB—head banging, arm banging, scratching, pinching, setting hair on fire	DRO	reversal	DRO decreased SIB; sympathetic comments given contingent on SIB increased it; effects did not generalize across settings
Nunes, Murphy, & Ruprecht, 1977	16-year-old boy severely mentally retarded institutionalized (A)	head hitting	vibration applied or withdrawn contingent on SIB (A) negative reinforcement (B) DRO	reversal, multiple baseline	vibration powerful enough reinforcer to reduce SIB when withdrawn contingent on occurrence and delivered as DRO
	12-year-old female severely mentally retarded institutionalized (B)				
Differential Reinforcement plus Timeout					
Peterson & Peterson, 1968	8-year-old boy profoundly mentally retarded institutionalized	multiple SIB—head hitting, head/hand banging, teeth hitting	combination—DRO and timeout	reversal	DRO and timeout decreased SIB; DRO did not have to be with an incompatible behavior
Dougherty & Lane, 1976	2½-year-old girl, not diagnosed	head banging	timeout and DRO	multiple baseline across settings	withdrawal of pacifier and parental attention contingent upon SIB eliminated SIB over a 30-day period

TABLE 12.7 (CONTINUED)

Reference	Subjects	Target Behavior	Treatment Technique	Design	Results
Lucero, Frieman, Spooring, & Fehrenbacher, 1976	3 profoundly mentally retarded girls: 10, 17, and 18 years institutionalized	head hitting (A) head banging (B) head hitting, eye gouging (C)	timeout, removal of food and adult attention, combination removal of food and attention	reversal	removal of food and combination food-attention removal reduced SIB; removal of attention increased SIB in 2 subjects, did not affect other subject
Timeout Lutzker, 1978	20-year-old male profoundly mentally retarded (PKU) institutionalized	head hitting	facial screening (timeout)	multiple baseline across settings	facial screening reduced SIB in each setting in which it was applied; regular teachers found procedure effective even when applied intermittently
Solnick, Rincover, & Peterson, 1977	16-year-old boy severely mentally retarded institutionalized	head banging	timeout with impoverished and enriched time in environments	reversal	SIB increased with timeout (removal of materials and examiner in impoverished time in situation and greatly reduced in enriched time in situation
Differential Reinforcement, Timeout, plus Verbal Reprimand					
Myers & Deibert, 1971	11-year-old institutionalized mentally retarded blind	head hitting	combination—DRO, timeout, and verbal reprimand	none	combination reduced SIB to 3 or 4 per day, effects did not generalize across settings
Repp & Deitz, 1974	2 severely/profoundly mentally retarded 1 male, 8 years old (A) 1 female, 13 years old (B) institutionalized	(A) unspecified SIB (B) scratching	(A) DRO and timeout (B) DRO and verbal punishment	reversal and baseline-intervention (AB)	DRO combined with timeout and aversive stimuli effective and usable by regular ward staff in reducing SIB
Overcorrection Measel & Alfieri, 1978	14-year-old male severely mentally retarded institutionalized	head hitting	overcorrection and DRO	started as reversal but changed to AB	procedure decreased SIB in one subject but increased SIB in other subject

Study	Subject	Behavior	Procedure	Design	Results
	16-year-old male severely mentally retarded institutionalized	head banging	overcorrection and DRO	reversal	combination procedure more effective than either procedure used alone, practical for use by regular staff in a variety of settings
DeCatanzaro & Baldwin, 1978	2 profoundly mentally retarded boys 8 and 12 years old institutionalized	head hitting	overcorrection and DRO		

Presentation of Aversive Consequences—Aversive Liquids and Odors

Study	Subject	Behavior	Procedure	Design	Results
Favell, McGimsey, & Jones, 1978	15-year-old girl	eye gouging	DRO with restraint and distraction combined with punishment by lemon juice squirts in mouth	reversal in Exp. 1	restraint as reinforcer for desirable behavior and punishment with lemon juice eliminated SIB in laboratory setting and in natural setting in one case
	8-year-old boy	head hitting/banging		multiple baseline across subjects in Exp. 2	
	27-year-old woman	hair pulling			
	all subjects profoundly mentally retarded institutionalized				
Sajwaj, Libert, & Agras, 1974	6-month-old girl, not diagnosed foster home	rumination	lemon juice squirted in mouth contingent on rumination	reversal	lemon juice effective in eliminating SIB in hospital and in reducing SIB at home; appropriate behavior increased
Tanner & Zeiler, 1975	20-year-old female autistic institutionalized	slapping	punishment with aromatic ammonia	reversal	reduction in SIB in natural setting by regular staff; no other changes in behavior

TABLE 12.7 (CONTINUED)

Reference	Subjects	Target Behavior	Treatment Technique	Design	Results
Presentation of Aversive Consequences—Shock					
Lovaas & Simmons, 1969	7-year-old boy, 8-year-old boy, 11-year-old girl, all psychotic/severely mentally retarded institutionalized	head banging	extinction, shock	AB, multiple baseline across subjects and experimenters	extinction and shock effective but shock immediate; effects not generalized; appropriate behavior increased; SIB increased with social attention
Romanczyk & Goren, 1975	7-year-old boy living at home autistic severely mentally retarded	head banging	combination—DRO and shock	none: baseline intervention (AB)	treatment totally eliminated SIB in laboratory setting and partially reduced SIB in natural setting
Multiple Treatments Including Shock as an Aversive Consequence					
Corte, Wolf, & Locke, 1971	3 female, 1 male adolescents institutionalized	multiple SIB—head banging/hitting, scratching, biting, hair pulling	extinction (2 subjects) DRO (2 subjects) shock (4 subjects)	multiple baseline across settings or experimenters	extinction not effective, DRO effective for 1 subject, shock effective for all subjects; effects did not generalize across settings
Tate, 1972	16-year-old girl severely mentally retarded institutionalized	multiple SIB—head banging/hitting, kicking	combination—DRO, shock, timeout, gradual withdrawal of restraints	none	combination treatment reduced SIB in one week in settings where applied; continued reduction after 7 months; recurrence after 3 years
Risley, 1968	6-year-old girl autistic living at home	dangerous climbing	timeout, extinction, punishment with shock	none: baseline intervention (AB)	shock eliminated climbing but effects did not generalize across behavior settings timeout and extinction ineffective; some side effects of shock; maintenance partial

340

destruction of property, and thrashing on the floor. Aggressive acts occur frequently in severely handicapped populations (Forehand & Baumeister, 1976). In fact, Ross (1972) reported that 27% of the institutionalized retarded individuals in California engaged in aggressive acts at least a monthly and in most cases more frequently (e.g., weekly or even daily).

The need to reduce aggression is obvious. In addition to the threat of physical harm to others, aggressive acts interefere with habilitation and educational programming and may even result in staff members avoiding the aggressive individual (Mithaug & Hanawalt, 1977).

Table 12.8 lists studies that are representative of those designed to decrease aggressive/disruptive behavior. The first category involves the modification of stimulus conditions. Boe (1977) evaluated the effects of room size, access to toys, and increasing positive interactions on the aggressive behavior of severely handicapped institutionalized people. Aggression decreased when toys were available and dramatically decreased when noncontingent positive attention was provided. This study supports an evaluation of ecological variables as an initial step in changing aggressive behavior. Perhaps increasing the number of positive interactions between staff and students would be sufficient to decrease aggressive/disruptive acts.

Differential reinforcement of other behavior has also been successful in decreasing aggression, and as stated previously, is a constructive and positive approach. In combination with timeout and response cost, DRO has strengthened alternative behaviors while decreasing aggressive/disruptive acts (e.g., Bostow & Bailey, 1969; Perline & Levinsky, 1968; Repp & Deitz, 1974).

Overcorrection has recently been shown to be effective in decreasing aggression and disruption. However, unlike self-stimulation, aggression usually disrupts the physical environment. Therefore, in addition to the positive practice involved in overcorrection for stereotypic behavior, overcorrection procedures used with aggression usually involve restitution as well (e.g., Foxx & Azrin, 1972). Another overcorrection procedure was used by Webster and Azrin (1973) to decrease aggressive/disruptive behaviors of mentally retarded adults. They made a 2-hour bed rest contingent on an aggressive/disruptive act. The purpose was to teach the aggressor to be calm and quiet when agitated.

Although these procedures have been successful, more research is needed. Furthermore, the demand on staff time in administering overcorrection is frequently unmanageable. These considerations must be made before beginning overcorrection. In addition, when using overcorrection, especially gradu-

ated guidance, care must be taken not to abuse the misbehavior physically with extreme force. With these considerations in mind, overcorrection procedures are potentially useful for eliminating chronic behavior problems that previously had not been considered manageable.

Finally, presenting aversive consequences such as physical punishment is a very intrusive technique for eliminating aggressive/disruptive acts. Again, the need for aversive consequences should be documented either by demonstrating the severity of the aggressive act or the ineffective application of less intrusive techniques.

Research needs in this area are similar to those for other problem areas. We need methodologically sound research that evaluates the relative contribution of components of treatment packages. In addition, further evaluation of the effects of stimulus conditions on aggressive/disruptive behavior would provide pertinent information for developing unintrusive environmental intervention techniques.

Eating Problems: Chronic Vomiting and Pica

Chronic vomiting and pica are serious and potentially life-threatening maladaptive behaviors. Chronic vomiting as a behavior problem is voluntary or self-induced regurgitation of food without illness. It involves either reswallowing the vomitus or ejecting it from the mouth (Davis & Cuvo, 1980; Kanner, 1972). Pica involves ingesting nonedible substances such as cigarette butts, paper, feces, and small objects, including any object that can be placed in the mouth.

Both chronic vomiting and pica are frequent problems of the severely handicapped (up to 9.5% of mentally retarded patients in California state hospitals engage in excessive vomiting [Ball, Hendrickson, & Clayton, 1974]) and pose serious health hazards. Malnutrition or dehydration may result from excessive vomiting (Davis & Cuvo, 1980); intestinal blockage, infection, disease, and perhaps poisoning may result from pica. Consequently, intervention to reduce these maladaptive behavior is usually necessary.

Table 12.9 lists representative studies designed to reduce excessive vomiting or pica in severely handicapped people. As in the preceding tables, the studies are arranged from least to most intrusive intervention techniques.

The first intervention category consists of modifying the presentation of food in a feeding setting. A special feeding technique consisting of stimulating the child's mouth and lips and presenting the food in a positive manner was used (Ball, Hendricksen, & Clayton, 1974). This procedure was selected based on the assumption that ruminating behaviors pro-

(Text continues on page 352.)

TABLE 12.8 Decreasing Aggressive/Disruptive Acts: Representative Intervention Studies

Reference	Subjects	Target Behavior	Intervention Techniques	Design	Results
Modifying Stimulus Conditions					
Boe, 1977	29 females severely/profoundly mentally retarded 8–19 years old, institutionalized	hitting, slapping, pushing, kicking, grabbing, pinching, biting, spitting, gouging, hair-pulling	comparison of size of room, availability of toys, and non-contingent reinforcement	reversal series	freely available toys did not decrease aggressive behavior; more space did decrease rate of aggressive behavior; noncontingent reinforcement dramatically decreased aggressive behavior
Differential Reinforcement of Other Behavior					
Carr, Newsom, & Binkoff, 1980	14-year-old male nonverbal autistic features institutionalized (A)	scratching, hitting, kicking, biting	(A) protective clothing worn; praise for 10 seconds without aggression (B) praise for correct response	reversal	aggressive high during demand situation and near zero during no demands
	9-year-old male mentally retarded nonverbal noninstitutionalized (B)	pinching, scratching, hair pulling	(B) toys and food for correct response	reversal	decrease of aggression when toys and food presented
			(A) leave chair contingent on a fixed ratio schedule of 5–25 acts, 25–45 acts, 45–65 acts	reversal	aggression increased as did an alternative behavior (hand tapping) as FR schedule increased
			(A) extinction	reversal	slow decrease of aggressive behavior
Wolf, Birnbrauer, Williams, & Lawler, 1965	9-year-old female MR, CP institutionalized	vomiting, tantrums	m & m and praise for no vomiting and tantrum, extinction	attempted reversal	decrease in both target behaviors

Timeout Plus Positive Reinforcement

Bostow & Bailey, 1969	58-year-old female nonambulatory institutionalized	loud and abusive verbal behavior	timeout on floor for 2 minutes, reinforcement when quiet on increasing time interval schedule	reversal	decrease of target behavior
	7-year-old male institutionalized	biting, hitting, kicking, scratching, head butting	timeout booth for 2 minutes, edible reinforcer for every 2 minutes without aggressive behavior	reversal	decrease of target behaviors
Burchard & Barrera, 1972	11 males—data for 6 reported 15–19 years old mentally retarded institutionalized	swearing, personal assults, property damage, etc.	0 timeout, 5 tokens taken; 0 timeout, 30 tokens; 5 minutes timeout, 0 tokens; 30 minutes timeout, 0 tokens	modified reversal	higher values more suppressive; higher became increased more suppressive over time
Repp & Deitz, 1974	12-year-old male severely mentally retarded ambulatory institutionalized	biting, hitting, scratching, kicking	differential reinforcement of other behavior (DRO)—candy timeout—30-second restraint	reversal	decrease of inappropriate behavior, increase of appropriate response
	8-year-old male mentally retarded ambulatory institutionalized	throwing, objects, hitting, biting, kicking, pinching, spitting, knocking over furniture, tearing papers	DRO—star traded for puzzle piece mild verbal punishment	reversal	decrease of aggression
	13-year-old male mentally retarded	leaving room, abusive language, threats, inappropriate body contact, aggressive use of furniture	DRO—stars in a book response cost—stars taken away mild verbal punishment	AB because it was felt behavior too dangerous to reverse	dramatic decrease of target behavior

TABLE 12.8 (CONTINUED)

Reference	Subjects	Target Behavior	Intervention Techniques	Design	Results
Vukelich & Hake, 1971	13-year-old female mentally retarded	choking, grabbing	timeout for choking, constant attention for nonaggression	baseline intervention$_1$, intervention$_2$, intervention$_3$ (AB$_1$B$_2$B$_3$)	rate of chokes decreased until last phase, then increased in phase 2, decreased in phase 3, and increased in last phase
			timeout for grab and choke, social attention for incompatible behavior		
			timeout for grab and choke, periodic social attention	none	chokes and grabs decreased
Weisen & Watson, 1967	6-year-old male severely mentally retarded institutionalized	grabbing, pulling, hitting	overcorrection—bed rest for 2 hours to become calm	none: baseline intervention (AB)	decreased disruptions in short period of time
Timeout Plus Response Cost Plus Positive Reinforcement					
Perline & Levinsky, 1968	4 residents of coed cottage severely mentally retarded 8–10 years old	aggression toward peers, aggression toward teacher, rising from chair, throwing objects, taking others' possessions	tokens given intermittently contingent on appropriate behavior; taken away when maladaptive behavior occurred; half of subjects received timeout for 5–15 minutes	not described	decrease of target behavior but no significant difference between subjects with and without timeout
Timeout					
Clark, Rowbury, Baer, & Baer, 1973	8-year-old female	chokes, armwraps, attacks on others, attacks to objects	timeout for 3 minutes	multiple baseline across behaviors	decrease of all behaviors
			timeout on a variable ratio schedule which increased	not described	larger percentage of respones punished, a greater decrease of frequency of that response
Hamilton, Stephens, & Allen, 1967	17-year-old female	head and back	timeout for 30 minutes	not described	decrease of target behavior

Study	Subject	Target behavior	Treatment	Design	Results
	24-yeard female	disrobing	timeout for 30 minutes	not described	decrease of target behavior
	16-year-old female	breaking windows	2-hour restraint in bed	not described	decrease of target behavior
	17-year-old female	pinching, slapping	timeout for 1 hour	not described	decrease of target behavior
	14-year-old female	fighting	timeout for 1 hour	not described	decrease of target behavior
White, Nielsen, & Johnson, 1972	20 mentally retarded persons 7–21 years 1/3 female institutionalized	vomiting, tantrums	timeout for 1 minute, 15 minutes, and 30 minutes	reversal	15 and 30 minutes equally effective and more effective than 1 minute
Overcorrection Polvinale & Lutzker, 1980	13-year-old male severely mentally retarded	assault, interpersonal sexual behavior	DRO—praise to subject or to peers overcorrection—apology to victims, peers, teacher	modified baseline across time of day and setting	decrease when both techniques used together
Foxx & Azrin, 1972	50-year-old female mentally retarded disabled institutionalized	destruction of property, attacks on others, screaming	household orderliness training, social reassurance training (overcorrection)	none: baseline intervention (AB)	decrease of target behavior
	22-year-old female profoundly mentally retarded institutionalized	physical attacks	oral hygiene training, medical assistance training, social reassurance training (overcorrection)	none: baseline intervention (AB)	decrease of target behavior
	56-year-old female brain damaged institutionalized	screaming, overturning furniture	quiet training, social reassurance training, household orderliness training, oral hygiene training, medical assistance training	none: baseline intervention (AB)	decrease of target behavior
Webster & Azrin, 1973	8 mentally retarded adults mean age 31 years 3 males 5 females	aggressive and disruptive behavior	overcorrection—bed rest for 2 hours to become calm	none: baseline intervention (AB)	decreased disruptions in short period of time

TABLE 12.8 (CONTINUED)

Reference	Subjects	Target Behavior	Intervention Techniques	Design	Results
Presentation of Aversive Consequences					
Paluck & Esser, 1971	21 males trainable mentally retarded or less ambulatory institutionalized	physical aggression, territorial aggression	verbal punishment for aggression, no punishment for aggression	none: baseline intervention (AB)	punishment decreased aggression; no punishment increased aggression
Negative Reinforcement					
Mithaug & Hanawalt, 1977	19-year-old female severely mentally retarded no functional expressive language	hitting	release of finger pressure for positive response, hand tapping	reversal	during finger pressure periods hits decreased and were eliminated; during verbal cue and hand tapping periods hits increased.
			verbal cue, removal of finger pressure	reversal	

TABLE 12.9 Decreasing Chronic Vomiting and Pica: Representative Intervention Studies

Reference	Subjects	Target Behavior	Treatment Technique	Design	Results
Modifying Task Presentation					
Ball, Hendrickson, & Clayton, 1974	11-year-old profoundly retarded male	vomiting	special feeding technique: oral stimulation during feeding	reversal	vomiting dropped to zero in first session and remained there
	6-year-old profoundly retarded male	vomiting		none: baseline intervention (AB)	only 1 occurrence of vomiting in 14 sessions
Food Satiation					
Jackson, Johnson, Ackron, & Crowley, 1975	29-year-old profoundly retarded male	vomiting	allowed to eat as much food as they desired at meals and were provided frequent snacks	reversal	number of vomiting occurrences dropped from an average of approximately 175 to about 35 on the first day of intervention and averaged approximately 10 per day during intervention
	27-year-old profoundly retarded male	vomiting		reversal	average number of vomiting occurrences during baseline was 12 per session and reduced to an average of 6 per session during intervention
Libby & Phillips, 1979	17-year-old profoundly retarded male	vomiting	served multiple portions of food during meals, and frequent snacks	none: baseline intervention (AB)	vomiting dropped to zero by second session and only occurred on 3 occasions after second session
Extinction plus Positive Reinforcement					
Wolf, Birnbrauer, Williams, & Lawler, 1965	9-year-old mentally retarded girl	vomiting	prior to treatment child was sent from classroom back to living unit when she vomited during extinction she was kept in class when vomiting occurred also, m & m's and praise were delivered for appropriate behavior	none: intervention only	gradual decline in vomiting to 0 after 6 weeks

TABLE 12.9 (CONTINUED)

Reference	Subjects	Target Behavior	Treatment Technique	Design	Results
Timeout plus Verbal Reprimand					
Ausman, Ball, & Alexander, 1974	14-year-old male nonverbal severely retarded ambulatory institutionalized	lengthy history of pica requiring surgery on 7 occasions	DRO with food rewards for abstention pica timeout helmet and verbal reprimand for pica behavior	none: intervention only	rate per hour of pica attempts dropped; criterion for extending training time: 3 "grab-free" sessions; training generalized to other settings and food items
Verbal Reprimand plus Restraint					
Bucher, Reykdal, & Albin, 1976	6-year-old profoundly retarded nonverbal ambulatory male	pica: grass, stones, dirt, food off floor, tiny objects	punishment: verbal reprimand, "No" and 30-second restraint when pica occurred	none: baseline intervention in settings: hallway with experimenter, without experimenter, and bedroom with and without experimenter	results for first subject incomplete
	6-year-old profoundly retarded nonverbal ambulatory female	pica: own feces; history of lead poisoning			second subject: decrease in rate of pica in 4 settings; zero frequency in settings when "No" and restraint followed earliest attempt at pica behavior
Overcorrection					
Azrin & Wesolowski, 1975	36-year-old profoundly retarded institutionalized female	vomiting, often precipitating disruptive behavior	required relaxation, timeout, positive practice and self-correction; practice correct vomiting and clean-up procedure	none: intervention only	baseline vomiting averaged 2 times daily required relaxation and timeout produced no change, positive practice and self-correction extinguished vomiting after 1 week; follow-up one year later showed vomiting was still extinguished
Duker & Seys, 1977	19-year-old profoundly retarded institutionalized female	vomiting, mostly after meals; timeout, extinction, DRO, and aversive gustatory stimulation tried with	restitutional overcorrection for vomiting: verbal reprimand, shown results of vomiting, 20 minutes restitution, washed face, cleaned vomit and part of room cleaned, removed clothes and dressed again, DRO—attention, contact privileges for nonvomiting behavior	reversal	number of vomiting responses dropped with treatment to 0 level vomiting responses occurred at higher level during reversal and dropped with reintroduction of treatment

Study	Subject	Behavior	Treatment	Design	Results
Foxx, Snyder, & Schroeder, 1979	25-year-old profoundly retarded male no teeth (meals are pureed) institutionalized	rumination after meals (for years)	verbal reprimand, oral hygiene following rumination: cleansing teeth and gums with Listerine for 2 minutes, satiation: eat until food refusal or until 2 meals had been consumed (lunch only)	multiple baseline across subjects	average % rumination during baseline of 89.5% dropped to 48.8% during satiation condition and to 3% during satiation plus oral hygiene condition
	22-year-old profoundly retarded female nonambulatory institutionalized	rumination after meals (for 6 years)			average % rumination during baseline of 49.9% dropped to 7.9% during satiation condition and to 1.4% during satiation plus oral hygiene conditions
Foxx & Martin, 1975	30-year-old profoundly retarded female	pica and coprophagy (feces eating)	overcorrection (30 minutes): spit out article, wash hands, fingernails, and anal area oral hygiene: brush teeth with mouthwash ward clean-up for pica	multiple baseline across behaviors	coprophagy was reduced by 95% during intervention pica reduced by 90% on first day of intervention
	31-year-old profoundly retarded female, 20-year-old profoundly retarded female	coprophagy	physical restraint conditions, overcorrection: same as above	multiple baseline across subjects	physical restraint reduced the behavior slightly, but when overcorrection applied behavior reduced to near zero level for both subjects
	33-year-old profoundly retarded male	pica: cigarette butts	overcorrection: same as above, with 10 minutes of emptying and wiping ashtrays	reversal: baseline intervention, with 2 one-day returns to baseline	baseline showed scavenging to be 100% of time first day of intervention reduced pica by 50% and after 4 days to zero

Presentation of Aversive Consequences—Aversive Liquids

Study	Subject	Behavior	Treatment	Design	Results
Becker, Turner, & Sajwaj, 1978	26-month-old retarded girl	lip smacking, choking, sucking to rumination	lemon juice (5–10 cc) squirted into mouth as soon as signs of rumination occurred	reversal	within 2 sessions rumination dropped to 20% level

TABLE 12.9 (CONTINUED)

Reference	Subjects	Target Behavior	Treatment Technique	Design	Results
Sajwaj, Libert, & Agras, 1974	6-month-old infant	rumination after feedings with weight loss and dehydration	punishment—lemon juice (5–10 cc squirted into mouth as soon as vigorous tongue movement preceding behavior occurred	reversal	baseline showed 40–70% rate of 10-second intervals of rumination 20 minutes after feeding treatment reduced behavior to 10% return to baseline showed high levels of behavior reinstitution of treatment dropped behavior to low level (.9–2.8%) weight gain documented with onset of treatment

Combinations of Differential Reinforcement plus Punishment Techniques

O'Neil, White, King, & Marek, 1979	26-month-old girl with seizure disorder and developmental delay	chronic rumination after feeding, involving severe weight loss	DRO: "Good" and honey and water given for every 15–30 without rumination, punishment: lemon juice in mouth contingent upon any ruminating behaviors, DRO and punishment combined, timeout and DRO fading for generalization, knuckle tapping punishment for hands in mouth	reversal	rumination frequency % interval: baseline 85–100% lemon juice 40–85% juice and DRO 0–95% DRO 0–35% baseline₂ 65–85% DRO₂ 0–18% baseline₃ 30–100% DRO₃ 0–65% timeout and fading 0–90% knuckle tapping 0–10%

Combinations of Aversive Techniques

Simpson & Sasso, 1978	10-year-old severely disturbed functionally retarded male in public school setting	rumination at mealtimes	verbal reprimand, physically forced to swallow vomit, lemon juice squirted into mouth, lips and mouth washed with soap (30 sec.), face cream on lips (45 sec.)	reversal	baseline showed mean % of time engaged during 20-minute session to be 44% treatment: behavior mean of .65% reversal showed increase in behavior to 53% mean treatment₂ showed 0% mean

Presentation of Aversive Consequences—Shock

Kohlenberg, 1970	21-year-old severely retarded nonverbal institutionalized female with mild quadriplegia	vomiting after meals and subsequent weight loss creating danger to subject	punishment: momentary shock contingent upon stomach tension, which preceded vomiting	none: intervention only	vomiting reduced from after every meal before treatment to 64/75 behavior-free sessions during treatment some spontaneous recovery required occasional shocks weight gain documented after treatment
Luckey, Watson, & Musick, 1968	6-year-old severely retarded male	vomiting	applied shock contingent on vomiting	none: intervention only	vomiting dropped to 0 within 6 days
Watkins, 1972	14-year-old severely retarded male	rumination	applied shock contingent on first signs of vomiting	none: baseline intervention (AB)	reduced vomiting, to 2 occurrences per week within 3 weeks
White & Taylor, 1967	23-year-old profoundly retarded nonverbal self-abusive institutionalized	excessive vomiting and rumination, often during or after meals (weight of 45 pounds)	punishment: electric shock contingent upon rumination	none: intervention only	reduction in behavior sporadic no functional relationship between decrease of behavior and treatment due to confounding variables
	14-year-old profoundly retarded male institutionalized	vomiting and rumination, often during or after meals (weight of 84 pounds)			

vided oral stimulation for the child; therefore, providing oral stimulation other than through rumination should minimize its occurrence. This technique was successful with the two subjects with whom it was tried.

A second treatment for excessive vomiting is food satiation. The basis for using food satiation is similar to that for using oral stimulation. If rumination results from hunger or from the reinforcing value of chewing and swallowing food, providing extra food should eliminate the need to vomit. Jackson, Johnson, Ackron, and Crowley (1975) and Libby and Phillips (1979) found that providing extra portions of food significantly decreased chronic rumination in three profoundly retarded subjects. The special feeding and food satiation techniques are potentially successful alternatives to more intrusive aversive techniques. More research is needed to evaluate environmental conditions (e.g., hunger, self-stimulating features of specific behaviors) that may affect excessive maladaptive behaviors such as vomiting.

More intrusive techniques such as extinction, timeout, verbal reprimands, restraint, and overcorrection have been effective in reducing pica and vomiting. Selection of procedures should depend on previously employed techniques and an ABC analysis of the problem behavior. For example, if attention is maintaining excessive vomiting, timeout may be effective in reducing it.

The use of aversive consequences such as distasteful liquids (e.g., lemon juice, tabasco sauce) or electric shock may be justifiable with these behaviors due to their life-threatening nature. Again, the necessity for using these most intrusive techniques must be documented.

Summary of Research Needs

Although the problem areas reviewed differ, the research needs are surprisingly similar. We need more research to evaluate the effects of the stimulus environment on maladaptive behavior. Perhaps an ecological approach to behavior reduction would prove most efficient as well as least intrusive.

All areas reviewed need more methodologically sound research (Davis & Cuvo, 1980; Horner & Barton, 1980). Sound experimental design, precise behavioral definitions, specific data collection procedures, and acceptable measures of interobserver reliability must be included in studies evaluating intervention techniques. Without all these components, results of research are questionable, and no definitive statements can be made.

Specific research should also be directed toward identifying the relative contributions of specific components of intervention packages. Teachers should not always assume that a package is more effective than a single procedure. Perhaps sufficient behavior change can be obtained with a single procedure which would require less preparation and staff time than a treatment package.

Finally, more attention should be focused on maintenance and generalization of behavior change (Davis & Cuvo, 1980; Horner & Barton, 1980). Reduction of maladaptive behavior is only successful if the behavior remains low across settings in the natural environment for long periods. Methods for facilitating behavior maintenance and generalization need extensive exploration.

SUMMARY

Appropriate social interaction skills are important for successful participation in all life skills. In fact, lack of appropriate social skills is a major reason for failure in community integration and community employment (Goldstein, 1964; Greenspan & Shoultz, 1981; Gaylord-Ross, 1979).

Severely handicapped people often do not have the social skills they need to interact successfully in a community setting. Therefore, a first step in increasing social competence is to *teach* the components of social interaction. These steps or skills range from a simple greeting response to participating in complex social interactions such as developing relationships with members of the opposite sex. Research in social skill instruction reflects the diverse range of skills involved. As a result, the research lacks continuity and is less than comprehensive. We need more research to tie together concepts and techniques and to validate the model proposed in this chapter.

In addition to social skill instruction, teachers must manage excessive maladaptive behaviors characteristic of severely handicapped students. Although a range of techniques have been effective in reducing maladaptive behavior, a teacher must carefully select a technique for intervention with a specific problem. A functional analysis of the target behavior in the natural environment will provide valuable information to help in selecting an intervention approach. In addition, the least intrusive but effective procedure should be selected for each specific maladaptive behavior. With a combination of social skill instruction and skillful management of excessive maladaptive behavior, severely handicapped people can become socially competent.

REFERENCES

Ausman, J., Ball, T.S., & Alexander, D. Behavior therapy of pica with a profoundly retarded adolescent. *Mental Retardation*, 1974, *12*, 16–18.

Axelrod, S., Brantner, J.P., & Maddock, T.P. Overcorrection: A review and critical analysis. *Journal of Special Education*, 1978, *12*, 367–392.

Azrin, N.H., Kaplan, S.J., & Foxx, R.M. Autism reversal: Eliminating stereotyped self-stimulation of retarded individuals. *American Journal of Mental Deficiency*, 1973, *78*, 241–248.

Azrin, N.H., & Wesolowski, M.D. Eliminating habitual vomiting in a retarded adult by positive practice and self-correction. *Journal of Behavior Therapy and Experimental Psychiatry*, 1975, *6*, 145–148.

Bachman, J. Self-injurious behavior: A behavioral analysis. *Journal of Abnormal Psychology*, 1972, *80*, 221–248.

Ball, T., Hendrickson, H., & Clayton, J. A special feeding technique for chronic regurgitation. *American Journal of Mental Deficiency*, 1974, *78*, 486–493.

Bandura, A. *Principles of behavior modification*. New York: Holt, Rinehart & Winston, 1969.

Bates, P. The effectiveness of interpersonal skills training on the social skill acquisition of moderately and mildly retarded adults. *Journal of Applied Behavior Analysis*, 1980, *13*, 237–248.

Bates, P., & Harvey, J. Social skills and the mentally retarded: An empirical analysis of the research. In O.C. Karan (Ed.), *Habilitation practices with the severely developmentally disabled*. Madison, Wisc.: R & T Center, 1978.

Bates, P., & Renzaglia, A. Language game instruction: Use of a table game. *Education and Treatment of Children*, 1982, *5*(1), 13–22.

Baumeister, A.A., & Forehand, R. Stereotyped acts. In N.R. Ellis (Ed.), *International review of research in mental retardation* (Vol. IV). New York: Academic Press, 1974.

Becker, J., Turner, S., & Sajwaj, T. Multiple behavioral effects of the use of lemon juice with a ruminating toddler-age child. *Behavior Modification*, 1978, *2*, 267–278.

Berkson, G., & Davenport, R.K. Stereotyped movements in mental defectives: I. Initial Survey. *American Journal of Mental Deficiency*, 1962, *66*, 849–852.

Boe, R.B. Economical procedures for the reduction of aggression in a residential setting. *Mental Retardation*, 1977, *15*(5), 25–28.

Bostow, D.E., & Bailey, J.B. Modification of severe disruptive and aggressive behavior using brief time-out and reinforcement procedures. *Journal of Applied Behavior Analysis*, 1969, *2*, 31–37.

Brown, L., Branston, N.B., Hamre-Nietupski, S., Pumpian, I., Certo, N., & Gruenewald, L. A strategy for developing chronological age appropriate and functional curricular content for severely handicapped adolescents and young adults. *Journal of Special Education*, 1979, *13*, 81–90.

Bucher, B., Reykdal, B., & Albin, J. Brief physical restraint to control pica in retarded children. *Behavior Therapy and Experimental Psychiatry*, 1976, *7*, 137–140.

Burchard, J.D., & Barrera, F. An analysis of time-out and response cost in a programmed environment. *Journal of Applied Behavior Analysis*, 1972, *5*, 271–282.

Carr, E.G., Newsom, C.D., & Binkoff, J.A. Stimulus control of self-destructive behavior in a psychotic child. *Journal of Abnormal Child Psychology*, 1976, *4*, 139–153.

Carr, E.G., Newsom, C.D., & Binkoff, J.A. Escape as a factor in the aggressive behavior of two retarded children. *Journal of Applied Behavior Analysis*, 1980, *13*, 101–117.

Clark, H.B., Rowbury, T., Baer, A.M., & Baer, D.M. Time-out as a punishing stimulus in continuous and intermittent schedules. *Journal of Applied Behavior Analysis*, 1973, *6*, 443–455.

Corte, H.E., Wolf, M.M., & Locke, B.J. A comparison of procedures for eliminating self-injurious behavior of retarded adolescents. *Journal of Applied Behavior Analysis*, 1971, *4*, 201–213.

Davis, P.K., & Cuvo, A.J. Chronic vomiting and rumination in intellectually normal and retarded individuals: Review and evaluation of behavior research. *Behavior Research of Severe Developmental Disabilities*, 1980, *1*, 31–59.

DeCatanzaro, D.A., & Baldwin, B. Effective treatment of self-injurious behavior through a forced arm exercise. *American Journal of Mental Deficiency*, 1978, *82*, 433–439.

Doleys, D., Wells, K., Hobbs, S., Roberts, M., & Cartelli, L. The effect of social punishment on noncompliance: A comparison of time-out and positive practice. *Journal of Applied Behavior Analysis*, 1976, *9*, 471–482.

Dougherty, E.H., & Lane, J.R. Naturalistic alternatives to extinction. An application to self-injurious bedtime behavior. *Journal of Behavior Therapy and Experimental Psychiatry*, 1976, *7*, 373–375.

Duker, P., & Seys, D.M. Elimination of vomiting in a retarded female using restitutional overcorrection. *Behavior Therapy*, 1977, *8*, 255–257.

Edmonson, B., Leland, H., & Leach, E. Increasing social cue interpretation by retarded adolescents through training. *American Journal of Mental Deficiency*, 1967, *71*, 1017–1024.

Eisler, R.M., Hersen, M., & Miller, P.M. Effects of modeling on components of assertive behavior. *Journal of Behavior Therapy and Experimental Psychiatry*, 1973, *4*, 1–6.

Favell, J.E., McGimsey, J.F., & Jones, M.L. The use of physical restraint in the treatment of self-injury and as positive reinforcement. *Journal of Applied Behavior Analysis*, 1978, *11*, 225–241.

Forehand, R., & Baumeister, A. Deceleration of aberrant behavior among retarded individuals. In M. Hersen, R.M. Eisler, & P.M. Miller (Eds.), *Progress in behavior modification*, 2. New York: Academic Press, 1976.

Foxx, R.M., & Azrin, N.H. Restitution: A method for eliminating aggressive-disruptive behavior of retarded and brain-damaged patients. *Behavior Research and Therapy*, 1972, *10*, 15–27.

Foxx, R.M., & Azrin, N.H. The elimination of autistic self-stimulatory behavior by overcorrection. *Journal of Applied Behavior Analysis*, 1973, *6*, 1–14.

Foxx, R., & Martin, E. Treatment of scavenging behavior (coprophagy and pica) by overcorrection. *Behavior Research and Therapy*, 1975, *13*, 153–162.

Foxx, R., Snyder, M., & Schroeder, F. A food satiation and oral hygiene punishment program to suppress chronic rumination by retarded persons. *Journal of Autism and Developmental Disorders*, 1979, *9*, 399–411.

Frankel, F., & Simmons, J.Q. Self-injurious behavior in schizophrenic and retarded children. *American Journal of Mental Deficiency*, 1976, *80*, 512–522.

Gardner, W.I. *Learning and behavior characteristics of exceptional children and youth: A humanistic behavioral approach.* Boston: Allyn & Bacon, 1977.

Gaylord-Ross, R.J. Mental retardation research, ecological validity, and the delivery of longitudinal education programs. *Journal of Special Education*, 1979, *13*, 69–80.

Gaylord-Ross, R.J. A decision model for the treatment of aberrant behavior in applied settings. In W. Sailor, B. Wilcox, & L. Brown (Eds.), *Methods of instruction for severely handicapped students.* Baltimore: Paul H. Brookes, 1980.

Gilhool, T.K., & Stutman, E.A. Integration of severely handicapped students: Toward criteria for implementing and enforcing the integration imperative of P.L. 94-142 and Section 504. In S. Sarason, D. Geller, & M. Klaber (Eds.), *Least restrictive alternatives: Moral, legal administrative dilemmas.* New York: Free Press, in press.

Goldstein, H. Social and occupational adjustment. In H. Stevens & R. Heber (Eds.), *Mental retardation: A review of research.* Chicago: University of Chicago, 1964.

Granger, C., & Wehman, P. Sensory stimulation. In P. Wehman (Ed.), *Recreation programming for the developmentally disabled person.* Baltimore: University Park Press, 1979.

Greenspan, S., & Shoultz, B. Why mentally retarded adults lose their jobs: Social competence as a factor in work adjustment. *Applied Research in Mental Retardation*, 1981, *2*, 23–38.

Hall, G., Sheldon-Wildgen, J., & Sherman, J. Teaching job interview skills to retarded clients. *Journal of Applied Behavior Analysis*, 1980, *13*, 433–442.

Hamilton, J., Stephens, L., & Allen, P. Controlling aggressive and destructive behavior in severely retarded institutionalized residents. *American Journal of Mental Deficiency*, 1967, *71*, 852–856.

Hamre-Nietupski, S., & Williams, W. Implementation of selected sex education and social skills to severely handicapped students. *Education and Training of the Mentally Retarded*, 1977, *12*(4), 364–372.

Haring, N.G., Liberty, K.A., & White, O.R. Rules for data-based strategy decisions in institutional programs. In W. Sailor, B. Wilcox, & L. Brown (Eds.), *Methods of instruction for severely handicapped students.* Baltimore: Paul H. Brookes, 1980.

Harris, S., & Wolchik, S. Suppression of self-stimulation: Three alternative strategies. *Journal of Applied Behavior Analysis*, 1979, *12*, 185–198.

Hill, J.W., Wehman, P., & Horst, G. Toward generalization of appropriate leisure and social behavior in se-

verely handicapped youth: Pinball machine use. *Journal of the Association for the Severely Handicapped*, 1982, *6*(4), 38–44.

Horner, R.D., & Barton, E.S. Operant techniques in the analysis and modification of self-injurious behavior: A review. *Behavior Research of Severe Developmental Disabilities*, 1980, *1*, 61–91.

Jackson, G., Johnson, C., Ackron, G., & Crowley, R. Food satiation as a procedure to decelerate vomiting. *American Journal of Mental Deficiency*, 1975, *80*, 223–227.

Kanner, L. *Child psychiatry.* Springfield, Ill.: Charles C Thomas, 1972.

Kaufman, M.E., & Levitt, H. A study of three stereotyped behaviors in institutionalized mental defectives. *American Journal of Mental Deficiency*, 1965, *69*, 467–473.

Kazdin, A.E. Acceptability of alternative treatments for deviant child behavior. *Journal of Applied Behavior Analysis*, 1980, *13*, 259–273. (a)

Kazdin, A. *Behavior modification in applied settings* (Rev. ed.). Homewood, Ill.: Dorsey Press, 1980. (b)

Kelly, J.A., Furman, W.F., Phillips, J., Hathorn, S., & Wilson, T. Teaching conversational skills to retarded adolescents. *Child Behavior Therapy*, 1979, *1*, 85–97. (a)

Kelly, J.A., Laughlin, C., Claireborne, M., & Patterson, J. A group procedure for teaching job interview skills to formerly hospitalized psychiatric patients. *Behavior Therapy*, 1979, *10*, 299–310. (b)

Kissel, R., & Whitman, T. An examination of the direct and generalized effects of a play-training and overcorrection procedure upon the self-stimulatory behavior of a profoundly retarded boy. *AAESPH Review*, 1977, *2*, 131–146.

Koegel, R.L., & Covert, A. The relationship of self-stimulation to learning in autistic children. *Journal of Applied Behavior Analysis*, 1972, *5*, 381–387.

Koegel, R.L., Firestone, R.L., Kramme, K.W., & Dunlap, G. Increasing spontaneous play by suppressing self-stimulation in autistic children. *Journal of Applied Behavior Analysis*, 1974, *7*, 521–528.

Kohlenberg, R. The punishment of persistent vomiting: A case study. *Journal of Applied Behavior Analysis*, 1970, *3*, 241–245.

Lamal, P. A simple technique for reducing self-stimulatory behavior of a retarded child. *Journal of Applied Behavior Analysis*, 1976, *9*, 140.

Leland, H. Theoretical considerations of adaptive behavior. In W.A. Coulter & H.W. Morrow (Eds.), *The concept and measurement of adaptive behavior within the scope of psychological assessment.* Austin: Texas Regional Resource Center, 1977.

Libby, D., & Phillips, E. Eliminating rumination behavior in a profoundly retarded adolescent: An explanatory study. *Mental Retardation*, 1979, *17*, 94–95.

Lovaas, O.I., & Simmons, J.Q. Manipulation of self-destruction in three retarded children. *Journal of Applied Behavior Analysis*, 1969, *2*, 143–157.

Lucero, W.J., Frieman, J., Spoering, K., & Fehrenbacher, J. Comparison of three procedures in reducing self-injurious behavior. *American Journal of Mental Deficiency*, 1976, *80*, 548–554.

Luckey, R., Watson, C., & Musick, J. Adversive conditioning as a means of inhibiting vomiting and rumination. *American Journal of Mental Deficiency*, 1968, *73*, 139–142.

Lutzker, J.R. Reducing self-injurious behavior by facial screening. *American Journal of Mental Deficiency*, 1978, *82*, 510–513.

Marchant, J., & Wehman, P. Teaching table games to severely handicapped students. *Mental Retardation*, 1979, *17*, 150–152.

Matson, J., & Andrasik, F. Training leisure-time and social-interaction skills to mentally retarded adults. *American Journal of Mental Deficiency*, 1982, *86*, 533–542.

Measel, C.J., & Alfieri, P.A. Treatment of self-injurious behavior by a combination of reinforcement for incompatible behavior and overcorrection. *American Journal of Mental Deficiency*, 1978, *81*, 147–153.

Mithaug, D.E., & Hanawalt, D. Employing negative reinforcement to establish and transfer control of a severely retarded and aggressive nineteen year old girl. *AAESPH Review*, 1977, *2*, 37–49.

Morris, R., & Dolker, M. Developing cooperative play in socially withdrawn retarded children. *Mental Retardation*, 1974, *12*, 24–27.

Murphy, R., Nunes, D., & Ruprecht, M. Reduction of stereotyped behavior in profoundly retarded individuals. *American Journal of Mental Deficiency*, 1977, *83*, 238–245.

Myers, J.J., & Deibert, A.N. Reduction of self-abusive behavior in a blind child by using a feeding response. *Journal of Behavior Therapy and Experimental Psychiatry*, 1971, *2*, 141–144.

Nelson, R., Gibson, F., Jr., & Cutting, D.S. Video-taped modeling: The development of 3 appropriate social responses in a mildly retarded child. *Mental Retardation*, 1973, *11*(6), 24–27.

Newman, R., Whorton, I., & Simpson, R. The modification of self-stimulatory verbalizations in an autistic child through the use of overcorrection procedures. *AAESPH Review*, 1977, *2*, 157–163.

Nunes, D.L., Murphy, R.J., & Ruprecht, M.L. Reducing self-injurious behavior of severely retarded individuals through withdrawal reinforcement procedures. *Behavior Modification*, 1977, *1*, 499–515.

O'Neil, P., White, J., King, C., & Marek, D. Controlling childhood rumination through differential reinforcement of other behavior. *Behavior Modification*, 1979, *3*, 355–372.

Paloutzian, R.F., Hasazi, J., Streifel, J., & Edgar, C. Promotion of positive social interaction in severely retarded young children. *American Journal of Mental Deficiency*, 1971, *75*, 519–524.

Paluck, R.J., & Esser, A.H. Controlled experimental modification of aggressive behavior in territories of severely retarded boys. *American Journal of Mental Deficiency*, 1971, *76*, 23–29.

Perline, I.H., & Levinsky, D. Controlling maladaptive classroom behavior in the severely retarded. *American Journal of Mental Deficiency*, 1968, *73*, 74–78.

Peterson, N., & Haralick, J.G. Integration of handicapped and nonhandicapped pre-schoolers: An analysis of play behavior and social interaction. *Education and Training of the Mentally Retarded*, 1977, *12*(3), 235–245.

Peterson, R.F., & Peterson, L.R. The use of positive reinforcement in the control of self-destructive behavior in a retarded boy. *Journal of Experimental Child Psychology*, 1968, *6*, 351–360.

Polvinale, R.A., & Lutzker, J.R. Elimination of assaultive and inappropriate sexual behavior by reinforcement and social restitution. *Mental Retardation*, 1980, *18*(1), 27–30.

Premack, D. Reinforcement theory. In D. Levin (Ed.), *Nebraska Symposium on Motivation*. Lincoln: University of Nebraska Press, 1965.

Quilitch, H.R., & Risley, T.R. The effects of play materials on social play. *Journal of Applied Behavior Analysis*, 1973, *6*, 575–578.

Rago, W.V., Jr., Parker, R.M., & Cleland, C. Effect of increased space on the social behavior of institutionalized profoundly retarded male adults. *American Journal of Mental Deficiency*, 1978, *82*, 554–558.

Repp, A., & Deitz, S.M. Reducing aggressive and self-injurious behavior of institutionalized retarded children through reinforcement of other behavior. *Journal of Applied Behavior Analysis*, 1974, *7*, 554–558.

Repp, A., Deitz, S., & Spier, N. Reducing stereotypic responding of retarded persons by the differential reinforcement of other behaviors. *American Journal of Mental Deficiency*, 1974, *79*, 279–284.

Rincover, A. Sensory extinction: A procedure for eliminating self-stimulatory behavior in developmentally disabled children. *Journal of Abnormal Child Psychology*, 1978, *6*, 299–310.

Rincover, A., Cook, R., Peoples, A., & Packard, D. Sensory extinction and sensory reinforcement principles for programming multiple adaptive behavior change. *Journal of Applied Behavior Analysis*, 1979, *12*, 221–233.

Rincover, A., Newsom, C., & Carr, E. Using sensory extinction procedures in the treatment of compulsive-like behavior of developmentally disabled children. *Journal of Consulting and Clinical Psychology*, 1979, *47*, 695–701.

Risley, T.R. The effects and side effects of punishing the autistic behaviors of a deviant child. *Journal of Applied Behavior Analysis*, 1968, *1*, 21–34.

Roberts, P., Iwata, B., McSween, T., & Desmond, E. An analysis of overcorrection movements. *American Journal of Mental Deficiency*, 1979, *83*, 588–594.

Rollings, J.P., Baumeister, A., & Baumeister, A. The use of overcorrection procedures to eliminate stereotyped behaviors in retarded individuals. *Behavior Modification*, 1977, *1*, 29–46.

Romanczyk, R.G., & Goren, E.R. Case studies—Severe self-injurious behavior: The problem of clinical control. *Journal of Consulting and Clinical Psychology*, 1975, *43*, 730–739.

Rose, H. Effectiveness and generalization of overcorrection procedures with the stereotyped behavior of a severely retarded adult. *AAESPH Review*, 1979, *4*, 196–201.

Ross, R.T. Behavioral correlates of levels of intelligence. *American Journal of Mental Deficiency*, 1972, *76*, 515–519.

Rychtarik, R.K., & Bornstein, P.H. Training conversational skills in mentally retarded adults. *Mental Retardation*, 1979, *17*(6), 289–293.

Sachs, D.A. The efficacy of time-out procedures in a variety of behavior problems. *Journal of Behavior Therapy and Experimental Psychiatry*, 1973, *4*, 237–242.

Sajwaj, T., Libert, J., & Agras, S. Lemon-juice therapy: The control of life-threatening rumination in a six-month-old infant. *Journal of Applied Behavior Analysis*, 1974, *7*, 557–563.

Schleien, S.J., Wehman, P., & Kiernan, J. Teaching leisure skills to severely handicapped adults: An age-appropriate darts game. *Journal of Applied Behavior Analysis*, 1981, *14*, 513–519.

Schroeder, S.R., Schroeder, C.S., Smith, B., & Dalldorf, J. Prevalence of self-injurious behaviors in a large state facility for the retarded: A three-year follow-up study. *Journal of Autism and Childhood Schizophrenia*, 1978, *8*, 261–269.

Serber, M. Teaching the non-verbal components of assertive training. *Journal of Behavior Therapy and Experimental Psychiatry*, 1972, *3*, 179–183.

Simpson, R., & Sasso, G. The modification of rumination in a severely emotionally disturbed child through overcorrection procedures. *AAESPH Review*, 1978, *3*, 145–150.

Smolev, S.R. Use of operant techniques for the modification of self-injurious behavior. *American Journal of Mental Deficiency*, 1971, *76*, 295–305.

Solnick, J.V., Rincover, A., & Peterson, C.R. Some determinants of the reinforcing and punishing effects of time-out. *Journal of Applied Behavior Analysis*, 1977, *10*, 415–424.

Sontag, E., Burke, P.J., & York, R. Considerations for serving the severely handicapped in the public schools. *Education and Training of the Mentally Retarded*, 1973, *8*(2), 20–26.

Stanfield, J.S. Graduation: What happens to the retarded child when he grows up. *Exceptional Children*, 1973, *39*, 548–552.

Strain, P. Increasing social play of severely retarded preschoolers. *Mental Retardation*, 1975, *13*(6), 7–9.

Sulzer-Azaroff, B., & Mayer, G.R. *Applying behavior-analysis procedures with children and youth.* New York: Holt, Rinehart & Winston, 1977.

Tanner, B.A., & Zeiler, M.D. Punishment of self-injurious behavior using aromatic ammonia as the aversive stimulus. *Journal of Applied Behavior Analysis*, 1975, *8*, 53–57.

Tate, B.G. Case study: Control of chronic self-injurious behavior by conditioning procedures. *Behavior Therapy*, 1972, *3*, 72–83.

Thoresen, C., & Mahoney, M. *Behavioral self-control.* Holt, Rinehart & Winston, 1974.

U.S. Office of Education, Bureau of Education for the Handicapped. Definition of severely handicapped children. *Code of Federal Register*, 1974, Title 54, Section 121.2.

Voeltz, L. Children's attitudes toward handicapped peers. *American Journal of Mental Deficiency*, 1980, *84*, 455–464.

Voeltz, L. Effects of structured interactions with severely handicapped peers on children's attitudes. *American Journal of Mental Deficiency*, 1982, *86*, 380–390.

Vukelich, R., & Hake, D.F. Reduction of dangerously aggressive behavior in a severely retarded resident through a combination of positive reinforcement procedures. *Journal of Applied Behavior Analysis*, 1971, *4*, 215–225.

Watkins, J.T. Treatment of chronic vomiting and extreme emaciation by an aversive stimulus: Case study. *Psychological Reports*, 1972, *31*, 803–805.

Webster, D.R., & Azrin, N.H. Required relaxation: A method of inhibiting agitative-disruptive behavior of retardates. *Behavior Research and Therapy*, 1973, *1*, 67–78.

Wehman, P. Effects of different environmental conditions on leisure time activity of the severely and profoundly handicapped. *Journal of Special Education*, 1978, *12*, 183–193.

Wehman, P. Teaching recreation skills to severely and profoundly handicapped persons. In E. Edgar & R. York (Eds.), *Teaching the severely handicapped* (Vol. 4). Seattle: American Association for the Education of the Severely/Profoundly Handicapped, 1979.

Wehman, P., & Schleien, S.J. *Leisure programs for handicapped persons.* Baltimore: University Park Press, 1981.

Weisburg, P., Passman, R., & Russel, J. Development of verbal control over bizarre gestures of retardates through imitative and nonimitative reinforcement procedures. *Journal of Applied Behavior Analysis*, 1973, *6*, 487–495.

Weisen, A.E., & Watson, E. Elimination of attention-seeking behavior in a retarded child. *American Journal of Mental Deficiency*, 1967, *72*, 50–52.

Wells, K., Forehand, R., & Hickey, R. Effects of verbal warning and overcorrection on stereotyped and appropriate behaviors. *Journal of Abnormal Child Psychology*, 1977, *5*(4), 387–403.

White, G.D., Nielsen, G., & Johnson, S.M. Time-out duration and the suppression of deviant behavior in children. *Journal of Applied Behavior Analysis*, 1972, *5*, 111–120.

White, J.C., & Taylor, D.J. Noxious conditioning as a treatment for rumination. *Mental Retardation*, 1967, *5*, 30–33.

Whitman, T., Mercurio, J., & Caponigri, V. Development of social responses in two severely retarded children. *Journal of Applied Behavior Analysis*, 1970, *3*, 133–138.

Wolf, M. Social validity: The case for subjective measurement or how applied behavior analysis is finding its heart. *Journal of Applied Behavior Analysis*, 1978, *11*, 203–214.

Wolf, M.M., Birnbrauer, J.S., Williams, T., & Lawler, J. A note on apparent extinction of the vomiting behavior of a retarded child. In L.P. Ullmann & L. Krasner (Eds.), *Case studies in behavior modification.* New York: Holt, Rinehart & Winston, 1965.

Wuerch, B.B., & Voeltz, L. *Longitudinal leisure skills for severely handicapped learners.* Baltimore: Paul H. Brookes, 1982.

Introduction to Chapter 13

In this chapter you will find an extensive review of current research on basic self-care instruction, particularly with retarded students. Undoubtedly some, if not all, of your students will have some deficiencies in either the basic skills of toileting, eating, and dressing or in more advanced self-help abilities such as grooming (hair and nail care, toothbrushing, bathing and showering, shaving), clothing care, and social eating skills (food passing, table manners).

Achieving the highest level of independence possible in basic self-care is critical for the moderately and severely handicapped. Not only will their care be simplified and more pleasant for their parents and teachers but, more importantly, to the extent a severely handicapped individual cares for his or her own personal needs, exclusion from educational programs and services is far less probable.

The younger or the more severely handicapped the learner, the more useful this chapter will be. To use the content described here, you will draw heavily from the observation and measurement techniques, the methods of task analysis, and the intervention strategies outlined in chapters 4 and 5.

13

Self-Care Skills

*This chapter was written by **Martha E. Snell,** University of Virginia.*

The development of self-care skills that begins early in the normal child's life represents a beginning of independence from parents. For handicapped children and adults this independence is of equal significance, though mental, physical, or behavioral deficiencies as well as environmental expectations may slow, limit, or indefinitely postpone the development of these basic adaptive skills. Feeding, dressing, and toileting are the most basic self-care skills. Early grooming skills supplement these basic abilities. They include hand-washing, face-washing, toothbrushing, nasal hygiene, and later bathing and showering, hair-combing and washing. Although most of these tasks are performed daily, all involve complex arrays of subskills learned in a highly organized sequence along with early cognitive, social, and motor abilities.

At the upper end of the continuum are nail care, skin care, use of deodorants and simple cosmetics, shaving, and hair setting and styling, in addition to menstrual hygiene for females. Furthermore, the ability to perform daily living tasks safely directly influences the quality of self-care. Clothing purchase and care (simple repair, selection and coordination of colors and style, clothing size, cleaning, ironing, storage), dressing appropriately (weather, stylishness, age-suited), careful use of prescription and nonprescription drugs and medications, healthy eating habits (balanced diet, adequate amounts, food purchase and preparation), and concepts of sexuality and sexual behavior (awareness of sexual differences, respect for privacy, male-female social interaction) are all important skills.

This chapter focuses on basic self-care—feeding, dressing, toileting, and early grooming skills—and how to measure and teach performance in these areas. Chapter 14, "Daily Living Skills," discusses more advanced personal maintenance, including showering, grooming habits, clothing combination, and clothing care.

BEHAVIORS INFLUENCING SELF-CARE SKILL LEARNING

Most severely handicapped children show delays in the mastery of self-care skills. Many causes beyond mental retardation may account for or contribute to this delay. For example, fine motor skills needed for self-care may be inadequate, or physical handicaps (visual, motoric) may aggravate the retardation or emotional disturbance. If a student's manipulative motor abilities are weak, reaching, grasping, and eye-hand coordination may need careful examination. Physical handicaps such as cerebral palsy (CP) require close guidance in assessment and training by a physical or occupational therapist to set realistic targets rather than encouraging dependency. For example, the athetoid CP student has problems of muscle control that are vastly different from the individual with severe spastic CP; these differences mandate procedural prescriptions for positioning, transporting, and specific movement requirements for eating, toileting, and dressing (Finnie, 1975).

If a student has not mastered some of the preverbal and early cognitive skills—visual attention, motor imitation, comprehension of simple commands and phrases—the training techniques a teacher uses will be quite different from those used with a verbal and attentive learner. For example, the use of verbal instructions ("Pick up your spoon") would be limited to the most relevant single word verb and noun requests with heavy reliance upon gestures (Bensberg, Colwell, & Cassel, 1965). At times it will be more efficient to work on attending and imitation first before turning to self-care. However, much successful self-care research has been carried out with individuals initially demonstrating little or no comprehension of verbal directions or cues (Bensberg et al., 1965; Minge & Ball, 1967). In many of these studies, gains in self-care skills were accompanied by increased comprehension of verbal requests to perform these skills. This same logic also may apply when the learner has extensive disruptive behaviors that result in inattention (repetitive hand staring, rocking) or aggressive behavior. Therefore, a teacher may elect to deal directly with the disruptive behaviors while reinforcing any improvements or even cooperation in self-care but not to teach new skills until self-control is more predictable. More often, training in self-care and behavior management will proceed simultaneously. Because of the differential reinforcement of self-help behaviors along with ignoring or timing-out of misbehaviors, the incidence of disruptive behavior will decrease (Azrin & Armstrong, 1973; Christian, Hollomon, & Lanier, 1973; Minge & Ball, 1967; O'Brien & Azrin, 1972; Song & Gandhi, 1974).

An additional class of behavior—noncompliance—may falsify assessment results and confuse teaching techniques. *Noncompliance* is the habitual tendency to refuse to perform skills or portions of skills which actually are in the individual's repertoire. This behavior is often inadvertently maintained by teachers who provide help at the least refusal to perform or complete a task or who inconsistently require the learner to perform self-care behaviors, alternating between firmness in task completion and "giving in" to extreme refusals or time constraints. For example, dressing training can be done at relevant times (right before dismissal) but enough time

must be available to ignore refusals to perform without necessitating dressing the student yourself.

The informal assessment should not only allow measurement of self-care skills but also estimate additional behaviors influencing training: physical handicaps and their effect on self-care behavior, level of fine motor development, attending, motor imitation, comprehension of simple commands (e.g., "Look here," "Eat with your spoon," "No," "Do this"), and disruptive or noncompliant behaviors that occur during meals, dressing periods, and toileting. In some cases a teacher can observe another teacher (parent or aide) working with a learner on self-care. These observations enable you to observe the student's response to commands, various prompts and reinforcement procedures, the learning situation, and so on, and to predict the success of changes in current antecedent or consequent events. Whenever possible, interviews with or observations of the parents' interaction with their child during self-care times are recommended. The teacher should gather information on the parents' expectations for performance, their understanding of analyzing tasks into small steps and reinforcing successive approximations, their consistency in approach, the use of imitative models, the appropriateness of the teaching materials (e.g., texture, flavor of food, level of toilet seat, size and complexity of clothing), and their feelings about the teaching program (Barnard & Powell, 1972). All of this information, along with the self-care skill data, will be valuable in creating and monitoring an individualized instructional program.

Summary of Self-Care Instructional Decisions

Chapters 4 and 5 discussed the steps involved in systematic instruction. The list below summarizes the instructional decisions involved in teaching feeding, toileting, dressing, and basic grooming skills.

1. What foods, toys, activities, and types of social attention and praise that are reinforcing to the learner and appropriate to his chronological and social age may be efficiently used in teaching?
2. What procedures may be used to control and reduce undesirable behaviors interfering with learning skills?
3. What self-help training objectives will be set?
   A. What behaviors are of most immediate importance to the individual, his home, or school setting?
   B. What is the student's current or baseline performance in these behaviors?
4. What instructional methods will be used to achieve the set objectives?
   A. Teacher instructions and requests,

B. Effective prompts,
C. Training setting and instructional materials,
D. Teaching times and frequency,
E. Task analysis of behavior,
F. Specific teaching techniques (shaping, backward chaining, dry pants check, positive practice, etc.).
5. How will changes in performance be monitored?
6. How will skill gains be maintained?
7. How will skill gains be generalized to other teachers, materials, and settings?

TOILET TRAINING

Independent toileting skills are all too often an unattained goal for the severely handicapped student. This failure often leads to exclusion from social and recreational programs and public schooling. It reduces teaching time between parent or ward attendant and the "accident prone" student, causes serious health hazards in the form of inadequate residential hygiene, dysentery, and intestinal infection, and makes the student less pleasant to be around. The high prevalence of daytime incontinence in this population is surpassed by nighttime incontinence or enuresis. While some have estimated that 40% of the institutionalized retarded adult population are enuretic at night (Smith, 1981), others (Azrin, Sneed, & Foxx, 1973; Sugaya, 1967) place this figure at 70%. Both estimates are in stark contrast to those reported for nonhandicapped 5-year-olds (17%), 11-year-olds (11%), and 15-year-olds (2%) (Kolvin, 1975).

In a 5-year survey of the toileting skill changes in a group of 3,427 institutionalized retarded individuals, Lohman, Eyman, and Lask (1967) discovered that 63% of the sample—those with the highest functioning capabilities (IQ 20)—were or became toilet trained during the 5 years rather easily by traditional methods without any special equipment or systematic operant techniques. However, 31% made no progress or regressed. Most members of this group had one or more of the following characteristics: IQ 10 or under, severely disturbed behavior, medically significant physical problems. The remaining 6.2% had an IQ between 10 and 20 and made progress during the 5 years toward daytime regulation (e.g., eliminated on toilet when taken but no self-initiation) with traditional methods of toilet training. The authors hypothesized that the unsuccessful group with "complex custodial problems" would probably never improve, where the smaller group of 6.2% would respond to intensive operant training.

Motivated by these statistics and their negative effect on further development of the handicapped, teachers and applied behavior analysts have in the last 15 years created, tested, and revised treatment procedures for incontinence. This section sets forth the basic elements of successfully documented toilet-training procedures, drawing heavily upon recent research and curricular applications in this area.

Entry Skills for Toilet Training

As with other tasks, toileting is learned in a logical developmental sequence building upon certain prerequisite behaviors. Developmental sequences reveal a number of important points.

1. Daytime regulation and training precedes nighttime training.
2. Bowel movements are regulated before urination, but toileting independence in both is generally learned at the same time.
3. The additional skills of undressing, dressing, and wiping "slow down" total independence in the normal child.
4. Nighttime bladder control is acquired only after daytime control.

Some entry behaviors, such as bladder and bowel regulation, are directly requisite to independent elimination. However, other entry skills such as walking, vision, comprehension of simple verbal commands, though not mandatory, will facilitate learning greatly.

Essential Entry Criteria

There are probably three essential characteristics of readiness for toilet training. They are interdependent and relate to physiological development—specifically the maturity of the central nervous system and the elimination sphincters.

1. The student should have a rather stable pattern of elimination. That is, urination and bowel responses occur within certain daily time periods (as illustrated in Figure 13.1) rather than "dribbling" throughout the day or having bowel movements at random times.

2. The student should have daily stable periods of dryness—the ability to withhold eliminations extending from 1 to 2 hours (as illustrated in Figure 13.1).

3. The moderately to profoundly retarded child should be 2½ years old or older. For retarded individuals, there appears to be a positive relationship between progress in training and chronological age (CA) relating to central nervous system (CNS) maturity; however, research results are somewhat inconsistent (Osarchuk, 1973). Hundziak, Maurer, and Watson (1965) noted that CA is less important because of the indirect relationship between CA and

the ability of the CNS to exert sphincter control. The relationship of mental age and success in toilet training is even less clear but recommendations reflect the rule: the greater the retardation, the longer you should wait before initiating training (Foxx & Azrin, 1974). The rationale for this rule concerns inadequate physiological readiness. For mildly retarded children, little or no delay appears necessary (Bensberg et al., 1965). Foxx and Azrin (1973a) recommended that moderately retarded children be at least 2½, while training may proceed best after a CA of 5 with the severely or profoundly retarded. However, *if a handicapped individual meets these three criteria, training should probably be attempted anyway, regardless of level of retardation.*

Additional Entry Skills

Although these skills are *not* essential indicators of readiness, they will facilitate learning. Their absence, in part or total, will mean the teacher must make special additions to the instructional procedure (e.g., instruction in wheelchair mobility and transfer; modification in wheelchair design; instruction in attending and sitting, sign language, or simple gestures; mobility training).

1. The student is ambulatory and can walk to and from the bathroom independently.
2. The student has the manipulative skills to learn the basic undressing and dressing tasks needed for independent toileting.
3. The student indicates a need to eliminate by facial expression or posture.
4. The student dislikes being wet or soiled and shows displeasure.
5. The student will remain seated for at least 5 minutes.
6. The student *understands* some simple commands (e.g., "Look at me," "Come here," "Sit," "Eat this").
7. The absence of behavior problems: aggressiveness, self-destructive behavior, withdrawal from social contact (Lohman et al., 1967).

Measurement of Entry Skills

Daytime regulation and dryness may be measured with the same elimination chart. The many toilet-training programs available for the handicapped provide a range of recommendations about how to record these baseline data with many consistencies.

Data Recording Form. Using a data collection form similar to that in Figure 13.1, check the student at the beginning of every half-hour from waking to bedtime and record whether he is wet (W or B) or dry (D or blank); if wet, is it due to bowel movement (B), urination or wetting (W), or both (W/B)? Furthermore, record whether the elimination occurred off the toilet (W, B, W/B) or on the toilet (W, B, W/B). As shown in Figure 13.1, accidents are indicated by circling the appropriate symbol. Additional symbols may indicate whether the toileting behavior was child-initiated (W+). If the student was placed on the toilet and no elimination occurred, an X could be recorded; while self-initiated toileting which resulted in no elimination would be recorded as X+.

Depending upon the student and the method of training, Fredericks, Baldwin, Grove, and Moore (1975) suggest additional codes—a small dot would indicate liquids were given to the student, M would be placed in those intervals where meals occurred, and naps would be marked on the chart with arrows extending from beginning to end. As long as the essential information is recorded in the appropriate time interval, any symbols may be used. If mechanical devices are going to be used to teach toileting, then additional records may be used during intervention.

During the collection of these data it is essential to change the student into dry clothing immediately after each accident with neutral teacher-student interaction (neither punishing or reinforcing) so that each accident will not be confused with earlier accidents. Clothing students in training pants rather than diapers will facilitate changing and detection of accidents.

Length of Data Collection. While some programs recommend a minimum of 3 (Foxx & Azrin, 1973b) to 7 days of baseline records (Copeland, Ford, & Solon, 1976), others use at least 15 days with a possible extension to 30 days if necessary to discover whether reliable toileting patterns exist (Fredericks et al., 1975; Giles & Wolf, 1966; Linford, Hipsher, & Silikovitz, 1972).[1]

---

[1] The purposes of baseline charting vary depending upon the method of toilet training. While all programs may use a 3- to 30-day baseline as a standard to evaluate the effectiveness of an intervention, some methods (referred to here as *the improved traditional methods*) rely upon baseline records to determine the expected time of elimination for each student. These expected times for urination and bowel movement become the training periods. However, in methods which use additional fluids and mechanical signaling devices (Azrin & Foxx, 1971; Foxx & Azrin, 1973b; Mahoney, VanWagenen, & Meyerson, 1971), pretraining accident and success records are kept as "an objective means of evaluating the seriousness of the incontinence problem and the need for the program" (Foxx & Azrin, 1973b, p. 25). Longer baselines revealing more accurate elimination schedules are probably most important for use with the improved traditional methods.

Name: _____   Date: _____

Time of Response	5/1	5/2	5/3	5/4	5/5	5/6	5/7	5/8	5/9	5/10	5/11	5/12	5/13	5/14
AM 7:00			W					W						
7:30	W			W		W					W		B	
8:00		W			W		W		W	W		W	W	W
8:30														
9:00	B		B		B		B		B		B			
9:30		B		B				B		B		B		B
10:00														
10:30														
11:00														
11:30						B								
PM 12:00														
12:30				W										
1:00	W	W	W		W		W	W		W		W		
1:30						W			W		W		W	W
2:00														
2:30														
3:00														
3:30		W				W		W		W				
4:00	W		W	W	W		W		W		W	W	W	W
4:30														
5:00														
5:30														
6:00												W		
6:30					W				W					W
7:00	W	W	W	W		W	W	W		W	W		W	
7:30														
8:00														
8:30		W							W					
9:00	W		W	W	W	W	W	W		W	W	W	W	W

Response Key:
Ⓦ Accident Wet   W+ Child-Initiated Wet   W− Teacher-Assisted Wet
Ⓑ Accident Bowel   B+ Child-Initiated Bowel   B− Teacher-Assisted Bowel

FIGURE 13.1
Sample Data Collection Chart for Toileting
SOURCE: *Systematic Instruction for Retarded Children: The Illinois Program, Part III Self-help Instruction,* by M. D. Linford, L. W. Hipsher, & R. G. Silikovitz, Danville, Ill.: Interstate, 1972, p. 146. Reprinted with permission.

Task Analysis of Toileting Skills

In 1963 Ellis proposed an analytical model of the stimuli and responses involved in toilet training which was the first task analysis. He reasoned that before toilet training, the elimination response (R_e) occurs in the presence of unpleasant bladder and rectal tension which act as discriminative stimuli (S^D) for these initially reflexive responses. R_e results in immediate reduction of the unpleasant tension, a process of negative reinforcement; however, as the child matures, the unpleasantness of wet and soiled clothes and parental disapproval are added. Ellis represented this as:

$$S^D \longrightarrow R_e \longrightarrow Consequences$$

Tension in bladder and rectum	Eliminatory response	1. Reduction of unpleasant tension (+)
		2. Wet clothing (−)
		3. Adult disapproval (−)

During toilet training a child is taught a variety of responses that precede elimination (R_A, approach to the toilet, preparation for toileting) and result in additional intermediate discriminative stimuli (S_A, cues generated by approach response; S_T, cues associated with toilet) in the presence of which the elimination occurs.

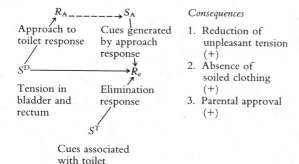

R_A - - - → S_A		Consequences
Approach to toilet response	Cues generated by approach response	1. Reduction of unpleasant tension (+)
S^D - - - - - → R_e		2. Absence of soiled clothing (+)
Tension in bladder and rectum	Elimination response	3. Parental approval (+)
	S^T	
	Cues associated with toilet	

This model not only stimulated toilet-training research with the institutionalized retarded, but also served as the first task analysis of elimination as a "conditionable" behavior.

A more detailed task analysis of the approach and the behaviors that immediately follow elimination (e.g., wiping, pants up and fastened) identifies the teachable steps and serves as a checklist assessment of baseline skill. Figure 13.2 provides a sequenced breakdown of the behavior chains before and after elimination. As with all task analyses, the number and order of the behaviors as well as the actual behaviors themselves will vary if one teacher's task analysis is compared to another's. For example, with younger children, a better method of teaching wiping requires that the child stand up and then wipe rather than remain seated. If skirts or dresses are worn, the pants down and up sequence will change. Some teachers will prefer to teach boys to stand and face the toilet bowl rather than sit during urination. Although this task analysis has eight behavior chains, some of which are subdivided, the number of components and their subdivisions depends upon the method selected to perform the task and the amount of detail imposed.

Multiple baseline observations should be made to obtain more accurate measurement. The teacher may also wish to use a more or less rigorous testing method than that described in Figure 13.2. The more rigorous method, referred to as the *single opportunity method* (see chapter 4), entails giving the student a single S^D or instructional cue (e.g., "Go to the bathroom"). The resultant performance would be scored without providing further assistance. Any errors or hesitations of more than 5 seconds would cause all remaining steps to be scored as errors. The less rigorous method, the *multiple opportunity* assessment procedure (see chapter 4), allows each erred or omitted response to be scored accordingly, then performed for the student by the teacher. This prepares the student to perform the next step in the chain and allows an observation of all steps. This method takes longer but often is more informative.

An assessment checklist, like this, should be used before toilet training and readministered regularly during training, where the toileting behavior chart (Figure 13.1) should be used before and *throughout* training. The information obtained from these two measurements is needed to set training objectives and evaluate progress during teaching.

General Elements of Toilet Training

After determining the learner's readiness for training, baseline elimination schedule, and current skills in the task analysis, the teacher must make instructional decisions about effective reinforcers and punishers as well as set instructional targets and specify methods to teach.

1. *What training objectives will be set?*

A. *Elimination.* Will bladder control *and* bowel control be taught together or separately? If separately, which will be taught first? Although teaching may proceed either way, the learner must have a stable pattern of elimination (in urination or bowel movement) in the areas selected for training. If only one area is selected, accidents in the other area must *not* be punished, though success certainly would be treated with the same reinforcing consequences as the targeted behavior.

FIGURE 13.2
Toileting Skill Checklist

Individual: _____ Date(s): _____

Directions: Test the student at least 3 times over a period of 2 or 3 days. Try to select a time when bladder or bowel tension is most likely. Give the first cue, observe and score the performance; give successive cues only if student hesitates for more than 5 seconds or omits a behavior after completion of the entire preceding behavior. Score as incorrect the first behavior in every chain which you must cue. Use a + if behavior is performed without help, a − if attempted but imperfect or incomplete, and a 0 if not tried.

Final Internal Cue (S^D) after Training	*Intermediate Training Cues (S^D)*	*Behavior*		*Date*				
Bladder and/or Bowel Tension	1. "Go to the bathroom" (gesture)	1. Walks directly to bathroom without more than a 3-second delay in initiating the response	1.					
	2. "Pull your pants down" (gesture)	2a. Unfasten buttons, zippers	2a.					
		b. Hooks thumbs into tops of underpants	b.					
		c. Removes under- and outerwear to at least mid-thigh	c.					
	3. "Sit on the toilet" (gesture)	3. Sits appropriately	3.					
	4. "Go *potty*"	4. Eliminates	4.					
	5. "Wipe yourself" (gesture)	5a. Reaches and grasps toilet paper	5a.					
		b. Pulls out and tears off an appropriate amount	b.					
		c. Bends and wipes self	c.					
		d. Drops paper into toilet	d.					
	6. "Flush the toilet" (gesture)	6a. Places hand on top of flusher	6a.					
		b. Pushes down until toilet flushes	b.					
	7. "Pull your pants up" (gesture)	7a. Grasps top band of underwear with both hands	7a.					
		b. Pulls underpants up and into place	b.					
		c. Grasps top band of outer pants with both hands	c.					
		d. Pulls pants up and into place	d.					
		e. Fastens buttons and zippers	e.					
	8. "Wash your hands" (gesture)	8a. Approaches sink	8a.					
		b. Turns water on	b.					
		c. Wets hands	c.					
		d. Picks up soap and rubs hands on and around soap	d.					
		e. Replaces soap	e.					
		f. Lathers hands	f.					
		g. Rinses hands	g.					
		h. Turns water off	h.					
		i. Reaches for towel and dries hands	i.					
	9. Leaves bathroom	9. Leaves bathroom	9.					

NOTE: Use language suited to student's CA.

B. *Daytime or Night Training.* Only after the student has mastered daytime toileting skills (e.g., eliminates on toilet most of the time when taken, and has few or no daytime accidents) should night training begin (Azrin & Foxx, 1974; Baller, 1975; Copeland et al., 1976; Finnie, 1975; Foxx & Azrin, 1973b; Linford et al., 1972). Fredericks et al. (1975) suggest that night training begin at this time regardless of whether the child has begun to express a need to go to the toilet or to initiate toileting.

C. *Related Toileting Skills.* What deficiencies are potential teaching targets? Does the learner need prodding to walk to the bathroom or restraining to remain seated on the toilet? Is he unable to manipulate his belt, snaps, and zippers? Does the child perform four of the nine steps in hand-washing but hesitate or fail on the remaining five? Choosing additional training targets beyond the elimination target relates partly to the teacher's time but primarily to the learner's deviation from performance expected at his age and with his mental and physical ability. Because elimination training requires at least five additional chains of behavior (toilet approach, pants removal, sitting, pants replacement, and leaving the bathroom), a teacher should identify how many of these behaviors a learner is capable of and, at the very minimum, require that level of performance while reinforcing any improvements.

Some orthopedically impaired students may focus on the portions of these skills they are physically capable of performing, while the teacher, a peer, or other care provider performs the remaining parts. This practice, referred to by Brown and his colleagues as *partial participation,* allows the student to attain dignity and profit from some independence in self-care rather than to remain totally dependent. (Refer to chapter 4 and to Brown, Branston-McClean, Baumgart, Vincent, Falvey, and Schroeder, 1979, for more on partial participation).

2. *What Instructional Methods Will Be Selected?* As discussed in the next section, there are two major daytime training methods: improved traditional training and rapid training procedures with intentionally increased elimination with or without the use of mechanical signals. Variations of both methods may be used for night training as well. Because teaching procedures should complement an individual learner's entry skills and learning characteristics, the teacher should specify the following elements of the teaching program. (Some of these will be determined by the method employed.)

A. *Instructions.* Verbal and gestural directions must be matched to the student's comprehension skills. Assessment of language skills will aid appro-

priate selection of meaningful instructions. For some, one-word commands accompanied by gestures are necessary; others may be able to follow more lengthy verbal instructions. With both extremes, consistency is of utmost importance. Instructions must be selected and standardized for each training objective.

B. *Effective Prompts.* At times a teacher will simply reinforce improvements in the toileting performance (shaping); but more often the need arises to prompt a nonoccurring behavior. Prompts may range from additional verbal directions (e.g., "Flush the toilet"), to demonstrations (e.g., by a teacher or peer models), to pointing and various amounts of physical assistance. Good instruction generally means providing the *least* assistance necessary to get the learner to perform. This allows the learner to perform more of the behavior and makes the eventual removal of assistance easier.

C. *Training Setting and Materials.* When a child is beginning to learn toileting skills, one bathroom area as close to the classroom as possible should be used. If the bathroom is too far away and if some students have difficulty walking, the teacher should consider moving portable toilets or potty chairs into a screened portion of the classroom. Some rapid methods involving signaling equipment (Azrin & Foxx, 1971; Foxx & Azrin, 1973a, 1973b) suggest moving the classroom into the bathroom. (This will be explained in more detail later.) Since there should be as many toilets or potty chairs as there are learners in a toileting program, the purchase of additional portable toilets may be necessary.

The type of toilet depends upon the learner. Those with weak muscle control (as in cerebral palsy) need toilet seats that provide support at the back, feet, and sides. Finnie (1975) provides examples of commercially available and adapted toilets.[2] If the toilet is adult size and the children are small, wooden steps and toilet seat insets should be used to allow independence in climbing up onto the toilet and to reduce fear and balance problems. The learner's feet should rest solidly on the floor or a step while he is seated on the toilet. The sinks also may need steps.

Once a student has learned to use one toilet and sink reliably, the training setting should be expanded to include other bathrooms. Although the need for adapted equipment may complicate this stage of teaching, it is essential that skill generalization be taught.

Reinforcers must be individually determined and their effectiveness tested before training begins. This determination may also include what *quantity* will be

---

[2]See also the list of commercial catalogues provided at the end of the chapter.

effective with different individuals (Osarchuk, 1973).

D. *Teaching Times and Frequency.* With the improved traditional method, toilet training will occur just before *every* normally expected time for urination and bowel movements (or one type of elimination, depending upon the objectives). With the rapid methods, additional fluids, milk of magnesia, or suppositories (Giles & Wolf, 1966) are given, creating the need for more elimination and more training sessions. However, with both methods, students may be taught various aspects of the toileting chains (e.g., pants up and down, toilet approach, hand-washing at times other than when bowel and bladder tension exist or are believed to exist). This extra training must only supplement that which is done in association with the internal bladder and bowel stimuli.

E. *Task Analysis.* The task analysis provided earlier may be used during assessment and as a teaching guide. Many teachers will need to modify it to suit the particular needs and additional handicaps of their students (e.g., shorten, lengthen, use entirely different behavior chains) as well as the training setting.

F. *Specific Training Techniques.* Although some techniques were developed as part of a larger toileting program, many can be used in the original or a modified form to create another program. For example, the "dry pants inspection," first described by Azrin and Foxx (1971), was one of many techniques in their rapid toilet-training method. Bender and Valletutti (1976) and Linford et al. (1972) include a less frequent dry pants inspection in their programs. Generally these *new* toilet-training "packages" have not been experimentally tested; however, if a teacher clearly understands the learning outcome of a particular procedure, can adjust the elements of that procedure to suit a specific student, and uses a data system of program evaluation, new combinations of techniques are justified.

Dry Pants Inspection

This technique (Azrin & Foxx, 1971; Foxx & Azrin, 1973b) consists of three steps.

1. Question the individual about dryness, using simple phrases and gestures (e.g., "Are you dry?").
2. Prompt the person to look at and feel the crotch area of the pants.
3. A. If the pants are dry, reinforce with praise for dryness (e.g., "Good, you have dry pants!") and an edible.
   B. If pants are wet, verbally chastise and withhold the edible (e.g., "No, you have wet pants, no candy!").

In a rapid training program where extra fluids are given, dry pants inspections are carried out every 5 minutes unless an accident occurs to delay the next inspection (Foxx & Azrin, 1973b). If dry pants inspection is part of a more traditional program, it would be less frequent.

Accident Treatment

Many accidents will be prevented by adhering strictly to a toileting schedule, maintaining a standardized eating and drinking pattern, and strongly reinforcing correct toileting behavior. However, not *all* accidents will be prevented, so a regular procedure for responding to accidents should be determined. The consequences may range from ignoring or extinction to punishment. Unless mandated by the program, select an accident treatment that best suits the learner. If, under the traditional method, daytime accidents continue after 2 months, a mild punishing accident consequence may be appropriate. Instead, the teacher may wish to systematically change some single element of the program at a time: reinforcers, toileting schedule, change to a more rapid method, addition of signaling equipment.

1. *Extinction.* Without talking to the student, change his pants and clean him, using lukewarm water. Be careful not to provide any reinforcing activity too soon after an accident.

2. *Mild Punishment.* As soon as an accident is discovered, approach the learner, have him feel and look at his pants, and provide verbal disapproval (e.g., "You wet your pants" or "No, you have wet pants"). The student may be left wet for a few minutes to experience the discomfort. The teacher then changes the student, using the extinction procedure. Smith (1979) successfully used a verbal reprimand and a 10-minute timeout from reinforcement in place of the Azrin and Foxx (1971) overcorrection procedures which he and others have found to be overly aversive.

A. *Cleanliness Training.* As soon as the accident is signaled, the student is grasped and told "No, you wet your pants!" Next he is told to undress and given a tepid shower. Then he is expected to dress in clean clothing, place his clothes in a sink, immerse them in water, wring out the water, spread them to dry, and clean the floor or chair where the accident occurred with a mop or cloth. Students resisting cleanliness training are physically assisted through every step. No reinforcers, social or edible, are given for an hour after an accident. A shortened version, which excludes clothing change and washing, is suggested for use during initial bladder training (Foxx & Azrin, 1973b). The expanded version just described is used once the student begins to toilet himself without a prompt (self-initiation stage). If the student is verbal, this overcorrection procedure may be enhanced by requiring him to verbalize the relationship between the overcorrection procedure and soiling with a statement such as "I am cleaning my pants because I soiled them and will have to do this each time it happens" (Doleys & Arnold, 1975, p. 16).

B. *Positive Practice.* Immediately after cleanliness training for an accident, Foxx and Azrin (1973b, 1974) use positive practice—the continuous repetition of movements related to toileting: toilet approach, pants down, sit for a few moments, rise, pants up, leave toilet area. Positive practice is continued, with prompting as needed, for the remainder of the half-hour cycle. If shortened cleanliness training is used, the student still has his wet pants on and a dry pants inspection follows at the end of every positive practice cycle. This means he feels his wet pants and is verbally chastised.

C. *Other Punishment Procedures.* Toileting accidents have been punished by spankings (Marshall, 1966), termination of meals, requirements that the child remain in soiled clothes, use of a restraining jacket (Giles & Wolf, 1966), and overcorrection (Barmann, Katz, O'Brien, & Beauchamp, 1981).

If used for accidents, aversive consequences must be chosen specifically for each learner, applied immediately and consistently following each accident, and used only in conjunction with strong positive reinforcement for appropriate behavior. The immediacy problem—discovering accidents as soon as they occur—is best solved by urine signaling equipment, but also may be decreased with frequent dry pants inspections.

Instruction of Related Behaviors

Most toilet training involves early shaping of behaviors preceding and following toilet elimination—walking to the toilet, pulling pants down, sitting on the toilet, etc. Although this training would naturally occur with every scheduled toileting, extra training also may be needed so the individual masters these skills before elimination control.

Using forward chaining in combination with prompting, fading, and shaping, Mahoney and colleagues (1971) taught normal and retarded youngsters first to approach the toilet when they heard an auditory signaling device. Next, reinforcement was made contingent upon toilet approach and pulling pants down; *then* approach, pants down and sitting (or standing). At this point fluid intake was increased and the signaling device modified so that each in-pants urination produced the auditory signal. Individuals who did not then go to the toilet were prompted by the experimenter—"No! Go potty!" If some urine was deposited in the toilet, the child was reinforced.

Giles and Wolf (1966) initially fed severely retarded individuals their meals contingent upon sitting on the toilet. Next, after suppositories and milk of magnesia were given to increase the probability of bowel movements, the students were reinforced only for sitting and eliminating on the toilet. Similarly, Marshall (1966) shaped the behavior of a young autistic boy by reinforcing correct performance of each successive component of the chain. Even in an institution where the attendant-resident ratio often was 1 to 10, this forward chaining to build the chain of responses was successful (Levine & Elliot, 1970).

The work of Azrin and Foxx also supports this practice of building behavior related to correct toileting. A recent application of their rapid training methods to normal children (Azrin & Foxx, 1974) uses imitation play; the child "teaches" a doll to potty herself. The child guides the doll through all the steps involved in the child's own training: giving the doll a drink, lowering the pants and placing on potty, reinforcing the doll for wetting (a wetting doll filled with water is used), emptying the potty, dry pants inspection, scolding for accidents, and positive practice. Although not tested with retarded individuals, the authors suggest that this procedure be used if the child seems to understand the meaning of the doll's actions, and they predict effectiveness of the doll-modeling procedure with some moderately and severely handicapped individuals.

Moisture-Signaling Devices

Regardless of whether extra fluids or moisture-signaling pants are used in a training program, reinforcement may be given more quickly if you know the moment of sphincter relaxation and elimination. Because training consists primarily of associating reinforcing consequences with sphincter control leading to elimination on the toilet, urine-signaling devices for the toilet let the teacher provide reinforcement without delay. Listening or looking for the movement of urination or defecation (even with aluminum foil placed in the potty to magnify the sound) are inaccurate and time consuming in comparison to moisture-detecting equipment.

Moisture-detecting devices may be built into a potty chair or into a plastic bowl which fits inside the regular toilet bowl (Figure 13.3). One way to build such a device involves fastening two snap studs about ½-inch apart to the bottom center of the plastic bowl. Next, following the circuit schematic pictured in the lower half of Figure 13.4, detachable insulated wires are connected to the studs and run to a circuit box with batteries. Urine or feces falling into the potty bowl complete a low voltage circuit between the two metal studs, which in turn produces a sound from a small speaker in the circuit box. Herreshoff (1973)

FIGURE 13.3

The Urine Alert. The plastic bowl fits into normal toilet bowl and rests on its top edge. The detachable wires connect the moisture-detecting snaps to the signal box, which can rest on the floor or top of the toilet. The signal box sounds a tone when urine or feces touches the snaps.

SOURCE: *Toilet Training the Retarded: A Rapid Program for Day and Nighttime Independent Toileting* by R.M. Foxx and N.H. Azrin. Champaign, Ill.: Research Press, 1973, p. 30. Reprinted with permission.

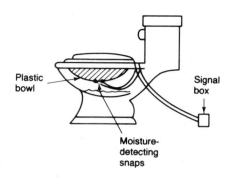

FIGURE 13.4

Schematic of Toilet-Signal Chair Circuit (top) and Wet-Alarm Pants Circuit (bottom)

Component identifications are as follows: R-1 and R-1a, 100 ohm, ⅛ watt resistor; R-2 and R-2a, 15,000 ohm, ⅛ watt resistor; R-3, 22,000 ohm, ⅛ watt resistor; C-1, 100 mfd capacitor, 15 volts; C-2, 22 mfd capacitor, 15 volt; T-1, T-1a, and T-3; transitor #GE-2; T-2, transitor #GE-7; S-1, "Bleep-tone" signal tone device available from C. A. Briggs Co., Glenside, Pa.; S-1a, speaker, 1.5 inch, 0.1 watt, 8 ohm; B-1 and B-1a battery, Eveready #216, 9 volt, or equivalent; snaps, Nu-Way, available from Burstein-Applebee Co., Kansas City, Mo. The A-snaps attach to matching snaps on the training pants; the B-snaps attach to matching studs on the toilet chair.

SOURCE: "Behavioral Engineering: Two Apparatuses for Toilet Training Retarded Children," by N.H. Azrin, C. Bugle, and F. O'Brien. *Journal of Applied Behavior Analysis,* 1971, *4*, 251. Reprinted with permission.

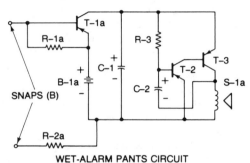

WET-ALARM PANTS CIRCUIT

TOILET-SIGNAL CHAIR CIRCUIT

FIGURE 13.5

The Pants Alarm.

The front view shows the moisture-detecting snaps fastened to the briefs. The back view shows the two flexible wires which lead from the snaps to the signal box. The snaps on the end of the wire are manually removable from the snaps on the clothing. The signal box is pinned to the back of the briefs (back view). A tone is sounded by the signal box when urine or feces moistens the area between the snaps.

SOURCE: *Toilet Training the Retarded: A Rapid Program for Day and Nighttime Independent Toileting* by R.M. Foxx and N.H. Azrin. Champaign, Ill.: Research Press, 1973, p. 32. Reprinted with permission.

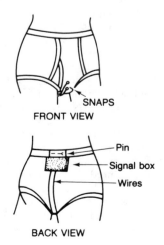

FRONT VIEW

BACK VIEW

describes two wiring plans for sensing devices connecting to a record player or a light. Sensing plates have also been used in place of snap studs (Training Resource Center, Note 1). As soon as the signal sounds, the teacher reinforces the student for a successful elimination and detaches the wires from the bottom of the bowl so that it may be emptied into the toilet, rinsed, dried, and reconnected in preparation for the next use.

Where a moisture-detecting potty chair signals the moment for positive reinforcement, moisture-detecting underpants (one design is pictured in Figure 13.5) signal the moment an accident occurs. Thus accident procedures can be implemented without delay. Wet pants are disconnected from the circuit box by unsnapping the wires. Dry pants are placed on the individual and reconnected. If both moisture-detecting pants and potties are part of the toileting program, as in Azrin and Foxx (1971) and Foxx and Azrin (1973b), two different signals need to be used so that the associated responses will not be confused. The wiring schematic for underpants, pictured in the upper portion of Figure 13.4 involves a somewhat similar circuit plan to the potty signal with the alarm box attached to the back of the pants or worn in a pocketed vest or chest harness.[3] Other designs (Van Wagenen & Murdock, 1966; Training Resource Center, Note 1) use cloth-encapsulated parallel wires running along the crotch of the pants and up the back to a circuit-box connection.

Mahoney et al. (1971) used more elaborate auditory signaling devices in combination with urine-detecting pants (Van Wagenen & Murdock, 1966). The experimenter in the study operated an FM radio transmitter while the child wore urine-detecting pants, an FM receiver, and an earphone. By pushing a button on the transmitter, a signal was generated in the child's receiver and sound transmitted through the earphone. In addition, the same signal could be triggered by urination. Training involved forward chaining; each step in the toilet approach chain was shaped, using prompts as needed, in response to the signal triggered from the transmitter. Once this chain was learned, elimination training began. Children were given extra fluids, radio devices were removed, and urination alone produced the signal. The child was reinforced for quickly going to and sitting on the toilet as long as some urine was deposited in the toilet. Although Mahoney et al. (1971) did not use toilet signaling devices or punishment for inappropriate eliminations, as was done by Azrin and Foxx (1971) and Azrin, Bugle, and O'Brien (1971), they were

successful in training severely and profoundly retarded individuals.

Improved Traditional Methods

A primary assumption of the more traditional methods of toilet training is that training proceeds best if you can accurately cue performance at the times when bladder and bowel tension are greatest. Various researchers have successfully used operant reinforcement principles combined with a regular elimination schedule with retarded learners (Baumeister & Klosowski, 1965; Bensberg, et al., 1965; Dayan, 1964; Giles & Wolf, 1966; Hundziak et al., 1965; Kimbrell, Lucky, Barberto, & Love, 1967; Levine & Elliot, 1970; Marshall, 1966; Smith, 1979).

Toileting records are kept for 15 or more days to identify these times, generally once daily for bowel movements and 3 to 5 times daily for urination. The learner is then cued to sit on the toilet and praised for any successful elimination. In a review of research on toileting with the severely retarded, Osarchuck (1973) stated that at best such records provide only "a very rough estimate of elimination probability" (p. 432). However, a number of toileting programs used with the severely handicapped describe additional techniques that may be added to this traditional method to increase its success rate (e.g., Baker, Brightman, Heifetz, & Murphy, 1977; Bensberg et al., 1965; Fredericks et al., 1975; Giles & Wolf, 1966; Hundziak et al., 1965; Levine & Elliot, 1970; Linford et al., 1972; Marshall, 1966). These techniques include dry pants check; teaching related responses such as approach, sitting, and pants down and up, before teaching elimination control or more intensively than simply preceding each elimination; use of urine-detection devices; specific accident procedures; consistent instructions and reinforcement for correct responses; and self-control training.

Linford et al. (1972) view toilet training as consisting of three stages: baseline (14 to 28 days), initial implementation, and development of self-control. During the second stage, after obtaining an accurate record of the child's eliminations, the trainer decides whether there is a consistent toileting pattern in urinations or bowel and selects the area(s) and times for instruction. Fredericks et al. (1975) recommend that the trainer choose only 2 times during the day during which to begin training. After the learner eliminates 75% of the time when taken at the 2 selected periods, another time period is added until the same 75% success rate is achieved. This practice continues until the entire day is covered. The rationale for the gradual expansion is the time commitment involved in each toileting (approximately 20 minutes).

Actual training proceeds according to the following steps.

---

[3]Urine-detecting training pants may be obtained commercially, already built or ready to assemble. Information on company, addresses, prices, and references is provided at the end of this chapter.

1. Approximately 10 minutes before an elimination typically will occur, the student is asked in simple terms to go to the bathroom. (For example the child charted in Figure 13.1 would be taken at 7:30 a.m., 8:50 a.m., 12:15 p.m., 3:50 p.m., 6:15 p.m., and 8:50 p.m. if both bowel and urine control were being taught for the entire day.)

2. If the student has not eliminated after sitting for 10 minutes, he may be asked to replace his clothes and continue his other activities for 5 minutes, without any criticism or praise. Next he is asked to go to the toilet; an interval of 5 minutes is allowed for elimination. If the learner is successful, he is immediately reinforced; if not, he is neutrally requested to leave the bathroom and return to his activities.

3. All eliminations (accidents, correct urinations, and bowel movements) are recorded on a chart posted in the bathroom. Symbols may record those times when no elimination occurred on the toilet.

4. Whenever the student is taken to the toilet, the trainer should teach the related skills (approach, pants down, etc.), providing, only when necessary, a minimum of prompts beginning with verbal instructions and proceeding to demonstration, then physical assistance as needed.

5. Since all correct elimination and related toileting behaviors must be reinforced immediately, the teacher needs to monitor the child's performance closely. Simple, specific praise throughout performance may be accompanied by activity or food reinforcers.

6. The routine is repeated for all the times selected for training.

The accident treatment procedure chosen should be used only during training periods. Simple extinction should be applied as a consequence for accidents at other times. Dry pants checks may be added to the routine, as may the other techniques described earlier.

In the third stage of training, the child is taught to develop self-control. The teacher gradually fades out all prompts (physical assistance, demonstrations, and verbal instructions) used during the second stage to teach related skills and to take the individual to the toilet at the scheduled times. Linford et al. (1972) suggest that the teacher ask the child if he needs to go to the bathroom and prompt a headshake or a yes or no response. Additionally all spontaneous indications to self-toilet must be reinforced vigorously, while the trainer should decrease the amount of time spent in the bathroom.

Rapid Toilet-Training Methods

Although toilet-training procedures have been used with moderately and severely handicapped individuals (Fredericks et al., 1975; Linford et al., 1972), no results have been reported by which to evaluate their effectiveness. The research cited earlier, which involved somewhat loosely described variations of traditional methods, generally has been poorly designed or inadequately described or has reported incomplete results. However, various rapid methods have extensive research supporting their application with moderately and severely handicapped persons.

"Rapid" toilet-training methods which involve procedures to increase elimination (increased fluid intake, milk of magnesia, suppositories) do not rely upon baseline schedules because the extra fluids or suppositories change the normal elimination pattern. Although these methods were originally developed for use with mechanical signaling equipment (Azrin & Foxx, 1971; Mahoney et al., 1971), rapid methods may be used with the handicapped without moisture-detecting devices (Azrin & Foxx, 1974; Williams & Sloop, 1978).[4]

Azrin and Foxx Procedure

Foxx and Azrin (1973b) describe four stages in their daytime rapid method: baseline, initial bladder training, self-initiation, and maintenance. After a 3-day minimum baseline period, the trainer may begin initial bladder training, which should last a minimum of 4 consecutive hours per day. The teaching ratio may vary from one trainer per student to one to three. The *average* time to achieve toileting independence for ambulatory, institutionalized, retarded individuals with this rapid method is 4 days (8 hours per day), with faster learning related to higher intellectual functioning. All training during the initial bladder stage takes place in the bathroom. Two chairs and liquid and food reinforcers must be available. The student should be wearing the urine-alert pants and the moisture-detecting toilet bowl insets must be in place. An hour before training, fluids are given so that urination might occur during the first half-hour. As described in Table 13.1 and illustrated in Figure 13.6, there is a sequence of nine steps to follow every half-hour. A prompting-fading procedure is used to guide the learner through the sequence, but once he independently carries out part of the chain (ap-

---

[4]See the original references for complete, detailed procedures (Azrin & Foxx, 1971, 1974; Foxx & Azrin, 1973b; Mahoney et al., 1971; Van Wagenen, Meyerson, Kerr, & Mahoney, 1969).

proaches the toilet, pulls pants down, etc.), no additional prompts are provided. Trainer-student interaction is kept to a minimum, until successful voiding occurs or the student is off the toilet seat. Accidents, of course, are signaled by the pants alarm and, after disconnecting the alarm, are followed by the brief cleanliness training and positive practice. Clean pants are provided and reconnected to the alarm at the end of the next scheduled toilet-approach trial.

Self-initiation training begins once the learner tries to toilet himself totally unprompted. This stage involves the following instructional modifications:

1. Give fluids immediately following an elimination.
2. No further toilet-approach prompts.
3. Continue to provide guidance and prompts for dressing and undressing and for flushing the toilet, if necessary, but never at a level greater than that needed on previous toiletings.
4. Move chair farther from toilet on each successful self-initiation.
5. Gradually lengthen the time between dry pants inspections.
6. Intermittently reward correct toileting.
7. When learner is self-initiating from the area where he spends most of his time, remove urine alert from the toilet bowl, pants alarm from briefs and the chair.
8. Require learner to show you that he can find the toilet from various other places.
9. Include learner on the maintenance program after nine self-initiations (Foxx & Azrin, 1973b, p. 54).

Reinforcement for dry pants and correct elimination is faded to an intermittent schedule, prompts are systematically faded, and the toilet approach distance is gradually increased, then varied to yield more generalized behavior. The brief cleanliness training consequence for accidents is replaced by full cleanliness training, and continues to be accompanied by positive practice.

A maintenance program is begun once the learner achieves nine self-initiated toiletings. In this stage of learning, six dry pants inspections are provided daily—before every meal and snack, before going to bed, and spontaneously, so that one occurs every 2 hours. While dry pants are praised, wet pants are followed by the full cleanliness procedure and positive practice; accidents detected before meals, snacks, and bedtime also result in a 1-hour delay of eating and sleeping. Maintenance training is terminated when no accidents have been recorded for 2 weeks.

Mahoney, VanWagenen, and Meyerson (1971) Procedure

This rapid procedure, also successful with severely and profoundly handicapped children, differs from Azrin and Foxx's procedure in a variety of ways. The toilet-approach responses are taught before elimination training in response to an auditory signal sounded by the trainer over an FM transmitter into an earphone worn by the subjects. A gradual prompting-fading process was used to teach these first three prerequisite phases.

1. The student learns to walk to the toilet in response to an auditory signal.

TABLE 13.1 Sequence of Steps in the Bladder Training Procedure. (Step one in the sequence is begun exactly on the half-hour)

1. Give as much fluid to the resident as he will drink while seated in his chair.
   A. Wait about 1 minute.
2. Direct resident to sit on toilet seat using the minimal possible prompt.
3. Direct resident to pull his pants down using the minimal possible prompt.
   A. When resident voids, give edibles and praise while seated, then direct him to stand.
   B. If resident does not void within 20 minutes after drinking the fluids, direct him to stand.
4. Direct resident to pull up his pants using the minimal possible prompt.
   A. If resident voided, direct him to flush the toilet using the minimal possible prompt.
5. Direct resident to his chair using the minimal possible prompt.
6. After resident has been sitting for 5 minutes, inspect him for dry pants.
   A. If pants are dry, give edible and praise.
   B. If pants are wet, only show him the edible and admonish him.
7. Check resident for dry pants every 5 minutes.
8. At the end of 30 minutes, begin the sequence of steps again.

NOTES: If self-initiation occurs at any time, start the self-initiation procedure. Continuously praise resident for being dry while he is seated in his chair.
SOURCE: *Toilet Training the Retarded* by R.M. Foxx and N.H. Azrin. Champaign, Ill.: Research Press, 1973, p. 45. Reprinted with permission.

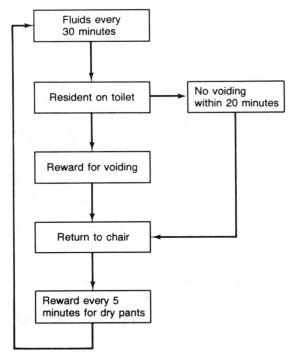

FIGURE 13.6
Flow Chart of the Bladder-Training Sequence (The specific steps involved in this flow chart are listed in Table 13.1.)

SOURCE: *Toilet Training the Retarded* by R.M. Foxx and N.H. Azrin, Champaign, Ill.: Research Press, 1973, p. 47. Reprinted with permission.

2. The student learns to walk to the toilet and lower his pants in response to an auditory signal.
3. The student learns to walk to the toilet, lower pants, and take male stance or sit on the toilet.

Next, extra fluids were given and the moisture-detecting pants signal connected for automatic triggering of the auditory signal. Students were both signaled by the experimenter for practice (sat on the toilet for 30 seconds) and by their own urinations. In the latter situation, the child who did not immediately go sit on the toilet was approached quickly and told, "No, go potty," and assisted if necessary. In either case, reinforcement was contingent upon the presence of *some* urine in the toilet. No toilet signaling devices were used nor were accidents followed by punishment.

At this phase, students were taught to pull up their pants after urinating or sitting on the toilet. By this time, trainers recognized behaviors preceding elimination (increase in movements, tugging at genitals, etc.) and at first signaled toilet approach with the

transmitted signal when it was not self-initiated. Next all signaling equipment was removed, and reinforcement was contingent upon unsignaled correct elimination. In the last phase, verbal students were taught to answer "potty" in response to the question "Where are you going?" Parents were taught to continue the training in the home.

In this study four of the five moderately to profoundly retarded children (three were 4 years old and one was 9) and all three normal preschoolers acquired toileting skills and attained bladder control with very few accidents over a 6-month period. An average of 29 hours of training and 262 training trials were required for the retarded children to reach criterion. Teaching the related toileting behaviors—walk to the toilet, lower pants, and assume the sex-appropriate stance—before teaching elimination training appears to be an effective alternative to teaching related behavior at the same time as bladder control.

Lancioni and Ceccarani (1981) Procedure

A recently reported study used a variation of the Azrin and Foxx toileting procedure successfully with nine profoundly retarded, institutionalized adolescents. In the first of two studies, Lancioni and Ceccarani (1981) were interested in discovering whether students with a history of toileting accidents could attain bladder independence with "a procedure that would not imply drastic changes in their daily programs or in the program of their trainers" (p. 80).

First they asked whether hourly toiletings, 6 days per week, increased liquids intake (0 to 14 glasses per day), toileting cues, success reinforcement, and accident punishment would constitute a successful intervention package. Toiletings took roughly 30 to 45 minutes daily, depending upon accidents and the use of an accident procedure. Students spent the remainder of the day in other scheduled instructional activities (unlike other intensive toileting programs that occupy the entire day). During the first study, all accidents were punished by 90-second exercises (knee walking or deep knee bends), during which students were prompted repeatedly to look at and touch their wet clothes. In addition, 25 toilet insert seats (equipped with urine-sensitive alarms) were scattered in conspicuous places in and outside the classroom and play area where the students spent their time. The first step in the hourly toileting chain was to get a toilet seat before going to the bathroom. Thus the toilet seats served as a visible reminder (discriminative stimulus) for toileting.

With this intervention, the accidents of five students were rapidly reduced (in roughly 10 to 12 days) and independent toileting appeared 7 to 10 days after baseline. Intervention procedures were gradually phased out over six successive phases:

1. Increased liquid, toilet seats present, increased assisted toileting, and punishments;
2. Assisted toileting reduced;
3. Assisted toileting discontinued;
4. Reinforcement reduced;
5. Gradual removal of toilet seats;
6. Reduction of liquids.

These changes let students acquire independence in toileting and return gradually to a normal routine with reduced assistance, fluids, and reinforcement; toileting was performed without insert toilet seats. Generally, students completed phase 3 (toileting assistance discontinued) after 20 days and phase 6 (reduction of liquids) after 40 days. A 60-day follow-up revealed that maintenance was good, with few or no accidents.

A second study with four similar students investigated whether the intervention would be effective if the accident punishment procedure were omitted. In particular, Lancioni and Ceccarani were interested in using this punishment-free procedure with students who were "regulated" and had very infrequent accidents (i.e., urinated at scheduled times of assisted toileting but never performed independently). Their reasoning was as follows:

Reduction in the rate of accidents increases the opportunities for pairing toileting activities and reinforcement. Even if punishment plays a role in the training of subjects who have a history of accidents, it could be superfluous in the training of subjects who have learned to urinate according to a schedule of assisted toileting, but who normally have no accidents. These subjects might display sporadic accidents at the beginning of the intervention when the amount of liquid increases, but they may then reacquire urinary control spontaneously. (p. 89)

All procedures and phases were identical except that the few accidents that occurred with the initial liquid increases were ignored. As in the first study, the end of phase 3 (the elimination of toileting assistance) occurred after roughly 16 to 20 days of intervention, with phase 6 (elimination of fluids) occurring in somewhat less than 40 days and only one accident during the 60-day maintenance period. For these students, punishment did not seem to have a direct effect on the acquisition of independent toileting; however, the authors concluded that students with a history of extensive accidents need the punishment to reduce the accident rate and provide more opportunity to associate toileting cues, toileting, and reinforcement.

While independence in toileting took longer with Lancioni and Ceccarani's modified approach than it takes with the original Azrin and Foxx version, the approach worked and was reported as being "less

stressful" for both students and personnel, since entire days were not spent in the bathroom and other instructional programs could continue uninterrupted.

A Comparison of Daytime Toileting Procedures

The success of either rapid methods or the traditional procedures will depend on the teacher's skills and the learner's handicapping conditions. However, there has not been any methodologically sound test of the traditional method nor, until recently, any formal comparisons of these procedures with the severely handicapped. While working with 15 institutionalized severely and profoundly retarded students (ages 5 to 18), Smith (1979) made a three-way comparison between the Azrin-Foxx procedure, the Mahoney et al. (1971) method, and a rapid group training method. A few modifications were made in the Azrin-Foxx rapid procedure, including the omission of overcorrection and positive practice for accidents, which have been reported to cause resistance and tantrums (Butler, 1976; Matson, 1975; Smith, Britton, Johnson, & Thomas, 1975). Instead, a sharp reprimand and timeout from reinforcement for 10 minutes was substituted. Second, rather than terminating prompts after the student made the first initiation, prompts were faded more gradually once self-initiations were reliable.

All three procedures used increased fluid intake and urine-sensing equipment. In the group procedure, one nurse worked with a group of five students and applied a version of Azrin-Foxx. These students were prompted to the toilet from the dayroom at regular 45-minute intervals, prompted individually to handle clothing and sit, immediately reinforced for correct eliminations, and given frequent dry pants checks. However, no pants alarms were used. Accidents resulted in 5 minutes of extinction and sitting in wet pants.

After 12 weeks of training, all five students on the Azrin-Foxx method were independent, while four using the Mahoney et al. (1971) method and one receiving group rapid training were independent. Independence meant both no wet pants and the ability to handle clothing and the tasks of approaching and leaving the bathroom. Thus, both individualized intensive methods were more effective than the group version of Azrin-Foxx. In terms of staff hours required, the Azrin-Foxx method took the most staff time (2,330 hours), with the Mahoney method requiring almost as many hours (2,079 hours) and the group method roughly half the longest time (1,260 hours). While the most effective method took almost twice as long as the group method, *it was* the most effective and thus the time was well spent in terms of outcome. Not only was the Mahoney method transistor equipment expensive, the staff members found the equipment difficult to maintain and use. Even though the Mahoney method was effective, because of these problems Smith concluded that the time savings and results would need to be substantially better before the Mahoney method would be recommended over the Azrin-Foxx individualized method.

While the rapid methods require equipment and more staff time, they have been shown to be more effective with severely handicapped learners. However, unmodified rapid methods eliminate time for instruction in anything else. These methods seem to take more time in most cases than that originally reported by Azrin-Foxx (1971), which means more staff time and even less variety in programming (Bettison, Davison, Taylor, & Fox, 1976; Smith, 1981). Thus, when choosing a procedure, a number of factors must be considered. First are the student's age and his or her toilet-training history. Generally with younger students (2 to 5 years), toilet training is a lower priority than at older ages, and thus training time need not to be so rapid. Most preschoolers do not have a long history or any history of failure in toilet training, which may mean that less intrusive procedures such as an improved traditional procedure should be tried before a rapid method.

However, students over 5 who appear physically capable of bladder control but are incontinent are likely to be excluded from programs, unpopular among their peers, and dependent upon teachers and parents. In these cases, toilet training should proceed rapidly. Thus you also must consider the programming and parental priorities for each student. If, for example, admission to a vocational or leisure program is denied due to incontinence, daytime control becomes more important. In these cases, time cannot be lost in achieving continence, and a more structured rapid procedure would be appropriate. Azrin-Foxx procedures have been implemented successfully by teachers of the retarded in the public school (e.g., Trott, 1977), with deaf-blind retarded individuals (Lancioni, 1980), and in shortened form with the elimination of the urine-sensing equipment (Williams & Sloop, 1978). The modified versions of Azrin and Foxx (Lancioni & Ceccarari, 1981; Smith, 1979) appear to be viable alternatives as well. While independence is likely to take longer with these alternatives—7 to 12 weeks versus 4 days—the benefits may include less disruption of other instructional programs, a reduction in punishment, and possibly less stress for students and staff.

Irregular Enuresis

Far less research has dealt with the problem of partial bladder control or intermittent wetting or enuresis.

Barmann, Katz, O'Brien, and Beauchamp (1981) used a shortened version of the Azrin-Foxx procedures with three young moderately to severely retarded boys using a multiple baseline design across subjects. They recorded toileting accidents in both the home and school during baseline, intervention, and follow-up for all three subjects. Since all the boys had self-initiated toileting in the past, initial bladder training procedures were not necessary. Instead the boys' pants were inspected hourly. If dry, they were praised verbally; when wet, *restitutional overcorrection* was employed. The child (a) obtained a towel, (b) cleaned up all traces of urine or feces, (c) went to his bedroom and obtained clean pants, and (d) placed the wet pants in a diaper pail. Immediately after these steps, *positive practice overcorrection* was required. The child (a) walked to the toilet, (b) lowered his pants, (c) sat for 3 to 5 seconds, (d) arose, (e) pulled up his pants, and (f) returned to the location of the accident. This sequence was repeated 10 times rapidly. Both forms of overcorrection together occupied roughly 20 minutes. The pants check and praise for dry pants was used in both the home and the school, while positive practice was required only at home to test whether its effects generalized into the classroom. Only the teacher and the boys' parents carried out the intervention.

The criterion for success was set at 13 of 14 consecutive days of no accident at home and in school. For all three subjects, the overcorrection led to substantial improvement over baseline accident levels (approximately 3¼ accidents daily). Once overcorrection was instituted, there was an immediate decline in accidents, followed by complete elimination. For all three boys, these results generalized from the home to the classroom and were maintained throughout a 2-month follow-up period. Thus it appears that irregular enuresis can be eliminated in the home and school by parents using Azrin-Foxx accident treatment overcorrection procedures in the home and the teacher using only pants checks and verbal praise for dry pants. Because others have reported problems with the Azrin-Foxx overcorrection methods (see the Smith study reviewed above), it would be interesting to see whether a less aversive and time-consuming treatment would be as effective. For example, Smith (1979) effectively used a verbal reprimand and a 10-minute timeout in place of overcorrection during an application of Azrin-Foxx initial bladder training methods.

Nighttime Toilet Training

After a student has achieved reliable toileting during 75% or more of the day, training may be extended to develop nighttime bladder control. As with daytime training, various methods have been successful with nonhandicapped enuretic children and adolescents, while these other methods have been effective with the severely handicapped. These methods include traditional procedures, the use of bed-wetting signaling equipment, and rapid methods.

Traditional Procedures

Linford et al. (1972) and Fredericks et al. (1975) described variations in traditional procedures found successful with the severely retarded, but unfortunately did not report any outcome data. Specific accident treatment procedures described earlier and urine-signaling devices for the bed and toilet may be added to improve these traditional methods. The parent follows the general steps listed below, taking special care to continue the daytime schedule, *reduce* fluids prior to bedtime, and keep accurate accident and toileting records so that a schedule may be prepared for parent-initiated toiletings at night.

1. Decrease the amount of liquids in the evening and give none within 1½ to 2 hours of bedtime. (Extra fluids may be provided during the day.)
2. Ask the child to go to the toilet just prior to a fixed bedtime.
3. Depending upon the parents' time, check the child as often as possible (every hour) to obtain a night schedule. Most parents will find this convenient only during their waking hours.
4. If the child understands, instruct him in simple language (perhaps showing him the reward) that a dry bed in the morning will be rewarded (special toy, activity, etc.). Check the bed in the morning and reinforce him if it is dry. Ignore wet beds.
5. About 1½ hours after the child has been in bed, awaken him and check for accidents or dryness, recording this on a nighttime chart.

   A. If dry, reinforce the child (dry pants inspection procedure may be used).

   B. If wet, either neutrally change the pants, pajamas, and sheets (extinction for accidents) or request his assistance. (A variation of the cleanliness training procedure may be used alone or accompanied by positive practice trips from the wet bed to the bathroom.)

6. Awaken the child before his usual accident time and direct him to go to the toilet. Require that the child sit on the toilet without sleeping for 5 minutes, or less if he urinates. Praise and chart successes; neutrally return the unsuccessful learner to bed, charting his failure to eliminate.

7. If the child is wet when awakened, chart the accident and awaken the child earlier the following

night. Fredericks et al. (1975) provide an example to clarify this step.

Take the case of Jane, who went through the procedure of being told about a reinforcer, reduced her fluid intake, was awakened before the parents' bedtime, but was still wetting during the night. The parents usually retired at 11:00; Jane usually wakened in the morning at 7:00; thus there was an 8-hour period of sleep. The parents divided the night in half (4 hours), set their alarm at 3:00 and woke Jane at that time. Jane was wet for the first 5 nights that they awoke her. The parents then decided to awaken Jane at 1:00; half way between 11:00 and 3:00. Awaking her at that time, they found that Jane was dry. If she had been wet, they would have awakened her at 12:00. However, since she was dry they had her go to the bathroom and eliminate. This procedure succeeded in keeping her dry for the entire evening (p. 13).

8. When the wake-up time that allows the child to be toileted once and remain dry has been identified, the child's ability to hold urine for longer periods each night should be strengthened by gradually moving back the wake-up time in intervals of 10 minutes, with continued charting to monitor accidents. Jane, for example, would be awakened at 12:50, then 12:40, then 12:30, etc.
9. The parents should continue to provide powerful reinforcers in the morning for dry beds while giving social praise at the least during the night for correct elimination or dry bed checks.

Bed-Wetting Signaling Equipment

A number of signaling apparatuses have been developed to treat enuretic individuals with or without the additional handicaps of deafness, blindness, or mental or emotional deficiencies (Coote, 1965; Lovibond, 1963, 1964; Mowrer & Mowrer, 1938; Seiger, 1952). There are two general designs.[5] The "sandwich" pad uses two pieces of screen or foil separated by fabric. Wet fabric results in contact between the positive and negative layers, completing an electric circuit. As with signaling underpants, this sounds a buzzer alarm and an optional light to wake the bedwetter. More expensive designs employ a one-piece pad which can be wiped dry after accidents, eliminating the need to replace the wet separating fabric.

The treatment procedure, which does not involve a reduction of fluid intake, tends to take several weeks or months to establish initial control but does so in about 80% to 90% of enuretics, though relapse is common (Jones, 1960; Lovibond, 1964; Sloop & Kennedy, 1973; Smith, 1981; Yates, 1970). Although the exact training procedure varies, a few similarities

---

[5]Commercially available bed-wetting signal devices are listed at the end of this chapter.

may be outlined (Baller, 1975). First, the student and parent should thoroughly understand the functioning of the equipment; "dry runs," especially important for the handicapped individual, will aid this process. This familiarization includes correct placement on the bed, turning off the signal once activated, and the steps followed by the parent and learner once urination is signaled (turn off alarm, go to the bathroom to complete or practice voiding, change sheets and pajamas, and reconnect signaling wires). A positive attitude should accompany the treatment, with social praise and perhaps more powerful reinforcers for dry beds. Records should be kept for accidents and successful urinations including the date, time, and perhaps size of the wet spot. Finally, criterion for dryness before discontinuation of the equipment is 10 to 14 dry nights (Baller, 1975). Apparatus can be reinstated if later accidents occur.

During an 11-week treatment period in an institutional ward, Sloop and Kennedy (1973) reported success with 52% of those moderately and severely retarded residents who were trained using bed-wetting signaling equipment. However, the relapse rate of 36% indicated a need for modification—perhaps of the type tested by Azrin et al. (1973) with profoundly retarded institutional residents, which will be summarized in the next section.

If a traditional method (no extra fluids) is adopted, signaling equipment can simplify the task of obtaining a baseline nighttime elimination schedule. After explaining the equipment to the learner, the parent, house parent, or ward attendant would simply record whenever the signal sounds, turn off the signal, wipe the pads dry, and return the dry learner to bed. Thus, hourly bedchecks are not needed. After a stable schedule is obtained, a reinforcement plan and possible accident treatment could be instituted, along with a wake-up procedure and continued use of the urine-sensing equipment. Like the traditional method, this particular combination of traditional method plus urine-sensing equipment has not been tested and thus may or may not prove effective.

Rapid Bedtime Training Procedures

Using methods similar to their rapid daytime bladder training program, Azrin et al. (1973) were able to reduce nighttime accidents in 12 profoundly retarded individuals by 85% during the first week following a single night of intensive training and then to 95% by the fifth week. Unlike other nighttime procedures, there was no relapse during a 3-month follow-up.

Because the procedure outlined in Table 13.2 was developed for institutional use, trainers were readily available on the midnight shift. Parents using this rapid procedure at home would need to modify it, as described in a later study (Azrin et al., 1974) with normal enuretic children. With further modifica-

tions, Bollard and Woodroffe (1977) found that parents of nonhandicapped and mildly retarded children could apply these (Azrin et al., 1974) steps and obtained more success with their bed-wetting children when signaling equipment was used.

A Variation of Azrin's Rapid Bedtime Procedure   Smith (1981) modified the nighttime training program used by Azrin and his colleagues, making it less intensive and thus more practical for most settings. All five institutionalized clients were severely or profoundly retarded, while three had serious behavior problems as well. Like Azrin, Smith used the enuresis alarm, increased fluids, and rewarded subjects for dryness; but also she reduced the punishment for accidents. Agreeing with other critics about the overcorrection accident treatment used by Azrin, Smith instead gave a sharp verbal reprimand for accidents and required the residents to feel the wet bed and use the toilet to finish urinating. Dry sheets were labeled ("nice clean dry sheets") and felt by the subjects to help them learn the difference between staying dry and having accidents. Wet sheets were left by the bed until the morning to emphasize the accident, when the subject placed them in the laundry. In addition, those who had accidents the night before were mildly reprimanded by the day staff and "rewards were withdrawn" (Smith, 1981, p. 69). While this treatment was not clearly defined, it was clear that positive reinforcement was emphasized both during the night and the following morning for those who had dry beds.

All five subjects attained the criterion of 4 consecutive dry weeks after 18 weeks (4½ months) to 92 weeks (1.7 years) of training, with a mean length of 47.6 weeks. Among the five subjects there was great variability and frequent 2- to 3-week periods of dryness followed by several relapse weeks of wetness. Thus a long criterion (4 or more weeks) was essential for obtaining long-term nighttime dryness. Follow-up checks on all five subjects at the same time revealed that all had remained dry without any relapses for 9 months to 2 years. While Smith's successes were obtained after a much longer training period, a few comments can be offered. First, it is questionable how many parents or staff members in residential programs can carry out the intensive all-night training used by Azrin et al. (1973). Second, Smith and others who have replicated Azrin and Foxx day and night training procedures (Bettison et al., Smith, 1979; Williams, Doleys, & Ciminero, 1978) have questioned the failure to replicate the rapid results of Azrin and his colleagues. Third is the interest of all researchers in long-term retention of bowel and bladder control and the absence in many studies of follow-up data. Thus, while Smith's variation of nighttime training did not yield rapid results,

TABLE 13.2 Dry-bed Procedure

I. *Intensive Training*
   A. Before bedtime
      1. Bedwetter drinks fluids
      2. Urine alarm placed on the bed
      3. Potty-alert placed in toilet bowl
   B. Hourly awakenings
      1. Minimal prompt given for awakening the resident
      2. Resident instructed or guided to the toilet
      3. Resident seated on toilet bowl
         a. If urination does not occur within 5 minutes
            (i) return resident to bed
            (ii) at bedside give resident fluids and praise as reinforcers
         b. If urination does occur within 5 minutes
            (i) give resident praise, snacks and fluids as reinforcers
            (ii) return resident to bed
      4. Praise resident for having dry bed (require resident to touch the dry sheets)
      5. Resident returns to sleep
   C. When accident occurs—45 min of cleanliness training and positive practice
      1. Disconnect the sound of the urine-alarm
      2. Awaken resident
      3. Reprimand resident for wetting and direct him to the toilet to finish urination
      4. Cleanliness training
         a. Bedwetter changes wet linen
         b. Attendant reactivates urine-alarm
      5. Positive practice in toileting
         a. Bedwetter lies down in bed for 3 minutes
         b. Bedwetter awakened with minimal prompt after 3 minutes
         c. Bedwett directed to toilet
         d. Repeat steps a, b, c about 9 times
      6. Bedwett returns to sleep when 45 minutes have elapsed since accident was detected
II. *Monitored post-training phase*
   A. Initiation of monitored post-training
      1. When resident has no more than 1 accident during a training night
      2. When the resident correctly toilets on at least 50% of all opportunities during a training night
   B. Procedure
      1. Urine-alarm on bed
      2. Whenever accident occurs, reprimand, cleanliness training and positive practice follow for 45 minutes
      3. No fluids, no hourly awakenings, no reinforcers
   C. Termination of monitored post-training
      1. Terminated 7 nights after last accident
III. *Normal procedure*
   A. Initiated after resident goes 7 nights without accident
   B. No urine-alarm, no reinforcers, no positive practice, etc.
   C. Bed inspected each morning
      1. If bed wet, resident remakes and cleans bed (cleanliness training)
      2. If 2 accidents occur within a given week, the monitored phase is reinstated

SOURCE: "Dry-Bed: A Rapid Method of Eliminating Bedwetting (Enuresis) of the Retarded," by N. H. Azrin, T. J. Sneed, and R. M. Foxx, *Behaviour Research and Therapy*, 1973, *11*, 430. Reprinted with permission.

the results appeared very resistant to relapse over time and the procedures were acceptable to those who had to implement them.

Given the success of repeated practice error correction in contrast to other, simpler correction procedures (Close, Irwin, Prehm, & Taylor, 1978), it would be particularly interesting to know whether a *shorter* period of repeated practice overcorrection for bed-wetting accidents would be as effective as the longer period used by Azrin (e.g. 2 to 5 trials of step

I.C.5 in Table 13.2 rather than 9). If this were so, many trainers might be less critical of repeated practice correction procedures; with their use, results might be obtained more rapidly.

Bowel and Bladder Management

Learners with immature or damaged central nervous systems may be unable to master voluntary bladder or bowel control (Snell, 1980). Included in this group are those with neural tube defects (such as myelomeningocele), spinal cord injuries, and multiple sclerosis that affects the relevant nerves. Students with extensive hypertonic cerebral palsy may have difficulty learning control due to problems with muscle relaxation; however, voluntary control or regulation may be mastered. In spite of these orthopedic handicaps, these students can be taught to manage some or all of their own toileting and related skills with the necessary medical consultation and educational intervention.

Depending upon the student's specific physical handicap, sex, age, and level of functioning, various surgical interventions (urinary diversions, ostomies) or less intrusive nonsurgical procedures may be employed to aid in bowel and/or bladder management. Nonsurgical techniques for bladder management include various types of urinary collection devices worn externally under the clothes (Bigge, 1982; Forrest, 1976; Hamilton, 1974; Swinyard, 1971) as well as a nonsterile self-catheterizing procedure which children may be taught to carry out independently (Altshuler, Meyer, & Butz, 1977). [See chapter 6.] A primary strategy to facilitate bowel management includes careful planning and regulation of the student's diet with plenty of roughage and adequate water, along with exercise. Stool softener medication and suppositories may be the only medical intervention needed, if any. In addition, parents and students will learn that certain routines will aid regular elimination (Bigge, 1982; Cheever & Elmer, 1975). (Snell, 1980, p. 57)

Frequently students with limited or no voluntary elimination control have skin breakdown in the genital and buttock region. This problem is caused by moisture from elimination or sweating, poor circulation, and excessive pressure from sitting. Skin sores heal slowly, and are often painful, inconvenient, and embarrassing. Thus the best solution to skin breakdown is prevention. The teacher and parents must help keep the student dry and clean after each elimination and conscientiously change the student's position at least hourly. Depending upon the student's handicap and type of equipment prescribed, using standing tables, prone boards, or scooter boards; walking or crawling to whatever extent possible; and wheelchair push-ups all offer means to improve circulation.

EATING SKILLS

Moderately and severely handicapped individuals may learn to feed themselves without complications or delay or with only slight delay when there are no behavioral, physical, or environmental inadequacies. However, motor or neurological handicaps, structural abnormalities in the oral cavity and musculature, attention problems, extreme disruptive behaviors, special dietary needs, sensory deficiencies, or inadequate learning environments (overprotective or uninterested parents, uninformed teachers, poor teacher-child ratio) may lead to delayed, incomplete, or abnormal development of eating skills (Bigge, 1982). Eating is perhaps the ideal skill for training because food is already a primary reinforcer. Related to this "built-in" reinforcement is the natural punishment for inappropriate eating—the removal, interruption, or postponement of eating (O'Brien, Bugle, & Azrin, 1972).

To promote independence in eating and related table skills, the teacher will make the instructional decisions listed earlier, individualizing the answers to suit the specific needs of each learner. Often assistance must be sought from physicians and physical and occupational therapists during observation and assessment, selection of adapted eating equipment, program development, and implementation.

This provides basic assessment and teaching techniques that have been successful with the severely handicapped. Although we will briefly discuss complications resulting from physical handicaps, curricular details must be sought in the references provided, as well as chapter 7.

Assessment of Eating Skills

In addition to using assessment devices based on task analysis and developmental information, there are a variety of techniques[6] to observe and directly measure baseline eating skills. As with toileting skills, if the assessment procedure allows you to measure performance of skills by observing finely analyzed steps comprising these skills, then selecting appropriate teaching targets and monitoring learning daily will be more precise and accurate. We will describe a few commercially available assessment procedures, though frequently teacher-constructed or -modified assessment devices are more useful.

---

[6]See, for example, Balthazar (1971); Barton, Guess, Garcia, and Baer (1970); Behavioral Characteristics Progression (1973); Bender and Valletutti (1976); Bowman, Calkin, and Grant (1975); Copeland et al. (1976); Ferneti, Lent, and Stevens (1974); Hanson (1977); Nelson, Cone, and Hanson (1975); O'Brien and Azrin (1972); van den Pol, Iwata, Ivancic, Page, Neef, and Whitley (1981).

Basic Eating Skills

The *Balthazar Scales of Functional Independence* (1971) measure eating abilities from dependent feeding to finger foods, spoon and fork usage, and drinking (Figure 13.7). The examiner unobtrusively observes the student eating a number of meals while assigning proportionate scores (0 to 10), based on the frequency of behavior occurrence. On the score sheet, behaviors within each skill class are arranged developmentally by increasing complexity. Indented behaviors are more complex than the items from which they are indented. Therefore, in scoring indented items, it is not possible to receive higher scores (better performance) on subscale items than on the preceding simpler items. For example, in the finger food class, "When a subject eats approximately half of his finger foods, he receives a score of '5' on item 1, 'Eats finger foods.' Consequently, the highest score he can receive on the indented item 2, 'Holds finger foods,' is a '5' also" (p. 16). A checklist, scored simply as "present," "not present," or "no opportunity to perform," roughly measures before-, during-, and after-meal activities.

For some students, it will be useful to time eating if it appears necessary to adjust the speed (slowing down or speeding up). In addition, as described by Balthazar (1971), the size of the bite, the amount placed in the mouth, and the extent of spilling, which are not easily measured, exemplify typical problems which should be measured.

Bowman, Calkin, and Grant (1975) described procedures for assessing and teaching spoon usage applicable in both home and school. A proficiency progress chart (Figure 13.8) is used both to assess entry skills and to monitor progress once a target has been selected and training is under way. To assess, the teacher observes the student during mealtime on one or more of the behaviors, which are indicated by checking the appropriate box. For example, when presented with a filled spoon, Jeff's mother noted that he opened his mouth correctly 9 out of 10 times. Thus she moved on to the next task. She would continue assessing until she identified a task on which performance was less than 90%. Suggestions also are provided on adapting utensils, teaching visually and motorically impaired students, and teaching techniques.

A curriculum developed by Tawney and his colleagues (1979) gives guidelines to assess and teach learners with and without physical impairments. Task analyses assess and direct the instruction of chewing, eating finger foods, drinking from a cup, and eating with a spoon and fork. Clearly specified are the physical arrangement, the instructional cue or command provided, and the response latency (how long the teacher waits for a response before either scoring the response when assessing or assisting when teaching).

Advanced Eating Skills

At more advanced levels, assessment of a wider range of related meal skills becomes relevant. For example, van den Pol and colleagues (1981) assessed and taught three mildly to moderately handicapped students to eat in McDonald's. Not only did they learn to stand in line, order, and pay for food, but their public eating skills were also shaped. A detailed task analysis of the responses involved was used to assess performance. (See chapter 14 for a discussion of this and other related studies.) Similarly Matson, Ollendick, and Adkins (1980) used task analytic assessment to measure 26 mealtime behaviors involved in a family-style dining program for 80 moderately to profoundly retarded adults. Table 13.3 lists various target behaviors observed in the five component skill clusters—orderliness, eating, utensil use, neatness, and table manners.

Measuring Food Intake

For some students the quantity of food eaten may need to be modified. Any extreme can be a difficulty. The obese student who eats excessively may develop related social and health problems that can adversely affect vocational opportunities, leisure-recreational skills, physical fitness, and community integration. The underweight student who eats very little, either because of extreme motor impairment or behavior problems, is threatened by reduced energy and related health complications. In both cases, careful baseline records should be kept to quantify and define the extent of the problem before setting instructional objectives. Consultation with a school nurse, nutritionist, or the student's physician should help verify whether intervention is necessary and may lead to more efficient ways to measure the weight problem initially.

Pipes (1976) suggests a procedure for taking a 7-day food record (Figure 13.9) with cooperation with the parents. Beverages and foods are measured before and after a meal to determine the actual amount consumed, which is then recorded. With some severely involved students who are fed and have extremely poor oral-motor ability, excessive spillage will confuse these measurements. In these cases a dry washcloth or damp sponge, weighed before feeding, can be held under the cup to catch spills. This amount is subtracted from the original quantity of liquid. Similarly, food that drops onto the table, plate, or bib may be weighed and thus separated from the quantity actually eaten.

As in other self-help skills, it may be useful to pinpoint and measure related behaviors. These may

EATING SCALES   Meal: _____   Date: _____

ITEM SCORING SHEET

CLASS I – DEPENDENT FEEDING

1___Mouth is open,
  2___voluntarily,
    3___without physical stimulation.
    4___Removes food with mouth,
      5___with lips.
      6___Allows spoon removal.
7___Retains food,
  8___in upright position.
Subtotal 9___Manipulates food in mouth.

CLASS II – FINGER FOODS

1___Eats finger foods.
  2___Holds finger foods.
    3___Hand to mouth movement.
    4___Reaches for finger food.
    5___Separates finger foods,
      6___with mouth.
      7___Does not stuff mouth with separated foods.
      8___Bites off appropriate sizes.
Subtotal   9___Does not stuff mouth with appropriate sizes.

CLASS III – SPOON USAGE

1___Eats tray foods.
  2___with spoon,
    3___held in finger position,
    4___palm up.
  5___Fills spoon independently.
    6___Attends to filling.
    7___Manipulates with precision.
    8___Fills appropriate amount.
  9___Directs spoon independently.
    10___Moves arm toward mouth.
    11___Directs spoon accurately.
    12___Does NOT spill from spoon.
Subtotal   13___Does NOT stuff mouth.

CLASS IV – FORK USAGE

1___Eats tray foods,
  2___with fork,
    3___held in finger position,
    4___palm up.
  5___Fills fork independently.
    6___Attends to filling.
    7___Manipulates with precision.
    8___Fills appropriate amount.
  9___Directs fork independently.
    10___Moves arm toward mouth.
    11___Directs fork accurately.
    12___Does NOT spill from fork.
Subtotal   13___Does NOT stuff mouth.

CLASS V – DRINKING

1___Takes liquids,
  2___from cup.
    3___Swallows liquids.
    4___Retains liquids,
      5___in upright position.
6___Contact with cup.
  7___Drinks from cup independently.
  8___Lifts cup off table with two hands.
    9___Does NOT spill while lifting.
    10___Does NOT spill while drinking.
    11___Lifts cup off table with one hand.
      12___Does NOT spill while lifting with one hand.
Subtotal   13___Does NOT spill while drinking with one hand.

FULL SCALE SCORE: _____

EATING CHECKLIST

A: Self Service

1___Pours own drink.
2___Gets own tray.
3___Selects own tray.
4___Carries own tray.
5___Serves self food.
6___Uses napkin.
7___Takes back dirty dishes.
8___Cleans off dirty dishes.
9___Proper dispensing of dirty dishes.

B: Assistive Devices

10___for drinking.
11___for eating.
12___eats with hand restraint.

C: Type of Food

13___Fed by gavage.
14___Drinks full liquids.
15___Blender-strained.
16___Blender foods.
17___Child bite-size.
18___Adult bite-size.

D: Positioning

19___Lying down.
20___Reclined position.
21___Upright with body restraint.
22___Upright alone.

E: Rate of Eating

23___Eats too fast.
24___Eats too slowly.

F: Advanced Utensil Usage

25___Uses spoon for correct foods.
26___Uses fork for correct foods.
27___Spreads with knife.
28___Cuts with knife.

G: Supervision

29___Eats without supervision.
30___Responds to supervision.
31___Maintains corrected behavior.
32___Does NOT respond to supervision.
  a. Eating skills.
  b. Stealing food.
  c. Behavior problem.
  d. Self induced emesis.
  e. Other_____

FIGURE 13.7

The Balthazar Scales of Functional Independence: Eating-Drinking Scales.

SOURCE: *Balthazar Scales of Adaptive Behavior for the Profoundly and Severely Mentally Retarded, Section 1,* by E.E. Balthazar. Champaign, Ill.: Research Press, 1971.

FIGURE 13.8
Sample Progress Chart.

Jeff was checked one day on the task of opening his mouth and as the sample progress chart shows, he did it correctly nine out of ten times. There was no need for training, so his mother filled in another chart and went on to check him on the next task, swallowing.

SOURCE: *Eating with a Spoon: How to Teach your Multi-Handicapped Child* by M. Bowman, A.B. Calkin, and P.A. Grant. Columbus: Ohio State University, National Center on Educ. Media and Materials for the Handicapped, 1975, p. 18. Reprinted with permission.

Name _____ *Jeff* _____   ☑ open mouth   ☐ pick up utensil

Date Started __*February 22, 1971*__   ☐ swallow   ☐ return spoon to plate

Date Stopped __*February 22, 1971*__   ☐ remove food from spoon   ☐ carry spoon to mouth

Code: X = successful   ☐ chew   ☐ carry spoon to food and fill it
　　　 O = unsuccessful

Date	Tries										Total X's	Comments
	1	2	3	4	5	6	7	8	9	10		
Test for competency: *2/22/71*	X	X	X	X	X	X	X	X	X	O	9	

TABLE 13.3 Hierarchical Classification of the 26 Mealtime Target Behaviors

Table Level	Target Behavior
Table Level 1: Orderliness	1. Picks up all utensils
	2. Appropriate noise level
	3. Appropriate line behavior
	4. Stays seated during meals
	5. Finishes eating before leaving table
	6. Returns tray and utensils properly
	7. Leaves dining room when finished eating
Table Level 2: Eating	8. Chews food before swallowing
	9. Takes small bites
	10. Swallows before next bite
	11. Drinks properly—glass in one hand
	12. Eats at normal pace—not too fast
Table Level 3: Utensil Use	13. Uses spoon appropriately
	14. Uses fork appropriately
	15. Uses knife appropriately
	16. Holds utensils properly
Table Level 4: Neatness	17. Eats neatly
	18. Wipes up spilled food
	19. Uses napkin
	20. Talks with mouth empty
	21. Has good posture
	22. Eats at normal pace
Table Level 5: Table Manners	23. Chews with mouth closed
	24. Elbows off table
	25. Hands in lap
	26. Pushes chair in

SOURCE: "A Comprehensive Dining Program for Mentally Retarded Adults" by J.L. Matson, T.H. Ollendick, & J. Adkins. *Behavior Research and Therapy*, 1981, *18*, 109, Pergamon Press, Ltd. Reprinted with permission.

include fine motor hand movements and object manipulation, sitting at the table, visual attending during utensil and cup use, comprehension of simple eating instructions and the words for training materials (spoon, cup, dessert, etc.), as well as disruptive mealtime behaviors (stealing or throwing food or utensils, aggressive behavior toward others at table, regurgitation of food, etc.).

To plan effective instruction, a teacher needs to know which types of prompts will work with a given student. Will verbal instructions be comprehended? Does the student imitate demonstrations or respond to gestures? Performance data collected on prompt categories as well as skill assessment data will help the teacher select initial teaching targets, monitor performance changes during training, and adjust instructional objectives as learning occurs.

Selection of Teaching Targets

Eating skills are learned in a general order, beginning with various aspects of dependent feeding (anticipates spoon, uses lips to remove food, etc.) to eating finger foods, to spoon and cup use, followed by fork use, then knife spreading and cutting, food serving, condiment usage, and table manners. Some of these skills are shown in Figure 13.10.

In general, selected targets should be both realistic in relation to the student's current performance and also immediately or subsequently relevant (i.e., prioritized by the parent or teacher as being needed on a regular basis). Thus, while it would be of immediate value to teach Mary to cut with a knife, she still has not mastered independent spoon use and should master this easier skill first. However, since she is mobile with a walker, it is not too early to teach her to use a napkin or to go through the lunch line and choose her food. Concurrent objectives and training may occur for fine motor skills (grasp, object manipulation, etc.) that may improve utensil and food manipulation. For example, Banerdt and Bricker (1978) identified a number of intermediate manual dexterity abilities relevant to independent feeding skills (Figure 13.11).

General Elements of Instruction

Teaching Times and Place

Depending upon the particular objectives, most instruction should occur before, during, and after eating in the school or home dining area. Azrin and Armstrong (1973) increased the number of daily training sessions by dividing meals into smaller por-

tions or "mini-meals" served hourly. This allowed more intensive instruction for the profoundly retarded learners and resulted in appropriate, independent eating after an average of 12 days of instruction. Others have replicated the effectiveness of mini-meals (Richman, Sonderby, & Kahn, 1980; Stimbert, Minor, & McCoy, 1977).

The literature on the best place to train basic eating skills is somewhat inconsistent. Azrin and Armstrong (1973) and Richman et al. (1980) found that eating instruction in a nondistracting setting produced a higher frequency of correct responses in less time than did instruction in the lunchroom. However, a study by Song and Gandhi (1974) supported the position that self-feeding skills learned in the natural setting are less likely to be forgotten or lost over time. Design and methodological problems in these and other feeding studies prevent us from drawing clear-cut conclusions about the relationship of training setting to skill acquisition and maintenance.

Certainly the ultimate goal is that the severely handicapped student be able to eat alongside others, handicapped and nonhandicapped, at home, at friends' homes, in the school cafeteria, and in public restaurants. At the same time, we know that they have difficulty generalizing learned skills from one setting to another. Both of these facts support instruction in the natural setting. A third related fact concerns those students with excessive behavior problems or movement difficulties due to upper motor neuron damage, primarily cerebral palsy. Two reasons are commonly cited to justify initial mealtime isolation of severely involved students. First is poor oral control, which results in excessive spillage even when the student is fed by a teacher. The second reason is the increased muscle tone that may result from cafeteria noise and distraction and thus may interfere with controlled movement, increase primitive reflexes, and reduce the amount actually eaten. In addition, many students' extreme behavior problems will increase with outside distraction. In spite of these problems, the decision to teach feeding skills in isolation must be made cautiously, since segregation eliminates social interaction, reduces the probability of skill generalization, and may mean less efficient use of staff time. In a few cases, either excessive mealtime behavior problems or extreme motor involvement may dictate temporary or partial isolation from the school cafeteria. For example, after conferring with the occupational therapist, a teacher decides to feed a student in a quiet corner of the classroom in two smaller meals before and after the noon meal, to facilitate greater food intake and more progress on cooperative feeding objectives. However, the same student would accompany the class to the school caf-

INSTRUCTIONS

1. Record *all* food or beverages immediately *after* they are eaten or drunk.

2. Measure the amounts of each food carefully in terms of standard measuring cups and spoons. Record meat portions in ounces or as fractions of pounds, for example: 8 ounces of milk; one medium egg; ¼ pound of hamburger; one slice of bread, white; ½ small banana.

3. Indicate method of preparation, for example: medium egg, fried; ½-cup baked beans with two-inch slice salt pork; four ounces steak, broiled.

4. Be sure to include any condiments, gravies, salad dressings, butter, margarine, whipped cream, relishes, etc., for example: ¼ cup mashed potatoes with 3 tablespoons brown gravy; ¼ cup cottage cheese salad with two olives; ½ cup cornflakes with 1 teaspoon sugar and ⅓ cup 2% milk.

5. Be sure to include all between meal foods and drinks, for example: coffee with 1 ounce of cream; 12 ounces of coke; four sugar cookies; one 10¢ candy bar (list brand).

6. If you eat away from home, please put a little symbol ★ beside the foods.

Date ———— Day of week ————

Weight ————

Time	Food	Amount	How prepared

FIGURE 13.9
Seven-Day Food Record

SOURCE: Assessing Food and Nutrient Intake by P.L. Pipes. In M.L. Erickson (Ed.), *Assessment and Management of Developmental Changes in Children*. St. Louis: C.V. Mosby, 1976, p. 140. Taken from Nutrition Department, Child Development and Mental Retardation Center, University of Washington, Seattle, 1975. Reprinted with permission.

383

FIGURE 13.10
Moderately Handicapped Young Students Are Learning to Negotiate the School Cafeteria Line Independently, Pour Milk from a Thermos Without Spilling, and Spread Butter on a Slice of Bread.

FIGURE 13.11
Training Lattice for Establishing Independent Feeding Skills
SOURCE: "A Training Program for Selected Self-Feeding Skills for the Moderately Impaired" by B. Banerdt and D. Bricker.
AAESPH Review, 1978, *3,* 224. Reprinted with permission.

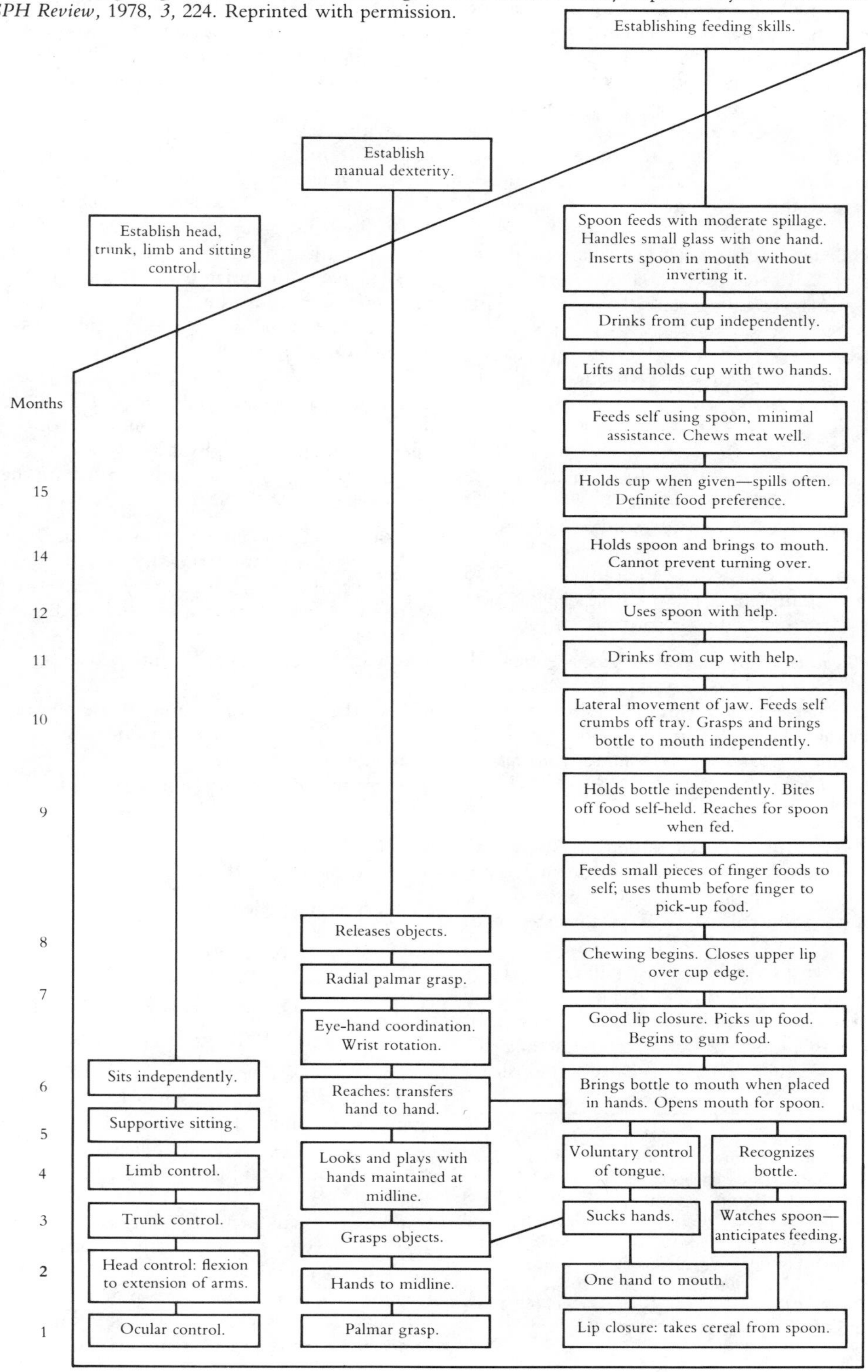

eteria at lunchtime, primarily for social interaction. A second student who steals and throws food, has little or no utensil use, and has frequent tantrums may eat in the classroom initially with one or two other students (who are more independent and are rotated so they do not always eat in isolation). Once some of the inappropriate behavior is under control, the student might eat in the cafeteria when no others except one or two classmates are present. Later this would be adjusted so the student would eat at the scheduled lunchtime.

Thus, while temporary mealtime isolation may be justified in special cases for a small number of students, the primary training setting for eating skills will be the school cafeteria, the student's home kitchen or dining room, or a local restaurant. In addition, using mini-meals may add additional trips to these lunch areas.

Teaching Materials

The food, utensils, and related eating materials are directly determined by the learner's particular instructional objectives and entry skills. For example, special individually prescribed considerations are necessary when feeding the cerebral palsied child and again when implementing the first steps toward self-feeding. Major feeding problems include the

lack of mouth, head and trunk control, lack of sitting balance and inability to bend his hips sufficiently to enable him to stretch his arms forward to grasp and to maintain that grasp irrespective of the position of his arms; finally his inability to bring his hands to his mouth and his lack of eye-hand coordination. (Mueller, 1975, pp. 114–115)

To overcome these problems when an individual is being fed by an adult, antecedent considerations will include selection of the appropriate sitting position, materials (glass, adaptations in the spoon, etc.), method of jaw control, as well as consistency of food.

The complexity of making these educational decisions means that consultation should be sought from additional references[7] and certainly from physical or occupational therapists. Again, when teaching the physically handicapped child to self-feed, the teacher

---

[7]For detailed information on positioning, feeding techniques, and nutritional considerations for cerebral palsied learners, see chapter 6 in this book; Banerdt and Bricker (1978); Bigge (1982); Bowman et al. (1975); Bricker and Campbell (1980); Campbell (1979); Campbell, Green, and Carlson (1977); Connor, Williamson, & Siepp (1978); Copeland et al. (1976); Finnie (1975); Hanson and Campbell (in press); Holser-Buehler (1966); Lemke and Mitchell (1972); Macey (1974); Mueller (1972, 1975); Morris (1977); Pipes (1976); Schmidt (1976); Tawney (1979); Utley, et al. (1977); and Sobsey (Note 2).

may use a nonslip mat under the place-setting, a bowl with steep sides for scooping food against rather than a plate, or temporary adaptive equipment such as spoons with built-up or curved handles, holding straps, or swivel bowls, and drinking cup holders or weighted cups with large handles. As is generally the case with the CP person, seating positions that facilitate head and trunk control are of central importance, as illustrated in Figure 13.12.

An evaluation will help the teacher specify the physically handicapped learner's entry skills and limitations so that teaching equipment and methods can be matched appropriately. Seriously handicapped children often must be taught to suck, swallow, chew, remove food from a spoon, and sip from a cup (Finnie, 1975; Stainback, Healy, Stainback, & Healy, 1976).

Utley, Holvoet, and Barnes (1977) list baseline information that should be sought through assessment conducted by a physical therapist, an occupational therapist, or a speech therapist with the teacher's assistance.

1. What is the student's muscular status (hypotonia, hypertonia, involuntary muscle actions, etc.)?
2. What pathological or primary reflexes are present (symmetrical tonic neck reflex, rooting reflex, etc.)?
3. What degree of head control does the student demonstrate?
4. Can the student grasp and release objects?
5. Does the child have hand-to-mouth movements?
6. Does the child's sitting balance require the use of his arms?
7. What particular mouth functions does the individual demonstrate?
   A. Tongue movements,
   B. Sucking reflex,
   C. Bite reflex,
   D. Gag reflex,
   E. Swallowing,
   F. Drooling and lip closure,
   G. Oral hypersensitivity.

The more severe the physical impairment, the more important it is that self-help instructional programs be formulated and evaluated by an interdisciplinary staff. (The references listed earlier give specific detail on techniques to teach rudimentary eating skills.)

When the handicapped learner is not cerebral palsied or otherwise disabled in body control, coordination, or balance, adaptive eating equipment and therapeutic positioning are not complex issues. However, the teacher must make some decisions concerning instructional materials. For example, the

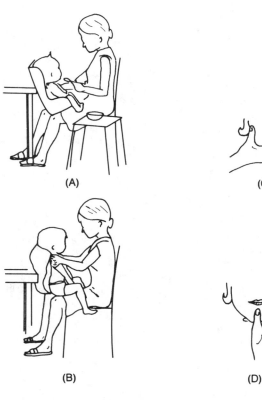

(A)

(C)

(B)

(D)

FIGURE 13.12
Techniques for feeding the cerebral palsied child
(A) Half-sitting position for the child with some sitting balance. Remember to put the food in front of him. If the child still needs support, an "Infant Seat" can be used resting against the table edge (p. 117).
(B) When sitting balance improves, sit the baby up straight with his legs abducted and his hips well flexed. You may still have to control him from the shoulders (p. 117).
(C) Jaw control as applied when the child is on your right side with your arm around his head; thumb on his jaw joint, index finger between chin and lower lip, middle finger behind chin applying constant firm pressure (p. 119).

SOURCE: From H. Mueller in Nancie R. Finnie (Ed.), *Handling the Young Cerebral Palsied Child at Home,* 2nd ed. Copyright © 1974 by Nancie R. Finnie, F.C.S.P.; additions for U.S. edition, copyright © 1975 by E.P. Dutton, Inc. Reprinted by permission of the publisher, E.P. Dutton, Inc.

chair and table height should match the learner's size and allow his feet to rest firmly on the floor or a foot block; utensil and cup size should fit the child, the food must be appealing, nourishing, and suited to the teaching goals (finger foods if this skill is targeted; slightly sticky foods when spoon instruction begins, etc.). For many beginning learners, placing a wet washcloth, suction cup, or rubber mat beneath plates and bowls will prevent slipping and allow easier spoon filling. After basic eating skills are mastered, other teaching materials will be added. Those may include forks and knives, paper napkins, salt and pepper shakers, serving bowls and spoons, milk cartons, cafeteria trays, straws, and specific types of food (e.g., thin soup, butter to spread, gravy to dip or pour, thermoses to pour from, spaghetti to eat, meat to cut). Finally, to facilitate generalization, a variety of materials and settings should be used. If a child has learned to use paper napkins, will he balk at the use of a cloth napkin? If a young man performs very well in the small school cafeteria where there are no food choices, how will he fare in the average cafeteria restaurant with many menu choices? This instructional concern moves beyond the mere learning of a skill (i.e. napkin usage); the generalization criterion deals with the successful use of the skill in realistic situations.

Basic Methods to Teach Self-Feeding

The primary procedures to teach basic eating skills and self-feeding include prompting targeted behaviors followed by fading or delay of prompts and shaping. Since many of the terminal goals actually involve chains of behavior (such as using utensils and going through a cafeteria line), the teacher will use both forward and backward chaining separately and in combination to "string together" the portions of these lengthy targeted skills. (See chapter 5 for clarification.)

Finger Foods
The first sign of independence in self-feeding is the predictably messy stage of eating finger foods. At this early stage, a child practices the pincer grasp to pick up food and refines hand-to-mouth movements (which already have been used extensively to explore objects by mouthing) in combination with the sucking, gumming, chewing, and swallowing of many soft foods such as bananas and saliva-softened toast. Finger feeding provides an essential opportunity to improve the movements necessary for learning utensil use later.

If baseline assessment reveals deficiencies in utensil use as well as poor coordination of grasp, lift, and placement of finger foods in the mouth, then finger food instruction should have priority. The teacher must specify the particular portion(s) of the finger food chain which are missing or weak: food location, grasp, lift from table to mouth, opening of mouth at appropriate time, putting food into open mouth, leaving food in mouth (releasing grasp or biting off a portion), chewing food, or swallowing food. In addition, the student's ability to deal with large pieces of food should be noted. Does she tear food into smaller pieces or does she gum or bite off smaller pieces from what she holds to the mouth (the more advanced method). Finally, if sloppiness is the primary problem, then its cause should be determined and targeted for instruction. For example, sloppiness may be caused by placing too much food in the mouth. Beginners should not be punished for sloppiness until they have developed the motor coordination needed for neatness.

Finger food self-feeding should be taught at the beginning of the meal when the child is hungry. Food consistency will depend on the presence or absence of teeth and the ability the student already has; for example, bananas and breads will be more easily placed in the mouth, chewed, and swallowed than will partially cooked vegetables and hot dog bits or raw vegetables. Guided assistance may be the most useful prompt since demonstrations require good attending and imitation skills (Nelson et al., 1975). However, this physical prompting should be provided from behind while sitting beside the learner so that the teacher's movements follow the natural pattern. The use of simple, consistent instructions ("Open;" "Chew, chew, chew") may be helpful paired with teacher modeling and gestures during the early stages of learning. Later, after prompts are faded, the simple instructions could be used to remind the learner.

Drinking from a Cup or Glass

Initially students will help the parent or teacher hold the cup or glass and lift it to the mouth. At this early stage and when an individual first drinks from a cup independently, both hands will be used. Straw drinking is not targeted until a student can drink from a cup. Also, as with finger feeding and utensil use, the learning process will be messy. As with all the self-care skills, a task analysis of drinking will help provide an accurate assessment of the beginning performance and needs.

For students with limited self-drinking abilities, manual guidance through the entire chain will be necessary, with fading proceeding backwards and forwards from points of successful performance in the chain. It is often easiest to begin fading assistance at the point after the glass is rested on the lower lip and before any liquid is tipped into the mouth. Especially if the student is thirsty and likes the liquid, success will be immediately reinforced. Assistance may be needed to complete the chain. Manual guidance would gradually be faded backward first and then forward to the last step in the chain (glass is placed back on table).

Utley et al. (1977) and Stainback et al. (1976) recommended some techniques for helping the dependent drinker to gradual independence. First, use a small (8-ounce), soft plastic or paper cup that is translucent so that the liquid is visible and you can more easily control positioning. Cutting a semicircle in the rim of the glass will let the student get liquid without having to tilt his head so he "fights" cup drinking less. At this stage, when a lot of assistance is provided, the glass should be fairly full. Do not use spouted or nipple cups which stimulate abnormal sucking (Mueller, 1975). Because sweet liquids stimulate drooling and milk thickens the saliva, other fluids such as unsweetened orange juice or cool to warm broth are better for initial training. Stainback suggests a slightly thickened liquid to stimulate swallowing and decrease spilling. So as not to encourage the learner to bite the edge of the cup, place the rim of the cup against the lower lip, not between the teeth. If it is necessary to help the student open her mouth, position the hand as in Figure 13.12 with the index finger on the chin, the third finger under the chin, and the thumb on the cheek or upper lip. Tilt the cup until liquid touches the upper lip and tongue, which encourages the learner to perform part of the task. Hold the cup in this position until a few swallows (with rests in between) have been taken. As you allow the student to perform more of the task alone, use smaller amounts of liquid to lessen spilling.

Only after the student learns to drink holding the handled cup or small glass with both hands should you begin to emphasize a reduction of spilling. Spilling will occur while drinking but may also happen as the glass is grasped, lifted, or replaced on the table. Handled or adapted cups may be more easily held, depending upon the student. Glasses with smaller circumferences filled with smaller amounts are also helpful. Eventually, as drinking and other self-feeding skills improve, the student should be reminded to lift the glass with only the dominant hand.

Stimbert et al. (1977) used six daily mini-meals and graduated guidance to teach six moderately to profoundly retarded students to drink from a glass and correctly use the hands and spoon to eat. The graduated guidance (described also in chapter 5) was physical assistance through the chain of drinking from a cup. Initially the trainer's hands were placed directly over the learner's hands, until pressure cues indicated that the student needed less than total assistance.

Then the trainer's hands were shifted to the student's wrists to provide some, but not total, guidance. Over successive trials, the trainer rotated the manual assistance to the forearm, the elbow, the upper arm, and finally the shoulders, giving at any point only as much guidance as was necessary to complete the task. Generally graduated guidance resulted in very few errors; however, when errors did occur the authors loudly reprimanded the student, stating specifically what was to be stopped (e.g., "No spilling"). As done by Azrin and Armstrong (1973), any spill or throwing of food was consequated with guided clean-up (restitutional overcorrection) and three practice trials of lifting the glass with guidance (positive practice overcorrection). All correct responses, initially whether prompted or not, were praised. Results indicated that the students learned independent drinking from a glass along with spoon use and eliminated inappropriate mealtime behavior rather rapidly, in 5 to 8 weeks. The new skills were still used after a 1-year follow-up.

Eating with a Spoon

Spoon use is the simplest of the utensil skills, followed in difficulty by eating with a fork, transferring spreads with a knife, spreading with a knife, cutting finger-grasped bread with a knife, and cutting meat with a fork and knife. When a learner has learned to grasp objects and demonstrates some success in manipulating finger foods, an assessment should be made of the ability to pick up and eat with a spoon.

Albin's (1977) rather simple task analysis of spoon use may be useful for assessment and later teaching. (Refer to chapters 4 and 5 for more detail on these procedures.)

1. Pick up the spoon,
2. Scoop,
3. Raise spoon to mouth,
4. Remove food,
5. Return spoon to bowl.

For other students, a slightly more detailed task analysis may be more suitable.

1. Pick up the spoon,
2. Move the spoon to the bowl,
3. Scoop some food with the spoon,
4. Take the spoon to your mouth,
5. Open your mouth,
6. Put the spoon in your mouth (Eat),
7. Remove the food with your lips,
8. Return the spoon to the bowl,
9. Chew and swallow,
10. Repeat steps 3–9 until done.

In this example, the specific verbal prompts, which are simplified versions of some of the steps, are underlined. In other words, the student will be trained on each step but verbally prompted only with the underlined phrases in steps 1, 3, 5, 6, and 9. (See chapter 4 for more information on task analysis.)

After field-testing a task analysis, the more difficult steps may need to be simplified; for example, food scooping has been identified as the most difficult step to teach severely retarded individuals (Song & Gandhi, 1974). In addition, it is important to note how often the spoon is abandoned in favor of the fingers, how much spilling occurs and why (e.g., on the way to the mouth due to poor wrist rotation), and how the spoon is grasped. Younger children with immature grasps will hold the spoon in a palm-down finger or fist position, while the more mature palm-up position will be learned only after the child makes gains in fine motor development.

Looking at and reaching for the spoon is best taught while the student is still in the dependent feeding stage—being spoon-fed by the parent or teacher. To do this the adult calls the student's name and, when he looks, places the spoon on the table within reach. The spoon may be gently tapped to cue attention. The food is presented as a consequence for looking at the spoon. Later the student will be expected to reach toward the spoon. Other guidelines for encouraging more active participation during dependent feeding (Mueller, 1975; Stainback et al., 1976) include:

1. A short and shallow-bowled spoon with a rounded end will not stimulate the gag reflex.
2. If the learner has a strong bite reflex and tends to bite the spoon, two procedures may be helpful. Present the filled spoon from the side of the mouth, moving it slowly toward a normal midline presentation as the learner is successful. Also, if the bite reflex is activated when the spoon is removed, do not wrench it from between the teeth; if pressure is applied under the chin near the base of the tongue, the bite often will be released.
3. Initially place food near the front of the spoon to facilitate its removal.
4. As the spoon is removed, use manual assistance if necessary to close the student's lips. This allows the tongue to move the food in rather than out of the mouth.
5. If you scrape the spoon against the lips or upper teeth as it is removed, two maladaptive consequences are apt to occur—tongue thrust may be stimulated and the learner is not expected to actively participate in food removal.

Progressing from dependent feeding to initial stages of teaching spoon use should be gradual, after the learner demonstrates some skill in eating finger foods, reaches for and holds the spoon, and can drink from a cup but not without spilling. Once baseline performance has been measured and an intervention plan initiated, instructional time should fill at least the initial part of most meals (if not the whole meal) when the student is hungry and progress to the entire mealtime. That is, you may choose to feed the student during the final third of a meal only after working on self-feeding. Eventually all dependent feeding should be replaced by instruction in self-feeding.

Several shaping and prompt-fade methods have been described to teach spoon use to severely and profoundly retarded individuals. O'Brien et al. (1972) divided spoon use into six steps and manually guided the child's hand through all the steps, fading the guidance backward systematically. Their task analysis of the steps and the teacher guidance included:

1. Place the spoon handle in the child's dominant hand while holding the same hand over the child's grasp;
2. Guide the spoon into the food, scoop food, and lift the spoon 1 inch above the bowl;
3. Guide the spoon to a point 2 inches from the student's mouth;
4. Open the student's mouth by applying gentle pressure on the chin;
5. Guide the spoon into the student's mouth;
6. Guide the student's hand upward and outward to remove the food against the student's upper teeth or lips.

An interruption-extinction procedure was used whenever an incorrect response occurred or when the student resorted to eating with his hands. That is, he was not allowed to put food into his mouth if he made an error while getting the food (used his hand, did not complete the step from which assistance had been faded, etc.). Instead the teacher emptied the food from his spoon or hand, cleaning the boy if necessary, and began the six-step sequence again.

The systematic fading of manual guidance proceeded as follows:

When training by manual guidance was first introduced, the teacher guided the child through all six of the steps. Whenever the sequence was completed correctly on three successive assisted trials, the child's hand was guided through one less step on the next assisted trial. Whenever an assisted trial was not completed correctly, it was interrupted and another guided trial was begun, which included one additional [guided] step. Whenever a step was eliminated [not guided], added [guided], eliminated, and added on three consecutive trials, the child's hand was guided through a point between that step and the next lower step (e.g., if step three was being added and eliminated, on the following trial the child's hand was guided to a point halfway between the bowl and her mouth). (p. 69)

Totally unguided trials were used after correct completions to probe independent performance.

This combination of manual guidance and interruption-extinction led to almost perfect independent performance after nine meals. However, O'Brien and his colleagues found that maintenance training consisting of interruption-extinction was essential to keep the student from reverting to eating without a spoon.

Azrin and Armstrong (1973) used a slightly different physical assistance (graduated guidance) and fading procedure called "hand-to-shoulder fading with constant contact." Napkin, glass, spoon, fork, and knife use were taught with this method, though one at a time and in this simple-to-complex order. To apply this method, a teacher would:

Begin guidance by having the trainer mold his hand around the student's and guide an entire response. As the student grasps the utensil himself, guidance is progressively reduced at the hand with a gentle touch. The locus of guidance is then faded up the arm to the forearm, elbow, upper arm then shoulder and upper back, always maintaining light touch unless more guidance is required. This constant contact serves as a reminder to the student that inappropriate responses will be prevented. (p. 11)

During this prompt-fade procedure, the trainer applied only enough movement assistance "to get a response going" and only enough restraint to stop an error. Verbal praise, specific to what the student was doing, was given throughout each trial. Mini-meals were served hourly. Initially, if needed, two trainers worked with a single learner—one to guide the utensil hand while the other guided the student's "lap hand" and head to prevent errors. In combination with these intensive training methods, Azrin and Armstrong (1973) applied overcorrective maintenance for errors made once a student learned to spoon-feed (or fork, etc.). For example, after a student was able to eat with a particular utensil, he cleaned up spills made with that implement. These restitutions were followed by a few positive practice trials. Therefore, spills from an overfilled spoon were first cleaned up and then the student was expected to practice scooping very small amounts of food into his spoon. With this intensive procedure, most of the 11 students learned correct utensil use in 5 days, with a few requiring 12 days of training.

The study on utensil use by Stimbert et al. (1977) replicated Azrin and Armstrong's procedures, using a single subject experimental design and a similar population. Although a similar frequency of daily training sessions was used, the subjects appeared to need an average of 29 training days (versus the 5- to 12-day range reported by Azrin and Armstrong, 1973). While the reason for these deficiencies is not clear, the trainer using these procedures should not modify the procedures, but continue their use if the skills are not mastered as rapidly as Azrin and Armstrong report.

Like Azrin and Armstrong (1973) and Stimbert et al. (1977), Albin (1977) used forward chaining on all the spoon-feeding steps; but he taught only one step at a time while totally assisting the student through the unlearned steps. With three profoundly retarded students, he successfully used a variation of graduated guidance to teach spoon use and later finger foods, fork, and bread plate use. First verbal cues plus firm hand control were used; they gradually were reduced to gentle hand control. Next verbal cues and firm wrist control were used and then replaced by gentle wrist control. After this, manual assistance was faded altogether, followed next by the discontinuation of verbal cues. Whenever the student failed to respond after 2 seconds with the level of assistance provided on a given step, a complete prompt was given. Continuous tactual reinforcement and praise was given for correctly performed steps, whether assisted or not.

At this point it should be clear that a rather wide variety of systematic procedures have been used to teach spoon usage as well as other self-feeding skills, including physical guidance (Albin, 1977; Azrin & Armstrong, 1973; Berkowitz, Sherry, & Davis, 1971; O'Brien et al., 1972), forward or backward chaining, praise and tactual reinforcement, and punishment of inappropriate behavior (which will be discussed in detail later). The more rapid and intensive procedures (e.g., Azrin & Armstrong, 1973; O'Brien et al., 1972; Stimbert et al., 1977) actually consist of a complex combination of precise techniques to schedule sessions; to shape, prompt, fade, and maintain correct responses; and to punish, ignore, and prevent errors. Most teachers may not be able to use such intensive interventions without additional help. However, simpler combinations of procedures have been effective when applied systematically (Barnard & Powell, 1972; Berkowitz et al., 1971; Christian et al., 1973; Song & Gandhi, 1974). Informal applications of a physical prompt with time delay fading (see chapter 5) indicate that this procedure may be particularly useful in place of graduated guidance. On the other hand, a system of least intrusive prompts incorporating verbal, model, and physical prompts has had only limited success with basic feeding skills (Kissel, Johnson, & Whitman, 1980), despite its documented success with more advanced daily living skills (putting on a hearing aid, housekeeping tasks, vocational assembly tasks, cooking, sewing, etc.) As discussed in chapter 5, prompting procedures must be matched to the learner's ability to respond to them. As is often the case with people needing instruction in basic feeding skills, the more sophisticated prompts of modeling or verbal instructions *without physical assistance* are not as effective as some form of physical assistance (Nelson et al., 1975).

Eating with a Fork

Although the fork grasp may be modified and its use to pick up food is different from spoon scooping, the procedures for teaching fork use are essentially identical to those for spoon use (Azrin & Armstrong, 1973; Nelson et al., 1975). Fork use should not be taught until after the student has mastered the spoon. The finger-hold, palm-up grip pictured at the top of Figure 13.13 is probably the best to teach for spearing and lifting food. Later, when fork cutting is taught, the grip will be modified and held sideways against the food (Nelson et al., 1975). To teach spearing and lifting, precut chunks or cubes of food will be needed, avoiding soupy food more appropriate for eating with a spoon. Azrin and Armstrong (1973) taught the use of one utensil at a time and did not present combinations of utensils until each utensil was learned.

Knife Usage

Table knives may be used (*a*) to transport a spread, such as butter, from one place to another, (*b*) to spread a substance on food, (*c*) to cut breads while holding the food with one hand, (*d*) to push foods onto a fork, and (*e*) with a fork to cut. These skills are taught and learned in this order.

As with spoon and fork use, Nelson et al. (1975) found that modeling was less effective than physical guidance during both instruction and correction of errors. O'Brien and Azrin (1972) and Ferneti et al. (1974) used three types of assistance to teach various knife skills and faded the assistance from manual guidance and instruction backward to modeling and instruction, to instruction only, and finally to no verbal reminders. If modeling is to be successful, the learner must be attentive and ready to imitate. The effectiveness of modeling is increased with imitative learners if they have already learned the behavior through shaping and physical guidance.

To simplify knife and fork cutting, a teacher may want to teach the continental style, which does *not* require switching the fork to the nondominant hand. To teach severely retarded individuals this method, Azrin and Armstrong (1973) first provided precut meat chunks and directed students to hold their forks in the dominant hand with tines pointed down to spear the food. Then they were instructed to pick up the knife in the other hand and use a sawing motion while stabilizing the meat with the fork. The Project MORE program for eating (Ferneti et al., 1974) suggests teaching the learner to switch the implement

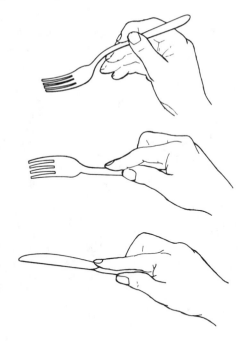

FIGURE 13.13
Correct Grips for Holding a Fork to Eat (top: palm-up finger grip) and to Cut (center), and For Spreading with a Knife (bottom)

SOURCE: "Training Correct Utensil Use in Retarded Children: Modeling vs. Physical Guidance" by G.L. Nelson, J.D. Cone, and C.R. Hanson, *American Journal of Mental Deficiency*, 1975, *80*, 115. Reprinted with permission.

from hand to hand; however, they do not provide performance data to support this recommendation with the severely handicapped.

Table Manners and Related Skills

Many inappropriate behaviors that prevent or interfere with self-feeding may occur during mealtime. For example, if a student is allowed to steal food or eat with his hands, he has little reason to learn or use the more difficult skills of utensil usage. Timeout from eating contingent upon inappropriate table behavior has been effective in improving mealtime behavior in retarded individuals (Barton et al., 1970; Christian et al., 1973; O'Brien & Azrin, 1972; Song & Gandhi, 1974). For some students a 30-second removal of the food tray is an aversive consequence strong enough to eliminate food stealing, food throwing, "pigging" or mouth stuffing, eating with hands, and inappropriately using utensils. With certain behaviors (food stealing), as with some students, tray removal is ineffective. Instead, the individual is

removed from the room for a time or for the remainder of the meal. These procedures quickly eliminate the misbehaviors (Barton et al., 1970). A successful method to reduce eating with fingers is to stop or interrupt the behavior before the individual can eat, remove the food from his hands, clean his hands, and manually guide correct spoon use (Azrin & Armstrong, 1973; O'Brien & Azrin, 1972). This interruption-extinction procedure prevents the child from reinforcing his own inappropriate responses. Finally, overcorrection and positive practice have been used to eliminate spilling and food and utensil throwing (Azrin & Armstrong, 1973).

Because of a high level of inappropriate mealtime behavior during baseline, Albin (1977) treated mealtime errors with a correction, a mild punishment, or both. For example, when a student's face came within 6 inches of the tray, the teacher said "NO!" and returned the head to an upright position. Eating with fingers was followed by a reprimand and 3 minutes in a timeout area, while spilling food, rubbing it on oneself, or pushing food off a utensil was reprimanded and the tray removed for 30 seconds. Additional instances of these behaviors during the same meal resulted in 3-minutes in timeout. A repeat of stealing terminated the meal. Once all three profoundly retarded students acquired basic eating skills and appropriate mealtime behavior, a maintenance plan was instituted. Initially staff left the eating area for 30-second intervals. Next they left for intervals of a few minutes. Then they stationed themselves in the back of the room, then moved outside an open door, and finally outside a closed door. This gradual fading of supervision enabled the students to maintain their improved mealtime behavior even under minimal supervision.

Excessively rapid eating can be a serious problem for some handicapped students because of social acceptability and potential health problems (vomiting, aspiration, and poor digestion). A survey of severely and profoundly institutionalized persons (McGimsey, Note 3) cited by Favell, McGimsey, and Jones (1980) defined "normal" eating rates as approximately eight bites per minute with total meal consumed in 15 to 20 minutes. "Rapid" eaters, however, "consumed food at rates sometimes exceeding 20 bites per minute, and finished their entire meal within 1 to 3 minutes" (p. 482).

Using a nonpunishing intervention, Favell et al. (1980) successfully reduced the eating rates of four profoundly retarded persons from an average of 10.5 bites per 30 seconds to 3 bites per 30 seconds. Other procedures such as increased meal portions, tray timeout, and removal from the dining area had failed to reduce eating rate. The successful intervention relied on two primary procedures: (*a*) social and edible reinforcement for increasingly longer unprompted pauses (up to 5 seconds) between bites; and (b) gradual reduction of physical prompts for pausing, contingent on instances of rapid eating. Once the goal was attained, a maintenance program of reinforcement and prompts for pausing was carried out by regular institutional staff. Side benefits of the training included a reduction in vomiting by one subject and sloppiness by another, appropriate weight gains in all, and an absence of misbehavior or undesirable alternatives to fast eating, such as the slower consumption of larger bites of food.

After the basics of self-feeding and utensil use are taught, a teacher should consider expanding mealtime instruction to include mixed utensil use, opening milk cartons, rotation eating (consuming small portions of the different foods in the meal in an alternating pattern), the use of salt and pepper and other condiments, passing and serving food, and other basic table manners. This advanced self-care instruction could be followed by basic cooking techniques, kitchen care, and dish-washing (described more fully in chapter 14).

The MORE eating program (Ferneti et al., 1974), Tawney (1979), Bender and Valletutti (1976), Matson et al. (1980), van den Pol et al., (1981), Marolin, O'Toole, Touchette, Berger, and Doyle (1979) and other references mentioned in chapter 14 provide task analyses and suggestions for teaching these more advanced skills. These skills are taught systematically if a teacher analyzes the skill; objectively measures student performance before, during, and after intervention; determines appropriate prompting and reinforcement procedures; uses realistic instructional materials and settings; and programs for skill maintenance and skill generalization to other eating situations.

DRESSING SKILLS

Just like eating with utensils, buttoning, snapping, buckling, zipping, lacing, and shoe tying involve refined eye-hand coordination and precise finger dexterity with controlled finger-thumb opposition. Dressing is more difficult than undressing for normal children as well as for handicapped individuals (Minge & Ball, 1967), as are buttoning, tying, snapping, etc. in contrast with unbuttoning, untying, and unsnapping.

Programs to teach dressing skills to severely handicapped individuals have involved prompting combined with shaping, backward chaining, and praise and food reinforcers. During short, daily training sessions, undressing usually has been taught before dressing. One garment is instructed at a time, beginning with loose-fitting socks, shirts, and pants and, if

part of the program, proceeding to buttons, laces, snaps, zippers, and belts (Ball, Seric, & Payne, 1971; Bensberg, 1965; Bensberg et al., 1965; Colwell, Richards, McCarver, & Ellis, 1973; Martin, Kehoe, Bird, Jensen, & Darbyshire, 1971; Minge & Ball, 1967). Although these combinations of training methods have been successful with the moderately and severely retarded, improvement in the dressing skills of institutionalized, profoundly retarded individuals taught by these traditional operant methods has been gradual. Learning is time-consuming and often temporary (Ball et al., 1971; Minge & Ball, 1967). This final section of the chapter describes dressing skill assessment and training procedures, with suggestions for improving instruction so that learning may be optimized for even the most severely handicapped individual.

Assessment

Dressing assessment involves observing a student's performance with a variety of garments, with or without increasing assistance whenever a failure is observed. Regardless of whether the assessment device allows you to evaluate the effect of prompts upon performance, it is essential that each task be stated in observable terms with specific directions so that with repeated applications you are giving the same test and results are comparable. While teacher-made assessment devices are frequently used to measure entry skills and monitor learning, a variety of criterion-referenced, informal tests and checklists may be of equal value (Ball et al., 1971; Balthazar, 1971; Behavioral Characteristics Progression, 1973; Bender & Valletutti, 1976; Copeland et al., 1976; Fredericks et al., 1975; Henderson & McDonald, 1973; McCormack, Hamlet, Dunaway, & Vorderer, 1976; Somerton & Turner, 1975; Tawney, 1979; etc.) Two of these are reviewed briefly, along with other informal methods, described earlier in chapter 4.

The dressing subscale of the *Balthazar Scales of Adaptive Behavior* (Balthazar, 1971) illustrated in Figure 13.14 uses a seven-point scoring system. Points earned are proportionate to independence in dressing and undressing. For each item, the learner is initially instructed by words and gestures to remove or put on, to fasten or unfasten, etc., each article of clothing or fastening. If the student does not begin or complete the task, a demonstration is given. Additional assistance is provided step-by-step whenever performance stops or errors occur. Therefore the learner is given credit for imitating a demonstration, for performing more than or less than half the task, and even for cooperating only by positioning his limbs. The time allowed for performance at each level of prompt is specified in Table 13.4, as is the score awarded for

Date: _____

DRESSING TALLY SHEET

Total Score	MALE ARTICLE/ACTIVITY	SCORE		FEMALE ARTICLE/ACTIVITY	SCORE	
		Right	Left		Right	Left
	Shoes			**Shoes**		
	PUT ON Shoes	1___	2___	PUT ON Shoes	1___	2___
	Tighten Laces	3___	4___	Tighten Laces	3___	4___
	Tie—single bow	5___	6___	Tie—single bow	5___	6___
	TAKE OFF Shoes	7___	8___	TAKE OFF Shoes	7___	8___
	Untie—start with a single bow	9___	10___	Untie—start with a single bow	9___	10___
	Socks			**Socks**		
	PUT ON Socks	11___	12___	PUT ON Socks	11___	12___
	TAKE OFF Socks	13___	14___	TAKE OFF Socks	13___	14___
	Pants			**Pants or Skirt**		
	PUT ON Pants		15___	PUT ON Pants or Skirt		15___
	Fasten		16___	TAKE OFF Pants or Skirt		16___
	Zip Up		17___	**Briefs**		
	Put Belt On		18___	PUT ON Briefs		17___
	Fasten Belt		19___	TAKE OFF Briefs		18___
	TAKE OFF Pants		20___	**T-Shirt/Undershirt**		
	Unfasten		21___	PUT ON T-Shirt		19___
	Unzip		22___	TAKE OFF T-Shirt		20___
	Take Belt Off		23___	**Blouse**		
	Unfasten Belt		24___	PUT ON Blouse		21___
	Briefs			Button		22___
	PUT ON Briefs		25___	TAKE OFF Blouse		23___
	TAKE OFF Briefs		26___	Unbutton		24___
	Shirt			**Dress**		
	PUT ON Shirt		27___	PUT ON Dress		25___
	Button		28___	Zip Up		26___
	TAKE OFF Shirt		29___	TAKE OFF Dress		27___
	Unbutton		30___	Unzip		28___
	T-Shirt/Undershirt			**Other:**		
				Brassiere		
	PUT ON T-Shirt		31___	PUT ON Brassiere		29___
	TAKE OFF T-Shirt		32___	TAKE OFF Brassiere		30___
		TOTAL SCORE	___		TOTAL SCORE	___

FIGURE 13.14
A Balthazar Scale for Adaptive Behavior in Dressing

SOURCE: *Balthazar Scales of Adaptive Behavior for the Profoundly and Severely Mentally Retarded, Section 1,* by E.E. Balthazar. Champaign, Ill.: Research Press, 1971.

various performances. The ability to remove and put on pants, shoes, and shirts is evaluated separately from skills in buttoning, zipping, buckling, lacing, and tying. To increase its usefulness, you should extend the Balthazar score sheet to include coats, hats, mittens, boots, bras, pantyhose, ties, etc. Although it may take some practice to obtain reliable results, it provides information relevant to selecting effective teaching strategies for each individual assessed.

Copeland et al. (1976) provide a less-structured checklist assessment of dressing skills (Figure 13.15), as well as a detailed list of steps to monitor performance during the instruction of each subtask. Their checklist allows you to note the student's particular method of completing each task (e.g., ineffectively uses flip-over method for jacket)—information that will be useful when devising a teaching procedure.

Assessment may include the related skills of discriminating front from back and inside-out from right-side-in; hanging clothes; putting away clean and dirty clothing; using a mirror to check appearance and adjust clothing; selecting clothes suitable to various occasions, seasons, and weather conditions;

and discriminating between clean and dirty (ripped, wrinkled, etc.) clothing. Although these skills will be taught only after an individual acquires the basics of dressing and undressing, each ability represents more advanced independence in self-care and may constitute a relevant goal for the older handicapped student. Assessment procedures also should include measuring skill maintenance and generalization (in various settings—in the school locker room, at home, and during summer camp—and under changing conditions—lacing boots as opposed to shoes, buttoning side and back buttons, etc.).

Again, when assessing the entry abilities of physically handicapped students, it will be helpful to obtain the assistance of a physical or occupational therapist. Positioning and support are of utmost importance; when appropriate, they will allow a more accurate measurement of the child's ability to dress or assist in dressing tasks (Campbell et al., 1977; Finnie, 1975). The related fine motor skills of grasping and releasing, when complicated by deformities, contractures, or spasticity, may need medical evaluation. These examinations will help you determine realistic goals for dressing skills and whether adaptive equip-

TABLE 13.4 Scoring Procedure for the Dressing-Undressing Scale of the Balthazar Scales of Adaptive Behavior

Score	Dressing/Undressing Performance	Testing Procedure
6	Perfect and independent	Give command and gesture, then wait 10 seconds for student to initiate. After student *finishes,* score and record time needed to complete task.
5	Imperfect but independent (e.g., shirt on backwards)	
4	Demonstration provided	If no progress is made for a second period and task still is incomplete, repeat command and gesture accompanied by a demonstration (put shirt on student, then remove). Repeat command and allow 1 minute to complete first step before giving any physical assistance.
3	Partially assisted (less than half of steps)	
2	Primarily assisted (more than half of steps)	
1	Cooperative (e.g., holds arm out for shirt sleeve)	In subsequent steps, if needed give command and allow 10 seconds for progress to begin. If no progress or if student stops, help student through that step. Remember to give student an opportunity to perform each step in every sequence listed in the manual.
0	No participation	

ment or modified clothing will increase independence.

Teaching the student to look at his hands when he tries to remove, put on, or fasten clothing is another important area that may need instruction. To obtain baseline performance, students may simply be asked to follow the cue "Look at this" while the teacher touches a garment, button, or zipper. If attending is deficient, contingent praise, pats, and possibly small food reinforcers on a more continuous schedule initially will be necessary to strengthen eye-hand behavior.

With the exception of awarding points for performance, the testing procedure used with the Balthazar dressing scale and with Copeland's assessment is similar to a multiple opportunity assessment with task analyses of dressing tasks. (This procedure and others are described in chapter 4.) If you want to individualize dressing task analyses to suit particular students and clothing rather than using prewritten ones like Balthazar's or Copeland's, it is best to avoid published assessment procedures. Instead you would write task analyses to suit the student and situation, perhaps field-test or validate the task analyses for accuracy, select the method of assessment to be used (refer to chapter 4), and proceed accordingly. Task analytic assessments, when conscienciously applied, yield the most useful information possible. Figure 13.16 illustrates an intentionally simple task analysis for removing an already unzipped jacket. The teacher chooses to use a single opportunity task analysis as

she plans to assess daily before instruction and knows this is faster than a multiple opportunity procedure but still accurate. The teacher has decided to assess and teach in the actual setting where coat removal is most relevant—near the coat hooks. In the single opportunity method, the instructional cue is given once when the student is attending, and he or she has 3 seconds to perform the first step. If no response is made during this period or if an error occurs, the assessment ends and all unperformed steps are scored as errors. However, the student is allowed to respond as long as no errors are made or no pauses longer than 3 seconds occur. If a multiple opportunity assessment had been chosen, the teacher would quickly perform each step not carried out or performed incorrectly. To avoid teaching during assessment, in neither procedure is the student's specific performance commented upon. However, the teacher would simply thank the student at the end of each assessment.

Selecting Teaching Targets

After examining the baseline performance, the teacher will choose instructional targets. The teacher should consult parents and others to determine any dressing priorities in the home or in other relevant settings. If consistent with priorities, easier skills should be targeted and taught before more difficult dependent skills. Therefore, instruction in removing a garment will precede instruction in putting on that same garment. Depending upon the amount of time

FIGURE 13.15
Test of Dressing Skills

SOURCE: *Occupational Therapy for Mentally Retarded Children,* by M. Copeland, L. Ford, and N. Solon, Baltimore: University Park Press, 1976, p. 95. © 1976 University Park Press. Reprinted with permission.

Child's name:

Date:

Pretest of Dressing Skills	Independent	Verbal Assistance	Physical Assistance	Description of Method Child Uses to Complete the Task
Undressing trousers, skirt				
1. Pushes garment from waist to ankles				
2. Pushes garment off one leg				
3. Pushes garment off other leg				
Dressing trousers, skirt				
1. Lays trousers in front of self with front side up				
2. Inserts one foot into waist opening				
3. Inserts other foot into waist opening				
4. Pulls garment up to waist				
Undressing socks				
1. Pushes sock down off heel				
2. Pulls toe of sock pulling sock off foot				
Dressing socks				
1. Positions sock correctly with heel-side down				
2. Holds sock open at top				
3. Inserts toes into sock				
4. Pulls sock over heel				
5. Pulls sock up				
Undressing cardigan				
1. Takes dominant arm out of sleeve				
2. Gets coat off back				
3. Pulls other arm from sleeve				
Dressing cardigan flip-over method				
1. Lays garment on table or floor in front of self				
2. Gets dominant arm into sleeve				
3. Other arm into sleeve				
4. Positions coat on back				
Undressing polo shirt				
1. Takes dominant arm out of sleeve				
2. Pulls garment over head				
3. Pulls other arm from sleeve				
Dressing polo shirt				
1. Lays garment in front of self				
2. Opens bottom of garment and puts arms into sleeves				
3. Pulls garment over head				
4. Pulls garment down to waist				
Undressing shoes				
1. Loosens laces				
2. Pulls shoe off heel				
3. Pulls front of shoe to pull shoe off of toes				
Dressing shoes				
1. Prepares shoe by loosening laces and pulling tongue of shoe out of the way				
2. Inserts toes into shoe				
3. Pushes shoe on over heel				

FIGURE 13.16
Teacher-Written Task Analysis for Removal of a Jacket

Teacher: Lesley Bain

Target Behavior: Remove the Jacket

Instructional Cue: "Take off your jacket."

Setting: Near coat hooks   Times: After all trips outside

Assessment Procedure: Single opportunity

STUDENT NAME AND DATE

	9-10	9-11	9-12	9-13	9-14
1. Grab the jacket (both lapels by neck)	+	–	+	+	–
2. Pull up and back	–	–	–	–	–
3. Let go	–	–	–	–	–
4. Straighten arms (at sides)	–	–	–	–	–
5. Wiggle arms (keep straight)	–	–	–	–	–
6. Grab jacket (before it falls)	–	–	–	–	–
	16%	0%	16%	16%	0%

Recording Key: + correct
 – incorrect

Criterion: 3 consecutive days 100% problems

Materials: Jacket (unbuttoned, unzipped) on student

Response Latency: 3 seconds

397

allowed for instruction, a student may be trained on a variety of targets simultaneously. Because it is easiest and often necessary to dress or undress completely during the day (gym, bedtime, etc.), a teacher and parent might determine undressing and dressing performance targets for underwear, pants, shirts, shoes, and socks as well as jackets or sweaters.

If undressing has been mastered and the student can grasp and release small objects, instruction could begin in unbuttoning and unzipping. As discussed in chapter 8, instructional objectives may be delineated for fine motor or manipulation abilities. Because improvement in grasp and release, finger-thumb opposition, and eye-hand coordination will positively influence a student's readiness to operate clothes fasteners, these fine motor activities should be scheduled before attempting to teach buttoning, zipping, and so on. Finally, visual attention during dressing may be targeted for instruction (Martin et al., 1971), as well as comprehension of clothing names. Learning both skills will speed attainment of dressing targets.

General Elements of Instruction

Teaching Times and Place

To maximize positive transfer of dressing skills, it is wise to teach in the places (bathroom, bedroom, locker room, coat area) and at least at the times when they are needed. However, to guarantee an unhurried training session, you must schedule sufficient time before the activity for which dressing and undressing are being carried out. If adequate time is alloted, you will not be tempted to overprompt to avoid being late.

Shorter training sessions of 10 to 20 minutes should be scheduled at various times throughout each day, rather than longer single sessions or sporadic training less than daily. However, Azrin, Schaeffer, and Wesolowski (1976) successfully used 3-hour sessions with profoundly retarded students where attention was prolonged by an intensive reinforcement and prompting procedure.

Teaching Materials

When working with the beginning self-dresser, success is more attainable with modified clothing. For example, some studies have used simple clothing two sizes larger than the student's usual size and without zippers and buttons (elastic waist bands, pull-over shirts) (Azrin et al., 1976; Minge & Ball, 1967). Others suggest color coding or marking clothes: the outside or front of the shirt is marked with colored tape, the right side of both shoestrings is red and the left is white (1 red and 1 white shoestring are cut in half;

each red half is joined with a white half to make the coded shoestrings).

If large buttons and buttonholes (snaps, zippers with large tabs) are taught first, the use of smaller fasteners will be learned more quickly. Kramer and Whitehurst (1981) found that retarded children could button larger buttons (38 mm) located at the top of a garment significantly more easily than smaller buttons (22 and 19 mm) in the middle or bottom of a garment. Some teachers have attached strings to front and back zippers to make pulling easier.

For some students who lack the necessary muscle control, more long-term clothing adaptations may be necessary. Velcro fasteners might replace buttons or simply be sewn beneath nonworking buttons; loose raglan sleeves, knitted fabrics, loafer shoes, elastic waistbands, and tubular socks without heels will present fewer dressing problems (Finnie, 1975).

While button, snap, and zipper boards or dolls with clothing seem to be useful, skill generalization may be a problem for the severely handicapped learner. The buttoning task is quite different when buttoning another's buttons, and zipping up a zipper attached to a horizontal board is not the same as looking down on a zipper. These materials should be used sparingly or replaced with "dress-up" or regular clothes with enlarged fasteners. As long as a training wooden shoe is positioned with toe facing away from the child, lacing and tying practice with it may not result in transfer problems. However, in the interest of generalization, it makes the most sense simply to use the student's own shoe.

Basic Methods to Teach Self-Dressing

Encouraging Active Involvement

Before teaching the learner the first independent steps in self-dressing, you should encourage active participation when the parent or teacher is dressing or undressing the child. Active participation means extending hands, arms, or feet in anticipation of being dressed or undressed, looking at or reaching for garments and body parts that are named and gestured toward by the teacher, and cooperating by moving limbs into or out of garments, as well as not resisting limb movement during dressing.

To teach these beginning dressing skills, you must create an unhurried, positive atmosphere during dressing times. Clothes should be pointed to and labeled repeatedly with simple phrases used to describe the activity (e.g., "Let's put on your shirt"). If the student's attention is not directed toward a particular garment before it is put on or removed, prompt attention by turning the student's head, moving the garment into view, or shaking it. At this time the garment should be labeled and the looking behavior reinforced with praise, hugs, noise toys (e.g., music box for a few seconds), or bits of food if necessary, making sure that reinforcers are suitable for the student's chronological age.

Once the learner demonstrates more visual attending to the teacher and garment, you could prompt her to move her limbs appropriately. During dressing this is done by holding the garment next to the corresponding limb (e.g., sock by foot) when the student is attending, and physically prompting movement of that limb in the direction of the garment. Getting the learner to push limbs into garments (or pull out of) is done by pushing the garment onto the extended limb in short, gently abrupt movements, allowing the student opportunity to push (or pull away from) between movements. Any beginning efforts should be encouraged.

The position of the student during dependent dressing should allow plenty of support, especially if he is weak in balance, unable to stand or sit, or has lack of muscle control (as with cerebral palsy). Finnie (1975) suggests that the younger athetoid student and the spastic student be laid tummy down across the teacher's lap to decrease the tendency to stiffen encouraged by a backlying position. As the physically handicapped individual grows larger, lying on one side will prevent the head from bending forward. If the student has some head and neck control, it might be best to support him from the back in a sitting position but at the hips with knees apart and bent and trunk well forward to maintain balance. Slippery sitting surfaces or pants should be avoided so that there is some friction between the student's buttocks and the seat, assuring stability. Once again, consult the advice of a physical or occupational therapist so that the teaching position may be individually prescribed. Additionally, chapter 7, Connor et al. (1978), Campbell et al. (1977), Finnie (1975), and Sternat, Messina, Lyon, and Nietupski (1977) are useful references.

Finnie (1975) provides some guidelines for dressing the cerebral palsied student.

1. Help the learner dress or undress the more affected arm or leg first.
2. Working from behind the seated child, try to position him symmetrically so the head is centered; this will allow more uniform ease in bending the limbs on both sides.
3. If a child has fallen too far forward while in a supported seated position, help him to a more upright angle (but still well forward) *before* beginning to dress.
4. To decrease stiffening of the foot and toes, bend

the child's leg before putting on shoes and socks.
5. Straighten the child's arm before putting on a sleeve; avoid pulling his fingers to get the arm through the sleeve as this causes the elbow to bend.
6. If a pillow is placed beneath the hips and head when changing diapers, the task of bending the hips and knees and keeping the knees together becomes easier. (pp. 94–95)

Applying "Partial Participation"

At times it will not be realistic to expect students to master all the steps in dressing (or other self-care tasks) due to motor impairments. For example, John has spastic cerebral palsy so severe that limited grasping is possible with only one hand; his upper mobility will allow him to perform some but not all of the steps in removing and putting on his shirt, which is required at least twice daily. In cases like John's, it is most appropriate to offer personal assistance on the steps he will be unable to perform, while teaching him to carry out the steps he can learn. Listed below are the steps in an adapted version of putting on a shirt suited to John's abilities. The steps prefaced with "teacher" are performed by the trainer, while steps written in **boldface** are taught to the student. Note that the weaker arm is placed into the shirt first. Adaptation of dressing task analyses for partial participation requires close consultation with an occupational therapist as well as subsequent field testing.

1. Teacher: "Put your shirt on."
2. Teacher positions shirt sleeve.
3. **Student lifts weak arm.**
4. Teacher slips shirt over wrist to elbow.
5. **Student grabs shirt sleeve with strong arm.**
6. **Student pulls shirt over elbow to shoulder.**
7. Teacher positions shirt neck on student's head.
8. **Student pulls shirt down over head.**
9. Teacher inserts student's strong hand into shirt sleeve.
10. **Student extends arm until shirt pops onto shoulder.**
11. Teacher pulls the shirt into place over student's body.[8]

This practice of partial participation allows a person to perform to the greatest extent he or she is capable

---

[8]This and other partial participation task analyses were contributed by Trice Lewis and Kathy Griffiths, teacher and graduate assistant in a community-based instruction program classroom at Woodbrook Elementary School in Charlottesville, Va.

of rather than promoting total dependence (Brown et al., 1979).

While there are many instances in which partial participation can be applied, the most frequently relevant to dressing tasks involve the use of personal assistance (such as with John) and adaptation of the skill sequence being taught (Baumgart, Brown, Pumpian, Nisbet, Ford, Sweet, Ranieri, Hansen, & Schroeder, 1980). To illustrate the latter instance, Baumgart et al. (1980) cite the routine task of using the toilet and the student who has extreme difficulty in motor skills and balance. When normally coordinated people perform this task, they just lower their pants and then sit down. However, this sequence of skills is rarely possible for those with balance problems. Instead, if the student is helped to transfer from her wheelchair to the toilet first and then lowers her pants, more independent toilet use may occur. Practicing partial participation in self-help instruction means maximizing each student's *useful* participation in the essential and routine tasks of dressing, eating, toileting, and grooming. This leads to reduced dependence upon others, which in turn is likely to increase the student's self-esteem as well as the respect received from others (Brown et al., 1979). (Chapter 4 elaborates upon this discussion of partial participation.)

Taking Off and Putting on Garments

The most common method for teaching a severely handicapped individual to undress or dress involves backward chaining. In this procedure the teacher first analyzes the dressing sequence into a series of small steps, as in Figure 13.16. Then the student is asked to remove the garment and is physically assisted through all the steps except the last step (e.g., grabs jacket before it falls). At this point the teacher encourages the learner to perform the last step by one or more of the following procedures: giving a direction ("Take off your jacket") while gesturing or touching the garment, demonstrating the last step on the learner or on the teacher and allowing the learner to imitate, or applying varying amounts of physical assistance. Praise and tangible reinforcers are given after completion. Training continues until the learner carries out the last step without any assistance. Then training is directed toward the next-to-last step by providing assistance and gradually fading it over trials. The learner continues to perform learned steps without help. Reinforcement is provided after the chain is completed. Gradually the learner learns each successive step until a single garment can be removed when requested. As illustrated by Figure 13.17, these general methods have been used to teach moderately and severely retarded individuals to undress as well as to dress (Baldwin, Fredericks, & Brodsky, 1973; Ball

et al., 1971; Bensberg, 1965; Bensberg et al., 1965; Colwell et al., 1973; Linford et al., 1972; Martin et al., 1971; Minge & Ball, 1967).

Forward chaining, which may be used to teach these same skills, has been applied less often (Azrin et al., 1976). The decision to use forward or backward chaining rests upon an understanding of the two processes, the skill being taught, and the performance of the student (Copeland et al., 1976). Forward chaining, described more fully in chapter 5, progresses from teaching the first step to the second, third, and so on in a manner similar to that for backward chaining. One difference occurs with the timing of reinforcement; though praise is given after successful performance of the teaching step, more extensive reinforcement is provided at the end of the chain after the student is assisted through all the unlearned steps. If a student's baseline performance shows more success early in the chain, then forward chaining may proceed more quickly than backward chaining. However, backward chaining has the advantage of associating reinforcement with task completion. Again forward and backward chaining also may be used together to teach dressing skills. Forward chaining is used at the beginning of the dressing or undressing sequence and advances forward while backward chaining starts at the end and proceeds backward over successive teaching sessions.

If the teacher elects to instruct one undressing skill at a time using forward or backward chaining, each daily session should begin with a review of the step just mastered rather than a new step. Assistance would be provided for the learned step, if needed, then faded before trying to teach the next step in the chain. The chain may be divided into more steps if a student has difficulty when prompts are faded on any single step. At this early stage of dressing instruction, loose, simple clothing should be used, preferably without zippers, hooks, or buttons. If fasteners are present, they should be opened and closed for the student since training at this stage focuses on the less-complicated skills of clothing removal and replacement.

Because the methods just described take weeks or months to produce functional skills, Azrin et al. (1976) developed a concentrated method for rapidly teaching these skills to profoundly retarded students. Dressing skills were taught after undressing skills had been mastered. However, each student learned to remove (and put on) five garments from outer- to underwear as an entire sequence (shoes, socks, pants, underpants, and shirt) rather than learning to remove one garment at a time. If a student had difficulty with one or two of the five garments, intensive training centered primarily on these garments. Seven students taught by this method learned to put on and remove

FIGURE 13.17

Learning to remove and hang up a coat and sweater independently will require some verbal demonstrative instruction by the teacher as well as lots of praise for improvements in performance. Soon John will be as independent as Glynis in his ability to remove and hang up a coat.

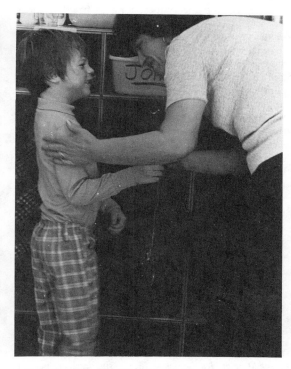

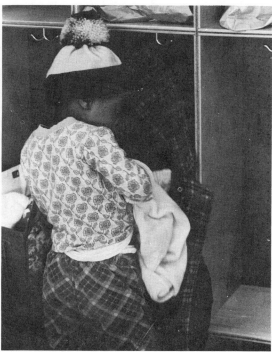

all five garments after a median training time of 10 hours or over 2 days.

This rapid success resulted from a combination of intense training techniques: long instructional sessions (3 hours); the instruction of all steps simultaneously in a forward progression; extensive use of manual guidance early in learning, which was graduated in intensity to match the student's responsiveness; systematic application and fading of prompts; continuous use of praise and stroking contingent upon any effort to follow instructions or guidance; the requirement of visual attention to the task; and the initial involvement of two trainers so that praise, stroking, and manual guidance could be provided. Azrin and his coworkers used slip-on clothing without fasteners which initially was two sizes larger than the student's regular clothes. After only touch assistance was needed to begin performance of the chain, clothing one size smaller was substituted. Students were taught to dress and undress while seated and to use both hands for all movements. Prompts were gradually increased until successful performance occurred.

The first instruction for each garment was simply verbal. If a few seconds passed with no action, the trainer pointed at or touched the garment. After a few seconds, the instruction was repeated and the trainer molded the student's hands around the garment. If a student still was not participating, the trainer then described each movement the student was to make as he guided the hands through the necessary motion. The instructions were very specific. This procedure provided multisensory information: verbal, visual, auditory, and tactual. (p. 30)

After manual guidance was faded for a garment, another student was encouraged to perform with pointing and instructional cues provided every 10 seconds as needed. If the response was not completed in 1 minute, manual guidance was reapplied. Some students, especially during early acquisition, resisted manual guidance. Although the trainer's hands were cupped around the student's, who in turn held the garment, the student was not forced to respond. After the student relaxed his resistance, manual graduated guidance was gently reinstated. As with methods to teach toileting and eating, Azrin and his coworkers have combined some of the best elements from the teaching technology to produce an instructional procedure that has yielded successful and swift results with profoundly retarded learners. While this method was not tested with physically handicapped retarded learners, such a rich combination of instructional elements applied under the direction of a physical or occupational therapist has potential for producing some skill development (Azrin et al., 1976, p. 33).

Fasteners

Skills in unfastening should be mastered before fastening. When oversized fasteners, visible to the learner, are used as the teaching materials, fastener instruction probably increases in complexity across the following skills: zipping (with front-opening zipper already securely attached at bottom), snapping (large, plastic snaps), buttoning, hooking, buckling. Learning to align the zipper tab with the zipper end on a front-opening jacket and to fasten buttons, snaps, or hooks located out of direct view is difficult for the handicapped (as well as for normal learners) and will be taught after the simple fasteners are mastered. Copeland et al. (1976), Linford et al. (1972), and Tawney (1979) provide useful task analyses of these skills with suggestions for teaching. For example, zipping unconnected front-opening jackets may be divided into seven steps, which Copeland suggests be taught with forward chaining.

1. First the learner grasps zipper tab and moves the slider with the dominant hand to the bottom of the track.
2. Then the pin is grasped between nondominant finger and thumb and is inserted into the slider (while holding onto both sides of the closure at the bottom).
3. The pin is pushed firmly into the slider box.
4. Nondominant hand grasps both sides of closure at bottom with thumb placed across zipper box (held through step 6).
5. With dominant hand the zipper tab is grasped.
6. Zipper tab is pulled up to top stop.
7. Zipper tab released and pushed with index finger to lock into position.

Some teachers will prefer subdividing the first two steps, while others may not teach the last step of locking the zipper. If a pull string is added to the zipper tab, the task is somewhat easier and the steps are modified slightly.

As illustrated by this example, hand dominance influences the teaching procedure. Hand dominance, if unknown, can be determined by simple observation during eating and play. Or the learner may be handed objects at midline while noting how often right- and left-hand grasps are used. To illustrate the importance of hand dominance, belt-buckling is easier if the learner is taught to grasp the buckle with the dominant hand and the strap with his other hand (Copeland et al., 1976). However, with the changing position of buttons and snaps, the matching of dominant hand to the logically dominant side of the task may create a problem. The position of buttons and buttonholes as well as bottom-fitting (under snap) and top-fitting snaps (over snap) is one way on boy's clothing and the opposite for girls. In boy's clothing, buttons are on the right edge and holes on the left, while bottom snaps are on the right and the top half is positioned on the left edge. The opposite arrangement occurs with girl's clothing. Since it may be easier to teach a child to grasp buttons as well as bottom snaps in the dominant hand (Copeland et al., 1976), boy's clothing would provide the appropriate arrangement for right handers while girl's clothing would be more suited to left handers. However, each sex must learn to fasten the corresponding clothing and perhaps learning both arrangements is best. Because the research is scanty in this area, girls and boys should begin on their own clothing, regardless of dominance and fastener arrangement. All beginning learning should involve the same arrangement of buttons, holes, and snaps. Once one arrangement is mastered, training could be provided with the opposite arrangement. However, if a child appears to be making slow progress during early learning and his hand dominance is not matched to the position of buttons on his clothing, you may want to try the opposite arrangement.

Shoe Tying

Baldwin et al. (1973), Copeland et al. (1976), Linford et al. (1972), and Martin et al. (1971) describe two nontraditional methods of teaching shoe tying to handicapped learners. The "rabbit ear" method involves tying a single knot, then forming two loops which are then tied together in another single knot (Figure 13.18). Martin and his coworkers used another procedure to teach the same skill: (a) tying a single knot, (b) tying a second knot which is not pulled tight, (c) making one loop by inserting one lace end into the hole between the knots. (d) pulling it to form a small loop, repeating steps (c) and (d) with the second lace end, and (e) grasping both loops and pulling the bow tight. (Refer to Figure 13.19.) While there are data supporting the use of this method with the severely retarded (Martin et al., 1971), the "rabbit ear" method, though reportedly used with the same population (Baldwin et al., 1973; Copeland et al., 1976; Linford et al., 1972), lacks such data.

The traditional method (single knot, form loop with one lace, wrap free lace around loop, etc.) is recommended less often for handicapped learners. This could be because of its nonsymmetrical formation as compared with the two untraditional methods—each lace is manipulated in a different way. Regardless of the method selected, the learner should be taught to untie bows and single knots first, then to tie single knots, and finally to tie bows.

Because of the complexity of shoe tying and the necessity of precise finger control, some handicapped learners should probably wear nontying shoes and

FIGURE 13.18
This teacher is using a backward chaining procedure to teach her student the traditional method of shoe tying. Jayne verbally instructs and manually helps Maude as needed with each step: tying a simple knot, making a loop with one lace, wrapping the free lace around the loop, switching position of fingers, pulling the second loop out through the opening, and pulling both loops tight. In the bottom picture, which illustrates the last step, Jayne has faded out her manual assistance by letting Maude tighten the bow on her own.

learning time should be directed to skills of a higher priority with a greater likelihood for success.

ADVANCED SELF-CARE ABILITIES

This chapter has discussed basic self-care. However, many field-tested instructional programs for teaching more advanced skills are available. The results of successful instruction in hair-washing, toothbrushing, and other aspects of self-care are illustrated in Figure 13.20.

Chapter 14 reviews the recent research in grooming, clothing selection, and clothing care (mending and washing). Other useful references in grooming instruction include Baker, Brightman, Heifetz, and Murphy (1976a, 1976b, and 1976c), *Be-*

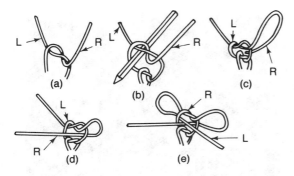

FIGURE 13.19
*Diagram of Steps for Tying a Bow. The letters "L"
and "R" indicate the hands (left or right) of the subject
that are holding the laces at the head of the arrows.*

SOURCE: "Operant Conditioning in Dressing Behavior of
Severely Retarded Girls" by G.L. Martin, B. Keogh, E.
Bird, V. Jensen, and M. Darbyshire, *Mental Retardation,*
1971, *9* (3), 29. Reprinted with permission.

havioral Characteristics Progression (1973), Bender
and Valletutti (1976), Copeland et al. (1976), Mc-
Cormack et al., (1976), and Tawney (1979). In addition, you may consult the following references for
teaching tooth-brushing and dental care (Abramson
& Wunderlich, 1972; Fowler, Johnson, Whitman, &
Zukotynski, 1978; Horner, Billionis, & Lent, 1975;
Horner & Keilitz, 1975; Tawney, 1979); nose-
blowing (Ingenthron, Ferneti, & Keilitz, 1975; Tawney, 1979); hand-washing (Stevens, Ferneti, & Lent,
1975; Tawney, 1979), use of deodorant (Lewis, Ferneti, & Keilitz, 1975b), complexion care (Fowler et
al., 1978; Keilitz, Horner, & Brown, 1975), hair-
washing (Fowler et al., 1978; Lewis, Ferneti, & Keilitz, 1975a), and sex education (Bender & Valletutti,
1976; Hamilton, Allen, Stephens, & Davall, 1969;
Hamre & Williams, 1974; Kempton, 1975).

SUMMARY

This chapter describes procedures to assess and teach
the basic self-care skills of independent toileting, eating, and dressing. It comments extensively on in-

FIGURE 13.20
*Hand-washing and tooth-brushing instruction can begin early and should include teacher demonstration. More
advanced grooming skills can best be taught in conjunction with a physical education program such as swimming.
Those skills include showering, hair-washing, -drying and -styling, skin and nail care, and, for girls, hygiene during
menstruation.*

structional prompts, shaping procedures, and materials, with a review of the research on teaching self-care skills to the moderately and severely handicapped.

The extent to which an individual attains independence in basic self-care clearly will influence his or her inclusion in educational programs, social activities, and vocational opportunities and certainly will affect the amount of time available to the parent and teacher and the self-esteem of the individual. The volume of research directed toward self-care instruction has been productive in providing methodological guidelines for parents and teachers. If educational programs individualize this information and successfully implement this technology, independence in the basic self-care abilities of the handicapped will be maximized.

REFERENCES

Abramson, E.E., & Wunderlich, R.A. Dental hygiene training for retardates: An application of behavioral techniques. *Mental Retardation*, 1972, *10*(3), 6–8.

Albin, J.B. Some variables influencing the maintenance of acquired self-feeding behavior in profoundly retarded children. *Mental Retardation*, 1977, *15*(5), 49–52.

Altshuler, A., Meyer, J., & Butz, M. Even children can do clean self-catheterization. *American Journal of Nursing*, 1977, *77*, 97–101.

Azrin, N.H., & Armstrong, P.M. The "mini-meal"—A method for teaching eating skills to the profoundly retarded. *Mental Retardation*, 1973, *11*(1), 9–11.

Azrin, N.H., Bugle, C., & O'Brien, F. Behavioral engineering: Two apparatuses for toilet training retarded children. *Journal of Applied Behavioral Analysis*, 1971, *4*, 249–253.

Azrin, N.H., & Foxx, R.M. A rapid method of toilet training the institutionalized retarded. *Journal of Applied Behavior Analysis*, 1971, *4*, 89–99.

Azrin, N.H. & Foxx, R.M. *Toilet training in less than a day*. New York: Simon & Schuster, 1974.

Azrin, N.H., Schaeffer, R.M., & Wesolowski, M.D. A rapid method of teaching profoundly retarded persons to dress by a reinforcement-guidance method. *Mental Retardation*, 1976, *14*(6), 29–33.

Azrin, N.H., Sneed, T.J., & Foxx, R.M. Dry bed: A rapid method of eliminating bedwetting (enuresis) of the retarded. *Behavior Research and Therapy*, 1973, *11*, 427–434.

Azrin, N.H., Sneed, T.J., & Foxx, R.N. Dry-bed training: Rapid elimination of childhood enuresis. *Behavior Research and Therapy*, 1974, *12*, 147–156.

Baker, B.L., Brightman, A.J., Heifetz, L.J., & Murphy, D.M. *Early self-help skills*. Champaign, Ill.: Research Press, 1976. (a)

Baker, B.L., Brightman, A.J., Heifetz, L.J., & Murphy, D.M. Intermediate self-help skills. Champaign, Ill.: Research Press, 1976. (b)

Baker, B.L., Brightman, A.J., Heifetz, L.J., & Murphy, D.M. *Advanced self-help skills*. Champaign, Ill.: Research Press, 1976. (c)

Baldwin, V.L., Fredericks, H.D.B., & Brodsky, G. *Isn't it time he outgrew this? or, A training program for parents of retarded children*. Springfield, Ill.: Charles C Thomas, 1973.

Ball, T.S., Seric, K., & Payne, L.E. Long-term retention of self-help skill training in the profoundly retarded. *American Journal of Mental Deficiency*. 1971, *76*, 378–382.

Baller, W.R. *Bed-wetting: Origins and treatment*. New York: Pergamon Press, 1975.

Balthazar, E.E. *Balthazar scales of adaptive behavior for the profoundly and severely retarded, Section 1*. Champaign, Ill.: Research Press, 1971.

Banerdt, B., & Bricker, D. A training program for selected self-feeding skills for the motorically impaired. *AAESPH Review*, 1978, *3*, 222–229.

Barmann, B.C., Katz, R.C., O'Brien, F., & Beauchamp, K.L. Treating irregular enuresis in developmentally disabled persons. *Behavior Modification*, 1981, *5*, 336–346.

Barnard, K.E., & Powell, M.L. *Teaching the mentally retarded child, a family care approach*. St. Louis: C.V. Mosby, 1972.

Barton, E.S., Guess, D., Garcia, E., & Baer, D.M. Improvement of retardates' mealtime behaviors by timeout procedures using multiple baseline techniques. *Journal of Applied Behavior Analysis*, 1970, *3*, 77–84.

Baumeister, A., & Klosowski, R. An attempt to group train severely retarded patients. *Mental Retardation*, 1965, *3*, 24–26.

Baumgart, D., Brown, L., Pumpian, I., Nisbet, J., Ford, A., Sweet, M., Ranieri, L., Hansen, L., & Schroeder, J. The principle of partial participation and individualized adaptations in educational programs for severely handicapped students. In L. Brown, M. Falvey, I. Pumpian, D. Baumgart, J. Nisbet, A. Ford, J. Schroeder, & R. Loomis (Eds.), *Curricular strategies for teaching severely handicapped students functional skills in school and non-school environments*. Madison: University of Wisconsin and Madison Metropolitan School District, 1980.

Behavioral characteristics progression, Palo Alto, Calif.: Vort Corp., 1973.

Bender, M., & Valletutti, P.J. *Teaching the moderately and severely handicapped* (Vol. 1). Baltimore: University Park Press, 1976.

Bensberg, G.J. (Ed.). *Teaching mentally retarded children*. Atlanta: Southern Regional Educational Board, 1965.

Bensberg, G.J., Colwell, C.N., & Cassel, R.H. Teaching the profoundly retarded self-help activities by behavior shaping techniques. *American Journal of Mental Deficiency*, 1965, *69*, 674–679.

Berkowitz, S., Sherry, P.J., & Davis, B.A. Teaching self-feeding skills to profound retardates using reinforcement and fading procedures. *Behavior Therapy*, 1971, *2*, 62–67.

Bettison, S., Davidson, D., Taylor, P., & Fox, B. The long-term effects of a toilet training programme for the retarded: A pilot study. *Australian Journal of Mental Deficiency*, 1976, *4*, 28–35.

Bigge, J.L. Self care. In J.L. Bigge (Ed.), *Teaching individuals with physical and multiple disabilities* (2nd ed.). Columbus, Ohio: Charles E. Merrill, 1982.

Bollard, R.J., & Woodroffe, P. The effect of parent-administered dry-bed training on nocturnal enuresis in children. *Behavior Research & Therapy*, 1977, *15*, 159–165.

Bowman, M., Calkin, A.B., & Grant, P.A. *Eating with a spoon: How to teach your multi-handicapped child*. Columbus: Ohio State University, National Center on Educational Media and Materials for the Handicapped, 1975.

Bricker, W.A., & Campbell, P.H. Interdisciplinary programming. In W. Sailor, L. Brown, & B. Wilcox (Eds.), *Teaching the severely handicapped*. Baltimore: Paul H. Brookes, 1980.

Brown, L., Branston-McClean, M.B., Baumgart, D., Vincent, L., Falvey, M., & Schroeder, J. Using the characteristics of current and subsequent least restrictive environments in the development of curricular content for severely handicapped students. *AAESPH Review*, 1979, *4*, 407–424.

Butler, J.F. The toilet training success of parents after reading 'Toilet training in less than a day,' *Behavior Therapy*, 1976, *1*, 185–191.

Campbell, P.H. Assessing oral-motor skills in severely handicapped persons: An analysis of normal and abnormal patterns of movement. In R.L. York and E. Edgar (Eds.), Teaching the severely handicapped (Vol. IV). Seattle: American Association for the Education of the Severely/Profoundly Handicapped, 1979.

Campbell, P.H., Green, K.M., & Carlson, L.M. Approximating the norm through environmental and child-centered prosthetics and adaptive equipment. In E. Sontag, J. Smith, & N. Certo (Eds.), *Educational programming for the severely and profoundly handicapped*, Reston, Va.: Council for Exceptional Children, 1977.

Cheever, R.C., & Elmer, C.D. *Bowel management programs*. Bloomington, Ill.: Accent Press, 1975.

Christian, W.P., Hollomon, S.W., & Lanier, C.L. An attendent operated feeding program for severely and profoundly retarded females. *Mental Retardation*, 1973, *11*(5), 35–37.

Close, D.W., Irvin, L.K., Prehm, H.J., & Taylor, V.E. Systematic correction procedures in vocational-skill training of severely retarded individuals. *American Journal of Mental Deficiency*, 1978, *83*, 270–275.

Colwell, C.N., Richards, E., McCarver, R.B., & Ellis, N.R. Evaluation of self-help habit training of the profoundly retarded. *Mental Retardation*, 1973, *11*(3), 14–18.

Connor, F.P., Williamson, G.G., & Siepp, J.M. (Eds.). *Program guide for infants and toddlers with neuromotor and other developmental disabilities*. New York: Teachers College Press, 1978.

Coote, M.A. Apparatus for conditioning treatment of enuresis. *Behavior Research and Therapy*, 1965, *2*, 233–238.

Copeland, M., Ford, L., & Solon, N. *Occupational therapy for mentally retarded children*. Baltimore: University Park Press, 1976.

Dayan, M. Toilet training retarded children in a state residential institution. *Mental Retardation*, 1964, *2*, 116–117.

Doleys, D.M., & Arnold, S. Treatment of childhood encopresis: Full cleanliness training. *Mental Retardation*, 1975, *13*(6), 14–16.

Ellis, N.R. Toilet training the severely defective patient: An S-R reinforcement analysis. *American Journal of Mental Deficiency*, 1963, *68*, 98–103.

Favell, J.E., McGimsey, J.F., & Jones, M.L. Rapid eating in the retarded: Reduction by nonaversive procedures. *Behavior Modification*, 1980, *4*, 481–492.

Ferneti, C.L., Lent, J.R., & Stevens, C.J. *Project MORE: Eating*. Bellevue, Wash.: Edmark, 1974.

Finnie, N.R. (Ed.). *Handling the young cerebral palsied child at home* (2nd ed.). New York: E.P. Dutton, 1975.

Forrest, D. Management of bladder and bowel in spina bifida. In G. Brocklehurst (Ed.), *Spina bifida for the clinician: Developmental medicine and child neurology*. (Sup. No. 57). Philadelphia: Lippincott, 1976.

Fowler, S.A., Johnson, M.R., Whitman, T.L., & Zukotynski, G. Teaching a parent in the home to train self-help skills and increase compliance in her profoundly retarded adult daughter. *AAESPH Review*, 1978, *3*, 151–160.

Foxx, R.M., & Azrin, N.H. Dry pants: A rapid method of toilet training children. *Behavior Research and Therapy*, 1973, *11*, 435–442. (a)

Foxx, R.M., & Azrin, N.H. *Toilet training the retarded: A rapid program for day and nighttime independent toileting*. Champaign, Ill.: Research Press, 1973. (b)

Foxx, R.M., & Azrin, N.H. *Toilet training in less than a day*. New York: Simon & Schuster, 1974.

Fredericks, H.D.B., Baldwin, V.L., Grove, D.N., & Moore, W.G. *Toilet training the handicapped child*. Monmouth, Ore.: Instructional Development Corporation, 1975.

Giles, D.K., & Wolf, M.M. Toilet training institutionalized severe retardates: An application of operant behavior modification techniques. *American Journal of Mental Deficiency*, 1966, *70*, 766–780.

Hamilton, J., Allen, P., Stephens, L., & Davall, E. Training mentally retarded females to use sanitary napkins. *Mental Retardation*, 1969, *7*(1), 40–43.

Hamilton, S. *My child has an ostomy*. Los Angeles: United Ostomy Association, 1974.

Hamre, S., & Williams, W. Family-life curriculum. In L. Brown, W. Williams, & T. Crowner (Eds.), *A collection of papers and programs related to public school services for severely handicapped students* (Vol. IV). Madison: University of Wisconsin, 1974.

Hanson, M.J. *Teaching your Down's Syndrome infant: A guide for parents*. Baltimore: University Park Press, 1977.

Hanson, M., & Campbell, P. *Teaching your motor delayed child*. Baltimore: University Park Press, in press.

Henderson, S., & McDonald, M. *Step-by-step dressing*. Champaign, Ill.: Suburban Publications, 1973.

Herreshoff, J.K. Two electronic devices for toilet training. *Mental Retardation*, 1973, *11*(6), 54–55.

Holser-Buehler, P. The Blanchard method of feeding the cerebral palsied. *American Journal of Occupational Therapy*, 1966, *20*, 31–34.

Horner, R.D., Billionis, C.S., & Lent, J.R. *Project MORE: Toothbrushing*. Bellevue, Wash.: Edmark, 1975.

Horner, R.D., & Keilitz, I. Training mentally retarded adolescents to brush their teeth. *Journal of Applied Behavior Analysis*, 1975, *8*, 301–309.

Hundziak, M., Maurer, R.A., & Watson, L.S. Operant conditioning in toilet training of severely retarded boys. *American Journal of Mental Deficiency*, 1965, *70*, 120–124.

Ingenthron, D., Ferneti, C.L., & Keilitz, I. *Project MORE: Nose blowing*. Bellevue, Wash.: Edmark, 1975.

Jones, G.H. The behavioral treatment of enuresis nocturna. In H.J. Eysenck (Ed.), *Behavior therapy and the neuroses*. Oxford: Pergamon Press, 1960.

Keilitz, I., Horner, R.D., & Brown, K.H. *Project MORE: Complexion care*. Bellevue, Wash.: Edmark, 1975.

Kempton, W. *Sex education for persons with disabilities that hinder learning: A teacher's guide*. Belmont, Calif.: Wadsworth, 1975.

Kimbell, D.L., Luckey, R.E., Barberto, P.F., & Love, J.G. Operation dry pants: An intensive habit-training program for the severely and profoundly retarded. *Mental Retardation*, 1967, *5*(2), 32–36.

Kissel, R.C., Johnson, M.R., & Whitman, T.L. Training a retarded client's mother and teacher through sequenced instructions to establish self feeding. *Journal of the Association for the Severely Handicapped*, 1980, *5*, 382–394.

Kolvin, I. Enuresis in childhood. *Practitioner*, 1975, *214*, 33–45.

Kramer, L., & Whitehurst, C. Effects of button features on self-dressing in young retarded children. *Education and Training of the Mentally Retarded*, 1981, *16*, 277–283.

Lancioni, G.E. Teaching independent toileting to profoundly retarded deaf-blind children. *Behavior Therapy*, 1980, *11*, 234–244.

Lancioni, G.E., & Ceccarani, P.S. Teaching independent toileting within the normal daily program: Two studies with profoundly retarded children. *Behavior Research of Severe Developmental Disabilities*, 1981, *2*, 79–96.

Lemke, H., & Mitchell, R.D. Controlling the behavior of a profoundly retarded child: A self-feeding program. *American Journal of Occupational Therapy*, 1972, *26*, 261–264.

Levine, M.N., & Elliot, C.B. Toilet training for profoundly retarded with a limited staff. *Mental Retardation*, 1970, *8*(3), 48–50.

Lewis, P.J., Ferneti, C.L., & Keilitz, I. *Project MORE: Hair washing*. Bellevue, Wash.: Edmark, 1975. (a)

Lewis, P.J., Ferneti, C.L., & Keilitz, I., *Project MORE: Use of deodorant*. Bellevue, Wash.: Edmark, 1975. (b)

Linford, M.D., Hipsher, L.W., & Silikovitz, R.G. *Systematic instruction for retarded children: The Illinois program. Part III: Self-help instruction*. Danville, Ill.: Interstate, 1972.

Lohman, W., Eyman, R., & Lask, E. Toilet training. *American Journal of Mental Deficiency*, 1967, *71*, 551–557.

Lovibond, S.H. The mechanism of conditioning treatment of enuresis. *Behavior Research and Therapy*, 1963, *1*, 17–21.

Lovibond, S.H. *Conditioning and enuresis*. New York: Macmillan, 1964.

Macey, P.G. *Mobilizing multiply-handicapped children: A manual for the design and construction of modified wheelchairs*. Lawrence: University of Kansas, Division of Continuing Education, 1974.

Mahoney, K., VanWagenen, R.K., & Meyerson, L. Toilet training of normal and retarded children. *Journal of Applied Behavior Analysis*, 1971, *4*, 173–181.

Marholin, II, D., O'Toole, K.M., Touchette, P.E., Berger, P.L., & Doyle, D.A. "I'll have a Big Mac, large fries, large Coke, and apple pie," . . . or teaching adaptive community skills. *Behavior Therapy*, 1979, *10*, 236–248.

Marshall, G.R. Toilet training of an autistic eight-year-old through conditioning therapy: A case report. *Behavior Research and Therapy*, 1966, *4*, 242–245.

Martin, G.L., Kehoe, B., Bird, E., Jensen, V., & Darbyshire, M. Operant conditioning in dressing behavior of severely retarded girls. *Mental Retardation*, 1971, *9*(3), 27–30.

Matson, J.L. Some practical considerations for using the Foxx and Azrin method of toilet training. *Psychological Reports*, 1975, *37*, 350.

Matson, J.L., Ollendick, T.H., & Adkins, J. A comprehensive dining program for mentally retarded adults. *Behavior Research and Therapy*, 1980, *18*, 107–112.

McCormack, J.E., Hamlet, C.C., Dunaway, J., & Vorderer, L.E. *Educational evaluation and planning package* (Vol. 1). Medford: Massachusetts Center for Program Development and Evaluation, 1976.

Minge, M.R., & Ball, T.S. Teaching of self-help skills to profoundly retarded patients. *American Journal of Mental Deficiency*, 1967, *71*, 864–868.

Morris, S.E. *Program guidelines for children with feeding problems*. Edison, N.J.: Childcraft Educational Corp., 1977.

Mowrer, O.H., & Mowrer, W.M. Enuresis: A method for its study and treatment. *American Journal of Orthopsychiatry*, 1938, *8*, 436–459.

Mueller, H. Facilitating feeding and pre-speech. In P. Pearson & C. Williams (Eds.), *Physical therapy services in developmental disabilities*. Springfield, Ill.: Charles C Thomas, 1972.

Mueller, H. Feeding. In N.R. Finnie (Ed.), *Handling the young cerebral palsied child at home*. New York: E.P. Dutton, 1975.

Nelson, G.L., Cone, J.D., & Hanson, C.R. Training correct utensil use in retarded children: Modeling vs. physical guidance. *American Journal of Mental Deficiency*, 1975, *80*, 114–122.

O'Brien, F., & Azrin, N.H. Developing proper mealtime behaviors of the institutionalized retarded. *Journal of Applied Behavior Analysis*, 1972, *5*, 389–399.

O'Brien, F., Bugle, C., & Azrin, N.H. Training and maintaining a retarded child's proper eating. *Journal of Applied Behavior Analysis*, 1972, *5*, 67–73.

Osarchuk, M. Operant methods of toilet behavior training of the severely and profoundly retarded: A review. *Journal of Special Education*, 1973, *7*, 423–437.

Pipes, P.L. Assessing food and nutrient in-take. In M.L. Erickson (Ed.), *Assessment and management of developmental changes in children*. St. Louis: C.V. Mosby, 1976.

Richman, J.S., Sonderby, T., & Kahn, J.V. Prerequisite vs. *in vivo* acquisition of self-feeding skill. *Behaviour Research and Therapy*, 1980, *18*, 327–332.

Schmidt, P. Feeding assessment and therapy for the neurologically impaired. *AAESPH Review*, 1976, *1*(8), 19–27.

Seiger, H.W. Treatment of essential nocturnal enuresis. *Journal of Pediatrics*, 1952, *40*, 738–749.

Sloop, W.E., & Kennedy, W.A. Institutionalized retarded nocturnal enuretics treated by a conditioning technique. *American Journal of Mental Deficiency*, 1973, *77*, 717–721.

Smith, L.J. Training severely and profoundly mentally handicapped nocturnal enuretics. *Behavior Research and Therapy*, 1981, *19*, 67–74.

Smith, P.S. A comparison of different methods of toilet training the mentally handicapped. *Behavior Research and Therapy*, 1979, *17*, 33–34.

Smith, P.S., Britton, P.G., Johnson, M., & Thomas, D.A. Problems involved in toilet training profoundly mentally handicapped adults. *Behavior Research and Therapy*, 1975, *15*, 301–307.

Snell, M.E. Does toilet training belong in the public schools? A review of toilet training research. *Education Unlimited*, 1980, *2*(3), 53–58.

Somerton, M.E., & Turner, K.D. *Pennsylvania training model: Individual assessment guide*. King of Prussia: Regional Resources Center of Eastern Pennsylvania for Special Education, 1975.

Song, A.Y., & Gandhi, R. An analysis of behavior during the acquisition and maintenance phases of self-spoon feeding skills of profound retardates. *Mental Retardation*, 1974, *12*(1), 25–28.

Stainback, S., Healy, H., Stainback, W., & Healy, J. Teaching basic eating skills. *AAESPH Review*, 1976, *1*(7), 26–35.

Sternat, J., Messina, R., Lyon, S., & Nietupski, J. Curricular suggestions for teaching severely handicapped students selected clusters of head control skills. In E. Sontag, J. Smith, & N. Certo (Eds.), *Educational programming for the severely and profoundly handicapped*. Reston, Va.: Council for Exceptional Children, 1977.

Stevens, C.J., Ferneti, C.L., & Lent, J.R. *Project MORE: Handwashing*. Bellevue, Wash.: Edmark, 1975.

Stimbert, V.E., Minor, J.W., & McCoy, J.F. Intensive feeding training with retarded children. *Behavior Modification*, 1977, *1*, 517–530.

Sugaya, K. Survey of the enureses problem in an institution for the mentally retarded with emphasis on the clinical psychological aspects. *Japanese Journal of Child Psychiatry*, 1967, *8*, 142–150.

Swinyard, C.W. *The child with spina bifida*. New York: Association for the Aid of Crippled Children, 1971.

Tawney, J.W. *Programmed environmental curriculum*. Columbus, Ohio: Charles E. Merrill, 1979.

Trott, M.C. Application of Foxx and Azrin toilet training for the retarded in a school program. *Education and Training of the Mentally Retarded*, 1977, *12*, 336–339.

Utley, B., Holvoet, J., & Barnes, K. Handling, positioning, and feeding the physically handicapped. In E. Sontag, J. Smith, & N. Certo (Eds.), *Educational programming for severely and profoundly handicapped*. Reston, Va.: Council for Exceptional Children, 1977.

van den Pol, R.A., Iwata, B.A., Ivancic, M.T., Page, T.J., Neef, N.A., & Whitley, F.P. Teaching the handicapped to eat in public places: Acquisition, generalization and maintenance of restaurant skills. *Journal of Applied Behavior Analysis*, 1981, *14*, 61–69.

VanWagenen, R.K., Meyerson, L., Kerr, N.J., & Mahoney, K. Field trials of a new procedure for toilet training. *Journal of Experimental Child Psychology*, 1969, *8*, 147–159.

VanWagenen, R.K., & Murdock, E.E. A transistorized signal-package for toilet training of infants. *Journal of Experimental Child Psychology*, 1966, *3*, 312–314.

Williams, C.L., Doleys, D.D., & Ciminero, A.R. A two-year follow-up of enuretic children treated with Dry Bed Training. *Journal of Behavior Therapy and Experimental Psychiatry*, 1978, *9*, 285–286.

Williams, F.E., & Sloop, W.E. Success with a shortened Foxx-Azrin toilet training program. *Education and Training of the Mentally Retarded*, 1978, *4*, 399–402.

Yates, A.J. *Behavior therapy*. New York: Wiley, 1970.

REFERENCE NOTES

1. Training Resource Center, *Toilet Training Equipment*. Unpublished manuscript, 1973. Available from Training Resource Center, Longley School, Mansfield Training School, Mansfield Depot, CT 06251.

2. Sobsey, D. *Facilitation of normal oral-motor responses in developmentally delayed and neurologically impaired children*. Final report to U.S. Department of Education, Office of Special Education. Morgantown: University of West Virginia, September, 1981.

3. McGinsey, J.F. *A brief survey of eating behaviors of 60 severe/profoundly retarded individuals*. Unpublished manuscript, Western Carolina Center, 1977.

TOILET-TRAINING SIGNALING EQUIPMENT

Signaling Pants, Potty Chairs, and Instructions for Building

1. BRS/LVE Tech. Serv., Inc.
   5301 Holland Drive
   Beltsville, MD 20705
   301-474-3400
   A. Potty Alert (#552-08)—$77.00 plus shipping
   B. Pants Alert (#552-09)—$77.00 plus shipping

2. Dr. A. Yonovitz
   Speech and Hearing Institute
   Health Service Center at Houston
   1343 Moursund
   The University of Texas
   Houston, TX 77025
   Construction Manual for Toilet Alarm and Body-Worn Alerting Unit—$2.00

3. Mr. Gil Langley
Northern Virginia Training Center
9901 Braddock Rd.
Fairfax, VA 22030
Construction manual for Toilet Alarm—free

4. C.A. Briggs Company
Cybersonic Division
P.O. Box 151
Glenside, PA 19038
215-805-2244
Bleeptone Audible Signalling Device—$9.94 plus shipping (for use with a body-worn alert or as part of a toilet alarm)

Bed-Signaling Equipment

1. Montgomery Ward Co.
Catalogue Sales
   A. Standard Wet Guard (#53 A 21530)—$37.99
      Unit with buzzer only; 2 bed packs; battery
   B. Deluxe Wet Guard (#53 A 21531)—$58.99
      Unit, 4 bed packs with 2 foil pads, 1 separating sheet, adjustable signal volume, battery.
   C. Replacement kit of 2 foil pad sets (#53 A 21532)—$7.99

2. Sears and Roebuck Co.
Catalogue Sales
   A. Lite-Alert Alarm (#8K-1301)—$59.99 plus shipping
   B. Wee Alarm (#8K-1300)—$37.99 plus shipping
   C. Extra Bedding Set (#8K-1172)—$7.49 plus shipping

Adaptive Equipment: Chairs and Self-Care Assistive Devices

Commercial catalogues

1. Abbey Medical Equipment Co.
Medical Catalog Sales Department
13500 South Figueroa Street
Los Angeles, CA 90061

2. Be OK Self Help Aids
Fred Sammons, Inc.
Box 32
Brookfield, IL 60513

3. Cleo Living Aids
3957 Mayfield Road
Cleveland, OH 44121

4. Contourpedic Corporation
1106 Edgewater Ave.
Ridgefield, NJ

5. Ortho-Kinetics, Inc.
1225 Pearl Street
Waukesha, WI 53186

6. J.A. Preston Corporation
71 Fifth Avenue
New York, NY 10003

7. Skill Development Equipment Co.
1340 North Jefferson
Anaheim, CA 92807

8. Rifton Equipment for the Handicapped
Rifton, NY 12471

References

1. *A Manual for Cerebral Palsy Equipment.* Chicago, Ill.: National Society for Crippled Children and Adults, Inc., 11 South LaSalle Street.

2. Finnie, N.R. *Handling the Young Cerebral Palsied Child at Home.* New York: E.P. Dutton, 1975.

3. Garee, B. (Ed.). *Accent on living: Buyer's Guide.* Bloomington, Ill.: Chewer, 1981.

4. Hoffman, R.B. *How to Build Special Furniture and Equipment for Handicapped Children.* Springfield, Ill.: Charles C Thomas, 1969.

Introduction to Chapters 14 and 15

In the next two chapters, Diane Browder and I address the instruction of daily living skills and functional reading. These areas span the many activities required to survive in the community. They are taught to expand our students' independence in all four domains—domestic living, leisure-recreational, vocational, and community living.

Your teaching approach must parallel the realities encountered by your students. Instructional materials cannot be traditional. Most workbooks, readers, commercial charts, flashcards, and dittoed worksheets are not practical because your students cannot relate the materials to the desired skills. Instead you will need materials such as newspapers, street signs, price tags from stores, and movie tickets. You will be unable to remain within the four walls of the classroom if you expect your students to develop functional skills. For example, students who have learned the basics of counting money must also be taught to count out and receive change in a store. They must have opportunities to use pay telephones, vending machines, and coin-operated washers and dryers. Students learning reading must use those skills in operating electric appliances, locating restrooms and exits, choosing foods in large supermarkets, reading office signs in public buildings, completing application forms, finding names, numbers, and addresses in telephone books, and comprehending directions on simple packaged foods.

With our population of students, it is not entirely clear how much, when, or with whom a teacher can effectively use simulated teaching situations in place of *in vivo* training or instruction in the actual setting. While the research reviewed in these chapters reveals some conflict on this issue, the safest approach appears to have a strong backing in the literature. And that approach is to teach and test daily living skills in their natural context. In this way teachers have more guarantee that their efforts will yield the competencies required of their students.

14

Daily Living Skills

*This chapter was written by **Diane M. Browder,** Lehigh University, and **Martha E. Snell,** University of Virginia.*

Daily living skills include all the competencies required to maintain your home and personal appearance, in addition to using related community resources such as a grocery store or bank. Instruction in daily living skills for the handicapped is crucial for several reasons. First, these skills are critical to success in a community placement (Schalock & Harper, 1978; Schalock, Harper, & Carver, 1981). Also, many of them are potentially useful for employment (e.g., as a custodian, short order cook). Another reason these skills are a priority is that they provide functional tasks for concurrent instruction in other areas such as reading, math, and fine motor skills. Depending on the age and functioning level of the student, the teacher might provide all academic instruction in a daily living context rather than as classroom or table-top instruction. For the teacher who provides instruction in general reading or math, daily living skills will provide practical opportunities to ensure that the student can apply the skills in natural settings. This chapter gives both an overview of daily living skill instruction and techniques for academic instruction in the context of these skills.

DAILY LIVING SKILLS FOR COMMUNITY SUCCESS

Snell (1981) has noted that the success of the handicapped in community placements is a function of three interrelated factors: (*a*) the characteristics of the placement itself and the skills it requires of its residents; (*b*) the daily living, vocational, and social skills of the handicapped clients; and (*c*) an absence of client behaviors that are bothersome to the community (Felsenthal & Scheerenberger, 1978; Gollay, Friedman, Wyngaarden, & Kurtz, 1978; Nihira & Nihira, 1975; O'Connor, 1976). This chapter focuses on one of these factors: daily living skills that enhance community success.

Nihira and Nihira (1975) interviewed over 100 caretakers of mentally retarded individuals to solicit incidents of positive adaptive behaviors. These interviews identified several daily living skills, including community travel, handling simple economic tasks, and use of community resources. Also cited were improved social skills.

Using a slightly different method to identify critical skills, Schalock & Harper (1978) monitored 131 borderline to severely retarded persons in community placements. Of these 131 clients, 13% "failed" (had to return to the institution) because they lacked skills in money management, meal preparation, and housekeeping. In a follow-up of 80% of the original clients, Schalock and colleagues (1981) found that success predictors still included personal maintenance, clothing care and use, and food preparation, as well as communication and community use, while failure was often associated with inadequate home maintenance, bizarre behavior, and nutritional problems. In a similar follow-up study of 400 deinstitutionalized retarded adults and children, Gollay et al. (1978) noted skills trained by the staff of community residences, including housekeeping, meal preparation, shopping, and money management. Other needed skills noted included traveling, using the telephone, handling emergencies, and using community agencies. Less than half of the clients received instruction in these skills because caretakers felt that they were not ready for the skills or the caretakers were not prepared to teach them.

Further support for the need for daily living skills was provided by Crnic and Pym (1979) in a follow-up of 17 mildly retarded adults trained in group homes for apartment placements. After 4 to 18 months of training, 14 of the clients made successful moves. Skills found to be essential to transition included personal maintenance, clothing care, home maintenance, food preparation, time management, social behavior, community utilization, communication, and functional academic skills. However, not all critical skills could be identified before the transition had been made. Also, generalization and maintenance of skills acquired in the homes did not always occur after the apartment placements. These two findings imply that training for independent living will need to continue after the placement. Crnic and Pym (1979) also noted that skill acquisition alone was not sufficient for community success. Clients who were highly motivated to live independently were the most successful. Factors that inhibited success were preplacement anxiety, a reduction in social contacts and support once available in the group home, and natural consequences for failure (e.g., job loss for tardiness, eviction for unclean apartment, and lack of funds for necessities due to overspending on pleasures). The implication of these studies is that, to ensure success in independent living, daily living skills programs will need both to train the critical skills identified and to use instructional procedures that encourage self-motivation and self-maintenance.

PLANNING DAILY LIVING SKILLS PROGRAMS

Like all programs for the moderately and severely handicapped, daily living skill programs should be individualized and systematically taught. We will review a few of the principles that guide all programs

for this population as they relate to daily living skills.

Self-Management and Maintenance

As noted by Crnic and Pym (1979), acquiring a skill does not ensure success for a handicapped person in the community. The person must be motivated to continue using the skill for a lifetime. When designing a daily living skills program for a moderately to severely handicapped student, we should consider the goal of long-term self-maintenance from the onset. Although initially a high ratio of tokens or tangible reinforcers may be required, these consequences should be faded and replaced by self-reinforcement before instruction ends. For example, Bauman and Iwata (1977) used self-scheduling of chores to enhance long-term maintenance of housekeeping skills by two mildly handicapped adults. With the severely handicapped, initial acquisition may be followed by maintenance training, where the student learns to correct and reinforce himself with graphs or praise in the teacher's presence and, eventually, independently. Although some severely handicapped adults will need ongoing monitoring of their work by nonhandicapped adults, self-scheduling and self-reinforcement will maximize their independence.

Another key to long-term maintenance is teaching the person to use naturally occurring cues that will be present in the environment in which a skill will be performed (Falvey, Brown, Lyon, Baumgart, & Schroeder, 1980). For example, a restaurant cashier might remind a customer to take her change after paying for her order. Unfortunately, there is no research literature illustrating or empirically validating systematic instruction based on naturally occurring cues. Research in this area could provide helpful suggestions for instruction.

Relying solely on naturally occurring cues may not be possible for early learning or for some tasks or task components without distinct cues. In the absence of distinct cues, the teacher might provide materials that the student can keep to cue responding during teacher absence (e.g., picture recipes, housekeeping schedule, laundry instruction cards). In early acquisition, a severely handicapped person may need more teacher-provided help that will be systematically faded. Several prompting/fading techniques have been used in teaching daily living skills, including a least to most intrusive prompt system (Cuvo, Leaf, & Borakove, 1978; Johnson & Cuvo, 1981), a most to least intrusive prompt system (Cuvo, Jacobi, & Sipko, 1981), time delay fading of a single prompt (Snell, 1981), and a less specific confirmation prompt for maintenance training (Cuvo, et al., 1981; Johnson

& Cuvo, 1981). (Chapter 5 describes these procedures.) The choice of prompting and fading techniques will depend on the learner and the task to be taught. The teacher should select a technique that provides *no more help than is essential* to correct performance. This may require using several instructional procedures like those implemented by Cuvo et al. (1981), in which the least intrusive prompt is provided for less difficult steps of a task, the most intrusive prompt is introduced only for steps with high error potential or dangerous steps (e.g., use of a butcher knife), and nonspecific prompts (e.g., "What's next?") are used for review. When a prompt is introduced before the student's response for the purpose of reducing errors, it may be faded using time delay (chapter 5). All dependence on teacher-provided prompts must be faded completely to develop self-management.

Program Selection

Selecting daily living skills for instruction can be difficult, given the scope of this program area. One tool that may help is the Independent Living Skills Inventory (Vogelsburg, Anderson, Berger, Haselden, Mitwell, Schmidt, Skowron, Ulett, & Wilcox, 1980). As shown in Table 14.1, this inventory guides the program staff in selecting the living situation, setting it up, and teaching skills for survival. Vogelsburg et al. (1980) emphasized that a published inventory can only suggest skill clusters; specific skills should be verified by an inventory of the student's own environment.

A survey of the student's own current and future least restrictive environments is called an *ecological inventory* or a *top-down curriculum* (Brown, Branston, Hamre-Nietupski, Pumpian, Certo, & Gruenewald, 1979). Relevant ecological inventories include a visit to the student's current domestic environments (e.g., family home, grandparents, babysitter) and future domestic environments (e.g., group home, apartment) to determine what skills are required. For example, home visits might reveal that one student has a home washer and dryer while another must use a public laundromat. Each of them will require slightly different instruction. The student who must use a laundromat will need to know how to choose coins and wait for an available dryer. Also relevant will be inventories of the student's current and potential future communities to determine, for example, the type of street crossing lights used, travel skills needed to use the public health clinic, and the directions for most local public phones (e.g., cost, insert coin before or after dialing). Comparing the student's current skills with the skills needed in a future setting will suggest numerous targets. Table 14.2 shows an ecological inventory for a severely handicapped ado-

TABLE 14.1 Outline of the Independent Living Skills Inventory

I. SELECTING AN INDEPENDENT LIVING SITUATION
   A. Individual Information Lists
   B. Legal Concerns
   C. Financial Considerations
   D. Where to Look for an Apartment
   E. Environmental Considerations
   F. Physical Setting
      1. Architectural Considerations
      2. Apartment Accessibility Survey
   G. Landlord Considerations
   H. Finalizing
II. SETTING UP AN INDEPENDENT LIVING SITUATION
   A. Initial Preparation
   B. Materials Inventory
   C. Acquisitions
III. SURVIVING IN AN INDEPENDENT LIVING SITUATION
   A. Scheduling
      1. Daily
         a. Monday–Friday
         b. Saturday
         c. Sunday
      2. Weekly
      3. Monthly
      4. Yearly
      5. Expenses
      6. Trainer Checklist
   B. Skills Specific Room by Room
      1. Living Room
      2. Bathroom
      3. Kitchen
      4. Bedroom
      5. Laundry Room/Laundromat
   C. Transportation
   D. Safety
   E. Money Management
   F. Communication
   G. Leisure Time
   H. Miscellaneous

SOURCE: "Programming for Apartment Living: A Description and Rationale of An Independent Living Skills Inventory" by R.T. Vogelsburg, J. Anderson, P. Berger, T. Haseldon, S. Mitwell, C. Schmidt, A. Skowron, D. Ulett, and B. Wilcox, *Journal of the Association for the Severly Handicapped*, 1980, *5*(1), 38–54. Reprinted with permission.

lescent who currently is living with her parents but who plans to live in a nearby group home at age 18. Priorities for her instruction in the domestic and community domains were set using the criteria discussed in chapter 4. These prioritized skills will then form her curriculum.

Setting and Schedules

Crnic and Pym (1977) observed that mildly retarded adults in a new home could not always use domestic skills that they had learned in another setting. Generalization will probably be even more difficult for the severely retarded adult. The following examples enhance generalization of daily living skills.

To maximize transfer to new times and settings, the teacher should teach daily living skills at the time and in the places they will be used. However, daily instruction in natural settings may not be feasible for all skills. Thus some training may be provided in the classroom using a simulation of the real setting. However, generalization will be enhanced if realistic materials are used. For example, the teacher might obtain lifesize photos of streetlights to teach pedestrian safety or use a home economics classroom to teach cooking. Whenever simulation is used, probes for generalization to the actual environment must be included.

Stokes and Baer (1977) have suggested that generalization could be improved with a mediating stimulus used across training tasks and settings. In daily living skills, the teacher might use written or pictorial instructions such as picture recipe cards (Johnson & Cuvo, 1981; Martin, Rusch, James, Decker, & Trytol, in press) or pictured weekly housekeeping schedules (Spellman, DeBriere, Jarboe, Campbell, & Harris, 1978). Students would learn to use these pictures as reminders of what housekeeping tasks to carry out each day and to alert them to the steps involved and materials needed. Even after a student mastered the skills, the pictures would be used as guides regardless of where the skill is performed.

Social Validation

Planning daily living skills instruction and writing task analyses may require more knowledge of domestic skills than the teacher has. For example, in planning food preparation programs, the teacher needs to consider each student's medical dietary restrictions, if any, and be able to plan nutritionally balanced, economical meals. Consultation with a home economics expert can help in developing the content of instruction. For example, Johnson and Cuvo (1981), Cuvo et al. (1981), and Cronin and Cuvo (1979) asked a professor of home economics with experience with developmentally disabled clients to review task analyses for mending, washing, and cooking and, in some cases, the finished products (e.g., food) of their programs. Consulting experts is social validation of the *procedures* (examining the task analyses for accuracy) and the *results* of the program (judging the quality of a sandwich or a repaired seam) (Cuvo, 1978; Kazdin, 1977).

Another technique of social validation, *normative comparisons*, also can be useful (Kazdin, 1977). For example, before teaching clothing matching to severely and profoundly retarded women, Nutter and Reid (1978) observed women in public settings to determine the most popular color combinations. This permitted them to teach color combinations which actually were popular in that area. Other examples are grooming (e.g., hair styling), household chores (identifying chores performed by the same age group), and use of community resources (e.g., popular restaurants or leisure settings for young adults). Also, an evaluation of the student's mastery might be based in part on comparison with nonhandicapped peers for skills like restaurant manners and bus riding.

Program Expense

Another demand upon special education teachers is minimizing expenses while maintaining program quality. Daily living skill programs can be especially expensive because of the materials required. Several program variations can cut expenses while leaving quality unthreatened.

Test Expense

The time taken to probe a student's mastery of a task as well as instructional materials can be expensive. Rather than daily probes, once or twice a week is often adequate to monitor progress objectively. Many teachers use only an AB design, in which a baseline for one skill is followed by training and ongoing probes. This design would be the least costly alternative and may well be preferable when using a program already validated by research. When a single subject design is used, a multiple probe (Horner & Baer, 1978) rather than a multiple baseline design allows more infrequent assessment. (See chapter 4 for more on design.) While most teachers will generally not employ single subject designs in teaching, using a proven design permits the evaluation of procedure effectiveness across a variety of skills and students.

Material Expense

The most obvious way to minimize material expense is to select the most economical materials available (e.g., generic brand laundry detergent, economical menus.) Another means is to reuse materials whose stimulus properties are not changed by performance of a task. For example, Johnson and Cuvo (1981) reused the same eggs to teach boiling over several sessions. Schleien, Ash, Kiernan, and Wehman's (1981) clients practiced baking a foil-covered but empty TV dinner tray. In some cases real materials may be used only during generalization probes. *If*

TABLE 14-2 A Sample Ecological Inventory for the Domestic and Community Domains for a Severely Retarded Adolescent Who Currently Lives at Home

I. DOMAIN Domestic

A. CURRENT ENVIRONMENT	FUTURE ENVIRONMENT
Parent's Home	Independent Group Home

B. SUBENVIRONMENTS

1. Kitchen	2. Laundry Room	3. Bathroom	4. Living Room/Den	5. Bedroom

C. ACTIVITIES

1.
a. Food preparation
b. Clean up
c. Food storage

2.
a. Wash clothes
b. Iron clothes
c. Mending

3.
a. Grooming
b. Cleaning

4.
a. Telephone
b. Recreation
c. Guest
d. Cleaning

5.
a. Dressing
b. Sleeping
c. Cleaning

D. SKILLS PRIORITIZED FOR INSTRUCTION

1a. Food Preparation
1. Drink
2. Sandwich
3. Tablesetting

1b. Clean Up
1. Wipe counters
2. Sweep
3. Load dishwasher

1c. Food Storage
1. Put away leftovers
2. Put away groceries

2a. Wash Clothes
1. Sort
2. Use washer
3. Use dryer

2b. Ironing
1. Flat (pillowcases)
2. Shirt

2c. Mending
1. Button
2. Seam

3a. Grooming
1. Wash hair
2. Style hair with blowdryer
3. Shave

3b. Cleaning
1. Mirror
2. Mop floor
3. Scrub tub
4. Scrub sink
5. Straighten after daily use

4a. Telephone
1. Emergencies
2. Social call

4b. Recreation
1. Television schedule
2. Checkers
3. Crocheting
4. Exercises

4c. Guest
1. Conversation
2. Cards
3. Serve snack

4d. Cleaning
1. Dust
2. Vacuum
3. Straighten

5a. Dressing
1. Selection of matching clothes
2. Hang up clean clothes
3. Fold clothes

5b. Sleeping
1. Make partially made bed
2. Strip bed

5c. Cleaning
1. Vacuum
2. Dust
3. Make stripped bed

II. DOMAIN *Community*

A. CURRENT ENVIRONMENTS 1. *Travel,* 2. *Family Doctor & Dentist,* 3. *Restaurant,* 4. *Shopping Center*
B. FUTURE ENVIRONMENTS 1. *Travel,* 2. *Public Health Services,* 3. *Restaurant,* 4. *Shopping Center*

B. SUBENVIRONMENTS
1. Travel
   a. In town
   b. In neighborhood
   c. Out of town
2. Doctor/Health Services
   a. Waiting room
   b. Examining room
3. Restaurant
   a. Waiting area
   b. Tables
   c. Cashier
   d. Restroom
4. Shopping Center
   a. Grocery store
   b. Department store

C. ACTIVITIES AND D. SKILLS PRIORITIZED FOR INSTRUCTION

1a. Town
   1. Bus riding
      a. Coin selection
      b. Reading bus names

1b. Neighborhood
   1. Walking
      a. Street crossing

1c. Out of Town
   1. Busriding
      a. Taking cab
      b. Purchase ticket

2a. Waiting Room
   1. Wait
      a. State name
      b. State doctor's name
      c. Telling time

2b. Examination Room
   1. Examination
      a. Name body parts where discomfort is
      b. Dressing
      c. Answer questions

3a. Waiting Area
   1. Wait
      a. State number in party

3b. Tables
   1. Order
      a. Read menu
      b. State order
   2. Eat
      a. Napkin use
      b. Conversation
   3. Leaving
      a. Request check
      b. Tip

3c. Cashier
   1. Pay check
      a. Identify spoken amount

3d. Restroom
   1. Grooming
      a. Wash hands
      b. Comb hair

4a. Grocery Store
   1. Select food
      a. Weigh produce
      b. Identify best price
      c. Select correct quantity
      d. Follow list

4b. Department Store
   1. Select clothes
      a. Identify size
      b. Try on clothes
   2. Select household items
      a. Locate department
      b. Find item on list
   3. Select leisure item
      a. Locate department
      b. Check prices
   4. Pay
      a. Put items on counter
      b. Select correct money

417

generalization occurs, the simulated materials may be far less expensive. For example, in daily laundry training with severely handicapped adolescents, Renzaglia (Note 1) used cardboard laundry appliance packaging cartons equipped with movable dials and painted realistically to look like washers and dryers, for a total cost of $6.00. Soap measured and placed in the simulated washer was reused, since it never was mixed with water. Generalization probes taken at regular intervals in a nearby apartment showed that, when given the real equipment, the students could perform the laundry skills without further instruction.

Instructional Arrangement

By using small group as well as one-to-one instruction, the teacher can more efficiently use the time and staff available. Small group instruction also may enhance motivation, provide peer models for observational learning, and enhance generalization (Brown, Holvoet, Guess, & Mulligan, 1980). Whether or not group instruction will be the most effective depends on the task to be taught and the group arrangement (Brown et al., 1980; Alberto, Jobes, Sizemore, & Doran, 1980). Smith and Meyers (1979) found small group instruction (five severely retarded students) more effective than one-to-one instruction in teaching telephone skills. In contrast, Alberto et al. (1980) found group instruction less effective than one-to-one ratio in teaching dressing, but equally effective for table-top instruction. Since many daily living skills do not lend themselves to table-top instruction, when using group instruction the teacher will need to organize the students and materials to ensure that all can observe each action clearly. Involving students in the presentations of instructional requests, prompts, and even dispensing reinforcers will facilitate learning (Matson, 1980; 1981).

FOOD PREPARATION SKILLS

Food preparation will be a priority for many daily living skills programs for several reasons (Johnson & Cuvo, 1981). First, being able to prepare meals enhances independent living (Schalock & Harper, 1978; Crnic & Pym, 1979). The alternatives to cooking—eating in restaurants or hiring a cook—can be quite expensive. Also, meal preparation provides social as well as survival benefits if the student cooks for family and friends. For some students, cooking might provide an employment alternative.

The development of a food preparation program will be similar to other daily living skills programs. (See Table 14.3.) Unique concerns are ensuring that the product is nutritious and edible and does not violate any dietary restrictions. Also, using kitchen utensils and appliances requires both skill and awareness of safety. Related skills like hand-washing, food storage, and trash disposal will be necessary for healthy food preparation. The discussion below addresses these unique needs but also provides a general example of the planning and implementation process for any daily living skills program.

Ecological Inventory for Food Preparation

To determine the needed food preparation skills, the teacher must obtain information on the student and the environment. Table 14.4 illustrates an inventory completed for a 12-year-old student named John who resides in an institution but was scheduled for a community placement soon. John's teacher surveyed all of John's current and future environments to determine what food preparation skills he could use in each setting. Currently there were three environments where he needed food-related skills—his dormitory, a store within walking distance of his dorm, and his parents' home. The teacher interviewed the staff at the dorm to determine what food preparation skills John could use there. At the dorm John used only two skills he knew well—pouring drinks and serving refreshments (Table 14.4). Next the teacher interviewed the clerk at the small grocery near the institution and watched other shoppers to find out what skills were required there. Subsequently she watched John at the store and noted in Table 14.4 that he could only (*a*) consume purchased items and (*b*) carry purchases back to his dorm, but he could not perform any of the other listed skills. The teacher also invited John's parents' home with him. Although John's parents did not let him help prepare food because of his lack of skills, they were eager for him to learn these tasks. So the teacher noted various family food preparation activities.

The teacher repeated this ecological inventory for each of the students in her class. She then obtained other information on the students, summarized in Table 14.5, before selecting skills for instruction. At this point the teacher consulted the students' parents and the institution's dietitian to determine dietary restrictions. Next, she observed the clients at mealtime and talked to their parents to ascertain food preferences. She listed this information along with the students' current skills on the same chart (Table 14.5). She then identified three or four skills as priorities for instruction. The criteria used for establishing priorities included (*a*) student, parent, and staff preference (e.g., for John these were cleaning up and making peanut butter crackers; (*b*) skills that would be used in the future as well as at present (e.g., preparation of snacks and clean up); (*c*) the student's chro-

TABLE 14.3 An Outline for Planning, Implementing, and Evaluating a Food Preparation Program

Development of Food Preparation Program
1. Ecological Inventories for Task Selection
   a. parents, practices and preferences
   b. student's current skills and preferences
   c. medical/diet considerations (doctor, dietician)
2. Scheduling
   a. group and/or individual
   b. prior to meals or as a snack
   c. clean up time is included
3. Instructional program
   A. Preparation Phase
      1. task analyze skill and obtain a validation from a home economist or other expert
      2. secure materials, ready appliances (adapt as needed)
      3. select recipe (make cards)
      4. outline prompting technique
      5. outline consequences and preparation (make histograms, secure tokens, etc.)
      6. make data sheets with TA, scoring, and graphs
   B. Baseline Assessment
      1. procedure specified
      2. stable performance obtained
   C. Acquisition/Generalization
      1. individual or group using procedures planned
      2. daily data/update graph
      3. teacher-delivered reinforcement thinned
      4. self-reinforcement introduced
      5. less specific prompts used in review sessions
      6. self-cuing (pictures) introduced
      7. generalization probed
      8. a new setting used (e.g., group home)
      9. similar skills (e.g., new recipe cards with same words) are probed and taught as needed
   D. Program Evaluation
      1. did learning occur? how efficiently?
      2. cost?
      3. social validation of learner's terminal performance?
      4. generalization/maintenance probes?

nological age (i.e., most nonhandicapped 12-year-olds prepare snacks, but not many prepare meals); (*d*) maintenance as well as acquisition of skills (e.g., independent sweeping); (*e*) skills that several students needed to enable her to use group instruction (e.g., make drinks); (*f*) tasks that included other target skills for the student (e.g., fine motor, counting,

matching); and (*g*) food items that are economical and met diet restrictions (use low-salt crackers and peanut butter, diet drink mix). These priority skills are noted in Table 14.5.

Scheduling

The next step in developing the program is to schedule time for teaching. To promote generalization, the teacher planned to teach the skills in the settings where they would be used. Meals were served in the dorm and often were confusing and noisy. The teacher decided to leave the classroom early at the end of each day and use the dining room when it was fairly quiet. An afternoon snack would be prepared and eaten there, allowing instruction in a realistic setting. Two students (Harold and Betty) capable of sweeping and table-washing but who needed regular practice to become more efficient helped the cafeteria staff clean up after the noon meal.

Instructional Program

Writing Task Analyses

The next step in the process is to plan an instructional program. First, each skill needs to be analyzed (refer to chapter 4). Johnson and Cuvo (1981) developed a task analysis using comprehensive validation. To determine what foods to teach and how to prepare them, they consulted cookbooks, people in the community with cooking skills, the students' parents, a professor of home economics who had experience with the developmentally disabled, a graduate student in food preparation, and the students themselves. Next they watched three people perform the cooking tasks. A written task analysis and a videotape of the cooking operations were submitted to the home economics professor for review. Her feedback was used to further refine the tasks. While these steps may seem rather involved, the quality of the task analysis is of utmost importance as it determines exactly what will be taught and evaluated.

Cookbooks and Recipe Pictures

After a task analysis is written and validated, the teacher needs to gather materials. Again a home economist might be consulted. If the teacher plans to use a recipe, it should be selected and perhaps adapted for the student's reading skills, motor skills (e.g., use of jig to open lid by physically handicapped student), and dietary restrictions (e.g., substitute another seasoning for salt).

Some cookbooks have been written for elementary school students (Better Homes and Gardens, 1972; Crocker, 1975; Moore, 1969; Parents Nursery

TABLE 14.4 Ecological Inventory of Food Preparation

Client's Name: __John__

I. Current or future environment

Place __Dorm__ (check skills client can perform)

Activity 1. Snack

Skills
1. make lemonade
2. peanut butter crackers
3. set table for snack
4. pour lemonade
5. serve snack
6. clean up snack table
7.

Activity 2. Birthday Party

Skills
1. set table for party
2. make punch
3. pour punch
4. cut cake
5. serve refreshments
6. clean up table
7. sweep floor

Activity 3.
1.
2.
3.
4.
5.
6.
7.

II. Current or future environment

Place __Mrs. Hill's Store__

Activity 1. Buy drink and snack

Skills
1. select drink
2. select nutritous snack
3. pay for items at counter
4. open and eat food items
5.
6.
7.

Activity 2. Buy food to fix snack

Skills
1. select drink mix
2. select crackers
3. select peanut butter
4. pay for items at counter
5. carry items back to dorm

Activity 3.
1.
2.
3.
4.
5.
6.
7.

III. Current or future environment

Place __Parent's home__

Activity 1. Snack

Skills
1. make Kool-aid
2. fix popcorn
3. fix peanut butter celery
4. pour Kool-aid
5. clean up counter
6.
7.

Activity 2. Mealtime

Skills
1. help set table
2. pour milk and tea
3. help clear table
4. wipe table
5. sweep floor
6.
7.

Activity 3.

Skills
1.
2.
3.
4.
5.
6.
7.

IV. Current or future environment

Place __Group Home__

Activity 1. Snack

Skills
1. make drink (e.g., instant tea)
2. fix popcorn
3. fix cheese and crackers
4. fix instant pudding
5. serve snack
6. clean up counter
7. wash dishes

Activity 2. Meal preparation

Skills
1. make drink
2. fix simple main dish, (e.g., sandwich)
3. pour drink
4. set table
5. serve food
6. clean up table
7. wash dishes

Activity 3. Grocery shopping

Skills
1. use picture list
2. fill basket with items on list
3. pay at check out
4. help carry bags to car
5. put groceries away
6.
7.

420

TABLE 14.5 Task Selection Worksheet for Planning Group Instruction in Food Preparation

CLIENT'S NAME	John	Harold	Betty	Dale
1. Dietary Restrictions	none	calories (weight problem)	low salt	none
2. Food Preferences	peanut butter	sweets and all foods	pudding peanut butter apples	chocolate
3. Current Food Preparation Skills	1. pour drinks 2. serve food 3. open food containers	1. open food containers 2. sweep floor (but needs reminders to finish) 3. serve food	1. clean table 2. sweep floor 3. pour drinks 4. serve food	1. serve food 2. open food containers 3. set snack table
4. Skills Needed (based on ecological inventory)	1. make drink from mix 2. fix crackers 3. set table 4. clean up	1. make drink from mix 2. fix crackers 3. pour drinks 4. clean up	1. make drink from mix 2. fix crackers 3. open food containers 4. set table	1. make drink from mix 2. fix crackers 3. clean up

School, 1974; and Sedgewick, 1967). Although these books do provide illustrations to clarify some steps and add interest, Robinson-Wilson (1977) noted several problems in using them with the severely handicapped, including their requirements for a 3rd or 4th grade reading level, measurement skills, and appliance use. Some cookbooks have been written specifically for the moderately retarded (Kahn, 1974; Staples, 1975; Steed, 1974; Yates, 1972). (Illustrations and a related discussion are found in chapter 15.) As Robinson-Wilson (1977) noted, these cookbooks may also be too difficult for some handicapped students because they require number recognition and a sight word vocabulary and because they sometimes require several steps in response to one picture.

However, for a few students, commercial cookbooks may be a good choice. If they are used, the teacher should include instruction in sight words, number comprehension, and picture reading as needed. For other students, simplified teacher-made picture recipes might be a better alternative. Robinson-Wilson (1977) used teacher-made picture recipes to teach the preparation of gelatin, hot dogs, and hot chocolate to three severely retarded adults. The pictures were drawn on 5 × 8 cards joined with two rings at the top. The first card contained a large color picture of the product. The next card illustrated the equipment and food items to be set out. Later cards illustrated the recipe, with three steps per card. Color coding was used for the stove burners and measuring utensils to simplify appliance use and measurement skills. The cards were plastic-coated and displayed on a wooden stand. Although Robinson-Wilson (1977)'s findings suggested the effectiveness of this system, the results were inconclusive due to a lack of experimental control (e.g., no baseline). Johnson and Cuvo (1981) and Martin et al. (in press) did establish experimental control in demonstrating the effectiveness of picture recipes in teaching food preparation to mentally retarded adults. Their studies suggested both effective materials and teaching techniques.

Teaching Procedures

Using a single subject design, Johnson and Cuvo (1981) taught several cooking skills to four moderately and mildly retarded adults in a sheltered workshop. The recipe cards had both written instructions and equivalent illustrations. The cooking skills taught were boiling eggs and vegetables, baking cornbread and biscuits, and broiling hot dogs and English muffins. Before each training session, the teacher readied the necessary materials and appliances (e.g., moving oven rack for broiling). During the session the teacher gave the participant the recipe and asked him or her to prepare that food item (e.g., "Using this recipe, bake the cornbread"). The student was permitted to initiate each step of the recipe independently. If the step was not begun, the teacher prompted the cooking behavior, using the least intrusive prompt necessary in the following order:

1. *Verbal Instruction*—The teacher verbalized the step (e.g., "Set the timer for 5 minutes");
2. *Verbal Instruction + Visual Cue*—The teacher repeated the verbal cue with a visual cue such as pointing to the equipment used or simulating the stimulus property for step completion (e.g., blowing through a straw in a pan of water to simulate boiling);
3. *Verbal Instruction + Modeling*—The teacher performed the step while verbalizing it;
4. *Verbal Instruction + Physical Guidance*—The teacher physically guided the student while repeating the step (e.g., "See how we pull out the oven rack").

In addition to praise during training, after a session, students received verbal and graphic feedback by filling in a bar graph that displayed the number of steps completed without prompting.

Maintenance was provided through review sessions. During review, additional less intrusive prompts were added, including *Confirmation* (the subject stated what came next and the trainer confirmed it) and a *Nonspecific Prompt* ("What's next?"). The consequences and materials used were the same as in acquisition training.

The study's results supported this procedure; the students improved in their performance of each subtask only after training. All four students reached the criterion of independent performance of all steps in each task. Generalization to untrained tasks occurred for three of the four students on both similar cooking processes (e.g., boiling eggs transferred to boiling vegetables) as well as to dissimilar cooking processes (e.g., improved performance on biscuit baking after mastering hot dog broiling). Only one or two review sessions were required for skill maintenance. The foods prepared by the students were rated by the home economist as being edible. And the cost of the program was fairly modest. Including the materials and trainer wages, the cost for each student ranged from $36.63 to $60.06, while testing cost an additional $30.00 per student.

Further support for the benefit of using a recipe was found by Martin et al. (in press). They compared cooking performance with verbal instruction and feedback to performance with this help plus picture recipe cards to assess the effectiveness of the recipe cards themselves. In contrast to Johnson and Cuvo (1981), who recruited mildly to moderately retarded adults, the subjects selected by Martin et al. (in press) were severely retarded adults. Target skills included preparing five nutritional meals (e.g. broiled fish, beans, and pudding). Training was conducted in the students' apartments. Martin et al. (in press) used black-and-white photographs bound in order rather than line drawings for the recipe cards. Each picture had a typed statement of the step and its number in the task analysis. Yellow stickers marked recipes that required preparation the evening before the meal.

A multiple baseline design across subjects was used. However, the baseline phase included simple instruction and feedback. The second phase (intervention) continued the instruction and feedback with the addition of the recipe cards. At the beginning of each session, the trainer verbalized all of the steps for the meal. Then, like Johnson and Cuvo (1981), the student was allowed to initiate each step before being prompted. If needed, verbal or physical cues were given, with praise provided for correct performance. During intervention, the procedure was the same except that, after preinstruction, the teacher gave the student the picture recipe cards. Once the pictures were introduced, all subjects immediately performed a higher percentage of steps independently. The results of this study are noteworthy for several reasons. First, they demonstrate the advantage of picture card instruction in contrast to trainer instruction and feedback alone. Second, this study taught severely retarded adults to prepare complex meals—not just one cooking skill. Unfortunately, this study did not measure generalization or maintainance and no social validation was reported.

In contrast, Schleien et al. (1981) did *not* use picture cards to cue cooking responses and still were successful in teaching a profoundly retarded woman three cooking skills. The woman, who lived at home, had no past training in cooking but reportedly enjoyed watching others cook. In a multiple baseline design across skills, she learned to boil an egg, broil an English muffin with cheese, and bake a TV dinner. A system of least intrusive prompts was used to teach the 10 to 14 steps in each of the three task analyses. The subject not only mastered the three skills but also generalized performance to her own home and to another day community facility. When asked to bake and boil other foods, she generalized adequately on most of the steps, though she was unable to generalize the broiling skill to another food. Schleien et al. (1981) demonstrated that pictures were not essential in teaching cooking skills, though systematic teaching certainly was.

Instructional Problems

Two problems not discussed in these studies but often encountered are making distinct pictures for some ingredients and procedures (e.g., sugar vs. salt, broil vs. bake) and teaching picture or word reading for the student who has not mastered this skill. For some students and some recipes, it might be best to teach sight words that will clarify steps difficult to illustrate. Also, if a teacher preferred to use a commercial cookbook like *A Special Picture Cookbook* (Steed, 1974), reading would be required. The essential response in word and picture reading is performing a verbal or motor action in reaction to a printed stimulus. For the nonreader, a printed stimulus is not an effective cue. However, other stimuli may be. For example, the teacher could tell the student what the picture or word says. To fade this help, the teacher might use time delay (see chapter 15). Time delay fading of a verbal model has been an effective and simple way to teach sight word reading (Browder, 1981) and picture reading for daily living skills (Spellman et al., 1978). Also, sight word instruction that facilitates daily living skills (e.g., recipes, laundry cards) can enhance generalization to similar, untrained materials (Browder, Hines, McCarthy, & Fees, Note 2).

PERSONAL MAINTENANCE

A second area of daily living skills is personal maintenance. Good personal maintenance is critical to securing a job and being accepted in the community. A training program here will incorporate the principles we have already discussed. A unique concern is the consideration of personal preferences as well as peer norms in determining what to teach. Nonhandicapped persons vary greatly in their clothing and hair styles, and the handicapped person should also have choices in these areas. However, certain jobs and communities may have a low tolerance for certain styles. If the student prefers or must secure a job that has dress guidelines, these norms will need to be taught.

Clothing Selection

Clothing selection skills follow after the basics of dressing. Although learning to put clothes on and fasten them may continue into adulthood for the handicapped person, additional skills are needed for an acceptable appearance. These skills include selecting clothes that match in color and design, buying clothes that fit, dressing appropriately for differing places (work, sports, church), and dressing appropriately for the weather. Also, like hair-styling, clothing selection varies, depending on current styles, personal preference, and culture.

Nutter and Reid (1978) solved the problem of differences in styles by teaching severely and profoundly retarded adult women the local fashion norms. The five women selected for this study all had independent dressing skills but could not select matching clothes. The author observed over 600 women in public settings in their community to determine the most popular matches. They only taught matching solids, since almost half the women observed wore no patterns. To teach clothing selection, a puzzle body with attachable clothing was used. They chose this simulated training over actual dressing because a greater number of training trials could be included in the alloted time. However, generalization was encouraged by verbal and visual reference to the clothes the women wore and reviews with actual clothes. Also, generalization probes were made of the women's selection of their own clothes. This training was successful; the women increased their selection of popular color combinations when dressing the puzzle and themselves.

The social validation procedure Nutter and Reid (1978) used to select popular color combinations is another normative comparison. An alternative procedure for selecting clothes that would fit and flatter the student would include consultation with an expert (Kazdin, 1977), such as a sales clerk or home economist.

Laundry

In addition to selecting clothes, the handicapped adult needs to keep them clean, which includes using a dry cleaner, sorting clothes to be washed, washing in a washer or by hand, drying in the dryer or on a line, folding, hanging, and polishing shoes.

Cuvo et al. (1981) reported a study focusing on laundry skills. Sorting, washing, and drying were taught to each of five moderately retarded students individually in a multiple baseline across subjects design. The laundry skills were socially validated through consultation with a home economist and observations of nonhandicapped adults performing the tasks. A system of least prompts was used for most steps, along with praise and histogram feedback on performance. This program led to rapid acquisition of the laundry skills by all five subjects.

Two academic skills that might further enhance this program are reading and coin selection (for coin laundry). Money skills will be discussed later in this chapter. Browder et al. (Note 2) found that using a written instruction card enhanced generalization of laundry skills to untrained clothing items.

Mending/Sewing

The ability to sew or mend clothes can be an asset to any adult. Mending clothes improves personal appearance and adds to the life of the clothes (Cronin & Cuvo, 1979). Sewing clothes can save considerable money, provides an enjoyable leisure-time skill, and may lead to employment.

Cronin and Cuvo (1979) taught five moderately retarded adolescents to mend clothes in school. Based on social validation using a sewing text, a home economics professor, and a wardrobe survey, they decided to teach sewing on buttons, hemming, and mending a seam by hand. The easiest, sturdiest hand stitches were selected for instruction. Students were assessed and taught both to identify the mending required and to mend the clothes. The prompting and consequences were similar to those in Johnson and Cuvo (1981); however, visual cues were related to the sewing discriminations. For example, the stitch length was marked with a dot, and the teacher said "Poke the needle down at the dot." Each student mastered all mending tasks after instruction and maintained the skills at the 100% criterion in a 2-week follow-up. Some generalization did occur between mending subtasks. Although setting generalization was not measured, the students reportedly used their mending skills at home.

Nettlebeck and Kirby (1976) taught more complex sewing skills to 36 mildly retarded women in a clothing factory. The women were trained initially in a secluded area of the shop and then supervised and retrained in the main shop area. Their procedures were not described specifically, but included task analysis, error prevention, feedback, and distributed practice. Although no experimental design was used, the skills had social validation. The supervisor reported that these women integrated more quickly into the shop and worked more independently than previously employed retarded women. Also, because

of their success, 11 of the women were permanently employed in the shop.

More research is needed in teaching sewing to the moderately and severely handicapped. Even in communities without a factory, this skill could provide self-employment.

Grooming

Grooming skills are an extension of basic self-help skills. Usually nonhandicapped persons learn grooming later than basic self-help skills, sometime between 6 and 16 depending upon the skill. One example of a grooming program was described by Hamre (1974). She taught hair-washing to 39 moderately retarded adolescents, some of whom had been labeled *aphasic, autistic,* and *cerebral palsied.* The students were grouped in classes of 11, 13, and 15 students with a teacher, student teacher, and aide. Only two students actually received instruction during each session because of the length of the task and the limited number of sinks. The teacher conducted a baseline assessment once for each student before training. In training, the teacher first modeled the entire procedure on herself, while describing it verbally. Then a student was asked to wash his or her hair. Each step performed correctly was praised; each error was corrected with modeling or physical assistance. By the end of the school year, 32 of the 39 students met criterion (3 consecutive errorless trials) on the hair-washing task. In discussing the results, Hamre noted that this was a time-consuming skill to teach and recommended instruction during the preteen years.

The daily task of showering or bathing is central to routine hygiene, regardless of how severely handicapped an individual is. Matson, DiLorenzo, and Esveldt-Dawson (1981) worked on showering with 36 adult residents of a state institution scheduled for placement in the community. After analyzing the tasks of showering, drying, and applying deodorant into a 27-step chain, subjects were assessed and matched by their baseline skills with control group subjects. All of the subjects had been previously assigned at random to a treatment or no treatment condition. Next, while the no treatment group continued to be showered as usual, the treatment group received independence training from one trainer in groups of five. The procedure involved the residents in the process; they were asked to praise other's successes, to prompt others in the group verbally, and to evaluate their own performance routinely. In addition, all self-evaluations were given feedback by the trainer. The trainer modeled all the steps at the beginning of each session.

After 4 months of hourly group training sessions 5 days a week, the treatment group clearly demonstrated more gains on the posttest and on a follow-up measure 3 months later. Average time required to master showering was 15 weeks, but ranged from 3 to 16 weeks. Both the independence methods and the efficient group training format were responsible for the rapid success.

In some cases students will have grooming skills but fail to use them, as Doleys, Stacy, and Knowles (1981) reported with seven moderately retarded clients living in one of two community-based group homes. Bathing, brushing teeth, washing hair, shaving, wearing clean clothes, and dressing appropriately were taught as essential daily grooming skills. In the morning each client was checked, praised, and awarded points that could be exchanged for a variety of reinforcers. For example, the men's faces were checked for whiskers; clothes were judged clean if pressed with no traces of dirt and stains. In order to be dressed appropriately, three criteria had to be met: (a) color and pattern coordinated, (b) attire suitable for weather and for (c) daily activity (e.g., work, leisure). Whenever a target grooming skill was observed, it was recorded. Results revealed a fairly rapid improvement in grooming after the implementation of the token program. Though not reported, it would be desirable to fade out the token reinforcement and teach the clients to respond to more natural contingencies.

Housekeeping

Acquiring housekeeping skills is likely to be essential for most severely handicapped people. Hiring someone to do all housekeeping is usually not economically feasible. In addition, the handicapped person who masters housekeeping skills will have a usable skill to earn additional income or as a main source of employment. Inadequate housekeeping can lead to eviction from an apartment (Crnic & Pym, 1979). Unfortunately, in some institutional settings and some families, the handicapped person is not expected to, or even permitted to, help clean house. This lack of experience makes transition to an independent setting difficult.

To determine what housekeeping skills to teach and to require of the handicapped persons, it may be useful to survey tasks most frequently performed by his or her age peers in similar living situations. For example, what chores do nonhandicapped 12-year-olds typically perform for their families? How is housekeeping handled in nonhandicapped young adult group homes (e.g., off-campus college housing)? Requiring a handicapped person to perform more housekeeping tasks than his or her peers without pay would be unfair; but requiring less work would also be unfair to the client's need for a normalized life. A second means for identifying skills is to survey the student's current and future residences and the housekeeping requirements and specific materials available.

Acquisition of Cleaning Skills

As mentioned previously, the system of prompts selected for training will depend on the student's ability to respond to various cues. If previous work indicates that the student will usually perform a step with verbal instructions, then a least intrusive prompt system would be appropriate (Cronin & Cuvo, 1979). However, students who do not frequently respond to verbal instruction early in a task and who tend to make errors if allowed to perform independently may need more assistance initially, with gradual fading. An example of this procedure is illustrated in one bed-making study (Snell, in press). Snell taught four institutionalized mentally retarded males bed-making skills using time delay fading of a model plus verbal prompt. The four tasks were making a partially unmade bed, stripping a bed, putting top and bottom sheets on a bed, and putting blanket, pillow, and spread on a bed.

Instruction included (a) forward chaining with all steps of each task taught simultaneously, (b) error correction procedures, and (c) model plus verbal prompts and physical plus verbal prompts. During the initial four trials, the teacher gave a model plus verbal prompt for the first step of the task analysis immediately after the instructional cue ("Make the bed") and then immediately guided the student to perform the step while repeating the verbal prompt. The model was given using a second bed parallel to the training bed. This procedure was repeated for all steps. After four trials, the trainer began to delay the prompts to encourage the student to perform independently.

Reinforcement was praise and a penny token system with age-appropriate materials (e.g., Velcro dart board, cassette tape player) and edibles that could be "purchased" at the end of the task. If a student made errors, either by failing to complete a step or by performing it inadequately, the trainer told the student that performance was not acceptable ("No, that's not how you make the bed"), withheld the penny, put the student through the step, and turned away from the student (timeout) for 10 seconds.

A multiple probe design across students showed a functional relationship between training and the acquisition of the skills. The students acquired from one to four of the skills in the time allocated for the study. Although training was conducted in a classroom, probes indicated that three of four subjects generalized their skills to their own beds. Two of the subjects maintained the skills with their own beds 7 weeks after training ended, despite the fact that staff policy prevented their daily use.

One of the few other studies in training housekeeping skills also overlaps with vocational preparation in janitorial tasks. Cuvo, Leaf, and Borakove (1978) trained six 13- to 15-year-old moderately retarded students to clean a school restroom. Social validation of their task analyses was based on an observation of the school janitor and a trained mentally retarded person cleaning the restroom. They used a least intrusive system of prompts similar to Johnson and Cuvo's (1981). They also used a most to least help sequence of prompts for more difficult steps that were frequently performed poorly, like spraying the mirror. Praise and candy, used as reinforcers, were thinned over sessions. All students rapidly acquired the cleaning skills, generalized to a second restroom, and maintained them for 2 weeks. An alternative to the edible reinforcer used in this study would be preferable in daily living skills training. Other daily living skills studies have supported the effectiveness of reinforcing with praise and self-graphing (Cuvo et al., 1981; Johnson & Cuvo, 1981), which are more age-appropriate for this population and may result in better skill maintenance.

Maintenance Housekeeping Skills

Before a student has mastered housekeeping, he or she must be able to determine when chores should be performed and must continue to perform them regularly. Emphasizing naturally occurring cues such as an unmade bed or a trash-covered restroom during training will encourage later independent skill performance (Falvey et al., 1980). However, these naturally occurring cues may not be sufficient for a severely handicapped person to maintain a clean home because they are numerous and often barely discernible (e.g., "dirty" sheets).

An added cue for housekeeping that is still normalized (i.e., used by some nonhandicapped persons) is a written schedule for chores (Spellman et al., 1978). Bauman and Iwata (1977) taught scheduling by initially providing this service for their clients and then gradually requiring them to make the schedule. Although their subjects were a nonretarded previously institutionalized man and a mildly retarded man, their technique might be replicable with severely handicapped clients.

A long-term housekeeping program for the severely handicapped student should include two instructional phases. In the first phase, acquisition, the teacher would be closely involved, providing systematic prompts and feedback. Once the skill is acquired, a maintenance phase should be implemented with gradually decreasing teacher checks and reinforcement for quality of performance until the student performs the skills under normal conditions (e.g., infrequent praise by visitors for a nice apartment).

USE OF COMMUNITY RESOURCES

The next section of this chapter focuses on skills needed to use community resources. Before leaving domestic skills, we will discuss a few skills used in the home that are related to using community resources. These include using the telephone and telling time.

Telephone Skills

Acquiring the skills to use a telephone can (a) save time (e.g., ordering over a phone), (b) save money (e.g., no transportation needed to shop by phone), (c) maintain communications with friends and family, and (d) allow the individual to get aid in an emergency. Using the telephone requires reading a phone book or a written number, matching numbers, recalling numbers, dialing, giving social greetings, stating a message, answering questions, and using coins (if a pay phone). For some students, telephone use may enhance academic and language skills. For less capable students, adjustments can be made to minimize the academic and language requirements and still permit phone use. For example, a personal phone book contains fewer words and pictures than the regular book and thus is easier to use. A card with money pictures showing the coin combinations acceptable for a pay call could be useful. Another technique would be to give the caller a set phrase to use in calling for a service, rather than relying on the individual to formulate a message. The studies that follow illustrate ways both to simplify the telephoning task and to teach the skills.

Aids and Organization

Studies by Leff (1974, 1975) and Smith and Meyers (1979) identify successful instructional arrangements that might be useful in teaching any telephone task. Leff (1974, 1975) developed a device called the Dial-A-Phone. Figure 14.1 shows a page from the Dial-A-Phone Book. The service or person to be called is illustrated with a picture and word. The number itself is color coded and has a window to guide dialing one number at a time. This device was tested in two studies teaching telephone skills to over 200 moderately retarded children and adults. Over 90% of the subjects learned to dial using this device.

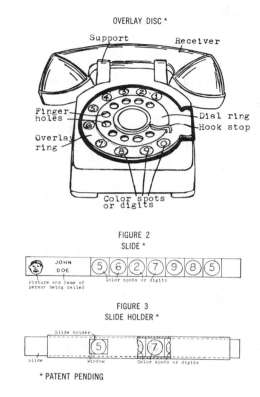

OVERLAY DISC *

Support   Receiver

Finger
holes
                Dial ring
Overlay   Hook stop
ring

Color spots
or digits

FIGURE 2
SLIDE *

JOHN
DOE   (5)(6)(2)(7)(9)(8)(5)
Picture and name of   Color spots or digits
person being called

FIGURE 3
SLIDE HOLDER *

Slide holder
        (5)   (7)
Slide   Window   Color spots or digits

* PATENT PENDING

FIGURE 14.1
Dial-A-Phone Device

SOURCE: *How To Use the Telephone,* by R.B. Leff. Copyright 1975, Instructo/McGraw-Hill, Paoli, Pennsylvania, 19301, Patent No. 3878623. Published in *Mental Retardation,* 1975, *13*(3), 10. Reprinted with permission of the author and the American Association on Mental Deficiency.

Another possible instructional arrangement is group instruction. Smith and Meyers (1979) compared demonstration with verbal summaries, demonstration alone, a no verbal instruction, and no demonstration practice control in both group and individual telephone instruction for 60 moderately to profoundly retarded adults. The telephone skills taught included identifying six parts of the telephone, dialing the operator to report a fire, calling for a doctor's appointment, and calling a drug store to ask the closing time. In group instruction, five adults were trained simultaneously but tested individually. All procedures improved the telephoning skills. However, in most cases, the group-trained individuals surpassed the performances of those trained individually. The demonstration and verbal summaries were not found to be greatly superior to practice. However, these cues were *not* step-by-step prompts but were lectures given before the students performed the skills. Based on this study, the teacher might maximize learning by using group instruction and step-by-step prompting rather than an initial lecture.

Using the Yellow Pages

For some students, using the telephone company phone book might be preferable to a teacher-made book, or this instruction might follow mastery of the simplified book. One of the advantages of using the regular directory is access to a greater number of persons and services. Kittelson and Certo (1975) taught five mildly retarded, orthopedically impaired students to use the local yellow pages to secure the delivery of selected goods and services. This program was particularly beneficial because of the students' difficulty in finding transportation to area businesses. The program was taught in six phases that focused on the components of Yellow Pages use, including locating the number (given a written cue), linking a needed product with its generic class (e.g., food for supper: grocers–retail), locating the number given a verbal cue, writing the number, dialing the number and making the request, and securing the product or service by performing all the tasks.

Before this program, these students had been taught related skills in reading, math, telephone use, and the use of the Yellow Pages. For example, they could locate the Yellow Pages in the directory and read the guide words. Teaching procedures followed the principles described in chapter 5, including task analysis, verbal and model prompts, reinforcement contingencies (praise and stars on a chart), and group instruction. One strategy this study used that may have been particularly helpful was alphabetical tab markers. These helped the student locate the guide words (e.g., cleaners, laundries, pizza, hospital equipment and supplies). A second technique employed was the instruction of verbal scripts to order items. A sample of these scripts is shown in Table 14.6. Sample scripts facilitated initial success as they eliminated the need for verbal spontaneity.

Emergency Phone Calls

Perhaps one of the most critical telephoning skills is the ability to call for help in an emergency. To place an emergency call, you must discriminate when help is required, whom to call, how to call, and what information to state. These skills were taught to three moderately retarded adults in a sheltered workshop by Risley and Cuvo (1980). As prerequisites, the subjects were required to state their name and address and correctly read five seven-digit numbers. The materials used included modified telephone directories containing a picture of the emergency person (e.g., fireman, police, or doctor), printed occupation, and a randomly selected seven-digit number.

TABLE 14.6 Sample Script Taught for Ordering A Service By Telephone after Using the Yellow Pages

Sample Script

Heading Word: *Cleaners*
Business: Good afternoon. Madison Steam and Dye.
John: *Hello. My name is John Hayes. I would like to have some clothes to be dry cleaned picked up at my school.*
Business: What is the name and address of the school?
John: *Lapham School. 1045 East Dayton Street. Room 117.*
Business: What is your name?
John: *John Hayes. The cleaning will be billed to my teacher, Mrs. Kittelsen.*
Business: When can we pick those up?
John: *Today or tomorrow before three.*
Business: We will take care of it. Thank you. Goodbye.
John: *Thank you. Goodbye.*

SOURCE: "Teaching Orthopedically Handicapped Adolescents to Secure Selected Products and Services From Their Community Through Functional Use of the Yellow Pages and Telephone" by E. Kittleson and N. Certo. In L. Brown, T. Crowner, W. Williams, and R. York (Eds), *Madison's Alternative for Zero Exclusion: A Book of Readings.* Madison, Wisc.: Madison Public Schools, 1975, p. 250. Reprinted with permission.

Also used were disconnected telephones and 18 pictures of emergency situations. These pictures showed scenes like a kitchen stove on fire, someone hurt, or someone in danger. A yellow posterboard "thermometer" showing the steps of the task analyses completed independently was used to give graphic feedback. The task analyses for the three types of calls were validated by watching someone make the calls, consulting the telephone company and the emergency departments, and viewing a telephone company film on dialing. During the test and training, the trainer showed one picture of an emergency and asked the student to use the telephone book and phone to demonstrate what to do in that situation. The "emergency person" on a second phone asked the vital questions identified earlier by social validation (e.g., "What is your name?"). During testing, each step of the task analysis was scored, with no help or feedback provided. During training the prompts used included (*a*) verbal instruction (e.g., "Put your index finger in the dial hole for the number three"), (*b*) verbal instruction plus modeling, and (*c*) verbal instruction plus physical guidance. Reinforcement consisted of praise after a predetermined set of steps and filling in the thermometer at the end of the task.

A multiple baseline design across subjects demonstrated the effectiveness of the procedure. Also, after one emergency was trained, generalization occurred to the other two emergencies.

Handling and Preventing Home Accidents

To the extent that a handicapped individual can recognize and escape fires and deal with simple injuries, the possibility of living in the community independently or semi-independently will be more likely. Matson (1980) taught these skills to five moderately retarded institutionalized adults being prepared for community living. Escaping a fire was taught through verbally rehearsing the steps and then modeling with a figure moved across a cardboard model of the living area. Both the verbal rehearsal and simulated role play were followed by teacher and peer praise and correction as needed. Students were taught in groups of two or three and mastered verbal rehearsal of the fire escape steps in 4 to 7 half-hour sessions with good retention after 7 months. Next, the same two groups learned to state and then role play with each other the first aid steps for simple cuts and injuries. Results revealed fairly rapid attainment of the two skills with good maintenance. However, with both the fire escape and the first aid steps, after the students could verbally rehearse the steps, *they still were unable to role play the behaviors* until taught to do so. However, once the steps were learned as role-played behaviors they were remembered well. Matson's (1980) comments on the use of role-play training are relevant here.

A note of caution about training persons with cognitive and adaptive skills similar to the subjects used in this study deserves mention. These subjects had previously received training in the role-playing of adaptive skills but for persons on the same ward, who were naive to such training, confusion resulted about how to role-play and the purposes for it. When asked to escape from a fire, typical comments have been "there is no fire." Thus, with subjects having little or no training in participant modeling or role-playing, a demonstration phase on the function of role-playing may be necessary. (p. 408)

Telling Time

Many programs designed to teach time telling to the handicapped require extensive prerequisites (O'Brien, Note 3). For example, one of the best-designed commercial programs (Bijou, 1973) requires students to (*a*) discriminate red and green, (*b*) count from 1 to 60, (*c*) read numbers from 1 to 60, (*d*) write numbers from 1 to 60, and (*e*) count by 5's to 55. O'Brien (Note 3) designed a program that does not require many prerequisites. To simplify the task, he taught 14 moderately retarded institutionalized

TABLE 14.7 Steps in the O'Brien Program for Telling Time

I. Reading the Hour Hand
  Step 1: Match number to clock face number
        Phase 1: 1   (numbers on the clock)
              2: 1, 8
              3: 1, 8, 5
              4: 1, 8, 5, 4
              5: 1, 8, 5, 4, 10
              6: 1, 8, 5, 4, 10, 9
              7: 1, 8, 5, 4, 10, 9, 2
              8: 1, 8, 5, 4, 10, 9, 2, 6
              9: 1, 8, 5, 4, 10, 9, 2, 6, 11
             10: 1, 8, 5, 4, 10, 9, 2, 6, 11, 7
             11: 1, 8, 5, 4, 10, 9, 2, 6, 11, 7, 3
             12: 1, 8, 5, 4, 10, 9, 2, 6, 11, 7, 3, 12
             13: 1, 8, 5, 4, 10, 9, 2, 6, 11, 7, 3, 12
  Step 2: "Point to number ___ on the clock face."
        Shown the number, point to its match on the clock.
        In 13 phases (see above), number held farther and farther away from clock.
  Step 3. "Point to number ___ on the clock face."
        (Not shown the number.)
  Step 4: Imitation of number name. "This is number ___.
        What number is this? Say ___." (Point to number on clock face.)
  Step 5: Number naming. "What number is this?" (Point to number on clock face.)
  Step 6: Reading the hour hand. "What number does the hour hand point to?"

II. Reading the Minute Hand
  Step 7: Discrimination of hour and minute hand. "Point to the hour hand." "Point to the minute hand."
  Step 8: Read minute hand—imitation. "What does the minute hand say. Say 'o'clock'." ("o'clock", "30", "15", "45")
  Step 9: Read the minute hand (no verbal prompt.)

III. Read the nearest quarter hour setting.
  Step 10: Read hour hand when not exactly on a number.
        Phase 1: Move hour hand clockwise.
              2: Only 2 numbers on clock. Hour hand between them. "Which number did the hour hand point to last?"
              3: All numbers showing.
              4: Hour hand between and minute hand on 9.
              5: Hour hand between and minute hand on 3.
              6: Hour hand between and minute hand on 6.
              7: Hour hand between or on and minute hand 12, 9, 3, 6.
                 Note S^D: "What number does the hour hand point to?"
                 "What number does the minute hand read?"
                 "What time is it? Say ___."
  Step 11: Read time to quarter hour. "What time is it?"
  Step 12: Read time between quarter hour as "It's about ___."
        S^D: "What time is it? Say about ___."
  Step 13: Read time between quarter hours. No prompt. "What time is it?"
        Phase   Distance from nearest quarter hour
          1   1 minute
          2   1, 3
          3   1, 3, 5
          4   1, 3, 5, 7
          5   0, 1, 3, 5, 7

SOURCE: "Instruction in Reading a Clock for the Institutionalized Retarded" by F. O'Brien. Unpublished manuscript, Southern Illinois University, 1974. Reprinted with permission.

adults to tell time to the nearest quarter hour and to say "about" when shown times between quarter hours (e.g., "It's about 8:15"). The only prerequisites necessary were adequate vision and some expressive language. A magnetic clock with detachable numbers was used. Reinforcement was praise and moving a slide counter ahead after each step. After eight slides of the counter, the subject received a sip of diet soda. When errors occurred, the trainer, who was a ward attendant, said a loud "No!" and moved the counter to zero. The phases of the O'Brien program are listed in Table 14.7. Note that the steps are based on an easy-to-hard discrimination sequence and introducing and withdrawing a verbal prompt. It would be possible to fade the verbal prompt more gradually, using time delay. Although O'Brien successfully taught telling time without using delay fading, this technique might enhance learning for other students.

As O'Brien noted, the skill he taught was only one of many possible time-telling skills. An ecological inventory of a student's environment will identify the precise skills needed, which may include reading written times in a movie ad or TV schedule, reading a digital clock (e.g., a watch or alarm clock), budgeting time to finish activities by a given time (e.g., getting to a bus stop, ending a break at work), and identifying a clock time, given a spoken time ("Take the roast out at 6:00, John"). When time-telling instruction is separate from its natural use in context (as O'Brien did), it will need to be probed and perhaps retrained in the natural situation. For some students it might be more efficient to teach a selected skill in the setting in which it is needed. For example, an adult in a sheltered workshop could be taught to return to a work station when "the long hand passes the two" without knowing how to read the time or any other number names.

When the task is reading written time, time delay fading of a verbal prompt may be an effective instructional strategy (see chapter 5). In an unpublished study, Chan (Note 4) taught a physically impaired, mildly retarded adult to read a TV schedule and a clock and identify when her favorite programs came on television. Chan taught three components of this skill: (a) reading a clock to the nearest half-hour (using the O'Brien sequence through step 11, omitting the "15" and "45" minutes), (b) reading the program names printed in the newspaper's TV schedule, and (c) reading the written time of the program printed in the newspaper. Using a multiple probe design across the three subtasks, Chan (Note 4) taught each task using delay fading of a verbal model and praise as a consequence. The student acquired each skill after instruction; however, maintenance was not measured. Because instruction in time telling can include

rather complex skills, it is essential, as Chan's work illustrates, that the aspects of telling time that are important for a given student be determined. This will require the teacher to become familiar with both current and subsequent vocational, leisure, community, and domestic environments.

Community Mobility Skills

Community mobility may be one of the most important sets of skills for a moderately or severely handicapped person. Walking or taking public transportation frees an individual from reliance on parents, friends, or special vans for access to employment, services, and recreation, thus providing a more normal life. The economic savings of agencies who teach the use of public transportation as compared to providing special transportation for all clients can be impressive (Cortazzo & Sansone, 1969). Descriptions of successful mobility training programs for this population document its feasibility as well as its benefits.

Orientation and mobility are critical skills for visually impaired people. Unfortunately, mobility training has not always been considered a priority for the sighted handicapped person, despite deficiencies in this area and need for these skills (Laus, 1977; Vogelsburg & Rusch, 1980). Laus (1977) emphasized the importance of mobility instruction in the real environment to avoid difficulty in generalizing from an artificial setting.

The major barriers to a community mobility program often are parental, staff, and community concern for the student's safety. Perske (1972) has defended the handicapped person's right to the "dignity of risk." Overprotection of handicapped people can bar them from opportunities for normal growth and development. Over the years, a handicapped person can learn incompetent or "helpless" behavior because service providers unintentionally deprive him of making decisions (Floor & Rosen, 1975).

Given the handicapped person's right to learn skills that involve some risk, it is still the instructor's responsibility to maximize safety. Sowers, Rusch, and Hudson (1979) included several safety precautions in their program to teach a severely retarded adult to ride a bus. They included having the client carry an emergency information card, notifying the local police about the program, and gradually fading supervision. To fade supervision, the instructor stopped riding the bus with the client after he performed all but one nonessential step independently. Next, the client's parents waited at the bus stop for him to check that he arrived on the right bus at the right time. In the next phase, neither parents nor the instructor were present, but an observer unknown to the client rode the bus. In the last phase, the client rode the bus with infrequent follow-up checks by the unknown observer. On one occasion, the client did miss his stop and rode the bus to the end of the route. The bus driver notified the police, who returned the client to his home. Vogelsburg and Rusch (1980) recommend that, because of the risks involved in mobility training, instructors should obtain parental or guardian consent, have professional liability coverage, and inform the mass transit system of the program. Vogelsburg and Rusch (1979) also used two instructors to teach one client to cross a street so that one could model the response while the other ensured that the client remained on the sidewalk. However, other studies (Matson, 1980; Page, Iwata, & Neef, 1976) have used one-to-one training or small group instruction successfully.

Goals for Community Mobility

Community mobility requires numerous skills—locating the destination, paying bus fares, crossing intersections, and handling variations in routine such as a late bus. Table 14.8 lists some of the community mobility skills, assuming that the student will be taught to travel in the community unassisted. However the goal for some individuals will probably be semi-independent travel.

To select a program goal from this list, the instructor should consider the student's age and environmental needs. Vogelsburg and Rusch (1980) recommend first teaching a student to travel to and from work. After this is mastered, the instructor might teach travel to needed services (e.g., health center) and next, travel to recreational facilities. Furthermore, the authors emphasized the importance of teaching any academic skills (e.g., coin identification) in the context of the mobility program. If a student is younger, not yet employed, and has some community mobility skills, a more comprehensive program might be taught. For example, Laus (1977) taught moderately retarded students mobility skills in the following order: (1) using stop/nonstop sign intersections, (2) traveling to a specific location, such as a neighborhood business, (3) crossing controlled intersections of many different types, and (4) traveling independently to and from home and on a school bus. Supplemental classroom instruction was provided in color recognition, numeral recognition, personal grooming, verbal communication, basic sign reading, and counting and exchanging money. To enhance generalization, these skills might be taught in the context of a bus-riding program.

One other consideration in selecting the mobility program goal is the need for reliable pedestrian skills as a prerequisite. Generally programs teaching bus riding to handicapped people with no community mobility skills have taught the related pedestrian skills as a component (cf., Cortazzo & Sansone, 1969; Neef, Iwata, & Page, 1978; Sowers, Rusch, & Hudson, 1979). Gruber, Reeser, and Reid (1979), on the other hand, selected walking to school as the priority goal for institutionalized profoundly retarded students. This priority was supported by the authors' survey of residences for the handicapped in 43 states, which indicated that transportation to school was a serious problem in most.

Instructional Procedures

Once the mobility goal is selected, the instructor must plan an effective program. A review of research on mobility instruction can suggest successful techniques.

Table 14.9 shows a detailed task analysis of bus riding which was tested by Neef et al. (1978). In an earlier study, Page et al. (1976) also task analyzed crossing intersections for five different types of intersections. For example, the pedestrian light skills consisted of four responses: student (a) stops upon arrival at the intersection; (b) starts across street within 5 seconds of the light changing to WALK, (c) turns head at least 45 degrees to the left and right at least once while in the street, and (d) does not stop walking until completely across the street (p. 437). Laus (1977) task analyzed the bus travel route itself to determine landmark cues for unboarding a bus. Gruber et al. (1979) task analyzed the walking route to determine successively longer starting points for the backward chaining of walking to school.

The earliest studies on community mobility training were comprehensive programs including classroom instruction in related skills such as social behavior and functional reading (Cortazzo & Sansone, 1969; Kubat, 1973; Laus, 1974). Although these authors did not agree on the predictive value of IQ for success in travel programs, all concluded that their own program success raised their expectations for retarded persons to master independent travel (Laus, 1977).

Subsequent research reports have offered more precision in teaching technique and evaluation of these techniques through experimental design. This precision has made independent mobility feasible for students who previously might not have been candidates for this instruction. For example, Gruber et al. (1979) taught independent walking skills to four institutionalized profoundly retarded men who were nonvocal, had toileting accidents, and exhibited self-stimulatory and self-abusive behavior. The target behavior was to walk from the living area to the school building, staying within defined but unmarked boundaries and without exhibiting inappropriate behaviors. To shape this behavior, the staff used backward chaining by initially bringing the stu-

TABLE 14.8 Skills for Community Mobility

USE OF PUBLIC TRANSPORTATION (bus)	CAR POOLING (if no public available)	GENERAL PEDESTRIAN SKILLS Cross Intersections (types)	ACADEMICS Optional
1. Walk to bus stop (see Pedestrian Skills)	1. Be ready and watch for car	1. Pedestrian light	1. Read bus schedule
2. Identify correct bus	2. Social behavior in car	2. Traffic light	2. Coin identification and summation
3. Signal bus	3. Pay share (more than driver's share)	3. Stop sign	3. Read community signs (bus names, numbers, street signs)
4. Board bus (pay fare)		(a) Cars cross pedestrian path	
5. Social behavior during bus ride		(b) Cars same direction as pedestrian	
6. Knowledge of route (identify landmarks)		4. Unmarked	*Essential*
7. Identify stop and pull buzzer			1. Leave home or work in time to catch bus
8. Depart bus		*Walking*	2. Present coins for fare
9. Bus transfer			3. (a) Recognition of correct bus numbers or name
10. Walk to destination		1. Within boundaries of sidewalk—correct side of road	(b) Use landmarks to follow correct route walking or identify bus departure site
11. Handling predictable variations: e.g., Bus does not arrive due to weather Bus late Someone stands blocking exit door No seats on bus		2. To destination (knowledge of route)	

dent three-fourths of the way to school and adding one-quarter distances after the student mastered each one. During the travel to school, the staff intermittently praised correct walking, verbally prompted remaining within boundaries, and reprimanded any inappropriate behaviors. Over training days, the staff faded themselves by increasing their distance from the clients.

Before instruction, the staff obtained a baseline measurement by watching each client walk to school. The assessment ended when the client walked out of bounds or engaged in an inappropriate behavior, at which time the student was returned to the living area. Once intervention began, the same procedure was repeated to probe independent walking at four program points (the four chaining distances). In a multiple baseline design across subjects, all four students learned to travel to school in 4 to 15 days. Without further training, all were able to walk back to the living area and maintained the travel skills when probed 8 weeks later.

Another school travel program was implemented by Spears, Rusch, York, and Lilly (1981), who taught school bus departure to a severely retarded, nonvocal boy with visual problems and no self-help skills. A multiple baseline design was employed across three target behaviors: (a) walking to the building from the bus, (b) locating the bedroom and putting down school bag and coat, and (c) locating and entering the playroom. The stimulus cue for this chain of behaviors was the school bus driver's command "Go in the building." The instructor used a least intrusive prompt system and verbal praise during baseline as well as intervention. The intervention technique was pacing prompts that were verbal reminders to prevent pausing on the next step (Bellamy, Horner, & Inman, 1979). A reversal design indicated the effectiveness of the pacing prompts. The student acquired the independent arrival (to living area) behavior in 46 days.

A more complex pedestrian skill is crossing intersections. Page et al. (1976) taught students to cross

TABLE 14.9 Correct and Incorrect Response Definitions for the Four Components of Bus Riding

Situation	Correct Response	Incorrect Response
1. Bus-stop location	1.1 Subject (S) walks directly to within 3 m of correct bus stop within 2 min of instruction.	(1) S is not within 3 m of correct bus stop within 2 min of instruction.
2. Boarding bus	2.1 S walks onto "West Main" bus before it departs.	(1) S walks onto other than "West Main" bus. (2) S does not board "West Main" bus before it departs.
	2.2 S puts 25¢ in meter or gives bus driver pass and waits for bus pass to be returned.	(1) S does not put 25¢ in meter. (2) S does not give pass to driver or wait for its return.
	2.3 S sits in any empty seat at or in front of back doors.*	(1) S sits in seat in back of back door. (2) S attempts to sit in a nonempty seat.
	2.4 S sits quietly on bus without disturbing others.	(1) S emits inappropriate verbal behavior in a manner to disrupt others or draw attention to himself. (2) S exhibits inappropriate motor behavior in a manner to disrupt others or draw attention to himself (e.g., rocking, smoking, staring, arms over front seat, not facing forward, etc.)
	2.5 S remains seated entire time bus is in motion until bus is ½ block from Maple Hill Mall.	(1) S gets out of seat while bus is in motion. (2) S gets out of seat when bus is stopped at location other than Maple Hill Mall.
3. Exiting bus	3.1 S pulls cord once, for 2 sec or less at location between Wards and Singers.	(1) S does not pull cord. (2) S pulls cord more than once. (3) S pulls cord for more than 2 sec. (4) S pulls cord when bus is 25 feet closer or further than target location.
	3.2 S stands up within 3 sec after bus stops.	(1) S stands up later than 3 sec after bus stops.
	3.3 S gets off bus within 7 sec after standing up.	(1) S does not get off bus within 7 sec after standing up.
	3.4 S steps on curb with no physical contact with bus within 3 sec after stepping off.	(1) S is in physical contact with bus within 3 sec after exiting. (2) S is standing in street within 3 sec after exiting.
4. Signaling bus**	4.1 S stands at least 0.6 m from curb, within 3 m of bus stop, facing street	(1) S stands closer than 0.6 m from curb. (2) S stands further than 3 m from bus stop. (3) S does not face street (within 90° of direction from which bus approaches).
	4.2 S raises hand when "Vine Lake" bus approaches from ½ block away.	(1) S does not raise hand when "Vine Lake" bus approaches.
	4.3 S stays at least 0.6 m from curb until bus comes to complete stop.	(1) S moves closer than 0.6 m from curb before bus is completely stopped.

* It was considered desirable for subjects to be in close proximity to the driver in the event of emergency situations.
** Since the first skill component involved boarding a bus already waiting at a central downtown location, signaling the bus was necessary only on the return trip and thus constituted the last skill component.

SOURCE: "Public Transportation Training: In Vivo Versus Classroom Instruction, by N.A. Neef, B.A. Iwata, and T.A. Page. *Journal of Applied Behavior Analysis*, 1978, *11*, 334–335. Copyright 1978 by the Society for the Experimental Analysis of Behavior, Inc. Reprinted with permission.

five types of intersections: (a) unmarked, (b) pedestrian lights, (c) traffic light, (d) stop sign—cars crossing the pedestrian's path, and (e) stop sign—cars going in same direction as the pedestrian. The students' level of functioning ranged from nonretarded to moderately retarded. Instruction occurred in the classroom and included a model representing four city blocks and a doll moved around on the simulated intersections. They also used frequent street probes to assess generalization to a real setting. Simulated training was used to minimize danger, to provide more training opportunities unhindered by weather, and to avoid the time and staff required for *in vivo* training. A multiple baseline across students and behaviors demonstrated that simulated training on each skill led to mastery of the simulated task. However, three of the five clients needed *in vivo* training on the first two types of intersections before generalizing to a real street. These results emphasize the value of teaching in realistic settings even with mildly retarded or nonretarded.

Vogelsburg and Rusch (1979) also taught street crossing, but their program was conducted *in vivo* and their students were severely mentally retarded, multiply handicapped adolescents. They selected only the first skill identified by Page et al. (1976)—unmarked intersections. The behavior was further analyzed into approach, look, step, and walk. Results of the multiple baseline design across subjects indicated that instructional feedback (least intrusive prompts) taught the students to approach and walk. However, it was necessary to use repeated practice (five repeated trials) to establish the looking responses. To fade reliance on prompts, the instructor rehearsed the entire skill with the student and then modeled the skill as the student watched. Next the student crossed the street alone. After 3½ months of daily 20-minute sessions, the students acquired the skill and generalized it to similar, untrained intersections.

The decision to use simulated or *in vivo* training may depend primarily on the client. The subjects of Page et al. (1976) were higher functioning as a group and learned rapidly in a simulated setting with minimal *in vivo* training (an average of 5.3 hours). In contrast, the subjects in the Vogelsburg and Rusch (1979) study, who were more severely handicapped, required substantially more time to acquire one street-crossing skill *in vivo*. Further clarification of setting selection can be found in the next few studies.

Neef et al. (1978) used both simulated and *in vivo* settings to teach bus riding skills to mildly and moderately retarded students. Five students were taught with a simulated bus, slides depicting correct and incorrect responses, and a street model identical to the one used by Page et al. (1976). Two students were trained *in vivo*. The simulated instruction was less expensive, less time-consuming (9 hours versus 33 hours), and generalized to an actual bus. Students also were able to generalize to a second bus, novel in contrast to the simulated bus, and maintained their skills over a year.

Another successful simulation program was implemented by Certo, Schwartz, and Brown (1975). Their simulation included videotapes of critical landmarks. The clients also received bus route cards to use permanently or temporarily. These cards listed the names of the two buses on the connecting routes and important landmarks. In contrast, Coon, Vogelsburg, and Williams (1981) did not find generalization from a similar simulated setting to an actual bus for a severely retarded woman. Only after training was given in the natural environment was the woman able to ride an actual bus.

Primarily using the natural environment, Sowers et al. (1979) trained bus riding to a severely retarded man in daily 3-hour sessions with supplemental classroom instruction on identifying the bus number. After 24 days, when the student had acquired all but one nonessential step (pulling the buzzer), training ended and covert observations were made to ensure maintenance and safety.

While no certain conclusions can be drawn from the research on pedestrian and bus-riding skills, simulated training alone appears less effective, the more severely handicapped the student. However, with mildly to moderately handicapped students, simulated training *may* result in generalization but may have to be supplemented with *in vivo* training. If a simulated setting is chosen, similarity to the actual task will enhance generalization (e.g., using videotapes of landmarks). For students with no community mobility skills, *in vivo* training may be worth the staff and time investment. Teaching pedestrian skills may be easier to train *in vivo* than bus riding, while teaching bus riding in the classroom may enhance, but not replace, *in vivo* training (cf. Coon et al., 1981).

Community mobility training requires a long time. Sowers, et al. (1979) scheduled daily 3-hour bus riding lessons (one trial to and from work) and concluded that more time might have resulted in faster acquisition. For safety, staffing may need to be one-to-one or even two-to-one for some clients trained *in vivo*. However, these temporary expenditures may be offset by the long-range savings when the client can travel independently.

Shopping

Goals for independent mobility probably include travelling to work, procuring community services, and using recreational facilities. Numerous community services might be selected for training, depending on the student's needs. A few examples are a health center, grocery stores, pharmacy, restaurants, clothing stores, and banks. After selecting the service, the instructor will write objectives specifying what items or services the student must learn to obtain. Ford, Opperman, and Weis (1975) listed hierarchies of objectives for teaching severely handicapped people to use clothing stores, grocery stores, and restaurants. For example, under clothing stores, they included objectives on getting to the store, finding the correct department, paying for the purchase, and leaving the store. The least sophisticated objective required the student to indicate which of several objects could be purchased there. The most sophisticated skill was to name or select a given clothing item.

Direct instruction in mobility is essential for learning. For example, Matson (1981) has shown that even mildly retarded adults will not acquire shopping skills unless taught to do so. Instead, uninstructed mildly retarded adults will pick items randomly or impulsively (Williams & Ewing, 1981).

In groups of five, Matson (1981) taught mildly retarded adults grocery shopping skills through classroom instruction which was followed by *in vivo* instruction. The 10 adults taught learned more than an untrained control group, maintained the skill for at least 2 months, and generalized the skills to an untrained store. During the first phase, training alternated between the classroom and the store.

Classroom training focused on selecting grocery items from a shopping list, staying within a $10.00 budget, and locating items using an aisle and department map of the store. By grouping grocery items in cost columns ($1.00 or $2.00), each client learned to select a total set of items under $10.00 since all were capable of counting to 10. In addition, clients rehearsed to the group the 14 grocery-buying steps listed in Table 14.10 and the basics of grocery item selection and location. On alternative sessions, training took place in the store, where food location was the primary skill taught during the first phase. During the second and third phases, clients were taught to buy their own weekly groceries, using the chain of steps. First the trainer modeled and described shopping tasks; then each client individually performed the task. Clients were asked to evaluate themselves; those that thought they'd done well also were given feedback about the accuracy of their evaluation. A client who stated that he or she needed to improve was asked to specify how and then given feedback on these comments. In addition to trainer modeling, self-evaluation, and trainer feedback, peer reinforcement in each group of five clients was also used. Although these subjects were mildly retarded, a similar instructional package was applied successfully in teaching showering skills to lower-functioning clients (Matson, 1981).

Nietupski, Certo, Pumpian, and Belmore (1976) taught grocery shopping to six severely handicapped students. Their skill sequence included labeling food, selecting food, generating a shopping list, transferring pictures from consumed food items to the grocery list, identifying the components of a supermarket, and using a portable shopping aid. After 16 weeks of instruction, two students mastered all skills in the sequence, while the remaining students required more training after acquiring two to four of the skills. As part of their training, students learned to use a cardboard prosthetic shopping aid (Figure 14.2), which helped them to compile a shopping list and determine the cost of selected items. Food items, which were sequenced by their location in the store, were shown pictorially, in written form, or both, depending upon the student. Extra space at the bottom of the card allowed new food items to be added; these varied according to the student's preferences. No product brand or sizes were indicated; instead students were taught to select the smallest can or package. Items to be purchased were checked beforehand located in each box.

As shown by each food item in Figure 14.2, the self-adhesive white squares represented $.50 intervals. Each item had as many squares as the number of $.50 intervals it cost (e.g., Spam cost between $.51 and $1.00). As an item was selected, the white squares were moved onto the money gauge—the black spaces in the upper left corner of the aid. Total grocery cost (up to $5.00) could be determined from the number below the last white square. Finally the aid, which was in a compact three-ring binder, could be placed open in the child seat of the shopping cart.

Use of Restaurants

Another community service that can be beneficial to a severely handicapped person is an inexpensive restaurant. Marholin, O'Toole, Touchette, Berger, and Doyle (1979) taught four moderately and severely retarded adults to travel to McDonald's and order a meal. This instruction was conducted *in vivo* and incorporated a least intrusive prompt system, social reinforcement, rehearsal, and brief timeouts (a few seconds withdrawal of teacher attention contingent on incorrect response). These adults increased their number of correct responses and generalized to an untrained fast-food hamburger restaurant. The authors defended the selection of a well-known chain as a target service because of convenient hours, location, and stimulus cues that are present across locations (e.g., "golden arches").

TABLE 14.10 Checklist of Grocery Shopping Skills

1. *Can Select the Store.* The client was able to pick out the grocery store from other stores on the block.
2. *Go into Correct Door.* The client could walk through the "in" door of the grocery store. (This step was important for decreasing congestion at the entrance of the store. Also, many grocery store doors are automated, making it impossible to go through the "out" door). Discriminative cues taught to the clients included going through the door to the right and identifying the words "in" and "out."
3. *Attend to Traffic Flow.* The client was able to follow traffic flow to the shopping carts. Attempts to go through the checkout area to reach the food shelves were scored as incorrect.
4. *Select a Shopping Cart.* The client was expected to obtain a cart from the storage area. No food items could be present in the cart.
5. *Look at Shopping List.* After obtaining a shopping cart, the client could look at his or her grocery list and determine where selected items were located in the store. Clients were then required to indicate verbally and/or gesturally zones specific foods were in. (A zone was defined as a discrete section of the grocery store, labeled with signs, where canned goods, meats, etc., were stored).
6. *Go to Zone of Store.* The client could successfully go to the store zone where grocery list items were located.
7. *Go to Additional Zones.* The client could go to all zones other than the first one in which food items on the shopping list were stored without trainer prompts.
8. *Find Individual Items.* The client could obtain all foods checked on the grocery list, unless the item was out of stock.
9. *Select Acceptable Quantity.* Based on the need and money available, the client could select an appropriate size and quantity of each item. (Quantities were predetermined and discussed with each resident receiving independence training before going to the store.)
10. *Check Grocery List.* Before checking out the items from the store, the clients could review his or her grocery list to ensure that all required items had been selected. This task was checked by the trainer, who observed the client while he or she verbally reviewed items after being asked to do so.
11. *Go to the Checkout Counter.* The client could line up at the checkout counter.
12. *Help Checker.* The client could take items from the grocery cart and place them on the checkout counter.
13. *Handle Money Appropriately.* After all items had been tabulated, the client could give the checker an amount of money greater than that required to pay for items purchased. The client could then wait until he or she received change and could safely deposit it in his or her pocket, purse, and/or wallet.
14. *Take Groceries.* The client could lift the groceries from the checkout counter and carry them out of the store.

SOURCE: "Use of Independence Training to Teach Shopping Skills to Mildly Mentally Retarded Adults" by J.L. Matson. *American Journal of Mental Deficiency,* 1981, *86,* 179. Reprinted with permission.

In a second study teaching the use of a fast-food restaurant, three mildly to moderately retarded and multiply handicapped high school students learned to use McDonald's (van den Pol, Iwata, Ivancic, Page, Neef, & Whitley, 1981). Classroom training using slides and a simulated ordering counter was combined with periodic *in vivo* probes. Follow-up generalization probes in a second fast-food restaurant (Burger King) were conducted both overtly and covertly (i.e., with and without the subjects' knowledge). Results indicated improved performance as well as extended maintenance a year after training and generalization to a novel restaurant.

MATH AND MONEY SKILLS

Throughout this chapter we have suggested ways in which functional academics like reading and math

might enhance the acquisition of daily living skills. For example, the ability to read recipes could aid in learning food preparation skills. Computational skills could expand shopping skills. However, daily living skills can and have been taught without teaching related academic skills. For example, a prosthetic shopping list or pocket calculator could substitute for computational skills while shopping (Nietupski et al., 1976; Smeets & Kleinloog, 1980; Wheeler, Ford, Nietupski, Loomis, & Brown, 1980). Also, a student could learn to pay a bus fare without having general money skills by learning to select the exact coins (without naming them or knowing their value) or to pay a restuarant bill by rounding off to the nearest dollar (van den Pol et al., 1981).

For some severely handicapped students, acquisition of general academic skills may be feasible and beneficial. For example, mastering matching coin

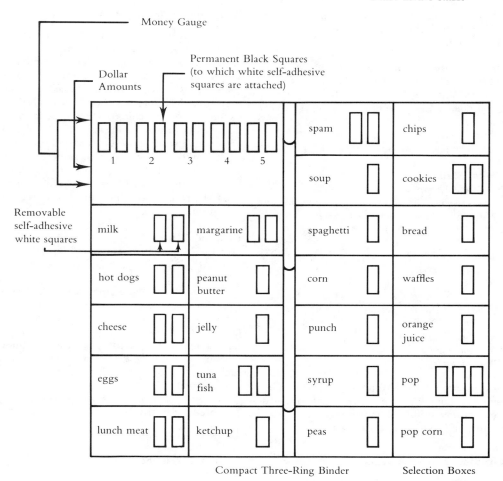

FIGURE 14.2
Prosthetic Shopping Aid

SOURCE: "Supermarket Shopping: Teaching Severely Handicapped Students to Generate a Shopping List and Make Purchases Functionally Linked with Meal Preparation" by R. Nietupski, N. Certo, I. Pumpian, and K. Belmore. In L. Brown, N. Certo, K. Belmore, and T. Crowner (Eds.), *Madison's Alternative for Zero Exclusion: Papers and Programs Related to Public Schools Services for Secondary Age Severely Handicapped Students* (Vol. 7, pt. 1). Madison, Wisc.: Madison Public Schools, University of Wisconsin, 1976, p. 229. Reprinted with permission.

combinations to a spoken or written amount would help students use a variety of services requiring coins (laundry, vending machine, small purchases, bus fare, etc.). To teach a general skill like money management, presenting skills in an easy-to-difficult sequence may be best. The sequence may be based on the order in which nonhandicapped persons acquire the skill (developmental) or on research that identifies a successful sequence for handicapped persons (remedial). When adapting a sequence for the severely handicapped person, tasks that are immediately useful (e.g., setting table, purchasing produce) should be chosen and grouped so that the person can master the general concept (e.g., counting an unordered set).

In grouping general math skills into functional tasks, the teacher may need to teach other skills at the same time. Grouping of skills within a task will result in distributed, rather than mass, practice on the math skill. Distributed practice may be a more efficient way to teach skills to the severely handicapped (Mulligan, Guess, Holvoet, & Brown, 1980). The following two illustrations contrast a nonfunctional, massed practice math lesson and a math skill incorporated in a functional task (a game for an *elementary-school-age* student):

Nonfunctional Massed Practice Math Lesson

T: *(presents 5 poker chips)* "Count the chips."
S: "One-two-three-four-five."
T: "Good counting!" *(Presents 3 poker chips)* "Count the chips."
S: "One-two-three."
T: "Good counting!" *(Presents 4 chips, etc...)*

Same Math Skill
Teacher-Made Shopping Game

T: *(Displays board game with photos of grocery store, picture grocery list, and displays real grocery items.)* "Let's go shopping. Who takes you shopping?" *(Language)*
S: "Mom and Dad."
T: "Yes, Mom and Dad." *(Hands list—picture reading).*
S: "We need potatoes." *Points to photo of produce aisle on game. Gets out real potatoes from bin.*
T: "How many potatoes?"
S: "One-Two-Three-Four-Five"
T: "Good counting! What's next?"
S: "We need apples." *(Etc.)*

This game would *not* substitute for instruction in a grocery store, but it would provide another opportunity to rehearse simple shopping behaviors (e.g., using a list) and to learn a leisure skill.

Longitudinal Math Sequence

A task analysis of an introductory mathematics curriculum was developed and validated for nonhandicapped children by Resnick, Wang, and Kaplan (1973). Table 14.11 presents the skills in this sequence. The level of difficulty increases with each successive unit. Within units, certain skills are of equal difficulty. For example, in Units 1 and 2, C and D are of equal difficulty, while skill D depends upon A through C. There is some evidence that the mentally retarded may learn these math skills in the same sequence as nonretarded learners (Spradlin, Cotter, Stevens, & Friedman, 1974). Following such a logical sequence might maximize transfer from one concept to the next (Resnick et al., 1973). To use this sequence, the teacher of the severely handicapped would select a set of functional tasks to teach each concept. Unit 8 probably would not be used for the severely handicapped because of its limited applicability to daily living.

Longitudinal Money Sequence

Table 14.12 presents a sequence for developing general money skills. This order is based on several theoretical assumptions: (a) matching precedes identification, (b) receptive precedes expressive labeling, (c) coins are easier than bills, and (d) concrete manipulations (touch coins) are easier than abstract ones (count without touching). When teaching coin addition, pennies are presented last, based on the successful teaching sequence researched by Lowe and Cuvo (1976). With the exception of the coin research of Cuvo and his colleagues, most of this sequence is based on theory and has not been validated by research. Thus teachers may find more efficient ways to order these skills.

Coin Summation

Lowe and Cuvo (1976) taught mildly and moderately retarded adolescents a finger-counting method to sum coins. The students were taught to place certain fingers on the table and tap them while counting by fives for each coin except pennies. For example, when counting a nickle, the index finger was used to tap once while saying "five." All five fingers were tapped in succession for a quarter. Pennies were introduced last; they were counted by tapping beside each penny and counting by ones from the amount already totaled (e.g., with a nickel and two pennies, "five" by the nickel, "six, seven" beside the pennies). The order of instruction was:

1. Count nickels;
2. Count dimes;
3. Sum nickels and dimes;
4. Count quarters;
5. Sum nickels, dimes, and quarters;
6. Count half dollars;
7. Sum nickels, dimes, quarters, half dollars;
8. Count pennies;
9. Sum all coins.

The instructional procedure was to model the counting while the student watched, count the coins with the student, and then require the student to count them alone. This sequence permits functional use from the onset, while learning to count pennies first may be less functional since many services, vending machines, and telephones will not take pennies.

An alternative would be a counting program that includes matching coins to prices to make small purchases. If students are young, teaching penny counting first may be a useful way to introduce the concept of counting and may also be involved in a token reinforcement system with other skills.

Table 14.11 Objectives of the Curriculum

*Units 1 and 2: Counting and One-to-One Correspondence**

A. The child can recite the numerals in order.
B. Given a set of moveable objects, the child can count the objects, moving them out of the set as he counts.
C. Given a fixed ordered set of objects, the child can count the objects.
D. Given a fixed unordered set of objects, the child can count the objects.
E. Given a numeral stated and a set of objects, the child can count out a subset of stated size.
F. Given a numeral stated and several sets of fixed objects, the child can select a set of size indicated by numeral.
G. Given two sets of objects, the child can pair objects and state whether the sets are equivalent.
H. Given two unequal sets of objects, the child can pair objects and state which set has more.
I. Given two unequal sets of objects, the child can pair objects and state which set has less.

*Units 3 and 4: Numerals***

A. Given two sets of numerals, the child can match the numerals.
B. Given a numeral stated and a set of printed numerals, the child can select the stated numeral.
C. Given a numeral (written), the child can read the numeral.
D. Given several sets of objects and several numerals, the child can match numerals with appropriate sets.
E. Given two numerals (written), the child can state which shows more (less).
F. Given a set of numerals, the child can place them in order.
G. Given numerals stated, the child can write the numeral.

Unit 5: Comparison of Sets

A. Given two sets of objects, the child can count sets and state which has more objects or that sets have same number.
B. Given two sets of objects, the child can count sets and state which has less objects.
C. Given a set of objects and a numeral, the child can state which shows more or less.
D. Given a numeral and several sets of objects, the child can select numerals which show more (less) than the set of objects.
E. Given two rows of objects (not paired), the child can state which row has more regardless of arrangement.
F. Given three sets of objects, the child can count sets and state which has most (least).

Unit 6: Seriation and Ordinal Position

A. Given three objects of different sizes, the child can select the largest (smallest).
B. Given objects of graduated sizes, the child can seriate according to size.
C. Given several sets of objects, the child can seriate the sets according to size.
D. Given ordered set of objects, the child can name the ordinal position of the objects.

Unit 7: Addition and Subtraction (sums to 10)

A. Given two numbers stated, set of objects, and directions to add, the child can add the numbers by counting out two subsets then combining and stating combined number as sum.
B. Given two numbers stated, set of objects, and directions to subtract, the child can count out smaller subset from larger and state remainder.
C. Given two numbers stated, number line, and directions to add, the child can use the number line to determine sum.
D. Given two numbers stated, number line, and directions to subtract, the child can use number line to subtract.
E. Given addition and subtraction word problems, the child can solve the problems.
F. Given written addition and subtraction problems in form: x or x; the child can complete the problems.
G. Given addition and subtraction problems in form: $x + \begin{matrix}+y\\ \overline{y}\end{matrix} = \square$, or $\begin{matrix}-y\\ \overline{x}\end{matrix} - y = \square$; the child can complete the equations.

TABLE 14.11 (CONTINUED)

Unit 8: Addition and Subtraction Equations

A. Given equation of form $z = \square + \triangle$, the child can show several ways of completing the equation.

B. Given equation of form $x + y = \quad + \quad$, the child can complete the equation in several ways.

C. Given equations of forms $x + y = z + \quad + z$, the child can complete the equations.

D. Given equations of forms $x + \square = y$ and $\square + x = y$, the child can complete the equations.

E. Given complete addition equation (e.g., $x + 7 = z$), the child can write equations using numerals and minus sign (e.g., $z - x = y$) and demonstrate relationship.

F. Given counting blocks and/or number line, the child can make up completed equations of various forms.

*Unit 1 involves sets of up to five objects: Unit 2 involves sets of up to 10 objects.

**Unit 3 involves numerals and sets of up to five objects; Unit 4 involves numerals and sets of up to 10 objects.

SOURCE: "Task Analysis in Curriculum Design: A Hierarchically Sequenced Introductory Mathematics Curriculum" by L.B. Resnick, M.C. Wang, and J. Kaplan. *Journal of Applied Behavior Analysis*, 1973, *6*, 679–710.

Whatever the order of coins selected, teaching counting can be more effective if the student initially displaces or moves the coin while counting. In a comparison of moderately retarded students taught with displacement and nondisplacement, Borakove and Cuvo (1976) found superior performance for those taught with the displacement method. This finding is consistent with Resnick et al.'s (1973) counting sequence.

Coin equivalency

To purchase an item, you must match coins equivalent to a price. To teach this skill, Trace, Cuvo, and Criswell (1977) used an adapted vending machine. Prices were illuminated on the front of the machine. The machine returned incorrect coin combinations and accepted correct coin combinations, for which it dispensed candy. Thus, the machine itself provided realistic feedback. The only exception was a coin equivalency test in which the machine was used to indicate prices only. Students were taught a variety of combinations to represent the prices on the machine, beginning with nickels alone and moving to larger coin combinations. Three specific responses were taught for using the machine: naming the price, selecting equivalent coins, and depositing coins. Although not included by Trace et al., (1977), the instructor could teach functional reading of the selection buttons—a fourth response required with most vending machines.

Change Computation

Computing change is more difficult than summing coins because it requires either subtraction or counting from one number (price) to another (money given). Change computation is primarily useful to the moderately or severely handicapped to prevent them from being taken advantage of by salespeople.

A study by Cuvo, Veitch, Trace, and Konke (1978) taught change computation to moderately retarded adolescents who were able to sum coins, read prices, and put together equivalent coins. The order of instruction was: 1¢ to 4¢, 2¢ to 25¢, 10¢ to 45¢ (using multiples of five), and 11¢ to 49¢ (not using multiples of five). The skill was taught by having the students make a purchase with available coins and then compute their change. The "counting back" procedure was used to make change. That is, the student learned to read the price ("10 cents") and count from the price to the coins given for purchase ("15, 20, 25,") and then to state the sum of the change ("15 cents").

The teacher of the severely handicapped who plans to teach either computation or general money skills should teach both as components of daily living, vocational, or leisure skills, not as isolated skills. Any skill presented solely in table-top instruction probably will not generalize to other settings or be maintained. To teach both concepts and functional activities, the teacher will want to consider first those activities most critical in the student's life. Then, by planning specific skills to teach within each activity, generalization across many situations can be taught to ensure concept mastery.

SUMMARY

Mastery of the routine life skills probably should constitute the majority of instructional time for most moderately to severely handicapped students. The literature on deinstitutionalization and community living indicates that survival for the severely handicapped adult in community-based, supervised, residential settings is clearly facilitated by skills in personal care, food preparation, home and clothing maintenance, and community use. This chapter re-

TABLE 14.12 Skill Sequence for Generalized Use of Money

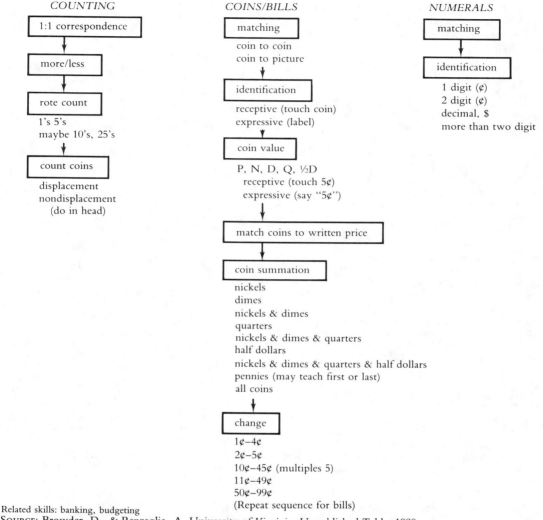

Related skills: banking, budgeting
SOURCE: Browder, D., & Renzaglia, A. University of Virginia, Unpublished Table, 1980.

views some of the recent literature in daily living skills instruction with this population, including food preparation, grooming, clothing selection and care, housekeeping, telephone skills, handling and preventing home accidents, time telling, pedestrian skills, use of public transportation, shopping, restaurant use, and coin skills. Some related program planning considerations are also addressed. These considerations are based on the following assumptions:

1. Self-management and long-term skill maintenance must be the ultimate goal of each daily living program.
2. Program goals should be selected only after a thorough inventory of the student's current and future environments (vocational, domestic, leisure, and community environments).
3. To maximize skill generalization, teaching should be done with realistic materials in natural settings as often as possible.
4. To maximize skill maintenance, daily living skills should be targeted that are most likely to be frequently needed and thus naturally retained.
5. Since the development of valid task analyses is central to skill acquisition, teachers should employ social validation techniques as programs are being developed.
6. To reduce program expense, teachers may want

to probe less frequently than daily and recycle materials whenever possible.

7. Group instruction as well as the active involvement of students in the teaching process appears to facilitate the acquisition and generalization of daily living skills.

REFERENCES

Alberto, P., Jobes, N., Sizemore, A., & Doran, D. A comparison of individual and group instruction across response tasks. *Journal of the Association for Severely Handicapped*, 1980, *5*, 285–302.

Bauman, K.E., & Iwata, B.A. Maintenance of independent housekeeping skills using scheduling plus self-recording procedures. *Behavior Therapy*, 1977, *8*, 554–560.

Bellamy, G.T., Horner, R.H., & Inman, D.P. *Vocational habilitation of severely retarded adults.* Baltimore: University Park Press, 1979.

Better Homes and Gardens junior cookbook. New York: Meredith Corp., 1972.

Bijou, S. *It's about time.* Bellevue, Wash.: Edmark, 1973.

Borakove, L.S., & Cuvo, A.J. Facilitative effects of coin displacement on teaching coin summation to mentally retarded adolescents. *American Journal of Mental Deficiency*, 1976, *81*, 350–356.

Browder, D. *A comparison of a stimulus prompt and a response prompt with four fading procedures to teach sight words to the moderately and severely retarded.* Unpublished doctoral dissertation, University of Virginia, 1981.

Brown, F., Holvoet, J., Guess, D., & Mulligan, M. The Individualized Curriculum Sequencing model (III): Small group instruction. *Journal of the Association of the Severely Handicapped*, 1980, *5*, 352–364.

Brown, L., Branston, M.B., Hamre-Nietupski, S., Pumpian, I., Certo, N., & Gruenewald, L. A strategy for developing chronological age appropriate and functional curricular content to severely handicapped adolescents and young adults. *Journal of Special Education*, 1979, *13*, 81–90.

Certo, N., Schwartz, R., & Brown, L. Community transportation teaching severely handicapped students to ride a public bus system. In L. Brown, T. Crowner, W. Williams, & R. York (Eds.), *Madison's alternative for zero exclusion: A book of readings.* Madison, Wisc.: Madison Public Schools, 1975.

Coon, M.E., Vogelsburg, T., & Williams, W. Effects of classroom public transportation instruction on generalization to the natural environment. *Journal of the Association of the Severely Handicapped*, 1981, *6*(2), 46–53.

Cortazzo, A.C., & Sansone, R. Travel training. *Teaching Exceptional Children*, 1969, *3*, 67–82.

Crnic, K.A., & Pym, H.A. Training mentally retarded adults in independent living skills. *Mental Retardation*, 1979, *17*(1), 13–16.

Crocker, B. *Cookbook for boys and girls.* New York: Golden Press, 1975.

Cronin, K.A., & Cuvo, A.J. Teaching mending skills to retarded adolescents. *Journal of Applied Behavior Analysis*, 1979, *12*, 401–406.

Cuvo, A.J. Validating task analysis of community living skills. *Vocational Evaluation and Work Adjustment Bulletin*, 1978, *11*(3), 13–21.

Cuvo, A.J., Jacobi, E., & Sipko, R. Teaching laundry skills to mentally retarded students. *Education and Training of the Mentally Retarded*, 1981, *16*, 54–64.

Cuvo, A.J., Leaf, R.B., & Borakove, L.S. Teaching janitorial skills to the mentally retarded: Acquisition, generalization and maintenance. *Journal of Applied Behavior Analysis*, 1978, *11*, 345–355.

Cuvo, A.J., Veitch, V.D., Trace, M.W., & Konke, J.L. Teaching change computation to the mentally retarded. *Behavior Modification*, 1978, *2*, 531–548.

Doleys, D.M., Stacy, D., & Knowles, S. Modification of grooming behavior in adult retarded: Token reinforcement in a community-based program. *Behavior Modification*, 1981, *5*, 119–128.

Falvey, M., Brown, L., Lynn, S., Baumgart, D., & Schroeder, J. Strategies for using cues and correction procedures. In W. Sailor, B. Wilcox, & L. Brown (Eds.), *Methods of instruction for severely handicapped students.* Baltimore: Paul H. Brookes, 1980.

Felsenthal, D., & Scheerenberger, R.C. Stability and attitudes of primary caregivers in the community. *Mental Retardation*, 1978, *16*(1), 16–18.

Floor, L., & Rosen, M. Investigation the phenomenon of helplessness in mentally retarded adults. *American Journal of Mental Deficiency*, 1975, *79*, 565–572.

Ford, A., Opperman, D., & Weis, J. Minimum objectives related to teaching severely handicapped students to use selected stores and services. In L. Brown, T. Crowner, W. Williams, & R. York (Eds.), *Madison's alternative for zero exclusion: A book of readings*, (Vol. 5). Madison, Wisc.: Madison Public Schools, 1975.

Gollay, E., Freedman, R., Wyngaarden, M., & Kurtz, N.R. *Coming back: The community experiences of deinstitutionalized mentally retarded people.* Cambridge, Mass.: Abt Books, 1978.

Gruber, R., Reeser, R., & Reid, D.H. Providing a less restrictive environment for profoundly retarded persons by teaching independent walking skills. *Journal of Applied Behavior Analysis*, 1979, *12*, 285–297.

Hamre, S. An approximation of an instructional model for developing home living skills in severely handicapped students. In L. Brown, W. Williams, & T. Crowner (Eds.), *A collection of papers and programs related to public school services for severely handicapped students.* Madison, Wisc.: Madison Public Schools, 1974.

Horner, R.D., & Baer, D.N. Multiple-probe techniques: A variation on the multiple baseline. *Journal of Applied Behavior Analysis*, 1978, *11*, 189–196.

Johnson, B.F., & Cuvo, A.J. Teaching mentally retarded adults to cook. *Behavior Modification*, 1981, *5*, 187–202.

Kahn, E.H. *Cooking activities for the retarded.* Nashville: Abingdon, 1974.

Kazdin, A.E. Assessing the clinical or applied importance of behavior change through social validation. *Behavior Modification*, 1977, *1*, 427–452.

Kittleson, E., & Certo, N. Teaching orthopedically handicapped adolescents to secure selected products and services from their community through functional use of the Yellow Pages and telephone. In L. Brown, T. Crowner, W. Williams, & R. York (Eds.), *Madison's alternative for zero exclusion: A book of readings.* Madison, Wisc.: Madison Public Schools, 1975.

Kubat, A. Unique experiment in independent travel. *Journal of Rehabilitation,* 1973, *2,* 36–39.

Laus, M.D. *Travel instruction for the retarded.* Springfield, Ill.: Charles C Thomas, 1977.

Leff, R.B. Teaching the TMR to dial the telephone. *Mental Retardation,* 1974, *12*(2), 12–13.

Leff, R.B. Teaching TMR children and adults to dial the telephone. *Mental Retardation,* 1975, *13*(3), 9–12.

Lowe, M.L., & Cuvo, A.J. Teaching coin summation to the mentally retarded. *Journal of Applied Behavior Analysis,* 1976, *9,* 483–489.

Marholin, II, D., O'Toole, K.M., Touchette, P.E., Berger, P.L., & Doyle, D.A. "I'll have a Big Mac, large fries, large coke, and apple pie," . . . or teaching adaptive community skills. *Behavior Therapy,* 1979, *10,* 236–248.

Martin, J., Rusch, F., James V., Decker, P., & Trytol K. The use of picture cues in the preparation of complex meals. *Journal of Applied Behavior Analysis,* in press.

Matson, J.L. Preventing home accidents: A training program for the retarded. *Behavior Modification,* 1980, *4,* 397–410.

Matson, J.L. Use of independence training to teach shopping skills to mildly mentally retarded adults. *American Journal of Mental Deficiency,* 1981, *86,* 178–183.

Matson, J.L., DiLorenzo, T.M., & Esveldt-Dawson, K. Independence training as a method of enhancing self-help skills acquisition of the mentally retarded. *Behavior Research and Therapy,* 1981, *19,* 399–405.

Moore, E. *The Seabury cookbook for boys and girls.* New York: Seabury Press, 1969.

Mulligan, M. Guess, P., Holvoet, J., & Brown, F. The Individualized Curriculum Sequencing model (I): Implications from research on massed, distributed or spaced trial training. *Journal of the Association for Severely Handicapped,* 1980, *5,* 325–336.

Neef, N.A., Iwata, B.A., & Page, T.A. Public transportation training: In vivo versus classroom instruction. *Journal of Applied Behavior Analysis,* 1978, *11,* 331–344.

Nettlebeck, T., & Kirby, N.H. Training the mentally handicapped to sew. *Education and Training of the Mentally Retarded,* 1976, *11,* 31–36.

Nietupski, R., Certo, N., Pumpian, I., & Belmore, K. Supermarket shopping: Teaching severely handicapped students to generate a shopping list and make purchases functionally linked with meal preparation. In L. Brown, N. Certo, K. Belmore, & T. Crowner (Eds.), *Madison's alternative for zero exclusion: Papers and programs related to public schools services for secondary age severely handicapped students* (Vol. 7, Pt. 1). Madison: Madison Public Schools, University of Wisconsin, 1976.

Nihira, L., & Nihira, K. Jeopardy in community placement. *American Journal of Mental Deficiency,* 1975, *79,* 539–544.

Nutter, D., & Reid, D.H. Teaching retarded women a clothing selection skill using community norms. *Journal of Applied Behavior Analysis,* 1978, *11,* 475–487.

O'Connor, G. Home is a good place: A national perspective of community residential facilities for developmentally disabled persons. *Monograph of the American Association of Mental Deficiency,* 1976 (Number 2).

Page, T.J., Iwata, B.A., & Neef, N.A. Teaching pedestrian skills to retarded persons: Generalization from the classroom to the natural environment. *Journal of Applied Behavior Analysis,* 1976, *9,* 433–444.

Parents Nursery School. *Kids are natural cooks.* Boston: Houghton-Mifflin, 1974.

Perske, R. The dignity of risk. In W. Wolfensberger (Ed.), *The principle of normalization in human services.* Toronto: National Institute on Mental Retardation, 1972.

Resnick, L.B., Wang, M.C., & Kaplan, J. Task analysis in curriculum design: A hierarchically sequenced introductory mathematics curriculum. *Journal of Applied Behavior Analysis,* 1973, *6,* 697–710.

Risley, R., & Cuvo, A.J. Training mentally retarded adults to make emergency telephone calls. *Behavior Modification,* 1980, *4,* 513–525.

Robinson-Wilson, M.A. Picture recipe cards as an approach to teaching severely and profoundly retarded adults to cook. *Education and Training of the Mentally Retarded,* 1977, *12,* 69–73.

Schalock, R.L., & Harper, R.S. Placement from community-based mental retardation programs: How well do clients do? *American Journal of Mental Deficiency,* 1978, *83,* 240–247.

Schalock, R.L., Harper, R.S., & Carver, G. Independent living placement: Five years later. *American Journal of Mental Deficiency,* 1981, *86,* 170–177.

Schleien, S.J., Ash, T., Kiernan, J., & Wehman, P. Developing independent cooking skills in a profoundly retarded woman. *Journal of the Association for the Severely Handicapped,* 1981, *6,* 23–29.

Sedgewick, V. *My learn to cook book.* New York: Golden Press, 1967.

Smeets, P.M., & Kleinloog, D. Teaching retarded women to use an experimental pocket calculator for making financial transactions. *Behavior Research of Severe Developmental Disabilities,* 1980, *1,* 1–20.

Smith, M., & Meyers, A. Telephone skills training for retarded adults: Group and individual demonstrations with and without verbal instruction. *American Journal of Mental Deficiency,* 1979, *83,* 581–587.

Snell, M.E. Daily living skills: Instruction of moderately and severely retarded adolescents and adults. In J.M. Kauffman & D.P. Hallahan (Eds.), *Handbook of special education.* Englewood Cliffs, N.J.: Prentice-Hall, 1981.

Snell, M.E. Teaching bedmaking to severely retarded adults through time delay. *Analysis and Intervention in Developmental Disabilities,* in press.

Sowers, J., Rusch, F.R., & Hudson, C. Training a severely retarded young adult to ride the city bus to and from work. *AAESPH Review,* 1979, *4,* 15–23.

Spears, D.L., Rusch, F.R., York, R., & Lilly, M.S. Training independent arrival behaviors to a severely mentally retarded child. *Journal of the Association for the Severely Handicapped;* 1981, *6*(2), 40–45.

Spellman, C., DeBriere, T., Jarboe, D., Campbell, S., & Harris, C. Pictorial instruction: Training daily living skills. In M.E. Snell (Ed.), *Systematic instruction of the severely and profoundly handicapped.* Columbus, Ohio: Charles E. Merrill, 1978.

Spradlin, J.E., Cotter, V.W., Stevens, C.M., & Friedman, M. Performance of mentally retarded children on pre-arithmetic tasks. *American Journal of Mental Deficiency,* 1974, *78,* 397–403.

Staples, K.S. *Cooking from pictures.* Fargo: North Dakota State University, 1975.

Steed, F.R. *A special picture cookbook.* Lawrence, Kans.: H & H Enterprises, 1974.

Stokes, T.F., & Baer, D.N. An implicit technology of generalization. *Journal of Applied Behavior Analysis,* 1977, *10,* 349–367.

Trace, M.W., Cuvo, A.J., & Criswell, J.L. Teaching coin equivalence to the mentally retarded. *Journal of Applied Behavior Analysis,* 1977, *10,* 85–92.

van den Pol, R.A., Iwata, B.A., Ivancic, M.T., Page, T.J., Neef, N.A., & Whitely, F.P. Teaching the handicapped to eat in public places: Acquisition, generalization, and maintenance of restaurant skills. *Journal of Applied Behavior Analysis,* 1981, *41,* 61–69.

Vogelsburg, R.T., Anderson, J., Berger, P., Hasleden, T. Mitwell, S., Schmidt, C., Skowron, A., Ulett, D., & Wilcox, B. Programming for apartment living: A description and rationale of an independent living skills inventory. *Journal of the Association of the Severely Handicapped,* 1980, *5,* 38–54.

Vogelsburg, R.T., & Rusch, F.R. Training severely handicapped students to cross partially controlled intersections. *AAESPH Review,* 1979, *4,* 264–273.

Vogelsburg, R.T., & Rusch, F.R. Community mobility training. In F.R. Rusch & D.E. Mithaug (Eds.), *Vocational training for mentally retarded adults.* Champaign, Ill.: Research Press, 1980.

Wheeler, J., Ford, A., Nietupski, J., Lommis, R., & Brown, L. Teaching moderately and severely handicapped adolescents to shop in supermarkets using pocket calculators. *Education and Training of the Mentally Retarded,* 1980, *15,* 105–112.

Williams, R.D., & Ewing, S. Consumer roulette: The shopping patterns of mentally retarded persons. *Mental Retardation,* 1981, *19,* 145–149.

Yates, J. *Look and cook.* Seattle: Bernie Straub Publishing Co. and Special Child Publications, 1972.

REFERENCE NOTES

1. Renzaglia, A. Personal Correspondence, May 1981.

2. Browder, D., Hines, C., McCarthy, L.J., & Fees, J. *Teaching sight words to promote generalization of daily living skills.* Unpublished manuscript, Lehigh University, 1981.

3. O'Brien, F. *Instruction in reading a clock for the institutionalized retarded.* Unpublished manuscript, Southern Illinois University, 1974.

4. Chan, C. *Using time delay to teach reading a clock and television schedule.* Unpublished manuscript, Lynchburg College, 1981.

*This chapter was written by **Martha E. Snell,** University of Virginia.*

15

Functional Reading

Education for the moderately and severely handicapped centers upon useful skills that increase independence in the tasks of daily living. Teachers of these students must operationalize this goal so that the curricula systematically build these skills. To do this, a teacher must ask how much reading ability is necessary.

Many would quickly state that the students should readily recognize and understand a basic "protective" vocabulary, including certain street signs (stop, walk, don't walk, etc.), building signs (danger, men, women, open, push, exit, entrance), and other cautionary words (poison, do not enter, private, danger), as well as their standard pictorial representations (i.e., the international sign system). The number of protective words would vary considerably from teacher to teacher, as would the words themselves. Other teachers would expand the list to include words pertaining to days and months, name and address, cooking, shopping, entertainment, and employment. This expansion quickly transforms a list of 15 to 50 words into one the size of a small dictionary. For example, the Oregon State curriculum for teachers of the trainable (*Curriculum-Cumulative Progress Report,* Note 1, page 1), in the cooking category, lists 52 verbs and adjectives from recipes: "wash," "cook," "cut," "saute," "scramble," "soft boil," etc. Then there are still food words, utensil words, and the common adjectives, adverbs, conjunctions, prepositions, and so on commonly found in even simple cookbooks. In short, while a list of cautionary words may be shorter than functional vocabulary lists, both sets lack specific definition, and their actual content varies by school district, teacher philosophy, and the student's specific vocational and daily living curriculum.

Some teachers would dodge the question altogether and state that reading instruction is unrealistic for this population, that it is too complex, and that success will not be forthcoming. Class time, they say, would be spent more profitably on other, less academic skills. This attitude is reflected by Kirk's words (1972).

In general, trainable children do not learn to read from even first grade books. Their ability is limited to reading and recognizing their names, isolated words and phrases, common words used for their protection, such as "danger," "stop," "men," "women" and other signs which they encounter in a community. Some trainable children with special abilities can learn to read. Most who learn to read, however, are probably educable mentally retarded children. (p. 231)

Kirk's comments represent the position that the task of reading relies upon mental abilities far beyond the capabilities of the moderately and severely retarded (Apffel, Kelleher, Lilly, & Richardson, 1975).

Fortunately, there has been a reasonable amount of research demonstrating successful procedures to teach reading to the moderately and severely handicapped. However, as with other complex skills, (a) the handicapped pupil's success is clearly a product of the teacher's ability to analyze and program instruction, (b) progress is usually slower than for learners with no mental or emotional handicap, and (c) the ultimate performance is lower for handicapped then normal learners. None of these three characteristics need prevent the development of reading as a useful skill.

TERMINOLOGY

Before delving into instructional methods, a few terms require further definition. "Functional" commonly describes the orientation of skill development for the severely handicapped. As it applies to reading vocabulary lists or to literacy, it takes on somewhat different meanings.

Functional Literacy

This term refers to minimal but practical competency in reading, indicating an ability to react appropriately to the daily reading and writing demands of modern life. These demands include using checks and bank statements; completing applications for jobs, driver's license, Medicaid, Social Security number, etc.; reading recipes, maps, personal letters, categorized listings such as the Yellow Pages and the want ads, food labels, warranties, and so on. In Figure 15.1, Lichtman (1974) lists common printed materials related to practical activities.

The question of what level of reading is functional has caused great debate in recent years (Harman, 1970), with educators identifying from 4th up to 7th-grade skills as minimal competency (Duffy & Sherman, 1977). However, most researchers agree upon the prevalence of the problem. The Survival Literacy Study (Heckler, Note 2) estimated that 13% of Americans are unable to complete common forms without making mistakes on 10% of the form's blanks, and one-third of these make errors on more than 30% of the form. For example, 34% of those interviewed had trouble reading a simplified Medicaid application and 8% could not accurately complete a driver's license form. While the exact overlap between functional illiterates and those classified as severely educationally handicapped or mentally retarded is unknown, it is probably considerable.

Realistic tools to measure functional literacy are still being developed and validated (Lichtman, 1974;

Nafziger, Thompson, Hiscox, & Owen, 1975; Stricht, Caylor, Kern, & Fox, 1972). Traditionally the tests used to assess reading ability in grade schools have been applied inappropriately to test unskilled adults. Although these tests do tap the necessary abilities of word recognition and comprehension and monitor type of reading errors and rate, practical reading tasks are omitted and test content is often geared to children. Because it is essential that teachers of the severely handicapped be able to assess functional literacy, this topic will be expanded later.

Functional Reading

The definition of "functional reading" is not specific across users. Brown and Perlmutter (1971) define it as "discrete and observable motor responses to printed stimuli" (p. 75), such that the student would learn two responses for any given printed stimulus: to read the word and to indicate the word's meaning in an observable way. "Functional" dictates the practical nature of the vocabulary, but its difficulty range as judged by grade level and its exact content is less clear than that covered by "functional literacy." Brown and his colleagues emphasize that the goal of functional reading instruction is a skill for survival in our word-dependent community—similar to functional literacy. However, fewer words are taught; they are selected by the needs of a given student. Words are not simply drawn from word lists. Rather, inventories or top-down curricula (see chapter 4) are the tools for determining which words need to be learned.

A second characteristic of functional reading concerns instruction. Although the term does not prescribe teaching methods, a "whole word" or visual approach is commonly used. Students are taught to memorize words through repeated drill, without placing emphasis upon sentence content, structural, or letter sound cues (Brown, Huppler, Pierce, York, & Sontag, 1974). The best instruction occurs in context, such as reading key words in simplified recipes while cooking, or locating the "In" door while learning to use a grocery store.

The vocabulary taught often includes a cautionary or protective vocabulary. Included are the words which normally appear on labels or signs in public places and often warn readers of potential risks, and the associated symbols (skull and crossbones to symbolize poisonous substances) or sign cues (red, hexagonal stop signs). Unless these words are taught *in context,* they are not likely to be functional. For example, a small group of words could be taught as part of a pedestrian skills program (walk, don't walk, stop), while another group might be taught in the context of a restaurant (in, out, men, women). When students have a limited potential for reading, in-

FIGURE 15.1

Categories of Commonly Used Printed Materials. [Items marked with an asterisk are included in a test of functional literacy: Reading/Everyday Activities in Life (R/EAL). The test is presented so that its appearance clearly resembles its actual printed form.]

1 Signs and Labels	2 Schedules and Tables	3 Maps	4 Categorized Listings and Indices	5 High-Interest, Factual Narrative
Road Signs*	T.V. Guide*	City/Street	Yellow Pages	Sports Events
Clothing Tags	Bus Schedule	Road*	Book Indices	News Report
Medicine Labels	Train/Plane Schedule	Global Weather	Want Ad*	Narcotics Article*
Billboards	Work/School Schedule		Dictionary	

6 Illustrated Advertisements	7 Technical Documents	8 Sets of Directions	9 Fill-in Blank Form
Department Store	Conditional Sales Contract	Recipe (Pizza)*	Banking Forms
Yellow Pages	Insurance Policies	Use of Tools/ Machinery/ Equipment	Job Application*
Food Store*	Guarantees	Sewing with Pattern	Car Registration
Magazine	Apartment Lease*		Credit Application
			Hospital Entry Form

*For each of these representative reading activities, detailed task analyses have been prepared, including terminal tasks and enabling tasks.

SOURCE: "The Development and Validation of R/EAL, An Instrument to Assess Functional Literacy," by M. Lichtman. *Journal of Reading Behavior*, 1974, *6*, 172. Reprinted with permission.

context instruction is most likely to let them learn the appropriate response to a given word.

LEARNING TO READ—A TASK ANALYSIS

Underlying all successful instruction is a clearly defined understanding of the task. When the task is complex, as reading is, the analysis is difficult. This section of the chapter borrows heavily from the work of others to describe a sequence of subtasks leading to reading skills. See also the portions of chapters 4 and 5 that detail behavior measurement, task analysis, and learning principles; these teaching skills are the basic tools for structuring learning in small, ordered steps, bolstering learning with cues and prompts, strengthening responses with an external motivation system, and measuring the learning stage and the extent of learning in each stage from acquisition and fluency to maintenance and generalization.

The analysis of a learning task relies upon the analyst's concept of how the task is learned. Even with simple motor chains like hand-washing, the task analysis will vary from teacher to teacher; the detail in the steps, their order, and the method used to complete the task will change depending upon the student, the materials used, and the teacher doing the analysis. With complex tasks like reading, many more conceptualizations of how the skill is acquired

are possible. The task analyst must determine what visual, auditory, and visual-auditory stimuli need to be discriminated, the corresponding responses, and the order of instruction.

This section describes three overlapping analyses of reading. The first is the simplest, but has been successful with retarded learners (Sidman, 1971; Sidman & Cresson, 1973). This learning process is a whole word or look-say approach that involves auditory and visual matching of pictures (their spoken and printed labels) and words (both spoken and printed). The second analysis is actually a series of simple analyses of specific *functional tasks* (Lichtman, 1972), such as interpreting the directions on a macaroni-and-cheese mix box. The task analysis simply evaluates the reading and direction-following skills. After the learner has mastered a set of vocabulary words, these functional task analyses suggest learning activities consistent with the development of useful reading skills. While the whole word instructional analysis details the steps to teach simple word acquisition, the functional analysis suggests steps for directing the learner to apply reading skills in everyday activities.

By necessity, the third analysis of reading is very detailed. It recognizes that reading involves both visual and auditory association and discrimination as well as visual memory and sequencing. Reading is not simply a process of visual memorization. The third analysis describes the behaviors necessary to take the learner from a level of no reading skills to a level of functional literacy—fluent reading at approximately 4th grade level with comprehension and an active use of word recognition strategies (Duffy & Sherman, 1973; Smith, Smith, & Brink, 1977). Although many of the early functional literacy skills have been successfully learned by the mildly and moderately mentally retarded (and will be reviewed later in this chapter), it is not clear how many of the remaining reading behaviors can be mastered by the moderately or severely handicapped. Thus, if we are to aim for functional literacy, instruction must begin in the primary years and be carried out in the context of realistic reading tasks and materials to enable generalization. Still, if student progress is not sufficient, goals must be reset before the student is too old to master some functional words or even picture reading.

The selection of a task analysis (simple or complex) to guide reading instruction will depend upon many variables. The teacher must consider the learner's prerequisite skills, chronological age or the number of schooling years remaining, and, depending upon the student's age, vocational potential (if a younger learner) or current need for reading in daily living and vocational activities (if older). For students weak in receptive language, reading instruction is obviously inappropriate. Other students with a good receptive repertoire will learn best with a whole word approach. And for some, if instruction begins early enough and prerequisite skills are there, the goal of functional literacy may be achieved with a more complex analysis.

Prerequisites

An essential precursor to reading is a *large receptive repertoire of meaningful words* without which "reading" could be conditioned but would remain meaningless. Reading and writing are abstract symbol systems whose entire meaning rests upon their corresponding verbal interpretation. As Staats (1968) has stated,

Bringing a vocal response under the control of a printed word stimulus imparts no additional functions to the printed word stimulus than just that—unless the vocal response (or the stimulus it produces) has already acquired other functions (meanings). If the vocal response already has other functions, that is, elicits other responses, then bringing the vocal response under the control of the printed word will impart these "functions" to the word according to the learning principles involved. At this point, the individual will read the printed word with comprehension. (p. 508)

Table 15.1 summarizes commonly identified, basic prerequisites to successful reading instruction. A physical handicap (manual dexterity, vision, or hear-

ing) alone does not eliminate the goal of learning to read or to express yourself in print. It does require, however, that the response modes be modified. For example, a motorically impaired student may learn to use a headwand-operated typewriter or a scanning aid (Harris-Vanderheiden & Vanderheiden, 1977) in place of handwriting, while manual communication would serve as an alternate response system during reading instruction with the deaf; and braille, though a complex tactual symbol system in itself, would replace printed words for the blind reader.

The mental and emotional handicaps of our students deter learning in both known and controllable ways as well as in unknown ways. We will review research on what is known and controllable for this population following the discussion on task analysis and testing.

Whole Word Approach

Sidman (1971) and Sidman and Cresson (1973, p. 521) viewed the task of learning to read as making a transfer from learned auditory-visual stimulus equivalences (teacher says "cat," student selects card with "cat" printed on it) to the purely visual equivalences that define simple reading comprehension (teacher shows student the word "cat" and student selects the cat picture from a group of choices). According to them, the barriers for most mentally retarded students who have been unsuccessful in learning to read *do not* concern the ability to understand spoken words (auditory comprehension, task 3 in Figure 15.2) or to name pictures (task 4). They generally master both tasks. However difficulties occur in "breaking through the 'sound barrier' " or transfering from auditory comprehension and picture naming to visual reading comprehension (tasks 6 and 7) and oral reading (task 8) (Sidman, 1971, p. 6). Sidman (1971) and Sidman and Cresson (1973) proposed and then

TABLE 15.1 Language and Sensory Skills Prerequisite for Reading

1. Intact visual and auditory sensory mechanisms[1]
2. The ability to respond to classroom stimuli which control and direct the learner's attentiveness
3. Meaningful receptive repertoire
4. A repertoire of vocal responses (repeating words, matching sounds and words, etc.) under the learner's immediate control[1]
5. Word associations leading to context cues

[1]While these behaviors are not mandatory, their absence necessitates the analysis of a more complex learning task with possible modifications in stimulus presentation format and response mode.

SOURCE: Adapted from Cohen, Gross, and Haring (1976); Duffy and Sherman (1973); Smith, Smith, and Brink (1977); Staats (1968).

demonstrated that if severely handicapped learners *first* were taught tasks 1 through 4 in which they were deficient and *second* were taught auditory receptive skills (task 5), then reading comprehension skills (tasks 6 and 7) and oral reading (task 8) emerged without any additional direct training.

The learners in these studies were moderately and severely retarded, demonstrated some skills in tasks 1 through 4 before teaching began, but essentially had no skills in tasks 5 through 8. They could not write, but were familiar with the automated teaching machine on which the teaching and testing was done. All three students learned to read 20 simple words after receiving instruction in the first 5 tasks. The majority of instruction was directed toward task 5

(auditory receptive reading), while tasks 2 and 3 (word matching and auditory comprehension) required a lot of instruction for two of the three students. The exact amount of instruction needed is difficult to quantify because it was sporadic; instruction ranged from 1 month of sessions for one student to a school year with sessions scheduled 1 to 3 times per week for another.

Depending upon the student's baseline performance in all the tasks, instruction began on one of the first five tasks and continued until the student had learned all 20 words at a given task level. Then instruction moved up to the next task in the first five tasks. The match-to-sample tasks (1, 2, 3, 5, 6, 7) were similar, except that the sample stimulus in tasks

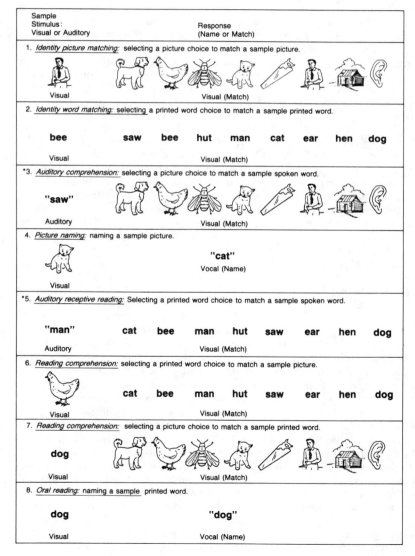

FIGURE 15.2
A Task Analysis of Learning to Read by a Whole Word Process
Once tasks 3 and 5 were mastered, subjects demonstrated successful learning transfer to tasks 6, 7, and 8—they demonstrated reading comprehension and oral reading without direct instruction on these skills.

SOURCE OF PICTURES: *Peabody Picture Vocabulary Test* by L.M. Dunn. Circle Pines, Minn.: American Guidance Services, 1959. Used with permission.
SOURCE OF TASK ANALYSIS: Drawn from Sidman, 1971; Sidman and Cresson, 1973.

1, 2, 6, and 7 was visual while in tasks 3 and 5 it was auditory. Visual samples appeared in an automated central window on the teaching machine which, when pressed by the learner, lighted the outer circle of eight choices to be lighted. Auditory samples were spoken over a speaker followed by the eight visual choices. In both cases, the student was to press the matching choice. In the two naming tasks (4 and 8) the center stimulus was lighted but outside choice panels remained blank since the task involved naming the stimulus rather than matching to a sample.

This method of teaching reading does not involve letter-sound association. Instead it emphasizes the whole word as a meaningful unit without any analysis of its parts. The main focus of instruction involves associating a spoken word with its printed word match (step 5), after prior visual discrimination of printed word similarities (step 2) and auditory comprehension of words (step 3). This analysis is more complete than other definitions of the same method; some whole word methods go from picture naming directly to oral naming of words with modeled prompts, a rather large shift in task complexity; other visual methods focus primarily on word-object matches followed by word-reading drill.

Two studies, which will be reviewed later (Hawker, 1968; Hawker, Geetz, & Shrago, 1964), suggest that steps 6 (picture stimulus–word choice) and 7 (word stimulus–picture choice) be reversed. This change would make the first task of reading comprehension involve a choice between meaningful items (pictures) rather than items with low meaning (words). More comparative study is needed to know whether all eight instructional steps in this order represent the most efficient way to teach words without any letter-sound analysis. Sidman's steps suggest one way to teach the reading of single words. Unfortunately this approach is limited to words that have picture counterparts.

Functional Reading Tasks

The best way to task analyze functional reading is to examine directly examples of reading found in common, everyday situations, such as those listed in Figure 15.1. A top-down approach for developing functional curricula (Brown, Branston, Hamre-Nietupski, Pumpian, Certo, & Gruenewald, 1979), discussed in chapters 4 and 14, perhaps is the best way to identify what reading skills a student actually needs in the relevant current and subsequent environments. While this approach is likely to yield more reading goals than can be taught, it is less likely to yield skills that, once learned, are forgotten through disuse.

After this list has been generated, priorities must be set and an instructional sequence determined.

Some objectives will have a logical order for instruction dictated by the easy-to-hard relationships among objectives as well as by the dependence of some tasks upon others. For example, before teaching a student to interpret a bus schedule or a television guide, the student must be able to read times and the days of the week and have a sizable sight vocabulary of words commonly used in television show titles and streets and places in the community. Therefore, time recognition and days of the week might be taught first. Realistic materials such as clocks, calendars, television guides, and bus schedules would still be used in teaching these skills.

Another consideration for sequencing objectives relates to the specific daily living and vocational needs of a given student. If a student lives in a boarding house, reading tasks related to cooking could be postponed while others may be of more immediate importance (e.g., operating automatic washers or dryers, using bus schedules, and reading street signs needed by pedestrians). For younger students living at home, functional reading instruction should also be tied to activities the student performs regularly at home and school to create practice opportunities and maximize motivation for learning.

Listing and ordering general objectives that directly relate to functional reading precede task analysis. Once a particular objective or small set of objectives has been informally selected, it must be analyzed to identify (a) how the terminal behavior will be measured, (b) the enroute instructional objectives leading to the terminal objective, (c) the instructional order of those objectives, and (d) the entry requirements or the skills prerequisite to the first enroute objectives.

Lichtman (1972) used a flow chart to display her task analyses of the reading comprehension and direction-following skills involved in some everyday activities. Task analyses were made to determine the reading, writing, and comprehension skills involved in one representative from each of the many categories of common printed materials listed in Figure 15.1. Then criterion-referenced tests were constructed to measure a student's functional use and understanding of nine materials: want ads, food store advertisement, television guide, road sign, road map, recipe, apartment lease, job application form, and high interest, factual article on narcotics.

Figure 15.3 shows the task analysis for following directions on a packaged pizza box. The analysis includes eight enroute objectives with an instructional sequence roughly identified from bottom to top by the three horizontal levels of objectives. Therefore, the two bottom objectives would be taught first and at the same time, though in different sessions with each measured separately. Furthermore, the eight objectives must be stated in measurable terms to evaluate performance on each. For example, the lower left-hand objective concerns recognizing and selecting ingredients and utensils needed to carry out the package instructions. A test of these skills like that in Figure 15.4 might be constructed. The student's baseline performance indicates a need for training on at least three items: can opener, cloth, and ½ cup warm water.

Once criterion is met (95% to 100% correct performance on three consecutive tests), the teacher may plan to teach additional enroute objectives using the same package mix. At the same time, other simple packaged mixes may be added to teach generalization of the new skill.

If reading instruction for the moderately handicapped does not include functional applications of skills as suggested by an inventory or relevant current and subsequent environments, it is not likely that reading skills will be used outside the classroom. However, a teacher must also teach the reading abilities underlying each practical life activity. Task analyses of the activity will identify the reading context, the comprehension involved, and behaviors related to carrying it out, but will not tell you how to teach the visual and auditory elements involved in word recognition. Therefore, the teacher must select or evaluate the learning steps involved in word recognition abilities.

Functional Literacy: Reading with Word Recognition and Comprehension Skills

In comparison to Sidman's whole word method, many additional skills must be learned to apply word recognition strategies to new words and to read with comprehension at a 4th-grade level. In other words, functional literacy is a far more comprehensive skill than acquiring a small set of sight words via the whole word procedure. Contrasting an analysis of the learning involved in functional literacy with that

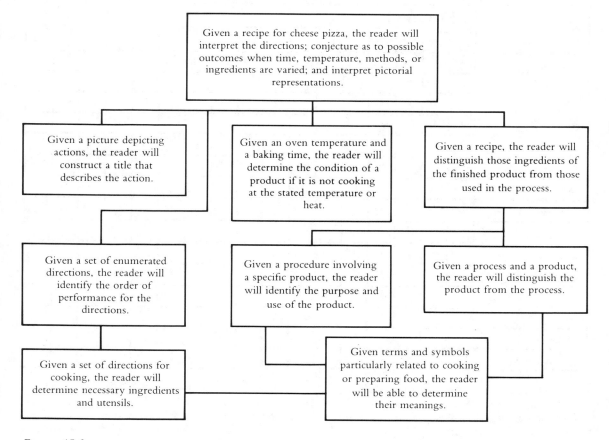

FIGURE 15.3
Task Analysis of Skill Involved in Preparing a Packaged Pizza Mix
SOURCE: *Reading/Everyday Activities in Life, Examiner's Manual,* by M. Lichtman. New York: CAL Press, 1972, p. 22. Reprinted with permission.

FIGURE 15.4

Recording Form for One Enroute Objective Leading to the Functional Reading Skill of Comprehending and Carrying Out Directions on a Packaged Food Mix (e.g., Pizza, Cake, Gelatine Mix)

Name	Nancy	Teacher	Susan
Date	*1-6-82*	Situation	Classroom Kitchen

Objective: Given a set of directions for cooking, the reader will determine the necessary ingredients and utensils.

Conditions: *Utensils:* measuring cup, bowl, fork, pizza pan, can opener, cloth to cover bowl. *Ingredients:* ½ c. warm water, grease, flour. *Appian Way* pizza mix is used. All items in kitchen, but put away.

Criterion: 95–100% correct responses on 3 consecutive tests. Then recycle objective for generalization (jello mix, canned soup, macaroni and cheese mix); check pizza mix performance one month after criterion (maintenance).

Key: Test + correct—error or no response
　　　Training Verbal prompt　M model prompt　P physical prompt
　　　+ correct unprompted

Behavior	Baseline																		
1. Gets utensils	1/6	1/7	1/8	1/9															
a. measuring cup	+	+	+	+															
b. bowl	+	+	+	+															
c. fork	−	+	+	+															
d. pan	+	+	+	+															
e. can opener	−	−	−	−															
f. cloth	−	−	−	−															
Score																			
2. Gets ingredients	1/6	1/7	1/8	1/9															
a. ½ c. warm water	−	−	−	−															
b. grease	+	−	+	+															
c. flour	+	+	+	+															
d.																			
e.																			
Score																			
Total Score %	55	55	67	67															

involved in functionally applying these skills reveals another large difference in complexity. That is, Lichtman's flow charts detour the question of *how* reading skills are first acquired. Instead they analyze the abilities involved in survival reading such as filling out applications, reading a movie or television schedule, and cooking from a recipe.

As shown in Figure 15.5, a comprehensive analysis of learning to read has to meet at least three broad objectives: it must (*a*) consider both visual and auditory elements; (*b*) program for more than simply visual discrimination learning (i.e., visual memory and sequencing, auditory discrimination, sound-symbol association and sound-symbol association with meaningful clues); and (c) sequence the skills for learning so that the learner with little or no ability to read learns the basic readiness skills and may progress systematically to initial mastery when the less efficient techniques of visual discrimination and memory are supplemented by a choice of word recognition strategies (Duffy & Sherman, 1973). Table 15.2 defines and gives examples of prerequisite word recognition skills.

Prerequisite Word Recognition Skills

The student learning the prerequisite word recognition skills actually will be building several smaller skills, each either primarily a visual task leading to recall and recognition of words or an auditory task leading to letter and sound association and context awareness. How the student is taught these skills depends upon the learning task involved. When teaching *discrimination*, the teacher will direct the

learner to note differences between stimuli; when teaching *memory*, the teacher will instruct the learner in various remembering strategies; *sequencing* tasks require the learner to attend to the order of stimuli and use memory strategies to retain that order; when the task involves *association*, the teacher will build on visual and auditory discrimination skills and direct the student to connect one type of stimulus (letter sound) to another (letter).

Because of the complexity of the task, analyses of reading (Duffy & Sherman, 1977; Gagne, 1965; Smith, 1976; Smith et al., 1977; Staats, 1968) do not correspond exactly. Not only does the wording of the steps, their number, and detail vary from one analysis to another, but their order and the type of learning targets specified also differ in ways reflecting the analyst's orientation toward learning itself. See Duffy and Sherman's task analysis because of its particular clarity and adaptability as an assessment and instructional guide. However, since there is inade-

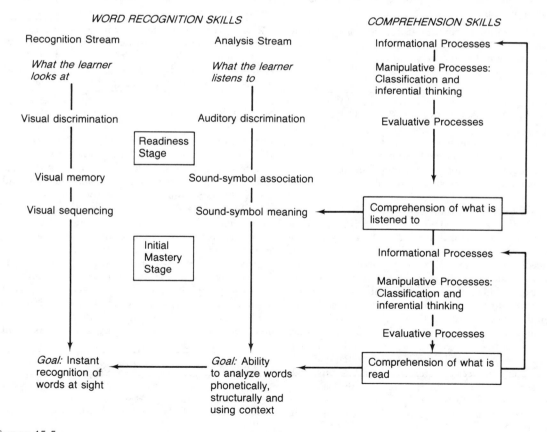

FIGURE 15.5
Word Recognition and Comprehension Skills Leading to Functional Literacy
SOURCE: Modified from *How to Teach Reading Systematically,* by G.G. Duffy and G.B. Sherman (originally published from *Durrell Analysis Reading Difficulty Test,* Harcourt, 1937). New York: Harper & Row, 1973, p. 136. Copyright © 1973 by Gerald G. Duffy and George B. Sherman. Reprinted with permission.

TABLE 15.2 Examples of Prerequisite Word Recognition Skills

Prerequisite Word Recognition Skills	Exemplifying Behaviors
Visual Discrimination—noting visual differences between geometric shapes, letters, and words.	"When given three geometric figures that are exactly alike and one that is clearly different, the learner will mark the one that is different." (p. 89)
Visual Memory—remembering the visual form and orientation of geometric figures, letters, and words. (May require a writing response mode.)	"When given a few seconds to examine a geometric figure, the learner will reproduce from memory, to the satisfaction of the teacher, a figure just like it." (p. 93)
Visual Sequencing—remembering the left-to-right order of letters and noting the first and last letter of a word.	"When presented with a card having his or her name printed on it, the learner will point to the first letter and to the last letter in his or her name." (p. 101)
Auditory Discrimination—noting differences in the beginning and ending sounds of words and in identifying specific beginning and ending sounds.	"Given spoken pairs of words, the learner will say 'yes' if the words begin alike and will say 'No' if they do not begin alike." (p. 128)
Sound-Symbol Association—establishing connections between alphabet letters (consonants and vowels) and the sounds they produce. Requires auditory discrimination.	"Given a stimulus word beginning with either m or d and a group of three other words one of which begins with m or d, the learner will pair the two words beginning with the same letter sound." (p. 135)
Sound-Symbol Meaning—using both letter-sound correspondence and the source of context to identify unknown words. Requires auditory discrimination and sound-symbol connection.	"When given an oral sentence with one word missing and being cued for the missing word with a card having printed on it the first letter of that word (m, d, l, c, s, h), the learner will say a word that fits the context and begins with that letter." (p. 147)

SOURCE: *Systematic Reading Instruction* (2nd ed.), by G.G. Duffy and G.B. Sherman. New York: Harper & Row, 1977. Copyright © 1972, 1977 by Gerald G. Duffy and George B. Sherman. Reprinted with permission.

quate research supporting any of these complex approaches with the more handicapped learner, you must adapt them cautiously, using realistic materials and reading tasks whenever possible.

Word Recognition Skills

To read fluently, a student must instantly recognize a large number of words as well as quickly determine new words through sound analysis and context clues. Since fluency is the goal of this stage of learning, the learner's talents in the auditory analysis stream are combined and used as specific analysis techniques. The three different techniques are *phonetic analysis* or sounding out words; *structural analysis* or recognizing meaning units such as parts of compound words, prefixes, suffixes, and parts of contractions; and *context analysis* or using the meaning of the sentence and preceding sentences to determine an unknown word. While the first two skills rely mainly upon auditory sense, context analysis is comprehension—a skill less dependent upon a single sense and more cognitive in nature.

Phonetic analysis includes three subskills: letter-sound correspondence, phonetic generalization, and syllabication (Duffy & Sherman, 1973). The prerequisite letter-sound associations focus upon single

consonants and consonant blends and digraphs[1] but do not teach symbol-sound associations for vowels. "Letter-sound correspondence" at this point focuses upon analyzing vowel sounds. To analyze the sound a vowel makes, you must know the letters that surround that vowel in any given word. Because a single vowel may have many sound associations depending upon the word it is in, you cannot identify its associated sound apart from seeing its position in a word. Instruction of vowel-sound correspondence proceeds in two stages. First the student is taught to recognize short-vowel phonograms[2] (*at, et, ot, ut, it,* etc.) within known words (*cat, pet, cot, nut, sit*) and then to replace the initial consonant with another to make a new word (*bat, set, rot, hut, pit*). Later the student

---

[1] A blend is the sound combination resulting from adjacent consonants without loss of either sound's identity, for example, *blue strike*. A digraph is two letters in succession which, when pronounced, represent a single sound rather than a blending of both letter sounds; for instance, *shoe, thirty*.

[2] A "phonogram" is a pronounceable sound unit beginning with a vowel (*ing, at, ot*) frequently found at the end of a word which may be combined with various initial consonants, consonants blends, or digraphs to make new words (*sing, bring, thing*).

learns to replace the final consonant in words with known phonograms with another consonant or a digraph to make new words with new phonograms (*cat—cap, can; met—men, mesh*).

In the English language there are some fairly consistent rules of sounding similar letter combinations in similar ways. These are called *phonetic generalizations*. Examples of these include the silent *e* (in the pronunciation of *smile, make, joke, ride, hole*) and the two vowels together—one syllable rule (*boat, plain, wheat, goat, suit*). Although these rules are not universally true, they are consistent enough to be taught as patterns to attend to in unknown words.

Syllabication is the third part of phonetic analysis—strategies to analyze sound units in an unknown word as a means of identifying that word. Syllabication breaks large, multisyllable words into smaller, more manageable units. The instructional progression for teaching various syllabication patterns (for example, vowel-consonant-consonant-vowel: *until, almost, after*; vowel-consonant-vowel: *even, between, tiger*) is first to teach auditory discrimination of the number of sound units, then to teach visual discrimination of the particular pattern of vowels and consonants and the rule for dividing a word into single sound units, and finally to teach generalization of the rule across many unfamiliar words with various patterns of letters.

Where in phonetic analysis the learner focuses on sound units to unlock unknown words, in *structural analysis* the learner must direct attention to those parts of the word that signal meaning as a method to analyze unknown words. Units of meaning that the student is taught to attend to include:

1. Root words plus inflectional endings, such as *-s, -ed,* and *-ing;*
2. Root words plus suffixes, such as *-ness, -able,* and *-ly;*
3. Prefixes plus the root word (*un-happy*);
4. Parts of compound words (*back-pack*);
5. Parts of contractions (*couldn't = could not*) (Duffy & Sherman, 1973, p. 169)

To use structural analysis, the reader must be able to look at unknown words and discover known parts, recognize the root word either instantly as a sight word or by sounding it out, sound the prefix, suffix, or the other portion of the compound, and finally blend the parts together as one word.

Context analysis allows a reader to determine unknown words from the meaning of known words and the clues provided by known letter sounds. Context analysis requires the student to read for meaning and, with the assistance of letter-sound correspondence, guess unknown words. When context clues are used without letter-sound analysis or vice versa,

guessing often is inefficient. For example, the unknown word in the sentence "She put the [unknown word] on her head" could be *cap, hat, helmet, scarf, shampoo,* etc. If an initial sound clue (*s . . .*) is recognized, identity becomes more likely. Additional phonetic or structural clues (i.e., *s . . . f*) may be used along with context to increase this likelihood (final consonant, syllabication, prefixes, etc.).

High Utility Words

To determine which words to teach in a functional literacy reading program when only a limited number will be taught requires an awareness of word frequency. Word lists such as Fry's list of 300 "Instant Words" (Fry, 1957, 1972), the Dolch list of 200 words (Dolch, 1950), and the revised Dale list of 769 useful words (Stone, 1956) all represent efforts to compile the most frequently appearing words in beginning reading material. Duffy and Sherman (1977) selected words common to the Fry, Dolch, and Stone lists as the most frequently appearing, and therefore most useful, words. Most of these are taught during the readiness phase. Next, they classified words by their phonetic and structural elements (i.e., compound words, words with the *sh* digraph, and those with the *-at* phonogram), ordered each classification in terms of frequency, eliminated words composed of infrequently occurring elements, and matched groups of words with teaching objectives. Words with a certain phonetic or structural element are taught at the time their corresponding rule is taught, where some frequently appearing but irregular words (those not employing the identified elements) are taught as sight words. In addition, some regularly spelled words (such as *cat* and *pen*) are taught in the prerequisite skills unit as sight words and are used again later as examples of phonetic or structural generalizations. In all, the reader who completes the prerequisite and word recognition skill units learns to recognize or analyze more than 900 words.

Comprehension Skills

While decoding new words is the most obvious half of reading, comprehension ultimately makes the skill functional. Most standardized and informal reading tests assess comprehension by asking factual, vocabulary, and inferential questions about a passage. In essence, these tests attempt to test comprehension—a skill that rests primarily upon the ability to conceptualize, to classify, or to determine relationships between concepts, and to answer factual questions about or make inferences from what is read. According to Duffy and Sherman's (1977) task analysis, teaching comprehension skills means teaching informational, manipulative, and evaluative processes. While instruction would parallel rather than follow instruction in prerequisite and word recognition abilities, it logically proceeds from the informational to the evaluative processes. For any given reading selection, comprehension activities must begin at the literal level—does the reader understand the factual content of what was read? If, as shown in Figure 15.5, the learner is in the readiness stage and cannot read enough to apply developing comprehension skills to a reading selection, listening comprehension is taught.

The informational processes that permit the reader to comprehend the basic facts in a selection include word meaning skills, understanding relationships, contextual prediction, and factual recall. For the functional reader, "concepts" or word meaning centers upon "content" and "function" words. Content words have a known referent and carry the meaning of a sentence—"Christmas," "mask," "dock," "wishbone." The specific meaning of a content word relates to its particular use in a sentence (e.g., "The man dove from the *dock*"; "Don't *dock* me for being late").

Function words describe the relationship between other words in a sentence; these relationships include (a) cause and effect ("since," "because," "if"), (b) chronological sequences ("during," "after," "finally," "first"), (c) contrast-comparison ("much more than," "either-or," "although"), (d) pronouns and their antecedents ("they" = John and the boys; "her" = Mary's), and (e) prepositions that refer to positional or time relationships ("across," "but," "on," "between," "until," "from").

Both function and content words are taught in three steps. First, provide an experience that serves as a basis for understanding the concept; second, identify the defining characteristics of the concept; third, associate the word label with the concept. Since functions words show relationships rather than the more "visible" referents of content words, they are often more difficult to teach. Therefore they should always be taught in context rather than isolated from content words. Understanding relationships between ideas read builds directly upon understanding the function and content words learned earlier. Once the student has learned the meaning of function words such as "because," "after," "next to," and many appropriate content words, she is taught to verbalize relationships among concepts. This is done by a variety of instructional activities—arranging pictures to retell a known story, completing analogies, and looking for sequential relationships, cause and effect, use, and composition similarities in sets of pictures, and so on.

Contextual prediction, a skill that accompanies fluent reading, allows the reader to predict the unknown elements of a paragraph or sentence from

what has been read. For example, the student who does not recognize the word "escalator" could understand its meaning from the following sentence: "It's fun to ride an escalator because it's like a moving staircase." Contextual predictions also may be made from clues of word order, punctuation, and intonation.

A final element of the informational processes includes factual recall, or memory. Once the reader has learned to identify the important facts, he must retain these facts before comprehension develops into manipulative and evaluative processes.

At the second level of comprehension, readers learn to manipulate ideas mentally. They are able to see relationships between facts, grasp the main idea of a selection, and make inferences from facts—to read between the lines. These mental operations enable readers to expand their comprehension beyond the literal level.

In the evaluative process, readers learn to use their past experiences as to judge the content of a selection and to recognize words that reflect the author's bias, mood, stereotype, or intent.

We do not know to what extent moderately handicapped learners may be taught comprehension skills beyond the basic level of information gathering. Advanced comprehension requires recognition of main ideas, mental classification, inference, and evaluation of content—skills which are far more abstract than simply understanding and remembering the literal meaning of a passage. The primary purpose of teaching moderately handicapped students to read is to increase their independence in daily life. Since the bulk of these activities requires reading for information, instruction will be directed toward these basic comprehension abilities.

Task Analysis Selection and Instructional Goals

If reading is a two-part skill (visual and auditory skills leading to word recognition abilities *and* understanding and thinking skills leading to comprehension), then it requires many more instructional steps than if it is simply a look-say process. Unlike the case of whole word task analysis, we do not know how many instructional steps contributing to word recognition and comprehension may be achieved by the moderately handicapped learner. Some steps have been tested and found successful with this population. The newness of systematic reading instruction for moderately handicapped learners contributes to our difficulty in evaluating the validity of this approach for these learners.

Despite validity problems, each task analysis supplies useful guidelines for teaching and testing the handicapped learner. Reading prerequisites for all three analyses are the same. The beginning elements of visual discrimination and initial mastery of sight words are identical to the whole word approach. Therefore, a teacher may start readiness instruction without having to select a particular analysis of reading. Then, depending upon the student's success and the number of remaining schooling years (i.e., the speed with which the student must achieve the *minimal* objective of a small cautionary vocabulary), a teacher will elect either (*a*) to continue to add sight words, limiting them to the essential protective vocabulary and giving particular attention to functional comprehension or (*b*) to work toward the goal of functional literacy. This would necessitate following a complex task analysis (e.g., Duffy & Sherman, 1977; Resnick & Beck, 1976; Smith, 1976) in part or total, while directing comprehension activities and reading materials toward functional reading tasks (e.g., Bender, Valletutti, & Bender, 1976; Lichtman, 1974).

Assessment

Traditional Tests

Traditional reading assessment includes presenting a series of graded word lists and paragraphs with comprehension questions asked on content.[3] The levels of difficulty correspond to grade levels, beginning with preprimer and primer levels (first part of 1st grade) and progressing through 1st grade, 2nd grade, and so on. Many tests allow two difficulty levels in the early grades so that the student's ability may be more closely pinpointed. Selections read aloud by the pupil are followed carefully by the examiner, with all errors coded by type (words omitted, substituted, misread, etc.) for later error analysis. After reading the paragraph aloud, the student is asked factual, inferential, and vocabulary questions; responses are scored and recorded before proceeding to the next graded paragraph.

In addition to the diagnostic information obtained on a student's word recognition and comprehension abilities, test data may be used to determine three levels of reading ability, based on the student's word recognition responses (percentage of words correctly read) and comprehension responses (percentage of questions answered correctly). These levels range from nearly error-free to an error frequency of 1 word recognition mistake every 10 or fewer words. They are referred to as the "independent reading level," the "instructional reading level," and the "frustration reading level." (See Table 15.3.) Some tests suggest that the student be read a series of graded paragraphs and then asked comprehension questions so that an "independent listening level" may be calculated. Listening level is generally higher than the frustration level of reading.

The use of graded word lists and paragraphs to determine the percentage of correct word recognition and comprehension ability and resultant reading and listening levels will have value for teachers of the severely handicapped only if the students have some reading ability. For these students, testing will be limited primarily to selections from primer to 4th or 5th-grade levels, though listening comprehension may be higher for some students. If reading inventories of this type are used, the content of the paragraphs must be interesting to the student. Since most tests draw primary-level selections from materials geared to young children, a teacher will need to seek out paragraphs from graded high interest–low vocabulary materials[4] (e.g., *Checkered Flag Series, SRA Pilot Library Series, Reader's Digest Skill Builders,* etc.) or construct graded selections with content suitable to the student's social age.

Word Lists

Word list tests may be made easily from graded lists of high utility words (e.g., Dolch, 1950; Fry, 1957, 1972; Stone, 1956), as illustrated in Figure 15.6. The rules for giving an informal test on isolated words are generally similar from test to test. Because the goal of word recognition is *instant* recognition, words are first systematically presented for 1 second; all error responses are repeated under untimed conditions. The simpler words are tested first, followed by more difficult lists.

If a teacher wants to teach a limited vocabulary of highly functional or protective words, informal tests may be simply constructed from lists composed of such words (e.g., *Curriculum-Cumulative Progress Report,* Note 1; Otto, McMenemy, & Smith, 1973) or from words surveyed by the teacher to be functional for a given student. Because such lists are difficult to grade, no estimates of grade reading levels will be obtained. However, since a criterion-referenced test such as a word list test or the oral reading of a paragraph may be constructed to measure exactly what is being taught, these tests are the most meaningful tools to monitor learning. Estimates of reading ability measured in often inexact grade levels are far less

---

[3]For additional reading or formal and information methods of reading assessment, see Bond and Tinker (1967), Cohen and Plaskon (1980), Duffy and Sherman (1973), Gillespie and Johnson (1974), Johnson and Kress (1965), Spache (1976), and Silvaroli (1973).

[4]For title and publisher information on high interest–low vocabulary materials refer to Appendix B in Duffy and Sherman (1977) and Appendix 1 in Gillespie and Johnson (1974).

TABLE 15.3 Levels of Reading and Listening Ability

Ability Level	Word Recognition (% of words correctly read)	Comprehension (% of questions answered correctly)	Behavioral Characteristics	Purpose of Level
Independent Reading Level	98–100%	90–100%	Level at which learner reads comfortably and with good comprehension; marked by expressive oral reading, observation of punctuation, and absence of lip movement, finger pointing, vocalization, head movement	Home work, worksheets and independent reading for enjoyment and information should be at this level
Instructional Reading Level	95%	75%	Makes 1 error every 20 words while only 3/4 of the content is understood; similiar characteristics as independent level	Level at which student can profit from directed reading instruction
Frustration Reading Level	90% or less	50% or less	Makes 1 error every 10 words or less while only half or less of the content is understood. May be marked by word-by-word reading without rhythm, lack of interest, pointing and lip movement, poor use of context cues	Material at this level of difficulty should be avoided
Independent Hearing Comprehension Level	Not applicable	75%	Highest level at which student satisfactorily understands materials read to him	Guide to level for verbal instruction and materials read to student; an index of student's level of speaking vocabulary and language structure

helpful in determining specific instructional targets and in measuring performance changes. In fact, in an extensive survey of high interest–low vocabulary reading materials used frequently by special education teachers, Lavely, Lowe, and Follman (1975) analyzed the accuracy of each publisher's grade level selections from all levels of each reading series examined. They found that the majority of publishers assigned grade levels much lower than their actual difficulty and that most books in series did not gradually increase in difficulty. Therefore, using these texts with their present designations to determine reading level would produce meaningless results.

Criterion-Referenced Tests

If an instructional objective is stated in observable terms and contains all the essential elements (conditions, behavior, and criteria), then a criterion-referenced test may be constructed to measure individual performance of the skill specified by the objective. This criterion-referenced testing does not compare a person's performance to a peer group, as with norm-referenced tests, but rather to an arbitrary criterion specified by the teacher. Because the tests are matched closely to what is being taught, they can measure the effectiveness of a given teaching pro-

FIGURE 15.6
Informal Word Recognition Test of Dolch Basic Words in Isolation

General Instructions:

The following steps should be followed to give an informal test of an individual's ability to recognize frequently used words (Dolch, 1950) in isolation of phrase or sentence context.

1. *Preparing word cards.* Type in primary-sized type or print clearly the high utility words selected for each grade level on separate 3 × 5 inch cards. A minimum of 25 words should be selected for at least each of the following grade levels: preprimer, primer, first, second, third.
2. *Ordering the words.* Order the words by level from preprimer on with a matched listing on which to score the student's responses (see test pages).
3. *Flashed exposure.* Make sure that the student is ready and attending; flash the words to the student one at a time allowing a 1-second exposure to each word. Unless you have information that the student "reads well" at levels above preprimer, start with preprimer words. The best method of flashing words is to hold a blank card over the word and move it up (or down), then back down after 1 second. Another way involves the use of a card with a window-opening in it or a tachistoscope.
4. *Scoring flashed words.* If the word is correctly read in the flashed condition, score a + in the appropriate blank and go to the next word. Immediate self-corrections are scored as incorrect because it indicates that the student's initial perception of the word was not accurate. If the word is not attempted, score a NR for no response to the word. For misread words, write the incorrect response in the blank. These mistakes will be analyzed after the test to detect any patterns in the student's incorrect responses.
5. *Untimed exposure.* Whenever an error is made in a flashed exposure, record the student's performance, then repeat the trial, allowing sufficient time (10 seconds) for the student to examine and analyze the word.
6. *Scoring untimed words.* The student's response to the untimed condition is listed in the untimed column: + for correct, NR for no response, and for errors the misread word is placed in the blank.
7. *Test ceiling.* Testing is stopped as soon as the student misses 10% (or more) at a given grade level (i.e. 2 of 20 words, 4 of 40, etc.). However, if one is interested in obtaining a larger baseline, one may test beyond a 10% error level as long as adequate reinforcement is made available.
8. *Determination of reading levels.* The results of a word list test can be used only to *roughly estimate reading levels* and tend to underestimate these levels because reading words in isolation is more difficult than in context. However, the highest grade level at which 98–100% of the words were correctly read may be regarded as an estimate of the student's independent reading level; 95% corresponds to instructional level and 90% or less signifies frustration level.

Name _____   Examiner _____

Date _____   School _____

Pre-Primer			Primer			First Grade		
---	Flashed	Untimed	---	Flashed	Untimed	---	Flashed	Untimed
1. and	_____	_____	1. all	_____	_____	1. after	_____	_____
2. run	_____	_____	2. am	_____	_____	2. again	_____	_____
3. up	_____	_____	3. are	_____	_____	3. an	_____	_____
4. down	_____	_____	4. at	_____	_____	4. any	_____	_____
5. where	_____	_____	5. ate	_____	_____	5. as	_____	_____
6. it	_____	_____	6. black	_____	_____	6. ask	_____	_____
7. come	_____	_____	7. do	_____	_____	7. by	_____	_____
8. red	_____	_____	8. eat	_____	_____	8. could	_____	_____
9. yellow	_____	_____	9. four	_____	_____	9. every	_____	_____

SOURCE: *Teaching Primary Reading,* (2nd ed.), by E.W. Dolch. Champaign, Ill.: Garrard Press, 1950. Reprinted with permission.

FIGURE 15.6 *(CONTINUED)*

	Pre-Primer			Primer			First Grade	
	Flashed	*Untimed*		*Flashed*	*Untimed*		*Flashed*	*Untimed*
10. big	___	___	10. get	___	___	10. fly	___	___
11. see	___	___	11. good	___	___	11. from	___	___
12. away	___	___	12. he	___	___	12. give	___	___
13. I	___	___	13. like	___	___	13. going	___	___
14. me	___	___	14. must	___	___	14. had	___	___
15. make	___	___	15. new	___	___	15. has	___	___
16. blue	___	___	16. no	___	___	16. her	___	___
17. help	___	___	17. now	___	___	17. him	___	___
18. one	___	___	18. on	___	___	18. his	___	___
19. for	___	___	19. our	___	___	19. how	___	___
20. a	___	___	20. out	___	___	20. just	___	___
21. little	___	___	21. please	___	___	21. know	___	___
22. funny	___	___	22. ran	___	___	22. let	___	___
23. go	___	___	23. saw	___	___	23. live	___	___
24. three	___	___	24. she	___	___	24. may	___	___
25. two	___	___	25. soon	___	___	25. of	___	___
26. to	___	___	26. that	___	___	26. old	___	___
27. said	___	___	27. there	___	___	27. once	___	___
28. my	___	___	28. they	___	___	28. open	___	___
29. the	___	___	29. this	___	___	29. pretty	___	___
30. look	___	___	30. too	___	___	30. put	___	___
31. here	___	___	31. under	___	___	31. round	___	___
32. is	___	___	32. want	___	___	32. some	___	___
33. in	___	___	33. was	___	___	33. stop	___	___
34. find	___	___	34. well	___	___	34. take	___	___
35. can	___	___	35. what	___	___	35. them	___	___
36. you	___	___	36. white	___	___	36. then	___	___
37. not	___	___	37. who	___	___	37. think	___	___
38. we	___	___	38. will	___	___	38. walk	___	___
39. jump	___	___	39. with	___	___	39. were	___	___
40. play	___	___	40. yes	___	___	40. when	___	___
TOTAL	___	___	TOTAL	___	___	TOTAL	___	___
PERCENT CORRECT	___	___	PERCENT CORRECT	___	___	PERCENT CORRECT	___	___

FIGURE 15.6 *(CONTINUED)*

	Flashed	Untimed		Flashed	Untimed
1. always			1. about		
2. around			2. better		
3. because			3. bring		
4. been			4. carry		
5. before			5. clean		
6. best			6. cut		
7. both			7. done		
8. buy			8. draw		
9. cold			9. drink		
10. does			10. eight		
11. don't			11. fall		
12. fast			12. far		
13. first			13. full		
14. gave			14. got		
15. goes			15. grow		
16. green			16. hold		
17. its			17. hot		
18. made			18. hurt		
19. many			19. if		
20. off			20. keep		
21. or			21. kind		
22. pull			22. laugh		
23. read			23. light		
24. right			24. long		
25. sing			25. much		
26. sit			26. myself		
27. sleep			27. never		
28. tell			28. only		
29. their			29. own		
30. these			30. pick		
31. those			31. seven		
32. upon			32. shall		
33. us			33. show		
34. use			34. six		
35. which			35. small		

FIGURE 15.6 (CONTINUED)

	Flashed	Untimed			Flashed	Untimed
36. why	_____	_____		36. ten	_____	_____
37. wish	_____	_____		37. today	_____	_____
38. work	_____	_____		38. together	_____	_____
39. would	_____	_____		39. try	_____	_____
40. write	_____	_____		40. warm	_____	_____
TOTAL	_____	_____		TOTAL	_____	_____
PERCENT CORRECT	_____	_____		PERCENT CORRECT	_____	_____

_____ independent reading level

_____ instructional reading level

_____ frustration reading level

Comments on student's word analysis methods:

gram by monitoring changes in the student's performance over time.

To construct criterion-referenced tests to measure reading skills, the teacher begins by task analyzing the skill and writing instructional objectives matched to the terminal and enroute behaviors. (Refer to Figure 15.3 where a daily living skill involving reading was task analyzed [Lichtman, 1972]. A test was constructed [Figure 15.4] to measure one of the enroute objectives [collecting utensils and ingredients specified in the instructions] and a criterion for that objective was established.)

Informal test construction and resultant teaching will require less trial and error if you begin with a task analysis already validated with the moderately handicapped. Such is the case with the whole word analysis (Sidman, 1971; Sidman & Cresson, 1973). Once a specific set of words has been selected, a student may be given informal tests to measure each of the eight tasks listed in Sidman's whole word method analyses (Figure 15.2). For example, to test task 2, identity word matching, you would first specify the instructional objective in more precise terms: "when shown a printed word sample stimulus, the student will select the single printed word match from a choice of eight printed words (coffee, milk, bread, meat, fruit, phone, police, fire) with 100% correct performance for three successive, randomly ordered tests on all eight words." Next, the testing materials must be made (two sets of printed word cards) and the testing directions and procedure stated (e.g., "Look at this card," sample stimulus word placed in front of student; "Now, find the word that matches this one in this group of words"; teacher places all

eight choices in random order below the sample word in front of student). Finally, a simple recording form and daily performance chart or graph is needed so results can be recorded accurately and progress toward achieving criterion can be monitored over time.

The complex task analyses of Duffy and Sherman (1977), Smith (1976), and Smith et al. (1977) do not have published applications with a moderately handicapped student population. Smith et al. (1977) *do* describe the validity of their criterion-referenced tests for general school and special project, or educationally delayed, populations. However, both objective lists contain criterion-referenced tests for each objective, thereby easing the teacher's task.

Testing for Functional Use of Skill

At some point after informal testing reveals that a skill is close to criteria, additional practice and testing using realistic materials and in applied situations will ensure the expansion of skills still impractical for functional reading. Many of the discrete skills listed in the Duffy and Sherman (1977) sequence exemplify this problem. By themselves they are not directly applicable at home, in the community, or in a vocational setting (e.g., matching the letters *t, b,* and *p* to spoken words beginning with these consonants). However, the same discrete skills are necessary elements for building reading ability. In addition, learning progresses best if, during the early instruction of a skill, the teaching task is held constant (materials remain the same, no change in stimuli presented and response requested) (Gagne, 1965; White & Haring, 1976). In fact, White and Haring suggest that during acquisition, the instructional task remain unchanged until the student responds correctly, without any assistance, about two-thirds of the time. Once this point is reached, generalization training must be programmed *in addition* to working with the basic task until the skill is fluently or proficiently performed and the criterion is met.

As applied to reading, generalization training may mean changing from less realistic materials (word cards, sentence building charts, word family wheels) to common printed materials (e.g., magazines; newspaper food ads; classified want ads; telephone book listings; slides of street signs, building directories, and bathroom signs; the writing on applicances and food boxes. If instruction was begun with more functional materials, then additional applications could be programmed. For example, the probe in Figure 15.4 suggests that, after criterion is met for selecting utensils and ingredients necessary for making a pizza mix, the student will be taught (and tested on) the same skill using gelatin mix, canned soup, and possibly a packaged macaroni-and-cheese mix. Besides changing materials, the teaching and corresponding test may change from a classroom with a familiar teacher to a grocery store, a department store, a restaurant, a street corner, or a workshop with a variety of individuals requesting the same reading skill or combination of learned reading skills. All of the objectives listed by Bender et al. (1976), as well as Lichtman's (1974) development of tasks to assess functional literacy, provide guidelines for building generalized functional reading skills. Informal tests are constructed in the same way as for examining less applied reading skills, except the conditions (materials, setting, individuals present) and the behaviors will be functional.

Besides teacher-made tests of functional skill use, there are available some tests of adult functional literacy, 36 of which have been summarized and evaluated by Nafziger et al. (1975). Among the instruments reviewed are informal reading tests, criterion-referenced tests, and standardized tests. Lichtman's (1972) criterion-referenced test, *Reading/ Everyday Activities in Life (R/EAL),* could be used by a teacher to collect performance data on such skills as reading want ads, understanding a lease, completing an application form, and reading traffic signs. Some of the testing materials are illustrated in Figure 15.7. Three additional criterion-referenced tests assess similar types of applied writing and reading skills such as filling out a check, ordering by mail, using a phone book, and addressing a letter. These are the *Adult Performance Level Functional Literacy Test* (Northcutt, Kelso, & Barron, 1975), the *Basic Reading Skills Mastery Test* (1974), and the *Wisconsin Test of Adult Basic Education* (1974).

IMPLICATIONS OF RESEARCH FOR TEACHING THE BASIC COMPONENTS OF THE READING TASK

Materials and procedures for reading programs that do not use research on the basic components of the reading task lead to error-ridden guesswork. However, this is not uncommon among authors and publishers of elementary school materials (Coleman, 1970). Consistent with the reading task analyses already reviewed (Duffy & Sherman, 1977; Sidman, 1971; Smith et al. 1977), the more logical and, in the long run, the more efficient approach to creating reading programs begins with isolating the components of associational learning involved in the reading task. Both Sidman's tasks, outlined in Figure 15.2, and Duffy and Sherman's breakdown of word recognition and comprehension skills (Figure 15.5) attempt to identify these components. The components that have been isolated (Samuels, 1971) include *attention, visual* and *auditory discrimination, short-* and *long-term memory,* and *mediation* (the often covert ability to act upon, classify, or analyze information or perceived stimuli to establish organizational systems or solve problems). The second step in the development of reading programs is to seek "empirically based information on the training and sequencing of the essential subskills" (Bilsky, Evans, & Martin, 1975, p. 259).

This two-step procedure of producing empirically based instructional methods in reading is even more essential when the learners are moderately and severely handicapped. This is because of the widespread evidence of deficiencies in the mentally retarded individual's ability to attend (Zeaman & House, 1963), to remember on a short-term basis (Ellis, 1970), and to mentally organize material into categories (Spitz, 1966, 1973). This section of the chapter describes the teaching implications of studies examining the components of learning to read with moderately retarded learners.

Creating Optimal Learning Conditions

An extensive review of learning research on retarded populations allowed Denny (1966) to define seven instructional conditions which maximize learning for these students. As you already know, success in reading relies upon attention, discrimination (visual and auditory), memory (long- and short-term), and mediation. The purposes of these maximizing practices are to (*a*) make the relevant stimuli more obvious, (*b*) decrease the tendency for error, (*c*) provide informative consequences for every response, and (*d*) encourage retention and skill generalization. To the extent that these principles result in these four outcomes,

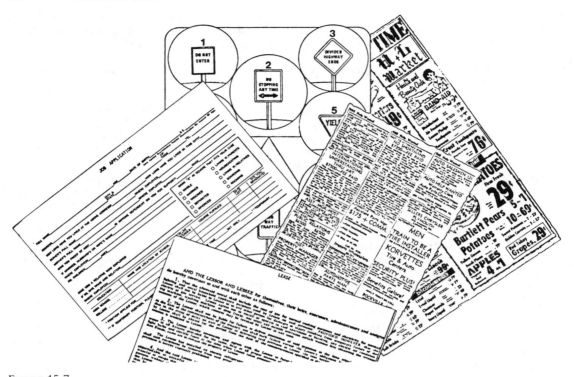

FIGURE 15.7
Examples of Testing Material Used in Lichtman's Test of Functional Literacy
SOURCE: *Reading/Everyday Activities in Life,* by M. Lichtman, New York: CAL Press, 1972, pp. 2, 10, 12, 16, 18. Reprinted with permission.

their application to reading instruction will facilitate attending, discimination, memory, and mediation. The principles are described in order of importance.

1. *Prevent uncorrect responses early in learning and increase the number of correct responses made.* This principle calls for two types of teaching during the initial stage—prompting to promote the correct response, thereby reducing errors, and providing many opportunities to repeat the same behavior in the presence of the relevant stimuli. Chapter 5 clearly defines the range of prompts that may reduce a student's uncertainty in responding; these include decreasing the number of choices, physical guidance, intercepting and stopping errors, redundancy cues or temporarily pairing of one dimension with the correct choice (color coding, size, or position cuing), match-to-sample cues, modeling a vocal or gestural response for imitating or physically cuing a response by tapping near or looking at the correct choice. Once these prompts have established the correct behavior, they must be gradually faded. Delay procedure (Tou-

chette, 1971; see chapter 5) has been useful for the errorless elimination of prompting cues with severely retarded students (Browder, 1980).

2. *Immediately provide knowledge of the accuracy of the response.* If a correct response is made, inform the learner as soon as the response has been completed; if an error is made, let the learner know in a nonaversive manner. Trials resulting in error should be repeated with prompting. If *noncompliancy* is suspected as the cause of error (i.e., the student is approaching criterion and the error is more indicative of a refusal to respond than uncertainty), response cost may be used as a consequence for errors. While the presentation and the absence of tangible reinforcers signal a correct or an error response, correct responses should be verbally affirmed if reinforcement is not being given continuously (e.g., "Good, that's right! The *B* goes with the *baseball* picture").

The *Language Master* recording–play back machine (Bell and Howell Company) to drill word recognition provides good immediate response feedback. Words or sentences are written on special cards with a strip of magnetic tape on the bottom. The cards are placed into a track in the *Language Master* and a pre-recorded voice reads the word as a check for the student.

3. *Whenever possible, provide differential feedback—feedback relevant to the meaning of the concept being taught.* Word meaning must be emphasized to promote comprehension. When teaching positional prepositions, familiar nouns, and verbs, have the learner perform each action or pair an object or picture with the word. The reading procedures that Brown and his colleagues have used with the moderately handicapped illustrate this principle well. For example, Brown et al. (1974) taught students to read action verbs by first requiring that they perform the action to indicate understanding and later match the word to a picture. Using realistic materials and teaching settings probably are the best means of applying this principle.

4. *To facilitate discrimination of the relevant stimuli and appropriate transfer of a learned response, first randomize all the irrelevant stimulus cues (e.g., the color, size, or position of an object, picture, or written word) and then program opportunities for stimulus generalization.* All the prompts used to get a response going during early learning need to be faded gradually so the student discriminates the stimuli in the presence of which a particular behavior is appropriate. For example, a teacher may have used red color cuing, as Egeland and Winer (1974) did with inner-city preschool children, to highlight the distinctive feature of similar letter pairs:

Then, using a match-to-sample, visual discrimination task, the teacher would say, "See this letter? [*R*] Now find all the letters that look the same in this group [*PRRPPRP*]." The color highlight certainly emphasizes the relevant feature of the letter and reduces the tendency for errors. However, until the color cue is faded, the child may simply be matching red marks with other red marks and not attending to the letter differences. Fading of cues is essential for discrimination to occur, but it must be done slowly or the student will become confused. Egeland and Winer (1974) found that 10 successive reductions of the red cue from bright red to no red cue at all enabled the children to master the discrimination without error.

Stimulus generalization is a somewhat opposite learning procedure. The learner who already discriminates the relevant stimuli must expand to include a broader class of stimuli. For example, once a student reads "Men" and "Women" without assistance at criterion, this skill should be generalized to the same words and to words with similar meaning despite variations in size, placement (on doors, walls, outside the classroom rather than word cards), and configuration (MEN, Gentlemen, Men, BOYS).

5. *To promote long-term retention, a student should have opportunities to overlearn—repeated practice or review distributed over time rather than massed into a brief period.* Some educators refer to this procedure as a maintenance period that begins *after* a student has achieved performance criterion. Review sessions are most efficient if they are scheduled at intervals (once a week, monthly, etc.) during a school year (as well as the summer).

6. *Keep the student's motivation for performance and interest in the task high.* Motivating students is important throughout all stages of learning. However, because students may be motivated in different ways (task novelty, reinforcement amount and schedule), teachers should be careful to match the method of motivation with the stage of learning (White & Haring, 1976). During acquisition stage, immediately providing reinforcers on a fairly frequent schedule is the best way to keep performance high. At this point it would not be appropriate to change the task materials or requests significantly, since the student is likely to become confused. However, during the generalization stage, task novelty is the primary mechanism for increasing interest because external reinforcers should have been reduced to an infrequent schedule.

All the classroom studies in which moderately and severely handicapped learners have been taught reading have employed contingent positive reinforcement. Bijou, Birnbrauer, Kidder, and Tague (1966), Staats (1968), and two studies with nonretarded populations (Staats & Butterfield, 1965; Staats, Minke, Finley, Wolf, & Brooks, 1964) established the importance of a strong motivational system upon the development of on-task behavior, reading, and other academic skills. These and more recent studies often use token economies. Bijou et al. (1966) identified three rules for the effective use of tokens in a classroom reading program for retarded students.

(1) The marks must be given as soon as possible consequent to the specific behaviors to be strengthened. (2) They must be given for increasingly larger units of behavior. (3) They must be given simultaneously, or almost so, with social stimuli from the teacher. (pp. 516–517)

Discussed more fully in chapter 5, the techniques for reinforcer selection, scheduling, and classroom use are relevant to effective reading instruction of the moderately handicapped learner.

7. *Determine the easy-to-hard sequence underlying the acquisition of a skill, so that instruction begins with prereq-*

uisites and gradually builds toward more difficult goals. This is especially common with handicapped learners. Sequential building relies upon empirically validated sequences for severely handicapped learners (such as Sidman's) and accurate task analyses, careful baseline and ongoing assessment, and precise determination of instructional targets from assessment data. The teacher must take a remedial approach when teaching functional reading by using the most efficient sequence of skill instruction. This sequence will not be the way most nonhandicapped students learn to read.

Implications of Basic Reading Research with Retarded Learners

Even though the more basic research in reading with moderately and severely retarded subjects is not carried out in classrooms, it has produced important educational implications. To present these implications efficiently, we will discuss several studies and summarize related recommendations.

Task Structure

Bilsky, Evans, and Martin (1975) investigated the effect of task format on the ability of mildly to severely retarded subjects to discriminate between "b" and "d." Tasks were presented to different groups in four ways in two studies: four-choice matching ("Find the one that looks like this," *b–b d d d*); two-choice matching ("Find the one that looks like this," *d–b d*); four-choice oddity ("Find the one that does not look like the others," *b d d d*); and two-choice discrimination ("Find the one that is right and gives you the candy" [e.g., "b" is correct], student sees: *b d*.) With two-choice discrimination tasks, none of the students learned to visually discriminate between the letters, while both the match-to-sample formats and the oddity format resulted in discrimination learning. In a second study a match-to-sample task arrangement with redundancy in its choices (*b–d b d d*) as compared with no redundancy (*b–b p d g*) did not make the discrimination easier for retarded learners. Also, when the choices (*b d d d* or *b g d p*) were delayed, that is, presented after the sample letter (*b*) had disappeared, the subject learned to discriminate more slowly than when both the stimulus and the choices were present simultaneously (*b–b g d p*) and visual memory was not required.

This study has several implications for promoting optimal learning in visual discrimination reading tasks.

1. Avoid two-choice discrimination tasks because of their difficulty; do not present two unknown stimuli with an unmeaningful request or no request at all and expect the student to learn that one choice is cor-

rect and leads to reinforcement and the other is incorrect. Avoid using worksheets or teaching tasks that make a choice response if either the preceding directions or printed stimuli or all of the choices are not meaningful. For example, if you hold up two or more last name cards and ask a student who *does not* recognize her last name to choose "her" card, she will probably guess. Because of the low number of choices she will be right half of the time without ever learning a visual discrimination. Trial-and-error learning is usually ineffective.

2. To facilitate visual discriminations, use match to-sample arrangements (*cat–bat cat toy cot*) or oddity tasks (*bat bat cat bat*). Both task formats make correct responding more probable because the skills of matching and selecting the single different stimulus are easier than selecting a choice from two (or more) different stimuli with no directions or unmeaningful directions.

3. Using redundancy in the choices of a match-to-sample match ($\triangle–\square\ \square\ \square\ \triangle$) may be more distracting than when all alternatives are different ($\triangle–\square\ \bigcirc\ \mathsf{X}\ \triangle$). Retarded learners do not readily use redundancy in the choices, and for some it is distracting.

4. To teach visual discriminations skills, first use simultaneous match-to-sample tasks in which the sample is presented along with the choices and no memory is required. Later teach the same discrimination on a delayed basis; that is, the choices follow the presentation of the sample. This will strengthen the discrimination in preparation for a more difficult task such as auditory association with the same visual stimulus. For example, task A should precede task B.

A. "Look at this word" (teacher points to BOY on left). "Now find the same word over here" (teacher points to choices).

BOY	BAT	BALL	BOY	TOY

B. "Look at this word and remember what it looks like" (teacher exposes card BOY). "Now find the same word you just saw" (teacher places four word cards in front of the student).

BAT	BALL	BOY	TOY

Hawker (1968) and *Hawker, Geertz, and Shrago (1964)* investigated the effects of instructional procedure (prompting or confirmation), grouping of response choices (same or different concepts), and method of stimulus presentation (word-pictures or picture-words) on 96 moderately to severely retarded individuals' ability to learn and retain a list of eight words (horse, duck, table, chain, etc.). The task itself was a simultaneous match-to-sample arrangement of words and pictures. Some learners had word samples and four picture choices ([horse]–[picture: pie] [picture: table] [picture: train] [picture: horse]), and others had picture samples and four word choices ([picture: horse]–[pie] [table] [train] [horse]). In the earlier study (Hawker et al., 1964), some students were given picture response choices that were all in the same class, such as all animals or all foods; for the different-concept group, all the choices were from different classes (e.g., pie, horse, table, ball). In the *prompting* procedure, the response choice was coded with a red arrow and the student was instructed to point to that item, then back to the matching stimulus and say the word aloud; students did not make errors in this condition. In the *confirmation* condition, students were shown the stimulus and instructed to point to the choice that was the same as the stimulus. If they made the correct choice, they were reinforced and asked to point to the word and say it aloud. If they made an incorrect choice, they were asked to try another choice until they were correct. Learning for all subjects was tested on recognition probes (multiple choice of words) and on recall probes (words alone) after each of the eight teaching sessions and 1 week later.

Although students made some errors with the confirmation procedure and none with the prompted procedure, neither one was superior to the other and both resulted in similar learning. Whether the picture choices were in the same class or a different class from the stimulus made no difference. It was felt that students did not attend to the similarity or difference; when incorrect response choices were in different categories from the stimulus, the task was not any easier. It was clear that a task is easier to learn if the response choices are meaningful for the student. Students in the word stimulus–picture choice condition learned to read the words more quickly than those with a picture stimulus and word choices, because the picture choices were meaningful and the word choices were not. Finally, because students were taught to *recognize* (to select the correct choice from four choices) rather than to *name* (read) single words, they showed no noticeable forgetting when given a recognition test a week after training, but did poorly on a word-naming test.

Four teaching implications for sight word instruction of the moderately retarded may be drawn from this work.

1. Prompting or confirmation in a multiple-choice (picture-word or word-picture) sight vocabulary task promotes learning. Both are good techniques; prompting reduces error and cues the correct choice, while confirmation provides immediate feedback and task repetition until the correct choice is made. A combination of prompting and confirmation would probably produce even faster learning.

2. If multiple-choice tasks are used to teach sight words, it is not important whether the choice pictures are of the same category as the stimulus picture. The category each picture choice belongs to should *not* be confused with visual similarity between the picture choices (e.g., pie, circle, ball, plate). Visual similarity *is* likely to make the task more difficult.

3. In multiple-choice (match-to-sample) tasks, position the most meaningful items as the choices rather than as the sample. Therefore, use pictures for the choices and a word as the stimulus *before* teaching the picture-word multiple-choice task. Note that Sidman's task analysis (1971) does not demonstrate this easy-to-hard sequence; in Figure 15.2, the order of steps 6 (picture-word match) and step 7 (word-picture match) should be reversed, according to Hawker's findings.

4. Match your probe to the reading skill you are teaching; for example, word list tests are harder than multiple-choice recognition tests and will underestimate a student's skill to recognize words that go with pictures or pictures that go with words.

Dorry and Zeaman (1973, 1975) also attempted to teach a simple reading vocabulary to 35 nonreading moderately and severely retarded individuals who were all able to label pictures corresponding to the vocabulary words. They experimented with four training procedures to determine which procedure resulted in the most learning. In the *standard* procedure, the subject was shown slides of a single vocabulary word and its picture and asked to say what was on the slide. Slides were repeated so that half of the eight words were each seen in one session a total of six times in random order; then the student was immediately tested on the first four words by being asked to read each word. The second four words were taught in the same way with an immediate test. Finally, word list 1 was tested again followed by a repeat test of list 2 (delayed tests). Standard procedure consisted simply of repeatedly viewing the pairs of pictures and their printed labels.

In the *faded* procedure, students began with the same picture-word pair slides but during training the pictures were gradually faded from very clear to hardly visible. The order of the four different picture-word slides was varied, but picture fading proceeded from visible to not visible. As with all groups, these students were also asked to say the stimulus word for each slide and the order of teaching and listing was the same: train on list 1, test on list 1; train on list 2, test on list 2; retest on lists 1 and 2.

In the *mixed* procedure, the training slides for each word alternated regularly over trials from a word-picture slide to a word slide and back. Describing the mixed training method, Dorry and Zeaman (1975) stated:

This sequence mimics three properties of fading: (a) it reduces generalization from training to test by interpolating test trials (word alone) among the training trials, (b) it provides a mixture of noncontingent (word-picture) trials and contingent (word) trials, and (c) it forces attention to the word on (word) trials, since these trials can be viewed as extreme instances of picture-fading. (p. 712)

The last teaching procedure was a control condition not meant to be effective. Control students were simply shown alternating slides of pictures alone and words alone (e.g., P_1, W_1, P_4, W_4, etc.).

The results clearly showed that the faded training procedure produced the *most* learning, followed in effectiveness by the mixed procedure, the standard procedure, and the very ineffective control procedure which resulted in almost no learning. Although all students performed better on the immediate test, when they did not have to remember, than they did on the delayed test, the order of procedural effectiveness on the delayed tests was still clearly the same. These studies suggest the following classroom practices.

1. If pictures are used as part of a procedure to teach a learner to read (verbally label) a printed word, learning will be greatest if the picture stimulus is always presented with the word stimulus and, over trials, the picture is gradually faded away. The learner should verbally label the picture-word pair on every trial.

2. If picture fading of some type is not used in sight-word instruction, learning will be poor. This is because nothing in the standard pairing approach (word-picture pairs with no picture fading) guarantees that the learner will attend to the word. To be correct, he simply must label the picture. On the other hand, fading the picture gradually decreases the picture's salience, resulting in more attention to the word. In the mixed procedure the learner's attention is also directed to the word on the "word only" trials, although attention to the word is less orderly.

The decision of whether to teach reading by an analytic (whole word) approach or a synthetic (small parts of word) approach is debated for normal as well as handicapped learners. A synthetic program starts by teaching the learner to associate single letter sounds with letters. A whole word program which starts by teaching the whole word and then presents single letter sounds may produce more rapid initial learning than a synthetic approach. However, the whole word learner must be taught new words because he is not likely to transfer or decode new combinations of previously introduced letters.

Neville and Vandever (1973) matched normal 6- and 7-year-olds with mild to moderately retarded persons of the same mental age and taught half of each group to read simple words written in a contrived alphabet somewhat analogous to the Roman alphabet:

$$a = ① \quad c = \ominus \quad f = \sqcap \quad t = \sqcup$$

The contrived alphabet was used to guarantee that high frequency words (e.g., "fan," "get") could be taught without any prior knowledge. Each child had two 45-minute, teaching-testing sessions. On the first day, six words were taught, after which the subjects were tested on those plus four similar transfer words. On the second day, they were taught eight words followed by a test of the eight and four more transfer words.

In the whole word method, words were presented in word families (e.g., fog, hog; get, met) in the following way:

1. One word (in contrived alphabet letters) was shown on a screen, pronounced, and used in a sentence.
2. Subjects were asked to count the number of letters.
3. Subjects' attention was drawn to tall letters and letters below the line.
4. A second word from the same word family was introduced (steps 1–3).
5. The two words were compared with configuration outlines (e.g., fog) which students were encouraged to use as an aid.
6. Students found words in booklets that matched spoken words and were given feedback.
7. The remaining word pairs were introduced similarly.
8. All words were reviewed.
9. All instructed words and new transfer words were tested—words were read aloud (e.g., "fog," "get," etc.) and students circled the printed word that corresponded to the spoken word from a choice of words.

Synthetic instruction was started with the presentation of several letters and proceeded as follows:

1. Several letters were shown on the screen and pronounced first in isolation and then in a word.
2. The letters were combined to form words.
3. Students found words in a booklet that matched words on screen.
4. Review was given on each of the letter sounds.
5. Words were presented orally and students sounded each out silently, then matched the corresponding word in their booklets.
6. Words were tested as in the last step of the procedure.

Both retarded and nonretarded synthetic learners learned more words and were able to read transfer words more often than subjects taught by the whole word approach. In addition, there was no difference in the amount of learning or transfer between retarded and the MA-matched nonretarded students except by the instructional procedure they received.

The major implication of this study, despite its short intervention time and use of a contrived alphabet, was that a synthetic method was more successful than a whole word method in teaching retarded learners a strategy to decode both instructed and new words. This study presents evidence somewhat contradictory to *traditional* practice—that a whole word approach is simpler than an analytic or "phonetic" approach for moderately handicapped learners. The results provide more support for starting reading instruction early and for teaching both the visual *and* auditory component skills.

Browder's dissertation (1980) compared four prompting-fading procedures to teach sight words to 80 moderately to severely retarded persons. Four randomly divided groups of 20 subjects each were taught by one of the following methods:

1. Graphic picture fading (reducing gradually the brightness and clarity of a picture prompt);
2. Delay picture fading (delaying the picture prompt by successively longer intervals);
3. Delay word fading (delaying the verbal model prompt by successively longer intervals);
4. Volume word fading (gradually reducing the volume of the verbal model prompts).

Thus, the two methods that used pictures as prompts faded them differently—one by diminishing the visibility of the picture across trials (as did Dorry) and the other by successively delaying presentation. Of the two methods that used verbal models as prompts, one was faded by gradually diminishing the volume of the model over successive trials and the other by successively delaying presentation. Time delay was therefore used to fade both a picture and a model prompt. Across the 12 training trials for each word, the delay increased from 0 seconds to 8 seconds between the presentation of the word and the model or picture prompt. In graphic and volume fading, prompts were reduced from normally perceived levels to being barely visible and audible.

The results indicated that delaying the verbal model was the most significantly effective method (as well as the most easily used), while delaying the picture prompt proved to be next effective. Graphic picture and word volume fading led to significantly less learning than the two delay methods. Not only

were the delay procedures more effective in teaching single sight words, but they seemed more easily applied since the trainer simply needed to count to herself to gauge the delay. By contrast, picture fading required six successively faded versions of the picture and volume fading required a prerecorded tape. No significant differences were found across the four groups in the number of errors made; each procedure increased correct responses.

The major implication of Browder's work is the documentation of time delay as effective and easily applied to fade either word models or picture prompts when teaching sight words. Delay necessitates no elaborate materials. It simply requires that the teacher initially prompt the student without delay and then wait progressively longer over successive trials on the same word, thus allowing the student to respond without the prompt, whether the prompt be the preferred verbal model or a picture of the word.

In a follow-up study with the same subjects, Browder, Snell, and Hines (Note 3) compared the effects of a delayed picture prompt, a delayed verbal model prompt, and an unfaded picture/verbal prompt on the acquisition and comprehension of sight words. The sight words were selected from the aisle signs of a nearby grocery store that the clients used. The training procedures for the delay word and delay picture groups were the same as those used by Browder (1980). The unfaded picture/verbal prompt procedure simply served as a comparison. In this procedure, both a verbal model and a picture prompt were given at 0 seconds delay on all 13 trials. Both the delay word and the delay picture methods were effective. No significant differences were found between the two methods in the students' ability to read or comprehend words. However, when the picture of verbal prompt was always present and not faded out (the comparison procedure), no learning took place.

In another follow-up to Browder (1980), Browder, Hines, McCarthy, and Fees (Note 4) used the delayed verbal model procedure to teach sight words in the context of daily living skills. Key words selected for instruction would assist in cooking, doing laundry, and using the telephone. In each task, the key words provided simplified directions for performing the task (e.g., recipe card with three key words and pictures). Generalization probes were made of the students' abilities to perform similar tasks using the key words with new materials. Instruction in each session included repeated practice on reading the key words, followed by instruction on using the directions to perform the tasks. All instruction was conducted in groups of two or three handicapped adults. All but one of the eight students mastered the words and used them to perform the tasks. In addition, the seven successful students were able to use the key words to perform *untrained tasks*. The authors concluded that the sight words had mediated generalization (Stokes & Baer, 1977).

Stimulus Materials

A number of studies have examined various ways of presenting letters and words to moderately handicapped learners that affect rate of learning. In the first study to be reviewed, the investigators were interested to learn whether special printing would facilitate learning.

Miller and Miller (1968) defined *symbol accentuation* as the conveyance of meaning by printing the letters of a particular word in a way that characterizes its meaning. For example, you could accentuate the letters of the word "candy" by coloring them with red and white stripes, the word "run" could be written with letters that slant forward, "up" written with the "p" raised above the line, and "look" with "o"'s that symbolize eyes ("look"). In two studies with a total of 48 mild to severely retarded individuals (mean IQ in the moderate range), Miller and Miller found that accentuated words were more rapidly learned.

In the *accentuated* condition the student saw the accentuated word and heard an explanation of its meaning ("This word is *candy*. A candy cane has red stripes," p. 202). The word was flashed quickly for a few seconds either by flipping a flashcard from the accentuated side to its conventionally written side or, in a later study, by alternating projected, overlapping slide images of the conventional form ("look") with the accentuated form ("look") 2 times per second for 15 seconds. In *conventional* training, no accentuated symbols were used but the meaning statement was still given. Even though the amount of time the word was viewed and the number of printed word–spoken word pairings were the same in both conditions, students in the accentuated condition learned to read the conventional form faster.

This study demonstrates the importance of emphasizing meaningful cues as a memory strategy and novel and interesting task presentation. Symbol accentuation (SA) must not be equated with picture-word pairs; they are different in many ways. Most importantly, words cued with SA still have the same basic form as their conventional word partner, while pictures do not incorporate the letter shapes of their printed labels. When the learner looks at an SA word, she is already attending to letter shape and position while being reminded of a familiar association of meaning. The clever alternation of SA and conventional words forced the learner to attend more closely

to the conventional form and served to fade the SA cues.

Of course, most words cannot be easily accentuated, making SA a very limited teaching technique. However, it may be useful for two types of handicapped learners: with beginning readers, SA is an interesting way to teach an initial, small set of content sight words; with older, nonreading students, SA might provide a quick and effective means to teach certain functional words (e.g., "stop," "poison," "entrance," "push," "pull," "walk").

Drinkwater (1972) reported that category words selected by the experimenter ("move," "wear," and "food") were learned more quickly by moderately retarded students when they were taught with pictures they preferred (boy sliding down slide, a watch, a hot dog) rather than with nonpreferred illustrations (boy walking, pair of school shoes, a potato). The implications from this simple study are clear. If task materials are interesting and have high meaning association for the learner, attention to those materials will increase. At the same time, the probability that an association between meaningful picture stimuli and nonmeaningful printed stimuli will be made and remembered increases.

Vandever and Neville (1974) reported a specific variation of their earlier study comparing whole word (visual emphasis) and synthetic (letter-sound emphasis) approaches. They examined the effect of various visual cuing procedures upon the word recognition skills of mildly retarded and nonretarded readers of the same chronological age (7 years). The same contrived alphabet used earlier was employed to insure that the children could not read any of the training words before instruction. Three cuing procedures were used to teach different groups the same set of eight words. Except for different letter cues, the basic instructional procedure for all three cuing techniques was a whole word approach.

The first two conditions emphasized word configuration both in instructional procedures, by calling attention to word shape, and in cues. While *outline cues* simply used a thick black line following the up-and-down shape of the letters, *contrast cues* used the same outline; but each word was set against a black background that followed the configuration contour. For example, in the experimental orthography, the

word "fat" with an outline cue appeared as: ⊓⊕⊔ ;

in the contrast condition it was presented as ⊓⊕⊔ ;

while the *letter cue* condition simply underlined each

word: ⊓⊕⊔ . Instruction for learners in this treatment was directed toward the "distinctive features" of each word's initial and final letters rather than to word shape. The student's attention was also drawn to the tall letters and those extending below the line. All three groups learned 1 word at a time, matched words presented on a screen to words in their booklets, and reviewed learned words.

While all the same-aged normal students learned more words, they were not affected by cuing condition. The retarded subjects taught with the letter cue recognized more words on a multiple-choice recognition test than did those learning with outline or contrast configuration cues. These findings suggest the following recommendations:

1. For young retarded learners who generally do not know what visual cues to look for when learning to read words, it is more effective to emphasize individual letter cues (position in word, ascending or descending parts, etc.) than word shape cues.

2. Cuing by shape or configuration outlines, whether they be simple line outlines or more obvious contrasting outlines, should be avoided. Configuration cues are not very utilitarian because many different words have identical shapes even though the ascending and descending letters may be different (e.g., "pad," "put," "got," "yet").

CLASSROOM READING INSTRUCTION

Applied Research, Reading Programs, and Materials

To the extent that classroom procedures to teach reading meet the following criteria, moderately handicapped students will learn functional reading skills more quickly: (*a*) derive their content from accurate task analyses (whether complex or simple), (*b*) incorporate functional materials and generalization activities, and (*c*) structure tasks to facilitate learning. This section describes reading programs which not only have been used in classrooms with the moderately handicapped but also incorporate two or all three of these criteria. Some of the programs were developed for slow learners but have been successful in varying degrees with moderately handicapped learners. Others were developed specifically for the moderately handicapped. These programs may be divided roughly into two types: visually oriented, emphasizing a whole word approach, and synthetic (phonetic), emphasizing both visual and auditory elements.

Some traditional remedial methods of teaching reading have been applied to mildly and moderately handicapped students. The research on the effectiveness of these methods is often inconclusive (Gillespie & Johnson, 1974). These techniques include the lan-

guage experience approach (Stauffer, 1970), the Fernald method (also called VATK for its visual, auditory, tactual, and kinesthetic emphases) (Fernald, 1943), Montessori's method (Montessori, 1912), various basal series procedures, and some programmed reading textbooks (e.g., *Sullivan Programmed Readers,* Buchanan, 1968).[5]

Rebus, Edmark, and DISTAR Reading Programs

Of these three commercially available programs, the Edmark Reading Program (1972) is the only one developed specifically for the mildly and moderately retarded nonreader (Bijou et al., 1966; Birnbrauer, Wolf, Kidder, & Tague, 1965). Because these programs are very different in approach and goals, they are described separately.

Peabody Rebus Reading Program

The Peabody Rebus Reading Program (Woodcock, Davies, & Clark, 1969) grew out of an experimental program that compared six different procedures for teaching young, mildly retarded children (Woodcock, 1968). Since that time it has been modified and used to teach non-English-speaking and hearing-impaired children, preschool through 1st grade children in regular grades, and Head Start classes. Its primary characteristic is the use of rebuses (pictures or symbols) to represent words before the introduction or printed words.

The rebuses introduced in the first two books are shown in Figure 15.8. After completing the two initial programmed books, the child has learned a vocabulary of 68 words and can decipher a series of rebuses arranged left-to-right with a normal down-the-page and page-to-page progression. Because the workbooks are programmed (Figure 15.9), they provide the student with immediate feedback on each response and advance in small steps with gradually increasing difficulty. In this readiness phase (the first two books), the student is exposed to the use of picture and context clues and structural analysis involving the -*ing* verb ending, the possessive -*'s,* and plural -*s* word endings. In the third book and two accompanying readers, the transition between traditional orthography and the rebuses takes place. Spelled words are gradually substituted for the rebuses by first being colored cued and paired with smaller rebuses; then spelled words appear alone but are color cued to a word key at the top of each page. At

---

[5]For more about these programs and their use with retarded learners, see original references and Gillespie and Johnson (1974) and Otto et al. (1973).

FIGURE 15.8
Rebus Vocabulary for the Two Introductory Books in the Peabody Rebus Reading Program

SOURCE: *The Peabody Rebus Reading Program Supplementary Lesson Kit: Manual of Lessons,* by R.W. Woodcock, C.O. Davies, and C.R. Clark. Circle Pines, Minn.: American Guidance Service, 1969, back cover page. Reprinted with permission.

the end of the transition, the student can read 172 words, with 122 of them being spelled words, and has been exposed to beginning sound-letter associations involving initial consonant sounds and some vowel-consonant combinations. The standardized picture vocabulary lets the learner represent to himself the necessary paired associates of sound and written form, taking advantage of the child's well-developed language skills.

Other Picture-Symbol Materials. The use of standardized picture systems with accompanying words *to substitute* for reading skills is quite different from those intended *to teach* reading. Recalling Dorry and Zeaman's research (1973, 1975), we could compare a more permanent picture-word system to the standard treatment where word and picture are viewed repeatedly without any picture fading. As you may remember, this teaching practice produced very little reading ability because the learner focused on the picture, not the word. Instruction that pairs pictures and words will lead to reading only if the pictures are faded out, directing the learner's attention away from the picture to the word. The more gradual the fading, the better the learning (Dorry & Zeaman, 1975).

Chapter 14 discusses picture recipes meant to substitute for reading rather than to teach reading. If such a system is standardized, the nonreading handicapped adult would be able to consult picture reference books for recipes, reminders on clean-up procedures, and the steps in common daily activities, reducing his or her dependence on memory or nonhandicapped adults. The international sign symbols used to mark restrooms and code traffic signs are meant as permanent word-picture pairs to facilitate comprehension for foreigners and nonreaders. A final example of a permanent picture-word system is the Blissymbols (Bliss, 1965). Blissymbols, some of which are illustrated in Figure 15.10, have been used effectively as communication systems for nonvocal, severely physically handicapped students (Vanderheiden & Grilley, 1975). Although each symbol card has the corresponding printed word on it, the word is meant primarily to remind readers of the symbol's meaning. (Review chapter 11 for more on Blissymbols.)

A wide variety of cookbooks do exist using various levels of picture symbols to either substitute for reading or aid the poor reader (*Cooking with Betty Crocker Mixes,* 1970; *Easy Menu Cookbook,* 1974; Kaman, 1974; Reed, 1973; Staples, 1975). Staples provides some useful guidelines for developing picture recipes based on the results of a project to teach recipes, basic nutrition, and cooking to moderately and

severely retarded students. She found that three difficulty levels of picture instructions were needed to match the varying skill levels of reading, attending, and memory encountered in the students. However, recipes at all levels are introduced with instruction. At *level one,* the directions were the simplest with generally not more than two pictures per page. At this level every utensil, ingredient, and action is pictured, with only a few words. In Figure 15.11, part of a level-one, 8-page recipe on making orange juice is illustrated. At level one, red and green traffic lights are useful to mark beginning and end of a recipe. *Level two* incorporates a utensil guide to refer easily to needed utensils; rather than picturing each spoon, bowl, etc. everytime, the recipe would state, for example, "For utensils needed, see utensil reference guide; page 1A, page 1B, page 7A, page 7B, page 8" (p. 24). This refers the cook to pictures of a wooden spoon, a paring knife, a measuring cup, etc., in the utensil guide. In level two, more than one step may

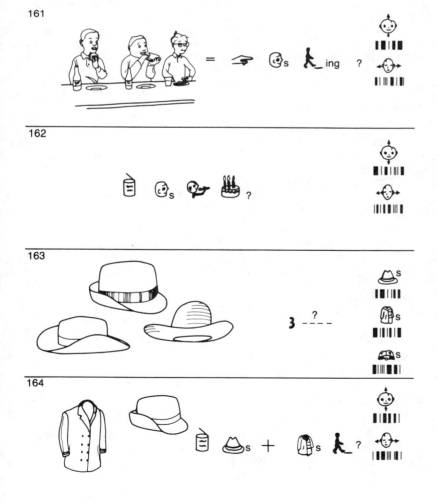

FIGURE 15.9
Example Response Frames from the Second Programmed Workbook in the Peabody Rebus Reading Program
Student reads frame, responds by touching a damp eraser to the markings below his selected answer in the right-hand column; color-changing inks provide immediate feedback—green means "correct," red means "try again."

SOURCE: *Introducing Reading, Book Two, Peabody Rebus Reading Program,* by R.W. Woodcock, C.O. Davies, & C.R. Clark. Circle Pines, Minn.: American Guidance Services, 1967, Frames 161–164. Reprinted with permission.

FIGURE 15.10

A Cerebral Palsied, Mentally Retarded Child using Blissymbols as a Means for Nonvocal Communication

SOURCE: *Non-vocal Communication Techniques and Aids for the Non-vocal, Severely Handicapped,* by G. Vanderheiden and K. Grilley. Baltimore, Md.: University Park Press, 1976, p. 129. Reprinted with permission.

be described per page, the recipes are often more difficult, and more words are used. The *third level* of difficulty is exemplified by two pages from a casserole recipe in Figure 15.12. As can be seen, this level depends more upon words but uses pictures for rein-

forcement. There may be six to eight ingredients pictured per page or three to four direction steps.

Staples (1975) provides additional suggestions for efficient and nonconfusing use of picture-word directions. Although her guidelines are directed toward

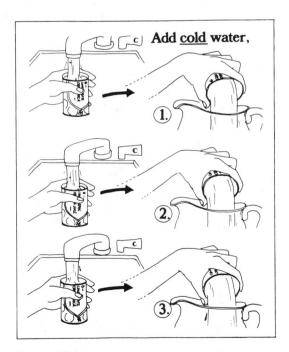

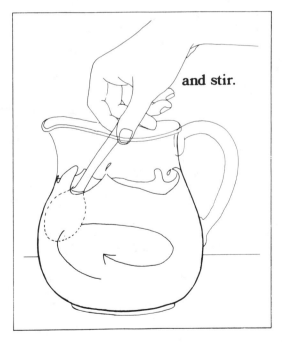

FIGURE 15.11

The Last 2 Pages from an 8-Page, Level 1 (Least Complex) Picture Recipe on Making Orange Juice from Frozen Condensed Juice

SOURCE: *Cooking from Pictures,* by K.S. Staples. Fargo: North Dakota State University, 1975, pp. 20–21. Reprinted with permission.

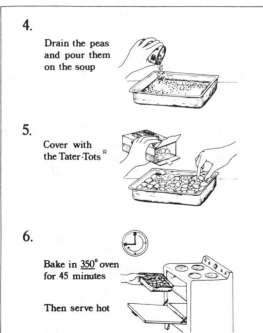

FIGURE 15.12
Two Pages of a 3-Page, Level 3 (Most Difficult) Casserole Recipe

SOURCE: *Cooking from Pictures,* by K.S. Staples. Fargo: North Dakota State University, 1975, pp. 38–39. Reprinted with permission.

the development of recipes, they can be used to develop other picture-word directions.

1. The finished product should be on the first page of an instruction booklet.
2. All ingredients (and utensils for level one) should be illustrated next.
3. Arrows should describe the direction of a movement (mixing, turning can opener, plugging in an appliance).
4. Steps are more easily followed if listed top to bottom rather than left to right.
5. All pages should be numbered, beginning with the front title page.
6. Stencils should be used to standardize pictures; a picture is best if it corresponds to the object's actual size (cup and spoon measures); color photographs or container labels corresponding to the actual brands used provide the most realistic pictures.
7. Picturing glass bowls, cups, and pitchers allows the illustration of their visible contents and avoids the use of cut-away pictures.
8. Time and temperature are clearly pictured by the use of shaded clocks and dials (Figure 15.12).

Because many severely handicapped individuals cannot read and others will not learn to read beyond a small functional vocabulary, simple, standardized picture-cued direction guides for vocational and daily living activities are an immediate materials need.

Edmark Reading Program

The Edmark Reading Program (1972) was developed by Sidney Bijou over a 10-year period with mildly and moderately retarded students at Rainier School in Washington (Bijou et al., 1966). It uses a whole word approach and a programmed response format for one-to-one word recognition instruction. As with DISTAR, the teacher's script is to be followed carefully so that error and correct responses are handled in a set manner, consistent with operant principles of learning. The program teaches a 150-word vocabulary of high utility words. The word-recognition program progresses from gross visual discrimination tasks (pictures and geometric shape matching) to finer and finer discriminations (single letters and word matching) in readiness for reading. Once a word is introduced and learned through the word-recognition programmed task, the student has independent activities that use the learned words. Direction books (Figure 15.13) request that the student locate and arrange pictures according to printed directions (e.g., "man on horse," "man in car"). In the Picture/Phrase Matching lessons, a student selects word and phrase cards to place beside their appropri-

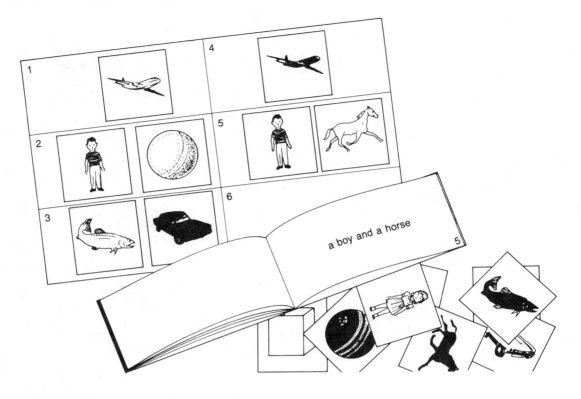

FIGURE 15.13

Direction Books: An independent reading activity in which the student reads the words on each page of directions, selects the corresponding picture from a group with a variety of distractor pictures, and places the pictures on the appropriate section.

SOURCE: *Edmark Reading Program* (Direction Book, Set B, Book 7). Seattle: Edmark, 1972. Reprinted with permission.

ate picture (Figure 15.14). Finally, Story Book lessons center on reading words the student can already independently decode.

Edmark has the advantages of being based upon some research, progressing sequentially, incorporating learning principles, providing opportunity for use of reading, requiring no special training to use, and allowing the teacher to monitor progress closely. Its disadvantages include its expense, the lack of supplemental reading materials, the less functional nature of vocabulary and reading activities, and the fact that word-recognition lessons are expected to be taught on a one-to-one basis. (Limited informal application of this program with groups of 2 and 3 students by the author suggests that this requirement may not be essential.)

DISTAR Reading Program

Designed to teach reading to slow learning and lower-income preschool children, the DISTAR Reading Program (Engelmann & Bruner, 1969) also

was developed from an empirical base and incorporates many of the principles for systematic learning (Bereiter & Engelmann, 1966). The program emphasizes the instruction of sound-symbol association, sound blending, rhyming, sequencing, and left-to-right visual progression. First, learners are taught to pronounce a set of 20 individual sounds; then they learn to sound out words ("say words slowly") and blend words by saying them fast. To simplify word-sounding tasks, DISTAR teaches a set of 9 visually and audibly distinct phonemes. These nontraditional letters (e.g., the digraph *th*) are used in words to represent sounds distinct from other sounds made by the same letters.

Instruction is done primarily in small, ability-matched groups. It moves in small steps and is fast-paced, lively, and dense with reinforcement and feedback from the teacher, who frequently uses hand signals to ensure that group responses begin and end together, to direct attention to visual stimuli, and to pace sound-blending activities.

FIGURE 15.14

Picture/Phrase Cards: An independent reading activity in which the student looks at the pictures on each section of the card, selects the appropriate word or phrase to label each picture from a group of phrases, and places the phrase card in the corresponding box under each picture.

SOURCE: *Edmark Reading Program* (Picture/Phrase Card 18). Seattle: Edmark Associates, 1972. Reprinted with permission.

Engelmann (1967) states that DISTAR reading instruction is not only appropriate for mentally retarded learners but should be begun early—at a mental age of 4.

The major implication of our work seems to be that children with relatively low mental ages (initially less than four years) can learn to read if the instruction is adequately geared to give them instruction in all of the subskills demanded by the complex behavior we call reading. Furthermore, virtually all children with mental ages of four or over can learn to read. Their progress is relatively slow, but all can progress from one subskill to the next until they are reading. With the emphasis on subskills, the teacher is in a position to know what skills a child has not learned. She therefore knows which skills to work on. When a child masters a given skill, the teacher can proceed to the next one. (p. 199)

Despite the assurances he provides, it is not clear how slowly a moderately retarded or otherwise handicapped student will progress through the DISTAR program and how many of the subskills will be mas-

tered. A few studies examining the effectiveness of the DISTAR, Edmark, and Rebus programs are described next.

Effectiveness of the Peabody Rebus, Edmark, and DISTAR Reading Programs with the Moderately Retarded

All three programs have been successful in teaching some reading skills to mentally retarded individuals at mild and moderate levels (*Rebus:* Apffel, et al., 1975; Woodcock, 1968; *Edmark:* Barrier, Note 5; Bijou et al., 1966; Birnbrauer, et al., 1965; Lent, 1968; Vandever, Maggart, & Nasser, 1976; Vandever & Stubbs, 1977; *DISTAR:* Apffel et al., 1975; Booth, Hewitt, Jenkins, & Maggs, 1979; Bracey, Maggs, & Morath, 1975; Engelmann, 1967; Williamson, 1970). Unfortunately few comparative studies allow critical evaluation of each program's effectiveness and identification of ways to match students to programs.

At the beginning and end of a school year, Vandever et al. (1976) pretested and posttested the word-recognition skills of 15 primary level classes for mildly retarded students. During the year five randomly selected classes were taught reading with the Edmark Reading Program, five with the Sullivan Programmed Readers (Buchanan, 1968), and five with the Merrill Linguistic basal series (Fries, Wilson, & Rudolph, 1966). Two word-recognition tests were used with each of the groups; one test was composed of the first 150 words taught by a respective reading program and the other was meant to measure reading transfer by testing a list of 50 words (15 words on this list were those common to all three programs and included on the first 150-word test, and the remaining 35 words were selected from the first 114 words on the Dolch list [Dolch, 1950] as those *not* appearing in any of the programs). Children who recognized more than 50 words on the pretest were eliminated from the study.

The Edmark program teaches a 150-word vocabulary by using a whole word, highly structured, programmed approach. The Merrill Linguistic Readers (Fries et al., 1966) teach words as members of word families (e.g., "mat," "fat," "pat," "sat"). Although the Linguistic Readers emphasize group instruction by the whole word approach, students are taught to attend to and contrast the distinctive features of separate letters (e.g., above or below the line) with the words initially presented in capital letters only. Sullivan Programmed Readers (Buchanan, 1968) take synthetic or phonetic approaches to teaching reading. Workbooks are programmed and present tasks involving question answering and sentence and word completion with multiple choices. The Sullivan series emphasizes sound–symbol associations with generalization of letter-sounding skills to phonetically regular words.

The test data revealed that students taught in the Edmark program recognized significantly more words on their 150-word test (an average of 49 words) than did those taught with either the Sullivan (average of 31 words) or the Merrill series (average of 39 words). However, all groups did equally poorly on the 50-word transfer test, mastering only about 20% of the words. The authors drew two important conclusions with related recommendations.

1. While Edmark was shown to be the most effective program of the three for mildly retarded students, its requirement of individual instruction demands that *(a)* peer tutoring or unpaid classroom volunteers supplement professional teaching staff so that one-to-one instruction is possible, and *(b)* classroom staff be skilled in behavior management techniques so that the individualized instruction and independent work required is feasible.

2. Unlike Edmark, the Merrill and Sullivan series teach words only of specific linguistic patterns. As the authors stated, "It may be particularly important, therefore, that children introduced to reading in a Merrill or Sullivan program complete the basic parts of that program before the attempt is made to transfer them to a more traditional basal reading program" (p. 32).

Apffel et al. (1975) closely monitored, rather than compared, the performance of 60 moderately to severely retarded students, aged 10 to 14, in two reading programs for one school year (DISTAR and Rebus). Performance was measured every 4 weeks using the program's own evaluation device. Student progress was recorded in terms of correct and error rates in relation to the difficulty level of the program in which a student was participating. While some students in both programs did not succeed, a majority made fair to good progress. Some students in both programs advanced to more conventional reading instruction; by contrast, some students needed "recycling" or repetition of lessons in their assigned group, and others were reassigned to less-advanced groups, depending upon the trends visible in their correct and error rates in relation to the program's pace. The authors concluded that, "These results give further evidence of the ability of the moderately retarded to cope with academic instruction. It is not suggested that all such children will profit from it, but clearly some can" (p. 235).

A final study addressed the comparative effectiveness of Dorry and Zeaman's picture-fading procedures (*not* a method used in any of the commercially available programs) and the errorless discrimination technique used by the Edmark reading program (Walsh & Lamberts, 1979). They selected 30 moderately retarded public school students who were unable to read any of the 20 targeted words but could name all of the corresponding pictures (e.g., balloon, telephone, chair, tree, airplane). All students were taught two lists of 10 words in varying orders, with one list taught in the picture-fading and one in the discrimination method. Figures 15.15 and 15.16 illustrate the stimulus progressions involved in the picture-fading and the errorless discrimination approaches respectively.

In either method on all presentations of the materials but the last, students were asked to "Point to the word _____" (mouse, horse, etc.); while on the last or fifth presentation they were asked to read the word. Errors were corrected by the teacher using the Edmark procedures ["No that is not _____. Point to _____ (or say _____)."]. Students were taught new words while reviewing old words, as the Edmark program suggests. Instruction was given daily on a one-to-one basis by the classroom teacher in 10-minute sessions.

Students learned significantly more when taught by the Edmark errorless discrimination methods than

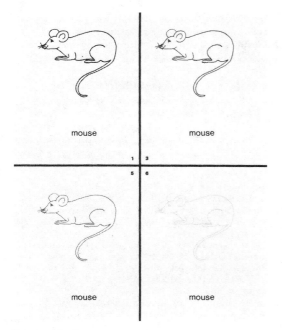

FIGURE 15.15
Stimulus Progression in Picture-Fading Approach
SOURCE: "Errorless Discrimination and Picture Fading as Techniques for Teaching Sight Words to TMR Students," by B.F. Walsh and F. Lambert. *American Journal of Mental Deficiency,* 1979, *83*(5), 474. Copyright, 1979, the American Association on Mental Deficiency. Reprinted with permission.

they did by picture-fading methods. These differences not only existed for word reading but also for word recognition (selecting a named word from a choice of three) and picture-word matching, neither of which were trained. The authors interpreted the

horse	---	---
ft	horse	un
ros	fuvx	horse
sho	horse	rwao
	horse	

FIGURE 15.16
Stimulus   Progression   in   Errorless-Discrimination Approach
SOURCE: "Errorless Discrimination and Picture Fading as Techniques for Teaching Sight Words to TMR Students," by B.F. Walsh and F. Lamberts. *American Journal of Mental Deficiency,* 1979, *83*(5), 474. Copyright, 1979, the American Association on Mental Deficiency. Reprinted with permission.

results as being due to a failure to attend to the printed word rather than only to the picture. Essentially stimulus control over the "reading" response was never shifted from the picture prompt to the printed word. These findings add further support for the Edmark procedures and caution about using successive picture fading as a means of teaching reading.

While it is unquestionably true that more systematic, applied research is called for before conclusions may be drawn comparing the DISTAR, Rebus, and Edmark programs with moderately handicapped individuals, there appears to be adequate evidence that a large fraction of these learners can learn some reading when taught with one of the three programs. The greatest potential danger in using these programs is that *functional* reading may not be the outcome due both to the specific words taught in a given program and to the generally nonapplied context in which words are taught.

Structured Whole Word Teaching Methods

Some examples of highly structured whole word teaching methods have already been discussed; a few were laboratory examples, most of which involved the use of some automated teaching equipment (Dorry & Zeaman, 1973, 1975; Hawker, 1968; Hawker et al, 1964; Sidman, 1971; Sidman & Cresson, 1973). Other studies (Bijou et al., 1966; Birnbrauer, Kidder, & Tague, 1964; Birnbrauer, et al., 1965), which laid the foundation for the Edmark reading program, were carried out systematically in classrooms with mild- and moderate-handicapped students. In addition, Brown and his colleagues have reported a series of successful variations of the whole word approach; these are described briefly along with a final example of a structured, visually directed reading program not supported by published data.

Work by Brown and Colleagues
Brown and Perlmutter (1971) defined functional reading as "discrete and observable motor responses to printed stimuli" (p. 75). This instructional definition includes the presentation of printed stimuli (words or sentences) followed by two student responses: reading the printed stimuli and demonstrating comprehension (e.g., by carrying out the actions indicated, by matching a word to its pictured referent).

In the first of three studies, Brown and Perlmutter (1971) taught seven moderately retarded teenagers to read nine sentences, a total of 71 words. The students were instructed in two small groups; each student received a total of 60 instructional hours. During this period, instruction was ordered according to the following steps, with performance measured before step 1 and after each step marked with an asterisk. All students were assessed on their ability to label single words, read sentences, and demonstrate reading comprehension by the following directions stated in each sentence.

1. Teaching students to label single words.
   A. Word card presented (Set I).
   B. Teacher labels word; student repeats.
   C. Teacher model is faded; training continues until criterion is reached on set being taught (criterion was three consecutive correct responses).
   D. Set II taught to criterion with steps A–C, while Set I is reviewed.
   *E. Set III taught to criterion with steps A–C, while Sets I and II are reviewed.
2. Teaching students to read words in sentences.
   A. Present sentence.
   B. Teacher reads sentence word by word as each word is pointed to in order; students repeat sentences.
   *C. Teacher model is dropped; training continues until criterion is reached.
3. Teaching students to demonstrate reading comprehension.
   A. Teacher reads each sentence and points to location directed by sentence (e.g., "The penny is on top of the box").
   B. Teacher reads one of the nine sentences; student carries out directions or indicates listening comprehension until criterion is reached (modeling prompts are used as needed, then omitted).
   *C. Repeat step B with remaining sentences to criterion.
   D. Student reads one sentence and carries out directions or demonstrates reading comprehension until criterion is reached (modeling prompts are used as needed, then faded).
   *E. Repeat step D with training sentences to criterion.

As with their other studies, this study used a response controlled progression. That is, students were not advanced to a more difficult level until criterion performance was attained at each earlier measured step. If the task analysis upon which instruction is based has small and properly sequenced steps leading to the target behavior and the measurement of performance is accurate, then students should progress with minimal errors. In addition, instruction in this and other studies involved contingent reinforcement, immediate feedback, error correction, prompts early in learning, and easy-to-hard learning sequences—which all promote optimal learning.

Note that model prompts were not gradually faded but instead simply omitted during the second and third phases. If this procedure is used with more severely handicapped students, gradual fading may be necessary to avoid excessive errors.

Brown et al. (1974) report the results of a program to teach three moderately retarded children to functionally read five action verbs ("color," "touch," "run," "walk," and "sit"). Their instructional procedure, which was successful, involved the following steps. As each behavior was taught, it was measured to control progression in the program by the student's performance.

1. Baseline measurement.
   A. Demonstrating spoken verb comprehension by performing action (e.g., "Walk to the chair").
   B. Labeling the actions illustrated in pictures.
   C. Demonstrating spoken verb comprehension by pointing to appropriate picture.
   D. Reading 5 printed verbs.
   E. Performing action indicated by a printed verb.
2. Teaching student to demonstrate comprehension of spoken verbs by carrying out requested action.
3. Teaching student to label action pictures.
4. Teaching student to demonstrate comprehension of spoken verbs by selecting a picture that illustrates that verb.
5. Teaching student to label verb word cards.
6. Teaching student to select a picture illustrating a printed verb.
7. Teaching student to perform action specified by a printed word.

In another study employing similar whole word methods, Brown, Jones, Troccolo, Heiser, Bellamy, and Sontag (1972) report a procedure by which two moderately retarded 5-year-olds learned to read 12 objective-noun phases (e.g., "big cup," "little cup," "red crayon," "blue crayon"). Progression through the following instructional steps depended on a student's measured performance in each step.

1. Baseline measurement.
   A. Labeling objects.
   B. Labeling printed words.
   C. Labeling words and touching corresponding object.
2. Labeling objects.
3. Reading printed stimuli for objects learned in step 2.
   A. With teacher model.
   B. Without teacher model.
4. Reading printed stimuli and touching corresponding object.

5. Second baseline measurement.
   A. Verbally labeling objects and their descriptors (e.g., "What is that?" "Yes, that is milk, but what kind of milk is it?").
   B. Reading adjective-noun phrases.
   C. Reading adjective-noun phrases and touching the corresponding object.
6. Labeling objects with descriptors (adjective-noun phrases).
7. Reading printed stimuli for adjective-noun phrases learned in step 6.
   A. With teacher model.
   B. Without teacher model.
8. Reading printed stimuli and touching corresponding object with appropriate description.

Data for both students indicated not only similar learning patterns but that as the student learned to read increasing numbers of words, they needed fewer trials to reach criterion for each additional word.

Brown's studies provide valuable evidence that the successful laboratory findings with whole word reading instruction for moderately retarded learners hold true in applied classroom settings. What is needed now are applications of these teaching procedures (along with Sidman's, Dorry's, and Browder's) with clearly functional words and in other settings where the reading must actually be done.

Curriculum-Cumulative Progress Report: Functional Reading Program

Oregon's state curriculum for teachers of the moderately and severely retarded (*Curriculum-Cumulative Progress Report,* Note 1) outlines a whole word instructional program that uses prompts to reduce errors, immediate feedback, overlearning, and generalization training. Although no supportive data are reported, its procedures do align well with the instructional principles and research implications outlined earlier. A protective vocabulary was taught with this procedure, but it could also be used to teach high utility sight words. The following steps represent the general instructional progression for each new word, though additional training suggestions have been added for procedural clarity. Throughout teaching, correct and error responses respectively are followed with positive reinforcement or repetition with assistance and correction. For example, in the matching tasks, student responses may be handled in the following ways. *Correct responses:* praise and repeat answer (e.g., "Yes they both say *men*"). *Error responses:* repeat with some assistance; increase assistance only as needed to evoke the correct response (e.g., reduce choices, use color cuing).

The student's word recognition performance is measured with flash cards before and after teaching for all old and new words taught.

1. Matching—Place 4 word cards in front of the student. (MEN, WOMEN, EXIT, ENTRANCE).
   A. Give the student a second MEN word card. Say "Match MEN; find the word that looks the *same* as this."
   B. Repeat with other three cards, one at a time.
2. Receptive reading—Select one word from the set of training words to begin with. This same word will be taught in steps 2–6 before any of the other words are taught in those steps.
   A. Place one word card in front of the student (MEN). Say "Point to MEN."
   B. Place two words in front of the student (the same correct choice and one distractor: MEN, PUSH) and repeat for the same word.
   C. Repeat for the same word with three choices, two of which are distractors.
3. Oral reading—Hold up card for word taught in step 2 and ask "What does this say?" (MEN)
4. Comprehension (receptive reading)—Place four word cards in front of student. Ask (for male student): "If you needed to go to the bathroom you would look for the sign that says MEN. Which sign would you look for?"
5. Generalization to new settings—Tape the MEN and WOMEN cards to the respective bathroom doors (over existing signs). Ask (for male student): "If you needed to go to the bathroom which sign would you look for?" Then ask, "What does that sign say?"
6. Generalization from word cards to new configurations—Locate bathroom doors with the words MEN and WOMEN printed on them (or use slides). Repeat question in step 5.

After student performs step 6 without errors. On first training word, repeat steps 2 through 6 with each additional word in the set of three to four new training words (WOMEN, EXIT, ENTRANCE). Drop back to matching step if student makes errors in step 2. Adjust comprehension and generalization requests, settings, and materials as appropriate to the target word (e.g., reword questions for males and females with words MEN and WOMEN; locate building signs marking ENTRANCE and EXIT to teach these words).

Testing and review. Introduce a new set of three to four words and teach as described above. Use old words as distractors. Review old words regularly both during teaching sessions and by testing. When testing, record the student's first response but provide feedback as during teaching so that testing provides maintenance training.

Teachers using the program are directed to alternate positions of the word-card choices whenever more than one choice is used to avoid reinforcing positional responses.

Synthetic or Phonetic Approach

Many researchers have recognized the limitations that whole word methods put upon reading achievement. Brown et al. (1974) comment,

It is quite probable that the whole-word method of teaching reading, at least as it has been discussed here, can result in substantial gains in reading achievement. However, it is doubtful that teachers will, by the use of this method, teach their students to read every word, every verb conjugation, and every plural and abbreviation that the students must learn. Hopefully it should be unnecessary to do this. Effective methods of teaching word-attack skills, phonetic, etc., must be delineated and verified empirically for use with this level student. (p. 58)

In order to achieve most of the functional reading goals described by Bender et al. (1976), the moderately handicapped reader must learn some word-recognition skills.

Some of the laboratory research already cited or described (Neville & Vandever, 1973; Staats, 1968), as well as some applied research with moderately retarded populations (Apffel et al., 1975; Vandever et al., 1976) and mildly handicapped learners (Lahey, Weller, & Brown, 1973; Lovitt & Hurlburt, 1974), has indicated the success of teaching readers to analyze words by sound, sight, and context rather than to read by sight alone. Two additional applied studies will be reviewed briefly, with some attention given to their techniques for teaching the functional application of phonics.

Direct Approach to Decoding (DAD)

Richardson, Oestereicher, Bialer, and Winsberg (1975) summarize an experimental program that was successful in teaching phonetic word-recognition skills to the handicapped. DAD was used with small group instruction and incorporated a criterion progression through the following four teaching steps:

1. Letter sounds: Student learns to associate a sound with single isolated letters (*p, s, m*).
2. Sound blending: Student learns to listen to sequences of sounds learned in step 1 (/p/, /an/) and to blend sounds to make words ("pan").
3. Phonetic analysis and blending: Student learns to look at printed words that were learned by blending (step 2) and to say each sound in sequence and then read the word.
4. Word reading: Student learns to look at, quickly analyze, and read new words in rapid succession.

While this (1975) program has been demonstrated successful, more research would be valuable to assess its comparable effectiveness with other sound-based reading programs as well as total reading achieved by DAD "graduates" as compared with students learning by a whole word approach.

Teaching Word Recognition Skills of Picture Cues, Context Cues, and Initial Sounds

Entrikin, York, and Brown (1977) report a well-defined sequence of objectives directed toward the instruction of elementary word recognition strategies: using picture cues, context cues, and initial consonant sounds to determine an unknown word. Three moderately retarded, 10-year-old students with varying motoric handicaps met the following six entry criteria for training and successfully used basic word recognition strategies with unknown words.

1. Imitation of teacher-provided consonant sounds;
2. Rudimentary speech;
3. A sight vocabulary of at least 50 words;
4. Left-to-right eye movement when reading;
5. A reliable and valid yes-no response;
6. A basic understanding of logical and absurd relationships. (Entrikin et al., 1977, p. 171)

The content of the instruction program is summarized by the detailed objectives that follow. For more definition of teaching procedure, see the original report (Entrikin, York, & Brown, 1975).

Phase I: When students are presented with a printed word they cannot label and four pictures that represent objects and actions with differing initial consonant sounds, they will determine the label of the unknown word by finding and labeling the picture which represents the object or action with the same initial consonant sound.

Part 1 – Teaching students to label object pictures and describe action pictures.

Part 2 – Teaching students to sound consonants presented on flashcards.

Part 3a – Teaching students to touch the first letter (color coded) in printed words.

Part 3b – Teaching students to touch the first letter (not color coded) in printed words.

Part 4 – Teaching students to sound initial consonants in selected printed words.

Part 5 – Teaching students to label object pictures, to describe action pictures, and to make the initial consonant sounds of the objects and actions represented in the pictures (e.g., Q–"What is this?" A–"(ball)" Q–"What is the first sound in (ball)" or Q–"What is the (boy) doing?" A–"(running)" Q–"What is the first sound in (running)?").

Part 6 – *Teaching students to label object pictures, to describe action pictures, and to make the initial consonant sounds of the objects and actions presented in those pictures (e.g., Q–"What is this?" A–"(ball)" Q–"What is the first sound in that word?" or Q–"What is the (boy) doing?" A–"(running)" Q–"What is the first sound in that word?")*

Part 7 – *Teaching students to make the initial consonant sounds of objects and actions represented in pictures (e.g., "What is the first sound in this?").[a]*

Part 8 – *Teaching students to touch the appropriate object or action picture in response to a consonant sound stated by the teacher (e.g., "Touch the thing that begins with (bb).").[b]*

Part 9 – *When students are presented with a printed word they cannot label and four pictures that represent objects and actions with differing initial consonant sounds, they will determine the label of the unknown word by finding and labeling the picture which represents the object or action with the same initial consonant sound.*

Phase II: When students are presented with a worksheet containing sentences composed of words they can label but which are missing one word in the subject, verb or object position (e.g., the_____hit the ball. The boy_____the ball. The boy hit the_____.) and three printed words above each sentence, they will mark the one word that logically completes the sentence.

Part 1 – *Teaching students to label object pictures and describe action pictures.*

Part 2 – *When students are presented with eight sets of two pictures, one component of each set depicting an absurd action (e.g., teacher combing hair with toothbrush) and the other component depicting a logical action (e.g., teacher combing hair with comb) and the question, "Does this picture make sense?", they will respond "yes" to pictures of logical actions and "no" to pictures of absurd actions.*

Part 3 – *When students are read sentences which are logical or absurd following the question, "Does this sentence make sense?" they will respond "yes" to logical sentences and "no" to absurd sentences.*

Part 4a – *When students are presented with a printed sentence read by the teacher with one word missing in the object position (e.g., The boy hit the_____.) and three object pictures, they will touch the one picture that represents the object which logically completes the sentence.*

Part 4b – *When students are presented with a printed sentence read by the teacher with one word missing in the verb position (e.g., The boy_____the ball.) and three action pictures, they will touch the one picture that represents the verb which logically completes the sentence.*

Part 4c – *When students are presented with a printed sentence read by the teacher with one word missing in the subject position (e.g., The_____hit the ball.) and three object pictures, they will touch the one picture that represents the subject which logically completes the sentence.*

Part 4d – *When students are presented with a printed sentence read by the teacher with one word missing (e.g., The_____the ball. The boy_____the ball. The boy hit the_____.) and three object or action pictures, they will touch the one picture that represents the subject, verb or object which logically completes the sentence.*

Part 5 – *When students are presented with a printed sentence read by the teacher with one word missing in the subject, verb or object position (e.g., The_____hit the ball. The boy_____the ball. The boy hit the_____.) and three printed words, they will touch the one word which logically completes the sentence.*

Part 6 – *When students are presented with a worksheet containing sentences composed of words they can label but which are missing one word in the subject, verb or object position (e.g., The_____hit the ball. The boy_____the ball. The boy hit the_____.) and three printed words above each sentence, they will mark the one word which logically completes each sentence.*

Phase III: When students are presented with a worksheet containing sentences composed of words they can label with the exception of one underlined word in the subject, verb or object position and four pictures above each sentence, they will determine the label of the underlined word by marking and naming the one picture which represents the object or action (A) with the same initial consonant sound as the underlined word and (B) which logically completes the sentence.

Part 1 – *Teaching sentences to label object pictures and describe action pictures as they are presented on worksheets.*

Part 2 – *When students are presented with a worksheet*

---

[a]Parts 5 and 6 differ in that the teacher repeats object labels and action descriptions in Part 5 but does not do so in Part 6. In Part 7, neither the teacher nor the student labels object pictures or describes action pictures.
[b](bb) as in boy.

containing sentences composed of words they can label with the exception of one underlined word in the subject verb or object position and four pictures above each sentence, they will determine the label of the underlined word by marking and labeling the one picture which represents the object or action (A) with the same initial consonant sound as the underlined word and (B) which logically completes the sentence. (Entrikin et al., 1975, pp. 451–454)

Not only do Entrikin et al. (1977) provide useful prerequisite and instructional guidelines for teaching fundamental word attack skills to the moderately handicapped learner, but also this study provides classroom data to support the relevance of the more complex task analyses for some learners in this population.

SUMMARY

Learning to read is one of the most complex tasks most students master in elementary school. For moderately and severely handicapped learners this same task is enormously more complicated, partly because of their weaknesses in attending, memory, and other thinking skills. More visible reasons for a lack of reading skills concern poor instruction (e.g., failure to teach prerequisite skills, excessive errors early in learning, an absence of generalization training with functional materials in realistic settings), not enough instruction, and a philosophy that the curriculum for these students should not include reading.

Fortunately we have adequate information concerning the sequence of skills that underlie word recognition and comprehension. In addition, the evidence provided by basic and applied research with moderately and severely retarded learners justifies the policy that teachers begin prerequisite or readiness instruction early and systematically direct their teaching toward the goal of functional literacy. For older students demonstrating no sight vocabulary or deficiencies in understanding spoken language, alternate instructional goals for reading should be selected. The first priority for students who have poor comprehension of spoken language is language instruction, not reading instruction, since verbal language understanding must precede written language. If the older student does have a strong receptive language repertoire but recognizes few sight words, then instruction in the remaining school years may be directed toward learning to recognize and understand a carefully chosen functional vocabulary. For these students, reading instruction will be taught by a whole word approach. Because their reading ability will be very limited, they should be taught to use pictoral cues in directions and picture reference books on a long-term rather than temporary basis. Finally, in many cases, spending the remaining school years on the most needed functional skills will mean that reading will not be taught at all.

A few remaining conclusions can be drawn from the reading research reviewed.

1. While language is required for reading, it may be taught immediately prior to reading.
2. Due to the complexity of the reading task and attentional deficits of severely handicapped, systematic prompting and fading as well as confirmation (i.e., error correction and reinforcement for correct responses) probably will be required.
3. The greater the demands of the reading task and the more severe the handicap, the more precise the prompting and fading procedures may need to be.
4. Response prompts (e.g., verbal models of words or a demonstration of a word's meaning) seem to be preferable to stimulus prompts (e.g., pictures), in that they are easier to fade, less distracting, and provide more vocabulary options.
5. If a teacher uses pictures, time delay may be a more effective and more practical fading procedure than a gradual reduction of the picture's clarity.
6. Teach only the most necessary "prerequisites" to reading, if any at all (e.g., Entrikin's [Entrikin et al., 1975] initial consonant sounds); teach these prerequisites in the context of functional activities (e.g., a leisure board game, vending machine use) words and materials.
7. The best strategy for teaching reading and assessing a student's performance in a given reading task (e.g., using a laundromat, a telephone directory, or a department store) is to analyze the task as it is actually performed in the real setting and use these same steps in both teaching and assessment.

REFERENCES

Apffel, J.A., Kelleher, J., Lilly, M.S., & Richardson, R. Developmental reading for moderately retarded children. *Education and Training of the Mentally Retarded,* 1975, *10,* 229–236.

Basic reading skills mastery test. Bloomington, Ind.: Services for Educational Evaluation, 1974.

Bender, M., Valletutti, P.J., & Bender, R. *Teaching the moderately and severely handicapped* (Vol. III). Baltimore: University Park Press, 1976.

Bereiter, C., & Engelmann, S. *Teaching disadvantaged children in the preschool.* Englewood Cliffs, N.J.: Prentice-Hall, 1966.

Bijou, S.W., Birnbrauer, J.S., Kidder, J.D., & Tague, C. Programmed instruction as an approach to teaching of reading, writing, and arithmetic to retarded children. *Psychological Record*, 1966, *16*, 505–522.

Bilsky, L.H., Evans, R.A., & Martin, P. Relative effectiveness of various letter discrimination procedures in directionality pretraining. *American Journal of Mental Deficiency*, 1975, *79*, 259–266.

Birnbrauer, J.S., Kidder, J.D., & Tague, C. Programmed reading from a teacher's point of view. *Programmed Instruction*, 1964, *3*, 1–2.

Birnbrauer, J.S., Wolf, M.M., Kidder, J.D., & Tague, C. Classroom behavior of retarded pupils with token reinforcement. *Journal of Experimental Child Psychology*, 1965, *2*, 219–235.

Bliss, C.K. *Semantography*. Sydney, Aust.: Semantography Publications, 1965.

Bond, G.L., & Tinker, M.A. *Reading difficulties: Their diagnosis and correction* (2nd ed.). New York: Appleton-Century-Crofts, 1967.

Booth, A., Hewitt, D., Jenkins, W., & Maggs, A. Making retarded children literate: A five year study. *Australian Journal of Mental Retardation*, 1979, *5*, 257–260.

Bracey, S., Maggs, A., & Morath, P. The effects of a direct phonic approach in teaching reading with six moderately retarded children: Acquisition and mastery learning stages. *The Slow Learning Child*, 1975, *22*, 83–90.

Browder, D.M. *A comparison of a stimulus prompt and a response prompt with four fading procedures to teach sight words to the moderately and severely retarded*. Unpublished doctoral dissertation, University of Virginia, 1980.

Brown, L., Branston, M.B., Hamre-Nietupski, S., Pumpian, I., Certo, N., & Gruenewald, L. A strategy for developing chronological age appropriate and functional curricular content for severely handicapped adolescents and young adults. *Journal of Special Education*, 1979, *13*, 81–90.

Brown, L., Huppler, B., Pierce, L., York, R., & Sontag, E. Teaching trainable-level students to read unconjugated action verbs. *Journal of Special Education*, 1974, *8*, 51–56.

Brown, L., Jones, S., Troccolo, E., Heiser, C., Bellamy, T., & Sontag, E. Teaching functional reading to young trainable students: Toward longitudinal objectives. *Journal of Special Education*, 1972, *6*, 237–246.

Brown, L., & Perlmutter, L. Teaching functional reading to trainable level retarded students. *Education and Training of the Mentally Retarded*, 1971, *6*, 74–84.

Buchanan, C.D. *Teacher's guide to programmed reading* (Book 1, Series 1, rev. ed., Sullivan Associates Program). St. Louis, Webster Division, McGraw-Hill, 1968.

Cohen, M.A., Gross, P.J., & Haring, N.G. Developmental pinpoints. In N.G. Haring & L.J. Brown (Eds.), *Teaching the severely handicapped* (Vol. 1). New York: Grune & Stratton, 1976.

Cohen, S.B., & Plaskon, S.P. *Language arts for the mildly handicapped*. Columbus, Ohio: Charles E. Merrill, 1980.

Coleman, E.B. Collecting a data base for reading technology. *Journal of Educational Psychology Monograph*, 1970, *61* (4, Pt. 2), 1–23.

Cooking with Betty Crocker mixes (large type edition). Minneapolis: General Mills, 1970.

Denny, M.R. A theoretical analysis and its application to training the mentally retarded. In N.R. Ellis (Ed.), *International review of research in mental retardation* (Vol. 2). New York: Academic Press, 1966.

Dolch, E.W. *Teaching primary reading* (2nd ed.) Champaign, Ill.: Garrard Press, 1950.

Dorry, G.W., & Zeaman, D. The use of a fading technique in paired-associate teaching of a reading vocabulary with retardates. *Mental Retardation*, 1973, *11*(6), 3–6.

Dorry, G.W., & Zeaman, D. Teaching a simple reading vocabulary to retarded children: Effectiveness of fading and nonfading procedures. *American Journal of Mental Deficiency*, 1975, *79*, 711–716.

Drinkwater, B.A. The significance of affect in verbal learning by subnormal children—An exploratory study. *Australian Journal of Psychology*, 1972, *24*, 327–329.

Duffy, G.G., & Sherman, G.B. *How to teach reading systematically*. New York: Harper & Row, 1973.

Duffy, G.G., & Sherman, G.B. *Systematic reading instruction* (2nd ed.). New York: Harper & Row, 1977.

Easy menu cookbook. Bristol, Ind.: Elkhart Jaycees-Auxilary of the Elkhart Jaycees, 1974.

Edmark reading program: Teacher's guide. Seattle: Edmark, 1972.

Egeland, B., & Winer, K. Teaching children to discriminate letters of the alphabet through errorless discrimination training. *Journal of Reading Behavior*, 1974, *2*, 143–150.

Ellis, N.R. Memory processes in retardates and normals. In N.R. Ellis (Ed.), *International review of research in mental retardation* (Vol. 4). New York: Academic Press, 1970.

Engelmann, S. Classroom techniques: Teaching reading to children with low mental age. *Education and Training of the Mentally Retarded*, 1967, *2*, 193–201.

Engelmann, S., & Bruner, E.C. *DISTAR reading: An instructional system*. Chicago: Science Research Associates, 1969.

Entrikin, D., York, R., & Brown, L. Teaching trainable level multiply handicapped students to use picture cues, context cues, and initial sounds to determine the labels of unknown words. In L. Brown, T. Crowner, W. Williams, & R. York (Eds.), *Madison's alternative for zero exclusion: A book of readings* (Vol. 5). Madison, Wisc.: Madison Public Schools, 1975.

Entrikin, D., York, R., & Brown, L. Teaching trainable level multiply handicapped students to use picture cues, context cues, and initial consonant sounds to determine the labels of unknown words. *AAESPH Review*, 1977, *2*, 168–190.

Fernald, G. *Remedial techniques in basic school subjects*. New York: McGraw-Hill, 1943.

Fries, C.C., Wilson, R., & Rudolph, M.K. *Merrill linguistic reader*. Columbus, Ohio: Charles E. Merrill, 1966.

Fry, E. Developing a word list for remedial reading. *Elementary English*, 1957, *33*, 456–458.

Fry, E. *Reading instruction for classroom and clinic*. New York: McGraw-Hill, 1972.

Gagne, R.M. *The conditions of learning* (2nd ed.). New York: Holt, Rinehart & Winston, 1965.

Gillespie, P.H., & Johnson, L. *Teaching reading to the mildly retarded child.* Columbus, Ohio: Charles E. Merrill, 1974.

Harman, D. Illiteracy: An overview. *Harvard Educational Review,* 1970, *40,* 226–243.

Harris-Vanderheiden, D., & Vanderheiden, G.C. Basic considerations in the development of communicative and interactive skills for non-vocal severely handicapped children. In E. Sontag, J. Smith, & N. Certo (Eds.), *Educational programming for the severely and profoundly handicapped.* Reston. Va.: Council for Exceptional Children, 1977.

Hawker, J.R. A further investigation of prompting and confirmation in sight vocabulary learning by retardates. *American Journal of Mental Deficiency,* 1968, *72,* 594–598.

Hawker, J.R., Geertz, U.W., & Shrago, M. Prompting and confirmation in sight vocabulary learning by retardates. *American Journal of Mental Deficiency,* 1964, *68,* 751–756.

Johnson, M.S., & Kress, R.A. *Informal reading inventories.* Newark: International Reading Association, 1965.

Kaman, M. *Cooking activities for retarded children.* Nashville: Abingdon, 1974.

Kirk, S.A. *Educating exceptional children* (2nd ed.). Boston: Houghton Mifflin, 1972.

Lahey, B., Weller, D., & Brown, W. The behavior analysis approach to reading: Phonics discriminations. *Journal of Reading Behavior,* 1973, *5,* 200–206.

Lavely, C., Lowe, A.J., & Follman, J. Actual reading levels of EMR materials. *Education and Training of the Mentally Retarded,* 1975, *10,* 271–275.

Lent, J.N. Mimosa cottage experiment and hope. *Psychology Today,* 1968, *52,* 51–58.

Lichtman, M. *Reading/everyday activities in life. Examiner's manual.* New York: CAL Press, 1972.

Lichtman, M. The development and validation of R/EAL, an instrument to assess functional literacy. *Journal of Reading Behavior,* 1974, *6,* 167–182.

Lovitt, T.C., & Hurlburt, M. Using behavior-analysis techniques to assess the relationship between phonics instruction and oral reading. *Journal of Special Education,* 1974, *8,* 57–72.

Miller, A., & Miller, E. Symbol accentuation: The perceptual transfer of meaning from spoken to printed words. *Journal of Mental Deficiency,* 1968, *73,* 200–208.

Montessori, M. *The Montessori method.* New York: Stokes, 1912.

Nafziger, D.H., Thompson, R.B., Hiscox, M.D., & Owen, T.R. *Tests of functional adult literacy: An evaluation of currently available instruments.* Portland, Ore.: Northwest Regional Educational Laboratory, 1975.

Neville, D., & Vandever, T. Decoding as a result of synthetic and analytic presentation for retarded and nonretarded children. *American Journal of Mental Deficiency,* 1973, *77,* 533–537.

Northcutt, N. Kelso, C., & Barron, W.E. *Adult functional competency in Texas.* Austin: University of Texas Press, 1975.

Otto, W., McMenemy, R.A., & Smith, R.J. *Corrective and remedial teaching* (2nd ed.). Boston: Houghton-Mifflin, 1973.

Reed, F.S. *A special picture cookbook.* Lawrence, Kans.: H & H Enterprises, 1973.

Resnick, L.B., & Beck, I.L. Designing instruction in reading: Interaction of theory and practice. In J.T. Guthrie (Ed.), *Aspects of reading acquisition.* Baltimore: Johns Hopkins University Press, 1976.

Richardson, E., Oestereicher, M., Bialer, I., & Winsberg, G. Teaching beginning reading skills to retarded children in community classrooms: A programmatic case study. *Mental Retardation,* 1975, *13*(1), 11–15.

Samuels, S.J. Success and failure in learning to read: A critique of the research. In F.B. Davis (Ed.), *The literature of research in reading, with emphasis on models.* New Brunswick, N.J.: Graduate School of Education, Rutgers University, 1971.

Sidman, M. Reading and auditory-visual equivalences. *Journal of Speech and Hearing Research,* 1971, *14,* 5–13.

Sidman, M., & Cresson, O., Jr. Reading and cross modal transfer of stimulus equivalences in severe retardation. *American Journal of Mental Deficiency,* 1973, *77,* 515–523.

Silvaroli, N.J. *Classroom reading inventory* (2nd ed.). Dubuque, Iowa: Wm. C. Brown, 1973.

Smith, D.E.P. *A technology of reading and writing, Volume I: Learning to read and write, a task analysis.* New York: Academic Press, 1976.

Smith, J.M., Smith, D.E.P., & Brink, J.R. *A technology of reading and writing, Volume 2: Criterion referenced test for reading and writing.* New York: Academic Press, 1977.

Spache, G.D. *Diagnosing and correcting reading difficulties.* Boston: Allyn & Bacon, 1976.

Spitz, H.H. The role of input organization in the learning and memory of mental retardates. In N.R. Ellis (Ed.), *International review of research in mental retardation* (Vol. 2). New York: Academic Press, 1966.

Spitz, H.H. Consolidating facts into the schematized learning and memory system of educable retardates. In N.R. Ellis (Ed.), *International review of research in mental retardation* (Vol. 6). New York: Academic Press, 1973.

Staats, A.W. *Learning, language, and cognition.* New York: Holt, Rinehart & Winston, 1968.

Staats, A.W., & Butterfield, W. Treatment of nonreading in a culturally deprived juvenile delinquent: An application of reinforcement principles. *Child Development,* 1965, *36,* 925–942.

Staats, A., Minke, K., Finley, J., Wolf, M., & Brooks, L. A reinforcer system and experimental procedure for the laboratory study of reading acquisition. *Child Development,* 1964, *35,* 209–231.

Staples, K.S. *Cooking from pictures.* Fargo: North Dakota State University, 1975.

Stauffer, R.G. *The language-experience approach to the teaching of reading.* New York: Harper & Row, 1970.

Stokes, T.F., & Baer, D.M. An implicit technology of generalization. *Journal of Applied Behavior Analysis*, 1977, *10*, 349–367.

Stone, C.R. Measuring difficulty of primary reading material: A constructive criticism of Spache's measure. *Elementary School Journal*, 1956, *6*, 36–41.

Stricht, T.G., Caylor, J.S., Kern, R.P., & Fox, L.C. Project REALISTIC: Determination of adult functional literacy skill levels. *Reading Research Quarterly*, 1972, *1*, 424–465.

Touchette, E.P. Transfer of stimulus control: Measuring the moment of transfer. *Journal of Experimental Analysis of Behavior*, 1971, *15*, 347–354.

Vanderheiden, G., & Grilley, K. *Non-verbal communication techniques and aids for the non-vocal severely handicapped*. Baltimore: University Park Press, 1975.

Vandever, T.R., Maggart, W.T., & Nasser, S. Three approaches to beginning reading. *Mental Retardation*, 1976, *14*(4), 29–32.

Vandever, T.R., & Neville, D.D. Letter cues vs. configuration cues as aids to word recognition in retarded and nonretarded children. *American Journal of Mental Deficiency*, 1974, *79*, 210–213.

Vandever, T.R., & Stubbs, J.C. Reading retention and transfer in TMR students. *American Journal of Mental Deficiency*, 1977, *82*, 233–237.

Walsh, B.F., & Lamberts, F. Errorless discrimination and picture fading as techniques for teaching sight words to TMR students. *American Journal of Mental Deficiency*, 1979, *83*, 473–479.

White, O.R., & Haring, N.G. *Exceptional teaching*. Columbus, Ohio: Charles E. Merrill, 1976.

Willamson, F. *DISTAR Reading—Research and experiment*. Urbana: University of Illinois, 1970.

Wisconsin test of adult basic education. Madison: University of Wisconsin, Rural Family Development Program, University Extension, 1974.

Woodcock, R.W. *Introducing reading. Book two, Peabody rebus reading prog*. Circle Pines, Minn.: American Guidance Services, 1967.

Woodcock, R.W. The Peabody-Chicago-Detroit reading project: A report of second year results. In J.R. Block (Ed.), *i.t.a. as a language arts medium*. Hempstead, N.Y.: The i.t.a. Foundation, Hofstra University, 1968.

Woodcock, R.W., Davies, C.O., & Clark, C.R. *The Peabody rebus reading program supplementary lessons kit: Manual of lessons*. Circle Pines, Minn.: American Guidance Service, 1969.

Zeaman, D., & House, B.J. The role of attention in retardate discrimination learning. In N.R. Ellis (Ed.), *Handbook of mental deficiency*. New York: McGraw-Hill, 1963.

REFERENCE NOTES

1. *Curriculum-cumulative progress report*. Salem, Ore.: Mental Health Division, Community Mental Retardation Section, 1972.

2. Heckler, M.M. How many Americans read well enough to survive? *Congressional Record*, Nov. 18, 1970, 38036-38–40.

3. Browder, D., Snell, M.E., & Hines, C. *A comparison of time delay procedures to teach sight words to moderately and severely retarded adults: Spoken versus picture prompt*. Unpublished manuscript, Lehigh University, 1982.

4. Browder, D., Hines, C., McCarthy, L.J., & Fees, J. *Teaching sight words to promote generalization of daily living skills*. Unpublished manuscript, Lehigh University, 1981.

5. Barrier, H.C. *The effectiveness of the Edmark reading program utilizing a single subject multiple probe design*. Unpublished manuscript, Pennsylvania State University, Division of Special Education and Communication Disorders, 1981.

In the next two chapters you will read information basic to vocational preparation of severely handicapped students. Traditionally special educators have had little to do with vocational training, and few know much of the mechanics and economics of a workshop. Similarly, teachers of higher functioning students have had minimal involvement with workshop programs. The severely handicapped (often the lower functioning students in classes for the trainable) generally could expect no vocational training.

When you stop and reflect on these practices, they are quite the opposite from what they should be. Students who are the least self-sufficient should never be abruptly or briefly "dumped" into a vocational training program or omitted altogether from that training. Because of these practices, many young adults have nothing to do when they leave school, except perhaps enroll in a nonprofitable activity center with no alternatives for vocational training.

While these practices have not disappeared, more generous funds for developing vocational training programs are now available; there is a supply of successful data-based models for vocational training of the severely handicapped; and competitive employment has been shown to be possible for this population.

What we need now are teachers ready to assume responsibility in accomplishing the task of vocational preparation. This task requires (a) developing a close working relationship with potential job placements and existing training settings in the community; (b) long-term planning of vocational preparation objectives with students' parents, beginning at age 10; (c) continually monitoring and adjusting these plans with parents and area employers and trainers during the students' remaining years in school; and (d) ideally, follow-up by the high school teacher of graduates, to facilitate continued success and improve the school's procedures.

In the next chapter you will be exposed to a comprehensive overview of the range of vocational options available to moderately and severely handicapped students after (and often before) the age of 21. Tom Bellamy and his colleagues explain the history, the legal framework, and the sometimes confusing workings of these agencies. This chapter provides critical information that will facilitate your interactions with these agencies.

Finally, Frank Rusch traces the more recent history of competitive employment of the moderately and severely handicapped. He sketches step-by-step procedures by which teachers may survey their community and develop training programs in cooperation with the private sector. These procedures are empirically based and thus, if conscientiously implemented, provide some guarantee of success.

Introduction to Chapters 16 and 17

16

Work and Work-Related Services: Postschool Options

G. Thomas Bellamy, Jo-Ann Sowers, and Philip E. Bourbeau are all with the Specialized Training Program, Center on Human Development, University of Oregon.

This chapter addresses vocational services and employment of severely handicapped adults with two purposes. The first is to foster your awareness of the vocational opportunities and services available to individuals with severe handicaps who leave school. The chapter analyzes postschool services and suggests several ways teachers can help students benefit from those services. The second purpose is to challenge special education, rehabilitation, vocational education, and related fields to develop a vocational service system that is more responsive to the unique needs of people with severe handicaps. We will outline some constraints on the design of such a system and some critical objectives the system should achieve.

The characteristics that render a person severely handicapped at school may or may not have similar effects in relation to employment. Consequently, it is not surprising that you can find a variety of definitions for terms like *severely handicapped, severely disabled,* and *developmentally disabled.* The confusion is not simply one of terminology. Individual characteristics and changing circumstances interact to produce different needs for educational, medical, vocational, and income maintenance services. For example, it is not unusual for people who have been considered moderately or severely handicapped in school to hold stable jobs as adults. It would be difficult to say that they were severely handicapped in relation to work. Similarly, some who fit in the educational mainstream may have extreme handicaps in relation to employment. From this perspective, a person's severe handicaps must be viewed as potentially temporary conditions that might be reversed by changes in environment.

Despite the definitional confusion, this chapter addresses vocational services and opportunities for adults who were labeled *severely handicapped* by the schools. As they leave school they represent only a part of several much larger groups of people considered severely handicapped or disabled by various social service providers, in relation to various environmental requirements and social services. Thus the adult experiences of severely handicapped school-leavers typically can only be estimated from the data available on the larger groups who receive adult services. While the heterogeneity of these groups may result in widely varied accounts of what can be predicted for severely handicapped students, the information should allow educators to estimate the probable range of vocational futures that face their students.

The importance of work for adults with severe handicaps has been broadly defended on personal, social, and economic grounds. Working appears to promote individual growth, expand one's social circle, enhance social status, provide the means to participate in normal activities, and allow one to contribute to the life of a community. It is much more difficult for most people to plan and lead a meaningful life without employment.

For many disabled people, normal access to opportunities in the job market are not sufficient to obtain and maintain employment. Joblessness may result from skill deficits, from unnecessary job entry requirements, from the particular way tasks are combined into jobs, from the architecture of the workplace, from the economics of employing people with various training needs or productivity levels, or from a variety of other characteristics. The United States and most other industrialized countries have developed an array of vocational services that aim to eliminate these barriers to employment. The vocational prospects for severely handicapped school-leavers must be seen in the context of both the employment opportunities in the economy and the vocational services that address individual needs.

We will first address the current status of vocational services from the perspectives of government policy and local practice. We then review recent program advances and analyze the discrepancy between practice and documented potential. Finally, we will discuss needed directions from both the perspective of an individual teacher and the field as a whole.

OVERVIEW OF VOCATIONAL SERVICES

The first U.S. federal program providing vocational habilitation services was the Soldier's Rehabilitation Act of 1918, passed in response to the large numbers of disabled veterans from World War I. This act marked the first government effort to assist and support its handicapped citizens (Rubin & Roessler, 1978). Since then there has been a gradual but steady addition of related programs extending both the range of service provided and persons served. Today there is an impressive array of vocational support services for the handicapped population.

Whatever patriotic or humanitarian interests prompted the initial legislation, the continuing investment in vocational services must be understood in terms of a fundamental difference between the economic interests of individual employers and society at large. It is almost always in an employer's best interest to channel out of the labor force anyone who is not maximally productive. On the other hand, with the high and escalating cost of unemployment compensation, disability insurance premiums, supplemental security income, medical assistance, and other social services, it is in the best interest of society as a whole to maintain as many people as possible in the work force. The United States and most other developed countries have met this conflict with a variety of regulations, incentives, and services designed to reduce unemployment of handicapped workers. Government expenditures and programs reflect two general strategies.

1. Incentives or requirements for potential employers that increase the likelihood that jobs will be available to job seekers with handicaps, and
2. Vocational services to handicapped individuals themselves.

Vocational Programs Affecting Employers

If joblessness among disabled individuals results in part from employers' hiring practices, one obvious way to address the problem is to establish contingencies that will change those practices. Two general methods have been used to affect the hiring practices of employers. The first involves government civil rights regulations and the associated possibility of legal action against employers by either job seekers or regulatory agencies. Until 1973, handicapped workers who believed they had been discriminated against in employment-related issues could only bring suit under the broad legal protection of the 14th Amendment or the Civil Rights Act of 1964, which does not specifically name handicapped persons as a protected group. The Rehabilitation Act of 1973, specifically Sections 503 and 504, provided the first clear mandate to protect people with handicaps from employment discrimination. Sections 503 and 504 apply to all public employers and to private companies that receive substantial government subsidies or contracts. The law requires the employer to make "reasonable accommodations" to hire handicapped persons and to not use employment criteria and pre-employment procedures that would have a discriminatory effect. The application of the law is still being determined in the courts (*Steiler v Spokane School District*, 88 Wn. 2d 68 (1977), *Milwaukee R. R. v Human Rights Commission*, 87 Wn. 2d 802 (1976), *Albertsons, Inc. v Washington Human Rights Commission*, 14 Wn. App. 697, 544 P. 2d 98 (1976)).

To date, the courts have not made a strong and inclusive statement regarding the law's intent, but instead support Kline's (1978) observation that "there is no civil rights violation in denying a job to a person who has not shown that he or she is qualified to perform it adequately. This should cause attorneys to assess carefully the merits of an employment discrimination action brought by a handicapped client." This focus on qualification for existing jobs may be of critical assistance to handicapped workers who have been denied employment on the basis of irrelevant factors. It does not, however, address the issue of job modifications that could allow other people, especially many with more severe handicaps, to be included in the work force.

Another limitation is simply the extent of federal regulatory authority. The vast majority of all U.S. employers are in the private sector. Antidiscrimination laws do not apply to these employers unless special circumstances, like doing business with the government itself, exist.

The second general method used to change the hiring practices of employers has been providing incentives to employers who do hire individuals. An example is the Targeted-Jobs Tax Credit. Under this program a private sector employer may receive tax reductions equivalent to 50% and 25% of a handicapped employee's 1st and 2nd year wages, respectively. Similarly, the Vocational Rehabilitation and CETA programs also reimburse employers with a percentage of a handicapped worker's wage during the first few months of employment to cover any related training cost.

These incentive programs appear well-designed to promote employment of workers who present initial excess costs, but who then perform as other workers. They do not, however, address the issue of employing individuals who may be productive, but present ongoing costs because of lower than average productivity or the need for additional supervision, retraining, equipment, or fixtures. The government provides no incentives for employers to hire workers who will not be normally productive at normal costs after the first few months on the job.

Vocational Services to Individuals

A disproportionately large number of disabled individuals, and practically all those labeled *severely handicapped* by the schools, remain jobless despite government incentives and regulations to increase employment opportunities. A variety of government programs seek to provide habilitation services for them that remove employment barriers associated with the individual. At this time there are five major federal laws that provide most vocational habilitation services to handicapped adults: The Rehabilitation Act, the Comprehensive Employment and Training Act (CETA), the Vocational Education Act, Titles XX and XIX of the Social Security Act, and the Developmental Disabilities Assistance and Bill of Rights Act. The programs associated with these acts share some basic administrative features. A federal agency provides general regulatory direction carried out by state or local government representatives, who in turn either deliver services directly or contract for services from local private providers.

The first three programs, Vocational Rehabilitation, CETA, and Vocational Education, are primarily transitional service programs. These services are meant to be short-term, time-limited services that result in client entry in competitive employment. Their intent is reflected in the eligibility requirements. Explicitly stated by Vocational Rehabilitation and implied by the other two programs is the entry criterion that an individual must show potential for competitive employment. In 1973 the Rehabilitation Act was amended to require that those with the most severe handicaps be given priority in services. However, the eligibility requirement of potential for employment remained intact, preserving the transitional nature of the program.

The three programs offer services such as vocational evaluation, work adjustment training, educational services, counseling, job placement, on-the-job training, and follow-up. Although some of these services are provided by the state or local government agency, most services are contracted from private providers, including rehabilitation companies, community colleges, technical schools, counselors, and sheltered workshops.

The remaining three programs, Title XX, Title XIX, and Developmental Disabilities, are primarily intended to provide extended, long-term services, often including some vocational services. Like the transition programs, the eligibility requirements for those programs reflect their intent. Eligibility for Title XX support is based on the presence of a handicap and low income level (usually, all recipients of SSI qualify), while Title XIX requires that an individual be "medically needy" and unable to afford medical services. Unlike the first two programs, the Developmental Disabilities program is intended specifically and exclusively for developmentally disabled persons. Eligibility for services requires that the individual have a significant functional impairment in at least two major life areas.

Service delivery in all three extended service programs relies to a great extent on private providers, like sheltered workshops and adult day programs—the same programs that deliver the transitional services as well. Private providers thus are the critical link in service delivery and deserve careful attention in any analysis of available services.

Private providers are often relatively free to establish entrance requirements and to determine the content and quality of services provided. Federal and state regulations often provide only broad guidelines for services, and with a few important exceptions exert only indirect control over the actual program offered. The bottom line is that local program representatives, such as vocational rehabilitation counselors and developmental disability case workers, can purchase services only from local providers. Consequently, the real impact of the various federal programs depends on the quality and local availability of services offered by private providers.

PRIVATE PROVIDERS

Private provision of vocational services to unemployed handicapped adults began long before government involvement. The sheltered workshop concept was introduced in the United States in 1838 by the Perkins Institute for the Blind (U.S. Department of Labor, 1977). The early workshop programs that followed were designed to provide supported employment for workers whose handicaps appeared to preclude competitive jobs.

The first major federal involvement came a century later. The 1938 amendments to the Vocational Rehabilitation Act permitted workshops to pay below-minimum wages to handicapped workers, thereby allowing them to compete more equally with other businesses for contracts. By the mid-1940s additional revisions to the act allowed the provision of services to retarded adults. Significant changes in workshop operation resulted from further amendments in 1954 that expanded funding for state rehabilitation programs and made grants available to private organizations to develop new techniques for serving handicapped people (U.S. Department of Labor, 1977). The resulting techniques turned attention away from workshop employment and toward preparation of handicapped adults to move into independent competitive jobs. Based on the research efforts of that time (Coakley, 1945; Engel, 1950; Warren, 1961), the new techniques emphasized the development of a general "work personality" and specific individual traits. Strategies designed to foster work readiness stressed evaluation, adjustment, and counseling services.

The Changing System

With increasing federal support for placement-related activities, workshops focused more on preparation for placement. Long-term employment for more severely handicapped individuals gradually became a secondary concern for private providers (DuBrow, 1959). The initial result was the development of dual objectives for workshops: Not only were they expected to provide sheltered employment, but they were supposed to move handicapped people into jobs in the competitive sector. Neff (1970) described this two-fold objective by distinguishing between "rehabilitation workshops," functioning as a transitional service fostering competitive placement, and "sheltered workshops," providing remunerative employment to those who presumably could not be hired independently. In reality, however, both functions were usually the goals of a single agency, and federal support encouraged staffing patterns and program objectives that gave greater emphasis to competitive placement. Work in these programs has increasingly been viewed as a therapy to build work tolerance and adjustment and prepare individuals to enter open employment (Ruegg, 1981).

A second major government influence on the services offered by private providers has occurred during the last two decades. Deinstitutionalization and related federal support for community day services have greatly expanded the group of consumers served by private providers. With this new government support, people have been included who earlier might have been denied entrance to workshop programs because of their apparent inability to participate in either sheltered work or employment preparation programs. To accommodate this influx of consumers, the system of service providers in most states developed a flow-through continuum of programs. Adults considered unable or not ready to benefit from job preparation are referred to more elementary training programs that are expected to lead to their "readiness" to benefit from workshop programs. As readiness develops, clients are expected to move through the continuum until they reach the goal of an independent competitive job. Gradually, this flow-through model has displaced the employment function of sheltered workshops to such an extent that only 5% of sheltered workshops in the country provide strictly remunerative employment for handicapped workers (Greenleigh, 1975).

The Present System of Private Providers

The current system of privately provided vocational services consists in most states of programs funded under the six major federal programs and administered by two state agencies, the vocational rehabilitation agency and a developmental disabilities or similar human service agency. There are differences in program characteristics and funding, but the objective of movement through the continuum toward competitive job placement is practically universal. State differences preclude precise national description of some services, but data are available on three general types of programs present in some form throughout the country: *regular program workshops* and *work activities centers,* two classes of sheltered workshops defined in the Fair Labor Standards Act as amended in 1966 and monitored by the Department of Labor; and *adult day programs,* managed by Developmental Disabilities Agencies in most states.

Regular Program Workshops

Regular program workshops (RPWs) are sheltered workshops designed to serve more capable or productive individuals. Department of Labor regulations require that clients served in RPWs earn no less than 50% of minimum wage when working. Nevertheless, the work provided is intended to be a therapeutic, tolerance-building activity designed to foster general vocational readiness. In 1976, 37,287 people were receiving services in regular program workshops (U.S. Department of Labor, 1979).

Work Activities Centers

Work activities centers (WACs) are defined as:

a physically separated department of a workshop . . . planned and designed exclusively to provide therapeutic activities for handicapped workers whose physical or mental impairment is so severe as to make their productive capacity inconsequential. Therapeutic activities include custodial activities (such as basic skills of living) and any purposeful activity so long as work is not the main purpose. (Federal Register, 1974, 17509)

Work activities centers are designed to serve more severely handicapped adults whose vocational evaluations indicate a lack of occupational readiness, but who need personal and social adjustment training. It is expected that the training will enable them eventually to move on to a regular program workshop. A wage ceiling of 50% of minimum wage has been set for WAC clients. In 1976 there were 85,550 individuals receiving services in WACs. (U.S. Department of Labor, 1979).

Adult Day Programs

A less well-defined but increasingly important option for severely handicapped people is adult day programs (ADPs). Adult day programs exist under a variety of labels, including activity centers, adult day activity programs, and developmental centers. These are generally nonvocational services administered by social service or developmental disabilities agencies in each state. No single federal agency funds or regulates the programs, and there is no national data base like that maintained by the Department of Labor for RPWs and WACs. Service consumers are generally those adults who are unserved or rejected for service by vocational rehabilitation agencies and sheltered workshops. Programs focus on basic education, motor skills, socialization, communication abilities, and basic work orientation, with the expectation that

acquiring these basic living skills and removing aberrant behaviors will facilitate movement into a more vocationally oriented program. In 1979 there were approximately 105,500 persons receiving services in ADPs (Bellamy, Sheehan, Horner, & Boles, 1980).

The step-wise progression of the vocational service system is evident in these program structures. The three types of programs are three distinct levels in many states. In others, there are only two levels, with various combinations of the three types. In each case, however, individuals are expected to move in the continuum from ADPs to WACs or RPWs and on to competitive employment. The face validity of this continuum is demonstrated by a survey of RPW, WAC, and ADP staff members conducted in Michigan (Lynch & Gerber, 1980), where 92% of the respondents indicated that their function was to move clients to progressively more sophisticated work settings.

System Effectiveness

Since privately provided vocational services are the primary link between federal programs and handicapped individuals, it is important to examine the effectiveness of the system. We look first at overall data on placement, interprogram movement, and wages as indices of success in preparing people for competitive jobs, providing sheltered employment, and moving people through a continuum of less restrictive services. We then look specifically at people with severe handicaps.

Placement in Open Employment

Volume II of the Department of Labor Sheltered Workshop Study (1979) reported that in 1976 4,213 (11%) of the 37,287 persons in RPWs and 6,328 (7%) of the 85,550 individuals in WACs were placed in competitive jobs. The total represents slightly less than 10% of the total consumer population that year. If these data are representative of other years, we could conclude that an average stay of 10 years (after leaving ADPs) would be required before competitive placement. The actual time required is even more revealing. Moss (1979) extracted data from Department of Labor reports (1977) that show that 75% of all clients placed in competitive employment are placed within 1 year of entering the program, and ⅓ of these are placed within their first 3 months. The frequency of placement for individuals who have been in RPWs longer than 2 years is less than 3%. Workshops appear successful at getting competitive jobs for those who can rapidly demonstrate competence in the program, but much less successful when longer training or preparation is needed.

Interprogram Movement

In 1976 2,340, or less than 3%, of the 85,550 people served in WACs moved on to RPWs; 7% of WAC participants were placed in competitive jobs during the year. These data are corroborated by a review of sheltered workshops by the California Department of Finance (1979), which reported that during 1978 placements in competitive jobs from California WACs occurred for 4.5% of the clients, while 3.3% moved on to programs in sheltered workshops. The same study shows that only 2.7% of California's ADP population moved on in the continuum during 1978. The State of New Jersey Bureau of Adult Training Services (Note 1) reports similar figures. In 1980 only 31 of 885 clients (3.5%) served in New Jersey ADPs moved on to more vocationally oriented programs. Of that number, 23 moved to WAC programs operated by Bureau of Adult Training Services itself.

These results give strong testimony that the flow-through model is not working for the severely handicapped. Consequently, rather than justify programs on the basis of what participants are being prepared to do, it seems more reasonable to ask what sort of services and benefits they enjoy in each program level.

Wages

Given that the majority of handicapped consumers in the adult service system remain in their programs for lengthy periods, their opportunity to generate meaningful wages assumes no small importance. Data reported by the Department of Labor (1979) indicate that in 1976 clients in sheltered workshops earned an average annual wage of $661. Those in RPWs earned an average annual wage over $2,000, while those in WACs averaged only $288 for the year, an average of $24 per month.

The inability of WACs to allow clients to generate meaningful wages further perpetuates their poverty. As Whitehead (1979) suggests, wages in sheltered workshops are so low that society may choose a total welfare instead of sheltered work and work preparation.

Clients With Severe Handicaps

The data on job placements, interprogram movement, and wages describe a significant national problem that has received increasing attention in the last few years (Bellamy, Horner, Sheehan, & Boles, 1981; Cobb, 1972; Conley, 1973; Lynch & Gerber, 1980; Whitehead, 1979). If the plight of handicapped adults in workshops and day programs is generally a problem, then the status of those with more severe handicaps presents an enormous problem within the problem. Information extrapolated from national surveys suggests that people considered severely handicapped in school have little likelihood of receiving vocational services, work opportunities, or assistance in locating open employment.

Exclusion from Services

In the absence of an entitlement to vocational services, local program providers and state agencies can establish entrance requirements that fit their fiscal constraints, special orientations, or staff interests. For example, a two-phase Wisconsin study assessed the postschool status of moderately and severely handicapped students. Phase I (Blessing & Samelian, 1972) assessed the postschool vocational involvement of 44 1961 graduates and found that, 11 years later, 28% had no job and were not involved in any work-oriented program. Phase II of the study (Blessing & Samelian, 1974) similarly assessed 196 former students 5 years after graduation and found that 24% were not involved in either a job or vocational program. Supportive data were reported by Lynch and Gerber (1980), who found that individuals were regularly excluded from Michigan workshops on the basis of behaviors unrelated to work.

Program Placement and Services

It should now be apparent that individuals with severe handicaps are served primarily in WACs and ADPs. In fact, the data on WACs probably provide an overly optimistic view. Of all retarded individuals served in certified workshops, 60% were served in WACs in 1976 (U.S. Department of Labor, 1979). Since the definition of *retardation* used in vocational programs at that time included anyone with measured IQ below 85, the group obviously includes more than that defined as *severely handicapped* in the schools. Those with severe handicaps probably have less than the annual 10% chance of advancement to employment or higher programs and earn less than the average $288 per year. Severely handicapped individuals in "vocational" services are likely to receive only a regimen of personal skill training, special developmental services, and structured leisure opportunities (Bellamy et. al., 1980).

Work Opportunities

The incredibly low wages earned by adults with severe handicaps reflects several restrictions on work opportunities. Some states specifically disallow work in ADPs that serve those with more severe handicaps. In other areas, ADP work is restricted by (a) lack of access to the business development capital that was available for some time to RPWs; (b) differences in wage payment methods between WACs and RPWs, which provide incentives to give available work to those with less severe handicaps; and (c) state and federal regulations that emphasize therapy and education to the practical elimination of accountability for vocational outcomes. Consequently, while work is in short supply for workshops generally, individuals with severe handicaps get the least access to what is available and have the least likelihood of participating in a program that is staffed and equipped to secure and perform work.

Summary

The picture that emerges when we analyze the status of people with severe handicaps in adult vocational services is one of lifelong preparation at the bottom of a continuum of services. While the goals of the continuum are impressive, the actual experiences of severely handicapped adults reflect limited access to work or work preparation, little chance of moving to more advanced programs or employment, and little or no access to meaningful wages.

DOCUMENTED POSSIBILITIES

In contrast to the current realities we have just looked at, there is much about which to be optimistic. Research and demonstration projects present strong evidence that severely handicapped individuals can learn the skills necessary for work, earn substantial wages, and even be integrated into nonsheltered work environments.

Skill Acquisition

Research literature dating back to the work of Loos and Tizard (1955) shows severely handicapped adults can learn to perform complex vocational tasks in sheltered environments. In the Loos and Tizard (1955) study, institutionalized severely retarded adults were trained to complete a nine-step cake box construction task. Since this first demonstration, research has continued to corroborate and extend this evidence of vocational competence with people having more severe handicaps and with more difficult tasks (Crosson, 1966; Hunter & Bellamy, 1976; Williams, 1967). Severely retarded adults have learned to perform such diverse tasks as assembly of pumps (Clarke & Hermelin, 1955), bicycle brakes (Gold, 1972), oscilloscope switches (Bellamy, Peterson, & Close, 1975), wiring harnesses (Hunter & Bellamy, 1976), nursery specimen cans (Karan, Eisner, & Endres, 1974), ballpoint pens (Martin & Flexer, 1975), and chain saw blades (O'Neill & Bellamy, 1978); agricultural gleaning jobs (Jacobs, 1976); and use of power equipment (Crosson, 1966). The range of skills learned, the variety of training strategies used, the different settings for training, and the range of individual learner characteristics leave little room

TABLE 16.1 Production Report October 1, 1980–March 31, 1981

Programs Using the STP Model	Total Commercial Revenue	Worker Generated Revenue	Number of Workers	Average Monthly Worker Wage	Hourly Wage in Production
STP, Eugene	$ 29,674	$21,690	15	$110	$1.33
Olympus, Seattle	$ 19,727	$16,989	17	$ 53	$1.02
Alpha, Reno	$ 7,865	$ 7,865	14	$ 46	$1.15
Dynatron, Bend	$ 11,654	$ 9,950	13	$ 62	$1.70
Qualitex, Tacoma	$ 6,600	$ 5,514	11	$ 41	$2.19
Desert Haven, Lancaster*	$ 7,331	$ 6,451	25	$ 29	$ .96
Benchworks, Anchorage	$ 14,024	$12,519	25	$ 33	$ .84
Precision Assembly, Boise**	$ 3,026	$ 3,026	14	$ 21	$1.40
Opportunity Center, Sweet Home†	$ 5,266	$ 5,071	16	$ 56	$1.59
STP Totals	$105,167	$89,075	150	$ 50	$1.35

Total Commercial Revenue: All revenue generated by the workshop
Worker Generated Revenue: All revenue generated by the severely handicapped (target) work force
Number of Workers: Number of severely handicapped (target) workers
Average Monthly Worker Wage: Average gross wage paid to workers
Straight Time Hourly Wage: Gross hourly wage while worker is at work station. Figures include time spent on simulated tasks
Production Hourly Wage: Gross hourly wage while worker is on remunerative tasks
* four months only
**five months only
† three months only

to doubt the ability of individuals with severe handicaps to learn requisite work skills.

Wage-Earning Potential

Skills, no matter how difficult or sophisticated, are useful in a vocational sense only if they result in work opportunities and wages. The research literature, however, shows considerably more professional interest in the process of teaching and learning than the factors that affect consumer economic benefits. As a result the literature left open until recently the possibility that severely handicapped adults might be incapable of using the skills they clearly could learn because of a lack of work tolerance, attention to task, quality, ability to change jobs as required, and so on. There are now an increasing number of reports that do include average wages of severely handicapped individuals in sheltered work settings. Two of the larger of these efforts are briefly described here.

The Specialized Training Program (STP) model, developed at the University of Oregon as a work-oriented alternative to ADPs, has been implemented in nine community programs across six western states. As of March 31, 1981, these programs served 150 individuals considered by state officials to be among the least capable adults receiving community services in each state. Table 16.1 summarizes wages earned and commercial revenue generated in these programs during the most recent 6-month period. Although we can safely assume that WACs generally serve a more capable group, hourly wages in STP model sites average over three times the national average of $.43 for WACs (individual programs range from 1.95 to 5.09 times the WAC average). Monthly wages are approximately double the national WAC average of $24, with individual programs ranging from 0.87 to 4.58 times the average.

Bourbeau (Note 2) described a work crew program operated by the New Jersey Bureau of Adult Training Services that employed moderately and severely handicapped individuals who had been rejected for vocational rehabilitation and sheltered work services. Workers were assigned to mobile crews that performed contract work throughout a community, thus avoiding much of the segregation that often occurs in sheltered work programs. In 1981 wages for 45 people in the programs averaged $50 per month, or about twice the national average for WAC participants.

Open Employment

The promise of research results on vocational skill acquisition and wage-earning performance is the possibility of securing and maintaining unsupported, unsheltered employment. Here, too, data are available to support the potential of individuals with severe handicaps. In response to a survey reported by Cook, Dahl, and Gale (1977), rehabilitation facilities reported that severely retarded adults were currently employed in the following occupations in competitive employment: collator, duplicating machine operator, maid, orderly, assembler, auto mechanic helper, porter, farm hand, hand packer, kitchen helper, laundry room helper, and building maintenance person.

More recently, several projects have focused directly on developing training and placement techniques for competitive employment, with a number of impressive employment demonstrations (Rusch & Mithaug, 1980; Sowers, Thompson, & Connis, 1979; Wehman, 1981). The projects described by these authors all are characterized by (a) specialization in preparing clients to move into competitive employment as quickly as possible; (b) the use of the best available training techniques; (c) training in applied settings; and (d) long-term follow-up to ensure job maintenance.

Outcome data support the investment in these projects. After 5 years of operation, the Food Service Vocational Training Program at the University of Washington had placed 30 individuals in part- or full-time jobs above minimum wages; all had held their jobs for 6 months or more. The majority of these people would be considered moderately and severely handicapped in school programs. The average cost of training, placing, and maintaining a client was approximately $6,000. Wehman (1981) reported similar results. In about 2 years this project placed in open employment 16 individuals, most of whom were severely or moderately retarded.

IMPROVING THE VOCATIONAL OUTLOOK

The discrepancy between the demonstrated vocational potential and the actual work success of adults with severe handicaps is a problem that has attracted considerable attention. The literature is replete with possible explanations, ranging from low professional expectations and lack of training in service programs to the structure of work that channels partially productive citizens out of the work force.

Whatever account you might accept, one thing is clear: The current paucity of vocational success cannot be attributed simply to individual readiness or potential to work. Too many different people with severe handicaps have shown the ability and desire to work, given opportunities and appropriate services.

Consequently, to improve the vocational outlook for our students, we should not simply attend to the skills and behaviors of individual students; rather, we must focus on the kinds of available work opportunities and the structure of services intended to help individuals take advantage of those opportunities. To continue to structure programs as if large groups of handicapped people had no vocational potential and to focus government and professional effort only on remediating deficits of individuals appear to reflect what Ryan (1971) describes as "blaming the victim," or attributing difficulties that result from work distribution to the shortcomings of individuals rather than to large social structures and processes.

The question now confronting us is not whether vocational participation is possible, but rather what combination of opportunities and services are needed to facilitate participation. Needed now is not simply further demonstrations of vocational potential, but rather a complete reassessment and redesign of government efforts to help people with handicaps obtain jobs. A broad agreement has emerged in the last few years that change is needed in existing services. Calls for reform have come from the public press (*Wall Street Journal,* 1979), the government (Whitehead, 1979), independent research groups (Greenleigh, 1975; Urban Institute, 1975), professionals and advocates (Bellamy et al., 1980; Pomerantz & Marholin, 1977), and service provider organizations (Lapidakis, Ansley, & Lowitt, 1980). A consensus is still emerging on the specific directions such changes should take, and it is critical that the interests of people with severe handicaps be represented in current discussions of program redesign.

To appreciate the complexity of any effort to improve existing services, we must understand the fundamental problems addressed by vocational programs. There is, first of all, an extremely high unemployment rate among handicapped people, and almost total unemployment or underemployment of those with more severe handicaps. At the same time, there is a political or social decision that many unemployed people with handicaps should receive publicly supported, out-of-home daytime services. Whether motivated from a concern for the individual, family, or community, these programs—the private providers—serve a diverse group of unemployed handicapped people. A value judgment made by individuals with handicaps, their families, and professionals stresses the importance of work in these programs, either through preparation for open employment or in supported work situations. The result is a set of goals and expectations for private providers that are incompatible in some basic ways. These programs are expected to simultaneously prepare people for competitive jobs, offer employment opportunities, and serve everyone in a community who qualifies and receives public support to attend. The result is a business that attempts to pay reasonable wages to employees, tries to place its best workers with competing firms, and is expected to include far more participants than the available work requires.

The inevitable conflicts over distribution of work and professional attention traditionally have been solved by adhering to the flow-through continuum of services. In the continuum, the most capable workers normally receive extra staff attention related to placement in open employment and first access to available work to support job preparation. Those considered less capable or less ready for competitive employment normally receive neither work nor services related to open employment, but rather services presumably to prepare them for these opportunities at higher program levels. The devastating results are that adults with severe handicaps are placed in lower program levels when they are fully capable of working if appropriate opportunities and services are provided. No readiness training may be needed at all.

The problem facing those concerned for the vocational futures of the severely handicapped is how to design an alternative to this flow-through continuum that provides equitable distribution of work opportunities and services. A community-scale solution is needed that integrates government policy, private provider practices, and changing employment possibilities into a reasonable support system for all citizens who have handicaps and experience employment problems. A successful redesign must resolve several problems and dilemmas in a fashion that is acceptable to diverse interests of consumers, professionals, parents, the business community, and the public at large. Among the most important of these are:

1. *Unemployment services and employment support*— The problems of providing employment-related services and services to unemployed people with handicaps are inextricably intertwined. We need a system of vocational services that recognizes and plans for both functions. Vocational services should be available to unemployed people with handicaps without assuming that their unemployment results from their inability or lack of potential. Designing vocational services simply to "fix" employment barriers associated with the individual though rehabilitation and training ignores realities of the labor market and blames people with handicaps for larger unemployment problems.

2. *Short work supply*—If vocational services are extended equitably to all handicapped individuals

who face employment problems, work will practically always be in short supply when viewed on a community, regional, or larger scale. Without public policies supporting full employment, it is unrealistic to expect that *all* the handicapped individuals in a community will be *fully* employed in either open or sheltered employment. Vocational services that have been successful in either job placement or well-paid sheltered work typically have restricted admission to the number of people for whom work was available. Other services were then needed to meet the needs of those who are not included. For program design to be successful, we need policies that equitably address how the available work is allocated to various groups of service recipients. Current practices concentrate sheltered work among those with least severe handicaps while others are served in prevocational or nonvocational alternatives. Since this priority can no longer be justified, a more just system of work allocation is needed.

3. *Accountability to consumers*—Policies are needed that make services accountable for benefits to consumers, for wage levels, job placements, and changes in lifestyles. Current government regulations and professional accreditation focus primarily on characteristics of services rather than on these consumer benefits. Since the diverse set of employment barriers faced by the handicapped will never be removed by any single set of professional services, we need evaluation standards that support effective services and encourage the development of different service approaches with different individuals.

4. *Opportunities as well as services*—Employment of individuals with handicaps in the open market is affected not only by individual disabilities and quality of services, but also by the economics of the work place. Disproportionately high unemployment can be expected to continue, regardless of service quality, as long as employers must bear excess costs associated with training, fixture development, job redesign, and so on. One way to reduce these excess costs is through expanded government incentives to employers. A balance must be achieved in government investment between services to enhance the individual's employability and incentives that expand the opportunities for employment.

5. *Participation before perfection*—Bagnasco (1980) suggests that severely handicapped people worldwide are victimized by an approach to vocational rehabilitation in which each individual is dependent on services until he or she can enter the work force needing no further support. The objective is to prepare people for complete independence and normal productivity. Those for whom this is a distant goal must endure extended, often lifelong preparation, with little opportunity to participate in the economic mainstream. Several authors have now argued for an alternative. Brown and his colleagues (Brown, Branston-McLean, Baumgart, Vincent, Falvey, & Schroeder, 1979) described a concept of "partial participation" to illustrate the value of normal life experiences whether or not complete independence is possible. A similar notion was applied to work in the structured employment proposal of Horner and Bellamy (1979). Structured employment is supported work, in a factory, cooperative, or workshop, in which work opportunities are provided together with public support for the training, supervision, engineering, and other ongoing services that promote individual productivity. If program redesign is to benefit those with severe handicaps, we need an alternative that provides an escape from perpetual preparation at the bottom of a service continuum.

6. *More practical research*—The research directions needed to support any system redesign extend beyond the vocational training and job placement studies that now appear frequently. These studies have been critically important in demonstrating that the problem of high unemployment among people with severe handicaps is not a necessary result of individual disabilities. That research provides the logical basis for the broad reforms advocated here. The research does not, however, point to an alternative solution that addresses the full scope of community service needs. Greater attention is needed to the design of solutions beyond the individual level: for local program design, community program management, and government funding and regulation. The issue is no longer whether or not behavioral technology works with severely handicapped individuals or in vocational contexts, but whether or not it can be combined successfully with business, management, and other service strategies to form workable, affordable programs at community levels. Program replication outside of demonstration or model project settings should become a basic criterion for program development research efforts (Paine & Bellamy, 1982).

7. *Effective specialization*—We need alternatives to private-provider approaches to vocational services. Organization of programs by business specialization rather than level of disability, separation of transitional services leading to open employment and extended supported or sheltered

work, and expansion of sheltered work in integrated work settings are but a few of the possibilities that should be explored.

Redesign of vocational services to allow severely handicapped individuals to participate in the work life of a community is a complex undertaking that will require a broad professional consensus. The fact that the most recent federal study of sheltered workshop improvement (Whitehead, 1979) eliminated from consideration the nation's day activity programs (in which most severely handicapped adults are now served) underscores the importance of their representation in the discussions and political processes that could produce system changes. Unless the full range of handicapping conditions is considered, severely handicapped students in school today will face a future of needless welfare, with both work and work-related services given to other, more vocal groups.

AN INDIVIDUAL PERSPECTIVE

The solution to our national problem of almost total and needless unemployment of people with severe handicaps is a matter of politics and system redesign. Solutions for severely handicapped students about to leave school are more individual and offer several more immediate avenues for teacher and parent support. At issue here is not so much the design of an effective service system or the total number of jobs available to individuals with handicaps, but rather how the existing opportunities and services are distributed among those who could benefit from them.

There are several strategies for teachers, parents, and others to increase the likelihood that their severely handicapped children are among the few who compete successfully for scarce job opportunities and effective vocational services. A few of the many possibilities are:

1. Help each student develop a work history while in school that documents successful performance of a variety of jobs. The history should be useful both in efforts to locate jobs and in attempts to secure placement in more advanced vocational services rather than ADPs.
2. Use the latter years of schooling to train students for jobs that have high turnover rates. Procedures described by Sowers, Thompson, and Connis (1979) and Rusch (chapter 17) could be applied in the schools to help students move directly from the schools to local employment. It may be possible to place many students in permanent work positions before they must leave school.

3. Help each student develop a social network of family, friends, and neighbors who will offer ongoing employment support. This network may greatly decrease the individual's dependence on social services at times of employment difficulties or personal transitions.
4. Evaluate the appropriateness of private provider services on the basis of actual benefits, not stated purposes. Before enrollment is considered, request and evaluate data on average wages in employment programs, number of job placements in work preparation services, and average length of job maintenance.
5. Develop individualized transition plans for each student, so that the move from school to work and adult life is systematically planned by everyone concerned with a student. Many of the decisions made in this period must necessarily reflect the values and best judgments of the student, family members, friends, and professionals.
6. Encourage the school district or state education agency to conduct regular follow-up studies of graduates. Public data on the employment status of graduates of school programs for severely handicapped students, such as that provided by Blessing and Samelian (1972, 1974), may be one of the most important means of expanding local vocational opportunities and improving local services.

SUMMARY

In the effort to reduce unemployment of handicapped individuals, government has invested in two general strategies: rehabilitation, education, and training to remediate barriers to employment associated with the individual; and incentives and regulations for employers to increase the available job opportunities. While both strategies have been effective with some groups, people considered severely handicapped by the schools have been largely unaffected. Instead of vocational preparation or work opportunities, they typically move from school to adult activity programs, where lifelong preparation substitutes for work participation.

Several illustrations of vocational competence indicate that this bleak vocational outlook cannot be attributed to the lack of vocational potential or readiness among the severely handicapped. Instead, causes and solutions must be sought in the design of vocational services and the type of work opportunities that government incentives create. While a real possibility of redesign of these opportunities and services exists, no clear solution has yet emerged to several important policy issues. People concerned for severely handicapped individuals are needed both to participate in the redesign of vocational policies and services and to help individuals leaving school to compete for scarce work opportunities and services.

REFERENCES

Bagnasco, V. *The integration of handicapped youth in open employment in Italy.* Working Paper, Organization for Economic Cooperation and Development, Paris, 1980.

Bellamy, G.T., Horner, R.H., Sheehan, M.R., & Boles, S.M. Structured employment and workshop reform: Equal rights for severely handicapped individuals. In J. Lapidakis, J. Ansley, & J. Lowitt (Eds.), *Work, services and change: Proceedings from the National Institute on Rehabilitation Facilities.* Washington, D.C.: National Association of Rehabilitation Facilities, 1981.

Bellamy, G.T., Peterson, L., & Close, D. Habilitation of the severely and profoundly retarded: Illustrations of competence. *Education and Training of the Mentally Retarded,* 1975, *10,* 174–186.

Bellamy, G.T., Sheehan, M.R., Horner, R.H., & Boles, S.M. Community programs for severely handicapped adults: An analysis of vocational opportunities. *Journal of the Association for Severely Handicapped,* 1981, *5,* 307–324.

Blessing, K., & Samelian, J. *Program accountability in special education: An eleven-year follow-up of adult former students of Wisconsin public school classes for the trainable mentally retarded.* Wisconsin Department of Public Instruction, 1972. (Monograph No. 1)

Blessing, K., & Samelian, J. *Program accountability in special education: A five-year follow-up of more recent enrollees of Wisconsin public school programs for the trainable mentally retarded.* Wisconsin Department of Public Instruction, 1974. (Monograph No. 4)

Brown, L., Branston-McLean, M.B., Baumgart, D., Vincent, L., Falvey, M., & Schroeder, J. Using the characteristics of current and subsequent least restrictive environments in the development of curricular content for severely handicapped students. *AAESPH Review,* 1979, *4,* 407–423.

California Department of Finance. *A review of sheltered workshops and related programs (Phase II): To assembly concurrent resolution No. 206, Volume II, Final Report.* Sacramento: State of California, 1979.

Clarke, A.D.B., & Hermelin, B.F. Adult imbeciles: Their abilities and trainability. *The Lancet,* August, 1955, 337–339.

Coakley, F. Study of feebleminded wards employed in war industries. *American Journal of Mental Deficiency,* 1945, *50,* 301–306.

Cobb, A.V. *The forecast of fulfillment: A review of research on predictive assessment of the adult retarded for social and vocational adjustment.* New York: Teachers College Press, 1972.

Conley, R. *The economics of mental retardation.* Baltimore: Johns Hopkins University Press, 1973.

Cook, P., Dahl, P., & Gale, M. *Vocational training and placement of the severely handicapped: Vocational opportunities.*

Palo Alto, Calif.: The American Institute for Research in the Behavioral Sciences, 1977.

Crosson, J. The experimental analysis of vocational behavior in severely retarded males (Doctoral dissertation, University of Oregon, 1966). *Dissertation Abstracts International,* 1966, *27,* 3304.

Dubrow, M. Sheltered workshops for the mentally retarded as an educational and vocational experience. In *New trends in rehabilitation.* Washington, D.C.: U.S. Department of Health, Education and Welfare, Office of Vocational Rehabilitation, 1959.

Engel, A.M. Employment of the mentally retarded. In S.G. DiMichael (Ed.), *Vocational rehabilitation of the mentally retarded.* Washington, D.C.: Federal Security Agency, Office of Vocational Rehabilitation, 1950.

Federal Register. Employment of handicapped clients in sheltered workshops, Chapter V, Part 525, May 17, 1974, 17509.

Gold, M. Stimulus factors in skill training of the retarded on a complex assembly task: Acquisition, transfer and retention. *American Journal of Mental Deficiency,* 1972, *76,* 517–526.

Greenleigh Associates, Inc. *The role of the sheltered workshop in the rehabilitation of the severely handicapped.* New York: Report to the Department of Health, Education, and Welfare, Rehabilitation Services Administration, 1975.

Horner, R.H., & Bellamy, G.T. Structured employment: Productivity and productive capacity. In T. Bellamy, G. O'Connor, & O. Karan (Eds.), *Vocational rehabilitation of severely handicapped adults: Contemporary service strategies.* Baltimore: University Park Press, 1979.

Hunter, J., & Bellamy, T. Cable harness construction for severely retarded adults: A demonstration of training technique. *AAESPH Review,* 1976, *1,* 2–13.

Jacobs, J.W. Retarded persons as gleaners. *Mental Retardation,* 1976, *14,* 42–43.

Karan, R.L., Eisner, M., & Endres, R.W. Behavior modification in a sheltered workshop for severely retarded students. *American Journal of Mental Deficiency,* 1974, *79,* 338–347.

Kline, A. Federal and state anti-discrimination law. In The Continuing Legal Education Committee, *Law of the Disabled.* Washington State Bar Association, 1978.

Lapidakis, J., Ansley, J., & Lowitt, J. (Eds.). *Work, services and change: Proceedings from the National Institute on Rehabilitation Facilities.* Washington, D.C.: National Association of Rehabilitation Facilities, 1980.

Loos, F., & Tizard, J. The employment of adult imbeciles in a hospital workshop. *American Journal of Mental Deficiency,* 1955, *59,* 395–403.

Lynch, K., & Gerber, P. A survey of community sheltered facilities: Implications for mandated school programs. *Education and Training of the Mentally Retarded,* 1980, *15,* 264–269.

Martin, A., & Flexer, R. *Three studies on training work skills and work adjustment with the severely retarded.* Lubbock: Texas Tech University, Rehabilitation Research and Training Center in Mental Retardation, 1975. (Monograph No. 5)

Moss, J.W. *Employment training of mentally retarded individuals: A proposed plan for national action.* Seattle: University of Washington, 1979.

Neff, W. Vocational assessment—Theory and models. *Journal of Rehabilitation,* 1970, *36*(1), 27–29.

O'Neill, C., & Bellamy, T. Evaluation of a procedure for teaching saw chain assembly to a severely retarded woman. *Mental Retardation,* 1978, *16*(1), 37–41.

Paine, S.C., & Bellamy, G.T. From innovation to standard practice: Developing and discriminating behavioral procedures. *Behavior Analyst,* Spring 1982, *5*, 29–44.

Pomerantz, D.J., & Marholin, D. Vocational habilitation: A time for change. In E. Sontag, N. Certo, & J. Smith (Eds.), *Educational programming for the severely and profoundly handicapped.* Reston, Va.: Council for Exceptional Children, 1977.

Rubin, S.E., & Roessler, R.T. *Foundations of the vocational rehabilitation process.* Baltimore: University Park Press, 1978.

Ruegg, P. The meaning and use of work as a modality in habilitation and rehabilitation of disabled persons in facilities providing vocational programs. In J. Lapidakis, J. Ansley, & J. Lowitt (Eds.), *Work, services and change: Proceedings from the National Institute on Rehabilitation Facilities.* Washington, D.C.: National Association of Rehabilitation Facilities, 1981.

Rusch, F.R., & Mithaug, D.E. *Vocational training for mentally retarded adults: A behavior analytic approach.* Champaign, Ill.: Research Press, 1980.

Ryan, W. *Blaming the victim.* New York: Vintage Books, 1971.

Sowers, J., Thompson, L., & Connis, R. The food service vocational training program. In T. Bellamy, G. O'Connor, & O. Karan (Eds.), *Vocational rehabilitation of severely handicapped persons: Contemporary service strategies.* Baltimore: University Park Press, 1979.

Urban Institute. *Report of the comprehensive service needs study.* Washington, D.C.: Urban Institute, 1975.

U.S. Department of Labor. *Sheltered workshop study.* Washington, D.C.: U.S. Department of Labor, 1977.

U.S. Department of Labor. *Study of handicapped clients in sheltered workshops* (Vol. 2). Washington, D.C.: U.S. Department of Labor, 1979.

Wall Street Journal, October 17, 1979.

Warren, F. Ratings of employed and unemployed mentally handicapped males on personality and work factors. *American Journal of Mental Deficiency,* 1961, *65*, 629–633.

Wehman, P. *Competitive employment: New horizons for severely disabled individuals.* Baltimore: Paul H. Brookes, 1981.

Whitehead, C.W. Sheltered workshops in the decade ahead: Work and wages, or welfare? In G.T. Bellamy, G. O'Connor, & O.C. Karan (Eds.), *Vocational rehabilitation of severely handicapped persons.* Baltimore: University Park Press, 1979.

Williams, P. Industrial training and remunerative employment of the profoundly retarded. *Journal of Mental Subnormality,* 1967, *13*, 14–23.

REFERENCE NOTES

1. New Jersey Bureau of Adult Training Services. *Movement of adult activities clients to vocational programs.* Paper presented at New Jersey Bureau of Adult Training Services Regional Supervisors Meeting, Trenton, June, 1981.

2. Bourbeau, P.E. *Community work crew programs in New Jersey.* Paper presented at the meeting of The Association of Severely Handicapped, Chicago, October, 1979.

This chapter was written by **Frank R. Rusch,** *University of Illinois at Urbana-Champaign. This manuscript was prepared while the author was with the Bureau of Educational Research, College of Education, University of Illinois. Special thanks are extended by the author to several students and colleagues for their willingness to help develop this manuscript, including Robert "Pete" Flexer, Lori Kopp, James Martin, Sister Diane Owens, Janis Rusch, and JoAnn Sowers.*

17

Competitive Vocational Training

Recent research and developments in teaching severely handicapped students complex, functional skills have changed our expectations about placing them in competition for jobs with the general public. Ten years ago we were boasting about our ability to teach them to stuff envelopes, form boxes, operate drill presses, and assemble bicycle brakes. These illustrations of competence were important, as they set the stage for the development of specialized programs for people for whom employment was never thought possible. Today, there is a new conceptual framework for the design of employment training programs. Because advances have been made in identifying employers' expectations regarding what must be learned by potential employees and in delineating guidelines to follow to promote severely handicapped people toward a wide variety of employment options, interest in serving these people in competitive employment has also grown.

There are several exemplary programs for research and development of guidelines to follow to employ severely handicapped persons in nonsheltered settings.[1] The published reports on competitive employment contain a consistent theme: employment in integrated, nonsheltered settings is realistic and attainable (Bates & Pancsofar, 1981; Connis, Thompson, & Sowers, 1981; Sowers, Thompson, & Connis, 1979; Sowers, Lundervold, Swanson, & Budd, Note 3). Four steps are important in securing nonsheltered employment for severely handicapped adults: (*a*) survey potential employers to determine important skills that need to be trained, (*b*) train students to perform these skills, (*c*) place trained clients into nonsheltered settings, and (*d*) provide long-term, follow-up training. With this *survey-train-place-train* framework, severely handicapped adults have been employed as porters, elevator operators, dishwashers, kitchen helpers, groundskeepers, janitors, and assembly line workers. This chapter presents the *survey-train-place-train* model and discusses how to identify job requisites for competitive employment

---

[1] See Wehman (1981) and reports by Bates and Pancsofar (Note 1), Rusch, Thompson, Sowers, and Connis (Note 2), Clarke, Greenwood, Abramowitz, and Bellamy (1980), Rusch and Schutz (1979), and Schutz and Rusch (1982) for a discussion of model programs.

in service and light industrial occupations, develop longitudinal curricula, establish community-based vocational training stations, identify placement options, and provide long-term, follow-up services. Because the term *competitive employment* is relatively new as it applies to severely handicapped people, we begin with a definition.

WHAT IS COMPETITIVE EMPLOYMENT?

Competitive employment is working for at least a minimum wage, or better, with nonhandicapped coworkers at a job that provides room for advancement in settings that produce valued goods or services. In contrast, *sheltered employment* is receiving subsidized wages or working for less than minimum wage, with handicapped coworkers at a job that provides limited advancement to competitive work settings and that is organized primarily for therapeutic habilitation or sheltered production.

Working for a Minimum Wage, or Better

Working for at least a minimum wage, or better, is taken for granted by most youths entering the job market. In contrast, working for minimum wages or even for any wage, has not been the primary goal for the severely handicapped. As Whitehead indicated in his 1979 study,

The typical client in the workshop in 1976 was a white, 25-year-old, mentally retarded male who had never married, and who lived in a dependent type arrangement (group home, residence operated by the workshop, or with parents). He worked about 20 hours a week at subcontract work in a work activities center as his first employment experience. His monthly earnings of about $31 were supplemented by public assistance (Supplemental Security Income) of $147. (p. 14)

In the United States, there are few major public or private efforts to train severely handicapped people for competitive employment. Although there are a few exemplary research and demonstration projects, the number of severely handicapped adults currently participating in the American work force is quite low. In fact, Rusch and Mithaug (1980), interpreting a nationwide study conducted by the U.S. Department of Labor, suggested that the:

Annual departure from sheltered workshops ranges from 12% to 15%, and that 75% of the persons are placed into competitive employment within one (1) year after entry into the workshop. In addition, the report indicated that 33% of this group were actually placed within the first three (3) months. The study pointed out that the longer individuals remained in the workshop setting, the less likely they were to be placed outside that setting. These data suggest that persons most frequently placed into com-

petitive employment were generally work ready when they entered the shop. (p. xv)

We can assume that those handicapped adults placed into competitive employment during the 1970s were primarily mildly handicapped or emotionally disturbed, not our target population. However, past efforts of sheltered workshops to place severely handicapped adults into competitive employment should not be used as the sole source to gauge whether they will be successful in nonsheltered employment. Typically, sheltered workshop staff members do not know what skills should be learned or how programs should be organized to promote clients toward nonsheltered settings.

Working With Nonhandicapped Coworkers

There are several reasons to stress the importance of nonhandicapped coworkers. Foremost is the opportunity for everyone, including those with severe handicaps, to lead a normal and dignified life with the expectation of being a contributing member of society. When training people to become contributing members of society, we must consider the society's values as we attempt to determine what to teach. Nonhandicapped coworkers provide a measure of what and how well we should teach. Training for competitive employment, by definition, requires training in performing tasks within tolerable, pre-established industrial norms. Once goals are determined, vocational training can focus upon training potential employees to work within the boundaries of "acceptable work performance."

Coworkers and employers can change society's acceptance of severely handicapped persons as a valued resource. Tax credit programs[2] offsetting the initial employment adjustment cost of training severely handicapped workers to enter the labor force have attracted employers' attention. If this attention is positively reinforced by acquiring a valued employee, employers should communicate these successes, which in turn will lead to additional jobs becoming available for other competent employees. Also, employees contribute to our federal tax base, which in turn supports the training costs of other people entering the labor market.

Jobs That Provide Room for Advancement in Settings that Produce Valued Goods or Services

This is important for several reasons. Sheltered workshops typically pay less than minimum wage

---

[2] The President's Committee on Employment of the Handicapped, Washington, DC 20210, has information related to taxes and resources related to the vocational preparation of youth and adults.

for work that has little or no value. Regrettably, these conditions often persist for the lifespan of the workshop client (Pomerantz & Marholin, 1977). If the purpose of employment is to make money or provide a valued community service, then accomplishments of the employee will always be stressed. In competitive employment, employees work for the profit or benefit of the employer. Therefore, competence is reinforced and incompetence is punished. These contingencies form the basis upon which employers advance employees. For example, a competent, probationary employee might be advanced to nonprobationary status, a helper to a laborer; an employee might receive adjusted, incremental pay increases, or an employee might have his or her position redesigned to better working conditions.

Nonsheltered, competitive employment is the normal and expected career path for the nonhandicapped. Competitively employing severely handicapped people challenges our traditional approach to career education for them. The opportunity to go to work every day and to be part of a work force that expects performance that results in profit is a new challenge to vocational training personnel. Employment in nonsheltered settings provides a guide, based upon normal expectations, for comprehensive training of severely handicapped individuals. This view complements that of Brown, Branston-McClean, Baumgart, Vincent, Falvey, and Schroeder (1979), who state:

Educational programs [should be] preparatory in nature, and severely handicapped persons should have access to the most comprehensive and longitudinal services available so that they can be prepared to function as independently and as productively as possible in a wide range of enhancing adult environments. (p. 422)

Competitive employment is an option that may not be suitable for every severely handicapped person; yet it should be available so that they can, if possible, enjoy and engage in work that may result in their becoming productive citizens. The ability of educators to change the attitudes and expectations of other educators, parents, and employers, as well as their own attitudes and expectations, remains the major roadblock to competitive employment.

SURVEY: EXAMINING COMMUNITIES FOR SURVIVAL SKILLS

Identification of possible community jobs and the skills needed results in a better understanding of what preschool, elementary, intermediate, and secondary students should learn in school. In this section we will look at the identification of potential job placements to determine job requisites, beginning with a discussion of survival skills and concluding with a

brief discussion of how to develop a community-based vocational curriculum.

Survival Skills

Much has been written in the past few years on developing age-appropriate and functional curricula for severely handicapped students. (See, for example, Brown, Pumpian, Baumgart, Vandeventer, Ford, Nisbet, Schroeder, & Gruenewald, 1981.) A pivotal concern is identifying relevant and functional skills that can increase the opportunity for severely handicapped people to enjoy the community, to obtain generic services (Kenowitz, Gallaher, & Edgar, 1977), and to interact with nonhandicapped persons (Brown et al., 1981.) We must teach relevant and functional vocational *and* social skills, called *survival skills,* with direct value to prospective employers (Rusch, 1979b). Obviously, curricula and associated instruction should be offered in domestic, recreation/leisure, and general community functioning to help severely handicapped students move into least restrictive settings (Brown, Branston, Hamre-Nietupski, Pumpian, Certo, & Gruenewald, 1979). With respect to vocational preparation, survival skills, such as completing a task or following instructions, are tantamount to success. *Social survival skills* include interactive behavior such as exchanging greetings, following directions, and complying to requests; *vocational survival skills* refer to behavior directly related to performing a task such as completing a sweeping or sorting task (Rusch & Schutz, 1981). Job survival depends upon valued social behavior as well as valued work behavior (Rusch & Schutz, 1981).

Identifying Potential Job Placements

Maintaining a job is usually the result of demonstrating valued behaviors (i.e., skills employers identify as important). The two broad categories of social and vocational survival skills should be the focus of our vocational training. Therefore, identifying them must be our initial concern. Logically, knowledge of a community's requirements for job survival is critical to developing a comprehensive employment training program. Because communities differ with respect to what is considered acceptable, survival and related programming may be a "local issue" (Thurman & Fiorelli, 1979). Thus, each community of employers must define what is important for survival, with training programs adjusting to these requirements. The primary role of training should be to prepare an individual for community integration; consequently, when developing programs, it is important to base goals and training objectives upon what the students will be expected to do on the job. Rusch and

Mithaug (1980) have outlined procedures to follow when surveying employers by mail or telephone. These surveys are particularly useful because a large number of prospective employers can be contacted at relatively low cost. Regardless of the approach taken, these initial contacts are fundamental to developing a community-based vocational training program.

Surveying Job Requisites—Social Validation

Again, social validation (see chapter 14) will identify the skills considered important for community integration (Kazdin, 1977; Kazdin & Matson, 1981; Van-Houten, 1979; Wolf, 1978). This methodology has been applied by Mithaug and his colleagues (Johnson & Mithuag, 1978; Mithaug & Hagmeier, 1978; Mithaug & Hanawalt, 1978) to identify the skills supervisors believe are necessary for entrance into sheltered workshops. It has been used to compare the work behavior of new employees with that of model employees. A number of recent studies centering upon rate of task completion (Crouch, 1981), continuous work (Rusch, 1979b; Rusch & Morgan, Note 4), and social interactions (Rusch, Weithers, Menchetti, & Schutz, 1980) exemplify this approach. In addition, social validation has been used to validate employers' acceptance of alternative training procedures that are typically used in competitive employment training with handicapped persons (Menchetti, Rusch, & Lamson, 1981).

Mithaug and Hagmeier (1978) used a structured questionnaire to examine the behavioral standards required for entrance into sheltered workshops in five northwestern states. In a replication of this original effort, Johnson and Mithaug (1978) compared the results of the original survey with data collected from 15 Kansas centers. This comparison provided a reliability check on the criterion categories. There was significant agreement between the two surveys, indicating that identified entry requirements were reliable across states and regions.[3]

The most striking finding of this research was that communicating basic needs, moving safely about the workshop, and participating vocationally were the three most agreed-upon job requisite skills. The ability to learn new tasks, referred to as *productivity*, was ranked seventh. Interestingly, the research literature on vocational training in sheltered settings has focused almost exclusively on vocational skill acquisition and production problems (Bellamy, Inman, & Schwarz, 1978; Rusch & Schutz, 1981; Rusch, Schutz, & Heal, in press). Consequently, the data presented by Mithaug and his colleagues suggest that

vocational training researchers have not necessarily addressed the same problems that may be confronted by those who will directly consume their efforts—the employers.

In an effort to avoid misdirection, we identified the job requisites Illinois employers believed would lead to competitive employment. Specifically, employers representing service (Rusch, Schutz, & Agran, Note 5) and light industrial occupations (Schutz & Rusch, Note 6) were surveyed. The combined results of these two surveys and how they can be used to develop a community-based training curriculum are discussed next.

Illinois Survey

Table 17.1 lists the vocational and social survival skills 80% of the respondents agreed were critical for entry into competitive employment. Vocationally, respondents unanimously agreed that prospective employees must demonstrate basic skill of addition. Socially, they unanimously agreed that prospective employees must recite their full name verbally upon request and follow at least one instruction at a time.

Employers believed that prospective employees should be able to learn new job tasks to minimum proficiency when provided a maximum of 1 to 6 hours of instruction (#49), by watching coworkers/supervisors perform the task (#35), or when explained by verbal instructions (#43). They also indicated potential employees should contact with supervisors or coworkers (#26) when they cannot perform a job and respond at least 50% of the time appropriately immediately after receiving an instruction (#9). Regarding compliance, these same employers indicated that potential employees should be able to respond to an instruction that requires compliance within at least 90 to 120 seconds (#36) with no more than one reminder (#21).

The results of this survey deserve a note of caution. The skills and standards listed in Table 17.1 were obtained from potential employers in Illinois. While it is quite possible that service and light industrial employers in other states may have similar expectations, it is also possible that they would differ markedly (Thurman & Fiorelli, 1979). Ideally, each community of employers should be surveyed to determine the skills required for employment entry. On the other hand, these findings may have general application. Many of these survival skills—such as those that refer to safety, compliance, time management, and grooming—are logical inclusions in any curriculum. However, while they may be universally applicable, the standards may vary. For example, specific placements may require a more constricted time frame for compliance or may require that an

---

[3] See Mithaug, 1981, for a complete overview of the identified behaviors.

TABLE 17.1 Competitive Employment Survival Skills

Skill	Percentage
1. Recites verbally upon request full name	100
2. Demonstrates basic arithmetic skills of addition	100
3. Follows (1) one instruction provided at a time	100
4. Recites verbally upon request home address	99
5. Recites verbally upon request home telephone number	99
6. Communicates such basic needs as sickness	99
7. Maintains proper grooming by dressing appropriately for work	99
8. Understands work routine by not displaying disruptive behaviors when routine task or schedule changes occur	99
9. Responds appropriately and immediately after receiving one (1) out of every two (2) instructions	98
10. Demonstrates basic arithmetic skills of subtraction	97
11. Moves safely about work place by paying attention to where they are walking	97
12. Works without displaying or engaging in major disruptive behaviors (e.g., arguments) more frequently than one (1)–two (2) times per month.	97
13. Communicates such basic needs as pain	96
14. Reaches places of work by means of own arrangement (walking, taxi, personal car)	96
15. Maintains proper grooming by cleaning self before coming to work	96
16. Initiates contact with coworkers when needs help on task	96
17. Initiates and/or responds verbally in three (3) to five (5) word sentences	96
18. Speaks clearly enough to be understood by anyone on the second transmission	96
19. Maintains personal hygiene by keeping teeth clean	96
20. Maintains personal hygiene by keeping hair combed	95
21. Remembers to respond to an instruction that requires compliance after a specified time interval with one (1) reminder	95
22. Works without initiating unnecessary contact with strangers more frequently than one (1)–two (2) times per day	95
23. Communicates need to use toilet	94
24. Follows instructions with words such as in, on	94
25. Continues working without disruptions when coworkers are observing	94
26. Initiates contact with supervisor when job cannot be done	94
27. Responds appropriately to safety signals when given verbally	93
28. Follows instructions with words such as under, over, through	93
29. Continues working without disruptions when supervisor observing	93
30. Writes three (3)–five (5) word sentences	93
31. Corrects work on task after second correction from supervisor	93
32. Communicates by means of verbal expression	92
33. Understands the purpose of money	92
34. Follows instructions with words such as to your right/left	92
35. Learns new job tasks explained by watching coworkers/supervisors perform task	92
36. Responds to an instruction requiring immediate compliance within 90–120 seconds	92
37. Works without initiating unnecessary contact with supervisor more frequently than three (3)–five (5) times per day	92
38. Moves safely about work place by identifying and avoiding dangerous areas	91
39. Wants to work for money	91
40. Manages time by completing an assigned task on time	91
41. Follows four (4) to six (6) word instructions	91
42. Communicates such basic needs as thirst	90
43. Learns new job tasks explained by verbal instruction	90
44. Wants to work for sense of accomplishment	90
45. Works without initiating unnecessary contact with coworkers (who are working) more frequently than six (6)–eight (8) times per day	90
46. Recites verbally upon request age	89
47. Communicates such basic needs as hunger	89

TABLE 17.1 (CONTINUED)

Skill	Percentage
48. Moves safely about work place by wearing appropriately safe work clothing	89
49. Learns to minimum proficiency new job task, provided one (1) to six (6) hours of instruction	89
50. Demonstrates understanding of rules (set down by supervisor) by not deviating from them more frequently than one (1)–two (2) times per month	89
51. Works without displaying or engaging in minor disruptive behaviors (e.g., interruptions) more frequently than one (1)–two (2) times per month	89
52. Adapts to new work routine, achieving normal levels of productivity within one (1)–five (5) days	88
53. Follows instructions with words such as press, hold, twist	88
54. Recognizes the importance of attendance and punctuality by not being late or absent from work more than an average of once per month	88
55. Maintains proper grooming by dressing appropriately after using restroom	86
56. Answers the telephone appropriately for self	85
57. Initiates contact with supervisor when a mistake is made	85
58. Participates in work environment for periods of five (5)–six (6) hours	85
59. Initiates contact with coworkers when needs task materials	84
60. Completes repetitive tasks previously learned to proficiency within 25–50% rate	84
61. Works at job continuously, remaining on task for one (1)–two (2) hour intervals	84
62. Reads 6–8 word sentences	83
63. Recites verbally upon request name of previous employer	83
64. Tells and follows time on the quarter hour	82
65. Adapts to new work routine, with the number of supervisory contacts being three (3)–four (4)	82
66. Maintains proper grooming by washing after using restroom	81
67. Maintains personal hygiene by using deodorant	81
68. Works alone and increase productivity on own	81
69. Works continuously without leaving job inappropriately (not having a good reason) more than one (1)–two (2) times per day	81
70. Responds appropriately to safety signals (e.g., buzzers, bells)	80
71. Works alone and increases productivity when asked to complete job by a specified time	80

employee acknowledge a request to comply (Karlan & Rusch, in press).

Developing a Longitudinal and Community-Based Vocational Curriculum

Severely handicapped students in public schools should move from one instructional level to the next (e.g., from intermediate to secondary classrooms), acquiring a continuum of skills leading to community placements. For example, if coming to work an average of 5 times a week has been identified as a skill needed to enter a community work setting, instruction should be directed toward developing this skill. Table 17.2 lists three vocational survival skills and Table 17.3 three social survival skills that are possible instructional goals beginning with the preschool classroom and advancing to the secondary classroom. The top of each table shows the chronological age of the student as well as the probable classroom

level. For example, regarding the goal "work continuously at the job for 1- to 2-hour intervals" (Table 17.1, #61), preschool students might be required to participate in direct instruction for at least 15 minutes and for increasingly longer periods as they move through public school until, eventually, they are working continuously for at least 30 to 60 minutes in job stations.

Social survival skills should also be subdivided into a sequence of instructional goals. For example, Table 17.3 lists the social survival skill "initiates contact with supervisor when cannot do job, feels sick, and needs to use the restroom." In the preschool classroom, the student goal might be to respond yes/no reliably when asked "need help" (Table 17.1, skills #16 and #26), "feel sick" (#6), and "need to use toilet" (#23). When the student reaches the secondary level, the goal should be "the student will independently initiate contact with supervisor and independently communicate wants/needs."

TABLE 17.2 Vocational Survival Skills

Preschool 3–5	Elementary 6–12	Intermediate 13–15	Secondary 16–21
Comes to Work on an Average of 5 Times per Week (see Table 17.1, Skill #54)			
Comes to school for a half-day at least 4 days per week	Comes to school for the entire day at least 4 days per week	Comes to school every day excluding holidays	Comes to work on an average of 5 times per week including days off for sick leave and vacation days
Works at the Job Continuously Remaining on Task for at Least 1–2 Hour Intervals (see Table 17.1, Skill #61)			
Participates in a 15-minute intensive instructional program.	Participates in a 30-minute intensive instructional program and, during the following 30 minutes works independently and continuously.	Works independently and continuously for a 60-minute period, at the same job station, 1–2 times during the work day.	Works independently and continuously for a 1–2 hour period, at the same job station, 2–3 times during the work day.
Wants to Work for Money (see Table 17.1, #39)			
Improves performances in all curricular areas when social praise and money are contingent upon correct responses	Improves and maintains performance in all curricular areas when social praise and money are contingent upon correct performance throughout each session	Improves and maintains performance in all curricular areas when social praise is contingent upon correct performance in entire self help and academic sessions, and money is contingent upon correct performance in all work related sessions (i.e., at the end of the day).	Improves and maintains performance in work related sessions when paid on a weekly basis

Each teacher's major responsibility is to teach skills required in future placements. Acquiring a list of the social and vocational survival skills potential employers believe are critical for job entry allows the teacher to develop a coordinated and longitudinal curriculum. Preschool, elementary, and intermediate classroom teachers should develop instructional programs that advance students through general applications of each skill to employer-specified task applications—the responsibility of secondary teachers.

Instructional content should be based on sequenced goals and on what is functional for each student. *Functionality* within the context of vocational training refers to teaching relevant applications of skills identified as important for eventual job entry. For example, a student might learn to move independently around the classroom, from the classroom to the cafeteria for lunch, then to the playground, and eventually from home to work. At the secondary level, all skills need to be taught on placement-specific tasks,

such as riding the bus to and from a community-based employment training program. In the preschool classroom, the level of instruction should be the more general application of the specific survival skill.

TRAIN: DEVELOPING COMMUNITY-BASED VOCATIONAL TRAINING STATIONS

It is not possible to simulate a real job with real expectations for real production. Consequently, avoid unnecessary training in simulated environments. Severely handicapped people rarely generalize newly acquired skills to new settings. Therefore, secondary instructional content and training should occur in community settings where they have immediate value. *Community-based vocational training* refers to training community-relevant behaviors (i.e., survival skills)

TABLE 17.3 Social Survival Skills

Preschool 3–5	Elementary 6–12	Intermediate 13–15	Secondary 16–21
Responds Appropriately to Safety Signals* when Given Verbally (see Table 17.1, skill #27)			
Follows teacher's verbal directions with physical assistance, to place of safety when safety signals occur	Follows teacher's verbal directions to place of safety when safety signals occur	Responds appropriately to safety signals when they occur during the school day	Responds appropriately to specified safety signals on the job
Responds to an Instruction that Requires Compliance within 90–120 Seconds (see Table 17.1, #36) With No More than One Reminder (see Table 17.1, #21)			
Follows an instruction which requires compliance when provided a model and given verbally with no more than two reminders	Follows an instruction which requires compliance when given verbally with no more than one reminder	Follows an instruction which requires complaince within 90–120 seconds with no more than one reminder	Independently responds to an instruction throughout the work day within 90–120 seconds with no reminders
Initiates Contact with Supervisors when Job Cannot be Done (see Table 17.1, #26) or Feels Sick (see Table 17.1, #6)			
Student reliably responds yes/no, when asked, "Need help?" Feel sick/tired?"	When asked, "Need help? Feel sick/tired"? the student responds, "yes or no," and then expresses want/need when given a model, e.g., "Yes, I need help."	The student independently communicates want/needs to teacher throughout the school day	The student independently initiates contact with supervisor and independently communicates want/need throughout the work day

*Safety signals include fire, tornado, danger, do not enter, caution, no smoking, etc.

in an environment that closely resembles probable job placements. We will now take a look at job station selection and organization and the training and management strategies that might be used to train social and vocational behavior.

Station Selection

Training stations which are likely community placement options and have nonhandicapped coworkers should be selected. Nonhandicapped workers provide a standard for evaluating the progress students make during training and serve as models. Nonstudent employees in training stations can also actually assist in training. For example, students could be taught how to interact with nonhandicapped coworkers during breaks and how to request assistance when the demands of the job increase (e.g., during peak work periods during the shift). Coworkers could be trained to follow prescribed instructional programs to assist in training.

Many communities contain hospitals; federal,

state, and local government offices; universities or colleges; restaurants; large factories; and other industries. These settings are ideal for training stations. If a local hospital needs bed-making staff, a training station could be set up in a similar setting to train bed makers. Or if maids are needed in a town, a teacher could approach the manager of a motel or hotel to establish a training program. The initial discussion to establish a training program should cover (a) the characteristics of the people to be served, (b) the association they have to the local public school, (c) the duration of training for each student, and (d) payment of wages.

Student Characteristics

Typically, employers, supervisors, and most other people have not worked with severely handicapped students, or perhaps even seen a severely handicapped person. Therefore, they need to be informed about the distinguishing characteristics of this group, emphasizing individual differences and abilities. It is important to establish that this population histori-

FIGURE 17.1.
A Student Learning to Ride the City Bus to and from a Community Training Station

cally has been underrepresented in our public schools and that new laws, combined with a developing teaching technology, suggest they can learn marketable skills. Severely handicapped students are complex people who require more time and possibly innovative teaching methods to learn new tasks. Stress that, with systematic instruction, they can be taught complex tasks such as riding a bus to and from work (Sowers, Rusch, & Hudson, 1979).

Public School Students

Nonhandicapped and mildly handicapped students have benefited from work-study programs by acquiring marketable skills. Work-study programs are not new (Halpern, 1974). Because severely handicapped people must acquire useful skills, employers should be told that they need to learn actual job-related skills on-the-job rather than in simulated work environments. Thus these students should have access to work-study programs.

Duration of Program

A probationary period of from one to several academic years or year round should be established. A probationary period may be helpful to both parties in that the employer and the school have a set period of time (e.g., 9 months) to evaluate the overall success of the station and the relationship. Also, holidays and breaks taken by schools but not most other institutions, number of students to be trained, number of supervisory staff, hours, and types of tasks should be discussed.

Payment of Wages

Payment of wages should be discussed in the initial meeting with the employer. The training stations we established have included three students working staggered hours during an 8-hour shift. The three students have typically worked for periods of 3 to 5 hours, receiving training in social survival skills for another 1 to 3 hours. These latter tasks have included learning to ride a city bus to and from work (Sowers, Rusch, & Hudson, 1979), travel training (Spears, Rusch, York, & Lilly, 1981; Vogelsberg & Rusch, 1979), and asking questions (Rusch, Karlan, Riva, & Rusch, Note 7).

Station Organization

Station organization ensures that all tasks needed for job completion are known and job performance is systematically checked. For example, if two training stations were developed in a performing arts and convention center, one group of students could clean stages, auditoriums, and entry ways; the other group could manage a different set of tasks (walkways, windows, floors). An aide might manage one station, with the teacher managing a second station and checking the aide's station.

Identifying Job Tasks and Monitoring Performance

Identifying job tasks is based upon a task analysis (Wehman, 1981). The task analysis should list the skills the student will perform and the method or particular way in which each should be performed (Gold, 1980). For example, the sequence of steps for sweeping and mopping a floor may be determined by directly watching a janitor perform the criterion task(s) (Cuvo, Leaf, & Borakove, 1978). (See chapter 4 for more discussion on task analysis.)

Table 17.4 shows a task performance sheet with kitchen laborer tasks for three students to complete during a work day. This sheet displays the time a task should be started, the tasks to be performed, the number of minutes each task should take (based upon data from watching employees perform the task), and a place to mark when the student started the task, total time on task, and whether the task was completed on time. In this example Student 1 is working a 4-hour shift; Student 2, a 4½-hour shift; and Student 3, a 2-hour shift. Both Students 1 and 2 are in the final stages of training and are being considered for actual placement. For Student 3, the majority of instruction is based on mobility skills, learning job-related skills (e.g., wiping, sorting, drying, carrying), and learning to cook and manage household chores at other times. Thus, Student 3 is still in the early stages of training.

TABLE 17.4 Kitchen Laborer Task Performance Sheet

Teacher _____   Date _____

Aide _____

		Min Allowed	Start Time	Total Time	On Time
Student 1					
Ready for work					
9:00 a.m.	Set up steam table	15			
9:15 a.m.	Clean small soup pot	20			
9:35 a.m.	Clean large soup pot	15			
9:50 a.m.	Clean soup drain	6			
9:56 a.m.	Clean windows	@ 3			
10:00 a.m.	Dry dishes	20			
10:30 a.m.	Wash dishes*	20			
10:50 a.m.	Polish and/or clean windows	@ 3			
11:45 a.m.	Fill sinks and wash dishes	7;20			
12:25 p.m.	Sweep floor	15			
12:40 p.m.	Mop floor	15			
1:00 a.m.	Clean sink	8			
Student 2					
Ready for work					
9:00 a.m.	Remove items from sink	1			
9:01 a.m.	Scrape pots and pans	2			
9:03 a.m.	Fill sinks w/water	8			
9:11 a.m.	Wash pots and pans*—1 load only	20			
9:30 a.m.	Laundry (M–W–F)	10			
9:40 a.m.	Wash dishes*—1 load only	20			
10:00 a.m.	Clean refrigerator (T–F)	20			
10:30 a.m.	Dry dishes*—1 load only	20			
11:00 a.m.	Wash dishes*—1 load only	20			
12:00 p.m.	Clean stove oven	30			
12:15 p.m.	Wash dishes & large plastic containers*	20			
1:20 p.m.	Mop kitchen area	15			
Student 3					
Ready for work					
10:00 a.m.	Clean cart	1			
10:01 a.m.	Clean mixer	5			
10:06 a.m.	Dry dishes*—1 load only	54			
11:00 a.m.	Wash dishes*—1 load only	20			
11:20 a.m.	Empty garbage	10			
11:30 a.m.	Wash dishes*—1 load only	20			
11:50 a.m.	Clean sink	10			

*Collect "looking busy" data.

The bottom of the task sheet indicates that the aide or teacher collects "looking busy" data. Our experience suggests that handicapped students sometimes receive unwarranted scrutiny when problems arise in work shifts. For example, once people are placed and trained, they work very hard at just those tasks for which they were trained. When they complete a task, such as sweeping a floor, they will often wait until it is time to begin the next task, standing idly rather than beginning a new task, slowing down on the task they are performing, or possibly finding a "filler task" to look busy. Standing idly is not a survival skill. Teaching prospective students to look busy (e.g., sweeping a floor, wiping surfaces, cleaning windows) should be included in the curriculum for each training station (Rusch, 1979a).

Training and Management Strategies

Menchetti et al. (1981) assessed college and university food service employers' acceptance of selected training and management strategies, grouping 68 survey items into six procedural categories. Table 17.5 lists the items 50% or more of the 29 respondents agreed could or could not be used when training on the job. The results of this survey suggest several guidelines for providing training and management in competitive employment settings. For example, these employers indicated that records could be kept, but not more frequently than once a week. Consequently, data should be collected unobtrusively and the purpose for data collection should be discussed with employers and nonhandicapped coworkers.

These employers felt that, when an employee made an error, varying levels of instructional assistance could be used, including asking the employee why he or she was behaving inappropriately. They also stipulated that employees must be paid money and that, if money was paid for work performed, other reinforcers could also be used (e.g., points, tokens). These employers indicated that instructions could be repeated, one task could be taught at a time, the easiest jobs could be taught first, and job-related equipment could be color coded. They also suggested several strategies they would never allow.

Techniques that are absolutely inappropriate for use in an actual job placement might be appropriate for use in a training station. For example, employers would most likely not allow the use of overcorrection (Agosta, Close, Hops, & Rusch, 1980; Rusch & Close, 1976; Rusch, Close, Hops, & Agosta, 1976). However, overcorrection might be used constructively in an instructional setting. Ultimately, however, the techniques used to control job-related behavior must be very similar to those that are tolerated on the job (Menchetti et al., 1981). For example, Schutz, Rusch, and Lamson (1979) used an employer validated procedure to train three individuals to quit verbally abusing their coworkers in an employment training station. The employer's procedure for misconduct on the job, a warning and one-day suspension, successfully reduced verbally abusive statements. The goal was to train potential employees to respond to the contingencies that would eventually be used by the employing agency. Failure to train potential employees to respond to normal working

TABLE 17.5 Selected Training and Management Strategies for Use in Competitive Employment

Employers would allow:
1. Keeping monthly records.
2. Keeping weekly records.
3. Telling the employee what he or she did wrong.
4. Verbally or physically instructing the employee while he or she corrects an error.
5. Asking the employee why he or she is acting socially inappropriately.
6. Allowing a performance rate of faster than 50% when the employee is receiving training.
7. Working for money.
8. Praise from a supervisor.
9. Immediate reinforcement.
10. A combination of food, points, access to preferred activities, physical contact, or praise and money.
11. Verbal instruction, demonstrations, and physical assistance when learning a new job.
12. Repeating an instruction.
13. Teaching one task at a time.
14. Teaching the easiest jobs first.
15. Color coding job-related equipment.

Employers would never allow:
1. Ignoring an error.
2. Yelling at an employee.
3. Yelling at the employee when acting socially inappropriately.
4. Ignoring socially inappropriate behavior.
5. Points for work which can later be traded for material objects.
6. Teaching all tasks at one time.

conditions, such as those related to staff supervision, will unnecessarily stigmatize the new employee.

PLACE: SURVEYING JOBS AND MONITORING TRAINING

The *place* step in the *survey-train-place-train* model is critical to the success of the two training steps. Training relies upon a coordinator's ability to survey potential jobs and identify survival skills, develop a secondary vocational curriculum, support students' progress in the community training stations, and place and monitor graduates' progress. Because job placement is the goal of vocational training, it is the primary criterion for evaluating the overall training effort.

Job placement has received extended attention in the literature (Brolin, 1976; Jacobs, Larsen, & Smith, 1979; Rubin & Roessler, 1978; Rusch & Mithaug,

1980; Wehman, 1981; Wehman & McLaughlin, 1980). Typically, placement includes follow-up services and, consequently, has been criticized for inadequately stipulating the steps to follow once students are employed (Schutz & Rusch, 1982; Wehman, 1981). To further complicate our understanding of placement, past research has examined job placement in relation only to disadvantaged and mildly handicapped persons. The knowledge obtained from over 30 years of placement literature lacks depth and a comprehensive perspective (Murphy, 1977). In practice, the placement process consists largely of a "place-and-pray" approach, with vocational rehabilitation personnel devoting only limited time to follow-up (Usdane, 1968). Recently, the vocational rehabilitation literature has addressed procedures to develop a comprehensive placement program emphasizing a community-based, vocational training program (Malik, 1979; Vandergoot & Worrall, 1979). In particular, Rusch and Mithaug (1980) and Wehman (1981) extend the job placement process to include a major, separate emphasis on long-term follow-up services. In this chapter, therefore, we present placement as separate from follow-up.

Supporting Student Progress

Placement staff members should serve as advocates for students, supporting their progress in the training stations and again when they have been employed. Placement staff should work with ancillary services (e.g., local sheltered workshops, community placement advisory committee) before students are employed because they likely need support services after they have been placed. This support might involve workshop personnel teaching nonhandicapped coworkers to train and manage handicapped workers or advocating for above-minimum wages and comprehensive benefits packages.

Establishing a community placement advisory committee to oversee secondary employment training programs is another level of advocacy. Often, school personnel need information and guidance about the local labor market. This committee might help a placement coordinator find job vacancies; gain entrance into various job sites; communicate with coworkers, supervisors, and employers; and conduct local surveys. Cooperation from potential community employers can be facilitated by an advisory committee. For example, committee members can make introductory telephone calls, allow the placement coordinator to use their letterheads, and write support letters for mailed surveys.

A third level of support can be established when reviewing progress made toward IEP goals. Traditionally, public schools assess student skills, specify

goals and objectives, develop instructional materials, incorporate procedures to reach these goals and objectives, and finally evaluate student progress. The *survey-train-place-train* model requires a parallel procedure. Once trained, the student can move along the placement continuum toward advanced settings (e.g., from the intermediate classroom to secondary community training stations teaching more advanced behaviors). When a placement is made, the previous instructional efforts are evaluated. Because the requisite skills are known and students are trained to perform those skills, the overall success of training can be monitored and evaluated. This approach to competitive employment relies upon teaching relevant skills in the classroom, with advancement from one classroom to a future classroom or job based upon acquiring these skills. The successes should be communicated to teachers and parents.

A final reason to support student progress is related directly to progress on the IEP. Because there is data on the functioning level of each student, the placement staff can select and make job placements based upon this knowledge. Severely handicapped students will have quite different levels of skill performance and may respond favorably under one set of contingencies (e.g., praise) and not under a second set (e.g., reprimands). With this knowledge, the staff can make appropriate placements based upon their understanding of probable placements and whether one placement option instead of another option will support some students.

Job Analysis

The placement process includes an analysis of employer expectations and development of a work performance evaluation form. Belmore and Brown (1978), Rusch and Mithaug (1980), and Wehman (1981) have delineated the components of a thorough job analysis. For example, Rusch and Mithaug (1980) outlined four components of a job analysis: (a) work environment (agency overview), (b) tasks to be completed (job task analysis), (c) conditions of employment (e.g., work hours per day, pay scale, travel requirements, insurance and other benefits), and (d) work requirements (e.g., educational requirements, tests, reasons for previous firings or abandonments).

Most employers will have a form and procedures developed to evaluate employees. In addition, the placement staff should design a list of social and vocational survival skills that have been determined to be important to employers. Service and light industrial occupations will have different "general categories" of important skills (social and vocational). Therefore, separate evaluation forms should be developed for these occupations and for any other occupations being considered. The work performance forms should include a third performance section listing the "specific categories" employers indicate are crucial for job entry or maintenance.[4]

One final note with regard to placement deserves consideration. Many communities, particularly smaller ones, may offer a restricted range of jobs. Therefore, it may be necessary to coordinate job placements with other social service agencies. In Champaign-Urbana, Illinois, for example, there are approximately 100 to 150 jobs that are reasonable options for severely handicapped workers. They offer flexible schedules, benefits, and good wages; have high employee turnover; and therefore need a stable working class. Thus, agencies seeking to employ severely handicapped adolescents and adults must coordinate their efforts with other service groups attempting to place handicapped or disadvantaged clients. Employers should not be contacted by several agencies, and no more than one thorough job analysis survey should be required of an employer in a given year. Service agencies, including schools, should collaborate on establishing a job placement office coordinating not only the placement of students from a public school but also placements from, for example, the local sheltered workshop.

Finally, employers should be told that jobs are being sought for trained workers and that, if a placement fails, another person will be placed in that job. By conceptualizing each community to include a designated number of "job slots," you reduce the number of times "new employers" must be found. When a person loses a job, the placement coordinator should provide feedback to the community training station and the follow-up staff about why the employee was terminated. The placement coordinator must also *preserve* the job slot in the community.

TRAIN: PROVIDING FOLLOW-UP SERVICES AFTER PLACEMENT

Developing a longitudinal, community-based vocational curriculum based on employer expectations, training functional survival skills, and placing students in actual jobs are processes that we are just beginning to understand. Unfortunately, how to best provide follow-up services is even less well understood. Our understanding of the best practices to follow to maintain employment is complicated by our

limited history in working with disadvantaged and mildly handicapped individuals. As we have said, traditional employment programs that serve the mildly handicapped use a "place-and-pray" method. This approach has been partly successful because the clients who are typically successful in holding their jobs beyond a trial period either have the requisite survival skills before they are placed or have benefited from follow-up services from the employing agency.

If schools train their secondary-aged, severely handicapped students in simulated work environments, the likelihood that these students will succeed in competitive employment is very low. No matter how well trained, they will need some initial daily guidance. To significantly influence the lives of severely handicapped students, the public school system must assume the follow-up training that these students need to adjust to the requirements of future adult environments—including competitive employment.

Final training should begin long before age 21. Most nonhandicapped students graduate and enter the work force when they are 18 years old. Child labor laws in all states require work permits for youths under the age of 16. Therefore, as a general rule, students need to be placed sometime between their 16th and 22nd birthdays. This decision should be based upon the student's competencies, the availability of follow-up personnel, and the selection of an appropriate placement. Most students, however, should receive *at least* 2 years of follow-up services before they graduate. In most (if not all) cases, the period should be longer. *Minimally, placement needs to be made at least by age 19.*

An effective follow-up program has many functions, including identifying problems, providing on-the-job training, seeking validation through significant others[5], planning intervention by others, and fading follow-up services. Identifying problems and providing on-the-job training rely upon general behavior analysis procedures requiring precise specification of survival skills before training. Once actual work performance standards are listed, a student's level of functioning can be evaluated. This evaluation identifies behavioral excesses or deficits that are then translated into instructional behavioral objectives. Mithaug and Haring (1977) proposed a similar approach which included, in part, these steps.

1. Analyzing the skills required to complete a job,
2. Pinpointing behaviors expected by the supervisor,

---

[4]Space here does not allow a thorough overview of conducting a job analysis survey, determining employers' expectations, and developing a work performance evaluation form. Again, see Belmore and Brown (1978), Rusch and Mithaug (1980), and Wehman (1981).

[5]*Significant others* refers to people who assess whether instructional goals, procedures, and results are appropriate for their intended purposes.

3. Specifying the motivational system on that job,
4. Encouraging conformity to rules,
5. Discouraging deviant behavior,
6. Assessing skill level relevant to the job,
7. Specifying behavioral objectives for each of the deficiencies identified,
8. Developing and implementing a training program.

We have already covered each of these steps. Seeking validation from significant others and developing a long-term follow-up program, however, have not yet been discussed.

Seeking Validation from Significant Others

One of four things happens when attempting to determine how well a placement is going (Rusch & Mithaug, 1980). Significant others (e.g., coworker, supervisor) either agree or disagree with direct, repeated measures of people competitively employed obtained by follow-up personnel; these same follow-up personnel either agree or disagree with indirect measures typically provided by supervisors or others on the job who have *designated* evaluation functions.

Identifying Discrepancies

Discrepancies between objective and subjective measures may be caused by several factors. The first is the person who serves as the evaluator, like the observer, being influenced by others. Investigators have been known to influence the performance of observers so as to confirm their expectations. This same problem can arise when an employer's wishes (either positive or negative) are made known to the evaluator.

Discrepancies between subjective and objective measures may also be due to the evaluator and the observer attending to similar, but not exactly the same, dimensions of behavior. Rusch et al. (1980) indicated that evaluators may use broader definitions of performance at other times of the work shift to influence their estimates of how well an employee is doing, where follow-up personnel focus on a target behavior during a constricted time period. They obtained the ratings of coworkers in conjunction with direct, repeated measures to determine whether coworkers agreed if preinstructions and feedback resulted in fewer topics being repeated during lunches and breaks in a kitchen setting. Interestingly, at the end of the training period, coworkers indicated that there was no change. Direct measures obtained by the observers, however, showed the new employee had not repeated topics for almost 3 weeks before the coworker ratings.

Regardless of the reasons for discrepancies, these data are the primary basis for follow-up services.

Typically, specific work settings will differ in what is considered acceptable behavior. As a result, follow-up personnel should use social validation to decide how placed students are doing (Kazdin & Matson, 1981). Social validation can include both descriptive and comparative validation.

Descriptive Validation

Descriptive validation refers to efforts to evaluate training consisting of judgments about qualitative aspects of behavior. For example, work behavior that has been changed by a teacher would be evaluated by significant others who are in a position to judge the effects of training. The placement staff should prepare a work performance evaluation form to be used by the follow-up training staff based upon their survey of probable jobs and their job analyses. Typically, employers evaluate staffs at least annually, with new staff evaluated during the first 3 to 6 months of employment. Sometimes existing work performance evaluations may be used as the sole descriptive validation measure. Often, however, existing forms are not sufficiently expansive or behaviorally oriented to provide information needed to develop training plans. Therefore, the placement staff should establish a work performance evaluation form that can be used during the first year *in addition* to the form that may be used by the employing agency.[6]

The work performance evaluation form should be completed by an employee who has responsibility for staff evaluations and, possibly, hiring and firing. This form should not be completed by coworkers in positions similar to the new employee nor by the new employee (or student) alone. Recent research has indicated that there are gross discrepancies between evaluations done by experienced staff and lower level employees (Riva & Rusch, Note 8). Handicapped people and their coworkers evaluated performance significantly higher than did supervisors.

We have asked employers to complete the work performance evaluation form once a week for the first month, then once a month for the remainder of the first year. After the first year, only the evaluation form originally used by the business is completed.

Descriptive validation can be obtained either verbally or with surveys. Thus far only surveys have been discussed. Asking significant others how well someone is doing or has done a particular job can be helpful. For example, Schutz, Jostes, Rusch, and Lamson (1980) asked shift supervisors to state whether they believed kitchen floors were adequately swept and mopped by two students being trained. In

---

[6]See Rusch and Mithaug (1980) for a detailed account of how to develop functional descriptive validation assessment instruments.

this study, supervisors identified baseline performance and performance during training. It is important to consider who is being asked to evaluate work performance verbally and how often. Several different employees with several different functions should not be asked to rate performance during the early stages of training. However, once a student has been trained to acceptable limits, he or she should meet the general expectancy of most coworkers. Thus, in a variety of ways, descriptive validation measures are crucial to the overall success of the survey-train place-train model.

Comparative Validation

Comparative validation refers to efforts to compare the student's or worker's target behavior (also goals and procedures) with that of peers (e.g., nonhandicapped coworkers). The primary goal is to determine whether the behavior is distinguishable from peer behavior. Comparative validation entails directly observing the work performance of an "established employee" to compare that performance with that of a new employee (see, for example, Rusch et al., 1980). The goal is *not* to train the new employee to work just like established employees. Rather, the goal is to adjust or manage the behavior so that the new employee works within tolerable limits. Employees behave variably (e.g., on some days they work faster). This variability may be due, in part, to setting conditions, subject characteristics, or a combination of the two. Thus, comparative validation should define the *boundaries* of acceptable work performance.

To use comparative validation correctly, you must know the student being compared and select an employee who is performing comparable tasks during similar work periods. Staff are typically compared along several dimensions. Table 17.6 lists many of the worker characteristics that have, in various combinations, been used for evaluation by agencies in the Champaign-Urbana area (Rusch, Note 9). Typically, employees are evaluated bimonthly, every 6 months, or annually, comparing new workers with nonprobationary employees with similar job descriptions. That is, helpers are not compared to laborers or laborers to dishwashers.

Selecting comparable work periods is also important. It is crucial to collect direct, repeated measures of work performed under very similar conditions. For example, it is appropriate to collect data on a target employee within 30 minutes of break if the comparison employee is also being observed during the same period. If both are working in the same location, the observer could either observe one employee for a brief period (e.g., 10 seconds), then a second employee for the same time period, alternating until the entire work sample is completed. If the two employees are working in separate locations in the same building, the observer could watch one person and then the other employee for exactly the same periods of time (e.g., for 10 minutes each). If a comparable employee is not working at the same time the new employee is, the peer should be observed performing the same tasks during the same periods when the target employee has a day off. That is, if the target employee works 5 days a week with a part-

TABLE 17.6 Worker Characteristics that Have Been the Subject of Employer Evaluations

Accepts criticism	Instructional assistance, level of
Acknowledgment	Maintains positive attitude about work
Arrival behaviors	Mopping responses
Asks for assistance	Noncompliance
Attending	Pages turned independently, percent of recipe
Not attending	Prompts and praises
Attending to task behavior	Producing—speed of task completion
Bus riding [from home to work]	Staff feedback
Complaining	Stereotypic behavior
Completes all assigned tasks	Sweeping responses
Completes job on time	Time management
Compliance	Topic repetition
Cooperates with employees & employers	Verbal abuse
Disagreements	Work behavior, compliant
Drooling	Works alone
Following a schedule	Works fast during rush times
In motion (looking busy)	Works safely
Not in motion	

time employee working his or her days off (or the reverse), observations should be made on both employees during the same week.

Comparative validation is useful when combined with descriptive accounts. As we have mentioned, subjective evaluations will be made in placement sites; these evaluations, particularly when poor, must be considered in determining whether the client is adjusting to the job. When supervisors provide subjective evaluations that are below standards, comparative validation is particularly useful. Instances where subjective evaluations show high performance but comparison measures show low performance are not as important as when subjective evaluations yield low performance and comparisons yield high or low. Simply stated, if the employer believes an employee is doing well and you disagree, based upon objective data, it is not essential to correct the employers' expectations. Only in those instances where the employer believes there is a problem is intervention crucial. For example, consider the situation in which the employer, who is also the supervisor, rates an employee poorly on "completes all assigned tasks." The follow-up staff should objectively evaluate "completes all assigned tasks" and, when (or where) a problem is found, remediate the difference. Perhaps a particular task is not being completed daily or a task is being completed differently than it has traditionally been. In either case, providing feedback to the employer and providing acceptable training should result in a higher evaluation on "completed all assigned tasks" the next time around. After you have attended to employer problems, then you can work on problems identified by the follow-up staff if time permits.

In some instances, the standard for a particular job will not be easily detectable and modifications in when or how the job is completed will not meet the expectations of the employer. In this case, you will need to make a comparison. For example, if the problem is one of speed, the objective is to determine four things: how fast the evaluator wants the job completed; how fast the job is being completed by an employee who is performing the job acceptably; how fast the target employee is completing the task; and how each of these assessments compare. Direct measures should be taken over 3 to 5 days. With this information, you could determine (a) if the problem is speed or speed along with other factors which are leading to lowered evaluations (e.g., how fast someone is doing a job and how much he talks to other employees) and (b) how the descriptive measures compare to the direct measures of the target employee receiving a lower rating and a comparable employee receiving a higher rating. Regardless of the problem, the difference is made up with training that reduces the discrepancy between what is expected and what is being done. In instances where the descriptive data are not reasonable, then the evaluator and the follow-up staff will need to negotiate for more time. If the evaluator has established a time line that is rarely if ever achieved by comparable employees, then this information should be shared with the evaluator, and the problem that is actually causing the low ratings must be identified.

Developing a Long-Term Follow-up Program

The recent literature pays considerable attention to maintaining a job (Kazdin, 1975) and evaluating job maintenance (Rusch & Kazdin, 1981). Our discussion provides only an overview of this topic, covering establishing a schedule to deliver follow-up services, using coworkers to support job maintenance, and withdrawing training and management strategies to enhance job maintenance.[7]

Establishing a Follow-up Schedule

Rusch and Mithaug (1980) have suggested two placement follow-up schedules: the adjusted follow-up schedule and the fixed follow-up schedule. The *adjusted follow-up schedule* is based exclusively on how well a new employee is performing on the job, with less and less time spent on follow-up as the employee adjusts to the demands of the job. This schedule assumes the new employee will meet the expectations of the employer, as determined by descriptive and comparative validation.

The *fixed follow-up schedule* is preset by the follow-up staff and reflects decreasing time spent by follow-up staff over an extended time. Because some employers believe they can provide "all necessary training," and therefore may ask the follow-up staff not to help them provide on-the-job training, it is crucial to establish a schedule for the follow-up staff for monitoring performance and providing training.

A placement should not be made if the employer will not, in advance, allow adjusted or fixed follow-up. As we have said, mildly and emotionally handicapped people have been the primary recipients of vocational rehabilitation, and they have adjusted largely due to their existing skills or the philanthropy of their employers. Severely handicapped people have *not* been a target rehabilitation population; consequently, employers have no experience working with them. Therefore, job advocacy based upon employee performance and employer perceptions of that performance will be

---

[7]See Kochany and Keller (1981) for an analysis of why some individuals placed by Wehman and his colleagues have failed to retain their employment.

crucial in termining whether a severely handicapped individual adjusts to a particular job.

Both the adjusted and fixed schedules include on-site and off-site services over periods longer than 6 months. The initial months might require daily services over the entire work schedule, including getting to and from the work site. On-site time should be spent training, managing, and evaluating behavior and perceptions of how others believe a placement is going (i.e., descriptive validation). This time should be divided into periods when the follow-up personnel are observable and not observable to the employee. Research suggests that employees may react to the observed presence of evaluators (Fisher, Wehman, & Young, Note 10; Rusch, Menchetti, Crouch, Riva, & Morgan, Note 11). Therefore, you should insure that newly placed students perform in the presence of coworkers just as they might perform in your presence.

Using Coworkers to Support Job Maintenance

Typically, follow-up staff observe and evaluate behavior and provide feedback based on their evaluations. This feedback usually takes the form of positive or negative statements. Therefore, we could say that those being observed, as in the Fisher et al. (Note 10) and Rusch et al. (Note 11) studies, were reacting to combined positive and negative reinforcement schedules. This leads logically to the conclusion that coworkers could help observe and evaluate and that these same coworkers could provide differential feedback based upon their evaluations.

To date, very little attention has been paid to job placement follow-up provided by coworkers. These coworkers could evaluate performance and be trained in short, in-service workshops to train and manage behavior. Short 10-minute sessions could be scheduled during breaks or before or after work to demonstrate effective training procedures and allow coworkers to practice. Behavior descriptions and the goal of work performance evaluation forms also could be discussed. In essence, the follow-up staff have the responsibility to monitor their *placements*. To this end, some time should be devoted to a well-planned and coordinated schedule of in-service activities directed toward all workers at the site. The topics of these miniworkshops should include employee adjustment to the work setting and to other employees.

Withdrawing Training and Management Strategies

Several methods of withdrawing training packages and evaluating these withdrawals have been discussed in the literature (Connis & Rusch, 1980; Rusch & Kazdin, 1981). Several factors should be considered when estimating how quickly to withdraw staff from the placement setting. Foremost is determining whether the newly placed employee can perform the job without any feedback from a trainer and in the trainer's absence. Rusch and Kazdin (1981) have suggested using partial withdrawal when estimating levels of dependence. *Partial withdrawals* withdraw one component of the training package or the complete training package from any combination and number of clients, behaviors, or settings. For example, Vogelsberg and Rusch (1979) used partial withdrawal to assess whether eliminating feedback from one of three severely handicapped adolescents who had learned to cross streets would lead to loss of acquired skills. In this study, when feedback was removed, one class of behaviors (looking left, right, in front, and behind) was not maintained. Therefore, they introduced a second training strategy, modeling, in place of feedback.

Rusch and Kazdin (1981) also recommended the use of sequential withdrawals to maintain responses. *Sequential withdrawals* withdraw one component of a multiple-component training package initially, then a second, and so on, until all components have been withdrawn. Rusch, Connis, and Sowers (1979) used this strategy with a mildly handicapped woman who was instructed to attend to task ("look busy"). The attending behavior was developed with prompts, praise, and a token economy. It required the woman to exchange her points twice a day. Therefore, the authors withdrew the token economy one component at a time, and then the prompts and praise, until the training package consisted of payment of wages every 2 weeks.

These withdrawal methods have only recently been introduced, and thus, there are few case studies using them. However, the strategies to withdraw training and management procedures are logical. We can say that trainers should evaluate whether the absence of intervention and the person(s) who introduced intervention results in loss of behavior. If so, the withdrawal approach must be (*a*) repeated more slowly so that the new employee eventually does not discriminate between the absence or presence of the trainer or intervention, (*b*) supplemented with a second strategy (e.g., self-monitoring) or possibly, (*c*) not totally withdrawn (i.e., part of the procedures remain). In the last instance, the strategy might include training people on the job to maintain performance (Rusch & Menchetti, 1981).

CONCLUSION

Identifying employers, jobs, survival skills, significant others, and the many other characteristics of a community that may influence the success of a community-based vocational training program is

FIGURE 17.2

Donna Graduated from a Community Training Program and Has Been Competitively Employed for over 3 Years as a Kitchen Laborer

crucial. We have suggested that placement staff consider a community of employers as a fixed commodity and identify and develop jobs for the purpose of employing handicapped workers. Communities offer limited job opportunities, and often several social service agencies appear to be competing for these jobs. Therefore, a placement office should coordinate the common goals of these agencies.

The concept of survival is important and logically points teachers toward those skills that may have value to employers. This chapter stresses how inappropriate it is to believe that employment conditions can be simulated in a classroom and suggests establishing the secondary classroom in the community.

Descriptive and comparative validation allows the staff to evaluate the new employee's work adjustment. We have provided guidelines to integrate the outcomes of subjective and objective evaluations and to withdraw follow-up services.

In conclusion, this chapter has presented the *survey-train-place-train* model for preparing severely handicapped students for competitive employment. We have not, however, discussed the importance of leisure and recreation, domestic, or self-help training as they relate to competitive employment. These topics and the skills they represent interact so as to appreciably influence individual success. Failure to

consider the entire student and his or her future environments in terms of the requirements of those environments will surely result in our failure to serve our severely handicapped students appropriately.

REFERENCES

Agosta, J.M., Close, D., Hops, H., & Rusch, F.R. Treatment of self-injurious behavior through overcorrection procedures. *Journal of the Association for the Severely Handicapped*, 1980, *5*, 5–12.

Bates, P., & Pancsofar, E. Longitudinal vocational training for severely handicapped students in the public schools. In R. York, W.K. Schofield, D.J. Donder, D.L. Ryndak, & B. Reguly (Eds.), *Organizing and implementing services for students with severe and multiple handicaps: Proceedings from the 1981 Illinois Statewide Institute for Educators of the Severely and Profoundly Handicapped*. Springfield: Illinois State Board of Education, Department of Specialized Educational Services, 1981.

Bellamy, G.T., Inman, D.P., & Schwarz, R.H. Vocational training and production supervision: A review of habilitation techniques for the severely and profoundly retarded. In N. Haring & D. Bricker (Eds.), *Teaching the severely and profoundly handicapped* (Vol. 3). Seattle: American Association for the Education of the Severely/Profoundly Handicapped, 1978.

Belmore, K., & Brown, L. Job skills inventory strategy for use in a public school vocational training program for severely handicapped potential workers. In N. Haring & D. Bricker (Eds.), *Teaching the severely handicapped* (Vol. 3). Seattle: American Association for the Education of the Severely/Profoundly Handicapped, 1978.

Brolin, D.E. *Vocational preparation of retarded citizens.* Columbus, Ohio: Charles E. Merrill, 1976.

Brown, L., Branston, M.B., Hamre-Nietupski, S., Pumpian, I., Certo, N., & Gruenewald, L.A. Strategy for developing chronological age appropriate and functional curricular content for severely handicapped adolescents and young adults. *Journal of Special Education*, 1979, *13*, 81–90.

Brown, L., Branston-McClean, M.B., Baumgart, D., Vincent, L., Falvey, M., & Schroeder, J. Using the characteristics of current and subsequent least restrictive environments in the development of curricular content for severely handicapped students. *AAESPH Review*, 1979, *4*, 407–424.

Brown, L., Pumpian, I., Baumgart, D., Vandeventer, P., Ford, A., Nisbet, J., Schroeder, J., & Gruenewald, L. Longitudinal transition plans in programs for severely handicapped students. *Exceptional Children*, 1981, *47*, 624–631.

Clarke, J.Y., Greenwood, L.M., Abramowitz, D.B., & Bellamy, G.T. Summer jobs for vocational preparation of moderately and severely retarded adolescents. *Journal of the Association for the Severely Handicapped*, 1980, *5*, 24–37.

Connis, R.T., & Rusch, F.R. Programming maintenance through sequential withdrawal of social contingencies. *Behavior Research of Severe Developmental Disabilities*, 1980, *1*, 249–260.

Connis, R.T., Thompson, L.T., & Sowers, J. (Ed.) *Training the mentally handicapped for employment: A comprehensive manual.* New York: Human Sciences Press, 1981.

Crouch, K.P. *Utilizing correspondence training to decrease time-spent completing vocational tasks.* Unpublished masters thesis, Department of Special Education, University of Illinois, 1981.

Cuvo, A.J., Leaf, R.B., & Borakove, L.S. Teaching janitorial skills to the mentally retarded: Acquisition, generalization, and maintenance. *Journal of Applied Behavior Analysis*, 1978, *11*, 345–355.

Gold, M. *Try another way training manual.* Champaign, Ill.: Research Press, 1980.

Halpern, A.S. Work-study programs for the mentally retarded: An overview. In Philip L. Browning (Ed.), *Mental retardation: Rehabilitation and counseling.* Springfield, Ill.: Charles C Thomas, 1974.

Jacobs, A.M., Larsen, J.K., & Smith, C.A. *Handbook for job placement of mentally retarded workers.* New York: Garland STPM Press, 1979.

Johnson, J.L., & Mithaug, D.E. A replication of sheltered workshop entry requirements. *AAESPH Review*, 1978, *3*, 116–122.

Karlan, G.R., & Rusch, F.R. Analyzing the relationship between acknowledgement and compliance in a non-sheltered work setting. *Education and Training for the Mentally Retarded*, in press.

Kazdin, A.E. *Behavior modification in applied settings.* Homewood, Ill.: Dorsey Press, 1975.

Kazdin, A.E. Assessing the clinical or applied importance of behavior change through social validation. *Behavior Modification*, 1977, *1*, 427–451.

Kazdin, A.E., & Matson, J.L. Social validation in mental retardation. *Applied Research in Mental Retardation*, 1981, *2*, 39–54.

Kenowitz, L.A., Gallaher, J., & Edgar, E. Generic services for the severely handicapped and their families: What's available? In E. Sontag, J. Smith, & N. Certo (Eds.), *Educational programming for the severely and profoundly handicapped.* Reston, Va.: Council for Exceptional Children, 1977.

Kochany, L., & Keller, J. An analysis and evaluation of the failures of severely disabled individuals in competitive employment. In P. Wehman (Ed.), *Competitive employment.* Baltimore: Paul H. Brookes, 1981.

Malik, K. Job accommodation through job restructuring and environment modification. In D. Vandergoot & J. Worrall (Eds.), *Placement in rehabilitation.* Baltimore: University Park Press, 1979.

Menchetti, B.M., Rusch, F.R., & Lamson, D.S. Employers' perceptions of acceptable training procedures for use in competitive employment settings. *Journal of the Association for the Severely Handicapped*, 1981, *6*, 6–16.

Mithaug, D.E. *Prevocational training for retarded students.* Springfield, Ill.: Charles C Thomas, 1981.

Mithaug, D.E., & Hagmeier, L.D. The development of procedures to assess prevocational competencies of severely handicapped young adults. *AAESPH Review*, 1978, *3*, 94–115.

Mithaug, D.E., & Hanawalt, D.A. The validation of procedures to assess prevocational task preference in retarded adults. *Journal of Applied Behavior Analysis*, 1978, *11*, 153–162.

Mithaug, D.E., & Haring, N.G. Community vocational and workshop placement. In N.G. Haring & L.J. Brown (Eds.), *Teaching the severely handicapped* (Vol. 2). New York: Grune & Stratton, 1977.

Murphy, S.A. A critical view of job placement inquiry. *Rehabilitation Counseling Bulletin*, December 1977, 166–175.

Pomerantz, D., & Marholin, D. Vocational habilitation. A time for change. In E. Sontag, J. Smith & N. Certo (Eds.), *Educational programming for the severely and profoundly handicapped.* Reston, Va.: Council for Exceptional Children, 1977.

Rubin, S.E., & Roessler, R.T. *Foundations of the vocational rehabilitation process.* Baltimore: University Park Press, 1978.

Rusch, F.R. A functional analysis of the relationship between attending to task and production in an applied restaurant setting. *Journal of Special Education*, 1979, *13*, 399–411. (a)

Rusch, F.R. Toward the validation of social/vocational survival skills. *Mental Retardation*, 1979, *17*, 143–145. (b)

Rusch, F.R., & Close, D. Overcorrection: A procedural evaluation. *AAESPH Review*, 1976, *1*, 32–45.

Rusch, F., Close, D., Hops, H., & Agosta, J. Overcorrection: Generalization and maintenance. *Journal of Applied Behavior Analysis*, 1976, *9*, 498.

Rusch, F.R., Connis, R.T., & Sowers, J. The modification and maintenance of time spent attending to task using social reinforcement, token reinforcement, and response cost in an applied restaurant setting. *Journal of Special Education Technology*, 1979, *2*, 18–26.

Rusch, F.R., & Kazdin, A.E. Toward a methodology of withdrawal designs for the assessment of response maintenance. *Journal of Applied Behavior Analysis*, 1981, *14*, 131–140.

Rusch, F.R., & Menchetti, B.M. Increasing complaint work behaviors in a non-sheltered work setting. *Mental Retardation*, 1981, *19* 107–112.

Rusch, F.R., & Mithaug, D.E. *Vocational training for mentally retarded adults: A behavior analytic approach*. Champaign, Ill.: Research Press, 1980.

Rusch, F.R., & Schutz, R.P. Non-sheltered competitive employment of the mentally retarded adult: Research to reality? *Journal of Contemporary Business*, 1979, *8*, 85–98.

Rusch, F.R., & Schutz, R.P. Vocational and social work behavior research: An evaluative review. In J.L. Matson & J.R. McCartney (Eds.), *Handbook of behavior modification with the mentally retarded*. New York: Plenum Press, 1981.

Rusch, F.R., Schutz, R.P., & Heal, L.W. Sheltered and nonsheltered work behavior: A discussion of behavioral research. In J.L. Matson & J.A. Mulick (Eds.), *Comprehensive handbook on mental retardation*. New York: Pergamon, in press.

Rusch, F.R., Weithers, J.A., Menchetti, B.M., & Schutz, R.P. Social validation of a program to reduce topic repetition in a non-sheltered setting. *Education and Training of the Mentally Retarded*, 1980, *15*, 208–215.

Schutz, R.P., Jostes, K., Rusch, F.R., & Lamson, D. The contingent use of pre-instruction and social validation in the acquisition, generalization, and maintenance of sweeping and mopping responses. *Education and Training of the Mentally Retarded*, 1980, *15*, 306–311.

Schutz, R.P., & Rusch, F.R. Competitive employment: Toward employment integration for mentally retarded persons. In K.L. Lynch, W.E. Kiernan, & J.A. Stark (Eds.), *Prevocational and vocational education for special needs youth: A blueprint for the 1980s*. Paul H. Brookes, 1982.

Schutz, R.P., Rusch, F.R., & Lamson, D.S. Evaluation of an employer's procedure to eliminate unacceptable behavior on the job. *Community Services Forum*, 1979, *1*, 4–5.

Sowers, J., Rusch, F.R., & Hudson, C. Training a severely retarded young adult to ride the city bus to and from work. *AAESPH Review*, 1979, *4*, 15–22.

Sowers, J., Thompson, L.E., & Connis, R.T. The food service vocational training program. In G.T. Bellamy, G. O'Conner, & O.C. Karan (Eds.), *Vocational rehabilitation of severely handicapped persons*. Baltimore: University Park Press, 1979.

Spears, D., Rusch, F.R., York, R., & Lilly, M.S. Training independent arrival behaviors to a severely mentally retarded child. *Journal of the Association for the Severely Handicapped*, 1981, *6*(2), 40–45.

Thurman, S.K., & Fiorelli, J.S. Perspectives on normalization. *Journal of Special Education*, 1979, *13*, 339–346.

Usdane, W. The placement process in the rehabilitation of the severely handicapped. *Rehabilitation Literature*, 1968, *78*, 283–284.

Vandergoot, D., & Worrall, J. *Placement in rehabilitation*. Baltimore: University Park Press, 1979.

Van Houten, R. Social validation: The evolution of standards of competency for target behaviors. *Journal of Applied Behavior Analysis*, 1979, *12*, 581–592.

Vogelsberg, R.T., & Rusch, F.R. Training severely handicapped students to cross partially controlled intersections. *AAESPH Review*, 1979, *4*, 264–273.

Wehman, P. *Competitive employment*. Baltimore: Paul H. Brookes, 1981.

Wehman, P., & McLaughlin, P. *Vocational curriculum for developmentally disabled persons*. Baltimore: University Park Press, 1980.

Whitehead, C. Sheltered workshops in the decade ahead: Work and wages, or welfare. In G.T. Bellamy, G. O'Connor, & O.C. Karan (Eds.), *Vocational rehabilitation of severely handicapped persons*. Baltimore: University Park Press, 1979.

Wolf, M.M. Social validity: The case for subjective measurement or how applied behavior analysis is finding its heart. *Journal of Applied Behavior Analysis*, 1978, *11*, 203–214.

REFERENCE NOTES

1. Bates, P., & Pancsofar, E. *Project EARN (Employment and Rehabilitation = Normalization): A competitive employment training program for severely disabled youth in the public schools*. Manuscript submitted for publication.

2. Rusch, F.R., Thompson, L., Sowers, J., & Connis, R.T. *Competitive employment of mentally retarded adults*. Unpublished manuscript, Department of Special Education, University of Illinois, Champaign, IL 1978.

3. Sowers, J., Lundervold, D., Swanson, M., & Budd, C. *Competitive employment training for mentally retarded adults: A systematic approach*. Specialized Training Program, 1590 Willamette, University of Oregon, Eugene, OR 97403.

4. Rusch, F.R., & Morgan, T.K. *The use of self-instruction to train workers to attend to task*. Unpublished manuscript, Department of Special Education, University of Illinois, Champaign, IL 61820.

5. Rusch, F., Schutz, R., & Agran, M. *Validating entry-level survival skills for service occupations: Implications for curriculum development*. Manuscript submitted for publication.

6. Schutz, R., & Rusch, F. *Assessing light and service industry employers' expectations for competitive employment*. Manuscript in preparation.

7. Rusch, J.C., Karlan, G.R., Riva, M.T., & Rusch, F.R. *Training mentally retarded adults conversational skills in employment setting*. Manuscript submitted for publication.

8. Riva, M., & Rusch, F.R. *Work supervisors', co-workers', and mentally retarded employees' work performance evaluations: A comparison*. Manuscript in preparation.

9. Rusch, F.R. *Glossary of dependent measures from the Employment Training Project*. Unpublished manuscript, Department of Special Education, University of Illinois,

Champaign, IL 61820.

10. Fisher, J., Wehman, P., & Young, R. *Reactivity and its effects on the performance of severely handicapped food service workers.* Manuscript submitted for publication.

11. Rusch, F.R., Menchetti, B.M., Crouch, K.P., Riva, M., & Morgan, T.K. *Assessing employee reactivity to naturalistic observation.* Manuscript submitted for publication.

Name
Index

Subject Index

Natural cues, 413, 426
Natural prompts, 122, 123, 125
Natural settings, for enhanced skill
    generalization, 419, 434, 435
    (*See also* In vivo training)
Neonatal mortality rates, 52
Neurodevelopmental assessment,
    180, 181
Neurodevelopmental treatment
    (NDT), 181, 187–89, 200
Neurological examination of infants,
    52
Neurological impairments, 47, 149,
    167
Nonhandicapped children, parents
    of, 23, 34
Nonhandicapped coworkers, 504,
    519
Nonhandicapped peers, 4, 79
    attitudes of, 33
    comparison of daily living skills
        with, 415
    integration with, 319–20
    interactions with, 6, 7, 8, 12–13,
        26, 32, 33, 34, 116, 314, 318,
        319
Nonsheltered employment, 503
Nonspeech communication, 289
    direct selection responses, 295–96,
        302
Nonverbal communication, gestural,
    289, 291, 292, 299, 301–2
Nonvocal communication,
    temporary, 302–3
Norm-referenced tests, 54, 55, 56,
    58, 59, 60, 61, 64, 66, 67, 68,
    78
Normative comparisons, 415, 423

Object control skills, 217, 284
Object differentiation, 279
Object–name associations, 242
Object permanence skills, 234, 236,
    237, 238, 239, 240–43, 255,
    265
Object relationship schemes, 233
Objectives
    functional, 83
    instructional (*see* Instructional
        objectives)
    long-term, 76, 79, 86, 110
    short-term, 76, 79, 84–86, 110
Occupational therapists, 69, 359,
    378, 394, 396, 399, 402
Occupational therapy, 2, 5, 36, 85,
    167, 180, 184, 185, 192
Occupations, 504, 506
Operant conditioning, 78 (*See also*
    Behavior modification)
Operational causality, 244, 253–55,
    258, 265
Oral-motor functions, 169, 183–84
Orientation, 276, 277
Orthopedic surgery, 149, 158
Osteoporosis, 149
Overcorrection procedures, 139, 142,
    366, 373, 374, 376, 377–78,
    389, 390, 392

Overprotection of handicapped
    people, 430
Overweight, 167

*PARC v. Commonwealth of
    Pennsylvania*, 3, 20
Parent advocates, 29, 39
Parental Behavior Inventory, 36
Parents of handicapped children, 17,
    23–24, 29, 33, 37
    classroom participation, 25, 38, 41
    guardianship, 34–35, 39, 40
    involvement in program planning,
        26, 28–29, 31–32, 35, 38, 50,
        52, 78, 142
    parent-child relationships, 36, 37
    parent-teacher interactions, 17–42,
        78
    rights and responsibilities, 20, 24,
        26, 29, 34–35
    support groups, 33, 35, 39
    training, 19, 36, 37–39, 257
Parents of nonhandicapped children,
    23, 34
Partial participation, principle of, 3,
    6, 13, 84, 365, 400, 499
Peabody Developmental Motor Scales,
    63
Peabody Picture Vocabulary Test
    (PPVT), 57, 449
Peabody Rebus Reading Program, 471,
    472, 473, 477–79
Pedestrian skills, 7, 80, 87, 313, 446
Peer interaction, 116, 117, 137, 138
Peers, nonhandicapped, (*see*
    Nonhandicapped peers)
*Pennsylvania Training Model:
    Individual Assessment Guide*,
    66, 69
Perceptual-motor skills, 219, 220
Personal-social skills, 40, 53
Phenylketonuria (PKU), 153
Physical fitness skills, 127, 203–4,
    208, 209, 210, 219–22, 223,
    380
Physical therapists, 69, 180, 184, 378,
    394, 399, 402
Physical therapy, 5, 22, 32, 70, 85,
    149, 185, 192
Physiological problems, 147
Piagetian concept development
    model, 55, 59, 66, 69, 227,
    230, 234, 265
Piagetian early human development
    model, 227, 228, 230, 237,
    244, 270
Piaget's stages of intellectual
    development, 231, 265, 290
Pictorial Test of Intelligence, 57
Placement, 24, 26, 27, 32, 45, 46–73,
    50, 51
Play skills, 37, 291
Positive reinforcement, 117–18, 121,
    140, 142, 211–12, 321, 327,
    345, 465
Postural fixations, 174–76, 196
Postural tone, 171, 173–74, 176, 181,
    182, 184, 185, 186–87, 196

normalization, 171, 176, 188–89,
    190, 192, 196, 199
Posture, 167, 171, 203, 210, 211,
    221–22, 293
Practical intelligence, 236
Preacademic performance, 27
Predictive validity of testing, 53
Prehension, 203
Premack's principle, 134–35, 236
Prenatal development, 46
Preschool Attainment Record, 54
Preschool Language Scale, 61
Preschool models for instructing
    adolescent students, 6, 12
Preschool programs, 35, 38
Prescription medication, 148
Primary reinforcers, 118, 119, 121,
    234
Privately provided vocational
    services, 2, 493–94, 499, 500
Problem-solving abilities, 234
Professional self-evaluation, 1
Professional service teams, 49
Program development for deaf-blind
    children, 65
Program development for
    multihandicapped children, 65
Programmed dependence, 6, 176,
    235, 430
Programming for independence, 13
Prompting applied to toilet training,
    365, 367, 370–71, 373
Prompting/fading techniques, 387,
    390, 413–14, 430, 434, 400,
    402
Prompting procedures, 122–29, 138,
    271, 308, 467, 469
Prompts, 78, 85, 123, 276, 277, 281,
    283, 287, 404, 519
    gestural, 127, 321, 382, 388, 400,
        402
    graduated physical guidance, 321,
        322
    least intrusive, 422, 423, 425, 426,
        432, 435
    model, 321, 422, 435
    molding, 398–99, 422, 428
    movement cues, 124
    natural, 122, 123, 125
    physical, 127, 128, 276, 284, 308,
        393
    systems, 125, 126, 127, 128, 427
        least to most intrusive, 413, 414
        most to least intrusive, 413
        time delay fading, 413, 425, 430
    verbal, 91–92, 123, 124, 135, 320,
        389, 391, 422, 425, 428
    visual, 422
"Protective" vocabulary, 445, 446
Psychomotor developmental indices,
    57
Psychomotor retardation, 168
Public funding, 2
Public Law (P.L.) 94-142, 2, 3, 8,
    17, 20–26, 27, 30, 35, 39, 41,
    50, 51, 70, 78, 116, 271
Punishment, 78, 138, 139–42, 328,
    329, 332, 335, 339, 341